South-East Asia

a Lonely Planet shoestring guide

Peter Turner
Joe Cummings
Hugh Finlay
James Lyon
Jens Peters
Robert Storey
Chris Taylor
Tony Wheeler

South-East Asia

8th edition

Published by
Lonely Planet Publications
Head Office: PO Box 617, Hawthorn, Vic 3122, Australia
Branches: 155 Filbert St, Suite 251, Oakland, CA 94607, USA
10 Barley Mow Passage, Chiswick, London W4 4PH, UK
71 bis rue du Cardinal Lemoine, 75005 Paris, France

Printed by
SNP Printing Pte Ltd., Singapore

Photographs by
Glenn Beanland (GB) Joe Cummings (JC) Hugh Finlay (HF) Richard I'Anson (RI)
Richard Nebesky (RN) Joanna O'Brien (JB) Jens Peters (JP) Tony Wheeler (TW)

Front cover: Rice workers at dusk, Kalibukbuk, Indonesia, Paul Ricketts, Horizons International Photo Library

First Published
1975

This Edition
October 1994

Although the authors and publisher have tried to make the information as accurate as possible, they accept no responsibility for any loss, injury or inconvenience sustained by any person using this book.

National Library of Australia Cataloguing in Publication Data

South-East Asia on a shoestring.

8th ed.
Includes index.
ISBN 0 86442 226 1.

1. Asia, Southeastern – Guidebooks. I. Turner, Peter.

915.90453

Peter Turner

Peter was born in Australia and his long-held interest in South-East Asia has seen him make numerous trips to the region. He joined Lonely Planet as an editor and now works as a full-time travel writer. He is the co-author of LP's guides to *Singapore* and *Malaysia, Singapore & Brunei*, and was last seen heading off to Indonesia yet again.

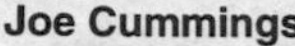

Joe Cummings

Joe has travelled in Asia over the last 15 years or so. Before becoming a full-time travel writer, he worked as a Peace Corps volunteer in Thailand, as an interpreter and translator of Thai, graduated with a MA in South-East Asian studies at UC Berkely, worked as a university lecturer in Malaysia, and a Lao bilingual consultant for Californian schools. Fluent in Thai and Lao, Joe is the author of Lonely Planet's *Laos* and *Thailand* guidebooks and a contributor to other LP guides to the region.

James Lyon

James is an Australian by birth, a social scientist by training and a sceptic by nature. He first travelled in Asia on the overland trail in the '70s and has returned numerous times since, in recent times accompanied by his wife Pauline and their two children. Formerly an editor with Lonely Planet, he is the author of LP's guide to *Bali & Lombok* and a contributor to LP's guides to *Indonesia* and *Mexico*.

Jens Peters

Jens was born in 1949 in West Germany, studied advertising, communications and arts education in Berlin. Since 1970 he has travelled for several months every year in countries outside Europe. He has visited the Philippines dozens of times and has spent several years living there. Since 1977 he has been involved in travel writing, and in particular is the researcher of LP's guide to the *Philippines*.

Robert Storey

Experienced budget traveller and renowned cheapskate, Robert has spent much of his time trekking around the world on a shoestring. During his travels, he survived a number of near-death experiences, including marriage and riding the subway in New York City. Robert now lives in Taiwan, where he has devoted himself to safe and serious pursuits like writing books, studying Chinese, computer hacking and bungee jumping. He has written or contributed to several LP books, including *China, Taiwan, Mongolia, Indonesia, Vietnam, Hong Kong, Macau & Canton* and *Beijing city guide*.

Chris Taylor

Chris Taylor grew up in England and Australia. After joining LP to edit our phrasebook series, he set off to work on our travel survival kit to *Japan*. He has since written city guides for *Tokyo* and *Seoul* and worked on the latest edition of our guidebook to *China*. Chris was dragged off to Cambodia, kicking and screaming all the way, while snowed under with work for the latest edition of our guide to *Japan*.

Tony Wheeler

Tony was born in England but spent most of his youth overseas. He returned to England to do a university degree in engineering, worked as an automotive design engineer, returned to university to complete an MBA, and then dropped out on the Asian overland trail with his wife, Maureen. They've been travelling, writing and publishing guidebooks ever since, having set up Lonely Planet Publications in the mid-'70s. Travel for the Wheelers is now considerably enlivened by by their daughter Tashi and their son Kieran.

From the Authors

From Chris Taylor Lisa Humphries of Phoenix Services in Hong Kong deserves a big thank you for last-minute info on Cambodia and putting up with my ever-changing travel plans. 'Glee', my indefatigable offsider in Phnom Penh deserves a job with LP. Thanks for whizzing me around Phnom Penh on the back of your bike and knowing exactly what I needed to know. Corrine and Hélène ('brains & brawn') were excellent companions to explore Angkor with. Lastly thanks to Murray White, who gave me a bed when I needed one.

This Book

This 8th edition of Lonely Planet's guide to *South-East Asia* and the year 1994 mark several milestones. It was 21 years ago in 1973 that Maureen and I published the very first Lonely Planet guide. It was 20 years ago in 1974 that we set off on the trip around the region that led to the first edition of this book. Looking back it's difficult to realise how much things have changed with both the book and the region. That first edition of *South-East Asia* was completely written, mapped and designed in a back room of the Palace Hotel in Singapore; check the Singapore section, the hotel is still there. A year later our friend and competitor Bill Dalton wrote his *Indonesia Handbook* in that same hotel room.

Edition one of this guidebook took Maureen and me a year to research and another three or four months to put together. It was all of 144 pages long. In contrast this latest edition has involved a team of talented writers and another team of equally talented editors and cartographers. It has involved the latest in technology from laptop computers in the field to computer-aided mapping equipment in our office.

But all that technology would be irrelevant if the writers out there travelling weren't enjoying themselves. And that is what still makes South-East Asia so special – it's simply fun to travel there. Over the 20 years this book has been going things have got better and worse, easier and harder. Visiting Angkor Wat, merely on our wish list 20 years ago, is now a reality. But Kuta Beach, a wonderfully laid-back little paradise, has become just another overpopulated resort.

Singapore has changed from exotic Asia to safe, prosperous and, let's face it, rather dull Asia. And the poor Burmese still have their ridiculous government.

What this edition of *South-East Asia* doesn't have is me. Over the years *South-East Asia* has grown much too big for one person to handle, but with every edition over the last 20 years I've always been back to the region to check things out and, very often, to discover new places I've not been to before. This time, for the very first time, I've left it entirely to other writers. I still love the region and I know I'll be back, but for a while my travels are taking me to other places. So this edition marks a number of milestones – 20 years, eight editions and over half a million copies in print; but *South-East Asia* will mark those milestones without me.

Tony Wheeler

This Edition

The comprehensive update of this book, the 8th edition of *South-East Asia*, required lots of people and lots of days on the road.

Hugh Finlay covered Peninsular Malaysia and Peter Turner covered Singapore, Brunei and East Malaysia for the new edition of *Malaysia, Singapore & Brunei*. Peter then wrote up the Singapore, Malaysia and Brunei sections for this book, and made a last-minute check on Singapore, and the major centres in Malaysia.

Indonesia, by virtue of its size, required a considerable effort to update. The Indonesia chapter draws on the work of the team of writers who have worked on the *Indonesia* guide over the years. For this book, Peter Turner went back to Indonesia and travelled the length of the archipelago, from Timor to Sumatra, and then on a second loop travelled down through Sumatra and across to Sulawesi and Maluku. He then put together the Indonesia chapter, and James Lyon updated the Bali and Lombok sections while researching the new *Bali & Lombok* guide.

Joe Cummings researched the Thailand and Laos chapters, as he travelled through the region researching Lonely Planet's *Thailand* and *Laos* guides. He also went across to Myanmar to update that chapter. Richard Nebesky also provided contributions to the Thailand chapter from his research on the latest edition of the *Thailand* guide.

Jens Peters, in the preparation of LP's *Philippines* guidebook, travelled throughout the country to update the Philippines chapter.

Robert Storey, from his base in North-East Asia, prepared the chapters on Hong Kong and Macau as he researched the latest guide to those countries. He also compiled the Vietnam chapter, which he updated from the 2nd edition of the *Vietnam* guide, based on Daniel Robinson's original research.

Finally, Chris Taylor updated the Cambodia chapter, originally researched and written by Daniel Robinson. Peter Turner coordinated the project and prepared the background chapters.

From the Publisher

This book was edited, proofed and indexed by Paul Smitz and Greg Alford. Additional proofing was done by Kristin Odijk. Mapping was done by Jacqui Saunders, who also coordinated design and layout. Thanks also to Tamsin Wilson for cover design. Additional mapping was by Sally Woodward and Sandra Smythe. And undying thanks to the ever-gracious Dan Levin, computer guru extraordinaire, who performed technological wonders in getting the Lao accents to do the circle dance.

Our thanks also to the many readers who wrote in to share their travelling adventures with us. A list of all your names is at the end of the book, after the index.

Warning & Request

Things change – prices go up, schedules change, good places go bad and bad places go bankrupt – nothing stays the same. So if you find things better or worse, recently opened or long since closed, please write and tell us and help make the next edition better. Your letters will be used to help update future editions and, where possible, important changes will also be included in a Stop Press section in reprints.

We greatly appreciate all information that is sent to us by travellers. Back at Lonely Planet we employ a hard-working readers' letters team to sort through the many letters we receive. The best ones will be rewarded with a free copy of the next edition or another Lonely Planet guide if you prefer. We give away lots of books, but, unfortunately, not every letter/postcard receives one.

Contents

SINGAPORE 658

THAILAND 689

Map Legend

BOUNDARIES

International Boundary

Internal Boundary

ROUTES

Freeway

Highway

Major Road

Unsealed Road or Track

City Road

City Street

Railway

Underground Railway

Tram

Walking Track

Walking Tour

Ferry Route

Cable Car or Chairlift

AREA FEATURES

Park, Gardens

National Park

Forest

Built-Up Area

Pedestrian Mall

Market

Cemetery

Reef

Beach or Desert

Rocks

HYDROGRAPHIC FEATURES

Coastline

River, Creek

Intermittent River or Creek

Lake, Intermittent Lake

Swamp

SYMBOLS

CAPITAL ....National Capital

Capital ....State Capital

CITY ....Major City

City ....City

Town ....Town

Village ....Village

Place to Stay

Place to Eat

Pub, Bar

Post Office, Telephone

Tourist Information, Bank

Transport, Parking

Museum, Youth Hostel

Caravan Park, Camping Ground

Church, Cathedral

Mosque, Synagogue

Buddhist Temple, Hindu Temple

Balinese Temple, Stupa

Hospital, Police Station

Airport, Airfield

Swimming Pool, Gardens

Shopping Centre, Zoo

A25 One Way Street, Route Number

Archaeological Site or Ruins

Stately Home, Monument

Castle, Tomb

Cave, Lighthouse

Mountain or Hill, Lookout

Pass, Spring

Underground Station (Singapore)

Ancient or City Wall

Rapids, Waterfalls

Cliff or Escarpment, Tunnel

Railway Station

Note: not all symbols displayed above appear in this book

Introduction

South-East Asia has so many highlights it is difficult to know where to begin. Volcanos, jungles, ancient cultures, thriving metropolises, pristine beaches and spellbinding ritual – you'll find them all. But perhaps it's easiest to sum it all up with a cliche – it's the people you meet that make it all worthwhile, and South-East Asia's greatest highlight is its peoples.

Chances are you'll arrive via one of the big Asian gateways. If Bangkok, Jakarta or almost any other capital city is your first taste of Asia, you may wonder why you bothered. Most Asian capitals are sprawling, congested, polluted boom towns. On arrival you can be guaranteed culture shock, but on departure, after a broader taste of the region, these places can be fascinating, vibrant microcosms of Asia. Hong Kong thrives with activity and commerce, Jakarta is the melting pot of Indonesia and Bangkok may shock but is guaranteed not to bore. Singapore is not so much 'shocking Asia' as 'shopping Asia', but a good place for Western delights and a bit of R & R. Or there are the quieter backwater capitals of Yangon and Hanoi. Yangon (Rangoon) is certainly a microcosm of Myanmar (Burma) – crumbling and antiquated with few signs of improvement since colonial days. Hanoi has unhurried French charm and wide, clean socialist boulevards.

South-East Asia has plenty of interesting cities nestling in the hills or on fine bays, but Asia's most likeable city is Georgetown on Penang (Malaysia). It is big enough to be exciting, small enough to be laid back. It is unmistakably Chinese, has predominantly British colonial architecture, good food and a ready supply of things to see.

But Asia's real sights are out in the countryside, and some are simply spectacular. For volcanos try Mayon, the 'most perfect', in the Philippines, or the moonscapes of Mt Bromo on Java. For mountain views they don't come much higher than Mt Kinabalu in Borneo; or for a hit-you-in-the-eye panorama the first views of Lake Toba in

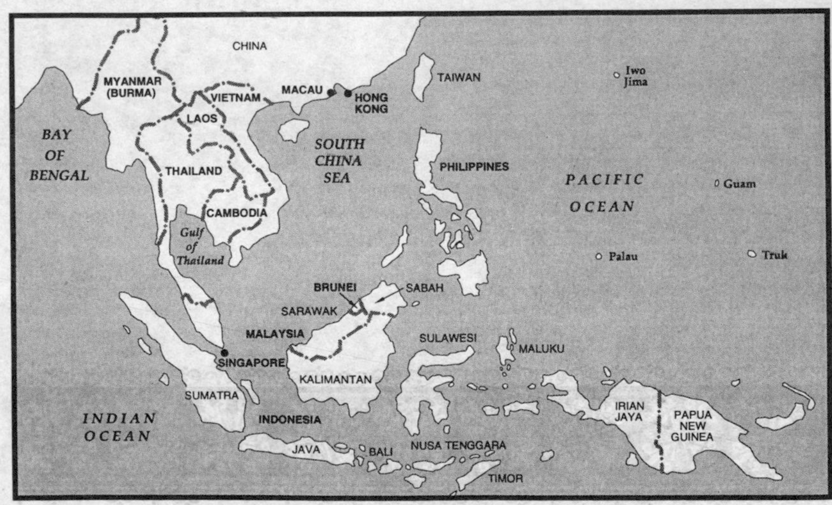

Sumatra are unforgettable. For a combination of mountain and lakes, one of South-East Asia's weirdest and most impressive sights is of the three-coloured lakes of Keli Mutu on Flores, Indonesia.

Trying to choose the best beaches is a good way to start an argument. Thailand probably takes the prize with Phuket and the islands of Ko Samui, Ko Samet, Ko Pha-Ngan, Ko Phi Phi...the list keeps growing. The east coast of Peninsular Malaysia has a few contenders, notably Tioman and the Perhentian islands. The Philippines is no slouch in the sea and sand department – Boracay is the most famed, or there's Puerto Galera, Malapascua or dozens of other resorts. Indonesia also has its fair share scattered around the archipelago, from Nias Island to Bali's Kuta Beach and the Gili Islands off Lombok. If you want to find that deserted paradise, Indonesia and the Philippines have thousands of islands. Vietnam is the new kid on the block with beaches like Nha Trang set to become big resorts.

South-East Asia specialises in ancient temple complexes, all competing to outdo each other for grandeur. Cambodia's Angkor Wat, Myanmar's Bagan, and Indonesia's Borobudur are massive structures and not to be missed. There are plenty of other temples of note, but the most fabulous is the Shwedagon Pagoda in Yangon, a gilded, jewel-encrusted treasure that dominates the city.

More? Well there's great food, jungle trekking, giant lizards, superb coral reefs...the list is endless.

A	B	C
D	E	F
G	H	I

A: Ratchaburi, Thailand (RN)
B: Dieng Plateau, Java, Indonesia (JC)
C: Chinatown, Singapore (RN)
D: Nong Khai, Thailand (JC)
E: Panay, Philippines (JP)
F: Angkor, Cambodia (GB)
G: Lantau, Hong Kong (TW)
H: Bangkok, Thailand (RN)
I: Singapore (RN)

CHINA
Mekong River
Ayeyarwady River
Guangzhou (Canton)
MACAU
HONG KONG
Mandalay
MYANMAR (BURMA)
Hanoi
Luang Phabang
Gulf of Tonkin
Hainan
Chiang Mai
Vientiane
Yangon (Rangoon)
Paracel Islands
Danang
THAILAND
Tavoy
Bangkok
Battambang
CAMBODIA
ANDAMAN SEA
Phnom Penh
Gulf of Thailand
Ho Chi Minh City
Cantho
SOUTH CHINA
Spratly Islands
Banda Aceh
Penang
Strait of Melaka
Peninsular Malaysia
Ipoh
Medan
Siantar
Kuala Lumpur
SINGAPORE
BRUNEI
Sarawak
Kuching
Pekanbaru
Pontianak
BORNEO
SUMATRA
Muaratembesi
Jambi
Palembang
Banjarmasin
Bandarlampung
JAVA SEA
INDIAN OCEAN
Jakarta
JAVA
Madura
Bandung
Semarang
Surabaya
Yogyakarta
Solo
Jember
Denpasar
100°
110°
Christmas Island (Australia)

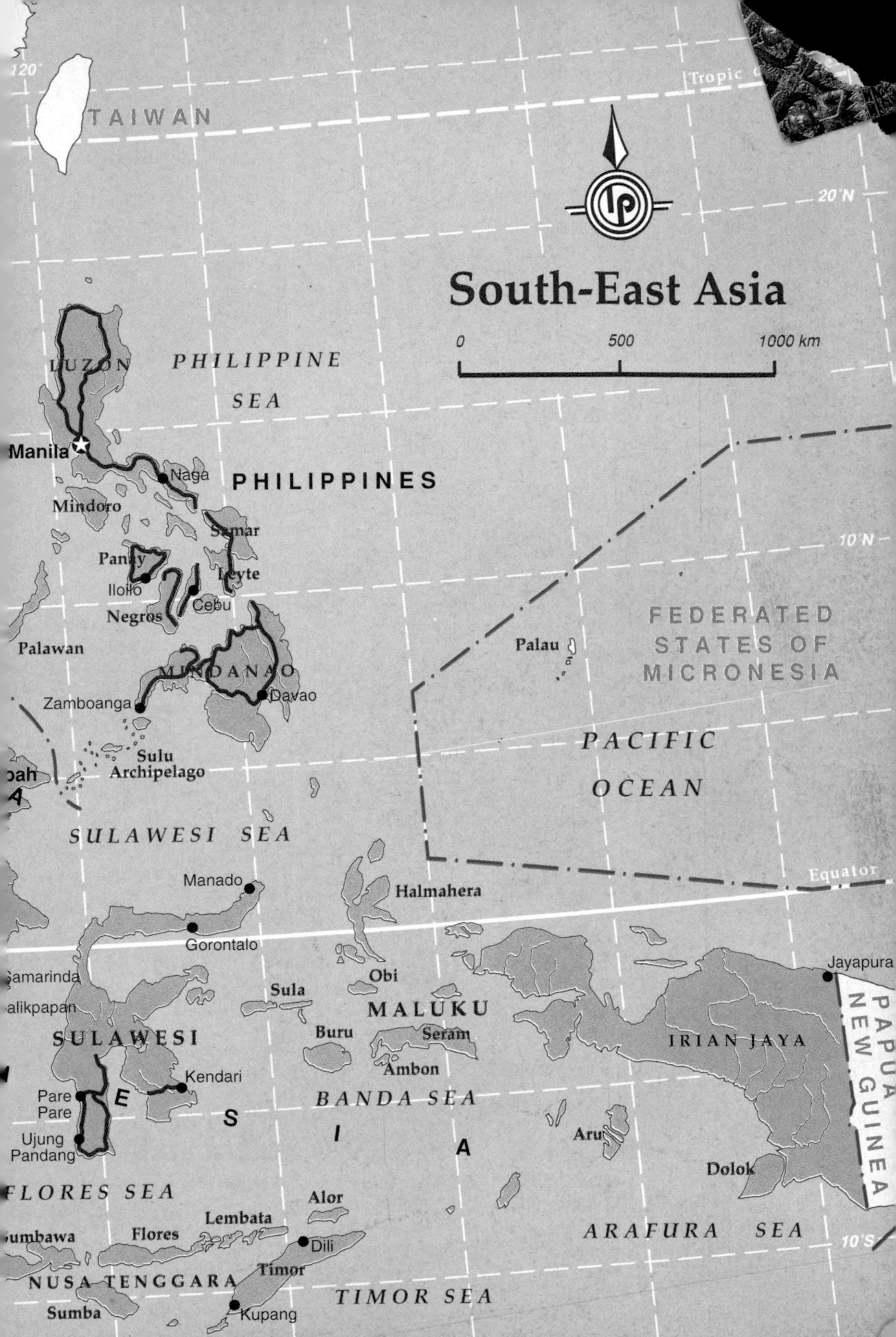
South-East Asia
0
500
1000 km
TAIWAN
Tropic
20°N
10°N
10°S
Equator
LUZON
PHILIPPINE
SEA
Manila
Naga
PHILIPPINES
Mindoro
Samar
Panay
Leyte
Iloilo
Cebu
Negros
Palawan
MINDANAO
Davao
Zamboanga
Sulu
Archipelago
FEDERATED
STATES OF
MICRONESIA
Palau
PACIFIC
OCEAN
SULAWESI SEA
Manado
Halmahera
Gorontalo
Obi
Sula
MALUKU
Buru
Seram
Ambon
SULAWESI
Kendari
Pare
Pare
Ujung
Pandang
BANDA SEA
IRIAN JAYA
Jayapura
PAPUA
NEW GUINEA
Aru
Dolok
FLORES SEA
Alor
Lembata
Flores
Dili
Timor
NUSA TENGGARA
Sumba
Kupang
TIMOR SEA
ARAFURA SEA

A	B	C
D	E	F
G	H	I

A: Bangkok, Thailand (JB)
B: Kampung Ayer, Brunei (HF)
C: Songkhla, Thailand (RN)
D: That Phanom, Thailand (JC)
E: Vientiane, Laos (RI)
F: Nha Trang, Vietnam (GB)
G: Hat Yai, Thailand (JC)
H: Philippines (JP)
I: Singapore (TW)

Regional Facts for the Visitor

PLANNING

When to Go?

Anytime for any amount of time might be the answer to this one. Although there are wet and dry seasons, the changes are not as distinct as they are on the Indian subcontinent. Nor are there seasons when you can and cannot do things (as for trekking in Nepal). The Climate sections of the various countries and regions detail what to expect and when to expect it, but anytime is the right time somewhere or other!

What to Bring

As little as possible is the best policy – but not so little that you have to scrounge off other travellers, as some of the 'super lightweight' travellers do. It's very easy to find almost anything you need along the way, and since you'll inevitably buy things as you go, it's better to start with too little rather than too much.

A backpack is still the most popular method of carrying gear as it is commodious and the only way to go if you have to do any walking. On the debit side, a backpack is awkward to load on and off buses and trains, it doesn't offer too much protection for your valuables, the straps tend to get caught on things and some airlines may refuse to be responsible if the pack is damaged or broken into. Fortunately, backpacks no longer have the 'pack equals hippy' and 'hippy equals bad' connotation they used to have.

Travelpacks, a combination of backpack and shoulder bag, are also popular. The backpack straps zip away inside the pack when not needed so you almost have the best of both worlds. Although not really suitable for long hiking trips, they're much easier to carry than a bag. They are also easier for accessing your gear – the top zips open and you don't have to take out everything to find something at the bottom of your pack – and easier to lock than a backpack. Another alternative is a large, soft zip bag with a wide shoulder strap so it can be carried with relative ease if necessary. Backpacks or travelpacks can be reasonably thief-proofed with small padlocks. Forget suitcases.

Once in the region you will, no doubt, be buying local clothes along the way (Levi jeans are cheaper in Hong Kong than most Western countries), so start light. My list of clothing to bring along would include:

- underwear & swimming gear
- a pair of jeans & a pair of shorts
- a few T-shirts & shirts
- a sweater for cold nights
- a pair of runners or shoes
- sandals or thongs
- a lightweight jacket or raincoat
- a dress-up set of clothes

Modesty is rated highly in Asian countries, especially for women. Wearing shorts away from the beach is often looked down upon as being rather 'low class'.

Other items I'd consider bringing include:

- washing gear
- a medical & a sewing kit
- sunglasses
- a padlock
- a sleeping bag
- a Swiss Army knife
- a sarong
- an umbrella

Sleeping bags are only necessary if you're going to be roughing it, getting well off the beaten track, climbing mountains and the like. They can also double as a coat on cold days, a cushion on hard train-seats, a seat for long waits at bus or railway stations and a bed top-cover, since hotels rarely give you one. A sarong is equally useful since it can be everything from a bedsheet to a towel, a beach wrap or a dressing gown.

A padlock is useful to lock your bag to a train or bus luggage rack or to fortify your hotel room – which often locks with a latch. I've made trips with an umbrella and it came in useful nearly every day I was on the road. I've also made trips without an umbrella and hardly missed it. Small folding umbrellas are readily available in Asia. Soap, toothpaste and so on are readily obtainable, but toilet paper can be impossible to find well off the beaten track. Tampons are also difficult to find away from the big cities.

There are two final considerations. The secret of successful packing is plastic bags, also called 'stuff bags' – they not only keep the items in your pack separate and clean but also dry.

Airlines do lose bags from time to time – you've got a much better chance of it not being yours if it is tagged with your name and address *inside* the bag as well as outside. Outside tags can always fall off or be removed.

Appearances & Conduct

If you want to have a smooth trip, attention to your appearance is most important. Throughout South-East Asia the official powers-that-be have a morbid hatred of 'hippies', 'freaks' and other similar low forms of life. When you arrive at embassies or consulates for visas, at the border to enter a country, or at docks or airports, you'll find life much more simple if you look neat and affluent. Particularly disliked are thongs (flip-flops), shorts, jeans (especially with patches on them), local attire, T-shirts – I could go on. It's advisable to have one set of conventional 'dress-up' gear to wear for these types of formal occasions.

Encounters with Asian officialdom are made much smoother if you keep repeating 'I must retain my cool' the more they annoy you! Displays of temper usually have a counterproductive effect. They just want to show you who's boss – if you imply that you realise they are but that you still insist (calmly) on your rights you'll probably manage OK. Exaggerated politeness can go a long way in Asia.

VISAS

Visas remain my pet Asian hate. Visas are a stamp in your passport permitting you to enter the country in question and stay for a specified period of time. They're generally pure red tape and another means of gouging a few more dollars out of you. If you spend much time travelling around the region you'll waste a lot of time, money, effort and passport pages on them, although I'm pleased to say that over the years the visa situation in South-East Asia has become much better. This is not so for Myanmar (Burma), however.

Several steps can make obtaining visas a little easier. As far as possible, get your visas as you go rather than all at once before you leave home. Two reasons – one, they often expire after a certain number of days, and two, it is often easier and very often cheaper to get them in neighbouring countries than it is from far away. Shop around for your visas – you'll hear on the grapevine that city A is far better than city B for such and such a visa.

Finally, there is the dreaded ticket-out problem. For some reason, several countries have this phobia that if you don't arrive clutching a departure ticket in your hand, you'll never leave. This is a real hassle if you intend to depart by some unusual means for which the tickets can only be bought after you arrive!

The answer is to just get the cheapest ticket out and get a refund on it later – make sure it's the cheapest and safest as there are some airlines who part with refunds like Scrooge with his pennies.

Of course, if you really intend to depart as planned, you will not have any problems. Note that in places where renewing visas can be difficult, a confirmed ticket out from the place you're trying to renew in will make your application much more acceptable to the authorities.

If you hit a sticky visa problem, shop around. In some other city or country, the situation concerning visas may be a lot better. See the Visas sections under the individual countries in this book for further information. And remember the most important rule: treat embassies, consulates and borders as formal occasions – dress up for them.

DOCUMENTS

There is one document you must have (a passport) and a number worth considering.

Passport

Make sure your passport is valid for a reasonably long period of time. In many countries, it is required that your passport has at least six months validity left, even if you're only staying for a few days.

Make sure it has plenty of space left for those rubber stamp-happy Asian bureaucrats to do their bit, too. It could be embarrassing to run out of blank pages although, in my experience, it is generally relatively easy to get a new passport in Asia (I've gotten one in Jakarta, and Maureen obtained one in Bangkok), so long as you haven't lost the old one. Some people (Americans for example) can simply have an extra concertina-section stuck in when their passport gets full.

The loss of your passport is a real hassle but it can be made a little easier if, somewhere else, you've got a record of its number and issue date, or even better, photocopies of the relevant data pages. A photocopy of your birth certificate can also be useful.

While you're compiling that info, add the serial number of your travellers' cheques and US$50 or more as emergency cash – keep all this emergency material totally separate from your passport, cheques and other cash.

International Health Certificate

This is a useful document to carry and a necessity if you're coming into the region from areas, such as Africa and South America, with yellow fever – see Immunisation in the following Health section for more details.

International Driving Permit

If you plan to be driving in the region, obtain one of these driving permits from your local automobile association. They are usually inexpensive and valid for one year only. These permits can make life much simpler, especially for hiring cars and motorbikes.

Hostelling International Card

These can be useful, even if you don't intend to use hostels. Although many Asian hostels do not require that you be a HI member, they will often charge you less if you have a card.

Student Cards

The most useful of these is the International Student Identity Card (ISIC), a plastic ID-style card with your photograph on it. It can perform all sorts of wonders, particularly when it comes to airline tickets, so it's no surprise that there is a worldwide industry in fake student cards.

Bangkok is a great centre for finding them – notices appear in all the relevant places! Of course some of the cards are of deplorably low quality, but airlines simply want to get you into their aircraft, even if it is with a student discount, and they're not too worried about how pretty the card is. Many places now also stipulate a maximum age for student discounts or, more simply, they've substituted a 'youth discount' for a 'student discount'.

Finally, remember that 'student' is a very respectable thing to be and if your passport has a blank space for occupation you are much better off having 'student' there than something nasty like 'journalist' or 'photographer'.

MONEY

Bring as much of this fine stuff as possible. Despite the ups and downs of international currencies, you will still generally find US dollars (US$) are the most easily exchanged but you may well decide that other currencies have better prospects of holding their value. The pound sterling (£) is nice to have in some places (Hong Kong, Malaysia and Singapore), the Deutschemark (DM) or the Japanese yen (¥) are well accepted everywhere, but when it comes down to day-in-day-out acceptability, the US dollar is the currency to carry. It's particularly good in the Philippines, Indochina, Thailand (where US influence is or has been strong) and in Indonesia, where the US$ often seems to enjoy a strange premium over the other currencies.

Travellers' Cheques

American Express or Thomas Cook travellers' cheques are probably the best to carry because of their wide acceptance and 'instant replacement' policies. The main idea of carrying cheques rather than cash is the protection they offer from theft, but it doesn't do a lot of good if you have to go back home first to get the refund. Amex have offices in most of the major cities but remember that 'instant replacement' may not be exactly instantaneous, although overall most people seem to be pretty satisfied with the service.

Keeping a record of the cheque numbers and the initial purchase details is vitally important. Without this you may well find that 'instant' is a very long time indeed. If you're going to really out-of-the-way places, it may be worth taking a couple of different brands of travellers' cheques since banks may not always accept all varieties. Once again, take well-known brands.

Take nearly all the cheques in large denominations, say US$100s. It's only at the very end of a stay that you may want to change a US$20 or US$10 cheque just to get you through the last day or two. A number of institutions charge a per-cheque service fee, so changing US$100 in 20s can end up five times as expensive as a single US$100 cheque. In many cases, the exchange rate for travellers' cheques is better than the exchange rate for cash.

Cash

Nothing beats cash for convenience...or risk. If you lose it, it's gone forever – very few travel insurers will come to your rescue. However, it is a good idea to take some cash with you. Often, it is much easier to change just a few dollars (when leaving a country for example) in cash rather than cheques – and more economical.

Cash is also very handy when banks are closed, or nonexistent. Even in remote villages it seems everyone knows what the greenback is worth, and you can often find someone who will accept US$ in an emergency.

In countries where there is a black market, cash is what's wanted, not travellers' cheques, but note that big denominations get a much better rate than small ones. Nobody wants US$1 notes. Of course, the odd dollar laid in the right place (the right hand) can perform wonders.

International Transfers

If you run out of cash, due to simply having spent it all or from more disastrous events, and need more, instruct your bank back home to send a draft to you (always assuming you've got some cash back home to send!). Specify the city and the bank – once I made the mistake of saying 'to your usual bank' and then spent a day trying to find out which was their 'usual bank'. If you don't know a bank to transfer money to, ask your bank to write and tell you where a suitable one is.

Money sent by telegraphic transfer should reach you in a couple of days, but by mail allow at least two weeks. When it gets there, it will most likely be converted into local currency – you can take it as it is or buy travellers' cheques. Singapore and Hong Kong are easily the best countries referred to in this book to transfer money to. Malaysia and Thailand are not bad either but even Indonesia and the Philippines are far easier than countries further west like India and Pakistan, where money transfers seem to drop into a bottomless pit, sometimes never to be seen again.

Credit Cards & ATMs

If you're very sound financially, an ideal travelling companion is a credit card. It always amuses me how many backpackers also have their credit cards! Credit cards are of limited use for day-to-day travel expenses in South-East Asia as only expensive hotels, restaurants and shops accept them, but they are very useful for major purchases like airline tickets.

Another major advantage is that they will allow you to draw cash over the counter at selected banks. If your credit card has a personal identification number (PIN) attached, you can also make cash withdrawals at automatic teller machines (ATMs) in the more developed countries of the region. In these countries it is also possible to access overseas savings accounts through ATMs – check with your bank at home before you leave.

Credit cards are a convenient way to carry your money. You don't have money tied up in travellers' cheques in a currency that is diving, you don't pay commission charges or transaction fees, and the exchange rates are often better than those offered by local banks for cash or travellers' cheques. The disadvantages are that interest is charged unless your account is always in the black, and credit limits can be too limited. Not all banks in South-East Asia will give cash advances on a credit card, and it can be difficult outside major cities. Don't rely on a credit card in Indochina or Myanmar.

Some travellers use credit cards exclusively for accessing money, but it is wise to also carry travellers' cheques or cash as back-up. It can be very disconcerting to see 'Funds unavailable – contact your bank' flash up on an ATM when your bank is thousands of miles away.

Visa is generally more widely accepted in the region, but you shouldn't have any problems with a MasterCard, and American Express has a large network of offices. A combination of two or three cards is better still.

Finally, always check purchases and receipts – when you buy something with a credit card, and against accounts when you get home. Credit card fraud, especially in Bangkok, is not unknown.

Cheques & Giro

There are other ways of carrying money or obtaining cash as well. In some places, you can cash Eurocheques or personal cheques with the appropriate identification, but this is less certain. Dutch travellers with a Dutch post office account can conveniently obtain cash from Indonesian post offices. These *girobetaalkaarten* are useful in the many Indonesian towns where there is no bank.

How Much Money?

Your budget is dependent upon how you live and travel. If you're moving around fast, going to lots of places, spending time in the big cities, then your day-to-day living costs are going to be quite high. People who tell you they spent six months on five dollars a day did it by sitting on the beach for five months and three weeks. Remember, you're not on some sort of travelling economy run – being tight with your money can mean you lose the whole purpose of being there.

See the cost comparison chart below for a comparison of prices between Western and South-East Asian countries.

Cost Comparison Chart
All figures in $US

	Aus	*HK*	*Indo*	*Mal*	*Phil*	*Sing*	*Thai*	*UK*	*USA*	*Vietnam*
Exchange Rates	0.72	7.57	2105	2.56	26.03	1.51	24.67	0.66	1	10945
Daily Paper	0.55	0.50	0.50	0.11	0.11	0.30	0.40	0.65	0.35	0.2
Kodacolor100	5	7.5	6	5	7.5	4	5	5	4	3.4
Cheap Hotel	25	15	7	8	7	15	5	34	25	5-8
Hostel Bed	10	6.5	3.5	3	3.5	5	2	10	12	n/a
Cheap Meal	7	5	3	3	3	4	1.25	8	6	1.50
Glass of beer	2	2	0.55	2	0.65	4	1.50	2.50	2	0.50
Big Mac	1.75	1.15	2	1.45	1.45	1.60	1.80	3.10	1.90	n/a
Litre of petrol	0.50	0.85	0.35	0.37	0.37	0.80	0.40	0.84	0.30	0.40
Local phone call	0.28	0.13	0.1	0.04	0.1	0.06	0.04	0.17	0.20	free
Time Magazine	2.10	3.25	2.2	2.00	2.2	3.15	3.00	2.57	2.50	4

ELECTRICITY

If you want to bring your ghetto blaster, notebook computer or hair dryer, try to make sure that it can handle different voltages and cycles, and bring socket adapters. Better still, make sure that it also runs on batteries.

The going voltage is 220 V at 50 cycles, except for the Philippines, which is 220 V at 60 cycles. Countries that used to have 110 V have made the switch but you may still occasionally come across 110 V in Indonesia, the Philippines and Indochina. Looking at the shape of the outlet on the wall gives no clue as to what voltage is flowing through the wires, so try to find a lightbulb or appliance with the voltage written on it. The best advice, however, is to ask before you plug in your appliances. Some appliances have built-in 110/220 V switches, and 240 V appliances will happily run on 220 V.

Reliability of supply is in direct relation to the affluence of the country. Myanmar, the Philippines and Indochina have frequent blackouts, Indonesia is generally reliable but not always, and elsewhere you shouldn't have any problems.

Sockets run the full range. Malaysia and Singapore use the flat three-pin type as used in the UK. Most other countries use the round two-pin type as found in Europe. Exceptions are the Philippines, which uses the flat, vertical, two-pin plug as in the USA, and Hong Kong, which has its own round three-pin socket. Outlets in Indochina generally take the European type, but some outlets take the US flat-pin type. Buy socket adapters before you leave – they are difficult to find in Asia.

POST

Poste restante (at almost any post office) is the best way of getting mail. American Express have client mail services but it's often not worth the effort. If you've got some definite contact point or know you will be at a certain hotel then use that. Nowadays, very few embassies will hold mail for their people – they'll just forward it on to poste restante. When getting people to write to you, ask them to leave plenty of time for mail to arrive and to print your name very clearly. Underlining the surname also helps. Remember, in some countries the surname comes first, so it's not surprising that many 'missing' letters are just misfiled.

When sending mail from the less affluent countries, it's often recommended that you have the stamps franked before your eyes, to prevent the stamps being stolen. However, this does not seem to be such a problem anymore, not in affluent South-East Asia anyway.

Aerograms are quite safe of course. I am very distrustful of 'mail it home' packaging services, however. I've sent parcels home from South-East Asia on a few occasions and (touch wood) they've always arrived – slightly battered and a long time later. If it's something you value, consider air freight. Inquire at the post office before you bring a parcel in as there may be special wrapping requirements or it may have to be inspected (as in Indonesia) before you wrap it.

TIME

Malaysia, in common with Brunei, Singapore, Hong Kong and Macau, is eight hours ahead of GMT/UTC (Greenwich Mean Time/Universal Time Coordinated). When it is noon in Malaysia, it is 8 pm the previous day in Los Angeles, 11 pm the previous day in New York, 4 am in London and 2 pm in Sydney. Like Hong Kong, the policy in Macau is to not observe daylight-saving time.

The Philippines is also eight hours ahead of GMT/UTC. Remember that most locals operate on 'Philippine time' with its attendant lack of punctuality. Allow flexibility in rendezvous times.

Vietnam, like the neighbouring countries of Thailand, Cambodia, Myanmar and Laos, is seven hours ahead of GMT/UTC. When it is noon in Vietnam, it is 5 am in London, 1 am in New York, 10 pm in Los Angeles and 3 pm in Sydney.

Myanmar is six and a half hours ahead of GMT/UTC, half an hour behind Bangkok time and an hour ahead of Dacca time. When it is noon in Yangon, it is 9.30 pm the previous day in San Francisco, 12.30 am in New York, 5.30 am in London and 3.30 pm in Sydney.

There are three time zones in Indonesia. Sumatra, Java and west and central Kalimantan are on West Indonesian Time, which is seven hours ahead of GMT/UTC. Bali, Nusa Tenggara, south and east Kalimantan and Sulawesi are on Central Indonesian Time, which is eight hours ahead of GMT/UTC. Irian Jaya and Maluku are on East Indonesian Time, which is nine hours ahead of GMT/UTC. Allowing for variations due to daylight saving, when it is noon in Jakarta, it is 9 pm the previous day in Los Angeles, 5 am in London, 1 pm in Ujung Pandang, 2 pm in Jayapura, 3 pm in Melbourne or Sydney and midnight in New York.

BOOKS

Guidebooks

In a guidebook of this size and scope we can't possibly cover every conceivable aspect of travel in South-East Asia. If you'd like more detailed information on a specific area or country, Lonely Planet produces a range of travel survival kits which are updated regularly and provide useful maps and a wealth of information for travellers.

The titles to look for are:

Bali & Lombok – a travel survival kit
Cambodia – a travel survival kit
Hong Kong, Macau & Canton – a travel survival kit
Indonesia – a travel survival kit
Laos – a travel survival kit
Malaysia, Singapore & Brunei – a travel survival kit
Myanmar (Burma) – a travel survival kit
North-East Asia on a shoestring
Philippines – a travel survival kit
Thailand – a travel survival kit
Vietnam – a travel survival kit

Look also for the following city guides:

Bangkok city guide
Singapore city guide

Phrasebooks

Also of interest to travellers in South-East Asia are Lonely Planet's range of phrasebooks which includes:

Burmese Phrasebook
Indonesian Phrasebook
Pilipino Phrasebook
Thai Phrasebook
Vietnamese Phrasebook
Mandarin Chinese Phrasebook
Thai Hill Tribes Phrasebook

FILM & PHOTOGRAPHY

You'll run through plenty of film in South-East Asia, and in Singapore and Hong Kong it's fairly cheap, particularly if you buy it in bulk – say a dozen at a time. Elsewhere, film is readily available (Malaysia, Thailand or Indonesia for example), but is slightly more expensive than in the West. Slide film is often difficult to obtain – Singapore and Hong Kong are good places to stock up.

Cameras are also cheap in Singapore or Hong Kong where the choice of camera equipment is literally staggering. If you have any difficulties, these are also the places to have your camera attended to.

Particular points to note when taking photos in the region are to compensate for the intensity of the light – for a few hours before and after midday the height of the sun will tend to leave pictures very washed out. Try to photograph early or late in the day. There will also be plenty of occasions when you'll want a flash, either for indoor shots or in jungle locations where the amount of light that filters through can be surprisingly low. When taking photographs of people, make sure they don't mind. They generally don't but it's polite to check first.

HEALTH

Travel health depends on your predeparture preparations, your day-to-day health care while travelling and how you handle any medical problem or emergency that does develop. While the list of potential dangers can seem quite frightening, with a little luck, some basic precautions and adequate information few travellers experience more than upset stomachs.

Travel Health Guides

There are a number of books available on travel health:

Staying Healthy in Asia, Africa & Latin America, Moon Publications. Probably the best all-round guide to carry, as it's compact but very detailed and well organised.

Travellers' Health, Dr Richard Dawood, Oxford University Press. Comprehensive, easy to read, authoritative and also highly recommended, although it's rather large to lug around.

Where There is No Doctor, David Werner, Hesperian Foundation. A very detailed guide intended for someone, like a Peace Corps worker, going to work in an undeveloped country, rather than for the average traveller.

Travel with Children, Maureen Wheeler, Lonely Planet Publications. Includes basic advice on travel health for younger children.

Predeparture Preparations

Travel Insurance A travel insurance policy to cover theft, loss and medical problems is a wise idea. There are a wide variety of policies and your travel agent will have recommendations. Some policies offer lower and higher medical expenses options but the higher one is chiefly for countries like the USA which have extremely high medical costs. Check the small print:

- Some policies specifically exclude 'dangerous activities' which can include scuba diving, motorcycling, even trekking. If such activities are on your agenda you don't want that sort of policy. A locally acquired motorcycle licence may not be valid under your policy.
- You may prefer a policy which pays doctors or hospitals direct rather than you having to pay on the spot and claim later. If you have to claim later make sure you keep all documentation. Some policies ask you to call back (reverse charges) to a centre in your home country where an immediate assessment of your problem is made.
- Check if the policy covers ambulances or an emergency flight home. If you have to stretch out you will need two seats and somebody has to pay for them!

Medical Kit A small and straightforward medical kit is a wise thing to carry. A possible kit list includes:

- Aspirin or Panadol – for pain or fever.
- Antihistamine (such as Benadryl) – useful as a decongestant for colds, allergies, to ease the itch from insect bites or stings or to help prevent motion sickness. Antihistamines may cause sedation and interact with alcohol so care should be taken when using them.
- Antibiotics – useful if you're travelling well off the beaten track, but they must be prescribed and you should carry the prescription with you. Some individuals are allergic to commonly prescribed antibiotics such as penicillin or sulfa drugs. It would be sensible to always carry this information when travelling.
- Kaolin preparation (Pepto-Bismol), Imodium or Lomotil – for stomach upsets.
- Rehydration mixture – for treatment of severe diarrhoea. This is particularly important if travelling with children, but is recommended for everyone.
- Antiseptic such as Betadine, which comes as impregnated swabs or ointment, and an antibiotic powder or similar 'dry' spray – for cuts and grazes.
- Calamine lotion – to ease irritation from bites or stings.
- Bandages and Band-aids – for minor injuries.
- Scissors, tweezers and a thermometer (note that mercury thermometers are prohibited by airlines).
- Insect repellent, sunscreen, suntan lotion, chap stick and water purification tablets.
- A couple of syringes, in case you need injections in a country with medical hygiene problems. Ask your doctor for a note explaining why they have been prescribed.

Ideally antibiotics should be administered only under medical supervision and should never be taken indiscriminately. Take only the recommended dose at the prescribed intervals and continue using the antibiotic for the prescribed period, even if the illness seems to be cured earlier. Antibiotics are quite specific to the infections they can treat. Stop immediately if there are any serious reactions and don't use the antibiotic at all if you are unsure that you have the correct one.

In many countries, if a medicine is available at all it will generally be available over the counter and the price will be much cheaper than in the West. However, be careful if buying drugs in developing countries, particularly where the expiry date may have passed or correct storage conditions may not have been followed. Bogus drugs are common and it's possible that drugs which are no longer recommended, or have even been banned, in the West are still being dispensed in many Third World countries.

In many countries it may be a good idea to leave unwanted medicines, syringes etc with a local clinic, rather than carry them home.

Health Preparations Make sure that you're healthy before you start travelling. If you are embarking on a long trip make sure your teeth are OK; there are lots of places where a visit to the dentist would be the last thing you'd want to do.

If you wear glasses take a spare pair and your prescription. Losing your glasses can be a real problem, although in many parts of Asia you can get new spectacles made up quickly, cheaply and competently.

If you require a particular medication take an adequate supply, as it may not be available locally. Take the prescription or, better still, part of the packaging showing the generic rather than the brand name (which may not be locally available), as it will make getting replacements easier. It's a wise idea to have a legible prescription with you to show you legally use the medication – it's surprising how often over-the-counter drugs from one place are illegal without a prescription or even banned in another.

Immunisations Vaccinations provide protection against diseases you might meet along the way. For some countries no immunisations are necessary, but the further off the beaten track you go the more necessary it is to take precautions.

Currently yellow fever is the only vaccine required by international health regulations to enter a country, and only then when coming from an infected area. Occasionally travellers face bureaucratic problems regarding cholera vaccine even though all countries have dropped it as a health requirement for travel. Other vaccinations are not required by law, but many are highly recommended for your own personal protection.

All vaccinations should be recorded on an International Health Certificate, which is available from your physician or government health department, for your own records as much as for any legal requirements.

Plan ahead for getting your vaccinations: some of them require an initial shot followed by a booster, while some vaccinations should not be given together. It is recommended you seek medical advice at least six weeks prior to travel.

Most travellers from Western countries will have been immunised against various diseases during childhood but your doctor may still recommend booster shots against measles or polio, diseases still prevalent in many developing countries. The period of protection offered by vaccinations differs widely and some are contraindicated if you are pregnant.

In some countries immunisations are available from airport or government health centres. Travel agents or airline offices will tell you where. The possible list of vaccinations includes:

Smallpox Smallpox has now been wiped out worldwide, so immunisation is no longer necessary.

Cholera Not required by law but occasionally travellers face bureaucratic problems on some border crossings. Protection is poor and it lasts only six months. It is contraindicated in pregnancy.

Tetanus & Diptheria Boosters are necessary every 10 years and protection is highly recommended.

Typhoid Available either as an injection or oral capsules. Protection lasts from one to three years and is useful if you are travelling for long in rural, tropical areas. You may get some side effects such as pain at the injection site, fever, headache and a general unwell feeling. A new single-dose injectable vaccine, which appears to have few side effects, is now available but is more expensive. Side effects are unusual with the oral form but occasionally an individual will have stomach cramps.

Infectious Hepatitis The most common travel-acquired illness which can be prevented by vaccination. Protection can be provided in two ways – either with the antibody gammaglobulin or with a new vaccine called Havrix. Havrix provides long-term immunity (possibly more than 10 years) after an initial course of two injections and a booster at one year. It may be more expensive than gammaglobulin but certainly has many advantages, including length of protection and ease of administration. It is important to know that being a vaccine it will take about three weeks to provide satisfactory protection – hence the need for careful planning prior to travel.

Gammaglobulin is not a vaccination but a ready-made antibody which has proven very successful in reducing the chances of hepatitis infection. Because it may interfere with the development of immunity, it should not be given until at least 10 days after administration of the last vaccine needed; it should also be given as close as possible to departure because it is at its most effective in the first few weeks after administration and the effectiveness tapers off gradually between three and six months.

Yellow Fever This is not required for Asia, unless you are coming from infected areas in Africa and South America.

Basic Rules

Care in what you eat and drink is the most important health rule; stomach upsets are the most likely travel health problem (between 30% and 50% of travellers in a two-week stay experience this) but the majority of these upsets will be relatively minor. Don't become paranoid; trying the local food is definitely part of the experience of travel, after all.

Water The number one rule is *don't drink the water* and that includes ice. In some places, such as Singapore, tap water is safe but if you don't know for certain that the water is safe always assume the worst. Reputable brands of bottled water or soft drinks are generally fine, although in some places bottles refilled with tap water are not unknown. Only use water from containers with a serrated seal – not tops or corks. Take care with fruit juice, particularly if water may have been added. Milk should be treated with suspicion, as it is often unpasteurised. Boiled milk is fine if it is kept hygienically and yoghurt is always good. Tea or coffee should also be OK to drink, since the water should have been boiled.

Water Purification The simplest way of purifying water is to boil it thoroughly. Vigorous boiling for five minutes should be satisfactory even at high altitude. Remember that at high altitude water boils at a lower temperature, so germs are less likely to be killed.

Simple filtering will not remove all dangerous organisms, so if you cannot boil water it should be treated chemically. Chlorine tablets (Puritabs, Steritabs or other brand names) will kill many but not all pathogens, including giardia and amoebic cysts. Iodine is very effective in purifying water and is available in tablet form (such as Potable Aqua), but follow the directions carefully and remember that too much iodine can be harmful.

If you can't find tablets, tincture of iodine (2%) can be used. Four drops of tincture of iodine per litre or quart of clear water is the recommended dosage; the treated water should be left to stand for 20 to 30 minutes before drinking. Iodine loses its effectiveness if exposed to air or damp so keep it in a tightly sealed container. Flavoured powder will disguise the taste of treated water and is a good idea if you are travelling with children.

Food There is an old colonial adage which says: 'If you can cook it, boil it or peel it you can eat it...otherwise forget it'. Salads and fruit should be washed with purified water or peeled where possible. Ice cream is usually OK if it is a reputable brand name, but beware of Third World street vendors and of ice cream that has melted and been refrozen. Thoroughly cooked food is safest but not if it has been left to cool or if it has been reheated. Shellfish such as mussels, oysters and clams should be avoided as well as undercooked meat, particularly in the form of mince. Steaming does not make shellfish safe for eating.

If a place looks clean and well run and if the vendor also looks clean and healthy, then the food is probably safe. In general, places that are packed with travellers or locals will be fine, while empty restaurants are questionable. Busy restaurants mean the food is being cooked and eaten quite quickly with little standing around and is probably not being reheated.

Nutrition If your food is poor or limited in availability, if you're travelling hard and fast and therefore missing meals, or if you simply lose your appetite, you can soon start to lose weight and place your health at risk.

Make sure that your diet is well balanced. Eggs, tofu, beans, lentils and nuts are all safe ways to get protein. Fruit you can peel (bananas, oranges or mandarins for example) is always safe and a good source of vitamins. Try to eat plenty of grains (rice) and bread. Remember that although food is generally safer if it is cooked well, overcooked food loses much of its nutritional value. If your diet isn't well balanced or if your food intake is insufficient, it's a good idea to take vitamin and iron pills.

In hot climates make sure you drink enough – don't rely on feeling thirsty to indicate when you should drink. Not needing to urinate or very dark yellow urine is a danger sign. Always carry a water bottle with you on long trips. Excessive sweating can lead to loss of salt and therefore muscle cramping. Salt tablets are not a good idea as a preventative, but in places where salt is not used much adding salt to food can help.

Everyday Health A normal body temperature is 98.6°F or 37°C; more than 2°C higher is a 'high' fever. A normal adult pulse rate is 60 to 80 per minute (children 80 to 100, babies 100 to 140). You should know how to take a temperature and a pulse rate. As a general rule the pulse increases about 20 beats per minute for each °C rise in fever.

Respiration (breathing) rate is also an indicator of illness. Count the number of breaths per minute: between 12 and 20 is normal for adults and older children (up to 30 for younger children, 40 for babies). People with a high fever or serious respiratory illness (like pneumonia) breathe more quickly than normal. More than 40 shallow breaths a minute usually means pneumonia.

In Western countries with safe water and excellent human waste disposal systems we often take good health for granted. In years gone by, when public health facilities were not as good as they are today, certain rules attached to eating and drinking were observed, like washing your hands before a meal. It is important for people travelling in areas of poor sanitation to be aware of this and adjust their own personal hygiene habits.

Clean your teeth with purified water rather than straight from the tap. Avoid climatic extremes: keep out of the sun when it's hot, dress warmly when it's cold. Avoid potential diseases by dressing sensibly. You can get worm infections through walking barefoot or dangerous coral cuts by walking over coral without shoes. You can avoid insect bites by covering bare skin when insects are around, by screening windows or beds or by using insect repellents. Seek local advice: if you're told the water is unsafe due to jellyfish, crocodiles or bilharzia, don't go in. In situations where there is no information, discretion is the better part of valour.

Medical Problems & Treatment

Potential medical problems can be broken down into several areas. First there are the climatic and geographical considerations – problems caused by extremes of temperature, altitude or motion. Then there are diseases and illnesses caused through poor environmental sanitation, insect bites or stings, and animal or human contact. Simple cuts, bites or scratches can also cause problems.

Self-diagnosis and treatment can be risky, so wherever possible seek qualified help. Although we do give treatment dosages in this section, they are for emergency use only. Medical advice should be sought where possible before administering any drugs.

An embassy or consulate can usually recommend a good place to go for such advice. So can five-star hotels, although they often recommend doctors with five-star prices. (This is when that medical insurance really comes in useful!) The ill-equipped village hospital may be cheap, but it is often better to pay for the best. In some places standards of medical attention are so low that for some ailments the best advice is to get on a plane and go somewhere else. You can usually find good medical facilities in Asia, especially in the major cities.

Climatic & Geographical Considerations

Sunburn In the tropics and at high altitude you can get sunburnt surprisingly quickly, even through cloud. Use a sunscreen and take extra care to cover areas which don't normally see sun – eg, your feet. A hat provides added protection, and you should also use zinc cream or some other barrier cream for your nose and lips. Calamine lotion is good for mild sunburn.

Prickly Heat Prickly heat is an itchy rash caused by excessive perspiration trapped under the skin. It usually strikes people who have just arrived in a hot climate and whose pores have not yet opened sufficiently to cope with greater sweating. Keeping cool but bathing often, using a mild talcum powder or even resorting to air-conditioning may help until you acclimatise.

Heat Exhaustion Dehydration or salt deficiency can cause heat exhaustion. Take time to acclimatise to high temperatures and make sure you get sufficient liquids. Salt deficiency is characterised by fatigue, lethargy, headaches, giddiness and muscle cramps and in this case salt tablets may help. Vomiting or diarrhoea can deplete your liquid and salt levels. Anhydrotic heat exhaustion, caused by an inability to sweat, is quite rare. Unlike the other forms of heat exhaustion it is likely to strike people who have been in a hot climate for some time, rather than newcomers.

Heat Stroke This serious, sometimes fatal, condition can occur if the body's heat-regulating mechanism breaks down and the body temperature rises to dangerous levels. Long, continuous periods of exposure to high temperatures can leave you vulnerable to heat stroke. You should avoid excessive alcohol or strenuous activity when you first arrive in a hot climate.

The symptoms are feeling unwell, not sweating very much or at all and a high body temperature (39°C to 41°C). Where sweating has ceased the skin becomes flushed and red. Severe, throbbing headaches and lack of coordination will also occur, and the sufferer may be confused or aggressive. Eventually the victim will become delirious or convulse. Hospitalisation is essential, but meanwhile get victims out of the sun, remove their clothing, cover them with a wet sheet or towel and then fan continuously.

Fungal Infections Hot weather fungal infections are most likely to occur on the scalp, between the toes or fingers (athlete's foot), in the groin (jock itch or crotch rot) and on the body (ringworm). You get ringworm (which is a fungal infection, not a worm) from infected animals or by walking on damp areas, like shower floors.

To prevent fungal infections wear loose, comfortable clothes, avoid artificial fibres, wash frequently and dry carefully. If you do get an infection, wash the infected area daily with a disinfectant or medicated soap and water, and rinse and dry well. Apply an antifungal powder like the widely available Tinaderm. Try to expose the infected area to air or sunlight as much as possible and wash all towels and underwear in hot water as well as changing them often.

Cold Too much cold is just as dangerous as too much heat, particularly if it leads to hypothermia. Sub-zero temperatures are rare in Asia, but if you are trekking at high altitudes be prepared. Expect it to get below 0°C on top of Mt Kinabalu, but it can be uncomfortably cold on lower peaks. In the north of the region – in the mountain areas of Vietnam and Laos, for example – temperatures do get down to freezing.

Altitude Sickness Acute Mountain Sickness or AMS occurs at high altitude and can be fatal. The lack of oxygen at high altitude affects most people to some extent.

It is very rare to contract AMS in South-East Asia, but you should be careful at Mt Kinabalu (4101 metres) and the peaks of Irian Jaya in Indonesia, such as Puncak Jaya, South-East Asia's highest peak at 5030 metres. There is no hard and fast rule as to how high is too high: AMS has been fatal at altitudes of 3000 metres, although 3500 to 4500 metres is the usual range. It is always wise to sleep at a lower altitude than the greatest height reached during the day, and generally acclimatise as much as you can.

To prevent acute mountain sickness, you should ascend slowly, have frequent rest days and drink extra fluids. Eat light, high-carbohydrate meals for more energy, and avoid alcohol and sedatives.

Motion Sickness Eating lightly before and during a trip will reduce the chances of motion sickness. If you are prone to motion sickness try to find a place that minimises disturbance – near the wing on aircraft, close to midships on boats, near the centre on buses. Fresh air usually helps, reading or cigarette smoke doesn't. Commercial anti-motion-sickness preparations, which can cause drowsiness, have to be taken before the trip commences; when you're feeling sick it's too late. Ginger is a natural preventative and is available in capsule form.

Diseases of Poor Sanitation

Diarrhoea A change of water, food or climate can all cause the runs; diarrhoea caused by contaminated food or water is more serious. Despite all your precautions you may still have a bout of mild travellers' diarrhoea but a few rushed toilet trips with no other symptoms is not indicative of a serious problem. Moderate diarrhoea, involving half-a-dozen loose movements in a day, is more of a nuisance. Dehydration is the main danger with any diarrhoea, particularly for children where dehydration can occur quite quickly. Fluid replacement remains the mainstay of management. Weak black tea with a little sugar, soda water, or soft drinks allowed to go flat and diluted 50% with water are all good. With severe diarrhoea a rehydrating solution is necessary to replace minerals and salts. Commercially available ORS (oral rehydration salts) is very useful; add the contents of one sachet to a litre of boiled or bottled water. In an emergency you can make up a solution of eight teaspoons of sugar to a litre of boiled water and provide salted cracker biscuits at the same time. You should stick to a bland diet as you recover.

Lomotil or Imodium can be used to bring relief from the symptoms, although they do not actually cure the problem. Only use these drugs if absolutely necessary – eg, if you *must* travel. For children Imodium is preferable, but under all circumstances fluid replacement is the main message. Do not use these drugs if the person has a high fever or is severely dehydrated.

In certain situations, a need for antibiotics may be indicated:

- Watery diarrhoea with blood and mucus. (Gut-paralysing drugs like Imodium or Lomotil should be avoided in this situation.)
- Watery diarrhoea with fever and lethargy.
- Persistent diarrhoea for more than five days.
- Severe diarrhoea (Use antibiotics if it is logistically difficult to stay in one place.)

The recommended drugs (adults only) would be either norfloxacin (400mg twice daily for three days) or ciprofloxacin (500mg twice daily for three days).

The drug bismuth subsalicylate has also been used successfully. It is not available in Australia. The dosage for adults is two tablets or 30mls and for children it is one tablet or 10mls. This dose can be repeated every 30 minutes to one hour, with no more than eight doses in a 24-hour period.

The drug of choice in children would be co-trimoxazole (Bactrim, Septrin, Resprim) with dosage dependent on weight. A three-day course is also given.

Ampicillin has been recommended in the past and may still be an alternative.

Giardiasis The parasite causing this intestinal disorder is present in contaminated water. The symptoms are stomach cramps, nausea, a bloated stomach, watery, foul-smelling diarrhoea and frequent gas. Giardiasis can appear several weeks after you have been exposed to the parasite. The symptoms may disappear for a few days and then return; this can go on for several weeks. Tinidazole, known as Fasigyn, or metronidazole (Flagyl) are the recommended drugs for treatment. Either can be used in a single treatment dose. Antibiotics are of no use.

Dysentery This serious illness is caused by contaminated food or water and is characterised by severe diarrhoea, often with blood or mucus in the stool. There are two kinds of dysentery. Bacillary dysentery is characterised by a high fever and rapid onset; headache, vomiting and stomach pains are also symptoms. It generally does not last longer than a week, but it is highly contagious.

Amoebic dysentery is often more gradual in the onset of symptoms, with cramping abdominal pain and vomiting less likely; fever may not be present. It is not a self-limiting disease: it will persist until treated and can recur and cause long-term health problems.

A stool test is necessary to diagnose which kind of dysentery you have, so you should seek medical help urgently. In case of an emergency the drugs norfloxacin or ciprofloxacin can be used as presumptive treatment for bacillary dysentery, and metronidazole (Flagyl) for amoebic dysentery.

For bacillary dysentery, 400mg of norfloxacin twice daily for seven days or 500mg of ciprofloxacin twice daily for seven days are the recommended dosages.

If you're unable to find either of these drugs then a useful alternative is co-trimoxazole 160/800mg (Bactrim, Septrin, Resprim) twice daily for seven days. This is a sulfa drug and must not be used in people with a known sulfa allergy.

In the case of children the drug co-trimoxazole is a reasonable first-line treatment.

For amoebic dysentery, the recommended adult dosage of metronidazole (Flagyl) is one 750mg to 800mg capsule three times daily for five days. Children aged between eight and 12 years should have half the adult dose; the dosage for younger children is one-third the adult dose.

An alternative to Flagyl is Fasigyn, taken as a two-gram daily dose for three days. Alcohol must be avoided during treatment and for 48 hours afterwards.

Cholera Cholera vaccination is not very effective. The bacteria responsible for this disease are waterborne, so that attention to the rules of eating and drinking should protect the traveller.

Outbreaks of cholera are generally widely reported, so you can avoid such problem areas. The disease is characterised by a sudden onset of acute diarrhoea with 'rice water' stools, vomiting, muscular cramps, and extreme weakness. You need medical help – treat for dehydration, which can be extreme, and if there is an appreciable delay in getting to hospital it will be necessary to begin taking tetracycline. The adult dose is 250mg four times daily. It is not recommended in children aged eight years or under nor in pregnant women. An alternative drug would be Ampicillin. Remember that while antibiotics might kill the bacteria, it is a toxin produced by the bacteria which causes the massive fluid loss. Fluid replacement is by far the most important aspect of treatment.

Viral Gastroenteritis This is caused not by bacteria but, as the name suggests, by a virus. It is characterised by stomach cramps, diarrhoea, and sometimes by vomiting and/or a slight fever. All you can do is rest and drink lots of fluids.

Hepatitis Hepatitis A is a very common problem amongst travellers to areas with poor sanitation. With good water and adequate sewage disposal in most industrialised countries since the 1940s, very few young adults now have any natural immunity and must be protected. Protection is through the new vaccine Havrix or the antibody gammaglobulin. The antibody is short-lasting.

The disease is spread by contaminated food or water. The symptoms are fever, chills, headache, fatigue, feelings of weakness and aches and pains, followed by loss of appetite, nausea, vomiting, abdominal pain, dark urine, light coloured faeces and jaundiced skin; the whites of the eyes may also turn yellow. You should seek medical advice, but in general there is not much you can do apart from rest, drink lots of fluids, eat lightly and avoid fatty foods. People who have had hepatitis must forego alcohol for six months after the illness, as hepatitis attacks the liver and it needs that amount of time to recover.

Hepatitis B, which used to be called serum hepatitis, is spread through contact with infected blood, blood products or bodily fluids - for example, through sexual contact, unsterilised needles and blood transfusions. Other risk situations include having a shave or tattoo in a local shop, or having your ears pierced. The symptoms of type B are much the same as type A except that they are more severe and may lead to irreparable liver damage or even liver cancer.

Although there is no treatment for hepatitis B, an effective prophylactic vaccine is readily available in most countries. The immunisation schedule requires two injections at least a month apart followed by a third dose five months after the second. Persons who should receive a hepatitis B vaccination include anyone who anticipates contact with blood or other bodily secretions, either as a health care worker or through sexual contact with the local population, particularly those who intend to stay in the country for a long period of time.

Hepatitis Non-A Non-B is a blanket term formerly used for several different strains of hepatitis, which have now been separately identified. Hepatitis C is similar to B less common. Hepatitis D (the ' particle') is also similar to B and alv occurs in concert with it; its occurrence currently limited to IV drug users. Hepatit E, however, is similar to A and is spread ir the same manner, by water or food contamination.

Tests are available for these strands, but are very expensive. Travellers shouldn't be too paranoid about this apparent proliferation of hepatitis strains; they are fairly rare (so far) and following the same precautions as for A and B should be all that's necessary to avoid them.

Typhoid Typhoid fever is another gut infection that travels the faecal-oral route – ie, contaminated water and food are responsible. Vaccination against typhoid is not totally effective and typhoid is one of the most dangerous infections, so medical help must be sought.

In its early stages typhoid resembles many other illnesses: sufferers may feel like they have a bad cold or flu on the way, as early symptoms are a headache, a sore throat, and a fever which rises a little each day until it is around 40°C or more. The victim's pulse is often slow relative to the degree of fever present and gets slower as the fever rises – unlike a normal fever where the pulse increases. There may also be vomiting, diarrhoea or constipation.

In the second week the high fever and slow pulse continue and a few pink spots may appear on the body; trembling, delirium, weakness, weight loss and dehydration are other symptoms. If there are no further complications, the fever and other symptoms will slowly go during the third week. However you must get medical help before this because pneumonia (acute infection of the lungs) or peritonitis (perforated bowel) are common complications, and because typhoid is very infectious.

The fever should be treated by keeping the victim cool and dehydration should also be watched for.

The drug of choice is ciprofloxacin at a

…one gram daily for 14 days. It is quite …nsive and may not be available. The …native, chloramphenicol, has been the …instay of treatment for many years. In …any countries it is still the recommended antibiotic but there are fewer side effects with Ampicillin. The adult dosage is two 250mg capsules, four times a day. Children aged between eight and 12 years should have half the adult dose; younger children should have one-third the adult dose.

People who are allergic to penicillin should not be given Ampicillin.

Worms These parasites are most common in rural, tropical areas and a stool test when you return home is not a bad idea. They can be present on unwashed vegetables or in undercooked meat and you can pick them up through your skin by walking in bare feet. Infestations may not show up for some time, and although they are generally not serious, if left untreated they can cause severe health problems. A stool test is necessary to pinpoint the problem and medication is often available over the counter.

Diseases Spread by People & Animals

Tetanus This potentially fatal disease is found in undeveloped tropical areas. It is difficult to treat but is preventable with immunisation. Tetanus occurs when a wound becomes infected by a germ which lives in the faeces of animals or people, so clean all cuts, punctures or animal bites. Tetanus is also known as lockjaw, and the first symptom may be discomfort in swallowing, or stiffening of the jaw and neck; this is followed by painful convulsions of the jaw and whole body.

Rabies Rabies is found in many countries and is caused by a bite or scratch by an infected animal. Dogs are noted carriers, as are monkeys and cats. Any bite, scratch or even lick from a warm-blooded, furry animal should be cleaned immediately and thoroughly. Scrub with soap and running water, and then clean with an alcohol solution. If there is any possibility that the animal is infected medical help should be sought immediately. Even if the animal is not rabid, all bites should be treated seriously as they can become infected or can result in tetanus. A rabies vaccination is now available and should be considered if you are in a high-risk category – eg, if you intend to explore caves (bat bites could be dangerous) or work with animals.

Meningococcal Meningitis This very serious disease attacks the brain and can be fatal – recurring epidemics have occurred in Vietnam. A scattered, blotchy rash, fever, severe headache, sensitivity to light and neck stiffness which prevents forward bending of the head are the first symptoms. Death can occur within a few hours, so immediate treatment is important.

Treatment is large doses of penicillin given intravenously, or, if that is not possible, intramuscularly (ie, in the buttocks). Vaccination offers good protection for over a year, but you should also check for reports of current epidemics.

Tuberculosis (TB) Although this disease is widespread in many developing countries, it is not a serious risk to travellers. Young children are more susceptible than adults and vaccination is a sensible precaution for children under 12 travelling in areas where the disease is endemic. TB is commonly spread by coughing or by unpasteurised dairy products from infected cows. Milk that has been boiled is safe to drink; the souring of milk to make yoghurt or cheese also kills the bacilli.

Diptheria Diptheria can be a skin infection or a more dangerous throat infection. It is spread by contaminated dust contacting the skin or by the inhalation of infected cough or sneeze droplets. Frequent washing and keeping the skin dry will help prevent skin infection. A vaccination is available to prevent the throat infection.

Sexually Transmitted Diseases Sexual contact with an infected sexual partner spreads these diseases. While abstinence is the only 100% preventative, using condoms is also effective. Gonorrhoea and syphilis are the most common of these diseases; sores, blisters or rashes around the genitals, and discharges or pain when urinating are common symptoms. Symptoms may be less marked or not observed at all in women. Syphilis symptoms eventually disappear completely but the disease continues and can cause severe problems in later years. The treatment of gonorrhoea and syphilis is by antibiotics.

There are numerous other sexually transmitted diseases, for most of which effective treatment is available. However, there is no cure for herpes and there is also currently no cure for AIDS.

HIV/AIDS HIV, the Human Immunodeficiency Virus, may develop into AIDS, Acquired Immune Deficiency Syndrome. HIV is a problem in countries like Thailand and the Philippines, and head-in-the-sand attitudes from some South-East Asian countries help make it a growing problem throughout the region. In these countries transmission is predominantly through heterosexual sexual activity, primarily in the sex industry. The second highest risk group is IV drug users. Any exposure to blood, blood products or bodily fluids may put the individual at risk. Apart from abstinence, the most effective preventative is always to practice safe sex using condoms. It is impossible to detect the HIV-positive status of an otherwise healthy-looking person without a blood test.

HIV/AIDS can also be spread through infected blood transfusions and dirty needles – they are as dangerous as intravenous drug use if the equipment is not clean. If you do need an injection, it may be a good idea to buy a new syringe from a pharmacy and ask the doctor to use it. You may also want to take a couple of syringes with you, in case of emergency.

Do not let the fear of contracting HIV/AIDS through blood transfusions or inappropriate medical practices stop you from seeking medical advice. The risk is very small, and many good facilities are found throughout the region. Some countries, such as Thailand, have extensive blood-screening programs.

Insect-Borne Diseases

Malaria This serious disease is spread by mosquito bites. Malaria is endemic throughout South-East Asia and it is extremely important to take malarial prophylactics. Parts of the region are low risk – malaria is virtually unheard of in Singapore, Hong Kong, Peninsular Malaysia and many of the major cities – but there are malarial areas throughout South-East Asia, including the remote parts of East Malaysia, Thailand, the Philippines, and much of Indochina and Indonesia. In South-East Asia, Irian Jaya is the most dangerous area. Anyone contemplating an extensive trip in South-East Asia should seek medical advice on the appropriate antimalarials to take. Antimalarial drugs do not prevent you from being infected but kill the parasites during a stage in their development.

Symptoms include headaches, fever, chills and sweating which may subside and recur. In its initial stages malaria can resemble nothing more than flu, and is then followed by the more severe symptoms of chills, high fever, and possibly vomiting and delirium. Without treatment malaria can develop more serious, potentially fatal effects. If you think you have malaria, seek treatment immediately. Major hospitals in Asia can provide good quality care and have expertise in dealing with malaria. Almost all deaths from malaria are a result of delay in diagnosis.

There are a number of different types of malaria. The one of most concern is falciparum malaria. This is responsible for the very serious cerebral malaria. Falciparum is the predominant form in many malaria-prone areas of the world, including parts of South-East Asia. Contrary to popular belief cerebral malaria is not a new strain.

The problem in recent years has been the emergence of increasing resistance to commonly used antimalarials like chloroquine, maloprim and proguanil. Newer drugs such as mefloquine (Lariam) and doxycycline (Vibramycin, Doryx) are now recommended for chloroquine and multidrug-resistant areas. Doxycycline is taken once a day and Lariam once a week. Lariam is now the main drug for treatment of malaria. Expert advice should be sought on antimalarials. Try to consult a doctor with expertise in tropical diseases – they should be able to inform you about high risk and resistent areas, and appropriate antimalarials for these areas and for the individual (eg, some antimalarials have been known to produce side effects, and some are inappropriate for pregnant women or for long-term use).

The main messages are:

- Primary prevention must always be in the form of mosquito avoidance measures. The mosquitos that transmit malaria bite from dusk to dawn and during this period travellers are advised to:
  *wear light coloured clothing
  *wear long pants and long sleeved shirts
  *use mosquito repellents containing the compound DEET on exposed areas
  *avoid highly scented perfumes or aftershave
  * use a mosquito net – it may be worth taking your own.
- While no antimalarial is 100% effective, taking the most appropriate drug significantly reduces the risk of contracting the disease.
- No one should ever die from malaria. It can be diagnosed by a simple blood test, so a traveller with a fever or flu-like illness should seek examination as soon as possible.

Contrary to popular belief, once a traveller contracts malaria he/she does not have it for life. One of the parasites may lie dormant in the liver but this can also be eradicated using a specific medication. Malaria is therefore curable, as long as the traveller seeks medical help when symptoms occur, either at home or overseas.

Dengue Fever There is no prophylactic available for this mosquito-spread disease; the main preventative measure is to avoid mosquito bites. A sudden onset of fever, headaches and severe joint and muscle pains are the first signs before a rash starts on the trunk of the body and spreads to the limbs and face. After a further few days, the fever will subside and recovery will begin. Serious complications are not common.

Typhus Typhus is spread by ticks, mites or lice. It begins as a bad cold, followed by a fever, chills, headache, muscle pains and a body rash. There is often a large painful sore at the site of the bite and nearby lymph nodes are swollen and painful.

Tick typhus is spread by ticks. Scrub typhus is spread by mites that feed on infected rodents and exists mainly in Asia and the Pacific Islands. You should take precautions if walking in rural areas in South-East Asia. Seek local advice on areas where ticks pose a danger and always check your skin carefully for ticks after walking in a danger area, such as a tropical forest. A strong insect repellent can help, and serious walkers in tick areas should consider having their boots and trousers impregnated with benzyl benzoate and dibutylphthalate.

Cuts, Bites & Stings

Cuts & Scratches Skin punctures can easily become infected in hot climates and may be difficult to heal. Treat any cut with an antiseptic such as Betadine. Where possible avoid bandages and Band-aids, which can keep wounds wet. Coral cuts are notoriously slow to heal, as the coral injects a weak venom into the wound. Avoid coral cuts by wearing shoes when walking on reefs, and clean any cut thoroughly with sodium peroxide if available.

Bites & Stings Bee and wasp stings are usually painful rather than dangerous. Calamine lotion will give relief or ice packs will reduce the pain and swelling. There are some spiders with dangerous bites but antivenenes are usually available. There are various fish and other sea creatures which can sting or bite dangerously or which are dangerous to eat. Again, local advice is the best suggestion.

Snakes To minimise your chances of being bitten always wear boots, socks and long trousers when walking through undergrowth where snakes may be present. Don't put your hands into holes and crevices, and be careful when collecting firewood.

Snake bites do not cause instantaneous death and antivenenes are usually available. Keep the victim calm and still, wrap the bitten limb tightly, as you would for a sprained ankle, and then attach a splint to immobilise it. Then seek medical help, if possible with the dead snake for identification. Don't attempt to catch the snake if there is even a remote possibility of being bitten again. Tourniquets and sucking out the poison are now comprehensively discredited.

Jellyfish Local advice is the best way of avoiding contact with these sea creatures with their stinging tentacles. The box jellyfish is found mostly in inshore waters around Australia, but is occasionally found in Borneo. It is potentially fatal, but stings from most jellyfish are simply rather painful. Dousing in vinegar will deactivate any stingers which have not 'fired'. Calamine lotion, antihistamines and analgesics may reduce the reaction and relieve the pain.

Bedbugs & Lice Bedbugs live in various places, but particularly in dirty mattresses and bedding. Spots of blood on bedclothes or on the wall around the bed can be read as a suggestion to find another hotel. Bedbugs leave itchy bites in neat rows. Calamine lotion may help.

All lice cause itching and discomfort. They make themselves at home in your hair (head lice), your clothing (body lice) or in your pubic hair (crabs). You catch lice through direct contact with infected people or by sharing combs, clothing and the like. Powder or shampoo treatment will kill the lice and infected clothing should then be washed in very hot water.

Leeches & Ticks Leeches may be present in damp rainforest conditions; they attach themselves to your skin to suck your blood. Trekkers often get them on their legs or in their boots. Salt or a lighted cigarette end will make them fall off. Do not pull them off, as the bite is then more likely to become infected. An insect repellent may keep them away. Vaseline, alcohol or oil will persuade a tick to let go. You should always check your body if you have been walking through a tick-infested area, as they can spread typhus. Leech socks are a worthwhile investment for those contemplating a lot of jungle trekking.

Women's Health

Gynaecological Problems Poor diet, lowered resistance due to the use of antibiotics for stomach upsets and even contraceptive pills can lead to vaginal infections when travelling in hot climates. Keeping the genital area clean, and wearing skirts or loose-fitting trousers and cotton underwear will help to prevent infections.

Yeast infections, characterised by a rash, itch and discharge, can be treated with a vinegar or even lemon-juice douche or with yoghurt. Nystatin suppositories are the usual medical prescription. Trichomonas is a more serious infection; symptoms are a discharge and a burning sensation when urinating. Male sexual partners must also be treated, and if a vinegar-water douche is not effective medical attention should be sought. Metronidazole (Flagyl) is the prescribed drug.

Pregnancy Most miscarriages occur during the first three months of pregnancy, so this is the most risky time to travel as far as your own health is concerned. Miscarriage is not uncommon, and can occasionally lead to severe bleeding. The last three months should also be spent within reasonable distance of good medical care. A baby born as early as 24 weeks stands a chance of survival, but only in a good modern hospital. Pregnant women should avoid all unnecessary medication, but vaccinations and malarial prophylactics should still be taken where possible. Additional care should be taken to prevent illness and particular attention should be paid to diet and nutrition.

Alcohol and nicotine, for example, should be avoided.

Women travellers often find that their periods become irregular or even cease while they're on the road. Remember that a missed period in these circumstances doesn't necessarily indicate pregnancy. There are health posts or Family Planning clinics in many small and large urban centres in developing countries, where you can seek advice and have a urine test to determine whether you are pregnant or not.

WOMEN TRAVELLERS

South-East Asia is generally a fairly straightforward region for women to travel in. In some places, the time honoured fixation that Western women are more easy-going (or of easy virtue) still exists but many parts of South-East Asia have really moved on from mere developing status to fully fledged developed, and people's ideas have also become more sophisticated.

Nevertheless, there are some places where a little extra care is needed and women should take precautions. South-East Asia does not have any really fundamentalist Muslim regions, so Muslim attitudes towards women do not present a major problem. Nevertheless, women travellers do experience more difficulty in Sumatra, along the east coast of Malaysia and in the southern Philippines so extra care should be taken there. Respectful dressing is certainly necessary – beachwear should be reserved for the beach and basically the less skin you expose the better. South-East Asia is not the sort of place where veils are required, however.

Attitude can be as important as what you wear. Never respond to come ons or rude comments. Completely ignoring them is always best. A haughty attitude can work wonders!

Of course, a husband (which equals any male partner) or children also confers respectability but the husband doesn't have to be present. Some women travellers wear a wedding ring simply for the aura it confers. The imaginary husband doesn't even have to be left at home – who is to say you're not meeting him that very day?

Some precautions are simply the same for any traveller, male or female, but women should take extra care not to find themselves alone on empty beaches, down dark streets or in other situations where help might not be available.

Look upon any holes in the walls of cheap hotels with deep suspicion, especially in showers. In some parts of the region, cheap hotels often double as brothels. If you find yourself in one of these, turning the haughty attitude up a notch may help but as often as not it's no problem; some people may be there because it's a brothel, but it's recognised that you're there because it's a cheap hotel. Nevertheless, you should take care, especially at night, and if you're uncomfortable move to another hotel.

Solo women travellers, just like solo male ones, should be wary when strangers are unexpectedly friendly. See the note in the following Dangers & Annoyances section about theft.

Tampons and other such necessities are reasonably widely available in the region. If you're worried that you won't be able to find something while you're in the back blocks of Borneo for a month, then stock up in a place like Singapore before you start out.

DANGERS & ANNOYANCES

Theft

I've made several trips through South-East Asia and not lost a thing – and one trip where every time I turned round something went missing. Theft is a problem but it's probably no more endemic than in Western countries. As a traveller, however, you're often fairly vulnerable and when you do lose things it can be a real hassle. Most important things to guard are your passport, papers, tickets and money. It's best to always carry these next to your skin or in a sturdy leather pouch on your belt.

You can further lessen the risks by being careful of snatch thieves in certain cities. Cameras or shoulder bags are great for these people. Be careful on buses and trains and even in hotels. Don't leave valuables lying around in your room. A very useful antitheft item is a small padlock – you can use it to double lock your room (there's often a latch for this purpose) or to tie your bag down to a train luggage rack.

A few years back there were a spate of druggings, particularly in Thailand. A solo traveller would be befriended by a local who would buy them a tea or coffee; a day later the unfortunate traveller wakes up with a splitting headache and with all their possessions gone. Food or drink on buses can also be risky – one traveller wrote of being drugged and robbed on a long-distance tour bus in Thailand! This particular technique seems to have moved on from South-East Asia to the subcontinent these days but be wary of sudden friendships. Also be wary of your fellow travellers as not all of them are scrupulously honest.

There are a variety of other ways of losing things apart from straightforward theft. Over the years, we've had letters from unfortunate travellers who have been the victims of just about every scam imaginable.

Two favourites have been airline-ticket rackets and buy-here, sell-there operations. Often people lose money on these deals through sheer stupidity.

Ask yourself, would you give somebody whose 'office' is a table in a coffee bar US$1000 to get you an airline ticket? Will they be there again tomorrow? And before you lay out large amounts of money for amazing gemstones (or some other high-value item) which you are assured you can sell at a huge profit back home, just ask yourself, 'If this is so easy why doesn't everybody do it?' Gambling rackets, 'losing' travellers' cheques, guaranteeing loans, they're all scams which unfortunate or foolish travellers have lost their shirts on.

Drugs

Always treat drugs with a great deal of caution. There is, of course, lots of dope available in the region but these days even a little harmless grass can cause a great deal of trouble. Also, as soon as you start messing with heavier stuff or trying to export it they'll land on top of you. There are a hell of a lot of travellers languishing behind bars and more have found themselves inside looking out after they've tried to bring stuff back home with them. Don't.

The days of paying off a few cops and then making a speedy exit from the country have pretty much disappeared. Even easy-going Bali now has a jail just down the road from Kuta Beach where a number of travellers are spending much longer enjoying the tropical climate than at first intended. In Indonesia, you can actually end up behind bars because your travel companion had dope and you didn't report them.

Other places can be a whole lot worse. A spell in a Thai prison is nobody's idea of a pleasant way to pass the time, while in Malaysia and Singapore, a prison spell may be supplemented with a beating with the *rotan*. In those countries, simple possession can have you dangling from a rope, as two Australians discovered in 1986. On a per capita basis, the Malaysians execute far more people for drug-related offences (and with far less publicity) than the Americans do for murder.

Don't bother bringing drugs home with you either. Back home in the West you may not get hung for possession but with the stamps you'll have on your passport you're guaranteed to be a subject of suspicion. I would have thought I had a fairly good reason for spending some time kicking around odd places, but for a couple of years every time I arrived home in Melbourne the customs guys always seemed glad to see me, to usher me off to a private room and to go through everything with a fine tooth comb.

ACTIVITIES

Diving & Snorkelling

South-East Asia is an underwater paradise and presents countless opportunities for diving and snorkelling. Indonesia, Malaysia and Thailand have the best facilities, and many easily accessible reefs, but the Philippines and even Vietnam also have some diving spots.

Many beach resorts rent out masks, snorkels and fins, so the many coral reefs are easy to explore, and require little outlay for novices. If you intend to do a lot of snorkelling, then it is worth bringing your own equipment. Rental gear is not always of good quality, and it soon becomes more economical to buy rather than rent. You don't have to hire boats or venture to far-flung islands to find some good snorkelling – Lovina Beach (Bali) and the Gili Islands (Lombok) in Indonesia, Perhentian and Tioman Islands on Malaysia's east coast, and Ko Pha-Ngan in Thailand are all popular beach resorts with easily accessible snorkelling.

Diving is generally cheap in South-East Asia and there are some very good operators around, but it isn't always the best place to get a diving certificate. Fewer operators are qualified to offer diving courses, and those that do are not always of the highest standards. It is usually better to get a certificate before arriving - eg, diving courses in Cairns, Australia, are often of high quality and cheaper than in South-East Asia.

Indonesia has extensive opportunities for diving. Bali, as the main tourist area, has a good supply of operators and some excellent dives. Between Komodo and Labuhanbajo in Flores are countless small islands and reefs. Maumere (Flores), Kupang (West Timor), Ambon and the Banda Islands (Maluku) all have good diving, while the 'sea gardens' of Sulawesi are legendary, particularly around Manado.

Malaysia has some diving on the west coast of the peninsula, but the east coast has better diving. The islands of Tioman, Kapas, Redang and the Perhentians are just some of the possibilities. Some of the best diving in Malaysia is found in Borneo. Sabah, in particular, has excellent diving and very professional dive outfits. Sipadan Island and its amazing wall is the most famous (and expensive) dive site.

In Thailand, Pattaya is crammed with dive shops and is popular because of its easy access and proximity to Bangkok. Phuket is the next most popular, and presents the best diving opportunities with plenty of nearby islands, including Ao Phang-Nga and the world famous Similan and Surin islands out in the Andaman Sea. Chumpon Province, just north of Surat Thani, has a dozen or so islands with undisturbed reefs.

Unfortunately many of the coral reefs in South-East Asia are under threat. Dynamite fishing has been a major culprit. Explosives are dropped into the water, stunning the fish, and then it is an easy matter to scoop up the catch from the surface. In the process the delicate coral is devastated. Other threats to coral reefs are silting caused by deforestation, overdevelopment in tourist areas and coral harvesting (live coral for boardroom fish tanks can bring big money). Moves are afoot to establish marine parks throughout the region, but it may be a case of too little too late.

Surfing

Indonesia is the big surfing destination in Asia, and for years surfers have been carting their boards to isolated outposts of the archipelago in search of long, deserted waves. Ulu Watu in Bali, Grajagan in Java and Nias in Sumatra are famous surfing destinations, but there is surf right along the southern coast of the inner islands from Sumatra through to Sumbawa, Sumba and across to Irian Jaya.

It is probably only a matter of time before new areas are opened up to surfing. Perhaps the famous surfing scene from *Apocalypse Now* will inspire a new invasion of Vietnam.

Trekking

Trekking in South-East Asia doesn't take on the same proportions as in Nepal, but there are plenty of good treks possible, particularly jungle hikes. Most visitors at least hike up a mountain or volcano somewhere in their travels – this inevitably involves a shivering, predawn climb to catch the sunrise.

Trekking in the hill tribe regions of Thailand features on many travellers' itineraries. It's no longer a unique experience, but despite mass tourism, many still find it rewarding. Shop around in Chiang Mai for a trek. Most last from three to seven days and may include rafting and elephant rides. Treks can also be organised in Chiang Rai, Mae Hong Son, and other northern centres.

One of Malaysia's highlights is its national parks, and Taman Negara National Park has some excellent walks. Some good treks can also be organised in East Malaysia, particularly in Sarawak at Gunung Mulu and around Bario for the more adventurous. No trip to Sabah is complete without visiting the towering summit of Mt Kinabalu, a relatively easy two-day climb.

In Indonesia, Sumatra has some good jungle treks, particularly in Gunung Leuser National Park, and it is easy to organise treks in Berastagi or Bukit Lawang. Java has some good walks in the national parks, but is more noted for its volcanic peaks. Mt Merapi can be a taxing climb, while spectacular Mt Bromo is more of a stroll. On Bali, Batur and Agung volcanos are popular day trips, or for an excellent three-day hike, go and try Gunung Rinjani on neighbouring Lombok. Indonesia's outer islands also have plenty of more adventurous jungle trekking opportunities, particularly Irian Jaya and Kalimantan.

In the Philippines, Mt Mayon is a 'must climb', but recent eruptions make it more difficult, as is also the case with Mt Pinatubo, another very active volcano. You can arrange walks around Banaue in North Luzon and Quezon National Park.

In Vietnam, Tam Dao has some of the best walks.

Wildlife

Ecotourism is catching on in South-East Asia – animals are becoming more profitable alive. Still, South-East Asia's national parks are not all that well developed, and there is nothing like the game parks of Africa. The variety of fauna is astonishing, but not all that easy to see.

Thailand has the most extensive national park network, but accommodation and facilities are limited. At the same time, they are relatively untouristic and if you have plenty of time and patience, they present good opportunities for exploring the countryside and seeking out wildlife.

Malaysia, with its excellent national parks, probably has the best set up in South-East Asia for observing wildlife. Taman Negara National Park has a system of hides to view the animals, and over in Borneo the Kinabatangan River and Danum Valley in Sabah are rich in wildlife.

Borneo is also home to all-but-one of the world's orang-utan rehabilitation centres (the other is in Sumatra). In Sabah, the Sepilok centre is very well organised, but also becoming very touristy, while the Semenggok centre in Sarawak is not as well organised and probably not tourist-oriented enough. In Central Kalimantan (Indonesian Borneo), Camp Leakey is one of the best places to see orang-utans but less accessible. Easiest to reach, and in a beautiful setting with plenty of budget accommodation, the Bohorok centre at Bukit Lawang in North Sumatra is the most popular.

Indonesia's best and most accessible national parks for wildlife are Gunung Leuser and Kerinci Seblat in Sumatra, Ujung Kulon and Baluran in Java, and of course there are those infamous 'dragons' on Komodo and nearby Rinca. Bali also has a national park in the west and Sulawesi's Lore Lindu park is rich in flora and fauna.

In the Philippines, Quezon National Park in South Luzon and the Mt Ilig-Mt Baco National Wildlife Sanctuary in Mindoro are worth a visit. Mt Kanlaon National Park on Negros is a major refuge for wildlife in the central Philippines, but visitor facilities are limited.

ACCOMMODATION

In most of South-East Asia, accommodation is no problem. About the only time you might have difficulty is over Chinese New Year, when finding a room can be a hassle in some places. Also, peak holiday periods like Christmas, when there is a mass exodus from Australia, can be a problem.

In Indonesia, cheap hotels are usually known as *losmen* – they're small, often family-run places. Elsewhere cheap hotels are often Chinese run – they're spartan, noisy, but in general clean and well kept.

Costs are variable, but in most of the region you can get a reasonable room for two from around US$5 to US$15 – it's more expensive in some of the big cities and sometimes less in remote areas.

If you arrive in a country by air, there is often an airport hotel booking desk, although they often do not cover the lower strata of hotels. Some airports (like Bangkok's) are better than others (like Singapore's) for this game. Otherwise, you'll generally find hotels clustered around the bus and train station areas – always good places to start hunting. Check your room and the bathroom before you agree to take it. If the sheets don't look clean, ask to have them changed right away.

If you think a hotel is too expensive, ask if they have anything cheaper. Often they may try to steer you into more expensive rooms, simply be trying it on a bit or even be open to a little bargaining. A very important point to remember in Chinese hotels is that a 'single' room usually has a double bed while a 'double' has two beds. A couple can always request a single room. Many cheaper hotels throughout the region only supply one sheet on the bed; if you want a top sheet (useful for keeping mosquitos away) you have to supply your own. I've been carrying the same Indonesian sarong around for this purpose for over 10 years now.

FOOD & DRINKS

Eat what you like when you want to would be my first advice. In general, food in South-East Asia is pretty healthy. A good rule of thumb is to glance at the restaurant or foodstall and its proprietor – if it looks clean and they look healthy then chances are the food will be OK too.

There are two main things to be careful about – water and fresh, uncooked food. Only in Singapore, Hong Kong and some other major cities can you drink water straight from the taps – elsewhere you should ensure that water is boiled or purified. It's no good avoiding the water if you then eat fruit or vegetables that have been washed in that unhealthy water. Ice can be a danger too as freezing things certainly doesn't kill all germs. Cooked food that has been allowed to go cold can also be dangerous.

In general, you should have few problems and, in places like Singapore, you can usually eat from street stalls with impunity. Of course, you'll also find Coke and other hygienically pure Western delights. McDonald's are spreading their tentacles through the region too and you'll find branches in Hong Kong, Macau, Malaysia, the Philippines, Singapore and Thailand. KFC have spread their influence even more widely.

Despite the pleasures of the local cuisine, some travellers feel there are benefits to be had by preparing their own food. This requires carrying cooking gear and a gas cooker (replacement cylinders are available in most places in the region) but you can save money this way and also eat well.

Fruit

South-East Asian travel can be a special taste treat when it comes to fruit. Apart from all those mundane bananas, pineapples and coconuts, there is a host of fruits that will do wonderful things for your taste buds. Fruit stalls are on hand all over the place to sell iced slices or segments of these fruits in season.

Durian – the most infamous fruit of the region, the durian is a large green fruit with a hard spiny exterior. Crack it open to reveal the biggest stink imaginable! Drains blocked up? No, it's just the durian season. If you can hold your nose you might actually learn to love them, although one traveller felt that I should come right out with it and admit that durians 'look like shit, smell like shit and taste like shit. On the other hand,' he went on, 'you can try durian in a milder form by having a durian ice cream – which also smells like shit and tastes like shit but looks like ice cream'. You can't satisfy everybody but as smelly as they are durians are reputed to be a phenomenal aphrodisiac!

Jeruk – the all-purpose term for citrus fruit. There are many kinds available including the huge *jeruk muntis* or *jerunga*, known in the West as a *pomelo*. It's larger than a grapefruit, has a very thick skin, but tastes sweeter, more like an orange.

Mangosteen – the small purple-brown mangosteen cracks open to reveal tasty white segments with a very fine flavour. Queen Victoria once offered a reward to anyone able to transport a mangosteen back to England while still edible.

Nangka – an enormous yellow-green fruit that can weigh over 20 kg. Inside are hundreds of individual bright yellow segments. Also called jackfruit, the taste is distinctive and the texture slightly rubbery.

Rambutan – a bright red fruit covered in soft, hairy spines, the name means Hairy. Break it open to reveal a delicious, white, lychee-like fruit inside.

Salak – found chiefly in Indonesia, the salak is immediately recognisable due to its brown 'snakeskin' covering. Peel the skin off to reveal segments that taste like a cross between an apple and a walnut. Bali salaks are much nicer than any others.

Starfruit – called belimbing in Indonesia and Malaysia, the name is obvious when you see a slice – it's star shaped. It has a cool, crispy, watery taste.

Zurzat – also spelt sirsak, also known in the West as soursop, a warty green skin covers a thirst-quenching interior with a slight lemonish taste. They are ripe when they feel squishy.

Other – the *sawo* looks like a potato and tastes like a pear. *Jambu* is pear shaped but has a radish-like crispy texture and a pink, shiny colour. *Papaya*, or *paw paw*, has a sweet, yellow pulp. Bananas are *pisang* and pineapples are *nanas* in Indonesia.

BUYING & SELLING

Making money out of selling things isn't what it used to be – in most cases, people can find pretty much everything you have and cheaper to boot. Obvious exceptions are places like Myanmar where almost everything has its demand and its price. Nor is there much opportunity for picking up casual work in the region. It is possible to teach English in Indonesia, but you have to get up to North-East Asia before you get into the lucrative 'English lessons' racket. In Hong Kong, for example, English teaching pays HK$50 an hour, but we've had warnings from people who have been ripped off by English-teaching schools.

Buying is a different game but don't get carried away with the idea of making your fortune with the goodies you bring back home with you. The people who buy art and handicrafts to profitably resell in the West are usually experts and the Asian clothes you see for sale in the West are usually brought in as a full-time business, not some one-off trip.

There are plenty of things you'll want to buy just for their own sake and it's worth having a few ground rules to follow. First of all, don't buy it unless you really want it. Secondly, outside of the odd 'fixed price' store, where prices are really fixed, the name of the game is bargaining. Food in markets, handicrafts, even transport are things you may have to bargain for. The secrets of successful bargaining are to make a game of it, to make a first offer that is sufficiently low to allow both buyer and seller room to manoeuvre (but not so low as to be laughable) and to be good humoured about it. Accept that you're simply going to have to end up paying more money than the locals, and remember that it's not a matter of life and death or personal honour!

FINAL THOUGHTS

It's people that make travel – seeing things may be great, doing things may be exciting, but it's the people who'll stay in your memory, so make the most of them. Go out of your way to meet people and get to know them. It's the only way you'll really get to know the countries you visit.

The same consideration applies to your fellow travellers. For perhaps obvious reasons, a cross-section of travellers seems to be a whole lot more interesting than a similar slice of the general population. Apart from making friends you'll run into time and again over the years, travel also provides a lot of immediate benefits through the friends you make. You rarely travel alone for long, it always seems that somebody else is going the same direction as you and you soon end up as part of a group heading to who knows where. Remember also, that your fellow travellers are the best source of information on what lies ahead.

Since the shoestring traveller seems to get a fair amount of flak from time to time, I'd better outline my philosophy of what he/she is not. They're not scroungers, or penniless layabouts, permanently high or rip-off merchants. If I had to define my belief in travel it's that if you've been some place and stayed in the local Hilton, you've probably not been there (sorry Conrad). Tourists stay in Hiltons, travellers don't.

The traveller wants to see the country at ground level, to breathe it, experience it – live it. This usually requires two things the tourist can't provide – more time and less money. If you're going to really travel, it's going to take longer and on a day-to-day basis cost less. So blend in, enjoy yourself, but most important of all, make it easy for the travellers who are going to follow in your footsteps.

Getting There & Away

Step one is to get to Asia and, in these days of severe competition between the airlines, there are plenty of opportunities to find cheap tickets to a variety of 'gateway' cities. You virtually have no choice apart from flying though – regular shipping services to South-East Asia are just about nonexistent and China-Vietnam is the only overland option.

AIR

The major Asian gateways for cheap flights are Singapore, Bangkok and Hong Kong. They are all good places to fly to and good places to fly from. Bangkok has long had a reputation as a bargain centre for cheap airline tickets, but first Singapore and then Penang (Malaysia) and Hong Kong joined the group.

Cheap tickets are available in two distinct categories – official and unofficial. Official ones are advance purchase tickets, budget-fares, Apex, super-Apex or whatever other brand name the airlines would care to tack on them in order to put, as it is so succinctly expressed, 'bums on seats'.

Unofficial tickets are simply discounted tickets which the airlines release through selected travel agents. Don't go looking for discounted tickets straight from the airlines. They are only available through travel agents. Generally, you can find discounted tickets at prices as low or lower than the Apex or budget tickets, plus there is no advance-purchase requirement nor should there be any cancellation penalty, although individual travel agents may institute their own cancellation charges.

It is necessary to exercise a little caution with discounted tickets. Make sure 'OK' on the ticket really means you have a confirmed seat, for example. Phone the airline and reconfirm again; it's better to find out immediately if the agent has made a firm booking.

Buying a Plane Ticket

Plane tickets will probably be the most expensive items in your budget, and buying them can be an intimidating business. There is likely to be a multitude of airlines and travel agents hoping to separate you from your money, and it is always worth putting aside a few hours to research the current state of the market.

Start early: some of the cheapest tickets have to be bought months in advance, and some popular flights sell out early. Talk to other recent travellers – they may be able to stop you making some of the same old mistakes. Look at the ads in newspapers and magazines (not forgetting the press of the ethnic group whose country you plan to visit), consult reference books and watch for special offers.

Then phone round travel agents for bargains. (Airlines can supply information on routes and timetables; however, except at times of inter-airline war they do not supply the cheapest tickets.) Find out the fare, the route, the duration of the journey and any restrictions on the ticket. (See Restrictions in the Air Travel Glossary in this chapter.) Then sit back and decide which is best for you.

You may discover that those impossibly cheap flights are 'fully booked, but we have another one that costs a bit more...' Or, the flight is on an airline notorious for its poor safety standards and leaves you in the world's least favourite airport in mid-journey for 14 hours. Or, they claim only to have the last two seats available for that country for the whole of July, which they will hold for you for a maximum of two hours. Don't panic – keep ringing around.

Use the fares quoted in this book as a guide only. They are approximate and based on the rates advertised by travel agents at the time of going to press. Quoted airfares do not necessarily constitute a recommendation for the carrier.

If you are travelling from the UK or USA,

you will probably find that the cheapest flights are being advertised by obscure bucket shops whose names haven't yet reached the telephone directory. Many such firms are honest and solvent, but there are a few rogues who will take your money and disappear, to reopen elsewhere a month or two later under a new name.

If you feel suspicious about a firm, don't give them all the money at once – leave a deposit of 20% or so and pay the balance when you get the ticket. If they insist on cash in advance, go somewhere else. And once you have the ticket, ring the airline to confirm that you are actually booked onto the flight.

You may decide to pay more than the rock-bottom fare by opting for the safety of

Air Travel Glossary

Apex Apex, or 'advance purchase excursion', is a discounted ticket which must be paid for in advance. There are penalties if you wish to change it.

Baggage Allowance This will be written on your ticket: usually one 20 kg item to go in the hold, plus one item of hand luggage.

Bucket Shop An unbonded travel agency specialising in discounted airline tickets.

Bumped Just because you have a confirmed seat doesn't mean you're going to get on the plane - see Overbooking.

Cancellation Penalties If you have to cancel or change an Apex ticket there are often heavy penalties involved; insurance can sometimes be taken out against these penalties. Some airlines impose penalties on regular tickets as well, particularly against 'no show' passengers.

Check In Airlines ask you to check in a certain time ahead of the flight departure (usually 1½ hours on international flights). If you fail to check in on time and the flight is overbooked the airline can cancel your booking and give your seat to somebody else.

Confirmation Having a ticket written out with the flight and date you want doesn't mean you have a seat until the agent has checked with the airline that your status is 'OK' or confirmed. Meanwhile you could just be 'on request'.

Discounted Tickets There are two types of discounted fares - officially discounted (see Promotional Fares) and unofficially discounted. The lowest prices often impose drawbacks like flying with unpopular airlines, inconvenient schedules, or unpleasant routes and connections. A discounted ticket can save you other things than money – you may be able to pay Apex prices without the associated Apex advance booking and other requirements. Discounted tickets only exist where there is fierce competition.

Full Fares Airlines traditionally offer first class (coded F), business class (coded J) and economy class (coded Y) tickets. These days there are so many promotional and discounted fares available from the regular economy class that few passengers pay full economy fare.

Lost Tickets If you lose your airline ticket an airline will usually treat it like a travellers' cheque and, after inquiries, issue you with another one. Legally, however, an airline is entitled to treat it like cash and if you lose it then it's gone forever. Take good care of your tickets.

No Shows No shows are passengers who fail to show up for their flight, sometimes due to unexpected delays or disasters, sometimes due to simply forgetting, sometimes because they made more than one booking and didn't bother to cancel the one they didn't want. Full fare passengers who fail to turn up are sometimes entitled to travel on a later flight. The rest of us are penalised (see Cancellation Penalties).

On Request An unconfirmed booking for a flight (see Confirmation).

a better known travel agent. Firms such as STA Travel, who have offices worldwide, Council Travel in the USA and Travel CUTS in Canada are not going to disappear overnight, leaving you clutching a receipt for a nonexistent ticket, and they offer good prices to most destinations.

Once you have your ticket, write its number down together with the flight number and other details, and keep this information somewhere separate and safe. If the ticket is lost or stolen, this will help you get a replacement.

It's sensible to buy travel insurance as early as possible. If you buy it the week before you fly, you may find, for example, that you're not covered for delays to your flight caused by industrial action.

Open Jaws A return ticket where you fly out to one place but return from another. If available this can save you backtracking to your arrival point.

Overbooking Airlines hate to fly empty seats and since every flight has some passengers who fail to show up (see No Shows) airlines often book more passengers than they have seats. Usually the excess passengers balance those who fail to show up but occasionally somebody gets bumped. If this happens guess who it is most likely to be? The passengers who check in late.

Promotional Fares Officially discounted fares like Apex fares which are available from travel agents or direct from the airline.

Reconfirmation At least 72 hours prior to departure time of an onward or return flight you must contact the airline and 'reconfirm' that you intend to be on the flight. If you don't do this the airline can delete your name from the passenger list and you could lose your seat. You don't have to reconfirm the first flight on your itinerary or if your stopover is less than 72 hours. It doesn't hurt to reconfirm more than once.

Restrictions Discounted tickets often have various restrictions on them – advance purchase is the most usual one (see Apex). Others are restrictions on the minimum and maximum period you must be away, such as a minimum of 14 days or a maximum of one year. See Cancellation Penalties.

Standby A discounted ticket where you only fly if there is a seat free at the last moment. Standby fares are usually only available on domestic routes.

Tickets Out An entry requirement for many countries is that you have an onward or return ticket, in other words, a ticket out of the country. If you're not sure what you intend to do next, the easiest solution is to buy the cheapest onward ticket to a neighbouring country or a ticket from a reliable airline which can later be refunded if you do not use it.

Transferred Tickets Airline tickets cannot be transferred from one person to another. Travellers sometimes try to sell the return half of their ticket, but officials can ask you to prove that you are the person named on the ticket. This is unlikely to happen on domestic flights; on an international flight tickets may be compared with passports.

Travel Agencies Travel agencies vary widely and you should ensure you use one that suits your needs. Some simply handle tours while full-service agencies handle everything from tours and tickets to car rental and hotel bookings. A good one will do all these things and can save you a lot of money but if all you want is a ticket at the lowest possible price, then you really need an agency specialising in discounted tickets. A discounted ticket agency, however, may not be useful for other things, like hotel bookings.

Travel Periods Some officially discounted fares, Apex fares in particular, vary with the time of year. There is often a low (off-peak) season and a high (peak) season. Sometimes there's an intermediate or shoulder season as well. At peak times, when everyone wants to fly, not only will the officially discounted fares be higher but so will unofficially discounted fares or there may simply be no discounted tickets available. Usually the fare depends on your outward flight – if you depart in the high season and return in the low season, you pay the high-season fare. ■

Round-The-World Tickets & Circle Pacific Fares

Round-the-World (RTW) tickets have become very popular in the last few years. The airline RTW tickets are often real bargains, and can work out no more expensive or even cheaper than an ordinary return ticket. Prices start from about £850, A$1900 or US$1400.

The official airline RTW tickets are usually put together by a combination of two airlines and permit you to fly anywhere you want on their route systems, so long as you do not backtrack. Other restrictions are that you (usually) must book the first sector in advance and cancellation penalties then apply. There may be restrictions on how many stops you are permitted. Usually the tickets are valid for a period of between 90 days and a year. An alternative type of RTW ticket is one where a travel agency combines a number of discounted tickets.

Circle Pacific tickets use a combination of airlines to circle the Pacific – combining Australia, New Zealand, North America and Asia. As with RTW tickets, there are advance purchase restrictions and limits to how many stopovers you can make. These fares are likely to be around 15% cheaper than Round-the-World tickets.

To/From the UK & Europe

Ticket discounting has been long established in the UK and it's wide open – the various agents advertise their fares and there's nothing under the counter about it at all.

Trailfinders in west London produce a lavishly illustrated brochure which includes airfare details. STA Travel also has branches in the UK. Look in the listings magazine *Time Out* plus the Sunday papers for ads. Also look out for the free magazines such as *TNT* and *Southern Cross* which are widely available in London. Start by looking outside the main railway stations.

The Globetrotters Club (BCM Roving, London WC1N 3XX) publishes a newsletter called *Globe* which covers obscure destinations and can help in finding travelling companions.

A couple of excellent agents to try are Trailfinders and STA. Trailfinders is at 194 Kensington High St, London W8 (☎ (071) 938 3939) and at 46 Earls Court Rd (☎ (071) 938 3366). STA is at 74 Old Brompton Rd, London W7 (☎ (071) 581 1022) and at Clifton House, 117 Euston Rd (☎ (071) 388 2261).

On the Continent, Amsterdam and Antwerp are among the best places for buying airline tickets. WATS, Keyserlei 44, Antwerp, Belgium, has been recommended. In Amsterdam, NBBS is a popular travel agent.

Many of the cheapest fares from Europe to South-East Asia are offered by Eastern European carriers. Garuda are also active fare cutters and you can find all sorts of interesting routes - simply to Jakarta or all the way to Australia - with stopovers in Indonesia.

Rock-bottom fares from London to South-East Asia for one way/return include Bangkok and Singapore for £225/£400, Jakarta £350/£620, Denpasar (Bali) £280/£450, Manila £280/£510 and Hong Kong from around £280/£490. From London to Malaysia, you're looking at UK£200 to UK£280 return. Fares to Bali or Jakarta are from around £300 one way or £600 return. Flights from London to Australia or New Zealand with stopovers in South-East Asia are available from £400 one way. You can get a London-Australia return ticket with a stopover in Jakarta or Bali, Singapore or Bangkok for around £950.

To fly to London from Penang in Malaysia, fares start from around RM830 with the less popular airlines such as Aeroflot. From Singapore, fares to London, or other European destinations, cost from S$590 one way with the Eastern European airlines and from S$700 one way with the better airlines. From Bangkok, European destinations cost from around US$350.

To/From Australia & NZ

Since there are far fewer airlines flying to and from Australia and New Zealand than there are to and from London, you won't find the same wide variety of fares. Nevertheless, bargains can still be found with a little shopping around. STA Travel and Flight Centre offices are major dealers in cheap airfares. Check them for starters or simply scan the ads in newspaper travel sections.

Regular excursion return fares from New Zealand and Australia usually have a low and a high-season period. The high season normally only applies for a limited time over the December-January school holiday period. There are also 'special fares' which are usually operated by airlines who are not regulars over that route (Alitalia or British Airways to Singapore for example) or by a more roundabout route (save money to Singapore by flying via Kuala Lumpur).

Return fares from Melbourne and Sydney include: Singapore, Kuala Lumpur and Bangkok from around A$700 to A$900; Hong Kong from A$900 to A$1300; Manila from A$750 to A$900. Logically it should be cheaper to fly to Denpasar, but its popularity as a holiday destination means that fares are around A$800 to A$1100, and the maximum stay is 90 days. Low fares quoted here are for specials available through travel agents and restrictions usually apply; high fares are for more flexible tickets of six to 12 months duration.

The cheapest flights to Asia are from Darwin and Perth. The flight from Darwin to Kupang (on the Indonesian island of Timor) costs A$198/330 one-way/return (A$248/407 in the high season) and is an economical and interesting way out of the country. This international connection is operated by Indonesia's main domestic carrier, Merpati, which has merged with Garuda. From Kupang, you can fly on to Denpasar for 224,000 rp (A$150), so it's cheaper to fly only as far as Kupang and buy another ticket there. The Merpati agent in Darwin is Natrabu (☎ 81 3695) at 12 Westlane Arcade off Smith St Mall – other agents also sell Merpati tickets. You do not need a visa to enter or leave Indonesia through Kupang. Other low-season fares from Darwin or Perth include Denpasar A$370/670, Singapore or Kuala Lumpur A$400/500, Bangkok A$420/870, Manila A$500/870 and Brunei A$360/680.

Qantas and Garuda both fly to Bali and Jakarta, while Ansett flies just to Bali. One-way fares from the east coast of Australia to Bali range from A$750 to A$860 depending on the season; return fares are A$900 to A$1070. Fares are less from Perth or Darwin and slightly more to Jakarta. The high season is essentially just the Christmas-January summer school holiday period in Australia.

From Auckland, you can get return flights to Denpasar for around NZ$1400 and to Bangkok for around NZ$1500.

From Penang in Malaysia, you can get one-way fares to Sydney from around RM1000 and returns from RM1500; Perth is about RM800 one-way. From Singapore, fares to Australia include Sydney or Melbourne for S$540 one way or Perth for S$620 return. From Bangkok, fares to Sydney/Melbourne are available for as low as US$324.

To/From North America

You can pick up interesting tickets to South-East Asia, particularly from the US west coast and Vancouver. In fact, the intense competition between Asian airlines has resulted in ticket discounting operations very similar to the London bucket shops.

The *New York Times*, the *Chicago Tribune*, the *LA Times*, the *San Francisco Examiner*, the *Vancouver Sun* and the *Toronto Globe & Mail* all produce weekly travel sections in which you'll find any number of travel agents' ads. Student travel specialists are Council Travel and Student Travel Network with offices in major US cities, while Travel CUTS has outlets throughout Canada. For discounted fares and ticketing, also contact CIEE or STA Travel offices in the USA.

The magazine *Travel Unlimited* (PO Box 1058, Allston, Mass 02134, USA) publishes details of the cheapest airfares and courier possibilities for destinations all over the world from the USA.

From the US west coast, fares to Singapore, Bangkok or Hong Kong cost around US$700/1000 one-way/return, while Bali flights cost from US$650/1100 in the low season (outside summer and Christmas). Flights to Malaysia are about US$800 one way. An interesting way to reach Indonesia is Garuda's Los Angeles-Honolulu-Biak-Denpasar flight for around US$700 one way, US$1200 return. There are plenty of competitive fares offered to Indonesia from the USA.

From Kuala Lumpur in Malaysia, you can fly to the US west coast for RM1100. From Singapore, one-way fares to the US west coast are around S$900 direct or with a stop in Manila. If you shop around the travel agents in Manila, you should be able get tickets to the US west coast for US$370 to US$450. There are always special multistop deals on offer such as Singapore-Jakarta-Sydney-Noumea-Auckland-Papeete-Los Angeles for S$1550. From Bangkok, one-way flights to Los Angeles or San Francisco cost from US$400 to US$500.

To/From Other Places

See the Indonesia Getting There & Away section for details of flights between Indonesia and Papua New Guinea.

LAND

To/From China

The only land borders between South-East Asia and the rest of Asia are the frontier that Myanmar shares with India, and the Chinese border with Burma, Laos and Vietnam. For decades these borders have been closed for foreign tourists, but at last it is possible to travel overland with the opening of the China-Vietnam border at Dong Dang on the way to Nanning in China, and at Lao Cai on the rail line between Hanoi and Kunming.

A special visa is required to enter Vietnam from China – it is not difficult to get but costs extra. No special requirements exist for exitng to China. See the Vietnam chapter for more details.

SEA

If you have ever wanted to jump a ship and see the world, some cargo ships have passenger services and stop in South-East Asia. Don't expect it be cheap – it can be many times more expensive than flying – but here are some suggestions:

NSB Frachtstiff-Touristik
: Niederlassung Bremen, Violenstrasse 22, 2800 Bremen, Germany (☎ (0421) 321668, fax (0421) 324089). This company is the main operator with ships out of Bremerhaven stopping in Felixstowe, Rotterdam, Antwerp, Le Havre and other European ports then via Saudi Arabia before reaching Singapore. Other routes are via Australia, Japan, New Zealand, the South Pacific and the USA.

Bankline
: Andrew Wier & Co, Dexter House, 2 Royal Mint Court, London EC3N 4XX, UK (☎ (071) 265 0808, fax (071) 481 4784). Has ships from Antwerp to French Polynesia, Fiji and Papua New Guinea before reaching Asia and returning to Rotterdam.

Leonhardt & Blumburg
: Hamburg-Sud Reiseagentur GmbH, Ost-West Strasse 59, 2000, Hamburg, Germany (☎ (040) 370 5593, fax (040) 370 5420). Has one of the most direct routes from Europe. It leaves from Hamburg and stops in European ports then Saudi Arabia before reaching Singapore.

ABC Containers
: The Strand Cruise & Travel Centre, Charing Cross Shopping Concourse, The Strand, London WC2N 4HZ, UK (☎ (071) 836 6363, fax (071) 497 0078). Via Europe, Israel, the Suez canal to Asia and then Australia.

Laeisz Line
: Freighter World Cruises Inc, 180 South Lake Ave, Suite 335, Pasadena, CA 91101, USA (☎ (818) 449 3106, fax (818) 449 9573). Operates from Long Beach via Oakland, Japan, Korea and Hong Kong to Singapore, before returning via Europe.

Getting Around

AIR

There are all sorts of ticket bargains around the region available to you once you arrive in South-East Asia. These inter-Asia fares are widely available, although Bangkok, Singapore, Penang and Hong Kong are the major ticket discounting centres.

A little caution is necessary when looking for tickets in Asia. First of all, shop around – a wise move anywhere, of course. Secondly, don't believe everything you are told – ticket agents in Penang (Malaysia) are very fond of telling people that tickets there are cheaper than in Bangkok or Singapore or wherever. In actual fact, they are often much the same price anywhere; if there is any difference it's likely to be in the favour of the originating city. For example, you're unlikely to find a Bangkok to Kathmandu ticket cheaper in Penang than in Bangkok. Or a Penang to

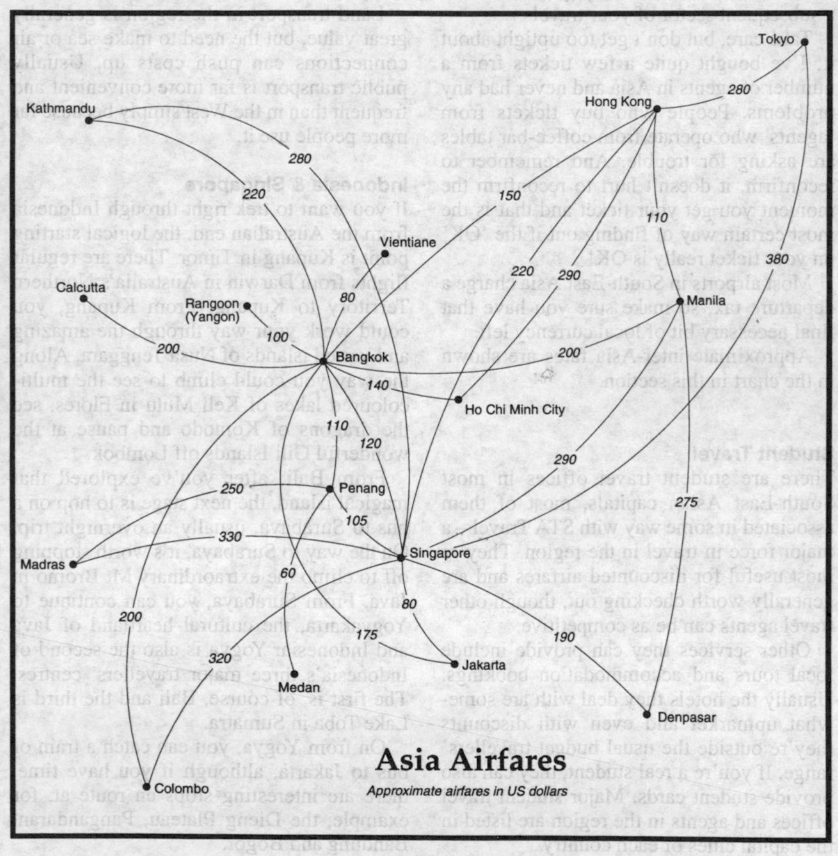

Asia Airfares

Approximate airfares in US dollars

Hong Kong ticket cheaper in Singapore than in Penang.

Most important of all, be very careful that you get what you want before handing over money and that the ticket is precisely what you pay for. Over the years, we have had many letters from people complaining that they were done by various agents.

Favourite tricks include tickets with very limited periods of validity when you have been told they are valid all year round. Or, you could find a ticket is marked 'OK', indicating that you have a seat reservation, when no reservation has been made. Also, that an airline will not accept your ticket for a subsequent sector of your travels.

Take care, but don't get too uptight about it; I've bought quite a few tickets from a number of agents in Asia and never had any problems. People who buy tickets from 'agents' who operate from coffee-bar tables are asking for trouble. And remember to reconfirm, it doesn't hurt to reconfirm the moment you get your ticket and that is the most certain way of finding out if the 'OK' on your ticket really is OK!

Most airports in South-East Asia charge a departure tax, so make sure you have that final necessary bit of local currency left.

Approximate inter-Asia fares are shown in the chart in this section.

Student Travel

There are student travel offices in most South-East Asian capitals, most of them associated in some way with STA Travel – a major force in travel in the region. They're most useful for discounted airfares and are generally worth checking out, though other travel agents can be as competitive.

Other services they can provide include local tours and accommodation bookings. Usually the hotels they deal with are somewhat upmarket and even with discounts they're outside the usual budget travellers' range. If you're a real student, they can also provide student cards. Major student travel offices and agents in the region are listed in the capital cities of each country.

OVERLANDING IN SOUTH-EAST ASIA

With all the water in the way 'overlanding' through South-East Asia seems a misnomer. However, if by the term overlanding you mean travelling from place to place by local transport with the minimum use of aircraft then South-East Asia offers enormous scope. Remember that it's by travelling that you actually meet the people.

If there are people in A and people in B, there will be transport between A and B. That's a simple rule which almost always seems to work. If you put your mind to it, you can always find a way of getting from one place to another.

Land transport in the region is generally great value, but the need to make sea or air connections can push costs up. Usually public transport is far more convenient and frequent than in the West simply because far more people use it.

Indonesia & Singapore

If you want to trek right through Indonesia from the Australian end, the logical starting point is Kupang in Timor. There are regular flights from Darwin in Australia's Northern Territory to Kupang. From Kupang, you could work your way through the amazing and varied islands of Nusa Tenggara. Along the way you could climb to see the multi-coloured lakes of Keli Mutu in Flores, see the dragons of Komodo and pause at the wonderful Gili Islands off Lombok.

From Bali, after you've explored that magical island, the next stage is to hop on a bus to Surabaya, usually an overnight trip. On the way to Surabaya, it's worth stopping off to climb the extraordinary Mt Bromo in Java. From Surabaya, you can continue to Yogyakarta, the cultural heartland of Java and Indonesia. Yogya is also the second of Indonesia's three major travellers' centres. The first is, of course, Bali and the third is Lake Toba in Sumatra.

On from Yogya, you can catch a train or bus to Jakarta, although if you have time, there are interesting stops en route at, for example, the Dieng Plateau, Pangandaran, Bandung and Bogor.

At Jakarta, you may be forced to make a decision. If your visa is running short, and unfortunately present Indonesian visa limitations make it virtually impossible to really explore the country in one bite, you have to leave. If you're in that situation, then head to Singapore from where you can then re-enter Indonesia and start again. There's no need to go right back to Jakarta though.

From Singapore ferries operate to Batam and Bintan islands in the Riau Archipelago, and from there speed boats go to Pekanbaru in Sumatra. If you're not embroiled in visa problems back in Jakarta, you could continue to Sumatra either by bus or train, and then by ferry.

Travel in southern Sumatra involves long bus trips to get to the north, so many people opt instead for the regular ship or flight from Jakarta to Padang. After Padang, the road through Sumatra continues north through delightful Bukittinggi, with perhaps a side trip to Nias Island and then a well-earned rest at relaxing Lake Toba.

Finally, you exit Sumatra by taking the ferry or flying from Medan to Penang in Malaysia. An alternative to this route would be to go from Singapore up to Penang and enter Sumatra at Medan then do the trip back down through Sumatra in reverse, finally exiting to Jakarta or to the Riau Archipelago and/or Singapore.

And of course, there are other Indonesian islands to the north and east, including Kalimantan (the southern half or Borneo), wonderful Sulawesi, the Maluku islands and Irian Jaya. To Sulawesi, Pelni passenger ships go from Java, Lombok, Sumbawa and Flores. It then possible to fly from Manado in northern Sulawesi to the Philippines, or you can go by boat from Sulawesi to Kalimantan and then cross overland to East Malaysia (visa problems notwithstanding – see the Indonesia chapter for details).

Malaysia & Thailand

Assuming you've followed the traditional path up through Indonesia, you're now in Penang and after enjoying yourself there you can head south to the hill stations like the Cameron Highlands, to Pulau Pangkor, to modern Kuala Lumpur, to historic Melaka and, finally, arrive at Singapore. Then you can head up the east coast and sample Malaysia's beaches and offshore islands. Travel in Malaysia is just about the most hassle-free of anywhere in Asia. There are excellent train and bus services, and very economical share-taxis; even the hitching is easy.

The northern Borneo states – Malaysia's Sabah and Sarawak and the independent kingdom of Brunei – are most easily visited from Singapore or Peninsular Malaysia since connections between north Borneo and Kalimantan are limited; but it can be done. You can fly from Sabah direct to Manila or Hong Kong.

There are a variety of ways of crossing to Thailand from Malaysia, but the usual routes are to take a taxi or train from Penang to Hat Yai if you're on the west coast, or to simply walk across the border from Rantau Panjang to Sungai Golok on the east coast.

From Hat Yai, the major city in the south of Thailand, you can continue by bus to Phuket, a resort island with superb beaches. Then continue north to Surat Thani and the equally beautiful island of Ko Samui, where you can wrestle with the important question of whether Phuket or Ko Samui is the better place to get away from it all. Finally, you reach hyperactive Bangkok and decide where to head next.

For most travellers, that decision will be to continue north to Chiang Mai, the second city of Thailand and another great travellers' centre. On the way, you could pause to explore the ancient cities of Ayuthaya and Sukhothai. From Chiang Mai, you can make treks into the colourful hill tribe areas or you can loop back to Bangkok through the north-east region. Bangkok is more than just the sin city of South-East Asia, it's also a centre for cheap airline tickets, so the next question is where to fly to – east or west.

Myanmar (Burma) & West

Since you can now get 30-day visas for Myanmar, it's a bit less of a rush around the attractions of that unusual country. Yangon (Rangoon) is the only entry point and you can either make a Myanmar visit as an out-and-back foray from Bangkok, or use Myanmar as a stepping stone between South-East Asia and West Asia. If the latter is your intention, then it's time to pack *South-East Asia on a shoestring* away and pick up other Lonely Planet guides on Bangladesh, India, Nepal and beyond.

Vietnam, Laos & Cambodia

This area of South-East Asia, often referred to as Indochina, has opened its doors to foreign travellers, but travel options for entering the area are still fairly limited. More border crossings should open, but as yet the only regular overland crossings are Thailand-Laos, China-Vietnam and Vietnam-Cambodia.

The main option is still to fly. To Vietnam there are a number of flights to and from Ho Chi Minh City's Tan Son Nhut or Hanoi's Noi Bai airports. Bangkok is the cheapest and most popular gateway.

The main overland option from Thailand is to enter Laos via the Nong Khai crossing. More border crossing options are available going the other way – see the Laos chapter for more details. With the possible exception of the Lao Bao exit point, it is still only possible to fly between Laos and Vietnam. There are no permitted border crossings between Laos and Cambodia, but regular buses run between Phnom Penh in Cambodia and Vietnam's Ho Chi Minh City.

The popular way to reach Vietnam from China is via the border at Dong Dang or Lao Cai. Travellers have reported other ways of reaching Indochina, notably by boat from Thailand to Cambodia by Ko Kong island, but these options are not strictly legal.

The most cost-effective way to tour Indochina is to take a flight from Bangkok to Phnom Penh or Ho Chi Minh City, then travel through Cambodia and up through Vietnam to the north. Then continue on to China or fly from Hanoi to Laos. From Laos you can continue back overland into Thailand.

Hong Kong & East

From Hong Kong, the frenetic city-state and gateway to China, you've got a choice of heading further east or west (in which case you need Lonely Planet's *North-East Asia on a shoestring* for China, Japan, Korea and Taiwan) or turning south for Vietnam or flying to the Philippines. Travelling across China to the far west and then down into Pakistan via the Karakoram Highway from Kashgar or into Nepal via Lhasa are adventurous routes.

The Philippines

Manila is overwhelmingly the gateway city to the Philippines, but there is an interesting short flight between Davao in Mindanao and Manado in Sulawesi (Indonesia). It is also possible to fly directly from Singapore to Cebu.

From Manila you can head north to the rice terraces and beaches of north Luzon, and south to the Mayon volcano and other attractions of south Luzon. Or, island hop off into the tightly clustered islands of the Visayas.

Eventually, you can hop back to Manila and decide where to next – on to Australia or further afield. A good loop through the region includes travelling from Australia to Indonesia, Singapore, Malaysia, Thailand, Indochina, Hong Kong, Philippines and, finally, back to Australia. But, of course, there are lots of other possibilities.

BUS

Bus travel can be absurdly comfortable, certainly by the standards further west in Asia, but there are always opportunities for crowded, bone-shaking bus rides shared with chickens, goats and all sorts of local produce.

Air-con luxury buses are widespread in Malaysia and Thailand (where they really are gigantic). In Indonesia air-con buses cover the main runs from north Sumatra right though to Flores, and the Philippines also has a number of air-con services. A host of cheaper, regular buses of a variety of standards cover the major and minor routes, while minibuses also operate and sometimes provide luxury services.

Regular buses tend to be cheap and frequent, but are often crowded and leg room is at a premium. They are usually fine for short to medium hops.

TRAIN

The main train services are to be found in Thailand, Malaysia, Vietnam, Myanmar, Cambodia and on Java in Indonesia. Buses are generally more convenient, more frequent, and often faster and cheaper, but the trains are still worth considering. Standards can vary enormously. In Thailand and Malaysia trains are very comfortable and a good alternative to the buses. Some of the crowded economy trains in Java are best avoided, but other services are excellent and cheap. Myanmar, Vietnam and Cambodia have dilapidated trains, but even they can be better than the dilapidated buses.

The only international train is the International Express that runs between Thailand and Malaysia.

Rail passes are offered in some countries, but unless you are travelling quickly and extensively by train, they are often not economic. See the individual country chapters for a full rundown of rail services.

CAR & MOTORBIKE

Of course, you can hit the road with your own transport, but you really cannot go that far in South-East Asia. It's not like the former Asian overland trip where you've got entire continents to cross. You could always buy a motorbike in Singapore, but once you've ridden it through Malaysia and Thailand you've come to the end of the road. Land borders to Myanmar are firmly shut so the idea of crossing Burma and heading across Asia to Europe is just a dream.

Remember too that many places (including Thailand and Indonesia) require a carnet – an expensive customs document which guarantees that you will later remove the vehicle from their country.

If you must have your own wheels, it's better to hire them when necessary. Car hire is becoming much more readily available in the region. Malaysia is like most countries in the West when it comes to car hire, and you can also easily hire cars in Indonesia and Thailand. Motorbikes can be hired in many places in Malaysia and Thailand; and, of course, in Bali, and other parts of Indonesia.

BICYCLE

Cycling is a cheap, convenient, healthy, environmentally sound and above all fun way of travelling. You can hire bicycles for day tripping in most tourist centres including Bali, Penang, Chiang Mai and Bagan in Myanmar, but they don't rent bicycles for long distance travel. Top quality bicycles and components can be bought in major cities like Singapore, but generally 10-speed bikes and fittings are hard to find and impossible in places like Vietnam. Bring your own.

Before you leave home, go over your bike with a fine-tooth comb and fill your repair kit with every imaginable spare. As with cars and motorbikes, you won't necessarily be able to buy that crucial gizmo for your machine when it breaks down somewhere in the back of beyond as the sun sets. A basic kit starts with allen keys, spoke key, tire levers and a small Swiss army knife.

Bicycles can travel by air. You can take them to pieces and put them in a bike bag or box, but it's much easier simply to wheel your bike to the check-in desk, where it should be treated as a piece of baggage. You may have to remove the pedals and turn the handlebars sideways so that it takes up less space in the aircraft's hold; check all this with the airline well in advance, preferably before you pay for your ticket.

Thailand is a good destination for bicycle touring and increasing numbers of travellers take their bicycles and continue through to Malaysia and Singapore. Road conditions are good enough for touring bikes in most places, but mountain bikes are recommended for off-the-beaten-track forays or for travel further afield in South-East Asia. Vietnam is a great place to take a (mountain) bicycle – traffic is relatively light, buses take bicycles and the entire coastal route is feasible, give or take a few potholes and hills. Indonesia is a less obvious destination – distances in Sumatra, congested roads in Java, hills in Bali, and poor road conditions in the outer islands, all conspire against it – but that doesn't stop a steady stream of dedicated cyclists.

HITCHING

Hitching is never entirely safe in any country in the world, and we don't recommend it. Travellers who decide to hitch should understand that they are taking a small but potentially serious risk. People who do choose to hitch will be safer if they travel in pairs and let someone know where they are planning to go.

BOAT

Ferry

Because many South-East Asian countries are often separated by water, you'll unavoidably have to spend more on transport than you would in other parts of Asia but some of these trips can be great experiences. There are not a lot of intercountry shipping services – most are between Indonesia and Malaysia or Singapore – although those that are available are often very interesting.

Indonesia and the Philippines are paradise if you love sea travel. Both countries have extensive ferry/passenger ship services.

Yacht

With a little effort, it's often possible to get yacht rides from various places in the region. Very often, yacht owners are just travellers too and they often need another crew member or two. Willingness to give it a try is often more important than experience and often all it costs you is a contribution to the food kitty. Check out anywhere that yachts pass through or in towns with Western-style yacht clubs.

On our first visit to Australia Maureen and I managed to get a yacht ride from Bali to Exmouth in Western Australia. Over the years we've had letters from people who've managed to get rides from Singapore, Penang, Phuket and (like us) Benoa in Bali.

Tony Wheeler

Brunei Darussalam

A comic-book little country, Brunei is blessed with a supply of that most prized commodity – oil. It shows from the grandiose public buildings of the capital, Bandar Seri Begawan (commonly called BSB or Bandar), and the airport terminal, large enough for a country 10 times Brunei's size, to the Sultan's fleet of exotic Italian cars.

The only reason most visitors come to Brunei is to pass through between the two Malaysian states of Sabah and Sarawak. For inveterate passport stamp collectors, Brunei is a must, otherwise its attractions are few. Brunei does have its own unique character though and Bruneians are some of the friendliest people you'll meet anywhere.

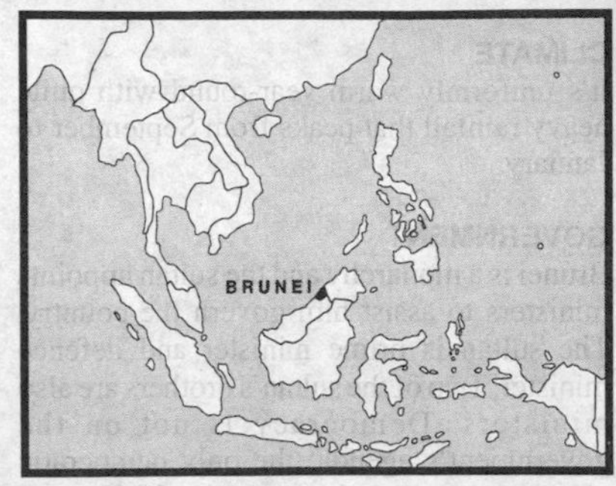

Facts about the Country

HISTORY

At one time, Brunei was a considerable power in these parts. Under the fifth sultan, Bolkiah (known as the 'singing admiral' for his love of music), Brunei's power extended throughout Borneo and into the Philippines. The arrival of the British, led by Rajah Brooke, under their excuse of wiping out piracy along the Borneo coast, spelt the end of this power.

Gradually, the country was whittled away. The final absurdity was when it was forced to cede Limbang to Sarawak, splitting the country into two halves. Then, in 1929, oil was discovered on the tiny bit of land left. That windfall allows Brunei to flourish with no income tax, pensions for all, magnificent and rather redundant public buildings and what must be the highest per capita consumption of cars in South-East Asia.

The current Sultan is the 29th of his line. His father pragmatically kept the country out of the Malaysian confederation before abdicating and now matches his son's sports cars with his own London taxi.

Rather reluctantly, in 1984, Brunei gained independence from Britain. The Sultan celebrated by building himself a new US$350 million palace and renaming the country Brunei Darussalam, or Haven of Peace. The *Guinness Book of Records* rates the Sultan among the richest men in the world, and his spending habits at exclusive London stores make great stories for the tabloids. He also had enough loose cash around the palace to chip in US$10 million for Ronald Reagan's Nicaraguan 'contra' fund but, unfortunately, the money ended up in the wrong Swiss bank account.

Recently, Brunei has shown an increasing trend towards Islamic fundamentalism. In 1991 the sale of alcohol was banned, stricter dress codes have been introduced and in 1992, Melayu Islam Beraja (MIB), the national ideology stressing Malay culture, Islam and monarchy, became a compulsory subject in schools.

GEOGRAPHY

Brunei covers an area of 5765 sq km and consists of two areas separated by the Limbang District of Sarawak. The western part of Brunei contains the main towns: Bandar Seri Begawan, the oil town of Seria and the commercial town of Kuala Belait.

The eastern part of the country, Temburong District, is much less developed. Brunei is mainly jungle; 75% of the country is covered by forest.

CLIMATE

It's uniformly warm year-round with quite heavy rainfall that peaks from September to January.

GOVERNMENT

Brunei is a monarchy and the sultan appoints ministers to assist him govern the country. The sultan is prime minister and defence minister. Two of the sultan's brothers are also ministers. Democracy is not on the government's agenda; the only democratic elections ever held were in 1962, and resulted in an attempted coup.

ECONOMY

Oil. Some diversification plans for the economy are now being instituted for that fearsome day when the pump runs dry, though Brunei has increased its oil production in the '90s. Brunei is also one of the world's largest exporters of liquefied natural gas; a small amount of rubber is also exported. About 80% of the country's food requirements have to be imported.

POPULATION & PEOPLE

The population of Brunei is about 260,000 and is composed of Malays (69%), Chinese (18%), Indians and around 14,000 Iban, Lun Bawang and other Dayak people of the interior. There are also around 20,000 expatriate workers from Europe and elsewhere in Asia.

ARTS & CULTURE

Traditional arts are not much in evidence in wealthy, modern Brunei, though during the height of the Brunei sultanates, brassware in the form of gongs, cannons and household vessels (such as kettles and betel containers) were prized throughout Borneo and beyond.

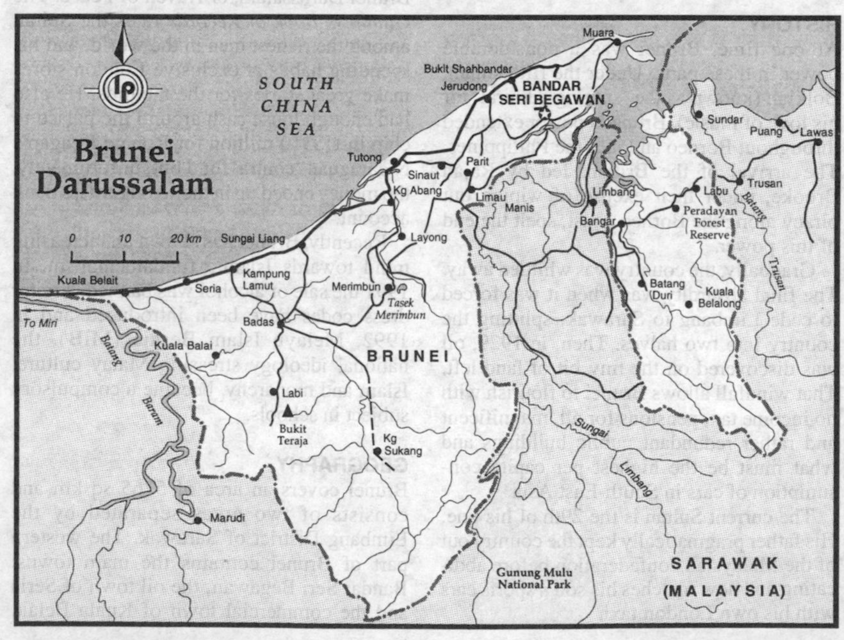

The lost wax technique used to cast brass declined with the fortunes of the Brunei sultanate and has become a lost art. Brunei's silversmiths also produced some exceptional work. Jong Sarat sarongs, using gold thread, are still prized for ceremonial occasions and this weaving art has survived.

Customs

Bruneians are mostly Malay and customs, beliefs and pastimes are very similar if not identical to the Malays of Peninsular Malaysia. *Adat*, or customary law, governs many of the ceremonies in Brunei, particularly in relation to royal ceremonies and state occasions.

The usual Asian customs apply – only the right hand should be used for offering or passing something, while beckoning someone is done with an open hand with the fingers waving downwards. Offering pork or alcohol to Muslims may not only cause offence, it is tempting them to break the law. When entering a mosque, or a house, remove your shoes first.

Muslim women are required to cover up from head to toe, with only the face and hands exposed, but Bruneian women are less cloistered than in other Islamic societies. Allowances are made for non-Muslim women, and because of the large expat population, many Bruneians are used to Western ways. For women travellers, dress should be conservative and not revealing – bare shoulders and short dresses are inappropriate.

RELIGION

Brunei is quite a strict Muslim country. Brunei has a Ministry of Religious Affairs, which has special officers who investigate breaches of Islamic law by Muslims, such as *khalwat*, the crime of unmarried couples standing or sitting too close to each other. The constitution does allow other religions to be practised in peace and harmony, and non-Muslim visitors need not worry about being abused for being infidels. Bruneians are very friendly and hospitable people, and generally more tolerant than government policies would suggest.

LANGUAGE

The official language is Malay but English is widely spoken. *Jawi*, Malay written in Arabic script, is taught in schools and most signs in the country are written in both Jawi and the roman script. Malay is virtually the same as Indonesian. See Lonely Planet's *Indonesian Phrasebook* and the Language section in the Indonesia chapter for an introduction to the language.

Facts for the Visitor

VISAS & EMBASSIES

For visits of up to 14 days, visas are not necessary for citizens of Switzerland, France, Canada, Thailand, the Philippines, Japan, Indonesia, the Netherlands, Belgium, Luxembourg, Germany and the Republic of Korea. British, Malaysian and Singaporean citizens do not require a visa for visits of 30 days or less.

All other nationalities, including British overseas citizens and citizens of British dependencies, must have visas to visit Brunei.

If entering from Sarawak or Sabah, there's no fuss on arrival – no money showing, no requirement for an onward ticket and it's unlikely your bags will even be looked at. A one-week stay permit is more or less automatic but, if you ask, you can usually get two weeks.

Brunei Embassies Abroad

Brunei Darussalam has diplomatic offices in neighbouring countries including:

Indonesia
: Bank Central Asia Building, Jalan Jenderal Sudirman, Jakarta (☎ 021-578 2180)

Malaysia
: Plaza MBF, Jalan Ampang, Kuala Lumpur (☎ 03-261 2828)

Singapore
: 7A Tanglin Hill, Singapore (☎ 474 3393)

Thailand
: Orakarn Building, 26/50 Soi Chitlon, Ploenchit Rd, Bangkok 10500 (☎ 02-515766)

MONEY

Currency

The official currency is the Brunei dollar (B$), which is worth exactly the same as the Singapore dollar (which can be used in Brunei). The B$ is worth about 40% more than the Malaysian ringgit. Banks give around 10% less for cash than they do for travellers' cheques. Cash advances can be obtained on credit cards over the counter at banks, or through the Hong Kong & Shanghai Bank's ATM.

Costs

Transport and food within the country are comparable with prices in the rest of East Malaysia – more expensive than Peninsular Malaysia but not outrageously expensive. The main problem is accommodation. There is only one cheap place to stay, and if that's full, Brunei can be fiercely expensive. It's cheaper to fly between Sabah and Sarawak than it is to pass through Brunei.

TOURIST OFFICES

There is an information desk at the airport, but the only decent publication available is the *Explore Brunei* booklet, which has a good map.

BUSINESS HOURS & HOLIDAYS

Government offices are open from 7.45 am to 12.15 pm and 1.30 to 4.30 pm, Monday to Thursday and Saturday. Private offices are generally open from 9 am to 5 pm, Monday to Friday, and until noon on Saturday, while banks are open from 9 am to 3 pm during the week and until 11 am on Saturday.

Many holidays and festivals in Brunei are religious celebrations and their dates are not fixed as they are based on the Islamic calendar.

Fixed holidays are New Year's Day (1 January), National Day (23 February), Anniversary of the Royal Brunei Armed Forces (31 May), Sultan's Birthday (15 July) and Christmas Day (25 December). Variable holidays include: Chinese New Year (January or February), Isra Dan Mi'Raj (February), Awal Ramadan (March), Anniversary of the Revelation of the Koran (April), Hari Raya Aidilfitri (April), Hari Raya Haji (June), First Day of Hijrah (July) and the Prophet's Birthday (July or August).

POST & TELECOMMUNICATIONS

Post offices are open from 7.45 am to 4.30 pm daily, except Friday and Sunday. International phone calls can be made at Telecom offices or by using phone cards at public booths. Faxes can be sent from Telecom offices or major hotels.

The Telecom office in Bandar Seri Begawan is next to the GPO.

BOOKS & MAPS

Books on Brunei are few and far between, and you are as likely to find books on Argentinian topiary in your local bookshop as titles about Brunei. Even Brunei bookshops stock few books on Brunei, simply because very few have been written and those that have are more than likely banned.

By God's Will – A Portrait of the Sultan of Brunei by Lord Chalfront is a measured look at the sultan and Brunei.

Brunei Darussalam, A Guide is an excellent, glossy publication produced by Brunei Shell. It was designed for the expat community and outlines a host of day trips and sights to be found around the country, though many of the excursions are of limited interest to international visitors. The government produces a number of publications about Brunei, such as *Brunei Darussalam in Profile*, *Brunei Darussalam in Brief* and *Selamat Datang*.

Getting There & Away

AIR

Airline offices in Bandar include: Malaysian Airline System (MAS) (☎ 02-224141), 144 Jalan Pemancha; Royal Brunei Airlines (☎ 02-242222), RBA Plaza, Jalan Sultan; Singapore Airlines (SIA) (☎ 02-227253), 49-50 Jalan Sultan; and Thai International (☎ 02-242299), 51 Jalan Sultan.

Royal Brunei Airlines connects Bandar Seri Begawan with Kuching (B$236), Kota Kinabalu (B$78), Kuala Lumpur (B$399), Singapore (B$377), Bangkok (B$510), Bali (B$457), Jakarta (B$574), Manila (B$444), Taipei (B$740) and Hong Kong (B$666). MAS, SIA, Thai International and Philippine Airlines also cover the routes to their home countries.

Discounts of up to 20% on the published rates quoted above are available through travel agents for most flights where Royal Brunei has competition. Discounts are not available on flights to Malaysia and Singapore, but because of the difference in exchange rates it is around 40% cheaper to fly to Brunei from Malaysia than vice versa.

Royal Brunei also has direct flights to Australia. From Darwin or Perth costs around A$400 one way or A$680 return.

LAND

To get to Miri in Sarawak from Bandar Seri Begawan, first take a bus to Seria (B$4, two hours), then another to Kuala Belait (B$1, 30 minutes) and from there five buses leave daily until 3.30 pm to Miri (B$9, 2½ hours). After going through Brunei customs, a Malaysian bus takes you to the Malaysian immigration checkpoint and then on to Miri. If you want to reach Miri in one day from BSB, start out early in the day.

The alternatives to all this bus hopping are the private minibuses that start picking up passengers from their hotels at 5 am and go direct to Miri. Mr Wong (☎ 228392 or 225643) is one operator who lives near the Pusat Belia (Youth Centre). The fare is B$25.

SEA

Apart from flying, the only viable way to get from Brunei to Sabah or the isolated eastern Sarawak outposts of Limbang or Lawas is to use launches or launch/bus combinations.

All international boats leave from the dock at the end of Jalan Roberts, where Brunei immigration formalities are taken care of.

To/From Sabah

Via Labuan Labuan is a duty-free island off Brunei from where you can get ferries to Sabah and then a bus to Kota Kinabalu, ferries direct to Kota Kinabalu, or flights to Sabah, Sarawak or Peninsular Malaysia.

From BSB there are four or five daily services to Labuan (B$20, 1½ hours). Tickets can be bought before departure at the ticket stalls on Jalan McArthur, or book in advance. Ratu Samudra Ticketing (☎ 02-243057), 201-213 Giok Tee Building, Jalan McArthur, is the main ticketing agent and has boats departing at 8 am. Other boats include the *Duta Muhibbah* (☎ 02-24803), departing at 1 pm, and the *Sri Labuan Tiga*, leaving at 3 pm – book at Halim Tours (☎ 02-226688) at 61 Jalan McArthur.

Via Lawas A daily express boat goes from BSB to Lawas (B$15, two hours) at 11.30 am. Book at Halim Tours. From Lawas, you can continue on to Sabah by bus.

Via Limbang Frequent *ekspres* boats from BSB do this run throughout the day and depart when full. The fare is B$10 and the trip takes about 30 minutes. From Limbang you can fly to Mulu, Miri, Lawas or Kota Kinabalu.

Getting Around

Transport around Brunei, for those poor unfortunates who don't have a Volvo or a BMW, is by bus or minibus, which are infrequent and unreliable – there are no fixed schedules and buses leave when full. Buses on the main highway from BSB to Kuala Belait are fairly regular. Hitchhikers are such a novelty in Brunei that the chances of getting a lift are good.

Bandar Seri Begawan

The capital, Bandar Seri Begawan (or simply BSB), is the only town of any size and really one of the few places to go in the country. All around are the signs of Arabia and oil money. Arabic script graces the street signs and copula domes and minarets dot the skyline. The huge, near-empty public buildings and stadiums, none more grand than the sultan's palace, are a folly that Brunei can easily afford. It is a spacious, overstated city, but most visitors are scratching around for something to do after a couple of days.

Things to See

The **Omar Ali Saifuddin Mosque**, named after the 28th Sultan of Brunei, was built in 1958 at a cost of about US$5 million. The golden-domed structure stands close to the Brunei River in its own artificial lagoon and is one of the tallest buildings in Bandar. It's one of the most impressive structures in the East.

Kampung Ayer, a collection of 28 water villages built on stilts out in the Brunei River, has been there for centuries and at present houses a population of around 30,000 people. It's a strange mixture of ancient and modern – old traditions and ways of life are juxtaposed with electricity, modern plumbing and colour TVs. A visit is probably the most rewarding experience you'll have in Brunei but the garbage floating around has to be seen to be believed. The villages are at their best at high tide. To get there, take the wooden walkways from behind the mosque or from the fish market near the customs wharf. Water taxi launches shuttle people back and forth for 50 sen to B$1, and they can be chartered.

The **Brunei Museum** is housed in a beautiful building on the banks of the Brunei River at Kota Batu, six km east from the centre, and is well worth a look. Historical treasures and a good ethnography section are the highlights. The adjoining **Malay Technology Museum** is also impressive. Take a Muara or Kota Batu bus for 50 sen, but remember they are not that frequent. You can hitch quite easily.

The **Royal Regalia Museum** is devoted to the Sultan of Brunei, and contains royal memorabilia and items relating to the coronation, including the enormous royal carriage. It is housed in a typically oversized building, aptly described by one traveller as looking like 'a giant hamburger with the ketchup dripping out'.

The magnificent sultan's palace, the **Istana Nurul Iman**, larger than the Vatican Palace, is an impressive sight, especially when illuminated at night. The Istana is open to the public only at the end of the fasting

PLACES TO STAY

1 Ang's Hotel
3 Sheraton Hotel
5 Capital Hostel
8 Pusat Belia (Youth Centre)
10 Jubilee Hotel
14 Princess Inn
25 Brunei Hotel
29 Government Rest House

PLACES TO EAT

13 Regent's Rang Mahal
27 Isma Jaya Restaurant
26 Tamu Kianggeh
28 Bus Station
30 Hua Hua Restaurant
40 Gerai Makan Food Centre

OTHER

2 Immigration
4 Royal Regalia Museum
6 Lapau
7 Dewan Majlis
9 Brunei History Centre
11 Post Office
12 Badiah Shopping Complex
15 Plaza Athirah
16 Yaohan Department Store
17 Royal Mausoleum
18 Omar Ali Saifuddin Mosque
19 Chinese Temple
20 Zura Travel Service
21 Hong Kong & Shanghai Bank
22 MAS
23 Malayan Bank
24 Wisma Jaya
31 Singapore Airlines
32 Giok Tee Building
33 Halim Tours
34 Teck Guan Complex
35 Darussalam Complex
36 Harrisons
37 Boat Ticket Stalls
38 Customs Wharf
39 Fish Market
41 Boats to Bangar

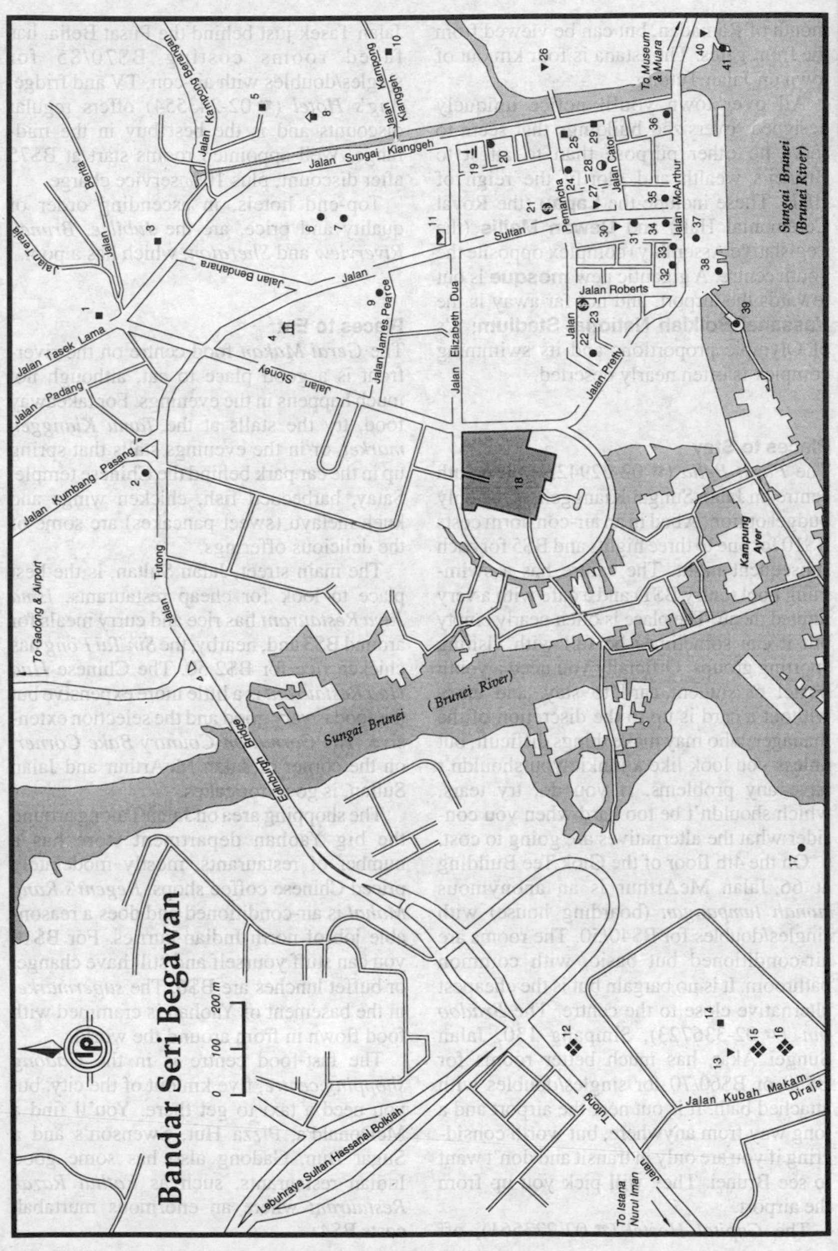
Bandar Seri Begawan
0 100 200 m
To Gadong & Airport
Jalan Kumbang Pasang
Jalan Padang
Jalan Tasek Lama
Jalan Tutong
Jalan Stoney
Jalan James Pearce
Jalan Elizabeth Dua
Jalan Bendahara
Jalan Berita
Jalan Teraja
Jalan Kampong Berangan
Jalan Sungai Kianggeh
Jalan Kampong Kianggeh
Jalan Sultan
Jalan Pemancha
Jalan Cator
Jalan McArthur
Jalan Roberts
Jalan Pretty
To Museum & Muara
Sungai Brunei (Brunei River)
Kampung Ayer
Edinburgh Bridge
Sungai Brunei
(Brunei River)
Lebuhraya Sultan Hassanal Bolkiah
Jalan Tutong
To Istana Nurul Iman
Jalan Kubah Makam Diraja

month of Ramadan, but can be viewed from the front gates. The Istana is four km out of town on Jalan Tutong.

All over town you'll notice uniquely designed, oversized buildings that seem to serve no other purpose than to attest to Brunei's wealth and glorify the reign of HRH. These include the **Lapau** (the Royal Ceremonial Hall) and **Dewan Majlis** (the Legislative Assembly) complex opposite the youth centre. A gigantic new **mosque** is out towards the airport, and not far away is the **Hassanal Bolkiah National Stadium**; it's of Olympic proportions and its swimming complex is often nearly deserted.

Places to Stay

The *Pusat Belia* (☎ 02-229423), the youth centre on Jalan Sungai Kianggeh, is the only budget option. A bed in an air-con dorm costs B$10 for one to three nights and B$5 for each subsequent night. The centre has a swimming pool (entry B$1) and a cafe with a very limited menu. The place is often nearly empty but it can sometimes be full with visiting sporting groups. Officially you need a youth hostel or student card to stay, and entry without a card is up to the discretion of the manager, who may make things difficult, but unless you look like a junkie you shouldn't have any problems. If you do, try tears, which shouldn't be too hard when you consider what the alternatives are going to cost.

On the 4th floor of the Giok Tee Building at 66 Jalan McArthur is an anonymous *rumah tumpangan* (boarding house) with singles/doubles for B$40/50. The rooms are air-conditioned but basic, with common bathroom. It is no bargain but is the cheapest alternative close to the centre. The *Bradoo Inn* (☎ 02-336723), Simpang 130, Jalan Sungei Akar, has much better rooms for B$50 or B$60/70 for singles/doubles with attached bath. It is out near the airport and a long way from anywhere, but worth considering if you are only in transit and don't want to see Brunei. They will pick you up from the airport.

The *Capital Hostel* (☎ 02-223561), off Jalan Tasek just behind the Pusat Belia, has faded rooms costing B$70/85 for singles/doubles with air-con, TV and fridge. *Ang's Hotel* (☎ 02-243554) offers regular discounts and is the best buy in the mid-range. Well-appointed rooms start at B$75 after discount, plus 10% service charge.

Top-end hotels, in ascending order of quality and price, are the *Jubilee*, *Brunei*, *Riverview* and *Sheraton*, which has a pool.

Places to Eat

The *Gerai Makan* food centre on the riverfront is a good place to eat, although not much happens in the evenings. For takeaway food, try the stalls at the *Tamu Kianggeh market*, or in the evenings stalls that spring up in the car park behind the Chinese temple. Satay, barbecued fish, chicken wings and kueh melayu (sweet pancakes) are some of the delicious offerings.

The main street, Jalan Sultan, is the best place to look for cheap restaurants. *Isma Jaya Restaurant* has rice and curry meals for around B$3 and, nearby, the *Sin Tai Pong* has chicken rice for B$2.50. The Chinese *Hua Hua Restaurant* is a little more expensive but the food is very good and the selection extensive. The *Carnation Country Bake Corner*, on the corner of Jalan McArthur and Jalan Sultan, is good for cakes.

The shopping area on Jalan Tutong around the big Yaohan department store has a number of restaurants, mostly moderately priced Chinese coffee shops. *Regent's Rang Mahal* is air-conditioned and does a reasonable job of north Indian curries. For B$10 you can stuff yourself and still have change, or buffet lunches are B$6. The *supermarket* in the basement of Yaohan is crammed with food flown in from around the world.

The fast-food centre is in the *Gadong shopping centre*, five km out of the city, but you need a taxi to get there. You'll find a McDonald's, Pizza Hut, Swenson's and a Sugar Bun. Gadong also has some good Indian restaurants, such as *Fathul Razak Restaurant* where an enormous murtabak costs B$4.

Getting There & Away

Buses that travel around Bandar Seri Begawan and to other parts of the country are few and far between and only leave when full. The bus station is beneath the parking lot on Jalan Cator. If you really want to see more of Brunei than BSB, then car hire starts at around B$90 – try Avis in the Sheraton Hotel.

Getting Around

Minibuses go to the airport, eight km from the city, but they usually pass by the airport on their way to other destinations and will only enter the airport to drop passengers off if requested. This means it is difficult to get a minibus from the airport and you may be in for a long wait. Taxis cost around B$20 – welcome to Brunei.

Around Brunei

The main land mass of Brunei in the western part of the country is quite small and any destination is only a few hours drive from the capital. The countryside has a lot of pristine forest with waterfalls and reserves that make pleasant day trips, but a car is essential to reach most of them. There are several other points of interest – decent beaches, some more impressive istanas, longhouses etc – but the only problem is getting to them because of the poor public transport system.

MUARA

Muara is a small town north-east of Bandar Seri Begawan at the top of the peninsula. It's an extensive container port of no interest but Muara Beach, two km from town, is a popular weekend picnic spot. Other beaches around Muara include Meragang Beach and Serasa Beach.

The bus from BSB to Muara town costs B$2, but the beach is about a one-km walk from the roundabout as you enter town.

JERUDONG

Jerudong is where the Sultan indulges his favourite pastime, polo. **Jerudong Park** is a huge complex with a polo stadium and luxurious stables that house polo ponies flown in from around the world. It is very grand and impressive, but uninvited visitors won't be able to tour the complex. Behind Jerudong Park is the wide **Jerudong Beach**, with stalls selling fresh fish. Buses to Seria pass the park, but it is a long walk to the beach. You won't see much of the area without a car.

SERIA

The area stretching along the coast between Seria and Kuala Belait is the main centre for oil production in Brunei. Shell Brunei has a number of big installations; the army is here to protect them and most expatriate workers live here in their suburban enclaves. Seria itself is an unremarkable oil town with a few modern blocks of shops and a market.

Places to Stay

The *Rumah Tumpangan Seria*, on Jalan Sharif Ali near the market, is an old, wooden Chinese hotel with spartan fan-cooled rooms for B$35 and air-con rooms for B$40.

Getting There & Away

There are about 10 buses a day to BSB taking two hours and costing B$4. From Seria there are frequent buses to Kuala Belait until 6.30 pm for B$1.

KUALA BELAIT

The last western town before Malaysia, Kuala Belait is where you get buses for Miri in Sarawak. The town has a lot more charm than Seria, though you won't miss much if you pass it by. The best place to change money is at the Hong Kong & Shanghai Bank opposite the bus station.

Places to Stay

At the cheap end of the scale there's the *Government Rest House* (☎ 03-334288) where, if you're permitted to stay, rooms are about B$12.

Otherwise, there is the *Sentosa Hotel*

(☎ 03-334341), 92 Jalan McKerron near the bus station, which is fully air-conditioned and has comfortable but way overpriced rooms for B$98. The *Seaview Hotel* (☎ 03-332651), Jalan Maulana, is two km from town on the beach road to Seria and costs B$130/155.

Getting There & Away

Five buses leave for Malaysia every day until 3.30 pm; the cost is B$9.

TEMBURONG DISTRICT

Temburong District is the eastern slice of Brunei surrounded by Sarawak. This quiet backwater, rarely visited by travellers, is reached by boat from Bandar Seri Begawan and can be visited on a day trip. Temburong has little industry or development, so much of the district is virgin rainforest.

Bangar, a sleepy town on the banks of the Temburong River, is the district centre. **Batang Duri** is an Iban longhouse on the Temburong River, 17 km south of Bangar. Two km before Batang Duri, is the **Taman Batang Duri**, a park and small zoo that is worth a quick look.

Kuala Belalong Field Studies Centre is a scientific research centre in the Batu Apoi Forest Reserve, a large area of primary rainforest that covers most of southern Temburong. It is primarily for scientists and school groups, though interested visitors can stay at the centre. Bookings must be made through the Biology Department of the Universiti Brunei Darussalam (☎ 02-427001).

The **Peradayan Forest Reserve** contains the peaks of Bukit Patoi and Bukit Peradayan, which can be reached along a walking trail – bring water and food. The one-hour walk through rainforest to Bukit Patoi and its fine views starts at the entrance to the park, 15 km from Bangar. Most walkers descend back along the trail, but it is possible to continue for another two hours along a harder, less distinct trail to Bukit Peradayan.

Places to Stay

The *Government Rest House* in Bangar is the only place to stay and costs B$12 per night. It is opposite the mosque, five minutes from the boat wharf.

Getting There & Away

Regular boats to Bangar leave from the wharf near the Gerai Makan food centre in BSB. They cost B$7 and take 45 minutes.

Getting Around

Taxis are the only form of transport around Temburong and they congregate around the Bangar wharf. Registered, metered taxis are available, as well as private taxis, which work out cheaper with some negotiation. A private taxi to Batang Duri should cost around B$20 for the return journey. For the Peradayan Forest Reserve and the walk to Bukit Patoi, taxis also charge B$20 to drop you off and pick you up at an arranged time. Hitching is possible though you may be in for a wait.

Cambodia

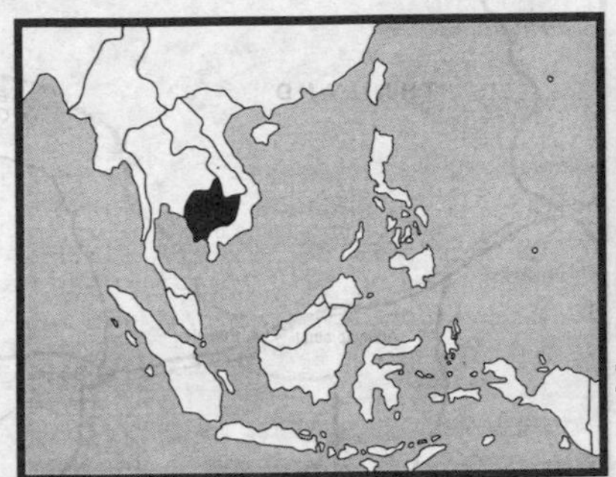

Modern-day Cambodia is the successor-state of the mighty Khmer Empire, which during the Angkorian period (9th to 14th centuries) ruled much of what is now Vietnam, Laos and Thailand. Among the accomplishments of the Khmer civilisation are the fabled temples of Angkor, one of humanity's most magnificent architectural achievements. These stunning monuments, surrounded by dense jungle, are only 152 km from the Thai border, which at the time of writing was reportedly open at Aranyaprathet (Poipet on the Cambodian side).

Cambodia is just emerging from two decades of continual warfare and violence, including almost four years (1975-79) of rule by the genocidal Khmer Rouge, who killed at least one million of Cambodia's seven million people and systematically sought to obliterate the country's prerevolutionary culture. Even today, all around the country you see mass graves and ruined structures.

Facts about the Country

HISTORY

From the 1st to the 6th centuries, much of present-day Cambodia was part of the kingdom of Funan, whose prosperity was due in large part to its position on the great trade route between China and India.

The Angkorian era, known for its brilliant achievements in architecture and sculpture, was begun by Jayavarman II around the year 800. During his rule, a new state religion establishing the Khmer ruler as a *devaraja* (god-king) was instituted. Vast irrigation systems facilitated intensive cultivation of the land around Angkor and allowed the Khmers to maintain a densely populated, highly centralised state.

For 90 years from 1863, the French controlled Cambodia as an adjunct to their colonial interests in Vietnam. Independence was declared in 1953. For 15 years King (later Prince, Prime Minister and Chief-of-State, and now King again) Norodom Sihanouk dominated Cambodian politics. But, alienating both the left and the right with his erratic and repressive policies, he was overthrown by the army in 1970 and fled to China.

From 1969 Cambodia was drawn into the Vietnam conflict. The USA secretly commenced carpet-bombing suspected Communist base camps in Cambodia and, shortly after the 1970 coup, American and South Vietnamese troops invaded the country to root out Vietnamese Communist forces. They failed. But the invasion did push Cambodia's indigenous rebels, the Khmer Rouge (Red Khmer in French), into the country's interior. Savage fighting soon engulfed the entire country, ending only when Phnom Penh fell to the Khmer Rouge on 17 April 1975, two weeks before the fall of Saigon.

Upon taking Phnom Penh, the Khmer Rouge, under leader Pol Pot, implemented one of the most radical, brutal restructurings of a society ever attempted. Its goal was the transformation of Cambodia into a Maoist, peasant-dominated, agrarian cooperative.

During the next four years, hundreds of

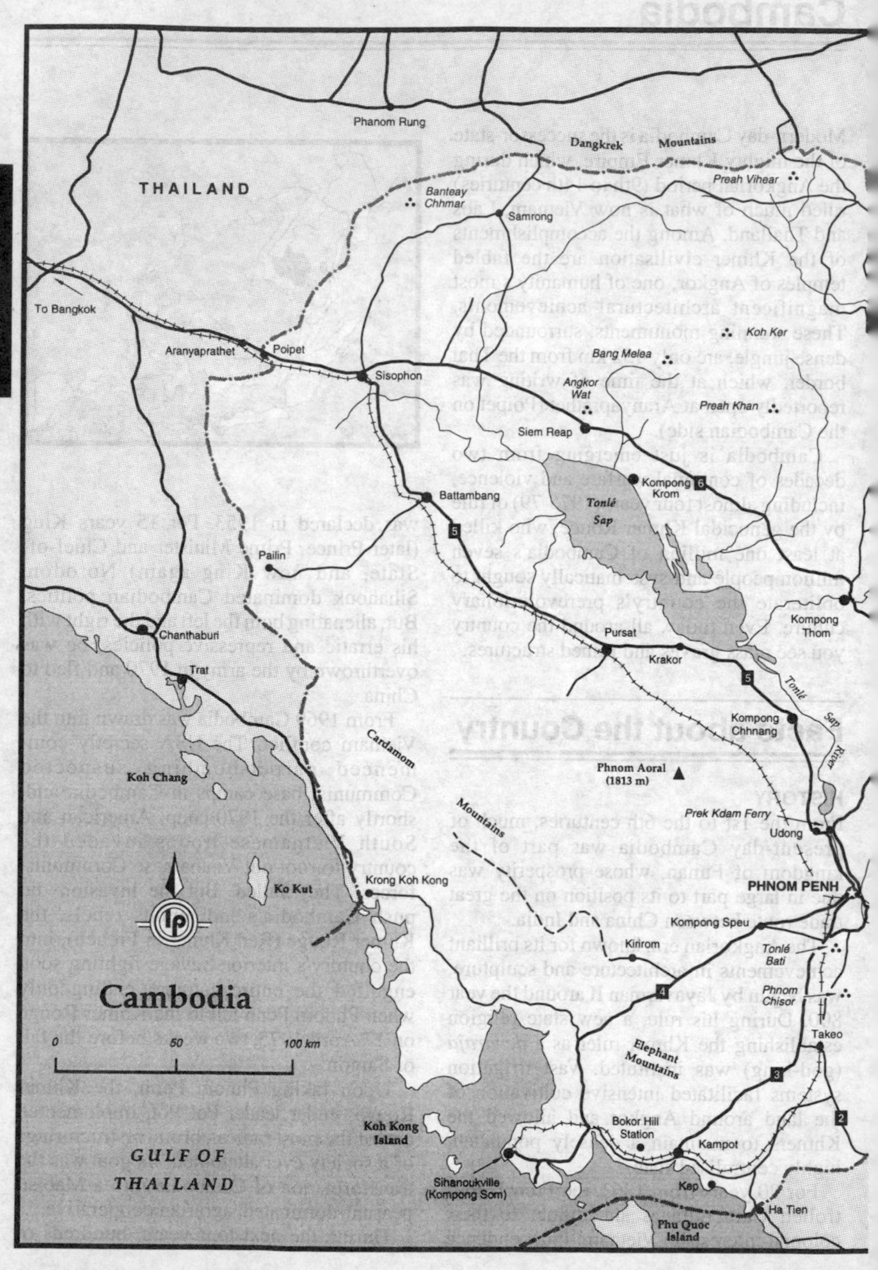

Cambodia
THAILAND
To Bangkok
Phanom Rung
Dangkrek Mountains
Preah Vihear
Banteay Chhmar
Samrong
Aranyaprathet
Poipet
Sisophon
Koh Ker
Bang Melea
Angkor Wat
Preah Khan
Siem Reap
Kompong Krom
Tonlé Sap
Battambang
Pailin
Kompong Thom
Chanthaburi
Pursat
Krakor
Trat
Tonlé Sap River
Kompong Chhnang
Cardamom Mountains
Koh Chang
Phnom Aoral (1813 m)
Prek Kdam Ferry
Udong
PHNOM PENH
Krong Koh Kong
Ko Kut
Kompong Speu
Kirirom
Tonlé Bati
Phnom Chisor
Takeo
Elephant Mountains
0
50
100 km
Koh Kong Island
Bokor Hill Station
Kampot
GULF OF THAILAND
Sihanoukville (Kompong Som)
Kep
Ha Tien
Phu Quoc Island
5
6
4
3
2

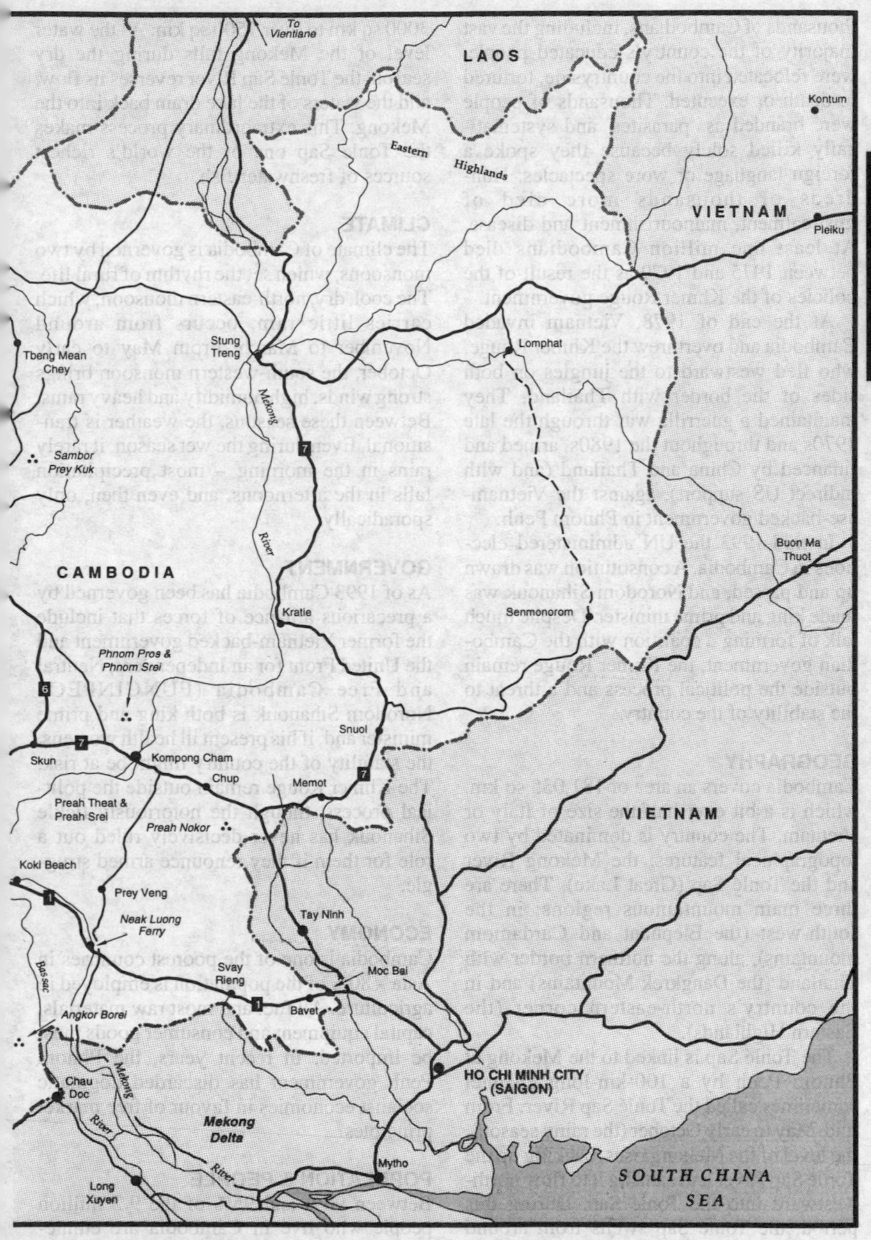
To Vientiane
LAOS
Kontum
Eastern Highlands
VIETNAM
Pleiku
Stung Treng
Lomphat
Tbeng Mean Chey
Mekong
River
7
Sambor Prey Kuk
Buon Ma Thuot
CAMBODIA
Kratie
Senmonorom
Phnom Pros & Phnom Srei
6
Snuol
Skun
7
Kompong Cham
Chup
7
Memot
Preah Theat & Preah Srei
Preah Nokor
VIETNAM
Koki Beach
1
Prey Veng
Neak Luong Ferry
Tay Ninh
Bassac
Svay Rieng
Moc Bai
1
Bavet
Angkor Borei
Mekong
Chau Doc
River
HO CHI MINH CITY (SAIGON)
Mekong Delta
River
Mytho
Long Xuyen
SOUTH CHINA SEA

thousands of Cambodians, including the vast majority of the country's educated people, were relocated into the countryside, tortured to death or executed. Thousands of people were branded as 'parasites' and systematically killed solely because they spoke a foreign language or wore spectacles. Hundreds of thousands more died of mistreatment, malnourishment and disease. At least one million Cambodians died between 1975 and 1979 as the result of the policies of the Khmer Rouge government.

At the end of 1978, Vietnam invaded Cambodia and overthrew the Khmer Rouge, who fled westward to the jungles on both sides of the border with Thailand. They maintained a guerrilla war through the late 1970s and throughout the 1980s, armed and financed by China and Thailand (and with indirect US support), against the Vietnamese-backed government in Phnom Penh.

In mid-1993 the UN administered elections in Cambodia. A constitution was drawn up and passed, and Norodom Sihanouk was made king and prime minister. Despite much talk of forming a coalition with the Cambodian government, the Khmer Rouge remain outside the political process and a threat to the stability of the country.

GEOGRAPHY

Cambodia covers an area of 181,035 sq km, which is a bit over half the size of Italy or Vietnam. The country is dominated by two topographical features: the Mekong River and the Tonlé Sap (Great Lake). There are three main mountainous regions: in the south-west (the Elephant and Cardamom mountains), along the northern border with Thailand (the Dangkrek Mountains) and in the country's north-eastern corner (the Eastern Highlands).

The Tonlé Sap is linked to the Mekong at Phnom Penh by a 100-km-long channel sometimes called the Tonlé Sap River. From mid-May to early October (the rainy season), the level of the Mekong rises, backing up the Tonlé Sap River and causing it to flow north-westward into the Tonlé Sap. During this period, the Tonlé Sap swells from around 3000 sq km to over 7500 sq km. As the water level of the Mekong falls during the dry season, the Tonlé Sap River reverses its flow, and the waters of the lake drain back into the Mekong. This extraordinary process makes the Tonlé Sap one of the world's richest sources of freshwater fish.

CLIMATE

The climate of Cambodia is governed by two monsoons, which set the rhythm of rural life. The cool, dry, north-eastern monsoon, which carries little rain, occurs from around November to March. From May to early October, the south-western monsoon brings strong winds, high humidity and heavy rains. Between these seasons, the weather is transitional. Even during the wet season, it rarely rains in the morning – most precipitation falls in the afternoons, and even then, only sporadically.

GOVERNMENT

As of 1993 Cambodia has been governed by a precarious alliance of forces that include the former Vietnam-backed government and the United Front for an Independent, Neutral and Free Cambodia (FUNCINPEC). Norodom Sihanouk is both king and prime minister and, if his present ill health worsens, the stability of the country might be at risk. The Khmer Rouge remain outside the political process, though the notoriously fickle Sihanouk has never decisively ruled out a role for them if they renounce armed struggle.

ECONOMY

Cambodia is one of the poorest countries in Asia – 80% of the population is employed in agriculture. All fuel and most raw materials, capital equipment and consumer goods must be imported. In recent years, the Phnom Penh government has discarded dogmatic socialist economics in favour of free market principles.

POPULATION & PEOPLE

Between 90% and 95% of the 9.2 million people who live in Cambodia are ethnic-

Khmers (ethnic-Cambodians), making the country the most homogeneous in South-East Asia. Only about 10% of Cambodia's population reside in the cities or towns.

The most important minority group in Cambodia is the ethnic-Chinese, who until 1975 controlled the country's economy and who, with the help of overseas Chinese investment, are once again making their presence felt. There is a great deal of mutual dislike and distrust between the Khmers and the country's ethnic-Vietnamese. Cambodia's Cham Muslims (Khmer Islam) currently number some 200,000. They suffered vicious persecution between 1975 and 1979 and a large part of their community was exterminated.

Cambodia's diverse ethnolinguistic minorities (hill tribes), who live up in the country's mountainous regions, numbered approximately 90,000 in 1975.

ARTS & CULTURE

Khmer architecture reached its zenith during the Angkorian era (the 9th to 14th centuries). Some of the finest examples of architecture from this period are Angkor Wat and the structures of Angkor Thom. Many of the finest works of Khmer sculpture are on display at the National Museum in Phnom Penh. Cambodia's highly stylised classic dance, adapted from Angkor dances (and similar to Thai dances derived from the same source), is performed to the accompaniment of an orchestra and choral narration.

Conduct

Proper etiquette in *wats* (pagodas) is mostly a matter of common sense. A few tips:

- Don't wear shorts or tank tops.
- Take off your hat when entering the grounds of the wat.
- Take off your shoes before going into the *vihara* (sanctuary).
- If you sit down in front of the dais (the platform on which the Buddhas are placed), sit with your feet to the side rather than in the lotus position.
- Never point your finger – or, heaven forbid, the soles of your feet! – towards a figure of the Buddha (or human beings either).

RELIGION

Hinayana Buddhism is the dominant religion in Cambodia and was the state religion until 1975. It was reinstated as the state religion in the late 1980s. Between 1975 and 1979, the vast majority of Cambodia's Buddhist monks were murdered by the Khmer Rouge, who also destroyed virtually all of the country's 3000 wats.

LANGUAGE

Cambodia's official language is Khmer. For most Westerners, writing and pronouncing this language proves confusing and difficult. For over a century, the second language of choice among educated Cambodians was French, which is still spoken by many people who grew up before the 1970s. English has recently surged in popularity.

Greetings & Civilities

excuse me
suom tous
good night
rear trei suor sdei
goodbye
lear heouy
hello
joom reab suor/suor sdei
How are you?
Tau neak sok sapbaiy jea te?
very well
sok touk jea thomada te
please
suom

Getting Around

I want a ticket to...
Khjoom junh ban suombuot teou...
When does it depart?
Tau ke jeng domneur moung ponmann?
When does it arrive here/there?
Tau ke teou/mouk doul moung ponmaan?
Where is a/the...?
Tau...nouv eir na?
railway station
sathani rout phleoung
bus station
ben lan

CAMBODIA

airport
veal youn huos
ticket office
kanleng luok suombuot
tourist office
kariyaleiy samrap puok tesajor
boat
kopal/tuok
bus
lan thom deouk monuos
train
rout phleoung

Accommodation

I want a...
Khjoom joung ban...
single room
bantuop kre samrap mouy neak
double room
bantuop kre samrap pee neak
room with a bathtub
bantuop deil meen thlang gnout teouk
bed
kre mouy
How much is a room?
Chnoul mouy bantuop tleiy ponmaan?

Other Useful Words & Phrases

no
te
thank you
ar kun
yes (used by men)
bat
yes (used by women)
jas

Numbers

1	*mouy*
2	*pee*
3	*bei*
4	*boun*
5	*bram*
6	*bram-mouy*
7	*bram-pee*
8	*bram-bei*
9	*bran-boun*
10	*duop*
11	*duop-mouy*
12	*duop-pee*
20	*maphei*
21	*maphei-mouy*
30	*samseb*
40	*sairseb*
100	*mouy-rouy*
500	*bram-rouy*
1000	*mouy-paun*
10,000	*mouy-meoun*

Emergencies

Please call...
Suom jouy hao...
an ambulance
lan peit
a doctor
krou peit
the police
police
a dentist
peit thmenh
It's an emergency.
Nees jea pheap ason.
I'm allergic to penicillin.
Khjoom min trouv theat neoung thanam peneecilleen.

Facts for the Visitor

VISAS & EMBASSIES

Cambodian visas are becoming increasingly easy to get hold of. Those arriving by air can obtain a visa on arrival at Pochentong airport, Phnom Penh. The cost is US$20 and the visa should be valid for one month (seven days was the norm until quite recently).

Those planning to enter the country overland from Vietnam or possibly from Thailand can apply in Saigon or in Bangkok (if you stop there first). Visas in Saigon should take two working days and cost US$20. In Bangkok, visas can be issued in one day and cost 650B. Most of the Khao San Rd travel agents can organise visas.

Cambodian Embassies Abroad

Cambodia's most useful consular sections are those in Laos and Vietnam. If you are arriving from anywhere else you will have to fly in and obtain your visa on arrival.

Laos
Thanon Saphan Thong Neua, Vientiane (☎ 2750, 4527)

Vietnam
71 Tran Hung Dao St, Hanoi (☎ 53788/9). The embassy is open Monday to Saturday from 8 to 11 am and from 2 to 4.30 pm.
41 Phung Khac Khoan St, Saigon (☎ 92751/2, 92744). The consulate is open Monday to Saturday from 8 to 11 am and from 2 to 5 pm.

Visa Extensions
Visa extensions are granted by the new Immigration Bureau at No 5, 200 St in Phnom Penh. Six-month visas are available for US$60.

Foreign Embassies
There are several useful foreign embassies in Phnom Penh.

The Laos embassy is at 245 St, midway between Monivong and Norodom Blvds (☎ 2.5181/2).

The Vietnamese embassy is on Monivong Blvd at 436 St, which is blocked off (☎ 2.5481, 2.5681). The consular section of this embassy (☎ 2.3142) is on the eastern side of Monivong Blvd opposite number 749 (between 422 St and Issarak Blvd). It is open weekdays (and on Saturday morning) from 7.30 to 11 am and from 2 to 5 pm. Two photos are required for a visa, which takes at least two days to issue and costs US$55.

MONEY
Currency
Cambodia's currency is the riel but by far the most useful foreign currency in Cambodia is US$ cash. Travellers' cheques in US$ can be changed at the official rate from the Foreign Trade Bank in Phnom Penh. Credit cards are not practical yet.

Exchange Rates
As Cambodia is effectively operating with two currencies – US dollars and riels – everybody is a black marketeer. When you use dollars to buy something with a riel price tag the price is calculated at that day's exchange rate. Change for amounts less than US$1 is given in riel at the appropriate exchange rate. The official exchange rates are as follows:

Australia	A$1	=	2524r
Canada	C$1	=	2598r
New Zealand	NZ$1	=	2078r
Britain	UK£1	=	5297r
USA	US$1	=	3500r
Japan	¥100	=	3416r
Germany	DM1	=	2148r
France	FF1	=	627r
Malaysia	M$1	=	1363r

Costs
Meals generally cost only a few US$, except in the fanciest restaurants. Hotel accommodation in Phnom Penh and Siem Reap costs between US$6 and US$25 per night (although you can spend lots more if you like). Public transport is cheap and dangerous and not off-limits to foreign travellers anymore. Hiring a car will set you back at least US$20 per day. All this will be included if you book a tour, for which you'll pay at least US$200 per day!

Tipping
Tipping is not expected but is very much appreciated. A person's monthly government salary may only total US$5 or less.

BUSINESS HOURS
Government offices are open Monday to Saturday from about 7.30 am to 4.30 pm, with a siesta from 11 or 11.30 am to 2 or 2.30 pm.

POST & TELECOMMUNICATIONS
Postal Rates
Cambodia's postal rates are cheaper than those in Vietnam (an aerogramme costs US$0.30) but service is excruciatingly slow because most international mail is routed via Moscow. Letters sent to Cambodia from abroad take two to three months to arrive.

Telephone
OTC Australia has set up Cambodia's international telephone network and there are

now numerous IDD telephones around Phnom Penh. Cards are available in denominations of US$20, US$50 and US$100. You'd be better off saving your calls for somewhere else though – rates are very high.

BOOKS

A number of superb works on Angkor have been published over the years. *Angkor: An Introduction* (Oxford University Press, Hong Kong, 1963; reissued in paperback by Oxford University Press, Singapore, 1986) by George Coedes gives excellent background information on the Angkorian Khmer civilisation.

The 3rd edition of *Angkor, Guide Henri Parmentier* (EKLIP/Albert Portail, Phnom Penh, 1959/1960) by Henri Parmentier, probably the best guidebook to Angkor ever written, was published under the same title in both English and French.

MEDIA

The best English-language newspaper is the *Phonm Penh Post*. It comes out every two weeks and costs 1200r. The *Cambodia Daily* costs 1000r and is also worth picking up.

Foreign radio services – Radio Australia, the BBC World Service and Voice of America – can be picked up on short-wave frequencies.

FILM & PHOTOGRAPHY

Do not put film of any speed or type through the ancient X-ray machines at the airport in Phnom Penh! Print film is readily available in hotels and photography shops around Phnom Penh and at Angkor. Processing is cheap and the results are OK.

HEALTH

Hospitals

If you have serious medical problems, the best advice is to jump on a flight to Bangkok or Hong Kong. The Calmette Hospital in Phnom Penh is partly French-run and will help with emergencies. Alternatively, World Access Medical Services at No 53B, 64 St (☎ 27045) has a Western doctor, a physiotherapist and nursing staff. They also have a pharmacy.

Infusions

Most intravenous (IV) solution used in Cambodian hospitals (other than the ones above) is *not* sterile. According to foreign aid workers, people often die from septicaemia (blood poisoning) caused by bacteria introduced into their blood during infusions. Visitors should not *under any circumstances* receive infusions. Be aware, also, that injections are routinely carried out using unsterilised equipment.

DANGERS & ANNOYANCES

Until the civil war definitely ends, travel outside areas under firm government control (of which there are few) will carry with it a certain degree of risk, especially in the evening and after dark. There is currently no curfew in Phnom Penh, but you can expect to be stopped by police occasionally if you stay out after 8 pm. Armed theft is a fairly common occurrence, even in Phnom Penh – take care.

Undetonated Mines, Mortars & Bombs

Never, ever touch any rockets, artillery shells, mortars, mines, bombs or other war material you may come across. In Vietnam, most of this sort of stuff is 15 or more years old (although not necessarily any less dangerous), but in Cambodia it may have landed there or been laid as recently as last night. In short: *do not* stray from well-marked paths under any circumstances, even around the monuments of Angkor.

Snakes

Visitors to Angkor and other overgrown archaeological sites should beware of snakes, especially the small but deadly light green Hanuman snake.

ACCOMMODATION

There has been a guesthouse boom in Cambodia over the last year or so, particularly in the Angkor area. Other places with tourist potential, like Sihanoukville, look set to follow. Phnom Penh now has a good range of places, from US$5 crash pads to US$10 to US$15 air-con guesthouses to upmarket monsters with room rates of US$160 upwards.

FOOD & DRINKS

In Phnom Penh, there is a growing number of decent restaurants. Both in the capital and in most towns there are foodstalls, often clustered in the marketplace.

Soda water with lemon is called *soda kroch chhmar* and the custom here seems to be to let the customer squeeze their own lemons. In Phnom Penh, ice *(tuk kak)* is produced by a factory that apparently uses treated water of some sort. Drinking tap water is to be avoided, especially in the provinces. Beware – some of the flavoured soda sold in bottles by kerbside vendors has been made cheaply by a process that renders the result toxic enough to cause headaches and stomach upset. Recent tests on locally produced bottled water found much of it to be 'not potable'.

Some useful words include:

Is there any...?
Tau ke mean...deir reou te?
meat
saach
fish
trei
chicken
maan
soup
suop
noodles
mee/kuy teav/noum banjuok

Getting There & Away

AIR

Cambodia's international air links are improving almost daily. There are currently direct connections with Bangkok (Siam Kampuchea Air, Bangkok Airways and Thai International), Hong Kong (Kampuchea Airlines and Dragon Air), Singapore (Silk Air), Kuala Lumpur (Malaysia Airlines), Saigon (Vietnam Airlines) and Vientiane (Lao Aviation).

Prices from Bangkok, which has the greatest frequency of flights and is the most popular place to fly to and from, are 4200B with Bangkok Airways, 4450B with Siam Kampuchea Air and 6650B with Thai International.

LAND

To/From Vietnam

Buses from Ho Chi Minh City to Phnom Penh, via the Moc Bai border crossing, leave early each morning, except Sunday, from Boi Xe 1A (☎ 93754) at 155 Nguyen Hue Blvd in Ho Chi Minh City. The trip, which costs about US$12, takes eight to 10 hours. Buses from Phnom Penh leave at around 5 am and tickets are best purchased the day before you leave. The ticket office is on the south-western corner of 211 and 182 Sts; it's open from 5 to 10 am and 2 to 5 pm and is closed on Sunday.

It's possible to rent a car and driver in Vietnam for trips into Cambodia. With Saigon Tourist the cost is around US$200 but will be a lot cheaper with independent agencies.

To/From Thailand

Despite continued Khmer Rouge activity in the border regions, rumours of possible border crossings from Thailand abound. Some travellers have been getting rides with boats from Trat in Thailand to Koh Kong Island, where they receive a Cambodian visa for US$20. It is not possible to get an exit visa in Trat however, making the venture somewhat illegal. From Koh Kong it is possible to get a ride with a fishing boat to Sihanoukville.

Before the war, there was a regular train service between Bangkok and Phnom Penh via Aranyaprathet and Poipet (Poay Pet). The road between Bangkok and Phnom Penh also crosses the Thai-Cambodian border at

Poipet. Some travellers are said to be using this route, taking a taxi from Aranyaprathet in Thailand to Poipet and on to Sisophon in Cambodia. Those who do so are taking a considerable risk, and would be well advised not to have too much cash or lots of valuables on them – too much of a temptation for anyone with a gun.

SEA

Passenger ferries link the Vietnamese port of Phu Chau (Tan Chau) in the Mekong Delta with Phnom Penh. For more information, see Getting There & Away in the Phnom Penh section.

Getting Around

AIR

There are a number of scheduled domestic flights around the country, but most travellers only use the Phnom Penh to Siem Reap service for Angkor. This takes around 25 minutes and costs US$43. Flights to Sihanoukville cost US$40, though most people hire a taxi for US$20. There are also flights to Koh Kong for US$50.

BUS

It is no longer forbidden to travel by bus in Cambodia, but you can expect services to be slow and *very* crowded. With the exception of all but the hardiest travellers, most people band together with a few others and hire a taxi for their destination.

TRAIN

Cambodia's rail system consists of about 645 km of single-track, metre-gauge lines. The 382-km north-western line, built prior to WWII, links Phnom Penh with Pursat, Battambang and, in peacetime, Poipet on the Thai border. The 263-km south-western line, completed in 1969, connects the capital with Takeo, Kep, Kampot and the port of Sihanoukville (Kompong Som).

Fares are calculated at the rate of about US$0.02 for each four km you travel. Recently, the country's rail system has often suffered from rebel sabotage. It is considered a more dangerous form of travel than bus travel.

CAR

The French colonials designed Cambodia's 15,000 km of roads to link the agricultural hinterlands of Cambodia with the port of Saigon. Even the small part of the network that was at one time surfaced (some 2500 km) has seriously deteriorated during the last two decades. Today, it is only marginally serviceable, and virtually impassable to passenger cars.

Phnom Penh

Phnom Penh (population one million), capital of Cambodia for much of the period since the mid-15th century (when Angkor was abandoned), is situated at Quatre Bras (literally, Four Arms in French) – the confluence of the Mekong, the Bassac and the Tonlé Sap rivers. Once considered the loveliest of the French-built cities of Indochina, Phnom Penh's charm is fast succumbing to the construction boom and the roar of traffic, but is still evident in parts of town.

Orientation

In 1993 most of Phnom Penh's main roads received a name change. The old names are listed in brackets here, just in case the new ones don't stick.

The most important north-south arteries are (from west to east): Monivong (Achar Mean) Blvd (where most of the hotels are), Norodom (Tou Samouth) Blvd, Samdech Sotharah (Lenin) Blvd (in front of the Royal Palace) and, along the riverfront (which is also oriented roughly north to south), Quai Karl Marx. Forming two rough semicircles in the quadrant south-west of the Central Market are Sivutha Blvd (which intersects Norodom Blvd at the Victory Monument) and Issarak (Keo Mony) Blvd (which intersects Norodom Blvd at the former US Embassy).

The most important east-west thoroughfares of the city are Pochentong (USSR) Blvd, which intersects Monivong Blvd near the railway station, and Kampuchea-Krom Blvd (128 St), which heads due west from the Central Market.

Unlike the major thoroughfares, which have names, smaller streets have numbers. In most cases, odd-numbered streets run more or less north-south (usually parallel to Monivong Blvd), with the numbers rising semisequentially as you move from east to west. Even-numbered streets run in an east-west direction and their numbers rise semisequentially as you move from north to south.

Information

Tourist Offices The head office of Phnom Penh Tourism (☎ 2.3949, 2.5349, 2.4059) is across from Wat Ounalom at the oblique intersection of Samdech Sotharah Blvd and Quai Karl Marx. Its two entrances are at 313 Quai Karl Marx and next to 2 Samdech Sotharah Blvd. Phnom Penh Tourism, which belongs to the Phnom Penh Municipality, largely restricts its activities to running expensive package tours.

The Ministry of Tourism (☎ 2.2107), at times referred to as Cambodia Tourism, is in a white, two-storey building across 232 St from 447 Monivong Blvd. The directorate rents cars, and guides are also available, but most travellers seem to arrange this privately (and more cheaply) at the Capitol Guesthouse.

Money The Foreign Trade Bank (☎ 2.2466), Banque du Commerce Extérieur du Cambodge in French, is at 24 Monivong Blvd. The exchange window (bureau de change) is open Monday to Saturday from 7.30 to 11 am and from 2.30 to 5 pm. Thai banks have also moved into Phnom Penh, and include the Bangkok Bank (☎ 2.6593), at 26 Norodom Blvd, and the Thai Farmers Bank (☎ 2.4035) on 114 St.

Post & Telecommunications The GPO (☎ 2.4511), which is on the western side of 13 St between 98 and 102 Sts, is open from 6.30 am to 9 pm daily. It offers postal services as well as domestic and international telegraph and telephone links. There is a 24-hour international telephone service, but these days you can make your calls from one of the upper-end hotels. There are also private operators around town offering international telephone services, as well as IDD public payphones.

Medical Services See the preceding Health section for information on the two best places in Phnom Penh to get emergency medical treatment.

Wat Phnom

Set on top of a 27-metre-high, tree-covered knoll, Wat Phnom was once visible from all over the city, and still makes for a good landmark. According to legend, the first pagoda on this site, which is at the intersection of Norodom Blvd and 96 St, was erected in 1373 to house four statues of the Buddha deposited here by the waters of the Mekong and discovered by a woman named Penh (thus the name Phnom Penh, The Hill of Penh).

At the bottom of the hill on the north-western side is a small zoo, though Wat Phnom's most endearing animal residents, its monkeys, live free in the trees, feasting on people's banana offerings. Elephant rides around the base of Wat Phnom are a favourite Sunday attraction.

Royal Palace

Phnom Penh's Royal Palace (☎ 2.4958) fronts Samdech Sotharah Blvd between 184 and 240 Sts. It is the official residence of King Norodom Sihanouk and is open from time to time to the public. A decision on regular opening hours doesn't seem to have been made yet.

Silver Pagoda

The spectacular Silver Pagoda is so named because the floor is covered with over 5000

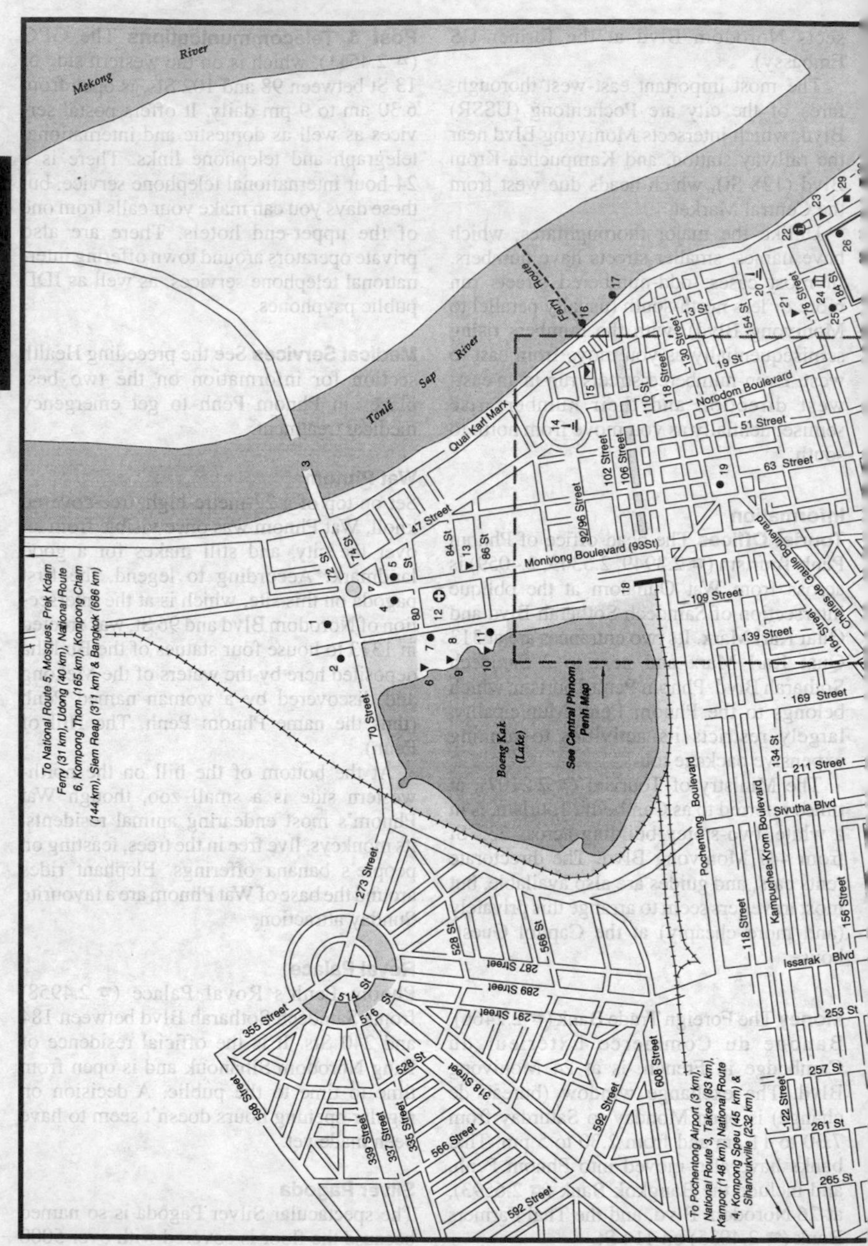
Mekong River
Tonlé Sap River
Ferry Route
Quai Karl Marx
To National Route 5, Mosques, Prek Kdam Ferry (31 km), Udong (40 km), National Route 6, Kompong Thom (165 km), Kompong Cham (144 km), Siem Reap (311 km) & Bangkok (686 km)
47 Street
72 St
74 St
5 St
80
84 St
86 St
70 Street
Monivong Boulevard (93St)
92/96 Street
102 Street
106 Street
110 St
118 Street
130 Street
13 St
154 St
178 Street
184 St
19 St
Norodom Boulevard
51 Street
63 Street
Charles de Gaulle Boulevard
164 Street
109 Street
139 Street
169 Street
See Central Phnom Penh Map
Boeng Kak (Lake)
Pochentong Boulevard
134 St
Kampuchea-Krom Boulevard
211 Street
Sivutha Blvd
118 Street
156 Street
Issarak Blvd
253 St
257 St
122 Street
261 St
265 St
273 Street
528 St
566 St
287 Street
289 Street
291 Street
608 Street
592 Street
514 St
516 St
355 Street
528 St
318 Street
598 Street
339 Street
337 Street
335 Street
566 Street
592 Street
To Pochentong Airport (3 km), National Route 3, Takeo (83 km), Kampot (148 km), National Route 4, Kompong Speu (45 km) & Sihanoukville (232 km)
1
2
3
4
5
6
7
8
9
10
11
12
13
14
15
16
17
18
19
20
21
23
24
25
26
29

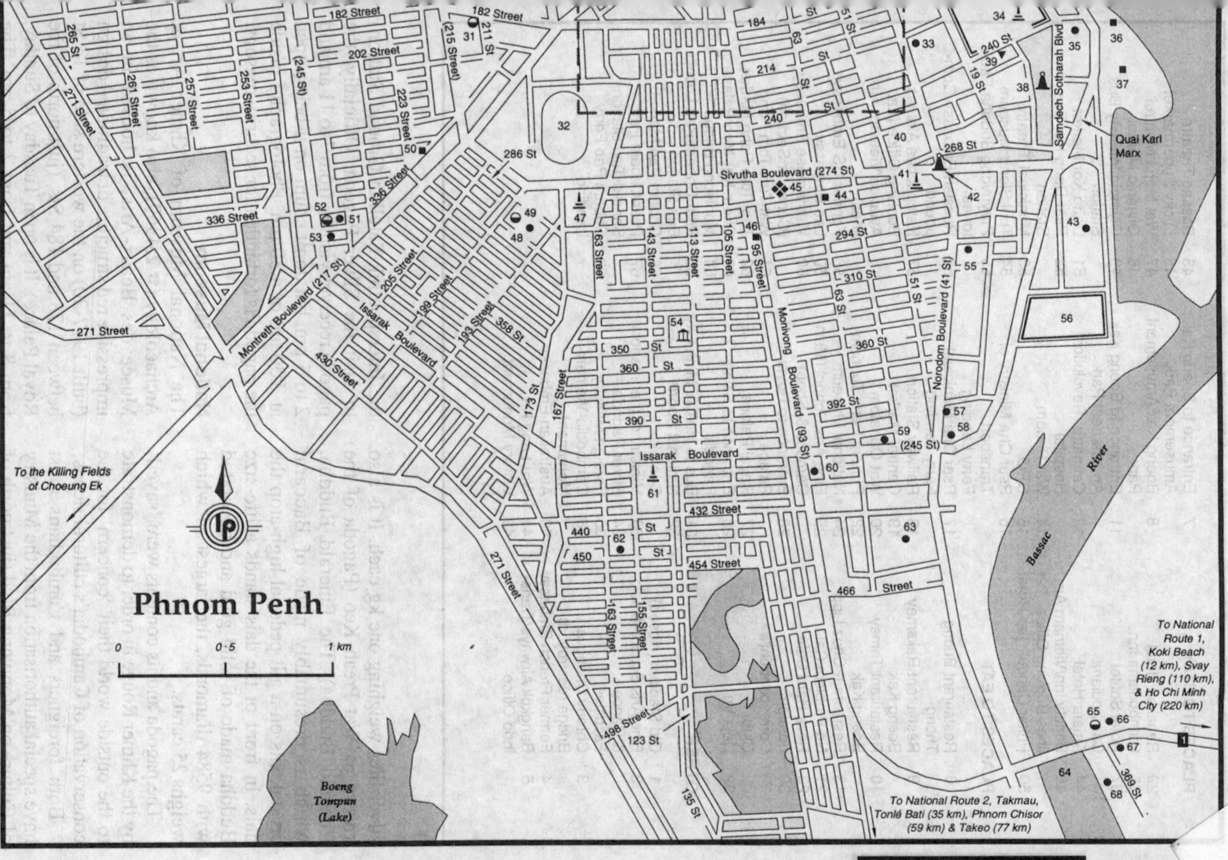
Phnom Penh
0
0·5
1 km
To National Route 1, Koki Beach (12 km), Svay Rieng (110 km), & Ho Chi Minh City (220 km)
To National Route 2, Takmau, Tonlé Bati (35 km), Phnom Chisor (59 km) & Takeo (77 km)
To the Killing Fields of Choeung Ek
Bassac River
Boeng Tompun (Lake)
Quai Karl Marx
Samdech Sotharah Blvd
Norodom Boulevard (41 St)
Monivong Boulevard (93 St)
Sivutha Boulevard (274 St)
Issarak Boulevard
Monireth Boulevard (217 St)
271 Street
498 Street
123 St
135 St
155 Street
163 Street
167 Street
173 St
105 Street
113 Street
143 Street
95 Street
182 Street
202 Street
223 Street
253 Street
257 Street
261 Street
265 St
286 St
336 Street
430 Street
432 Street
454 Street
466 Street
268 St
240 St
19 St

PLACES TO STAY

29 Renakse Hotel
36 Cambodiana Inn
37 Hotel Sofitel Cambodiana
44 Amara Hotel
46 Beauty Inn/Vietnam Airlines Booking Office
50 Phkar Chhouk Tep Hotel

PLACES TO EAT

6 Restaurant Buong Thong
9 Restaurant Raksmey Boeng Kak
10 Restaurant Thmey Boeng Kak
13 Restaurant Chez Lipp
21 No Problem Café
23 Rock Hard Café
30 Foreign Correspondent's Club
39 Déja Vu

OTHER

1 Old Stadium (closed)
2 Fine Arts School (Music & Dance Faculties)
3 Chrouy Changvar Bridge (destroyed)
4 Former French Embassy
5 Bangkok Airways/Transindo Office
7 Entrance to Boeng Kak Amusement Park
8 Boeng Kak Amusement Park
11 Entrance to Boeng Kak Amusement Park
12 Calmette (Revolution) Hospital
14 Wat Phnom
15 GPO
16 Psar Cha Ministry of Transport Ferry Landing
17 Psar Cha Municipal Ferry Landing
18 Railway Station
19 Central Market
20 Wat Ounalom
22 Phnom Penh Tourism
24 National Museum
25 Fine Arts School (Main Campus & Shop)
26 Entrance to Royal Palace
27 Royal Palace
28 Entrance to Silver Pagoda
31 Bus to Ho Chi Minh City
32 National Sports Complex
33 Ministry of the Interior
34 Silver Pagoda
35 Foreign Ministry
38 Cambodia-Vietnam Monument
40 Australian Embassy
41 Wat Lang Ka
42 Victory Monument
43 Bassac Theatre
45 Lucky Supermarket
47 Wat Moha Montrei
48 Olympic Market
49 Olympic Intercity Bus Station
51 Dang Kor Market
52 Psar Dang Kor Bus Station
53 Municipal Theatre
54 Tuol Sleng Museum
55 Prayuvong Buddha Factories
56 Russian Embassy Compound
57 Kampuchea Airlines Booking Office (Lao Aviation/Vietnam Airlines)
58 Former US Embassy
59 Lao Embassy
60 Vietnamese Embassy (Consular Section)
61 Wat Tuol Tom Pong
62 Tuol Tom Pong Market
63 Cham Kar Mon Palace
64 Monivong Bridge
65 Psar Chbam Pao Local Bus Station
66 Chbam Pao Market
67 Psar Chbam Pao Shared-Taxi Station
68 Chbam Pao Ferry Landing

silver tiles weighing one kg each. It is also known as Wat Preah Keo (Pagoda of the Emerald Buddha). The Emerald Buddha, which is presumably made of Baccarat crystal, sits on a gilt pedestal high atop the dais. In front of the dais stands a life-size Buddha made of solid gold and decorated with 9584 diamonds, the largest of which weighs 25 carats.

The pagoda and its contents were 'saved' by the Khmer Rouge in order to demonstrate to the outside world their 'concern' for the conservation of Cambodia's cultural riches.

Both foreigners and Cambodians must have special authorisation from the Ministry of Culture on Monivong Blvd (just north of the Interspoutnik Satellite Ground Station) to visit the Silver Pagoda. Officially, the pagoda receives visitors from 7 to 11 am and 2 to 5 pm, but don't count on it being open at 7.30 am or 4.30 pm. Photography inside the pagoda is forbidden for security reasons.

National Museum

The National Museum of Khmer Art & Archaeology (☎ 2.4369), also known as the Musée des Beaux-Arts, is housed in an impressive red structure of traditional design (built 1917-20) on the western side of 13 St between 178 and 184 Sts, (just north of the Royal Palace). It is open Tuesday to Sunday, from 8 to 11 am and from 2 to 5 pm. The entry fee for foreigners is US$2, and English and French-speaking guides are available. Photography is prohibited inside. The Fine Arts School (École des Beaux-Arts) is in a structure behind the main building.

The National Museum exhibits numerous masterpieces of Khmer art, artisanship and sculpture dating from the pre-Angkor period of Funan and Chenla (4th to 9th centuries AD), the Indravarman period (9th and 10th centuries), the classical Angkor period (10th to 14th centuries) and the post-Angkor period (after the 14th century).

Tuol Sleng Museum

In 1975, Tuol Svay Prey High School was taken over by Pol Pot's security forces and turned into a prison known as Security Prison 21 (S-21). It soon became the largest such centre of detention and torture in the country. Almost all the people held at S-21 were later taken to the extermination camp at Choeung Ek to be executed. Detainees who died during torture were buried in mass graves in the prison grounds. During the first part of 1977, S-21 claimed an average of 100 victims per day.

S-21 has been turned into the Tuol Sleng Museum (☎ 2.4569), which is a testament to the crimes of the Khmer Rouge. The museum, whose entrance is on the western side of 113 St just north of 350 St, is open daily from 7 to 11.30 am and 2 to 5.30 pm.

Wat Ounalom

Wat Ounalom, headquarters of the Cambodian Buddhist patriarchate, is on the south-western corner of the Samdech Sotharah Blvd and 154 St intersection (across from Phnom Penh Tourism).

Under Pol Pot, the complex, which was founded in 1443 and includes 44 structures, was heavily damaged and its extensive library destroyed. Wat Ounalom was once home to over 500 monks. Now there are only 30, including all of the Buddhist hierarchy.

Other Wats

Other wats in Phnom Penh worth visiting include **Wat Lang Ka**, which is on the southern side of Sivutha Blvd just west of the Victory Monument; **Wat Koh**, which is on the eastern side of Monivong Blvd between 174 and 178 Sts; and **Wat Moha Montrei**, which is one block east of the Olympic Market on the southern side of Sivutha Blvd between 163 and 173 Sts.

Chrouy Changvar Bridge

The 700-metre Chrouy Changvar Bridge over the Tonlé Sap River, just off Monivong Blvd at 74 St, was the country's longest until it was blown up in 1975. It has since become something of a meeting place for young lovers. Refreshments are on sale near the unfenced drop-off.

Boeng Kak Amusement Park

Lakeside Boeng Kak Amusement Park has a small zoo, paddleboats for hire and a few restaurants. Its two entrances are 200 metres west of Monivong Blvd on 80 and 86 Sts.

English St

This is a cluster of private language schools that teach English (and some French). It is one block west of the National Museum on 184 St between Norodom Blvd and the back part of the Royal Palace compound. Between 5 and 7 pm, the whole area is filled with students who see learning English as the key to making it in postwar Cambodia. This is a good place to meet local young people.

Victory Monument

Victory Monument, which is at the intersection of Norodom and Sivutha Blvds, was built in 1958 as Independence Monument. It is now a memorial to Cambodia's war dead (or at least those the present government considers worthy of remembering).

Festivals

The Festival of the Reversing Current (Bon Om Touk or Sampeas Prea Khe in Khmer) is also known as the Water Festival (Fête des Eaux). It corresponds with the moment in late October or early November when the Tonlé Sap River (which since July has been filling the Great Lake with the waters of the

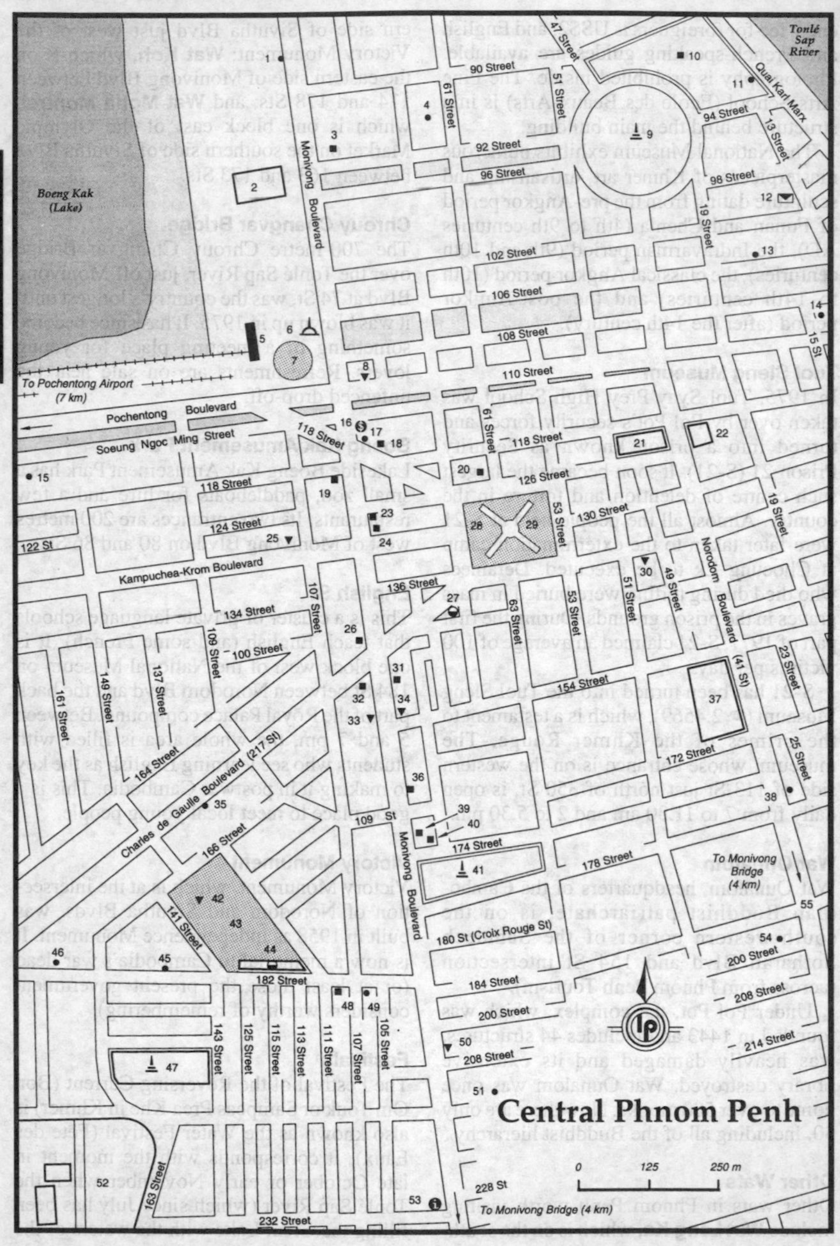
Central Phnom Penh
Tonlé Sap River
Boeng Kak (Lake)
47 Street
90 Street
61 Street
51 Street
Quai Karl Marx
94 Street
13 Street
92 Street
96 Street
98 Street
Monivong Boulevard
19 Street
102 Street
106 Street
108 Street
15 St
110 Street
To Pochentong Airport (7 km)
Pochentong Boulevard
Soeung Ngoc Ming Street
118 Street
126 Street
53 Street
130 Street
124 Street
122 St
Kampuchea-Krom Boulevard
136 Street
134 Street
107 Street
109 Street
100 Street
49 Street
63 Street
Norodom Boulevard (41 St)
23 Street
154 Street
161 Street
149 Street
137 Street
164 Street
Charles de Gaulle Boulevard (217 St)
172 Street
25 Street
109 St
166 Street
174 Street
178 Street
To Monivong Bridge (4 km)
141 Street
180 St (Croix Rouge St)
182 Street
184 Street
200 Street
208 Street
214 Street
143 Street
125 Street
115 Street
113 Street
111 Street
105 Street
163 Street
228 St
232 Street
To Monivong Bridge (4 km)
0
125
250 m
1 2 3 4 5 6 7 8 9 10 11 12 13 14 15 16 17 18 19 20 21 22 23 24 25 26 27 28 29 30 31 32 33 34 35 36 37 38 39 40 41 42 43 44 45 46 47 48 49 50 51 52 53 54 55

PLACES TO STAY

3 Hotel Le Royal
10 Hotel Wat Phnom
18 Hotel Dusit
19 Hotel Monorom
20 Hotel Apsara
23 Hotel Sukhalay
24 Hotel D'Asie
26 Hotel Paradis
31 Pacific Chai Hotel
32 Pailin Hotel
36 Phka Chhouk Hotel
39 Hotel Mittapheap
40 Hotel Orchidee
48 Capitol Guesthouse

PLACES TO EAT

7 Night Market
8 Happy Herb's Pizza
25 Small Restaurants & Pastry Shops
28 Food Stalls
30 Small Restaurants
33 Cheers Pub & Restaurant
34 Night Market
42 Food Stalls
50 Asia Soup Restaurant

OTHER

1 Ministry of Culture
2 Interspoutnik Satellite Ground Station
4 National Library
5 Railway Station
6 Stupa
9 Wat Phnom
11 Entrance to Hotel Wat Phnom
12 GPO
13 Thai International/Silk Air/Dragon Air Booking Offices
14 Old Market
15 Council of Ministers
16 Foreign Trade Bank
17 Phnom Penh Airways Office
21 Customs House
22 Former National Bank Site
27 Psar Thmei Local Bus Terminal
29 Central Market
35 Motorbike Parts Shops
37 Military Museum (closed)
38 Kampuchea Airlines Booking Office
41 Wat Koh
43 O Russei Market
44 O Russei Local Bus Station
45 Bicycle Shops
46 Motorbike Parts Shop
47 Wat Sampao Meas
49 Bicycle Shops
51 Bangkok Airways
52 National Sports Complex
53 Ministry of Tourism
54 Immigration Bureau
55 English Street

flood-swollen Mekong) reverses its flow and begins to empty the Tonlé Sap back into the Mekong. Pirogue (long canoe) races are held in Phnom Penh.

Ethnic-Chinese and Vietnamese living in Cambodia celebrate New Year in late January or early February.

Places to Stay

There is a lot more choice of accommodation in Phnom Penh these days, though the bottom end of the market is still poorly served.

Bottom End Most backpackers head straight to the *Capitol Guesthouse* (also known as the Hotel Capitol). It's a grotty kind of place in a grotty part of town, but for the moment it's the cheapest place in town. Singles range from US$4 to US$6 and doubles from US$8 to US$10. The *Happy Guesthouse*, next door, is run by the same management, has the same rates and takes the overflow from the Capitol.

Elsewhere, rates rise significantly from those offered by the Capitol, though it's worth considering that you do at least get value for money. The *Amara Hotel & Restaurant* (☎ 2.7240) is a quiet and friendly place, where clean air-con singles/doubles with attached bathroom cost US$12/15. It's just south of Sivutha Blvd, around the corner from the Lucky Supermarket.

Another reasonably priced option is the *Phkar Chhouk Tep Hotel* (☎ 2.7446), just off Montreth Blvd on 336 St. Air-con singles/doubles with attached bathroom and TV cost US$15. Not far from the Capitol Guesthouse, at 258 Monivong Blvd, is the *Phka Chhouk Hotel* (☎ 2.6696), another place with clean air-con rooms with attached bathroom. Singles range from US$15 to US$20 and doubles range from US$20 to US$25. Also on Monivong Blvd, south of Sivutha Blvd, is the *Beauty Inn* (☎ 2.7426), where singles are US$16 and doubles are US$22.

Middle There's mid-range accommodation scattered all over Phnom Penh these days,

CAMBODIA

but the highest concentration of places is on Monivong Blvd between Sivutha and Pochentong Blvds. All the places listed in this category have air-con rooms with attached bathrooms. Standards seem to be fairly similar.

About a five-minute walk from the Capitol Guesthouse is the *Hotel Orchidee* (☎ 6.2090), with singles from US$20 to US$30 and doubles at US$40. The similar *Hotel Mittapheap* (☎ 2.6492) is next door and is cheaper: singles/doubles cost only US$20/25. Going further north on Monivong is the *Pacific Chai Hotel* (☎ 015.911097), a friendly place with the same rates as the Mittapheap. Diagonally across the road from here is the *Hotel Paradis* (☎ 2.2951) where singles/doubles cost US$20/30. Slightly north again is the *Hotel D'Asie* (☎ 2.7037), which has singles and doubles from US$28.

Those looking for some decaying colonial ambience might want to check out the *Hotel Le Royal* (☎ 2.4151). The phone was out of order when we called in, and that's fairly representative of the state of affairs in this hotel. The staff are all asleep and the place is falling apart, but it's been around for a while (part of the film *The Killing Fields* was set here). Singles/doubles are US$29/36. The hotel is on the corner of Monivong Blvd and 92 St. Better value in the colonial ambience category is the *Renakse Hotel* (☎ 2.2457), a fine old building which has singles/doubles at US$25/30.

Top End On Monivong Blvd is the *Pailin Hotel* (☎ 2.6696/7), a hotel that's undergone a bit of a facelift recently. Standard singles/doubles are US$33/44, but upmarket suites and deluxe doubles are available at US$66 and US$55.

The *Cambodiana Inn* (☎ 2.6771), on Quai Karl Marx near the foot of 240 St, has a collection of bungalows (each with two rooms) in the grounds of the huge Hotel Cambodiana, under construction since about 1967. The rooms are big, air-conditioned but a little overpriced at US$55 to US$70. It's arguably worth spending the money just for the peacefulness of the well-kept grounds the bungalows are in, though. Next door is the *Hotel Sofitel Cambodiana* (☎ 2.6392), *the* place for visiting dignitaries, UN representatives and the idle rich. It has a collection of shops, restaurants, a cabaret (Filipino entertainers) and a swimming pool. Room rates range from US$160 for a single and US$190 for a double.

Places to Eat

Restaurants – Central Market Area For the latest travellers' gossip, the place to hang out, eat and drink coffee or Angkor beer is the *Capitol Restaurant* beneath the Capitol Guesthouse. The food is nothing to write home about and you'll be racing with the flies to see who finishes it first, but it's a popular place all the same.

Not far away, on the north-eastern corner of the Monivong Blvd and 208 St intersection, is the *Asia Soup Restaurant*, a restaurant known by locals for Vietnamese beef soup made with white vermicelli. North of here on Monivong Blvd, you can sample the eclectic menu of *Cheers Pub & Restaurant* for a few dollars a main course. It advertises itself as preparing Japanese and Thai food – not bad.

It's worth splashing out and spending US$5 to US$10 on a good meal with a couple of drinks while you are in Phnom Penh. There are a few restaurants around with great atmosphere and an interesting mix of Western and Asian cuisine. On 178 St is the *No Problem Café* in a beautifully restored old colonial building. Equally tasteful is *Déja Vu*, an excellent French restaurant run by a friendly foreign couple. It's at No 22, 240 St.

Restaurants – Boeng Kak Area There are at least three restaurants in the lakeside Boeng Kak Amusement Park, whose two entrances are one long block west of Monivong Blvd at 80 St and 86 St. A delicious meal at the two most expensive and popular of them, *Restaurant Thmey Boeng Kak* and *Restaurant Buong Thong*, costs about US$5 per person, though you can spend more if you splash out. The frogs' legs and lobster are excellent.

Just south-east of Boeng Kak, near the corner of Pochentong and Monivong Blvds, is *Happy Herb's Pizza*, a friendly place that is a popular expat hangout. It's about the only place in town you can get a decent pizza, though reckon on spending at least US$6 per head.

Restaurants – Riverfront Redevelopment along the riverfront area is sweeping away a number of popular restaurants. On the other side of Quai Karl Marx though are a couple of popular places to eat and meet people. The foreign-run *Rock Hard Café* has meals from around US$4 and is a *cool* place to lounge around in – look out for the item of Madonna's underwear in a mounted glass cabinet. Just down the road at No 363 is the *Foreign Correspondent's Club* (FFC). You don't need to be a foreign correspondent to hang out here, and there are snacks and drinks at reasonable prices.

Foodstalls Foodstalls can be found in and around the Central Market (on the western side, which faces Kampuchea-Krom Blvd), O Russei Market (along 141 St, midway between 182 and 166 Sts), Tuol Tom Pong Market, the Olympic Market (along 286 St), Dang Kor Market (in the middle), the Old Market (Psar Cha) and near the Psar Cha Ministry of Transport ferry landing.

In the evening and at night, foodstalls pop up between the railway station and Pochentong Blvd. There is a small night market on the corner of Monivong Blvd and 154 St (next to 232 Monivong Blvd).

Things to Buy

The Art-Deco, dark yellow Central Market has four wings filled with shops selling gold and silver jewellery, antique coins, fake name-brand watches and other such items. Antiques, silver items and jewellery are also available from shops at 163, 139, 105 and 99 Monivong Blvd, and on the street that links the Hotel Monorom with the Central Market.

'Luxury' foodstuffs, costume jewellery and imported toiletries are sold in hundreds of stalls at O Russei Market, which is on 182 St between 111 and 141 Sts. Tuol Tom Pong Market, bound by 155 St on the east, 163 St on the west, 440 St on the north and 450 St on the south, is the city's best source of real and fake antiquities.

A great deal of wholesaling is done at the Olympic Market (Marché Olympique), which is near the National Sports complex and Wat Moha Montrei. Dang Kor Market is just north of the intersection of Issarak and Montreth Blvds, where the Municipal Theatre building stands.

Household goods, clothes and jewellery are on sale in and around the Old Market (Psar Cha), which is bound by 13, 15, 108 and 110 Sts. Small restaurants, food vendors and jewellery stalls are scattered throughout the area.

The École des Beaux-Arts (Fine Arts School) shop on the corner of 19 and 184 Sts (at the back of the National Museum complex) is open daily (except Sunday afternoon) from 7 to 11.30 am and from 2 to 5.30 pm. The shop sells traditional-style works made by the school's students, who share in the proceeds.

The checked cotton scarves everyone wears on their heads, around their necks or, if bathing, around their midriffs, are known as *kramas*. Fancier coloured versions are made of silk or a silk-cotton blend. They can be purchased at the Central Market (in the eaves of the main building), at other marketplaces and from the Hotel Monorom giftshop. You can request that unhemmed silk kramas be hemmed on the spot.

Bolts of colourful cloth for sarongs and *hols* (variegated silk shirts) are on sale at Nay Eng, a shop at 108, 136 St (opposite the southern side of the Central Market). It is open from 7 am to 9 pm.

There are a number of photo stores selling Kodak and ORWO print film. These are found along Monivong Blvd (try numbers 149 and 203 and around the White Hotel); most of them also have one-hour colour print processing available these days.

Finally, those hanging out for Arnott's

CAMBODIA

assorted creams or Cadbury chocolates should head over to the Lucky Supermarket on Sivutha Blvd – it has an excellent supply of foreign goods.

Getting There & Away

Air The Kampuchea Airlines booking office (☎ 2.5887) is at 62 Norodom Blvd, just north of Issarak Blvd. Official hours are from 7 to 11 am and from 2 to 5 pm Monday to Saturday. The office represents Lao Aviation and Vietnam Airlines but, while you can buy Vietnam Airline tickets here, to reconfirm them you'll need to go to the main Vietnam Airlines office, which is at 537 Monivong Blvd.

Other offices around town for purchasing international tickets include Bangkok Airways (☎ 2.2335), Silk Air (☎ 2.2034), Thai International (☎ 2.6406) and Dragon Air. The latter three can all be found at No 19, 106 St, just south-east of Wat Phnom. Most airline offices are closed Sunday, open in the morning on Saturday and are open 9 am to 5 pm weekdays. Thai International has a two-hour lunch break from noon to 2 pm.

Bus Buses to points north, east and west of Phnom Penh depart from Olympic Intercity bus station (☎ 2.4613), which is on 199 St next to the Olympic Market (Marché Olympique). Most buses to destinations south and south-west of Phnom Penh depart from Psar Dang Kor bus station, which is on Issarak Blvd next to Dang Kor Market (between 336 St and Montreth Blvd). At both stations, you would be wise to purchase tickets a day before departure. Intercity bus transport is in a state of flux and departure stations may be changed.

Buses leave for Ho Chi Minh City daily at 5 am from an office (☎ 2.3139) on the south-western corner of 211 and 182 Sts. The office is open from 5 to 10 am and from 2 to 5 pm daily except Sunday. One-way passage costs the equivalent of US$12.

Train The Phnom Penh railway station is on the western side of Monivong Blvd between 106 and 108 Sts (☎ 2.3115). Tickets can be purchased the day before departure, between 3 and 5 pm, and on the morning that you intend to travel from 5.55 am. The trip to Battambang is supposed to take 12 hours but, because of frequent attacks and the bad condition of the tracks, rarely does.

Taxi Most travellers organise taxi hire at the Capitol Restaurant beneath the Capitol Guesthouse. This place offers the cheapest rates in town (US$3 out to the airport as opposed to US$5 elsewhere). Some examples include Udong for US$20 and Tonlé Bati for US$15 for up to four people.

Boat Large government-run ferries to Kompong Cham, Kratie, Stung Treng, Kompong Chhnang and Phnom Krom (about 25 km south of Siem Reap) depart from the Psar Cha Ministry of Transport ferry landing (☎ 2.5619), which is on Quai Karl Marx between 102 and 104 Sts. Services to Phnom Krom are irregular and prices vary from around US$5 to US$10 depending on the boat. This is the most popular way to reach Angkor apart from flying.

Passenger ferries to Kompong Cham (and ports along the way) depart from the Psar Cha Municipal ferry landing which is on Quai Karl Marx between 106 and 108 Sts (next to Tonlé Sap 1 Restaurant).

Passenger and goods ferries to Vietnam leave from the Chbam Pao ferry landing. To get there, walk a few hundred metres south from Chbam Pao Market on 369 St and turn right, down an unmarked alleyway, opposite number 210, 369 St.

Getting Around

To/From the Airport Pochentong international airport is seven km west of central Phnom Penh via Pochentong or Kampuchea-Krom Blvds. Official taxis cost US$10, but you can negotiate a taxi (before you leave customs!) for US$5 or less. For a couple of dollars or less you can get a ride on the back of a motorbike.

Bus Buses and small passenger trucks serving Phnom Penh's suburbs (including Chbam Pao Market, which is across the river, the mosques of Chraing Chamres and Pochentong international airport) depart from a parking lot on 182 St next to O Russei Market. The station operates from about 5.30 am until sundown.

The Psar Thmei local bus terminal is 100 metres south-west of the Central Market at the intersection of Charles de Gaulle Blvd and 136 St. Buses leave for Chbam Pao, Chraing Chamres and Takmao from about 5.30 am to 5 pm.

Buses from the lot in front of Chbam Pao Market go to O Russei Market and the Central Market.

Motorbike & Bicycle Bicycles are available for hire at US$2 per day and motorbikes at US$5 per day at the Capitol Restaurant.

Cyclo Cyclos (samlors), which can be found cruising around town and at marketplaces, are a great way to see the city. Some of the drivers who hang out near major hotels speak a bit of English or French.

Around Phnom Penh

NUR UL-IHSAN MOSQUE

This mosque, seven km north of downtown Phnom Penh on National Route 5 and in Khet Chraing Chamres, was founded in 1813. According to local people, it was used by the Khmer Rouge as a pigsty and was reconsecrated in 1979. It now serves a community of 360 Cham and ethnic-Malay Muslims. Next to the mosque is a *madrasa* (religious school). Shoes must be removed before entering the mosque.

Getting There & Away

To get to Nur ul-Ihsan Mosque, take a bus, Lambretta or *remorque-moto* (a trailer pulled by motorbike) heading towards Khet Prek Phnou from O Russei Market. Newly rebuilt **An-Nur An-Na'im Mosque** is about one km north of Nur ul-Ihsan Mosque.

KILLING FIELDS OF CHOEUNG EK

Between 1975 and December 1978, about 17,000 men, women and children (including nine Westerners), detained and tortured at S-21 prison (now Tuol Sleng Museum), were transported to the extermination camp of Choeung Ek to be executed. They were bludgeoned to death to avoid wasting precious bullets.

The remains of 8985 people, many of whom were found bound and blindfolded, were exhumed in 1980 from mass graves in this one-time longan orchard. Some 43 of the 129 communal graves here have been left untouched. Fragments of human bone and bits of cloth are scattered around the disinterred pits. Over 8000 skulls, arranged by sex and age, are visible behind the clear glass panels of the Memorial Stupa, which was erected in 1988.

Getting There & Away

The Killing Fields of Choeung Ek are 15 km south-west from downtown Phnom Penh. The Capitol Guesthouse has a taxi service for US$4 for one person and U$10 for five people.

UDONG

Udong, 40 km north of Phnom Penh, served as the capital of Cambodia under several sovereigns between 1618 and 1866. Phnom Udong, a bit south of the old capital, consists of two parallel ridges, both of which offer great views of the Cambodian countryside and its innumerable sugar palm trees. The larger, uneven ridge, Phnom Preah Reach Throap (Hill of the Royal Fortune), is so named because a 16th-century Khmer monarch is said to have hidden the national treasury here during a war with the Thais.

The most impressive structure on Phnom Preah Reach Throap is **Vihear Preah Ath Roes**, or Vihara of the 18-Cubit (nine-metre) Buddha. The vihara and the Buddha, dedicated in 1911 by King Sisowath, were blown up by the Khmer Rouge in 1977.

CAMBODIA

At the north-west extremity of the ridge stand three large **stupas**. The first one you come to is the final resting place of King Monivong (ruled 1927-41). Nearby, a staircase leads down the hill to the access road and a **pavilion** decorated with graphic murals of Khmer Rouge atrocities. Across the street is a **memorial** containing the bones of some of the people who were buried in approximately 100 mass graves found on the other side of the hill.

Getting There & Away

Most travellers get together with a couple of others and hire a taxi from the Capitol Restaurant for US$20, but you could also hire a motorbike and do it yourself by heading north out of Phnom Penh on National Route 5. Continue on past Prek Kdam Ferry for 4½ km and turn left (southward) at the roadblock and bunker. Udong is 3½ km south of the turn-off.

By bus, take any vehicle heading from Phnom Penh towards Kompong Chhnang or Battambang and get off at the roadblock and bunker.

TONLÉ BATI

South of Phnom Penh, the laterite **Ta Prohm Temple** was built by King Jayavarman VII (ruled 1181 to 1201) on the site of a 6th-century Khmer shrine. The main sanctuary consists of five chambers. In each is a statue or linga (or what is left of them after the destruction wrought by the Khmer Rouge). The site is open all day, every day. A Khmer-speaking guide can be hired for around US$1 a day.

About 300 metres north-west of Ta Prohm Temple, a long, narrow peninsula juts into the Bati River. On Sunday, it is packed with picnickers and vendors selling food, drink and fruit.

Getting There & Away

The access road to Ta Prohm Temple, which is in the Tonlé Bati district of Takeo Province, intersects National Route 2 at a point 33 km south of Phnom Penh, 21 km north of the access road to Phnom Chisor and 44 km north of Takeo. The temple is 2½ km from the highway. Any bus linking Phnom Penh with the town of Takeo by way of National Route 2 will pass by the access road. Taxis taking up to four people are available at the Capitol Restaurant for US$15.

PHNOM CHISOR

There is a spectacular view of the surrounding countryside from the top of Phnom Chisor. The main temple, which stands at the eastern side of the hilltop, was constructed in the 11th century of laterite and brick. The carved lintels are made of sandstone. On the plain to the east of Phnom Chisor are two other Khmer temples, **Sen Thmol** (at the bottom of Phnom Chisor) and **Sen Ravang** (further east), and the former sacred pond of **Tonlé Om**. All three form a straight line with Phnom Chisor.

Getting There & Away

The intersection of National Route 2 with the eastward-bound access road to Phnom Chisor is marked by the two brick towers of Prasat Neang Khmau (Temple of the Black Virgin), which may have once served as a sanctuary to Kali, the dark Hindu goddess of destruction.

Prasat Neang Khmau is on National Route 2 at a point 55 km south of central Phnom Penh, 21 km south of the turn-off to Tonlé Bati and 23 km north of Takeo. The distance from the highway to the base of the hill is a bit over four km.

There are two paths up the 100-metre-high ridge, which takes about 15 minutes to climb. A good way to see the view in all directions is to go up the northern path and to come down the southern stairway.

Angkor

The world-famous temples of Angkor, built between seven and 11 centuries ago when the Khmer civilisation was at the height of its extraordinary creativity, constitute one of humanity's most magnificent architectural achievements. From Angkor, the kings of the Khmer Empire ruled over a vast territory that extended from the tip of what is now southern Vietnam northward to Yunnan in China, and from Vietnam westward to the Bay of Bengal.

The 100 or so temples constitute the sacred skeleton of a much larger and spectacular administrative and religious centre whose houses, public buildings and palaces were constructed out of wood – now long decayed – because the right to dwell in structures of brick or stone was reserved for the gods.

SIEM REAP

The town of Siem Reap is only a few km from the temples of Angkor and serves as a base for visits to the monuments. The name Siem Reap (pronounced 'see-EM ree-EP') means Siamese Defeated.

Siem Reap is 6.4 km south of Angkor Wat and 9.7 km south of the Bayon.

Information

The offices of Angkor Tourism, the government tourism authority in the Angkor area, are in a small building next to the Villa Princière, the structure just east (towards the Siem Reap River) of the Grand Hotel d'Angkor. There's also an office at the airport, but there's no need to deal with either of them.

Angkor Conservation (☎ 82), also referred to as Angkor Conservancy, which has official responsibility for the study, preservation and upkeep of the Angkor monuments, is in a large compound between Siem Reap and Angkor Wat. Over 5000 statues, lingas and inscribed steles found in the vicinity of Angkor are stored here for safekeeping. Special permission is required to view the items here. Inquire at the front desk of the Grand Hotel d'Angkor.

Fees Each of the sights in the Angkor area has a separate entry fee. These are grouped together into sections: Angkor Wat (US$13); Angkor Thom (US$15); Petit Circuit (US$13); Grand Circuit (US$11); Outside Angkor (US$14); Roluos Group (US$5). You pay at a gate about halfway between the Grand Hotel and Angkor Wat but, no matter what you pay to visit, once you are through the gate there seems to be no policing of the sights for fee payment.

Dangers Some areas in and around the temple complexes have been mined. Visitors should *not* stray from clearly marked paths.

Places to Stay

The venerable *Grand Hotel d'Angkor* (☎ 15), built in 1928, charges US$30/40 for singles/doubles. Plans to renovate this place seem to have floundered on apathy or incompetence – perhaps both. The *Villa Apsara*, an extension of the Grand, sports a swimming pool that looks like a good location for a remake of *The Blob*. The rooms are mildewy and cost US$50/60 for singles/doubles – avoid it.

Most travellers skip the Grand and head off to one of the many guesthouses that have sprung up around town. There are dozens of them, most without names – just numbers. Most of them are on the sidestreets running off National Route 6. A good starting place is on the second street to the right just over the bridge from the Grand (heading towards the Central Market). Around the Bayon Restaurant, you'll find *Mom's* and the *Sunrise Guesthouse*. Both charge US$5 for a room with shared bathroom.

There are also numerous guesthouses around town charging from US$15 to US$20 for a room with air-con and attached bathroom. Try the *Sony Guesthouse* or the *Ban Thai*. Taxi drivers coming in from the airport all know the current prices of guesthouses and can drop you off at one.

Places to Eat

The restaurant of the *Grand Hotel d'Angkor* has set meals for US$10, but you can eat cheaper by choosing only one or two of the dishes. It's worth eating there at least once, if only to witness the incredible incompetence of the waiters. There are a number of other places to eat around town, including

CAMBODIA

the *Bayon Restaurant*, just off National Route 6 about 100 metres east of the Siem Reap River. One of the best places around is the *Samapheap Restaurant* (take the first street to the right over the Siem Reap River from the Grand). The food is cheap and tasty, and the service is friendly.

Getting There & Away

Air There are two flights daily to and from Phnom Penh and Siem Reap. A round-trip costs US$86. The flight takes around 25 minutes by a jet Turpolev Tu134. There's a US$4 departure tax at Phnom Penh airport.

Siem Reap airport is seven km north-west of town and four km due west of Angkor Wat.

Bus & Car Some travellers are reportedly coming from Thailand to Angkor by road (from Poipet by way of Sisophon). Angkor is only 418 km from Bangkok via the border crossing between Poipet, in Cambodia, and Aranyaprathet, in Thailand. It would be an arduous trip on bad roads and would entail considerable risk of armed robbery by the Khmer Rouge. Once the civil war really ends, it should be a much more viable proposition.

Because the road from Phnom Penh to Angkor is in a state of extreme dilapidation, the 311-km drive takes two days.

Train Some travellers make their way by train to Battambang from Phnom Penh (2500r) and then travel onwards to Siem Reap by hire taxi (US$20-30). You'll need to overnight in Battambang, where there is basic accommodation. The trip to Battambang will probably take around 14 hours. Theft is a very real risk on the train – armed attacks also occur from time to time. The Cambodian authorities do not advise foreigners to use this train service, though it is not forbidden.

Boat Ferries from Phnom Penh to Phnom Krom, about 25 km south of Siem Reap, depart from the capital's Psar Cha Ministry of Transport ferry landing. The trip takes two days, with an overnight stop at Kompong Chhnang. There is an irregular 'fast' service that does the trip in one day for around 30,000r. Breakdowns are frequent, and locals report that boats have been known to overturn – bring your water wings.

Getting Around

Angkor Tourism hires out taxis for US$20 per day, but you can come to a cheaper arrangement with the taxi drivers that hang around at the airport. Many of the guesthouses around town hire out motorbikes for US$5 per day, and this is probably the most popular way of getting around for backpackers. Bicycles are available for hire, but it's hot work cycling around Angkor.

TEMPLES OF ANGKOR

Between the 9th and the 13th centuries, a succession of Khmer kings who ruled from Angkor utilised the vast wealth and huge labour force of their empire to carry out a series of monumental construction projects. Intended to glorify both the kings and their capitals, a number were built in the vicinity of Siem Reap.

The successive cities at Angkor were centred on a temple-mountain identified with Mt Meru, home of the gods in Hindu cosmology, which served as both the centre of the earthly kingdom over which the king ruled and the symbolic centre of the universe within which the kingdom existed.

Many of the temples around Angkor were built to serve as foci for cults through which various important personages were identified with one of the gods of the Indian pantheon and thus assured immortality. The grandest such structure was Angkor Wat.

The 'lost city' of Angkor became the centre of intense European popular and scholarly interest after the publication in the 1860s of *Le Tour du Monde*, an account by the French naturalist Henri Mouhot of his voyages. A group of talented and dedicated archaeologists and philologists, mostly French, soon undertook a comprehensive programme of research.

Under the aegis of the École Française

d'Extrême Orient, they made an arduous effort – begun in 1908 and interrupted at the beginning of the 1970s by the war – to clear away the jungle vegetation that was breaking apart the monuments and to rebuild the damaged structures, restoring them to something approaching their original grandeur.

The three most magnificent temples at Angkor are the Bayon, which faces east and is best visited in the early morning; Ta Prohm, which is overgrown by the jungle; and Angkor Wat, the only monument here facing westward and at its finest in the late afternoon.

If you've got the time, all these monuments are well worth several visits each. Angkor's major sites can be seen without undue pressure in three full days of touring.

Angkor Thom

The fortified city of Angkor Thom, some 10 sq km in extent, was built in its present form by Angkor's greatest builder, Jayavarman VII (reigned 1181 to 1201), who came to power just after the disastrous sacking of the previous Khmer capital, centred around the Baphuon, by the Chams.

Angkor Thom, which may have had a million inhabitants (more than any European city of the period), is enclosed by a square wall eight metres high and 12 km in length. It is also encircled by a moat 100 metres wide said to have been guarded by a number of fierce crocodiles.

The city has five monumental gates, one each in the north, west and south walls and two in the east wall.

The Bayon The most outstanding feature of the Bayon, which was built by Jayavarman VII in the exact centre of the city of Angkor Thom, is the eerie and unsettling third level, with its 49 towers projecting 172 icily smiling, gargantuan faces of Avalokitesvara.

Almost as extraordinary are the Bayon's 1200 metres of bas-reliefs, incorporating over 11,000 figures. The famous carvings on the outer wall of the first level depict vivid scenes of life in 12th-century Cambodia.

The Baphuon The Baphuon, a pyramidal representation of Mt Meru, is 200 metres north-west of the Bayon. It was constructed by Udayadityavarman II (reigned 1050 to 1066) at the centre of his city, the third built at Angkor.

The decor of the Baphuon, including the door frames, lintels and octagonal columns, is particularly fine. On the western side of the temple, the retaining wall of the second level was fashioned – apparently in the 15th century – into a reclining Buddha 40 metres in length.

Terrace of Elephants The 350-metre-long Terrace of Elephants was used as a giant reviewing stand for public ceremonies and served as a base for the king's grand audience hall. The middle section of the retaining wall is decorated with human-size Garudas (mythical human-birds) and lions. Towards either end are the two parts of the famous Parade of Elephants.

Terrace of the Leper King The Terrace of the Leper King, just north of the Terrace of Elephants, is a platform seven metres in height on top of which stands a nude (though sexless) statue (actually a copy). The figure, possibly of Shiva, is believed by the locals to be of Yasovarman, a Khmer ruler whom legend says died of leprosy.

The front retaining walls are decorated with five or so tiers of meticulously executed carvings of seated *apsaras* (shapely dancing women).

On the southern side of the Terrace of the Leper King (facing the Terrace of Elephants) is the entry to a long, narrow trench excavated by archaeologists. This passageway follows the front wall of an earlier terrace that was covered up when the present structure was built. The figures look as fresh as if they had been carved yesterday.

Angkor Wat

Angkor Wat, with its soaring towers and extraordinary bas-reliefs, is considered by many to be one of the most inspired and

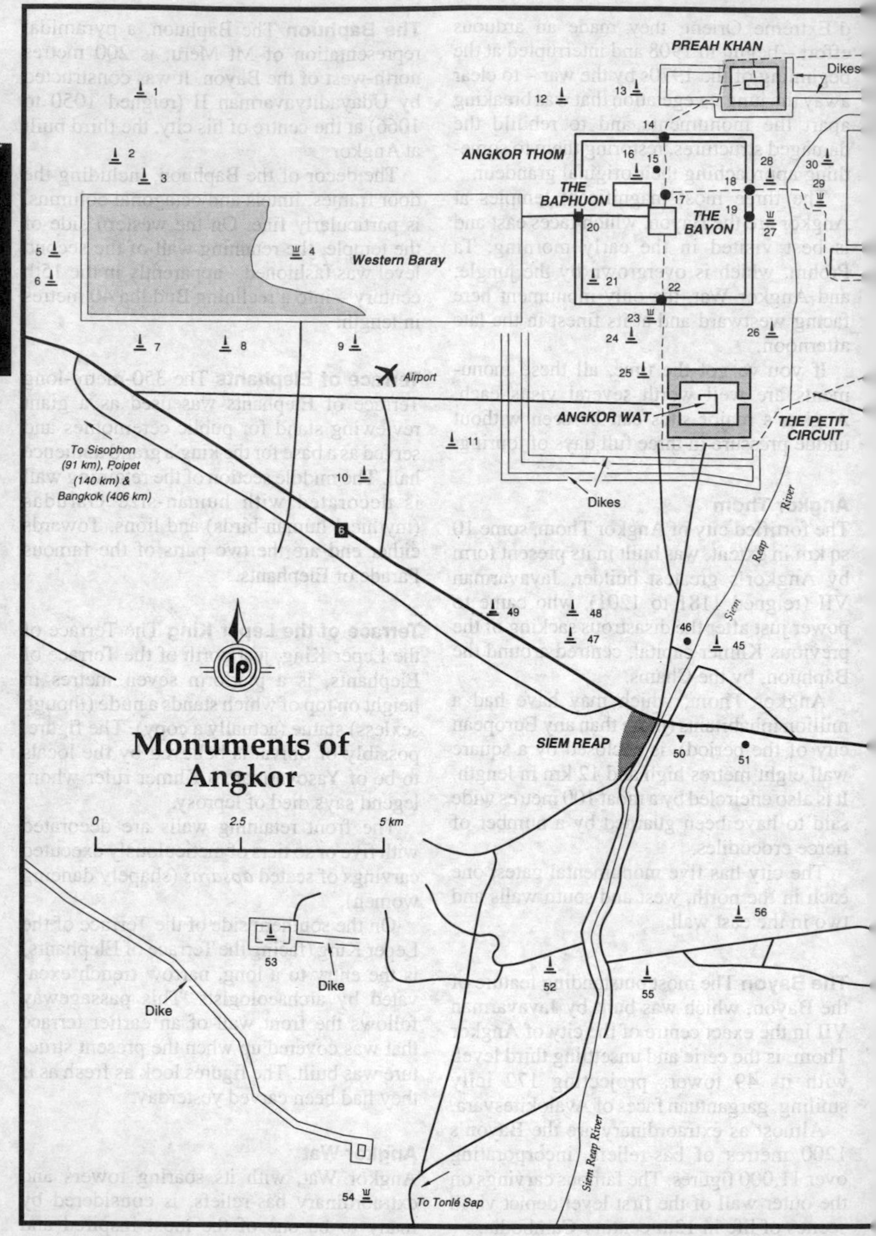
Monuments of Angkor
PREAH KHAN
Dikes
ANGKOR THOM
THE BAPHUON
THE BAYON
Western Baray
Airport
ANGKOR WAT
THE PETIT CIRCUIT
To Sisophon (91 km), Poipet (140 km) & Bangkok (406 km)
Dikes
Siem Reap River
SIEM REAP
0
2.5
5 km
Dike
Dike
Siem Reap River
To Tonlé Sap
1
2
3
4
5
6
7
8
9
10
11
12
13
14
15
16
17
18
19
20
21
22
23
24
25
26
27
28
29
30
45
46
47
48
49
50
51
52
53
54
55
56

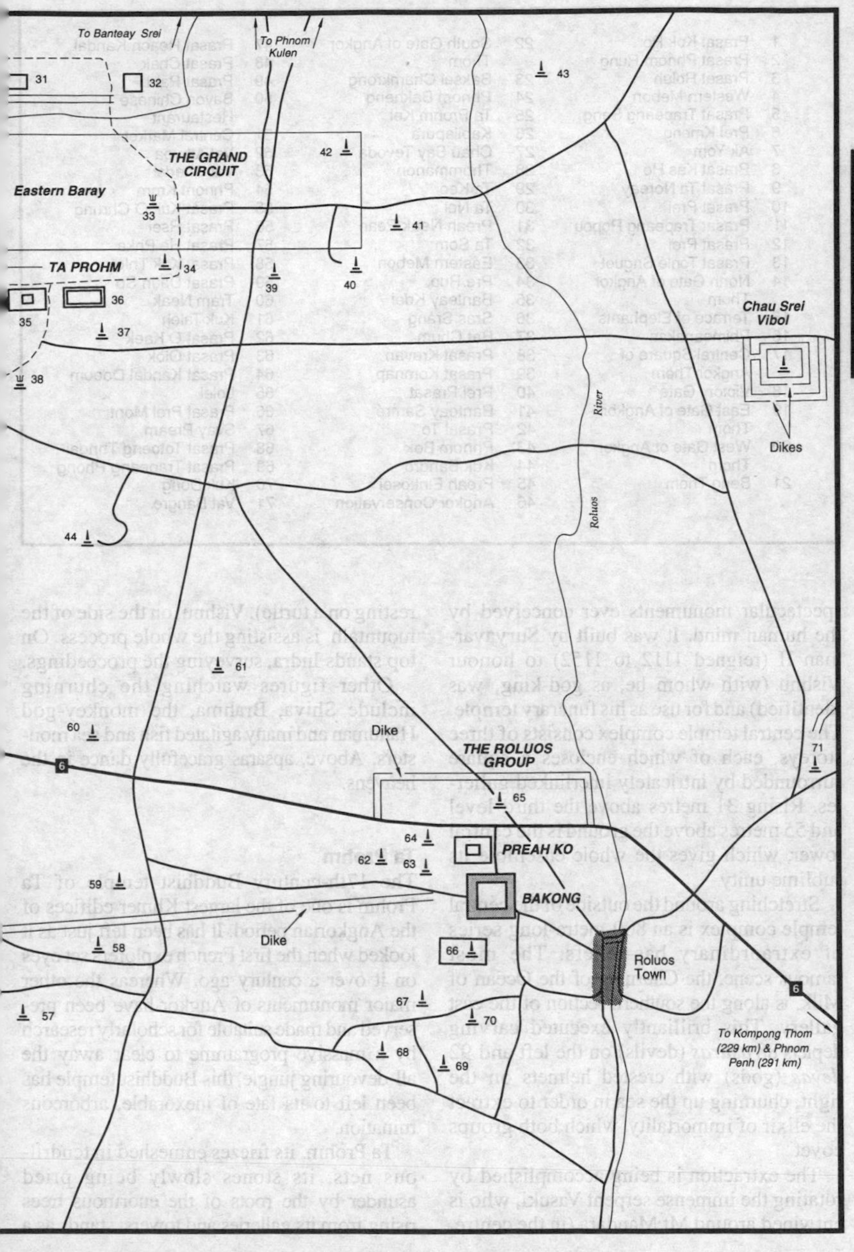
To Banteay Srei
To Phnom Kulen
THE GRAND CIRCUIT
Eastern Baray
TA PROHM
Chau Srei Vibol
Dikes
River
Roluos
Dike
THE ROLUOS GROUP
PREAH KO
BAKONG
Dike
Roluos Town
To Kompong Thom (229 km) & Phnom Penh (291 km)
6
31
32
33
34
35
36
37
38
39
40
41
42
43
44
57
58
59
60
61
62
63
64
65
66
67
68
69
70
71

1 Prasat Kok Po
2 Prasat Phnom Rung
3 Prasat Roluh
4 Western Mebon
5 Prasat Trapeang Seng
6 Prei Kmeng
7 Ak Yom
8 Prasat Kas Ho
9 Prasat Ta Noreay
10 Prasat Prei
11 Prasat Trapeang Ropou
12 Prasat Prei
13 Prasat Tonlé Snguot
14 North Gate of Angkor Thom
15 Terrace of Elephants
16 Phimeanakas
17 Central Square of Angkor Thom
18 Victory Gate
19 East Gate of Angkor Thom
20 West Gate of Angkor Thom
21 Beng Thom
22 South Gate of Angkor Thom
23 Baksei Chamkrong
24 Phnom Bakheng
25 Ta Prohm Kel
26 Kapilapura
27 Chau Say Tevoda
28 Thommanon
29 Ta Keo
30 Ta Nei
31 Preah Neak Pean
32 Ta Som
33 Eastern Mebon
34 Pre Rup
35 Banteay Kdei
36 Sras Srang
37 Bat Chum
38 Prasat Kravan
39 Prasat Komnap
40 Prei Prasat
41 Banteay Samré
42 Prasat To
43 Phnom Bok
44 Kuk Bangro
45 Preah Einkosei
46 Angkor Conservation
47 Prasat Reach Kandal
48 Prasat Chak
49 Prasat Patri
50 Bayon Chinese Restaurant
51 Central Market
52 Vat Athvea
53 Vat Chedei
54 Phnom Krom
55 Prasat Kuk O Chrung
56 Prasat Rsei
57 Prasat He Phka
58 Prasat Kok Thlok
59 Prasat Daun So
60 Tram Neak
61 Kuk Taleh
62 Prasat O Kaek
63 Prasat Olok
64 Prasat Kandal Doeum
65 Lolei
66 Prasat Prei Monti
67 Svay Pream
68 Prasat Totoeng Thngai
69 Prasat Trapeang Phong
70 Kuk Dong
71 Vat Bangro

spectacular monuments ever conceived by the human mind. It was built by Suryavarman II (reigned 1112 to 1152) to honour Vishnu (with whom he, as god-king, was identified) and for use as his funerary temple. The central temple complex consists of three storeys, each of which encloses a square surrounded by intricately interlinked galleries. Rising 31 metres above the third level and 55 metres above the ground is the central tower, which gives the whole ensemble its sublime unity.

Stretching around the outside of the central temple complex is an 800-metre-long series of extraordinary bas-reliefs. The most famous scene, the Churning of the Ocean of Milk, is along the southern section of the east gallery. This brilliantly executed carving depicts 88 *asuras* (devils) on the left and 92 *devas* (gods) with crested helmets on the right, churning up the sea in order to extract the elixir of immortality, which both groups covet.

The extraction is being accomplished by rotating the immense serpent Vasuki, who is entwined around Mt Mandara (in the centre, resting on a turtle). Vishnu, on the side of the mountain, is assisting the whole process. On top stands Indra, surveying the proceedings.

Other figures watching the churning include Shiva, Brahma, the monkey-god Hanuman and many agitated fish and sea monsters. Above, apsaras gracefully dance in the heavens.

Ta Prohm

The 17th-century Buddhist temple of Ta Prohm is one of the largest Khmer edifices of the Angkorian period. It has been left just as it looked when the first French explorers set eyes on it over a century ago. Whereas the other major monuments of Angkor have been preserved and made suitable for scholarly research by a massive programme to clear away the all-devouring jungle, this Buddhist temple has been left to its fate of inexorable, arboreous ruination.

Ta Prohm, its friezes enmeshed in tendrilous nets, its stones slowly being pried asunder by the roots of the enormous trees rising from its galleries and towers, stands as a monument to the awesome fecundity and power of the jungle. It is not to be missed.

ROLUOS GROUP

The monuments of Roluos, which served as the capital of Indravarman I (reigned 877 to 889), are among the earliest large, permanent temples built by the Khmers and mark the beginning of Khmer classical art.

Preah Ko

Preah Ko was erected by Indravarman I in the late 9th century. The six brick *prasats* (towers), aligned in two rows and decorated with carved sandstone and plaster reliefs, face eastward. Sanskrit inscriptions appear on the doorposts of each temple.

Bakong

Bakong, constructed by Indravarman I and dedicated to Shiva, was intended to represent Mt Meru. The eastward-facing complex consists of a five-tier central pyramid of sandstone flanked by eight towers of brick and sandstone (or their remains) and other minor sanctuaries.

Getting There & Away

The Roluos Group is 13 km east of Siem Reap along National Route 6. Preah Ko is 600 metres south of National Route 6 (to the right as you head away from Siem Reap). Bakong is about a km further south.

South Coast

KAMPOT

The pretty riverside town of Kampot (population 14,000) is on the Tuk Chhou River (also called the Prek Thom River), five km from the sea. Although many buildings in town were damaged by the Khmer Rouge, Kampot retains much of its charm. The **To Chu Falls** are north of Kampot towards the hills.

Places to Stay & Eat

Hotels include the *Phnom Kamchai Hotel* and the *Phnom Khieu Hotel* (Blue Mountain Hotel) near the central plaza, and the *Kampot Province Hotel* on the river.

There are foodstalls in the main market and elsewhere around town.

Getting There & Away

Because of the road's dilapidated state, the 148-km drive from Phnom Penh to Kampot along National Route 3 takes five hours.

BOKOR HILL STATION

The now-ruined mountaintop hill station of Bokor (elevation 1080 metres), 41 km west from Kampot and 190 km south-west from Phnom Penh, is known for its pleasant climate, rushing streams, forested vistas and stunning panoramas of the sea.

The best time of year to visit Bokor, which is in the Elephant Mountains, is said to be between November and May. The two **waterfalls** of Popokvil, 14 and 18 metres high, are not far from the access road to Bokor Hill Station.

KEP

The seaside resort of Kep (Kep-sur-Mer), with its six-km palm-shaded corniche, was once a favourite vacation spot for Cambodia's Frenchified elite.

Under the Khmer Rouge, the town (founded in 1908) and its many villas were completely destroyed – not neglected and left to dilapidate, but intentionally turned into utter ruins. The Khmer Rouge also turned the underground petrol tank of the old Shell station into a mass grave. By 1979, not a single building remained intact in Kep.

Although there are plans to rebuild Kep and re-establish it as a beach resort, at present it is a ghost town with only one basic guesthouse.

Getting There & Away

If you take the train, get off at the Damnak Chang Aeu railway station, which is a few km from Kep. By road, Kep is 24 km south-east of Kampot and 49 km from the Vietnamese town of Ha Tien. There is a border crossing eight km north of Ha Tien but it is not presently open to foreigners.

CAMBODIA

KIRIROM

The hill station of Kirirom, set amidst pine forests and 675 metres above sea level, is 112 km south-west of Phnom Penh. It is in the Elephant Mountains to the west of National Route 4.

SIHANOUKVILLE (KOMPONG SOM)

Sihanoukville (also known as Kompong Som), Cambodia's only maritime port, had a population of 16,000 in the mid-1960s and probably has the same population now. Near town, there are superb beaches and, for diving enthusiasts, shoals and reefs teeming with multicoloured fish.

Places to Stay & Eat

Sihanoukville looks set to take off as a popular travellers' destination. There are a few guesthouses around town charging US$5 for a basic room with shared bathroom. *Doctor Zog Seaview* is on Independence Beach, is foreign run and is the cheapest place around. It has dorm beds for US$3 and two doubles for US$10. It's signposted from town. On Sokha Beach there are a number of run-down French *bungalows* for around US$40.

In town is the *Café Rendezvous*, a foreign-run French restaurant. Locals report that the best seafood in Cambodia is available at the beachfront *Koh Pos Restaurant*.

Getting There & Away

Sihanoukville is 232 km south-west from Phnom Penh via one of the best roads in the country, National Route 4. Hire taxis from Dang Kor Market in Phnom Penh cost US$20. Sihanoukville can also be reached from the capital by train, but very few travellers come this way. Flights are available for US$40.

Warning

We currently recommend that visitors do not travel to the Cambodian port of Sihanoukville, previously known as Kompong Som, by road or rail. The kidnapping and subsequent murder in April 1994 of three visitors (two British and one Australian) travelling by road and the more recent kidnapping in July of three more visitors (one British, one French, one Australian) travelling by train indicates that this area is not safe. ■

Hong Kong

Precariously perched on the edge of China, Hong Kong is a curious anomaly. It's an energetic paragon of the virtues of capitalism but nevertheless gets the unofficial blessing of the largest Communist country in the world – on which it is dependent for its very existence. The countdown to 1997, when Hong Kong is due to be handed back to the People's Republic, has made it an even more volatile and intriguing enigma.

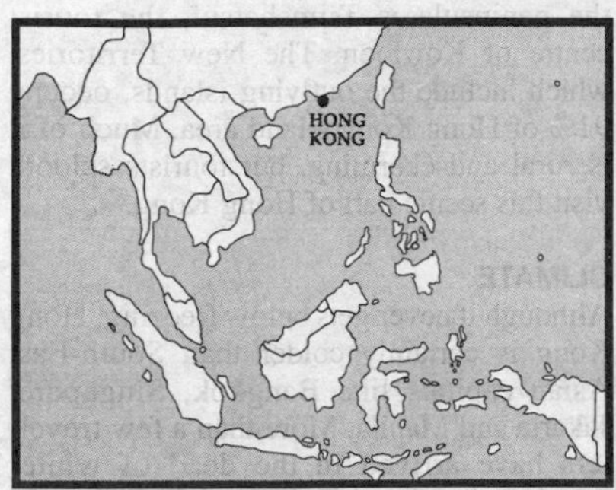

Facts about the Country

HISTORY

Hong Kong must stand as one of the more successful results of dope running. The dope was opium and the runners were backed by the British government. European trade with China goes back over 400 years. As the trade mushroomed during the 18th century and European demand for Chinese tea and silk grew, the balance of trade became more and more unfavourable to the Europeans – until they started to run opium into the country.

The Middle Kingdom grew alarmed at this turn of events and attempted to throw the foreign devils out. The war of words ended when British gunboats were sent in. There were only two of them, but they managed to demolish a Chinese fleet of 29 ships. The ensuing First Opium War went much the same way and, at its close in 1842, the island of Hong Kong was ceded to the British.

Following the Second Opium War in 1860, Britain took possession of the Kowloon Peninsula. Finally, in 1898, a 99-year lease was granted for the New Territories. What would happen after the lease ended on 1 July 1997 was the subject of considerable speculation. Although the British supposedly had possession of Hong Kong Island and the Kowloon Peninsula for all eternity, it was pretty clear that if they handed back the New Territories, China would want the rest as well.

Late in 1984, an agreement was finally reached that China would take over the entire colony lock, stock and skyscrapers, but that Hong Kong's unique free-enterprise economy would be maintained for at least 50 years. It would be a tiny enclave of all-out capitalism within the Chinese sphere. However, many of Hong Kong's population – well aware of China's broken promises and erratic policies of the past – aren't yet buying it. The emigration queues at the embassies of Australia, Canada, New Zealand and the USA grow longer all the time.

The reality of the situation has always been, of course, that China could reclaim Hong Kong any time it wanted to. Hong Kong has survived so long already simply because it's been useful. It acts as a funnel for Chinese goods to the West and for Western goods into China. Also, it is a valuable source of both foreign exchange and information, without the need for China to let corrupting foreign influences across the border.

GEOGRAPHY

Hong Kong's 1070 sq km is divided into four main areas – Kowloon, Hong Kong Island, the New Territories and the outlying islands.

Hong Kong Island is the economic heart of the colony, but only 7% of Hong Kong's land area. Kowloon is the densely populated peninsula to the north. The southern tip of the peninsula is Tsimshatsui, the tourist centre of Kowloon. The New Territories, which include the outlying islands, occupy 91% of Hong Kong's land area. Much of it is rural and charming, but tourists seldom visit this scenic part of Hong Kong.

CLIMATE

Although it never gets below freezing, Hong Kong is certainly colder than South-East Asian capitals like Bangkok, Singapore, Jakarta and Manila. More than a few travellers have arrived in the dead of winter wearing shorts and T-shirts and barely survived the experience! Summer is hot and humid, and thunderstorms often force visitors to scamper for cover. From June to October, Hong Kong is occasionally hit by typhoons. Autumn (October to November) is the most pleasant time of the year.

GOVERNMENT

Hong Kong is not a democracy, and China is determined that it doesn't become one. At the moment, Hong Kong is a British colony.

Heading Hong Kong's administration is a governor who presides over meetings of both the Executive Council (EXCO) and the Legislative Council (LEGCO). The Urban Council and Regional Council are in charge of the day-to-day running of services like street cleaning and garbage collection. The enormous Hong Kong Civil Service does the rest.

ECONOMY

Trade with both the West and China has always been the cornerstone of the Hong Kong economy. Service industries like banking, insurance, telecommunications and tourism now employ 75% of Hong Kong residents. All the polluting sweatshop factories have moved just across the border to China.

Part of the reason for Hong Kong's prosperity is that it is a capitalist's dream; it has lax controls and a maximum tax rate of 15%. Even with just three years to go until the handover, fortunes are still being made, new skyscrapers are still being hurled up, and new BMWs and Mercedes are still pouring out of the showrooms. You can smell wealth in the air.

POPULATION & PEOPLE

At the end of WW II, Hong Kong's population was slightly over half a million. Today it stands at six million, most of it squeezed onto Hong Kong Island, Kowloon and the so-called 'new towns' in the New Territories.

About 98% of the people are ethnic Chinese, most of whom have their origins in China's Guangdong Province. About 60% were born in the colony.

ARTS & CULTURE

Hong Kong is Chinese, but with a Cantonese twist. Traditional Chinese arts such as operas are performed in the Cantonese language. Hong Kong's homegrown variety of music largely consists of soft-rock love melodies sung in Cantonese, collectively known as Canto-Pop.

Of all the Chinese, the Cantonese have probably been the most influenced by the rest of the world. Hong Kong is a very Westernised place that immediately latches on to the latest crazes in disco, punk, rock, new wave, break dancing, the Lambada or whatever it happens to be this week.

RELIGION

In Chinese religion as it's now practised, Taoism, Confucianism and Buddhism have become inextricably entwined. Ancestor-worship and ancient animist beliefs have also been incorporated into the religious milieu. Foreign influence has been heavy in Hong Kong, which explains why 9% of the population is Christian. The cosmopolitan population also incorporates a smattering of Muslims, Jews, Sikhs and Hindus.

LANGUAGE

Cantonese is the most common Chinese dialect spoken in Hong Kong. Mandarin

Chinese, or *putonghua*, is the official language in China, and about half the people in Hong Kong can also understand it. For more information, consult LP's *Cantonese phrasebook* and *Mandarin phrasebook*.

Although English is widely spoken in Hong Kong, it is on the decline. With 1997 approaching, those educated in English have the easiest time emigrating and are taking advantage of this fact.

Cantonese is difficult for *gwailos* (foreign devils) because it's tonal – the meaning varies with the tone. Few gwailos gain fluency, but here are a few phrases to try.

Civilities

hello, how are you
nei hou ma
good morning
jou san
goodbye
joi gin
thank you
m goi
you're welcome
m saihaakhei
I'm sorry/excuse me
deuimjyu

Other Useful Phrases

How much does it cost?
Gei siu chin?
too expensive
taai gwaige
Waiter, the bill.
Wogei, maai daan.

Facts for the Visitor

VISAS & EMBASSIES

Most visitors do not need a visa for a stay of less than one month. British passport holders are permitted to stay visa-free for 12 months, citizens of all Western European nations, Canada, Australia and New Zealand can stay for three months, and citizens of the USA and most other countries get one month. Visas are still required for Eastern Europeans and all Communist countries.

Hong Kong is the usual launchpad for excursions into China, though Macau is also a possibility. Chinese visas can be obtained in Hong Kong in one or two days.

Visa Extensions

For visa extensions, you should inquire at the Immigration Department (☎ 8246111), 2nd Floor, Wanchai Tower Two, 7 Gloucester Rd, Wanchai. In general, the department does not like to grant extensions unless there are special circumstances – these include cancelled flights, illness, registration in a legitimate course of study, legal employment and marriage to a local.

HONG KONG

DOCUMENTS

Visitors and residents are advised to carry identification at all times in Hong Kong. It needn't be a passport – anything with a photo on it will do.

MONEY

Hong Kong is a dream come true for moneychanging. Any major trading currency, and even many insignificant currencies, can be exchanged. All major international credit cards are accepted.

Banks give the best exchange rates by far, but they vary. One of the best is Wing Lung Bank, 4 Carnarvon Rd, Tsimshatsui, next to the New Astor Hotel. Another good bank for changing money is Hang Seng Bank, which has numerous branches all over the city. The main Tsimshatsui branch is at 18 Carnarvon Rd. The small branches in the Mass Transit Railway (MTR) stations do not change money.

The HongkongBank gives relatively poor rates for a bank, and in addition tacks on a HK$20 service charge for each transaction.

Licensed moneychangers in the tourist districts operate 24 hours a day, but give relatively poor exchange rates which are clearly posted. However, you can almost always get a much better rate by bargaining! Moneychangers are no longer allowed to charge commissions.

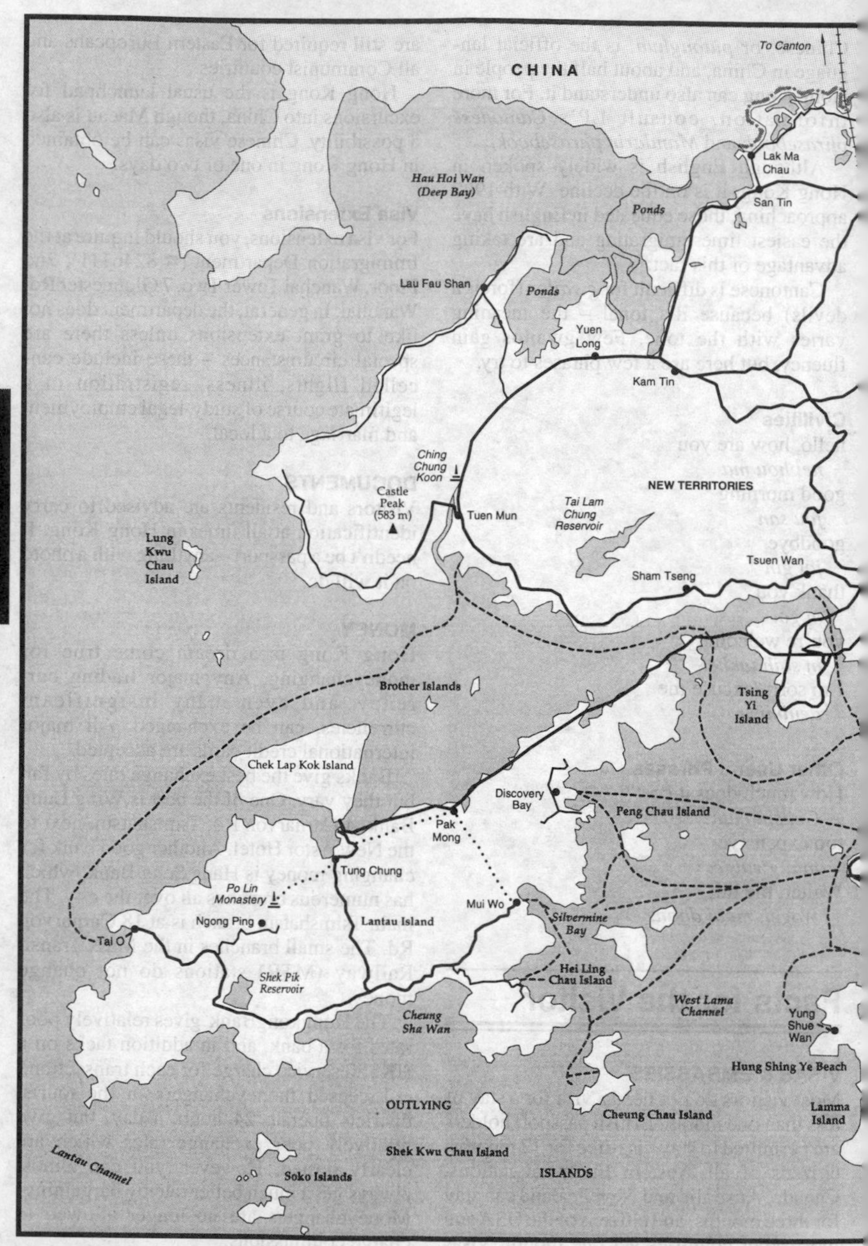
To Canton
CHINA
Hau Hoi Wan
(Deep Bay)
Lak Ma
Chau
San Tin
Ponds
Lau Fau Shan
Ponds
Yuen
Long
Kam Tin
Ching
Chung
Koon
Castle
Peak
(583 m)
Tuen Mun
NEW TERRITORIES
Tai Lam
Chung
Reservoir
Lung
Kwu
Chau
Island
Sham Tseng
Tsuen Wan
Brother Islands
Tsing
Yi
Island
Chek Lap Kok Island
Discovery
Bay
Peng Chau Island
Pak
Mong
Tung Chung
Po Lin
Monastery
Ngong Ping
Lantau Island
Mui Wo
Silvermine
Bay
Tai O
Shek Pik
Reservoir
Hei Ling
Chau Island
West Lama
Channel
Cheung
Sha Wan
Yung
Shue
Wan
Hung Shing Ye Beach
OUTLYING
Cheung Chau Island
Lamma
Island
Shek Kwu Chau Island
Lantau Channel
Soko Islands
ISLANDS

HONG KONG

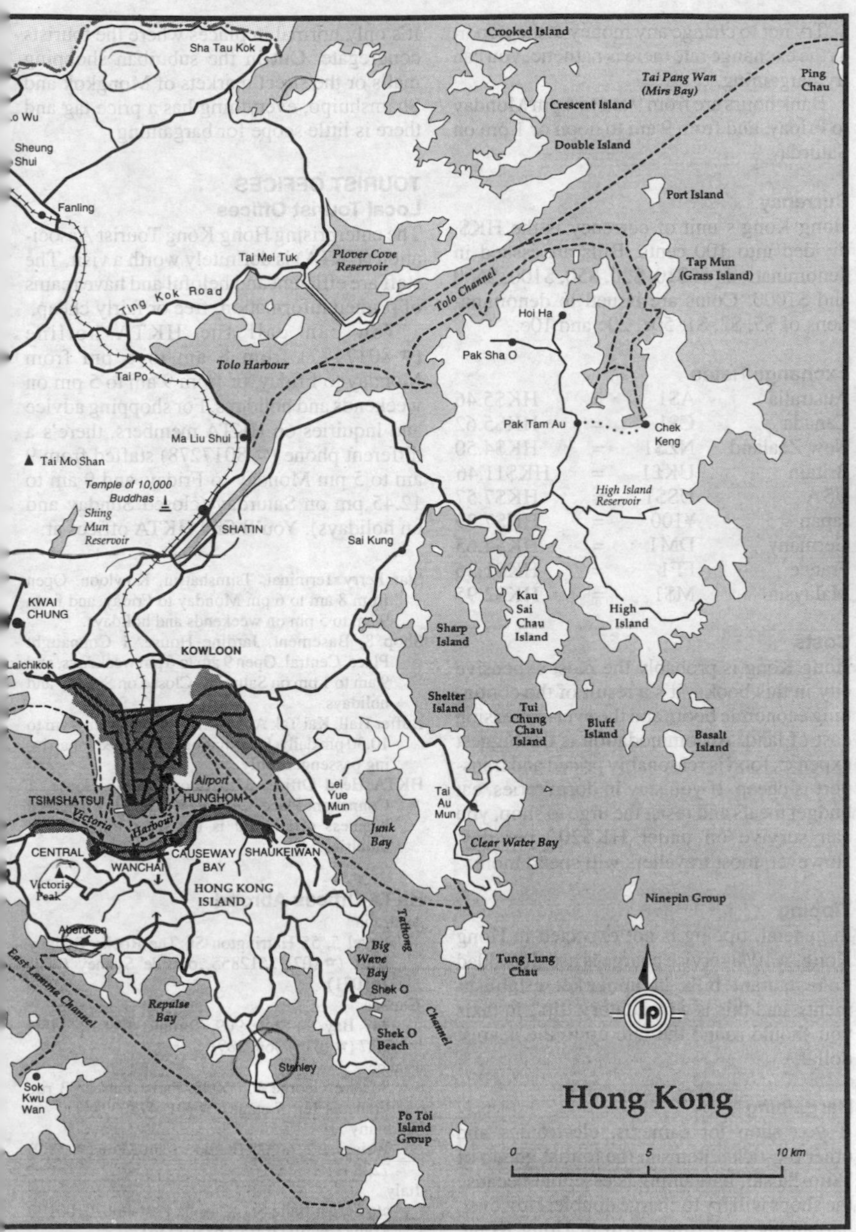

Crooked Island
Sha Tau Kok
Tai Pang Wan (Mirs Bay)
Ping Chau
Crescent Island
Double Island
Lo Wu
Sheung Shui
Port Island
Fanling
Tai Mei Tuk
Plover Cove Reservoir
Tap Mun (Grass Island)
Ting Kok Road
Tolo Channel
Hoi Ha
Pak Sha O
Tai Po
Tolo Harbour
Pak Tam Au
Chek Keng
Ma Liu Shui
Tai Mo Shan
Temple of 10,000 Buddhas
High Island Reservoir
Shing Mun Reservoir
SHATIN
Sai Kung
KWAI CHUNG
Sharp Island
Kau Sai Chau Island
High Island
KOWLOON
Laichikok
Shelter Island
Tui Chung Chau Island
Bluff Island
Basalt Island
Airport
TSIMSHATSUI
HUNGHOM
Lei Yue Mun
Tai Au Mun
Victoria Harbour
Junk Bay
Clear Water Bay
CENTRAL
WANCHAI
CAUSEWAY BAY
SHAUKEIWAN
Victoria Peak
HONG KONG ISLAND
Ninepin Group
Aberdeen
Tathong Channel
East Lamma Channel
Big Wave Bay
Tung Lung Chau
Shek O
Repulse Bay
Shek O Beach
Stanley
Sok Kwu Wan
Hong Kong
Po Toi Island Group
0
5
10 km
HONG KONG

Try not to change any money at the airport as the exchange rate there is pathetic; you can try bargaining.

Bank hours are from 9 am to 4 pm Monday to Friday, and from 9 am to noon or 1 pm on Saturday.

Currency

Hong Kong's unit of currency is the HK$, divided into 100 cents. Bills are issued in denominations of $10, $20, $50, $100, $500 and $1000. Coins are issued in denominations of $5, $2, $1, 50c, 20c and 10c.

Exchange Rates

Australia	A$1	=	HK$5.46
Canada	C$1	=	HK$5.62
New Zealand	NZ$1	=	HK$4.50
Britain	UK£1	=	HK$11.46
USA	US$1	=	HK$7.57
Japan	¥100	=	HK$7.39
Germany	DM1	=	HK$4.65
France	FF1	=	HK$1.36
Malaysia	M$1	=	HK$2.95

Costs

Hong Kong is probably the most expensive city in this book – it's a result of the continuing economic boom and the ever-increasing cost of land. Accommodation is the biggest expense; food is reasonably priced and transport is cheap. If you stay in dormitories, eat budget meals and resist the urge to shop, you can survive on under HK$200 per day. However, most travellers will spend more.

Tipping

In general, tipping is not expected in Hong Kong. A 10% service charge is usually added to restaurant bills in upmarket establishments, and this is a mandatory 'tip'. In taxis you should round the fare up to the nearest dollar.

Bargaining

If you shop for cameras, electronics and other big-ticket items in the tourist ghetto of Tsimshatsui, bargaining is essential because the shops will try to charge double. However, bargaining is *not* the norm in Hong Kong. It's only normal in places where the tourists congregate. Out in the suburban shopping malls or the street markets of Mongkok and Shamshuipo, everything has a price tag and there is little scope for bargaining.

TOURIST OFFICES

Local Tourist Offices

The enterprising Hong Kong Tourist Association (HKTA) is definitely worth a visit. The staff are efficient and helpful and have reams of printed information, free or fairly cheap.

You can call the HKTA hotline (☎ 8017177) from 8 am to 6 pm from Monday to Friday, or from 9 am to 5 pm on weekends and holidays. For shopping advice and inquiries on HKTA members, there's a different phone (☎ 8017278) staffed from 9 am to 5 pm Monday to Friday, and 9 am to 12.45 pm on Saturday (closed Sunday and on holidays). You'll find HKTA offices at:

Star Ferry Terminal, Tsimshatsui, Kowloon. Open from 8 am to 6 pm Monday to Friday, and from 9 am to 5 pm on weekends and holidays.

Shop 8, Basement, Jardine House, 1 Connaught Place, Central. Open 9 am to 6 pm weekdays, and 9 am to 1 pm on Saturday. Closed on Sunday and holidays.

Buffer Hall, Kai Tak Airport, Kowloon. Open 8 am to 10.30 pm daily. Information is provided for arriving passengers only.

HKTA Head Office, 35th floor, Jardine House, 1 Connaught Place, Central (☎ 8017111). This is a business office and is not for normal tourist inquiries.

HKTA Offices Abroad

Australia
Level 5, 55 Harrington St, The Rocks, Sydney 2001 (☎ (02) 2512855, outside Sydney (008) 251071)

Canada
347 Bay St, Suite 909, Toronto, Ontario M5H 2R7 (☎ (416) 3662389)

France
38 Ave George V, 75008, Paris (entree 53 rue Francois 1er, 7 etage) (☎ (01) 47203954)

Germany
Weisenau 1, 60323 Frankfurt-am-Main (☎ (069) 722841)

Italy
c/o Sergat Italia Sr1, Casella Postale 620, 00100 Roma Centro (☎ (06) 68801336)

Japan
4th floor, Toho Twin Tower Building, 1-5-2 Yurakucho, Chiyoda-ku, Tokyo 100 (☎ (03) 35030735)
8th floor, Osaka Saitama Building, 3-5-13 Awaji-machi, Chuo-ku, Osaka 541 (☎ (06) 2299240)

Korea
c/o HK PR, Suite 1204, Sungji Building, 538 Dowha-Dong, Mapo-gu, Seoul (☎ (02) 7065818)

New Zealand
PO Box 2120, Auckland (☎ (09) 5203316)

Singapore
13th floor, 13-08 Ocean Building, 10 Collyer Quay, Singapore 0104 (☎ 5323668)

South Africa
c/o Development Promotions Pty Ltd, PO Box 9874, Johannesburg 2000 (☎ (011) 3394865)

Spain
c/o Sergat Espana SL, Pau Casals 4, 08021 Barcelona (☎ (3) 4141794)

Taiwan
7th floor, 18 Chang'an E Rd, Section 1, Taipei (☎ (02) 5812967)
Hong Kong Information Service (☎ (02) 5816061)

UK
5th floor, 125 Pall Mall, London, SW1Y 5EA (☎ (071) 9304775)

USA
333 North Michigan Ave, Suite 2400, Chicago, IL 60601-3966 (☎ (312) 7823872)
5th floor, 590 Fifth Ave, New York, NY 10036-4706 (☎ 212-8695008)
10940 Wilshire Blvd, Suite 1220, Los Angeles, CA 90024 (☎ (213) 2084582)

BUSINESS HOURS & HOLIDAYS

Office hours are Monday to Friday from 9 am to 5 pm, and on Saturday from 9 am to noon. Lunch hour is from 1 to 2 pm and many offices simply shut down and lock the door at this time.

Stores and restaurants that cater to the tourist trade keep longer hours, but almost nothing except 7 Eleven opens before 9 am. Even tourist-related businesses shut down by 9 or 10 pm, and many will close for major holidays, especially Chinese New Year.

Western and Chinese culture combine to create an interesting mix of holidays. The first day of the first moon (late January or early February) is Chinese New Year. Only the first three days of this are a public holiday, but everything pretty much shuts down for a week and all flights out of Hong Kong are booked solid for at least two weeks.

The other big public holiday to avoid is Ching Ming (visits to ancestors' graves) which falls around Easter time.

The mid-year Dragon Boat (Tuen Ng) Festival is a dramatic sight culminating in the international races. The time to enjoy moon cakes is during the Mid-Autumn Festival (15th night of the eighth moon).

The last public holidays are Christmas (25 December) and Boxing Day (26 December), when the lights of Hong Kong are bright and the streets are packed.

Some colourful nonpublic holidays include the birthdays of Tin Hau (the goddess of fisherfolk), Tam Kung (another patron saint of seafarers) and Lord Buddha. The Cheung Chau Bun Festival features raucous fun on the island of Cheung Chau. Then there's the Yue Lan Festival of Hungry Ghosts (late August or September) which is a great time to visit Taoist temples.

POST & TELECOMMUNICATIONS

Post

All post offices are open Monday to Saturday from 8 am to 6 pm, and are closed on Sunday and public holidays. The GPO is where you go to collect poste restante letters – it's in Central just to the west of the Star Ferry Terminal. In Tsimshatsui, there are two convenient post offices just east of Nathan Rd: one at 10 Middle Rd and another in the basement of the Albion Plaza, 2-6 Granville Rd.

Telephone

If you want to phone overseas, it's cheapest to use an IDD (International Direct Dialling) telephone. You can place an IDD call from most phone boxes but you'll need stacks of coins. An alternative is to buy a phonecard, which comes in denominations of HK$50, HK$100 or HK$250. You can find the card phones in shops, on the street or at a Hong Kong Telecom office. There's an office at 10 Middle Rd in Tsimshatsui and another at Exchange Square No 1 Building, west of the GPO in Central. To make an IDD call from

Hong Kong, first dial ☎ 001, then the country code, area code and number. When calling Hong Kong from abroad, the country code is ☎ 852.

For calls to countries that do not have the IDD service, you can call from a Telecom office – first pay a deposit and you will be hooked up (minimum call is for three minutes) and given your change after the call is completed.

Fax, Telex & Telegraph

All your telecommunication needs can be taken care of at Hong Kong Telecom. Many hotels and even hostels have a fax and will allow you to both send and receive for a reasonable service charge.

BOOKS & MAPS

The government's annual report is entitled *Hong Kong 1993*, *Hong Kong 1994* etc. In addition to the excellent photographs, the text is a gold mine of information.

A cynical antidote to the government's upbeat version of events is *The Other Hong Kong Report* (Chinese University Press).

Maurice Collis' *Foreign Mud* (Faber & Faber UK) tells the sordid story of the Opium Wars.

Novels to dip into include the readable *Tai-pan* by James Clavell, which is (very) loosely based on the Jardine-Matheson organisation in its early days. Richard Mason's *The World of Suzie Wong* is also interesting – after all, she was Hong Kong's best known citizen.

If you want more information on Hong Kong and the surrounding area, look for the Lonely Planet guidebook *Hong Kong, Macau & Canton – a travel survival kit* (Canton is now known in China as Guangzhou).

The giveaway maps provided by the HKTA are adequate for finding your way around most places in Kowloon or the city part of Hong Kong Island. The Government Publications Centre in the GPO sells far more detailed maps.

Bookshops

Good outlets for browsing and buying books in Hong Kong include:

Bookazine Company, basement, Jardine House, Connaught Rd, Central (opposite HKTA office)
Government Publications Centre, GPO building, Central (near Star Ferry pier)
South China Morning Post Bookshop, Star Ferry pier, Central
Wanderlust Books, 30 Hollywood Rd, Central (good travel book section)
Peace Book Company, 35 Kimberley Rd, Tsimshatsui
Swindon Books, 13 Lock Rd, Tsimshatsui
Times Books, Shop C, 96 Nathan Rd, entrance on Granville Rd, Tsimshatsui

HIGHLIGHTS

The trip on the Peak Tram to Victoria Peak has been practically mandatory for visitors since it opened in 1888. A 30-minute ride in a sampan through Aberdeen Harbour is equally intriguing. Lunch at a good dim sum restaurant is one of the great pleasures of the Orient, and of course, shopping is what Hong Kong is all about. The relatively undeveloped outlying islands are in some ways the most surprising and enjoyable part of Hong Kong.

ACCOMMODATION

Accommodation prices are rising to absurd levels. There are a couple of youth hostel dormitories which charge only HK$40 per bed, but most are very inconveniently located. The same is true for camping sites – they exist, but you'll spend an hour or more commuting to/from the city.

You'll need a hostel card to stay at any of the hostels. If you arrive in Hong Kong without a hostel card and wish to join, the local representative is Hong Kong Youth Hostels Association (☎ 7881638), Room 225, Block 19, Shek Kip Mei Estate, Kowloon. The annual membership fee for Hong Kong residents is HK$60; nonresidents pay HK$150.

Guesthouses are the salvation for most budget travellers. Some guesthouses (not many) have dormitories where beds go for HK$70 to HK$100, with discounts for long-term (one week or more) rentals. Private rooms the size of closets are available for as little as HK$150 but you can easily spend twice that. It definitely pays for two people to share a room as this costs little or no extra. Mid-range hotels start around HK$400 and go up to around HK$800.

For information on exactly where to stay in Hong Kong, see Places to Stay in the Around Hong Kong section.

FOOD & DRINKS

Hong Kong offers incredible variety when it comes to eating. By all means you should try *dim sum*, a uniquely Cantonese dish served only for breakfast or lunch, but never dinner. Dim sum delicacies are normally steamed in a small bamboo basket. Typically, each basket contains four identical pieces, so four people would be an ideal number for a dim sum meal. You pay for the number of baskets you order. The baskets are stacked up on pushcarts and rolled around the dining room. You choose whatever you like from the carts, so no menu is needed.

In Chinese restaurants tea is often served free of charge, or at most you'll pay HK$1 for a big pot which can be refilled indefinitely. On the other hand, coffee is seldom available except in Western restaurants or coffee shops, and is never free.

Beer is extremely popular among the Chinese. The brands made in China are excellent, the most popular being Tsingtao, now a major export.

THINGS TO BUY

Oh yeah, shopping – some people do come to Hong Kong for that. 'Shop till you drop' is the motto of many tourists, but you should pause before embarking on a buying binge. It's very easy in Hong Kong to decide suddenly that you need all sorts of consumer goods you don't really need at all.

Hong Kong resembles a gigantic shopping mall, but a quick look at price tags should convince you that the city is not quite the bargain it's cracked up to be. Imported goods like Japanese-made cameras and electronic gadgets can be bought for roughly the same price in many Western countries. However, what makes Hong Kong shine is the variety – if you can't find it in Hong Kong, it probably doesn't exist.

The worst neighbourhood for shopping happens to be the place where most tourists shop. Tsimshatsui, the tourist ghetto of Kowloon, is the most likely place to be cheated. Notice that none of the cameras or other big-ticket items have price tags. This is *not* common practice elsewhere in Hong Kong. If you go out to the Chinese neighbourhoods where the locals shop, you'll find price tags on everything.

Clothing is the best buy in Hong Kong. All the cheap stuff comes from China and most is decent quality, but check zippers and stitching carefully – there is some real junk around. You'll find the best buys at the street markets at Tong Choi St in Mongkok and Apliu St in Shamshuipo. If you want to search around Tsimshatsui, the best deals are generally found on the eastern end of Granville Rd. Another good place for clothes is the mezzanine floor of Chungking Mansions (not the ground floor). Two Chinese chainstores with Italian names, Giordano's and Bossini, offer quality clothing at reasonable prices.

Yue Hwa Chinese Products at 301 Nathan Rd, Yaumatei (corner of Nathan and Jordan Roads) is a good place to pick up everyday consumer goods. It's also one of the best places to have spectacles made.

The Golden Shopping Centre, Basement, 146-152 Fuk Wah St, Shamshuipo, has the cheapest collection of computers, accessories and components that can be found in Hong Kong.

If it's a camera you need, don't even bother wasting your valuable time on Nathan Rd in Tsimshatsui. Photo Scientific (☎ 5221903), 6 Stanley St, Central, is the favourite of Hong Kong's resident professional photographers. But if you're in a hurry and want to buy in Tsimshatsui, the best seems to be Kimberley Camera Company (☎ 7212308), Champagne Court, 16 Kimberley Rd.

Apliu St in Shamshuipo has arguably the

best collection of electronics shops selling personal stereos, CD players and the like.

You can find cheap CDs and music tapes in the night markets of Temple St, Tong Choi St and Apliu St, but the selection in these places is very limited. Tower Records (☎ 5060811), 7th floor, Shop 701, Times Square, Matheson St, Causeway Bay, offers the widest selection of recorded music in Hong Kong.

Another good place for finding discounted CDs and tapes is KPS, a chain store with shops at: Prince's Building, 9-25 Chater Rd, Central; Far East Finance Centre, Central, just next to the Admiralty MTR station; Ocean Gallery, No 233-235 Harbour City on Canton Rd, Tsimshatsui; and at Inter-Continental Plaza, Granville Rd, Tsimshatsui East.

The sports-minded might want to visit Flying Ball Bicycle Shop (☎ 3815919), 201 Tung Choi St, Mongkok (near Prince Edward MTR station).

Hong Kong is a good place to pick up a decent backpack, sleeping bag, tent and other gear for hiking, camping and travelling. Mongkok is by far the best neighbourhood to look for this stuff, though there are a couple of places in nearby Yaumatei. Some of the places worth checking out include:

Grade IV Alpine, 13 Saigon St, Yaumatei (☎ 7820202)

Mountaineer Supermarket, 395 Portland St, Mongkok (☎ 3970585)

Rose Sporting Goods, 39 Fa Yuen St, Mongkok (☎ 7811809)

Sportsman Shop, 72 Sai Yee St, Mongkok (☎ 3956405)

Tang Fai Kee Military, 248 Reclamation St, Mongkok (☎ 3855169)

Three Military Equipment Company, 83 Sai Yee St, Mongkok (☎ 3914019, 7894326)

Finally, if you want to see a good shopping mall, where all the locals choose to congregate, go and visit Cityplaza in Quarry Bay. To get there, take the MTR to the Tai Koo station.

HONG KONG

Getting There & Away

AIR

For most travellers, the normal arrival point will be Kai Tak airport – with its runway sticking out from Kowloon into the harbour it makes a pretty dramatic entrance.

Hong Kong is a good place to buy discounted air tickets, but watch out! There are a few real swindlers in the travel business. The most common trick is a request for a non-refundable deposit on an air ticket. So you pay a deposit for the booking, but when you go to pick up the tickets they say that the flight is no longer available, but that there is another flight at a higher price, sometimes 50% more!

It is best not to pay a deposit, but rather to pay for the ticket in full and get a receipt clearly showing that there is no balance due, and that the full amount is refundable if no ticket is issued. Tickets are normally issued the day after booking, but for the real cheapie tickets (actually group tickets), pick them up yourself at the airport from the tour leader (who you will never see again once you've got the ticket). One caution: when you get the ticket from the tour leader, check it carefully. Occasionally, there are errors, such as your being issued a ticket with a return portion valid for only 60 days when you paid for a ticket valid for one year.

Some budget fares available in Hong Kong are listed in the table, but realise that these are discounted fares and will have various restrictions upon their use.

Travel Agencies

Some agencies we've tried and found to offer competitive prices include:

Phoenix Services, Room B, 6th floor, Milton Mansion, 96 Nathan Rd, Tsimshatsui (☎ 7227378; fax 3698884)

Shoestring Travel, Flat A, 4th floor, Alpha House, 27-33 Nathan Rd, Tsimshatsui (☎ 7232306; fax 7212085)

Traveller Services, Room 1012, Silvercord Tower 1, 30 Canton Rd, Tsimshatsui (☎ 3752222; fax 3752233)

Airfares from Hong Kong

Destination	*One Way*	*Return*
Auckland	US$574	US$898
Bangkok	US$155	US$220
Beijing	US$267	US$532
Frankfurt	US$375	US$725
Guam	US$455	US$476
Guangzhou	US$57	US$114
Ho Chi Minh City	US$294	US$589
Honolulu	US$376	US$727
Jakarta	US$227	US$415
Kuala Lumpur	US$188	US$314
London	US$375	US$725
Manila	US$115	US$193
New York	US$496	US$870
Phnom Penh	US$272	US$532
San Francisco	US$428	US$675
Seoul	US$201	US$272
Singapore	US$216	US$275
Sydney	US$570	US$825
Taipei	US$127	US$214
Tokyo	US$279	US$487
Vancouver	US$392	US$678
Yangon	US$367	US$735

Victoria Travel, connected to Victoria Hostel, 1st floor, 33 Hankow Rd, Tsimshatsui (☎ 3760621; fax 3762609)

Departure Tax

Airport departure tax is now HK$50, but you're excused from paying if you can convince them that you're under the age of 12. If you are departing by ship to Macau or China, departure tax is HK$26, but it's included in the purchase price of the ticket.

LAND

If you just want a brief guided visit to the People's Republic of China, you can do that quite easily. There are plenty of one-day across-the-border jaunts available from Hong Kong or Macau, and slightly longer Guangzhou quickies which give you a few days in the neighbouring city.

A train to Lo Wu at the border will cost you just HK$37. You walk across the border to the city of Shenzhen, and from there you can take a local train to Guangzhou and beyond.

Alternatively, you can take an express train straight through from Hunghom station in Kowloon to Guangzhou for HK$182.

SEA

Hong Kong has one of the most spectacular harbours in the world, so it's a shame that there's not much of a chance of arriving by boat – unless you're rich and on a cruise liner. It may still be possible though for budget travellers, if they want to take a boat from China. The Shanghai-Hong Kong ferry is very popular with travellers, and it's a great way to leave China.

You can go to Shenzhen in China by hoverferry from the China Hong Kong City Ferry Terminal in Tsimshatsui. Perhaps cheapest (HK$160) and most pleasant is to take the overnight ferry from Tsimshatsui to Guangzhou. You are able to sleep in dorm beds and save a night's accommodation charge at a hotel.

Getting Around

Hong Kong has a varied and frequent public transport system. The fastest is the Mass Transit Railway (MTR), but slower and much more fun are the ferries. Before setting out to travel anywhere by bus, ensure you have a good pocketful of small change – the exact fare normally must be deposited in a cash box and nobody has change. However, change is readily available for the MTR and ferries.

TO/FROM THE AIRPORT

There is an A5 bus to Quarry Bay from the airport, which runs from 9 am to midnight every day.

BUS

There are plenty of buses with fares starting from HK$1.80 and going up to HK$12 for the longest ride you can take in the New Territories. You pay the fare as you enter the bus so make sure you have the exact change ready. The double-decker buses are blue and cream on Hong Kong Island (operated by China Motor Bus) or red and cream in Kowloon (operated by Kowloon Motor Bus).

Most services stop around 11 pm or midnight but bus Nos 121 and 122 are 'Cross Harbour Recreation Routes' which operate through the Cross-Harbour Tunnel every 15 minutes from 12.45 to 5 am. Bus No 121 runs from Macau Ferry Terminal on Hong Kong Island, then through the tunnel to Chatham Rd in Tsimshatsui East before continuing on to Choi Hung on the east side of the airport.

Bus No 122 runs from North Point on Hong Kong Island, through the Cross-Harbour Tunnel, to Chatham Rd in Tsimshatsui East, the northern part of Nathan Rd and on to Laichikok in the north-western part of Kowloon.

MINIBUS & MAXICAB

Small red and yellow minibuses supplement the regular bus services. They are a little more expensive (generally HK$2 to HK$6). They generally don't run such regular routes but you can get on or off almost anywhere. If you know where you are going and where they are going, you may well find them both fast and convenient.

Maxicabs are just like minibuses, except they are green and yellow and do run regular routes. Two popular ones are from the carpark in front of the Star Ferry in Central to Ocean Park or from HMS Tamar (east of the Star Ferry) to the Peak. Fares are between HK$1 and HK$8.

TRAIN

The Kowloon-Canton Railway (KCR) runs right up to the border, where visitors to China usually walk across the bridge and change trains. There are also four express trains daily which run to Guangzhou. Apart from being one of the best ways of entering China, it's also an excellent alternative to buses for getting into the New Territories. The last stop before China is Lo Wu but you are only supposed to go there if you plan to enter China.

MASS TRANSIT RAILWAY (MTR)

Opened in 1979-80, the MTR operates from Central across the harbour and up along Kowloon Peninsula. This ultramodern, high-speed subway system has been quite a hit with office commuters. The ticket machines do not give change (get it from the ticket windows) and the tickets are valid only for the day they are purchased. Once you go past the turnstile, you must complete the journey within 90 minutes or the ticket becomes invalid. The MTR operates from 6 am to 1 am.

If you use the MTR frequently, it's very useful to buy a Common Stored Value Ticket for HK$70, HK$100 or HK$200. These can also be used on the KCR except for the Lo Wu station on the China border. The MTR Tourist Ticket is a rip-off at HK$25 because it gives you only HK$20 worth of fares!

Smoking, eating or drinking are not allowed in the MTR stations or on the trains (makes you wonder about all those Maxim's Cake Shops in the stations!). The fine for eating or drinking is HK$1000, while smoking will set you back HK$2000. Busking, selling and soliciting are forbidden. There are no toilets in the MTR stations.

TRAM

There is just one main tram line, running east-west along the northern side of Hong Kong Island. As well as being ridiculously picturesque and fun to travel on, the tram is quite a bargain at HK$1 for any distance. You pay as you get off.

Apart from the main line, there is a spur route off to Happy Valley. Some trams don't run the full length of the line, but basically you can just get on any tram that comes by. They pass frequently and there always seem to be half a dozen trams actually in sight.

CAR & MOTORBIKE

Should you cross the border from Hong Kong (left-side driving) into China, you will have to switch to the right. But many will prefer to avoid the hassles of driving in Hong Kong (which is actively discouraged by high registration fees, tough standards and heavy penalties for driving breaches). If undeterred, you can drive for up to 12 months in Hong Kong on an international permit, but to stay on the road for longer you will need a Hong Kong licence from the Transport Department. Motorbikes are not favoured in the crowded road conditions and are difficult to rent, although car rental deals (self-drive or chauffered) often come with free unlimited km.

TAXI

On Hong Kong Island and Kowloon, the flagfall is HK$10 for the first two km and an extra HK$1 for every additional 0.2 km. In the New Territories, flagfall is HK$9 for the first two km, thereafter 90c for every 0.2 km. There is a luggage fee of HK$5 per bag but not all drivers insist on this.

If you go through either the Cross-Harbour Tunnel or Eastern Harbour Tunnel, you'll be charged an extra HK$20. The toll is only HK$10, but the driver is allowed to assume that he won't get a fare back so you have to pay.

BICYCLE

Bicycling in Kowloon or Central would be suicidal, but in quiet areas of the islands or the New Territories a bike can be quite a pleasant way of getting around. The bike rental places tend to run out early on weekends.

Some places where you can rent bikes and ride in safety include: Shek O on Hong Kong Island; Shatin and Tai Mei Tuk (near Tai Po) in the New Territories; Mui Wo (Silvermine Bay) on Lantau Island; and the island of Cheung Chau.

BOAT

Star Ferries

There are three routes on the Star Ferry, but by far the most popular shuttles between Tsimshatsui and Edinburgh Place in Central. Costing a mere HK$1.20 (lower deck) or HK$1.50 (upper deck), it's a real travel bargain. It's often said that this is one of the most picturesque public transport journeys in the world. The schedules for all three ferries are as follows:

Tsimshatsui-Central (Edinburgh Place)
every five to 10 minutes from 6.30 am up until 11.30 pm
Tsimshatsui-Wanchai
every 10 to 20 minutes from 7.30 to 10.50 pm
Hunghom-Central (Edinburgh Place)
every 12 to 20 minutes (every 20 minutes on Sunday and holidays) from 7 am to 7.20 pm

Hoverferries

Three hoverferry services link with Central on the following schedules:

Tsimshatsui East-Central (Queen's Pier)
every 20 minutes from 8 am to 8 pm
Tsuen Wan-Central (Government Pier)
every 20 minutes from 7.20 am to 5.20 pm
Tuen Mun-Central (Central Harbour Services Pier)
every 10 to 20 minutes from 6.45 am to 7.40 pm

Kaidos

A *kaido* is a small to medium-sized ferry which can make short runs on the open sea. Few kaido routes operate on regular schedules, preferring to adjust supply according to demand. There is a sort of schedule on popular runs like the trip between Aberdeen and Lamma Island. Kaidos run most frequently on weekends and holidays when everyone tries to get away from it all.

A *sampan* is a motorised launch which accommodates only a few people. A sampan is too small to be considered seaworthy, but can safely zip you around typhoon shelters like Aberdeen Harbour.

Bigger than a sampan, but smaller than a kaido, is a *walla walla*. These operate as water taxis on Victoria Harbour. Most of the customers are sailors living on ships anchored in the harbour.

Outlying Island Ferries

The HKTA can supply you with schedules for ferries to outlying islands. Fares are higher on weekends and holidays and the boats can get crowded. From Central, most ferries go from the Outlying Island piers between the Star Ferry and Macau Ferry terminals.

The main island destinations from Central are:

Cheung Chau
: 21 ferries daily from 6.25 to 12.30 am, five hoverferries Monday to Friday only between 9 am and 4 pm

Lamma Island
: two destinations, Yung Shue Wan (14 ferries between 6.50 and 12.30 am) and Sok Kwu Wan (seven ferries between 8 am and 11 pm), plus a kaido service between Sok Kwu Wan and Aberdeen

Lantau Island
: to the port of Mui Wo (Silvermine Bay), 20 ferries daily between 6.10 and 12.20 am, four of which stop at Peng Chau en route; also four hoverferries daily between 9.40 am and 4.25 pm, all of which stop in Peng Chau

Peng Chau
: 18 ferries daily between 7 and 12.20 am, plus an inter-island ferry to Cheung Chau and Lantau Island

HONG KONG

TOURS

There are dozens of tours, including boat tours. All can be booked through the HKTA, travel agents, large tourist hotels or directly from the tour company.

Around Hong Kong

KOWLOON

Kowloon, the peninsula pointing out towards Hong Kong Island, is packed with shops, hotels, bars, restaurants, nightclubs and tourists. Nathan Rd, the main drag, has plenty of all. Some of the ritziest shops are in the Ocean terminal beside the Star Ferry. There always seems to be one ocean liner moored here which is full of elderly millionaires.

The tip of the peninsula, the area most popular with tourists, is known as Tsimshatsui. If you continue north up Nathan Rd you come into the tightly packed Chinese residential and business districts of Yaumatei and Mongkok.

Start your exploration from Kowloon's southern tip. Adjacent to the Star Ferry terminal is the **Cultural Centre**. Just next door is the **Hong Kong Museum of Art**. Both are closed on Thursday, otherwise operating hours are weekdays (including Saturday) from 10 am to 6 pm, and Sunday and holidays from 1 pm to 6 pm.

Adjacent to the preceding is the **Space Museum**, which has several exhibition halls and also a **Space Theatre** (planetarium). Opening times for the exhibition halls are weekdays (except Tuesday) from 1 pm to 9 pm, and from 10 am to 9 pm on weekends and holidays. The Space Theatre has about seven shows each day (except Tuesday), some in English and some in Cantonese, but headphone translations are available for all shows. Check times with the museum.

Hidden behind Yue Hwa's Park Lane Store on Nathan Rd is **Kowloon Park**, which every year seems to become less of a park and more like an amusement park. The swimming pool is perhaps the park's finest attribute – it's even equipped with waterfalls.

The **Museum of History** is in Kowloon Park near the Haiphong Rd entrance. It covers all of Hong Kong's existence from prehistoric times (about 6000 years ago, give or take a few) to the present and contains a large collection of old photographs. The museum is open Monday to Thursday and Saturday from 10 am to 6 pm, and Sunday and public holidays from 1 to 6 pm. It is closed on Friday. Admission costs HK$10.

The **Kowloon Mosque** stands on Nathan Rd at the corner of Kowloon Park. It was opened in 1984 on the site of an earlier mosque constructed in 1896. Unless you are Muslim, you must obtain permission to go inside. You can inquire by ringing up (☎ 7240095).

The **Hong Kong Science Museum** is in Tsimshatsui East at the corner of Chatham and Granville Roads. This multilevel complex houses over 500 exhibits. Admission costs HK$25 for adults and HK$15 for students and seniors. The hours are 1 to 9 pm Tuesday through Friday, and 10 am to 9 pm on weekends and holidays. The museum is closed on Monday.

The most exotic sight in the Mongkok district is the **Bird Market**. It's located on

Hong Lok St, an obscure alley on the south side of Argyle St, two blocks west of Nathan Rd. The Hong Kong government says it will have to move, but there is so far no word as to when and where.

The **Wong Tai Sin Temple** is a very large and active Taoist temple built in 1973. It's right near the Wong Tai Sin MTR station. Adjacent to the temple is an arcade filled with about 150 booths operated by fortune tellers. Some of them speak good English, so if you really want to know what fate has in store for you, this is your chance to find out. The temple is open daily from 7 am to 5 pm.

The **Laichikok Amusement Park** has standard dodgem cars, shooting galleries and balloons for the kiddies, but the ice-skating rink may be of interest for the sports-minded. There is a theatre within the park's grounds that has Chinese opera performances. Operating hours for the park are Monday to Friday from noon to 9.30 pm, and from 10 am to 9.30 pm on weekends and holidays. From the Kowloon Star Ferry bus terminal take bus No 6A, which terminates near the park. Otherwise, it's a 15-minute walk from the Mei Foo MTR station. Admission is HK$15.

Adjacent to the Laichikok Amusement Park is the **Sung Dynasty Village**, which is hyped up as an authentic recreation of a Chinese village from 10 centuries ago. The village is open from 10 am to 8.30 pm daily. Admission costs HK$120. It drops to HK$80 on weekends and public holidays between 12.30 and 5 pm.

HONG KONG ISLAND

The north and south sides of the island have very different characters. The north side is an urban jungle, while much of the south is still surprisingly rural (but developing fast). The central part of the island is incredibly mountainous and protected from further development by a country park.

North Side

Central is the bustling business centre of Hong Kong. A free shuttle bus from the Star Ferry Pier brings you to the lower station of the famous Peak Tram on Garden Rd. The tram terminates at the top of **Victoria Peak**. It's worth repeating the peak trip at night – the illuminated view is something else if the weather cooperates. Don't just admire the view from the top – wander up Mt Austin Rd to **Victoria Peak Garden** or take the more leisurely stroll around Lugard and Harlech Roads – together they make a complete circuit of the peak. You can walk right down to Aberdeen on the south side of the island or you can try Old Peak Rd for a few km return to Central. The more energetic may want to walk the **Hong Kong Trail**, which runs along the top of the mountainous spine of Hong Kong Island from the Peak to Big Wave Bay.

There are many pleasant walks and views in the **Zoological & Botanical Gardens** on Robinson Rd overlooking Central. Entry is free to the **Fung Ping Shan Museum** in Hong Kong University (closed Sunday).

Hong Kong Park is just behind the city's second tallest skyscraper, the Bank of China. It's an unusual park, not at all natural but beautiful in its own weird way. Within the park is the **Flagstaff House Museum**, the oldest Western-style building still standing in Hong Kong. Inside, you'll find a Chinese tea ware collection. Admission is free.

Between the skyscrapers of Central you'll find **Li Yuen St East** and **Li Yuen St West**, which run parallel between Des Voeux Rd and Queen's Rd. Both streets are narrow alleys, closed to motorised traffic and crammed with shops and stalls selling everything imaginable.

The **Hillside Escalator Link** is a mode of transport that has become a tourist attraction. The 800-metre moving walkway (known as a 'travelator') runs from the Vehicular Ferry Pier alongside the Central Market and up Shelley St to the Mid-Levels.

West of Central in the Sheung Wan district is appropriately named **Ladder St**, which climbs steeply. At the junction of Ladder St and Hollywood Rd is **Man Mo Temple**, the oldest temple in Hong Kong. A bit further north near the Macau Ferry Pier is the indoor **Western Market**, a four-storey red brick

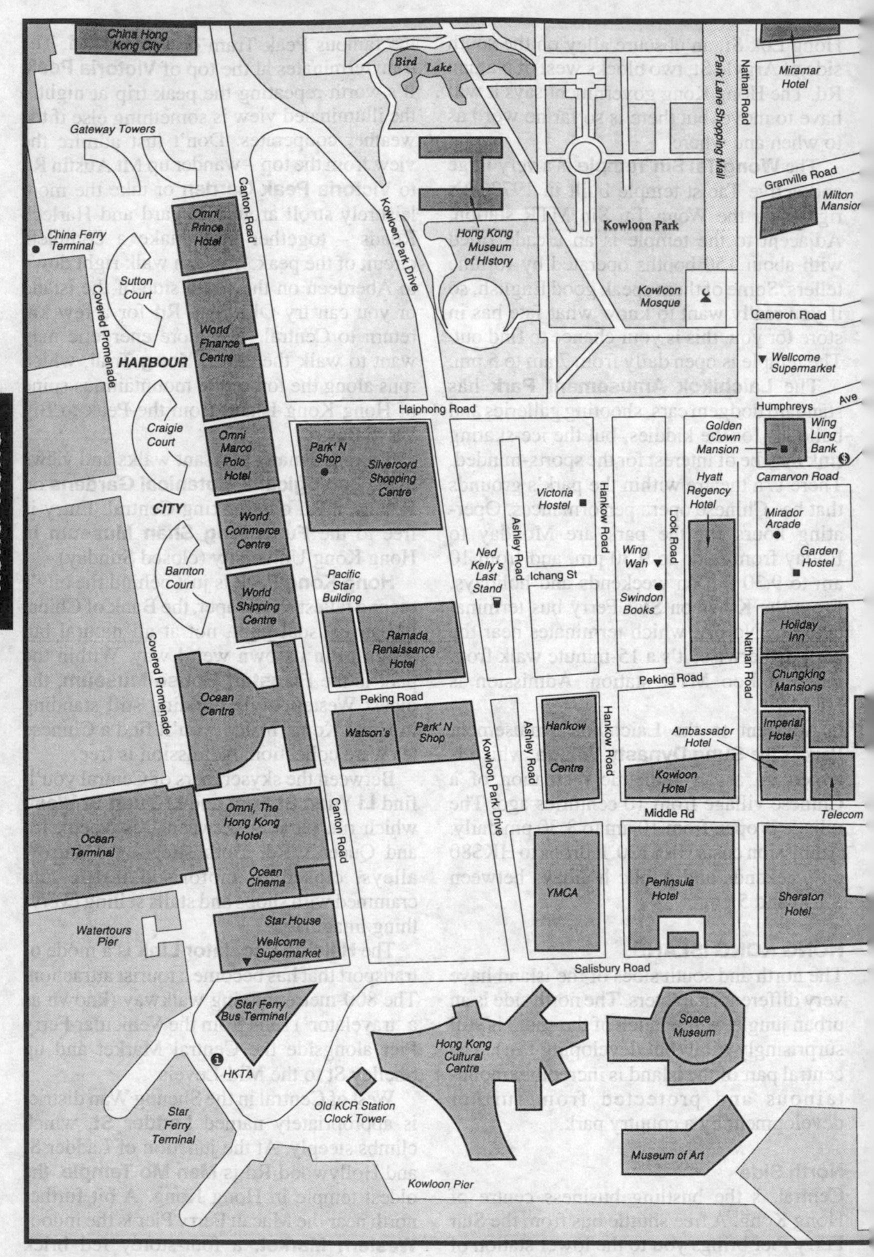
China Hong Kong City
Bird Lake
Miramar Hotel
Park Lane Shopping Mall
Nathan Road
Gateway Towers
Canton Road
Kowloon Park Drive
Granville Road
Milton Mansion
Omni Prince Hotel
China Ferry Terminal
Hong Kong Museum of History
Kowloon Park
Sutton Court
Covered Promenade
World Finance Centre
Kowloon Mosque
Cameron Road
HARBOUR
Wellcome Supermarket
Haiphong Road
Humphreys Ave
Golden Crown Mansion
Wing Lung Bank
Craigie Court
Omni Marco Polo Hotel
Park' N Shop
Silvercord Shopping Centre
Hyatt Regency Hotel
Carnarvon Road
CITY
World Commerce Centre
Victoria Hostel
Hankow Road
Ashley Road
Lock Road
Mirador Arcade
Garden Hostel
Ned Kelly's Last Stand
Wing Wah
Ichang St
Barnton Court
Pacific Star Building
World Shipping Centre
Swindon Books
Holiday Inn
Ramada Renaissance Hotel
Peking Road
Chungking Mansions
Ocean Centre
Watson's
Hankow Centre
Ambassador Hotel
Imperial Hotel
Kowloon Hotel
Middle Rd
Telecom
Omni, The Hong Kong Hotel
Ocean Terminal
Ocean Cinema
YMCA
Peninsula Hotel
Sheraton Hotel
Star House
Wellcome Supermarket
Watertours Pier
Salisbury Road
Star Ferry Bus Terminal
Space Museum
Hong Kong Cultural Centre
HKTA
Old KCR Station Clock Tower
Star Ferry Terminal
Museum of Art
Kowloon Pier

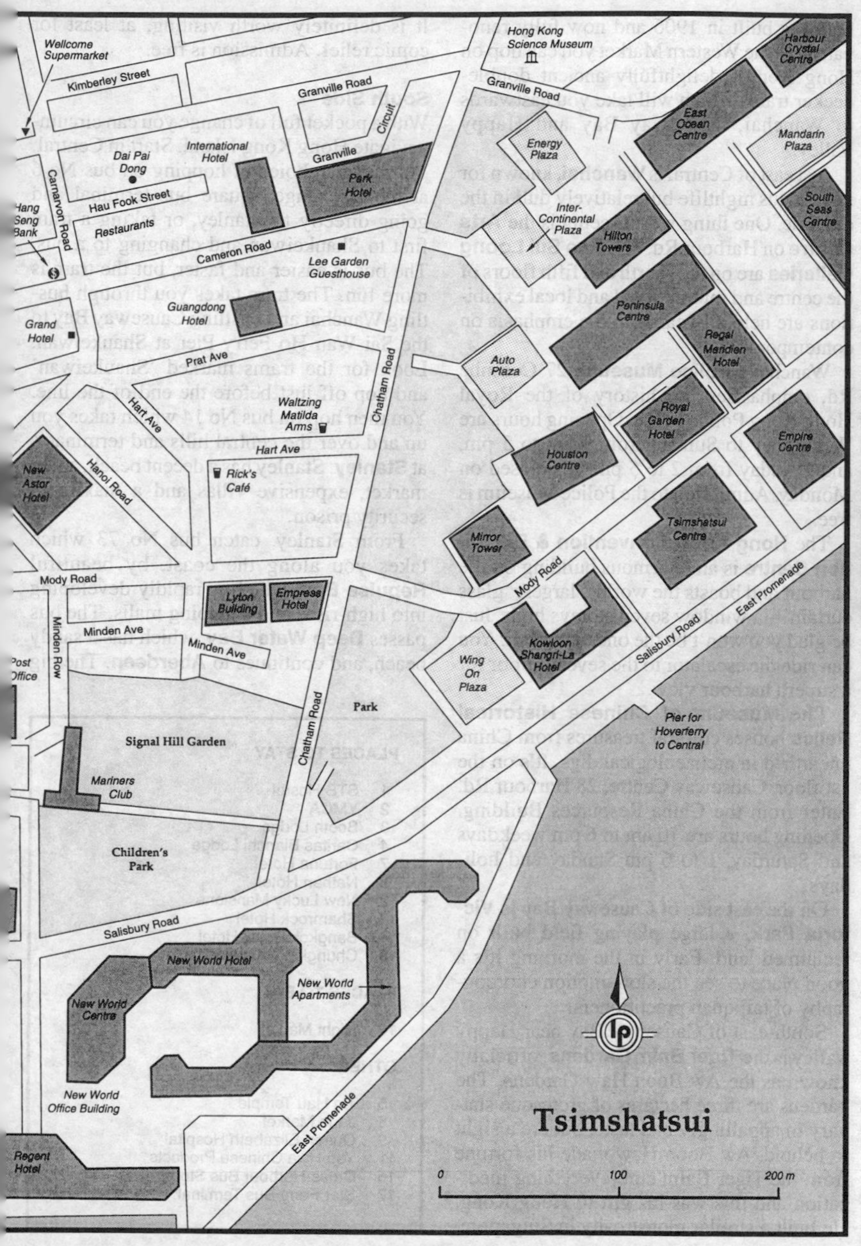
Wellcome Supermarket
Kimberley Street
Granville Road
Circuit
Granville
Hong Kong Science Museum
Granville Road
Harbour Crystal Centre
East Ocean Centre
Mandarin Plaza
Energy Plaza
Dai Pai Dong
International Hotel
Park Hotel
Carnarvon Road
Hau Fook Street
Hang Seng Bank
Restaurants
Cameron Road
Lee Garden Guesthouse
Inter-Continental Plaza
Hilton Towers
South Seas Centre
Peninsula Centre
Guangdong Hotel
Grand Hotel
Prat Ave
Auto Plaza
Regal Meridien Hotel
Chatham Road
Hart Ave
Waltzing Matilda Arms
Hart Ave
Royal Garden Hotel
Empire Centre
Houston Centre
New Astor Hotel
Hanoi Road
Rick's Café
Tsimshatsui Centre
Mirror Tower
Mody Road
Mody Road
East Promenade
Lyton Building
Empress Hotel
Kowloon Shangri-La Hotel
Salisbury Road
Minden Ave
Minden Row
Minden Ave
Post Office
Wing On Plaza
Park
Pier for Hoverferry to Central
Chatham Road
Signal Hill Garden
Mariners Club
Children's Park
Salisbury Road
New World Hotel
New World Apartments
New World Centre
New World Office Building
East Promenade
Regent Hotel
Tsimshatsui
0
100
200 m

HONG KONG

building built in 1906 and now fully renovated. At the Western Market you can hop on Hong Kong's delightfully ancient double-decker trams which will take you eastwards to Wanchai, Causeway Bay and Happy Valley.

Just east of Central is **Wanchai**, known for its raucous nightlife but relatively dull in the daytime. One thing worth seeing is the **Arts Centre** on Harbour Rd. The **Pao Sui Loong Galleries** are on the fourth and fifth floors of the centre and international and local exhibitions are held all year with the emphasis on contemporary art.

Wanchai's **Police Museum**, 27 Coombe Rd, emphasises the history of the Royal Hong Kong Police Force. Opening hours are Wednesday to Sunday from 9 am to 5 pm, and Tuesday from 2 to 5 pm. It's closed on Monday. Admission to the Police Museum is free.

The **Hong Kong Convention & Exhibition Centre** is an enormous building on the harbour and boasts the world's largest 'glass curtain' – a window seven storeys high. Just be glad you won't be the one to wash it. You can ride the escalator to the seventh floor for a superb harbour view.

The **Museum of Chinese Historical Relics** houses cultural treasures from China unearthed in archaeological digs. It's on the 1st floor, Causeway Centre, 28 Harbour Rd. Enter from the China Resources Building. Opening hours are 10 am to 6 pm weekdays and Saturday, 1 to 6 pm Sunday and holidays.

On the east side of Causeway Bay is **Victoria Park**, a large playing field built on reclaimed land. Early in the morning it's a good place to see the slow-motion choreography of taijiquan practitioners.

South-east of Causeway Bay near Happy Valley is the **Tiger Balm Gardens**, officially known as the Aw Boon Haw Gardens. The gardens are three hectares of grotesque statuary in appallingly bad taste, but are a sight to behold. Aw Boon Haw made his fortune from the Tiger Balm cure-everything medication and this was his gift to Hong Kong. He built a similar monstrosity in Singapore. It is definitely worth visiting, at least for comic relief. Admission is free.

South Side

With a pocket full of change you can circumnavigate Hong Kong Island. Start in Central. You have a choice of hopping on bus No 6 at the Exchange Square bus terminal and going directly to Stanley, or taking a tram first to Shaukeiwan and changing to a bus. The bus is easier and faster, but the tram is more fun. The tram takes you through hustling Wanchai and bustling Causeway Bay to the Sai Wan Ho Ferry Pier at Shaukeiwan. Look for the trams marked 'Shaukeiwan' and hop off just before the end of the line. You then hop on bus No 14 which takes you up and over the central hills and terminates at **Stanley**. Stanley has a decent beach, a fine market, expensive villas and a maximum security prison.

From Stanley, catch bus No 73 which takes you along the coast, by beautiful **Repulse Bay**, which is rapidly developing into high-rises and shopping malls. The bus passes **Deep Water Bay**, which has a sandy beach, and continues to **Aberdeen**. The big

PLACES TO STAY

1 STB Hostel
2 YMCA
3 Booth Lodge
4 Caritas Bianchi Lodge
7 Fortuna Hotel
8 Nathan Hotel
12 New Lucky Mansions
13 Shamrock Hotel
14 Bangkok Royal Hotel
16 Chungking Mansions

PLACES TO EAT

10 Night Market

OTHER

5 Tin Hau Temple
6 Jade Market
9 Queen Elizabeth Hospital
11 Yue Hwa Chinese Products
15 Cross-Harbour Bus Stop
17 Star Ferry Bus Terminal

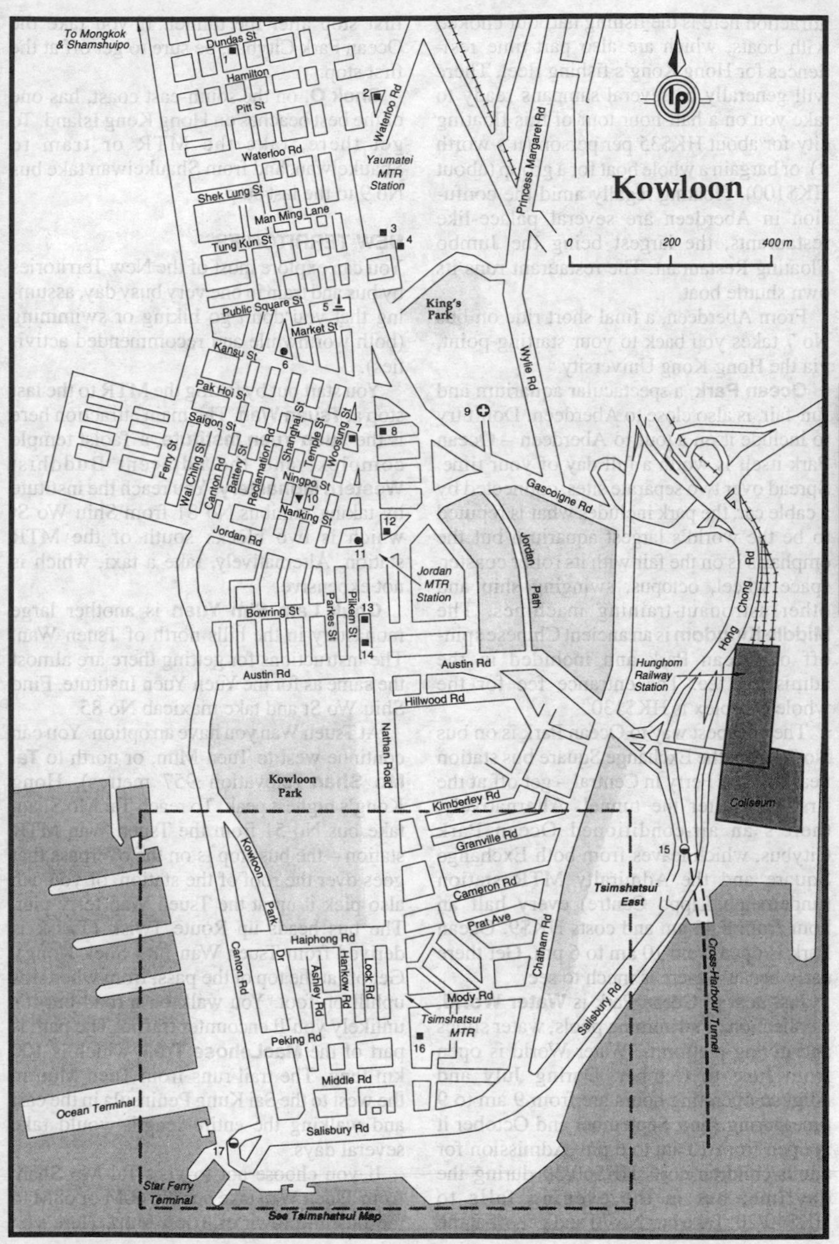
Kowloon
0
200
400 m
To Mongkok & Shamshuipo
Dundas St
Hamilton
Pitt St
Waterloo Rd
Waterloo Rd
Yaumatei MTR Station
Shek Lung St
Man Ming Lane
Tung Kun St
Public Square St
Market St
Kansu St
Pak Hoi St
Saigon St
Ferry St
Wai Ching St
Canton Rd
Battery St
Reclamation Rd
Shanghai St
Temple St
Woosung St
Ningpo St
Nanking St
Jordan Rd
Jordan MTR Station
Bowring St
Parkes St
Pilkem St
Austin Rd
Hillwood Rd
Nathan Road
Kowloon Park
Kowloon Park Dr
Canton Rd
Haiphong Rd
Hankow Rd
Ashley Rd
Lock Rd
Peking Rd
Middle Rd
Salisbury Rd
Ocean Terminal
Star Ferry Terminal
See Tsimshatsui Map
Tsimshatsui MTR
Mody Rd
Prat Ave
Cameron Rd
Granville Rd
Kimberley Rd
Austin Rd
Chatham Rd
Salisbury Rd
Tsimshatsui East
Cross-Harbour Tunnel
Coliseum
Hunghom Railway Station
Hong Chong Rd
Jordan Path
Gascoigne Rd
Wylie Rd
King's Park
Princess Margaret Rd
1
2
3
4
5
6
7
8
9
10
11
12
13
14
15
16
17

HONG KONG

attraction here is the fishing harbour choked with boats, which are also part-time residences for Hong Kong's fishing fleet. There will generally be several sampans ready to take you on a half-hour tour of this floating city for about HK$35 per person (it's worth it), or bargain a whole boat for a group (about HK$100). Floating regally amid the confusion in Aberdeen are several palace-like restaurants, the largest being the Jumbo Floating Restaurant. The restaurant runs its own shuttle boat.

From Aberdeen, a final short ride on bus No 7 takes you back to your starting point, via the Hong Kong University.

Ocean Park, a spectacular aquarium and fun-fair, is also close to Aberdeen. Don't try to include it on a tour to Aberdeen – Ocean Park itself is worth a full day of your time. Spread over two separate sites, connected by a cable car, the park includes what is reputed to be the world's largest aquarium but the emphasis is on the fair with its roller coaster, space wheel, octopus, swinging ship and other astronaut-training machines. The **Middle Kingdom** is an ancient Chinese spin-off of Ocean Park and included in the admission fee. The entrance fee for the whole complex is HK$130.

The cheapest way to Ocean Park is on bus No 70 from the Exchange Square bus station near the Star Ferry in Central – get off at the first stop after the tunnel. Alternatively, there's an air-conditioned Ocean Park Citybus, which leaves from both Exchange Square and the Admiralty MTR station (underneath Lippo Centre) every half an hour from 8.45 am and costs HK$9. Ocean Park is open from 10 am to 6 pm. Get there early because there is much to see.

Just next to Ocean Park is **Water World**, a collection of swimming pools, water slides and diving platforms. Water World is open from June to October. During July and August, operating hours are from 9 am to 9 pm. During June, September and October it is open from 10 am to 6 pm. Admission for adults/children costs HK$60/30 during the daytime, but in the evening falls to HK$40/20. Take bus No 70 and get off at the first stop after the tunnel. If you take the Ocean Park Citybus, be sure to get off at the first stop.

Shek O, on the south-east coast, has one of the best beaches on Hong Kong Island. To get there, take the MTR or tram to Shaukeiwan, and from Shaukeiwan take bus No 9 to the last stop.

NEW TERRITORIES

You can explore most of the New Territories by bus and train in one very busy day, assuming that you don't go hiking or swimming (both worthwhile and recommended activities).

You start out by taking the MTR to the last stop at **Tsuen Wan**. The main attraction here is the **Yuen Yuen Institute**, a Taoist temple complex, and the adjacent Buddhist **Western Monastery**. You reach the institute by taking minibus No 81 from Shiu Wo St which is two blocks south of the MTR station. Alternatively, take a taxi, which is not expensive.

Chuk Lam Sim Yuen is another large monastery in the hills north of Tsuen Wan. The instructions for getting there are almost the same as for the Yuen Yuen Institute. Find Shiu Wo St and take maxicab No 85.

At Tsuen Wan you have an option. You can continue west to Tuen Mun, or north to **Tai Mo Shan** (elevation 957 metres), Hong Kong's highest peak. To reach Tai Mo Shan, take bus No 51 from the Tsuen Wan MTR station – the bus stop is on the overpass that goes over the roof of the station, or you can also pick it up at the Tsuen Wan ferry pier. The bus heads up Route Twisk (Twisk is derived from Tsuen Wan Into Shek Kong). Get off at the top of the pass, from where it's uphill on foot. You walk on a road but it's unlikely you'll encounter traffic. The path is part of the **MacLehose Trail**, which is 100 km long. The trail runs from Tuen Mun in the west to the Sai Kung Peninsula in the east and walking the entire length would take several days.

If you choose not to visit Tai Mo Shan, from Tsuen Wan take bus No 60M or 68M to the bustling town of **Tuen Mun**. Here you can visit Hong Kong's largest shopping mall, the Tuen Mun Town Centre. From here, hop on the Light Rail Transit (LRT) system to reach **Ching Chung Koon**, a temple complex on the north side of Tuen Mun.

You then get back on the LRT and head to Yuen Long. From here, take bus No 54, 64K or 74K to the nearby walled villages at **Kam Tin**. These villages with their single stout entrances are said to date from the 16th century. There are several walled villages at Kam Tin but most accessible is **Kat Hing Wai**. Drop about HK$5 into the donation box by the entrance and wander the narrow little lanes. The old Hakka women in traditional gear require payment before they can be photographed.

The town of Sheung Shui is about eight km east on bus No 77K. Here you can hop on the Kowloon-Canton railway (KCR) and go one stop south to **Fanling**. The main attraction in this town is the **Fung Ying Sin Kwun Temple**, a Taoist temple for the dead.

At Fanling, get on the KCR and head to Tai Po Market station. From here, you can walk 10 to 15 minutes to the **Hong Kong Railway Museum**. You can get back on the KCR and go south to the Chinese University where there's the Art Gallery at the **Institute of Chinese Studies**. Admission is free.

The KCR will bring you to Shatin, a lively, bustling city where you can visit the huge **Shatin Town Centre**, one of Hong Kong's biggest shopping malls. Also, from here you begin the climb up to the **Temple of 10,000 Buddhas** (which actually has over 12,000).

All this should fill your day, but there are other places to visit in the New Territories. The **Sai Kung Peninsula** is one of the least spoilt areas in the New Territories – great for hiking and you can get from village to village on boats in the Tolo Harbour. Also, the best beaches in the New Territories are in the eastern New Territories around the Sai Kung Peninsula, including **Clear Water Bay**.

OUTLYING ISLANDS

There are 235 islands dotting the waters around Hong Kong, but only four have bedroom communities and are thus readily accessible by ferry. Although very tranquil during the week, the islands pack out on weekends and holidays. Cars are prohibited on all of the islands except Lantau, and even there vehicle ownership is very restricted.

Cheung Chau

This dumbbell-shaped island has a large community of Western residents who enjoy the slow pace of island life and relatively low rents. Were it not for the Chinese signs and people, you might think you were in some Greek island village.

The town sprawls across the narrow neck connecting the two ends of the island. The bay on the west side of the island (where the ferry lands) is an exotic collection of fishing boats much like Aberdeen on Hong Kong Island. The east side of the island is where you'll find **Tung Wan Beach**, Cheung Chau's longest. There are a few tiny but remote beaches that you can reach by foot, and at the southern tip of the island is the hideaway **cave** of notorious pirate Cheung Po Tsai.

The big gwailo nightlife spot is the *Garden Cafe Pub* (☎ 9814610) at 84 Tung Wan Rd, in the centre of the island.

Lamma

This is the second largest of the outlying islands and the one closest to the city. Lamma has good beaches and a very relaxed pace on weekdays, but on weekends it's mobbed like anywhere else. There are two main communities here, Yung Shue Wan in the north and Sok Kwu Wan in the south. Both have ferry services to Central.

Both Yung Shue Wan and Sok Kwu Wan are lined with seafood restaurants, so you won't starve. The *Waterfront Bar* in Yung Shue Wan is a lively place for nightlife and good food, or you can try its quieter competiton, the *Island Bar*.

Lantau

This is the largest of the islands and the most sparsely populated – it's almost twice the size of Hong Kong Island but the population is only 30,000. You could easily spend a

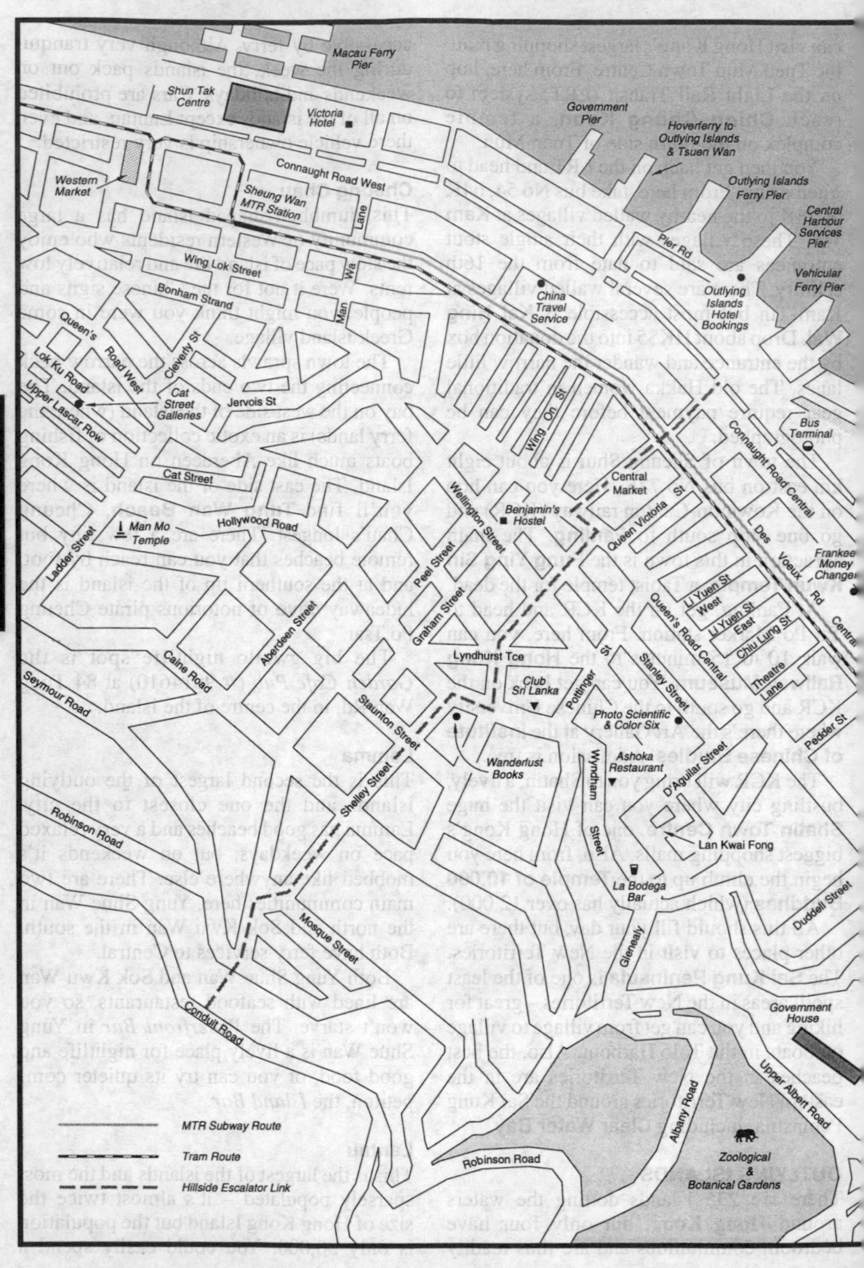
Macau Ferry Pier
Shun Tak Centre
Victoria Hotel
Government Pier
Hoverferry to Outlying Islands & Tsuen Wan
Outlying Islands Ferry Pier
Central Harbour Services Pier
Vehicular Ferry Pier
Western Market
Connaught Road West
Sheung Wan MTR Station
Lane
Wa
Man
Wing Lok Street
Bonham Strand
Pier Rd
China Travel Service
Outlying Islands Hotel Bookings
Queen's Road West
Lok Ku Road
Upper Lascar Row
Cleverly St
Cat Street Galleries
Jervois St
Wing On St
Connaught Road Central
Bus Terminal
Cat Street
Central Market
Queen Victoria St
Des Voeux Rd Central
Man Mo Temple
Hollywood Road
Wellington Street
Benjamin's Hostel
Frankee Money Changer
Ladder Street
Peel Street
Li Yuen St West
Li Yuen St East
Chiu Lung St
Queen's Road Central
Graham Street
Aberdeen Street
Lyndhurst Tce
Club Sri Lanka
Pottinger St
Stanley Street
Theatre Lane
Caine Road
Seymour Road
Staunton Street
Photo Scientific & Color Six
Pedder St
Ashoka Restaurant
Wanderlust Books
Wyndham Street
D'Aguilar Street
Shelley Street
Robinson Road
Lan Kwai Fong
La Bodega Bar
Duddell Street
Mosque Street
Glenealy
Government House
Conduit Road
Albany Road
Upper Albert Road
MTR Subway Route
Tram Route
Hillside Escalator Link
Robinson Road
Zoological & Botanical Gardens

HONG KONG

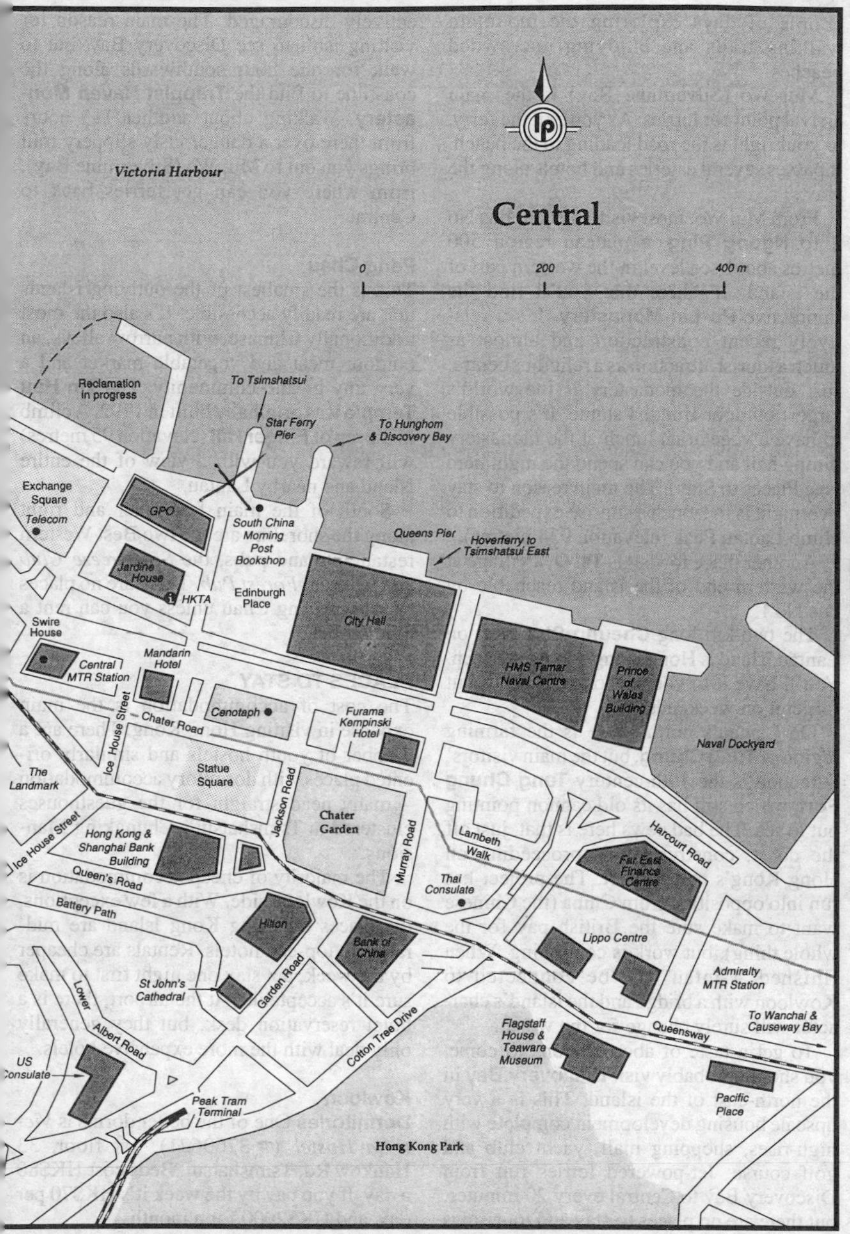
Central
0
200
400 m
Victoria Harbour
Reclamation in progress
To Tsimshatsui
Star Ferry Pier
To Hunghom & Discovery Bay
Exchange Square
Telecom
GPO
South China Morning Post Bookshop
Queens Pier
Hoverferry to Tsimshatsui East
Jardine House
HKTA
Edinburgh Place
City Hall
Swire House
Central MTR Station
Mandarin Hotel
HMS Tamar Naval Centre
Prince of Wales Building
Cenotaph
Furama Kempinski Hotel
Chater Road
Ice House Street
Naval Dockyard
The Landmark
Statue Square
Jackson Road
Chater Garden
Murray Road
Lambeth Walk
Harcourt Road
Ice House Street
Hong Kong & Shanghai Bank Building
Queen's Road
Far East Finance Centre
Thai Consulate
Battery Path
Hilton
Bank of China
Lippo Centre
Admiralty MTR Station
St John's Cathedral
Garden Road
Lower Albert Road
Cotton Tree Drive
Queensway
To Wanchai & Causeway Bay
Flagstaff House & Teaware Museum
US Consulate
Peak Tram Terminal
Pacific Place
Hong Kong Park

couple of days exploring the mountain walking trails and enjoying uncrowded beaches.

Mui Wo (Silvermine Bay) is the main arrival point for ferries. As you exit the ferry, to your right is the road leading to the beach. It passes several eateries and hotels along the way.

From Mui Wo, most visitors board bus No 2 to **Ngong Ping**, a plateau region 500 metres above sea level in the western part of the island. It's here that you'll find the impressive **Po Lin Monastery**. It's a relatively recent construction and almost as much a tourist attraction as a religious centre. Just outside the monastery is the world's largest outdoor Buddha statue. It's possible to have a vegetarian lunch at the monastery dining hall and you can spend the night here (see Places to Stay). The main reason to stay overnight is to launch a sunrise expedition to climb Lantau Peak (elevation 934 metres).

Another place to visit is **Tai O**, a village at the western end of the island reachable by bus No 1.

The two-km long **Cheung Sha Wan** on Lantau Island is Hong Kong's longest beach. You'll have it to yourself on weekdays, but forget it on weekends.

On Lantau's north shore is the farming region of **Tung Chung**, but the main visitors' attraction is the 19th-century **Tung Chung Fort**, which still has its old cannon pointing out to sea. The bad news here is that, just off the coast, construction is proceeding on Hong Kong's new airport. The project has run into opposition from China (the Chinese want to make sure the British pay for the whole thing), but work is continuing. When finished, Lantau will be connected to Kowloon with a bridge and the island's character will surely change for the worse.

To get a taste of abominations to come, you should probably visit **Discovery Bay** in the north-east of the island. This is a very upscale housing development complete with high-rises, shopping mall, yacht club and golf course. Jet-powered ferries run from Discovery Bay to Central every 20 minutes, but there are no places to stay and tourism is actively discouraged. The main reason for visiting isn't to see Discovery Bay, but to walk for one hour southwards along the coastline to find the **Trappist Haven Monastery**. Walking about another 1½ hours from there over a dangerously slippery trail brings you out to Mui Wo (Silvermine Bay), from where you can get ferries back to Central.

Peng Chau

This is the smallest of the outlying islands that are readily accessible. It's also the most traditionally Chinese, with narrow alleys, an outdoor meat and vegetable market and a very tiny gwailo community. The **Tin Hau Temple** was originally built in 1792. A climb to the top of **Finger Hill** (elevation 95 metres) will reward you with a view of the entire island and nearby Lantau.

South of the main ferry pier and right along the shoreline are the two Best Western restaurants and pubs, the *Sea Breeze Club* and adjacent *Forest Pub*. There are no places to stay in Peng Chau unless you can rent a holiday flat.

PLACES TO STAY

The cost of accommodation is the main expense in visiting Hong Kong. There are a number of youth hostels and similarly oriented places with dormitory accommodation – many head straight for the guesthouses clustered in Tsimshatsui's Chungking Mansions.

The majority of cheap accommodation is on the Kowloon side. With a few exceptions, the places on Hong Kong Island are mid-range to top-end hotels. Rentals are cheaper by the week, but stay one night first to make sure it's acceptable. At the airport, there is a hotel reservation desk, but they generally only deal with the more expensive hotels.

Kowloon

Dormitories One of the better dorms is *Victoria Hostel* (☎ 3760621), 1st floor, 33 Hankow Rd, Tsimshatsui. Beds cost HK$80 a day. If you pay by the week it's HK$70 per day, and HK$2000 for a month.

There is probably no other place in the world like Chungking Mansions, the bottom-end accommodation ghetto of Hong Kong. It's a huge high-rise dump at 30 Nathan Rd in the heart of Tsimshatsui. It's divided into five blocks labelled A through E, each with its own lift. Each block has numerous guesthouses, including a few dormitories.

On the 16th floor of A Block in Chungking Mansions is *Travellers' Hostel* (☎ 3687710), a Hong Kong landmark. You may have to queue for 20 minutes to get up the lift, but when you finally arrive beds are just HK$60 *if* it's not full. Double rooms with/without attached bath cost HK$150/170. The management also operates a cheap beachside hostel at Ting Kau in the New Territories.

The 12th floor of A Block is where you'll find the friendly *Super Guest House* where dormitory beds start at HK$60.

On the sixth floor of A Block is the *New World Hostel* (☎ 7236352). Dormitories are HK$60 and double rooms go for HK$180. *Friendship Travellers Hostel* (☎ 3110797, 3112523), B Block, 6th floor, has mixed dormitory accommodation. The first night costs HK$80, the second HK$70 and anything thereafter is HK$60.

Around the corner from Chungking Mansions is the *Garden Hostel* (☎ 7218567). It's in Mirador Arcade, 58 Nathan Rd, but it's easier to find if you enter from Mody Rd. Turn right as you come out of the main entrance to Chungking and then right at Mody Rd (the first street). On the left side of the street is an obvious sign. Follow the stairs to the third floor. Beds cost HK$80 in the dorm, but drop to HK$65 per night if paid by the week.

On the 13th floor of Mirador Arcade, 58 Nathan Rd, you'll find the *Kowloon Hotel* (☎ 3112523) and *New Garden Hotel* (same phone and same owner). Dormitories are HK$60. Singles with shared bath are HK$150, rising up to HK$200 for rooms with private bath. Ask about discounts if you want to rent long-term.

The *Golden Crown Guest House* (☎ 3691782), Golden Crown Mansion, 5th floor, 66-70 Nathan Rd, Tsimshatsui, has dormitory beds for HK$100; singles start from HK$250 and doubles from HK$300.

Guesthouses The already-mentioned Chungking Mansions has more than just dorms. There are approximately 60 licenced guesthouses plus a few illegals. The price range for a private room is roughly HK$150 to HK$250. Some of the better places to stay are:

A Block – *Park Guest House* (☎ 3681689), 15th floor; *New Hawaii Guest House* (☎ 3666127), 14th floor; *Peking Guest House* (☎ 7238320), 12th floor; *New International Guest House* (☎ 3692613), 11th floor; *New Mandarin Guest House* (☎ 3661070), 8th floor; *Welcome Guest House* (☎ 7217793), 7th floor; and *London Guest House* (☎ 7245000), 6th floor.

B Block – *Astor Guest House*, 16th floor; *Carlton Guest House* (☎ 7210720), 15th floor; *New Washington Guest House* (☎ 3665798), 13th floor; *Grand Guest House* (☎ 3686520), 9th floor; *New York Guest House* (☎ 3395986), 7th floor; and *Dragon Inn*, 3rd floor.

C Block – *Tom's Guest House* (☎ 3679258), 16th floor; *New Grand Guest House* (☎ 3111702), 13th floor; *Marria Guest House*, 11th floor; *Garden Guest House* (☎ 3687414), 7th floor; *New Brother's Guest House* (☎ 7240135), 6th floor; and *Maharaja Guest House*, 4th floor.

D Block – *Four Seas Guest House* (☎ 3687469), 15th floor; *Guangzhou Guest House* (☎ 7241555), 13th floor; *China Town* (☎ 7213723), 10th floor; *Fortuna Guest House* (☎ 3664524), 8th floor; *Royal Plaza Inn* (☎ 3671424), 5th floor; *Mt Everest Guest House*, 4th floor.

E Block – *Far East Guest House* (☎ 3681724), 14th floor; *Chungking Mansion Mandarin Guest House*, 13th floor; *Regent Guest House* (☎ 7220833), 6th floor.

You can avoid the stigma of staying in Chungking Mansions by checking out Mirador Arcade at 58 Nathan Rd. On the 14th floor in Flat F2 you'll find the *Man Hing Lung* (☎ 7220678). All rooms come equipped with private bath, air-con and TV. Singles cost HK$260 to HK$280 and doubles are HK$320 to HK$360. If you arrive by yourself and want a roommate, the management can put you in with another traveller. On the 12th floor in Flat B5 is *Ajit*

Guest House (☎ 3691201), which is very friendly and clean with rooms for HK$150. On the 7th floor in Flat F2 is *Mini Hotel* (☎ 3672551), under renovation during our visit so no one could quote a price.

Tourists Home (☎ 3112622) is on the 6th floor, G Block, Champagne Court, 16 Kimberley Rd. Doubles are from HK$280 to HK$320. All rooms have an attached private bath.

The New Lucky Mansions, 300 Nathan Rd (entrance on Jordan Rd), Yaumatei, is in a better neighbourhood than most of the other guesthouses. There are eight guesthouses to choose from. The rundown from top floor to bottom is:

Great Wall Hotel, 14th floor, very posh doubles for HK$450 (☎ 3887645)
Ocean Guest House, 11th floor, singles/doubles HK$300/350 (☎ 3850125)
Nathan House, 10th floor, under renovation at time of research so no price available (☎ 7801302)
Overseas Guest House, 9th floor, singles/doubles with shared bath HK$180/190, clean and friendly
Tung Wo Guest House, 9th floor, singles HK$150, cheap but not so nice
Hoi Pun Uk House, 5th floor, doubles HK$280, good but at present there is no English sign, the owner speaks Mandarin (☎ 7807317)
Hitton Inn, 3rd floor, double with private bath HK$230, good value (☎ 7704880)
Hakkas Guest House, 3rd floor, doubles HK$250, nice rooms and the owner speaks good English (☎ 7701470)

Hotels – bottom end The *YMCA International House* (☎ 7719111), 23 Waterloo Rd, Yaumatei, has 29 cheap rooms with shared bath for HK$150 for men only. The majority of their rooms are rented to both men and women, but these are not terribly cheap at HK$450 to HK$660. There are some suites for HK$800.

The *YWCA* (☎ 7139211) is badly located near Pui Ching Rd and Waterloo Rd in Mongkok. The official address is 5 Man Fuk Rd, up a hill behind a Caltex petrol station. Single rooms for women only are HK$250 to HK$400, while doubles and twins are HK$500.

King's Hotel (☎ 7801281), 473 Nathan Rd, Yaumatei, has 72 rooms and is one of the better deals. Singles cost HK$340 to HK$360, doubles and twins cost HK$400 to HK$430.

The Salvation Army runs *Booth Lodge* (☎ 7719266), 11 Wing Sing Lane, Yaumatei, where doubles/twins are HK$380/680. Just around the corner is *Caritas Bianchi Lodge* (☎ 3881111), 4 Cliff Rd, Yaumatei, where singles are HK$450 and doubles range from HK$520 to HK$640. There is another *Caritas Lodge* (☎ 3393777), 134 Boundary St, Mongkok (take MTR to Prince Edward Station), where singles/doubles are HK$330/390.

Hotels – middle By Kowloon standards, a mid-range hotel is defined as one in which you can find a room costing approximately HK$400 to HK$800. Some travel agencies can get you a sizeable (up to 50%) discount if you book through them. One such place is Traveller Services (☎ 3752222) but a few other agents do it as well. Some places in the mid-range include:

Bangkok Royal, 2-12 Pilkem St, Yaumatei (Jordan MTR station), 70 rooms, singles HK$350 to HK$450, doubles and twins HK$460 to HK$580 (☎ 7359181)
Concourse, 22 Lai Chi Kok Rd, Mongkok (Prince Edward MTR station), 359 rooms, doubles and twins HK$780 to HK$1280, suites HK$1680 (☎ 3976683)
Eaton, 380 Nathan Rd, Yaumatei (near Jordan MTR station), 392 rooms, doubles and twins HK$630 to HK$1250, suites HK$1450 (☎ 7821818)
Fortuna, 355 Nathan Rd, Yaumatei (near Jordan MTR station), 187 rooms, singles HK$600 to HK$1000, doubles and twins HK$900 to HK$1100 (☎ 3851011)
Grand Tower, 627-641 Nathan Rd, Mongkok, 549 rooms, singles HK$760 to HK$1000, doubles and twins HK$830 to HK$1100 (☎ 7890011)
Guangdong, 18 Pratt Ave, Tsimshatsui, 245 rooms, doubles and twins HK$800 to HK$990 (☎ 7393311)
Imperial, 30-34 Nathan Rd, Tsimshatsui, 214 rooms, singles HK$720 to HK$920, doubles and twins HK$800 to HK$1000, suites HK$1400 to HK$1700 (☎ 3662201)
International, 33 Cameron Rd, Tsimshatsui, 89 rooms, singles HK$380 to HK$680, twins

HK$500 to HK$880, suites HK$1100 to HK$1400 (☎ 3663381)

Metropole, 75 Waterloo Rd, Yaumatei, 487 rooms, doubles and twins HK$720 to HK$1250, suites HK$2200 to HK$4200 (☎ 7611711)

Nathan, 378 Nathan Rd, Yaumatei, 186 rooms, singles HK$550, doubles and twins HK$650 to HK$700, suites HK$850 (☎ 3885141)

New Astor, 11 Carnarvon Rd, Tsimshatsui, 151 rooms, doubles and twins HK$780 to HK$1080, suites HK$1500 to HK$2400 (☎ 3667261)

Newton, 58-66 Boundary St, Mongkok, 176 rooms, singles HK$700 to HK$950, doubles and twins HK$750 to HK$1000 (☎ 7872338)

Prudential, 222 Nathan Rd, Yaumatei (near Jordan MTR station), 434 rooms, singles HK$480 to HK$1280, twins HK$550 to HK$1350, suites HK$1680 to HK$1800 (☎ 3118222)

Shamrock, 223 Nathan Rd, Yaumatei, 148 rooms, singles HK$380 to HK$650, doubles and twins HK$450 to HK$750, suites HK$800 to HK$850 (☎ 7352271)

YMCA, 41 Salisbury Rd, Tsimshatsui, singles HK$590, doubles and twins HK$690 to HK$860, suites HK$1150 to HK$1350 (☎ 3692211)

Hong Kong Island

Hostels *Ma Wui Hall* (☎ 8175715) on top of Mt Davis on Hong Kong Island offers stunning views and is the most accessible of the YHA hostels. The drawback is that it's centrally located in the relative sense only. From the Star Ferry pier in Central it's still a good hour's journey but travellers say it's almost worth it. Before embarking on the trek, ring up to be sure a bed is available. To get there, take a No 5B bus to the end of the line, walk back 100 metres and look for the YHA sign. You've then got a 20 to 30-minute climb up the hill! There are 112 beds here and the nightly cost is HK$40. You need a youth hostel card to stay, the hostel is closed from 10 am to 4 pm and it's lights out by 11 pm.

Guesthouses *Noble Hostel* (☎ 5766148) is surely one of the best guesthouses in Hong Kong, but is often full. Due to popular demand, the owner has expanded to five locations. There are two offices where you can check in – one is at Flat C1, 7th floor, 37 Paterson St, Paterson Building, Causeway Bay, and the other is nearby at Flat A3, 17th floor, 27 Paterson St. Singles with shared bath are HK$200 to HK$220; doubles with shared bath are HK$260 to HK$280; doubles with private bath are HK$330 to HK$350. If the guesthouse is full, the manager will try to help you find another place to stay.

The Phoenix Apartments, 70 Lee Garden Hill Rd, Causeway Bay, (look for New Phoenix Shopping Centre on the ground floor) has a number of elegant and reasonably priced guesthouses. The catch here is that most are short-time hotels where rooms are rented by the hour. One hotel proudly advertises 'Avoidance of Publicity & Reasonable Rates'. Nevertheless, rooms are available for overnighters, and as long as they have changed the sheets recently it's not a bad place to stay. The *Sunrise Inn* (☎ 5762419) on the 1st floor advertises rooms for HK$128 if you stay overnight, or HK$58 for two hours. Another cheapie is *Garden House* (☎ 5777391), on the 2nd floor, which has rooms for HK$160. The *Hoi Wan Guest House* (☎ 5777970), on the 1st floor, Flat C, has plush rooms starting at HK$250. The 1st floor also has the *Baguio Motel* (☎ 5761533) where very fancy rooms go for HK$400. The *Fulai Hotel* on the 5th floor also charges HK$400. There are numerous other guesthouses in Phoenix Apartments where you might be able to negotiate a cheaper rate for a longer term (or shorter term).

Nearby is *Emerald House* (☎ 5772368), 1st floor, 44 Leighton Rd, where clean doubles with private bath and round beds (no kidding) are HK$350. Enter the building from Leighton Lane just around the corner. Guesthouses are plentiful in this section of Leighton Rd, but some are pretty grotty.

Leishun Court, at 116 Leighton Rd, Causeway Bay, is another cheap option. The building houses a number of low-priced guesthouses, mostly on the lower floors. *Fuji House* (☎ 5779406), 1st floor, is excellent value at HK$250 for a room with private bath. On the same floor is the *Villa Lisboa Hotel* (☎ 5765421). On the 3rd floor is *Sam Yu Apartment*.

Hotels In terms of mid-range hotels, there's even less available on Hong Kong Island than in Kowloon. Estimate HK$450 at the minimum. Again, check with Traveller Services (☎ 3752222) or other travel agents for discounts. Some places to check out include:

China Merchants, 160-161 Connaught Rd West, Sheung Wan, 285 rooms, doubles and twins HK$650 to HK$950, suites HK$1800 (☎ 5596888)

Emerald, 152 Connaught Rd West, Sheung Wan, 316 rooms, singles HK$500, doubles and twins HK$600 to HK$800, suites HK$850 to HK$1200 (☎ 5468111)

Harbour, 116-122 Gloucester Rd, Wanchai, 200 rooms, singles HK$500 to HK$800, doubles and twins HK$680 to HK$950, suites HK$1400 (☎ 5118211)

Harbour View International, 4 Harbour Rd, Wanchai, 320 rooms, with doubles and twins HK$620 to HK$850, and suites from HK$950 to HK$1050 (☎ 8021111)

New Cathay, 17 Tung Lo Wan Rd, Causeway Bay, 223 rooms, singles HK$550 to HK$800, doubles and twins HK$690 to HK$850, suites HK$1300 to HK$1500 (☎ 5778211)

New Harbour, 41-49 Hennessy Rd, Wanchai, 173 rooms, doubles and twins HK$680 to HK$1050, suites HK$1100 to HK$1400 (☎ 8611166)

Newton, 218 Electric Rd, North Point (Fortress Hill MTR station), 362 rooms, with singles HK$700 to HK$1050, doubles and twins from HK$750 to HK$1100, and suites HK$1750 to HK$1800 (☎ 8072333)

Wesley, 22 Hennessy Rd, Wanchai, 251 rooms, doubles and twins HK$650 to HK$950 (☎ 8666688)

YWCA-Garden View International, 1 MacDonnell Rd, Central, 131 rooms, with doubles and twins from HK$480 to HK$580, suites HK$780 (☎ 8773737)

New Territories

Travellers' Hostel (☎ 3687710), Chungking Mansions, 16th floor, A Block, Tsimshatsui, also operates a *Beachside Hostel* (☎ 4919179) at Ting Kau near Tsuen Wan, opposite Tsing Yi Island. Dorm beds at the hostel cost HK$80 a night. A private room with shared/private bath costs HK$150. You get there by taking the MTR to Tsuen Wan, then minibus No 96 or 96M. It's hard to find this place so ring first and the staff will send someone to meet you.

The Hong Kong Youth Hostel Association (HKYHA) operates several hostels in the New Territories. All are in fairly remote locations and it isn't practical to stay in these places and commute to the city. The only reason for staying would be to enjoy the countryside and do a bit of exploring and hiking. For all of these places, you need a hostelling card. You are also strongly advised to ring up first to make sure that a bed is available. The following three places are all HKYHA operated.

Sze Lok Yuen (☎ 4888188) is on Tai Mo Shan Rd. Beds cost HK$40 and camping in tents is permitted. Take the No 51 bus (Tsuen Wan Ferry Pier-Kam Tin) at Tsuen Wan MTR station and alight at Tai Mo Shan Rd. Follow Tai Mo Shan Rd for about 45 minutes, then turn on to a small concrete path on the right-hand side which leads directly to the hostel. This is a good place from which to climb Tai Mo Shan, Hong Kong's highest peak. Because of the elevation, it can get amazingly cold at night, so be prepared.

Pak Sha O Hostel (☎ 3282327) charges HK$40 a bed and also permits camping. Take bus No 92 from the Choi Hung Estate bus terminal and get off at the Sai Kung terminal. From Sai Kung, take bus No 94 towards Wong Shek Pier, but get off at Ko Tong village. From there, find Hoi Ha Rd and a road sign 30 metres ahead showing the way to Pak Sha O.

Also on the Sai Kung Peninsula is *Bradbury Hall* (☎ 3282458), in Chek Keng. From Choi Hung Estate bus terminal, take bus No 92 to the Sai Kung terminal. From Sai Kung, take bus No 94 to Yellow Stone Pier, but get off at Pak Tam Au. There's a footpath at the side of the road leading to Chek Keng village. The hostel is right on the harbour just facing the Chek Keng Ferry Pier. An alternative route is to take the ferry from Ma Liu Shui (adjacent to the Chinese University railway station) to Chek Keng Pier.

Outlying Islands

Cheung Chau Cheung Chau has one upmarket hotel, the *Warwick Hotel* (☎ 9810081). Doubles cost HK$920 on a weekday and HK$1050 on a weekend, plus a 10% service charge and 5% tax.

Star House Motel (☎ 9812186) at 149 Tai Sun Bak St has double rooms starting at HK$200 on weekdays and costing between HK$600 and HK$700 a night on weekends.

There is a solid line-up of booths offering flats for rent opposite the ferry pier. Small flats for two persons begin at HK$200 but prices double to HK$400 on weekends and holidays.

Lamma Island There are several places to stay in Yung Shue Wan. Right by the Yung Shue Wan ferry pier is the *Man Lai Wah Hotel* (☎ 9820220), where doubles cost HK$300 on weekdays, rising to HK$500 to HK$600 on weekends. *Lamma Vacation House* (☎ 9820427) is at 29 Main St and offers coffin-sized rooms for HK$120 or reasonably cushy flats for HK$200.

Lantau Island As you exit the ferry in Mui Wo, turn right and head towards the beach. Here you'll find several hotels with a sea view. The line-up of places to stay includes *Sea House* (☎ 9847757) which has rather dumpy-looking rooms that start from HK$200 on weekdays, HK$400 on weekends. One of the best deals around is the *Mui Wo Inn* (☎ 9841916) with doubles from HK$243 to HK$435 on weekdays, and HK$435 to HK$565 on weekends. Top of the line is the *Silvermine Beach Hotel* (☎ 9848295) which has doubles from HK$680 to HK$980 plus a 15% surcharge.

There are two places to stay in Ngong Ping. The *Po Lin Monastery* offers dormitory beds for HK$200 (the price includes vegetarian meals), but it's not a friendly place. A better deal is the nearby *S G Davis Youth Hostel*, which costs HK$40, but a youth hostel card is required.

PLACES TO EAT

Hong Kong has just about every dining choice you can think of from McDonald's to Mexican or Sichuan to spaghetti. It's not a fantastically cheap food trip like Bali but you can still eat well at a reasonable price. But if you're really economising, you might find yourself eating more Big Macs than you might have expected.

Kowloon

Breakfast The window of the *Wing Wah Restaurant* (☎ 7212947) is always filled with great-looking cakes and pastries. It's at 21A Lock Rd near Swindon's Bookstore and the Hyatt Regency. Either take food away or sit down with some coffee. Prices are very reasonable and this place has kept me alive for years. Inexpensive Chinese food is also served and – a rare treat for a Hong Kong budget Chinese cafe – there is an English menu.

A very similar cafe with cakes, coffee and other delicacies is the nearby *Kam Fat Restaurant* at 11 Ashley Rd. Prices here are slightly higher than Wing Wah but the atmosphere is also better.

Deep in the bowels of *every* MTR station you can find *Maxim's Cake Shops*. The cakes and pastries look irresistible, but don't sink your teeth into the creamy delights until you're back on the street as it is prohibited to eat or drink anything in the MTR stations or on the trains – it's a HK$1000 fine if you do.

There is a chain of bakeries around Hong Kong with the name *St Honore Cake Shop*, but there's no English sign on their stores although you'll soon recognise their ideogram. You can find one at 221 Nathan Rd, Yaumatei, and a much smaller one at 8 Canton Rd, Tsimshatsui.

If you're up before the aforementioned places open, *7 Eleven* operates 24 hours and does good coffee, packaged breads and microwave cuisine.

Dim Sum The Chinese dim sum is normally served from around 11 am to 3 pm, but a few places have it available for breakfast. Nothing in Hong Kong is dirt cheap, but the following places are chosen for reasonable prices:

Canton Court, Guangdong Hotel, 18 Prat Ave, Tsimshatsui, dim sum served from 7 am to 4 pm (☎ 7393311)

HONG KONG

Harbour View Seafood, 3rd floor, Tsimshatsui Centre, 66 Mody Rd, Tsimshatusi East, dim sum served from 11 am to 5 pm, restaurant closes at midnight (☎ 7225888)
New Home, 19-20 Hanoi Rd, Tsimshatsui, dim sum served from 7 am to 4.30 pm (☎ 3665876)
Orchard Court, 1st and 2nd floors, Ma's Mansion, 37 Hankow Rd, Tsimshatsui, dim sum served from 11 am to 5 pm (☎ 3175111)
Tai Woo, 14-16 Hillwood Rd, Yaumatei, dim sum served from 11 am to 4.30 pm (☎ 3699773)
Eastern Palace, 3rd floor, Omni The Hongkong Hotel, Shopping Arcade, Harbour City, Canton Rd, Tsimshatsui, dim sum served from 11.30 am to 3 pm (☎ 7306011)
North China Peking Seafood, 2nd floor, Polly Commercial Building, 21-23 Prat Ave, Tsimshatsui, dim sum served from 11 am to 3 pm (☎ 3116689)

Chinese Street Stalls The cheapest place to enjoy authentic Chinese cuisine is the *Temple St Night Market* in Yaumatei. It starts at about 8 pm and begins to fade at 11 pm. There are also plenty of mainstream indoor restaurants with variable prices.

Filipino The *Mabuhay* (☎ 3673762), at 11 Minden Ave, serves good Filipino and Spanish food though it is not really cheap.

Indonesian *Java Rijsttafel* (☎ 3671230), Han Hing Mansion, 38 Hankow Rd, Tsimshatsui, is a good place to enjoy a rijsttafel, literally meaning a rice table. This place packs out with Dutch expats.

There is also the *Indonesian Restaurant* (☎ 3673287), 66 Granville Rd, Tsimshatsui.

Malaysian The *Singapore Restaurant* (☎ 3761282), 23 Ashley Rd, Tsimshatsui, is a great bargain. It's coffee-shop style, but forget the decor because the food is excellent and cheap. Malaysian, Chinese and Western food costs about HK$45 for a set dinner. It's open from 11 am until midnight.

Thai Thai food is devastatingly hot but excellent. A reasonably priced and good Thai restaurant is *Royal Pattaya* (☎ 3669919), 9 Minden Ave, Tsimshatsui. Also good is the *Sawadee* (☎ 3763299), at 6 Ichang St, Tsimshatsui.

Korean There are several excellent and easily accessible Korean restaurants. A good one is *Seoul House* (☎ 3143174), 35 Hillwood Rd, Yaumatei.

Another place is *Manna*, a chain restaurant with outlets in Tsimshatsui at 83B Nathan Rd (☎ 7212159); Lyton Building, 32B Mody Rd (☎ 3674278); and 6A Humphrey's Rd (☎ 3682485).

Two other centrally located Korean restaurants are *Arirang* (☎ 7352281), ground floor, room 9, Sutton Court, Harbour City, Canton Rd, Tsimshatsui, and *Korea House* (☎ 3675674), Empire Centre, 68 Mody Rd, Tsimshatsui East.

Indian The greatest concentration of cheap Indian restaurants is in Chungking Mansions on Nathan Rd. Despite the grotty appearance of the entrance to the Mansions, many of the restaurants are surprisingly plush inside. A meal of curried chicken and rice, or curry with chappatis and dahl, will cost around HK$30 per person.

Start your search for Indian food on the ground floor of the arcade. The bottom of the market belongs to *Kashmir Fast Food* and *Lahore Fast Food*. These open early, so you can have curry, chapatis and heartburn for breakfast. Neither of these two offers any kind of cheery atmosphere, so it's no place to linger.

Upstairs in Chungking Mansions are many other places with better food and a more pleasant atmosphere. Prices are still low, with set meals from HK$35 or so. The following are presented in order from A to E blocks, from top floor to bottom, rather than by order of price and quality:

Nanak Mess, 11th floor, flat A-4, decent but not one of the top spots
Kashmir Club (☎ 3116308), 3rd floor, A Block, highly rated and even offers free home delivery
Centre Point Club (☎ 3661086), 6th floor, B Block, also highly recommended
Ashok Club, 5th floor, B Block, Nepalese food, atmosphere could stand some improvement
Taj Mahal Club Mess (☎ 7225454), 3rd floor, B Block, excellent

Sher-I-Punjab Club Mess (☎ 3680859), 3rd floor, B Block, Nepalese and Indian food
Mumtaj Mahal Club (☎ 7215591), 12th floor, C Block, good if you're staying in this block
Islamabad Club (☎ 7215362), Indian and Pakistani halal food, looks decent
Delhi Club (☎ 3681682), 3rd floor, the best in C Block
New Madras Mess (☎ 3685021), 16th floor, Muslim and vegetarian halal food, grotty atmosphere
Royal Club Mess (☎ 3697680), 5th floor, D Block, Indian and vegetarian, offers free home delivery and is my personal favourite in Chungking Mansions
Karachi Mess (☎ 3681678), halal food, looks like you've stepped right into Pakistan
Khyber Pass Club Mess (☎ 7212786), 7th floor, E Block, looks decent

Vegetarian The *Bodhi* (☎ 7392222), ground floor, 56 Cameron Rd, Tsimshatsui, is one of Hong Kong's biggest vegetarian restaurants with several branches: 36 Jordan Rd, Yaumatei; 1st floor, 32-34 Lock Rd (you can also enter at 81 Nathan Rd), Tsimshatsui; and 56 Cameron Rd, Tsimshatsui. Dim sum is dished out from 11 am to 5 pm.

Also excellent is *Pak Bo Vegetarian Kitchen* (☎ 3662732), 106 Austin Rd, Tsimshatsui. Another to try is *Fat Siu Lam* (☎ 3881308), 2-3 Cheong Lok St, Yaumati.

Fast Food *Oliver's* is on the ground floor at Ocean Centre on Canton Rd. It's a great place for breakfast – inexpensive bacon, eggs and toast. The sandwiches are equally excellent, though it gets crowded at lunchtime.

McDonald's occupies key strategic locations in Tsimshatsui. Late-night restaurants are amazingly scarce in Hong Kong, so it's useful to know that two McDonald's in Tsimshatsui operate 24 hours a day: at 21A Granville Rd, and 12 Peking Rd. There is also a McDonald's at 2 Cameron Rd, and another in Star House just opposite the Star Ferry pier.

Domino's Pizza (☎ 7650683), Yue Sun Mansion, Hunghom, does not have a restaurant where you can sit down to eat. Rather, pizzas are delivered to your door within 30 minutes of phoning in your order.

Other fast-food outlets in Kowloon include:

Cafe de Coral, mezzanine floor, Albion Plaza, 2-6 Granville Rd, Tsimshatsui; 54A Canton Rd
Fairwood Fast Food, 6 Ashley Rd, Tsimshatsui; basement two, Silvercord Shopping Centre, Haiphong and Canton Rds
Hardee's, arcade of Regent Hotel, south of Salisbury Rd at the very southern tip of Tsimshatsui
Jack in the Box, Cameron Plaza, 21 Cameron Rd, Tsimshatsui; Tsimshatsui Centre, Mody Rd, Tsimshatsui East
Ka Ka Lok Fast Food Shop, 55A Carnarvon Rd, Tsimshatsui; 16A Ashley Rd (but enter from Ichang St), Tsimshatsui; 79A Austin Rd, Yaumatei; Peninsula Centre, Mody Square, Tsimshatsui East
Kentucky Fried Chicken, 2 Cameron Rd, Tsimshatsui; 241 Nathan Rd, Yaumatei
Pizza Hut, Lower Basement, Silvercord Shopping Centre, Haiphong and Canton Roads, Tsimshatsui; Shop 008, Ocean Terminal, Harbour City, Canton Rd, Tsimshatsui; 1st floor, Hanford House, 221C-D Nathan Rd, Yaumatei; Port A, Basement 1, Autoplaza, 65 Mody Rd, Tsimshatsui East
Spaghetti House, 3B Cameron Rd; 1st floor, 57 Peking Rd; basement, 6-6A Hart Ave; 1st floor, 38 Haiphong Rd, Tsimshatsui; 1st floor, Imperial Hotel, 30-34 Nathan Rd, Tsimshatsui; 001-2, Phase I, Barton Court, Harbour City, Canton Rd, Tsimshatsui
Wendy's, basement, Albion Plaza, 2-6 Granville Rd, just off Nathan Rd, Tsimshatsui

American *Dan Ryan's Chicago Grill* (☎ 7356111), shop 200, Ocean Terminal, Harbour City, Canton Rd, Tsimshatsui, is a trendy spot with prices to match.

Mexican *Someplace Else* (☎ 3691111, ext 5), Sheraton Hotel, 20 Nathan Rd, is part bar and part Mexican restaurant. The tex-mex luncheons are worth trying, but in the evening it becomes very busy. Operating hours are from 11 am until 1 am.

Kosher The *Beverley Hills Deli* (☎ 3698695), level 2, shop 55, New World Centre, Salisbury Rd, is where you'll find gefilte fish and lox. It's good, but not cheap.

Italian *Mama Italia* (☎ 7233125), 2A Hart Ave, Tsimshatsui, is mostly takeaway Italian treats at very low prices. There are just a couple of stools if you want to eat the pizza and lasagna on the spot.

A great Italian restaurant is *Valentino* (☎ 7216449) at 16 Hanoi Rd. Also highly rated is *La Taverna* (☎ 3761945), Astoria Building, 36-38 Ashley Rd, Tsimshatsui.

Pizza World (☎ 3111285), ground floor, New World Centre, 22 Salisbury Rd, is extremely popular and has the best salad bar in Hong Kong – the large-size salad for HK$30 is a meal in itself.

Self-Catering If you're looking for the best in cheese, bread and other imported delicacies, check out the delicatessen at *Oliver's* on the ground floor of Ocean Centre on Canton Rd. Another branch is on the ground floor of the Tung Ying Building, Granville Rd (at Nathan Rd).

Numerous supermarkets are scattered about. A few in Tsimshatsui and Yaumatei to look for include:

Park 'n Shop, south-west corner, Peking Rd and Kowloon Park Drive; 2nd basement, Silvercord Shopping Centre, 30 Canton Rd; 3rd floor, Ocean Terminal, 3 Canton Rd (near the Star Ferry terminal)

Wellcome, inside the Dairy Farm Creamery (ice-cream parlour), 74-78 Nathan Rd; north-west corner of Granville and Carnarvon Rds

Yue Hwa Chinese Products, basement, 301 Nathan Rd, Yaumatei (north-west corner of Nathan and Jordan Rds), both Western products and Chinese exotica (tea bricks and flattened chickens)

Hong Kong Central

The place to go for reasonably priced eats and late-night revelry is the neighbourhood known as Lan Kwai Fong. However, it's such a conglomeration of pubs and all-night parties that it's covered in the Entertainment section.

Breakfast To save time and money, there are food windows adjacent to the Star Ferry that open shortly after 6 am. They serve standard commuter breakfasts consisting of bread, rolls and coffee and have no place to sit except on the ferry itself. As you face the ferry entrance, off to the right is a *Maxim's* fast-food outlet, also with no seats.

If you'd prefer something better, *Jim's Eurodiner* (☎ 8686886), Paks Building, 5-11 Stanley St, does outstanding morning meals between 8 and 10.30 am for around HK$20 to HK$30. From noon until 10 pm it's standard Western fare.

Dim Sum All of the following places are in the middle to lower price range:

Tai Woo, 15-19 Wellington St, dim sum served from 10 am to 5 pm (☎ 5245618)

Luk Yu Tea House, 26 Stanley St, dim sum served from 7 am to 6 pm (☎ 5235464)

Zen Chinese Cuisine, LG 1, The Mall, Pacific Place Phase I, 88 Queensway, dim sum served from 11.30 am to 3 pm (☎ 8454555)

Malaysian If you like Malaysian food, try the *Malaya* (☎ 5251675), 15B Wellington St. It has Western food too, but it's considerably more expensive.

Indian The ever-popular restaurant *Ashoka* (☎ 5249623) is at 57 Wyndham St. In the basement at 57 Wyndham St is the excellent *Village Indian Restaurant* (☎ 5257410).

Greenlands (☎ 5226098), 64 Wellington St, is another superb Indian restaurant offering all-you-can-eat buffets for HK$68.

Club Sri Lanka (☎ 5266559) in the basement of 17 Hollywood Rd (almost at the Wyndham St end) has great Sri Lankan curries. The fixed price all-you-can-eat deal is a wonderful bargain – HK$66 for lunch and HK$75 for dinner.

Vegetarian If you crave curry dishes of the Indian and Sri Lankan variety, check out the *Club Lanka II* (☎ 5451675) in the basement at 11 Lyndhurst Terrace. The all-you-can-eat luncheon buffet costs HK$65 (free drinks), and dinner is HK$70 (includes one drink).

Fast Food *Domino's Pizza* (☎ 8109729), 9 Glenealy Rd, has no restaurant facilities but delivers to any address within a two-km radius.

Famous fast-food chains have the following outlets in Central:

Cafe de Coral, 10 Stanley St; 18 Jubilee St; 88 Queen's Rd
Fairwood, Ananda Tower, 57-59 Connaught Rd
Hardee's, Grand Building, 15 Des Voeux Rd
Kentucky Fried Chicken, 6 D'Aguilar St; Pacific Place
Maxim's, Sun House, 90 Connaught Rd
McDonald's, Hang Cheong Building, 5 Queen's Rd; basement, Yu To Sang Building, 37 Queen's Rd; Sanwa Building, 30-32 Connaught Rd; Shop 124, Level 1, The Mall, Pacific Place, 88 Queensway
Pizza Hut, B38, basement 1, Edinburgh Tower, The Landmark, 17 Queen's Rd
Spaghetti House, lower ground floor, 10 Stanley St

Kosher The *Shalom Grill* (☎ 8516300), 2nd floor, Fortune House, 61 Connaught Rd, serves up kosher and Moroccan cuisine. If you're in the mood for a Jerusalem falafel or a Casablanca couscous, this is the place.

French Wine, cheese, the best French bread and bouillabaisse can be found at *Papillon* (☎ 5265965), 8-13 Wo On Lane. This narrow lane intersects with D'Aguilar St (around No 17) and runs parallel to Wellington St.

Self-Catering A healthfood store with great bread and sandwiches is *Eden's Natural Synergy* (☎ 5263062), 2nd floor, 226-227 Prince's Building, 10 Chater Rd, Central.

For imported delicacies, check out *Oliver's Super Sandwiches* which has three locations: Shop 104, Exchange Square II, 8 Connaught Place; Shop 233-236, Prince's Building, 10 Chater Rd (at Ice House St); and Shop 8, lower ground floor, The Mall, Pacific Place, 88 Queensway.

The largest stock of imported foods is found at the Seibu Department Store, Level LG1, Pacific Place, 88 Queensway (near Admiralty MTR station). Besides the imported cheeses, breads and chocolates, tucked into one corner is the Pacific Wine Cellar. This is *the* place to get wine, and there are frequent sales on wine by the case. It's open from 11 am until 8 pm.

Of special interest to chocolate addicts is *See's Candies* with two stores in Central: B66 Gloucester Tower, The Landmark, 11 Pedder St; and Shop 245, Pacific Place, Phase II, Queensway (near Admiralty MTR station).

ENTERTAINMENT

Kowloon

Rick's Cafe (☎ 3672939), Basement, 4 Hart Ave, is popular with the backpacker set.

Jouster II (☎ 7230022), Shops A and B, Hart Ave Court, 19-23 Hart Ave, Tsimshatsui, is a fun multistorey place with wild decor. Normal hours are noon to 3 am, except on Sunday when it's from 6 pm to 2 am. The happy hour is anytime before 9 pm.

Ned Kelly's Last Stand (☎ 3760562), 11A Ashley Rd, open 11 am to 2 am, became famous as a real Australian pub complete with meat pies. Now it is known mainly for its Dixieland jazz and Aussie folk bands.

Amoeba Bar (☎ 3760389), 22 Ashley Rd, Tsimshatsui, has local new wave live music from around 9 pm, and the place doesn't close until about 6 am.

The *Red Lion* (☎ 3760243), 15 Ashley Rd, is just down the street from the Amoeba. A feature of this pub is that customers are invited to sing along with the band.

The *Kangaroo Pub* (☎ 3120083), 1st and 2nd floors, 35 Haiphong Rd, Tsimshatsui, is an Aussie pub in the true tradition. This place does a good Sunday brunch.

Mad Dog's Pub (☎ 3012222), basement, 32 Nathan Rd, is a popular Aussie-style pub. From Monday through Thursday it's open from 7 am until 2 am, but from Friday through Sunday it's a 24-hour service.

Blacksmith's Arms (☎ 3696696), at 16 Minden Ave, Tsimshatsui, is a British-style pub with darts and barstools.

Hong Kong Island

Lan Kwai Fong Running off D'Aguilar St in Central is a narrow L-shaped alley closed to cars. This is Lan Kwai Fong, and along

HONG KONG

with neighbouring streets and alleys it is Hong Kong's No 1 eating, drinking, dancing and partying venue. Prices range from economical to outrageous.

One place which plays a cat-and-mouse game with the safety inspector-type authorities is *Club 64* (☎ 5232801), 12-14 Wing Wah Lane, D'Aguilar St. The bureaucrats' complaint is also the pub's greatest asset – it's one of the few places in Hong Kong where you can sit outside while eating, drinking and chatting.

As you face the entrance of Club 64, off to your left are some stairs (outside the building, not inside). Follow the stairs up to a terrace to find *Le Jardin Club* (☎ 5262717), 10 Wing Wah Lane. This is an excellent place to drink, relax and socialise.

Facing Club 64 again, look to your right to find *Bon Appetit* (☎ 5253553), a Vietnamese restaurant that serves up cheap but scrumptious meals.

Top Dog (☎ 8689195, 8689196), 1 Lan Kwai Fong, produces every kind of hot dog imaginable. Opening hours are late and the management's policy is to stay open 'until nobody is left in the street'.

As the name implies, late-night hours are kept at *Midnight Express* (☎ 5255010, 5234041), 3 Lan Kwai Fong. This place has a combination menu of Greek, Indian and Italian food, with deliveries available from Monday to Saturday. The kebabs are outstanding and cost from HK$35 to HK$45. Opening hours are 11.30 am to 3 am the next day, except on Sunday, when it opens at 6 pm.

While glasnost is already becoming yesterday's buzzword, you can still find it at *Yelt's Inn* (☎ 5247796), 42 D'Aguilar St. This place boasts Russian vodka, a bubbly party atmosphere and extremely loud music.

If it's fine Lebanese food, beer and rock music you crave, there is no better place to find it than *Beirut* (☎ 8046611). It's at 27 D'Aguilar St.

If you prefer Europe to the Middle East, visit *Berlin* (☎ 8778233), 19 Lan Kwai Fong. This place features loud disco music with members of the audience invited to sing along – think of it as disco karaoke.

Post 97 (☎ 8109333), 9 Lan Kwai Fong, is a very comfortable eating and drinking spot. During the daytime it's more of a coffee shop, and you can sit for hours to take advantage of the excellent rack of Western magazines and newspapers. It can pack out at night, and the lights are dimmed to discourage reading at that time.

Next door in the same building and under the same management is *1997* (☎ 8109333), known for really fine Mediterranean food. Prices are mid-range.

Graffiti (☎ 5212202), 17 Lan Kwai Fong, is a very posh and trendy restaurant and bar, but high drink prices don't seem to have hurt business.

It's raging revelry at the *Acropolis* (☎ 8773668), on the ground floor of Corner II Tower, 21 D'Aguilar St. Shoulder-to-shoulder crowds, loud music and reasonably cheap drinks contribute to the party atmosphere.

The California Entertainment Building is at the corner of Lan Kwai Fong and D'Aguilar St. There are numerous places to eat here at varying price levels, but it tends to be upmarket. Note that the building has two blocks with two separate entrances, so if you don't find a place mentioned in this book be sure to check out the other block.

Top-flight food at high prices can be found at *Koh-I-Noor* (☎ 8779706), an Indian restaurant. *Il Mercato* (☎ 8683068) steals the show for Italian food. Both are in the California Entertainment Building. Prices are mid-range.

The *California* (☎ 5211345), also in the California Entertainment Building, is perhaps the most expensive bar mentioned in this book. Open from noon to 1 am, it's a restaurant by day, but there's disco dancing and a cover charge from Wednesday to Sunday night from 5 pm onwards.

The American Pie (☎ 5213381) is *the* locale for desserts in Hong Kong; not only pies, but all sorts of killer desserts like cakes, tarts, puddings and everything else containing sinful amounts of sugar, not to mention superb coffee and tea. If you're on a diet, don't even go near the place. Despite its very

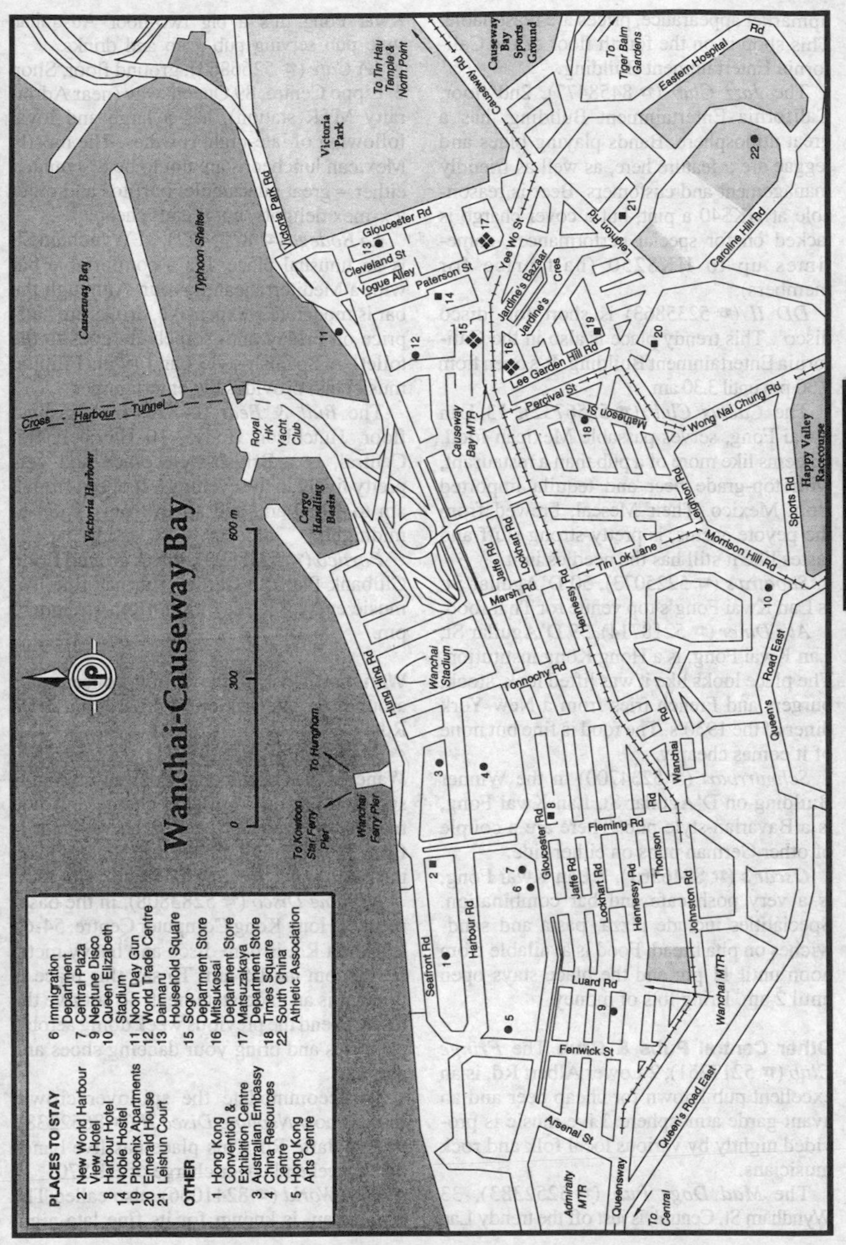
Wanchai-Causeway Bay
PLACES TO STAY
2 New World Harbour View Hotel
8 Harbour Hotel
14 Noble Hostel
19 Phoenix Apartments
20 Emerald House
21 Leishun Court
OTHER
1 Hong Kong Convention & Exhibition Centre
3 Australian Embassy
4 China Resources Centre
5 Hong Kong Arts Centre
6 Immigration Department
7 Central Plaza
9 Neptune Disco
10 Queen Elizabeth Stadium
11 Noon Day Gun
12 World Trade Centre
13 Daimaru Household Square
15 Sogo Department Store
16 Mitsukosai Department Store
17 Matsuzakaya Department Store
18 Times Square
22 South China Athletic Association
0
300
600 m
Victoria Harbour
Causeway Bay
Cross Harbour Tunnel
Typhoon Shelter
Royal HK Yacht Club
Cargo Handling Basin
To Kowloon Star Ferry Pier
To Hunghom
Wanchai Ferry Pier
Victoria Park
Victoria Park Rd
To Tin Hau Temple & North Point
Causeway Bay Sports Ground
To Tiger Balm Gardens
Eastern Hospital Rd
Caroline Hill Rd
Happy Valley Racecourse
Sports Rd
Wong Nai Chung Rd
Morrison Hill Rd
Leighton Rd
Tin Lok Lane
Queen's Road East
Wanchai Rd
Wanchai MTR
Admiralty MTR
Queensway
To Central
Arsenal St
Fenwick St
Luard Rd
Fleming Rd
Thomson Rd
Johnston Rd
Hennessy Rd
Lockhart Rd
Jaffe Rd
Gloucester Rd
Harbour Rd
Seafront Rd
Hung Hing Rd
Wanchai Stadium
Tonnochy Rd
Marsh Rd
Causeway Bay MTR
Percival St
Matheson St
Lee Garden Hill Rd
Jardine's Bazaar
Jardine's Cres
Yee Wo St
Causeway Rd
Paterson St
Vogue Alley
Cleveland St

HONG KONG

upmarket appearance, prices are reasonable. This shop is on the fourth floor of the California Entertainment Building.

The *Jazz Club* (☎ 8458477), 2nd floor, California Entertainment Building, has a great atmosphere. Bands playing blues and reggae are a feature here, as well as friendly management and customers. Beer is reasonable at HK$40 a pint, but a cover charge is tacked on for special performances, sometimes up to HK$250 (half-price for members).

DD II (☎ 5235863) is short for 'disco disco'. This trendy place is also in the California Entertainment Building. It's open from 9.30 pm until 3.30 am.

The *Cactus Club* (☎ 5256732), 13 Lan Kwai Fong, serves passable Mexican food. It seems like more of a pub than a restaurant, with top-grade beer and tequila imported from Mexico. Their Mescal, brewed from the peyote cactus, is pretty strong stuff and tastes like it still has the needles in it.

Supatra's (☎ 5225073), 50 D'Aguilar St, is Lan Kwai Fong's top venue for Thai food.

Al's Diner (☎ 5218714), 39 D'Aguilar St, Lan Kwai Fong, is a Hong Kong institution. The place looks like it was lifted lock, stock, burgers and French fries from a New York diner of the 1930's. The food is fine but none of it comes cheaply.

Schnurrbart (☎ 5234700) in the Winner Building on D'Aguilar St, Lan Kwai Fong, is a Bavarian-style pub. There are a couple of other German pubs on either side.

Oscar's (☎ 8046561), 2 Lan Kwai Fong, is a very posh cafe and bar combination. Specialities include pizza, pasta and sandwiches on pita bread. Food is available from noon until 11 pm and the place stays open until 2 am. Bring lots of money.

Other Central Pubs & Grub The *Fringe Club* (☎ 5217251), 2 Lower Albert Rd, is an excellent pub known for cheap beer and an avant-garde atmosphere. Live music is provided nightly by various local folk and rock musicians.

The *Mad Dogs Pub* (☎ 5252383), 33 Wyndham St, Central, is just off the trendy Lan Kwai Fong. It's a big two-floor Australian style pub serving pub grub and drinks.

LA Cafe (☎ 5266863), ground floor, Shop 2, Lippo Centre, 89 Queensway (near Admiralty MTR station), has a large and loyal following of late-night rowdies. The mostly Mexican luncheons are not to be discounted either – great guacamole, burritos and other tex-mex delights, but it isn't cheap.

La Bodega (☎ 8775472), 31 Wyndham St, is an unusual place. It's a comfortable bar with a Mediterranean flavour. Although the bar is moderately expensive, drinks are half-price on Friday until somebody goes to the toilet! A Spanish-style band (with Filipino musicians) provides the entertainment.

The *Bull & Bear* (☎ 5257436), ground floor, Hutchison House, 10 Harcourt Rd, Central, is a British-style place and gets pretty lively in the evenings. It opens from 8 am to 10.30 am, and again from 11 am to midnight.

Portico (☎ 5238893), lower ground floor, Citibank Plaza, 3 Garden Rd, has fine live music every Saturday night from around 10 pm.

Wanchai Most of the action concentrates around the intersection of Luard and Jaffe Rds.

Joe Bananas (☎ 5291811), 23 Luard Rd, Wanchai, has become a trendy disco nightspot and has no admission charge, but you may have to queue to get in. Happy hour is from 11 am until 9 pm (except Sunday) and the place stays open until around 5 am.

Neptune Disco (☎ 5283808), in the basement of Hong Kong Computer Centre, 54-62 Lockhart Rd, is pure disco and heavy metal from 4 pm until 5 am. To say this place is popular is an understatement. To survive the night, spend the previous week doing aerobic exercises and bring your dancing shoes and earplugs.

To accommodate the spillover crowd, there is now *Neptune Disco II* (☎ 8652238), 98-108 Jaffe Rd. This place has live bands and a weekend cover charge of HK$70.

West World (☎ 8241066), also called The Manhattan, is known for its fine late-night dancing music. Admission is free, except on Friday and Saturday when it costs HK$140 (one drink included). It's on the fourth floor of the New World Harbour View Hotel – ask at the front desk where to find the lift.

JJ's (☎ 5881234, ext 7323), Grand Hyatt Hotel, 1 Harbour Rd, Wanchai, is known for its rhythm and blues bands. There is a cover charge after 9 pm.

The Big Apple Pub & Disco (☎ 5293461), 20 Luard Rd, is thumping disco. There is a weekend cover charge of HK$60 for men and HK$40 for women. From Monday to Friday it operates from noon until 5 am, and on weekends and holidays it's open from 2 pm until 6 am.

Old Hat (☎ 8612300), 1st floor, 20 Luard Rd, keeps some of the latest hours around – it's open 24 hours on Friday and Saturday night, so you can stay up all evening and have breakfast there. There are daily set lunches Monday to Friday from noon until 2.30 pm, happy hours, crazy hours, satellite TV and takeaway burgers, French fries, pizza and satay.

Crossroads (☎ 5272347), at 42 Lockhart Rd, Wanchai, is a loud disco that attracts a young crowd. Dancing is from 9 pm to 4 am. There is a cover charge, but one drink is included.

At 54 Jaffe Rd, just west of Fenwick Rd, is the *Wanchai Folk Club* (☎ 5590058), better known as The Wanch. It stands in sharp contrast to the more usual Wanchai scene of hard rock and disco. This is a very pleasant little folk-music pub with beer and wine at low prices, but it can be packed out.

HONG KONG

Indonesia

Indonesia is a long chain of tropical islands offering a mixture of cultures, people, scenery, prospects, problems and aspirations unmatched in South-East Asia. For the budget traveller, Indonesia is a kaleidoscope of cheap food, adventurous travel and every sort of attraction – the tropical paradise of Bali, the untouched wilderness of Sumatra, the historical monuments of Yogyakarta, with the unbelievable squalor of Jakarta thrown in to leaven the mix.

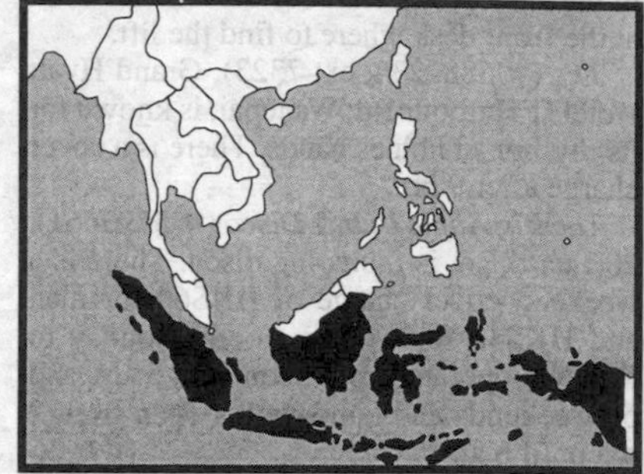

Facts about the Country

HISTORY

It is generally believed that the earliest inhabitants of the Indonesian Archipelago came from India or Burma, while later migrants, known as Malays, came from southern China and Indochina. This second group is believed to have populated the archipelago gradually over several thousand years.

Powerful kingdoms began to appear in Java and Sumatra towards the end of the 7th century. The Buddhist Srivijaya Empire ruled southern Sumatra and much of the Malay Peninsula for six centuries, whilst the Hindu Mataram Kingdom presided over Java. The two developed side by side as both rivals and partners and, between them, raised inspiring monuments like Borobudur.

The last important kingdom to remain Hindu was the Java-based Majapahit, founded in the 13th century. It reached its peak under Prime Minister Gajah Mada, and although it is reputed to have ruled over a vast area of the archipelago, it probably controlled only Java, Bali and the island of Madura, off Java's north coast.

The spread of Islam into the archipelago spelt the end of the Majapahits – satellite kingdoms took on the new religion and declared themselves independent of the Majapahits. But unlike the fanatical brand exported initially by the Arabs, the Islamic religion was considerably mellowed by the time of its arrival in Java. The Majapahits retreated to Bali in the 15th century to found a flourishing culture while Java split into separate sultanates.

By the 15th century, a strong Muslim empire had developed with its centre at Melaka (Malacca) on the Malay Peninsula, but in 1511 it fell to the Portuguese and the period of European influence in the archipelago began. The Portuguese were soon displaced by the Dutch who began to take over Indonesia in the early 1600s. A British attempt to oust the Dutch in 1619 failed – Melaka fell to the Dutch in 1641 and by 1700 they dominated most of Indonesia by virtue of their supremacy at sea and their control of the trade routes and some important ports. By the middle of the 18th century, all of Java was under their control.

The Napoleonic Wars led to a temporary British takeover between 1811 and 1816 in response to the French occupation of Holland, and Java came under the command of Sir Stamford Raffles.

Indonesia was eventually handed back to the Dutch after the cessation of the wars in Europe, and an agreement made whereby the

English evacuated their settlements in Indonesia in return for the Dutch leaving India and the Malay Peninsula.

But while the Europeans may have settled their differences, the Indonesians were of a different mind – for five years from 1825 onwards the Dutch had to put down a revolt led by the Javanese Prince Diponegoro. It was not until the early 20th century that the Dutch brought the whole of the archipelago – including Aceh and Bali – under control.

Although Dutch rule softened, dissatisfaction still simmered and a strong nationalist movement – whose foremost leader was Sukarno – developed despite Dutch attempts to suppress it. The Japanese occupied the archipelago during WW II. After their defeat, the Dutch returned and tried to take back control of their old territories. For four bitter years, from 1945 to 1949, the Indonesians fought an intermittent war with the Dutch and, in the end, the Dutch were forced to recognise Indonesia's independence.

Weakened by the prolonged struggle and without the government structure bequeathed to British colonies, the transition to independence did not come easily. The first 10 years of independence saw Indonesian politicians preoccupied with their own political games until, in 1957, President Sukarno put an end to the impasse by declaring Guided Democracy and investing more power in himself. Sukarno proved to be less adept as a nation-builder than as a revolutionary leader. Grandiose building projects, the planned 'socialisation' of the economy and a senseless confrontation with Malaysia led to internal dissension and a steady deterioration of the national economy.

As events came to a head, there was an attempted coup in 1965 led by an officer of Sukarno's palace guard, and several of Indonesia's top army generals were killed. The coup was suppressed by the Indonesian army under the leadership of General Suharto. The reasons for the coup are unclear but it was passed off as an attempt by the Communists to seize power and thousands of Communists, suspected Communists and sympathisers were killed or imprisoned. Suharto eventually pushed Sukarno out of power and took over the presidency himself. In stark contrast to the turbulent Sukarno years, things have, on the whole, been more stable under Suharto.

The invasion of Portuguese Timor, in 1975, stands as much to the world's discredit as Indonesia's, and it's surely no coincidence that Henry Kissinger left Jakarta the day before the invasion. Recently, Indonesia has shown signs of coming to grips with its internal economic problems and some of the worse excesses have been curbed, though the Dili massacre in 1991 has severely embarrassed Indonesia's international standing.

Large oil exports and other substantial natural resources seem to offer the promise of better days but graft and corruption are still very much a way of life. The economy is growing dramatically and while some people get very rich, the lot of the average Indonesian, particularly in parts of overcrowded Java, is very hard. The main political question facing Indonesia is what

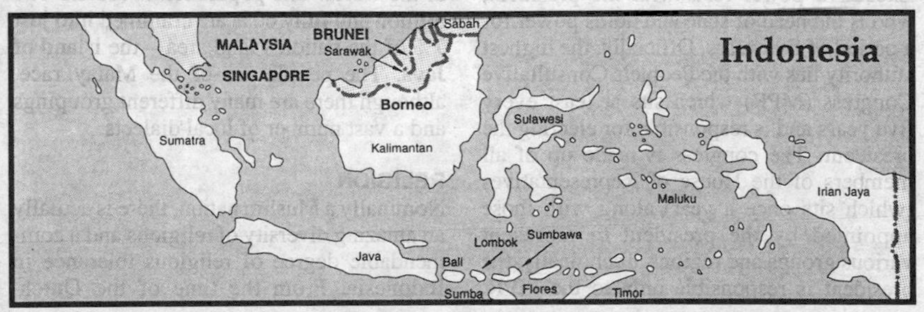

will happen after Suharto's likely retirement in 1998, at the end of his current five-year term.

GEOGRAPHY

Indonesia has an area of 1,475,000 sq km scattered over about 13,700 islands. It is a far less compact mass of islands than the nearby Philippines, the other island nation of the region. Parts of Indonesia are still vast, barely explored regions of dense jungle and many islands have extinct, active or dormant volcanoes.

CLIMATE

Draped over the equator, Indonesia is hot year round – hot and wet during the wet season, and hot and dry during the dry season. Coastal areas are often pleasantly cool, however, and it can get extremely cold in the mountains.

Generally, the wet season starts later the further south-east you go. In north Sumatra, the rain begins to fall in September, but in Timor it doesn't fall until November. Sumatran seasons have been fairly described as the wet and the wetter. The wet seasons are roughly as follows: Sumatra, September to March; Java, October to April; and Bali and further south, November to May.

In January and February it can rain often, and an umbrella is an excellent item to have stuffed in your backpack. The odd islands out are those of Maluku (the Moluccas) where the wet season is from the beginning of April to the end of August.

GOVERNMENT

Executive power rests with the president, who is the head of state and holds power for a period of five years. Officially, the highest authority lies with the People's Consultative Congress (MPR) which sits at least every five years and is responsible for electing the president. The congress is made up of all members of the House of Representatives (which sits once a year) along with those appointed by the president to represent various groups and regions. Technically, the president is responsible only to the MPR. The MPR will elect the president and the vice-president. The president then appoints ministers, who are responsible only to the president, to a cabinet.

Party politics, what there is of it, continues under the one-group/two-party system devised by Suharto in the early 1970s. This involves the government-run Golkar, which is technically not a political party, the Muslim United Development Party (PPP) and the Indonesian Democratic Party (PDI). Distinctions between the parties are deliberately blurred.

The enforced acceptance of the Pancasila (Five Principles) Democracy as the sole philosophical base for all political, social and religious organisations is also aimed partly at diffusing and suppressing dissent. The five principles are Faith in God, Humanity, Nationalism, Representative Government and Social Justice.

ECONOMY

Indonesia still has a basically rural subsistence economy but it has large mineral resources which it is only now starting to tap. It has good oil reserves, although a unique combination of corruption and inefficiency allowed the huge Pertamina conglomerate to go bankrupt in the 1970s!

The fortunate combination of fertility and rainfall allows Indonesia to approach self-sufficiency in food production but, often, the food potential isn't where the population is, and every year the population increases.

POPULATION & PEOPLE

Indonesia is the fifth most populous country in the world. The population is around 180 million and fully 60% are crammed into just 7% of the nation's land area – the island of Java. The people are of the Malay race, although there are many different groupings and a vast number of local dialects.

RELIGION

Nominally a Muslim nation, there is actually an amazing diversity of religions and a commendable degree of religious tolerance in Indonesia. From the time of the Dutch, pockets of Christianity have continued to exist on the islands of Timor and Flores, and in the Lake Toba region of north Sumatra and the Tanatoraja area of Sulawesi. At one time, Sumatra was predominantly Buddhist and Java was predominantly Hindu – this was before the spread of Islam and its eventual dominance of the region. The last remnants of Hinduism are found in Bali.

LANGUAGE

Although there are a vast number of local languages and dialects in the country, Bahasa Indonesia, which is all but identical to Malay, is promoted as the one national language.

Like most languages, Indonesian has its simplified colloquial form and its more developed literate language. *Pasar*, or market Indonesian, is very easy to learn. It's rated as one of the simplest languages in the world as there are no tenses, no genders, and often one word can convey the meaning of a whole sentence. There are often no plurals, or it is only necessary to say the word twice – child is *anak*, and children are *anak anak* or *anak dua*. Book is *buku* and books are *buku dua*. With other words, the context makes it clear that it's plural.

Indonesian can also be a delightfully poetic language with words like *mata hari*, or 'sun', derived from *mata* (eye) and *hari* (day), so the sun is literally the eye of the day.

Lonely Planet's *Indonesian Phrasebook* is a pocket-sized introduction to the language, intended to make getting by in Bahasa as easy as possible.

Greetings & Civilities

good morning
selamat pagi
good day
selamat siang
good afternoon/evening
selamat sore
good night
selamat malam
goodbye (to person staying)
selamat tinggal
goodbye (to person going)
selamat jalan
How are you?
Apa kabar?
I'm fine.
Kabar baik.
please
silakan
thank you (very much)
terima kasih (banyak)

Getting Around

I want to go to...
Saya mau ke...
What time does the...leave/arrive?
Jam berapa...berangkat/tiba?
How far?
Berapa jauh?
bus
bis
ship
kapal
train
kereta api
bus station
setasiun bis/terminal
ticket
karcis

Accommodation

guesthouse
losmen
Is there a room available?
Adakah kamar kosong?
Can I see the room?
Boleh saya melihat kamar?
bed
tempat tidur
one night/two nights
satu malam/dua malam
toilet
WC ('way say') or *kamar kecil*
bathroom
kamar mandi
key
kunci

Around Town

Where is...?
Dimana...?
bank
bank

INDONESIA

post office
kantor pos
tourist office
dinas parawisata
here/there
disini/disana
left/right
kiri/kanan
near/far
dekat/jauh
straight ahead
terus

Time
When?
Kapan?
At what time...?
Jam berapa...?
open/close
buka/tutup
today
hari ini
tonight
nanti malam
tomorrow
besok
yesterday
kemarin

Other Useful Words & Phrases
yes/no
ya/tidak
excuse me
permisi
I don't understand.
Saya tidak mengerti.
How much (price)?
Berapa (harga)?
expensive
mahal
What is this?
Apa ini?

Numbers

½	*setengah*
1	*satu*
2	*dua*
3	*tiga*
4	*empat*
5	*lima*
6	*enam*
7	*tujuh*
8	*delapan*
9	*sembilan*
10	*sepuluh*
12	*duabelas*
20	*duapuluh*
21	*duapuluh satu*
30	*tigapuluh*
50	*limapuluh*
100	*seratus*
1000	*seribu*

Emergencies
Help!
Tolong!
doctor
dokter
police
polisi

Facts for the Visitor

VISAS & EMBASSIES

Visitors from most Western countries can enter Indonesia without a visa, for a stay of up to 60 days, so long as they enter and exit through certain recognised airports or seaports. Officially (but not always in practice), you must have a ticket out of the country when you arrive. Officially (and almost certainly), you cannot extend your visa beyond 60 days. If you really intend to explore Indonesia in some depth, then 60 days is inadequate and you will have to exit the country and re-enter.

One possibility is to start from north Sumatra and travel down to Pekanbaru, then exit via Batam to Singapore for rest and refreshment. From there, you can start with a fresh 60 days and continue to Java and Bali, which still leaves Nusa Tenggara and the outer islands to worry about!

The 'ticket out' requirement seems to be less strictly enforced these days, and evidence of sufficient funds is usually acceptable in lieu. US$1000 seems to be the magic number. If you don't have it, dress as if you do, otherwise say you are only making a short visit – a 60-day entry permit is standard regardless of the length of stay. If you fly to Kupang (in Timor) from Darwin, or take the ferry to Batam from Singapore, it's unlikely that any great fuss will be made. In Kupang, they may ask to see a wad of travellers' cheques, but Batam is a breeze. Expect to flash your cash if arriving in Medan (in Sumatra) on the ferry from Penang (in Malaysia).

In the more 'normal' entry points, like Bali or Jakarta, they may still ask to see a ticket but most Bali visitors are on short-stay package trips, so you're unlikely to be troubled. The main problem is likely to be with airlines overseas, who may strictly enforce official requirements and not let you on flights to Indonesia without an onward ticket.

If you want a simple solution, the Malaysian Airline System (MAS) flight between Medan and Penang is straightforward, reasonably cheap and able to be refunded if you don't use it. The various flights between Jakarta and Singapore are also safe bets.

The real problem with the visa-free entry system is for that tiny minority of travellers who plan to arrive or depart through an unrecognised 'gateway', such as Dumai in Sumatra or Jayapura in Irian Jaya. If you fall into that category then you have to get an Indonesian visa before arriving and visas are only valid for one month. Extensions on a one-month visa are usually only for two weeks and cost around 50,000 rp.

The recognised 'no visa' entry and exit points are the airports of Ambon, Bali, Batam, Biak, Jakarta, Kupang, Manado, Medan, Pontianak and Surabaya, and the seaports of Bali, Balikpapan, Batam, Jakarta, Kupang, Medan, Pontianak, Semarang and Tanjung Pinang.

The list of approved gateways does change, so if you're planning an odd entry or exit find out the latest story. However, the official list published by Indonesian authorities is often inaccurate, and not all Indonesian consular offices know the full story. If you want to enter Indonesia at an airport not on the list, check with the airline. As a general rule, entering by air on a regular flight is not a problem, but entering or leaving Indonesia overland or by unusual sea routes requires a visa.

Finally, check your passport expiry date. Indonesia requires that your passport has six months of life left in it on your date of arrival.

Indonesian Embassies Abroad

Indonesian embassies, consulates and diplomatic offices in the region include:

Hong Kong
  Consulate-General, 127-129 Leighton Rd, Causeway Bay, Hong Kong (☎ (5) 890 4421)
Malaysia
  233 Jalan Tun Razak, Kuala Lumpur (☎ 03-9842011)
  467 Jalan Burma, Penang (☎ 04-374686)
  5A Pisang Rd, Kuching, Sarawak (☎ 082-241734)
  Jalan Karamunsing, Kota Kinabalu, Sabah (☎ 088-219578)
  Jalan Apas, Tawau, Sabah (☎ 089-765930)
Philippines
  Embassy, 185/187 Salcedo St, Legaspi Village, Makati, Manila (☎ 285 5061 to 67)
Singapore
  7 Chatsworth Rd, Singapore (☎ 737 7422)
Thailand
  Embassy, 600-602 Petchburi Rd, Bangkok (☎ 252 3135 to 40)

Foreign Embassies

Countries with diplomatic relations with Indonesia will generally have their consular offices in Jakarta, the capital. Some of the foreign embassies in Jakarta include:

Brunei
  9th Floor, Central Plaza Building, Jalan Jenderal Sudirman (☎ 517990)
India
  Jalan Rasuna Said 51, Kuningan (☎ 5204150)
Malaysia
  Jalan Imam Bonjol 17 (☎ 323750)
Myanmar
  Jalan H Augus Salim 109 (☎ 320440)
Papua New Guinea
  6th Floor, Panin Bank Centre, Jalan Jenderal Sudirman (☎ 711218)
Philippines
  Jalan Imam Bonjol 6-8 (☎ 348917)
Thailand
  Jalan Imam Bonjol 74 (☎ 343762)

Vietnam
Jalan Teuku Umar 25 (☎ 347325)

MONEY

Currency

The Indonesian rupiah is a floating currency but has remained fairly stable against the US$ over the past few years. In areas with many tourists, like Bali, even quite modest hotels quote prices in US$ and so some prices in this edition are also quoted in US$.

Exchange Rates

US dollars are easily the most widely accepted foreign currency and often have a better exchange rate than other currencies – this is especially so outside of Jakarta and the major tourist areas. If you're going to be in really remote regions, carry sufficient cash with you as banks may be scarce. Even those you do come across may only accept certain varieties of travellers' cheques – stick to the major companies. Dutch travellers can cash their giros (girobetaalkaarten) at all major post offices for up to 75,000 rp.

Exchange rates tend to vary a bit from bank to bank – shop around. The rates also tend to vary between cities – Jakarta and Yogyakarta seem to have better rates than Surabaya for example. In some remote regions, the rate can be terrible – or there may be no banks at all!

There are moneychangers in many locales and they're open longer hours and change money (cash or cheques) much faster than in the banks. In places like Bali, they offer extremely competitive rates.

The official exchange rates are as follows:

Australia	A$1	=	1518 rp
Britain	UK£1	=	3185 rp
Canada	C$1	=	1562 rp
France	FFr1	=	377 rp
Germany	DM1	=	1291 rp
Japan	¥100	=	2054 rp
Malaysia	M$1	=	819 rp
New Zealand	NZ$1	=	1250 rp
Singapore	S$1	=	1390 rp
USA	US$1	=	2105 rp

Credit Cards

Credit cards are of limited usefulness. Fancy shops and restaurants, big hotels and most airline offices accept them. Outside of major cities, many banks will not give cash advances, even in some of the main regional centres.

Costs

Indonesian costs are variable – similar places to stay can be four times as expensive in some places (like Maluku and Irian Jaya) than in others (like Bali). What it costs you depends on where you go. If you follow the well-beaten tourist track through Bali, Java and Sumatra, you may well find Indonesia one of the cheapest places in the region. Travellers' centres like Bali, Yogyakarta and Lake Toba are superb value for accommodation and food.

Fuel is cheap in Indonesia, so transport costs are also pleasantly low, particularly if you've got your own motorbike to travel around on. Fuel prices are pretty much the same throughout the country, and only in the outer islands and remote places (like the interior of Irian Jaya) do prices skyrocket.

TOURIST OFFICES

The National Tourist Organisation of Indonesia (the Directorate General of Tourism) produces a *Calendar of Events* for the entire country and a useful *Indonesia Tourist Map* booklet which includes some good maps and helpful travel information. They're available from the Directorate General of Tourism office at Jalan Kramat Raya 81, Jakarta, where you should be able to get brochures on most tourist destinations.

Otherwise, Indonesian tourist offices are generally the poorest in South-East Asia in terms of the utility of the information they offer to visitors. The usefulness of individual tourist offices in Indonesia often depends on who works there, and who you get to talk to.

Some of the regional tourist offices produce local information, or useful items such as the festival calendar available from the office in Denpasar, Bali. The Jakarta regional office, run by the Jakarta city government and located in the Jakarta Theatre Building on Jalan Thamrin (next to the Sarinah department store), is fairly helpful. Bandung, Yogyakarta and Solo also have good tourist offices. Other good regional offices can be found in Bukittinggi and Padang in Sumatra and Mataram in Lombok. There's also an excellent independent tourist office in Ubud, Bali. Outside of these areas, it often isn't worth the effort.

BUSINESS HOURS & HOLIDAYS

Most government offices are open Monday to Thursday from 8 am to 3 pm, Friday from 8 to 11 am, and Saturday from 8 am to 2 pm. Private business offices have staggered hours: Monday to Friday from 8 am to 4 pm or 9 am to 5 pm, with a break in the middle of the day. Some offices are also open on Saturday morning till noon. Banks are usually open Monday to Friday from 8 am to 3 pm, and on Saturday morning.

Shops tend to open about 8 am and stay open until around 9 pm. Sunday is a public holiday but some shops and many airline offices open for at least part of the day.

As most Indonesians are Muslims, many holidays and festivals are associated with the Islamic religion.

Ramadan (Bulan Puasa) – This is the traditional Muslim month of daily fasting from sunrise to sunset. It falls in the ninth month of the Muslim calendar. Many restaurants shut down during the day.

Lebaran (Idul Fitri) – This marks the end of Ramadan and is a noisy celebration at the end of a month of gastric austerity. It is a national public holiday of two days duration.

Kartini Day – This falls on 21 April and commemorates the birthday of Raden Ajeng Kartini. She was an early nationalist and Indonesia's first woman emancipationist.

Independence Day (Hari Proklamasi Kemerdekaan) – On 17 August 1945, Sukarno proclaimed Indonesian independence in Jakarta. It is a national public holiday.

Christmas Day, Good Friday & New Year's Day – These are national public holidays.

POST & TELECOMMUNICATIONS

The postal service in Indonesia is generally good and the poste restante service at Indonesian *kantor pos* (post offices) – at least in the major travellers' centres like Jakarta, Yogyakarta, Bali, Medan and Lake Toba – is efficiently run. Expected mail always seems to arrive.

Overseas parcels can be posted, insured and registered *(tercatat)* from a main post office but they'll usually want to have a look at the contents first so there's not much point in making up a tidy parcel before you get there. If you are going on to Singapore, postage is cheaper from there.

International calls are easy to make from Wartel (Warung Telekomunikasi) offices, which have sprung up all over the country. Many Wartels have card phones where you can directly dial overseas calls. Reverse-charge calls can be made from Telkom offices and Wartels free of charge, though private Wartels usually charge for the first minute or don't offer the service at all.

Direct Home Phones (press one button to get through to your home country operator) can be found in international terminals at major airports, some big hotels and some Telkom offices.

BOOKS & MAPS

For more detailed information on the whole archipelago, or just on Bali and neighbouring Lombok, look for the following Lonely Planet guidebooks: *Indonesia – a travel survival kit* and *Bali & Lombok – a travel survival kit*.

For an introduction to the country, read *Indonesia* by Bruce Grant, *Indonesia since Sukarno* by Peter Polomka and *Suharto's Indonesia* by Hamish McDonald. *Sukarno – An Autobiography*, as related to Cindy Adams, captures the charisma and ego of the man.

Twilight in Jakarta, by the Indonesian journalist Mochtar Lubis, is an outspoken condemnation of political corruption and one of the best documentations of life in the capital, particularly of Jakarta's lower depths – the prostitutes, becak (trishaw) drivers and rural immigrants. Lubis has twice been imprisoned for his political convictions and the book goes on and off the list of banned books.

Pramoedya Ananta Toer, who spent more than 17 years imprisoned by colonial and Indonesian governments, is Indonesia's most celebrated novelist. His novels *This Earth of Mankind, Child of all Nations, The Fugitive* and *House of Glass* are all available in English translations.

The award-winning Australian novel *The Year of Living Dangerously* by Christopher Koch is an evocative reconstruction of life in Jakarta during the final chaotic months of the Sukarno period.

Oxford in Asia have a number of books on Indonesian subjects. *Indonesia, Between Myth & Reality* by Lee Khoon Choy is an excellent compilation of some of the intriguing religious, social and mystical customs of Indonesia.

Locally produced maps are often surprisingly inaccurate. The Nelles Verlag map series covers most of Indonesia in a number of separate sheets, and they're usually quite good.

ACCOMMODATION

When you're trying to find accommodation, look for *losmen* or *penginapan* or just say you want to *tidur* (sleep). The word *wisma*, akin to guesthouse, is also worth watching out for and in some places you'll simply see the word *'kosong'* posted up; it means 'empty'.

Losmen are usually very basic, rarely containing more than a bed and a small table. In compensation, tea or coffee is usually provided gratis a couple of times a day. Traditional washing facilities consist of a *mandi*, a large water tank from which you scoop water with a dipper. Climbing into the tank is very bad form! Toilets may also be the traditional hole-in-the-floor variety but in places like Bali, showers and Western sit-up toilets are now common. Don't expect hot water in budget-priced places though.

Prices in Indonesia vary considerably – Yogyakarta, Bali and Lake Toba are much cheaper than other places in the country. In Bali, the austerity of the rooms is often balanced by pleasant gardens and courtyards. There are some really nice places around and finding rooms for US$2 to US$4 a night is often quite possible, particularly in Bali and Yogyakarta.

FOOD & DRINKS

A *rumah makan*, literally 'house to eat', is the equivalent of a restaurant, whereas a *warung,* or foodstall, is a supposedly less grand eating place – the dividing line is hazy. In Bali, where food is cheap, the cost difference is minimal. In more expensive Java, food is often much cheaper in warungs. The *pasar* (market) is a good food source, especially the *pasar malam* (night market).

As with food in the rest of Asia, Indonesian food is heavily based on rice. *Nasi goreng* is the national dish: it's fried rice, with an egg on top in deluxe *(istimiwa)* versions. *Nasi campur*, rice with whatever is available, is a warung favourite, often served cold. The two other real Indonesian dishes are *gado gado* and *sate*. Gado gado is a fresh salad with prawn crackers and peanut sauce. It tends to vary a lot, so if your first one isn't so special try again somewhere else. Sate are tiny kebabs served with a spicy peanut dip.

The Dutch feast *rijsttafel*, or rice table, consists of rice served with everything imaginable – for gargantuan appetites only. Some big hotels still do a passable imitation. Indonesians are keen snackers, so you'll get plenty of *pisang goreng* (banana fritters), peanuts in palm sugar or shredded coconut cookies.

Padang food, from the Padang region in Sumatra, is popular throughout Indonesia. In a Padang restaurant, a bowl of rice is plonked in front of you, followed by a whole collection of small bowls of vegetables, meat, fish and eggs. Eat what you want and your bill is added up from the number of empty bowls. In Sumatra, food can be hot enough to burn your fingers. Spicy hot, that is.

Drinking unboiled water is not recommended in Indonesia – the iced juice drinks can be good, but take care! Indonesian tea is fine and coffee is also good. Soft drinks are quite expensive compared to those in other Asian countries. Local beer is good – Bintang is Heineken supervised and moderately expensive. Bali Brem rice wine is really potent, and the more you drink the nicer it tastes. *Es buah* or *es campur* is a strange concoction of fruit salad, jelly cubes, syrup, crushed rice and condensed milk. It tastes absolutely *enak* (delicious).

Warning

In South-East Asia, this is the country where the most travellers get the most stomach upsets, in some cases pretty serious ones. A lot of this is due to poor hygiene and contaminated drinking water. Take extra care with cold drinks – the drink itself may be made from boiled water but how about the ice?

The same warning applies to seafood, which is really susceptible to contamination. If you aren't positive it is safe and, equally important, fresh, then leave it alone. Don't be overly worried though – apart from my own trips to Indonesia, my children have also notched up numerous visits without an upset stomach between them.

Food *(makan)*

beef
daging
chicken
ayam
crab
kepiting
egg
telur
sweet & sour omelette
fu yung hai
fish
ikan
frog
kodok
noodle soup
mie kuah
fried noodles
mie goreng
with crispy noodles
tami
pork
babi
potatoes
kentang
prawns
udang
rice with odds & ends
nasi campur
fried rice
nasi goreng
white rice
nasi putih
soup
soto
vegetables
sayur
fried vegetables
cap cai

Drinks *(minum)*

beer
bir
coffee
kopi
cordial
stroop
drinking water
air minum
milk
susu
orange juice
air jeruk
tea with sugar
teh manis
plain tea
teh pahit

THINGS TO BUY

There are so many regional arts and crafts in Indonesia that they're dealt with under the separate regional sections. For an overview of the whole gamut of Indonesian crafts, pay a visit to the Sarinah department store or the art market of Pasar Seni at Ancol in Jakarta. They've got items from all over the archipelago. While you may not find all the most interesting products, you'll certainly see enough for a good introduction as to what is available.

Getting There & Away

AIR

Indonesia's two main international gateways are Denpasar in Bali and Jakarta in Java. Although Bali is by far Indonesia's major tourist attraction, the Indonesians limit the number of flights into Bali, so many visitors have to arrive in Jakarta and transfer there. Airport tax for international departures varies from 17,000 rp from Jakarta to 12,000 rp from Bali.

In Borneo, Malaysian Airline System (MAS) flies between Pontianak in Kalimantan and Kuching in Sarawak, and Bouraq flies between Tarakan in Kalimantan and Tawau in Sabah. See the Kalimantan Getting There & Away section.

Bouraq has flights from Manado in Sulawesi to Davao in the Philippines – you can enter or exit Manado without an Indonesian visa. Flights to Davao go on Wednesday and Saturday and cost US$150.

From Singapore, the usual route is to Jakarta. There are all sorts of flights with all sorts of fares from as low as US$70 to US$100. Garuda has flights between Singapore and Balikpapan in Kalimantan, but these go via Jakarta. A much cheaper trip between Singapore and Kalimantan is to fly between Batam and Pontianak (148,000 rp) and take the ferry between Batam and Singapore.

Another popular 'local hop' into Indonesia is the 20-minute leap over the Melaka Straits from Penang in Malaysia to Medan in Sumatra – the fare is about US$60.

A lesser known route is the one between Irian Jaya and Papua New Guinea. From PNG, the only way of getting to Irian Jaya is the once-weekly flight on Sunday between Vanimo and Jayapura with Douglas Airways, which connects with Air Nuigini flights between Vanimo and Wewak. Fares from Vanimo to Jayapura are 50 PNG kina or roughly US$50. They're worried about guerrilla activity in the border area, so strolling across the border is definitely not on.

If you are arriving from PNG, you must have a visa for entry to Indonesia. If you are flying from Jayapura to Vanimo in PNG, you must also have a visa for PNG. PNG has a consulate in Jayapura that issues visas, or you can obtain one in Jakarta. You can only leave from Jayapura if you have entered Indonesia on a visa rather than a tourist pass, though some travellers have reported that they have been able to exit Jayapura on a tourist pass.

LAND

Only two countries – Malaysia and Papua New Guinea – have land borders with Indonesia. It is possible to cross overland between the Malaysian city of Kuching in Sarawak and the Indonesian city of Pontianak in Kalimantan, but a visa is required. The land border between Papua New Guinea and Irian Jaya is still closed.

SEA

Most sea connections are between Malaysia and Sumatra (see Sumatra Getting There & Away for full details). The most popular ferry service is between Penang (Malaysia) and Medan (Sumatra) but ferries also connect Medan with Port Kelang and Lumut in Malaysia, and Dumai (Sumatra) with Melaka and Port Kelang. Another alternative is to take a boat from Pasir Gudang (near Johor Bahru in Malaysia) to Batam, Bintan or Surabaya in Java (see the Surabaya Getting There & Away section).

From Singapore to Batam in Indonesia's Riau Archipelago is less than half an hour by ferry, and from Batam boats go through to Pekanbaru in Sumatra. Ferries also run between Singapore and nearby Bintan Island, from where passenger boats go on to Jakarta. See the Sumatra Getting There & Away section for more details.

It's possible to go from Manado in Sulawesi via Tahuna and Marore to Mindanao in the Philippines, but it's not advisable – pirates are still a way of life in Philippine waters.

Getting Around

AIR

Indonesia has a number of airlines flying to some pretty amazing places. Fares are often the same between airlines, but some fares vary and it pays to shop around.

Garuda, named after the mythical man-bird vehicle of the Hindu god Vishnu and a hero of the *Ramayana*, operates all the long-distance international connections and major domestic routes using jet aircraft. Merpati, which has merged with Garuda, is the country's main domestic carrier.

Garuda and Merpati issue the Visit Indonesia Decade Pass. It starts at US$300 for three sectors, and each additional sector is US$100. You must buy the air pass overseas or within 14 days of arrival in Indonesia, and you must enter the country on Garuda or Merpati. If your travel is restricted to Java and Sumatra, you might not save any money with these passes but if you're going to fly way out to Irian Jaya, Maluku or Sulawesi, they can soon start to look very attractive.

Other airlines include Sempati, which has a fleet of jet aircraft and a reputation for efficiency and the best service. Bouraq have some useful flights to Kalimantan, Sulawesi and Nusa Tenggara; their slogan is 'fly to the most unreachable destinations'. It sounds distinctly dangerous! Mandala has an interesting fleet of vintage prop aircraft, most of which seem to spend most of the time stationary at Jakarta airport.

Merpati, and most other airlines, offer 25% discount for students up to 26 years of age.

Domestic air tickets attract a 10% tax and an airport tax that varies with the airport – usually 4400 or 5500 rp. Airfares quoted in this book are at the base rate and do not include tax. Airport tax is usually included on your ticket so check if you are asked to pay the airport tax at check-in – close inspection of the *small* print on your ticket may show that it has already been paid for.

It is cheaper to buy tickets for domestic flights in Indonesia. Fares bought overseas are quoted in US$, and are up to 50% more than the rupiah fare.

BUS

Indonesia has a huge variety of bus services – from trucks with wooden seats in the back to air-con deluxe buses with TV and karaoke – that will take you all the way from Bali to Sumatra. Java and Sumatra have the greatest variety of bus services. Local buses are the cheapest; they leave when full and stop on request. Then there is a variety of different classes and prices, depending on whether buses have air-con, reclining seats, TV, on-board toilets etc. The deluxe express buses often do the night runs, when traffic is lighter and travel is faster.

Minibuses often do the shorter runs. In Sumatra, and especially Java, deluxe minibuses also operate on the major routes and are the most comfortable buses of all. Bali also has tourist buses plying the popular routes.

In the outer islands, the options for bus travel are much more limited and often only bemos or local buses or bemos (see the Local Transport section) are available.

TRAIN

There is a pretty good railway service running the length of Java. In the east, it connects with the ferry to Bali, and in the west with the ferry to Sumatra. Otherwise, there's just a bit of rail into Sumatra but most of that vast island is reserved for buses. Trains vary – there are slow, miserable, cheap ones and fast, comfortable, expensive ones, and some in-between. So check out what you're getting before you pay.

Some major towns (eg Surabaya and Jakarta) also have several stations, so check where you'll be going to and from as well. Student discounts are generally available but tend to vary from about 10% to 25%.

BOAT

Indonesia is an island nation, so ships are important. If you're going to really explore you'll have to use them.

Indonesian Airfares
(Selected Merpati, Sempati & Bouraq Flights)
0
400
800 km
SOUTH CHINA SEA
INDIAN OCEAN
Airfares are in '000 rp (excluding 10% tax & departure tax)
Banda Aceh
Medan
Pekanbaru
Padang
Batam
Palembang
Jakarta
Pontianak
Tarakan
Balikpapan
Banjarmasin
Surabaya
Yogyakarta
Denpasar
Ujung Pandang
Palu
Manado
Ternate
Ambon
Sorong
Biak
Jayapura
Bima
Waingapu
Maumere
Kupang
Dili
108
131
119
114
148
204
218
215
117
174
201
133
97
84
215
277
293
128
161
111
53
106
183
136
151
233
83
136
110
200
476
137
114
125
125
125
104
77
65
69
117
199

Pelni Ships

Pelni is the biggest shipper with services almost everywhere. They have modern, all air-con ships, operate regular two-weekly or monthly routes around the islands and are surprisingly comfortable. The ships usually stop for four hours in each port, so there's time for a quick look around. Schedules change every few months and cannot be quoted here – get a copy of the schedule from any Pelni office.

The fleet is comprised of the ships *Kerinci*, *Kambuna*, *Rinjani*, *Umsini*, *Tidar*, *Ciremai*, *Dobonso*, *Kelimutu*, *Lawit*, *Tatamailau*, *Sirimau* and *Awu*. The good news is that Pelni is adding more ships to its fleet, which means more services and more ports to be covered. The bad news is that as new ships start operation, the routes are reviewed, so Pelni services are in a state of flux – the routes may change.

Following is a listing of Pelni boats and the seaports that make up their respective routes (initials in parentheses indicate the area of Indonesia in which the port is located):

Awu
Nunukan (K), Tarakan (K), Toli Toli (Sul), Balikpapan (K), Pare Pare (Sul), Batulicin (K), Surabaya (J), Benoa (B), Bima (NT), Ujung Pandang (Sul), Kendari (Sul), Kolonedale (Sul), Luwuk (Sul), Gorontalo (Sul), Bitung (Sul), Lirung (Sul), Tahuna (Sul)

Ciremai
Jakarta (J), Ujung Pandang (Sul), Bau Bau (Sul), Banggai (Sul), Bitung (Sul), Ternate (M), Sorong (IJ), Manokwari (IJ), Biak (IJ), Jayapura (IJ)

Dobonsolo
Jakarta (J), Surabaya (J), Bima (NT), Kupang (NT), Dili (NT), Ambon (M), Sorong (IJ), Manokwari (IJ), Biak (IJ), Jayapura (IJ)

Kambuna
Belawan (Sum), Jakarta (J), Surabaya (J), Ujung Pandang (Sul), Balikpapan (K), Pantoloan (Sul), Toli Toli (Sul), Bitung (Sul)

Kelimutu
Banjarmasin (K), Surabaya (J), Benoa (B), Bima (NT), Waingapu (NT), Maumere (NT), Ujung Pandang (Sul), Kupang (NT), Dili (NT), Kalabahi (NT)

Kerinci
Belawan (Sum), Jakarta (J), Surabaya (J), Ujung Pandang (Sul), Bau Bau (Sul), Ambon (M), Ternate (M), Bitung (Sul)

Lawit
Sibolga (Sum), Gunung Sitoli (Sum), Padang (Sum), Jakarta (J), Pontianak (K), Semarang (J), Banjarmasin (K)

Rinjani
Dumai (Sum), Kijang (Sum), Muntok (Sum), Jakarta (J), Surabaya (J), Ujung Pandang (Sul), Bau Bau (Sul), Ambon (M), Banda (M), Tual (M), Fak Fak (IJ)

Sirimau
Jakarta (J), Pontianak (K), Semarang (J), Banjarmasin (K), Surabaya (J), Lembar (NT), Ujung Pandang (Sul), Kendari (Sul), Ambon (M), Sorong (IJ), Manokwari (IJ), Biak (IJ), Nabire (IJ), Seru (IJ), Jayapura (IJ)

Tatamailau
Jakarta (J), Pontianak (K), Cirebon (J), Banjarmasin (K), Surabaya (J), Labuhanbajo (NT), Larantuka (NT), Dili (NT), Saumlaki (M), Tual (M), Dobo (M), Merauke (IJ), Kaimana (IJ), Fak Fak (IJ), Sorong (IJ)

Tidar
Surabaya (J), Balikpapan (K), Ujung Pandang (Sul), Pantoloan (Sul), Tarakan (K)

Umsini
Jakarta (J), Ujung Pandang (Sul), Kwandang (Sul), Bitung (Sul), Sorong (IJ), Manokwari (IJ), Jayapura (IJ)

Travel on Pelni ships is comprised of four cabin classes, followed by Kelas Ekonomi which is the modern version of the old deck class. There you are packed in a large room with a space to sleep; but, even in ekonomi, it's air-con and can get pretty cool at night, so bring warm clothes or a sleeping bag. There are no locker facilities in ekonomi, so you have to keep an eye on your gear.

Class I is luxury plus with only two beds per cabin and a price approaching air travel. Class II is a notch down in style, with four to a cabin and no TV, but still very comfortable. Class III has six beds and Class IV has eight beds to a cabin. Class I and II have a dining room while in ekonomi you queue up to collect a meal on a tray and then sit down wherever you can to eat it.

Ekonomi is fine for short trips. Class IV is the best value for longer hauls, but some ships only offer Class I & II in addition to ekonomi. Prices quoted in this book are for ekonomi – as a rough approximation Class IV is 50% more than ekonomi, Class III is

INDONESIA

100% more, Class II is 200% more and Class I is 400% more.

You can book tickets up to 10 days ahead; it's best to book at least a few days in advance. Pelni is not a tourist operation, so don't expect any special service, although there is usually somebody hidden away in the ticket offices who can help foreigners.

As well as their luxury liners, Pelni have Perinitis (Pioneer) ships that visits many of the other ports not covered by the passenger liners. They can get you to just about any of the remote outer islands, as well as the major ports. The ships are often beaten up old crates that also carry cargo. They offer deck class only, but you may be able to negotiate a cabin with one of the crew.

Other Ships

The inner islands – Sumatra, Java, Bali and Nusa Tenggara – are all connected by regular ferries and you can use them to island hop all the way from Sumatra to Timor.

Getting a boat in the outer islands is often a matter of hanging loose until something comes by. Check with shipping companies, the harbour office or anyone else you can think of. For these interisland services, when the ship arrives it's usually better to negotiate your fare on board rather than buy tickets from the office in advance (apart from big centres like Jakarta and Surabaya).

If you're travelling deck class, unroll your sleeping bag on the deck and make yourself comfortable. Travelling deck class during the wet season can prove to be extremely uncomfortable. Either get one person in your party to take a cabin or discuss renting a cabin from one of the crew (it's a popular way for the crew to make a little extra). Bring some food of your own.

It's also possible to make some more unusual sea trips. Old Makassar schooners still sail the Indonesian waters and it's often possible to travel on them – from Sulawesi to other islands, particularly Java and Nusa Tenggara.

LOCAL TRANSPORT

There's a great variety of local transport in Indonesia. This includes the ubiquitous *bemo*, a pick-up truck with two rows of seats down the sides, or else a small minibus. Bemos usually run standard routes like buses and depart when full but can also be chartered like a taxi. A step up from the bemo is the small minibus known either as an *opelet, mikrolet* or a *colt*, since they are often Mitsubishi Colts. In some towns bemos are now known as *angkots*, from *angkutan* (transport) and *kota* (city). Bali has an extensive bemo network.

Then there's the *becak*, or bicycle-rickshaw – they're just the same as in so many other Asian countries, but are only found in towns and cities. Increasingly, they are being banned from the central areas of major cities. There are none in Bali. The *bajaj*, a three-wheeler powered by a noisy two-stroke engine, is only found in Jakarta. They're identical to what is known in India as an autorickshaw. In quieter towns, you may find *dokars* and *andongs* – horse or pony carts with two or four wheels respectively.

In Bali, Yogyayakarta and some other centres you can also hire bicycles or motorbikes. Many towns, of course, have taxis (they even use their meters these days in the big cities in Java). You can also hire drive-yourself cars in Jakarta and Bali. Then there are all sorts of oddities: you can hire horses in some places.

Java

Indonesia's most populous island presents vivid contrasts of wealth and squalor, majestic open country and crowded filthy cities, quiet rural scenes and bustling modern traffic. For the traveller, it has everything from live volcanos to inspiring 1000-year-old monuments.

Java is a long, narrow island that can be conveniently divided into three sections – West, Central and East Java. The western region, also known as Sunda, is predominantly Islamic, and it is here that you will find the capital, Jakarta.

Other important historic centres of the

Sunda region were Banten, Bandung and Cirebon. Today, the most visited places, other than Jakarta, are Bogor, Bandung and the relaxing beach centre of Pangandaran. This is an area noted for its *wayang golek* (wooden puppets).

Central Java is the most Indonesian part of Indonesia and the centre for much of the island's early culture. The two great Hindu/Buddhist dynasties were centred here and they constructed the immense Borobudur Temple and the complex of temples at Prambanan. Later, the rise of Islam carried sultans to power and their palaces, or *kratons*, at Yogyakarta and Solo (Surakarta) can be visited. This is a region for dance drama, or *wayang orang*, *gamelan* orchestras and *wayang kulit* shadow puppet performances.

Finally, there is East Java or Java Timur, the area most likely to be rushed through by travellers in their haste to get to Bali. The major city here is the important port of Surabaya. Although East Java's attractions include the ruins at Trowulan and around Malang, the main interest in the region is natural rather than man-made: the settings of the many hill stations and the superb Mt Bromo volcano.

Most people travelling through Java follow the well-worn route of Jakarta-Bogor-Bandung-Pangandaran-Yogyakarta-Solo-Surabaya-Bali, with short diversions or day trips from points along that route. Many only stop at Jakarta and Yogyakarta! There are also a number of major towns along the north coast, but they attract few visitors.

Things to Buy

Yogyakarta is the place in Java where your money deserves to be spent, but it's worth checking out the Sarinah department store on Jalan Thamrin in Jakarta. The 3rd floor of Sarinah is devoted to handicrafts from all over the country. It can be a little variable – you might not be able to find certain items that really interest you or you might find one area badly represented – but, overall, it's a great place for an overview of Indonesian crafts. The art market, Pasar Seni, at Ancol in Jakarta, is also worth a visit.

Batik The art of batik is one of Indonesia's best known crafts, and it has been a Yogyakarta speciality since who knows when. Batik is the craft of producing designs on material by covering part of it with wax and then dyeing it. When the wax is scraped or melted off, an undyed patch is left. Repeated waxing and dyeing can produce colourful and complex designs. Batik pieces can be made by a hand-blocked process known as *batik cap*, in which a copper stamp is used to apply the wax, or they can be hand drawn *(batik tulis)* using a wax-filled pen known as a *canting*.

Batik can be bought as pieces of material, cushion covers, T-shirts, dresses, dinner sets and as paintings. An easy check for quality is to simply turn the item over to ensure the design is of equal colour strength on both sides of the material – that makes it batik and not just printed material. In Yogyakarta, you can buy batik in shops, in the market or from the many galleries.

Solo, Pekalongan and Cirebon are major centres for batik.

Other Crafts Silverwork can be found in the Kota Gede area, a few km south-east of Yogyakarta. Wayang puppets can be found all over Yogyakarta but wayang golek puppets are more frequently found in the area around Bandung and Bogor. *Kebayas*, those flimsy lace jackets, are now outdated as a fashion but you can find lots of them in Yogyakarta along with other popular Western clothing. At Prambanan and Borobudur, look for bamboo whistling tops as they make great presents for children.

Leatherwork in Yogyakarta is cheap but the quality is not always high. Very good lampshades and other cane craft can be found in Yogyakarta but they're hard to transport.

Getting There & Away

You can get to Java by a number of means and from a variety of directions. People usually come to Java from:

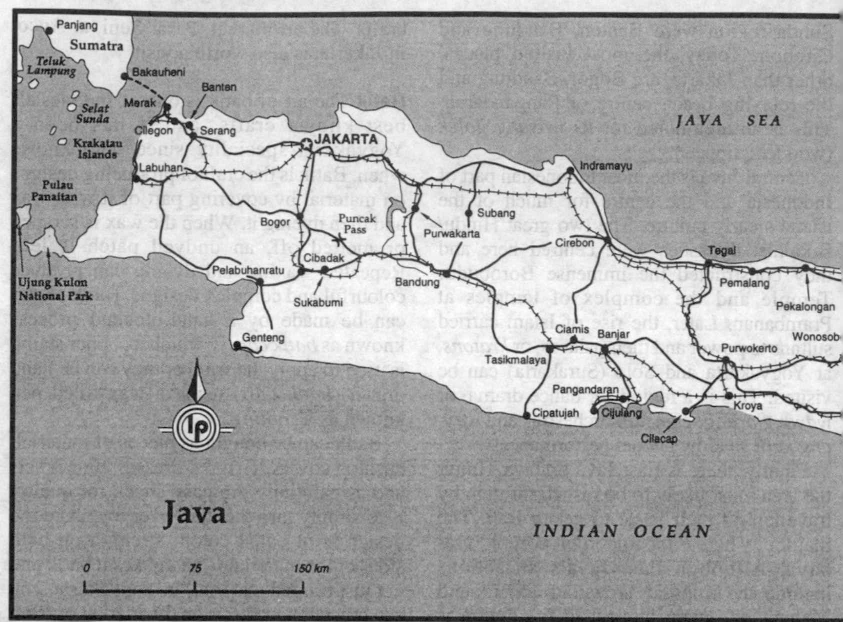

Sumatra – either by the Padang to Jakarta shipping service or the short trip across the Sunda Strait from Bakauheni in Sumatra to Merak in Java.

Bali – take the very short ferry trip from Gilimanuk in Bali to Banyuwangi at the eastern end of Java.

The outer areas – like Sulawesi, Kalimantan, Maluku or Irian Jaya, by air or sea.

From Singapore – see the Getting There & Away section at the start of this chapter for details.

Air Jakarta is a reasonably good place for shopping around for airline tickets, although it is not as good as Singapore. See the Jakarta Getting There & Away section for further information.

Some sample Merpati flights are: Jakarta to Denpasar for 195,000 rp, Yogyakarta to Denpasar for 104,000 rp and Surabaya to Denpasar for 78,000 rp.

Sea There are, of course, shipping services from other Indonesian islands. See the introductory Indonesia Getting Around section for more information on the regular Pelni shipping services, most of which operate from, or through, Jakarta and Surabaya.

For details on how to get to Java from Malaysia or Singapore, see the Getting There & Away section at the start of this chapter.

Getting Around

Air There's no real need to fly around Java, unless you're in a real hurry or have money to burn – there's so much road transport available. If you do decide to take to the air, you will get some spectacular views of Java's many mountains and volcanos.

Flying Merpati, fares include Jakarta to Yogyakarta for 111,000 rp and Jakarta to Surabaya for 161,000 rp.

Bus Daytime bus travel is often slow and nerve-racking. It is probably just as bad for your nerves at night (if you are awake), but at least travel is much faster. Although buses

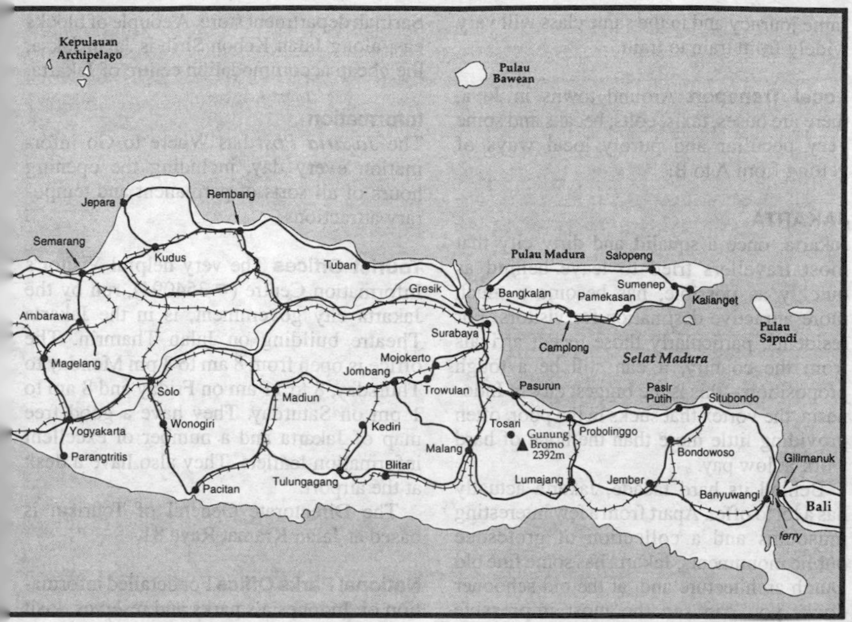

run all over Java, you're generally better off taking trains for the long hauls and using buses on the shorter trips. In some places, there are good reasons for taking the bus, as on the scenic Jakarta to Bandung trip over the Puncak Pass.

As with trains, there can be variations in fares and bus types. Where the fare isn't ticketed or fixed, it's wise to check the fare with other passengers – bemo drivers are the worst culprits for jacking up fares for foreigners. Beware of the practice of taking your money and not giving you your change until later.

The cheapest buses are the big public buses. There are also private bus companies, some of which run air-con deluxe services on important routes. Small minibuses run the shorter routes more frequently and more comfortably than the big public buses. The most comfortable version of all are the deluxe air-con minibuses which operate on the major runs. There are also share-taxi services from Jakarta to Bogor, Bandung, Cirebon and a few other destinations.

Train Choose your trains for comfort, speed and destination. There is a wide variety ranging from cheap, slow trains to reasonably cheap fast trains, very expensive expresses and squalid all-ekonomi-class cattle trains. The schedules change frequently and although departures may be punctual, arrivals will be late for most services and very late for others.

In Jakarta and Surabaya in particular there are several stations, some of them far more convenient than others. Bear this in mind when choosing your trains. Student discounts are generally available, but not for the expensive *Bima* and *Mutiara* night express trains. Try going straight to the stationmaster for speedier ticketing, and to get tickets even when, officially, the train is booked out. Remember, once again, that fares for the

INDONESIA

same journey and in the same class will vary widely from train to train.

Local Transport Around towns in Java, there are buses, taxis, colts, becaks and some very peculiar and purely local ways of getting from A to B.

JAKARTA

Jakarta, once a squalid and dirty city that most travellers tried to leave behind as quickly as possible, has become a much more attractive destination for visitors. For residents, particularly those recent arrivals from the country, it can still be a tough proposition – this is the biggest city in Indonesia, the vortex that sucks in the poor, often providing little more than the hope of hard work at low pay.

Behind its hard facade, Jakarta actually has a lot to offer. Apart from a few interesting museums and a collection of grotesque public monuments, Jakarta has some fine old Dutch architecture and, at the old schooner dock, you can see the most impressive reminder of the age of sailing ships to be found anywhere in the world.

The Dutch took Jakarta and renamed it Batavia back in 1619; the name reverted to Jakarta after independence. You may still occasionally see it spelt Djakarta.

Orientation

Jakarta is a sprawling city; it's 25 km from the docks to the suburb of Kebayoran Baru. Sukarno's towering national monument (Monas) in Merdeka Square is an excellent landmark for Jakarta. You can always get your bearings from it. North of the monument is the older part of Jakarta, including the Chinatown area of Glodok, the old Dutch area of Kota, then the waterfront and the old harbour area known as Sunda Kelapa. The modern harbour, Tanjung Priok, is several km along the coast to the east. The more modern part of Jakarta is to the south of the monument.

Jalan Thamrin is the main north-south street of the new city and this wide boulevard has Jakarta's big hotels, big banks and the Sarinah department store. A couple of blocks east along Jalan Kebon Sirih is Jalan Jaksa, the cheap accommodation centre of Jakarta.

Information

The *Jakarta Post* has Where to Go information every day, including the opening hours of all sorts of permanent and temporary attractions.

Tourist Offices The very helpful Visitor's Information Centre (☎ 354094), run by the Jakarta city government, is in the Jakarta Theatre building on Jalan Thamrin. The office is open from 8 am to 3 pm Monday to Thursday, 8 to 11 am on Friday and 8 am to 1 pm on Saturday. They have a good free map of Jakarta and a number of excellent information leaflets. They also have a desk at the airport.

The Directorate General of Tourism is based at Jalan Kramat Raya 81.

National Parks Office For detailed information on Indonesia's parks and reserves, visit the PHPA (the Directorate-General of Forest Protection and Nature Conservation), which is in the Forestry Department (Departemen Kehutanan) building, Jalan Gatot Subroto. Take bus No 210 or 213 from Jalan Jenderal Sudirman, which is south of Jalan Thamrin.

Post & Telecommunications The main post office, with its efficient poste restante service, is behind Jalan Pos Utara, to the north-east of Monas. It is open from 8 am to 4 pm Monday to Friday, and from 8 am to 1 pm on Saturday. It's a good half-hour walk from the city centre or you can take a No 12 bus from Jalan Thamrin.

International phone calls can be made from the 24-hour phone office in the Jakarta Theatre building, where you'll also find the tourist office. The Warpostal on Jalan Jaksa, next to Anedja cafe and opposite Nick's Corner, is convenient but charges around 4500 rp for a reverse-charge call.

Bookshops Most of the big hotels have bookshops. Singapore's Times Bookshop chain has a branch in the Plaza Indonesia shopping centre, next to the Grand Hyatt Hotel on Jalan Thamrin. On the other side of the roundabout, the Hotel Indonesia also has a good bookshop.

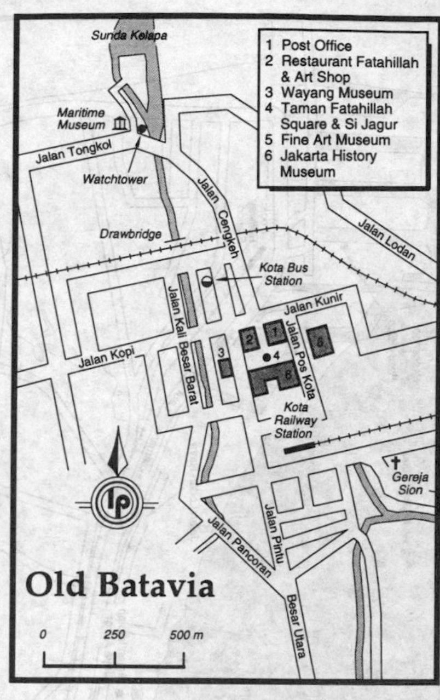

Sunda Kelapa

This is the best sight in Jakarta – it is the old **Dutch port** where you will see more sailing ships, the magnificent Buginese Makassar schooners, than you ever thought existed. To get there, take a blue No 70 bus (or the less crowded P11 express bus) from Jalan Thamrin down to Kota, and then walk (or take the unique local transport – a ride on a 'kiddie seat' on the back of a pushbike). Admission to the harbour is 200 rp. Old men will take you in row boats around the schooners for about 2000 rp.

The early morning fish market, **Pasar Ikan**, is close by. In the same area, one of the old Dutch East India Company warehouses has been turned into a **Museum Bahari** (Maritime Museum). Admission is 150 rp (100 rp on Sunday) and it's open from 9 am every day, except Monday, and closes at 3.30 pm Tuesday to Thursday, at 3 pm on Friday and Sunday and at noon on Saturday. You can climb up inside the old **watchtower** near the bridge for a good view of the harbour.

Old Batavia (Kota)

There's still a Dutch flavour to this old part of town. It's gradually being restored, but cleaning up the stinking canals is a superhuman task. Take a Kota bus to the Kota bus terminal. Next to the terminal is the last remaining old Dutch **drawbridge**, across the Kali Besar Canal. Walk south along the canal, past fine 18th-century houses, then cross the canal again and you can cut through to the Taman Fatahillah Square.

Standing on the open cobbled square is the old City Hall, dating from 1710, that is now the **Jakarta History Museum** (Museum Sejarah Jakarta), with furniture and paintings from Dutch colonial life. The city hall was also the main prison compound of Batavia – in the basement there are cells and 'water prisons' where often more than 300 people were kept. Admission to the museum is 150 rp. It opens at 9 am every day except Monday, and closes at 4 pm from Tuesday to Friday, at 1 pm on Saturday, and at 4 pm on Sunday.

The old Portuguese cannon **Si Jagur**, or Mr Fertility, opposite the museum, was believed by women to be a cure for barrenness because of its strange clenched fist (a symbol of fertility) and Latin inscription ('Ex me ipsa renata sum' – 'Out of myself I was reborn'). Women used to offer flowers to the cannon and sit on top of it in the hope of bearing children.

Across the square on Jalan Pintu Besar Utara, the **Wayang Museum** has a good display of puppets from Indonesia and other parts of Asia. Wayang golek or wayang kulit performances are put on every Sunday between 10 am and 2 pm. The museum is open from 9 am every day except Monday and closes at 3 pm Tuesday to Thursday and

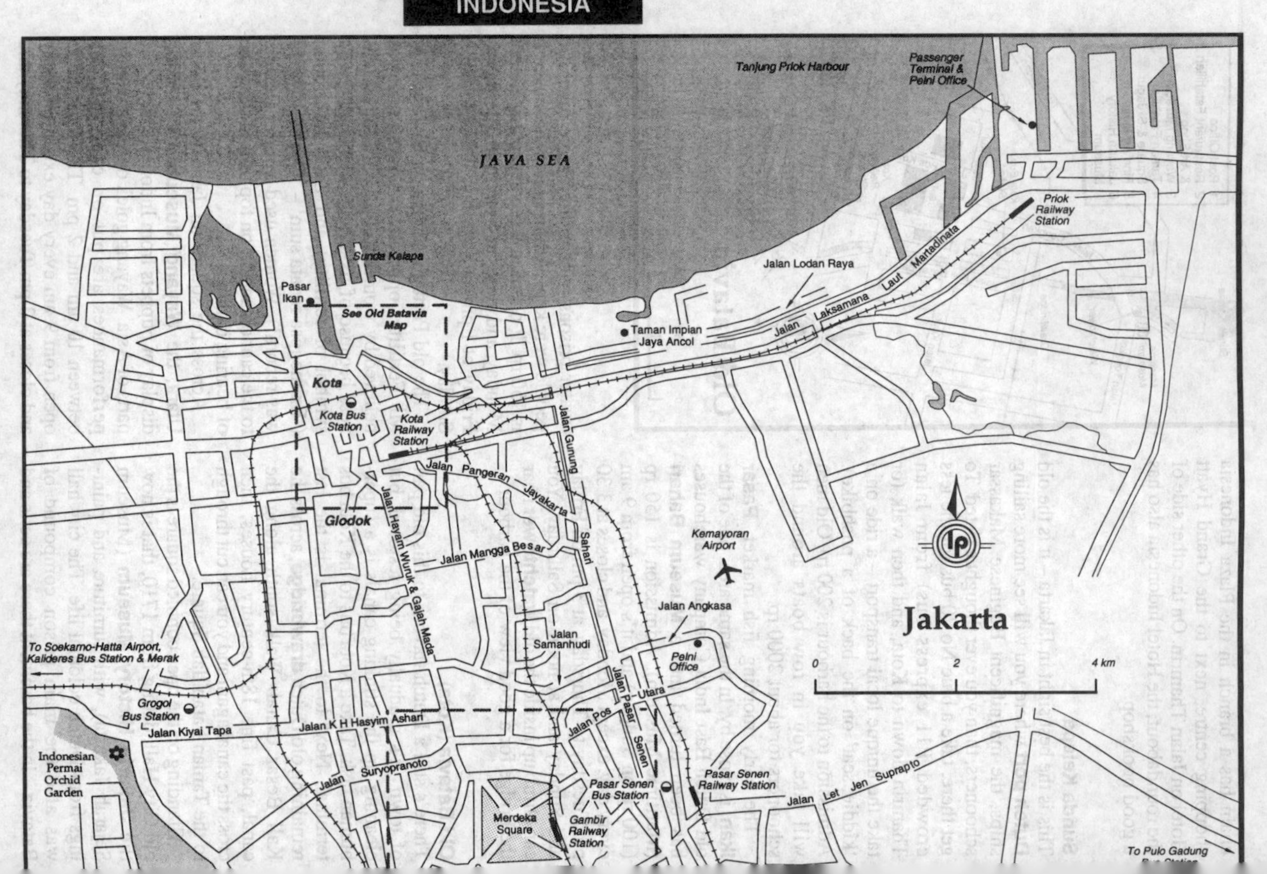
Jakarta
0
2
4 km
JAVA SEA
Tanjung Priok Harbour
Passenger Terminal & Pelni Office
Priok Railway Station
Jalan Laksamana Laut Martadinata
Jalan Lodan Raya
Taman Impian Jaya Ancol
Jalan Gunung Sahari
Sunda Kelapa
Pasar Ikan
See Old Batavia Map
Kota
Kota Bus Station
Kota Railway Station
Jalan Pangeran Jayakarta
Glodok
Jalan Mangga Besar
Jalan Hayam Wuruk & Gajah Mada
Kemayoran Airport
Jalan Angkasa
Jalan Samanhudi
Pelni Office
Jalan Pasar Senen
Utara
Jalan Pos
To Soekarno-Hatta Airport, Kalideres Bus Station & Merak
Grogol Bus Station
Jalan Kiyai Tapa
Jalan K H Hasyim Ashari
Indonesian Permai Orchid Garden
Jalan Suryopranoto
Pasar Senen Bus Station
Pasar Senen Railway Station
Jalan Let Jen Suprapto
Merdeka Square
Gambir Railway Station
To Pulo Gadung

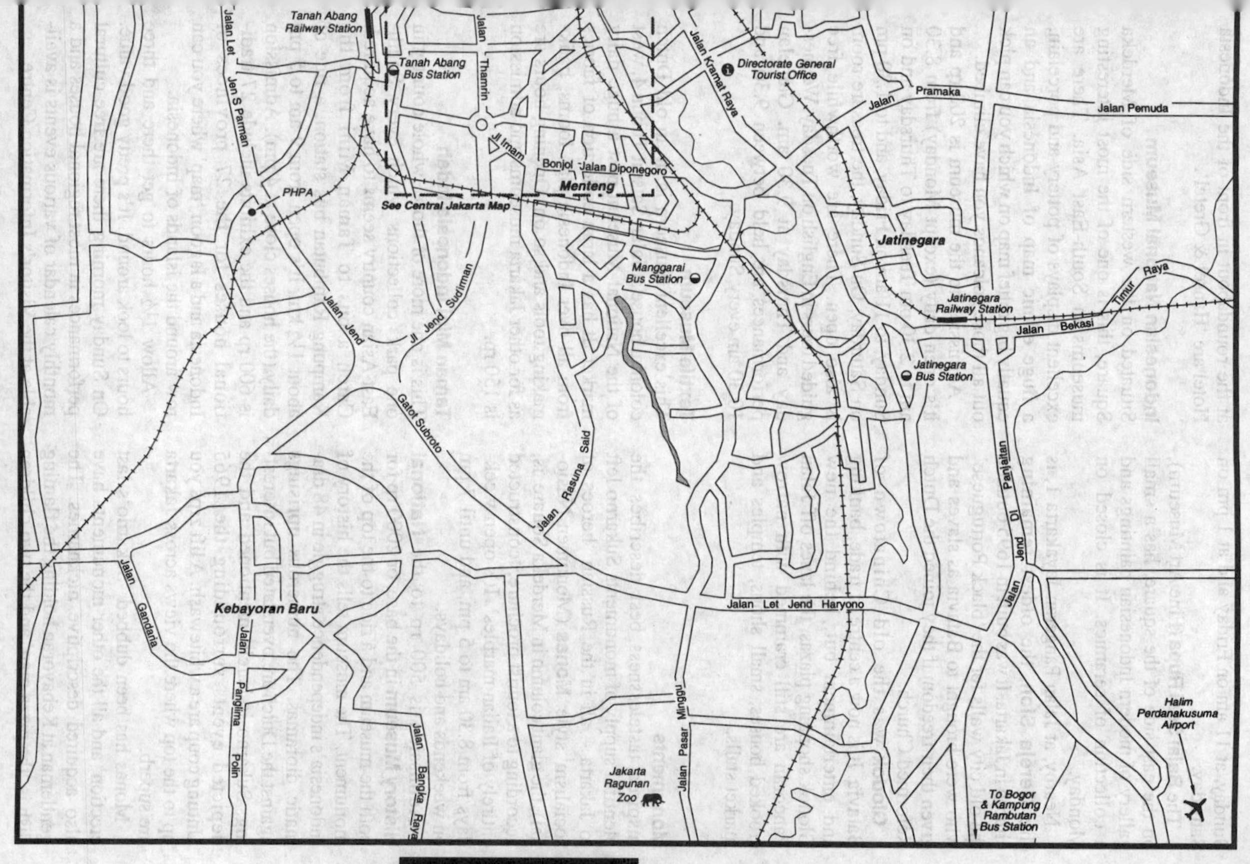
Tanah Abang Railway Station
Jalan Let Jen S Parman
Tanah Abang Bus Station
Jalan Thamrin
Jalan Kramat Raya
Directorate General Tourist Office
Jalan Pramaka
Jalan Pemuda
Jl Imam
Bonjol
Jalan Diponegoro
Menteng
See Central Jakarta Map
PHPA
Jatinegara
Manggarai Bus Station
Timur Raya
Jatinegara Railway Station
Jalan Bekasi
Jalan Jend
Jl Jend Sudirman
Jatinegara Bus Station
Gatot Subroto
Jalan Jend DI Panjaitan
Jalan Rasuna Said
Kebayoran Baru
Jalan Gandaria
Jalan Let Jend Haryono
Jalan Panglima Polin
Jalan Pasar Minggu
Jalan Bangka Raya
Jakarta Ragunan Zoo
Halim Perdanakusuma Airport
To Bogor & Kampung Rambutan Bus Station

INDONESIA

Sunday, at 11 am on Friday and at 1 pm on Saturday.

The **Balai Seni Rupa** (Fine Art Museum), on the east side of the square, has a small gallery of modern Indonesian paintings and a collection of ceramics. It is closed on Monday.

Nearby, at Jalan Pangeran Jayakarta 1, is the **Gereja Sion**, the oldest remaining church in Jakarta. It was built in 1695 outside the old city walls for the 'black Portuguese' who were brought to Batavia as slaves and given their freedom if they joined the Dutch Reformed Church.

Glodok was the old Chinatown of Batavia. It is now a centre of trade, banking and entertainment but, behind the new Glodok shopping plazas, the lanes off Jalan Pancoran are still crammed with narrow crooked houses, small shops, temples and market stalls.

Monuments

Inspired tastelessness best describes the plentiful supply of monuments Sukarno left to Jakarta – all in the Russian 'heroes of socialism' style. **Monas** (Monumen Nasional), the giant column in Merdeka Square, is, according to a tourist brochure, 'constructed entirely of Italian marbles'. It's open weekdays from 8.30 am to 5 pm, and until 7 pm on weekends and holidays.

Admission is 500 rp to the **National History Museum** in the base, or 2000 rp for both the museum and a ride to the top of the monument. The museum tells the history of Indonesia's independence struggle in 48 dramatic dioramas. The numerous uprisings against the Dutch are overstated but interesting, Sukarno is barely mentioned and the depicted events surrounding the 1965 Untung coup are a whitewash. A lift zips you up to the top where the views across Jakarta are superb.

Monas has been dubbed 'Sukarno's last erection' and all the other monuments have also acquired descriptive nicknames. The gentleman at Kebayoran holding the flaming dish is 'the pizza man' and the two children at the roundabout in front of the Indonesia Hotel are 'Hansel & Gretel'.

Indonesian National Museum

Situated on the western side of Merdeka Square, this is one of the most interesting museums in South-East Asia. There are excellent displays of pottery and porcelain, a huge ethnic map of Indonesia and an equally big relief map on which you can pick out all those volcanos you have climbed.

Admission to the museum is 200 rp and it's open daily (except Monday) from 8.30 am to 2.30 pm Tuesday to Thursday and on Sunday, to 11 am on Friday, and to 1.30 pm on Saturday. On Sunday, the treasure room is also open. There are worthwhile free guided tours in English on Tuesday, Wednesday and Thursday at 9.30 am. Gamelan performances are held between 9.30 and 10.30 am every Sunday.

Textile Museum

This excellent museum is in an old Dutch colonial house at Jalan Satsuit Tubun 4, west of the National Museum past a huge daily market. It has a large collection of fabrics from all over Indonesia plus looms, batik-making tools and so on. Opening hours are as for other Jakarta museums and admission is 150 rp.

Taman Mini Indonesia Indah

This is one more of those 'whole country in one park' collections which every South-East Asian country seems to have acquired. Catch a bus to Taman Mini from the Kampung Rambutan bus station, a ride of about 1½ km. It's open from 9 am to 5 pm daily (the houses close at 4 pm). Admission is 600 rp and the exhibits include 27 traditional houses for the 27 provinces of Indonesia and a lagoon 'map' where you can row around the islands of Indonesia.

Allow 1½ hours to get there and three hours to look around. It's pretty good value. On Sunday morning there are free cultural performances in most regional houses and a monthly calendar of various events is available at the Visitor's Information Centre.

Taman Impian Jaya Ancol
Dreamland is on the bayfront between Kota and Tanjung Priok Harbour. This huge amusement complex has an oceanarium, an amazing swimming pool complex with wave-making facilities, an Indonesian Disneyland and the excellent Pasar Seni Art Market with its numerous small shops, an exhibition gallery and sidewalk cafes.

The park is open from 9 am to midnight daily; admission is 850 rp on weekdays but more on weekends when it can get crowded. The various attractions have extra charges and are open at different times. The pool is open from 7 am to 9 pm.

The 'Disneyland' is Dunia Fantasi (Fantasy World) and if you've got children it's really quite good. It's closely modelled on Disneyland and although it's much smaller, the 9000 rp for an unlimited ride passport makes it excellent value. The Small World ride, a favourite with children at the original Disneyland, is much better in the Jakarta version! Dunia Fantasi is open Monday to Friday from 2 to 9 pm, Saturday from 2 to 10 pm and Sunday from 10 am to 9 pm.

To get there, take a Tanjung Priok No 60 bus, or a bus to Kota and then bus No 64 and 65 or a M15 minibus.

Other Attractions
To the north of Merdeka Square you'll see the gleaming white **Presidential Palace**. To the north-east is the vast **Istiqlal Mosque**, the largest mosque in South-East Asia.

The **Jakarta Ragunan Zoo**, in the Pasar Minggu district south of the city, has Komodo dragons, orang-utans and other interesting Indonesian wildlife. The **Sarinah department store**, with its fine handicrafts section, is always worth a browse. There are **market stalls** selling antiques on Jalan Surabaya, and at Jalan Pramuka there is a **bird market**.

Places to Stay
There's a hotel booking counter at Soekarno-Hatta airport, 35 km west of the city, but the slightly upscale Djody Hotel on Jalan Jaksa is about the cheapest place they handle.

Jalan Jaksa Jakarta's cheap accommodation is almost all centred around Jalan Jaksa, a small street centrally located in the newer part of Jakarta, a few blocks over from Jakarta's main drag – Jalan Thamrin.

Once, *Wisma Delima*, at Jalan Jaksa 5, was the only cheap place to stay. Now there are lots of alternatives and Wisma Delima is still popular but quieter. Dorm beds are 5500 rp (5000 rp for YHA members), or small but spotless doubles are 12,000 rp. Food and cold drinks are available, as is good travel information.

Moving down Jalan Jaksa from No 5, the *Norbek (Noordwijk) Hostel* (☎ 330392) at No 14 has rooms for 9000/12,000 rp, but most are around 12,000 rp to 15,000 rp. It's a dark rabbit warren, and one of those places which likes to have lists of rules posted on every vertical surface.

Nick's Corner (☎ 336754) at No 16 advertises itself as the 'cleanest' in town, and it's hard to disagree. A dorm bed costs 7500 rp in immaculate, if somewhat cramped, eight and 12-bed air-con dorms. Good doubles are 30,000 rp and 35,000 rp, or 45,000 rp and 65,000 rp with bathroom. Breakfast is included.

Continue down the street to the *Djody Hostel* at Jalan Jaksa 27. This is another old standby with dorm beds for 7500 rp, and double rooms from 20,000 to 27,500 rp, but it is getting overpriced. A few doors further up, the related *Djody Hotel* (☎ 332368) at No 35 has rooms without bath for 15,000 rp and 20,000 rp. Rooms with bath and air-con cost 45,000 rp and 60,000 rp.

The *International Tator Hostel* (☎ 325124, 323940), Jalan Jaksa 37, is a small place and a notch up in quality. Rooms start at 17,500 rp with bath and go up to 32,500 rp with air-con. *Hotel Karya* (☎ 320484) at Jalan Jaksa 32-34 is a full-blown mid-range hotel. Most rooms cost 87,500 rp, but cheaper, dismal rooms with attached bath are available for 29,000 rp.

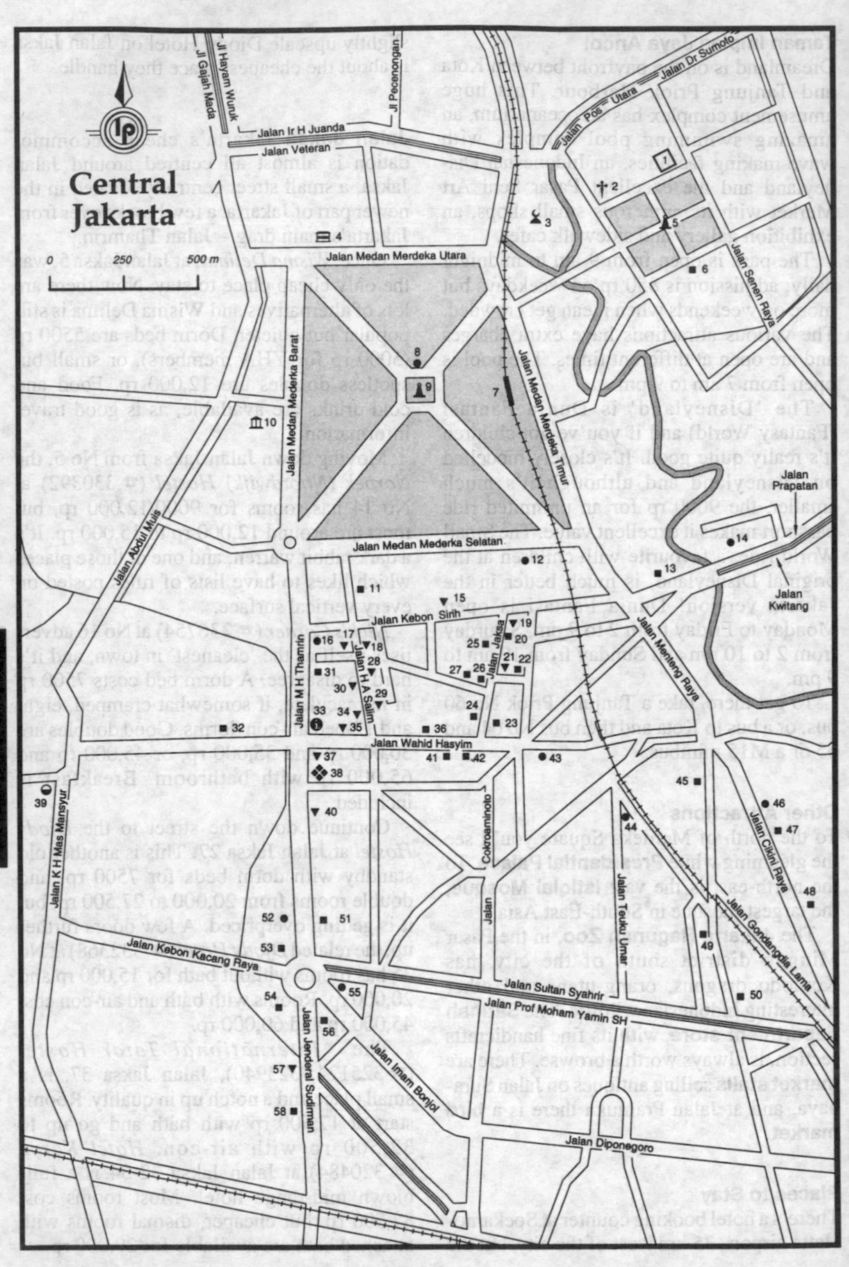
Central Jakarta
0
250
500 m
Jl Gajah Mada
Jl Hayam Wuruk
Jl Pecenongan
Jalan Ir H Juanda
Jalan Veteran
Jalan Dr Sumoto
Jalan Pos Utara
Jalan Senen Raya
Jalan Medan Merdeka Utara
Jalan Medan Merdeka Barat
Jalan Medan Merdeka Timur
Jalan Medan Mederka Selatan
Jalan Abdul Muis
Jalan Prapatan
Jalan Kwitang
Jalan Kebon Sirih
Jalan M H Thamrin
Jalan H A Salim
Jalan Jaksa
Jalan Menteng Raya
Jalan Wahid Hasyim
Jalan Cokroaminoto
Jalan Teuku Umar
Jalan Cikini Raya
Jalan Gondangdia Lama
Jalan K H Mas Mansyur
Jalan Kebon Kacang Raya
Jalan Sultan Syahrir
Jalan Prof Moham Yamin SH
Jalan Jenderal Sudirman
Jalan Imam Bonjol
Jalan Diponegoro
1
2
3
4
5
6
7
8
9
10
11
12
13
14
15
16
17
18
19
20
21
22
23
24
25
26
27
28
29
30
31
32
33
34
35
36
37
38
39
40
41
42
43
44
45
46
47
48
49
50
51
52
53
54
55
56
57
58

INDONESIA

PLACES TO STAY

6 Borobudur Intercontinental Hotel
11 Sabang Metropolitan Hotel
13 Aryaduta Hyatt Hotel
20 Wisma Delima
22 Bloem Steen & Kresna Homestays
23 Djody Hotel & International Tator Hostel
24 Hotel Karya
25 Norbek Hostel
26 Nick's Corner
27 Borneo Hostel
31 Hotel Sari Pacific
32 Wisma ISE Guest House
36 Bali International Hotel
41 Hotel Indra International
42 Cipta Hotel
45 Hotel Menteng I
47 Hotel Cikini Sofyan
48 Hotel Menteng II
49 Losmen Luhandydan
50 Hotel Marcopolo
51 President Hotel
53 Grand Hyatt Hotel
54 Hotel Indonesia
56 Mandarin Hotel
58 Kartika Plaza Hotel

PLACES TO EAT

15 Shalimar & Ikan Bakar Kebon Sirih Restaurants
17 Paradiso 2001 Restaurant
18 Sakura Anpan Bakery
19 Senayan Satay House
21 Angie's Cafe
28 Natrabu Restaurant
29 Budi Bundo Restaurant
30 A & W Hamburgers
34 Lim Thiam Kie Restaurant
35 Pizza Hut
37 MacDonald's
40 Bakmi Gajah Mandah & Studio 21
57 George & Dragon Pub

OTHER

1 Post Office
2 Cathedral
3 Istiqlal Mosque
4 Presidential Palace
5 Unchained Statue
7 Gambir Railway Station
8 Entrance To Monas
9 Monas
10 Indonesian National Museum
12 US Embassy
14 4848 Taxis
16 Qantas & Thai International
33 Jakarta Theatre Building & Visitor's Information Centre
38 Sarinah Department Store
39 Tanah Abang Bus Station
43 Media Taxis
44 Immigration Office
46 Taman Ismail Marzuki (TIM)
52 Australian Embassy
55 British Embassy

More places can be found in the small streets running off Jalan Jaksa. Gang 1 is a small alley connecting Jalan Jaksa to Jalan Kebon Sirih Timur. The *Kresna* (☎ 325403) at No 175 and the *Bloem Steen*, right next door at No 173, are a bit cramped but popular and good value for Jakarta. Rooms at the Kresna cost 12,000 rp or 18,000 rp with bath, or the Bloem Steen has rooms for 9000/12,000 rp and 15,000 rp.

At Kebon Sirih Barat Dalam 35, running west off Jalan Jaksa, *Borneo Hostel* (☎ 320095) packs them in and has a lively cafe, despite the mediocre food. The dorm beds at 5000 rp are about the cheapest around. The rooms for 15,000 rp to 20,000 rp are well kept but no bargain. Still, it's popular, well run and friendly. Avoid the annexe next door, which is under different management – it's boring and the rooms are badly in need of maintenance. Other less popular possibilities down this lane are the *Bintang Kejora*, the *Hostel Rita*, *Pondok Wisata* and the *Wisata Jaya*.

Other Central Jakarta Places If you go along Jalan Wahid Hasyim, at the southern end of Jalan Jaksa, and keep going across Jalan Thamrin, at No 168 is the *Wisma ISE Guest House* (☎ 333463), with spartan rooms at 9900/15,400 rp, or 25,000 rp with bath or 35,000 rp with bath and air-con. It's a clean and friendly place with a pleasant balcony bar at the back where you can look out over Jakarta.

Looking for a pool and air-con close to the centre of things? Then try the *Sabang Metropolitan Hotel* (☎ 3857621) at Jalan H A Salim 11. Singles cost from US$45 to US$70, doubles from US$60 to US$85, and there is a 15% tax and service. The *Cipta Hotel* (☎ 3904701), Jalan Wahid Hasyim 53, is right opposite the southern end of Jalan Jaksa. Good mid-range rooms in this new hotel cost US$63 to US$68, plus 17.5%.

There's an enclave of mid-range hotels just south-east of the city centre, along Jalan Cikini Raya and Jalan Gondangdia Lama. There are three Hotel Mentengs – *Menteng I*

INDONESIA

(☎ 325208) is at Jalan Gondangdia Lama 28, *Menteng II* (☎ 325543) is at Jalan Cikini Raya 105 and the newest, *Grand Menteng* (☎ 881863), is at Jalan Matraman Raya 21. Rooms are around 100,000 rp. *Hotel Marcopolo* (☎ 325409) at Jalan Cik Ditiro 19 is slightly cheaper. These places all have a pool and other amenities.

Airport The new Soekarno-Hatta airport at Cengkareng is a long way from central Jakarta. The terminal buildings seem to be shut up at night so there's probably no chance of sleeping there overnight.

The other option is the *Cengkareng Transit Hotel* (☎ 611964, 614194) at Jalan Jurumudi Km 2.5, Cengkareng. There's nothing fancy about it – air-con rooms with bath are 47,000/63,000 rp and there's a 24-hour coffee shop. They operate a free minibus service which takes about 20 to 30 minutes from the airport.

Places to Eat

There's no shortage of eating places in Jakarta. They range from the cheap travellers' centres along Jalan Jaksa to a diverse collection of Western fast-food purveyors and some fancy local restaurants.

Popular places along Jalan Jaksa, all dishing out the standard travellers' menu, include *Angie's Cafe, Memories Cafe, Anedja Cafe* and, topping the popularity polls, *Nick's Corner Restaurant*, next to the hotel of the same name. The food is so-so, but they have video movies in the evening and the disco at the back can get pretty lively.

At the top end of Jalan Jaksa, on Jalan Kebon Sirih, is the *Senayan Satay House* at No 31A. It is comfortable, air-con and more expensive but the food is good. Further west at No 40, *Ikan Bakar Kebon Sirih* specialises in that popular Sulawesi dish Makassar-style roast fish (ikan bakar).

Jalan H A Salim is probably the food centre of Jakarta and boasts many types of restaurants. For Padang food try the *Budi Bundo* or the more expensive, but still moderately priced *Natrabu*, where the Padang food is excellent. If you only try Padang food once in your whole stay in Indonesia, then this is an excellent place to do it.

Sakura Anpan, a Japanese bakery at No 25/27, has a truly mind-blowing selection of cakes, pastries and ice creams. *Lim Thiam Kie* at No 53 serves excellent and economical Chinese food, while *Paradiso 2001*, just down an alley off Jalan H A Salim, is a vegetarian restaurant.

Western fast food along this strip includes *KFC*, *A&W* and *Sizzlers*; home-grown varieties include *Kim's Hamburgers* and *Jakarta Ayam Goreng*. *Hoka Hoka Bento*, a popular Japanese fast-food chain, is also represented.

For more fast food, the Jakarta Theatre building on Jalan Thamrin has *Pizza Hut*, *California Fried Chicken* and the *Cafe A&A* upstairs. On the ground floor, the *Green Pub*, a popular expat hang-out, has Mexican food and live music at night – Indonesians dressed in the outfits of Mexican wranglers seem a bit odd at first but you soon get used to it. Happy hour is from 3 to 6 pm. Of course, you can have a big mac in Jakarta. Indonesia's first *McDonald's* is at the front of the Sarinah department store on Jalan Thamrin. The *Sarinah department store* also has a supermarket and a very expensive but good foodstall area in the basement.

Continue down Jalan Thamrin to the very popular, neat and clean *Bakmi Gajah Madah* with its extensive menu of noodle and rice dishes from around 4000 rp. There's more Western fast food further down Jalan Thamrin under the Grand Hyatt.

For real Indonesian food at a rock-bottom price, there are lots of *night stalls* along Jalan Kebon Sirih and Jalan Wahid Hasyim. Some of them are of dubious cleanliness, so inspect them first.

You'll find plenty of *Chinese restaurants* in the Glodok area, numerous places along Jalan Gajah Mada (north-west of Monas), and the Blok M shopping centre, way down Jalan Thamrin in Kebayoran Baru, also has a wide variety of places to eat.

On Jalan Thamrin, between the Hotel Indonesia and the Kartika Plaza Hotel, the *George & Dragon Pub* looks as properly British as suggested by its name. It's a good

INDONESIA

place for a beer and they also do some of the best Indian food in Jakarta.

Cross Jalan Thamrin and go down Jalan Blora, turn left along Jalan Kendal (which runs beside the railway line) and you'll come to a string of interesting *foodstalls*.

Entertainment

The Jakarta cultural centre, *Taman Ismail Marzuki* or TIM, hosts all kinds of cultural performances – Western and Indonesian. Here you can see everything from Balinese dancing to poetry readings, movies to gamelan concerts, a batik exhibition or the planetarium. Events are listed in the TIM monthly programme and in the daily *Jakarta Post*. Bus No 34 from Jalan Thamrin for Megaria/Rawamangun will get you to TIM (☎ 322606) at Jalan Cikini Raya 73.

At 8.15 pm every evening, except Monday and Thursday, wayang orang can be seen at the *Bharata Theatre*, Jalan Kalilio 15 near the Pasar Senen. Ketoprak (Javanese folk theatre) performances also take place here on Monday and Thursday evening.

Getting There & Away

Jakarta is the main travel hub for Indonesia. From here, ships depart for ports on the other islands, flights fan out all over the archipelago, trains come and go for other parts of Java and buses depart for destinations not only throughout Java but also for Bali and the towns in Sumatra.

Air Most flights go from the newer Soekarno-Hatta international airport although some domestic flights (eg to Bandung, Bandar Lampung, Cirebon) use the more centrally located Halim airport. Airport tax is 17,000 rp on international flights (payable at check-in) and 5000 rp on domestic flights (usually included in the ticket price).

The domestic airline offices are dotted around the city. Garuda has several offices around town including one in the BDN Building (☎ 334425), Jalan Thamrin 5, and another in the Hotel Indonesia (☎ 3100568, 3100570). Mandala (☎ 4246100) is at Jalan Garuda No 79, out near the Pelni office. Merpati (☎ 413608) is at Jalan Angkasa 2, and Bouraq (☎ 6295150) is at Jalan Angkasa 1-3, both in Kemayoran. Any Garuda office can handle Merpati bookings. Sempati have several offices, including one at Jalan Merdeka Timur 7 (☎ 3851450) and at the Plaza Indonesia (☎ 3100575) on Jalan Thamrin. Travel agents can also sell domestic tickets – it pays to shop around.

For international flights, Travel International (☎ 330103), in the Plaza Indonesia next to the Hyatt Hotel on Jalan Thamrin, is a good place to look for cheap tickets, as is Vayatour (☎ 3100720) next door. Pacto Ltd (☎ 320309), Jalan Cikini Raya 24 (south-east of Monas), is one of Indonesia's largest travel agents, and the agent for STA Travel is Indo Shangrila Travel (☎ 632703), Jalan Gajah Mada 219G (north-west of Monas). Sea Breeze Travel (☎ 326675) and Balimaesti are two agents conveniently located on Jalan Jaksa. Discounting has seen the one-way fare to Singapore as low as US$70 – Sempati is often one of the cheapest.

Within Indonesia, published Merpati fares from Jakarta include Biak for 598,000 rp, Batam for 204,000 rp, Denpasar for 195,000 rp, Jayapura for 662,000 rp, Kupang for 393,000 rp, Medan for 300,000 rp, Padang for 215,000 rp, Pontianak for 174,000 rp, Surabaya for 161,000 rp, Ujung Pandang for 293,000 rp and Yogyakarta for 111,000 rp.

Bus There are city bus stations in all the main districts of Jakarta – Grogol in the west, Kampung Rambutan way out in the south and Pulo Gadung in the east – and buses radiate out from them to the suburban inter-city stations. Prices quoted below are the average for non-air-con buses. Dozens of bus companies operate the major routes and offer a variety of services – eg air-con services to Yogyakarta start at around 17,500 rp and run up to 28,000 rp for super luxury buses.

Buses to towns south of Jakarta go from the Kampung Rambutan bus station out past Halim Perdanakusuma airport. Buses from here go to Bogor (800 rp), Puncak, Sukabumi, Pelabuhanratu, Bandung (2800 rp) and Banjar (5000 rp).

Buses to Central and Eastern Java operate from the Pulo Gadung station. Destinations include Cirebon (4100 rp, five hours), Yogyakarta (11,000 rp, 13 hours) and Surabaya (13,500 rp, 15 hours).

Buses for Merak (2000 rp, three hours) depart every 10 minutes between 3 am and midnight from the Kalideres bus station in the north-west. This is also the place for buses to Labuhan (for Carita Beach, seven km to the north of Labuhan) (3000 rp) and Sumatran destinations such as Palembang (12,500 rp), Pekanbaru (23,000 rp) and Padang (24,000 rp).

Train Jakarta has a number of train stations, the most convenient of which is Gambir, on the eastern side of Merdeka Square and within walking distance of Jalan Jaksa. Gambir handles trains to Bogor, Bandung, Yogyakarta, Solo and Semarang. Pasar Senen, to the east, has mostly local trains to eastern destinations including Semarang, Surabaya, Yogyakarta and Solo. Jakarta Kota is in the old city area in the north and departures include the luxury express trains *Bima* and *Mutiara* to Surabaya via Yogyakarta or Semarang. Tanah Abang, to the west, has trains to Merak (1600 rp, 3½ hours). The morning train is faster and connects with the daytime ferry service from Merak to Bakauheni in Sumatra.

The bajaj and taxi drivers at Gambir are a mercenary lot. It shouldn't cost more than 1000 rp to Jalan Jaksa, but after waiting for who-knows-how-long for a fare, they want more for the short trip – either pay over the odds or walk to the road and hail a taxi or bajaj. Allow plenty of time to get to Kota station during the rush hour – a metered taxi is about 3500 rp from Jalan Jaksa.

To Bogor The train to Bogor runs every 20 minutes or so from Kota, stopping at Gambir on the way through. Trains can be horribly crowded during rush hour, but otherwise provide a good service. The fare is 700 rp from Kota and 650 rp from Gambir for the 1½ hour trip.

To Bandung The *Parahyangan* service departs roughly every hour between 5 am and 8 pm from Gambir station and takes three hours. Fares are 12,000 rp in bisnis class. There is also the Galuh service from Pasar Senen at 2.20 pm which costs 4500 rp ekonomi and 11,000 rp bisnis.

To Cirebon Most trains that run along the north coast leave from Gambir. Cirebon trains take three to four hours and vary from 6000 rp in ekonomi to 31,000 rp in bisnis on the *Mutiara Utara*. There are also services continuing on to Semarang, Yogyakarta and/or Surabaya.

To Yogyakarta Jakarta to Yogyakarta takes nine to 12 hours and most departures are from Gambir station. Fares vary from 5000 rp in ekonomi, and from 7500 rp in bisnis. The deluxe *Bima Express* costs from 36,000 rp in bisnis up to 94,000 rp for a sleeper.

To Surabaya Trains between Jakarta and Surabaya either take the shorter northern route via Semarang or the longer southern route via Yogyakarta. The trip takes 10 to 17 hours although, in practice, the slower 3rd-class trains can take even longer. Fares start at 10,000 rp in ekonomi and 26,000 rp in bisnis.

Taxi There are fast and convenient, but rather more expensive, intercity taxis and minibuses to Bandung. Fares start from 11,000 rp and they depart as soon as they have five passengers. You can book ahead and they will pick you up from your hotel as well as drop you off at your hotel when you get there.

Media Taxis are at Jalan Johar, near Jalan Jaksa. The 4848 Taxis (☎ 364488) are at Jalan Prapatan 34, just beyond the Aryaduta Hyatt Hotel.

Boat See the Indonesia Getting Around section for information on the Pelni shipping

INDONESIA

services which operate on a regular two-week schedule to ports all over the archipelago. Most of them go through Jakarta (Tanjung Priok Harbour). The Pelni ticketing office (☎ 4211921) is at Jalan Angkasa No 18, to the north-east of the centre. Pelni agents charge a small premium but are much more convenient – try Panintama Tour & Travel (☎ 3902076), in the Sarinah department store building on Jalan Thamrin.

Ships go from Jakarta to Tanjung Pinang in the Riau Archipelago, from where it is just a short ferry ride to Singapore. As well as the Pelni boats, the MV *Bintan Permata* leaves Jakarta every Wednesday and Saturday at 4 pm for Tanjung Pinang, arriving at 2 pm the following day. It costs 91,500 rp in economy or 111,500 rp in 1st class. Bookings can be made through travel agents or PT Admiral Lines, 21 Jalan Raya Pelabuhan, right on Tanjung Priok Harbour.

Getting Around

To/From the Airport Soekarno-Hatta is a long way out to the west of the city at Cengkareng. Allow at least an hour to cover the 35 km although you can do it in half an hour when it is quiet, eg Sunday morning. Getting into and out of Jakarta is the problem; once you're on the toll highway it's plain sailing.

There's a Damri bus service every 30 minutes between the airport and Gambir station (close to Jalan Jaksa) in central Jakarta. This quick and convenient service costs 3500 rp. Alternatively, a metered taxi costs about 25,000 rp, including the 6000-rp road toll and the additional airport surcharge. Some Jalan Jaksa hostels have minibuses to the airport for 25,000 rp. They are convenient but no bargain, and they may not use the toll road.

To/From Tanjung Priok Harbour The Pelni ships all use Pelabuhan (dock) No 1. The Tanjung Priok bus station is two km from the dock, past the harbour Pelni office. From Tanjung Priok, bus P14 runs along Jalan Kebon Sirih for Jalan Jaksa before terminating at Tanah Abang, west of the centre. Tanjung Priok is quite a distance from the centre of the city, so allow at least an hour to get there. A taxi will cost around 6000 rp.

Bus The regular big city buses charge a fixed 250 rp, and the express Patas buses, which are usually less crowded, charge 600 rp. The Pasar Senen bus station, to the east of Merdeka Square, is the most central bus terminal. There are also a number of other stations for suburban and intercity buses, like the Grogol and Pulo Gadung bus stations. The regular bus service is supplemented by orange metro-minis (minibuses) and, in a few areas, by pale blue mikrolet buses.

Be warned that Jakarta's crowded buses are notorious for their pickpockets and bag slashers. They will gang up on you, and the buses will often be so crowded you can't do anything anyway. Bus No 70 between Kota railway or Kota bus stations and the Jalan Thamrin area is particularly bad and many guesthouses have signs recommending that you completely avoid this bus and take a taxi, despite the cost. The air-con Patas are generally safer.

Tourist office handouts have useful information on getting to Jakarta's main attractions by public transport. Buses all have their ultimate destination on the front. The Sarinah department store on Jalan Thamrin is a popular landmark and within easy walking distance of Jalan Jaksa. Some of the useful buses which will drop you off there include:

No	*From*
408 & P11*	Kampung Rambutan bus station
59	Pulo Gadung bus station
16	Kalideres bus station
70, P1* & P11*	Kota railway station
10	Pasar Senen bus & railway stations
34	TIM on Jalan Cikini Raya
10, 12 & 16	Blok M, Kebayoran

*P is for Patas or express
Bus Nos 10, 12 & 110 go by the post office

Taxi The taxis in Jakarta are modern, well-kept, and have air-con and working meters which are used without argument (those at Gambir station are about the only exception – see the information on trains in the previous Getting There & Away section). Flagfall is 900 rp, then 50 rp more for each additional 100 metres. The Bluebird Taxis have a good reputation.

Local Transport Bajaj are nothing less than Indian auto-rickshaws – three wheelers that carry two passengers (three at a squeeze) and are powered by noisy two-stroke engines. You can get most places for less than 1000 rp but bajaj are not allowed along Jalan Thamrin.

Becaks (bicycle rickshaws) are banned from Jakarta and the authorities seized thousands of them and dumped them in the sea, creating a becak reef. Around Sunda Kelapa, the old port area north of Kota, you can get around on bicycles with padded 'kiddy carriers' on the back. A rider will dink you from Sunda Kelapa to Taman Fatahillah Square in Old Batavia for 500 rp!

AROUND JAKARTA

Pulau Seribu

Pulau Seribu, or Thousand Islands, start only a few km out in the Bay of Jakarta. Some of them are virtually deserted and have fine beaches but others can be very crowded, particularly on weekends. Many have resorts. The Visitor's Information Centre produces a useful pamphlet listing resort and transport prices for the islands.

Getting There & Away Daily boats go to some islands, or boats can be hired, from the Marina at Ancol. You can also reach some of the islands by light aircraft. It's a one-hour boat trip (15 km) from the Marina to Pulau Bidadari, and you can reach other islands from there. Boats leave at 10 am and 5 pm during the week, returning at 7 am and 3 pm.

Phinisi Nusantara (☎ 7396602) is a Bugis schooner that does day trips (US$35) and weekend packages (US$145) to the islands from Sunda Kelapa.

MERAK

This is the port at the western end of Java, from where the ferry crosses to Sumatra. It's a small place and the bus and train stations are within easy walking distance of each other.

Places to Stay

If you have to spend the night in Merak, there are a couple of reasonable losmen just across the railway line and opposite the bus station, on Jalan Florida. The *Hotel Anda* has rooms from 12,500 rp, and the *Hotel Robinson* is right next door.

Getting There & Away

Buses for Merak depart frequently from the Kalideres bus station in Jakarta. Trains leave at 6 am and 5 pm from the Tanah Abang railway station.

Ferries to Bakauheni in Sumatra depart every hour from the dock near the bus station; the trip takes 1½ hours and costs from 1500 rp. Refer to the Sumatra Getting There & Away section for more details.

BANTEN

En route to Merak from Jakarta, you pass through Serang, which marks the turn-off for the historic town of Banten – this is where the bedraggled Dutch first set foot on Java in 1596. In the 16th and 17th centuries, the town was the centre of a great and wealthy sultanate but it's hardly splendid now.

There's not a lot to see around this small coastal village but Banten has an interesting mosque, the **Mesjid Agung**, and a great white lighthouse of a minaret which was designed by a Chinese Muslim in the early 17th century. The old palaces are now in ruins and the Dutch **Speelwijk Fortress**, built in 1682, is equally decayed.

WEST COAST

There are good beaches along the west coast, between Labuhan and Merak, at **Anyer**, **Karang Bolong** and **Carita**. Labuhan has no bank – change money beforehand.

Carita, seven km north of Labuhan, is a good base for visits to the **Krakatau Islands**

INDONESIA

in the Sunda Strait, about 50 km from Carita and Labuhan. Boat hire to the site of the world's biggest explosion is expensive and difficult to find during the wet season.

The **Ujung Kulon National Park** is home to the near-extinct Javan rhinoceros and the near-extinct Javan rainforest. Get park permits and book accommodation at the Labuhan PHPA office, about two km from the centre of town on the road to Carita.

Places to Stay

Anyer has a couple of luxury beach hotels, and further south at Carita the rustic *Carita Krakatau Beach Hotel* has rooms from as low as US$9, rather more on weekends; beds are US$4 in the associated *Hostel Rakata*. The Visitor's Information Centre in Jakarta can arrange discounts. Another budget alternative is the *Losmen Grogana*, one km away from the Carita Krakatau, with rooms for 10,000 rp.

Accommodation at Ujung Kulon is in *PHPA bungalows* at two islands off the mainland – Gili Peucang, the most popular place, and Gili Handeuleum – and at Taman Jaya, on the edge of the park.

Getting There & Away

Carita is a pleasant place if you want to escape from Jakarta for a few days but it's close enough to the capital for it to get crowded at weekends. Buses go hourly from the Kalideres bus station in Jakarta to Labuhan (3000 rp, four hours), and colts run from Labuhan to Carita. Anyer, Carita and Labuhan can also be reached from Merak. First take a bus to Cilegon and then another bus along the coast road.

Boats to Krakatau can be chartered from the PHPA in Labuhan or from Carita Krakatau Beach Hotel for around 400,000 rp. This can work out to be about 30,000 rp per person, depending on the number of people going. Fishing boats, which have a poor reputation, will cost about 240,000 rp.

Inquire at a PHPA office about getting to Ujung Kulon. Boats can be chartered or a regular boat goes to the park and its offshore islands on Monday and Friday for 60,000 rp per person one way from Labuhan. It is also possible to hire transport to go overland to Taman Jaya.

BOGOR

The **Kebun Raya** are huge botanical gardens in the centre of Bogor, which is just 60 km from Jakarta. Sir Stamford Raffles founded them in 1817, during the British interregnum, and they have a huge collection of tropical plants. A monument to Raffles' wife, Olivia, is near the main entrance to the gardens. The gardens are open from 8 am to 5 pm every day. Admission is 1100 rp. The gardens get very crowded on Sundays and public holidays.

The **Presidential Palace**, built by the Dutch and much favoured by Sukarno (Suharto has ignored it), stands beside the gardens and deer graze on its lawns. The palace is not normally open to the public but tours can be arranged through the tourist office.

Near the garden entrance, the **Zoological Museum** exhibits a blue whale skeleton and other interesting items. If you ever heard about the island of Flores having a rat problem, one glance at the stuffed Flores version in the showcase of Indonesian rats will explain why. Admission to the museum is 400 rp and it's open from 8 am to 4 pm daily.

Information

Bogor's Visitor's Information Centre is at Jalan Ir H Juanda 10, west of the gardens. In the same government complex is the headquarters of the PHPA, the administrative body for all of Indonesia's wildlife reserves.

Places to Stay

Bogor has a good selection of family-run places which make staying in Bogor a real pleasure, even though they're a little expensive. Most budget travellers head for the Abu or Firman pensiones.

Abu Pensione (☎ 322893), near the railway station at Jalan Mayor Oking 15, is clean, attractive and pleasantly situated. It overlooks the river and has a nice garden.

PLACES TO STAY

1 Wisma Mirah
2 Wisma Teladan
5 Elsana Transit Hotel
7 Wisma Karunia
8 Sempur Kencana Hotel
9 Hotel Pangrango
10 Bogar Inn
12 Hotel Salak
15 Abu Pensione
22 Wisma Permata
24 Homestay Puri Bali & Pensione Firman
25 Wisma Ramayana
30 Wisma Duta

PLACES TO EAT

3 Bogar Permai Coffee House
4 Night Market
6 Lautan Restaurant
16 Food Court
17 Singapore Bakery
18 Night Market
19 Hidangan Trio Masakan Padang & Hidangang Puti Bungsu
21 Pizza Hut
28 Kentucky Fried Chicken
31 Adem Ayem Restaurant
32 Dunia Baru Restaurant
33 No 99 Restaurant

OTHER

11 Presidential Palace
13 Visitor's Information Centre
14 Train Station
20 Orchid House
23 Post Office
26 Zoological Museum
27 Botanical Gardens Entrance
29 Bus Station
34 Gong Foundry

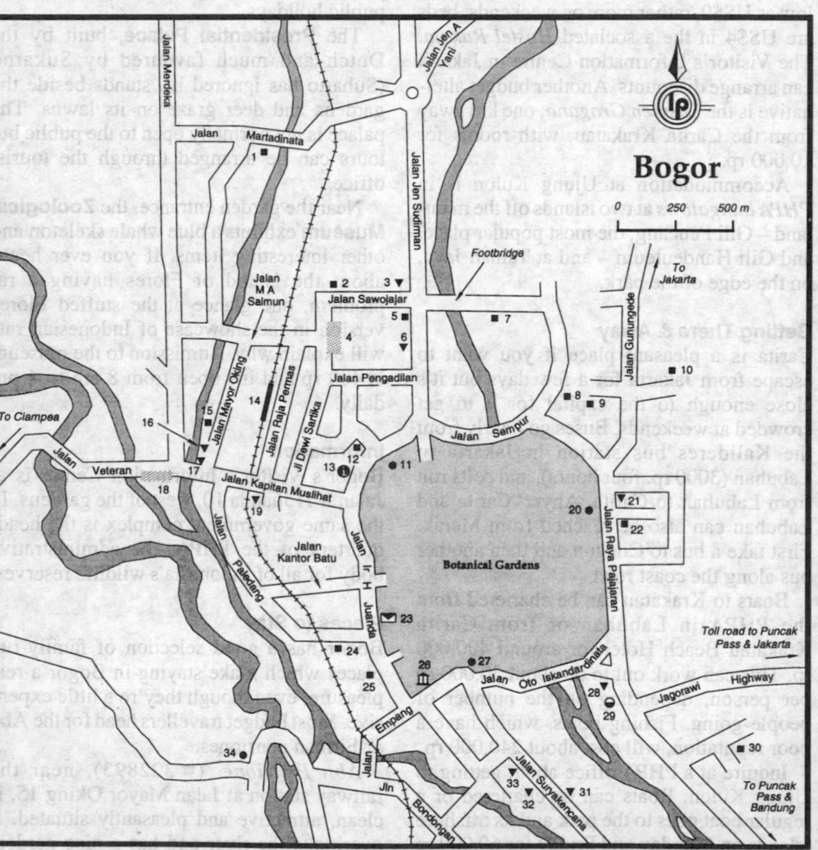

INDONESIA

Dorm beds cost 5000 rp or doubles are 15,000 rp in the rickety old section. Rooms with a bath in the new section start at 20,000 rp. Another relatively cheap alternative near the railway station is the well-run *Efita Hotel* (☎ 335327) at Jalan Sawojajar 5. Rooms without bath cost 12,500 rp, or from 15,000 rp for rooms with bath.

Just across from the gardens at Jalan Ir H Juanda 54 is the very colonial *Wisma Ramayana* (☎ 320364) which has a variety of singles/doubles from 17,000/18,000 rp without bath, and better rooms with bath from 28,000 rp to 43,000 rp. Breakfast is included.

Round the corner at Jalan Paledang 50 is the *Homestay Puri Bali* (☎ 317498) with rooms for 13,000/17,500 rp and 15,000/20,000 rp. All rooms have a bath and there is an attractive garden restaurant. Next door at No 48, *Pensione Firman* (☎ 323426) is the cheapest around with dorm beds at 6000 rp, and rooms for 10,000/13,000 rp or 15,000/20,000 rp with bath, all including breakfast.

On the other side of the gardens, but a little difficult to get to, are a number of very good mid-range guesthouses, similar to the Ramayana. Try *Wisma Duta* (☎ 328494) on Jalan Baranangsiang II, Kav 7, *Wisma Karunia* (☎ 323411) at Jalan Sempur 35-37, or *Sempur Kencana Guest House* (☎ 328347, 326584) at Jalan Sempur 6.

Places to Eat

The guesthouses all try hard to keep their guests well fed. Otherwise, the best cheap eats in Bogor are the *night markets* which set up on Jalan Dewi Sartika and Jalan Veteran.

On the corner of Jalan Veteran and Jalan Mayor Oking, there's the *Singapore Bakery*, and next door is the *Food Court* with several foodstalls. More places can be found behind the adjacent Muria Plaza shopping centre including *Es Teler KK*, a good place for lunch. Near the railway station, on Jalan Kapitan Muslihat, the *Hidangan Trio Masakan Padang* and the *Hidangan Puti Bungsu* are good bets for Padang food.

Up Jalan Sudirman, some distance north of the town centre, the *Lautan Restaurant* is a big, modern, featureless place with rather dull and expensive fare. The nearby *Bogor Permai Coffee House* has a similar menu but also has a supermarket area, a bakery and a more expensive restaurant.

Getting There & Away

Bus Buses can do the trip in 30 minutes if the traffic is not too heavy, are generally more comfortable and cost 800 rp. The only problem is that they go from/arrive at the Kampung Rambutan station in Jakarta, which is too far out to be convenient. A Jalan Tol (expressway) bus is faster than the buses which go via Cibinong.

Buses depart frequently from Bogor to Bandung (2200 rp, three hours). On weekends, buses are not allowed to go via the scenic Puncak Pass (it gets very crowded) and have to travel via Sukabumi. Not only does the trip take much longer, it's also more expensive at 2600 rp.

Train Trains to/from Jakarta leave about every 20 minutes until 8.20 pm and take about 1½ hours. They cost 650 rp to/from Gambir station or 700 rp to Kota. The trains are reasonably efficient but are best avoided during peak hours when they can be horribly crowded.

Taxi From Bogor, taxis and door-to-door minibuses also go to Bandung for 11,000 rp – the guesthouses such as Abu Pensione can arrange them.

Getting Around

Bemos shuttle around town, particularly between the bus and railway station, in an anticlockwise loop around the gardens. The three-wheelers cost 250 rp and the four-wheelers 300 rp. Becaks are banned from the main road encircling the gardens – in any case, getting them to go where you want to go is not always easy! You can rent bicycles from the Abu Pensione.

AROUND BOGOR

There are a number of small resort towns and tea plantations on the way up and over the beautiful Puncak Pass, between Bogor and Bandung. You can make pleasant walks from Tugu and Cisarua on the Bogor side of the pass, or from Cibodas and Cipanas on the other side.

On the way up to the Puncak summit from Bogor, you can stop at the **Gunung Mas Tea Plantation** and tour the tea factory or visit the pleasant lake of **Telaga Warna** (just before the summit).

At **Cibodas**, just over the Puncak Pass, there is a cooler, high-altitude extension of the Bogor botanical gardens. The gardens are four km off the main road and only a short distance from Cipanas. From here, you can climb **Gunung Gede**, a volcano peak offering fine views of the surrounding area. You have to obtain permission first from the PHPA office at the entrance to the gardens, and they provide good maps of the route. The walk takes all day, so start as early as possible.

Places to Stay

The *Kopo Hostel* (☎ 0251-4296) at Jalan Raya Puncak 557 in Cisarua is on the main Bogor-Bandung road. It has its own garden, dorm beds for 6000 rp and rooms from 12,500 rp; blankets are provided. It's about 45 minutes by bus or colt from Bogor.

Also in Cisarua, *Chalet Bali International* is affiliated with the Bali International in Jakarta and has dorm beds and rooms but it is not as good as the Kopo Hostel.

In Cibulan, the *Hotel Cibulan* is an old-world Dutch hotel – it's run-down but friendly. Rooms cost from around 7500 rp – they're more expensive on weekends when people from Jakarta flock up here to escape the heat.

The *Pondok Pemuda Cibodas*, near the Cibodas PHPA office, is comfortable, friendly and has dorm beds and rooms.

In the village, 500 metres down the hill, you can stay with *Mohammed Saleh Abdullah* (also known as Freddy) for rock-bottom prices.

Getting There & Away

You can get up to the towns on the pass by taking a colt or any Bandung bus from Bogor.

PELABUHANRATU

From Bogor, you can continue south-west of the small town of Sukabumi to Pelabuhanratu, a popular coastal resort where swimming, surfing and walking are possible. There are rocky cliffs, caves and gorges to explore and a fine beach but the sea here is treacherous and signs warn swimmers away. You're best off in the hotel pool.

Places to Stay & Eat

Pelabuhanratu is very crowded on weekends and it's expensive. There are a number of *beach bungalows* to rent along the four km between the big Samudra Beach Hotel and Pelabuhanratu's fish market, but prices are likely to be over 15,000 rp. The *Bayu Amrta* (also known as the Fish Restaurant or Hoffman's), at the edge of a cliff, has doubles from 25,000 to 32,000 rp and the restaurant is known for its good seafood.

Getting There & Away

Take a bus or train from Bogor to Cibadak or Sukabumi, then take a colt, or there are buses from Bandung.

BANDUNG

The capital of west Java and the third largest city in Indonesia, Bandung's chief claim to fame is that it was the site for the first (and so far only) Afro-Asian conference back in 1955. Third World leaders from a variety of countries converged on Bandung but not much seems to have happened since. The city's 750-metre altitude makes the climate cool and comfortable. Treat it as a short stop between Jakarta and Yogyakarta.

It's worth a brief pause to visit the nearby volcano, Tangkuban Perahu, and there are several interesting museums. If you travel between Bandung and Bogor take the bus so you can see the beautiful Puncak Pass. Bandung is a big university town which is surprisingly go-ahead and affluent.

Information

The very helpful Visitor's Information Centre is on the corner of Alun Alun Square, the main square on Jalan Asia-Afrika.

The Golden Megah Corp moneychanger is an easy place to change cash and travellers' cheques and it stays open later than the banks.

Museums

At Jalan Diponegoro 57, in the northern part of the city, the **Geological Museum** has some interesting exhibits including relief maps and volcano models.

If the Afro-Asian conference really fascinates you, then visit the **Freedom Building** (Gedung Merdeka) for the full story of the meeting between Sukarno, Chou En-Lai, Ho Chi Minh, Nasser and other figureheads of the Third World of the 1950s. It's on Jalan Asia-Afrika near the city centre.

Other museums include the **Army Museum** on Jalan Lembong, with its grim and explicit photographs of the Darul Islam rebellion. The **West Java Cultural Museum** is south-west of the city centre on Jalan Oto Iskandardinata (Jalan Otista for short). It is closed Monday.

Jeans St

Bandung is a centre for clothing manufacture and shops on a km-long strip of Jalan Cihampelas compete for the most outrageous shopfronts and decor. It's definitely worth seeing, and the jeans and T-shirts are cheap.

Other Attractions

Bandung is noted for its fine Dutch Art-Deco architecture. The expensive **Savoy Homann Hotel** and the restored **Grand Hotel Preanger** are worth a look. Also take a look at the magnificent **Regional Government Building** near the Geological Museum. It's known as Gedung Sate, or the Sate Building, because it's topped by what looks like a sate stick.

Bandung's ITB or Institute of Technology is one of the most important universities in Indonesia – it's on the north side of the city. On Jalan Taman Sari, close to the ITB, Bandung's **zoo** has Komodo dragons, open park space and a wide variety of Indonesian bird life. Once a fortnight, on Sunday morning, traditional ram-butting fights are held at Ranca Buni, near Ledeng to the north of the city.

Places to Stay

Jalan Kebonjati, near the railway station and the city centre, is the place to head for. *By Moritz* (☎ 437264), Kompleks Luxor Permai 18, Jalan Kebonjati, is an excellent, well-managed travellers' hotel, and even has a computerised billing system. Dorm beds cost 5000 rp and immaculate rooms are 10,500/15,000 rp. Breakfast is included.

Le Yossie Homestay (☎ 4205453), 53 Jalan Kebonjati, is another new, excellent place and good value. The four-bed dorm costs 4000 rp per person; singles/doubles/triples are 8500/12,000/15,000 rp.

Other options are the two Sakadarnas. At Jalan Kebonjati 34, the *Sakardana International Travellers Homestay* used to be Bandung's No 1 travellers' place but is looking a little tired. It's clean with dorm beds at 4000 rp or basic doubles at 10,000 rp. The original *Losmen Sakardana* (☎ 439897) is down a little alley beside the Hotel Melati at No 50/7B. Basic but well-kept rooms are 7000/11,000 rp.

Jalan Kebonjati also has a few hotels, though Bandung's hotels are quite expensive. The *Hotel Surabaya* (☎ 444133) at No 71 is a rambling, older-style hotel which has recently had a facelift. Rooms start at 10,000/17,500 rp or 12,500/17,500 rp with bath.

Jalan Kebonjati has two Melati Hotels. *Hotel Melati*, right by the Losmen Sakardana, is tatty and costs 12,500 rp or 15,000/20,000 rp with bath. Across the road, the *Hotel Melati II* (☎ 446409) is better with singles at 20,000 rp and doubles from 30,000 rp.

Across the railway tracks at Jalan Oto Iskandardinata 3, the *Hotel Sahara* (☎ 51684) costs 12,000/19,000 rp, or doubles with bath cost 25,000 to 45,000 rp.

INDONESIA

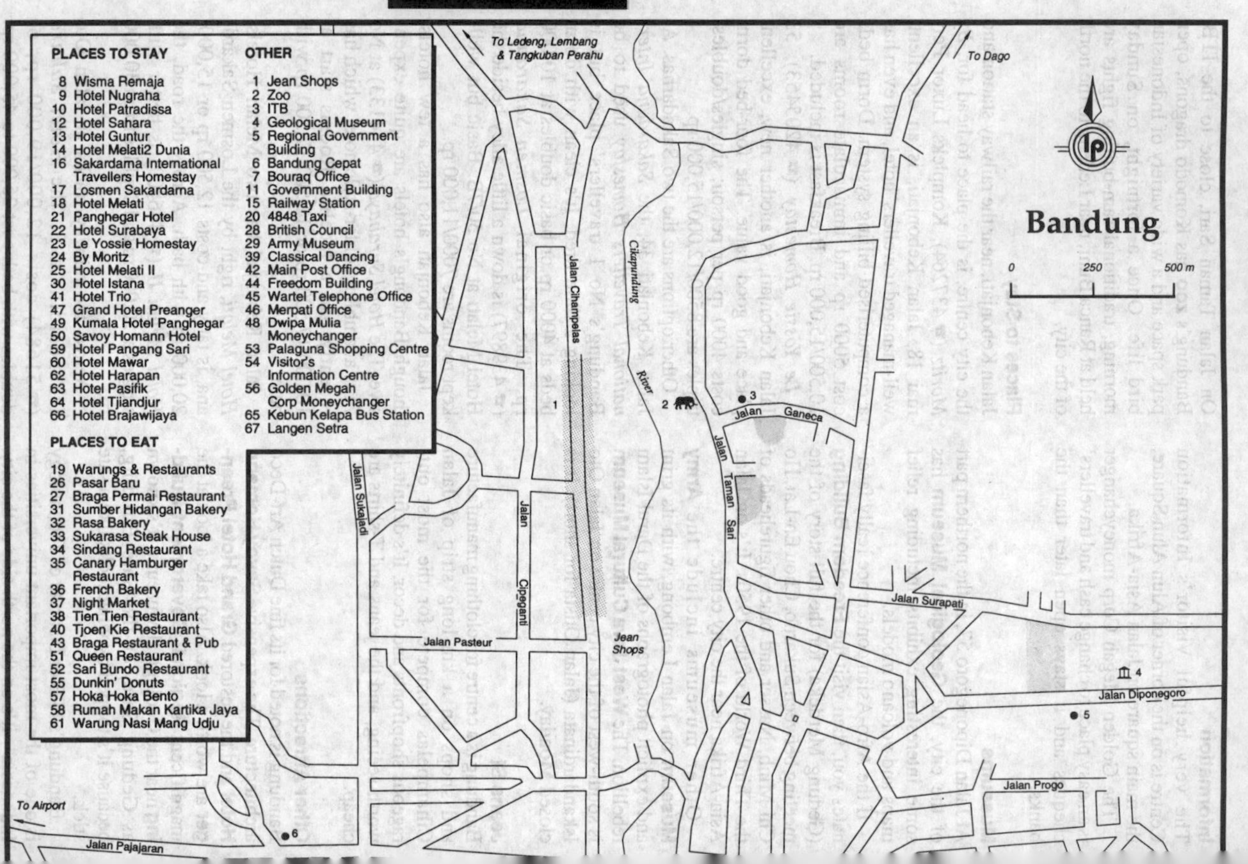
Bandung
0
250
500 m
To Ledeng, Lembang
& Tangkuban Perahu
To Dago
To Airport
Jalan Pajajaran
Jalan Sukajadi
Jalan Pasteur
Jalan Cipeganti
Jalan Cihampelas
Cikapundung River
Jean Shops
Jalan Ganeca
Jalan Taman Sari
Jalan Surapati
Jalan Diponegoro
Jalan Progo
PLACES TO STAY
8 Wisma Remaja
9 Hotel Nugraha
10 Hotel Patradissa
12 Hotel Sahara
13 Hotel Guntur
14 Hotel Melati2 Dunia
16 Sakardama International Travellers Homestay
17 Losmen Sakardama
18 Hotel Melati
21 Panghegar Hotel
22 Hotel Surabaya
23 Le Yossie Homestay
24 By Moritz
25 Hotel Melati II
30 Hotel Istana
41 Hotel Trio
47 Grand Hotel Preanger
49 Kumala Hotel Panghegar
50 Savoy Homann Hotel
59 Hotel Pangang Sari
60 Hotel Mawar
62 Hotel Harapan
63 Hotel Pasifik
64 Hotel Tjiandjur
66 Hotel Brajawijaya
PLACES TO EAT
19 Warungs & Restaurants
26 Pasar Baru
27 Braga Permai Restaurant
31 Sumber Hidangan Bakery
32 Rasa Bakery
33 Sukarasa Steak House
34 Sindang Restaurant
35 Canary Hamburger Restaurant
36 French Bakery
37 Night Market
38 Tien Tien Restaurant
40 Tjoen Kie Restaurant
43 Braga Restaurant & Pub
51 Queen Restaurant
52 Sari Bundo Restaurant
55 Dunkin' Donuts
57 Hoka Hoka Bento
58 Rumah Makan Kartika Jaya
61 Warung Nasi Mang Udju
OTHER
1 Jean Shops
2 Zoo
3 ITB
4 Geological Museum
5 Regional Government Building
6 Bandung Cepat
7 Bouraq Office
11 Government Building
15 Railway Station
20 4848 Taxi
28 British Council
29 Army Museum
39 Classical Dancing
42 Main Post Office
44 Freedom Building
45 Wartel Telephone Office
46 Merpati Office
48 Dwipa Mulia Moneychanger
53 Palaguna Shopping Centre
54 Visitor's Information Centre
56 Golden Megah Corp Moneychanger
65 Kebun Kelapa Bus Station
67 Langen Setra

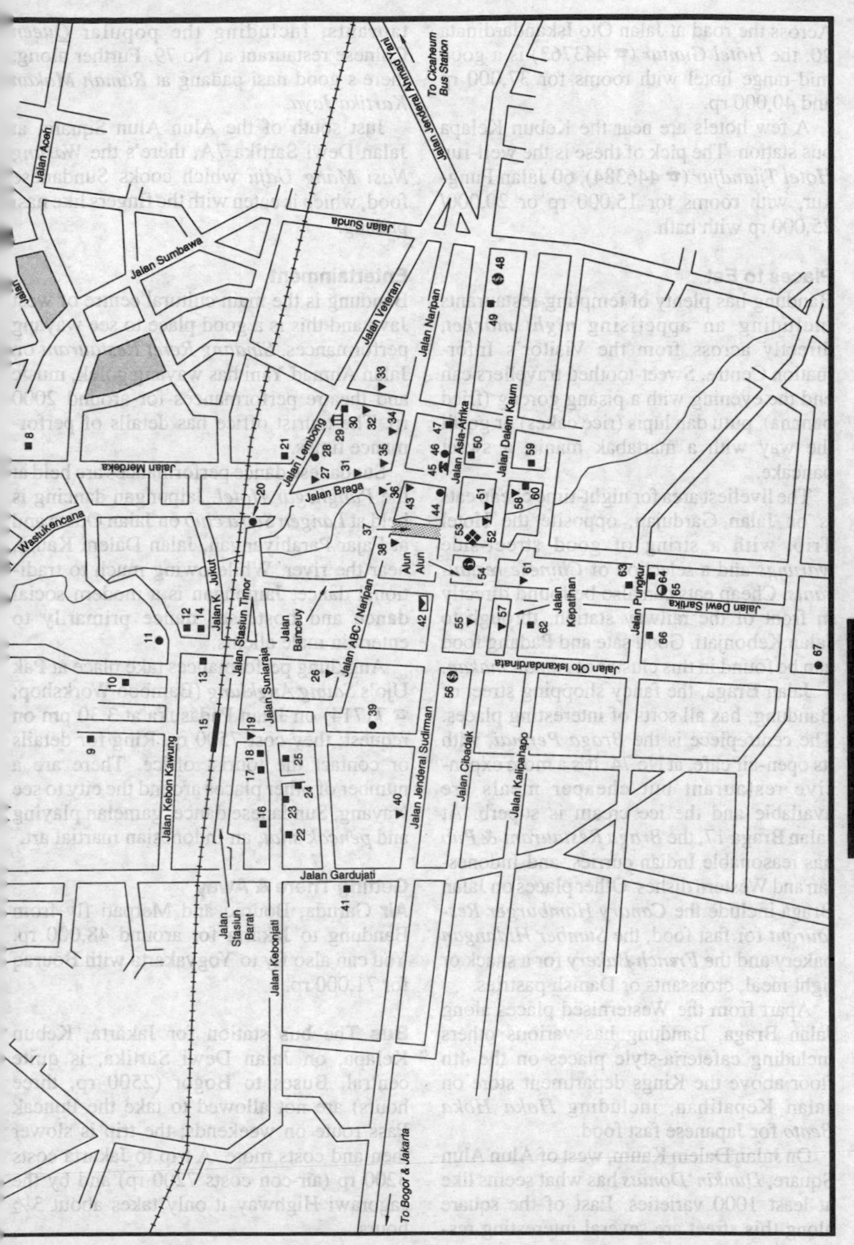

To Cicaheum Bus Station
Jalan Jenderal Ahmad Yani
Jalan Aceh
Jalan Sunda
Jalan Sumbawa
Jalan Veteran
Jalan Naripan
Jalan Merdeka
Jalan Lembong
Jalan Braga
Wastukencana
Jalan Asia-Afrika
Jalan Dalem Kaum
Alun Alun
Jalan ABC / Naripan
Jalan Banceuy
Jalan Suniaraja
Jalan Stasiun Timor
Jalan K. Jukut
Jalan Kebon Kawung
Jalan Stasiun Barat
Jalan Kebonjati
Jalan Gardujati
Jalan Jenderal Sudirman
To Bogor & Jakarta
Jalan Cibadak
Jalan Kalipahapo
Jalan Oto Iskandardinata
Jalan Kepatihan
Jalan Pungkur
Jalan Dewi Sartika

Across the road at Jalan Oto Iskandardinata 20, the *Hotel Guntur* (☎ 443763) is a good mid-range hotel with rooms for 37,000 rp and 40,000 rp.

A few hotels are near the Kebun Kelapa bus station. The pick of these is the well-run *Hotel Tjiandjur* (☎ 446384), 60 Jalan Pungkur, with rooms for 15,000 rp or 20,000/25,000 rp with bath.

Places to Eat

Bandung has plenty of tempting restaurants including an appetising *night market*, directly across from the Visitor's Information Centre. Sweet-toothed travellers can end the evening with a pisang goreng (fried banana), putu dan lupis (rice cakes) or go all the way with a martabak manis, a sweet pancake.

The liveliest area for night-time cheap eats is on Jalan Gardujati, opposite the Hotel Trio, with a string of good street-side *warungs* and a selection of *Chinese restaurants*. Cheap eats can also be found directly in front of the railway station, through to Jalan Kebonjati. Good sate and Padang food can be found in this cluster of *rumah makan*.

Jalan Braga, the fancy shopping street of Bandung, has all sorts of interesting places. The centrepiece is the *Braga Permai*, with its open-air cafe, at No 74. It's a more expensive restaurant but cheaper meals are available and the ice cream is superb. At Jalan Braga 17, the *Braga Restaurant & Pub* has reasonable Indian curries, and Indonesian and Western dishes. Other places on Jalan Braga include the *Canary Hamburger Restaurant* for fast food, the *Sumber Hidangan* bakery and the *French Bakery* for a snack or light meal, croissants or Danish pastries.

Apart from the Westernised places along Jalan Braga, Bandung has various others including cafeteria-style places on the 4th floor above the Kings department store on Jalan Kepatihan, including *Hoka Hoka Bento* for Japanese fast food.

On Jalan Dalem Kaum, west of Alun Alun Square, *Dunkin' Donuts* has what seems like at least 1000 varieties. East of the square along this street are several interesting restaurants, including the popular *Queen* Chinese restaurant at No 79. Further along, there's good nasi padang at *Rumah Makan Kartika Jaya*.

Just south of the Alun Alun Square, at Jalan Dewi Sartika 7A, there's the *Warung Nasi Mang Udju* which cooks Sundanese food, which is eaten with the fingers like nasi padang.

Entertainment

Bandung is the main cultural centre of west Java and this is a good place to see wayang performances. *Sindang Reret Restaurant* on Jalan Ahmad Yani has wayang golek, music and theatre performances for around 2000 rp. The tourist office has details of performance times.

Sundanese dance performances are held at the *Panghegar Hotel*. Jaipongan dancing is held at *Langen Setra club* on Jalan Otista and at Fajar Parahiyangan, Jalan Dalem Kaum, near the river. While owing much to traditional dance, Jaipongan is a modern social dance and hostesses dance primarily to entertain male clients.

Angklung performances take place at Pak Ujo's *Saung Angklung* (Bamboo Workshop; ☎ 71714) on Jalan Padasuka at 3.30 pm on request; they cost 7500 rp. Ring for details or contact the tourist office. There are a number of other places around the city to see wayang, Sundanese dance, gamelan playing and *pencak silat*, an Indonesian martial art.

Getting There & Away

Air Garuda, Bouraq and Merpati fly from Bandung to Jakarta for around 48,000 rp. You can also fly to Yogyakarta with Bouraq for 71,000 rp.

Bus The bus station for Jakarta, Kebun Kelapa, on Jalan Dewi Sartika, is quite central. Buses to Bogor (2500 rp, three hours) are not allowed to take the Puncak Pass route on weekends; the trip is slower then and costs more. A trip to Jakarta costs 3200 rp (air-con costs 7200 rp) and by the Jagorawi Highway it only takes about 3½ hours.

INDONESIA

For buses to Yogyakarta and other places to the east, it's a lengthy bus ride or bemo trip to the Cicaheum station east of the city. Most buses to Yogyakarta leave around 3 to 7 pm. Bandung Cepat, 5 Jalan Dr Cipto, has air-con buses at 6 pm for 15,000 rp.

For Pangandaran, take a bus to Banjar or Tasikmalaya (2100 rp) and then another to Pangandaran. A door-to-door taxi service is provided by 4848 Taxi for 7500 rp or Sari Harum (☎ 78110) has less cramped, air-con minibuses (11,000 rp, four hours).

Train The Bandung-Jakarta *Parahyangan Express* is the main service with 14 departures throughout the day to Jakarta's Gambir station. It takes under three hours and the cheapest class is bisnis for 12,000 rp. Slower trains pass through in the morning for Jakarta's Pasar Senen or Tanah Abang stations. Fares cost from 3300 rp in ekonomi.

Several daily trains also operate between Yogyakarta and Bandung. The journey takes about nine to 10 hours and the fare varies from around 3500 rp in ekonomi, and from 14,000 rp in bisnis. Trains to Surabaya include the *Badra Surya* which costs 7500 rp in ekonomi, and the luxurious *Mutiara Selatan* which starts at 23,000 rp for bisnis class.

Getting Around

Bandung's airport is only four km north-west of the city centre, about 4000 rp by taxi. In Bandung, bemos are called *angkot*. They cost a standard 300 rp around town for most destinations and depart from the terminal outside the railway station or from the bus stations. The Damri city bus No 1 runs from west to east down Jalan Asia-Afrika to Cicaheum.

Metered taxis are common in Bandung. As in other cities, the becaks are being relegated to the back streets and are no longer seen in great numbers.

AROUND BANDUNG

Tangkuban Perahu Area

The 'overturned perahu' **volcano crater** stands 30 km north of Bandung. Legend tells of a god challenged to build a huge boat during a single night. His opponent, on seeing that he would probably complete this impossible task, brought the sun up early and the boat builder turned his nearly completed boat over in a fit of anger.

Tangkuban Perahu isn't really that special if you've seen Bromo or other volcanos. It's very commercial up at the crater – car parks, restaurants, an information centre and an admission fee. To get there, take a Subang minibus (1500 rp) from Bandung's train station, which goes via Lembang to the park entrance.

At weekends, a minibus goes from the gate up to the main crater but on other days you'll have to hitch or walk the four km. A more interesting, two-km short cut goes through the jungle to an area of steaming and bubbling geysers and another steep path cuts up to the main crater. Start up the road and take the first turning on the right.

Lembang, 16 km north of Bandung, has a planetarium. There are hot springs at **Ciater**, a few km beyond the Tangkuban Perahu entrance point, and **Maribaya**, five km beyond Lembang. Ciater has the better hot springs for a swim on a cold, rainy day but both are commercialised.

You can extend your Tangkuban Perahu trip by walking from the bottom end of the gardens at Maribaya down through a brilliant river gorge (there's a good track) to **Dago**, an exclusive residential suburb of Bandung with a famous teahouse. Allow about two hours for the walk to Dago. It's a good spot to watch the city light up and you can then get back into the city on the local bemos, which run to/from the train station in Bandung.

BANDUNG TO PANGANDARAN

Garut

This pleasant town is between Bandung and Banjar. There are popular **hot springs** *(air panas)* just five km north of Garut at Cipanas village, Tarogong. From Garut, you can climb **Gunung Papandayan**.

Places to Stay *Hotel Mulia* at Jalan Kenanga 17 is probably better than the *Hotel Nasional* nearby. There are more places at Tarogong.

Tasikmalaya & Cipatujah
Tasikmalaya is midway between Bandung and Pangandaran. **Gunung Galunggung**, 17 km north-west of Tasikmalaya, is a volcano that exploded dramatically a few years ago. You can get to Galunggung by motorbike from Tasikmalaya, although the locals will think you're nuts for wanting to climb it. In Tasikmalaya you can stay at the *Santosa Hotel*.

The beach at Cipatujah is 74 km south of Tasikmalaya. There's a **coral beach** at Sindangkerta, 14 km away, and minibuses run there from Cipatujah. In Cipatujah you can stay at the *Pantai Indah Losmen*. Buses run from Bandung to Tasikmalaya, where you get another bus to Cipatujah.

PANGANDARAN
This coastal resort is one of the few places on the south Java coast with good swimming. A coral reef cuts down the surf and dangerous undertows on the eastern beach, but caution is necessary on the western beach. The Pangandaran Nature Reserve is part of this small fishing town and the focus for travellers.

Pangandaran is centrally located between Yogyakarta and Bandung – Banjar, on the Yogyakarta to Bandung road, is where you turn off.

Information
Pangandaran has a tourist office and another information centre at the national park visitor's centre, but information is limited. You're charged a once-only 1000 rp fee when you enter the accommodation area from the bus station area. Entry to the national park is another 1000 rp.

Avoid weekends and holidays – Christmas and after Ramadan, in particular – when it gets very crowded and prices soar. At other times, this is a peaceful and relaxing place to take a break from travel.

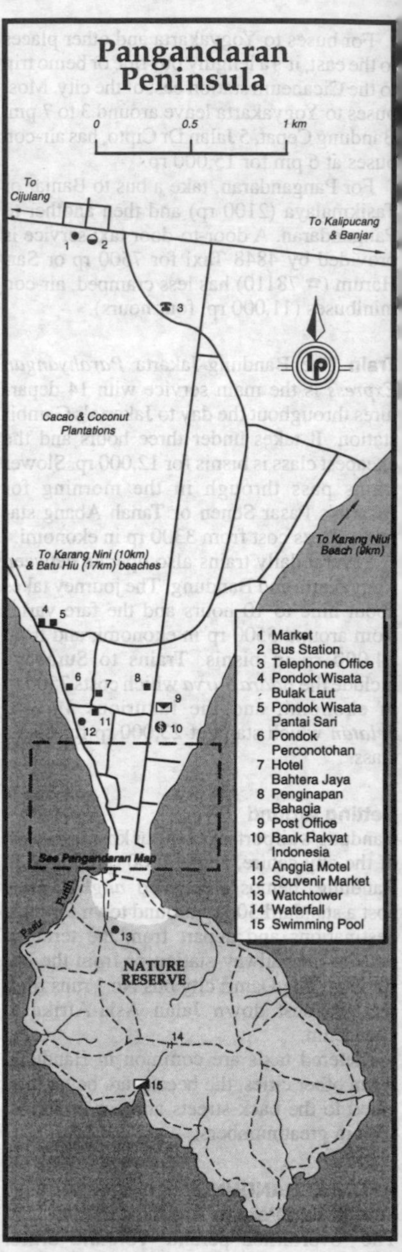

Things to See

Pangandaran has beaches on both sides of the peninsula, right by the town. The western beach is wide but overused and there are better beaches in the national park. **Pasir Putih**, the beach on the western side of the peninsula, about a half-km walk from town, has good sand and snorkelling. The beaches on the eastern side are pleasant but the water is very shallow.

The **national park** is right next to the town and there are good walks through the headland reserve which is cloaked in thick jungle and home to many monkeys and buffalo. There's a watchtower where you can see wildlife.

Places to Stay

Pangandaran has many places to stay in all price categories. Simply wander around and look in a few places. With the great variety, this can be the best way of finding a good room. Look for the sign 'kosong', which means 'rooms available'.

Popular cheaper places include the *Losmen Mini* on the main road. It is clean, convenient and popular and singles/doubles cost from 7500/10,000 rp, including a good breakfast. Turn off the main road and towards the west beach, and then turn again to the north to find a second Mini, *Losmen Mini Dua*, which is a more basic place with slightly cheaper rooms. Between the Minis is the *Rawamangun Lodge*, a basic place; but it's clean, welcomes travellers and is about the cheapest in Pangandaran at 4000/6000 rp.

Nearby, *Pondok Pelangi* is close to the west beach and has comfortable individual bungalows with two or three bedrooms for 80,000 rp or 25,000 rp per room. They're great for families. They also have an annexe with a block of good rooms with bath and pleasant veranda for 10,000 rp to 15,000 rp.

On the main road, the *Losmen Laut Biru* has singles from 10,000 rp or singles/doubles for 10,000/15,000 rp with bath. The rooms are large but a little grotty and nothing special. Also on the main road, the *Hotel Samudra* is a pleasant and clean place with rooms for 25,000 rp.

Of the places on the eastern beach, the *Losmen Panorama* has good veranda rooms right on the beach from 15,000 rp and rooms behind from 9000 rp. Next door, the more expensive *Sunrise Homestay* is pleasant and has a pool, and further south is the uninspiring *Penginapan Adem Ayem*.

All the new development is on the western beach, where you'll find most of the big hotels and mid-range accommodation. A cheap, local place at the southern end of this beach is the *Penginapan Saputra*, with tree-house-style bungalows for 7500 rp and 'suites' with bath for 10,000 rp.

Further north, *Pondok Wisata Bulak Laut* on Jalan Pamugaran has very nice bungalows for 15,000 rp including breakfast, tea and coffee. Each bungalow has a living room, open-air bathroom and a bedroom with a large double bed. *Pondok Wisata Pantai Sari* is next door and has similarly priced bungalows and a small Chinese restaurant. A number of new, more upmarket places are north of the Bulak Laut, and this area is now Pangandaran's Côte d'Azur. They provide very good accommodation for 15,000 rp and up. Good places include the *Sandaan*, *Bayu Indah* and yet another mini – *Mini 3*. A very nice but expensive place is *Adam's Homestay*. It is Mediterranean-influenced with eclectic architecture and cappuccinos.

Right away from the action at the northern end of the western beach road is *Delto Gecko Village*, a travellers' hangout costing 7,500 rp per person. It can be reached from the bus station without going into Pangandaran. It has a vegetarian restaurant, bicycles, an art shop and more.

Places to Eat

Restaurants are also in plentiful supply in Pangandaran, and the fish here is often superb. Usually, when you order fish you're invited back to the kitchen to see what's available and the price is dependent on weight.

INDONESIA

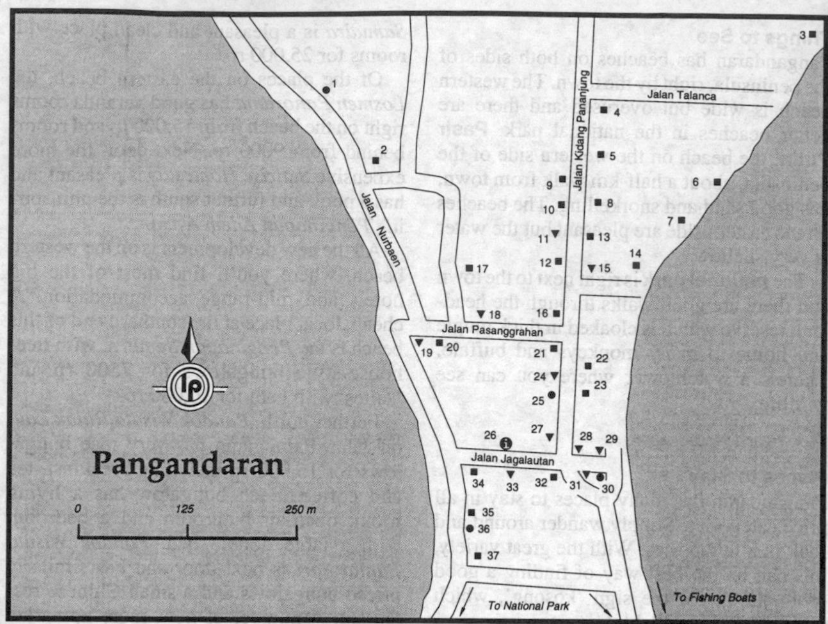

INDONESIA

On the main road, *Cilicap Restaurant* is a very popular and busy place with fairly standard prices and excellent fresh fish. In fact, all their food is very good, particularly the pancakes, and they provide good travel information. Further down the road, the *Sympathy Cafe* is a basic little place with surprisingly good food at pleasing prices.

Across the street from the Sympathy Cafe, the big *Inti-Laut* restaurant serves grilled fish and Indonesian fare. It's quite popular with Indonesians on holiday. Heading east from the Inti-Laut, you will find the *Lonely Planet* restaurant! I wish I could say that the fish and Chinese food served here was out of this world, but it's not bad and, given the eatery's name, at least the prices are budget.

Looking out on the west beach, at the end of Jalan Pasangrahan, is *Nanjung Restaurant* with a pleasant open-air dining area and excellent food including great barbecued fish. There are numerous other restaurants around and plenty of food carts and late-night warungs along the beaches. There are even food carts where croissants are for sale!

Getting There & Away

Bus & Train Access to Pangandaran is normally by Banjar on the main highway.

From Jakarta, buses from Kampung Rambutan bus station go directly to Banjar, via Bogor and Bandung. From Bandung, take a bus or a train to Banjar (4000 rp, four hours), then take a bus or colt (2000 rp, two hours) to Pangandaran. Pangandaran can also be reached from Tasikmalaya.

The most comfortable and easiest way to reach Bandung is take the door-to-door minibus service for 11,000 rp.

When leaving Pangandaran, frequent buses go to Tasikmalaya and Ciamis, all of which pass Banjar for onward connections. Ekonomi trains from Banjar to Bandung leave at 5.15 am (4500 rp, three hours), 12.45 pm (2500 rp, five hours) and 3.15 pm (4400 rp, three hours). For Yogyakarta, the 12.10

PLACES TO STAY

2 Hotel Bumi Nusanatra
3 Hotel Bumi Pananjung
4 Penginapan Pantai Indah
5 Hotel Pamordian
6 Pantai Indah Timur
7 Losmen Panorama
8 Losmen Srihana
9 Hotel Flamboyan
10 Pantai Indah Bahrat
12 Hotel Samudra
13 Sunrise Homestay
14 Penginapan Adem Ayam
16 Penginapan Damai
17 Losmen Mini Dua
20 Pondok Pelangi
21 Rawamangun Lodge
22 Penginapan Setia Famili
23 Losmen Mini Losmen
32 Laut Biru
34 Hotel Mangkabumi
35 Penginapan Saputra
37 Pangandaran Beach Hotel

PLACES TO EAT

11 Rumah Makan Budi Jaya
15 Cilicap Restaurant
18 Rumah Makan Sari Harum
19 Nanjung Restaurant
24 Ayem Goreng & Bakar Restaurant
27 Sympathy Cafe
28 Inti-Laut Restaurant
29 Lonely Planet Restaurant
31 Warungs
33 Rumah Makan Mambo

OTHER

1 Star Meridian Disco
25 Books for Sale
26 Tourist Office & Guide Service
30 Fish Auction
36 Aquarium

pm train from Banjar costs 2700 rp ekonomi and takes six hours.

Boat The most popular way to reach Yogyakarta is via the interesting backwater trip between Cilacap and Kalipucang. This starts with a 17-km bus trip east from Pangandaran to Kalipucang. From Kalipucang the ferry travels across the wide expanse of Segara Anakan and along the waterway sheltered by the island of Nusa Kambangan. It's a fascinating trip, hopping from village to village in a rickety 25-metre wooden boat. There's usually plenty of room for people and baggage but it's a popular service with plenty of local use. It takes four hours to Cilacap and costs 1100 rp. The last boats leaves at noon. From the Cilacap jetty you can get a becak and then a bemo to the Cilacap bus station, and then a bus to Yogyakarta.

The trip is made very easy by the door-to-door services between Pangandaran and Yogyakarta that will drop you at the ferry and pick you up on the other side for 12,500 rp, including the ferry ticket. It costs more from Yogya, sometimes much more! All up the journey takes about eight hours.

CIREBON

Cirebon, midway between Jakarta and Semarang, gets few visitors. The town has Javanese and Sundanese influences and is an important port with a busy fishing fleet. It is also a major centre for batik.

Things to See

In the south of the city, the **Kraton Kanoman** dates from 1681 but is sadly neglected. It's approached through the colourful Pasar Kanoman outdoor market. The more recent **Kraton Kesepuhan** is still in use as the home of the Sultan of Kesepuhan, but parts of it can be visited. There's an interesting, if somewhat run-down, museum.

Four km south-west of town is the **Gua Sunyaragi**, a bizarre 'cave' honeycombed with chambers, doors and staircases leading nowhere. The **Tomb of Sunan Gunungjati** is another of the town's claims to fame – he was one of the nine *walis* (holy men) who spread Islam through Java.

The harbour area is always an interesting place to visit, and Cirebon is famed for its distinctive batik, particularly from the nearby village of **Trusmi** (try Ibu Masina's) or from Indramayu, which is further out.

Places to Stay

Hotel Asia (☎ 2183) at Jalan Kalibaru Selatan 15 has a variety of rooms with and without mandi from around 13,000 rp. It's about a 15-minute walk from the railway station alongside the quiet tree-lined canal near Pasar Pagi.

Cirebon's other low-budget places are along Jalan Siliwangi between the railway station and the canal. Walking from the station towards Jalan Siliwangi, the *Palapa Hotel* looks rather dreary but it's actually a pretty good place for 9000 rp. On the corner of the same street, at Jalan Siliwangi 66, the *Hotel Famili* has adequate rooms from 10,000 rp.

Slightly more expensive are the *Hotel Slamet* at Jalan Siliwangi 66, the *Hotel Cordova* at No 77, the *Hotel Langensari* at No 117 and the *Hotel Priangan* at No 108. At Jalan Siliwangi 98, next to the town square, the *Grand Hotel Cirebon* (☎ 2014/5) is an old-fashioned but pleasant hotel with rooms from around 50,000 rp up – a long way up!

Places to Eat

Nasi lengko, a rice dish with bean sprouts, tahu, tempe, fried onion and cucumber, is a local speciality. *Rumah Makan Jatibarang*, on the corner of Jalan Karanggetas and Jalan Kalibaru Selatan, is a good place for this dish. Nearby on Jalan Karanggetas is the clean and reasonable *Kopyor Restaurant*. The *Hong Kong Restaurant* at Jalan Karanggetas 20 has decent Chinese food.

Seafood restaurants along Jalan Bahagia, towards Jalan Pasekutan, include the well-known *Maxim's* at No 45-47. The Chinese *seafood market*, in the small square at the south end of Jalan Bahagia, has great food although not at rock-bottom prices. The *Pasar Pagi Market* has good fruit and foodstalls. Nearby is *Toko Famili* at Jalan Siliwangi 96 which has good baked snacks.

Getting There & Away

Buses from Jakarta take about five hours, or 3½ hours from Bandung – the bus station is a 15-minute minibus trip south-west of the town centre.

Cirebon is on the railway line from Jakarta for both Surabaya in the north and Yogyakarta in the south, so there are frequent trains. From Jakarta, it takes four hours and costs 9000 rp in bisnis class.

Getting Around

The minibus or taxi kota service costs a flat 300 rp, and there are also plenty of becaks.

YOGYAKARTA

The most popular city in Indonesia, Yogya is easy-going, economical and offers plenty for the budget traveller. Long a centre of power, the Mataram Kingdom's control extended as far as Sumatra and Bali over 1000 years ago. The final Hindu/Buddhist kingdom of the Majapahits also controlled this area until the

PLACES TO STAY

7 Ambarrukmo Palace Hotel

PLACES TO EAT

5 Holland Bakery
15 Pasar Beringharjo

OTHER

1 Colt Station to Kaliurang & Prambanan
2 Bus Stop For Borobudur
3 Monument
4 Army Museum
6 Affandi Museum
8 Yogyakarta Craft Centre
9 Monumen Diponegoro
10 Gramedia Bookshop
11 Telephone Exchange Office
12 Railway Station
13 Tourist Information Office
14 ISI (Institute of Arts)
16 Museum Bekas Benteng Vredeburg
17 Senopati Shopping Centre & Colt Station
18 Paku Alam Kraton
19 Batik Research Centre
20 Nitour
21 Museum Sono-Budoyo
22 Post Office
23 Taxi Stand
24 Wartel Telephone Office
25 Mesjid Besar
26 Museum Kareta Kraton
27 Yogya Kraton
28 Zoo
29 Pasar Ngasem Bird Market
30 Taman Sari
31 Sasono Hinggil
32 THR (People's Amusement Park)
33 Batik Galleries
34 Dalem Pujokusuman Theatre
35 Agastya Institute
36 Bus Station

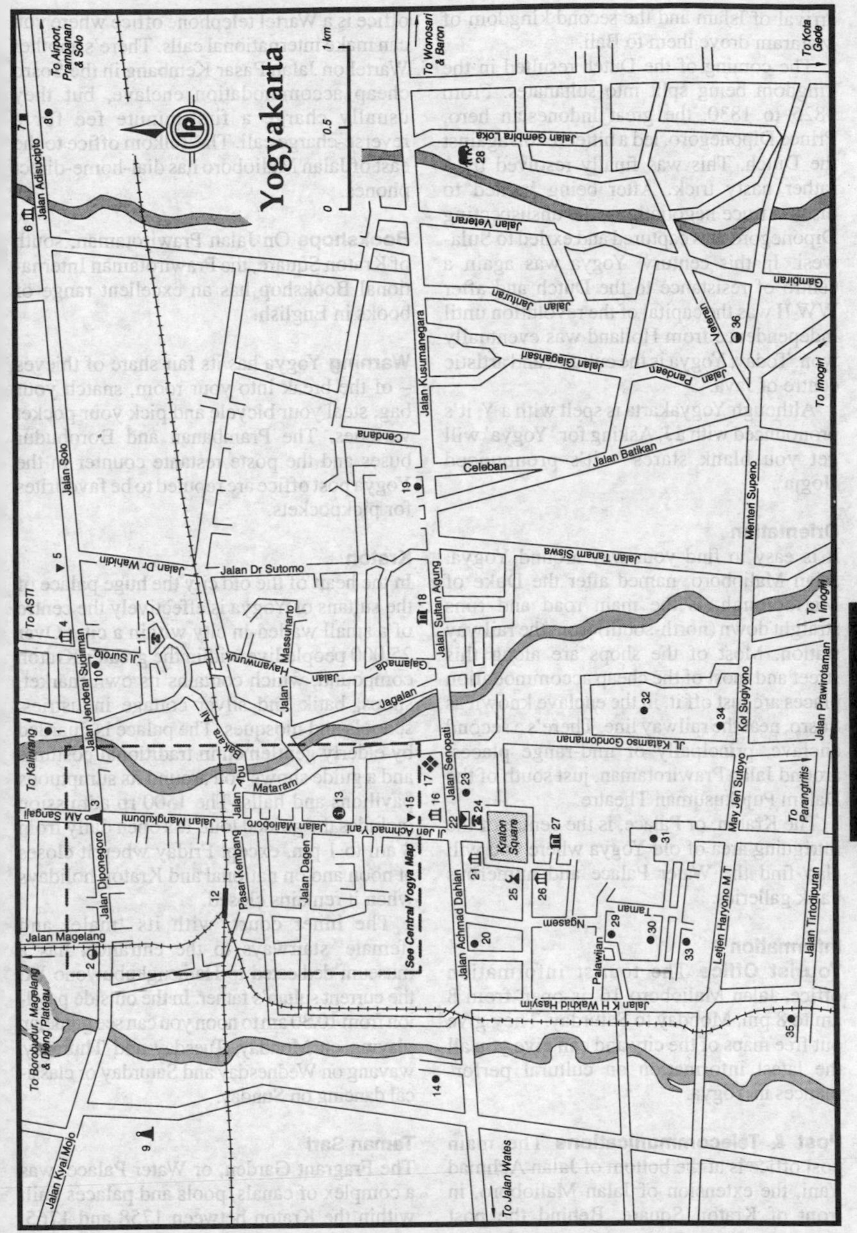
Yogyakarta
0
0.5
1 km
To Airport, Prambanan & Solo
Jalan Adisucipto
To Wonosari & Baron
To Kota Gede
Jalan Gembira Loka
Jalan Veteran
Gambiran
Jalan Janturan
Veteran
Jalan Glagahsari
Jalan Pandean
To Imogiri
Jalan Kusumanegara
Cendana
Celeban
Jalan Batikan
Menteri Supeno
Jalan Taman Siswa
Jalan Dr Wahidin
Jalan Dr Sutomo
To ASTI
Jalan Solo
Jalan Jenderal Sudirman
Jl Suroto
Jalan Hayamwuruk
Jalan Massuharto
Gajamada
Jagalan
Jalan Sultan Agung
Jalan Senopati
Jl Katamso Gondomanan
Kol Sugiyono
Jalan Prawirotaman
To Parangtritis
May Jen Sutoyo
To Kaliurang
AM Sangaji
Jalan Mangkubumi
Jalan Diponegoro
Jalan Malioboro
Mataram
Jalan Abu Bakar Ali
Pasar Kembang
Jalan Dagen
Jl Jen Achmad Yani
Kraton Square
Jalan Achmad Dahlan
Ngasem
Taman
Palawijan
Letjen Haryono M T
Jalan Tirtodipuran
Jalan Magelang
See Central Yogya Map
Jalan K H Wakhid Hasyim
To Borobudur, Magelang & Dieng Plateau
To Jalan Wates
Jalan Kyai Mojo

arrival of Islam and the second kingdom of Mataram drove them to Bali.

The coming of the Dutch resulted in the kingdom being split into sultanates. From 1825 to 1830, the great Indonesian hero, Prince Diponegoro, led a bitter revolt against the Dutch. This was finally resolved by a rather nasty trick. After being invited to discuss truce negotiations, the unsuspecting Diponegoro was captured and exiled to Sulawesi. In this century, Yogya was again a centre of resistance to the Dutch and after WW II was the capital of the revolution until independence from Holland was eventually won. Today, Yogya is the cultural and artistic centre of Java.

Although Yogyakarta is spelt with a Y, it's pronounced with a J. Asking for 'Yogya' will get you blank stares – it's pronounced 'Jogja'.

Orientation

It is easy to find your way around Yogya. Jalan Malioboro, named after the Duke of Marlborough, is the main road and runs straight down (north-south) from the railway station. Most of the shops are along this street and most of the cheap accommodation places are just off it, in the enclave known as Sosro, near the railway line. There's a second enclave, principally of mid-range places, around Jalan Prawirotaman, just south of the Dalem Pujokusuman Theatre.

The Kraton, or Palace, is the centre of the intriguing area of old Yogya where you will also find the Water Palace and numerous batik galleries.

Information

Tourist Office The tourist information office, Jalan Malioboro 16, is open from 8 am to 8 pm, Monday to Saturday. They give out free maps of the city and can give you all the latest information on cultural performances in Yogya.

Post & Telecommunications The main post office is at the bottom of Jalan Achmad Yani, the extension of Jalan Malioboro, in front of Kraton Square. Behind the post office is a Wartel telephone office where you can make international calls. There's another Wartel on Jalan Pasar Kembang in the Sosro cheap accommodation enclave, but they usually charge a first-minute fee for a reverse-charge call. The Telkom office to the east of Jalan Malioboro has dial-home-direct phones.

Bookshops On Jalan Prawirotaman, south of Kraton Square, the Prawirotaman International Bookshop has an excellent range of books in English.

Warning Yogya has its fair share of thieves – of the break into your room, snatch your bag, steal your bicycle and pick your pocket varieties. The Prambanan and Borobudur buses and the poste restante counter in the Yogya post office are reputed to be favourites for pickpockets.

Kraton

In the heart of the old city the huge palace of the sultans of Yogya is effectively the centre of a small walled-in city within a city. Over 25,000 people live within the greater Kraton compound, which contains its own market, shops, batik and silver cottage industries, schools and mosques. The palace is guarded by elderly gentlemen in traditional costume and a guide shows you around its sumptuous pavilions and halls. The 1500 rp admission includes the guided tour. It's open daily from 8 am to 1 pm, except Friday when it closes at noon and on national and Kraton holidays when it remains closed.

The inner court, with its 'male' and 'female' stairways to the entrance, has a museum dedicated to Hamengkubuwono IX, the current sultan's father. In the outside pavilion from 10.30 am to noon you can see gamelan playing on Monday, Tuesday and Thursday, wayang on Wednesday and Saturday or classical dancing on Sunday.

Taman Sari

The Fragrant Garden, or Water Palace, was a complex of canals, pools and palaces built within the Kraton between 1758 and 1765.

Damaged first by Diponegoro's Java War and then further by an earthquake it is, today, a mass of ruins, crowded with small houses and batik galleries. Parts are being restored but not very well. Admission is 500 rp to the restored area, and it's open from 7 am to 5 pm daily.

On the edge of the site is the interesting Pasar Ngasem bird market.

Museum Sono-Budoyo

Close to the Kraton, on the north-western corner of the Kraton Square, this museum has excellent exhibits including palace furnishings, jewellery, bronze statues and wayang puppets. It is open from 8 am to 1.30 pm Tuesday to Thursday, to 11.15 am Friday and to noon on weekends. Entry is 300 rp and it's well worth a visit.

Other Museums

On the south-western corner of Kraton Square, between the Kraton entrance and the Sono-Budoyo Museum, the **Museum Kareta Kraton** has a collection of palace carriages, some of them extravagantly ornate, and hearses are displayed. The museum is open from 8 am to 4 pm daily.

At the bottom of Jalan Achmad Yani, the **Museum Bekas Benteng Vredeburg** is built in the old Dutch fort and has interesting displays about the history of Yogya and its role in Indonesia's struggle for independence. The museum is open from 8.30 am to 1.30 pm Tuesday to Thursday, to 11 am Friday, and to noon on weekends.

Monumen Diponegoro

This reconstruction is of Prince Diponegoro's residence, destroyed by the Dutch in 1825. The hole in the wall through which

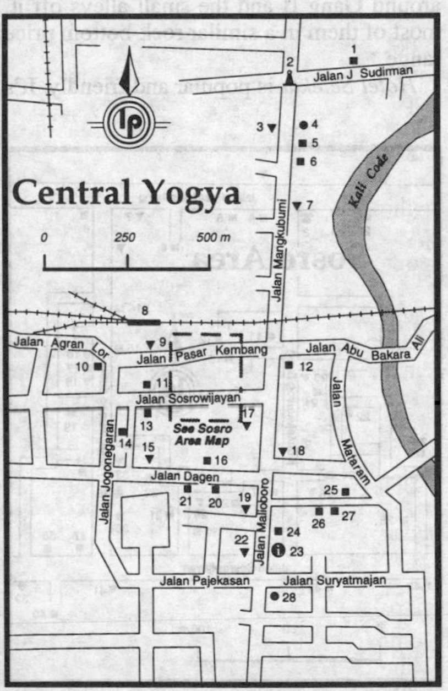

PLACES TO STAY

1 Hotel Santika
5 Arjuna Palace Hotel
6 Batik Palace Hotel
10 Hotel Kota
11 Hotel Karunia
12 Garuda Hotel
13 Hotel Oryza
14 Ella Homestay
16 Hotel Blue Safir
20 Hotel Sri Wibowo
21 Peti Mas Guesthouse
24 Mutiara Hotel
25 Hotel Zamrud
26 Wisma Hasta Wisata
27 Hotel Puri

PLACES TO EAT

3 Malioboro Restaurant & Zangrandi Ice Cream Palace
7 Tip Top Ice Cream
9 Mama's Warung
15 Bladok Coffee House
17 Kentucky Fried Chicken
18 Legian Restaurant
19 Shinta Restaurant
22 Colombo Restaurant

OTHER

2 Monument
4 Garuda Airways Office
8 Railway Station
23 Tourist Information Office
28 Terang Bulan Batik Shop

INDONESIA

the prince escaped is still there. The site is open from 7.30 am to 4 pm daily. It's four km out of Yogya – bus No 2 along Jalan Mataram will get you there, and bus No 1 will get you back to Jalan Malioboro.

Other Sights

The **Ambarrukmo Palace** is in the grounds of the Ambarrukmo Palace Hotel, on the Solo road. It's another interesting example of Javanese palace architecture.

The **Yogyakarta Craft Centre**, opposite the Ambarrukmo Palace Hotel, is promoted by the government and has a good display of high-quality crafts which are reasonable in price.

The main street of **Kota Gede**, five km south-east of Yogya, is the silverwork centre of Yogya, and the **grave** of Senopati, the first king of Mataram, can also be seen here.

Swimming Pools

If the heat in Yogya gets too much you can, for a fee, use the swimming pool at the luxurious Ambarrukmo or Mutiara hotels. A number of the mid-range hotels at Jalan Prawirotaman also have pools.

Places to Stay

Accommodation in Yogya is remarkably good value and there is a superb choice. It's certainly the best city in Java for places to stay and places to eat. There are two particularly popular enclaves – the central Sosro area for the really cheap places and the Prawirotaman area, a couple of km south of the Kraton, for mid-range places.

Sosro Area The real cheapies are almost all in the Sosro area, defined by Jalan Pasar Kembang (immediately south of the railway station) and Jalan Sosrowijayan (a block south again). Connecting the two, and just a couple of doors down from Jalan Malioboro, is the narrow alleyway known as Gang Sosrowijayan I and a maze of other little alleys including Gang Sosrowijayan II. Numerous small guesthouses and restaurants are dotted around these alleys.

Gang Sosrowijayan I has some very low-cost places but make sure your room is secure as Yogyakarta is notorious for theft. At the northern end, the first place is *Losmen Sastrowihadi*, about as basic as you can get with singles/doubles for 4000/5000 rp. *Losmen Beta* is similar in price and standards but is more geared to travellers. A bit further along this gang is *Sari Homestay*, a new place with immaculate rooms built around a courtyard. Rooms with bath cost 7000/10,000 rp and are good value.

Just around the corner is *Losmen Lucy*, which is quite salubrious – good rooms are 7500/10,000 rp. The *Hotel Rama* has reasonable doubles for 6000 rp and the *Hotel Jogja* is clean and well kept but no bargain at 7500/10,000 rp. *Lima Losmen*, in the alley east of Gang I, is a dive but they don't come any cheaper at 3000/4500 rp.

On Gang Sosrowijayan II, the next alley back, is the clean, good value and popular *Hotel Bagus*. It's built around a central courtyard and rooms with fan cost from 5000/6000 rp. There are a host of small losmen around Gang II and the small alleys off it, most of them in a similar rock-bottom price range.

Hotel Selekta is popular and friendly. It's

roomier and lighter than most, and good value at 5000 rp or 7500 rp with bath. Nearby the *Losmen Wisma Wijaya* has a friendly and helpful manager but little else to recommend it. Singles/doubles are 7000/10,000 rp. Other cheap but less popular places are the *Utar Pension* and *Isty Losmen* with good rooms from 5000 rp, the *Losmen Setia* with very basic rooms from 3500/4000 rp, the overpriced *Losmen Setia Kawan* costing 7500 rp and the good value *Supriyanto Inn* with bright rooms for 4000/5000 rp.

Between Gang I and Gang II, the friendly *Dewi Homestay* is a brighter place with a garden and is deservedly popular. Rooms start at 6000 rp, and rooms with bath are 10,000 rp.

On Jalan Sosrowijayan, between Gang I and Malioboro, is the security-conscious *Aziatic*, an old Dutch-style hotel. Large but slightly rundown doubles are 10,000 rp and there's a wide central hallway/cafe where you can sit and chat. Across the road from the Aziatic, the large *Hotel Indonesia* has nice courtyard areas and good-sized rooms at 6000 rp, or rooms with bath for 7500 rp, 9000 rp and 12,000 rp.

Other places along Jalan Sosrowijayan include the *Wisma Gambira*, which is a colonial-style place with spotless rooms for 8500/10,500 rp or 14,000/22,000 rp with bath. The owners of Gambira also run the slightly ritzier *Oryza Hotel*, at 49 Jalan Sosrowijayan. Jalan Sosrowijayan also has a number of mid-range places including the very new and flash *Marina Palace* with rooms starting at 30,000 rp. At the western end of the street, 100 metres down an alley, is the popular and well run *Ella Homestay*. It's good value with rooms from 5000/7000 rp up to 7000/9000 rp with bath, including breakfast.

Jalan Pasar Kembang, at the northern end of the Sosro area, also has a number of hotels. Most of the cheap places are very seedy and some specialise in 'massage', but the street has a few reasonable mid-range hotels. The *Asia-Afrika* (☎ 66219), 21 Jalan Pasar Kembang, has a variety of rooms with bath from 12,500/15,000 rp, then 17,500/22,500 rp up to 27,500/32,500 rp or more for air-con. The rooms are nothing special for the price but the hotel has a pool and an attractive garden cafe at the back. The *Ratna* is a pleasantly quiet place set back from the road. Reasonable doubles are 11,000 rp, or 17,500 rp and 20,000 rp with mandi and toilet.

Other, more expensive hotels include the

PLACES TO STAY

2 Hotel Mendut
4 Batik Palace Hotel
5 Hotel Asia-Afrika
6 Hotel Ratna
8 Kencana Hotel
10 Losmen Setia
11 Hotel Bagus
12 Supriyanto Inn
13 Losmen Setia Kawan
14 Losmen Sastrowihadi
15 Losmen Beta
17 Sari Homestay
19 Losmen Lucy
21 Losmen Betty
22 Utar Pension Inn
23 Hotel Selekta
24 Jaya Losmen
25 Losmen Wisma Wijaya
27 Losmen Gandhi
28 Losmen Atiep
30 Dewi Homestay
31 Losmen Happy Inn
34 Lima Losmen
35 Hotel Jogja
36 Hotel Rama
37 Hotel Kartika
38 Hotel Aziatic
39 Marina Palace Hotel
40 Hotel Indonesia
42 Wisma Gambira

PLACES TO EAT

1 Mama's
7 Borobudur Bar & Restaurant
9 Cheap Warungs
16 Old Superman's Restaurant
18 Bu Sis Restaurant
20 Anna's Restaurant
26 Heru Jaya Restaurant & Losmen
29 Lovina Coffee Shop
32 Eko Restaurant
33 New Superman's Restaurant
41 Ris Restaurant & Bakery
43 Caterina Restaurant

OTHER

3 Wartel Telephone Office

Batik Palace Hotel (☎ 63824) at Jalan Pasar Kembang 29, with rooms starting at US$19/23. There are two other Batik Palaces, the best being the cottages down an alley south off Jalan Sosrowijayan with a large pool and bungalows from US$22/27. The *Hotel Mendut* (☎ 3114) at Jalan Pasar Kembang 49 also has air-con rooms and a swimming pool.

Other Central Hotels Cross Jalan Malioboro and follow the alley further down from the Legian Restaurant. You'll soon come to the extremely well-kept and very quiet *Hotel Puri* (☎ 4107) at No 22, with rooms starting at 6000/7500 rp and free tea or coffee in the morning and evening.

The nearby *Hotel Wisma Hasta Wisata* (WHW) at No 16 is similarly priced but not so good. Or there's the *Prambanan Guest House* at No 18-20, also in the same price bracket. Further down, the *Hotel Zamrud* at No 47 is the best in the street, and costs 12,000/17,500 rp including breakfast.

Jalan Dagen, south of the Sosro area, has a number of mid-range hotels such as the *Peti Mas* (☎ 2896) at No 39. Fan-cooled rooms range from 16,000/20,000 rp, and air-con ones from 50,000/60,000 rp. There's a pool and a pleasant garden with a restaurant area in this centrally located and attractive hotel.

Jalan Prawirotaman This street, a couple of km south of the city centre, has developed into a second, more upmarket enclave than Sosro. Many of the hotels have swimming pools and the rooms may be built around pleasant gardens. There are also a number of restaurants, so it's a self-sufficient, quieter area, though not so central or interesting as Sosro. A becak from the central Jalan Malioboro area is likely to cost 1500 rp. Alternatively, take the blue and white No 14 from Jalan Malioboro. The orange bus No 2 on Jalan Parangtritis will take you back for 250 rp.

This area does have some cheaper places like the neat, clean and helpful *Vagabond Youth Hostel* (☎ 71207) at Jalan Prawirotaman MG III/589, where dormitory beds cost 5000 rp, singles/doubles cost 7000/10,500 rp, slightly more for larger rooms. Student and YHA card holders can get a 1000 rp discount.

The *Perwita Sari* (☎ 77592), 32 Jalan Prawirotaman, is one of the cheapest in the area with singles/doubles/triples for 10,000/15,000/21,000 rp and 15,000/20,000/28,000 rp with attached bath. Breakfast is included, and while the rooms won't win any awards, it's comfortable and good value considering it has a pool. *Sartika Homestay* (☎ 87399) at No 44A doesn't have some of the glitz of its neighbours, but it is friendly and reasonable value. Doubles with bath cost 15,000 rp and 20,000 rp, including breakfast.

Duta Guesthouse (☎ 75219) at No 20 is popular and has rooms without bath for 10,000/14,000 rp or with bath for 20,000 rp and up. Breakfast is included and it has a pool. *Agung Guest House* (☎ 75512) is also popular and they will pick you up from the train station. It has a pool and rooms start at 10,000/12,500 rp, but most are 15,000/17,500 rp with bath up to 30,000/37,500 rp with bath and air-con. Look around Prawirotaman as there are many more options to suit all tastes, and some of the more expensive old villas like the *Kirana Guest House* (☎ 76600) have real colonial style.

The next street south, Jalan Prawirotaman II, also has a few places. The *Muria Guesthouse* (☎ 87211) at MGIII/600 is reasonable at 12,500 rp for doubles with attached bathroom. Other cheaper places include the *Pelupi*, *Merapi* and the well-run *Post Card Guesthouse*. The *Delta Homestay* (☎ 55135) at No 597A is a cut above these and good value. It has a pool and very good rooms for 10,500/15,000 rp or 21,000/25,000 rp with bath.

Places to Eat

There is as wide a variety of eating places as there are losmen in Yogya and most of them cater very much to the standard travellers' tastes.

INDONESIA

Sosro Area Everybody seems to pay a visit to either Mama's or Superman's. You'll find both the original *Superman's* and its new larger offshoot on Gang Sosrowijayan I. They're both very popular and trendy and the food is good and reasonable in price. All the regular travellers' specials appear on the long menu, ranging from fruit salad to banana pancakes.

On Jalan Pasar Kembang, beside the railway line, *Mama's* is definitely the number-one warung. Evening time is when it comes into full swing with good food and salads. *Borobudur Bar & Restaurant* has average fare at higher than average prices – the sometimes seedy bar atmosphere is the reason to come here.

There are plenty of other little eating places in the alleys and lanes of Sosro, such as the *N & N*, a popular and cheap eatery on Gang I. Other good places include *Anna's* and *Eko Restaurant*. For cheap eats, head to the little cluster of gang-side *warungs* at the station end of Gang I.

Jalan Sosrowijayan has a number of good restaurants. *Caterina* has good food at low prices and you can dine lesahan-style (on mats) at the back. *Apapaya*, further west along Jalan Sosrowijayan at No 45, is more upmarket with tasteful decor; it has steaks and Italian food. At the other end of street and quality scale, the *Ris Restaurant* is badly in need of improved food and service.

Jalan Malioboro There are a number of places along Jalan Malioboro serving Western-style food. They include survivors like the *Shinta* at No 57 and the *Colombo* at No 25. Both are popular for their ice juice. The *New Happy* is at Jalan Achmad Yani 95, on the corner with Jalan Gandekan.

On the corner of Jalan Malioboro and Jalan Perwakilan, the unusual *Legian Restaurant* is hidden away upstairs. It has Indonesian, Chinese, French and Italian food served by Balinese waiters in a garden setting. It's very chic, with most mains costing 3000 rp to 5000 rp.

Late at night, after 9 pm, *foodstalls* replace the souvenir stands on Jalan Malioboro and you can take a seat on the woven mats along the pavement. Most of them serve the speciality of Yogya – nasi gudeg (rice with young jackfruit cooked in coconut milk).

Jalan Malioboro changes names across the railway line and becomes Jalan Mangkubumi. At No 28, you'll find the *Tip Top* with excellent ice cream and cakes.

Jalan Prawirotaman Restaurants are popping up to complement the guesthouses on Jalan Prawirotaman. On the corner with Jalan Parangtritis, the *Tante Lies* is simple and deservedly popular.

One Prawirotaman restaurant to which it's worth making a special excursion is the excellent *Hanoman's Forest Restaurant* at No 9B. This fine restaurant has good food at reasonable prices, along with wayang kulit, wayang golek or classical dance performances for 2000 rp.

Other restaurants along the street include *Galunggung*, *Griya Bujana*, the *Prambanan Restaurant* and the popular *La Beng Beng Restaurant*. The bigger restaurants here are glossy affairs, more akin to the restaurants at Kuta Beach in Bali.

Entertainment

There are an enormous number of cultural performances. The tourist information office can advise you of what's on, or check in the tourist newspapers. There are classical dancing and gamelan rehearsals in the *Kraton*. Performances also take place in hotels, restaurants and a variety of performing arts centres.

Wayang kulit (leather shadow puppets) can be seen at several places around Yogya on virtually every night of the week. The *Agastya Art Institute* has afternoon performances every day except Saturday. The *Yogyakarta Craft Centre* puts on evening performances every day. The *Museum Sono-Budoyo* has performances every evening except Monday. The *Arjuna Palace Hotel* has performances every Tuesday evening. Every second Saturday of the month, all-night performances are held at the southern square *(Sasono Hinggil)* of the Kraton area.

Wayang golek (wooden puppet) plays are also performed frequently. The *Agastya Art Institute* has performances on Saturday afternoon and there is a daily Nitour performance, except on Sunday. Wayang orang or wayang wong are Javanese dance dramas; and these can also be seen at a variety of venues.

Excellent performances of the great Ramayana ballet are held at the *Purawisata Theatre* at the THR, Jalan Katamso, every night from 8 to 10 pm. Also see the upcoming Prambanan section.

Things to Buy

Batik cloth is sold all over Yogya but the Terang Bulan shop, before the market as you walk south on Jalan Malioboro, will give you a good idea of what is available. The prices are fixed but reasonable, and the quality is reliable.

Yogya has dozens of batik art galleries. Top of the scale is Amri Yahya's flash gallery at Jalan Gampingan 67 – his beautiful modern batiks can cost over US$1000. Nearby, on the same street, is ISI (Institute of Arts), open to visitors in the mornings from Monday to Saturday.

Carry on up Jalan Wates (the western extension of Jalan Achmad Dahlan which runs past Kraton Square) to other interesting – and more reasonably priced – places. Another good place for top-quality, but expensive, batik is Kuswadji's, in the north square near the Kraton. Or, there's Bambang Utoro to the east of town off Jalan Kusumanegara, the continuation of Jalan Sultan Agung. There are also a number of batik workshops and galleries along Jalan Tirtodipuran and Jalan Prawirotaman in the south of Yogya.

Affandi, Indonesia's internationally renowned painter, has an interesting modern gallery about five km out of Yogya on the Solo road. Paintings are for sale but the gallery is also a permanent museum displaying the works of Affandi, his daughter Kartika and other artists. It's open from 9 am to 4 pm, and an admission fee of 300 rp is charged.

The Water Palace is the site for most of the cheaper galleries but the great percentage of them are very poor quality and very 'me too' in their style. Look carefully and be very selective as original work can always be found. Try to avoid the touts and 'guides' who follow you – you'll end up paying commission on anything you buy. Yogya is crawling with batik sellers and many scams are tried. Don't believe the tales about huge ASEAN exhibitions in Singapore which empty the city of batik and that today is your last chance to buy!

If you want to have a go at batik yourself, Yogya has plenty of batik courses. Many teachers are self-proclaimed 'experts' out to make some easy money so it's a good idea to ask other travellers who may have just completed a course.

The Yogya government-run Batik Research Centre at Jalan Kusumanegara 2 is an interesting place to visit – they explain the batik process in detail and have some unusual batiks on display and for sale. It's expensive but the quality is high. The centre also conducts comprehensive batik courses for foreigners, and can recommend other courses.

See the Java Things to Buy section for more information on batik.

Getting There & Away

Air There are air connections between Yogyakarta and Jakarta (111,000 rp), Surabaya (53,000 rp), Denpasar (104,000 rp) and many other centres.

Bus The bus station is four km south-east from the city centre, east of the Jalan Prawirotaman area. Ticket agents along Jalan Sosrowijayan sell tickets for the various bus companies and, in some cases, their own services, but their commission can be excessive. Bus company offices are also found along Jalan Mangkubumi, the northern extension of Jalan Malioboro across the railway line.

Colts for Solo can be caught as they run up Jalan Mataram, a block east from Jalan Malioboro. Regular buses are 1200 rp, or there's a door-to-door minibus service.

INDONESIA

Buses from the station include Prambanan (700 rp), Parangtritis (1000 rp), Borobudur (1000 rp) and Kaliurang (1000 rp). The bus for Borobudur can also be caught along Jalan Magelang to the north; a city bus No 5 will drop you there. Colts to Prambanan and Kaliurang also leave from Jalan Simanjuntak, near the corner with Jalan Jenderal Sudirman.

Further afield, fares from Yogya to Jakarta cost from 11,500 rp for the economy service. Air-con buses cost from 19,000 rp up to 32,000 rp for the deluxe services, which take about 14 hours. Buses to Bandung cost from 8000 rp or from 13,500 rp with air-con. Buses to Surabaya cost from 6000 rp or 10,000 rp with air-con, and buses to Malang will cost 6500 rp. It takes about 16 hours to Denpasar, Bali – it's 13,000 rp by public bus or from 22,000 to 38,000 rp, depending on the bus and the company, for the better private buses.

Door-to-door minibus services operate to a number of centres, such as Solo, Surabaya and Malang. To Pangandaran, the popular bus/ferry/bus service costs around 15,000 rp at the Sosro agents. There is little difference between the services offered, but the prices can vary enormously – especially at the agents in the Prawirotaman area.

Train Unlike Jakarta and Surabaya, there is only one station in Yogya and it is very conveniently located in the centre of town. The secret to catching economy trains is to take those originating in Yogya – not the through trains that can be horribly crowded. For Bandung (4500 rp, 9¼ hours) and Banjar (3500 rp, five hours) the *Cepat* departs at 8 am. To Surabaya (3700 rp, seven hours) and Banyuwangi (7000 rp, 15 hours) the *Argopuro* departs at 7.15 am. Solo is on the main Yogya to Surabaya railway line, only about an hour out of Yogya.

Trains to Jakarta take nine to 12 hours and cost from 7000 rp in ekonomi and from 15,000 rp in bisnis. The *Senja Ekonomi* leaves at 5.10 pm; for express trains, the *Fajar Utama* leaves at 7 am and the Senja Utama leaves at 6 pm.

The most luxurious way to travel is on the deluxe trains, like the *Bima Express* or *Mutiara*, which pass through Yogya as they run between Jakarta and Surabaya. Book as far in advance as possible.

Getting Around

To/From the Airport Taxis from the airport to Yogya, about 10 km, cost 6000 rp. You can walk out to the main road and turn left, only 200 metres from the terminal, and catch any colt or minibus into town for about 250 rp. The airport is on the main road to Prambanan and Solo, so they come by in a steady stream.

Local Transport Bis Kotas are bright orange minibuses operating on eight set routes around the city for a flat 250 rp fare. From the bus station, a No 2 bus will drop you on Jalan Mataram, a block over from Malioboro. Bus No 1 from Jalan Malioboro will get you out to the bus station, about 20 minutes from the city centre.

You can hire bicycles and motorbikes but lock them up very securely. Theft is big business in Yogya. There's an enormous supply of becaks for around 1000 rp an hour but fares are dependent on the time of day, difficulty of the trip, weight of the passengers and assorted other factors.

Tours to Prambanan, Borobudur and the Dieng Plateau are run by numerous agents around the Sosro hotels. Trips to climb Merapi for the sunrise are also organised.

AROUND YOGYAKARTA

There are a whole series of places to visit around Yogyakarta. Best known, of course, are the great temple complex of Prambanan and the huge Buddhist centre at Borobudur, but there are a number of others worth a visit.

Prambanan

The biggest Hindu temple complex in Java, Prambanan is 17 km east from Yogya on the Solo road. Of the original group, the outer compound contains the ruins of 224 temples, only two of which have been restored. Eight minor and eight main temples stand in the central court. The largest of these, the **Shiva**

temple, has been restored and others are being reconstructed. The 50-metre-high temple bears 42 scenes from the *Ramayana*.

The statue of Shiva stands in the central chamber and statues of the goddess Durga, Shiva's elephant-headed son Ganesh and Agastya the teacher stand in the other chapels of the upper part of the temple. The Shiva temple is flanked by the Vishnu and Brahma temples, the latter carrying further scenes from the *Ramayana*. In the small central temple, opposite the Shiva temple, stands a fine statue of the bull Nandi, Shiva's mount.

Built in the 9th century AD, possibly 50 years after Borobudur, the complex at Prambanan was abandoned soon after its completion when its builders moved east. Many of the temples had collapsed by the last century and not until 1937 was any form of reconstruction attempted. Other temple ruins can be found close to Prambanan and on the road back to Yogya.

There is a 4000 rp admission charge to the temple complex. It's open from 6 am to 6 pm and the temples are at their best in the early evening light or in the early morning when it's quiet. If you are here at the right time

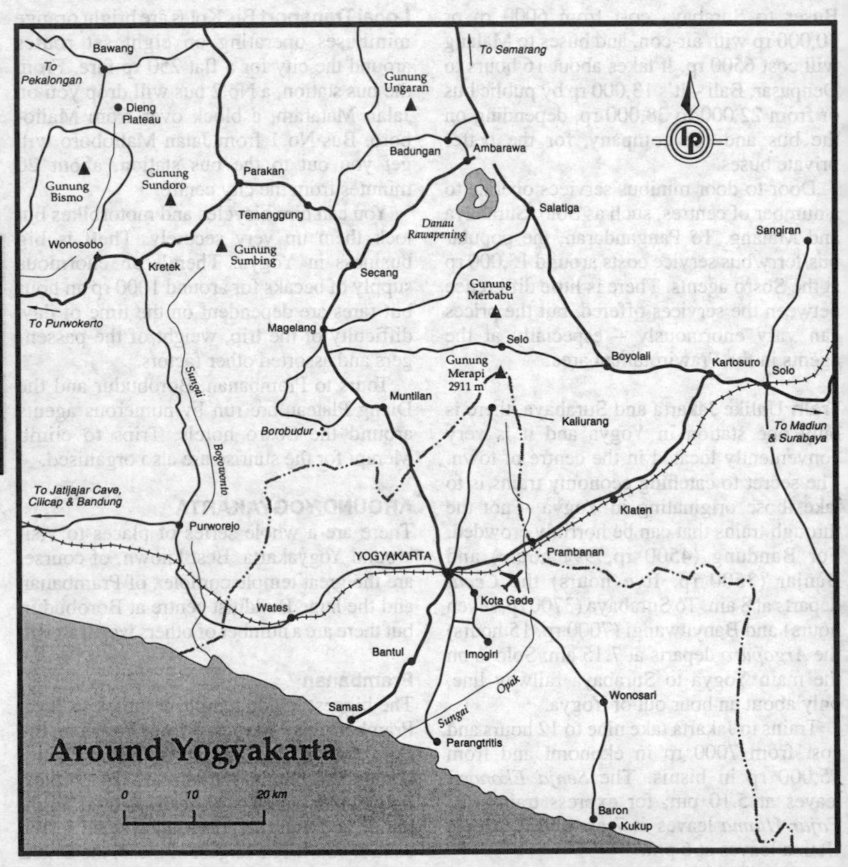

don't miss the great Ramayana ballet performance. It takes place over the full moon nights from May to October. Prambanan's Trimurti Theatre has performances throughout the year on Tuesday, Wednesday and Thursday nights from 7.30 to 9.30 pm.

Getting There & Away To get to Prambanan, take a Solo bus or colt from Yogya for 700 rp. A bicycle roadway runs all the way to Prambanan from Yogya, so this can be an interesting place to visit by hired bicycle.

Borobudur & Mendut

Ranking with Bagan and Angkor Wat as one of the greatest South-East Asian Buddhist monuments, **Borobudur** is an enormous construction covering a hill, 40 km from Yogya. With the decline of Buddhism, Borobudur was abandoned and only rediscovered in 1814 when Raffles governed Java.

The temple consists of six square bases topped by three circular ones and it was constructed roughly contemporaneously with Prambanan in the early part of the 9th century AD.

Over the centuries, the supporting hill became waterlogged and the whole immense stone mass started to subside at a variety of angles. A US$12 million restoration project has returned it to its former glory.

Nearly 1500 panels on the terraces illustrate Buddhist teachings and tales while over 400 Buddha images sit in chambers on the terraces. On the upper circular terraces there are latticed stupas which contain 72 more Buddha images.

The **Mendut Temple**, three km east of Borobudur, has a magnificent statue of Buddha seated with two disciples. He is three metres high and sits with both feet on the ground, rather than in the usual lotus position. It has been suggested that this image was originally intended to top Borobudur but proved impossible to raise to the summit.

Entry to Borobudur is 4000 rp. There's an additional fee to the Mendut Temple.

Places to Stay & Eat *Losmen Citra Rasa* is cheap with rooms from 7000 rp with mandi. *Losmen Saraswati* is good with rooms from 12,000 rp or there's the straightforward and similarly priced *Villa Rosita* to the west of the monument. *Bhumi Sambhara* is new and very comfortable with doubles for 15,000 rp with breakfast.

There are many warungs near the temple and in the village. *Mamy's Warung* (look for the sign 'Rice Stall 2M') is at the temple end of the road from the bus terminal.

Getting There & Away From Yogya a direct bus is 1000 rp or take a bus to Muntilan for 500 rp and then it's another 300 rp bus ride to the site.

The bus from Muntilan passes first Mendut and then the smaller Pawon Temple en route to Borobudur. So, if you don't feel like walking, you can use the bus to hop from one temple to the next.

Kaliurang

Kaliurang is a pleasant mountain resort on the slopes of volcanically active Mt Merapi, 26 km north from Yogya. It makes an interesting alternative to the better known trip to the Dieng Plateau, which is north of Wonosobo. There are great views of the mountains, lovely walks, waterfalls and a rather chilly swimming pool. It's pleasant to feel the crisp mountain air after the sweaty heat of the plains.

The climb of **Mt Merapi** takes about eight hours up and back for experienced walkers, and more like 15 hours for the less fit. You need to start at about 3 am to get the sunrise. Merapi is a difficult climb from Kaliurang (it's easier from Selo to the north of the volcano) and it's worth contacting the owner of Vogels for information and advice. It's only a one-hour climb to the volcano observation point from where you can watch Merapi when it's active.

Places to Stay & Eat This is basically a local resort but you can get rooms for less than 5000 rp in the delightful *Vogels*. A number of travellers have written to recommend this little place. You can also eat at Vogels and the food is excellent. The new rooms are much better than the old ones in the original building.

Kaliurang has over 100 other places to stay. Most of them are basic, cheap losmen where rooms start at 6000 rp. Try the *Berlian, Garuda, Bumi Putra* or *Gadjah Mada*.

Imogiri

The **Royal Cemetery of the Sultans of Mataram**, 20 km south-east from Yogya, sits high on a hillside at the top of 345 steps. Imogiri is a sacred site and many local people visit to pay their respects at the royal graves, especially that of the great Sultan Agung.

It's an interesting place to visit but you are expected to follow the strict etiquette of the kraton rules. All visitors have to sign the Visitor's Book, pay a small donation and hire traditional Javanese dress before they enter the graveyard. Men have to wear a sarong, women have to be bare-shouldered and wear kain (cloth) and kebayan (a Chinese long-sleeved blouse with a plunging front and embroidered edges). If you follow everyone else you will know what to do.

They don't seem to mind you entering the tomb of Sultan Agung, although it could be a problem if you're tall – it's a matter of crawling inside and keeping on your knees. Cameras are not allowed in the graveyard. Imogiri is only open on Monday from 10 am to 1 pm and on Friday from 1.30 to 4 pm.

INDONESIA

Parangtritis

The best known of the beaches south of Yogya, Parangtritis is 27 km away. Cheap accommodation and food are available and although the currents and undertows are reputed to be dangerous here, several travellers have written to say that swimming is possible. Perhaps it's seasonal.

You can, however, swim in freshwater pools at the base of the hill. This is a centre for the worship of Nyai Lara Kidul, the Queen of the South Seas. A sultan of Yogya is supposed to have taken her as his wife. Avoid Friday and the weekend when Parangtritis is crowded.

Places to Stay & Eat There are plenty of more or less similar *losmen* along the main street in this Yogya beach resort. Prices are low but facilities are limited and a bit unhealthy.

Away from the main street, *Penginapan Parang Endong* has simple rooms for 4000 rp and a good swimming pool. *Losmen Widodo* is in the middle price bracket with rooms from around 10,000 rp. The *Agung Hotel & Garden Restaurant* is similarly priced. There are cheap *warungs* along the promenade.

Getting There & Away From Yogya, it's 1000 rp and one hour from the bus station on Jalan Senopati, and this includes the 'entry' fee. The last bus back to Yogya leaves at 6 pm.

Bandungan & Ambarawa

Between Yogya and Semarang, you can stop at Bandungan to see the **Gedung Songo** (Nine Buildings in Javanese), which are a collection of small but beautifully sited Hindu temples on the slopes of Mt Ungaran.

The town of Ambarawa, on the main central route, is the turn-off point for Bandungan and anyone who's fascinated by railway engines will enjoy the **Ambarawa Railway Museum**. The collection of 20 or so railway engines at the old depot includes a 1902 cog locomotive which is still in working order.

Places to Stay Places to stay in Bandungan include the cheap *Losmen Riani I* from 8000 rp and *Wisma Kereta Api* with comfortable bungalows which are similar in price. The modern *Madya Hillview Inn* is economical but watch out for the cockroaches. Other places include the pleasant *Losmen Pojok Sari* and the more expensive *Rawa Pening Hotel*. Avoid weekends when Bandungan gets very crowded.

Getting There & Away From Ambarawa to Bandungan, it's half an hour by colt, and from the market place (also worth a visit) in Bandungan you have to get another colt to travel about six km to the actual site of the temples. To visit all of the temples could take up to six hours – you can go on horseback.

Other Attractions

Magelang was formerly a Dutch military garrison and it was here that the Javanese hero, Prince Diponegoro, was tricked into captivity in 1829. There's a small museum in the house where he was captured.

The **Jatijajar Cave** is 20 km south of Gombang, which is 130 km west of Yogya on the main road and railway line to Bandung or Cilacap. There are remarkable life-sized statues around the sides of the cave. Near the caves is the coastal resort of **Karang Bolong** where swallows nests are collected for that famous Chinese delicacy, bird's nest soup. Gombang has lots of losmen.

WONOSOBO

This is a pleasant place en route from Yogya to the Dieng Plateau or as a break between Bandung and Yogya.

Places to Stay & Eat

Hotel Jawa Tengah, on Jalan Ahmad Yani next to the market and the colt terminal for Dieng, is a good, clean place with rooms from 8000 rp. Others include the *Losmen Petra*, 200 metres down from the Jawa Tengah at Jalan Achmad Yani 81, with rooms with mandi from 8000 rp and cheaper rooms without. The *Losmen Famili* at Jalan Sumbing 6 is clean, comfortable and priced about the same.

The *Dieng Restaurant* and the *Asia*, on Jalan Kawedanan near the Jawa Tengah, both have good food. You can also eat well and cheaply at the *Rumah Makan Klenyer*, in the small grocery shop next to Losmen Petra.

Getting There & Away

It's a short bus or colt trip from Yogya to Magelang and then a much longer one from there to Wonosobo. Allow at least three hours from Magelang to Wonosobo – it can take longer and there's inevitably some hanging around waiting for a full passenger load to assemble. The Wonosobo bus station is about a km out of town.

If you intend to visit Borobudur on the way, start out as early as possible to make all the connections. Direct buses from Wonosobo to Cilacap don't arrive early enough to catch the last ferry to Kalipucang (for Pangandaran), but by departing at the crack of dawn you can get to Cilacap in time via Purwokerto.

DIENG PLATEAU

About 130 km from Yogya, this 2000-metre-high plateau has a number of interesting temples, some beautiful scenery, good walks and (at night) freezing temperatures. Come prepared for the night-time cold, Dieng's basic losmen and unexciting food, and you'll probably find it interesting.

Dieng is the collapsed remnant of an ancient crater. In the centre, where it is very swampy, there are five **Hindu/Buddhist temples**. These temples are thought to be the oldest in Java, predating Borobudur and Prambanan. There are a number of other temples scattered around. **Candi Bima**, to the south, is particularly fine but, like all too many places in Indonesia, has been defaced by graffitists.

The road forks at Bima. The right fork goes on to an area which smells of sulphur because of the frantically bubbling **mud ponds**. The left fork goes to placid **Lake Warna** with Semar Cave, an old meditation spot. The energetic can walk to many other places around the area, including the highest village in Java.

The kiosk next to Losmen Bu Jono, as you enter Dieng, sells hand-drawn maps of the area but you can ignore them and get a free map at the tourist office, almost next door.

If you're feeling fit, you can walk out to Bawang and continue from there by bemo to

Pekalongan on the north coast. It's downhill nearly all the way and takes about four hours. If it has been raining, this route can be very slippery but if you start early from Dieng you can be in Pekalongan in the afternoon. It's a quiet, friendly, hassle-free town where you can buy interesting and colourful batik.

Places to Stay & Eat

Dieng's losmen are all very basic. The *Losmen Asri* is the most popular with rooms from 6000 rp. *Losmen Bu Jono* has small, airy rooms from around 5000 rp, blankets and really cold mandi water. It's good value in Dieng. The *Dieng Plateau Homestay* is the best place, and has rooms for 6000 rp, a good-value cafe and plenty of information on the area.

Food is available at Bu Jono's, or there's the very friendly *Warung Sederhana*, close by on the road to the mushroom factory. It's OK for a cheap and spicy nasi goreng or noodles.

Getting There & Away

From Yogya, take a bus or colt to Magelang (800 rp, one hour) and another to Wonosobo (1200 rp, two hours). From the Wonosobo marketplace, take a colt (800 rp, 1½ hours) up the winding road to the plateau.

It is possible to visit Borobudur on the way, although you need to start out very early to complete the trip by night. You've got to travel Yogya-Muntilan-Borobudur-Magelang-Wonosobo-Dieng Plateau, so there are a lot of connections to make. Day tours to Borobudur and Dieng are also available from Yogya.

SOLO

Situated between Yogya and Surabaya, Solo (Surakarta or Sala) was for a time the capital of the Mataram Kingdom. The sultanate had shifted its capital several times from Kota Gede to Plered and then to Kartasura. The court of Kartasura was devastated by fighting in 1742 and the capital was moved east to the small village of Sala on the Bengawan Solo River.

It's a relatively quiet, easy-going and hassle-free town with two royal palaces where you are allowed to visit the pavilions and museums. Solo is also a good source of high-quality batik.

Information

The helpful tourist office at Jalan Slamet Riyadi 275 has a useful Solo guide map and a great many leaflets.

Kratons

The Susuhunan of Mataram, Pakubuwono II, finally moved from Kartasura into his new

PLACES TO STAY

2 Hotel Yayakarta
5 Solo Inn
6 Hotel Putri Ayu
9 Sahid Solo Hotel
10 Kusuma Sahid Prince Hotel & Garuda Office
12 Hotel Dana
16 Ramayana Guesthouse
18 Hotel Cakra
22 Solo Homestay
23 Losmen Nirwana
26 Hotel Central
29 Losmen Kota
32 Relax Homestay
34 Bamboo Homestay
35 Happy Homestay
38 Westerners
39 Mama Homestay

PLACES TO EAT

7 Swensen's & KFC
8 Adem Ayam Restaurant
17 Cipta Rasa Restaurant
19 American Donut Bakery
20 Jalan Teuku Umar Night Market
21 Warung Baru
24 Pasar Gede
27 Superman's Restaurant
28 Kasuma Sari Restaurant
31 New Holland Bakery

OTHER

1 Balapan Railway Station
3 RRI Radio Station
4 Bus Stop
11 Puro Mangkunegaran
13 Radya Pustaka Museum
14 Tourist Office
15 Sriwedari Amusement Park
25 Post Office
30 Wartel Telephone Office
33 Singosaren Plaza
36 Taxi Stand
37 Vihara Rahayu Chinese Temple
40 Mosque
41 Pasar Klewer
42 Kraton Surakarta
43 Solo Kota Railway Station

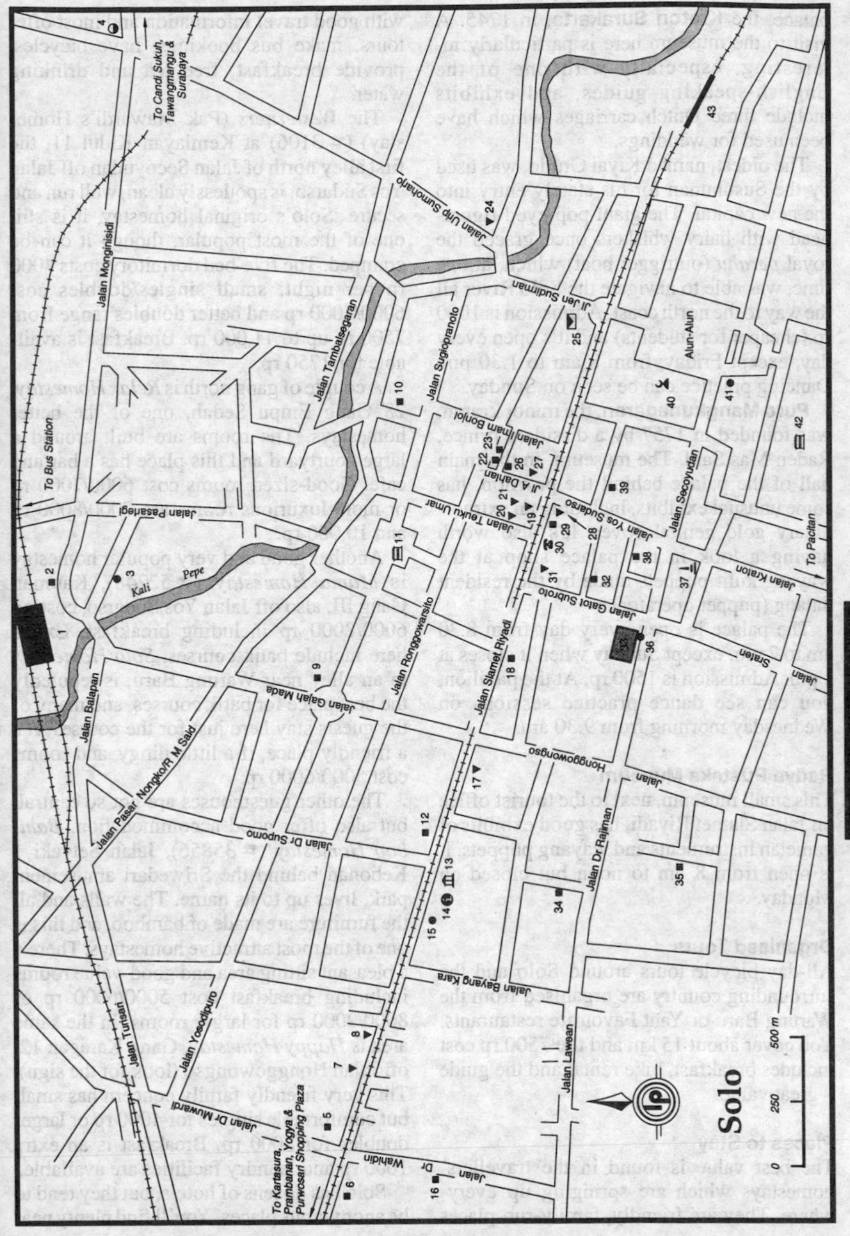
Solo
0
250
500 m
To Candi Sukuh, Tawangmangu & Surabaya
To Bus Station
Jalan Monginsidi
Jalan Pasar Legi
Jalan Urip Sumoharjo
Jalan Tambalsegaran
Kali Pepe
Jalan Balapan
Jalan Pasar Nongko/R M Said
Jalan Turisari
Jalan Yosodipuro
Jalan Dr Muwardi
To Kartasura, Prambanan, Yogya & Purwosari Shopping Plaza
Jalan Dr Wahidin
Jalan Dr Supomo
Jalan Gajah Mada
Jalan Ronggowarsito
Jalan Slamet Riyadi
Jalan Teuku Umar
Jalan Sugiopranoto
Jalan Imam Bonjol
Jl Dahlan
Jl Jen Sudirman
Jalan Yos Sudarso
Jalan Gatot Subroto
Jalan Secoyudan
Alun-Alun
Jalan Kraton
To Pacitan
Jalan Honggowongso
Jalan Dr Rajiman
Jalan Bayang Kara
Jalan Lawean

palace, the **Kraton Surakarta**, in 1745. A visit to the museum here is particularly interesting, especially with one of the English-speaking guides, and exhibits include three Dutch carriages which have been used for weddings.

The oldest, named Kiyai Grudo, was used by the Susuhunan for his stately entry into the new capital. The giant pop-eyed figurehead with hairy whiskers once graced the royal *perahu* (outrigger boat) which, at one time, was able to navigate the Solo River all the way to the north coast. Admission is 1000 rp (cheaper for students) and it's open every day, except Friday, from 8 am to 1.30 pm. Dancing practice can be seen on Sunday.

Puro Mangkunegaran, the minor kraton, was founded in 1757 by a dissident prince, Raden Mas Said. The museum, in the main hall of the palace behind the pavilion, has some unusual exhibits, including an extraordinary gold genital cover. It's also worth having a look in the palace shop at the wayang kulit puppets made by the resident dalang (puppet operator).

The palace is open every day from 8.30 am to 2 pm, except Sunday when it closes at 1 pm. Admission is 1500 rp. At the pavilion, you can see dance practice sessions on Wednesday morning from 9.30 am.

Radya Pustaka Museum

This small museum, next to the tourist office on Jalan Slamet Riyadi, has good exhibits of gamelan instruments and wayang puppets. It is open from 8 am to noon but closed on Monday.

Organised Tours

All-day bicycle tours around Solo and the surrounding country are organised from the Warung Baru or Yant Favourite restaurants. You cover about 15 km and the 7500 rp cost includes breakfast, bike rental and the guide – great value.

Places to Stay

The best value is found in the travellers' homestays which are springing up everywhere. They are friendly, family-run places with good travel information and most offer tours, make bus bookings, have bicycles, provide breakfast, free tea and drinking water.

The *Westerners* (Pak Mawardi's Homestay) (☎ 3106) at Kemlayan Kidul 11, the first alley north of Jalan Secoyudan off Jalan Yos Sudarso, is spotlessly clean, well run and secure. Solo's original homestay, it is still one of the most popular, though it can be cramped. The five-bed dormitory costs 4000 rp per night, small singles/doubles cost 6000/7000 rp and better doubles range from 7500 rp up to 11,000 rp. Breakfast is available for 1750 rp.

A couple of gang north is *Relax Homestay*, 28 Gang Empu Sedah, one of the better homestays. The rooms are built around a large courtyard and this place has a bar and cafe. Good-sized rooms cost 6000/7000 rp or more luxurious rooms are 7000/8000 rp and 10,000 rp.

Another good and very popular homestay is *Mama Homestay* (☎ 52248), Kauman Gang III, also off Jalan Yos Sudarso, costing 6000/8000 rp including breakfast. Extras here include batik courses. *Solo Homestay*, in an alley near Warung Baru, is reputedly the best place for batik courses, and many of the guests stay here just for the courses. It's a friendly place, if a little dingy, and rooms cost 5000/6000 rp.

The other guesthouses are not so central, but also offer good accommodation. *Bamboo Homestay* (☎ 35856), Jalan Setyaki 1 Kebonan behind the Sriwedari amusement park, lives up to its name. The walls and all the furniture are made of bamboo, and this is one of the most attractive homestays. There's a pleasant sitting area and good-value rooms including breakfast cost 5000/6000 rp or 8000/9000 rp for larger rooms. In the same area is *Happy Homestay*, Gang Karagan 12, off Jalan Honggowongso (look for the sign). This very friendly family concern has small but comfortable singles for 4000 rp or larger doubles for 8000 rp. Breakfast is an extra 1000 rp and laundry facilities are available.

Solo has dozens of hotels, but they tend to be anonymous places. You'll find plenty near the Balapan railway station but you are better off heading into town to a central location. The long-running *Losmen Kota*, Jalan Slamet Riyadi 125, is very central. It's a double-storey place built around a large open courtyard. Rooms cost from 7000/10,000 rp to 12,500/20,000 rp for singles/doubles with mandi. At Jalan Achmad Dahlan 32 is the open and airy *Hotel Central*. With its very fine Art-Deco woodwork, a thorough restoration would turn this hotel into a real showpiece. Meanwhile the rooms, all without bath, are 6000 rp and 7500 rp for doubles.

Around the corner the *Losmen Nirwana* at Jalan Ronggowarsito 59 has doubles for the same price. For something more luxurious, the *Ramayana Guesthouse* (☎ 32814), 22 Jalan Dr Wahidin, has quite good doubles with bath for 25,300 rp including breakfast, though it's the garden and stylish dining/lobby area decorated with objets d'art that make this place special.

Places to Eat

There are countless warungs and rumah makans including several serving Padang food. Jalan Teuku Umar, which runs north from Jalan Slamet Riyadi, has a row of stalls where you can get fresh milk, *susu segar* or *minuman sehat* (healthy drink), from some of the warungs – hot or cold or with honey. *Nasi gudeg* is popular but the speciality of Solo is *nasi liwet*, rice with chicken and coconut milk. On fine evenings, straw mats are laid out on the pavement on Jalan Slamet Riyadi near Jalan Yos Sudarso and the sate is superb. Another local speciality to try at night is *srabi*, the small rice puddings served up on a crispy pancake with banana, chocolate or jackfruit on top – best eaten piping hot.

Jalan Achmad Dahlan is quite a travellers' centre and the extremely popular *Warung Baru* turns out all the travellers' favourites. *Superman's*, opposite at No 22, is also good but definitely second in the popularity stakes.

Places along Jalan Slamet Riyadi include the *American Donut Bakery* and the *New Holland Bakery*. The latter has a bewildering array of baked goods and delicious savoury martabak rolls. At Jalan Slamet Riyadi 111, on the corner with Jalan Yos Sudarso, the *Kusama Sari* has air-con, good grills and ice creams. Other possibilities include the *Cipta Rasa*, west from the town centre on Jalan Slamet Riyadi.

Things to Buy

Solo, a batik centre rivalling Yogya, has its own individual style. Many people find it better value for batik and handicrafts than Yogya, quite possibly because it attracts fewer tourists. There are hundreds of cheap batik stalls at Pasar Klewer, or try the numerous shops for more sophisticated work (most of these shops are marked on the Solo guide map). Batik Semar is one good place and you can see the batik being made. The Trisne Batik and Artshop has some fine traditional batik tulis and other crafts.

There is also a good antiques market on Jalan Diponegoro. Look for old batik 'cap' stamps here. They're much cheaper than in Yogya but check that they are not damaged.

Entertainment

You can see wayang orang performances every evening, except Sunday, at the *Sriwedari amusement park theatres* on Slamet Riyadi. The costumes are stunning and the seats are cheap, starting from around 400 rp.

Other cultural performances are sometimes held at the *RRI*, the local radio broadcasting station – the tourist office will have details. Dance and gamelan rehearsals can be seen at the *Sasono Mulyo* building, near the Kraton Surakarta, every afternoon, except Sunday, between 2 and 4 pm.

Getting There & Away

Air There are air connections with a number of cities including Surabaya, less than an hour away. The airport is eight km west of town.

Bus & Train Solo is on the main Yogya to Surabaya rail and road route. The main bus station (Tirtonadi) is about three km from the town centre, not far from the Balapan railway station. Yogya is two hours away and costs 1000 rp. Buses to Semarang, Prambanan and Yogya are cheaper from Kartasura (west of the centre), reached by double-decker city bus. To Malang takes nine hours and costs around 6500 rp by bus. It's around 5000 rp for a public bus from Surabaya to Solo; it takes six to seven hours by day but half that time by night. The better air-con buses are more like 9000 to 12,000 rp.

By train Surabaya takes about five hours on the *Argopura*, which departs at 9.20 am and costs 3700 rp.

Deluxe door-to-door minibuses cost 3500 rp to Yogya or 13,000 rp to Surabaya or Malang. The Gilingan minibus station is right near the main bus station; the homestays and agents next to Losmen Kota or Warung Baru sell tickets.

Getting Around

A becak from the Balapan railway station or the bus station into the town centre is around 1000 rp. The orange minibus No 06 costs 250 rp to Jalan Slamet Riyadi.

The city double-decker bus runs between Kartasura in the west and Palur in the east, directly along Jalan Slamet Riyadi, and costs a flat fare of 200 rp. Bicycles can be hired from the homestays.

Solo has metered taxis. The main taxi stand is at the corner of the Singosaren Plaza shopping centre; ☎ 45678 to book a taxi.

AROUND SOLO

Sangiran

Prehistoric Java Man was discovered at Sangiran, 15 km north of Solo, and there is a small museum with fossil exhibits including some amazing 'mammoth' bones and tusks.

They are still finding things and if you wander up the road past the museum and have a look in some of the exposed banks you may find shells or fossil bones and crabs. To get there take a bus to Kalijambe (400 rp) and it's a three-km walk from there.

Candi Sukuh & Tawangmangu

Candi Sukuh is a primitive-style temple on the slopes of Mt Lawu, 36 km east of Solo. It dates from the 15th or 16th century and has a curious Inca-like look. To get there, take a Tawangmangu bus to Karangpandan (600 rp), then catch a minibus to Candi Sukuh (450 rp). On market days the minibus stops right beside the temple, but on other days it's an uphill walk of a few km to the site. It is about 1½ hours travelling by bus in total but it's worth it for the superb views and atmosphere.

Tawangmangu, a mountain resort about a 1½ hour ride out of Solo, has an impressive **waterfall** (the Grojogan Sewu) where you can take a dip in the very chilly pool. You can catch a bus from Karangpandan but it's possible to walk to Tawangmangu from Candi Sukuh. It's a very pleasant 2½ hour stroll along well-worn cobblestoned paths, and from Tawangmangu you can bus back to Solo for around 750 rp. Some people find the walk more interesting than Tawangmangu or Candi Sukuh.

Places to Stay & Eat In Tawangmangu, you can stay at the *Pak Amat Losmen* which has a garden. The rooms, from 8500 rp, are individual little houses with bathrooms and veranda. Further up the hill, the *Losmen Pondok Garuda*, next to the mosque, has a variety of rooms with and without bathroom at similar prices, some with a good view over the valley. On the main street, Jalan Lawu, about a km up from the bus station, *Hotel Lawu* has doubles from 22,000 rp. There's good food in the warungs further up the hill.

SEMARANG

This north coast port is the capital of central Java. It's about 120 km north of Yogya and about two-thirds of the way from Jakarta to Surabaya.

Information

There is a Semarang tourist office in the Wisma Pancasila building on Simpang Lima, the town square. There is also a central

Java tourist office, Kantor Dinas Pariwisata, at Jalan Pemuda 171.

Things to See

The **Sam Po Kong Temple** in the south-west of the city is dedicated to Admiral Cheng Ho – the famous Muslim eunuch of the Ming dynasty who led many expeditions from China to Java and other parts of South-East Asia in the early 15th century. He is particularly revered in Melaka (Malaysia), and the Chinese temple in Semarang is the largest in Indonesia, honoured by both Chinese Buddhists and Muslims.

It's better known as Gedong Batu (Stone Building) and is in the form of a huge cave. To get there, take a bemo from Terminal Baru in the centre of town to Karang Ayu, and then another to Gedong Batu. The temple is about half an hour from the city centre.

There isn't a great deal to do or see in Semarang itself except for a sprinkling of old buildings from the Dutch colonial era. On Jalan Let Jen Suprapto, south of Tawang railway station, there's the 1753 **Gereja Blenduk** church with its huge dome and baroque organ. Behind Poncol railway station there is the ruin of an old **Dutch East India Company fort** and there are numerous old warehouses around Tawang. The **Tay Kak Sie Temple** is on Gang Lombok, off Jalan Pekojan in Semarang's old Chinatown. Semarang also has an interesting day market, **Pasar Johar**, on the square at the top of Jalan Pemuda.

Places to Stay

Some of the bottom-end places at Semarang are of very low standard. Most places are in the centre of town, near Pasar Johar, and the old bus terminal, now a shopping centre.

The *Losmen Jaya* at Jalan M T Haryono 85-87, about a km south of the bus station, has rooms with fan from 9000 rp, more with mandi but breakfast is included. *Losmen Agung*, in the same area at Jalan Petolongan 32-34, is a colonial relic with rooms from 6000 rp; it gets decidedly mixed reports. *Losmen Djelita* at Jalan M T Haryono 34-38 is better although similarly priced.

Other cheap hotels are scattered along or just off Jalan Imam Bonjol. Try and get a room back from the street. The *Losmen Singapore* at Imam Bonjol 12 is reasonably central, near Pasar Johar, and has rooms from 9000 rp. The nearby *Hotel Oewa-Asia* at Jalan Kol Sugiono 12 is a former colonial hotel. It's a friendly, comfortable place with rooms from 12,000 rp including breakfast. There are more expensive rooms with bathroom and fan or air-con.

Further west, near the Poncol railway station, is the fairly comfortable and friendly *Losmen Ardjuna* at Jalan Imam Bonjol 51, and the *Losmen Rahayu* at No 35. Much further out at Jalan Imam Bonjol 144 is the *Bali* with clean if somewhat overpriced rooms from 16,500 rp. Becak riders may try to steer you here for the commission.

The *Dibya Puri* (☎ 27821) at Jalan Pemuda 11 is a rambling old place with a pleasant courtyard with trees. They have a restaurant, a bar and a laundry service, and large, airy rooms start from around 30,000 rp with shared bathrooms, including breakfast.

Places to Eat

The *Toko Oen* at Jalan Pemuda 52, a short walk from the Pasar, is a wonderfully genteel old place. It's not cheap but well worth a visit – the food is good and they have a terrific selection of exotic ice creams.

Restaurants along Jalan Gajah Mada include the reasonably priced *Gajah Mada* at No 43 with good Chinese food and seafood. On Gang Lombok, off Jalan Pekojan in Chinatown, there are good Chinese eating places. At *Pasar Ya'ik*, the night market next to Pasar Johar, there are plenty of cheap foodstalls.

The *Hotel Dibya Puri* restaurant on Jalan Pemuda serves European and Indonesian food and their set Indonesian meal, complete with fruit and coffee, is good value. The *Ritzeky Pub* on Jalan Sinabung Buntu is an expat hang-out.

Entertainment

Every evening there are wayang orang performances in the *Ngesti Pandowo Theatre* at

Jalan Pemuda 116. Performances start at 8 pm. Or, take a city bus out to Gombel, the 'new town' on the hills to the south, and have a drink at the *Sky Garden Hotel* from where there is a fine view of the city and ships at sea. To get there, take a bus down Jalan Pemuda bound for Jatingalen and ask for Bukit Gombel, which is just past the hotel.

Getting There & Away

Semarang is on the main north coast train route between Jakarta and Surabaya and can also be reached from those towns by bus. Tawang is the main railway station in Semarang.

The Jurnatan bus station on Jalan M T Haryono is close to Tawang and fairly central. Most bus ticket agents are near the bus station along the same street. There are public buses to Yogya (2000 rp, 3½ hours) and Solo, or air-con services and door-to-door minibuses.

An air-con 4848 Taxis' minibus operates from Cirebon to Semarang, again door-to-door. Semarang to Surabaya costs about 6000 rp by public bus and from 9500 rp by night bus and takes about eight hours. Buses to Jakarta cost from around 8000 rp for the cheapest public buses but it's better to take the train. The night buses arrive at ungodly hours at the remote Pulo Gadung bus station.

Getting Around

You can get around town by fixed-price city buses or minivans for 250 rp. Minivans depart from Terminal Baru on Jalan H A Salim behind Pasar Johar.

PEKALONGAN

The small town of Pekalongan is on the north coast between Semarang and Cirebon. Few travellers pause here but there's some fine local batik and a **batik museum**.

Places to Stay & Eat

Directly opposite the railway station, at Jalan Gajah Mada 11A, the *Hotel Gajah Mada* (☎ 41185) is clean, basic and good value. Nearby, you'll find the *Losmen Ramayana* and the *Losmen Damai*.

The *Hotel Istana* (☎ 61581) at Jalan Gaja Mada 23 is a more expensive hotel with rooms from around 25,000 rp.

Near the railway station, the *Rumah Makan Saiyo* has reasonable Padang food. Try the *Buana Restaurant* at Jalan Mansyur 5 for seafood or the *Purima* on Jalan Hayam Wuruk for snacks and ice cream.

KUDUS

An important Islamic centre, Kudus is north-east of Semarang towards Surabaya near the north coast. The **Al-Manar Mosque** in the centre of the old town dates from 1549. Kudus is also noted for its *kretek* (clove-flavoured cigarette) manufacturing.

Places to Stay & Eat

Within walking distance of the bus station, the *Hotel Notasari* (☎ 21245) at Jalan Kepodang 12 has rooms with mandi from 26,000 rp. The cheaper and more spartan *Losmen Slamet* is in the town centre at Jalan Sudirman 63.

The *Hotel Notasari* has a good restaurant or try the *Garuda* on Jalan Sudirman 1 for Chinese, Indonesian or Western food. The *Rumah Makan Hijau*, near the bus station at Jalan Achmad Yani 1, is cheap and has good food and fruit juices.

AROUND KUDUS

The town of **Mayong**, 12 km north-west of Kudus on the road to Jepara, was the home of Raden Ajeng Kartini, a noted Indonesian writer who died in 1904. **Jepara** is the centre for Java's best traditional woodcarvers. **Rembang**, further east from Kudus, has a good beach.

MALANG

Malang is a big country town on the alternative 'back route' between Yogyakarta and Banyuwangi. The countryside on this run is particularly beautiful and Malang is a nice city with just enough altitude to take the edge off the heat. It gets few Western visitors, although it has good parks and trees and a large central market.

Places to Stay

Surabaya's *Bamboe Denn* has a branch hostel (☎ 24859) at Jalan Semeru 35, only a 10-minute walk from the bus or railway station. It's very cheap and has dorm beds for 4000 rp, but is often full. You'll probably get roped into English conversation lessons too!

The *Hotel Santosa* is central at Jalan H A Salim 24, just off the main square, and has basic but clean rooms with private mandi from around 18,000 rp. The *Hotel Malang* on Jalan Zainul Arifin, off Jalan H A Salim, is also central but rather noisy. Better value is the pleasantly old-fashioned *Hotel Malinda*, also on Jalan Zainul Arifin, with rooms with private mandi from 18,000 rp and up – and ceilings that must be seven metres high! The excellent *Hotel Helios* on Jalan Pattimura is similarly priced and has a very pleasant garden.

Hotel Aloha (☎ 26950) at Jalan Gajah Mada 7 is nice but expensive. Rooms with bath cost 20,000 rp and 40,000 rp with air-con. *Hotel Pelangi*, a very large old Dutch hotel building right on the town square, is good but expensive.

Places to Eat

One of the good places to eat is the anachronistically colonial *Toko Oen* on the town square, but it's rather expensive. *Rumah Makan Padang Minang Jaya* at Jalan Basuki Rachmat 111 has terrific Padang food, or try *Depot Pangsit Mie Gadjah Mada* on Jalan Pasar Besar for good cheap noodles. Malang also has an excellent cheap night market, *Pasar Senggol*, along Jalan Majapahit by the river.

Getting There & Away

Buses to or from Yogyakarta or Solo take about nine hours and cost 6500 rp, or around 13,000 rp by air-con express bus. Buses leave regularly to and from Surabaya (1700 rp, 2½ hours). The ekonomi-class only train from Surabaya takes about the same time and is similarly priced.

The bus to Probolinggo from Malang (1800 rp) takes about two hours. Buses to or from Banyuwangi cost 5200 rp and take about nine hours. Night buses to Bali cost around 16,000 rp. Bali Indah has an office on Jalan Pattimura, and Pemuda Express at Jalan Basuki Rachmat 1 operates night buses to Bali and other destinations.

AROUND MALANG

For an interesting trip in this area take a train from Solo to Jombang, then colts to Blimbing, Kandangan, Batu and, finally, Malang.

High mountains around Malang include **Gunung Semeru**, the highest point in Java at 3678 metres. It takes three or four days to climb to the top and back; it is a real climb, not an easy walk. Selekta (see Around Surabaya), a hill resort, is just 16 km north-west of Malang – take a colt to Batu and from there another colt will drop you right at the Selekta swimming pool.

Malang has some excellent ruins. A good, roughly circular day trip is to go 12 km north of Malang to **Candi Singosari** (the temple is to the right in Singosari, 500 metres from the main Malang to Surabaya road). Return to the village of Blimbang, north of Malang, and then travel east to **Candi Jago** at Tumpang, and then to **Candi Kidal** in the small village of Kidal. Finally, you can complete the circle back to Malang via Tajinan. For transport, first take a bemo to the terminal at Blimbing, and from Blimbing you can take bemos all the way.

SURABAYA

A big, busy and not particularly interesting place, the capital of east Java is a major port and the second largest city in Indonesia. For most people, it's just a short stop between central Java and Bali, although it is probably the most 'Indonesian' of all the large cities. People who do find Surabaya interesting, and to be fair quite a few people do, generally enjoy the Indonesian atmosphere of the place.

Information

The East Java regional tourist office is at Jalan Pemuda 118, across from the Surabaya Delta Plaza. The small office is open from 8

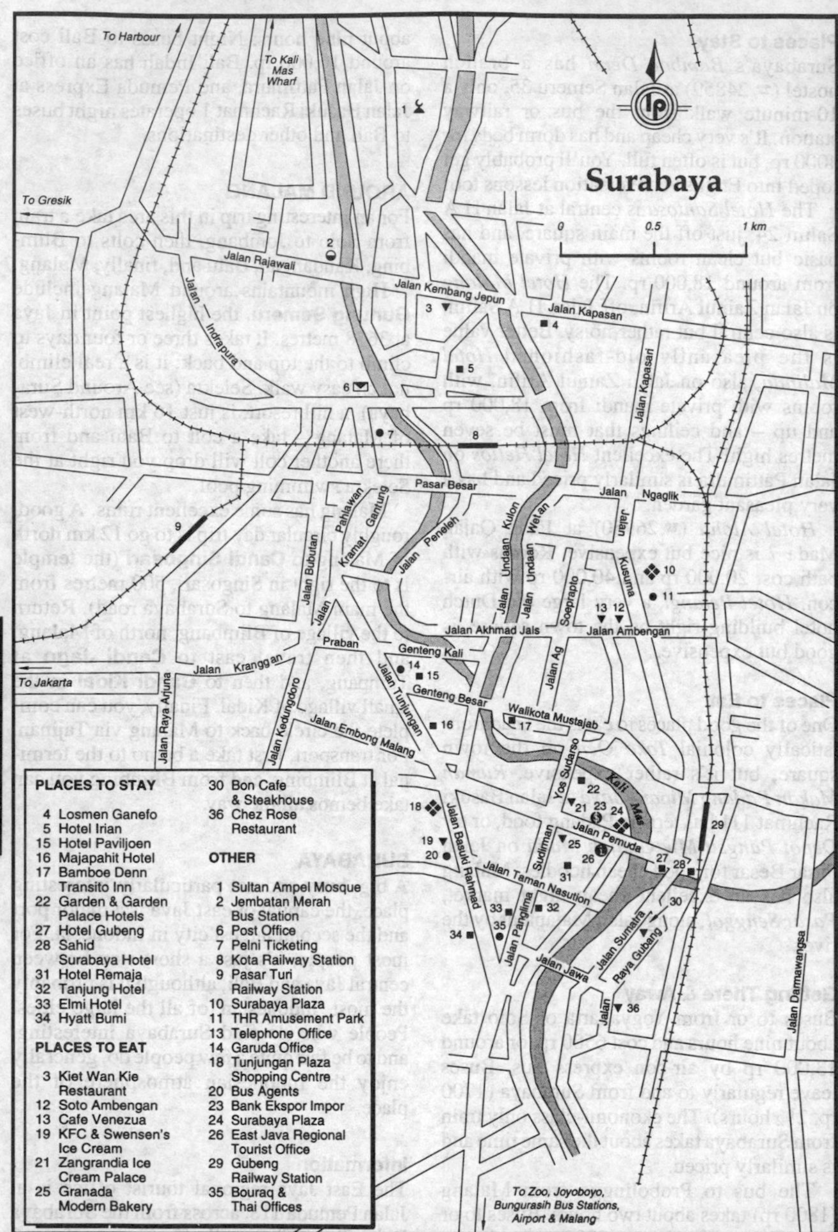
Surabaya
0
0.5
1 km
To Harbour
To Kali Mas Wharf
To Gresik
To Jakarta
To Zoo, Joyoboyo, Bungurasih Bus Stations, Airport & Malang
Jalan Rajawali
Jalan Indrapura
Jalan Kembang Jepun
Jalan Kapasan
Jalan Kapasari
Pasar Besar
Pahlawan
Kramat Gantung
Jalan Peneleh
Jalan Bubutan
Jalan Undaan Kulon
Jalan Undaan Wetan
Jalan Ngaglik
Jalan Kusuma
Soeprapto
Jalan Akhmad Jais
Jalan Ambengan
Jalan Praban
Genteng Kali
Jalan Kranggan
Jalan Raya Arjuna
Jalan Kedungdoro
Jalan Tunjungan
Genteng Besar
Jalan Embong Malang
Jalan Ag
Walikota Mustajab
Yos Sudarso
Kali Mas
Jalan Pemuda
Sudirman
Jalan Basuki Rahmad
Jalan Taman Nasution
Jalan Panglima
Jalan Sumatra
Raya Gubang
Jalan Jawa
Jalan Darmawangsa
INDONESIA
PLACES TO STAY
4 Losmen Ganefo
5 Hotel Irian
15 Hotel Paviljoen
16 Majapahit Hotel
17 Bamboe Denn Transito Inn
22 Garden & Garden Palace Hotels
27 Hotel Gubeng
28 Sahid Surabaya Hotel
31 Hotel Remaja
32 Tanjung Hotel
33 Elmi Hotel
34 Hyatt Bumi
PLACES TO EAT
3 Kiet Wan Kie Restaurant
12 Soto Ambengan
13 Cafe Venezua
19 KFC & Swensen's Ice Cream
21 Zangrandia Ice Cream Palace
25 Granada Modern Bakery
30 Bon Cafe & Steakhouse
36 Chez Rose Restaurant
OTHER
1 Sultan Ampel Mosque
2 Jembatan Merah Bus Station
6 Post Office
7 Pelni Ticketing
8 Kota Railway Station
9 Pasar Turi Railway Station
10 Surabaya Plaza
11 THR Amusement Park
13 Telephone Office
14 Garuda Office
18 Tunjungan Plaza Shopping Centre
20 Bus Agents
23 Bank Ekspor Impor
24 Surabaya Plaza
26 East Java Regional Tourist Office
29 Gubeng Railway Station
35 Bouraq & Thai Offices

am to 3 pm daily, except Friday when it closes at 11 am.

There are plenty of banks around including a huge and flashy Bank Ekspor Impor office on Jalan Pemuda. The main post office is on Jalan Kebon Rojo. The easiest place to make telephone calls is at the Wartel in Tunjungan Plaza. There are swimming pools at the Garden Hotel and the Hotel Simpang, at Jalan Pemuda 1-3.

Things to See

The Surabaya **zoo** is reputed to be the largest in South-East Asia. It is well organised and has a couple of big Komodo dragons, who seem to spend half the time fast asleep. Admission is 1000 rp and it costs 200 rp more for the aquarium (worth it) or the nocturama. The zoo is only a short ride south by city bus No 2 or bemo V from Jalan Panglima Sudirman in the centre of town.

The small **MPU Tantular Museum** has interesting archaeological exhibits and is across the road from the zoo. Close to the town centre is the **THR amusement park**, open in the evenings, but usually dead unless a special event is on. Plenty of Makassar schooners can be seen at the **Kali Mas wharf**. The **Sultan Ampel Mosque** is dedicated to one of the Wali Songo, the nine holy men that brought Islam to Java. Around the mosque are the colourful winding streets of Kampung Arab.

Places to Stay

The *Bamboe Denn* (☎ 40333), Jalan Ketabang Kali 6A, a 20-minute walk from Gubeng railway station, is a Surabaya institution and has been the No 1 travellers' centre in Surabaya for over 20 years. Beds in the large dorm are 4000 rp and tiny singles/doubles are 5000/7500 rp.

Apart from the Bamboe Denn, there isn't a great choice of cheap accommodation in Surabaya. Then again, not many people pause here. The *Hotel Gubeng* at Jalan Sumatra 18 is only 100 metres from the Gubeng station and has reasonable rooms from 18,000 rp.

If you continue beyond the Bamboe Denn and cross the river to Jalan Genteng Besar, you'll come to *Hotel Paviljoen* (☎ 43449) in an old colonial house at No 94. Older rooms without bath are 14,000 rp, which is reasonable value for Surabaya – larger renovated rooms with bath are 27,000 rp.

Well north of the town centre, near the Kota railway station, is *Losmen Ganefo* (☎ 311169) at Jalan Kapasan 169-171. This spacious old hotel has some real character with rooms from 16,000 rp, or 25,000 rp with bath. In the same area, a similar cheap hotel with colonial style is the *Hotel Irian* (☎ 20953), Jalan Samudra 16, which has doubles for 16,500 rp or rooms with bath for 30,000/35,000 rp. Jalan Samudra has a number of other hotels including the cheaper *Hotel Rejeki* and the much more upmarket *New Grand Park Hotel*.

There aren't many bargains in the mid-price range either but one place definitely worth trying is the fine old *Majapahit Hotel* (☎ 43351) at Jalan Tunjungan 65. Dating from 1910, there's a surprisingly good garden, considering its central location, and economy rooms from US$40. The *Tanjung Hotel* (☎ 42431) at Jalan Panglima Sudirman is a more modern mid-range hotel with rooms from around 65,000 rp.

Places to Eat

Apart from night-time foodstalls, Surabaya seems to be dominated by Western-style fast-food places. Surabaya Delta Plaza, near the Gubeng station, has *Pizza Huts* (two of them!), *McDonald's*, plenty of local fast-food outlets, and a pretty good air-con foodstall centre on the 4th floor.

There's more fast food in the *Tunjungan Plaza* – a collection of restaurants on the top floor plus *Kentucky Fried Chicken* and *Swensen's Ice Cream* downstairs.

On Jalan Pemuda, right at the corner with Jalan Sudirman, there's the *Granada Modern Bakery*, a good breakfast place. The *Zangrandia Ice Cream Palace*, at the front of the Garden Palace Hotel, is a very grand and expensive ice cream parlour.

For cheap eats, patronise the *stalls* around the Gubeng station or off Jalan Tunjungan.

There are *night markets* near the flower market on Jalan Kayoon and on Jalan Pandegiling. The market on Jalan Genteng Besar, just across the river from the Bamboe Denn, has good roadside *warungs* – sate ular (snake sate) is sometimes available.

Up near the Jembatan Merah bus station, *Kiet Wan Kie*, Jalan Kembang Jepun 51, serves excellent Chinese fare at reasonable prices considering the fancy decor and agreeable air-conditioning.

Getting There & Away

Air There is an hourly shuttle service to Jakarta for 161,000 rp. Other fares include Bandung for 128,000 rp, Denpasar for 78,000 rp, Ujung Pandang for 183,000 rp and Yogyakarta for 53,000 rp.

Bus The main bus station in Surabaya is the Bungurasih terminal, 10 km south of the centre. Take bus P1 from Jalan Pemuda or Jalan Sudirman to the bus station for 400 rp.

There are many bus company offices at the station for public and private buses. Fares for ordinary buses include Probolinggo (1700 rp, two hours), Banyuwangi (6000 rp), Malang (1700 rp, two hours), Solo (6000 rp, eight hours) and Yogya (8000 rp, nine hours).

For the longer trips to Solo, Yogya or Denpasar, the express buses are much quicker and more comfortable, and many go at night when traffic is lighter. Express buses to Yogya cost around 15,000 rp and take about seven hours. Night buses to Denpasar cost from around 15,000 to 21,000 rp and take 10 hours. There are buses going straight through to Bandung and even Jakarta but that's a long trip by bus (859 km; 15 hours). It's better to take a train if you want to go there directly.

Tickets for air-con buses and door-to-door minibuses can also be bought at the bus agents on Jalan Basuki Rahmad in the centre of the city. Minibuses to Solo or Yogya cost around 15,000 rp, to Semarang it's 16,000 rp and to Denpasar it's 25,000 rp.

If you're heading to the north coast of Java, buses and colts depart from the Jembatan Merah station, north of the Kota railway station. Buses to Semarang cost 5800 rp. Buses run direct from Surabaya to various towns on the island of Madura.

Train Trains from Jakarta, taking the northern route via Semarang, arrive at the Pasar Turi station. Trains taking the southern route via Yogya, and trains from Banyuwangi and Malang, arrive at Gubeng and carry on to Kota. The Gubeng station is much more convenient for central places than Kota or Pasar Turi.

The trip from Jakarta takes 12 to 17 hours although in practice, the slower ekonomi trains can take even longer. Fares vary from 10,000 rp in ekonomi class, from 26,000 rp in bisnis and from 44,000 rp in eksekutif. The best services are with the deluxe *Bima Express* via Yogya or the slightly quicker *Mutiara Utara* via Semarang. The cheapest are the ekonomi services like the *Gaya Baru Malam Utara* (14 hours) or the *Parcel* (14 hours) on the northern route, or the *Gaya Baru Malam Selatan* (17 hours) on the southern route.

Trains to or from Solo (4½ to six hours) and Yogyakarta (5½ to seven hours) cost from 3700 rp in ekonomi and from 14,000 rp in bisnis. The train is faster and cheaper than the buses. The 8.25 am *Purbaya* and the faster 1 pm *Argopura* are good ekonomi services.

Apart from services to the main cities, there are trains to Malang (two hours) and Banyuwangi (seven hours) for the ferry to Bali. The fare to Banyuwangi costs from 3500 rp in ekonomi and from 7000 rp in bisnis.

Boat Surabaya is an important port and most of the regular Pelni services operate through here. See the Indonesia Getting Around section for more details. Connections to Kalimantan and Sulawesi are particularly popular.

Ekonomi fares include Ujung Pandang for 35,000 rp, Jakarta for 24,000 rp, Banjarmasin for 30,000 rp, Balikpapan for 45,000 rp, Waingapu for 62,000 rp and Kupang for

76,000 rp. Boats depart from Tanjung Perak harbour; bus P1 or C will get you there.

The Pelni ticket office (☎ 21041) at Jalan Pahlawan 112 is open from 9 am to 1.30 pm Monday to Friday, and from 8 am to 1 pm Saturday. The front ticket counter is chaotic but you can go round to the back office where the staff are more helpful. For information on cargo boats, try the harbourmaster at Kalimas Baru 194, Tanjung Perak.

Kalla Lines (tel 21024), Jalan Perak Timur 158, also have a ship once a week to Pasir Gudang, just outside Johor Bahru in Malaysia. The cost is around US$80 per person for the cheapest eight-berth cabins, and the journey takes 60 hours.

From the harbour there is also a ferry to Madura for 400 rp.

Getting Around

To/From the Airport Juanda airport is 18 km south of the city centre, and an air-con taxi costs around 9000 rp. To reach the airport by bus take any J bus (400 rp) and then an Alloha-Juanda bus for 2300 rp.

Local Transport Surabaya has plenty of air-con metered taxis and flagfall is 800 rp. Typical fares from central Surabaya include the Pelni office for 3000 rp, the harbour for 4500 rp, Bamboe Denn to Gubeng station for 2000 rp and the airport for 9000 rp. Becaks are useful for local transport and there are plenty of them around town. Bemos are labelled A, B, C etc and all charge a standard 250 rp. Patas (fast) buses are labelled P and charge a fixed 400 rp fare.

AROUND SURABAYA

Gresik

The **tomb** of the Muslim saint, Sunan Giri, one of the nine wali songo credited with introducing Islam to Java in the 13th century, is in this town. It is 25 km north-west of Surabaya.

Trowulan

Scattered around Trowulan, 60 km south-west from Surabaya on the Surabaya to Solo road, are the remains of the ancient Majapahit Kingdom. The Majapahits were the final Hindu kingdom to rule on Java until the Muslims drove them out to Bali in the early 1500s.

The **Trowulan Museum** has a large map indicating the locations of the *candis* (shrines of original Javanese design), tombs and graves. The museum is open from 7 am daily (except Monday) and closes at 2 pm Tuesday to Thursday and Sunday, at 11 am on Friday and 12.30 pm on Saturday.

Some of the temple remains are very impressive in their shattered grandeur and a few of the sites are within walking distance of the museum. If you're going somewhere else, you can leave your gear at the museum office. Or hire a becak – a three to four-hour trip costs about 8000 rp and the ride along the country lanes is easily as good as the temples themselves. A bus from Surabaya (1000 rp) will drop you right at the museum on the main road, and it's another 1400 rp on to Madiun.

Pandaan

The open-air **Candra Wilwatikta Theatre** at Pandaan, 40 km south of Surabaya on the road to Malang, is the site of the east Java classical ballet festival held during the dry season on the first and third Saturday nights of the months of May to October.

Mountain Resorts

At **Tretes**, 55 km south of Surabaya, and nearby **Prigen** there is a network of footpaths and trails and many waterfalls. I wouldn't recommend it for a special trip but if you have to kill time in Surabaya, this is a good escape. On the other side of the same mountain, the similar resorts of **Selekta** and **Batu** are easily accessible from Malang. Selekta has an excellent swimming pool and **Songgoriti**, near Batu, is a spa town with relaxing hot sulphur baths. Others are **Tosari** and **Wendit**, which has a lake where you can swim and lots of monkeys.

Places to Stay & Eat There are lots of cottages or individual rooms available in Tretes and in Prigen – somebody will find

INDONESIA

you a place, although this is principally a local resort where few foreigners are seen. Prices are not cheap and go sky-high. There are some good and cheap places to eat around the market. The situation is similar in Batu and Selekta.

MADURA

Only half an hour from Surabaya by ferry, the relatively untouristic island of Madura has fine beaches and picturesque remote countryside. Coming up from Bali, Madura is also accessible by daily ferry from Jangkar, north of Banyuwangi, to Kalianget on the island's eastern tip – you could make a trip through Madura and exit from Kamal to Surabaya.

Madura is a flat and rugged island, much of it dry and sometimes barren, and it's a contrast to Java in both landscape and lifestyle. Cattle raising is important rather than rice growing. The production of salt is another major industry – much of Indonesia's supply comes from the vast salt tracts around Kalianget in the east.

During the dry season, particularly in August and September, Madura is famed for its colourful **bull races**, the *kerapan sapi*, which climax with the finals held at Pamekasan. The bulls are harnessed in pairs, two teams compete at a time and they're raced along a 120-metre course in a special stadium. Races don't last long – the best time recorded is nine seconds over 100 metres, which is faster than the men's world track record. Bull races for tourists are sometimes staged at the Bangkalan Stadium. The east Java tourist board can supply details of where and when the bull races will be held.

Apart from beaches and the bull races, there are a number of interesting places to visit dotted around the island. Near the village of Arasbaya, on the west coast, is **Air Mata** (Water of the Eye or Tears) where the old royal cemetery of the Cakraningrat family is perched on the edge of a small ravine, with beautiful views along the river valley and across the terraced hills. To get there from Kamal, which is south of Bangkalan, take a colt for Arasbaya (28 km north) and ask for the turn-off to Air Mata. From there, it's a four-km walk inland.

Along the south coast road to Pamekasan, 100 km east of Kamal, there are fields of immaculately groomed cattle, small fishing villages and a sea of rainbow-coloured perahus (boats). **Camplong**, about 15 km short of Pamekasan, has a fine sweeping beach and calm water. From Pamekasan, the capital of Madura, you can visit the strange natural fire resources of **Api Abadi** (Eternal Fire), where 'fire spouts out of the earth'.

Sumenep is an old and attractive town, 53 km north-east of Pamekasan in the more isolated hills of the interior. Sumenep is more interesting than Pamekasan and a good base for visiting remoter parts of the island. You can see Sumenep's 18th-century mosque, the kraton and its small, interesting museum of royal family possessions. **Asta Tinggi**, the royal cemetery, is only about three km from the town centre.

At **Salopeng**, 21 km from Sumenep and near the fishing village of Ambunten on the north coast, there are great yellow sand dunes, palm trees and rough seas. Further west, **Pasongsongan** is the beach to head for as it has accommodation. The beach at **Lombang**, 30 km from Sumenep near the eastern tip of the island, is reputed to be even more beautiful but less accessible.

Places to Stay

In Pamekasan, you could try the *Hotel Garuda*, on Jalan Masigit near the town square, with rooms at around 7000 rp. The cheaper *Losmen Bahagia* is further down Jalan Trunojoyo and costs 5000/8000 rp. Or there's the more expensive *Hotel Trunojoyo*, round the corner and down a small alley off Jalan Trunojoyo. They're all in the centre of town and a 300 rp becak ride from the bus station.

In Sumenep, *Losmen Wijaya I* and *II*, both near the main bus station, are good with rooms from around 8000 rp. Or try the cheaper *Losmen Damai* or *Losmen Matahari* near the town square on Jalan Sudirman.

If you want to stay out on the beach, *Taufik's Homestay* is at Pasongsongan, on

INDONESIA

the north coast about 30 km north-west of Sumenep. It is geared for travellers and costs 5000/8000 rp.

Getting There & Away

It's only half an hour by ferry from Surabaya to Kamal, the harbour town in Madura. From the ferry terminal in Kamal you can take a bus or colt to other main towns, including Pamekasan (2000 rp, 2½ hours) and Bangkalan (600 rp, half an hour).

There is also a ferry between Kalianget and Jangkar in the very north-east of Java. Ferries depart in either direction at 7 am, take four to five hours and cost 2500 rp.

MT BROMO

A visit to this fantastic, and still far from extinct, volcano is easy to fit in between Bali and Surabaya. The usual jumping-off point for Bromo is the town of Probolinggo on the main Surabaya to Banyuwangi road. From there, you have to get to Ngadisari or Cemoro Lawang, high on the slopes of an ancient volcano.

You can stay with one of the villagers in Ngadisari or you can continue up the very steep final three km to Cemoro Lawang at the rim of the crater – jeeps do the trip for 1000 rp. Alternatively, direct bemos run from Probolinggo to Cemoro Lawang. At Ngadisari pay the 1550 rp entry fee.

Cemoro Lawang is the most popular place to stay because you've got a shorter and easier walk in the morning. On Bromo, as at so many other mountains, it's being there for the sunrise which is all-important!

As at Mt Batur in Bali, Bromo is a crater within a crater. The outer one is vast and across to Bromo and nearby Mt Batok is a scene of utter desolation. Get up at 5 am or earlier for an easy stroll across and just follow the path down into the crater and the white markers across the lava sand to Bromo. Take a torch (flashlight) or the descent in the dark can be fairly dodgy. There is no need for a guide or horses although, if you want to, you can ride across for about 10,000 rp.

By the time you've crossed the lava plain and started to climb up Bromo (246 steps, one traveller reported) it should be fairly light. From the top you'll get an unreal view of the sun sailing up over the outer crater. Bromo continuously pours out some very smelly white smoke – New Zealanders will find it familiar!

A number of travellers have sent in more suggestions about the Bromo trip, almost all noting that it's definitely worthwhile and that it's worth staying a day or two and doing more walking. In the wet season, the dawn and the clouds often arrive simultaneously so at that time of year you might just as well stay in bed and stroll across later in the day when it's much warmer.

In January or February, the big annual Kesada festival is held and at that time of year getting up the mountain involves fighting your way through the crowds. One visitor even suggested that if you're really crazy, you could climb right down inside the crater. Another nutcase suggested climbing it at night while it's erupting, adding that it 'scares the shit out of you'!

As an alternative to the usual return to Probolinggo, you can walk right around Bromo across the lava plain and climb up over the opposite edge to Ngadas. You can walk down from village to village until you eventually get a ride into Malang. It entails six or seven hours of walking, so start early in order to get to Malang by evening.

Places to Stay & Eat

Mt Bromo In Ngadisari, *Yoschi's* is the most popular place to stay. Basic rooms cost 6000 to 10,000 rp and more expensive cottages are available. There are plenty of other places to stay in Ngadisari, although the quality varies a lot and security is not always so great. Prices vary from around 3500 rp.

At Cemoro Lawang, right on the rim of the Tengger crater, the *Cafe Lava Hostel & Restaurant* is the No 1 travellers' place. Singles/doubles cost 7000/10,000 rp, a dorm bed is 4000 rp and YHA and student discounts are offered. *Hotel Bromo Permai* has comfortable dorm beds for 5000 rp (cheaper for students or YHA members) and rooms ranging from 12,000 rp right up to 65,000 rp.

The hotel has a bar and restaurant – food here is also pricey but they're quite substantial meals. At night, it's very cold at the top (it is in Ngadisari too) but staying up here does save an hour or so of walking before dawn!

Probolinggo This town is a useful mid-point between Surabaya and Banyuwangi as well as being the jumping-off point for Mt Bromo. There are hotels and some cheap restaurants along the main street, Jalan Raja P Sudirman, less than a 10-minute walk from the bus station. The *Hotel Bromo Permai II*, opposite the bus station, is a good source of information on Bromo and transport for Bali. It's open all hours – nice if your bus arrives in the middle of the night – and has dorm beds at 3500 rp and doubles for 10,000 rp.

At the other end of the street, on a corner, you'll find the imposing *Hotel Victoria* with a variety of rooms from 7000 rp all the way to 25,000 rp and more. Tea on arrival and breakfast are thrown in too.

Hotel Tampiarto Plaza at Jalan Suroyo 16, just round the corner from Jalan Raja P Sudirman, is a pleasant place and good value with rooms from 6000 rp. *Hotel Ratna* at Jalan Raja P Sudirman 94 is also good with rooms from 7000 rp up to 30,000 rp with bath and fan; the tariff includes breakfast. The *Hotel Kamayoran*, almost opposite the Victoria, is cheap but also rather dirty.

Getting There & Away

To Probolinggo there are buses from Surabaya (1700 rp/3000 rp air-con, 2½ hours), Malang (1750 rp, 1½ hours) and Banyuwangi (3500 rp, four hours). If coming from Bali, direct buses from Denpasar take around eight hours to Probolinggo. By train costs 2700 rp ekonomi from Surabaya or Banyuwangi, or from Yogya the 11-hour trip costs 5000 rp.

Bemos from Probolinggo to Ngadisari (1500 rp, 1½ hours) and Cemoro Lawang (2500 rp, two hours) go from the bus station, five km from town on Jalan Sukapura – take a yellow 'G' bemo (300 rp) from the train station. Avoid rip-off 'tourist office' bus agents. From Probolinggo, it's 28 km to Sukapura and another 14 km from there to Ngadisari.

From the mountain, direct minibus services operate to Malang, Solo and Yogya in the tourist season.

BLITAR

Blitar is a small town on the Malang to Kediri road. The very beautiful **Panataran Temple** complex is 10 km north of Blitar and can be reached by motorbike or an expensive and infrequent colt service. On the way out to Panataran, you can visit Sukarno's elaborate **grave.**

Places to Stay

The *Hotel Sri Lestari*, a 10-minute walk from the bus station at Jalan Merdeka 173, has rooms for 7000 rp.

GEMPOL

Take a bus from Malang to Bondowoso and on from there to Gempol, a tiny village in a coffee-growing area. You can spend the night there and climb the nearby small but beautiful volcano **Ijen** in the morning. There's a house near the top where you can leave your gear, retrieve it on the way down and continue walking until you reach the road leading to Banyuwangi.

PASIR PUTIH

Some distance east of Probolinggo on the Surabaya to Banyuwangi road, Pasir Putih is East Java's main coastal resort and it can be mobbed at weekends. The name means White Beach but the sand is more grey-black than white. No matter – there's clear water, pleasant swimming and lots of picturesque outrigger boats. But compared to Lovina Beach, only a few hours away on Bali, it's no big deal. Scuba diving at Pasir Putih can be organised from Surabaya.

Places to Stay

There are a number of hotels jammed between the highway and the beach. The *Pasir Putih Inn* is the pick of the bunch with rooms from 11,000 rp. Next door to the Oriental Restaurant, the *Hotel Bhayangkara*

Beach is one of the cheapest. Rooms facing the highway cost around 8,000 rp or better rooms face the beach.

BANYUWANGI

Banyuwangi is the ferry port for Bali but the actual ferry departure point is eight km from the town at Ketapang, where the railway station is also located. Colts run between the ferry terminal in Ketapang and the Blambangan bus terminal in Banyuwangi.

Places to Stay & Eat

The *Hotel Baru* (☎ 21369) at Jalan Pattimura 82-84 is friendly and good value with big airy rooms with and without bath from around 7000 rp to 12,000 rp (which includes breakfast). The excellent warung next door is run by the same family. *Hotel Slamet* also has a good restaurant.

In the centre of town, the *Hotel Baru Raya* at Jalan Dr Sutomo 32 has reasonable and very cheap rooms from 5000 rp. The *Hotel Anda* at Jalan Basuki Rachmat 36, a five-minute walk from the bus terminal for Ketapang, is adequate with rooms from about 6000 rp.

Bali

To Westerners, Bali has been both a tropical paradise and an example of the destructive effects of tourism. It has a rich culture, beautiful landscapes and coastline, a small bustling capital, several interesting towns, and hundreds of rural villages, where most Balinese live. The most conspicuous effects of tourism are confined to a few areas, and it's not hard to find fascinating places where tourists are a novelty.

Bali's unique culture is a legacy of the great Java-based Majapahit dynasty, which consolidated control of Bali in 1343, under chief minister Gajah Mada. With Muslim power on the rise in Java, there was a progressive movement of the Hindu Majapahit court to Bali, complete with its entourage of scholars, intelligentsia and artists.

Balinese dancing, mu architecture are unique and a itors. Religion is central to Bali the temples, festivals and offering quitous.

Information

There are tourist offices at the airport, Kuta, Denpasar and Ubud. There are many moneychangers and travel agents in tourist areas and you can travel for as little as US$5 to US$6 per day.

Poste restante mail can be sent to post offices or agents in the main tourist centres or in Denpasar. Most larger towns have Telkom wartels (Warung Telekomunikasi) and/or private telephone offices, for local and international phone calls and faxes. Denpasar and all the tourist areas of south Bali are in the 0361 telephone district; 0362 covers the north coast.

Dangers & Annoyances Violent crime is uncommon, but there is some bag-snatching, pickpocketing (especially on bemos) and theft from losmen rooms. Touts and hawkers can be a major annoyance, and overcharging can border on the criminal.

There's no drug scene – ignore any offers on the street. Magic mushrooms *(oong)* appear at certain times of the year, but for legal and psychological reasons they can't be recommended.

Things to Buy

There's a lot of junk, but you can buy really nice woodcarvings, leather goods, paintings, silverwork and clothing. Other possibilities include carved coconut shells, bone work, temple umbrellas, kites, model boats, bronze castings, stone statues, musical instruments, cassettes and coffee-table books.

Getting There & Away

Air See the Indonesia Getting There & Away section for details of international flights to Bali. Reconfirm tickets because flights out of Bali are often full. Most of the airlines have offices at the airport and in the Grand

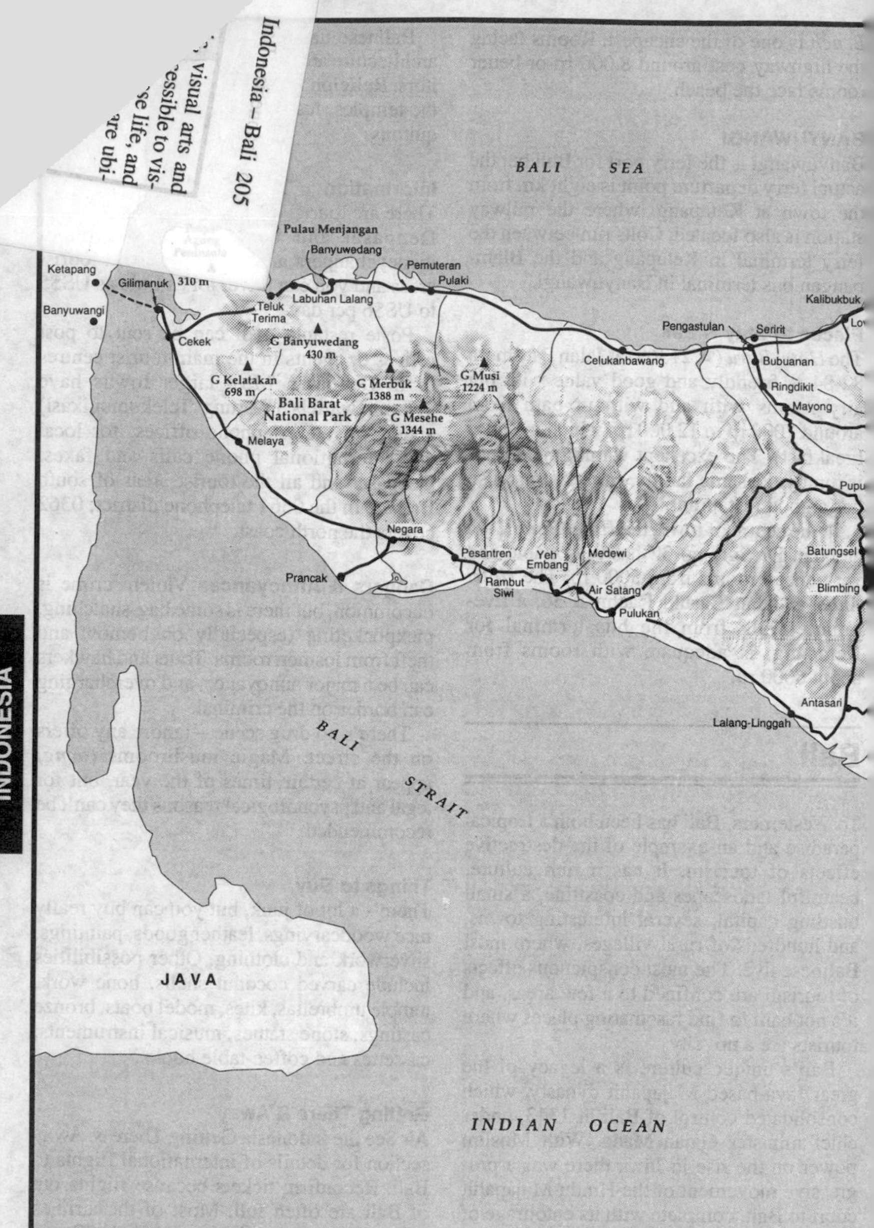

BALI SEA
Pulau Menjangan
Banyuwedang
Pemuteran
Pulaki
Ketapang
Gilimanuk
310 m
Banyuwangi
Teluk Terima
Labuhan Lalang
Cekek
G Banyuwedang 430 m
G Kelatakan 698 m
G Merbuk 1388 m
G Musi 1224 m
G Mesehe 1344 m
Bali Barat National Park
Melaya
Negara
Prancak
Pesantren
Yeh Embang
Medewi
Rambut Siwi
Air Satang
Pulukan
Kalibukbuk
Pengastulan
Seririt
Celukanbawang
Bubuanan
Ringdikit
Mayong
Pupu
Batungsel
Blimbing
Antasari
Lalang-Linggah
BALI STRAIT
JAVA
INDIAN OCEAN

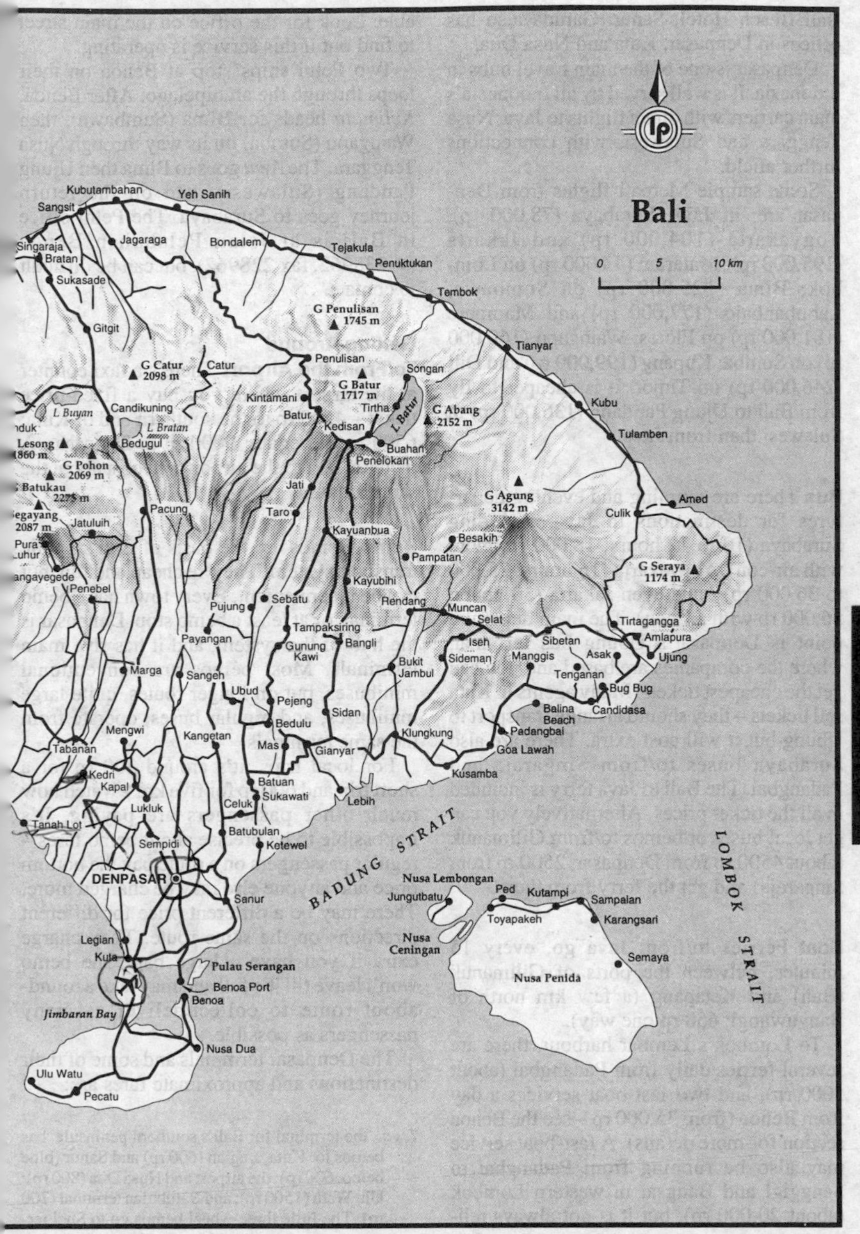
Bali
0 5 10 km
Kubutambahan
Yeh Sanih
Sangsit
Singaraja
Bratan
Jagaraga
Bondalem
Tejakula
Penuktukan
Sukasade
Tembok
G Penulisan
1745 m
Gitgit
Tianyar
G Catur
2098 m
Catur
Penulisan
Songan
G Batur
1717 m
Kintamani
L Buyan
Candikuning
Batur
Tirtha
L Batur
G Abang
2152 m
Kubu
L Bratan
Kedisan
Lesong
1860 m
Bedugul
Buahan
Penelokan
Tulamben
G Pohon
2069 m
Batukau
2276 m
Jati
G Agung
3142 m
Amed
Culik
Pacung
Taro
Jatuluih
Kayuanbua
Besakih
Pura Luhur
Pampatan
G Seraya
1174 m
Penebel
Kayubihi
Sebatu
Rendang
Muncan
Selat
Pujung
Tirtagangga
Tampaksiring
Bangli
Iseh
Sibetan
Amlapura
Payangan
Gunung Kawi
Bukit Jambul
Sideman
Manggis
Asak
Ujung
Marga
Sangeh
Tenganan
Ubud
Bug Bug
Pejeng
Sidan
Candidasa
Balina Beach
Mengwi
Bedulu
Kangetan
Klungkung
Padangbai
Tabanan
Mas
Gianyar
Goa Lawah
Kedri
Kusamba
Kapal
Batuan
Sukawati
Lukluk
Celuk
Lebih
Tanah Lot
Batubulan
Ketewel
Sempidi
BADUNG STRAIT
LOMBOK STRAIT
DENPASAR
Nusa Lembongan
Jungutbatu
Ped
Kutampi
Sanur
Sampalan
Toyapakeh
Karangsari
Legian
Nusa Ceningan
Kuta
Semaya
Pulau Serangan
Nusa Penida
Benoa Port
Benoa
Jimbaran Bay
Nusa Dua
Ulu Watu
Pecatu

INDONESIA

Bali Beach Hotel, Sanur. Garuda also has offices in Denpasar, Kuta and Nusa Dua.

Denpasar is one of the main travel hubs in Indonesia. It is well served by all Indonesia's main carriers with direct flights to Java, Nusa Tenggara and Sulawesi, with connections further afield.

Some sample Merpati flights from Denpasar are: in Java, Surabaya (78,000 rp), Yogyakarta (104,000 rp) and Jakarta (195,000 rp); Mataram (43,000 rp) on Lombok; Bima (125,000 rp) on Sumbawa; Labuhanbajo (177,000 rp) and Maumere (181,000 rp) on Flores; Waingapu (160,000 rp) on Sumba; Kupang (199,000 rp) and Dili (246,000 rp) on Timor. It is cheaper to fly from Bali to Ujung Pandang (136,000 rp) in Sulawesi than from Java.

Bus There are morning and evening departures for destinations in Java, including Surabaya (10 to 12 hours; 18,000 rp, more with air-con), Yogyakarta (16 hours; 25,000 to 36,000 rp) , and even Jakarta (30 hours; 56,000 rp with air-con). The main departure point is Denpasar's Ubung bus terminal, where the companies are based and you can get the cheapest tickets. Many agents in Kuta sell tickets – they should arrange transport to Ubung but it will cost extra. There are also Surabaya buses to/from Singaraja and Padangbai. The Bali to Java ferry is included in all the ticket prices. Alternatively you can get local buses or bemos to/from Gilimanuk (about 4500 rp from Denpasar, 2500 rp from Singaraja) and get the ferry from there.

Boat Ferries to/from Java go, every 15 minutes, between the ports of Gilimanuk (Bali) and Ketapang (a few km north of Banyuwangi; 650 rp one way).

To Lombok's Lembar harbour, there are several ferries daily from Padangbai (about 5000 rp), and two fast-boat services a day from Benoa (from 35,000 rp – see the Benoa section for more details). A fast-boat service may also be running from Padangbai to Senggigi and Bangsal in western Lombok (about 20,000 rp), but it is not always reliable. Look for the office on the main street to find out if this service is operating.

Two Pelni ships stop at Benoa on their loops through the archipelago. After Benoa, *Kelimutu* heads for Bima (Sumbawa), then Waingapu (Sumba) on its way through Nusa Tenggara. The *Awu* goes to Bima then Ujung Pandang (Sulawesi), and on the return journey goes to Surabaya. The Pelni office in Bali is at Jalan Pelabuhan Benoa (☎ 238962, fax 228962), but can be difficult to contact.

Getting Around

To/From the Airport There's a taxi counter at the airport where you buy a fixed-price ticket – 4500 rp to the southern end of Kuta; 6500 rp to Legian; 9000 rp to Denpasar. A metered taxi to the airport will cost about the same amount.

Bemo Bemos are the basis of Bali's public transport system. They're cheap and fun, but can be inconvenient. Every town has a bemo terminal, or at least a bemo stop. Denpasar is the hub of the system, and it has five main terminals. Most bemos are conventional minibuses, but on longer routes, quite large minibuses, and regular buses, operate from the same terminals.

For local trips, it's around 300 rp for a short trip and 600 rp for five km – watch how much other passengers are paying. It's impossible to be precise about bemo fares – regular passengers on a route pay the bottom price and anyone else may be charged more. There may be a different price for different directions on the same route. They charge extra if you have a large bag. The bemo won't leave till it's full and may take a roundabout route to collect/deliver as many passengers as possible.

The Denpasar terminals and some of their destinations and approximate fares are:

Tegal, the terminal for Bali's southern peninsula, has bemos to: Kuta, Legian (600 rp) and Sanur (blue bemo, 600 rp); the airport and Nusa Dua (800 rp); Ulu Watu (1500 rp); and Batubulan terminal (700 rp). The little three-wheel bemos go to Suci ter-

INDONESIA

minal (300 rp), Ubung terminal (500 rp) and Kereneng terminal (500 rp).

Ubung, for the north and west of Bali, and also the main terminal for destinations in Java, has bemos to: Kediri (1000 rp); Mengwi (900 rp); Negara (3500 rp) and Singaraja (2000 rp); Gilimanuk (4500 rp); Bedugul (1600 rp); Tegal, Kereneng and Batubulan terminals (500 rp).

Batubulan terminal is actually several km north-east of Denpasar, and it serves destinations in the east and central area of Bali: Ubud and Gianyar (1000 rp); Tampaksiring, Klungkung and Bangli (1000 rp); Padangbai (2000 rp); Candidasa (2200 rp); Amlapura (3000 rp); Kintamani (1700 rp).

Suci terminal is mainly for connections to Benoa Port (600 rp), but the offices of many of the Surabaya bus lines and agents for shipping lines are also here.

Kereneng is just an urban transfer terminal and a hub for the little three-wheelers which beetle around Denpasar: Tegal, Ubung and Suci (500 rp); Batubulan (600 rp).

Bemos are licensed to work particular routes or areas. In tourist areas, white minibuses are available for charter – for a trip, by the hour, or by the day. The cost depends on time and distance; work on 40,000 to 60,000 rp per day. Outside tourist areas you can charter unlicensed bemos for lower rates, but petrol is extra and the driver won't speak English. For longer charters, you should buy the driver some nasi campur and a bottle of water when you stop for a break.

Tourist Shuttle Buses Direct shuttle buses run between the main tourist areas on Bali, with connections to Java, Lombok and Sumbawa. They are more expensive than public bemos and buses, but much cheaper than car rental, charter or a tour. Perama is the most established operator, with a wide network and offices in Kuta, Candidasa, Lovina and Ubud, and agents in other places. Typical fares from Kuta are: Padangbai and Candidasa for 10,000 rp; Ubud for 7500 rp; and to Lovina Beaches for 12,500 rp.

Taxi Metered taxis are becoming more common in Kuta, Denpasar and Sanur – they're blue with a yellow top. The fare is 800 rp flagfall and then 800 rp for the first km or so, but this drops to about 500 rp per km on longer trips. They won't pick up passengers on Jalan Legian, the main road between Seminyak, just north of Legian, and Kuta.

Car The most popular rental vehicle is the little Suzuki mini-jeep (Jimny) which typically costs from around 35,000 rp a day, including insurance. It's cheaper by the week – around 210,000 rp. Bigger groups could get a Kijang, which seats six in some comfort, and costs from 55,000 rp for a day. Get an international driving permit before you leave home – even if the rental company doesn't insist on you having one, it is still a legal requirement and insurance may not be valid without it. Driving is hazardous though, and a car not only intrudes on the environment but isolates you from it. Parking can be a hassle in busier centres, and usually costs 200 to 500 rp in a town or near a tourist attraction.

Motorbike A rented motorbike is much cheaper than a car (around 10,000 rp per day; less by the week), and in many ways is more pleasant, more convenient and less intrusive. It's dangerous though; don't do it unless you're a reasonably experienced rider. Check the machine first, and ride sensibly. Get an international driving permit, endorsed for motorbikes, before you depart. Otherwise you'll have to get a Balinese visitors' licence in Denpasar at the police station, valid for one month. It's easy but it can take a whole morning and costs 50,000 rp. Police do occasional roadside licence checks – the fine is 200,000 rp.

Bicycle Bicycles rent from around 4000 to 5000 rp per day. They're handy transport in towns, and an ideal way to explore the countryside. Most are multi-gear mountain bikes, but long uphill stretches can still be arduous – put your bike on a bemo.

Tours

Tours can be good value if time is short, or for places like Besakih where public transport is difficult. Day tours cost from around

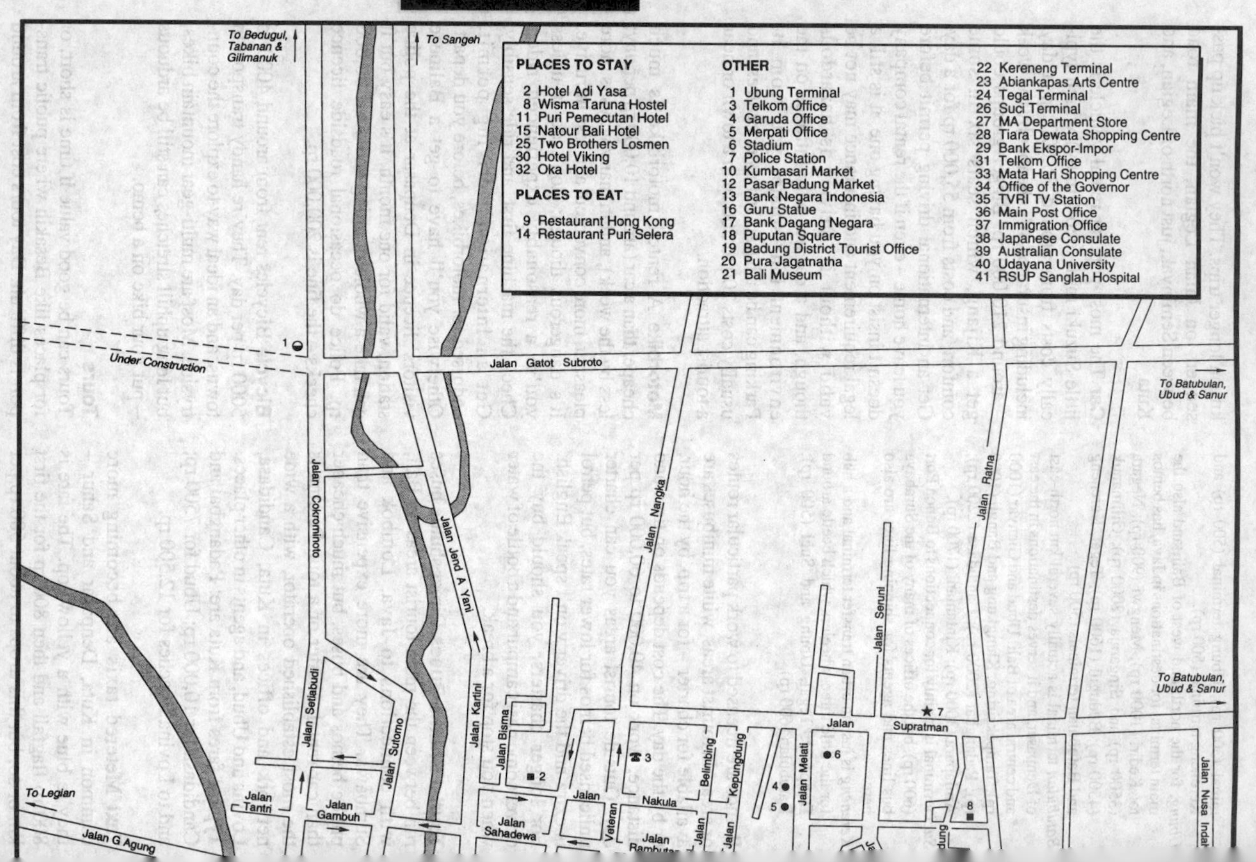
PLACES TO STAY
2 Hotel Adi Yasa
8 Wisma Taruna Hostel
11 Puri Pemecutan Hotel
15 Natour Bali Hotel
25 Two Brothers Losmen
30 Hotel Viking
32 Oka Hotel
PLACES TO EAT
9 Restaurant Hong Kong
14 Restaurant Puri Selera
OTHER
1 Ubung Terminal
3 Telkom Office
4 Garuda Office
5 Merpati Office
6 Stadium
7 Police Station
10 Kumbasari Market
12 Pasar Badung Market
13 Bank Negara Indonesia
16 Guru Statue
17 Bank Dagang Negara
18 Puputan Square
19 Badung District Tourist Office
20 Pura Jagatnatha
21 Bali Museum
22 Kereneng Terminal
23 Abiankapas Arts Centre
24 Tegal Terminal
26 Suci Terminal
27 MA Department Store
28 Tiara Dewata Shopping Centre
29 Bank Ekspor-Impor
31 Telkom Office
33 Mata Hari Shopping Centre
34 Office of the Governor
35 TVRI TV Station
36 Main Post Office
37 Immigration Office
38 Japanese Consulate
39 Australian Consulate
40 Udayana University
41 RSUP Sanglah Hospital
To Bedugul, Tabanan & Gilimanuk
To Sangeh
Under Construction
Jalan Gatot Subroto
To Batubulan, Ubud & Sanur
To Batubulan, Ubud & Sanur
Jalan Cokrominoto
Jalan Jend A Yani
Jalan Nangka
Jalan Ratna
Jalan Seruni
Jalan Supratman
Jalan Setiabudi
Jalan Sutomo
Jalan Kartini
Jalan Bisma
Belimbing
Kepundung
Jalan Melati
Jalan Nakula
Veteran
Jalan Tantri
Jalan Gambuh
Jalan Sahadewa
To Legian
Jalan G Agung

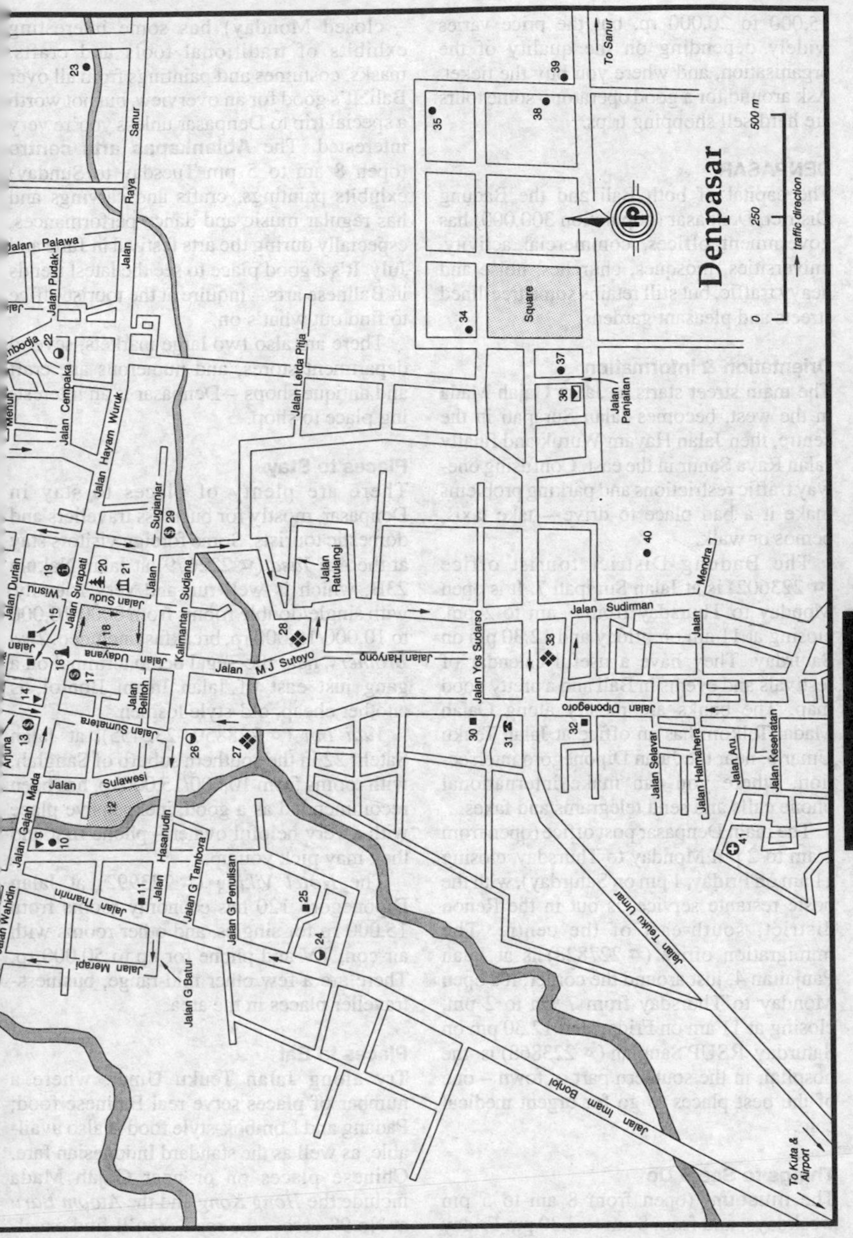
Denpasar
0
250
500 m
traffic direction
Square
To Sanur
To Kuta & Airport
Jalan Teuku Umar
Jalan Imam Bonjol
Jalan Sudirman
Jalan Diponegoro
Jalan Yos Sudarso
Jalan Panjaitan
Jalan Mendra
Jalan Selavar
Jalan Halmahera
Jalan Aru
Jalan Kesehatan
Jalan M J Sutoyo
Jalan Hayang
Jalan Ratulangi
Jalan Letda Pitja
Jalan Kalimantan
Sudjana
Jalan Belitoh
Jalan Hasanudin
Jalan G Tambora
Jalan G Penulisan
Jalan G Batur
Jalan Merapi
Jalan Thamrin
Jalan Wahidin
Jalan Gajah Mada
Jalan Sulawesi
Jalan Sumatera
Jalan Udayana
Jalan Surapati
Jalan Sudu
Jalan Durian
Wisnu
Arjuna
Jalan Sugianjar
Jalan Hayam Wuruk
Jalan Cempaka
Jalan Pudak
Jalan Palawa
Jalan Raya Sanur
Menuri
Kambodja

15,000 to 20,000 rp, but the price varies widely depending on the quality of the organisation, and where you buy the ticket. Ask around for a good operator – some tours are hard-sell shopping trips.

DENPASAR

The capital of both Bali and the Badung District, Denpasar (population 300,000) has government offices, commercial activity, universities, mosques, churches, noise and heavy traffic, but still retains some tree-lined streets and pleasant gardens.

Orientation & Information

The main street starts as Jalan Gajah Mada in the west, becomes Jalan Surapati in the centre, then Jalan Hayam Wuruk and finally Jalan Raya Sanur in the east. Confusing one-way traffic restrictions and parking problems make it a bad place to drive – take taxis, bemos or walk.

The Badung District tourist office (☎ 223602) is at Jalan Surapati 7. It is open Monday to Thursday from 7 am to 2 pm, closing at 11 am on Friday and 12.30 pm on Saturday. They have a useful calendar of festivals and events in Bali and a pretty good map. The banks are mostly along Gajah Mada. Telkom has an office at Jalan Teuku Umar 6, near the Jalan Diponegoro intersection, where you can make international phone calls and send telegrams and faxes.

The main Denpasar post office (open from 8 am to 2 pm Monday to Thursday, closing 11 am on Friday, 1 pm on Saturday), with the poste restante service, is out in the Renon district, south-east of the centre. The immigration office (☎ 227828) is at Jalan Panjaitan 4, just around the corner; it's open Monday to Thursday from 7 am to 2 pm, closing at 11 am on Friday and 12.30 pm on Saturday. RSUP Sanglah (☎ 223868) is the hospital, in the southern part of town – one of the best places to go for urgent medical care.

INDONESIA

Things to See & Do

The **museum** (open from 8 am to 5 pm weekdays, and from 8 am to 3.30 pm Friday – closed Monday) has some interesting exhibits of traditional tools and crafts, masks, costumes and paintings from all over Bali. It's good for an overview, but not worth a special trip to Denpasar unless you're very interested. The **Abiankapas arts centre** (open 8 am to 5 pm Tuesday to Sunday) exhibits paintings, crafts and carvings and has regular music and dance performances, especially during the arts festival in June and July. It's a good place to see the latest trends in Balinese arts – inquire at the tourist office to find out what's on.

There are also two large markets, several department stores, and numerous art, craft and antique shops – Denpasar is an interesting place to shop.

Places to Stay

There are plenty of places to stay in Denpasar, mostly for business travellers and domestic tourists. Some foreign visitors stay at the *Adi Yasa* (☎ 222679) at Jalan Nakula 23B, which is well run and very friendly, with single/double rooms from 8000/10,000 to 10,000/15,000 rp, breakfast included. *Two Brothers*, near the Tegal bemo terminal on a gang just east of Jalan Imam Bonjol, is another cheap, old-style losmen.

Yuai Inn (☎ 228850, 232455), at Jalan Satelit 22 in the southern suburb of Sanglah, with rooms from 10,000/15,000 rp, has been recommended as a good, inexpensive place with a very helpful owner – phone first and they may pick you up.

The *Hotel Viking* (☎ 223992) at Jalan Diponegoro 120 has economy rooms from 15,000 rp for singles, and other rooms with air-con, TV and phone for up to 50,000 rp. There are a few other mid-range, business-traveller places in the area.

Places to Eat

Try along Jalan Teuku Umar, where a number of places serve real Balinese food; Padang and Lombok-style food is also available, as well as the standard Indonesian fare. Chinese places on or near Gajah Mada include the *Hong Kong* and the *Atoom Baru* at No 98 across the road. You'll find excellent and cheap food at the *stalls* by the Suci terminal and at the other markets, especially in the evenings. The food court in the *Tiara Dewata* shopping centre is very clean, and has a good selection of typical street-stall food.

Getting There & Away
See the Bali Getting Around section for details of the bus and bemo network centred in Denpasar.

Getting Around
Within town, the little three-wheeler bemos shuttle between the bemo terminals and all over the place (500 rp), but it's hard to know which ones go where. The larger minibus bemos go between some terminals but aren't allowed in the centre of town. Horse-drawn dokars are fun, but slow and restricted from some streets.

KUTA & LEGIAN

Kuta is the biggest low-budget beach area of Bali, and the closest place to the airport. It's great for cheap accommodation, Western food, shopping, surf, sunsets and partying, and there is a Balinese society here, beneath the brash, touristic surface.

Kuta beach is a pleasant strip of white sand, with some fine surf and a dangerous undertow that takes away a few swimmers every year. Beach-selling is restricted to the upper part of the beach, away from the water. Inland from the beach is a network of roads and tiny alleys (known as gangs) with hundreds of small hotels (losmen), restaurants, bars, foodstalls and shops. Legian is the next beach north of Kuta, but the developments have merged. Legian also merges into Seminyak, further north, where a lot of long-term visitors stay. Kuta is moving upmarket – the beery, boisterous nightlife remains, but there are more sophisticated alternatives. Shopping is the big growth area.

Orientation
Most of the banks, moneychangers, post offices, restaurants, bars, travel agents and smaller shops are along Jalan Legian, the main road which runs south from Seminyak to Kuta; most of the cheap accommodation is in the lanes between Jalan Legian and the beach. Bemo Corner is at the southern end of Jalan Legian, at the intersection with Jalan Pantai Kuta. Many of the roads are one way – traffic goes southwards on Jalan Legian and northwards on the road along the beach.

Information

Tourist Office The Bali government tourist information service (☎ 753540) is in the foyer of a new building on Jalan Benesari in Legian; they have some printed information and can answer any questions.

Money The numerous moneychangers are faster than banks, open longer hours and give just as good a rate. There are banks too, for money transfers, credit card advances, or if the moneychangers don't like your brand of travellers' cheques.

Post & Telecommunications The post office is on a small back road near the night market, off the airport road, with a sort-it-yourself poste restante service. It's open Monday to Saturday from 8 am to 2 pm, closing at 11 am on Friday. There is also a postal agent on Jalan Legian, about half a km north of Bemo Corner – have mail addressed to 'Kuta Postal Agent, Jalan Legian, Kuta'.

Wartels (telephone offices) are on Jalan Bakung Sari next to the supermarket, off Jalan Legian in the side street to Peanuts disco, opposite the Alas Arum supermarket in Seminyak, and at the south end of Jalan Kartika Plaza (which runs along Kuta Beach) towards Tuban. You can dial international calls yourself, but reverse-charge calls can be difficult. There are card phones at some bigger hotels, including the Natour Kuta Beach Hotel, and several at the airport.

Other The Garuda office (☎ 751179) is in the Natour Kuta Beach Hotel. Numerous agents sell bus tickets and arrange tours. Perama (☎ 751551) is near the southern end of Jalan Legian. For English-language books, try the Karta Bookshop on Jalan Legian.

Places to Stay – bottom end

As Kuta moves upmarket, more and more middle and upper-bracket hotels cater to package tourists. Many of these have been thrown together cheaply, to maximise the number of rooms on the site, and turn over as many rupiah as quickly as possible. Old, cheap places are expanded or renovated – most losmen rooms have private bathrooms and you won't find many with a squat toilet.

Generally the cheaper places are away from the beach on tiny alleys, and can be quite difficult to find. The more expensive hotels are closer to the beach, and have bigger signs out the front. Look for a place far enough off the main road to be quiet but close enough so that getting to the shops and restaurants is no problem. Cheaper losmen still offer breakfast, even if it's only a couple of bananas and a cup of tea, but it is charged as an extra as you move up the price scale. Clean but basic rooms cost from around 8000/10,000 rp a single/double. An extra few thousand rupiah will get you a considerably nicer place, and for around 20,000 to 25,000 rp you can find a really nice place, with a garden and possibly a pool.

Prices quoted in US dollars on a printed sheet are the 'publish rates' for the package-tour market – this rate is always negotiable, up to 50% off in the low season. Cheaper places with rupiah prices may also negotiate, especially when a lot of rooms are empty. All but the cheapest places add 15% for tax and service, but this is an element in the negotiations – make sure before you agree on the price.

The places that follow are just a sample of the cheap accommodation available, grouped by location so if the first place you see is full or unappealing, you can find others nearby. The list starts at the southern end, closest to the airport. The references in paratheses indicate the number on the relevant map.

Mandara Cottages (☎ 751775; Kuta No 119) – friendly and spacious with a pool, from 20,000/25,000 rp; some noise from the airport and the road.

Flamboyan Inn (☎ 752610; Kuta No 109) – south of Kuta in one of the lanes off Kartika Plaza; one of several newer places in the area which have good rooms but an uninteresting location. They ask about US$20, but come down to 25,000 rp a double in the low season.

Bamboo Inn (☎ 751935; Kuta No 97) – a traditional little losmen in central Kuta, some distance from the beach but close to the restaurants and bars. Good rooms cost from 12,000/17,000 rp including breakfast.

Jesen's Inn II (☎ 752647) & *Zet Inn* (both Kuta No 97) – pleasant little places near the Bamboo Inn, costing around 17,500/20,000 rp.

Anom Dewi Youth Hostel (☎ 752292; Kuta No 77) – close to Bemo Corner, a cheap but well-run youth hostel-associated losmen with standard rooms at 10,000 and 12,000 rp and superior rooms at 12,000/15,000 rp, with a supplement of 3000 rp in the high season.

A number of cheap places are on Jalan Pantai Kuta, between Bemo Corner and the beach. Rooms away from the road aren't too noisy.

Budi Beach Inn (☎ 751610; Kuta No 66) – an old-style losmen with a garden and rooms from 10,000/15,000 rp up to 20,000/25,000 rp.

Kodja Beach Inn (☎ 752430; Kuta No 64) – with some rooms well away from the road; fan-cooled rooms are 10,000/12,500 rp and rooms with air-con and hot water are up to 36,000 rp.

Suci Bungalows (☎ 753761; Kuta No 65) – well established with a good restaurant, not too noisy, and with singles/doubles from 12,000/15,000 rp to 17,500/25,000 rp.

Yulia Beach Inn (☎ 751893; Kuta No 63) – this standard small hotel has been going for years and offers a central location with bungalows from US$10/12 to US$22/25, and rooms at US$5/6. Tax, service and breakfast are extra.

The gangs between the beach and Jalan Legian are a maze, and a hassle to drive a car through. There are many cheap places to stay in these blocks, only a short walk from the shops and the surf, but still nice and quiet.

Komala Indah I (Kuta No 53) – in Poppies Gang right opposite Poppies Cottages but much more basic. It's clean, and great value for the location at 10,000 rp for a room.

Kempu Taman Ayu (Kuta No 50) – round the corner

INDONESIA

from TJ's and Poppies, this long-running and friendly little place has fairly standard cheap rooms from 9000 to 12,000 rp.

Berlian Inn (Kuta No 28) – just off Poppies Gang, with rooms from 16,000/20,000 rp including breakfast; this place is good value.

Arena Bungalows & Hotel (Kuta No 26) – a new place, with a pool, a bit of style and rooms from 15,00/25,000 rp upwards.

Sorga Cottages (☎ 751897; Kuta No 24) – there's a pool, the location is quiet and the rooms cost from 17,500 to 25,000 rp with fan, or from 25,000 to 35,000 rp with air-con.

Bali Sandy Cottages (Kuta No 9) – still manages to be in a coconut plantation close to the beach and Poppies Gang II; small, nice and inexpensive at 15,000/20,000 rp.

Puri Ayodia Inn (Kuta No 30) – this small and very standard losmen is in a quiet but convenient location and has rooms for just 10,000 rp.

Jus Edith (Kuta No 19) – A basic place, but quiet and central, with rooms at 7000/10,000 rp to 12,000/15,000 rp.

There are more cheap places on Poppies Gang II, and the gangs running north from it. It's about the best place to look for budget accommodation – ask for the cheapest rooms if that's what you want.

Palm Gardens Homestay (☎ 752198; Kuta No 14) – a neat and clean place, good value from 15,000 to 20,000 rp including breakfast, and the location is quiet but convenient.

Bali Dwipa & Bali Indah (Kuta No 4) – located on the gang going north of Poppies Gang II. They don't have a lot of character or comfort, but they're well located and cheap at around 12,000 rp a double.

Bendesa I & II, Meka Jaya (Kuta Nos 1 to 3) & *Bene Yasa Beach Inn* – all on the same gang, and with cheap rooms from 12,000/15,000 rp including breakfast and tax.

Kuta Suci Bungalows (Kuta new 11) – on a cul-de-sac off Poppies Gang II, this is a plain two-storey place with rooms from 12,500/15,000 rp.

Cheap accommodation in Legian tends to be north of Jalan Padma. There's no road along the beach up here, so there are places fronting the beach. The swimming can be very dangerous here, and there's not much public transport up north. Some places up in Seminyak are for longer term rentals – ask around.

Legian Beach Bungalows (Legian No 60) – in the centre of Legian on busy Jalan Padma, with singles from US$10 to US$15 and doubles from US$12 to US$18. The rooms are OK, and back from the street in a nice garden.

Puri Damai Cottages (Legian No 57) – also on Jalan Padma, this budget place has doubles from 16,000 rp to 20,000 rp.

Sinar Indah (Legian No 45) – on Jalan Padma Utara, the rough lane between Jalan Padma and Jalan Pura Bagus Taruna, in north Legian, this standard-style losmen has singles/doubles from 12,000/15,000 rp (without breakfast), plus bigger rooms with kitchen facilities.

Sinar Beach Cottages (Legian No 42) – east of Jalan Padma Utara at the north end of Legian, this pleasant little place has a garden and rooms at 15,000 rp.

Sari Yasai Beach Inn (Legian No 31) – on Jalan Pura Bagus Taruna, this small losmen has rooms at 7000/12,000 rp.

LG Beach Club Hotel & Restaurant (☎ 751060; Legian No 15) – well located behind the beachfront restaurant, this is budget accommodation near Legian beach, at 25,000 rp for a room. There are other places to stay behind the beachfront bars/restaurants around here.

Mesari Beach Inn (☎ 751401; Legian No 5) – one of the few budget places up in Seminyak, with single/double rooms for 12,000/15,000 rp, and bungalows at around 140,000 rp per week.

INDONESIA

Places to Stay – middle

There are a great many mid-range hotels, which at Kuta means something like US$15 to US$60. A 17½% tax and service charge is usually tacked on as well. The best of these places are former budget places which have become popular and gone upmarket. Others are cheaply built package-tourist places, with air-con and a swimming pool, but no character or family atmosphere.

Mutiara Bungalows (Kuta No 47) – conveniently located on Poppies Gang, the Mutiara is excellent value with a pool, a spacious and lush garden, and straightforward, if slightly tatty, fan-cooled rooms with veranda at US$12/15.

Poppies Cottages II (☎ 751059; Kuta No 13) – the original Poppies (despite the name) is not as fancy nor as central as the newer Poppies I, but they are pretty cottages, at US$23/28. Guests can use the pool at Poppies I.

Bruna Beach Hotel (☎ 751565; Legian No 77) – this simple place has a good central location near the beach. The rooms are nothing special but they're

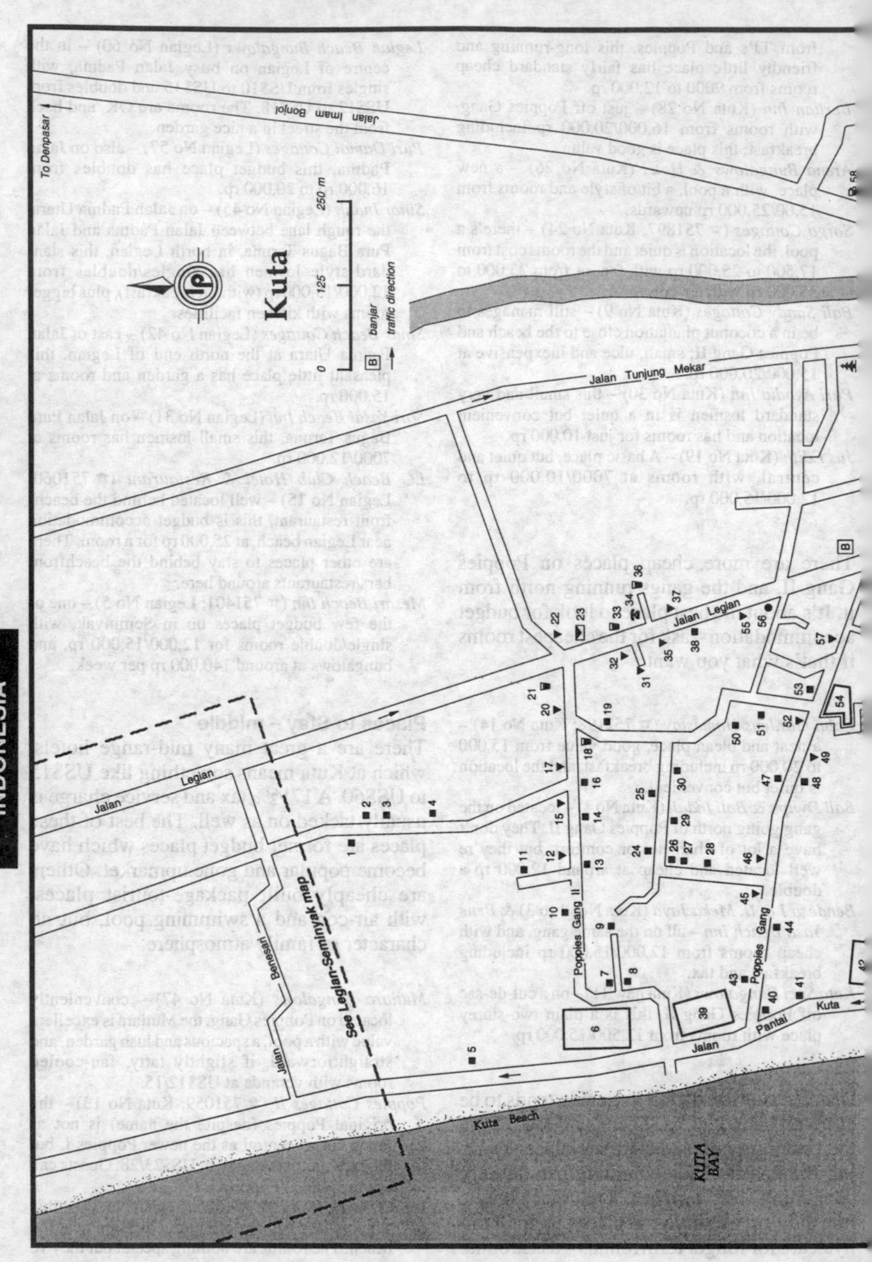
Kuta
0
125
250 m
banjar
traffic direction
To Denpasar
Jalan Imam Bonjol
Jalan Tunjung Mekar
Jalan Legian
Jalan Legian
Poppies Gang II
Poppies Gang
Jalan Pantai Kuta
Jalan Benesari
See Legian-Seminyak map
Kuta Beach
KUTA BAY
INDONESIA

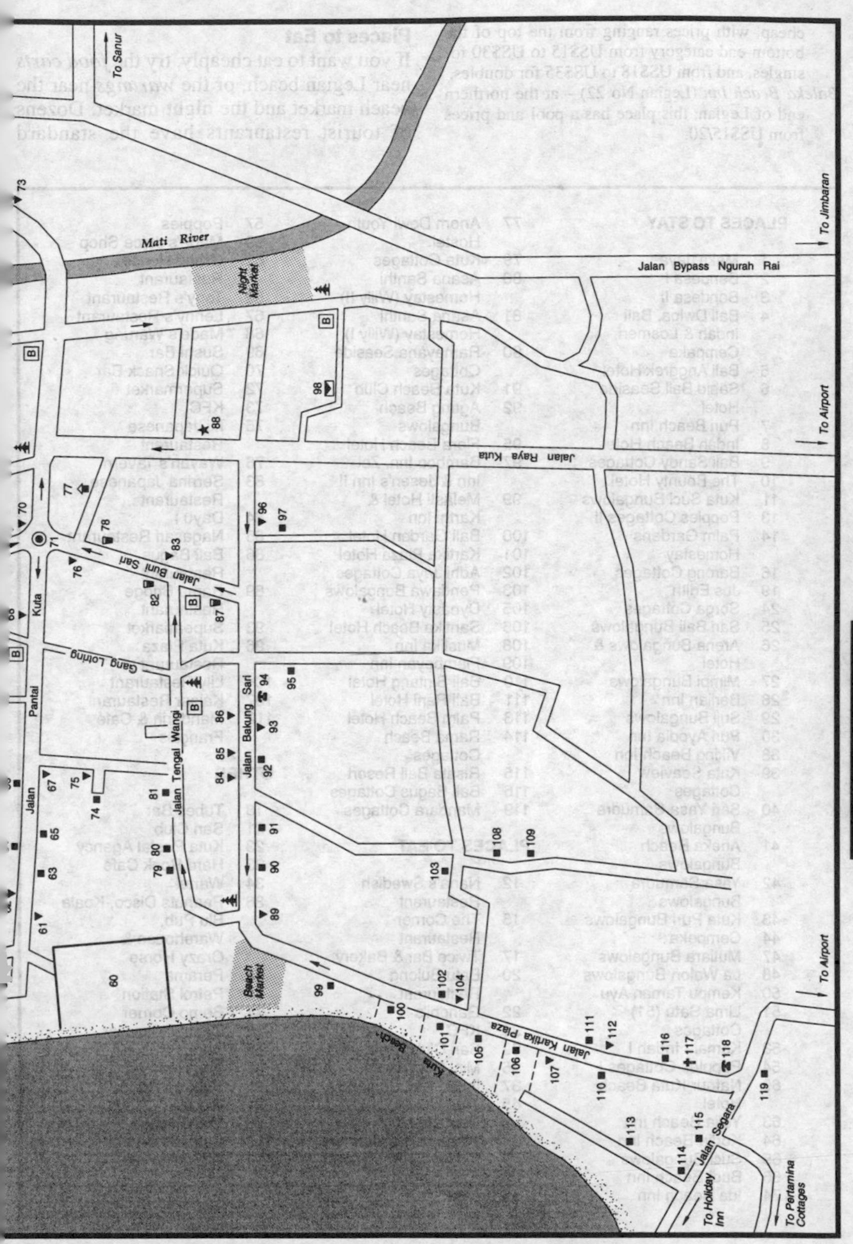
To Sanur
Mati River
Night Market
Beach Market
Jalan Bypass Ngurah Rai
To Jimbaran
To Airport
To Airport
Jalan Raya Kuta
Jalan Buni Sari
Gang Lolting
Jalan Bakung Sari
Jalan Tengal Wangi
Jalan Pantai Kuta
Jalan Kartika Plaza
Kuta Beach
Jalan Segara
To Holiday Inn
To Pertamina Cottages

cheap, with prices ranging from the top of the bottom-end category from US$15 to US$30 for singles, and from US$18 to US$35 for doubles.

Baleka Beach Inn (Legian No 22) – at the northern end of Legian, this place has a pool and prices from US$15/20.

Places to Eat

If you want to eat cheaply, try the *food carts* near Legian beach, or the *warungs* near the beach market and the night market. Dozens of tourist restaurants have the standard

PLACES TO STAY

1 Meka Jaya
2 Bendesa I
3 Bendesa II
4 Bali Dwipa, Bali Indah & Losmen Cempaka
5 Bali Anggrek Hotel
6 Sahid Bali Seaside Hotel
7 Puri Beach Inn
8 Indah Beach Hotel
9 Bali Sandy Cottages
10 The Bounty Hotel
11 Kuta Suci Bungalows
13 Poppies Cottages II
14 Palm Gardens Homestay
16 Barong Cottages
19 Jus Edith
24 Sorga Cottages
25 Sari Bali Bungalows
26 Arena Bungalows & Hotel
27 Mimpi Bungalows
28 Berlian Inn
29 Suji Bungalows
30 Puri Ayodia Inn
38 Viking Beach Inn
39 Kuta Seaview Cottages
40 Sari Yasa Samudra Bungalows
41 Aneka Beach Bungalows
42 Yasa Samudra Bungalows
43 Kuta Puri Bungalows
44 Cempeka
47 Mutiara Bungalows
48 La Walon Bungalows
50 Kempu Taman Ayu
51 Lima Satu (51) Cottages
53 Komala Indah I
54 Poppies Cottages I
60 Natour Kuta Beach Hotel
63 Yulia Beach Inn
64 Kodja Beach Inn
65 Suci Bungalows
66 Budi Beach Inn
74 Ida Beach Inn
77 Anom Dewi Youth Hostel
79 Kuta Cottages
80 Asana Santhi Homestay (Willy II)
81 Asana Santhi Homestay (Willy I)
90 Ramayana Seaside Cottages
91 Kuta Beach Club
92 Agung Beach Bungalows
95 Flora Beach Hotel
97 Bamboo Inn, Zet Inn & Jesen's Inn II
99 Melasti Hotel & Karthi Inn
100 Bali Garden Hotel
101 Kartika Plaza Hotel
102 Adhi Jaya Cottages
103 Pendawa Bungalows
105 Dynasty Hotel
106 Santika Beach Hotel
108 Mustika Inn
109 Flamboyan Inn
110 Bali Bintang Hotel
111 Bali Rani Hotel
113 Palm Beach Hotel
114 Rama Beach Cottages
115 Risata Bali Resort
116 Bali Bagus Cottages
119 Mandara Cottages

PLACES TO EAT

12 Nana's Swedish Restaurant
15 The Corner Restaurant
17 Twice Bar & Bakery
20 Batu Bulong Restaurant
22 Gandhi's
31 KFC
32 Sari Club Restaurant
35 Mini Restaurant
37 Indah Sari Seafood
45 Tree House Restaurant
46 Warung Transformer
49 Fat Yogi's Restaurant
52 TJ's
55 Aleang's
57 Poppies
59 Made's Juice Shop
61 Green House Restaurant
62 Tony's Restaurant
67 Lenny's Restaurant
68 Made's Warung
69 Sushi Bar
70 Quick Snack Bar
72 Supermarket
73 KFC
75 Iki Japanese Restaurant
76 Wayan's Tavern
83 Serrina Japanese Restaurant
84 Dayu I
85 Nagasari Restaurant
86 Bali Bagus Restaurant
89 Rama Bridge Restaurant
93 Supermarket
96 Kuta Plaza Restaurant
104 Lily Restaurant
107 Kaiser Restaurant
112 Mandarin & Café Français

OTHER

18 Tubes Bar
21 Sari Club
23 Kuta Postal Agency
33 Hard Rock Cafe
34 Wartel
36 Peanuts Disco, Koala Blu Pub, Warehouse & Crazy Horse
56 Perama
58 Petrol Station
71 Bemo Corner
78 Casablanca Bar
82 Bagus Pub
87 The Pub
88 Police Station
94 Wartel
98 Post Office
117 Catholic Church
118 Telkom Wartel

Indonesian items (nasi goreng, nasi campur etc), as well as hamburgers, jaffles, spaghetti and salads (costing between 2000 rp and 4500 rp at most places). A good pizza, seafood or steak dish will cost between 6000 rp and 10,000 rp.

For fancier food, you'll find French, German, Italian, Japanese, Korean, Mexican and Swiss restaurants. Wine is expensive, but some places have Australian wine by the glass for around 4000 rp. Beer goes well with most meals, and is a fair index of prices – in cheap places a large beer is around 3000 rp; in expensive places it costs from 4000 rp upwards.

Jalan Kartika Plaza, south of Kuta, has a couple of interesting places. The *Café Français* is good for croissants (1300 rp) and coffee. *Bali Seafood*, opposite the Bali Bintang Hotel, is a big place where you can select your main course while it's still swimming, and the Chinese restaurant in the *Dynasty Hotel* is well regarded. On Bakung Sari there are several standard restaurants including *Dayu I* and *Nagasari*, and a supermarket with many Western-style foods.

Jalan Buni Sari, which runs north of Bakung Sari, has some more long-term survivors including the *Bali Indah, Wayan's Tavern* and *Dayu II*. *D'Este* restaurant has good Italian food.

Along Jalan Pantai Kuta, near Bemo Corner, popular *Made's Warung* is an open-fronted place which is good for people-watching – the food is good though a touch expensive. The *Suci Restaurant*, on the south side of Pantai Kuta, is good value with delicious fruit drinks.

Poppies Gang, the tiny lane between Jalan Legian and the beach, is named for *Poppies*, one of the oldest and most popular restaurants in Kuta. The garden setting and the atmosphere are delightful, and the food is consistently good, though not cheap. A few steps west is *TJ's*, a deservedly popular Mexican restaurant, with a good ambience and main courses from 8000 to 12,000 rp. Further towards the beach are several popular places, including *Fat Yogi's*, with good pizzas, *Warung Transformer*, and the pleasant *Tree House Restaurant*, a good place for a cheap breakfast.

Right on Bemo Corner is the *Quick Snack Bar*, for a snack or breakfast – their yoghurt is particularly good. Further up busy Jalan Legian, the *Sushi Bar* has excellent sushi for 1200 rp to 3000 rp, and sashimi from 7000 rp to 10,000 rp. *Twice Bar & Bakery* is good for breakfast, and the huge *Mini Restaurant* is a busy place with basic food at low prices. The *Sari Club Restaurant* is similar in style, price and quality. *Indah Sari* is a big seafood place, but pricey and of variable standard, and there's a new *KFC* on a side alley near here. Round the corner in Poppies Gang II there are quite a few places that are popular with budget travellers, like the *Batu Bulong*, with a varied menu, and *Nana's Swedish Restaurant*, which has good guacamole.

Continue north into Legian, where *Mama's German Restaurant* has pretty authentic German food with main courses for around 8000 rp. The *Depot Viva* is a cheap and popular Indonesian and Chinese place with good food despite its basic appearance. *Za's Bakery & Restaurant* is a good spot for breakfast, and has a varied menu.

Further north, *Il Pirata* is noted for its good pizzas (5000 to 7000 rp) and its late hours. Continue north to the ever-popular *Do Drop Inn*, the well-regarded *Warung Kopi*, and the long-standing *Restaurant Glory*.

On Jalan Melasti is the big *Orchid Garden Restaurant*, the *Legian Garden Restaurant* and the *Restaurant Puri Bali Indah*, with excellent Chinese food. Jalan Padma also has some tourist restaurants, and more Aussie-oriented bars.

Further north, things get more expensive but the standards are higher – this is the trendy end of town. Some of the most interesting places are on Jalan Pura Bagus Taruna (also known as Rum Jungle Road). The *Topi Koki Restaurant* does French food and is about the most expensive place around. The nearby *Swiss Restaurant* is also classy and expensive. Others include the *Sawasdee Restaurant, Yudi Pizza* and the distinctive

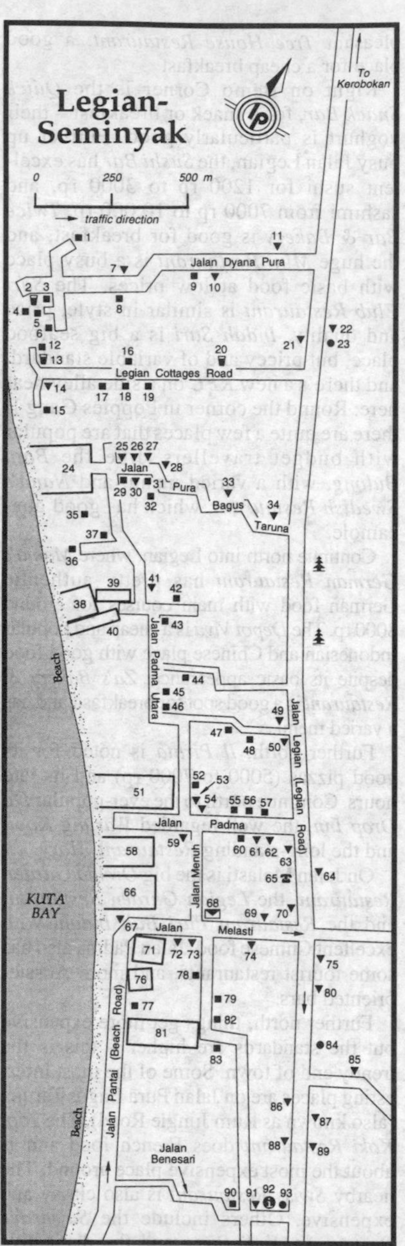

PLACES TO STAY

1 Bali Agung Village
3 Dhyana Pura Hotel
4 Nusa di Nusa Hotel
5 Mesari Beach Inn
6 Bali Holiday Resort
8 Tjendana Paradise Hotel
9 Surya Dharma Cottages
12 Sheraton Hotel
15 LG Beach Club Hotel
16 Legian Garden Cottages
17 Sing Ken Ken
18 Bali Subak
19 Suri Bunga Bungalows
24 Kuta Palace Hotel
29 Orchid Garden Cottages
31 Sari Yasai Beach Inn
32 Baleka Beach Inn
35 Mabisa Beach Inn
36 Puri Tantra Beach Bungalows
37 Mabisa Hotel
38 Bali Niksoma Inn
39 Bali Coconut Hotel
40 Maharta Beach Inn
42 Sinar Beach Cottages
43 Adika Sari Bungalows
44 Surya Dewata Beach Cottages
45 Sinar Indah
46 Bali Sani Hotel
47 Sri Ratu Cottages
48 Three Brothers
51 Bali Padma Hotel
52 Garden View Cottages
55 Legian Village Hotel
56 Puspasari Hotel
57 Puri Damai Cottages
58 Bali Mandira Cottages
60 Legian Beach Bungalows
66 Legian Beach Hotel
71 Bali Intan Cottages
76 Kul Kul Resort
77 Bruna Beach Hotel
78 Ocean Blue Club
79 Legian Mas Beach Inn
81 Kuta Jaya Cottage
82 Puri Tanah Lot
83 Sayang Beach Lodging
90 Kuta Bungalows

PLACES TO EAT

7 Pino Lotus Restaurant
10 Jimbaro Cafe
11 Benny's Cafe II
14 Puri Naga
21 Luna Cafe
22 Goa 2001 Pub Restaurant
25 Topi Koki Restaurant
26 Swiss Restaurant
27 Twice Cafe
28 Rum Jungle Road Bar & Restaurant
30 Sawasdee Thai Restaurant
33 Bamboo Palace Restaurant

34 Benny's Caf
41 Poco Loco Mexican Restaurant
49 Restaurant Glory
50 Warung Kopi
53 Legian Snacks
54 Joni Sunken Bar & Restaurant
59 Padma Club Restaurant
61 Rama Garden Restaurant
62 Norman Garden Restaurant
63 MS Restaurant
64 Ned's Place
67 Karang Mas Restaurant
69 Gosha Restaurant
70 Do Drop Inn
72 Restaurant Puri Bali Indah
73 Legian Garden Restaurant
74 Orchid Garden Restaurant
75 Manhattan Restaurant & Bar
80 Made's Restaurant
85 Il Pirata
86 The Bounty
87 Depot Viva
88 Za's Bakery & Restaurant
89 Mama's German Restaurant
91 Midnight Oil Restaurant

OTHER

2 Chez Gado Gado
13 66 Club
20 Strand Bar
23 Jaya Pub
65 Wartel
68 Postal Agent
84 Peanuts II
92 Government Tourist Information
93 Krishna Bookshop

and very popular *Bamboo Palace Restaurant*. On the corner, *Benny's Café* has good pastries and coffee.

Good, though not cheap, places to eat in Seminyak include the *Ibiza* Italian restaurant and *Goa 2001*, both on Jalan Legian. *Benny's Cafe II* and *Jimbaro Cafe* are mid-range places. On a beach track past the Oberoi, *La Lucciato* is an Italian place with food that people rave about, and prices which aren't excessive.

Entertainment

Nightspots are scattered around Kuta, Legian and Seminyak, many along Jalan Legian. The wild, drunken excesses of Kuta are mostly a scene for young Australians on cheap package holidays. The scene centres around a short side alley off Jalan Legian, with *Peanuts Disco* at the far end, and bars like *Crazy Horse*, the *Warehouse* and *Koala Blu Club* on either side. Peanuts gets going around 11 pm, and charges about 6000 rp admission, which includes one drink. The bars start earlier and finish later, and entry is free. The whole Peanuts complex is to be redeveloped as a shopping centre (a sign of the times!) and the owners have established *Peanuts II*, up in Legian, to continue the reputation (or notoriety) of the original. Other Aussie drinking places include the *Sari Club* (or SC for short), just up the road, and *Tubes Bar*, for surfers. The glossy new *Hard Rock Cafe* will doubtless prove popular.

In Kuta *Un's Pub*, near Bemo Corner, is central and popular. On Jalan Buni Sari you'll find, in order of noisiness, *The Pub*, one of Kuta's original bars, the *Bagus Pub* and *Casablanca*. In Legian there are more Aussie drinking places on Jalan Padma.

In Seminyak, the trendy expatriates start with drinks and/or dinner at *Goa 2001*. They move on for drinks at the *Jaya Pub*, or coffee at *Luna Cafe*. Well after midnight, the action shifts to the beachside *66 Club* (pronounced 'double six'), or *Chez Gado Gado*, at the beach end of Jalan Dyana Pura.

Large-screen video (or laser disk) movies are featured at some of the restaurants/pubs, including the *Batu Bulong*, the *Twice Bar* and the *Bounty*. Only go if you want to see the movie – it will be impossible to ignore.

Getting There & Away

Kuta has lots of travel agencies but there are no bargain airfares. Agents sell bus tickets to destinations on Java, Lombok and Sumbawa, and to all the tourist centres on Bali, but it might be cheaper to buy tickets at the appropriate Denpasar bus terminal. Sightseeing tours to Balinese dances, craft centres and other tourist attractions are available. Public bemos do a circuitous loop from Denpasar's Tegal terminal to the airport via Kuta and Legian.

INDONESIA

Getting Around

It's hard to get around Kuta and Legian by public transport. There's only one bemo route and it doesn't go very far north into Legian. The guys with minibuses to rent are trying to monopolise the transport business, and discourage both public bemos and metered taxis from taking passengers, especially along Jalan Legian.

BUKIT PENINSULA

The southern peninsula, known as Bukit (Hill) is dry and quite sparsely populated. Just south of the airport, **Jimbaran Bay** is a superb crescent of white sand and blue sea, with a fishing village selected for luxury hotel development. There's only one cheaper place, on the east side of the road, the *Puri Indra Prasta* bungalows, with a murky pool, restaurant and grubby rooms at 25,000 rp.

A sealed road goes south from Jimbaran to **Ulu Watu**, where an important temple perches on the tip of the peninsula, and sheer cliffs drop into the sea. Just before the temple car park, there's a sign to **Pantai Suluban** (Suluban Beach), famous for its great surf. Other surf breaks are at **Oalangan**, **Bingin**, **Padang** and **Nyang Nyang**, some of which have secluded beaches. Guys on motorbikes will take you to the more isolated ones, where there are usually warungs but no places to stay.

INDONESIA

Nusa Dua

Nusa Dua is Bali's most expensive beach resort – a luxury enclave for tourists who want to experience Bali in very small and sanitised doses, if at all. There's a very ritzy shopping centre, which sometimes has sales, and a consistent right-hand surf break on the reef.

The nearest thing to budget accommodation is the *Lancun Guesthouse* (☎ 71983/5), run by the Hotel & Tourism Training School, which has very ordinary rooms for about US$25 a double. Go north to Benoa village for cheaper hotels.

Benoa

Labuhan Benoa, the wide but shallow bay east of the airport, is one of Bali's main harbours. Benoa is actually in two parts. Benoa Port, with a wharf and some offices, is on the north side, with a two-km long causeway connecting it to the main Kuta-Sanur road. There's a Pelni office here – see the Indonesia Getting Around section for details of their services. The fast *Mabua Express* boat to Lombok leaves Benoa Port at 8.30 am and 2.30 pm. A number of touristy excursion boats also operate from Benoa Port, and private yachts anchor here.

Benoa village is on a point at the south side of the bay, and is a centre for watersports. There are some mid-price places to stay, as well as the cheap *Homestay Hasam*, with singles from 17,0000 rp.

SANUR

Sanur is an upmarket resort for package tourists after sea, sand and sun. The water is safe for kids, but very shallow at low tide, and there's sometimes an excellent right-hand surf break on the reef. The main road, Jalan Danau Toba/ Jalan Danau Tamblingan, runs parallel to the beach, and has restaurants, shops, travel agencies, moneychangers and other facilities. American Express and a number of airlines have offices in the big Bali Beach Hotel at the northern end of town. Nearby is the former home of prewar Belgian artist Le Mayeur, now a **museum**.

Places to Stay

The few low-budget places to stay are away from the beach, mostly at the northern end of town. Side by side on Jalan Segara, west of the main road, are three cheapies – the *Hotel Sanur-Indah*, *Hotel Taman Sari* and *Hotel Rani* (☎ 288578). They have rooms from around 12,500/17,000 rp, up to 45,000 rp with air-con and hot water. At the northern end of Sanur Beach, the *Ananda Hotel* (☎ 288327) is neat and clean with rooms from 25,000/30,000 rp. The *Watering Hole* (☎ 288289), opposite the Bali Beach Hotel entrance, is friendly and well run with good food, a bar and rooms from 25,000 rp.

Three basic homestays, the *Yulia*, the *Luisa* and the *Coca* are at the northern end of Jalan Danau Toba, behind shops at numbers 38, 40 and 42. Clean, simple rooms with private mandi go for around 20,000 rp per night. Other places on the main road, with budget-priced non-air-con rooms, include the *Laghawa Beach Inn* (☎ 288494), *Swastika Bungalows* (☎ 288699) and *Hotel Ramayana* (☎ 288429), all with pools. The *Wirasana* (☎ 288632) is cheaper at 20,000/40,000 rp, but doesn't have a pool. On a side road to the beach is the *Werdha Pura* (☎ 288171), a government-run 'beach cottage prototype', with single/double rooms at 25,000/50,000 rp.

Places to Eat

From north to south, the *Watering Hole*, *Borneo Restaurant*, *Warung Aditya*, *Swastika I Restaurant* and *Donald's Cafe & Bakery* are good mid-range places, but there are plenty of others. You can get cheap meals at the warungs on the bypass road, where there is also a *Kentucky Ayam Goreng* and a *Swensen's Ice Cream* place. The cheapest food is from the food carts and warungs in the *night market*, or at the northern end of the beach, near where the boats go to Nusa Lembongan.

UBUD

Situated in the hills north of Denpasar, Ubud is the centre of 'cultural tourism' on Bali. In recent years, Ubud has been developing nearly as fast as the beach resorts, and now has traffic problems in the centre and urban sprawl on the edges. But it's still a wonderful place to see Balinese arts, handicrafts, dance and music.

Orientation & Information

The intersection of Jalan Raya and Monkey Forest Rd is the centre of Ubud, which now encompasses the neighbouring villages of Campuan, Penestanan, Padangtegal, Peliatan and Pengosekan.

The friendly and helpful tourist office (Bina Wisata) is on Jalan Raya in the centre of town, and there are numerous moneychangers. The small post office has a good poste restante service and therer are a couple of places to make international phone calls – one near the Nomad Restaurant and another on the main road at the east end of town. The colourful produce market operates every third day.

Things to See & Do

The **Puri Lukisan Museum**, in the middle of town, displays fine examples of all schools of Balinese art. It's open daily; admission is 500 rp. The superb **Museum Neka**, in Campuan, displays modern Balinese art and fine pieces by Western artists who have resided or worked in Bali. There are many commercial galleries, but the Neka Gallery on Jalan Raya, and the Agung Rai Gallery in Peliatan, are two of the largest and most important.

You can visit the home of the late Gusti Nyoman Lempad, a pioneering Balinese artist, and Antonio Blanco, a well-known artist who still works here. The home of Walter Spies, an influential German artist from the 1930s, is now one of the rooms at the Campuan Hotel, and Han Snel's work can be seen in his restaurant.

The **Monkey Forest** in Ubud's south has monkeys which provide entertainment and demand peanuts – they can get aggressive if you don't hand them over. Other interesting **walks** are: east to Pejeng, across picturesque ravines; north to Petulu, where herons roost at dusk; and west to Sayan, with views over the Ayung River gorge.

Places to Stay

Ubud has many small homestays, where a simple, clean room in a pretty garden will cost around 10,000 to 12,000 rp for a single/double, with private bathroom and a light breakfast. More basic places can cost less, especially outside the high seasons. For around 25,000 to 35,000 rp, you can get a very nice room or bungalow, decorated with local artworks, perhaps with a view of rice fields, jungle or garden. At most cheaper and mid-price places, breakfast is included in the price. Some of the accommodation is geared to longer stayers (several weeks at least) and offers cooking facilities rather than meals.

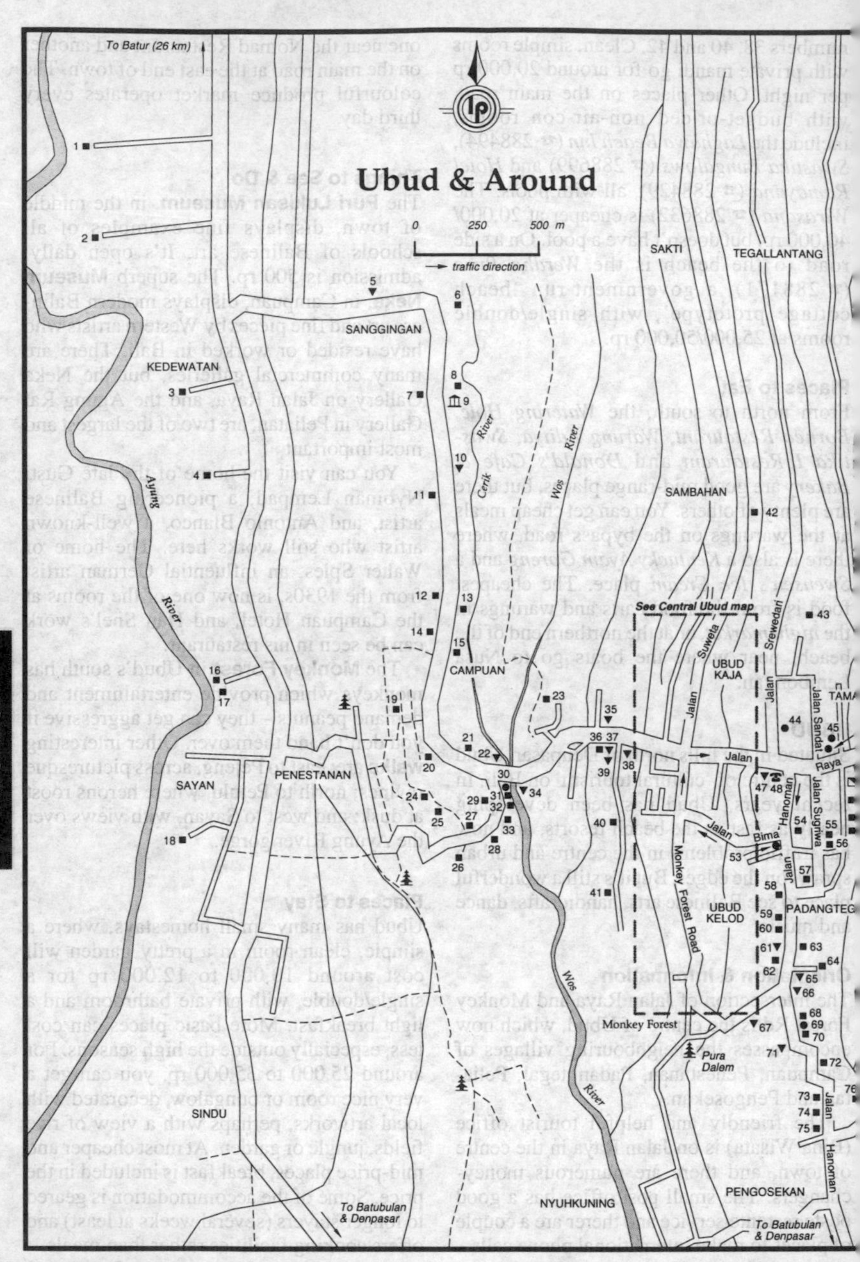

Ubud & Around
0
250
500 m
traffic direction
To Batur (26 km)
SAKTI
TEGALLANTANG
SANGGINGAN
KEDEWATAN
SAMBAHAN
Ayung River
Cerik River
Wos River
See Central Ubud map
Jalan Suweta
Jalan Sriwedari
UBUD KAJA
CAMPUAN
SAYAN
PENESTANAN
Jalan Raya
Jalan Sandat
Jalan Hanoman
Jalan Sugriwa
Jalan Bima
UBUD KELOD
Monkey Forest Road
PADANGTEG
Monkey Forest
Pura Dalem
Wos River
SINDU
NYUHKUNING
PENGOSEKAN
Jalan Hanoman
To Batubulan & Denpasar
To Batubulan & Denpasar

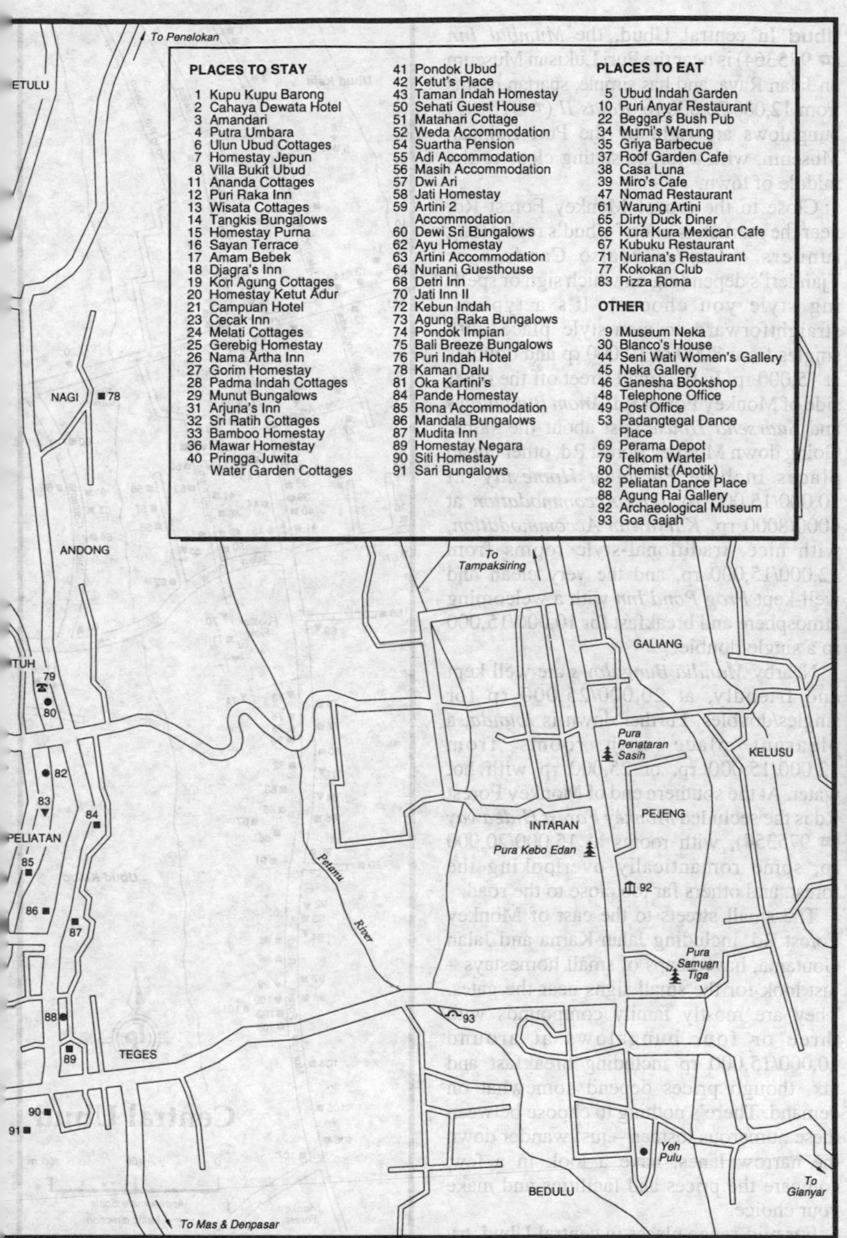
To Penelokan
PLACES TO STAY
1 Kupu Kupu Barong
2 Cahaya Dewata Hotel
3 Amandari
4 Putra Umbara
6 Ulun Ubud Cottages
7 Homestay Jepun
8 Villa Bukit Ubud
11 Ananda Cottages
12 Puri Raka Inn
13 Wisata Cottages
14 Tangkis Bungalows
15 Homestay Purna
16 Sayan Terrace
17 Amam Bebek
18 Djagra's Inn
19 Kori Agung Cottages
20 Homestay Ketut Adur
21 Campuan Hotel
23 Cecak Inn
24 Melati Cottages
25 Gerebig Homestay
26 Nama Artha Inn
27 Gorim Homestay
28 Padma Indah Cottages
29 Munut Bungalows
31 Arjuna's Inn
32 Sri Ratih Cottages
33 Bamboo Homestay
36 Mawar Homestay
40 Pringga Juwita Water Garden Cottages
41 Pondok Ubud
42 Ketut's Place
43 Taman Indah Homestay
50 Sehati Guest House
51 Matahari Cottage
52 Weda Accommodation
54 Suartha Pension
55 Adi Accommodation
56 Masih Accommodation
57 Dwi Ari
58 Jati Homestay
59 Artini 2 Accommodation
60 Dewi Sri Bungalows
62 Ayu Homestay
63 Artini Accommodation
64 Nuriani Guesthouse
68 Detri Inn
70 Jati Inn II
72 Kebun Indah
73 Agung Raka Bungalows
74 Pondok Impian
75 Bali Breeze Bungalows
76 Puri Indah Hotel
78 Kaman Dalu
81 Oka Kartini's
84 Pande Homestay
85 Rona Accommodation
86 Mandala Bungalows
87 Mudita Inn
89 Homestay Negara
90 Siti Homestay
91 Sari Bungalows
PLACES TO EAT
5 Ubud Indah Garden
10 Puri Anyar Restaurant
22 Beggar's Bush Pub
34 Murni's Warung
35 Griya Barbecue
37 Roof Garden Cafe
38 Casa Luna
39 Miro's Cafe
47 Nomad Restaurant
61 Warung Artini
65 Dirty Duck Diner
66 Kura Kura Mexican Cafe
67 Kubuku Restaurant
71 Nuriana's Restaurant
77 Kokokan Club
83 Pizza Roma
OTHER
9 Museum Neka
30 Blanco's House
44 Seni Wati Women's Gallery
45 Neka Gallery
46 Ganesha Bookshop
48 Telephone Office
49 Post Office
53 Padangtegal Dance Place
69 Perama Depot
79 Telkom Wartel
80 Chemist (Apotik)
82 Peliatan Dance Place
88 Agung Rai Gallery
92 Archaeological Museum
93 Goa Gajah
ETULU
NAGI
ANDONG
TUH
PELIATAN
TEGES
To Tampaksiring
GALIANG
Pura Penataran Sasih
KELUSU
PEJENG
INTARAN
Pura Kebo Edan
Petanu River
Pura Samuan Tiga
Yeh Pulu
BEDULU
To Gianyar
To Mas & Denpasar

INDONESIA

Ubud In central Ubud, the *Mumbul Inn* (☎ 975364) is near the Puri Lukisan Museum on Jalan Raya, and has simple, spartan rooms from 12,000/20,000 rp. *Rojas II* (☎ 975107) bungalows are right by the Puri Lukisan Museum, with a jungle setting close to the middle of town.

Close to the top of Monkey Forest Rd, near the market, is one of Ubud's really long runners – *Canderi's* (also Candri's or Tjanderi's depending on which sign or spelling style you choose). It's a typical, straightforward losmen-style place with singles from 8000 to 10,000 rp and doubles at 15,000 rp. In the small street off the other side of Monkey Forest Rd, *Anom Bungalows* and *Suarsena House* cost about the same. Going down Monkey Forest Rd, other cheap places include *Pandawa Homestay* at 10,000/15,000 rp, *Igna Accommodation* at 6000/8000 rp, *Karyawan Accommodation*, with nice, traditional-style rooms from 12,000/15,000 rp, and the very clean and well-kept *Frog Pond Inn* with a welcoming atmosphere and breakfast for 10,000/15,000 rp a single/double.

Nearby *Mandia Bungalows* are well kept and friendly, at 20,000/25,000 rp for singles/doubles. Further down is *Ibunda*, a pleasant place with rooms from 12,000/15,000 rp, or 25,000 rp with hot water. At the southern end of Monkey Forest Rd is the secluded *Monkey Forest Hideaway* (☎ 975354), with rooms at 15,000/20,000 rp, some romantically overlooking the forest, and others far too close to the road.

The small streets to the east of Monkey Forest Rd, including Jalan Karna and Jalan Goutama, have heaps of small homestays – just look for the small signs near the gates. They are mostly family compounds with three or four bungalows at around 10,000/15,000 rp including breakfast and tax, though prices depend somewhat on demand. There's nothing to choose between these numerous losmen – just wander down the narrow lanes, have a look in a few, compare the prices and facilities and make your choice.

For mid-range places in central Ubud, try

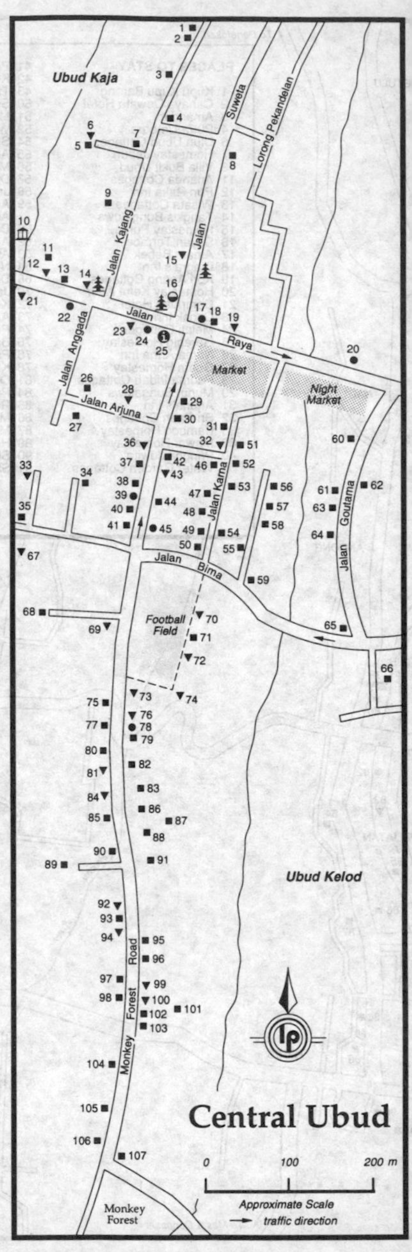

PLACES TO STAY

1 Kajeng Home Stay
2 Gusti's Garden Bungalow
3 Lecuk Inn
4 Arjana Accommodation
5 Siti Bungalows
7 Shanti's Homestay
8 Suci Inn
9 Roja's Homestay
11 Mumbul Inn
13 Puri Saraswati Cottages
18 Sudharsana Bungalows
26 Anom Bungalows
27 Suarsena House
29 Happy Inn
30 Canderi's Losmen & Warung
31 Yuni's House
34 Oka Wati's Sunset Bungalows
35 Igna 2 Accommodation
37 Alit's House
38 Puri Muwa Bungalows
40 Dewa House
41 Igna Accommodation
42 Pandawa Homestay
44 Badra Accommodation
46 Gandra House
47 Sudartha House
48 Seroni Bungalows
49 Mertha House
50 Surawan House
51 Widiana's House Bungalows
52 Sania's House
53 Wija House
54 Ning's House
55 Devi House
56 Sayong's House
57 Dewi Putra House
58 Raka House
59 Esty's House
60 Wayan Karya Homestay
61 Wena Homestay
62 Shana Homestay
63 Nirvana Pension
64 Agung's Cottages
65 Sidya Homestay
66 Ramasita Pension
68 Bendi's Accommodation
71 Wahyu Bungalows
75 Accommodation Kerta
77 Karyawan Accommodation
79 Frog Pond Inn
80 Ubud Village Hotel
82 Mandia Bungalows
83 Puri Garden Bungalow
85 Pertiwi Bungalows
86 Adi Cottages
87 Rice Paddy Bungalows
88 Sri Bungalows
89 Jati 3 Bungalows & Putih Accommodation
90 Villa Rasa Sayang
91 Nani House (Karsi Homestay)
93 Jaya Accommodation
95 Ibunda Inn
96 Ubud Bungalows
97 Dewi Ayu Accommodation
98 Ubud Tenau Bungalows
101 Sagitarius Inn
102 Fibra Inn
103 Ubud Inn
104 Lempung Accommodation
105 Pande Permai Bungalows
106 Monkey Forest Hideaway
107 Hotel Champlung Sari

PLACES TO EAT

6 Han Snel's Garden Restaurant
12 Mumbul's Cafe
14 Lotus Cafe
15 Coconut's Cafe
19 Restaurant Puri Pusaka
21 Menara Restaurant
23 Ary's Warung
28 Satri's Warung
32 Seroni's Warung
33 Oka Wati's Warung
36 Ayu's Kitchen
43 Gayatri Restaurant
67 Beji's Cafe
69 Bendi's Restaurant
70 Legian Cafe & Video
72 Ubud Dancer Restaurant
73 Ibu Rai Restaurant
74 Cafe Bali
76 Dian Restaurant
81 Coco Restaurant
84 Cafe Wayan
92 Jaya Cafe
94 Yudit Restaurant & Bakery
99 Warsa's Cafe
100 Ubud Restaurant

OTHER

10 Puri Lukisan Museum
16 Bemo Stop
17 Palace & Hotel Puri Saren Agung
20 I Gusti Nyoman Lempad's home
22 Supermarket
24 Ubud Bookshop
25 Tourist Office
39 Bookshop
45 Ibu Rai Gallery
78 Batik Workshop & Crackpot Cafe

Oka Wati's Sunset Bungalows (☎ 975063), near the top of Monkey Forest Rd and off to the left, still with a rice paddy in view but being built out. The rooms range from US$25/30 to US$45/55. There's a swimming pool and a restaurant here. Further south, the *Ubud Inn* (☎ 975188) is a well-established place with a variety of bungalows and rooms dotted around a spacious garden area with a swimming pool; rooms cost US$25/35 with fan, US$30/40 with air-con, and two-storey family rooms cost US$45.

If you want some rural tranquility, look for a place on the outskirts of town. There are a few places on roads that run north of Jalan Raya. Jalan Kajang has a number of more expensive places with great views over the river gorge to the west, and a few budget places like *Roja's Homestay*, with rooms at 8000/10,000 rp and 12,000/15,000 rp. Jalan Suweta has the *Suci Inn*, across from the banyan tree, a very straightforward losmen-style place with simple rooms with bath from 9000 rp in front and 12,000 rp in the back. The rooms look out on to the central garden, and it's a friendly, relaxed place, quiet yet very central.

Continue up this road for about 10 minutes to Sambahan, where there's a small group of places, best known of which is *Ketut's Place* (☎ 975304). It has rooms in a family compound from 10,000/15,000 rp for singles/doubles in the front to 25,000 rp for cottages at the back, or 35,000 rp with hot water. *Sambahan Village Guest House* has also been recommended. A really secluded place is *Taman Indah Homestay*, a walk into the rice fields at the north end of Jalan Sandat, with three rooms at 8000/10,000 rp.

Around Ubud More accommodation can be found in the streets east of central Ubud in Padangtegal. Jalan Hanoman, Jalan Sugriwa and Jalan Jembawan all run south off Jalan Raya. *Puri Asri*, on Hanoman, has six rooms at 20,000/25,000 rp, while *Nuriani Guesthouse* (☎ 975346), just off to the east side on the rice fields, costs 25,000 rp to 30,000 rp a double. Hanoman continues south to Pengosekan, past the pleasant *Jati Inn* which has two-storey rooms for only 8000/10,000 rp, and the *Bali Breeze* with bungalows at 30,000 rp. Further east is Peliatan, where Jalan Tebesaya has some possibilities, including the popular *Rona Accommodation*, a very nice place with rooms at 10,000/12,000 rp and 17,000/20,000 rp.

On the main road south, *Mudita Inn* has two rooms in its shady garden for 8000/10,000 rp for singles/doubles, and there are other places nearby. At the junction, where the road bends sharply left to Denpasar, you'll see a sign for the *Sari Bungalows*, just 100 metres or so off the road. It's a pleasantly quiet location and good value with singles from 5000 to 6000 rp and doubles from 8000 rp, all including a 'big breakfast'. Nearby is the pleasant *Siti Homestay*, with a garden and rooms at 8000/12,000 rp.

Heading west on Jalan Raya brings you to Campuan, where the Wos and Cerik rivers meet. This is expensive artist country, but the *Cecak Inn* is good value at around 25,000 rp for an attractive, well-located bungalow. Cross the suspension bridge by Murni's, and take the steep road uphill by Blanco's house to Penestanan, a quiet but arty area. Along this road you'll find a pretty little group of homestays including the attractive *Arjuna's Inn*, run by the artist's daughter, with rooms at 15,000 to 20,000 rp.

There are more places further up into the rice paddies – you have to walk to get to them. The asking price is from around 15,000/20,000 rp for singles/doubles and up to around 40,000 rp per night for a larger bungalow, but many people stay much longer and negotiate a much lower rate. Further west is Sayan, where there are a few small places with great views over the Ayung River, costing from around US$25 per night.

Places to Eat

Ubud's many restaurants offer the best and most interesting food on the island. Well-prepared Indonesian and Balinese food is available, and a great selection of international dishes. Jalan Raya, the main east-west road, offers plenty of interesting possibilities, starting with the popular and dirt-cheap night market *(pasar malam)* which sets up at dusk right beside the main market area. Just east of the pasar malam, the *Nomad Restaurant* opens later than most places. Going west on Jalan Raya you'll find numerous restaurants, and you can get an excellent meal in any of them. *Ary's Warung*, right in the centre of town, is one of the cheaper places, with good nasi campur and many other dishes.

On the north side of Jalan Raya, *Lotus Cafe* is fashionable and pricey but still a relaxed place for a light lunch or a snack. *Mumbul's Cafe*, on the same side, is small with friendly service and excellent food, and even a children's menu.

Opposite Mumbul's, *Menara Restaurant* has good Balinese food and laser disk video entertainment.

Continuing west on Jalan Raya, *Casa Luna* has a superb international menu which is worth blowing your budget on, and the *Roof Garden Cafe* has good food, and views from its elevated position. Also a few steps up from the main road, *Miro's Cafe* has tasty food in a cool garden.

In Campuan, *Murni's Warung* is right beside the suspension bridge – it offers a beautiful setting and consistently excellent food; not cheap, but good value. The *Beggar's Bush*, a bit further west on the opposite side, is like an English pub, but has good food and is a local meeting place.

Monkey Forest Rd has many possibilities (these ones are listed from north to south). *Satri's Warung* is an inexpensive place with good food, while *Canderi's Warung* is an old Ubud institution and still worth trying. Another long-running place is the *Ubud Restaurant*, with some authentic local dishes. Just off the Monkey Forest Rd, *Oka Wati's* is a pleasant, friendly and economical place to eat, and a good source of information.

Back on Monkey Forest Road, down past the football field, *Cafe Wayan* is more expensive but has some of the best food in town; it also has delightful open-air tables at the back. Further down, the *Yudit Restaurant & Bakery* has pretty good pizzas for 6500 rp and good bread, rolls and other baked goods.

Entertainment

The main entertainment in Ubud is *Balinese dancing*. Even the tourist dances show a high degree of skill and are wonderfully presented. Entry is about 5000 rp; see the tourist office for information. Some restaurants run video movies, which are becoming popular. *Casa Luna* sometimes has a kids session at 4.00 pm.

Getting There & Away

Bemos from the Batubulan bus terminal, outside Denpasar, are 1000 rp. They arrive and depart from the middle of town, just north of Jalan Raya. You can get bemos from here to nearby villages like Kedewaten, Pejeng, Bedelu, Mas, Sakah and Blahbatuh (from around 350 rp). To get a bemo to southern or western Bali, you'll probably have to go via Batubulan and one of the other Denpasar terminals. For bemos to eastern or northern Bali, go via Gianyar.

Tourist shuttle buses go directly to other tourist areas: Sanur, Kuta, the airport, Padangbai, Candidasa or Kintamani cost 7500 rp; to Singaraja or Lovina it's 12,500 rp. The Perama depot (☎ 975513) is way down south towards Pengosekan. Some companies pick up closer to town – try the place at the Nomad Restaurant.

Getting Around

You can rent a bicycle (5000 rp for a day, cheaper for longer), motorbike (10,000 to 12,000 rp) or car (from 38,000 rp per day, including insurance).

AROUND UBUD

Two km along the main road to Gianyar is the heavily touristic **Goa Gajah**, or elephant cave, discovered in the 1920s and believed to have been a Buddhist hermitage. Nearby is **Yeh Pulu** with its carved bas relief. Go a couple of km north to the **Pura Penataran Sasih**, a temple with a huge bronze drum said to be 2000 years old. A legend tells of it falling to earth as the Moon of Pejeng.

Off to the eastern side of the road, near Tampaksiring, **Gunung Kawi** is a group of large stone memorials cut into cliffs on either side of a picturesque river valley. They're one of the best sights in Bali, impressive both for their sheer size and their setting.

A bit further north, in the shadow of the Sukarno-era presidential **palace**, is the holy spring and temple of **Tirta Empul**. An inscription dates the spring from 926 AD. There are fine carvings and Garudas on the courtyard buildings.

BESAKIH

Nearly 1000 metres up the side of mighty Gunung Agung, this is Bali's mother temple. It's big, majestically located and very well kept. Your contribution is 300 rp per car to park, 550 rp to enter and 1000 rp to rent a temple scarf. You can also pay for a guide, but you don't need one. The inner part of the temple is closed to visitors. There are regular bemos from Klungkung.

From Besakih you can climb to the top of Gunung Agung in around six hours. Take a guide and start very early. The *Arca Valley Inn*, about five km below Besakih, would be a convenient place to stay for an early start.

DENPASAR TO KLUNGKUNG

The traffic is heavy from Denpasar to Klungkung, but then becomes much lighter. There are some things to see in the main towns, and interesting detours to the coast and the mountains.

In **Gianyar**, the capital of Gianyar regency, there are weaving workshops, where hundreds of young workers prepare and dye threads and weave sarongs. You are welcome to visit, and of course to buy.

North of the main road, halfway up the slope to Penelokan, is **Bangli**. This place is usually reached from Gianyar, but is also accessible from Ubud via Tampaksiring, or by a very pretty small road from just below Rendang. Bangli has two fine temples, Pura Kehen, with a massive banyan tree, and Pura Dalem Penunggekan, a temple of the dead with gruesome sculpture panels along the front. You can stay at the *Artha Sastra Inn*, a former palace residence, for 10,000 to 20,000 rp. A little further north is the youth-hostel affiliated *Losmen Dharmaputra*, with rather basic singles/doubles at only 5000/7000 rp.

INDONESIA

KLUNGKUNG

Once the centre of an important Balinese kingdom, Klungkung is noted for its **water palace** and the adjacent **Kherta Ghosa**, or Hall of Justice. Disputes that could not be settled locally were brought here, and the accused could study lurid paintings on the roof, of wrongdoers suffering in the afterlife.

Places to Stay & Eat

The *Ramayana Palace Hotel* (☎ (0366) 21044), on the Candidasa side of town, is pleasant, with a good restaurant and spartan rooms at 10,000 rp; bigger and better rooms cost 20,000 rp. The basic *Losmen Wisnu* is near the bus terminal. There's quite good food at the *Restaurant Bali Indah* and *Restaurant Sumber Rasa*, both near the market.

NUSA PENIDA

Nusa Penida is the largest of three islands which comprise the administrative area of Nusa Penida within Klungkung District. Nusa Penida itself has few visitors and few facilities, and tiny Nusa Ceningan is virtually uninhabited. Nusa Lembongan, to the north-west, attracts visitors for its surf and seclusion.

Nusa Penida

The hilly island of Nusa Penida (population 40,000) was once used as a place of banishment for criminals from the Kingdom of Klungkung. The main town, **Sampalan**, is on the north coast; the only *losmen* is opposite the police station, a couple of hundred metres to the east.

Fast, twin-engined fibreglass boats run between Padangbai and Buyuk Harbour, Sampalan. The trip takes less than an hour and costs 3000 rp. Boats also cross from Kusamba, loaded with supplies; they're much slower and no safer. A boat from Nusa Lembongan can drop you on the beach at **Toyapakeh**, where you can stay at *Losmen Terang*.

Nusa Lembongan

The offshore coral reef is where the surf breaks, and it protects the arc of white beach. There's no jetty; the boats beach at **Jungutbatu**, or a little further north-east where most of the accommodation is. The most conspicuous place is the two-storey *Main Ski Restaurant & Cottages*, right on the beach, with good food, a great view and rooms from 12,000 rp. Other places to stay include *Agung's Lembongan Lodge*, *Nusa Lembongan Restaurant & Bungalows*, and *Ta Chi*.

Boats to Nusa Lembongan cost 15,000 rp per person, and leave from the north end of

Sanur Beach, where there's a ticket office. The boats leave early, 8.30 am at the latest, and take at least 1½ hours. The trip can be very rough. Local boats go between Jungutbatu and Nusa Penida, particularly on market days.

PADANGBAI

The port town of Padangbai, east of Klungkung, is on a perfect bay two km off the main road. The frequent ferries to Lombok leave from here, and visiting cruise ships anchor offshore. West of Padangbai, near the fishing village of Kusamba, sea salt is extracted by evaporation from hundreds of shallow wooden troughs. Also nearby is **Goa Lawah**, where thousands of bats line the cave behind the temple. It's not very interesting and the smell is overpowering.

Places to Stay & Eat

There are several pleasant places to stay on the beach-front. *Rai Beach Inn* has thatched two-storey cottages at 20,000 rp, and standard single-storey rooms with bath at 15,000 rp. The *Kerti Beach Inn* and the *Padangbai Beach Inn* both have basic rooms facing the sea from about 8000 rp. At the far end of the beach, *Topi Restaurant & Inn* has small, plain rooms at 8000/10,000 rp, and a dorm for 2000 rp per person. In the town, there's the neat and tidy *Homestay Dharma*, at about 8000 rp for a double. *Pantai Ayu Homestay* is back from the beach but in a good location; rooms cost 6000/10,000 rp.

On the beachfront the *Pantai Ayu Restaurant* is popular, and the *Apple Cafe* and the *Celagi Restaurant* are both good. And it's worth a walk down the beach to the *Topi Restaurant*, with its sand-floor dining area and colourful menu.

Getting There & Away

There are frequent ferries to Lombok's Lembar harbour – see the Bali Getting There & Away section for details. The ticket office is down by the pier, near where the buses arrive. Buses meet the ferry and go straight to Denpasar. Orange bemos go to Candidasa (500 rp) and Amlapura, while blue ones go to Klungkung – they're more frequent in the morning.

A fast catamaran service to Senggigi and Bangsal (for the Gili Islands) on Lombok was operating for some months (advertised trip time was two hours, but it sometimes took much longer; 20,000 rp). Look for the office on the main street to find if it is operating.

There are also bus connections from Padangbai right through to Surabaya and Yogya in Java, for slightly more than the fares from Denpasar; you'll find the buses in the parking area near the pier, and the touts will find you.

The fast, fibreglass boats to Nusa Penida (about 3000 rp) leave from the beach near the eastern corner of the carpark next to the pier.

BALINA BEACH

About 11 km along the main road from the Padangbai turn-off, Balina Beach is a scuba-diving centre on a quiet bit of the coast. It is in the process of acquiring its first large hotel, and losing its nice beach to erosion.

Places to Stay

The *Balina Beach Bungalows* (☎ 0361-88451) rent diving equipment and organise snorkelling and diving trips all around Bali. They have a pool, and rooms at a host of prices from as low as US$16/20. The *Puri Buitan* (☎ 0361-87182), on the opposite side of the access road, is less attractive. Two *homestays*, about 200 metres to the east along the beach, have bungalows at about 15,000/20,000 rp.

TENGANAN

North-west of Candidasa, about five km from the main road, is Tenganan, a Bali Aga village with walled homes, a symmetrical layout and unique crafts. The Bali Aga were the original inhabitants of Bali, before the arrival of the Hindu Javanese. The village is a bit commercialised, but it is still a fascinating place and you don't get hassled. Try to visit during a festival. Get a lift from the main

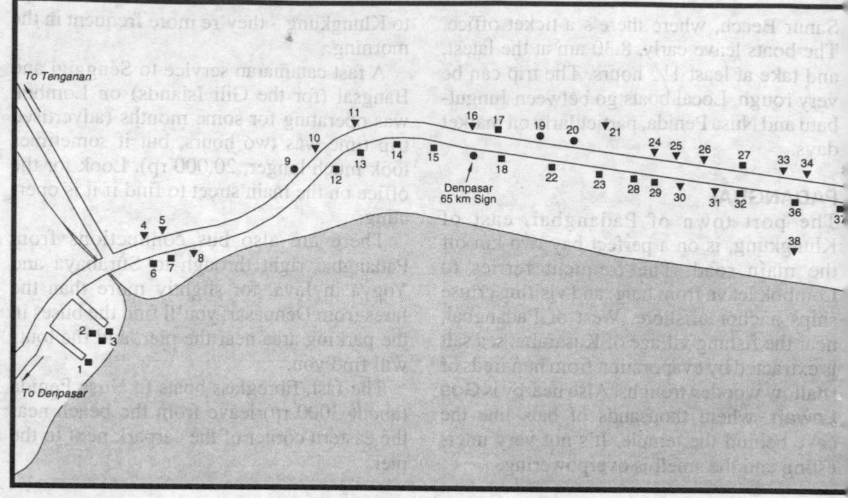

road by motorbike (about 1000 rp) and walk back; it's a good excursion from Candidasa. A donation is requested as you enter.

CANDIDASA

Candidasa changed from a quiet fishing village to a new beach resort with astonishing speed during the '80s. In that time its beach eroded away almost completely, partly because the fringing reef was destroyed by taking coral to make lime for concrete. T-shaped concrete piers have been constructed to save what little sand is left, and they now provide some nice little bathing areas if the tide is right. Candidasa seems overbuilt and lacking in charm, but some visitors like it – it's quieter than Kuta, cheaper than Sanur, and a good base from which to explore East Bali or do scuba trips.

Information

All the tourist facilities are along the main street, including moneychangers, travel agents, postal agents, bookshops and car rental places. You can make phone calls from the Kubu Bali Restaurant.

Places to Stay

Mid-range mass tourism has arrived, and there are a number of larger places with air-con, swimming pools and pretentious lobbies, but there are still plenty of low-cost, basic losmen at around 10,000/12,000 rp for a single/double, especially in the off-season. It's worth looking at a few places before deciding where to stay, if only to get a good feel for prices – they're not afraid to try out a high first price here.

Starting from the Denpasar (western) side, there are places off the main road several km before you reach Candidasa. Even this far out, the beach is still eroded. Most places are secluded, mid-range package-tour hotels like the *Candi Beach Cottage* at US$60/70, but the nearby *Amarta Beach Inn* has a great location and is good value at 15,000 rp a double, including breakfast. The *Nusa Indah Beach Bungalows* are the same price, but they are isolated with no restaurant, so you really need your own transport to get into town for meals.

As you approach Candidasa there are a few cheapies on the beach side of the road. *Sari Jaya Seaside Cottage* is OK and quiet, and costs 10,000 rp for singles or doubles,

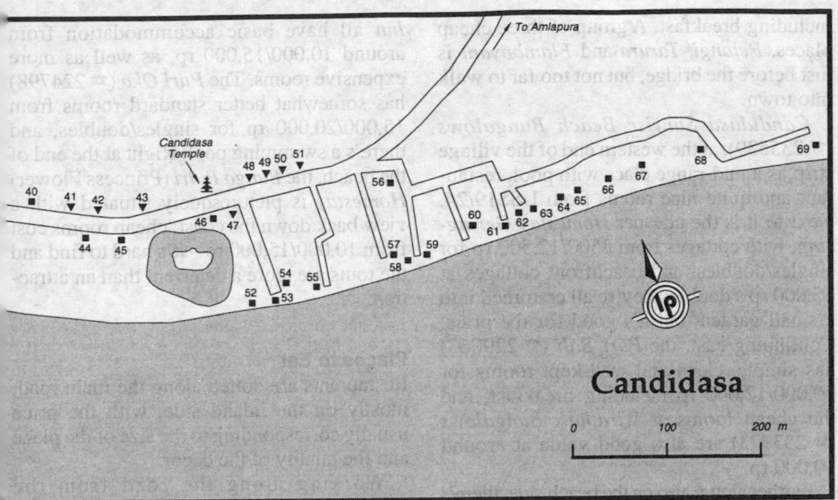

PLACES TO STAY

1 Sari Jaya Seaside Cottage
2 Flamboyant
3 Pelangi & Tarura
6 Bali Samudra Arirang Hotel
7 Homestay Catra
12 Candidasa Sunrise Beach Bungalows
13 Homestay Geringsing
14 Homestay Segara Wangi
15 Homestay Ayodya
17 The Watergarden (Taman Air)
18 Puri Bali
22 Wiratha's Bungalows
23 Puri Pandan Losmen & Restaurant
27 Homestay Sasra Bahu
28 Candidasa Beach Bungalows II
29 Homestay Lilaberata
32 Agung Bungalows
36 Pondok Bamboo Seaside Cottages
37 Dewa Bharata Bungalows
39 Homestay Natia
40 Cantiloka Beach Inn
44 Homestay Ida
45 Homestay Kelapa Mas
46 Dewi Bungalows
52 Rama Bungalows
53 Sindhu Brata Homestay
54 Pandawa Homestay
55 Srikandi Bungalows
56 Satria
57 Barong Beach Inn
58 Ramayana Beach Inn
59 Dutha Homestay
60 Nani Beach Inn
61 Genggong Cottages
62 Puri Tinarella Hotel
63 Puri Oka
64 Ida Beach Village
65 Puri Pudak Bungalows
66 Asoka Beach Bungalows
67 Sekar Orchid Bungalows
68 Puri Bagus Beach Hotel
69 Bunga Putri Homestay

PLACES TO EAT

4 Restaurant Flamboyant
5 Molly's Garden Cafe
8 Baliku Restaurant
10 Arie's Restaurant
11 Candidasa Restaurant
16 TJ's Restaurant
21 Ciao Restaurant
24 Chez Lilly Restaurant
25 Restaurant Candra
26 Hawaii Restaurant
30 Restaurant Sumber Rasa
31 Tirtanadi Restaurant
33 Sanjaya Beer Garden
34 Kubu Bali Restaurant
35 Murni's Cafe
38 Pondok Bamboo Restaurant
41 Legend Rock Cafe
42 Warung Srijati
43 Warung Rasmini
47 Kusuma Restaurant
48 Raja's Restaurant
49 Pizzeria Candi Agung
50 Ngandi Restaurant
51 Mandara Giri Pizzaria

OTHER

9 Perama
19 Bookshop
20 Pandan Harum

including breakfast. A group of three cheap places, *Pelangi, Tarura* and *Flamboyant* is just before the bridge, but not too far to walk into town.

Candidasa Sunrise Beach Bungalows (☎ 235539), at the western end of the village strip, is a mid-range place with pool, restaurant and quite nice rooms from US$19/24. Next to it is the cheaper *Homestay Geringsing*, with cottages from 8500/12,500 rp for singles/doubles, and beachfront cottages at 15,000 rp a double; they're all crammed into a small garden, but it's good for the price. Continuing east, the *Puri Bali* (☎ 229063) has simple, clean and well-kept rooms for 10,000/12,000 rp including breakfast, and the cheap rooms at *Wiratha's Bungalows* (☎ 233973) are also good value at around 10,000 rp.

Further along, also on the beach side, there's *Puri Pandan* (☎ 235541), at 15,000/20,000 rp for a room with breakfast, and the popular but rock-bottom *Homestay Lilaberata*, at 8000/10,000 rp, with a good location, squat toilets and chickens. The *Pondok Bamboo Seaside Cottages* (☎ 235534) is fancier, with rooms at 27,000/32,000 rp and a beach-front restaurant.

Homestay Ida, close to the lagoon, is spacious, with pleasantly airy, bamboo cottages dotted around a grassy coconut plantation. Smaller rooms are 20,000 rp, and larger rooms with a mezzanine level are 40,000 rp, including breakfast and tax. The *Homestay Kelapa Mas* (☎ 233947), next door, is also well kept and spacious, and costs 10,000 rp for the smallest rooms to 15,000, 17,000 and 25,000 rp for larger ones – the seafront rooms are particularly well situated.

Beyond the Kelapa Mas is the lagoon, and there are plenty of small losmen further along the beach, as well as some newer, more expensive places. Three fairly standard losmen east of the lagoon are *Dewi Bungalows, Rama Bungalows*, and the *Sindhu Brata Homestay*, all with rooms from 15,000/20,000 rp upwards. Nearby is the cheaper *Pandawa Homestay*.

Further along the beach, *Barong Beach Inn*, *Ramayana Beach Inn*, and *Nani Beach Inn* all have basic accommodation from around 10,000/15,000 rp, as well as more expensive rooms. The *Puri Oka* (☎ 224798) has somewhat better standard rooms from 15,000/20,000 rp for singles/doubles, and there's a swimming pool. Right at the end of the beach, the *Bunga Putri* (Princess Flower) *Homestay* is picturesquely situated with a view back down the coast; cheap rooms cost from 10,000/15,000 rp – it's hard to find and the touts are more a deterrent than an attraction.

Places to Eat

Restaurants are dotted along the main road, mostly on the inland side, with the price usually corresponding to the size of the place and the quality of the decor.

Working along the road from the Denpasar end, some of the more interesting places include *Molly's Garden Cafe*, and *TJ's Restaurant*, which is related to the popular TJ's in Kuta, but the food is not as Mexican, nor as good. *Ciao Restaurant* serves good Italian food, while *Chez Lilly* is a newer place which already has a reputation for excellent food. *Restaurant Candra* is good for Indian dishes, while *Sumber Rasa* and the *Hawaii Restaurant* are both long-term survivors. *Tirtanadi Restaurant* (The TN) is one of the few eating places on the beach side of the road, and has a cheerful atmosphere and a long cocktail list.

Back on the north side of the road, the *Kubu Bali Restaurant* is a big place built around a pond, with an open kitchen in front, turning out Indonesian, Chinese and seafood dishes. It's in the middle price range, but usually worth it. For cheaper eating, try *Warung Srijati* and *Warung Rasmini*, on the north side of the road but closer to the lagoon. Just beyond the lagoon, the *Pizzeria Candi Agung* and the *Mandara Giri Pizzaria* display different approaches to spelling although pizza is definitely on the menu at both places!

Entertainment

Balinese dances are staged at 9 pm on Tuesday and Friday at *Pandan Harum*, in the centre of the Candidasa strip. Entry is 4000 rp.

Getting There & Away

A bemo from the Batubulan terminal in Denpasar should cost about 2200 rp. Tourist shuttle buses also operate from Candidasa; to the airport, Denpasar or Kuta it costs 10,000 rp, to Ubud it's 7,500 rp, or to Lovina it's 20,000 rp.

AMLAPURA

Amlapura was called Karangasem, the same as the district, but the name was changed after the 1963 eruption of Agung, to get rid of any nasty associations which might provoke a recurrence! It's an attractive little town with a fine old **palace**, once the seat of the old Raja of Karangasem. The uninspiring ruins of the **Ujung Palace** are near the coast about three or four km south of town.

Losmen Sidha Karya, on the road into town about 200 metres past the statue, has cheap, basic rooms. There are regular buses to and from Denpasar and less frequent connections around the east coast to Singaraja.

AMLAPURA TO RENDANG

From Amlapura, you can follow the slopes of Gunung Agung, through some very pretty countryside, to Rendang. It's easy with your own transport, but time-consuming by bemo. You can stay at *Losmen Kembang Ramaja*, just out of Amlapura on the Rendang road, or at the pretty and secluded *Homestay Lila*, three km further along the same road.

About 11 km beyond Bebandem there's a turnoff to Putung, right at the top of the ridge. The land drops away to the coast, and you can see ships anchored off Padangbai. You can rent a bungalow here for about 20,000 rp. A short detour south goes to **Iseh**, where German artist Walter Spies and Swiss painter Theo Meier both lived.

TIRTAGANGGA

Just before Amlapura, turn inland and continue to Tirtagangga, where there's a delightful **Water Palace**, which dates from 1947 but looks much older. Admission is 550 rp, plus 2000 rp to use the lower swimming pool or 1000 rp for the upper one. The rice terraces around Tirtagangga are particularly picturesque, and this is a very relaxing and peaceful place to stay.

Places to Stay & Eat

Within the palace compound, the *Tirta Ayu Homestay* has pleasant individual bungalows from 20,000/25,000 rp, including admission to the water palace swimming pools. Near the palace, *Losmen Dhangin Taman Inn* has rooms at 10,000/12,000 rp up to 20,000 rp, including breakfast, and the *Good Karma* restaurant has good food and music. Across the road from the palace, the *Rijasa Homestay* is a small, simple place with clean single/double rooms at 10,000/15,000 rp, with breakfast and tea.

Kusuma Jaya Inn, the Homestay on the Hill, 300 metres beyond the water palace and up the steep steps, has a fine view over the rice paddies and rooms from 25,000 to 40,000 rp including breakfast and tea. Another 600 metres brings you to the steps to *Prima Bambos Homestay*, a new 'homestay on the hill', with a great outlook and rooms at 11,000/16,000 rp including breakfast.

TULAMBEN & AMED

North beyond Tirtagangga the road descends through some spectacular terraced rice fields to the coast. Head north to reach Tulamben, where the wreck of the USS *Liberty* is a major attraction for divers and snorkellers, and where there are bungalows at around 20,000 to 25,000 rp. Continue around the good-quality coast road for about 70 km to reach Singaraja.

After descending from Tirtagangga you can also go east, where there are some isolated places to stay on the coast near Amed. The road round the south-east peninsula is a narrow, winding switchback, but it's sealed, scenic, and quite passable right round to Ujung and Amlapura again.

SOUTH-WEST BALI

North of Seminyak, the road doesn't follow the coast, but you can detour to beaches at **Petingan** (on the fringe of the Kuta-Legian development), **Berewa** (with some nice hotels) and **Canggu** (with a famous surf break). Further north, **Tanah Lot** is a temple spectacularly balanced on a rocky islet. It's probably the most photographed temple in Bali, particularly at sunset; it's also horrifically touristy.

At **Mengwi**, north of the main road, there's an impressive royal water palace and temple. About 10 km north again is the monkey forest and temple of **Sangeh** – watch out, as the monkeys will snatch anything from peanuts out of your pocket, to your sunglasses or camera for good measure.

The large town of **Tabanan** is in the heart of the fertile south Bali rice-belt. It's also the capital of Tabanan District and a centre for dancing and gamelan playing. **Krambitan**, south-west of Tabanan, has a royal palace, and you can stay nearby at *Bee Bees* in Tibubiyu.

Eventually the main road swings south to the coast, but doesn't actually follow it. Numerous side roads lead to villages with black-sand beaches, some beautiful scenery and very little tourist development. **Lalang-Linggah** is a get-away-from-it-all place. You can stay at the *Balian Beach Club*, overlooking the river and surrounded by coconut plantations. Rooms are from 35,000 to 50,000 rp, but there is some cheaper bunk accommodation.

The turn-off to the **Medewi** surfing point is just west of Pulukan village – there's a large but faded sign on the main road. The *Medewi Beach Cottages* have cheaper rooms from 23,000 rp. A bit further west, *Tinjayya Bungalows* cost 20,000 rp downstairs and 25,000 rp for bigger upstairs rooms.

The beautiful temple of **Rambut Siwi** is just south of the main road, high on a cliff top overlooking the sea.

Bullock races are held at **Negara** between July and October each year, but otherwise it's very quiet. There're a few losmen on the main street – the *Hotel Ana* is about the cheapest, with rooms from around 6000 rp. The *Wira Pada* (☎ 41161) is probably the best, costing from 10,000/12,500 rp.

Off the main road about seven km north of Melaya, **Blimbingsari** and **Palasari** are (respectively) the main Protestant and Catholic communities on Bali, each with an impressive church.

Right at the western end of the island, **Gilimanuk** is the port for ferries to and from Java (650 rp per person). There's a bus terminal behind the market on the main street, about a km from the dock. There are several places to stay along the main road, including *Homestay Surya* and *Lestari Homestay*. Only 200 metres from the port, and well to the east of the main drag, *Nusantara II* is a bit quieter, with small rooms from 10,000 rp.

GUNUNG BATUR AREA

The volcanic cone of Gunung Batur, and Lake Batur, which fills half of the huge surrounding caldera, form a spectacular landscape which is one of Bali's natural wonders. Unfortunately, it is also an area where visitors can experience some hassles, from very persistent hawkers to downright rip-offs. You have to buy a 500 rp entry ticket, and a car costs another 400 rp.

There are several routes up Gunung Batur (1717 metres) – from Tirtha (Toyah Bungkah), Songan, Kedisan or even Kintamani on the outer rim. Ideally, you should get to the top for the sunrise – a magnificent sight. Mist and cloud can obscure the view later in the day. The easiest route is up the north-east ridge, from a new access trail and parking area near Songan. From Tirtha it's longer (a round trip of four or five hours) and the track is not quite as easy to follow, especially before dawn. Lots of locals will offer to be your guide, sometimes for outrageous amounts – 6000 rp is a fair price. Cooking eggs, bananas and other items in the hot fissures on the summit has been a source of litter – bring a snack you can eat cold, or get something from the warung on top. For reliable trekking information, see Jero Wijaya, near Arlina Bungalows as you enter Tirtha.

Around the Crater Rim

From the south, **Penelokan** is the first place you'll come to on the rim of the caldera. Be prepared for wet, cold and cloudy conditions and some aggressive souvenir selling.

The *Lakeview Restaurant & Homestay* (☎ 32023) has brilliant views and asks US$8 for very small 'economy' rooms. A little further north, past the road down into the crater, *Losmen & Restaurant Gunawan* also has great views and quite high prices for small rooms (about 20,000 rp). The bigger restaurants along here are geared for buffet-style lunches for the tour groups which arrive by the bus-load. The *Restaurant Mutiari* is better value, and there are cheap *warungs* along the main road.

Further north-west is the town of **Batur**, which merges into **Kintamani**, the main town on the rim of the caldera. The original town of Batur, down in the crater, was engulfed in the 1926 eruption. Batur was rebuilt up on the caldera rim, and its temple was relocated to the impressive site it now occupies. The *Hotel Miranda*, at 6000 to 8000 rp for basic rooms with breakfast, has a friendly atmosphere and helpful owners. Further north, *Losmen Sasaka* has clean, spacious rooms and great views for 15,000/20,000 rp with breakfast.

Just beyond Kintamani is **Penulisan**, site of the highest temple in Bali and the Bali TV relay-station tower. The road descends from here through misty villages to Kubutambahan, on the north coast.

Around Lake Batur

A steep side road winds down from Penelokan to Kedisan on the shore of the lake. From there, you can take a boat across to the Bali Aga village of Trunyan, or follow the quaint little road across the lava fields to the hot springs at Tirtha (Toyah Bungkah). The road continues to Songan, under the north-eastern rim of the crater, and a side road goes around to the north side of Gunung Batur until it is stopped by a huge 'flow' of solidified black lava.

Turning left as you enter **Kedisan**, you come first to the *Segara Bungalows*, with basic rooms from 8000/10,000 rp, including breakfast, and better rooms at higher prices. A bit further on is the *Surya Homestay & Restaurant*, with a similar variety of rooms at similar prices. Turn right as you come into town and you'll reach the cheaper and more basic *Segara Homestay*, from 6000 rp. Further round is **Buahan**, where you can stay at *Baruna Cottages*, with a restaurant and single/double rooms with mandi from 8000/10,000 rp.

Trunyan There's very little to see in this Bali Aga village – a few remaining old-style buildings, an old temple and an enormous banyan tree. Beyond Trunyan is the cemetery, where bodies are laid out in bamboo cages to decompose. It's a pretty morbid tourist trap. To get there, take a boat from the jetty near the middle of Kedisan, where there is a ticket office and a fenced car park. There's a fixed price for a boat and guide for a round-trip from Kedisan to Trunyan, the cemetery, Tirtha and back – 37,500 rp with two or three people; 39,500 rp with seven.

Tirtha (Toyah Bungkah) This small settlement is named for its hot springs (Tirtha and Toyah both mean Holy Water). You can climb Gunung Batur in the early morning, and soak your aching muscles in the hot springs afterwards. The hot springs are channelled into a concrete bathing pool (surrounded by litter), which you can use for 1000 rp. To enter Tirtha costs 550 rp for an adult, 400 rp for a car and 250 rp for a child.

There are quite a few places to stay, and more are under construction. None of them are anything special, and some are pretty grimy. The going price is between 8000/10,000 rp and 10,000/15,000 rp for a basic single/double – it's definitely worth looking at the room and discussing the price. *Arlina Bungalows* are better than the average, and *Tirta Yastra* is cheap and near the lake. There are a number of warungs and restaurants, mostly with similar menus and prices. Fresh fish from the lake is a local speciality.

LAKE BRATAN AREA

Next to pretty Lake Bratan, **Bedugul** is on the most direct north-south route between Denpasar and the north coast. Three km north of Bedugul at **Candikuning**, the picturesque temple of Pura Ulu Danau stands partly on an island at the lake's western shore. There are some pleasant hikes around the lake, which is also good for swimming.

Upmarket watersports, such as waterskiing and parasailing, are available in the **Taman Rekreasi** (Leisure Park) at the southern end of the lake – entry and parking costs 500 rp. There's a big **flower market** near the temple on Sunday, and the cool, attractive **Botanical Gardens** (entry 500 rp) are on the slopes of Gunung Pohon.

There are several places to stay in the area, but the best options are the well-located *Lila Graha* (☎ (0362) 23848), up a steep drive from the lakeside road, with singles/doubles from 25,000/30,000 rp, and the popular *Hotel Ashram* (☎ (0362) 22439), right by the lake, with ordinary rooms from 15,000 rp.

To get to Bedugul, take a bemo between Singaraja and Denpasar (Ubung terminal), and tell the driver where you want to get off.

OTHER MOUNTAIN ROUTES

West of the road down from Bedugul to Mengwi is Gunung Batukau, with the remote temple **Pura Luhur** perched on its slopes. Interesting trips can be made to the west round Lake Buyan and Lake Tamblingan, through Munduk and on to Seririt.

There's a scenic but little-used road which winds up from the south, through Blimbing and Pupuan, to the north coast. Another route starts from near Pulukan on the south coast and climbs through spice-growing country and picturesque paddy fields until it joins the other road at Pupuan.

SINGARAJA

Singaraja is Bali's principal north-coast town, and the capital of Buleleng District. Its colonial-era port has closed, but it is still a thriving town (85,000) with a substantial student population, some broad tree-lined streets and quite a few old Dutch buildings.

Places to Stay & Eat

Hotels mainly cater to Indonesian business travellers. *Hotel Sentral* (☎ 21896), on Jalan Achmad Yani, is a well-run place, with basic singles/doubles from 7000/10,000 rp. *Hotel Garuda* (☎ 41191), at Jalan Achmad Yani No 76, is similarly priced. On Jalan Imam Bonjol, the street that continues south to Bedugul and Denpasar, you'll find the friendly, funky *Tresna Homestay* which is cheap, and has an antique collection and good information.

There are several places to eat on Jalan Achmad Yani, including the *Restaurant Gandhi*, a popular Chinese place, and the *Restaurant Segar II*, across the road. *Gaguk Cafe* (☎ 25111), just west of the western bus terminal, has tasty food, is popular with local students and is a good place to find out what's going on.

Getting There & Away

Singaraja has two bus terminals: Terminal Banyualit in the west and Terminal Penarunan about three km to the east. Minibuses to Denpasar (Ubung terminal) via Bedugul leave every half-hour from the western terminal, and cost around 2000 rp. There are also direct buses to Surabaya on Java (20,000 rp). For Yogyakarta you can get a local bus to Gilimanuk (2000 rp) and then change to a Denspasar-Yogyakarta bus.

EAST OF SINGARAJA

There are a number of places of interest just to the east of Singaraja. The soft local stone has allowed temple sculptors to produce some extravagantly whimsical scenes. **Pura Beji** at Sangsit, on the coast side of the main road, has a whole Disneyland of demons and snakes on its front panels. **Jagaraga temple**, a few km inland, features vintage cars, a steamship and even an aerial dogfight between early aircraft. About a km east of the Kintamani turn-off, the **Pura Maduwe Karang**, on the coast side of the road, has the famous relief of a gentleman riding a bicycle with flower-petal wheels.

Fifteen km east of Singaraja, at **Yeh Sanih** (also called Air Sanih), freshwater springs

INDONESIA

are channelled into a fine **swimming pool** (entry 400 rp; children 200 rp). It's set in attractive gardens right by the sea, and the water is cool and refreshing. You can stay at *Bungalow Puri Sanih*, in the springs complex; doubles cost 20,000 to 40,000 rp. They have a restaurant overlooking the gardens, and there are a number of warungs and a restaurant across the road. *Puri Rena* is up the hillside on the southern side of the road, with rooms from 10,000/15,000 rp and great views from the restaurant.

LOVINA BEACHES

To the west of Singaraja is a string of coastal villages which have become a popular budget beach resort collectively known as Lovina. The beaches are black volcanic sand, and a reef keeps the water calm. You can take a boat out to see dolphins cavorting in the sea at sunrise, or for snorkelling. You can also make day trips to nearby waterfalls, the Bali Barat National Park, or the temples and craft centres around Singaraja. The atmosphere is relaxed, despite the hawkers, and there's a lively night life in the tourist season. The accommodation is stretched out over seven or eight km, but the main focus is at Kalibukbuk, 10½ km from Singaraja, where there are restaurants, shops, bars and other tourist facilities.

Places to Stay

There are so many places to stay along the Lovina beach strip that it's impossible to list them all. Generally, the cheapest places are away from the beach, some on the southern side of the main road. When accommodation is tight the prices are a bit higher. Upstairs rooms are cooler and a bit more expensive, especially if they have a view. A light breakfast is sometimes included, as is the 5% tax on accommodation.

Singaraja to Anturan Starting from the Singaraja end are the higher-priced *Baruna Beach Cottages* and *Bali Taman Beach Hotel*. On the side road, between these two places and close to the beach, are the plain but clean *Jati Reef Bungalows*, with double rooms from around 12,000 rp. The nearby *Happy Beach Inn* is a cheerful place, with rooms from 7000 to 10,000 rp. Just inland, *Permai Beach Bungalows* have ordinary rooms at 10,000/15,000 rp; 20,000/25,000 rp with air-con.

Anturan There are three places in this little fishing village. *Mandhara Cottages*, on the right side of the road to the beach, have basic singles/doubles at 10,000/12,000 rp. The friendly *Gede Homestay*, just behind, is about the same price. Walk a short distance east along the beach to the refurbished *Simon's Seaside Cottages*, with comfortable rooms for 20,000 rp. Next door to Simon's is *Homestay Agung*, with rooms at around 10,000 rp.

Anturan to Kalibukbuk Continuing west you reach the *Hotel Perama* (☎ 21161) on the north side of the main road, with a restaurant and rooms for about 10,000 rp. This is also the office for the Perama shuttle buses and tours, and they are a useful source of information.

The next turn-off goes down to the beach and the *Lila Cita*. It's simple, but very friendly and popular. Rooms range from 8000/10,000 rp up to 15,000/20,000 rp for a room with a mandi and the sea just outside your window. On the way there, you'll pass the *Celuk Agung Cottages* – another flashy new place.

The next side road down to the beach has quite a few places to stay. The pleasant *Kali Bukbuk Beach Inn* is down by the beach on the left side, with rooms from 15,000 rp to 35,000 rp. Other places here include the *Banyualit Beach Inn*, *Yudhistra Inn*, and *Janur's Dive Inn*. Back on the main road, on the southern side, is the *Adi Homestay*, with rooms from 6000 rp, and on the north side, the new *Palma Beach Hotel*, which costs over US$60; but you can use the pool for just 5000 rp.

Kalibukbuk Just past the 10 km marker, this is the 'centre' of Lovina. Here you'll find *Ayodya Accommodation*, a traditional place in a big old Balinese house, with simple

INDONESIA

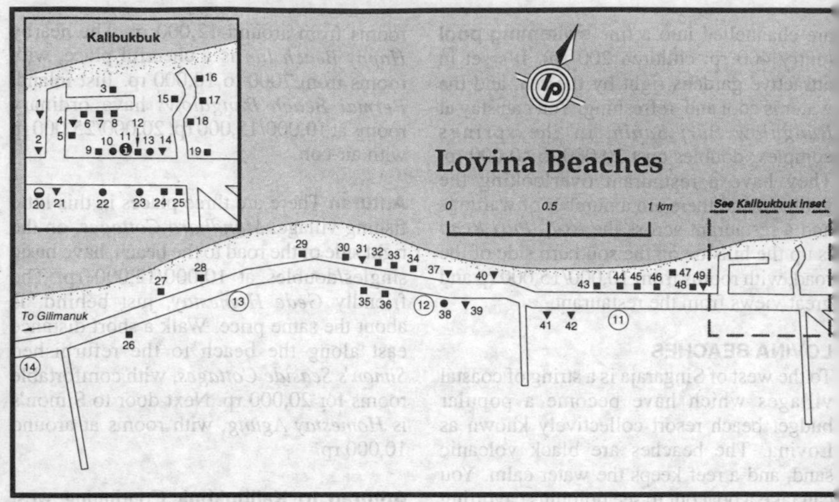

rooms from 7000 to 8000 rp. Follow the track beside Ayodya down towards the beach and you come to the well-run *Rambutan Cottages* (☎ 23388), with pretty gardens, a pool, and clean, comfortable rooms from 30,000 rp, but 5000 rp more in peak seasons.

Closest to the beach is another good place, the *Rini Hotel* (☎ 23386). It's very clean and well run, with a good restaurant and double rooms from 20,000 to 30,000 rp. In between these two are the *Puri Bali Bungalows* which are good value for this location at 8000/10,000 rp for standard singles/doubles. Opposite Rini are the *Astina Cottages*, in a pretty garden setting with a variety of rooms and bungalows from 9000 to 15,000 rp.

Along the main road west of Ayodya, you'll find the *Khi Khi Hotel & Restaurant* on the south side, with a murky pool and ordinary rooms at 20,000 rp. A bit further along is the small *Wisata Jaya Homestay*, one of the cheapest around, with basic but satisfactory rooms for 8000 rp. On the other side of the road you'll find the *New Srikandi Hotel, Bar & Restaurant*, which is also cheap, and the more expensive *Chono Beach Cottages*.

The next turn-off to the beach takes you down to the carpark of the well-established *Nirwana Cottages* (☎ 22288), with double rooms from 20,000 to 45,000 rp, and two-storey Bali-style cottages for good family accommodation. It's a great location but some readers don't find it good value. Right behind Nirwana is *Angsoka* (☎ 22841), which advertises 'luxury on a shoestring' but only has a couple of cheap rooms – most are over 35,000 rp. *Susila Beach Inn 2*, beside the Angsoka, is a small, straightforward losmen with cheap rooms for 7000/8000 rp.

Back on the main road, there is a string of cheap places beyond the Nirwana/Angsoka turn-off, with prices from about 8000 rp a double. They include the *Purnama Homestay*, *Mangalla Homestay* and *Susila Beach Inn*, which are all grouped together on the north side the road. Some of the places here extend through to the beach so you can get away from the road noise. *Lovina Beach Hotel* (☎ 23473) has a variety of rooms extending to the beach – pretty basic ones are US$5. *Puri Tasik Madu* extends to the beach and costs 12,000 to 15,000 rp.

Beyond Kalibukbuk Continuing further west along the road, there's the pricey *Aditya Bungalows & Restaurant*, with beach front-

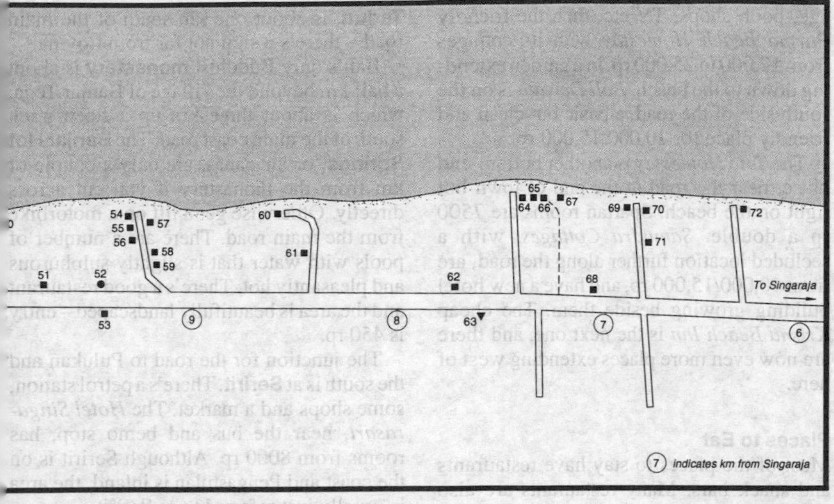

PLACES TO STAY

- 3 Nirwana Cottages & Restaurant
- 5 Palestis Hotel
- 6 Ray Beach Inn
- 7 Susila Beach Inn 2
- 8 Angsoka Cottages & Restaurant
- 9 Chono Beach Cottages & Restaurant
- 12 New Srikandi Hotel, Bar & Restaurant
- 15 Astina Cottages
- 16 Rini Hotel
- 17 Puri Bali Bungalows
- 18 Rambutan Cottages & Restaurant
- 19 Ayodya Accommodation
- 24 Wisata Jaya Homestay
- 25 Khi Khi Hotel & Restaurant
- 26 Ayu Pondok Wisita
- 27 Krisna Beach Inn
- 28 Samudra Cottages
- 29 Toto Homestay
- 30 Billibu Cottages
- 32 Miami
- 33 Parma Beach Homestay
- 34 Aditya Bungalows & Restaurant
- 35 Bali Dewata
- 36 Billibu Restaurant & Homestay
- 43 Puri Tasik Madu
- 44 Mangalla Homestay & Restaurant
- 45 Susila Beach Inn
- 46 Purnama Homestay
- 47 Lovina Beach Hotel
- 48 Bali Lovina Cottages
- 50 Las Brisas
- 51 Palma Beach Hotel
- 53 Adi Homestay
- 54 Kali Bukbuk Beach Inn
- 55 Suma's Guesthouse & Pringga Guesthouse
- 56 Yudhistra Inn
- 57 Banyualit Beach Inn
- 58 Janur's Dive Inn
- 59 Awangga Inn
- 60 Lila Cita
- 61 Celuk Agung Cottages
- 62 Hotel Perama & Postal Agency
- 64 Mandhara Cottages
- 65 Gede Homestay
- 66 Simon's Seaside Cottages
- 67 Homestay Agung & Restaurant
- 68 Bali Taman Beach Hotel
- 69 Happy Beach Inn
- 70 Jati Reef Bungalows
- 71 Permai Beach Bungalows
- 72 Baruna Beach Cottages

PLACES TO EAT

- 1 Bali Bintang Restaurant
- 2 Puri Taman Restaurant
- 4 Kakatua Bar & Restaurant
- 14 Surya Restaurant
- 21 Arya's Cafe
- 31 Karina Restaurant
- 37 Johni's Restaurant
- 39 Restaurant Adi Rama
- 40 Marta's Warung
- 41 Superman Restaurant
- 42 Singa Pizza Restaurant
- 49 Wina's Bar & Restaurant
- 63 Harmoni Restaurant

OTHER

- 10 Perama Office
- 11 Tourist Office & Police Station
- 13 Malibu Club
- 20 Bus Stop
- 22 Moneychanger
- 23 Air-Brush T-Shirt Shop
- 38 Spice Dive
- 52 Radio Mast

age, pool, shops, TV etc, then the friendly *Parma Beach Homestay* with its cottages from 12,000 to 25,000 rp, in a garden extending down to the beach. *Bali Dewata* is on the south side of the road, a basic but clean and friendly place for 10,000/15,000 rp.

The *Toto Homestay* is another bottom-end place, near the road at the end of town but right on the beach. Spartan rooms are 7500 rp a double. *Samudra Cottages*, with a secluded location further along the road, are from 10,000/15,000 rp, and have a new hotel building growing beside them. The cheap *Krisna Beach Inn* is the next one, and there are now even more places extending west of here.

Places to Eat

Most of the places to stay have restaurants and snack bars. Many restaurants are also bars, especially later at night. With all these, plus a handful of warungs, there are dozens of places to eat and drink. *Arya's Cafe*, *BU Warung*, *Chono's*, *Surya Restaurant*, *Warung Made* and *Kakatua* are current local favourites, but you'll do well just looking around and eating anywhere that takes your fancy.

Getting There & Away

To get to Lovina from the south of Bali, go to Singaraja and take a bemo out from there (500 rp). The direct buses between Singaraja and Surabaya (in Java) stop at Lovina – you don't have to go into Singaraja first. The Perama depot (☎ 21161) is at the Perama Hotel in Anturan; they have another office near the police station, or will pick you up from your losmen if you book ahead. Buses to/from Gilimanuk cost about 2000 rp.

NORTH COAST TO GILIMANUK

The road from Singaraja to Lovina continues along the north coast to the Bali Barat National Park, then swings south to connect with Gilimanuk at Bali's western tip. There are a number of sights along the way, and the route is quite scenic in places.

Daybreak Waterfall, or **Singsing Air Terjun**, is about one km south of the main road – there's a sign not far from Lovina.

Bali's only Buddhist **monastery** is about a half km beyond the village of Banjar Tega, which is about three km up a steep track south of the main coast road. The **Banjar Hot Springs**, or air panas, are only a couple of km from the monastery if you cut across directly. Otherwise get a lift on a motorbike from the main road. There are a number of pools with water that is slightly sulphurous and pleasantly hot. There's a good restaurant and the area is beautifully landscaped – entry is 450 rp.

The junction for the road to Pulukan and the south is at **Seririt**. There's a petrol station, some shops and a market. The *Hotel Singarasari*, near the bus and bemo stop, has rooms from 8000 rp. Although Seririt is on the coast and Pengastulan is inland, the area is usually just referred to as Seririt.

Celukanbawang is now the main port for north Bali. You may see Bugis schooners anchored here, and there's also a small beach. The *Hotel Drupadi Indah*, a combination losmen, cinema, bar and cafe, is the only place to stay.

The temple at **Pulaki** is on a pretty stretch of coast, and has lots of monkeys and grape vines nearby. The Pemuteran **hot springs**, a few hundred metres north of the road, are uninspiring.

BALI BARAT NATIONAL PARK

Taman Nasional Bali Barat (West Bali National Park), with the park extension and the adjacent coral reef and coastal waters, protects nearly 80,000 hectares of western Bali. Information and facilities for visitors are quite limited, but this may improve as the area becomes better known. A 2000 rp day ticket allows you to stop at all the places of interest – they're called 'visitor objects' – but you don't have to pay any entrance fees just to drive through.

Labuhan Lalang & Pulau Menjangan

The office in Labuhan Lalang has some information and a good relief model of the area. You can buy your 2000 rp day ticket here, to enter the foreshore area where there's a pleasant white-sand beach and a warung (it's another 2000 rp to park a car).

There's a jetty for boats to **Pulau Menjangan** (Deer Island), an unspoilt and uninhabited island reputed to offer the best diving in Bali (arrange a trip with Spice Dive, in Lovina). Excursions start at 42,000 rp for a boat for a four-hour trip – it's cheaper with a group of up to ten people.

Jungle Treks

Treks must be accompanied by a guide, which can be arranged through the national park office office at Labuhan Lalang – it costs 15,000 rp for a three-hour trek with one to four people. Arrange it the day before, and be at the office at 7.30 am. A variety of animals and birds can be seen. Trekking is currently restricted on Menjangan Island and the Prapat peninsula because of a project to re-establish the Bali starling. Other treks can be arranged at the office in Cekik (open 7.30 am to 2 pm daily except Sunday), at the southern entrance to the park.

Teluk Terima

This is the site of Jayaprana's grave, a 10-minute walk up some stone stairs from the southern side of the road. Jayaprana, the foster son of a 17th-century king, and his girlfriend, Layonsari, are Bali's answer to Romeo and Juliet.

Sumatra

Sumatra is one of Indonesia's 'new frontiers'. It has vast wealth in natural resources but is comparatively unpopulated and undeveloped, despite major resettlement projects, or 'transmigration', from Java. Sumatra offers wild jungle scenery. The Bukit Barisan, or Marching Mountains, do just that – right down the west coast – and there is a diverse collection of highly individual cultures and peoples. In 1958, Sumatra tried to break away from the rest of Indonesia in an abortive rebellion.

Getting There & Away

The most conventional way to reach Sumatra is to take the ferry from Penang in Malaysia to Medan, then travel by bus down through the island to Padang. From Padang you can travel by ship to Jakarta or continue down via Palembang to the southern tip of Sumatra and take the ferry across to Merak in Java.

Other variations include arrival or departure via the Riau Archipelago, flying to or from various cities in Sumatra or taking the ferry service between Melaka (Malaysia) and Dumai.

Air Penang to Medan flights for the short 40-minute hop across the Melaka Straits are operated by MAS and Sempati for around US$60. This is a popular flight to satisfy the 'ticket out' requirement of Indonesian visas.

Garuda and Silk Air have flights from Singapore to Medan for US$127, and MAS has direct flights from Kuala Lumpur to Medan. Pelangi Air and Sempati have direct flights from Kuala Lumpur to Pekanbaru and Padang.

Merpati have flights from Jakarta to all sorts of destinations in Sumatra including flights to Banda Aceh (394,000 rp), Bengkulu (142,000 rp), Medan (300,000 rp), Padang (215,000 rp) and Pekanbaru (218,000 rp).

Boat The Penang-Medan ferry is a convenient way to enter Sumatra, and the Singapore-Batam-Pekanbaru route is also popular.

Penang to Medan This is the easiest way into or out of Sumatra and since most of Sumatra's attractions are up at the northern end of the island, many people arrive and depart Sumatra via this route. The comfortable, high-speed ferries, the *Ekspres Selasa* and *Ekspres Bahagia*, between them have departures every day except Friday and Sunday from Penang for RM90. From Medan (actually Belawan, Medan's port), the ferries go to Penang on Tuesday, Wednesday, Friday and Sunday for 78,500 rp. See the Medan section for details.

Port Kelang & Lumut to Medan From Port Kelang, near Kuala Lumpur, ferries go to Belawan (RM120, six hours) at 10 am on Sunday, and from Belawan at 11 am on Monday and Wednesday.

Ferries from Lumut to Belawan (RM90, four hours) leave on Wednesday, Friday and Sunday at 9 am.

Melaka to Dumai A ferry runs between Melaka (Malaysia) and Dumai every day except Sunday for RM80. Dumai is a small port where the only thing to do is get on a bus and head south for 158 km to Pekanbaru. From Pekanbaru, buses depart regularly for Bukittinggi. You need a visa to enter or leave Indonesia through Dumai.

Ferries also leave Port Kelang for Dumai at 10 am on Tuesday (RM180, four hours).

Singapore to Sumatra via the Riau The Riau Archipelago is the scattering of Indonesian islands immediately south of Singapore – they can make an interesting and

convenient stepping stone to Sumatra or to other destinations in Indonesia. Batam and Bintan are the main islands, and both are 'visa free' entry or exit points.

Ferries operate from Singapore to Sekupang on Batam Island where you go through Indonesian immigration. From Sekupang speedboats go via Selat Panjang on Pulau Tebingtinggi to Tanjung Buton on the Sumatran coast in about four hours. From Tanjung Buton buses go to Pekanbaru in about three hours. Tickets cost 35,000 rp from Batam, including the bus fare to Pekanbaru. Alternatively, a slow ferry also does the run between Pekanbaru and Batam in 24 hours. From Pekanbaru, there are plenty of buses to Bukittinggi, other Sumatran destinations or right through to Java.

The journey from Batam can be done in stages, but you run the risk of missing connections. Selat Panjang is a grotty, bustling, oversized water village with a strong Chinese influence – interesting for an hour or so and it has hotels (the *Wisma Holiday* is cheap) but there is no reason to stay. Tanjung Buton is just a bus/ferry terminal with no facilities.

The other Riau option is to take a ferry from Singapore to Tanjung Pinang on Bintan Island, and then catch a boat to other parts of Sumatra or to Jakarta (see under Bintan for more details). Pelni's KM *Rinjani* and KM *Umsini* call in every two weeks on their way between Jakarta and Dumai in Sumatra, and the twice-weekly MV *Bintan Permata* goes between Tanjung Pinang and Jakarta. See under Tanjung Pinang, Bintan, for details of these ships.

Jakarta to Sumatra Pelni has five ships operating between Jakarta and ports in Sumatra on a regular two-weekly schedule. The Jakarta-Padang-Sibolga-Gunung Sitoli-Padang-Jakarta route serviced by the KM *Lawit* is the one most used by travellers. The overnight journey from Jakarta to Padang takes 41 hours and fares vary from 37,000 rp ekonomi to 126,000 rp 1st class. See the Indonesia Getting Around section for more details of the ships and routes.

Merak to Bakauheni Ferries shuttle across the narrow Sunda Strait between Java and Sumatra from Merak to Bakauheni; they depart every hour or so, take about 1½ hours and cost from 1,250 to 2,250 rp. If you travel by bus between Jakarta and destinations in Sumatra, the price of the ferry is included in your ticket.

Getting Around

Air It's possible to fly around Sumatra and save a lot of time and trouble compared to travelling at surface level. Since most of the interest in Sumatra is in the north, many visitors fly from Jakarta to Padang for 215,000 rp and skip the southern part of Sumatra completely.

Merpati fares include Bengkulu to Palembang for 77,000 rp, Palembang to Padang for 136,000 rp, Padang to Medan for 131,000 rp and Medan to Gunung Sitoli for 100,000 rp. Sempati and Mandala also have flights through Sumatra.

Bus Travelling through Sumatra by bus is the most popular method. The distances are long and it can be hard going but the Trans-Sumatran Highway has made a huge improvement in speed and pleasure. The old travellers' tales of Sumatra's notorious bus trips and their hours of bone-shaking horror are fading into history, at least on the main highway. On the back roads, travelling around Sumatra by bus can still be grindingly slow, diabolically uncomfortable and thoroughly exhausting, particularly during the wet season when bridges are washed away and the roads develop huge potholes.

If your only travel is on the Trans-Sumatran Highway, then the big air-con buses and tourist coaches can make travel a breeze, as long as you take it in manageable stages. The best express air-con buses have reclining seats, toilets, video and even karaoke. The only problem is that many of them do night runs, so you miss out on the scenery. The non-air-con buses are in many cases just older versions of the air-con buses. They rattle more, the air-con no longer works and they can get very crowded, but they are fine for short trips.

From major towns, many bus companies cover the popular routes and bus prices can vary greatly, depending on the quality and comfort of the bus. Ticket agents may charge 10% or more than the bus companies, but they are more convenient and in some cases the only place to buy tickets. In some places, especially in the heavily touristic areas, agents charges can be excessive – it pays to shop around.

Many travellers take the convenient tourist coaches that do the Bukit Lawang-Berastagi-Prapat-Bukittinggi run. They pick up and drop off at hotels, travel during the day so you can see the scenery, and stop at points of interest on the way. While you feel like you're in a tour group at times, they certainly are comfortable and take some scenic routes that normal buses don't cover. The cost and journey times are about the same as air-con buses.

Trans-Sumatran Highway You can take an air-con bus right through from **Jakarta to Padang**. The trip takes as little as 32 hours. To break the journey and see something of south Sumatra, you can venture off the main highway and take a bus from Jakarta to Palembang (20 hours), or through to Jambi, Pekanbaru or Bengkulu. From Palembang to Padang (24 hours) the road runs through superb jungle. Rivers are muddy, wide, winding facsimiles of the Amazon. The road from Lubuklinggau – the end of the railway line north – to Padang runs along the eastern side of the mountains and is one of the most scenic in Sumatra.

Most people make one or more stops on the **Padang to Parapat** sector – usually Bukittinggi and/or Sibolga. The Padang-Bukittinggi road is excellent and this scenic sector takes less than two hours. The Bukittinggi-Parapat road is sealed all the way, though narrow and winding for much of the journey. Air-con buses do it in 12 to 13 hours, most running at night, while public buses take 16 hours or more. The special tourist minibuses do the trip in 12 to 13 hours during the day.

Buses from **Parapat to Medan** operate frequently and take about four hours. Buses also operate frequently between Medan and Berastagi but, unless you take the tourist buses, the trip from Berastagi to Parapat is time-consuming and involves changes at Kabanjahe and Siantar.

From **Medan to Banda Aceh** the road is surfaced. The bus trip takes about 14 hours, mainly because of prolonged stops along the way.

Train There only two regular train services in Sumatra. The more useful one is in the south between Bandarlampung (Tanjungkarang) and Palembang, and then on to Lubuklinggau. The second one runs between Medan, Tanjungbalai and Rantauprapat.

BAKAUHENI & BANDARLAMPUNG

Bakauheni, on Sumatra's southern tip, is the terminal for ferries from Java. Ferries from Bakauheni to Merak in Java operate roughly every hour, 24 hours a day, take 1½ hours and cost 1250 rp.

From Bakauheni buses travel the 90 km to Bandarlampung (1400 rp) for connections to the rest of Sumatra. Bandarlampung has a wide variety of accommodation if you get stuck. The Tanjungkarang train station is in the north of Bandarlampung, and the main Rajabasa bus depot is further out past the railway station.

WAY KAMBAS

The Way Kambas Reserve is a lowland forest and swamp park, noted mostly for its **elephant training centre**. As well as daily elephant performances, the park affords the best opportunity to view elephants in the wild, and other wildlife is found in the reserve.

Getting There & Away

From the Rajabasa bus station in Bandarlampung, take a bus to Metro (1000 rp, one hour), then to Way Jepara (1500 rp, one hour) and then another bus to the reserve

(1500 rp, one hour). Metro has some cheap losmen.

PALEMBANG

Standing on the Musi River, only 50 km upstream from the sea, Palembang made an abrupt leap into the 20th century when oil was discovered in Sumatra earlier this century. Palembang quickly became the main export outlet for south Sumatra, and today it is a heavily industrialised city with tin-mining operations and a petrochemical refinery. It's also the capital of south Sumatra but as it's a rather dull place to visit it attracts few travellers.

A thousand years ago, Palembang was the centre of the highly developed Srivijaya civilisation but, unfortunately, few relics remain from this period. Nor is there much of interest from the early 18th century when Palembang was an Islamic kingdom. Most of the buildings from that era were destroyed in battles with the Dutch – the last battle was in 1811.

Coming into Palembang from the south, you pass plantations of rubber, coffee, pepper and pineapples. In complete contrast are the smokestacks of the Sungai Gerong refinery and the petrochemical complex at Plaju, which impart a kind of futuristic look to the landscape, particularly at night.

Orientation & Information

The city is split in half by the Musi River and sprawls along both banks. The two halves of the city are connected by the Ampera Bridge. A hotchpotch of wooden houses on stilts crowd both banks, but the south side, known as Ulu, is where the majority of people live.

The 'better half', Ilir, is on the north bank and there you find most of the government offices, shops, hotels and the wealthy residential districts. Jalan Sudirman is the main street of town, running right to the bridge.

The Palembang city tourist office (☎ 28450) is at the Museum Sultan Machmud Badaruddin II on Jalan Sudirman.

There are various bank branches including the Bank Bumi Daya on Jalan Sudirman and the Bank Ekspor Impor on Jalan T P Rustam Effendy. Dharma Perdana is a moneychanger at Jalan Kol Atmo 446.

Things to See

There is very little reason to hang around Palembang. It's not an interesting city to wander around and there's very little to see.

In town, there's a floating market which operates like an extension of the main market, **Pasar 16 Ilir**. There's usually lots of activity on the river and you can overlook it from the **Ampera Bridge**. Near the bridge and the Ampera opelet station is the **Museum Sultan Machmud Badaruddin II**. There are three rooms, each showing a different traditional room of Palembang royalty. Behind it is a curious monument and then the large and imposing **Grand Mosque**, built by Sultan Machmud Badaruddin in the 18th century.

The **Museum Sumatera Selatan** is about five km out from the town centre, off the airport and Jambi road. It really doesn't have much of interest apart from the traditional Sumatran house, or Rumah Bari.

Places to Stay

Cheap hotels in Palembang are nothing special. At Jalan Sudirman 45E, close to the intersection with Jalan Diponegoro, the *Hotel Asiana* is bare and basic with singles/doubles at 7000/10,000 rp. It's clean and not as noisy as it might be as it's elevated.

Two hotels with similar prices and style are the *Penginapan Riau* (☎ 22011), Jalan Dempo 409C, and the *Hotel Segaran* at Jalan Segaran 207C. It is another decidedly bottom-end hotel with rooms from around 6000 rp. The street numbers of Jalan Segaran follow no discernible pattern.

Almost down to the river at Jalan Sayangan 769, *Losmen Jakarta* is also cheap at 5000/9000 rp but this is a real rock-bottom, survival-only place. Across the road at No 669, *Hotel Surabaya* (☎ 26874) is a mid-range hotel with rooms from 20,000 rp.

Other mid-range hotels are the *Hotel Sriwidjaja* (☎ 24193), Jalan Letkol Iskandar 31/488, and at Jalan Letkol Iskandar 17, in

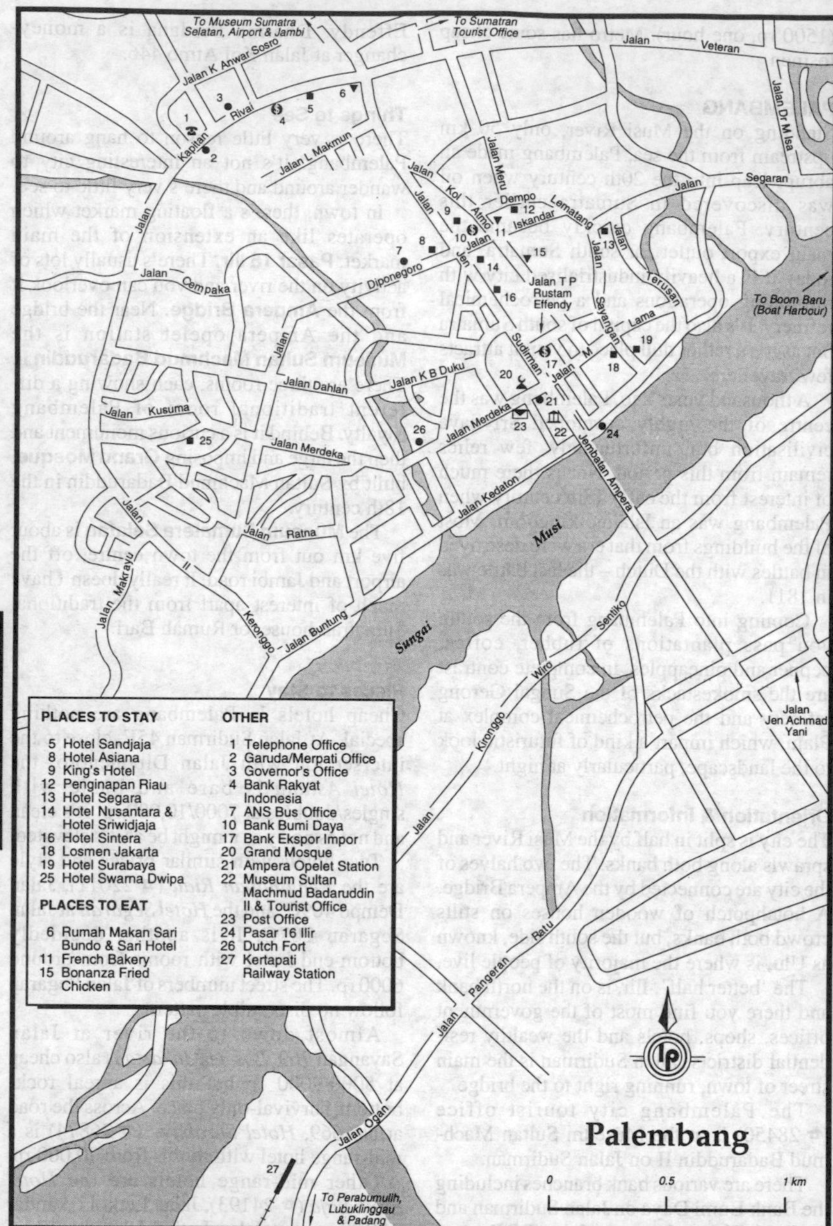
To Museum Sumatra Selatan, Airport & Jambi
To Sumatran Tourist Office
Jalan Veteran
Jalan K Anwar Sosro
Jalan Dr M Isa
Jalan Kapitan Rivai
Jalan L Makmun
Jalan
Jalan Meru
Jalan Kol Atmo
Jalan Segaran
Dempo
Lematang
Iskandar
Jalan Jalan
Jalan Jen
Jalan Cempaka
Diponegoro
Jalan T P Rustam Effendy
Terusan
To Boom Baru (Boat Harbour)
Jalan Sayangan
Lama
Sudirman
Jalan M
Jalan Dahlan
Jalan K B Duku
Jalan Kusuma
Jalan Merdeka
Jalan Merdeka
Jalan Kedaton
Jembatan Ampera
Musi
Jalan Makrayu
Jalan Ratna
Jalan
II
Kerongo – Jalan Buntung
Sungai
Sentiko
Wiro
Kironggo
Ratu
Pangeran
Jalan
Jalan
Jalan Jen Achmad Yani
Jalan Ogan
To Perabumulih, Lubuklinggau & Padang
Palembang
0
0.5
1 km
PLACES TO STAY
5 Hotel Sandjaja
8 Hotel Asiana
9 King's Hotel
12 Penginapan Riau
13 Hotel Segara
14 Hotel Nusantara & Hotel Sriwidjaja
16 Hotel Sintera
18 Losmen Jakarta
19 Hotel Surabaya
25 Hotel Swarna Dwipa
PLACES TO EAT
6 Rumah Makan Sari Bundo & Sari Hotel
11 French Bakery
15 Bonanza Fried Chicken
OTHER
1 Telephone Office
2 Garuda/Merpati Office
3 Governor's Office
4 Bank Rakyat Indonesia
7 ANS Bus Office
10 Bank Bumi Daya
17 Bank Ekspor Impor
20 Grand Mosque
21 Ampera Opelet Station
22 Museum Sultan Machmud Badaruddin II & Tourist Office
23 Post Office
24 Pasar 16 Ilir
26 Dutch Fort
27 Kertapati Railway Station

the same little alley off the main road, the *Hotel Nusantara* (☎ 23306).

Places to Eat

At night, Jalan Sajangan, parallel to Jalan Sudirman, is crowded with Chinese *food stands* and sate places. This is a great area to eat with some excellent food. Round the corner on Jalan T P Rustam Effendy, there are fruit stalls and *stands* selling pisang goreng (fried bananas) and other snacks.

On Jalan Iskandar, near Jalan Sudirman, there are a cluster of places including *Yohan Bakery & Fried Chicken* and the *Warna Warni* ice-cream parlour next door. There are a number of bakeries around the centre which also do mie, or noodle, dishes and other simple meals. You'll find them along Jalan Sudirman. Or, try the *French Bakery* at Jalan Kol Atmo 481B, opposite King's Hotel.

Nasi padang restaurants can be found all over town. The *Rumah Makan Sari Bundo* on the corner of Jalan Sudirman and Jalan Kapitan Rivai is good, but more expensive. Finally, *Bonanza Fried Chicken* is Palembang's closest thing to a Western fast-food joint. It's upstairs at Jalan Kol Atmo 425, in the Yuppies Centre!

Getting There & Away

Few travellers bother with Palembang as it's off the Trans-Sumatran Highway; you can skip right by it on a direct Jakarta to Padang bus, fly right over it, or take the Jakarta to Padang ship and sail right around it.

Air If you do want to fly to Palembang there are regular flights with Garuda/Merpati. Merpati has an office in the Sandjaja Hotel, Jalan Kapitan Rivai 35.

Bus ANS is at Jalan Iskandar 903C, just off Jalan Sudirman. Other bus companies are in the same area, and the bus station is at Km 5. There are frequent departures for Jakarta and the 18-hour trip costs 21,000 rp, or 34,000 rp with air-con. Buses to Padang range from 18,000 rp for non-air-con, while air-con buses start at 30,000 rp.

Train The Kertapati railway station is on the south side of the river, eight km from the town centre.

Boat Daily ferries operate from Palembang to Muntok, Bangka Island. The air-con boat takes 2½ hours and is 20,000 rp. Boats also go to Tanjung Pandan on Pulau Belitung.

Getting Around

To/From the Airport Talang Betutu airport is 12 km north of town and a taxi costs a standard 10,000 rp from the town. The road runs right in front of the terminal and you can get into town on a Talang Betutu-Ampera opelet for 400 rp.

Local Transport Opelets around town cost a standard 200 rp. Most routes start or finish at Ampera, the opelet stop at the northern end of the Ampera Bridge. Take a Kertapati opelet for the railway station or a Km 5 opelet for the Jambi buses and the nearby museum.

AROUND PALEMBANG

You can hire a boat and take a look at the **Chinese temple** on Kemaro Island. It's near the junction of the Musi, Oghan and Komering rivers. About 100 years old, its architectural design and ornamentation could only be Chinese, and statues of dragons and monkeys guard the entrance. You can also take a boat up to the refinery, **Sungai Gerong**, if you're interested. Or, cross the river and take an opelet to **Kayuagung** on the banks of the Komering to see the local pottery manufacture. Boats go from right by the bridge.

JAMBI

There's nothing much to be said for this unexciting riverine town – it's just there. The surrounding province, however, is populated by a polyglot mix of Chinese, Arabs, Malays, Minangkabaus, Bataks and the original inhabitants of Jambi, the forest-dwelling Kubus.

Information

The tourist office (☎ 25330) is on Jalan Basuki Rachmat in Kota Bharu.

Things to See

The **Museum of Jambi** is on the corner of Jalan Urip Sumobaryo and Jalan Dr Sri Sudewi. It is a small but interesting museum which exhibits tools, costumes and handicrafts from Jambi Province, and some Hindu sculptures.

The **Muara Jambi Temples** are 25 km from Jambi and can easily be visited in one day. The easiest way to see them is by boat – on Sunday there are public boats for 5000 rp for a return trip, otherwise it costs 25,000 rp to charter a boat.

Places to Stay & Eat

The cheaper places are generally drab and unpleasant and the more expensive ones are...more expensive. *Hotel Merpati Inn* (☎ 24861) at Jalan Y Leimena 71 has stuffy and very basic rooms with mandi for 5000 rp, and airier rooms with windows for 6000 rp. The *Penginapan Sumatera* on Jalan R A Kartini is a rock-bottom, survival-only place where rooms cost 7000 rp. A reasonable place, where rooms start from 22,500 rp, plus tax, is the *Hotel Marisa* (☎ 23533) at Jalan Kol Abun Jami 12.

Of course, nasi padang is what you'll find to eat, and there are branches of the *Simpang Raya* restaurant at Jalan Wahidin 11 and Jalan Thamrin 22. There are also lots of *stalls* selling slices of chilled fruit, including delicious pineapple. *Safari* at Jalan Veteran 29 is also worth a try.

Getting There & Away

Like Palembang, the Trans-Sumatran Highway does not run through Jambi so it requires a definite decision to go there. Garuda flies to Jambi regularly, connecting directly with Jakarta and other centres via Palembang. Buses to and from Palembang cost 7000 rp. From Jambi, you can continue on to Padang.

BENGKULU (Bencoolen)

Bengkulu was Raffles' foot in the door to Indonesia but this British attempt to displace the Dutch was half-hearted and never really successful. The British actually first established themselves here in 1685. Raffles didn't arrive until 1818 but, in 1824, Bengkulu was traded for Melaka on the Malay coast. From then on the British and Dutch stared at each other across the Melaka Strait.

There are still some reminders of the British presence in Bengkulu but overall the town is of little interest and, like Palembang and Jambi, getting there requires a detour off the Trans-Sumatran Highway.

Orientation & Information

Although Bengkulu is right by the sea, it only really touches it near Fort Marlborough. Otherwise, the town is set back from the coast. Jalan Suprapto and the nearby Pasar Minggu Besar are the modern 'town centre', separated from the old town area around Fort Marlborough by the long, straight Jalan Achmad Yani. The coast is surprisingly quiet, rural and only a km or so from the centre.

The post office and telephone office are opposite Pasar Barukoto, near the fort. There's another telephone office on Jalan Suprapto near the modern town centre but it's open shorter hours.

Fort Marlborough

Raffles' fort, Benteng Marlborough, was originally built between 1714 and 1719. It was restored in 1983 and reopened to the public in 1984 after a long period of use by the army. There are a few small and uninteresting exhibits about the restoration, together with a pile of cannonballs and a couple of old British gravestones.

Sukarno's House

Don't miss Rumah Bung Karno, where Sukarno was exiled by the Dutch from 1938 until the Japanese arrived in 1941. Throughout the '30s he had a grand tour of Indonesia at Dutch expense. You can see a few faded photos, the wardrobe where his clothes used

INDONESIA

to hang and, not to be missed, the Bung's bicycle! Like any real Indonesian bicycle, the brakes don't work.

Other Attractions

Pantai Panjang, the Bengkulu beach, is long, grey, wide, featureless and decidedly unattractive. The **Bengkulu Museum Negeri**, at Jalan Pembangunan P D Harapan, is south of the town centre. **Dendam Taksuda** is a reserve area four km south of the town.

Bengkulu has a few reminders of the British besides Fort Marlborough, including the **Thomas Parr Monument** in front of the Pasar Barukoto and a couple of Monumen Inggris. The one near the beach is to Captain Robert Hamilton who died in 1793, 'in command of the troops'.

Places to Stay

Like other towns in south Sumatra, the cheap hotels are no great bargain. *Penginapan Surya* (☎ 21341) at Jalan K H Abidin 26 is just off the main road, Jalan Suprapto. It's a rock-bottom place with rooms from 6000 to 10,000 rp. Right across the road, at No 18, is *Penginapan Damai* (☎ 22912), with slightly better rooms with mandi at 7000 rp.

Wisma Rafflesia (☎ 21650) at Jalan Achmad Yani 924, halfway between the town centre and Fort Marlborough, and *Losmen Aman*, behind the market near the fort, are other basic survival places with rooms from 5000 rp.

Wisma Bumi Endah (☎ 21665) at Jalan Fatmawati 29 is better and still convenient to the town centre. It's quite pleasant; small but clean rooms cost from 10,000 rp.

There are a number of mid-range hotels, some of them quite pleasant. *Nala Beach Cottages* (☎ 31855) at Jalan Pantai Nala 133 is right by the beach, below the expensive Pantai Nala Samudra Hotel. The individual cottages are good value, costing from 15,000 rp to 30,000 rp, but it's a km-plus walk from the centre. *Wisma Balai Buntar* (☎ 31254), Jalan Khadijal 122, near the fort, is a similarly priced guesthouse. Close to the town centre, at Jalan Sudirman 245, the *Hotel Samudera Dwinka* (☎ 31604) is big, clean, well kept and virtually deserted. Rooms cost from 20,000 rp with fan.

Places to Eat

There are a number of restaurants along Jalan Suprapto including the neat, clean little *Buffet Sisters*, with the usual mie and nasi menu. The *Bengkulu Restoran*, also on Jalan Suprapto, is similar, or you can try the *Gandhi Bakery* with its amazing selection of ice creams.

Halfway along Jalan Achmad Yani, between the town centre and the fort, there is a small cluster of restaurants opposite the Garuda office and Hotel Asia. They include *Cafe Trully*, the seafood specialist *Asia Restaurant* and the *Rumah Makan Srikandi*.

Overlooking the beach, at the corner right next to the Nala Beach Cottages and the Pantai Nala Samudra Hotel, the *Kafeteria Nala* is a good place for drinking cold beer, looking out to sea and wondering what brought you here in the first place!

Getting There & Away

Air Merpati has direct flights to Jakarta (142,000 rp) and Palembang (77,000 rp).

Bus Terminal Panorama, the long-distance bus terminal, is several km south of town and costs 200 rp by opelet. Buses run to Lubuklinggau, the junction town 110 km away on the Trans-Sumatran Highway, for 5000 rp. Other fares include Jakarta for 25,000 rp, Palembang for 9000 rp and Padang for 14,000 rp. Most of the long-distance bus operators also have offices in the centre of town, like Bengkulu Indah at Jalan Suprapto 5.

Getting Around

The airport is 14 km south of town and the standard taxi fare is 8000 rp. You can walk 100 metres out to the road, from where you should be able to get a bemo or bus into Bengkulu.

There are countless tiny mikrolets shuttling around town at a standard fare of 250 rp.

KERINCI

Kerinci is a mountain valley accessible by bus from either Jambi or Padang – the road from Padang is more beautiful and also a better road. It's a rich, green area with two very dominating features – Gunung Kerinci, the highest mountain in the Sumatra-Sunda island chain and Danau Kerinci, a lake at the other end of the valley. Sungai Penuh is the largest town with some 200 small villages in the area. Its matrilineal social structure is similar to that found in west Sumatra.

Things to See & Do

In Sungai Penuh there is a large, pagoda-style **mosque** with carved beams and old Dutch tiles. It is said to be over 400 years old but you need permission to go inside. **Sungai Tetung** is nationally renowned for its basket weaving. All over the area there are stone carvings which have not really been carefully investigated. Locals have a legend of a great kingdom here a long time ago. The carvings are very different from those of the Majapahit or Srivijaya areas. It's easy to find a cheap guide for day trips from Sungai Penuh.

Tours around **Danau Kerinci** are good and the best starting points are at Jujun or Keluru (20 km from Sungai Penuh and half a km apart). Make sure to ask to see **Batu Gong**. About 40 km out of Sungai Penuh, on the way to **Gunung Kerinci**, there is a tea plantation called **Kayo Aro**, worth going to see if you've never been over one before. There are hot springs nearby – too hot for swimming in the main pool, but you can get a private room with a hot mandi.

Watch for tigers as there are said to be many still around. If you are lucky you might be able to catch a magic dance or a pencak silat performance.

This was the last area to fall to the Dutch in 1902, the Japanese had a hard time here and, in Sukarno's time, it was a Communist stronghold – and we know what happened then.

Places to Stay & Eat

In Sungai Penuh the *Mata Hari Losmen* is cheap and clean. One of the best restaurants in Sungai Penuh is the *Minang Soto*, which has good Padang food and is cheap and clean. For a taste treat, try dendeng batokok, a speciality of the region – these are strips of beef smoked and grilled over a fire and which, someone reported, taste like charcoal.

PADANG

This is the centre of the matrilineal Minangkabau area where the eldest female is the boss and property is inherited through the female line. Beautiful examples of the high-peaked Minangkabau houses can be seen on the pastoral, tranquil road down to Padang from Solok. As you start the final descent down to Padang there are spectacular sweeping views along the coast.

Padang is a fairly easy-going town with Chinese making up about 15% of the population. Padang itself does not have much to offer apart from Padang food, although in the harbour you can see the rusting remains of Dutch ships, sunk by the Japanese when they entered WW II.

Orientation & Information

It is easy to find your way around Padang; the central area is quite compact. Jalan Prof M Yamin – which runs from the bus terminal corner at Jalan Pemuda to Jalan Azizcham – is the main street of town. The main bus terminal and the opelet terminal across from the market are both very centrally located.

Padang has two helpful tourist offices: the provincial tourist office at 43 Jalan Jenderal Sudirman, and the regional office further north at 22 Jalan Khatib Sulaiman (take an opelet along Jalan Jenderal Sudirman). Both are open from 8 am to 2 pm Monday to Thursday, 8 to 11 am on Friday, and 8 to 12.30 pm on Saturday.

For changing money, Padang has a phenomenal number of extremely large and imposing banks. Building huge new bank buildings seems to be a current Indonesian craze but it's taken to extremes in Padang.

The post office is at Jalan Azizcham 7, and the Telkom office is at Jalan Veteran 47.

INDONESIA

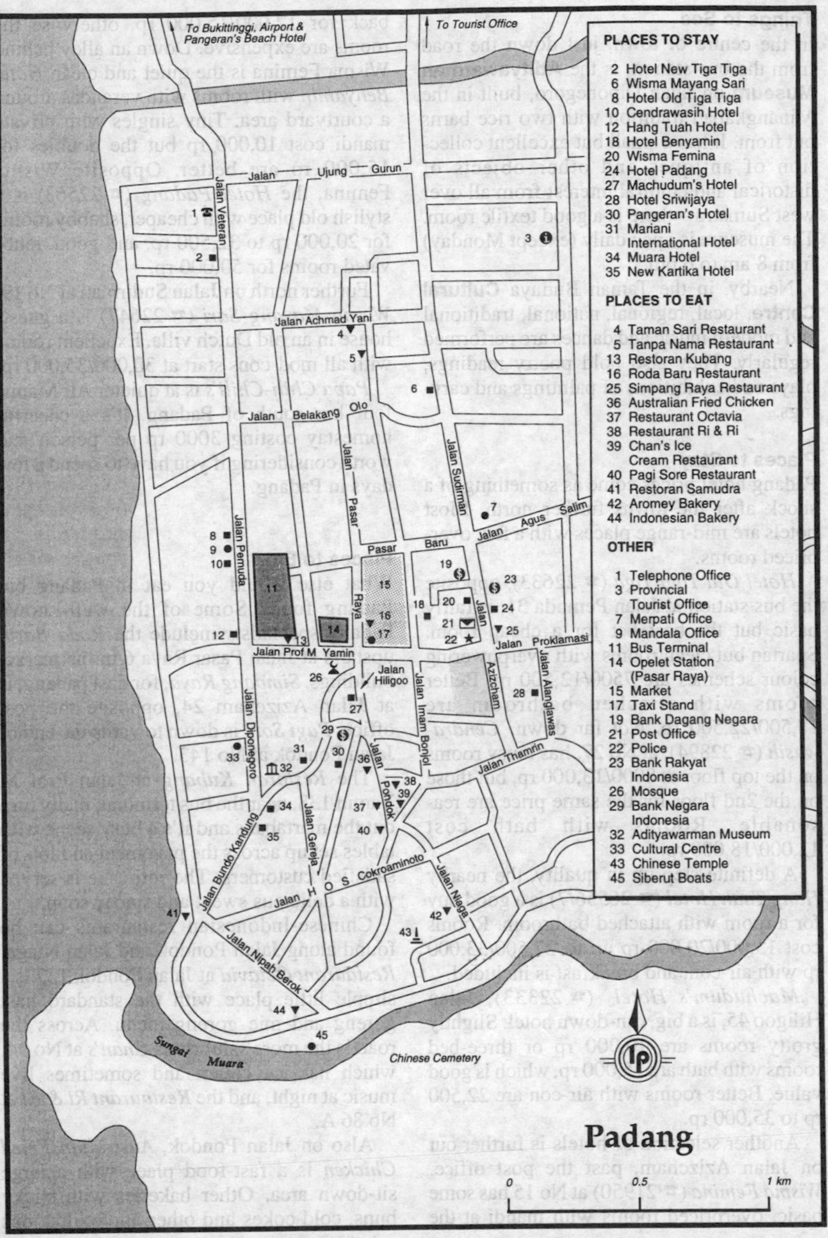
To Bukittinggi, Airport & Pangeran's Beach Hotel
To Tourist Office
PLACES TO STAY
2 Hotel New Tiga Tiga
6 Wisma Mayang Sari
8 Hotel Old Tiga Tiga
10 Cendrawasih Hotel
12 Hang Tuah Hotel
18 Hotel Benyamin
20 Wisma Femina
24 Hotel Padang
27 Machudum's Hotel
28 Hotel Sriwijaya
30 Pangeran's Hotel
31 Mariani International Hotel
34 Muara Hotel
35 New Kartika Hotel
PLACES TO EAT
4 Taman Sari Restaurant
5 Tanpa Nama Restaurant
13 Restoran Kubang
16 Roda Baru Restaurant
25 Simpang Raya Restaurant
36 Australian Fried Chicken
37 Restaurant Octavia
38 Restaurant Ri & Ri
39 Chan's Ice Cream Restaurant
40 Pagi Sore Restaurant
41 Restoran Samudra
42 Aromey Bakery
44 Indonesian Bakery
OTHER
1 Telephone Office
3 Provincial Tourist Office
7 Merpati Office
9 Mandala Office
11 Bus Terminal
14 Opelet Station (Pasar Raya)
15 Market
17 Taxi Stand
19 Bank Dagang Negara
21 Post Office
22 Police
23 Bank Rakyat Indonesia
26 Mosque
29 Bank Negara Indonesia
32 Adityawarman Museum
33 Cultural Centre
43 Chinese Temple
45 Siberut Boats
Jalan Ujung Gurun
Jalan Veteran
Jalan Achmad Yani
Jalan Belakang Olo
Jalan Pasar Raya
Jalan Sudirman
Jalan Agus Salim
Jalan Pasar Baru
Jalan Permuda
Jalan Prof M Yamin
Jalan Hiligoo
Jalan Azizcham
Jalan Proklamasi
Jalan Alanglawas
Jalan Imam Bonjol
Jalan Thamrin
Jalan Diponegoro
Jalan Pondok
Jalan Bundo Kandung
Jalan Gereja
Jalan H O S Cokroaminoto
Jalan Niaga
Jalan Nipah Berok
Sungai Muara
Chinese Cemetery
Padang
0
0.5
1 km

INDONESIA

Things to See

In the centre of town, just down the road from the bus station, is the **Adityawarman Museum** on Jalan Diponegoro, built in the Minangkabau tradition with two rice barns out front. It has a small but excellent collection of antiques and other objects of historical and cultural interest from all over west Sumatra – there is a good textile room. The museum is open daily (except Monday) from 8 am to 6 pm.

Nearby, in the Taman Budaya **Cultural Centre**, local, regional, national, traditional and modern music and dances are performed regularly. They also hold poetry readings, plays and exhibitions of paintings and carvings.

Places to Stay

Padang hotel prices come as something of a shock after the towns further north. Most hotels are mid-range places with a few overpriced rooms.

Hotel Old Tiga Tiga (☎ 22633), opposite the bus station at Jalan Pemuda 31, is fairly basic but the best bet for a cheap room. Spartan but clean rooms with overpowering colour schemes are 7500/12,500 rp. Better rooms with attached bathroom are 17,500/22,500 rp. Not far down, *Cendrawasih* (☎ 22894), at No 27, has lousy rooms on the top floor at 8000/13,000 rp, but those on the 2nd floor for the same price are reasonable. Rooms with bath cost 12,000/18,000 rp.

A definite step up in quality, the nearby *Hang Tuah Hotel* (☎ 26556/7) is a good buy for a room with attached bathroom. Rooms cost 15,000/20,000 rp up to 27,500/33,000 rp with air-con, and breakfast is included.

Machudum's Hotel (☎ 22333), Jalan Hiligoo 45, is a big, run-down hotel. Slightly grotty rooms are 10,000 rp or three-bed rooms with bath are 15,000 rp, which is good value. Better rooms with air-con are 22,500 rp to 35,000 rp.

Another selection of hotels is further out on Jalan Azizcham, past the post office. *Wisma Femina* (☎ 21950) at No 15 has some basic, overpriced rooms with mandi at the back for 12,000/15,000 rp, otherwise the rooms are expensive. Down an alley behind Wisma Femina is the quiet and clean *Hotel Benyamin* with rooms with verandas around a courtyard area. Tiny singles with private mandi cost 10,000 rp but the doubles for 15,000 rp are better. Opposite Wisma Femina, the *Hotel Padang* (☎ 22563) is a stylish old place with cheaper, shabby rooms for 20,000 rp to 32,500 rp, and good, renovated rooms for 50,000 rp.

Further north on Jalan Sudirman at No 19, *Wisma Mayang Sari* (☎ 22647) is a guesthouse in an old Dutch villa. Excellent rooms with all mod-cons start at 30,000/35,000 rp.

Papa Chili-Chili's is at quieter Air Manis, four km south of Padang. It's a cheerful homestay costing 3000 rp per person and worth considering if you have to spend a few days in Padang.

Places to Eat

What else would you eat in Padang but Padang food? Some of the well-known Padang specialists include the *Roda Baru*, upstairs at Jalan Pasar Raya 6 in the market buildings. *Simpang Raya*, for nasi padang, is at Jalan Azizcham 24, opposite the post office. *Pagi Sore* is down towards the end of Jalan Pondok at No 143.

The *Restoran Kubang* at Jalan Prof M Yamin 138, near the bus terminal, really turn out the martabaks and it's a busy scene with tables set up across the pavement and lots of satisfied customers. The roti cane is served with a delicious sweet and spicey soup.

Chinese-Indonesian restaurants can be found along Jalan Pondok and Jalan Niaga. *Restaurant Octavia* at Jalan Pondok 137 is a simple little place with the standard nasi goreng and mie goreng menu. Across the road is the more salubrious *Chan's* at No 94, which has ice cream and sometimes live music at night, and the *Restaurant Ri & Ri* at No 86 A.

Also on Jalan Pondok, *Australian Fried Chicken* is a fast-food place with a large sit-down area. Other bakeries with sticky buns, cold cokes and other approximations of Western food are the *Indonesian Bakery* and the *Aromy Bakery*.

At night, along the beachfont south of Jalan Mohammed Yamin, basic *warungs* set up tables and chairs on the pavement. Further along the beach, Taman Ria Pantai Padang is a more upmarket version with a few foodstalls and the *Restoran Samudra*, which has seafood and beer.

Getting There & Away

Air Padang is well served on Merpati's network, including Pekanbaru (51,000 rp), Batam (114,000 rp), Jakarta (215,000 rp) and Medan (131,000 rp). Sempati and Mandala also have flights to and from Padang, and Sempati and Pelangi Air have international flights to Kuala Lumpur.

The Merpati office (☎ 32010) is at Jalan Sudirman 2. Once a week, they fly from Padang to Pulau Sipora in the Mentawai Islands. Mandala (☎ 32773) is at Jalan Pemuda 29A, opposite the bus station.

Bus The Padang bus terminal is conveniently central and there are frequent departures for buses north and south. Buses to Bukittinggi, the prime destination for travellers passing through Padang, cost 1500 rp (2500 rp air-con) and take about two hours along a fine road with wonderful scenery. If you arrive in Padang by air there's no need to go into town – the main road, with buses bound for Bukittinggi, is only 100 metres from the terminal.

From the city terminal, buses include Jambi for 8500 rp and Palembang for 12,000 rp. To Pekanbaru is 6,500 rp, or 10,000 rp with air-con, but you go via Bukittinggi. Parapat, again via Bukittinggi, is 19,000 rp. To get all the way to Jakarta, fares start at 35,000 rp, or with air-con range from 50,000 rp up to 72,000 rp for the super-luxury buses. The trip takes 32 hours or more.

Train The railway line from Padang to Bukittinggi used to be quite an attraction for railway enthusiasts, but now the line is only for freight trains. However, there is a Sunday tourist train at 8 am to Pariaman, 70 km north of Padang along the coast. It costs 2000 rp in economy or 3000 rp in air-con and returns to Padang at 2pm.

Boat The Pelni ship KM *Lawit* operates a regular Jakarta-Padang-Sibolga-Gunung Sitoli and return service every two weeks. This is probably the shipping route most frequently used by travellers visiting Indonesia. Jakarta to Padang takes about 41 hours and costs from 37,000 rp ekonomi to 126,000 rp in 1st class. It continues on to Sibolga and Gunung Sitoli on Pulau Nias. The Pelni office (☎ 22109) is on Jalan Tanjung Priok, Teluk Bayur.

There are other occasional ships from Padang to Bengkulu, Nias or, more regularly, to Siberut Island.

Getting Around

To/From the Airport Padang's Tabing airport is nine km north of the town centre on the Bukittinggi road. A metered taxi to the airport costs around 5000 rp, or take opelets or the yellow bus 14A for 250 rp. From the airport the standard fare is 8000 rp but you can walk 100 metres out to the road and catch any opelet heading into town for 250 rp.

Local Transport Opelets and buses around town cost from 150 rp to 300 rp. The opelet station is Pasar Raya, next to the main bus station. Blue opelets run from here to Teluk Bayur (for Pelni boats) and cost 250 rp. Metered taxis ply the streets of Padang for 800 rp flagfall and 400 rp per km. *Bendis* (horsecarts) cost around 1000 rp per trip to anywhere in town.

AROUND PADANG

Beaches

At **Bungus**, 22 km south of Padang, is a good beach, palm-fringed and, at one time, postcard-pretty – there is now a big Korean timber mill on the beach. Opelets run there and you can hire a perahu and paddle out to a nearby island. There are a number of homestays or *Carolina's Beach Hotel*.

Other good beaches are **Pasir Putih**, only 24 km from Padang, where you can stay at

Losmen Tin Tin, and **Taman Nirwana**, 12 km out. To get to Pasir Putih, take an opelet or bus to the university at Air Tawar. There are some interesting fishing villages north along the beach.

From where the Siberut boats leave, you can take a sampan across the Muara River and walk up to the **Chinese cemetery** overlooking the town. A km walk will take you to the fishing village of Air Manis and, at low tide, you can wade out to a small island or take a sampan to a larger one. Climb the nearby hill for a good view of **Teluk Bayur**, Padang's port. Air Manis can also be reached by bus.

Islands

There are a number of islands close offshore from Padang. **Pulau Pisang Besar** (Big Banana Island) is the closest, only 15 minutes out; boats run there from the Muara River Harbour. Others islands include **Pagang**, **Pasumpahan**, **Sirandah**, and **Sikoai** (where you can stay at the expensive *Pusako Island Resort)*. Boats can be chartered from Muara, though Pantai Bungus is the usual departure point.

SIBERUT ISLAND

The Mentawai Islands are a chain of islands off the coast of Sumatra from Padang. Siberut, the largest island, attracts a growing number of adventurous travellers. There are few facilities for visitors but the island has outstanding beaches, big surf along the long west-coast beach and some fine diving opportunities.

The island's isolation has led to a unique culture and some unusual endemic wildlife, including several species of monkey. Unfortunately, despite its scientific interest, the wildlife is not easily seen.

Information

The tourist office in Padang has information about the island. *Saving Siberut* is a booklet on this interesting island by the World Wildlife Fund. The only losmen is *Syahruddin's Home Stay* at Muarasiberut, and travel around the island is difficult.

Organised Tours

Most travellers opt for one of the 10-day, US$125 tours on the island offered by various guides in Bukittinggi. The tour price includes guide service and accommodation (in village huts), food (usually prepared by the guide) and transport to and from the island.

Tours usually don't go during the months of June and July when the seas are too rough for safe sailing. May is generally the best month for suitable weather. At any time of the year you can expect heavy rains on Siberut. The treks usually include plenty of mud-slogging, river crossings and battles with indigenous insects, so it's definitely not a casual hiking experience.

The return on your suffering is the chance to experience unspoiled rainforest and the local culture of Siberut.

Getting There & Away

If you want to try and reach Siberut on your own, boats from Padang go to the island, a distance of approximately 150 km, about three times a week. Inquire around the harbour area on the Muara River or at the office of PT Rusco Lines (☎ 21941) at Jalan Batang Arau 31, or Nusa Mentawai Indah (☎ 28200), Jalan Batan Arau 88. The better boats cost from 15,000 economy to 20,000 rp, and the journey takes 10 to 12 hours. Sometimes people get groups together to charter a boat across and back, giving them transport around the coast as well.

PADANG TO BUKITTINGGI

It's a beautiful 90-km trip from Padang to Bukittinggi. There are rice paddies, mountains, Minangkabau houses and plenty of other scenery along the road as well as numerous possible diversions if you're in the mood. **Padangpanjang** is the main town through which the road passes and it has a conservatorium of Minangkabau culture. The Padangpanjang Monday market is worth visiting – it's not as big as the one in Bukittinggi but just as interesting and there are lots of good taste treats.

Near Padangpanjang, at Panyalaian, **bull-**

fights are held every Tuesday afternoon. In the village of Padang Lawas, there's a bull-fight on Saturday at 4 pm. Venues do change so check with the tourist offices in Bukittinggi or Padang. The fight is known as *adu sapi* and involves two water buffalo, of roughly the same size and weight, locking horns under the keen eyes of their respective owners and gathered gamblers. The bull-fights are nothing like those in Spain as there's no bloodshed and the bulls don't get hurt. Once the fight starts it continues until one of the bulls breaks away and runs out of the ring. This usually results in two bulls chasing each other around and the on-lookers running in every direction.

Located about 45 km south-east of Bukittinggi, off the Padangpanjang-Solok road, is the village of Batu Sangkar. Turn off the road towards the village of Pagaruyung (four km distance) and you'll see many **Minangkabau houses**. Along the roadside are **stone tablets** inscribed in Sanskrit.

BUKITTINGGI

This cool, easy-going mountain town is one of the most popular travellers' centres in Sumatra. Often called Kota Jam Gadang, the Big Ben Town, because of the clocktower that overlooks the large market square, Bukittinggi is also known as Tri Arga or the Town of Three Mountains. It stands at 930 metres above sea level and is encircled by the three majestic mountains – Merapi, Singgalang and Sago. Bukittinggi is a centre for Minangkabau culture and has a small university.

Orientation

The centre of town is compact, and the rusty iron roofs make it look remarkably like the hill station towns in India. Like them, the changes in level, connected by steps, initially make it a little confusing.

Information

Tourist Office The excellent tourist office is beside the market car park, overlooked by the clocktower. It is open Monday to Thursday from 8 am to 2 pm, Friday from 8 to 11 am and Saturday from 8 am to 12.30 pm.

Money There's a Bank Negara Indonesia branch in the Pasar Atas Market building and you can also change money at the lower rate at Toko Eka, Jalan Minangkabau, by the market. If you are heading north, change plenty of money – rates are generally poor between Bukittinggi and Medan.

Market

Bukittinggi's large and colourful market is crammed with stalls of fruit and vegetables, clothing and handicrafts. Market days are Wednesday and Saturday. There are several interesting antique shops and craft shops in the market streets near the clocktower.

Museum & Zoo

On a hilltop site, right in the centre of town, is Taman Bundokanduag, a museum and zoo. The museum, which was built in 1934 by the Dutch Controleur of the district, is a superb example of Minangkabau architecture, with its two rice barns (added in 1956) out front. It is the oldest museum in the province and has a good collection of Minangkabau historical and cultural exhibits. It also has a weird collection of stuffed, freak buffalo more suited to the adjoining zoo – a depressing Third World zoo with sadly neglected animals kept captive in miserable conditions.

There is a 1000 rp entry fee to the gardens and zoo and a further 300 rp to the museum. This includes entry to Fort de Kock, reached by footbridge.

Fort de Kock

Except for the defence moat and a few cannons, not much remains of Bukittinggi's old Fort de Kock. Built during the Padri Wars (1821-37) by the Dutch, it provides fine views across the town and surrounding countryside from its hilltop position.

Panorama Park & Japanese Caves

On the southern edge of the town, Panorama

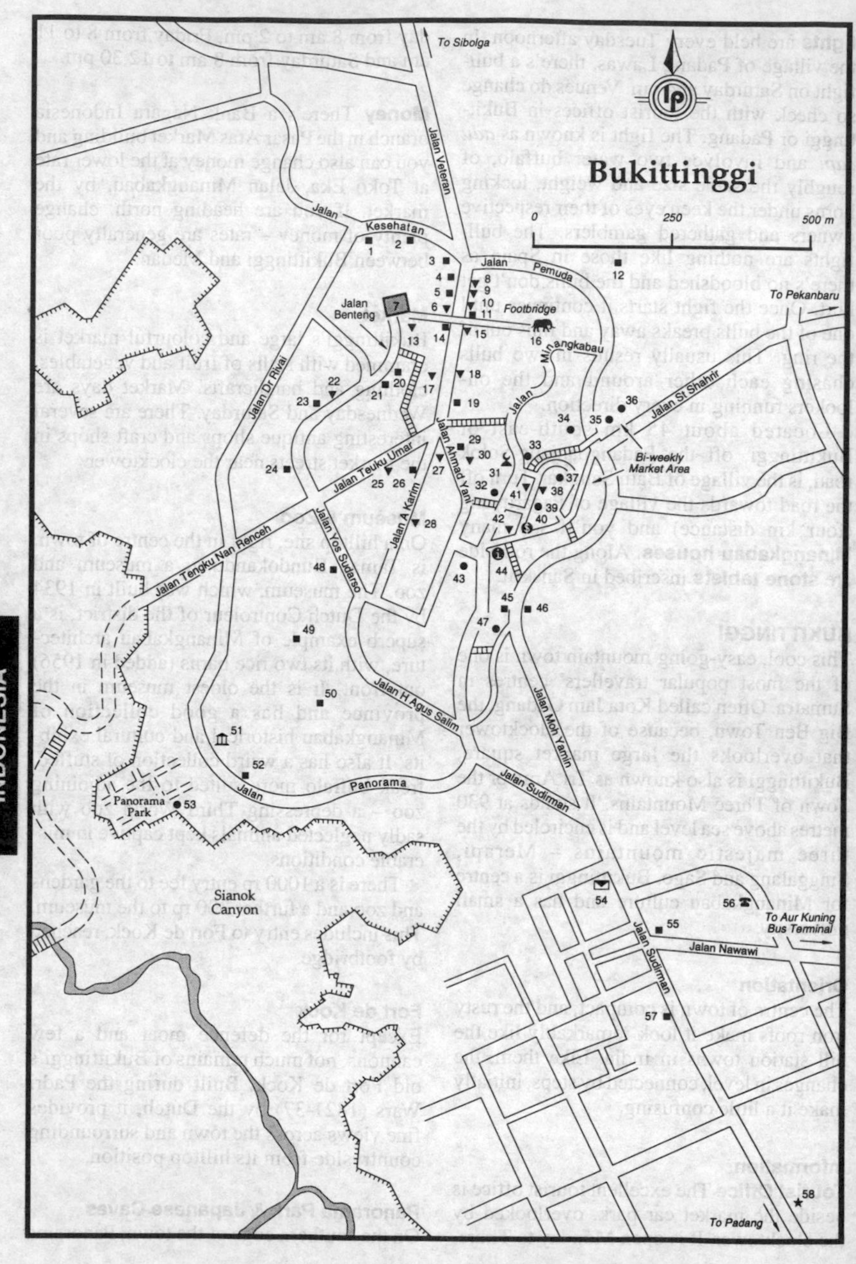
Bukittinggi
0
250
500 m
To Sibolga
Jalan Veteran
Jalan Kesehatan
Jalan Pemuda
To Pekanbaru
Jalan Benteng
Footbridge
Jalan Minangkabau
Jalan St Shahrir
Jalan Dr Rivai
Jalan Teuku Umar
Jalan Ahmad Yani
Jalan A Karim
Jalan Yos Sudarso
Jalan Tengku Nan Renceh
Bi-weekly Market Area
Jalan H Agus Salim
Jalan Moh Yamin
Jalan Sudirman
Jalan Panorama
Panorama Park
Sianok Canyon
To Aur Kuning Bus Terminal
Jalan Nawawi
Jalan Sudirman
To Padang

PLACES TO STAY

1 Hotel Denai
2 Lima's Hotel
3 Sri Kandi Hotel
4 Murni's Hotel
5 Hotel Nirwana
11 Singgalang Hotel
12 Tropic Hotel
14 Hotel Yany
19 Wisma Tigo Balai
20 Benteng Hotel
21 Suwarni Guest House
23 Mountain View Guest House
24 Wisma Bukittinggi
26 Surya Hotel
29 Gangga Hotel
45 Hotel Jogja
46 Hotel Antokan
48 Hotel Sari
49 Gallery Hotel
50 Sumatera Hotel
52 Minang Hotel
55 Dymen's Hotel
57 Bagindo Hotel

PLACES TO EAT

6 The Coffee House
8 Rendezvous Coffee Shop
9 Three Tables Coffee House
10 Mexican Coffee Shop
13 Family Restaurant
15 Bukittinggi Coffee Shop
17 Jazz & Blues Coffee Shop
18 Bouganville Coffee Shop
22 Restaurant Sari
25 Canyon Coffee Shop
27 Singgalang Coffee Shop
28 ASEAN Restaurant
30 Mona Lisa Restaurant
38 Roda Group Restaurant
41 Simpang Raya Restaurant
42 Simpang Raya Restaurant

OTHER

7 Fort de Kock
16 Zoo & Museum
31 Mosque
32 Toko Eka
33 Gloria Cinema
34 Roda Barn
35 Pasar Bawah (Market)
36 Bemo & Opelet Station
37 Pasar Wisata
39 Pasar Atas
40 Bank Negara Indonesia
43 Clocktower
44 Tourist Office & Small Post Office
47 Medan Nan Balituduang (Saliguri Dance Group)
51 Military Museum
53 Japanese Cave Entry
54 Post Office
56 Telephone Office
58 Police

Park overlooks the deep Sianok Canyon that cuts right into Bukittinggi. In the park is the entry to the extensive grid of caves which the Japanese tunnelled out during WW II. Many of the tunnels look out from the cliff faces over the canyon. At the entrance to the caves, or Lobang Jepang, there's a bas relief showing the Japanese herding the helpless Indonesians inside.

Military Museum

Right across the road from Panorama Park, this museum has weapons and pictures of the struggle against the Dutch in the 1940s. It's open daily from 8 am to 5 pm.

Places to Stay

Jalan Ahmad Yani, right in the centre of town, is 'bule (Whites) row', with cheap hotels, travel agents and coffee shops with travellers' menus. Bukittinggi's cheap hotels are a dull and charmless lot, although they are cheap.

Working down that street from the top, *Murni's* at No 115 has plain but clean singles/doubles at 4000/6000 rp and a nice sitting area upstairs. The similar *Hotel Nirwana* (☎ 21292) is right next door at No 113. Across the road, there's the *Hotel Rajawali* with rooms for 4000/5000 rp, and you can have an outside sitting area if you take the rooms on the roof. The *Singgalang Hotel* (☎ 21576), Jalan Ahmad Yani 130, is a light and airy place with rooms at 6000 rp.

The *Hotel Yany* (☎ 22740) at No 101 has overpriced rooms for 10,000 rp, while the *Wisma Tigo Balai* (☎ 21824) at Jalan Ahmad Yani 100 is about as cheap and as basic as they come with rooms at 3500/5000 rp. The *Gangga Hotel* (☎ 22967) at No 70 is a sprawling place and costs 3500/6000 rp for basic rooms; better rooms are 5000/8000 rp with shower and top-of-the-range rooms cost 10,000/15,000 rp up to 20,000/25,000 rp.

A good alternative to Jalan Ahmad Yani are the places on the way up to Fort de Kock. The quiet *Suwarni Guest House* is in an old Dutch house and has a lot more character than the cheap hotels. Food is served and you can get good information on the attractions around Bukittinggi. Dorm beds are 3500 rp or rooms cost 7000 rp to 10,000 rp, all with shared bathrooms. Another good old-style guesthouse is the *Wisma Bukittinggi* with small rooms for 4000 rp and larger rooms for 7500 rp or 10,000 rp with attached bathroom. The *Mountain View Guest House* (☎ 21621) at Jalan Yos Sudarso 3 is a more modern place with well-kept rooms from 14,000 rp with mandi. There are indeed mountain views and an excellent restaurant next door. Similar are the *Gallery Hotel*, Jalan H Agus Salim 25, with rooms from 10,000 without bath or 15,000 rp with bath, and the *Hotel Sari*, with rooms with bath starting at 12,500 rp.

The *Benteng Hotel* (☎ 21115), up towards the top of Fort de Kock hill, is a very pleasant mid-range place. Rooms cost from 28,000/36,000 rp up to 67,000/72,500 rp. There's a restaurant and bar, great views over the town and showers have hot water.

Places to Eat

In amongst the cheap hotels along Jalan Ahmad Yani are two very popular restaurants with menus which feature all those familiar travellers' specials, from fruit salad to banana pancakes. The *Coffee House* at No 103 has a pleasant outdoor area overlooking the street. The *Three Tables Coffee House* at No 142 is a bit bigger (there are more than three tables) and equally popular. Another popular place is the *Bouganville Coffee Shop*.

Off by itself, on Jalan Teuku Umar, is the delightful *Canyon Coffee Shop* with good food and atmosphere. Further down at Jalan Ahmad Yani 58 is the *Mona Lisa*, a tiny place with a Chinese-influenced menu. The *ASEAN Restaurant* on Jalan A Karim 12A has better Chinese food. *Restaurant Sari* has excellent food and juices on its mostly Chinese menu and is moderately priced for the quality on offer. You can dine outside in the thatched area, with commanding views of the surrounding valley and hills.

Of course, Padang food is important in Bukittinggi and the *Roda Group Restaurant*, in the Pasar Atas Market building, has good food and a menu, so you know what you're paying for. In the Pasar Wisata building, right next to the Pasar Atas building, there are more restaurants and warungs including a branch of the *Simpang Raya* nasi padang restaurants at each end of the block. They also have a menu, unusual in Padang restaurants. Up on the Fort de Kock hill, right at the top of the road, the *Family Restaurant* also does pretty good Padang food.

A number of places in Bukittinggi, including the Western-oriented coffee houses, do the local speciality, dadiah campur, a tasty mixture of oats, coconut, fruit, molasses and buffalo yoghurt.

Getting There & Away

Padang is only two hours south of Bukittinggi, a pleasant trip costing 1500 rp. The road north to Sibolga and Parapat is twisting and narrow for much of the way. Regular buses can make the trip to Parapat in 16 hours, or the air-con buses do it in 13 hours.

The Aur Kuning bus station is about two km from the town centre but you can get there easily on the local opelets. Typical fares from Bukittinggi include Medan for 20,000 rp (25,000 rp air-con), Parapat for 17,500 rp (22,500 rp air-con), Sibolga for 8500 rp and Pekanbaru for 5000 rp. You can get also get buses through to Bengkulu, Jambi or Palembang but most people travel via Padang. You can buy tickets at the bus station, and the tourist office has a list of bus companies and ticket prices. Some Bukittinggi travel agents have been known to charge high prices for poor buses, so shop around if you deal with an agent.

The tourist coaches leave for Parapat every morning at 7.30 am and cost 20,000 rp. Tickets can be booked at a number of places in town. The bus picks up from some hotels and travel agents that sell tickets.

If you're arriving in Bukittinggi from the north (Parapat) or east (Pekanbaru) get off the bus near the town centre, saving the 200 rp opelet ride back from the bus terminal south of the centre.

Getting Around

Opelets around Bukittinggi cost a flat 150 rp for three-wheelers or 200 rp for the four-wheel variety. The four-wheelers run to the

INDONESIA

bus station. Bendis cost from 500 to 1000 rp depending on the distance.

AROUND BUKITTINGGI

A path through the Sianok Canyon leads to the village of **Koto Gadang**. Turn left at the bottom of the road just before the canyon and keep going. Don't cross the bridge there because if you do it's a 12-km walk (instead of a relatively short five-km one). Koto Gadang is noted for its silverwork which, though exquisite, is limited in range.

There are several other villages around Bukittinggi which are still producing traditional crafts, one of the more interesting being **Pandai Sikat**, 13 km away. It's a centre for weaving and wood carving.

Ngalau Kamanga, 15 km to the east of Bukittinggi, was the scene of armed resistance against the Dutch in the 19th and early 20th centuries. Apparently, the villagers used a 1500-metre-long local cave as a hideout from the Dutch and conducted effective guerrilla attacks in the surrounding country from this base. The cave is dripping with stalactites and stalagmites and has a small, clear lake.

There is a **Rafflesia sanctuary** about 15 km north of town; a sign at the village of Batang Palupuh indicates the path. Rafflesia are giant, cabbage-sized flowers named after Sir Stamford Raffles. Rafflesia bloom between August and December.

Further north, on the way to Sibolga, a large globe which indicates the position of the **equator** stands in a rice paddy beside the road.

Lake Maninjau

About 30 km south-west of Bukittinggi is Lawang Top and, directly below it, Lake Maninjau. Lake Maninjau is warmer than Toba and is an extremely beautiful crater lake. You can zip around it by speedboat or water scooter if you wish. The final 12-km descent to the lake twists and turns through 44 numbered hairpin bends.

Places to Stay & Eat Most guesthouses are basic but good, with friendly owners. One of the best is *Beach Guest House* with rooms for 3000 rp per person and bungalows, on the edge of the lake, for 6000 rp. *Amai Cheap* in the centre of the village is an old teak house with large rooms from 4000 rp.

Pasir Panjang Permai is an expensive place about one km from the centre of town but of high standards, with rooms starting from 40,000 rp. All rooms overlook the lake and there are hot/cold showers and TV. *Palentha Guest House*, which is past the Pasir Panjang Permai Hotel, is a popular place to stay with rooms from 4000 rp. The *Maninjau Indah* is another upmarket hotel but it is starting to look a bit run-down. The *Pilli Guest House* is another cheapie.

The *Three Tables Coffee House* and *Srikandi* are the best places to eat.

Getting There & Away You can catch a bus there directly from Bukittinggi for 800 rp or get off at Matur, climb to Lawang for the view and then walk down to the lake, which takes a couple of hours if you're fit but is much longer if you're not.

PEKANBARU

Pekanbaru is a grubby oil town with a sleazy port. There's no particular attraction to the place and it's simply somewhere to pass through on the way to or from Singapore via the Riau Archipelago. If arriving from Singapore you can usually get a bus straight out to Bukittinggi, but in the other direction you may have to spend the night.

Information

There is no tourist office as such – the local government department in the Governor's office (☎ 25301) on the corner of Jalan Gajah Mada 200 and Diponegoro handles this service. You can change money at the airport, in Bank Negara Indonesia at Jalan Sudirman 63 or in Toko Firmas at Jalan Sudirman 27.

Places to Stay

If you have to stay overnight, *Tommy's Place*, half a km from the bus station on

Gang Nantongga at Jalan Nangka 41D, is the place to head for. Rooms cost 5000 rp and they can arrange tickets for the Batam boats. From the bus station, turn right and Gang Nantongga is the second gang on your right side. Walk down it and keep asking for Tommy's until you get to it.

There are numerous other losmen around the bus terminal on Jalan Nangka. *Penginapan Linda*, with clean rooms from 7500 rp, is one of the better places in this area. If you're departing by boat, there are a couple of run-down and depressing hotels with little to recommend them except for their proximity to the port. The *Nirmala* at Jalan Yatim 11 is typical with rooms from 7000 rp.

Better mid-range places with rooms from 20,000 rp include the *Hotel Anom* on Jalan Gatot Subroto, (Riau Hotel, Jalan Dipoengoro 26, and the more expensive *Hotel Rauda*.

Getting There & Away

Merpati has direct flights to Batam, Tanjung Pinang, Medan and Jakarta. Sempati also fly to Jakarta, Padang, Tanjung Pinang and Kuala Lumpur in Malaysia. Buses to Bukittinggi take about six hours and cost from 5000 rp for non-air-con.

Boats to Batam & Singapore Agents all around town sell tickets for the boats to Batam. Tickets include the bus fare to Tanjung Buton and the speedboat from there to Batam, usually via Selat Panjang. There is not a lot of difference between the speedboat services, though the prices vary from around 28,000 to 35,000 rp. Garuda Express goes by speedboat down the river to Perawang, then by bus to Tanjung Buton and then another speedboat to Batam. It is an interesting trip, though no quicker despite the claims. It is slightly cheaper to do the trip in stages yourself, but you may miss connections.

The other alternative is the slow boat on Monday, Wednesday and Friday at 5 pm, travelling down the Siak River and then on to Selat Panjang (9500 rp, 12 hours), Batam (25,000 rp, 24 hours) and Bintan. Buy tickets at the wharf – an extra 3000 rp will get you a 'cabin', which is just a bare, wooden sleeping platform, but a luxury compared to deck class. It is certainly a *Heart of Darkness* adventure, but definitely a once in a lifetime experience. See the Sumatra Getting There & Away section for more details on the Pekanbaru-Batam-Singapore run.

DUMAI

On the coast, 158 km north from Pekanbaru, Dumai is of interest only for the ferry service between here and Melaka in Malaysia (see the Sumatra Getting There & Away section for details). Dumai is strictly a one-street town and once you arrive the only thing to do is catch a bus to Pekanbaru. When you get to Pekanbaru there's not much to do either! You need a visa to arrive in or depart Indonesia through Dumai.

SIBOLGA

There's no attraction to bring you to this rather dirty and drab little port, except as an overnight stop between Bukittinggi and Parapat or a jumping-off point to Nias. Sibolga is north of Bukittinggi, where the road turns inland to Parapat and Lake Toba. The descent into Sibolga – approaching from Parapat – is very beautiful, particularly at sunset. The harbour itself is attractive and there are some good beaches nearby.

Places to Stay & Eat

The losmen in the central area are generally dirty and/or unfriendly. An exception is the new, well-run *Pasar Baru Inn*, Jalan Suprapto 41. Very clean rooms start from 8000 rp and go up to 30,000 rp, and the management are very helpful. Others include the *Hotel Sudi Mampir* and the *Subur*, with rooms from around 6000 rp. *Hotel Indah Sari*, Jalan Achmad Yani 29, is slightly more expensive with rooms from 7000 rp but at least it's reasonable – they also have rooms with air-con and bathrooms from 15,000 rp. The *Maturi*, opposite the Indah, is dirt cheap.

Off to the north of town, *Hotel Tapian Nauli* is much nicer – rooms from 18,000 rp have bathrooms and a balcony. *Hotel Hidup Baru* (☎ 21957) at Jalan Suprapto 123 has rooms from 8000 to 13,000 rp with bath or at 22,000 rp with air-con – all prices include breakfast.

To compensate for Sibolga's other drawbacks, there are some good restaurants and an ice-cream place on the corner across from the cinema. The *Telok Indah* at Jalan Achmad Yani 63-65 is an expensive but good Chinese restaurant.

Getting There & Away

Sibolga is on the Bukittinggi-Parapat-Medan route, so all the buses pass through here. See the following Nias section for details of sea connections.

NIAS ISLAND

Off the west coast of north Sumatra, Nias is interesting for its traditional megalithic villages, unique customs and fine beaches. The points of interest are in the south, where the most interesting villages and good, easy jungle treks can be made, most of which follow stone tracks. Surfers have discovered some of the best breaks in Indonesia here along the southern shore, and Lagundi is a popular beach hangout.

Orientation & Information

The roads on Nias are really shocking although, fortunately, the two most interesting towns in the south of the island are fairly close together. Gunung Sitoli is the main town in the north and Teluk Dalam is the port and main town in the south. You can cash travellers' cheques at a poor rate in both towns. Chloroquine-resistant malaria has been reported on Nias so take appropriate precautions.

Gunung Sitoli has a tourist information office (☎ 21545) on Jalan Sukarno 6.

Things to See

At **Gunung Sitoli** there is little to offer apart from a walk to some traditional houses uphill from Hilimbawodesolo, about 14 km from town. **Teluk Dalam** is a transit point to the island's main points of interest.

With its perfect horseshoe bay, **Lagundi**, 12 km from Teluk Dalam, is a popular hangout for surfies and Sumatra's No 1 beach resort. There's not much to do here except surf, swim, walk and bask in the sun.

From Lagundi you can make treks to traditional villages such as **Bawomataluo**, 14 km from Teluk Dalam. It is reached via an impressive entrance of 480 stone steps and has high-roofed traditional houses and the fine 'palace' of the tribal chief. It's worth exploring, but tourist prices apply for statues, dances, photographs etc. **Hilisimaetano** is a larger but newer village, 16 km north-west from Teluk Dalam, with 140 traditional houses. Stone-jumping is performed here – once a form of war training, the jumpers had to leap over a two-metre-high wall of stones surmounted by pointed sticks (nowadays left off).

Places to Stay & Eat

Lagundi There are dozens of places to stay at Lagundi, most costing from around 1000 rp to 2000 rp per person for a room, or double that for a bungalow. All the losmen provide food, the menu in most being exactly the same – mie goreng, omelettes, fried rice and vegetables, gado gado, pancakes, chips and so on. The ridiculously cheap accommodation is subsidised by the food, so losmen owners can get peeved if their lodgers eat somewhere else. Places to stay include the *Damai, Friendly, Rufas, Happy Beach, Jamburae, Sea Breeze, Purba, Amagumi, Manuel* and *Tolong Menolong*.

There are more losmen, including the *Risky, Magdalena* and the *Yanti*, near the centre of the horseshoe. All three are good places to stay as they're cheap and the losmen owners are friendly, knowledgeable and helpful.

Teluk Dalam *Wisma Jamburae* is on the waterfront with basic and clean rooms for 8000 rp. The more expensive *Hotel Ampera* on Jalan Pasar has clean rooms with mandi from 15,000 rp. You are better off heading straight to Lagundi.

Gunung Sitoli Cheap accommodation in this town is expensive, dirty and depressing. The best place to stay is the *Wisma Soliga*, although it's four km from the town centre on the main road into the township. It's clean, spacious and has good Chinese food. Rooms cost from around 10,000 rp, even less with bargaining.

In the centre of town at Jalan Gomo 148, the *Hotel Gomo* has cheap rooms upstairs from 8000 rp. They are bright and airy compared to the dark and more expensive air-con rooms downstairs. *Hotel Wisata*, Jalan Sirao 2 is a better alternative to Hotel Gomo with rooms for 7500 and 10,000 rp but none of them are air-con.

The cell-like *Hotel Beringin* on Jalan Beringin has rooms for 5000 rp. Cheaper and even sadder is the *Penginapan Banuada* on Jalan Kopri.

Getting There & Away

Air Merpati flies from Medan to Nias for 100,000 rp. The airport is 19 km from Gunung Sitoli and the taxi costs 4000 rp.

Boat Boats run daily from Sibolga to Gunung Sitoli; the eight to 10-hour journey

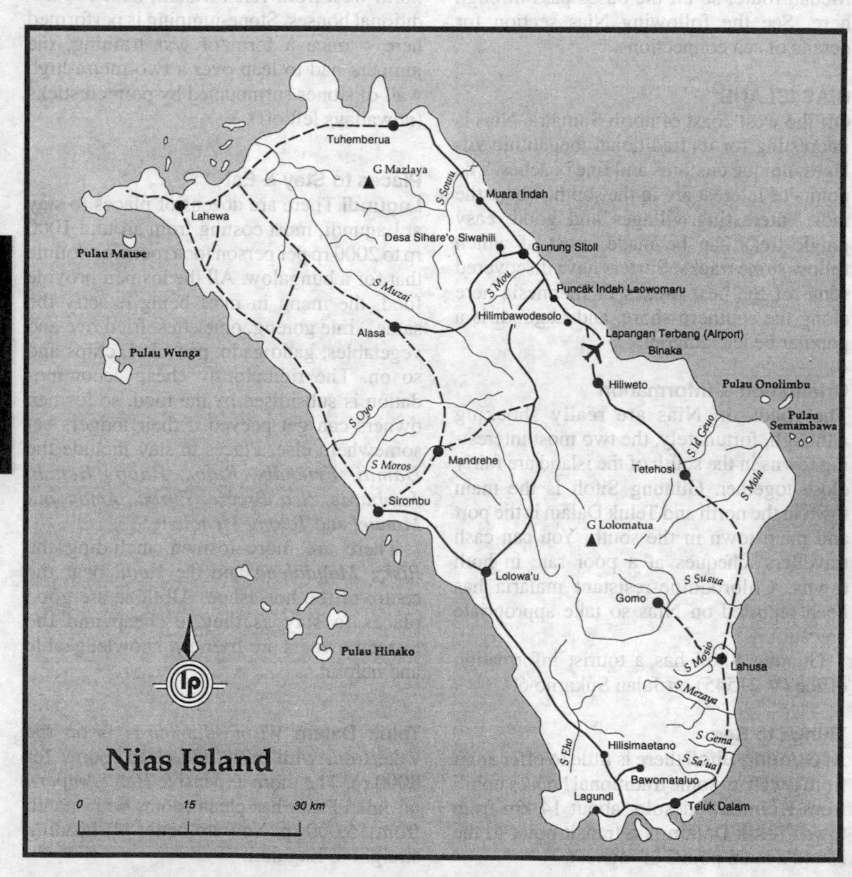

costs 7500 rp in deck class and 11,500 rp for a cabin.

Once every two weeks Pelni's KM *Lawit* runs from Padang to Sibolga (15 hours) and then across to Gunung Sitoli (six hours) before returning to Padang (16 hours). From Padang to Sibolga costs from 15,000 rp ekonomi.

Most of the places of interest are down in the south so if you arrive in Gunung Sitoli, you have to take a bus to Teluk Dalam (5000 rp). Boats also do the run on Monday, Wednesday and Friday but they take 10 hours. The bus trip takes about six hours, but can take all day if you're unlucky. The bus will drop you six km from Lagundi before going into Teluk Dalam. Special 'tourist' buses sometimes go to the beach for 500 rp, or you can continue there by motorbike for 1000 rp.

PARAPAT

Located on the shores of Lake Toba, between Medan and Bukittinggi, this is the arrival and departure point for ferries to Samosir Island in Lake Toba. Parapat is quite a pleasant place, but there's no reason to stay here, unless you miss the ferries to the island or have to catch an early morning bus.

The expensive Parapat Hotel sometimes put on **performances** of Batak singing or other local culture for tour groups. Parapat is also a good place to get Batak **handicrafts**. Parapat's Saturday **market**, right near the ferry jetty, is always lively and worth a visit. The village of **Labuhan Garaga**, 25 km from Parapat, is noted for its fine Batak blankets.

Orientation & Information

Parapat is essentially in two parts, the line of restaurants and shops on the Trans-Sumatran Highway (Jalan Sisingamangaraja) and, one km away, the area down by the lake from where ferries to Samosir Island depart.

Just where Jalan Pulau Samosir turns off from the Trans-Sumatran Highway, there's a small tourist office with some limited information about Parapat and the lake. Further along this road is the Sejahtera Bank Umum which changes cash and travellers' cheques. The Telkom office, on the back road between the ferry terminal and the bus station, has a dial-home-direct phone for international calls, or there is a Wartel on Jalan Sisingamangaraja. The bus station is about two km from the ferry wharf on the main road towards Bukittinggi.

Places to Stay

Parapat has plenty of places to stay, some of them quite pleasant, but Samosir Island is such a bargain that Parapat ends up looking very expensive. The main reason travellers spend the night in Parapat is to catch the early morning tourist buses. The travel agents, never ones to miss out on a rupiah, arrange accommodation. *Andilo Nancy* has rooms at their losmen right near the ferry dock, as well as at their bus station office, for 5000/7500 rp. It's reasonable value. *Dolok Silau* also provides rooms. They have an office at Jalan Sisingamangaraja 56 on the main road and opposite Andilo Nancy at the ferry dock.

Down at the lakeside, there are several places along Jalan Haranggaol including the popular *Pago Pago Inn*, close to the harbour, at No 50. The rooms are quite simple and not as flash as the lobby, but they are clean and good value at 6000/10,000 rp and there are fine views across the lake.

Opposite, the *Riris Inn* (☎ 41392) at No 39 has simple, well-kept rooms with mandis for a steep 15,000/20,000 rp. Just down from it, at Jalan Haranggaol 47, the *Hotel Soloh Jaya* has very small rooms, some windowless, from 7500 rp. Better rooms with mandi cost from 17,500 rp.

Go right down to the ferry dock at the end of the road, turn the corner and *Wisma Gurning* is right by the lakeside, a simple place with rooms with two beds and a mandi for 10,000 rp. The big hotels in Parapat are much more expensive and rooms at the *Hotel Parapat* cost around 100,000 rp.

Places to Eat

Parapat has plenty of places to eat including a host of nasi padang specialists along the main road. At No 80/82, right by the Sudi

INDONESIA

Mampir, the *Asia Restaurant* does good Chinese food as does the clean, neat and modern *Singgalang Restaurant* underneath the Singgalang Hotel.

Down towards the lake, there are several restaurants along Jalan Haranggaol including the *Restaurant Hong Kong* and the *Restaurant Bali* opposite. They have very similar Chinese menus which are not cheap, but chicken with lychees at the Bali is delicious.

Getting There & Away

For bus tickets, Andilo Nancy (☎ 41548) and Dolok Silau (☎ 41467) are the main agents and generally provide a good service, despite some annoying hard-sell practices. Parapat agents tend to charge higher than average commission and have been known to bungle bus and flight reservations from Medan – Parapat is not a major travel hub, so do most of your business in Medan if possible. Public buses leave from the bus station, but some express buses stop at the agents on Jalan Sisingamangaraja.

Public buses to or from Medan (3500 rp, four to five hours) leave throughout the day, but most departures are in the morning. Other public bus services generally depart up until noon and include Sibolga (7000 rp, four hours), Bukittinggi (17,000 rp, 18 hours), Padang (19,000 rp, 20 hours) and Pekanbaru (17,000 rp).

Most express buses run from Medan to Bukittinggi or Padang. The best air-con luxury buses to Bukittinggi run at night and cost 25,000 rp. They bypass Sibolga, take 12 or 13 hours and are much less arduous than the public buses. ALS and ANS buses both have a good name.

Andilo Nancy and Dolok Silau between them have tourist minibuses every day to Bukittinggi (22,500 rp, 13 hours). They leave early in the morning so you get to see the scenery, and they stop at points of interest on the way. The buses are looking a little worn, but are still comfortable, and the most convenient way to travel.

For Berastagi, you have to change buses at Siantar and Kabanjahe, and it takes up to six hours. The daily tourist buses do the direct trip in three hours or more and cost 12,000 rp. They take a spectacular route that winds around the lake for much of the way. These buses continue on to Bukit Lawang for 20,000 rp.

Getting Around

Opelets around Parapat cost 200 rp and do an anticlockwise circle of the town from the ferry terminal, past the telephone office to the bus station and then back to the ferry terminal.

LAKE TOBA

Lake Toba is a spectacular crater lake, bang in the middle of north Sumatra, 176 km south of Medan. It is high up (800 metres), big (1707 sq km) and deep (450 metres). Out of the middle of this huge inland lake rises Samosir Island, almost as big as Singapore.

Parapat, on the shore of the lake, is the principal town of the area and a popular resort for Medan with its many restaurants, hotels, beaches and amusements. The real interest, however, starts on Samosir Island, centre for the likeable Batak people. You can see plenty of their high-peaked Batak houses in the villages around the island. Greet people with a hearty 'horas'. The Christian tombs of the Batak are scattered in the fields of this very beautiful island and the deep green lake invites swimming.

Tourism is also big on Samosir, and mammon is sometimes more noticeable than Christianity, especially at the popular resort of Tuk Tuk. Those with an interest in the Toba Batak will gain more satisfaction from getting out and exploring the rest of the island.

Information

Change money before you get to Lake Toba, as exchange rates are poor. The bank Sejahtera Bank Umum at Parapat is reasonable for US$ but is more severe on other currencies.

Beware of theft and keep your door locked. There have been a number of reports of thieves quietly sneaking into rooms at night and stealing cash or cameras – almost always the result of carelessness. Samosir is also one of the few places in Indonesia where ganja is readily available, but caution and discretion are essential.

Tomok

If you follow the road away from the lakefront and the dozens of souvenir stalls in the village you will come to the **Tomb of King Sidabatu**, one of the last animist kings before the arrival of Christianity. Although Tomok is the main village it has few places to stay and Tuk Tuk, a few km away, is where all the action is. It is possible to trek from Tomok to Pangururan on the other side of the island.

Tuk Tuk

This once small village is now a string of hotels and restaurants stretching around the peninsula, just above the lake's waters. Pointed Batak roofs are plonked on many of the new concrete-block hotels, but otherwise traditional Batak culture is not much in evidence. Still, the living is easy and very cheap,

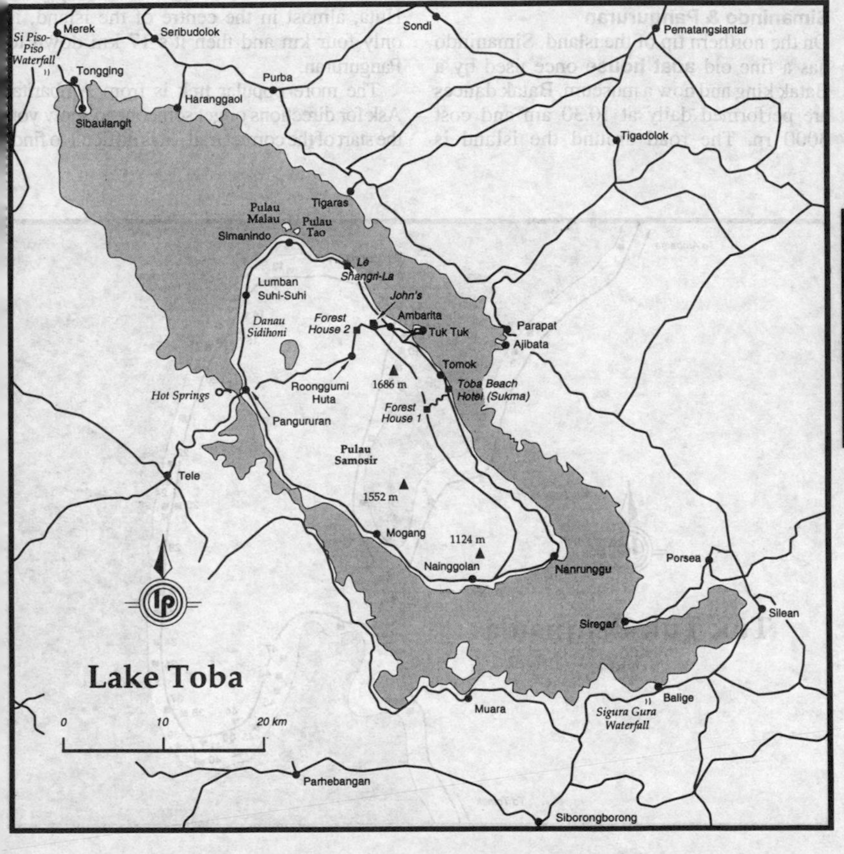

and Tuk Tuk is a pleasant place to relax and use as a base from which to visit the rest of the island.

Ambarita

A couple of km north of the Tuk Tuk Peninsula, Ambarita has a group of **stone chairs** where important matters and disputes were once settled. Until the arrival of Christianity about 250 years ago, serious wrongdoers were led to a further group of stone furnishings in an adjoining courtyard and despatched from this world by application of an axe to the back of the neck, and then supposedly chopped up and consumed.

Simanindo & Pangururan

On the northern tip of the island, Simanindo has a fine old **adat house** once used by a Batak king and now a museum. Batak dances are performed daily at 10.30 am and cost 3000 rp. The road around the island is improving and irregular bemos run all the way from Tomok.

At Pangururan, the island is only divided from the mainland by a canal. You can travel by bus from here to Berastagi but the road to Sidikalang is very poor. There are hot springs to relax in five km beyond Pangururan.

Across Samosir

The hardy can walk right on up and over the island from Tomok in a day's hard walking. It's 13 km from Tomok to Pasanggrahan (Forest House 1) where you can stay if you wish. Then it's a further 16 km down to Forest House 2 – you can short-cut to here from Ambarita. From here to Roonggurni Huta, almost in the centre of the island, is only four km and then it's 17 km down to Pangururan.

The more popular trek is from Ambarita. Ask for directions or get someone to show you the start of the correct trail – it is difficult to find.

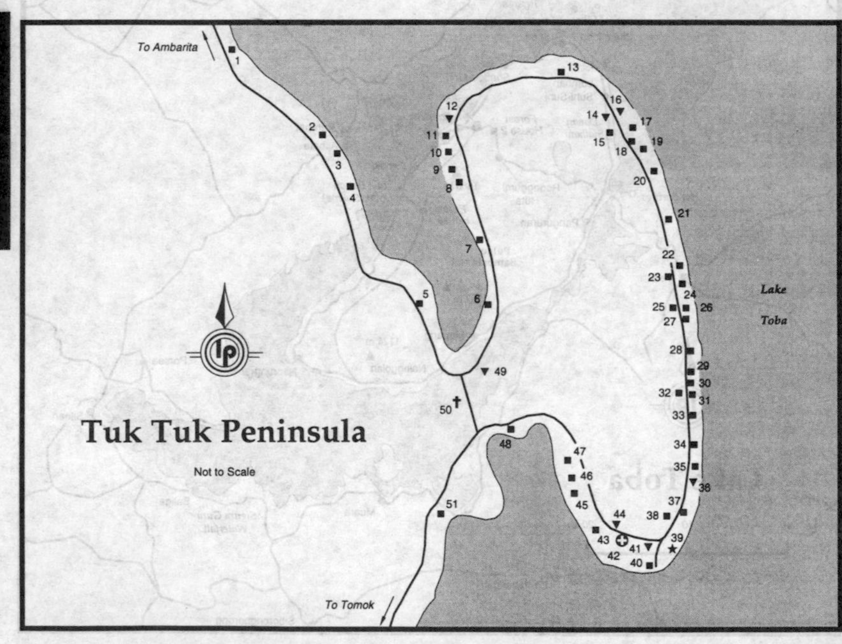

After the hard, steep climb to the top the path leads to Dolok, where you can stay at *John's Losmen*. It is possible to do the walk in a day if you start early, but it's best to stay overnight. From Dolok you can continue on to Pangururan via Roongguni and Lake Sidihoni, or via a shorter, easier route. Easiest of all is to do the trek from Pangururan, thus avoiding the initial steep climb and problems finding the trail.

Places to Stay

Samosir is a great place to rest up if you've just suffered the rigours of long-distance Sumatran buses. Although it's no longer the traffic-free, primitive place it once was, Samosir is certainly easy-going and carefree enough to suit most people.

Samosir has some of the best value accommodation in Indonesia. You can still find some very spartan places at 2000 rp a single or 4000 rp a double, some still in wooden Batak-style buildings. Most places tend to be of the concrete box variety these days, but you'll get a good-sized, clean box, usually with attached mandi, from around 3000 rp a single or 5000 rp a double. A room with a balcony overlooking the lake can be had for 4000 to 5000 rp a single or 5000 to 7500 rp a double.

Most of the accommodation is concentrated around the Tuk Tuk Peninsula and nearby Ambarita. Tomok, the main village a couple of km south of Tuk Tuk, also has a couple of places to stay.

Tuk Tuk has some larger hotels appealing to wealthy north Sumatrans or tourists from Singapore, but *Carolina's* is still the longest-running and most popular 'upmarket' place. Rooms range from simple ones at 12,500 rp and 15,000 rp up to 50,000 rp for the deluxe rooms with balconies overlooking the lake. There's a restaurant, bar and even a diving board into the lake. Carolina's is usually the first stop for the ferries. *Bagus Bay* is a quiet, less expensive mid-range place on the neck of the peninsula towards Tomok. Rooms cost 15,000 rp.

Around the peninsula from Carolina's, the big *Silintong Hotel* is expensive and somewhat overpriced, while on a hill above the road, *Maduma* is pleasant but not on the lake and the so-so rooms cost 15,000 rp. Then there's *Bernard's* and *Matahari's*, two of the longest-running places on Samosir. Basic rooms without mandi are 6000 rp, while bungalows at Bernard's cost 10,000 rp. Other cheap places in this area include *Marraon*, *Romlan* and *Rudy's*.

After this cluster of places more are scat-

PLACES TO STAY

1 Tuktuk Timbul
2 Mas
3 Miss Nina
4 Sony
5 Christina's
6 Antonius
7 Murni
8 Sibayak
9 Tony's
10 Abadi's
11 Caribien
13 Toledo Inn
15 Dewi's
17 Samosir Losmen
18 Junita
19 Popy's
20 Endy's
21 Lekjon
22 Toledo 2
23 Ambaroba Resort Hotel
24 Pos
25 Rudy's
26 Rodeo
27 Hotel Silintong
28 Hotel Sumber Polo Mas
29 Marraon
30 Hisar's
31 Bernard's
32 Lenny's
33 Matahari's
34 Rosita
35 Elsina's Losmen on the Beach
37 Silintong Hotel
38 Maduma
40 Carolina's
43 Mafir
45 Dumasari
46 Sahatma
47 Linda's
48 Bagus Bay
51 Smiley's

PLACES TO EAT

12 Reggae Restaurant
14 Brando's Blues
16 Anju Restaurant
36 Franky Restaurant
41 Pepy's Restaurant
44 Roy's Pub
49 Romlans Beer Garden

OTHER

39 Police Station
42 Health Centre
50 Church

INDONESIA

tered along the road, like *Pos*, one of the cheapest around with basic rooms for 2000/4000 rp or reasonable rooms with bath by the lake for 3500/7000 rp. Pos is mostly surrounded by big package-tour places like the *Amaroba*, which has rooms for 40,000 rp and 60,000 rp.

Further along, *Lekjon* gets mixed reviews but the lakeside rooms for 5000 rp are good value. *Endy's* is a Batak-style place with rooms at 3500 rp. *Samosir* is on its own point with mid-range bungalow-style rooms from 7000 rp. It is more attractive than most and has a good restaurant. The *Toledo Inn* is a big package-tour hotel with rooms at 30,000 rp. After another gap is a tightly packed string of basic places, built on the hillside between the road and the lake and looking like a downmarket Riviera resort. *Abadi's*, with its good restaurant and fine views, is probably the pick of these. Rooms cost 3000/5000 rp or 5000/7000 rp for larger rooms. *Tony's* is a big place that has consumed most of its neighbours in the local monopoly game, while Antonius is a basic, traditional Batak-style place.

Continue on towards Ambarita and a trail descends down from the road to the popular *Sony* and, further on, *Tuktuk Timbul* by the lakeside. These quiet, isolated places have rooms for around 4000 rp to 6000 rp. They're fine if you want to get away from it all.

Further away from it all, *Gordon's* is a couple of km beyond Ambarita on the way to Simanindo, and right next to it is the flashy, high-security *Sopotoba*. For something really isolated, the friendly *Le Shangri-La* is six km past Ambarita (300 rp on a Simanindo-bound bus). Clean Batak-style bungalows front a sandy beach and cost 4000/5000 rp, or dorm accommodation is 2000 rp.

Few people stay in Tomok, although there are plenty of restaurants and warungs here for day-trippers who come across on the ferry from Parapat. *Roy's Restaurant* on the main street, right near the track to the royal tombs, has accommodation on the edge of town in large Batak houses for 3000 rp per person. Tomok also has two other basic losmen. Regular bemos depart from Tomok to other parts of Samosir Island.

Round at Pangururan, on the other side of the island, *Mr Barat Accommodation* is close to the wharf at Jalan Sisingamangaraja 2/4; 'he's a friendly guy with a maniac laugh'. The rooms are 3500 rp.

Places to Eat

Most places have their own restaurants and the food is much like that at any other travellers' centre. There are no real surprises although most places still run a book for each guest, with each banana pancake or fruit salad added to a list which can stretch to a surprising length over a week or two.

Around Samosir Losmen, there are a few independent eating places like *Miduk, Anju* and the fancy *Gokhi Bar Club* and *Brando's Blues*, which stand out above the rest. *Carolina's* restaurant is the best and most popular restaurant in Tuk Tuk, though prices are a bit higher than elsewhere. Nearby, the long-running *Pepy's Restaurant* is a Tuk Tuk institution that is now often empty. The sign advertising magic mushroom omelettes is the only reminder of its heyday.

Tuk Tuk also has a few bar/restaurants such as *Franky*, which pumps out the music, and *Roy's Pub*, which has bands – sometimes. *Romlans Beer Garden* is pleasant enough if you are staying nearby but otherwise not worth a special visit.

Getting There & Away

See the Parapat section for information on bus travel to and from Lake Toba. There is also a daily bus service from Pangururan to Berastagi but the road is very poor. Every Monday a 7 am ferry goes from Ambarita to Haranggaol, a market town at the northern tip of the lake, and meets a bus that goes on to Berastagi. The total cost is around 2500 rp and trip time is about 2½ hours from Ambarita. On Thursday, a similar ferry leaves from Simanindo at 9 am and also meets a bus from Haranggaol to Berastagi.

The ferries between Parapat and Samosir operate roughly every hour, sometimes more, especially on Saturday market days.

INDONESIA

The last ferry to Samosir leaves around 5.30 pm, and the last one to Parapat around 4.30 pm. The fare is 800 rp one way. Most boats go to Tuk Tuk and then continue on to Ambarita, but four or five boats per day go directly to Ambarita. Tell them where you want to get off on Samosir when you pay your fare, or sing out when your hotel comes around – you'll be dropped off at the doorstep or nearby. When leaving for Parapat, just stand out on your hotel jetty and wave a ferry down.

Ferries to Tomok leave from Ajibata, about one km from the market and the Tuk Tuk ferry jetty. Car ferries operate throughout the day.

Getting Around

Minibuses run between Tomok and Ambarita with some regularity – these often continue to Simanindo with less frequency but not to Tuk Tuk. There is no specific time schedule but services are more frequent in the morning and it is difficult to find anything after 3 pm. Infrequent buses also run around the island from Tomok to Pangururan.

You can rent motorbikes in Tuk Tuk for around 20,000 rp a day or bicycles from 5000 rp – rates are negotiable, like everything else.

BERASTAGI

On the back road from Medan to Lake Toba is Berastagi (Brastagi), a centre of the Karo Batak. Their traditional horned-roof houses can be seen in surrounding villages. This cool hill town is a pleasant base from which to organise treks. The marquisa, a passionfruit variety, is grown only here and in Sulawesi; it makes a very popular drink.

Orientation & Information

Berastagi is essentially one main road, Jalan Veteran. There are some interesting antique and souvenir shops along this road and Crispo Antiques has interesting items for sale.

It is best to change money before you come to Berastagi. Wisma Sibayak offers bad rates. The large Bukit Kuba Hotel or Hotel International Sibayak have better exchange rates than the Bank BNI 1946 in Kabanjahe, the closest bank to Berastagi.

The helpful tourist office is near the fruit market.

Places to Stay

Wisma Sibayak is at the Kabanjahe end of the main street, in an old colonial house surrounded by gardens. Dorm beds cost 2500 rp, and singles/doubles start at 4000/6000 rp for small rooms and range up to 10,000 rp for larger doubles. It's always packed with travellers and has excellent travel information and a popular restaurant area.

Their backup establishment is the *Losmen Sibayak Guesthouse* in the centre of town on Jalan Veteran. It is also good, but not as salubrious. Dorms cost 2500 rp and rooms are 3000/5000 rp or 7500 rp with attached bath.

Wisma Ikut, 24 Jalan Gundaling, is popular and also in a fine old colonial house on a hill above the town with views of Gunung Sibayak. Cheaper, rather dreary rooms cost 3000/5000 rp or pleasant doubles are 7500 rp. It's a friendly, well-run place but in need of some maintenance.

If you continue past Wisma Ikut you'll find *Kaliaga Bungalow*, a good mid-range place near the big Hotel International Sibayak. Rooms cost 20,000/25,000 rp including attached bathroom with hot-water showers.

The *Ginsata Hotel* is at Jalan Veteran 79. This hotel is clean and quite OK with rooms with mandi for 6500 rp and a nasi padang restaurant downstairs. Other cheap places include the neat and clean *Crispo Losmen*, above the antique shop on the main street, the modern *Torong Inn* further down at Jalan Veteran 128, or just off the main road, there's the *Losmen Mepati*.

Places to Eat

There is a surprising number of interesting eating possibilities to be found along Jalan Veteran. They include the simple Chinese *Rumah Makan Terang* at No 369, which has food that is simple, but tasty. Right across the

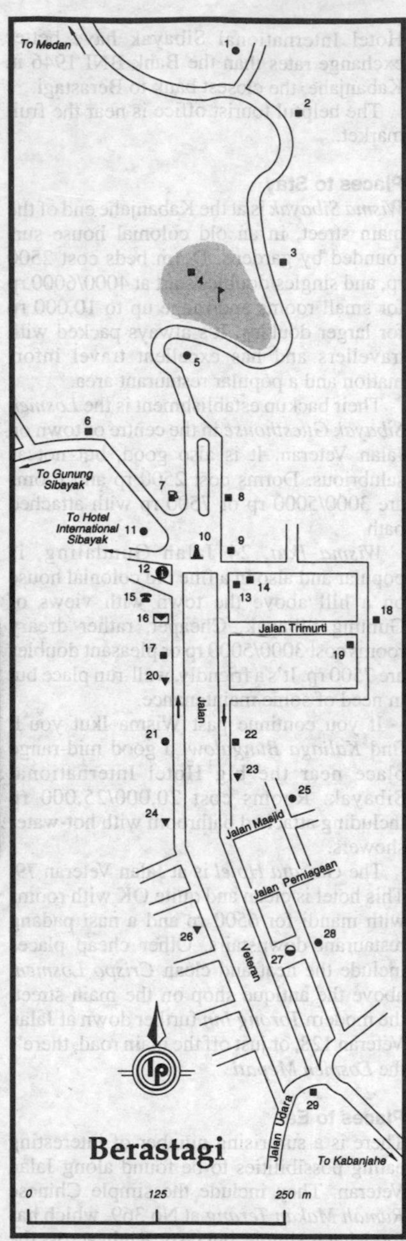

PLACES TO STAY

2 Rose Garden Hotel
3 Rudang Hotel
4 Hotel Bukit Kubu
6 Wisma Ikut
8 Crispo Losmen
9 Ginsata Hotel
13 Losmen Timur
14 Hotel Anda
17 Torong Inn
18 Losmen Trimurty
19 Losmen Merpati
22 Losmen Sibayak Guesthouse
29 Wisma Sibayak

PLACES TO EAT

20 Asia Restaurant
23 Rumah Makan Terang
24 Eropah Restaurant
26 Restaurant Ora et Labora

OTHER

1 Peceren Traditional Longhouse
5 Power Station
7 Petrol Station
10 Memorial
11 Fruit Market
12 Tourist Office
15 Telephone Office
16 Post Office
21 Public Health Centre
25 Ria Cinema
27 Bus & Opelet Station
28 Market

street from here is the equally bright and cheerful *Eropah Restaurant* at 48G.

The *Asia Restaurant*, which you can find at Nos 9 and 10, is a bigger, more expensive Chinese place that is quite popular with travellers.

There are several nasi padang places, including one at the *Ginsata Hotel*, and the food is deservedly popular at the *Wisma Sibayak*. You can buy your own food from the fruit and vegetable market that is off Jalan Veteran, or you can go and try the local market that's further up the road. At nighttime, try some of the delicious cakes made from rice flour, palm sugar and coconut steamed in bamboo cylinders; they are available from a *stall* that is located right outside the cinema.

Getting There & Away
Buses run regularly to and from Medan (1200 rp, 1½ hours).

Getting to or from Parapat by public bus is less straightforward. The first stage from Parapat is to take a regular Medan bus as far as Siantar (600 rp, one hour). From Siantar, it's a rough ride to Kabanjahe (1750 rp, 3½ hours) and then a short 12-km jaunt from Kabanjahe to Berastagi in a minibus, which costs 250 rp. This trip takes most of the day so start early. You can also reach Samosir via Haranggaol – see the Lake Toba Getting There & Away section for details.

The easy alternative is one of the tourist buses that pick you up at your hotel in Berastagi and drop you at the Parapat jetty three hours later. They cost 12,000 rp and depart every day except Monday at 3 pm. The bus stops at points of interest on the way and takes a spectacular route with fine views of Lake Toba.

The tourist buses also go to Bukit Lawang for 12,000 rp, or a public bus (4000 rp, five hours) takes the longer route, going almost into Medan.

AROUND BERASTAGI

From Berastagi, you can climb **Gunung Sibayak**, a 2094-metre-high volcano and have a soak in the hot springs on the way back. Wear good walking boots because the path is wet and slippery all year round. Also, start early as the walk takes all day. Bring food and water and a torch (flashlight), just in case it takes more than all day.

The guest books at Wisma Sibayak in Berastagi have a lot of useful information about this climb and various other walks in the area.

There is a great deal of interesting Karo Batak architecture in and around Berastagi. Included is the **Peceren traditional long-house** which is within walking distance of the town centre. Go to Kabanjahe and, from there, walk four km to the traditional village of **Lingga**. The design of these houses, with their horn-shaped roofs, has remained unchanged for centuries. You'll also find Karo Batak houses in nearby **Barusjahe**.

Kutacane and the **Leuser National Park** is good trekking and wildlife country. The park is beyond Kutacane, which is 106 km from Kabanjahe. First take a bus to Kabanjahe, then a bus takes six to seven hours (3200 rp) to Kutacane, where you take an opelet (200 rp) to the PHPA office in nearby Tanah Merah for park permits. Kutacane has a few cheap hotels.

Gunung Sinabung, a 2451-metre-high volcano, is also reached from Kabanjahe. Twenty-four km from Kabanjahe, just off the main road, are the impressive **Si Piso-Piso Falls**, with spectacular views of Lake Toba. The tourist buses stop here on the way to Toba and then continue on to **Rumah Bolon Museum Simalungan**, the Simalungan raja's house, now a museum (500 rp entry).

BUKIT LAWANG AREA

Eighty km from Medan, near Bukit Lawang, is an **orang-utan rehabilitation centre** where these extraordinary and fascinating creatures are retrained to survive in the wild after a period of captivity. Apart from the wildlife, the country around here is wild and enchanting with dense jungle, a clear, fast-flowing river and cascading waterfalls.

The number of visitors to the reserve is limited so avoid Sunday when there are lots of day-trippers from Medan. A permit to visit the reserve is issued at the PHPA office near the bus station and entry costs 4000 rp.

It's a 20-minute walk to the reserve along the Bohorok River, where you then cross by boat, which is free. Take your permit to the second PHPA office on the other side of the river. The trail in the reserve is easy to pick up and follow. The orang-utan feeding times are from 8 to 9 am and from 3 to 4 pm.

Bukit Lawang is turning into a travellers' centre with a host of cheap accommodation and organised activities. While many visitors only stay overnight (the tour groups only come for the morning or afternoon feeding sessions) Bukit Lawang is a beautiful spot to stay awhile and use as a base to explore the Gunung Leuser National Park.

The going rate for **jungle treks** is 20,000 rp per person for one day, or a three-day trek

INDONESIA

to Berastagi is 30,000 rp per day. A host of other treks are organised, and caving expeditions are also offered. Another activity in the area is **tube rafting** down the Bohorok River, but ask about the water level first – tubing can be dangerous when the river is swollen by rains.

Places to Stay & Eat

Bukit Lawang has a string of good, cheap losmen spread out along the river from the Visitor Centre to the river crossing for the rehabilitation centre. Rooms start at 2000 rp, but most are 3000 rp to 5000 rp, usually with attached mandi.

Wisma Leuser Sibayak, across the river from where the buses pull in, is the closest thing to a resort. It has dozens of rooms ranging from basic but decent singles/doubles for 3000/5000 rp up to the fanciest rooms in town for 15,000 rp. The big *restaurant* is popular with tour groups and even has slides into the river. On the same side of the river, quieter places nearby are the *Wisma Bukit Lawang Cottages*, *Wisma Bukit Lawang Indah* or *Yusman*.

The other losmen are on the same side of the river as the bus station, along the trail towards the rehabilitation centre. The first ones you come to are *Fido Dido* and the popular *Eden Homestay*, which has rooms upstairs for 2000/3000 rp and fancier rooms with attached bath for 7000 rp; best are the bungalows by the river for 4000 rp. If you keep walking past the campground, you'll come to a cluster of places leading up to the river crossing. It's a long haul from the bus station, but worth it for the quiet location if you intend to stay a few days. Here you'll find the *AM Guesthouse*, *Queen Emerald*, with basic rooms from 2000 rp, *Indrah Inn*, *Sinar Guesthouse*, *Back to Nature*, the very popular *Jungle Inn* and, right by the river crossing, the *Losmen Bohorok River*. The last three are probably the pick of this very similar bunch.

Getting There & Away

Buses run between Medan and Bukit Lawang (1300 rp, three hours) every half-hour until 5 pm. The local bus to Berastagi (9000 rp, five hours) leaves at 9 am but it goes via Medan. There are also tourist buses everyday at 7.30 am to Berastagi for 12,000 rp and they stop at attractions on the way, such as a crocodile farm, and rubber and palm oil plantations. The tourist buses continue on to Lake Toba every day except Monday for 20,000 rp.

MEDAN

Although it's the capital of Sumatra and a major entry or exit point for the area, for many travellers Medan conjures up images of belching becaks belting towards you and the pungent attack of their noxious fumes on the nostrils. It's actually not a bad city but apart from some good antique shops, a mosque, a museum, a palace, air-con malls and lots of people, it has little to offer beyond the remnants of a Dutch planter aristocracy.

Orientation

Finding your way around Medan is no problem, although it's sprawling and the traffic can be horrendous – a good map is essential. Street names can be confusing: one of the main city-centre arterial roads is Jalan Ahmad Yani, which changes to Jalan Pemuda and, finally, Jalan Brigjen Katamso as it stretches south-east from the city centre.

Information

Tourist Offices The Medan tourist office or Dinas Pariwisata Sumatera Utara (☎ 51 1101) is at Jalan Ahmad Yani 107 and has maps and information. It's open Monday to Thursday from 8 am to 2.30 pm, Friday from 8 am to noon and Saturday from 8 am to 2 pm.

There is also an information centre at the arrival terminal at Polonia international airport.

Money There are a number of banks in Medan, particularly along Jalan Pemuda, Jalan Ahmad Yani and Jalan Balaikota, which is really one continuous street. Medan has the best exchange rates in Sumatra, so it pays to change a reasonable amount of money here. If you are heading south, you won't find good exchange rates until you hit Bukittinggi.

Post & Telecommunications The GPO, a wonderful old Dutch building, is on the main square in the middle of town. To make international direct dial phone calls, you go to PT Indosat at the junction of Jalan Ngalengko and Jalan Thamrin.

Mosque & Palace

The Great Mosque, or Mesjid Raya, is on Jalan Sisingamangaraja while the Istana Maimoon, or Maimoon Palace, is nearby on Jalan Katamso. The large and lovely mosque dates from 1906 and the palace from 1888. They were both built by the Sultan of Deli.

Museums

Diagonally opposite the Danau Toba International Hotel, at Jalan Zainul Arifin 8, is the **Bukit Barisan Military Museum**. This museum features a collection of weapons and memorabilia from WW II, the War of Independence and the Sumatra rebellion of 1958.

The **Museum of North Sumatra**, Jalan H M Joni 51, north-east of the zoo, is open Tuesday to Sunday from 8 am to 5 pm and costs 200 rp. It's a good and quite extensive cultural and historical museum of North Sumatra. There is a good guide here who happily explains most of the items.

Other Attractions

The **Parisada Hindu Dharma Temple** is on Jalan Zainul Arifin, on the corner with Jalan Diponegoro. A number of cultural performances are put on at **Taman Budaya** on Jalan Perintis Kemerdekaan, near PT Indosat. The tourist office has a list of what's on.

The **amusement park** (Taman Ria) on Jalan Binjai is the site for the Medan Fair which is held each year around May to June. Medan's **zoo** (Taman Margasawata) is a bemo ride further along Jalan Katamso.

Belawan is the port for Medan through which most of the area's exports flow – it's 27 km east of the city. This is also where you catch the ferry to Penang.

Places to Stay

The *Losmen Irama*, in a little alley at Jalan Palang Merah 1125, is the best bet close to the centre. It's well kept and well set up for travellers – they even have a dial-home-direct phone for international calls. Dorm beds cost 3500 rp or doubles are 7000 rp to 10,000 rp, all with common bath.

Another good place is the *Penginapan Taipan Nabaru* (☎ 51 2155), at Jalan Hang Tuah 6 and right by the river, charging the same rates as the Irama. It's quiet and somewhat off the beaten track.

G's Koh I Noor (☎ 513953), 21 Jalan Mesjid, is an Indian restaurant, but a few dorm beds are available upstairs for 5000 rp. The manager speaks excellent English and this family-run homestay is conveniently located.

Only a few doors down from the Garuda office, the *Sigura Gura*, 2K Jalan Suprapto above the travel agent, is rather dull and the rooms are dark but it's reasonable value with rooms for 6000 rp.

The *Shahibah Guest House* (☎ 718528), 3 Jalan Armada, to the south off Jalan SM Raja, gets the most business because their touts meet the ferries from Penang. Dorm beds cost 5000 rp, rooms are 10,000 rp, or 15,000 rp and 20,000 rp with attached bath. It's well run and arranges coach transport, but it's no bargain and a long walk from the centre. The less crowded *Sarah's Guest House*, Jalan Pertama 10, is a nearby alternative. It's basic and similarly priced to the Shahibah.

Other cheapies in town include the *Hotel Melati* (☎ 51 6021), Jalan Amaluin 6, or the very basic *Hotel Waringin*, right across the road.

Jalan Sisingamangaraja has a string of middle and upper-range hotels where better rooms with attached bath start at around 20,000 rp. These include the *Hotel Sumatera* (☎ 24973) at No 21, the *Hotel Garuda* (☎ 20213) at No 18 and the *Dhaksina Hotel* (☎ 324561) at No 20.

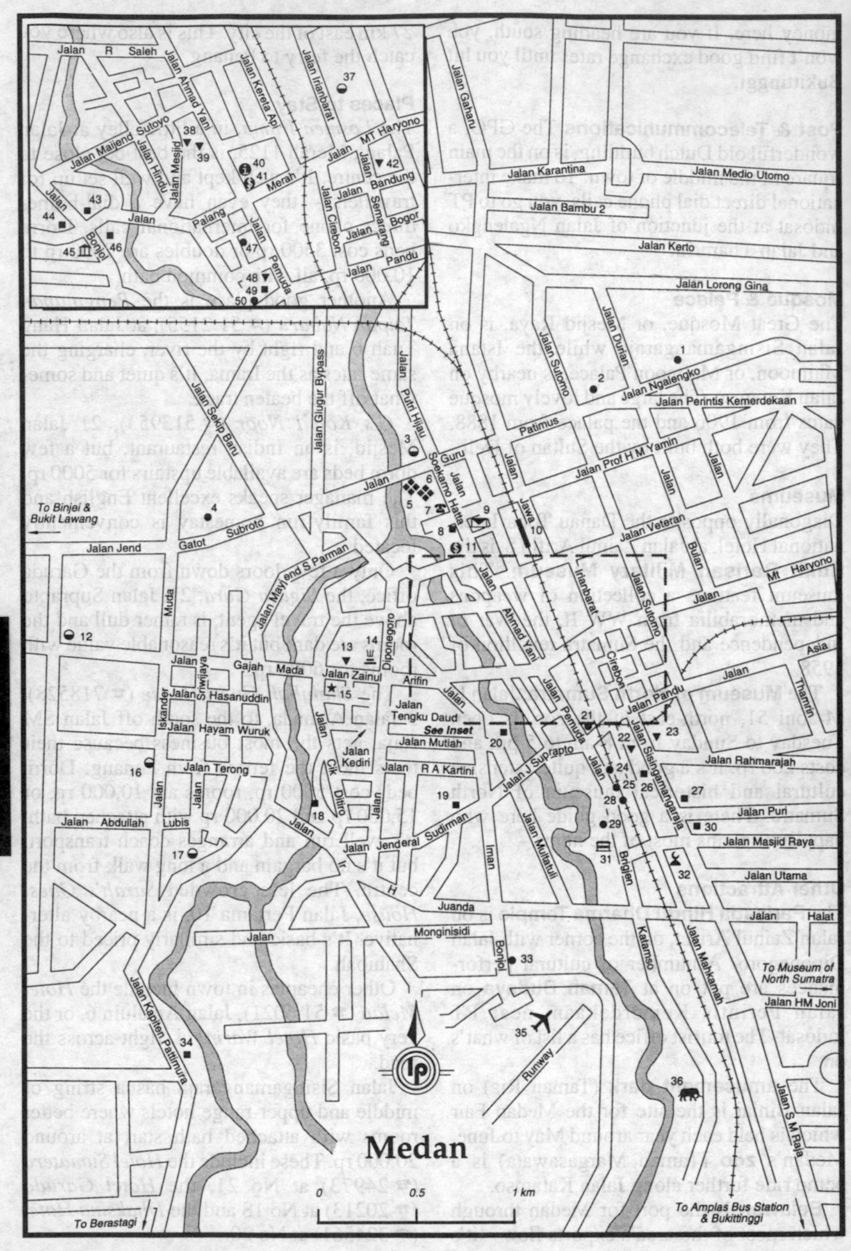
Medan
See Inset
Jalan R Saleh
Jalan Ahmad Yani
Jalan Kereta Api
Jalan Irianbarat
Jalan Majiend Sutoyo
Jalan Hindu
Jalan Mesjid
Jalan MT Haryono
Jalan Bandung
Jalan Merah
Jalan Cirebon
Jalan Semarang
Jalan Bogor
Jalan Palang
Jalan Pemuda
Jalan Pandu
Jalan Bonjol
Jalan Gahanu
Jalan Karantina
Jalan Medio Utomo
Jalan Bambu 2
Jalan Kerto
Jalan Lorong Gina
Jalan Sutomo
Jalan Durian
Jalan Ngalengko
Jalan Perintis Kemerdekaan
Patimus
Jalan Prof H M Yamin
Jalan Jawa
Jalan Veteran
Jalan Putri Hijau
Jalan Glugur Bypass
Jalan Sekip Baru
Jalan Guru
Soekarno Hatta
To Binjei &
Bukit Lawang
Jalan Gatot Subroto
Jalan Jend
Jalan Mayjend S Parman
Jalan Bulan
MT Haryono
Irianbarat
Jalan Asia
Jalan Thamrin
Jalan Muda
Jalan Sriwijaya
Jalan Iskander
Jalan Gajah Mada
Jalan Zainul Arifin
Diponegoro
Jalan Hasanuddin
Jalan Hayam Wuruk
Jalan Terong
Jalan Tengku Daud
Jalan Mutiah
R A Kartini
Jalan Kediri
Jalan Cik Ditiro
Jalan Abdullah Lubis
Jalan Jenderal Sudirman
Jalan Imam Bonjol
Jalan J Suprapto
Jalan Multatuli
Jalan Sisingamangaraja
Jalan Rahmarajah
Jalan Puri
Jalan Masjid Raya
Jalan Utama
Jalan Halat
Brigjen Katamso
Jalan Mahkamah
Juanda
Monginisidi
To Museum of
North Sumatra
Jalan HM Joni
Runway
Jalan Kapiten Pattimura
Jalan S M Raja
To Amplas Bus Station
& Bukittinggi
To Berastagi
0
0.5
1 km

PLACES TO STAY

- 8 Hotel Dharma Deli & Garuda
- 18 Penginapan Taipan Nabaru
- 19 Polonia Hotel & Singapore Airlines
- 20 Hotel Tiara Medan & Garuda
- 26 Hotel Dhaksina & Hotel Garuda Plaza
- 27 Hotel Sumatera
- 30 Hotel Garuda
- 34 Wisma Sibayak
- 43 Losmen Irama
- 44 Hotel Dirga Surya
- 46 Danau Toba International Hotel & MAS
- 49 Sigura Gura

PLACES TO EAT

- 13 Westin Fried Chicken
- 22 Rumah Makan Gembira
- 23 Rumah Makan Famili
- 38 G's Koh I Noor Restaurant
- 39 Tip Top Restaurant
- 42 Chinese Foodstalls
- 48 France Modern Bakery

OTHER

- 1 PT Indosat
- 2 Taman Budaya
- 3 Bus to Belawan
- 4 Medan Fair
- 5 Sinar Plaza
- 6 Deli Plaza Shopping Centre
- 7 Telkom
- 9 Post Office
- 10 Railway Station
- 11 Bank Negara Indonesia
- 12 Kurnia Bus
- 14 Parisada Hindu Dharma Temple & Medan Bakers
- 15 Police Office
- 16 Bus Station for Berastagi
- 17 Sei Wempa & Buses to Binjei
- 21 Garuda Office
- 24 Selasa Ekspres Office
- 25 Pacto
- 28 Merpati Office, Eka Sukma Wisata Tour & Mandala Office
- 29 Inda Taxi
- 31 Istana Maimoon
- 32 Mesjid Raya
- 33 SMAC
- 35 Polonia International Airport
- 36 Medan Zoo
- 37 Old Central Bus Station
- 40 Tourist Office
- 41 Bank Dagang Negara
- 45 Bukit Barisan Military Museum
- 47 Pelni Office
- 50 Garuda Office

Places to Eat

One of Medan's saving graces is Jalan Semarang, which in the evening becomes a traffic jam of Chinese food. During the daytime, it's just a dirty back alley but come nightfall *foodstalls* set up along the street across Jalan Bogor between Jalan Pandu and Jalan Bandung. Jalan Semarang is the third block beyond the railway line.

Kampung Keling on Jalan Zainul Arifin is an area with lots of small gangs and numerous *warungs* specialising in different kinds of food – Chinese, Indian, Indonesian and European.

The *Tip Top Restaurant* at Jalan Ahmad Yani 92 has a large veranda for people-watching, consistently good food and they also do breakfasts, baked goods and ice cream. A few doors down at No 98 is *Lyn's Cafe & Restaurant*, a gathering place for Medan businesspeople and expats. It's dim and cool, and the menu is predominantly Western. They actually ask how you like your steak done.

A good and cheap Indian restaurant is *G's Koh I Noor* at Jalan Mesjid 21. It is a family-run place with good curries and biriyanis. They also provide travel information.

There are several Padang *restaurants* near the junction of Jalan Sisingamangaraja and Jalan Pandu. Or try the *Rumah Makan Famili* at Jalan Sisingamangaraja 21B, or the *Rumah Makan Gembira* by the railway line.

There are all sorts of eating possibilities in the big *Deli Plaza* shopping centre on the corner of Jalan Balaikota and Jalan Getah, including bakeries and Western fast food.

Things to Buy

The city has a number of interesting arts and crafts shops, particularly along Jalan Ahmad Yani. Try Toko Asli at No 62, Toko Rufino at No 64, and Toko Bali Arts at No 68. There is a good selection of antique weaving, Dutch pottery, Batak carvings and other interesting pieces in all of these shops.

Getting There & Away

Medan is the major travel centre of Sumatra and an important overseas arrival or departure point.

Air Internationally, you can fly from Medan to Penang (Malaysia), Singapore or Kuala Lumpur. See the Sumatra Getting There &

Away section for details. Medan is also a major domestic air-travel centre with flights by Garuda, Mandala and Merpati.

Bus & Taxi Medan is the major crossroads for bus travel in north Sumatra. Parapat is the main destination from Medan; buses depart very regularly, take four hours or more and cost 3500 rp. The buses depart from the Amplas bus station in South Medan on Jalan Pertahanan, off Jalan S M Raja. Buses from Amplas depart to all destinations south and east, including Bukittinggi, Padang, Pekanbaru and Jakarta.

Pinang Baris is the other main station, 10 km west of the centre, with buses to the north and west, including Bukit Lawang (1300 rp), Berastagi (1200 rp) and Banda Aceh (22,000 rp air-con). Kurnia also have buses to Aceh.

Shahibah Guest House arranges direct minibuses to Bukit Lawang (10,000 rp), Berastagi (10,000 rp) and Parapat (15,000 rp), if there is enough demand. It's convenient but not cheap.

Medan has a number of long-distance taxi operators, including Inda Taxi (☎ 516615), Jalan Brigjen Katamso 60. Taxis take five people and operate on a share basis, but demand is light to the tourist spots, except to Parapat on the weekends. A whole taxi costs 60,000 rp to Parapat, to Berastagi it's 50,000 rp and they also run to Sibolga and Pekanbaru.

Boat The high-speed ferries to Penang can be booked at the agents on Jalan Brigjen Katamso. Selasa Ekspres (☎ 514888), Jalan Brigjen Katamso 35C, has a service leaving on Wednesday, Friday and Sunday at 1 pm. The fare for the five-hour journey is 78,500 rp, including the bus fare to Belawan. They also handle the ferries to Lumut (78,500 rp, four hours), which depart on Tuesday, Thursday and Saturday at 2 pm.

Express Bahagia (☎ 720954), Jalan Sisingamangaraja 92A, has ferries to Penang on Tuesday, Friday and Sunday at 11 am, and Wednesday at 1.30 pm. Tickets can also be bought at Pacto (☎ 510081), Jalan Brigjen Katamso 35G, which also sells tickets for the Belawan-Port Kelang ferries which leave on Monday and Wednesday at 10 am and cost 87,000 rp.

Pelni ships connect Medan (ie Belawan) with Jakarta and on to other ports in Indonesia. The Pelni office in Medan is at Jalan Sugiono, a block back from Jalan Pemuda and close to the tourist office and Garuda office.

Getting Around

Airport taxis charge 5000 rp from the airport, and are reluctant to use their meters.

Belawan Harbour (for the ferries to Malaysia or Pelni boats) is 27 km north of Medan. The ferries provide buses from Medan, otherwise take an opelet or Damri Patas bus to Belawan and then take an opelet for the last 1½ km to the harbour.

There are plenty of opelets or angkot travelling around town and to the bus stations for a standard 250 rp, but they often charge 500 rp if you have a large backpack.

Medan also has plenty of motorised and human-powered becaks. Just as inexpensive (often much more inexpensive for foreigners) are the metered taxis that ply the streets in large numbers.

BANDA ACEH

The capital of Aceh province, Banda Aceh is right at the northern tip of Sumatra. Fiercely independent and devoutly Islamic, Aceh was once a powerful state in its own right and later held out against the Dutch longer than almost anywhere else in the archipelago. In recognition of this, it is now designated as a Special Territory by the Indonesian government, which gives it the freedom to pursue its own religious, cultural and educational policies.

Still the most staunchly Muslim part of the country, Aceh is run under Islamic law, but despite their rigid religious conservatism, the Acehnese are friendly and helpful people.

You can make trips from Banda Aceh to the seaside at Lhok Nga, 12 km from the city, or take a ferry to Sabang, on Pulau We off the coast.

INDONESIA

Orientation & Information

The centre of town is marked by an imposing five-domed mosque. Across the Krueng Aceh River is Jalan Achmad Yani, where most of the hotels are.

The tourist office (☎ 21377) is on Jalan T Nyak Arief 92. The Bank Negara Indonesia is on Jalan Merduati and the post office on Jalan Kuta Alam, one block from Simpang Tiga.

Mosque

With its stark white walls and licorice-black domes, the stunning Mesjid Raya Baiturrahman is like an oasis in the dust and fumes of central Banda Aceh. Ask the keeper to let you climb the staircase to one of the minarets so you can get a good view over the city.

Gunongan

For a contrast in architectural styles, go and see Gunongan on Jalan Teuku Umar, near the clocktower. This 'stately pleasure dome' was apparently built for the wife of a 17th-century sultan, a Malayan princess, as a private playground and bathing place.

The building itself is a series of frosty peaks with narrow stairways and a walkway leading to hummocks which are supposed to represent the hills of her native land so she could take an evening stroll – a liberty not permitted in Banda Aceh in that era.

Directly across from the Gunongan is a low **vaulted-gate** in the traditional Pintu Aceh style, which gave access to the sultan's palace and was supposed to have been used by royalty only. Nearby is the **cemetery** for more than 2000 Dutch soldiers who fell in battle against the Acehnese. The entrance is about 250 metres from the clocktower on the road to Uleh-leh.

Museum

Banda Aceh has a large museum at Jalan Alauddin Mahmudsyah 12 which exhibits weapons, household furnishings, ceremonial costumes, everyday clothing, gold jewellery and books.

In the same compound is the **Rumah Aceh**, a fine example of traditional architecture, which is built without nails and held together with cord and pegs. It contains more Acehnese artefacts and war memorabilia. In front of the Rumah Aceh is a large cast-iron **bell**, which was given to the Acehnese by a Chinese emperor in the 1st century AD.

Places to Stay

Accommodation in Banda Aceh is relatively expensive and not that good. The decent *Losmen International* on Jalan Achmad Yani, opposite the night market, has small rooms for 5000 rp and larger rooms with mandi for 7500 rp. Ask for one of the quieter rooms at the rear. There are a number of other hotels along this road including the *Hotel Medan* at No 9, with rooms with mandi from 15,000 rp, or the similarly priced *Wisma Parapat* at No 11.

On nearby Jalan Khairil Anwar are the *Losmen Palembang* at No 8 and the *Losmen Aceh Barat*, with rooms in the 8000 to 15,000 rp range. Other places to try include the clean *Wisma Lading* at Jalan Cut Meutia 9 with accommodation from 5000 to 10,000 rp.

The colonial *Losmen Aceh*, opposite the mosque on Jalan Muhammed Jam, has basic rooms from 6000 rp, or 17,500 rp with private bath and air-con. Near the market, at Jalan Muhammed Jam 1, is the fairly dreary *Losmen Yusri*.

Places to Eat

Jalan Ahmad Yani is a good place to look for food. There are many moderately priced Padang-style places along this street, and along nearby Jalan Cut Nyak Dhien and Jalan Panglima. For seafood and kindergarten decor, try the *Restoran Happy* at Jalan Ahmad Yani 74-76. At present they have karaoke so it is very noisy in the evenings. Close by is *Restoran Tropicana* at Nos 90-92. *Aroma* at Jalan Cut Nyak Dien has good Chinese food.

The night market at the corner of Jalan Ahmad Yani and Jalan Kharil Anwar is a good place for cheap food, and has a lively atmosphere.

Like other Sumatran cities there are also

many bakeries around the middle of town. Try *Satyva Modern Bakery* at Kharil Anwar 3, *Toko Muara* at Jalan K H A Dahlan 17 and *Toko Setia Baru* across from the Pasar Setui on Jalan Teuku Umar.

Getting There & Away

Air Merpati flies between Medan and Banda Aceh (108,000 rp, one hour).

Bus If the road is dry, the trip from Medan takes 12 to 14 hours by bus. Fares vary around 22,000 rp – try Kurnia. The road is in good condition and takes you through numerous villages, mountains, rice fields and rolling country. The Setui bus terminal, on Jalan Teuku Umar, is where buses depart for Medan, Meulaboh or Tapaktuan.

You can get smaller bemos from Jalan Dipenogoro near the big mosque for places like Ulee Lheu, Pelabuhan Malahayati and Lhok Nga.

PULAU WE

This small island north of Banda Aceh has lots of attractive, palm-fringed beaches and very good snorkelling nearby, especially at Pulau Rubiah, one hour away. Stingray Dive Centre, at the Losmen Pulau Jaya, rents out diving and snorkelling equipment and can organise transport. Remember that June to October is the wet season and not the best time to go.

Places to Stay

Sabang, the main town, has a number of losmen. *Losmen Pulau Jaya* at Jalan Teuku Umar 17 has basic, good clean rooms from 5000 rp, 10,000 rp including mandi and 15,000 rp with air-con. They have plenty of information about hiking as well as snorkelling around the island. It is possible to stay at their deserted beach, Tupin Gapang, (18 km from Sabang) for 5000 rp plus meals.

Losmen Irma is on the same street at No 3 and it has rooms at similar prices. They also have bungalows on two different beaches, Iboih and Balik Gunung (closed June to October because of high winds), for 2000 rp per person.

Holiday Losmen is tucked away in a side lane down Jalan Perdagangan so it is quieter than the above two but also more expensive with rooms at 6000/10,000 rp and air-con rooms for 25,000 rp. Mr Amin, a regular in the hotel, is a guide who can also organise hiking, snorkelling and diving trips.

Two other cheap losmen are *Raja Wali* and *Sabang Merauke*.

Places to Eat

There are numerous coffee places in Sabang but one of the best is *Rilzky Restaurant* on Jalan Teuku Umar and Perkapalan. It has good seafood, Chinese and Indonesian meals. *Café Ban* has a traveller's type of menu at higher prices.

Getting There & Away

Boats leave every afternoon from the old Banda Aceh port of Pelabuhan Malahayati at Kreung Raya and arrive at Sabang about two hours later. The port is 35 km from the centre of Banda Aceh (catch a bemo for 1200 rp for a 45-minute trip from Jalan Diponegoro) and the cost over to the island is 3400 rp or 4500 rp in 1st class, one way.

Getting Around

Sabang town is 12 km from the harbour – you can get there by opelet (1000 rp) or taxi. The taxi station is in front of Toko Sahabar on Jalan Perdagangan. Ask there about renting motorbikes and boats.

Riau Archipelago

Immediately south of Singapore are the islands of the Riau Archipelago. There are hundreds of islands but only a few of them are inhabited. Much of the Riau is still explorer territory, unexploited and unspoilt, but it's also one of the richest areas in Indonesia due to its oil and tin exports. Islands which are closest to Singapore are also becoming economic development zones and weekend retreats for residents of that increasingly wealthy city-state.

Batam and Bintan are the two major islands close to Singapore, and the main stepping stones to other parts of Indonesia. You do not need a visa to enter or leave Indonesia through these ports. Furthermore, you do not have to show an onward or return ticket on entry. If they ask for one, you could always buy a ferry ticket back to Singapore for less than US$10. There are very frequent ferry services to Batam from Singapore but less frequent services to Bintan. From Batam, boats go to Pekanbaru and other Sumatran mainland destinations (see the Sumatra Getting There & Away section for more details). There are also regular flights to Jakarta and other parts of Indonesia.

BATAM

Batam is being heavily developed to become a virtual industrial suburb of Singapore. Already, there are resorts on the north coast and there will soon be factories, warehouses and even a huge reservoir to supply water to the nearby city-state. Meanwhile, there's a distinct frontier town atmosphere to the place, with high prices, ugly construction sites and no reason to pause longer than you have to.

Sekupang is the arrival port and the place to get boats to other parts of Sumatra. After you clear immigration, there are counters for money exchange, taxis and hotels, but most travellers catch another boat straight out.

Nagoya, the main town, is a boom town, complete with shopping centres, bars and prostitutes that are there to appeal mostly to Singaporean visitors. Nagoya's port area is Batu Ampar. **Kabil** is the tiny port from where boats cross to Tanjung Uban and Tanjung Pinang on Bintan. **Batu Besar** is a small fishing village on the east coast from which the airport takes its name. **Nongsa** is the centre for the Singapore beach-resort hotels on the north-eastern corner of the island.

Information

Singapore dollars are easier to spend than Indonesian rupiah on Batam. Change money at the Sekupang ferry building or in Nagoya.

Places to Stay

There is no pressing reason to stay on Batam but if you must Nagoya has a variety of overpriced places.

About a km out of town at Blok C, Jalan Teuku Umar, there's a line-up of utterly rock-bottom and extremely basic losmen or penginapan. The *Minang Jaya* (☎ 457964) is the best of a bad bunch with bare, partitioned singles for 15,000 rp, and although they may bargain it's still absurdly expensive compared to almost anywhere else in Indonesia.

Wisma Star International (☎ 457372), Jalan Komplek Sriwijaya Abadi 9/10A, is a better choice close to the town centre. It's no bargain but has decent rooms from 20,000 rp. In the town centre, there are plenty of mid-range hotels charging around S$50 to S$75 per room. These include the *Holiday Hotel* (☎ 458616), Jalan Imam Bonjol, the bigger *Batam Jaya Hotel* (☎ 458707) on Jalan Raja Ali Haji, with a few dismal economy rooms for S$30, and the better *Horisona Hotel* (☎ 457111) at Blok E, Kompleks Lumbung Rezeki. The pick of the bunch is probably the pleasant *Bukit Nagoya Hotel* (☎ 452871) at Jalan Sultan Abdul Rahman 1, with rooms from S$40.

The beach resorts around Nongsa are mainly for visitors from Singapore. The fancy *Batam View* and *Turi Beach Resort* both cost over US$100 a night for a double. The *Nongsa Beach Cottages* are plain, cost from S$80 and include breakfast.

Places to Eat

The best eating in Nagoya is found at the night *foodstalls* which are set up along Jalan Raja Ali Haji or at the big, raucous and noisy *Pujasera Nagoya* food centre. There are some good nasi padang places like *Mak Ateh Nasi Padang*.

There are a number of waterfront seafood places dotted around the coast of the island, particularly around the Singapore resorts at Nongsa. They include *Setia Budi* and *Sederhana* near the Nongsa Beach Cottages and *Selera Wisata* at Batu Besar.

INDONESIA

Getting There & Away

Merpati and Sempati have flights to a variety of cities in Sumatra, Java and Kalimantan including Pekanbaru (78,000 rp), Palembang (112,000 rp), Padang (114,000), Medan (169,000 rp), Pontianak (148,000 rp) and Jakarta (204,000 rp).

The main reason most travellers come to Batam is to catch a boat to Pekanbaru from Sekupang. The *Dumai Express* is one of the best services, departing at 9.30 am. Most departures to Pekanbaru or Selat Panjang depart before noon. See the Sumatra Getting There & Away section for full details of this route. From Batam boats also go to Karimun (13,000 rp), Kundur (15,000 rp), Tembilahan (40,000 rp), Kuala Tungkal for Jambi (50,000 rp) and Dumai (45,000 rp).

Ferries also go from the tiny port of Kabil, on Batam's south-eastern coast, to Tanjung Pinang on Bintan Island. An assortment of other boats also shuttle across, taking 30 minutes for the fastest boats (12,500 rp), one hour for the medium-speed boats (10,000 rp) and three to four hours for the slow boats (6000 rp). Ferries also operate on the shorter route between Kabil and Tanjung Uban, on Bintan's north-western coast. Operated by the slow boats, this trip takes 45 minutes and costs just 3000 rp. From Tanjung Uban, there's a bus to Tanjung Pinang, taking two hours and costing 3000 rp.

To/From Singapore Frequent ferries go between Singapore's World Trade Centre and Sekupang (S$16, 25 minutes) until around 7 pm. A few ferries also go to Batu Ampar for S$12 – these are handy for Nagoya, but not for boat connections to other parts of Sumatra.

Getting Around

There is a hard-to-find bus service from Sekupang to Nagoya for 600 rp but otherwise the only transport around Batam is taxi and you have to bargain hard. Between Sekupang and Nagoya or between Nagoya and Kabil, you should be able to get a share taxi at around 2000 rp per person, otherwise pay 5000 rp for the whole taxi. From Nagoya to the airport should be a bit less. Don't believe cards showing 'official' fares.

BINTAN

Bintan is larger than Batam and much more interesting. Singaporean development is, at present, on a much lower key on Bintan but a mega-resort is on the drawing boards for the north coast.

For visitors, the island has three areas of interest – the town of Tanjung Pinang and nearby Penyenget Island; the relatively untouched beaches along the east coast; and Tanjung Pinang's useful role as a departure point for ships bound to other parts of the country.

Tanjung Pinang

Tanjung Pinang is the biggest town in the Riau Archipelago and there is a constant stream of boats arriving and departing. These vary from large freighters to tiny sampans. An old and quite picturesque wooden section of the town juts out over the sea on stilts but there are also some lush parks and gardens on dry land.

The town is famed for its two red-light villages – Batu Duabelas and Batu Enambelas – no prizes for guessing that they are respectively 12 *(duabelas)* km and 16 *(enambelas)* km out of town.

Information PT Info Travel, one of the shipping agents at the main wharf, is used to dealing with visitors and has all the shipping information. They also rent motorbikes. The post office is on Jalan Merdeka, near the harbour.

Tanjung Pinang is not a good place to change money; the banks are either choosey about what currencies they accept or offer bad rates.

Tanjung Pinang has a reputation for shady deals and theft so take notice of the *'awas copet'* ('beware of pickpockets') signs.

Things to See The piers and market are colourful places to explore. There is a **Chinese temple** right in town. Not far from the city centre is the small **Riau Kandil**

Museum with its curious collection of old bits and pieces, some dating from the Riau Kingdom.

Across the river from the town is the village of **Senggarang**. Walk up the pier and turn left to a building totally overgrown by a banyan tree and now used as a Chinese temple. Continue half a km along the waterfront to a big square fronting three side-by-side Chinese temples.

It's only a short sampan ride to Senggarang from Tanjung Pinang but is much further by road. A sampan can also take you up the **Snake River** through the mangroves to another Chinese **temple** with graphically gory murals on the trials and tortures of hell.

Places to Stay At the end of Lorong Bintan II, which runs off Jalan Bintan in the centre of town, is the very popular *Bong's Homestay* at No 20. A bed costs 3000 rp, includes breakfast, and the friendly Mr and Mrs Bong make this a great place to stay. Next door, at No 22, *Johnny's Homestay* is a good overflow.

The *Hotel Surya* (☎ 21811/293) on Jalan Bintan is a good average losmen with rooms from 12,000 rp. Around the corner on Jalan Yusuf Khahar, the *Penginapan Sondang* is very bare, basic and similarly priced.

There's a string of mid-range places on Jalan Yusuf Khahar including the simple but modern *Sampurna Inn* where rooms cost from 15,000 rp with fan or from 25,000 to 45,000 rp with air-con.

Places to Eat Tanjung Pinang has a superb *night market* with a tantalising array of foodstalls offering delicious food at bargain prices. It sets up in the bus and taxi station on Jalan Teuku Umar. More night-time *foodstalls* can be found at the Jalan Pos and Lorong Merdeka intersection.

During the day, there are several pleasant cafes with outdoor eating areas in front of the stadium (Kaca Puri) on Jalan Teuku Umar. Try *Flipper* or *Sunkist*.

Penyenget Island

Tiny Penyenget Island is in the harbour across from Tanjung Pinang. It was once capital of the kingdom and the whole place is steeped in history. After 1721, the island played an important political and cultural role in the history of the Riau as one of the two seats of government.

It is believed to have been given to Sultan Raja Riau-Lingga VI in 1805 by his brother-in-law Sultan Mahmud Lingga-Riau IV as a wedding present. The place is littered with reminders of its past and there are ruins and graveyards wherever you walk.

On arrival, take the road to the right and head north-east – most of the kampungs are along the shoreline but the ruins of the **old palace** of Raja Ali and the **tombs and graveyards** of Raja Jaafar and Raja Ali are slightly further inland. The sulphur-coloured **mosque** has a historic library and is also worth seeing.

Frequent boats go from Bintan's main pier for 500 rp per person. There's a 500 rp entry charge on weekends. You won't be allowed into the mosque if you're wearing shorts or a short skirt.

Beaches

Bintan's beaches are relatively untouched apart from the inevitable overlay of bottles and other drift-plastic. There's a fine 30-km-long beach strip along the east coast, although getting there can be a problem.

Pantai Trikora is the main east-coast beach with some accommodation. Snorkelling is fine most of the year except during the November to March monsoon period.

Off the north-eastern end of the island, a sunken 1754 Dutch VOC (Vereenigde Oost-Indische Compagnie) vessel was, to the considerable consternation of the Indonesian authorities, discovered and salvaged in the mid-80s by a team of scuba divers.

The main beach stretch is 40 to 50 km from Tanjung Pinang. Getting there costs 4000 rp per person by the share taxis, which mainly operate in the morning.

Places to Stay & Eat *Yasin's Guest House*, at the Km 46 marker, has simple wooden huts with a bed, mosquito nets, veranda and not much else. It's situated on a beach cum trash heap and costs 15,000 rp per day including three meals. At the Km 38 marker, the flashier *Trikora Country Club* at Pantai Trikora has singles from S$50 to S$70 and doubles from S$60 to S$80.

Getting There & Away

Bintan is usually a stopover while travelling by boat between Singapore and Jakarta. Two ferries per day operate between Singapore and Bintan (S$51, two hours). Ferries also go every day to Pasir Panjang, near Johor Bahru in Malaysia, for 50,000 rp.

Pelni's KM *Rinjani* and KM *Umsini* call in every two weeks on their way between Jakarta and Dumai in Sumatra. Sailings are from Kijang, the port at the south-eastern corner of the island. Pelni schedules are constantly changing, so check departures in Singapore before arrival to avoid a long wait on Bintan. In Singapore, schedule information is available from Pelni agents (☎ 272 6811 in Singapore) or the Indonesian Tourist Promotion Office (☎ 534 2837), 15-07 Ocean Building, 10 Collyer Quay. It costs 38,000 rp in economy up to 143,000 rp in 1st class from Bintan to Jakarta.

A new service to Jakarta on the MV *Bintan Permata* leaves Tanjung Pinang every Tuesday and Friday at 8 am, arriving 6 am the following day. It costs 91,500 rp in economy and 111,500 rp in 1st class. The ship leaves Jakarta on Wednesday and Saturday. Bookings can be made through Primkopal, 18 Jalan Samudra, Tanjung Pinang.

It is also possible to go from Tanjung Pinang to Pekanbaru in Sumatra, though most boats go from Batam – see the Sumatra Getting There & Away section.

Three ferries go to Dabo on Singkep Island – fares range from 16,000 rp (10 hours) to 25,000 rp (four hours). Ferries also operate every day to Tanjung Balai on Karimun (17,000 rp), and to Daik on Lingga Island (12,500 rp).

SINGKEP

Well to the south of Tanjung Pinang, Singkep is the third-largest island in the archipelago. It has a big Chinese population and is the headquarters of the Riau Tin and Timah mining companies. Few outsiders visit here, but it's fairly easy to get to and has most of the services of a much larger place.

Dabo, the main town, is shaded by lush trees and gardens and is clustered around a central park. Nearby, and on the road to Sungeibuluh, a large **mosque** dominates the skyline. **Batu Bedua**, not far out of town, is a white-sand beach fringed with palms. It's a good place to spend a relaxing few hours; there are a couple of others nearby called **Sergang** and **Jago**. You get fine views if you walk to the top of the hill just past the residential district of Bukit Asem.

The fish and vegetable markets down near the harbour are interesting and Jalan Pasar Lamar is a good browsing and shopping area.

Information

Bank Dagang Negara changes money at quite good rates. The post office is on Jalan Pahlawan and there is also an overseas telephone office about three km out of town on the road to Sungeibuluh.

Places to Stay & Eat

Wisma Sri Indah on Jalan Perusahaan has rooms from 15,000 rp. It's spotlessly clean and has a comfortable sitting-room. Similar places are the *Wisma Gapura Singkep*, on the opposite side of the street and a bit north, and *Wisma Sederhana*. The *Wisma Pemda* is the top place in town.

Eat at the *markets* behind Wisma Sri Indah or try any of the *warungs* on Jalan Pasar Lama and Jalan Merdeka. Foodstalls and warungs pop up all over the place at night.

Getting There & Away

The boat trip from Tanjung Pinang crosses the equator and passes several shimmering islands on the way. The boat docks at Sunggai Buluh, from where buses go to Dabo. Ferries also go to Daik on Pulau Lingga and once a week to Jambi.

Nusa Tenggara

Nusa Tenggara refers to the string of islands which starts to the east of Bali and ends with Timor. Some of the most spectacular attractions of Indonesia can be found in Nusa Tenggara – Mt Rinjani on Lombok, the dragons of Komodo, the immense stone tombs of Sumba and the coloured volcanic lakes of Keli Mutu on Flores.

Whilst a steady stream of people pass through the islands, there's nothing like the tourist hordes you find in Bali or Java. In one way, this is an advantage because the reaction of the local people is generally more natural, but it does create one headache – you can be a constant centre of attraction.

If you don't mind this, then travelling in Nusa Tenggara is fairly easy-going. People are very friendly, and there's been a great deal of improvement in recent years – there are more surfaced roads, losmen, flights, ferries and regular road transport. Just stick to the main routes, avoid travel in the wet season when some of the roads turn to slush, and you shouldn't have any trouble.

You need at least a month to get a reasonable look around the whole chain.

Money & Costs

Nusa Tenggara's islands are marginally more expensive for food, accommodation and transport than Bali and Java, but by any standards, costs are still low. It's probably wise to allow for a couple of flights; one for getting back to Bali or Java, rather than backtracking all the way through the islands by road and ferry, and another if you want to go to Timor and/or Sumba.

Nusa Tenggara has fewer places to change money than in Bali and Java but there will generally be at least one bank in each of the main towns that will change foreign cash and travellers' cheques. Stick to the major brands of travellers' cheques – US$ are preferable, but Australian dollars, Deutsche marks, pounds sterling and Netherlands florin are OK.

Getting There & Away

Denpasar in Bali is the usual jumping-off point for the islands of Nusa Tenggara – from Denpasar you can go by ferry, hydrofoil or plane across to Lombok, or fly to one of the other islands. You can also fly directly to some destinations in Nusa Tenggara from Java or Sulawesi. Flights from Nusa Tenggara generally terminate in Surabaya (Java) or Bali, but you can usually make same-day connections on to other parts of Indonesia.

Merpati have a twice-weekly connection between Kupang in Timor and Darwin in Australia's Northern Territory. This is an excellent way to travel to Indonesia from Australia. You can then island-hop through Nusa Tenggara to Bali without having to backtrack, as you would on a return trip into the islands from Bali.

The Pelni ship KM *Kelimutu* comes through the islands every two weeks and there are regular ferries between all the islands. Sometimes, the Bugis Makassar schooners find their way right down into Nusa Tenggara – so if you want a really different way to get to Sulawesi...!

Getting Around

Most of the islands are now connected by regular ships and ferries, thus making a loop through the islands from Bali and back fairly easy. You can even charter sailing boats or small motor boats for short hops at fairly reasonable prices, for example to Komodo from Labuhanbajo on the west coast of Flores.

Most of the flights in this group of islands are handled by Merpati, although Sempati and Bouraq are also operating a few services in the area.

Boats and planes are the means of getting from island to island but on the islands you usually travel by bus. There are now many more surfaced roads and, consequently, bus travel has become much more reliable and comfortable.

Nevertheless, buses are not as regular and reliable as you might wish, and a motorbike would probably be the ideal way to explore Nusa Tenggara. Except for Lombok, the act of hiring a motorbike is not the easiest thing

to do in Nusa Tenggara, so this is really only an option for people who have their own transport. The situation is the same for bicycles.

Lombok

Lombok has uncrowded beaches, a spectacular volcano, tranquil countryside and one main urban area. The people are mostly Muslim, though some are Balinese Hindu and a few follow the indigenous Wektu Telu religion. Balinese princes ruled Lombok from the mid-1700s until the 1890s when the Dutch took control.

Getting There & Away

Air There are frequent connections between Lombok and nearby islands. Merpati have direct flights to Bima (86,000 rp), Sumbawa Besar (50,000 rp), Denpasar (43,000 rp) and Surabaya (93,000 rp), with connections to other parts of Indonesia.

Bus Buses go directly from Sweta terminal to Sumbawa destinations including Sumbawa Besar (9000 rp, 10,000 rp with air-con) and Bima (18,000 rp, 22,000 rp with air-con). Other destinations are Taliwang, Dompu and Sape. You can buy tickets from various agents, which may include transport to Sweta, but it's cheaper to get them at the terminal. Buses from Lembar Harbour through to Sumbawa will probably stop at Sweta anyway.

Tourist shuttle buses go to Lembar, Mataram, Senggigi, the Gili islands, Labuhan Lombok, and Kuta beach on Lombok, from various tourist centres on Bali, and also connect to Java and Sumbawa. A Perama ticket from south Bali to Mataram or Senggigi is 20,000 rp, including the ferry. From Mataram to Bima (Sumbawa) is 25,000 rp.

Boat Regular passenger ferries go to/from Lombok:

To/From Bali
: Padangbai (Bali) to Lembar Harbour (Lombok), departures are scheduled every two hours from 4 am. Actual times vary from both ports. Ekonomi costs 4800 rp and the trip takes at least four hours.

To/From Sumbawa
: Ferries to Poto Tano on Sumbawa depart from Labuhan Lombok every one to 1½ hours. Fares are 3100 rp in A class (air-con) and 2000 rp in B

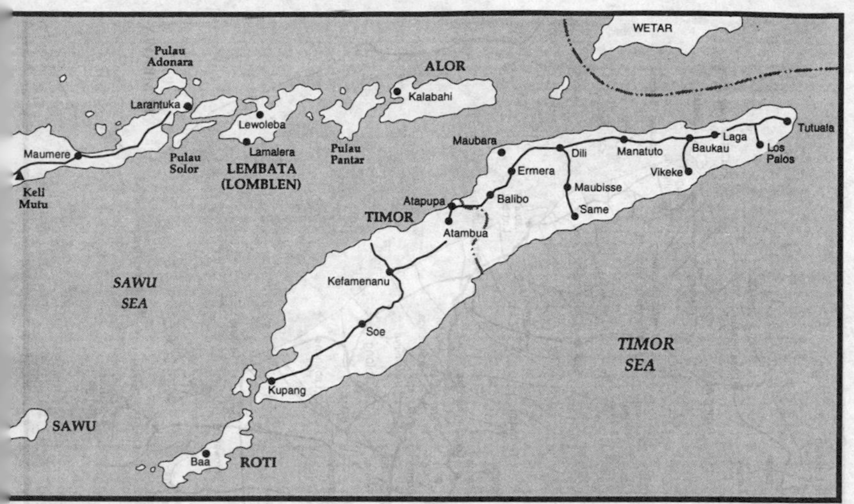

class; it's 2500 rp for a bicycle. The trip takes about 1½ hours.

The *Mabua Express* is a fast luxury catamaran going between Bali's Benoa Port and Lembar Harbour on Lombok. It leaves Benoa at 8.30 am and 2.30 pm, and leaves Lembar at 11.30 am and 5 pm; the trip takes about two hours and costs 35,000 rp for the cheapest class.

A fast, small-boat service may also be running from Padangbai (Bali) to Senggigi and Bangsal in west Lombok (about 20,000 rp), but it is not always reliable. It's supposed to take two hours but some travellers have reported four-hour crossings.

Pelni's KM *Sirimau* calls at Lembar on its scheduled loop to and from Ujung Pandang in Sulawesi and Surabaya in Java. The Pelni office is at Jalan Industri 1 in Ampenan (☎ 21604).

Tours

Agents offer boat trips to Flores with stops at Komodo and perhaps some uninhabited island as well. Some of these trips are pretty rough, with minimal safety provisions. Perama's seven-night, boat and bus Land-Sea Adventure, from Mataram to Labuhanbajo on Flores via Komodo and Rinca, is expensive at 525,000 rp.

A cheaper offering is the Reef Explorer tour from Bangsal to Flores, lasting seven days and six nights, and including a number of locations for US$125. Boat trips around islands are much cheaper if you take them from Labuanbajo on Flores, but they involve smaller fishing boats with lower standards of comfort and safety.

Getting Around

Bemos & Buses There are several terminals on Lombok, the main one at Sweta and others at Praya and Kopang. Away from main roads, take a dokar or *cidomo*, a motorbike or walk.

Car & Motorbike On Jalan Gelantik in Mataram, near the junction of Jalan Selaparang and Jalan Hasanuddin, motorbike owners hang around with bikes to rent from 9000 to 12,000 rp a day.

The cheaper car rentals cost about 45,000 rp per day for a Suzuki Jimny-type vehicle. Larger 4WD Toyotas are cheaper to rent, but you'll spend more on petrol. Hotels can often

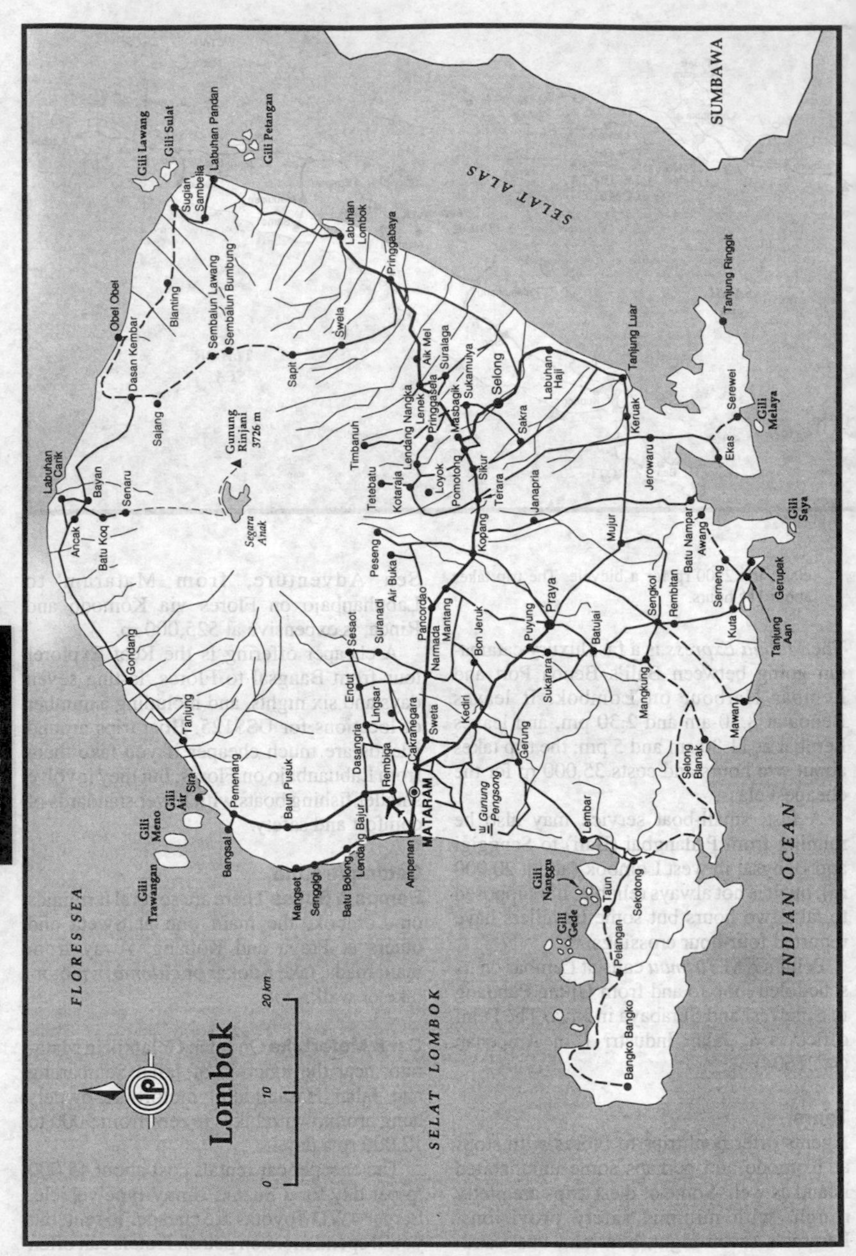

Lombok
0
10
20 km
FLORES SEA
SELAT LOMBOK
SELAT ALAS
INDIAN OCEAN
SUMBAWA
Gili Trawangan
Gili Meno
Gili Air
Bangsal
Pemenang
Sira
Tanjung
Gondang
Ancak
Batu Koq
Labuhan Carik
Bayan
Senaru
Segara Anak
Gunung Rinjani 3726 m
Sajang
Dasan Kembar
Obel Obel
Blanting
Sembalun Lawang
Sembalun Bumbung
Sugian
Sambelia
Gili Lawang
Gili Sulat
Labuhan Pandan
Gili Petangan
Labuhan Lombok
Pringgabaya
Swela
Sapit
Timbanuh
Tetebatu
Kotaraja
Lendang Nangka
Lenek
Pringgasela
Aik Mel
Suralaga
Sukamulya
Masbagik
Loyok
Pomotong
Sikur
Selong
Sakra
Labuhan Haji
Tanjung Luar
Keruak
Jerowaru
Ekas
Serewei
Gili Melaya
Tanjung Ringgit
Terara
Janapria
Kopang
Mujur
Batu Nampar
Awang
Gili Saya
Gerupak
Tanjung Aan
Kuta
Semeng
Rembitan
Sengkol
Mangkung
Batujai
Praya
Puyung
Sukarara
Bon Jeruk
Mantang
Pancordao
Air Buka
Peseng
Narmada
Suranadi
Sesaot
Endut
Lingsar
Dasangria
Rembiga
Baun Pusuk
Cakranegara
Sweta
Kediri
Gerung
Gunung Pengsong
MATARAM
Ampenan
Lendang Bajur
Batu Bolong
Senggigi
Mangset
Lembar
Gili Nanggu
Gili Gede
Taun
Sekotong
Pelangan
Bangko Bangko
Selong Blanak
Mawan

organise cars, or try Metro Photo (☎ 22146), Jalan Yos Sudarso 79 in Ampenan.

Chartering Only some vehicles are registered to take passengers all over Lombok; it costs about 40,000 rp a day, more for a long trip.

MATARAM

Ampenan-Mataram-Cakranegara-Sweta is the four-part capital, port and main town of Lombok. The four towns have virtually merged. Ampenan, once the main port of Lombok, has several budget places to stay and eat, moneychangers and transport connections. Mataram is the administrative capital of Nusa Tenggara Barat (West Nusa Tenggara) which covers all of Lombok and Sumbawa. Cakranegara (Cakra) is the main commercial centre, and Sweta is the main transport terminal of Lombok and the largest market.

Orientation

Ampenan-Mataram-Cakra-Sweta is spread over 10 km along one main road, variously called Jalan Yos Sudarso, Jalan Langko, Jalan Pejanggik and Jalan Selaparang. It's a one-way road, from west to east, for most of its length. A parallel road, Jalan Sriwijaya-Jalan Majapahit, brings traffic back towards the coast.

Information

The helpful West Nusa Tenggara government tourist office (☎ 21866, 31730) is at Jalan Langko 70 in Mataram. They open from 7 am to 2 pm Monday to Thursday, 7 to 11 am Friday and 7 am to 12.30 pm on Saturday.

Most banks are along the main road, and will change travellers' cheques, though it can take some time. Bank Ekspor-Impor seems to be open longer than the others – weekdays from 7.30 am to noon and 1 to 2 pm. Other places that change money are in Ampenan, the airport and the Perama office.

The Mataram GPO on Jalan Sriwijaya is the main post office and the place for poste restante mail. There's a Telkom telephone office on Jalan Langko, from which you can make overseas calls and faxes at any time.

Things to See

There's an interesting **museum** on Jalan Banjar Tilar Negara in Ampenan with exhibits on the geology, history and culture of Lombok and Sumbawa. It's open Tuesday to Sunday from 8 am to 4 pm and costs 200 rp.

The **Mayura Water Palace**, in Cakra, was built in 1744 and was part of the royal court of the former Balinese kingdom on Lombok.

Opposite the water palace is the **Pura Meru**, the largest Balinese temple on Lombok.

Places to Stay

Ampenan Most of the cheapies are in Ampenan. Near the central intersection, the friendly *Hotel Zahir* (☎ 22403) is at Jalan Koperasi 12. It's a simple place with singles/doubles at 6000/7500 rp, or 8000/10,000 rp with bathroom. Also in the centre of town is the basic *Losmen Pabean* (☎ 21758) at Jalan Pabean 146, where rooms with shared mandi cost 4500/7000 rp for singles/doubles.

Losmen Horas (☎ 21695), at Jalan Koperasi 65, is basic but OK, with rooms at 5000/7500 rp with Indonesian bathrooms. *Losmen Wisma Triguna* (☎ 21705), on Jalan Koperasi, a little over a km from central Ampenan, is spacious, with helpful staff and rooms at around 10,000 rp, breakfast included. The nearby *Losmen Angin Mammire* is cheap, but OK.

Mataram The *Hotel Kambodja* (☎ 22211) is at Jalan Supratman 10 on the corner with Jalan Arif Rahmat. It's pleasant and has rooms for about 8500 rp.

Cakranegara There are some mid-range business-traveller hotels on Jalan Pejanggik, with a variety of rooms from 15,000 to 25,000 a double and more. They include the *Selaparang Hotel* (☎ 32670), the *Mataram Hotel* (☎ 23411) and the *Hotel Kertajoga* (☎ 21775). Just south of the main drag, at Jalan Maktal 15, is the *Hotel & Restaurant*

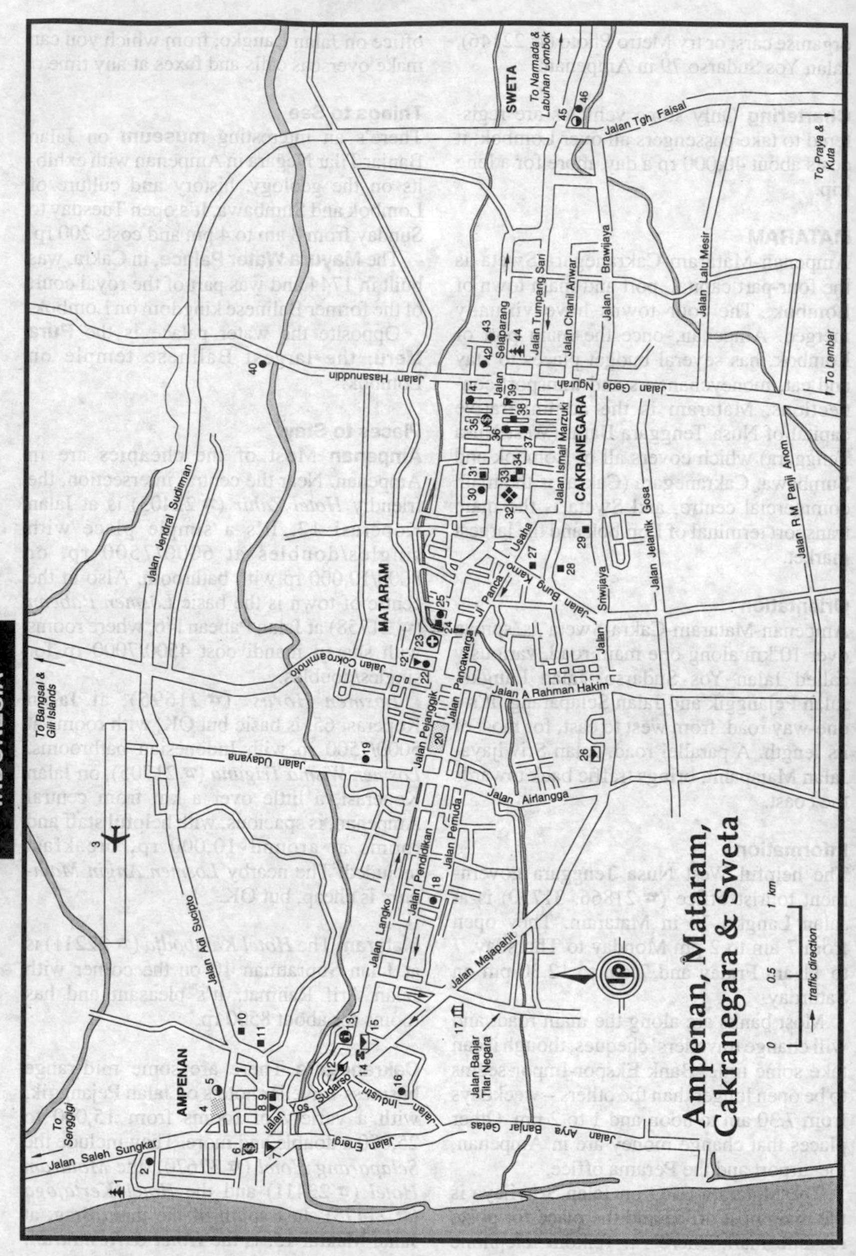
Ampenan, Mataram, Cakranegara & Sweta
SWETA
To Narmada & Labuhan Lombok
Jalan Tgh Faisal
To Praya & Kuta
To Lembar
Jalan Lalu Mesir
Brawijaya
Jalan Chanil Anwar
Jalan Tumpang Sari
Jalan Selaparang
Jalan Gede Ngurah
Jalan Ismail Marzuki
CAKRANEGARA
Jalan R M Panji Anom
Jalan Jelantik Gosa
Jalan Sriwijaya
Usaha
Jalan Bung Karno
Jl Panca
Jalan Hasanuddin
Jalan Jendral Sudirman
MATARAM
Jalan Cokroaminoto
Jalan Pejanggik
Jalan Pancawarga
Jalan A Rahman Hakim
Jalan Airlangga
Jalan Pemuda
Jalan Pendidikan
Jalan Langko
Jalan Majapahit
Jalan Udayana
To Bangsal & Gili Islands
Jalan Adi Sucipto
AMPENAN
To Senggigi
Jalan Saleh Sungkar
Jalan Yos Sudarso
Jalan Energi
Jalan Industri
Jalan Banjar Tilar Negara
Jalan Arya Banjar Getas
0 0.5 1 km
traffic direction

PLACES TO STAY		PLACES TO EAT			
9	Hotel Zahir	7	Pabean & Cirebon Restaurants	18	Mataram University
10	Losmen Wisma Triguna	8	Kiki Restaurant	19	Immigration Office
11	Losmen Horas	21	Garden House Restaurant	20	Main Square (Lampangan Mataram)
12	Nitour Hotel & Restaurant	39	Sekawan Depot Es	22	Governor's Office
24	Hotel Kertajoga			23	Hospital
27	Hotel Granada			25	Perama Office
28	Graha Ayu		**OTHER**	26	GPO
29	Puri Indah Hotel			30	Rinjani Hand Woven
31	Selaparang Hotel	1	Pura Segara Temple	32	Cilinaya Shopping Centre
33	Hotel & Restaurant Shanti Puri	2	Sudirman Antiques	35	Bank Ekspor-Impor
		3	Selaparang Airport	36	Merpati Office
34	Oka Homestay	4	Ampenan Market	40	Lombok Handicraft Centre
37	Losmen Ayu	5	Ampenan Terminal		
38	Adiyuna Homestay	6	Moneychangers	41	Motorbike Rental
		13	Tourist Office	42	Selamat Riady
		14	Telephone Office	43	Mayura Water Palace
		15	Post Office	44	Pura Meru Temple
		16	Pelni Office	45	Sweta Terminal
		17	Museum	46	Sweta Market

Shanti Puri (☎ 32649) with comfortable rooms up to 12,000/15,000 rp. In the blocks east of here are a number of Balinese-style losmen, like the *Oka*, *Adiyuna* and the friendly *Losmen Ayu* (☎ 21761), with cheap rooms at about 10,000 rp a double.

If you want some comfort, the *Puri Indah* (☎ 37633) on Jalan Sriwijaya has a restaurant, pool and good rooms from 15,000/20,000 rp, or 25,000/30,000 rp with air-con.

Places to Eat

There are several Indonesian/Chinese restaurants in Ampenan, including the *Cirebon* at Jalan Pabean 113, and the *Pabean* next door. *Kiki Restaurant*, upstairs at the top end of Jalan Yos Sudarso, has a more interesting menu, and balcony tables overlooking the main intersection.

In Mataram, near Jalan Pejanggik, are the *Garden House Restaurant*, an open-air place, and the *Taliwang*, with local dishes.

In Cakranegara, the *Sekawan Depot Es* has cold drinks downstairs and a seafood and Chinese restaurant upstairs. Round the corner on Jalan Hasanuddin, a few places serve Padang and Sasak food. There are also a handful of bakeries, plenty of cheap, spicy food at the *Cakra Market*, and even a *KFC*.

Things to Buy

Some weaving factories still operate in Mataram, where you can see and buy *ikat* weaving – ikat is cloth in which the pattern is produced by dyeing the individual threads before weaving. Ampenan has some craft and antique shops; also check the Lombok Handicraft Centre at Sayang Sayang.

Getting There & Away

See the Lombok Getting There & Away section for details of flights and ferry services to and from Lombok. The main Merpati office (☎ 23762) in Ampenan, at Jalan Yos Sudarso 6, also handles bookings and enquiries for Garuda flights. Perama (☎ 22764, 23368) is at Jalan Pejanggik 66.

From Sweta, bemos go to Lembar (1000 rp), Praya (700 rp), Labuhan Lombok (2000 rp) and Bayan (1800 rp). For Senggigi, go to the bus station next to the market in Ampenan.

Getting Around

From the airport, frequent No 7 bemos come by and run to the Ampenan bemo terminal. Bemos shuttle up and down the two main routes between the Ampenan terminal at one end and the Sweta terminal at the other. The fare is a standard 250 rp regardless of dis-

INDONESIA

tance. You can also rent good bicycles for about 5000 rp a day from near the Cirebon Restaurant.

SENGGIGI BEACH

Senggigi is really a string of beaches, between seven and 12 km north of Ampenan, which has become the most developed tourist area on Lombok. The plan is to promote three and four-star hotels along the beachfront, and restrict budget accommodation to the inland side of the road. The new sealed road, the assorted new buildings, and the fenced-off construction sites detract greatly from the tropical beach atmosphere. There's some good snorkelling, sea views and sunsets over Bali.

The Graha Beach Hotel and several travel agents will arrange tours, confirm flights, and change money or travellers' cheques. Perama will also provide information and change money. There's a Telkom telephone office, and the new supermarket complex will have most other things you'll need.

Places to Stay

There's not a great deal for those on low budgets. The most popular travellers' place at Senggigi is the *Pondok Senggigi* (☎ 93273), with a good restaurant and a variety of accommodation including cheap rooms at 10,000/13,000 rp with shared bathroom, and better rooms, with Western-style bathrooms, from 15,000/20,000 rp. A 15% tax is added to your food and room bill. The rooms are on long verandas which face the tropical garden.

One of the cheapest places is *Pondok Sederhana*, with rooms staggered up the hillside and sharing a communal mandi and toilet. They're pretty grotty but cheap, from about 7000 rp. On the beach side a little further north, *Lina Cottages & Restaurant* (☎ 93237) is reasonable value at 25,000/30,000 rp including tax – it's central, but feels cramped.

Coming from Ampenan, one of the first places you'll strike is the *Asri Beach Cottages*, with standard rooms at 12,500 rp and bungalows at 17,500 rp, including tax and breakfast. They're basic, but clean and near the beach. Just north of Asri is *Atitha Sangraha*, a nice new place with similar prices. Further north, the pricier *Batu Bolong Cottages* (☎ 24598) have bungalows on both sides of the road. *Melati Dua Cottages* (☎ 93288), close to the middle of the strip, has standard single/double rooms at 20,000/22,000 rp plus tax. *Pondok Rinjani*, further north but still central, has cottages with bathrooms from 20,000 rp plus tax. *Pondok Sinta Cottages*, a bit north of the central part of Senggigi, are cheap at 10,000/12,000 rp (less with shared facilities), basic but well located and breakfast is included.

Windy Cottages (☎ 93161) are out by themselves, beyond Senggigi in an area known as Mangset. It's a great location if you want to get away from it all, and the restaurant is good value. Rooms start at 20,000 rp, including breakfast and tax.

Places to Eat

Most of the places to stay have their own restaurants, and of course you can eat at any one you like. The restaurant at the central *Pondok Senggigi* is an open-air place, popular from breakfast time until late at night. The *Sunshine Restaurant*, also in the central strip, has a typical tourist menu with seafood. Further north, *Arlina Restaurant* is a good value-for-money place, and the *Princess of Senggigi Restaurant* has also been recommended.

Coming in from the south, *Flamboyant II* is relocated from Mataram and retains its good reputation. *Cafe Wayan* has the same management as its namesake in Ubud, so it has to be worth a try. A bit further on, the *Dynasty Restaurant & Bar* is by itself near the sea, but organises transport in the evening so you can enjoy the music and a few drinks.

Entertainment

Local rock bands often perform at the *Pondok Senggigi* and the *Graha Beach Hotel*. Also check *Bananas Disco* and *Dynasty Restaurant & Bar*.

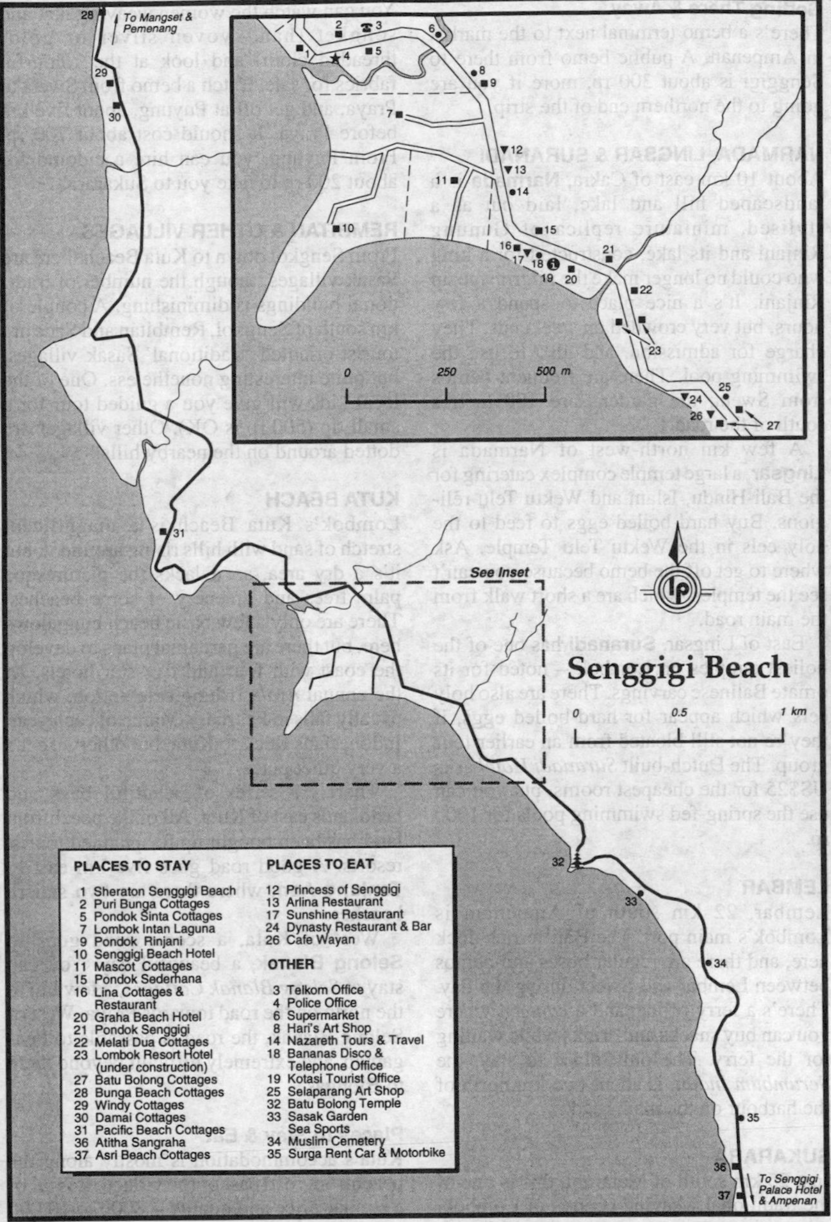
Senggigi Beach
0 0.5 1 km
0 250 500 m
See Inset
To Mangset & Pemenang
To Senggigi Palace Hotel & Ampenan
PLACES TO STAY
1 Sheraton Senggigi Beach
2 Puri Bunga Cottages
5 Pondok Sinta Cottages
7 Lombok Intan Laguna
9 Pondok Rinjani
10 Senggigi Beach Hotel
11 Mascot Cottages
15 Pondok Sederhana
16 Lina Cottages & Restaurant
20 Graha Beach Hotel
21 Pondok Senggigi
22 Melati Dua Cottages
23 Lombok Resort Hotel (under construction)
27 Batu Bolong Cottages
28 Bunga Beach Cottages
29 Windy Cottages
30 Damai Cottages
31 Pacific Beach Cottages
36 Atitha Sangraha
37 Asri Beach Cottages
PLACES TO EAT
12 Princess of Senggigi
13 Arlina Restaurant
17 Sunshine Restaurant
24 Dynasty Restaurant & Bar
26 Cafe Wayan
OTHER
3 Telkom Office
4 Police Office
6 Supermarket
8 Hari's Art Shop
14 Nazareth Tours & Travel
18 Bananas Disco & Telephone Office
19 Kotasi Tourist Office
25 Selaparang Art Shop
32 Batu Bolong Temple
33 Sasak Garden Sea Sports
34 Muslim Cemetery
35 Surga Rent Car & Motorbike

Getting There & Away

There's a bemo terminal next to the market in Ampenan. A public bemo from there to Senggigi is about 300 rp, more if you are going to the northern end of the strip.

NARMADA, LINGSAR & SURANADI

About 10 km east of Cakra, **Narmada** is a landscaped hill and lake, laid out as a stylised, miniature replica of Gunung Rinjani and its lake, constructed for a king who could no longer make the pilgrimage up Rinjani. It's a nice place to spend a few hours, but very crowded on weekends. They charge for admission, and also to use the swimming pool. There are frequent bemos from Sweta; the gardens are 100 metres south of the road.

A few km north-west of Narmada is **Lingsar**, a large temple complex catering for the Bali-Hindu, Islam and Wektu Telu religions. Buy hard-boiled eggs to feed to the holy eels in the Wektu Telu Temple. Ask where to get off the bemo because you can't see the temples, which are a short walk from the main road.

East of Lingsar, **Suranadi** has one of the holiest temples on Lombok – noted for its ornate Balinese carvings. There are also holy eels which appear for hard-boiled eggs, if they're not still bloated from an earlier tour group. The Dutch-built *Suranadi Hotel* asks US$25 for the cheapest rooms, but you can use the spring-fed swimming pools for 1000 rp.

LEMBAR

Lembar, 22 km south of Ampenan, is Lombok's main port. The Bali ferries dock here, and there are regular buses and bemos between Lembar and Sweta during the day. There's a ferry office, and a *canteen* where you can buy snacks and drinks while waiting for the ferry. The only place to stay, the *Serumbum Indah*, is about two km north of the harbour on the main road.

SUKARARA

Just 25 km south of Mataram, this is one of the traditional weaving centres of Lombok. You can watch the women weaving ikat and songket (hand-woven silver or gold-threaded cloth) and look at the colourful fabrics for sale. Catch a bemo from Sweta to Praya, and get off at Puyung, about five km before Praya. It should cost about 700 rp. From Puyung, you can hire a cidomo for about 200 rp to take you to Sukarara.

REMBITAN & OTHER VILLAGES

From Sengkol down to Kuta Beach there are Sasak villages, though the number of traditional buildings is diminishing. A couple of km south of Sengkol, Rembitan and Sade are tourist-oriented 'traditional' Sasak villages, but quite interesting nonetheless. One of the local kids will give you a guided tour for a small tip (500 rp is OK). Other villages are dotted around on the nearby hills.

KUTA BEACH

Lombok's Kuta Beach is a magnificent stretch of sand with hills rising around it, but it's a dry area, so it lacks the picturesque palm trees and greenery of some beaches. There are only a few basic beach bungalows here, but there are perennial plans to develop the coast with four and five-star hotels. At the annual *nyale* fishing celebration, which usually falls in February-March of each year, Indonesians flock to Kuta, but otherwise it's a very quiet place.

There's a series of beautiful bays and headlands east of Kuta. All of the beachfront land has been bought up for planned tourist resorts. A good road goes five km east to **Tanjung Aan**, where there are two superb beaches.

West of Kuta, a scenic road goes to **Selong Blanak**, a beautiful bay. You can stay at *Selong Blanak Cottages*, a few km to the north on the road towards Praya. West of Selong Blanak, the road is passable to Pengantap, and extremely difficult beyond there to Blongas.

Places to Stay & Eat

Kuta's accommodation is mostly along the beachfront road east of the village. It is all of a similar price and quality – 8000 to 10,000 rp a double for a bamboo box on stilts with its own roofless bathroom, breakfast and tea on request. Most places also have bigger, more expensive rooms. From the west, after the police station, you come to *Rambitan*, *Wisma Segara Anak*, with a restaurant, *Pondok Sekar Kuning*, where upstairs rooms have a view, and *Anda Cottages*, the original place at Kuta, with a garden and a good restaurant.

A bit further along are *Florida Bungalows*, with good food, and *Rinjani Agung Beach Bungalows*. *Mascot* is just a pub and music place, and *Cockatoo Cottages & Restaurant* is the last place along the beach.

On the eastern edge of the village, *Kuta Beach Bungalows* is a friendly place, and the *Losmen Mata Hari*, near the market on the road to Mawan, is also clean and good value.

Getting There & Away

To get to Kuta by public transport, first get a bemo to Praya, then wait for one to Sengkol (500 rp) and then another down to Kuta (300 rp). Market day in Sengkol is Thursday, and there may be more transport then. Shuttle buses are about 10,000 rp from Mataram or Senggigi.

KOTARAJA AREA

The villages of **Kotaraja** and **Loyok** in eastern Lombok are renowned for their handicrafts, particularly their basketware and plaited mats. You may also come across intricate metal jewellery, vases, caskets and other decorative objects. The area is cooler than the lowlands, and a great place to walk through rice fields, jungle and unspoilt villages.

Tetebatu is a mountain retreat on the southern slopes of Gunung Rinjani, seven km north of Kotaraja. **Lendang Nangka**, a few km east, is an interesting Sasak village and a good base from which to explore the surrounding area. Nearby is **Tojang**, the biggest spring in Lombok. **Pringgasela**, about 10 km east of Kotaraja, is a centre for weaving blankets and sarongs.

Places to Stay & Eat

Wisma Soedjono in Tetebatu has a variety of single/double rooms and bungalows from around 15,000 rp to 35,000 rp. *Diwi Enjeni*, in the rice fields on the right as you come in from the south, is a good place, with rooms at 5000/7500 rp. Other bungalows are sprouting in the rice fields around here.

At Lendang Nangka, you can stay with Hadji Radiah, the local primary school teacher who speaks good English and is a mine of information on the area. It costs 10,000/15,000 rp per day for a simple room with three meals. There's another losmen west of the village, and other small homestay places are appearing in villages like Loyok, Pringgasela, Repo (near Masbagik), Lenek and Sapit.

Getting There & Away

It's easy to get around this area, only 40 km or so from Sweta, with your own transport. By public transport, take a bemo from Sweta to Pomotong (about 950 rp) or Masbagik (1000 rp) and then head north by cidomo (500 rp), or on the back of a motorbike.

EAST COAST

The east coast is dry and sparsely populated, with little tourist interest and few facilities. There's a nearly deserted beach bungalow at **Labuhan Haji**, the former harbour, and a pungent fishing port at **Tanjung Luar**.

The black sand beach at **Pulo Lampur**, 14 km north of Labuhan Lombok, is popular with locals on Sunday and holidays. *Siola Cottages*, near the sea at **Labuhan Pandan**, are secluded and cost 12,000/20,000 rp for singles/doubles, including three meals. From here you can charter a boat out to explore the uninhabited offshore islands.

Labuhan Lombok

This is the port for ferries to Sumbawa, visible from here in clear weather. Look around the houses on stilts near the old port, or climb the hill on the south side of the harbour. Stay at *Losmen Munawar*, on the road round to the ferry port, which is simple but quite OK at 2500/5000 rp.

…here & Away There are regular … between Labuhan Lombok and Sweta (69 km; 2000 rp; about two hours). The ferry to Poto Tano on Sumbawa departs from a jetty about three km away on the north side of the harbour – take a bemo for 250 rp. The ferry ticket office is beside the car park. See the Nusa Tenggara Getting There & Away section for details. The actual departure times are flexible – you're unlikely to have to wait more than an hour. There are foodstalls at the port, and guys come on the boat selling snacks. Take some water – it's a hot trip.

NORTH COAST

The road around the north coast is still being worked on. It's rough, but there are public bemos and it's definitely passable in a Suzuki Jimny, at least in the dry season. From the main road you can detour to **Sembalun Lawang** and **Sembalun Bumbung**, traditional villages on the eastern slopes of Rinjani. The main road is still a bit rough until Bayan, near the turn-off for Senaru and the Rinjani trek, but it's very good for the rest of the way to Pemenang, where you turn off for the Gili Islands.

GUNUNG RINJANI

At 3726 metres, Gunung Rinjani is the highest mountain in Lombok and the third highest in Indonesia. It is an active volcano – the last eruption was in 1901 – and it has a huge half-moon crater with a large green lake, hot springs and a number of smaller volcanic cones. It's sacred to both Sasaks and Balinese, and many make pilgrimages here – it can get crowded. In the wet season the paths are slippery and dangerous.

The easiest route up Rinjani, and the most frequently used, is from Senaru, on the northern slopes. Access is via Bayan to Batu Koq, just below Senaru. There are a number of places to stay along here – they're nothing fancy, but cheap from around 5000/10,000 rp for singles/doubles including breakfast, and some have views of the valley below and Rinjani above. Most can provide information, supplies and equipment, and arrange trekking guides. Equipment rental is around 15,000 rp for a sleeping bag, tent, stove and cooking gear.

From Senaru, it's about a six-hour walk to the base camp just below the rim at Pos III. From there make an early start for the two-hour climb to the rim for sunrise, then descend for another four hours down into the crater. After walking around part of the lake's northern shore, most people camp near the hot springs and return all the way to Batu Koq the next day. You need three clear days to do it – up and back down again – and probably at least another day to recover.

To get to the actual summit of Rinjani takes at least an extra day from Senaru. The track to the summit branches off about a two-hour walk east of the hot springs. From the junction (about 2400 metres altitude), it's a difficult three or four-hour climb over loose ground to the top (3726 metres). Another option is to traverse the whole mountain by continuing east from the hot springs, then descending to Sembalun Lawang and Sembalun Bumbung on the eastern slopes of Rinjani.

Getting There & Away

Several buses a day go from Sweta to Bayan, the first leaving around 9 am, and some continue to Batu Koq (it costs about 1800 rp for the three-hour trip). On the eastern side, there is transport from Sembalun Lawang and Sembalun Bumbung to the north-coast road. Going south, you'd have to walk to Sapit, from where bemos connect to Pringgabaya and Labuhan Lombok.

GILI ISLANDS

Off the north-west coast of Lombok are three small coral-fringed islands – Gili Air, Gili Meno and Gili Trawangan – known as the Gili Islands by the thousands of visitors who come here for the very simple pleasures of sun, snorkelling and socialising. There are white sandy beaches, clear water and coral reefs. There are also some small shops (with souvenirs, beachwear and basics), telephones, moneychangers and 'pubs', but no sellers and no motor vehicles. There are ome scuba-diving operators – Blue Marlin has an office on each island and can do a cash advance on credit cards. Note that topless (for women) or nude sunbathing is offensive to the local people.

Gili Air is the closest island to the mainland. Beaches run round most of the island and there's a small village at the southern end. Homes and small farms are dotted amongst the palm trees, along with losmen and a couple of 'pubs'.

Gili Meno, the middle island, has the smallest population and the fewest tourists.

The largest island, with a local population of about 400, Trawangan also has the most visitors, the most facilities, and a reputation as the party island. The accommodation and restaurants/bars are clustered (cramped?) mostly on the east and south-east coast beaches. Some places may be rebuilt in the north-east of the island, but not right on the beach.

There are proposals to build golf courses on two of the islands, and a resort on the mainland at Sira. This plan is not supported by many of the locals who lease the land on which the very successful low-budget tourist development is built. In 1992 bungalows on Trawangan were closed and/or relocated by the authorities; it's not clear whether this was to permit a grand development project, or because the bungalows contravened the lease conditions, or because they did not meet environmental and health standards. Some are to be rebuilt further inland at the northern end of the beach.

Places to Stay & Eat

The price of accommodation, a standard bungalow on stilts with a concrete bathroom out the back, is pretty well fixed. There is some cost-cutting in the low season and some better places charge more. The low season price is about 9000/15,000 rp for singles/doubles with bed and breakfast only, or 15,000/22,000 rp with three meals – add 2000/5000 rp for the high season. Most places provide bed and breakfast only, but you can order dinner as an extra, or eat somewhere else. Rooms with shared bathroom are cheaper, but becoming rare.

Gili Air Most of the accommodation on Gili Air is scattered round the southern end of the island at the harbour, though there are losmen near the east, north and west coasts. Some places on the west side may have to move to accommodate the golf course.

Gili Indah is one of the bigger places on Gili Air, and contains the Perama office, telephone office and moneychanger. They have rooms from US$7/10 up to US$20/30. Only slightly more expensive than the norm, *Coconut Cottages* are very nice, with excellent food. *Han's Bungalows*, at the northern end of the island, are above average in price at 15,000/20,000 rp, but they have been upgrading their accommodation and installing a swimming pool. *Bulan Madu* is expensive at 50,000/60,000 rp, but has very attractive rooms.

The other places to stay, about 15 of them, are all similar – pick one in a location you like, or that's been recommended by other travellers.

Gili Meno The accommodation here is mostly on the east beach, with a couple of places which are pretty upmarket by Gili standards. *Zoraya Pavillion* (☎ 33801) has a variety of rooms from 15,500 to 40,000 rp a double, with various watersports and a tennis court. *Gazebo Hotel* (☎ 35795) has tastefully decorated Bali-style bungalows with private bathrooms, air-con and electricity (if it's working). It costs about US$45 a double for bed and breakfast. Anyone can change cash or travellers' cheques here, make phone calls or eat in the fancy balcony restaurant.

Kontiki has a variety of rooms and prices, and *Casa Blanca* has fan-cooled rooms at US$25/30, but seems overpriced, even with its tiny swimming pool. The other half-dozen places have standard Gili Islands bungalows and charge standard prices.

Gili Trawangan The accommodation and prices on Gili Trawangan are even more standardised than on the other islands.

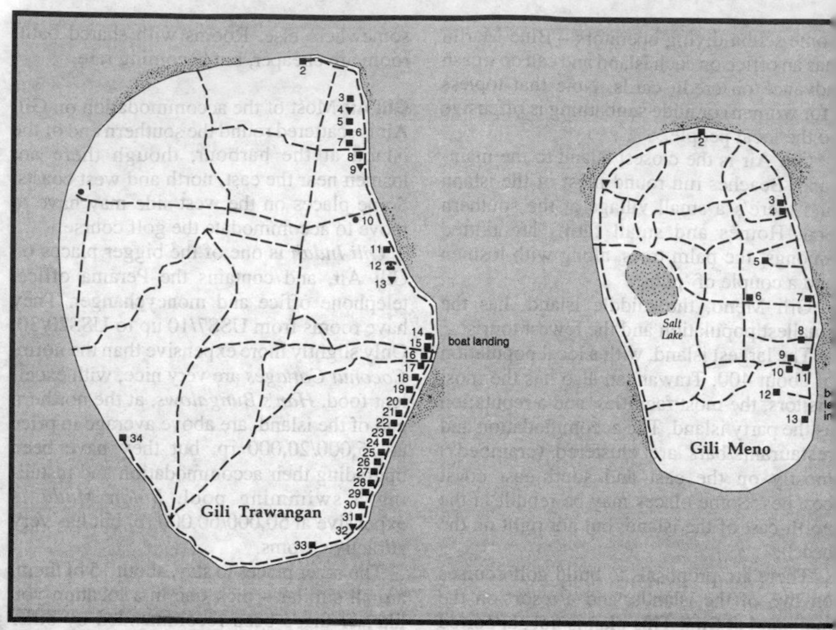

GILI TRAWANGAN

1 Navigation Light
2 Nusa Tiga
3 Coral Beach *
4 Borobudur Restaurant *
5 Good Heart *
6 Mountain View *
7 Creative *
8 Sudi Nampir
9 Excellent Restaurant
10 Blue Marlin Dive Centre
11 Mountain View
12 Wartel
13 Borobudur Restaurant
14 Danau Hijau Bungalows
15 Fantasi Bungalows
16 Pak Majid's
17 Sandy Beach Bungalows
18 Dua Sekawan I
19 Paradise Cottages
20 Damai Indah
21 Rudy's Pub & Cottages
22 Dua Sekawan II
23 Trawangan Cottages
24 Halim
25 Holiday Inn
26 Pasir Putih
27 Homestay Makmur
28 Melati Losmen
29 Majestic Cottages
30 Rainbow Cottages
31 Mawar Accommodation
32 Simple Food
33 Pondok Santi
34 Mawar II

GILI MENO

1 Good Heart Restaurant
2 Blue Coral Bungalows
3 Pondok Meno
4 Zoraya Pavillion
5 Casa Blanca
6 Pondok Wisata
7 Janur Indah Bungalows

Typical basic bungalows cost 10,000/15,000/20,000 rp for singles/doubles/triples, with breakfast and private mandi. *Pondok Santi* is a bit more expensive, but probably worth the extra. Most of the places to stay also serve food, but there's a few convivial restaurants which are more like bars in the evening. There's usually music and dancing in at least one of them.

Getting There & Away

From Ampenan or the airport, take a bemo north to Rembiga (about 200 rp), then a bus

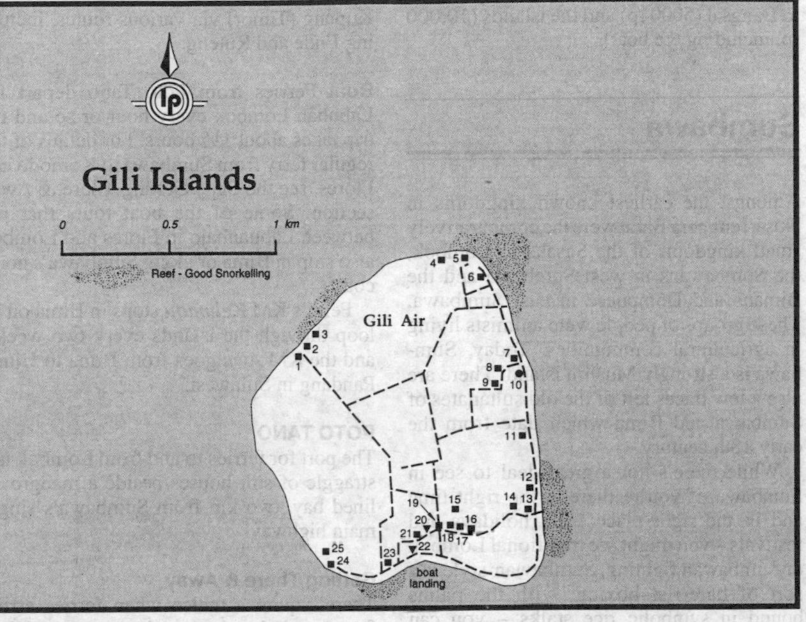

8 Matahari Bungalows
9 Fantastic Cottages
10 Rawa Indah
11 Malia's Child Bungalows
12 Gazebo Hotel
13 Kontiki Cottages & Restaurant

GILI AIR

1 Hink Bungalows *
2 Muksin Cottages *
3 Rose Cottages
4 Lombok Indah
5 Han's Bungalows & Restaurant
6 Gusung Indah Bungalows
7 Fantastic Bungalows
8 Coconut Cottages
9 Gili Air Cottages
10 Ozzy's Shop
11 Bulan Madu
12 Gita Gili Sunrise
13 Corner Cottages
14 Nusa Tiga Bungalows
15 Bupati's Cottages
16 Sederhana Losmen
17 Resorta Cottages
18 Garden Cottages
19 Pondok Gili Air
20 Go Go Pub
21 Bamboo Cottages
22 Fanta Pub
23 Gili Indah Cottages & Perama Office
24 Lucky Cottages *
25 Salabose Cottages *

* These businesses will be re-established in the positions indicated

INDONESIA

to Pemenang (600 rp). From there it's a 200-rp cidomo ride to the harbour at Bangsal. Some bemos from Sweta go directly to Pemenang (700 rp). Boat tickets are 900 rp to Gili Air, 1000 rp to Gili Meno and 1200 rp to Gili Trawangan. You have to wait until there's a full boatload, about 20 people, or pay the extra fares between you. Try to get to Bangsal by 10 am.

You can charter a whole boat, but it's expensive – 60,000 rp to visit all three islands. There's a boat shuttle service between the islands twice a day. Perama shuttle buses go from Mataram or Senggigi to Bangsal (5000 rp) and the islands (10,000 rp, including the boat).

Sumbawa

Amongst the earliest known kingdoms in Nusa Tenggara Barat were the comparatively small kingdoms of the Sasaks in Lombok, the Sumbawans in west Sumbawa and the Bimans and Dompuese in east Sumbawa. These groups of people were animists living in agricultural communities. Today, Sumbawa is a strongly Muslim island. There are also a few traces left of the old sultanates of Sumbawa and Bima which date from the early 18th century.

While there's not a great deal to see in Sumbawa, if you're there at the right time and in the right place – on holidays and festivals – you might see traditional Lombok or Sumbawan fighting. Sumbawan-style is a sort of bare-fist boxing, with the palms bound in symbolic rice stalks – you can possibly see it in east Bali as well. Lombok-style is called Peresehan and is a more violent type of combat involving leather-covered shields and bamboo poles. Most matches seem to end in draws. Water buffalo races take place at one festival, but they are not exactly the Grand National.

With the advent of good bus services from Lombok straight to Bima and Sape, and interesting boat tours between Lombok and Flores, most travellers quickly pass through Sumbawa or skip it all together. Pulau Moyo is an island nature reserve with good coral reefs and Huu is a surfing destination, but elsewhere off the main highway jaws will drop at the sight of a foreigner.

Getting There & Away

Air Merpati have flights from Denpasar via Mataram to Sumbawa Besar (76,000 rp from Denpasar) and direct to Bima (116,000 rp). Merpati also connect Bima with Bajawa, Ende, Labuhanbajo, Ruteng (all in Flores) and Tambolaka (Sumba). Flights operate to Kupang (Timor) via various routes, including Ende and Ruteng.

Boat Ferries from Poto Tano depart for Labuhan Lombok every hour or so and the trip takes about 1½ hours. For details of the regular ferry from Sumbawa to Komodo and Flores, see the Sape Getting There & Away section. Some of the boat tours that ply between Labuanbajo in Flores and Lombok also stop in Bima or along Sumbawa's north coast.

Pelni's KM *Kelimutu* stops in Bima on its loop through the islands every two weeks, and the KM *Awu* goes from Bima to Ujung Pandang in Sulawesi.

POTO TANO

The port for ferries to and from Lombok is a straggle of stilt houses beside a mangrove-lined bay, two km from Sumbawa's single main highway.

Getting There & Away

There's quite a melee when ferries arrive from Lombok as bus conductors try to fill up all the waiting buses quickly. Buying a bus ticket from the touts on the ferry can save some hassle, but overcharging can occur. Fares and journey times are: Taliwang (1000 rp, one hour), Sumbawa Besar (2000 rp, 2½ hours) and Bima (8000 rp, 10 hours).

About a dozen ferries run daily between Lombok and Poto Tana. The crossing takes about 1½ hours and costs 2000 rp or 3100 rp with air-con.

SUMBAWA BESAR

Sumbawa Besar is a ramshackle collection of concrete-block houses, thatch-roofed and woven-mat-walled stilt bungalows and shacks which cling to the sides of the hills and have paths leading up to them made of small boulders. The place has a distinct Asian feel about it, with numerous dokars rattling down the streets and Muslim men flooding out of the mosques after midday prayer. The 'hello mister' cult reaches its peak here.

The chief attraction is the **Dakam Laka,**

he interesting, wooden, barn-like Sultan's 'alace.

nformation

The Bank Negara Indonesia is at Jalan Kartini 10.

For information on Pulau Moyo (Moyo sland), contact the Direktorat Jenderal Kehutanan (☎ 21358), Jalan Garuda 12.

Places to Stay

Central Sumbawa Besar is a compact place and there's a cluster of losmen along Jalan Hasanuddin, just a five-minute walk from he bus terminal. Walk down Jalan Kaboja, which is opposite the bus station, to get to Jalan Hasanuddin. All these hotels are within ange of the 5 am wake-up call from the nosque – experience indigenous culture at ts loudest.

The best of these hotels is the *Hotel Suci* ☎ 21589) with rooms around an attractive courtyard and garden, which keeps out much of the traffic noise. Rooms cost from 5000 to 11,000 rp – they are all clean and have a fan, mandi and toilet. The *Losmen Tunas* (☎ 21212) on the same side of the street is a reasonable place with rooms from 5000 rp. The *Losmen Dewi* (☎ 21170) is a little quieter and has rooms for 5000 rp with mandi. The *Losmen Saudara* (☎ 21528) can be horribly noisy but has a decent restaurant. Singles/doubles are 6000/8000.

The best hotel in Sumbawa Besar is the *Hotel Tambora* (☎ 21555), just off Jalan Garuda on Jalan Kebayan II, a 15-minute walk or a short trip in a dokar from the bus terminal. Rooms cost from 7000 rp with mandi to around 60,000 rp for a suite.

Places to Eat

The *Rumah Makan Surabaya* is a minute's walk from the bus terminal and serves cheap dishes like nasi campur and nasi goreng. They close very early, around 5.30 pm. On Jalan Wahiddin, the *Rumah Makan Anda* stays open until around 9 pm and has similar prices, standards and food. *Rumah Makan Rukun Jaya* on Jalan Hasanuddin is a newish, clean place. The *Hotel Tambora* has a pleasant restaurant set in a garden and a rather more varied menu.

There are numerous night-time satay *stalls* along Jalan Wahiddin, near the junction with Jalan Merdeka.

Getting There & Away

Air Merpati have flights to Mataram (50,000 rp) with connections to Denpasar, Surabaya, Semarang and Yogyakarta.

Bus The long-distance bus terminal is on Jalan Diponegoro. Fares include Dompu for 5500 rp, Bima for 6000 rp and Poto Tano for 2000 rp. The bus ride to Bima is a six-hour journey (including a half-hour lunch break) and the road is surfaced the whole way. Alternatively the much more comfortable express buses offer a combined bus/ferry ticket to Mataram, or catch them to Bima for around 10,000 rp. Buy tickets from the Toko Titian Mas or Toko Hari Terang, both on Jalan Kartini.

Getting Around

Sumbawa Besar is very small – you can walk around much of it with ease. The bus terminal is, in essence, the centre of town. Bemos operate on a flat rate of 250 rp per person including to the airport, post office or to Labuhan Sumbawa, Sumbawa's port, three km west of town.

PULAU MOYO

Two-thirds of Pulau Moyo, three km off Sumbawa's north coast, is a reserve noted for its excellent snorkelling and abundant fish. The boat tours between Lombok and Flores (see the Labuhanbajo section) usually stop here or Moyo can be reached by boat from Labuhan Sumbawa. Alternatively, you can charter a boat for around 10,000 rp one way from Air Bari on the coast, half an hour north of Sumbawa Besar. The Forestry Department are helpful for arranging a visit.

HUU

Sumbawa's south coast has some beautiful beaches and good surf. Huu, south of Dompu, is Sumbawa's surfing Mecca. *Mona*

Lisa and *Indah Lestari* are two hotels with accommodation from 5000 rp per person, and there are other surfing camps. Buses to Huu leave Bima at 8 am and noon and cost 2500 rp, or catch a bus from Dompu.

BIMA

This is Sumbawa's main port and the major centre at the eastern end of the island. It's really just a stop on the way through Sumbawa, and there's nothing much to see or do. The only notable attraction of Bima is the large former **sultan's palace**, now a museum that's worth a look. Guides will show you around and expect a 1000 rp 'donation', but they are useless if you don't speak Indonesian, and not much use if you do. The Jalan Flores **night market** is worth a wander – vendors display posters of Western pop stars side by side with posters of President Suharto.

Information

The Bank Negara Indonesia will change major travellers' cheques and foreign currencies.

The post office is on Jalan Kampung Salama, which is out in the suburbs, way past the palace – take a bemo. Perama (☎ 3510), 50 metres from the Losmen Lila Graha, is good for travel information and expensive tours.

INDONESIA

Places to Stay

Like Sumbawa Besar, Bima is compact and the losmen are all grouped together in the middle of town around the palace.

The *Losmen Lila Graha* (☎ 2740) on Jalan Belakang Bioskop, a 10-minute walk from the central bus station, has long been the most popular hotel and has clean rooms and a good restaurant. Rooms cost 8000/11,500 rp or 13,500/16,000 rp with bath. Breakfast is included but it is getting overpriced. Try bargaining or head for the friendly *Wisma Komodo* (☎ 2070) on Jalan Sultan Ibrahim, just along from the sultan's palace. Large, faded rooms with a hint of the colonial cost 7500 rp a double without bath or 10,000 rp with bath.

Losmen Pelangi (☎ 2878) is a reasonable place a few doors away from the Lila Graha and is good value at 6000 rp for doubles or 7500 rp with bath. The *Losmen Kartini* (☎ 2072) on Jalan Sultan Kaharuddin is a dinghy place with spartan rooms for 3500 per person if you are desperate.

Places to Eat

The Chinese-oriented food in the *Restaurant Lila Graha* is good and moderately priced. Another very good Chinese restaurant with seafood specialities is the *Depot Sembilan Sembilan*, just around the corner from the Lila Graha. The *Bima Cafe*, on Jalan Soekarno Hatta, near the sports field at the opposite end from the sultan's palace, is Bima's answer to cafe society. This convivial place has average fare but the owner, Sil, is good for travel information.

There are various cheap little warungs around the centre of town and the *night market* has some foodstalls serving tasty sweets and snacks. For cheap rumah makan, try the area around the market and the long-distance bus ticket offices on the road to the bus station.

Getting There & Away

Air The Merpati office (☎ 2697) is at Jalan Sukarno Hatta No 60, a few doors from the upmarket Hotel Parewa. Bima is well serviced with direct flights between here and Denpasar, Ende, Labuhanbajo, Mataram, Maumere, Ruteng and Tambulaka, as well as connections to points further afield.

Bus Buses to destinations west of Bima depart from Bima's central bus station, just 10 minutes' walk from the centre of town. Day buses to Sumbawa Besar cost 6000 rp. The numerous express night-bus agents are near the centre of town on the way to the bus station, and air-con buses cost 10,000 to 12,500 rp to Sumbawa Besar or 22,000 rp to Mataram (18,000 rp without air-con) – shop around. Buses leave around 7.30 pm and arrive in Mataram around 9 am.

Minibuses to the east and Pelabuhan Sape – from where you catch the ferry to Flores and Komodo – depart from Kumbe in Raba, a 20-minute bemo ride (250 rp) east from

Bima. It costs 1200 rp to Sape, but for the early-morning ferry take the special 2000 rp buses – catch them in the centre of town or hotels can arrange pick up.

Boat The Pelni office (☎ 35402) is at Jalan Martadinata 73, near the Losmen Kartini. Every two weeks the KM *Kelimutu* calls at Bima on the way to Waingapu (17,000 rp ekonomi), Ende (21,100 rp) and Kupang (36,000 rp). In the reverse direction, it stops in Bima en route to Lembar on Lombok (20,000 rp) and Surabaya (40,000 rp). Pelni's KM *Awu* sails around Kalimantan and Sulawesi and stops in Bima before sailing to Ujung Pandang (19,000 rp).

Getting Around

Bima has plenty of bemos and dokars for short trips. Both cost 250 rp per person. Bima's airport is 16 km out of town; bemos are cheap but infrequent while taxis cost 10,000 rp.

SAPE

Sape is a pleasant enough little town but it is only a transit point. The ferry to Komodo and Flores leaves from Pelabuhan Sape, two km from Sape.

The PHPA office for Komodo information is 1½ km from the town towards Pelabuhan Sape.

Places to Stay & Eat

Losmen Ratna Sari is cheerful, cheap and the most popular at 4000 rp per person. *Losmen Give* is the most basic but the cheapest at 3500 rp per person and *Losmen Friendship* is the best choice for a better room, which cost from 4000 to 10,000 rp with bath. Take a dokar there from the bus station.

As for eating, the best choice is the *Sape Cafe*. Otherwise a couple of rumah makan are only memorable for some of the worst variations of nasi campur in all Indonesia!

Getting There & Away

Bus Buses go to Sape from the Kumbe bus station in Bima-Raba for 1200 rp. Buses meet the ferry from Komodo and Labuhanbajo, and you can pick up the air-con express buses all the way to Mataram (26,000 rp) or even through to Jakarta. Tickets can be bought on the ferry.

Boat Ferries for Komodo and Flores depart from Pelabuhan Sape – take a dokar from Sape for 250 rp per person. Pelabuhan Sape is nothing more than one street leading down to the dock, lined by stilt houses. The chief hobby here is building anything from a canoe to a galleon beside your house.

The ferry leaves every day except Friday at 8 am and stops at Komodo before continuing on to Labuhanbajo in Flores. It takes around seven hours to Komodo and 10 hours to Labuhanbajo, a little less if the conditions are favourable. The fare to both destinations is 9000 rp and tickets can be purchased at the pier one day before departure.

Komodo & Rinca

Komodo is a hilly, dry, desolate island neatly sandwiched between Flores and Sumbawa. Komodo's big attraction is lizards – four-metre, 130-kg lizards, appropriately known as Komodo dragons. From June to September, in the dry season, is the best time to see the dragons as there are more of them out looking for food then. They are carnivores and a goat is the recommended *makan bwaya*, or dragon food. Normally, the dragons eat the deer and wild pig which are found on the island. The only village on the island is **Kampung Komodo**, a fishing village on the east coast of the island and worth a look. Also on the coast and a half-hour walk north of the village is **Loh Liang**, the site of the PHPA tourist camp.

Some people prefer to visit Rinca because it is closer to the Flores coast and less visited. Dragon-spotting is less organised and the chances of seeing them less certain. The PHPA also has a tourist camp on Rinca at **Loh Buaya**.

Permits
You get your permit for Komodo on the island itself, at the PHPA camp at Loh Liang, or on Rinca at Loh Buaya. PHPA is the Indonesian government organisation responsible for managing the country's nature reserves and national parks. Permits cost 2000 rp per person.

Dragon-Spotting
The most accessible place to see the dragons has been set up like a little theatre. The PHPA guides will take you to a dried up river bed about a half-hour walk from Loh Liang. A clearing has been made here overlooking the creek. Wednesday and Sunday are the official goat sacrifice days and a goat costs 50,000 rp, but there are usually large groups around on these days. A dead goat is dangled from a pulley strung over the river and it's not uncommon to see several dragons clambering over each other to get at the last legs of a goat. If this gory sight doesn't appeal, go on other days when you will still be certain of seeing these monsters.

A guide costs 2500 rp for up to five people.

Around Komodo
Other things to do on Komodo include climbing up the hills at the rear of Kampung Komodo for a sweeping view across Komodo village and the other islands in the region.

If you go trekking around the island – climbing **Gunung Ara** for example – be warned that this place is very hot! If you really want to trek into the uplands, then make sure you're the sort of person who runs up and down a volcano before breakfast every morning. The PHPA will provide you with a guide. Sights around the island include wild deer and large, poisonous (though not deadly) spiders.

As for swimming, the PHPA people say that the sea snakes only come out at night and that you'll only attract sharks if you cut yourself on the coral and bleed. Land snakes are supposed to infest the island – signs are posted around the PHPA camp to warn you to wear trousers and shoes and to watch fo[r] snakes.

Wild pigs are commonly seen, often clos[e] to the camp, and the Komodo dragons occa[-]sionally wander into the PHPA camp, bu[t] they avoid the kampung because there ar[e] too many people. Good snorkelling can b[e] found at **Pantai Merah** (Red Beach) and th[e] small island of **Pulau Lasa** near Kampun[g] Komodo. Boats can be hired, as can a snorke[l] and mask from the PHPA, but if you want t[o] go snorkelling it's best to bring your ow[n] equipment.

Places to Stay & Eat
The PHPA camp at Loh Liang is a collectio[n] of large, spacious, clean wooden cabins o[n] stilts. Each cabin has four or five rooms an[d] cost 5000 rp per person per night. Accom[-]modation on Rinca is similar and costs th[e] same.

Bring your own food! The PHPA restau[-]rant is limited to below-average mie goren[g] and nasi goreng, plus expensive beverages[.] For other food, try in Kampung Komodo.

Getting There & Away
You can get to Komodo on the regular ferr[y] that runs between Labuhanbajo in Flores[,] Komodo and Pelabuhan Sape on Sumbawa[.] Cheap day tours from Labuhanbajo also tak[e] in Rinca and Pulau Kalong (or Bat Island)[,] and three to five-day boat tours betwee[n] Lombok and Flores stop at Komodo an[d] Rinca. See the Labuhanbajo section fo[r] details of tours.

Flores

One of the most beautiful islands in Indonesia, Flores is an astounding string of active and extinct volcanos. The name is Portuguese for Flowers, as the Portuguese were the first Europeans to colonise the island. They eventually sold it to the Dutch. The most notable feature of Flores is Catholicism; 95% of the population is Catholic. The church dominates every tiny village and only in the ports will you find any number of Muslims.

Flores was rocked by earthquakes in December 1992. Maumere was devastated and the damage can still be seen in other towns in central Flores such as Ende, but travel in Flores is back to normal – the crowded bus trips can still be arduous.

Getting There & Away

Air Maumere has the best connections for getting to or from Flores by air. Book well in advance for flights from other towns in Flores and always reconfirm, at least once. If you have heard bad reports about Merpati, chances are it was from someone who had been to Flores. The problem is that the airfields in Ende, Labuhanbajo and Bajawa only accommodate small aircraft and so seating is limited. Merpati's short-wave radio booking system on Flores also leaves a lot to be desired.

Bouraq connect Maumere in Flores with Denpasar in Bali (180,000 rp) and Kupang in Timor (65,000 rp). Merpati also connect Maumere with Bima in Sumbawa and Ujung Pandang in Sulawesi, as well as Kupang in Timor. They also connect Bajawa, Labuhanbajo and Ruteng with Bima in Sumbawa, and Ende with Kupang in Timor. From these centres, there are flights on to other parts of Indonesia.

Boat Pelni's KM *Kelimutu* on its regular two-weekly sweep through Nusa Tenggara's islands travels from Waingapu in Sumba to Ende, then Kupang, Dili, Kalabahi, Maumere, Ujung Pandang and then back. The KM *Tatamailau* calls at Labuhanbajo and Larantuka on its way between Surabaya and Dili (Timor), Maluku and Irian Jaya.

Regular ferries connect Labuhanbajo in western Flores with Komodo and Sumbawa. From Larantuka in eastern Flores there are ferries to Kupang in Timor and the eastern islands of Adonara, Solor and Lembata. From Ende regular boats go to Waingapu in Sumba and to Kupang in Timor. As well as the regular services, cargo ships visit the main Flores ports of Labuhanbajo, Reo, Maumere, Larantuka, Ende and Mborong.

Getting Around

Air Merpati has flights connecting Ende with Bajawa, Labuhanbajo and Ruteng.

Bus The Trans-Flores Highway loops and tumbles nearly 700 scenic km from Labuhanbajo to Larantuka. The highway connects all the major centres and most of the road is now surfaced. Ende-Bajawa still has some long, bone-shaking sections and Moni-Maumere does suffer from the occasional landslide, but travel is now much easier and more reliable. Travel in the wet season can still be problematic, especially off the highway when vehicles on the unsealed roads get bogged; a trip that might take hours in the dry season can take days.

Public buses run regularly between all the major towns. They are cheap, leave when full (sometimes very full) and stop at all stations. Tickets can usually be bought the day before departure from agents or from the drivers. The big air-con luxury buses you'll find on Sumatra or Java don't exist on Flores. The highway is too narrow and winding to accommodate big buses, and the road would quickly turn any 'delux' bus into 'ekonomi'. Open-sided trucks with wooden seats also cover the local runs.

Boat Irregular boats ply the water from Labuhanbajo to Reo, and a regular boat runs from Ende to Nggela (see the Ende section).

LABUHANBAJO

This fishing village at the extreme western end of Flores is a jumping-off point for Komodo. If you've got a few days to while away, then Labuhanbajo is a pleasant enough village to do it in. It's a pretty place with a harbour sheltered by several small islands. There are reasonable beaches such as Waecicu just outside town, good snorkelling and a host of tours on offer.

INDONESIA

Information

The Bank Rakyat Indonesia branch in Labuhanbajo changes travellers' cheques at low but acceptable rates. The ferry ticket office is near the ferry dock. The PHPA office is a five-minute walk along the airport road from the Hotel Wisata.

Organised Tours

Labuhanbajo is also inundated with boat tours to Komodo, Rinca and further afield. Boat hire for a day tour to Komodo, Rinca and Kalong (Bat Island) costs around 60,000 to 70,000 rp, for a fishing boat which will take eight to 10 people. A boat to Pulau Sabolo, reputed to have the best snorkelling, will cost 30,000 rp for the day. Many hotels, such as Waecicu Beach, arrange boats for guests. Competition is fierce and two-day/one-night boat tours to Komodo and Rinca are available for as low as 25,000 rp per person.

Other tours continue on to Sape or around the north coast of Sumbawa, stopping at Moyo Island before continuing on to Lombok. Prices range from around 50,000 rp for three days to 100,000 rp for five days. Don't expect luxury or Swiss-watch organisation – these are small boats run by local operators and overnight stops are often spent on the boat. The bigger companies like Perama have bigger boats and are more comfortable, but are also much more expensive.

Places to Stay & Eat

Hotel prices in Labuhanbajo are very fluid and bargaining is the rule, but you can expect to pay up to 50% more when they are busy. Breakfast is usually included. The *Mutiara Beach Hotel* boasts a sitting area and restaurant with a fine harbour view. With singles/doubles at 3000/6000 rp with private bath it is hard to beat. The nearby *Bajo Beach Hotel* is the big operator in town. Very clean rooms range from 3500 rp for windowless boxes and 6000/8000 rp for rooms with bath to 12,500 rp and more for fancier rooms favoured by tour groups.

On the hill above town, *Chez Felix Homestay* is run by a friendly family that speaks good English. It has a pleasant porch area for sitting and good rooms with attached bath cost 5000/8000 rp. Just nearby, *Sony Homestay* has reasonable rooms with bath for 4000 rp per person. *Oemathonis Homestay*, on the road leading towards the airport, is clean and airy. Rooms cost 3500 rp per person.

Other cheap but very basic, local losmen include the *Bahagia Homestay* (3500 rp per person), past the wharf away from town, and *Homestay Gembira* (3000 rp) near the mosque. At the other end of the scale, *Hotel Wisata* has the best rooms in town for 10,000/15,000 rp.

If you want to spend some time in Labuhanbajo, head for the *Waecicu Beach Hotel*, a 20-minute boat ride away. This popular travellers' retreat has simple cabins on the beach for 7500 rp and 10,000 rp per person including three excellent meals. It's comfortable enough but the lack of fresh water is a drawback. *Batu Kolok* is a new place further along the same beach. Further out still, *Batu Gosok Beach Hotel* is 12,500 rp per person including meals and while the rooms are not so good, the white-sand beach and clear waters are the best. However, plans are afoot to turn it into an upmarket resort.

Both Waecicu and Batu Gosok are reached by the hotel boats, free for guests, from the far end of the main street, just past the jetty. For non-guests the return trip to Waecicu costs 2000 rp.

Most of the hotels have meals; alternatively, the no-frills *Banyuwangi* has cheap food, and the *Sunrise* has a pleasant aspect and good meals. Whole grilled fish is a cheap treat in Labuhanbajo and the *Restaurant New Tenda Nikmat* does it better than anyone.

Getting There & Away

Air Merpati has direct flights between Labuhanbajo and Ende (97,000 rp), Ruteng (42,000 rp) and Bima (53,000 rp), with connections on to Mataram (138,000 rp), Denpasar (177,000 rp) and further afield.

The airfield is 2½ km from the town and hotels can arrange a taxi (5000 rp) to get you there. The Merpati office is between

INDONESIA

Labuhanbajo and the airport, about 1½ km from the town.

Bus Buses go to Ruteng (4000 rp, four hours) around 7.30 am and 3 pm and some of the morning buses continue through to Bajawa (9000 rp, nine hours). Buy advance tickets from hotels or from the bus drivers the evening before, and get them to pick you up from your hotel. One bus goes right through to Ende, but you travel at night and miss out on the scenery, and it has been known to stop in the middle of nowhere while the driver gets some sleep.

Boat The ferry to Komodo and then Sape (Sumbawa) departs Labuhanbajo at 8 am every day except Sunday, and costs 9000 rp to Sape or 2800 rp to Komodo. Get tickets from the harbourmaster's office near the pier at the northern end of the main street. You can also ask at the harbourmaster's office about cargo boats to other destinations – something sails to Reo every few days.

Pelni's KM *Tatamailau* calls at Labuhanbajo once a month on its way from Surabaya and Badas and goes on to Larantuka, Dili, Maluku and Irian Jaya. It calls back at Labuhanbajo two weeks later travelling the reverse route.

REO

Located on an estuary, a little distance up from the sea, is the oversized village of Reo. The large Catholic mission in the middle of the town is Reo's focal point. Few travellers bother visiting Reo but if you want to get off the beaten track, hunt around Labuhanbajo's port for a boat there. The journey takes about 10 hours, or Reo can easily be reached by bus from Ruteng (1500 rp, three hours). Reo has a few basic *losmen*.

RUTENG

Ruteng is basically just another stop on the way through Flores. For spectacular views of the rice paddies and terraced slopes of the hills and valleys to the north, climb the hill to the north of Ruteng early in the morning. Take the Reo road, and about 10 minutes from Wisma Agung, you will come to a small bridge across a stream. Turn right and head up the track immediately after the bridge. **Mt Ranaka**, an active volcano that erupted in 1989, is just outside town. It can be climbed, though the adjacent peaks such as **Nampar Mos** are easier and safer.

Information

The Bank Rakyat Indonesia will change foreign cash (like US$ and A$) and major travellers' cheques. The post office is at Jalan Baruk 6.

Places to Stay & Eat

The *Wisma Dahlia* is one of the best places in town and has an excellent restaurant. Rooms cost from 8000 rp or 12,000 rp with mandi. The similarly priced *Hotel Sindha* on Jalan Yos Sudarso is also good, and serves Chinese food.

The *Wisma Agung I* (☎ 80) at Jalan Wae Cos 10 has lost its shine a little but is still reasonable with rooms from 6000 rp, and the restaurant is cheap. The *Wisma Agung II*, behind Toko Agung on Jalan Motang Rua, is more central but darker, shabbier and more expensive with rooms from 8000 rp. The *Losmen Karya* is a decent little place but it always seems to be 'full' – rooms cost from 5000 rp.

Apart from the hotels, for Chinese food, try the *Rumah Makan Dunia Baru* or, for nasi padang, the *Rumah Makan Beringin*. The *Rumah Makan Indonesia* at the bus station is cheaper and does decent, filling food, although the menu is rather limited. There's a string of little *warungs* by the adjacent market.

Getting There & Away

Air Merpati (☎ 147) is on Jalan Pertiwi 15, about a 10-minute walk from town in the rice paddies. Merpati connects Ruteng with Bima (85,000 rp) and Kupang (121,000 rp) and there are onward connections from those centres. Two flights a week go to Labuhanbajo (42,000 rp).

INDONESIA

Road Buses and trucks depart from the station next to the market and do the usual pick-up around town. Fares and distances are: Bajawa (5000 rp, six hours), Labuhanbajo (4000 rp, four hours) and Ende (9000 rp, 12 hours).

BAJAWA

Bajawa is a little town nestled in the hills and is also the centre for the Ngada people of the Bajawa Plateau area. Coming in on the road from Ruteng, you'll see the great volcanic **Gunung Inerie** – a spectacular sight in the setting sun. Nearby is **Gunung Wolobobor**, an extinct volcano with the top half shaved off.

Bajawa is a pleasant enough place for a short stop, but the main attraction is the Ngada villages around Bajawa. **Bena**, 19 km north of Bajawa, is one of the most traditional and interesting villages. It has also had the greatest exposure to tourism and visitors' fees are expected. **Soa** has an interesting Sunday afternoon market, while **Langa**, **Boawae**, **Wogo** and **Ogi** are other villages worth visiting.

The area has many traditional houses and the odd *ngadhu*, basically a carved pole supporting a conical thatched roof, rather like a large umbrella. Ngadhu are a male symbol used in ancestor worship, and to guard against sickness and preserve fertility – both human and agricultural. The female counterpart of this all-round 'tree of life' is the *bhaga*, a structure that looks something like a miniature thatched-roof house. You can see a ngadhu in Bajawa at the end of Jalan Satsuitubu.

Places to Stay & Eat

The *Hotel Sunflower* (☎ 236) on Jalan H Waruk is one of the first places as you enter town. It is deservedly the most popular with good rooms and views from the porch overlooking the valley. Rooms cost 5000/8000 rp with attached bathroom, and excellent, cheap tours to the surrounding villages are organised from here.

Just below the Sunflower on the main road, the *Hotel Modest Dagalos* is cheap at 5000 rp per double but bare and unattractive. A better bet is to walk a bit further up the road to the *Hotel Korina*, a friendly family-run hotel with comfortable rooms for 6000/9000 rp.

Hotel Johny on Jalan Gajah Mada out towards the post office is a reasonable place but not so conveniently located. Rooms are 7500/10,000 rp with bath. For the same price, the *Hotel Virgo* is one of the better budget places in town and has clean rooms with bath around a courtyard. Other places include the *Hotel Kambera* and the *Hotel Anggrek*, both on Jalan El Tari just around the corner from the Virgo, and the *Hotel Kembang*, one street over on Jalan Marta Dinata.

The popular *Restoran Carmellya* is a cosy travellers' restaurant on Jalan Ahmad Yani, just across from the Hotel Korina. *Rumah Makan Wisata*, near the market, is similar with a varied menu and good information on the area. The friendly *Rumah Makan Kasih Bahagia*, near the market on Jalan Achmad Yani, has cold beer and inexpensive Indonesian food.

Getting There & Away

Air Merpati flies from Bajawa to Bima and Ende, with onward connections. The Merpati office (☎ 21051) is opposite the Bajawa Market.

Bus The long-distance bus station is a few km outside of town near the highway. Take a bemo for 300 rp. Buses to Ende (4000 rp, five hours) leave at 7 am and noon. More frequent buses go to Ruteng (5000 rp, six hours). The bus to Labuhanbajo (9000 rp, 10 hours) also leaves at 7 am. Bus tickets can be bought the previous evening from the bus drivers around the market, or from agents such as Toko Sinar Mustika near the market on Jalan Pasar Rahmat. On arrival in Bajawa, buses will drop you off at your hotel.

For surrounding villages, small buses and trucks leave from the market.

INDONESIA

RIUNG

Riung, on the coast north of Bajawa, has beaches and giant iguanas – not quite komodo dragons, but impressive beasts nonetheless and more colourful. The off-shore reserve of **Pulau Tujuh Belas** (Seventeen Islands) offers excellent snorkelling. Riung is well off the beaten tourist track but two homestays, the *Liberti* and *Tamri*, have opened up and cater for travellers. They cost 8000 rp per person including all meals.

A direct bus to Riung leaves Ende at 7 am. From Bajawa it is possible to travel the rough road north to Riung in stages, but it is a roundabout route; buses and trucks from Bajawa take the highway to Aegela, about 50 km east of Bajawa, and then the better road to Riung.

ENDE

The capital of Flores is a dull and dusty town – it's easy to see why the Dutch exiled Sukarno here in the 1930s. You can visit the house he lived in but there's nothing much to see. The revolting beach improves as you walk west from the town centre. Ende has it's own distinctive style of ikat weaving, and examples of Jopu, Nggela and Wolonjita weaving can also be found in the main street market near the waterfront.

Orientation & Information

Gunung Meja's perfect cone provides a useful landmark to the south-west of the airport. Ende straddles a narrow peninsula with the port and airport on the east side and the town on the west. The Bank Rakyat Indonesia offers reasonable exchange rates and has a temporary branch next to the Hotel Dwi Putra, while their bank on Jalan Sudirman is being rebuilt after the earthquake.

Places to Stay

Near the airport, the *Losmen Ikhlas* on Jalan Achmad Yani is in a class of its own. Singles/doubles/triples cost 4500/7500/10,000 rp or 6000/9000/12,000 rp with mandi. The place is often run by a bevy of tourism students who don't know what they're doing, but otherwise it is well set up for travellers, with good meals and excellent travel information. Next door is the more upmarket *Losmen Safari* at Jalan Achmad Yani 3, where rooms, all with mandi, cost 8000/13,000 rp.

Between the airport and the town centre, on Jalan Achmad Yani close to the harbour turn-off, is the rock-bottom *Losmen Rinjani* with rooms for 4500/7500 rp. Not far from the airport, towards the town on Jalan Kelimutu, the *Wisma Wisata* is pleasant but overpriced at 11,000/15,000 rp or 14,000/17,500 rp with bath.

Starting from the town side, the *Hotel Dwi Putra* (☎ 21465) on Jalan K H Dewantara is the top hotel in town, though the earthquake has left it a little frayed. Rooms cost 15,000/20,000 rp with fan or 30,000/35,000 rp with air-con. The *Sandalwood Hotel* on Jalan Sukarno near the market area is a clean, well-run hotel with rooms for 6000/9000 rp. The *Hotel Amica* at Jalan Garuda 15 is on the airport side of the town centre. It is dead quiet and dreary rooms cost 6500/12,000 rp with bath.

Other good hotels, a little out from the centre to the north, are the *Hotel Nirwana* at Jalan Pahlawan 29, and the nearby *Losmen Solafide*, Jalan One Kore 2, and *Hotel Merlin*.

Places to Eat

Many *warungs* set up in the evening around the market, serving satay, rice and boiled vegetables. The *Kambera Restaurant*, next to the bemo stand at the market, has bamboo decor and Indonesian dishes at reasonable prices. At Jalan Sudirman 6, *Depot Ende* is a bit dreary but the Chinese and Indonesian food is good.

Look for the *alus manis* man who plays a calypso tune on the tins hanging around his neck. He sells a sticky pink sweet, like coarse fairyfloss with a coconut flavour – it's 100 rp for a small serve.

Getting There & Away

Air Merpati (☎ 21355) is on Jalan Nangka, a 15-minute walk from the airstrip. Ende's short airstrip means that only small aircraft service the town and few seats are available to or from Ende.

Bus Buses to the east leave from Terminal Ende, four km from town. Buses to Moni (2000 rp, 2½ hours) depart at 6 am and 2 pm or you can also take a Wolowaru bus. Regular trucks go to Moni on market days, Monday and Tuesday. Buses to Maumere (5000 rp, 6½ hours) leave in the morning around 8 am and in the afternoon at 5 pm. Maumere buses will drop you in Moni but charge for the full fare to Maumere.

Buses to the west leave from Terminal Ndao, two km north of town on the beach road. Buses to Bajawa (4000 rp, six hours) leave at 7 am and noon. Buses to Ruteng (9000 rp, 12 hours) leave at 8 am.

Boat Ships dock at Pelabuhan Ipi, the main port, which is about 2½ km from the town. Pelni's KM *Kelimutu* stops in Ende every two weeks as it comes in from Waingapu in Sumba (12,000 rp ekonomi, seven hours) and continues on to Kupang in Timur (15,000 rp, 10 hours). It then reverses direction and heads back along the same route.

A regular ferry runs to Kupang (15,300 rp, 17 hours) departing Sunday at 1 pm. It leaves Kupang for Ende on Monday and then continues on to Waingapu (Sumba) on Wednesday at 7 pm (10,400 rp). Small boats chug between Ende and Nggela, 55 km east of Ende, leaving at 7 am every day except Friday and taking 3½ hours.

INDONESIA

Getting Around

Bemo fares around town are a flat 300 rp. This includes trips to the airport, to the bus stations and to Pelabuhan Ipi.

KELI MUTU

This extinct volcano is the most fantastic sight in Nusa Tenggara, if not all of Indonesia. The crater has three lakes – the largest is bright turquoise and next to it there is a pale green lake and a bit further away a black lake. Chemicals in the soil account for this weird colour scheme and it changes with time (the green lake was a deep maroon/brown in the mid-70s).

The best time to see Keli Mutu is in the early morning as clouds usually settle down later on and you need strong sunlight to bring out the colours of the lakes. If you get a really bad day – or if you get to the top too late in the day – the clouds will have rolled in covering the lakes and you won't be able to see anything at all.

Getting There & Away

Most visitors base themselves in Moni, the village at the foot of the volcano, and make their way up to the top with the 3500 rp truck which departs for the summit at 4 am. Hotels in Moni can arrange this the night before. You can set out at 2 am and walk the 13 km to the top in three to four hours, arriving in time for the sunrise. Or, you can hire a horse but it will probably be slower than walking. Enterprising locals sell breakfast at the top for suitably inflated prices. The truck goes down the mountain at 7 am, but most travellers walk back.

If you walk up, there's a park entry post halfway up the road where you pay a 400 rp entry fee. It probably won't be open on your way up so you pay on your way down. Coming down, there's a shortcut from just beside the entry post which comes out by the hot springs and waterfall. It's fine going down but would be difficult to find, in the dark, on your way up. Coming down takes two to three hours.

MONI

Moni (Mone) is a little village and mission on the Ende to Maumere road at the base of Keli Mutu. It is cooler than the lowlands, scenic and a good place for walks. About one km before Moni, on the Ende side, is the turn-off to the top of Keli Mutu. This turn-off is a 15-minute walk from the centre of Moni. Moni's Tuesday **market** (it starts on Monday) is a major local event and attracts a large and colourful crowd.

Places to Stay & Eat

Moni is a good stop for a few days and has a

collection of small, cheap homestays along the road through town. *Homestay Daniel* is one of the most popular, largely because this is where most buses stop. Rooms cost 4000 rp per person and good, all-you-can-eat meals are an extra 2500 rp. Clustered nearby are *Homestay Moni Indah* (5000 rp with bargaining, *Homestay John* (3500 rp) and *Homestay Amina Moe II* (4000 rp). *Friendly Homestay* has good rooms for 4000 rp per person but is less frequented, while just back from the main road is *Amina Moe I*, with basic rooms for 3500 rp per person, good views from the porch and the irrepressible Mina as hostess.

Other, quieter homestays away from the market are *Nusa Bunga* with singles/doubles for 5000/8000 rp, the *Regal Jaya* with good rooms for 5000 rp per person and the *Wisata Restaurant*, which has cute thatched rooms for the same price.

Most of the homestays provide good meals. The *Lovely Rose*, *Cafe Ankerma* and the *Restaurant Kelimutu*, perched up above the town near the Keli Mutu turn-off, are good alternatives with local and Western dishes.

Getting There & Away

Moni is 52 km north-east of Ende and 96 km west of Maumere. For Ende, the truck to Keli Mutu descends the mountain and goes to Ende at 8 am. The buses from Maumere to Ende come through from around 10 am until noon, and then there may be nothing until the evening. Many buses and trucks leave on market days, Monday and Tuesday.

For Maumere (3000 rp, four hours) the first buses start coming though at around 9 or 10 am. As most of the buses stop in Moni mid-route, it's first-come, first-served for a seat.

WOLOWARU AREA

Wolowaru is an oversized village 13 km from Moni on the road to Maumere. As you come into Wolowaru from Ende, note the complex of five traditional houses, or *rumah adat*, distinguished by their high sloping roofs.

From Wolowaru, a road leads to the coast and the villages of **Jopu**, **Wolonjita** and **Nggela**. Beautiful and intricately woven sarongs and shawls can be found in these and other small villages. The villages are an interesting and pleasant walk from Wolowaru, so long as you avoid the heat of the day. The volcano-studded skyline is beautiful and near Nggela, which is perched on a clifftop, there are fine views of the ocean. Nggela has a number of traditional houses but the town's chief attraction is the stunning weaving.

Places to Stay

It is possible to stay in Wolowaru at the *Losmen Kelimutu* and *Losmen Setia* for around 5000 rp per person, though most visitors stay in Moni and visit Wolowaru on a day trip.

Getting There & Away

A couple of buses based in Wolowaru go to Maumere (3000 rp, four hours), Ende (2100 rp, three hours) and Moni (500 rp, half an hour). It is advisable to book at the agents in town. Otherwise, hail down buses on the Ende to Maumere road.

A rough road leads all the way from Ende to Nggela via Wolowaru, Jopu and Wolonjita. Irregular vehicles run from Ende to Nggela and you may be able to hitch, otherwise walk from Wolowaru. At Wolowaru, a dirt road leads off to Jopu, four km away, and on to Wolonjita, a further four km away. From Wolonjita, a dirt track leads downhill and across the paddy fields to Nggela – about an hour's walk. You can easily get from Wolowaru to Nggela and back in a day, even if you have to walk both stretches.

A boat leaves Ende for Nggela every day except Friday at 7 am and returns from Nggela around noon.

MAUMERE

Maumere is a medium-size port on the north-east coast and a stopover on the route between Ende and Larantuka. This is still an important mission centre and the Maumere area also has strong ikat-weaving traditions. In December 1992, Maumere was devastated by the earthquakes that hit Flores and also went under a 20-metre-high tsunami. It will take years before Maumere loses its war-zone look.

Information

The Bank Rakyat Indonesia at Jalan Soekarno Hatta changes travellers' cheques.

The post office is next to the soccer field on Jalan Pos, and the Telkom office is further south from the town centre on Jalan Soekarno Hatta.

Things to See

The walls of the **cathedral** near the Losmen Bogor are adorned with an unusual series of pictures illustrating the crucifixion of a very Indonesian-looking Jesus. Behind the cathedral is an interesting old **cemetery**. On Jalan Pasar Baru, opposite the market, the Harapan Jaya Art shop has an excellent selection of ikat cloth.

Places to Stay

A number of Maumere's hotels disappeared in the quake and accommodation can sometimes be tight.

Losmen Wini Rai (☎ 388) is near the bus station for Moni and Ende, a bit of a walk south of the centre along Jalan Gajah Mada. Singles/doubles in this popular and very well-kept place are 7500/12,500 rp or 20,000/25,000 rp with mandi and fan. A mediocre breakfast is included.

Possibilities around the centre include *Losmen Bogor II* (☎ 271) which is next to the Pelni office at Jalan Slamet Riyadi 1-4, near the waterfront. Rooms are comfortable and cost 7500/12,500 rp and a few singles are 5500 rp. Right across the road, *Hotel Bogor* is a dive and costs 3500 rp per person in share rooms.

Losmen Beng Goan III, south of the centre on Jalan K S Tubun, is cheap at 3500 per person but deserted and half-destroyed by the quake.

A little out of the town centre is the *Gardena Hotel* (☎ 489) on Jalan Pattirangga, three blocks east from the market. Reasonable rooms with mandi cost 10,000/12,500 rp, including breakfast. The *Hotel Malwali*, Jalan Raja Don Tomas, is the best place in town with rooms from 10,000/20,000 rp to 32,000/56,000 rp.

Places to Eat

In the evenings, *warungs* set up around the edge of the market and offer the cheapest fare in town. The best place to hunt out a restaurant is Jalan Pasar Baru Barat, which runs beside the market down to the waterfront. *Rumah Makan Surya Indah* has Chinese food and does good squid; and opposite, *Rumah Makan Sumber Indah* is a little more expensive and has seafood dishes. Stevani, with a bamboo bar and huts spread around a garden, seems more suited to Kuta in Bali than Maumere, but it's a good place for a drink.

Getting There & Away

Air Bouraq and Merpati fly to Maumere and both connect with Kupang (65,000 rp) and Bali (181,000 rp). Merpati fly via Bima (Sumbawa) en route to Bali and also have a direct flight to Ujung Pandang (125,000 rp). Bouraq's office (☎ 21467) is on Jalan Nong Meak. The Merpati office (☎ 147, 242) is at Jalan Don Thomas 18.

Bus The bus station for westbound buses is 1½ km from the centre on the road to Moni and Ende. Buses to Ende (5000 rp, 6½ hours) leave early in the morning and at 5 pm, and usually stop for a meal at Wolowaru, just 13 km before Moni. You can catch these buses to Moni but you may have to pay the full fare to Ende. Buses also run to Wolowaru for 3000 rp.

For eastbound buses, Terminal Timur is five km east of town. Buses to Larantuka (5000 rp, four hours) leave until around 4 pm and this is also the terminal for buses to Waiara (500 rp, 45 minutes).

Boat Pelni's KM *Kelimutu* sails to and from Ujung Pandang in Sulawesi (21,000 rp, 22 hours) and Kalabahi on Alor (11,000 rp, 12 hours). The Pelni office is on Jalan Slamet Riyadi, next to Losmen Bogor II.

Getting Around

The airport is three km from the town centre, off the Maumere to Larantuku road. Count on around 5000 rp for a taxi or chartered bemo to the airport. The standard bemo fare around town and to the bus terminals is 300 rp.

AROUND MAUMERE

Just off the Larantuka road, 13 km east of Maumere, **Waiara** is becoming increasingly popular for the scuba diving around offshore islands. There are diving schools associated with the two places to stay at Waiara Beach. *Saowisata* caters mostly to tour groups and rooms start at US$35/40. A full day's dive costs US$55. The *Sea World Club* is a cheaper alternative with rooms from US$20.

The village of **Sikka** has its own distinctive style of weaving and can be reached in an hour by bus from Maumere. **Ladalero,** about 24 km from Maumere, is a major Catholic seminary from where many Florinese priests are ordained. Father Piet Petu's museum with its ikat and artefacts from all over Indonesia is the village's chief attraction. Buses run regularly to Ladalero from Maumere.

LARANTUKA

This little port nestles at the base of a high hill at the eastern end of Flores. From here, you can see the islands of Solor and Adonara across the narrow strait. There's not a great deal to see in town, although outside the Holy Mary Church you will find an old Portuguese cannon and a bell – both painted a ghastly silver.

Information

The only place to change money is the Bank Rakyat Indonesia.

Places to Stay & Eat

Hotel Rulies must be one of the friendliest and most convivial places in Indonesia; it has rooms at 6000 rp per person. Although it's clean and relatively new, *Hotel Tresna* looks better from the outside than it actually is. Its basic rooms are similarly priced.

Losmen Kartika is a rather seedy looking place but if the Tresna or the Rulies are full, or you want something cheaper, then it's OK, although it can be noisy from the street. Rooms are 4000 rp per person.

There's a cluster of anonymous *warungs* near the wharf.

Getting There & Away

Air The Merpati office is diagonally opposite the large church on the street running parallel to Jalan Niaga. Flights out of Larantuka go to Lewoleba in Lembata and Kupang in Timor. A chartered bemo to the airport is around 3500 rp.

Bus Buses between Maumere and Larantuka cost 5000 rp and take four hours. If you're coming in by boat from the Solor Archipelago, enthusiastic tours will be waiting to whisk passengers away to Maumere.

Boat A ferry runs twice a week between Larantuka and Kupang (12,400 rp, 12 hours) and these ferries also run to Weiwerang on Adonara (1900 rp) and Lewoleba on Lembata (3400 rp). Departures are from the wharf five km south-west of Larantuka (300 rp by a yellow-lamp bemo). Smaller boats depart almost every day from Larantuka to the islands of Lembata, Adonara and Solor. Ask at the harbourmaster's office and at the Pelni office on Jalan Niaga for information on services out of Larantuka.

Pelni's KM *Tatamailau* calls at Larantuka on its way between Labuhanbajo and Dili in Timor.

Lembata

The terrain of Lembata Island (also referred to as Lomblen Island) in the Solor Archipelago is strongly reminiscent of Australia, the palm trees of the coast giving way to gum trees in the hills. Fine ikat comes from villages on the slopes of Ili Api, a smoking volcano near Lewoleba.

LEWOLEBA

Lewoleba is the island's chief settlement and is a relaxed, easy-going place despite the proximity of Ili Api. Between the pier and town is a Bugis **stilt village**. Some of the inhabitants are pearl divers. Lewoleba's banks do not change money.

Places to Stay & Eat

Hotel Rejeki, opposite the market in the centre of town, is a pleasant place to stay and has rooms for 6000 rp. Meals here can be excellent. For an extra charge, you can get three meals a day with rice, fish, meat, squid, vegetables and egg.

Alternatively, the very basic *Losmen Rachmat*, on the end of Jalan Aulolon and at the back of the market, costs 3800 rp per person but there's no food service. A row of *warungs* nearby offer basic sustenance.

Getting There & Away

Air Merpati flies from Larantuka to Lewoleba (33,000 rp) and on to Kupang (84,000 rp) twice a week.

Boat Boats to Lewoleba depart daily from Larantuka at 7 am. The four-hour trip, which costs 3400 rp, usually includes a 45-minute stop to load and unload passengers at Waiwerang. Boats also run to Kalabahi on Alor, usually via Balauring and Wairiang in north-east Lembata, but this trip can take up to 2½ days – bring plenty of food and drinking water. From Kalabahi a ferry then runs to Kupang twice a week for 14,900 rp.

LAMALERA

On the south coast, Lamalera is a whaling village where the villagers still hunt whales. They use small rowboats and hand-thrown harpoons. If you want to stay, you can try the missionary or ask the kepala desa (village head).

Getting There & Away

Walking There are two roads from Lewoleba – the long one and the short one. For the short one, you head out of Lewoleba and ask directions for the nearby village of Namaweke. If you simply ask for the road to Lamalera, you could end up being directed along the main road which follows a wide circular route around the island. Even by the short route, the walk takes about seven hours.

Boat There's a regular boat each Monday from Lewoleba to Lamalera.

Timor

The Portuguese were the first Europeans to land in Timor, in the early 16th century. The Dutch occupied Kupang in the middle of the 17th century and after a lengthy conflict, the Portuguese finally withdrew to the eastern half of the island in the middle of the 18th century. When Indonesia became independent in 1949, the Dutch half of Timor became part of the new republic but the Portuguese still retained the eastern half.

On 25 April 1974, there was a military coup in Portugal and the new government set about discarding the Portuguese colonial empire. Within a few weeks of the coup, three major political parties had been formed in East Timor. After the UDT attempted to seize power in August 1975, a brief civil war between the rival parties, Fretilin and UDT, saw Fretilin come out on top.

However, a number of top generals in the Indonesian army opposed the formation of an independent East Timor and, on 7 December 1975, Indonesia launched a full-scale invasion of the former colony. It can hardly be a coincidence that this happened just one day after US Secretary of State Henry Kissinger had cleared out of Indonesia after a brief visit – presumably having put the US seal of approval on the invasion.

By all accounts, the Indonesian invasion was brutal. Fretilin fought a guerrilla war with marked success in the first two or three years but after that began to weaken considerably. The cost to the Timorese people was horrific, many dying through starvation or disease due to the disruption of food and medical supplies. By 1989, Indonesia had things firmly under control and opened East Timor to tourism, but on 12 November 1991 army troops opened fire on protestors at the Dili cemetery, once again alerting the world to East Timor's plight.

Fretilin activity is still sporadically reported but East Timor (or Timor Timur) is very quiet and the army has firm control. The hangover from the 1991 massacre is that travellers are not allowed overland across the border without a travel permit from the army in Kupang, which is rarely issued. Some travellers have been able to convince the border guards that they are not journalists and made it through without a permit. Check the latest developments in Kupang – the situation may well change. For the moment Dili can only be reached by air or sea, though once in Dili it is possible to travel around the province and back overland to Kupang.

Getting There & Away

Air Kupang, the capital of Timor, is well connected by air with other parts of Indonesia – Merpati, Sempati and Bouraq all fly there with connections to a number of other islands in Nusa Tenggara and other parts of the country. A good way to explore Nusa Tenggara is to fly directly from Denpasar (Bali) to Kupang for 199,000 rp and then island-hop back.

Merpati have a twice-weekly service (currently Wednesday and Saturday) between Darwin in Australia's Northern Territory and Kupang. See the Indonesia Getting There & Away section for more details. This is a terrific way of getting to Indonesia; the flight is popular but usually not heavily booked.

Kupang is on the no-visa-required entry list. On arrival you will be asked to show an onward ticket or a significant wad of cash or travellers' cheques (US$1000 is very acceptable), though immigration here is usually easy going.

Boat Pelni's KM *Kelimutu* operates a service down through the Nusa Tenggara islands to Kupang and Dili and back every two weeks – see the Getting Around section at the start of this chapter for details of Pelni boats. The KM *Dobonsolo* runs directly between Surabaya and Kupang and on to Dili and Ambon in Maluku. Pelni's Perintis cargo line also takes passengers and operates boats to many other destinations in the region.

Perum ASDP has twice-weekly ferries between Larantuka in Flores and Kupang, and these boats continue on to Waiwerang and Lewoleba, east of Flores. Boats depart from Kupang to Larantuka the day after the Darwin flight arrives. Perum ASDP ferries also operate once a week to Ende on Flores and then on to Waingapu on Sumba, twice a week to Kalabahi on Alor Island, and other services operate to the islands of Roti and Sawu.

Getting Around

Prior to the Indonesian takeover, the roads in Timor were really rotten. It was debatable whether the Portuguese half was more or less neglected than the Indonesian half. The road from Kupang to Atambua via Soe and Kefamenanu is now well surfaced. In eastern Timor, many of the roads are now in good condition.

KUPANG

Kupang is the biggest town on the island and capital of the southern province of Nusa Tenggara. If you've been on the other islands of Nusa Tenggara for any length of time, then Kupang comes as something of a shock. Compared to the sedate little towns of Flores or Sumbawa, this is a booming metropolis.

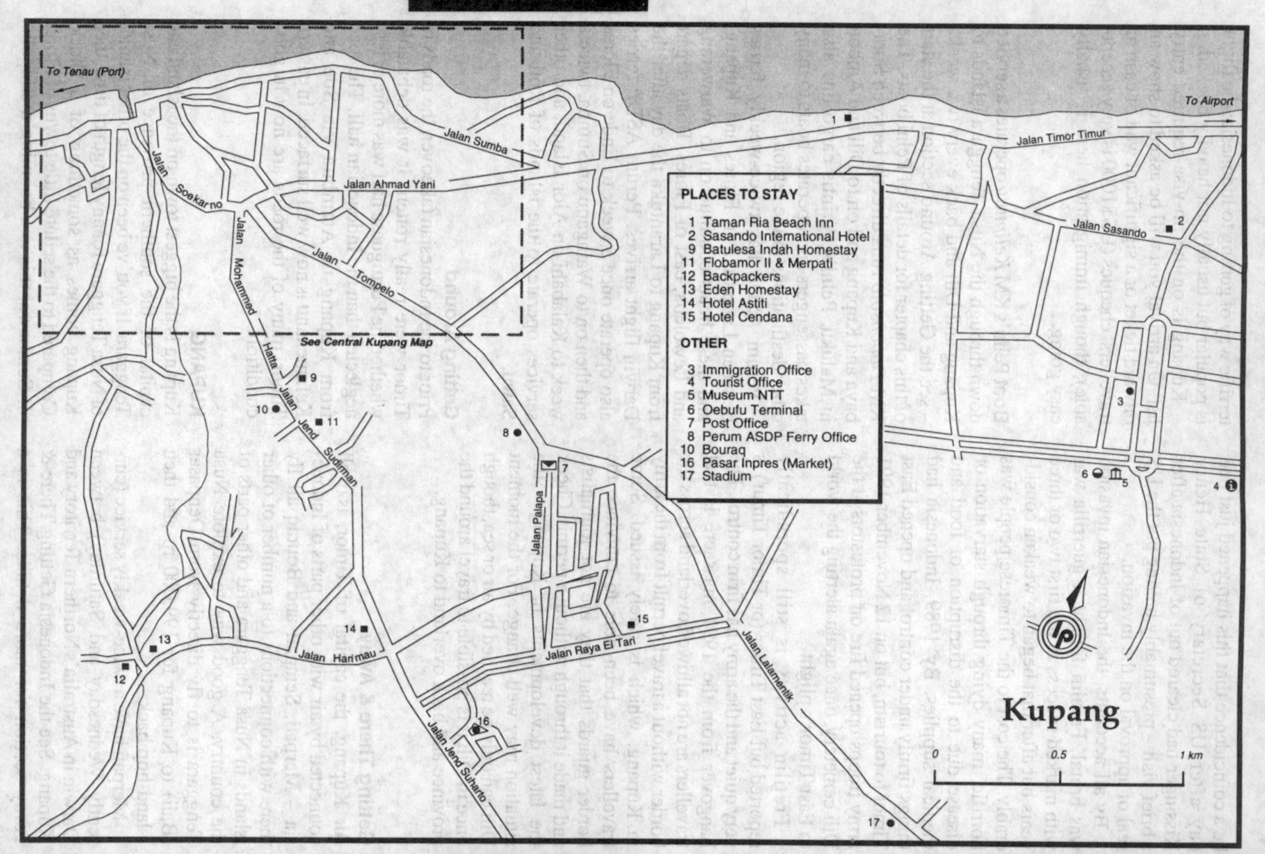
To Tenau (Port)
To Airport
Jalan Sumba
Jalan Timor Timur
Jalan Ahmad Yani
Jalan Soekarno
Jalan Mohammed Hatta
Jalan Tompelo
Jalan Sasando
See Central Kupang Map
Jalan Jend Sudirman
Jalan Palapa
Jalan Harimau
Jalan Raya El Tari
Jalan Lalamentik
Jalan Jend Suharto
PLACES TO STAY
1 Taman Ria Beach Inn
2 Sasando International Hotel
9 Batulesa Indah Homestay
11 Flobamor II & Merpati
12 Backpackers
13 Eden Homestay
14 Hotel Astiti
15 Hotel Cendana
OTHER
3 Immigration Office
4 Tourist Office
5 Museum NTT
6 Oebufu Terminal
7 Post Office
8 Perum ASDP Ferry Office
10 Bouraq
16 Pasar Inpres (Market)
17 Stadium
Kupang
0
0.5
1 km

It's not a bad place to hang around – Captain Bligh did, after his *Bounty* misadventures.

Information

Tourist Office The Kupang tourist office is right out in the sticks near the Walikota bemo terminal – it's not really worth the effort.

Money The Bank Dagang Indonesia, down near the waterfront on Jalan Soekarno, will change cash and travellers' cheques. Bank Negara Indonesia on Jalan Sumatera, next to Wisma Maliana, also has a good foreign exchange service. The currency exchange office at Kupang airport is open when flights arrive from Darwin.

Post & Telecommunications Poste restante mail goes to the central post office, Kantor Pos Besar, at Jalan Palapa 1. A branch post office is on Jalan Soekarno, diagonally across from the Bank Rakyat Indonesia. The Telkom office is on Jalan Urip Sumohardjo.

Permits For overland travel permits to East Timor, you have to go to Korem (Komando Resor Militer) about 2½ km beyond the main post office on Jalan Lalamentik. Best of luck.

Places to Stay

Accommodation in Kupang is spread out, but the efficient bemo system makes everywhere easily accessible.

Taman Ria Beach Inn (☎ 31320), at Jalan Tim Tim 69, three km from the Terminal Kota Kupang, is popular for its cheap 4000-rp dorm prices, or singles/doubles are 8000/11,000 rp. Taman Ria fronts the beach, and there's a cafe and bar. To get there, catch a No 10 bemo.

The very popular *Backpackers* (☎ 31291) at Jalan Kancil 37B, Air Nona, is about four km from the city centre – catch a No 3 bemo. It costs 3000 rp per person for doubles or beds in small dorms with outside bath. It's a friendly if basic place, and the setting is peaceful; it even has a small swimming pool. Just a one-minute jog from the Backpackers is *Eden Homestay* (☎ 21921) at Jalan Kancil 6. They have bungalows with private bath and also charge just 3000 rp per person. You can swim in the large pond nearby.

Fatuleu Homestay (☎ 31374) is very clean, good value and conveniently close to the centre. Rooms with shared bath are 7000/10,000 rp, or relatively luxurious doubles with private bath are 15,000 rp.

Sea Breezes Homestay is on Jalan Ikan Tongkol (Tuna Fish St) next to Teddy's Bar. It's very basic, but the location is very convenient with views over the sea. Rooms are 5000/8000 rp.

The central *Pitoby Lodge* (☎ 32910) on Jalan Kosasih 13 is popular and gets most of its trade from Ivan's backpackers in Darwin. You'll pay premium prices in Darwin, but it includes pick up from the airport. Walk-in rates for very good rooms with tasteful decor cost 5000 rp in the four-bed dorm, or doubles are 15,000 up to 30,000 rp with attached bath.

Batulesa Indah Homestay (☎ 32863), Gang Johar 1/5 Jalan Sudirman, is a new, immaculate place where rooms with attached bath cost 5000/10,000 rp. It is down an alley just around the corner from the Hotel Flobamor II.

Places to Eat

There are no gourmet delights in Kupang but there are some good *foodstalls* which set up at the night market along Jalan Garuda, near the Garuda office on Jalan Kosasih. One of the best places in town is the *Restaurant Lima Jaya Raya* at Jalan Soekarno 15, near the bus terminal. The Chinese-Indonesian menu is extensive and reasonably priced.

Visiting Darwinites like to hang out at *Teddy's Bar*, Jalan Ikan Tongkol 1-3. The food is good but a bit pricier than elsewhere in town. The menu includes Western dishes and seafood, and it is right on the beach. The *Pantai Laut Restaurant* nearby and its amiable staff serve a variety of chicken, seafood and beef dishes.

For seaside ambience, try the *Restaurant Karang Mas* at Jalan Siliwangi 88, a short walk from the terminal near the corner of Jalan Soekarno. The *Rumah Makan Beringin*

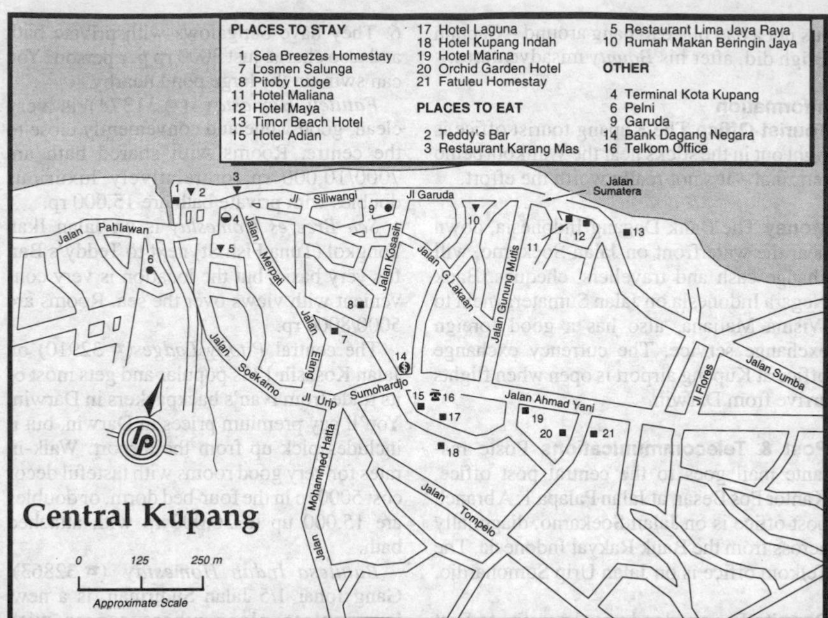

Jaya is on Jalan Garuda and has Padang food at reasonable prices.

Getting There & Away

Air The Bouraq (☎ 21421) office is at Jalan Sudirman 20; Garuda (☎ 21205) is at Jalan Kosasih 13; Merpati (☎ 21961) is at Jalan Sudirman 21; and Sempati (☎ 33044) is in the Hotel Marina, Jalan Ahmad Yani 79. All airlines have flights to Denpasar (199,000 rp) and on to Jakarta, as does Mandala, and Sempati also fly to Dili (69,000 rp). It pays to shop around. Apart from their many flights to other places in Indonesia, Merpati also has flights from Kupang to various parts of Timor including Atambua, Dili and to the islands of Roti and Sawu.

Merpati also flies between Darwin (Australia) on Wednesday and Saturday. From Kupang the fare is US$150, or a 90-day return excursion fare is US$250 – it's cheaper from Darwin. You won't be allowed on the plane without an Australian visa – obtainable in Denpasar or Jakarta, not Kupang.

Bus Long-distance buses depart from the Oebufu terminal out near the museum – take a No 10 bemo. Buses go to Soe (3000 rp, two hours), Kefamenanu (5000 rp, five hours) and Atambua (8500 rp, eight hours). Bemos to villages around Kupang go from the central terminal, Kota Kupang.

Boat Pelni is at Jalan Pahlawan 3, near the waterfront. The harbourmaster's office is at the harbour at Jalan Yos Sudarso 23. The Pelni ship KM *Kelimutu* passes through every two weeks to and from Ende (15,000 rp) in Flores and Dili (17,000 rp). The KM *Dobonsolo* goes direct from Surabaya to Kupang and then on to Dili, Ambon and Irian Jaya, returning back through Dili and Kupang. Pelni's cargo ships also take passengers but are much less comfortable. The *Elang* loops around Timor and the small islands to the north. The *Baruna Eka* and/or *Baruna Fajar* service Sawu, Ende and Waingapu.

Perum ASDP ferries (☎ 21140), Jalan Cak Doko 20, has ferries to Larantuka (Flores) on Thursday and Sunday at 2 pm for 12,400 rp. These ferries continue on to Waiwerang (Adonara) and Lewoleba (Lembata). The ferry to Kalabahi (Alor) departs Thursday and Saturday at 1 pm and cost 14,900 rp. The ferry to Ende (Flores) departs Monday at 2 pm and costs 15,300 rp. This ferry continues on to Waingapu (Sumba).

Perum ASDP also have ferries departing to Roti (4400 rp) from Wednesday to Saturday at 9 am, Sawu (11,900 rp) on Monday and Friday at 2 pm, and Naikliu on Timor's west coast on Wednesday at 7 am.

Getting Around

To/From the Airport Kupang's El Tari airport is 15 km east of the centre. Taxis cost a fixed 7500 rp. You might get a bemo from just outside the airport gates, a 200-metre walk, but it's a good half-km to the main road where bemos pass by regularly. From there, it's just 300 rp into town.

Local Transport Kupang's bemo terminal is at the waterfront, on the corner of Jalan Soekarno and Jalan Siliwangi. Kupang Harbour is about seven km from the bus terminal. A bemo from the bus terminal will take you straight to the harbour for 300 rp, and drop you off right at the harbourmaster's office.

Around town, bemos cost a standard 250 rp and are identified by the number of lamps on the roof – you take a one-lamp bemo, a two-lamp bemo or whatever. The bemos are fast, efficient, brightly painted and incredibly noisy – drivers like the bass turned up high and a multi-speaker stereo system is de rigueur.

AROUND KUPANG

Past the airport, about 18 km east of town, **Baumata** has a swimming pool and caves with stalactites and stalagmites. The beaches around town are dirty and unappealing but **Pantai Lasiana**, nine km east of town, is a pleasant sandy stretch and popular on weekends. It's a km off the main road and, as an alternative to taking a bemo back, you can walk along the coast.

SOE

Soe is a dull sprawl of wooden and corrugated-iron-roofed houses. Despite its appearance it would be worth taking a day trip up here to get a look at the western Timorese countryside. There are frequent bemos and buses between Kupang and Soe, leaving from around 7 or 7.30 am. The trip takes anything from 2½ to four hours.

You can stay in *Hotel Bahagia* on Jalan Diponegoro, where rooms cost from 11,000 rp. *Losmen Anda*, around the corner on Jalan Kartini, is friendly but basic with rooms from just 4000 rp.

KEFAMENANU

Kefamenanu is a forgettable (and forgotten) place – just a through town on the way to east Timor. If you stop here, the *Losmen Ariesta* has rooms from around 9000 rp and up, or the *Losmen Soko Windu* is a basic but cheap alternative with rooms for 6000 rp.

ATAMBUA

Atambua is the major town and resting place on the overland Dili-Kupang route. Nearby, **Atapupa** is a major port where you may find boats to other islands.

Places to Stay

Atambua has five losmen, including at least one that dates back as far as the 1975 edition of *South-East Asia on a shoestring*. The long-running *Losmen Sahabat* is at Jalan Merdeka 7 and offers very basic accommodation from around 4500 rp per person. Better value is the more expensive *Losmen Nusantara* from around 7500 rp per person with breakfast.

DILI

The old capital of the Portuguese half of the island is a pleasant, lazy place with a few reminders of Portugal, such as the villas on

INDONESIA

the beach road and the Mercado Municipal (now closed). Check out the **Integration Monument** near the waterfront which has a Timorese rapturously breaking his chains of colonial bondage. It looks like a relic from Sukarno's Jakarta statuary collection. Just along from the monument, the **craft centre** features a traditional house from the Los Palos region. A gigantic **cathedral** is another post-Indonesian addition.

The army presence is everywhere and patrols cruise the streets after dark – most of Dili is asleep by 9 pm. Be wary of discussing politics.

Information

The tourist office, west of the Mercado Municipal on Jalan Kaikoli, has brochures with maps.

Toko Dili is a souvenir shop beside the telephone office and has maps. The Turismo Beach Hotel has a dial-home-direct phone in the lobby for international calls.

Places to Stay

Dili has no accommodation bargains. *Villa Hormonia* (☎ 22065), four km from town, is the only place under 10,000 rp but it is now off-limits to foreigners. The best choice is the *Wisma Taufiq* (☎ 21934), on Jalan Comoro and close to the centre, with habitable rooms at 10,000/16,500 rp or 15,000/22,000 rp with bath. The *Losmen Basmery Indah* (☎ 2731), on Jalan Estrade de Balide near the university, isn't value at 13,500/16,500 rp with bath.

If these are full, and they often are, the 'top end' is the only choice. The *Turismo Beach Hotel* (☎ 22029), on Jalan Avenida Marechal Carmona by the waterfront, has a certain neglected charm. Room rates, including breakfast, start at 20,000/24,000 rp, then go to 31,000/35,000 rp with balcony and bathroom or 36,000/41,000 rp with air-con. On the same road, a bit closer to the town centre, the *Hotel Dili* (☎ 22094) has rooms at 20,000 rp but is quiet and as dull as a morgue. More expensive places include the *New Resende Inn* (☎ 22098) and the *Wisma Cendana* (☎ 21141), both with rooms from 35,000/45,000 rp.

Places to Eat

Pasar Bidau is a string of cheap, basic *warungs* next to the river that are lively at night (for Dili) and friendly. On Jalan Jose Maria Marques in the town centre, the *Golden Bakery* is good for baked produce. *Rumah Makan Jakarta* just around the corner has good food but is a little expensive, while the *Rumah Makan Seroja* is cheaper and has Chinese dishes. Nasi padang places can be found near the telephone office and stadium. The restaurants at the *New Resende Inn* have good food at moderate prices, and you can still get Portuguese Mateus Rosé wine at around 20,000 rp! They also have karaoke some nights, about the closest thing Dili has to nightlife.

Getting There & Away

Overland travel from West Timor to East Timor is not permitted but you can go back the other way. This may change – check in Kupang. For the moment, entry to Dili is by the short flight from Kupang, or by sea. Travel around East Timor is officially open, but you may still be asked to show a travel permit *(surat jalan)* in some areas. Check with the tourist office in Dili.

Air Merpati and Sempati have flights between Dili and Kupang for 69,000 rp. Merpati (☎ 21880), in the New Resende Inn, also flies to Suai, Atambua, Maliana and Oecussi.

Bus Going to Kupang, most people stay overnight in Atambua. Buses to Atambua (5000 rp, five hours) leave from Terminal Tasitolo to the west of town past the airport. Buses to the east and south leave from Terminal Becora, four km east of town. Buses to Baukau (4000 rp, four hours) leave at 7 and 8 am and 1 pm. Journey times and prices may increase in the wet season, especially for trips on the back roads.

Hotels can arrange bus tickets and may be able to get the buses to pick you up from the hotel. Regional buses also go *keliling* (driving around, sometimes endlessly, for passengers) and can be picked up at the roundabout by the stadium and Mercado Municipal, but with these buses you have less chance of getting a seat.

Boat Inquire at the harbour about boat departures. Pelni (☎ 21415), Jalan Sebastian de Costa 1, is back from the road a little way out towards the airport. The KM *Kelimutu* travels from Kupang to Dili (17,000 rp, 13 hours) and on to Kalabahi (9000 rp, seven hours) and returns doing this route in reverse. The KM *Dobonsolo* travels from Kupang to Dili and on to Ambon (28,000 rp, 18 hours). The new KM *Tatamailau* comes from Larantuka to Dili and continues on to southern Maluku and Irian Jaya, and then reverses its route. Pelni's Perintis ships also have some interesting routes.

Getting Around

Dili's Comoro airport is five km west of the town; the standard taxi fare is 5000 rp. Buses A or B stop on the main road outside the airport and they also go to Terminal Tasitolo. For Terminal Becora take bus D or mikrolet I from the roundabout by the stadium. The beat-up buses and better mikrolets cost 200 rp. Taxis generally cost a flat 750 rp around town.

AROUND DILI

From Dili, you can take a sidetrip to the hill town of **Maubisse**, where the losmen costs 5000 rp, and on to **Same**, a spectacular trip south. **Ermera** is a coffee-growing centre on the road towards the Indonesian half of the island. On the coast beyond Dili, there's an old Dutch fort in the town of **Maubara**.

BAUKAU

The second-largest town in the Portuguese half, Baukau is a charmingly run-down old colonial town. In pre-invasion times, it was the site of the international airport (now a military airbase). The altitude makes it pleasantly cool and the **beaches**, five km sharply downhill from the town, are breathtakingly beautiful.

The old *Hotel Flamboyan*, a hangover from Portuguese days, is still in operation but seems to have had zero maintenance since the Portuguese left – rooms are 12,000 rp. Baukau also has a cheaper *losmen* near the bus station.

BEYOND BAUKAU

An interesting sidetrip from Baukau is to **Tutuala** on the eastern tip of the island. This village has interesting houses built on stilts, plus spectacular views out to sea. There are plans to convert the police station at Tutuala into a losmen. Meanwhile, bring your own food and supplies. Just before Tutuala is **Los Palos** where the old raja's house now has *accommodation* for 6000 rp.

There is an old Portuguese fort at **Laga**, a town on the coast en route to Tutuala. Another sidetrip is down to **Vikeke** (Viequeque), close to the south coast. On the way you pass **Venilale**, with Japanese WW II bunkers outside the town.

Roti & Sawu

Roti (also spelled Rote) is the southernmost island in Indonesia, and has linguistic ties with nearby Timor. Further west, Sawu (also spelled Sabu) has closer linguistic and cultural ties to Sumba. These small dry islands are seldom visited, but a steady trickle of visitors make it to Roti, which is fairly easily accessed from Kupang. As is often the case with obscure Indonesian islands, it is surfers that have 'discovered' Roti and opened it up to tourism. Nambrala Beach on the west coast is the surf centre with cheap accommodation and meals, or you can stay in the main town of Baa. Sawu also has a few cheap losmen.

Getting There & Away

Merpati flies a Kupang-Roti-Sawu-Roti-Kupang route on Tuesday and Saturday.

Fares from Kupang are Roti for 35,000 rp and Sawu for 72,000 rp.

See the Kupang Getting There & Away section for details on ferries to Sawu and Roti. On Roti, the ferry docks at Pantai Baru from where waiting buses will take you to Baa. From Baa, trucks and buses make the bone-shaking trip to Nambrala.

Sumba

This dry island, one of the most interesting in the Nusa Tenggara group, is noted for the large, decorated stone tombs found in the graveyards. Its isolation has helped preserve one of the country's most bizarre animist cultures. Sumba is also famous for its ikat blankets with their interesting motifs, including skulls hanging from trees, horse riders, crocodiles, dragons, lions, chickens, monkeys and deer.

Sumba Blankets

Most blankets are blue, red and white – the pastel oranges and browns are only occasionally seen. There's a band of almost incredibly persistent middle-men working the streets of Waingapu with sacks full of blankets. They lay siege to your hotel, hanging around all day and half the night. Every blanket is the 'number one' blanket but artificial dyes are used to make instant 'antique' blankets and asking prices are exorbitant, although you can bargain. If you want a good blanket then *wait* – they'll eventually bring out the better stuff.

Getting There & Away

Air Flights operate from Bali, Flores, Timor and Sumbawa to the main centres of Tambolaka (the airport for Waikabubak) and Waingapu. Merpati operate a Denpasar-Bima-Tambolaka-Waingapu-Kupang route, while Bouraq fly Denpasar-Waingapu-Kupang.

Boat Pelni's KM *Kelimutu* operates through Nusa Tenggara every two weeks and sails from Padangbai (Bali) to Lembar, Ujung Pandang (Sulawesi), Bima, Waingapu (Sumba), Ende (Flores), Kupang (Timor) and return. There are occasionally other ships plying between Waingapu and Ende.

WAINGAPU

There's nothing much to do in Waingapu, but it has some reasonable hotels and restaurants and is a good place for day-tripping to the interesting villages in the surrounding area, where the blankets are made and where the stone tombs can be found.

Orientation & Information

The town has two centres, one around the harbour and one around the bus station about a km to the south-east. The Bank Rakyat Indonesia on Jalan Achmad Yani is the only place on Sumba that will change major travellers' cheques and cash.

Places to Stay

Losmen Permata is a small but pleasant place with only five rooms for 4000 rp per person for a room with attached mandi. *Hotel Sandle Wood* (☎ 117) at Jalan Panjaitan 23 near the bus terminal is the top place in town with rooms ranging from 8000 rp to 40,000 rp.

Just down the road from the Sandle Wood is the amiable *Losmen Kaliuda*, a small, quiet and new place with a pleasant garden. Rooms with shared bath are 7000/9000 rp, or it's 8000/11,000 rp for rooms with attached bath.

Hotel Elim (☎ 462) at Jalan Ahmad Yani 55 is somewhat old and faded, but it's still the number-two place in town. Rooms start at 7000 rp or 23,000 rp with air-con.

Hotel Lima Saudara (☎ 83), in the northern part of town at Jalan Wanggameti 2, is tatty but has large rooms with attached bath for 8000/15,000 rp and a nice front porch.

Hotel Surabaya (☎ 125) at Jalan El Tari 2 is uncomfortably near the mosque and bus station and costs from 6000/10,000 rp.

Places to Eat

For cheap food, try the night *warungs* around the corner of Jalan Hatta and Jalan Sudirman. *Restaurant Rajawali* is popular and as well as having good food, the place organises tours and jeep rental. Otherwise, eat at the hotels – the best and most expensive food is found at the *Hotel Sandle Wood*. The *Hotel Surabaya* is cheaper and even offers Chinese takeaways.

Getting There & Away

Air Merpati (☎ 21323), Jalan Achmad Yani 73, and Bouraq (☎ 363), Jalan Yos Sudarso 57, between them have direct flights to/from Bima (77,000 rp), Kupang (117,000 rp), Tambolaka (Waikabubak – 48,000 rp), and Denpasar (160,000 rp).

Bus Buses to Waikabubak (3500 rp, five hours) depart at 7 am, noon and 3 pm. Try to book a day or two in advance. The hotels will usually book you a ticket or go to one of the bus agents.

Boat Pelni (☎ 27), Jalan Hasanuddin 1, is located at the Waingapu harbour. The KM *Kelimutu* calls in every two weeks at a special dock at the other end of the harbour – a bemo to this pier is 250 rp per person. From Waingapu it runs to/from Ende or Bima. A regular ferry also operates once a week from Ende (see the Ende section) and Pelni Perintis ships also call at Waingapu.

Getting Around

Bemos from the town centre to the airport, six km out, cost 300 rp while a chartered bemo will be about 3000 rp. There are regular bemos to villages around Waingapu.

AROUND WAINGAPU

Rende

Rende village has several traditional-style buffalo horn-adorned Sumba houses and a number of massive carved stone graves. You may be charged 2000 rp as a sort of 'admission fee' to the village. Take a bus at around 7 am from Waingapu to Rende (1200 rp, two hours).

Umabara

Umabara has several traditional Sumba houses and tombs. A few minutes' walk down the track from Umabara is the village of **Pau**, which also has traditional houses.

Umabara is a half-hour walk from the village of Melolo, which is split by a river. The road to Umabara leads off from the Waingapu side. Have the colt driver drop you off at the start of this road.

Kaliuda

Kaliuda is one of the ikat-weaving centres of the area, though the place where most of the weaving is done is just before the village. To get to Kaliuda, take a bus at around 7 am from Waingapu. You can then spend about two hours looking around Kaliuda before catching the same bus as it returns through Kaliuda. It will probably be packed by the time it arrives there, so you may have to insist on being picked up.

WAIKABUBAK

Waikabubak is a neat little town with many traditional houses and old graves carved with buffalo-horn motifs. One of the attractions of western Sumba is the *Pasola*, or mock battle ritual, held near Waikabubak each year. It's a kind of jousting match on horseback and is rather dangerous.

At the village of **Lamboya**, traditional Sumba horseback mock battles are held every year during February – this village is 20 km from Waikabubak. At **Wanokaka**, the battles are held in March. At **Rua Beach**, 30 km south of Waikabubak, the festival is also held in March.

Places to Stay & Eat

Hotel Aloha on Jalan Gajah Mada is most popular with budget travellers. Comfortable rooms start at 7000/9000 rp, including a simple breakfast. The restaurant serves up some of the better food in town and is a good place to collect travel information.

Close by, *Hotel Manandang* (☎ 197, 292), Jalan Pemuda 4, is relatively upmarket with rooms around 15,000 rp but it has a few budget rooms.

Hotel Pelita (☎ 104) on Jalan Achmad Yani is basic but clean with rooms at 4500 rp per person. The *Hotel Rakuta* on Jalan Veteran is a somewhat musty place with large rooms, big double beds, mandis and toilet from around 5000 rp.

Hotel Mona Lisa on Jalan Adhyaksa is the luxury resort of Waikabubak. It's 2½ km from town and mainly used by tour groups. Rooms cost a breathtaking 50,000 rp or more.

There are lots of basic *rumah makan* along Jalan Ahmad Yani and some *warungs* set up here at night, but hotels are the best places to eat.

Getting There & Away

The Merpati agent is in the centre of town, on Jalan Ahmad Yani. The nearest airport is at Tambolaka, 42 km north. There are direct flights to Bima (50,000 rp) and Waingapu.

There are regular bemos to villages around Waikabubak and a few buses throughout the day to Waingapu.

Getting Around

The Bumi Indah goes to the airstrip at Tambolaka for 1500 rp, but is not always reliable. Otherwise, a taxi costs a whopping 35,000 rp.

The Hotel Aloha rents motorbikes for around 15,000 rp per day and can arrange jeep trips around western Sumba for up to five people from 50,000 rp per day.

AROUND WAIKABUBAK

Anakalang

Twenty-two km from Waikabubak is the village of Anakalang with its large **graveyard**. Anakalang is also the site of the Purung Takadonga – a mass marriage **festival** held once every two years. The date is determined by the full moon and is different each time. There are regular bemos from Waikabubak to Anakalang and the trip takes about one hour and costs 600 rp.

Galubakul

Almost opposite the Anakalang graveyard is the road leading to the village of Galubakul (formerly Prai Bokul), an hour's walk away. In this village, you'll find the **Umbu Sawola Tomb**, a structure carved out of a single piece of rock and mounted on supports. The slab cost four million rp, weighs 70 tonnes and took three years to carve. The base of the stone is about five metres long, four metres wide and a bit less than a metre thick.

Kalimantan

Kalimantan, the southern two-thirds of the island of Borneo, is a vast, jungle-covered, undeveloped wilderness. Apart from the area around Pontianak and the region from Samarinda to Banjarmasin there are few roads. The boats and ferries of the numerous rivers and waterways are the chief form of long-distance transport, although there are also plenty of flight connections.

Some of the coastal cities have their own remarkable attractions – the canals of Banjarmasin and the fiery orange sunsets over Pontianak, for example. On the whole, however, apart from its being a diversion between Sulawesi and Java, it is the native Dayak tribes of the inland areas that are the main reason for coming to Kalimantan.

Getting There & Away

To/From East Malaysia Despite the long land border with the East Malaysian states of Sabah and Sarawak, options for crossing between the two countries are limited. The only real options are by air or land between Kuching in Sarawak and Pontianak, and by air or sea between Tawau in Sabah and Tarakan.

MAS has flights twice a week between Pontianak and Kuching, or a daily express bus does the trip in about 10 hours. See under Pontianak for details. Pontianak airport is a visa-free port but you must have an Indonesian visa to cross overland at the Tebedu/Entikong border.

Bouraq flies from Tarakan to Tawau, or boats run between Tarakan and Nunukan, and from Nunukan regular boats go to/from Tawau. Tarakan is not a visa-free entry/exit point and an Indonesian visa is required for arrival by air or sea. See under Tarakan for details of this route.

Indonesian visas can be easily obtained at the consulates in Kuching, Kota Kinabalu or Tawau. Most nationalities do not require a visa to enter Malaysia.

To/From Other Parts of Indonesia Kalimantan has a variety of air and sea connections with other places in Indonesia.

Air Bouraq, Merpati, Garuda and Sempati all fly into Kalimantan and there are lots of flights from other parts of Indonesia. Fares include: Jakarta to Banjarmasin for 215,000 rp, Jakarta to Pontianak for 174,000 rp, Jakarta to Balikpapan for 277,000 rp and Ujung Pandang to Balikpapan for 151,000 rp.

Boat There are shipping connections to Java and to Sulawesi, both with Pelni and other shipping companies. Most of Pelni's ships stop at Kalimantan somewhere along their routes. See the introductory Indonesia

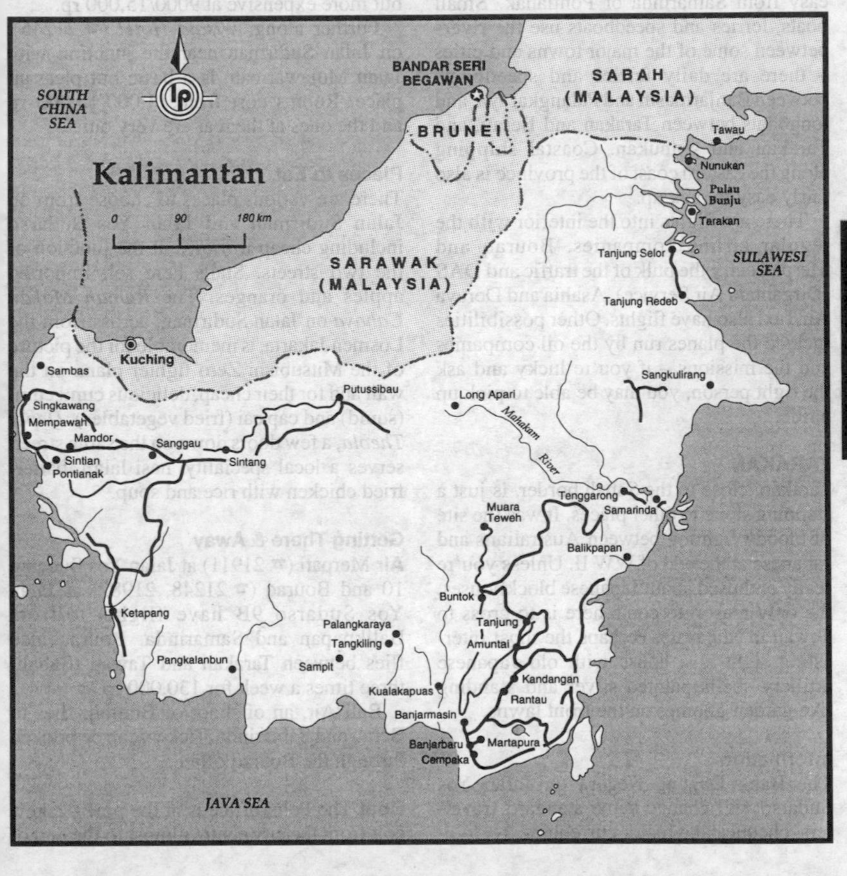

INDONESIA

Getting Around section for details of Pelni ships and the routes they take.

There are also regular ships from the ports on the east coast of Kalimantan to Pare Pare and Palu in Sulawesi. Mahakam Shipping, Jalan Kali Besar Timur 111 in Jakarta, may be worth trying for more information on other ships to Kalimantan.

Getting Around

There are roads in the area around Pontianak and in the region from Banjarmasin to Balikpapan and Samarinda, but boat is the main form of transport. Going upriver by boat into some of the Dayak regions is fairly easy from Samarinda or Pontianak. Small boats, ferries and speedboats use the rivers between some of the major towns and cities – there are daily ferries and speedboats between Banjarmasin and Palangkaraya, and longboats between Tarakan and Berau, and Tarakan and Nunukan. Coastal shipping along the eastern coast of the province is also fairly easy to pick up.

There are flights into the interior with the regular airline companies. Bouraq and Merpati carry the bulk of the traffic and DAS (Dirgantara Air Service), Asahia and Deraya Air Taxi also have flights. Other possibilities include the planes run by the oil companies and the missions – if you're lucky and ask the right person, you may be able to pick up a ride.

TARAKAN

Tarakan, close to the Sabah border, is just a stepping stone to other places. It was the site of bloody fighting between Australians and Japanese at the end of WW II. Unless you're really enthused about Japanese blockhouses, the only reason to come here is to cross to Tawau in Malaysia. Perhaps the most interesting sight is a house with old Japanese artillery shells painted silver and standing like garden gnomes on the front lawns.

Information

The Bank Dagang Negara on Jalan Yos Sudarso will change some standard travellers' cheques and major currencies.

Places to Stay

There is a line of cheap and mid-range losmen and hotels along Jalan Sudirman (also known as Jalan Kampung Bugis). These include the *Losmen Jakarta* (☎ 21919) at No 112 which has little boxes for rooms but is otherwise quite a reasonable place to stay at 7000/9000 rp.

The *Barito Hotel* (☎ 435), Jalan Sudirman 133, is basic, clean and relatively new with rooms from 8000 to 14,000 rp. The *Losmen Herlina* is basic but habitable so long as you avoid the dark, dismal downstairs rooms. Rooms cost 6000/7000 rp. The *Orchid Hotel* is OK (although the mandis could be cleaner) but more expensive at 9000/15,000 rp.

Further along, *Wisata Hotel* (☎ 21245), on Jalan Sudirman near the junction with Jalan Mulawarman, is a basic but pleasant place. Rooms cost from 11,000/15,000 rp and the ones at the rear are very quiet.

Places to Eat

There are various places to choose from on Jalan Sudirman and Jalan Yos Sudarso including cheap *warungs* at the junction of the two streets. Stalls here sell imported apples and oranges. The *Rumah Makan Cahaya* on Jalan Sudirman, across from the Losmen Jakarta, is memorable for the picture of the Mitsubishi Zero fighter plane on the wall and for their cheap, delicious cumi cumi (squid) and cap cai (fried vegetables). *Depot Theola*, a few doors down on the same street, serves a local speciality, nasi lalap, batter-fried chicken with rice and soup.

Getting There & Away

Air Merpati (☎ 21911) at Jalan Yos Sudarso 10 and Bouraq (☎ 21248, 21987) at Jalan Yos Sudarso 9B have flights to/from Balikpapan and Samarinda. Bouraq also flies between Tarakan and Tawau (Sabah) three times a week for 130,000 rp.

Bali Air, an offshoot of Bouraq, flies to Berau and Samarinda. Tickets can be booked through the Bouraq office.

Boat The Pelni office is at the port – take a colt from the city centre almost to the end of

Jalan Yos Sudarso. The KM *Awu* calls into Tarakan on its route around Sulawesi and Kalimantan, and continues on to Nunukan. The KM *Tidar* runs between Balikpapan, Tarakan and Pantoloan in Sulawesi.

To/From Malaysia Boats leave Tarakan for Nunukan (14,000 rp, 12 hours) or speedboats do the run in four to five hours for 25,000 rp. If you have to overnight in Nunukan, the Losmen Nunukan costs around 6000 rp. From Nunukan there's a boat at noon to Tawau (10,000 rp, four to five hours). Departure tax is 1000 rp. The *K M Samudra Express* goes from Tarakan to Tawau via Nunukan but operates on a changing schedule.

Clear immigration in Nunukan – get there well before departure in case you have hassles. An Indonesian visa is essential to enter Indonesia through Nunukan. If exiting to Tawau, you'll have no problems if you entered Indonesia on a one-month visa but if you came in on a 60-day tourist pass through a visa-free gateway, in theory you need an exit permit from Jakarta. Nunukan immigration has been known to issue exit stamps after lengthy deliberation, but there are no guarantees. Some travellers report Tarakan immigration as being more helpful.

Getting Around

From the airport, tickets for taxis at the taxi counter cost 4000 rp to the city, or walk down the airport turn-off road to the main road and wait for a bemo. You should be able to get one going to the city (300 rp, 10-minute drive).

Bemos around town cost a 300 rp flat rate.

SAMARINDA

Samarinda is another old trading port on one of Kalimantan's mighty rivers. Balikpapan is the place for oil and Samarinda is the place for timber so, in both, there are large and suitably insulated communities of foreign workers and management. If you want to get a look at a timber mill, there's a giant one on the road to Tenggarong, not far out from Samarinda.

Samarinda is also the most commonly used jumping-off point for trips up the river to the inland Dayak areas.

Orientation & Information

The main part of Samarinda is laid out along the northern bank of the Mahakam River. The centre of town is the enormous mosque on the riverfront. Running east along the riverfront is Jalan Yos Sudarso and to the west is Jalan Gajah Mada. Most of the offices and hotels are in these two streets or in the streets behind them.

The tourist office (Kantor Parawisata) is just off Jalan Kesuma Bangsa at Jalan AI Suryani 1.

The Bank Dagang Negara on Jalan Mulawarman changes cash and travellers' cheques.

Places to Stay

The *Hotel Hidayah* on Jalan K H Khalid is central with clean, spartan rooms for 10,000/16,000 rp. The upstairs rooms are quieter than those downstairs.

Further north, along the same road, is the similar *Hotel Rahayu* where rooms range from 12,000 to 20,000 rp and include breakfast.

The *Hotel Andhika* (☎ 22358) at Jalan Haji Agus Salim 37 has clean, quiet economy doubles from 22,000 rp (ask for a room away from the foyer), and a good restaurant.

Cosier are the two inns on Jalan Pirus, just off busy Jalan Sudirman – the *Wisma Pirus* (☎ 21873) and *Hotel Hayani* (☎ 22653). Wisma Pirus has rooms with shared mandi for 11,600/16,000 rp and rooms with private mandi in the 20,000 rp range. Hayani, on the other side, has similar rooms with mandi.

Places to Eat

Samarinda is fruit city and people sit outside along Jalan Mas Tenggarong carving giant nangka into manageable segments. Zurzats are cheap and there are also pineapples, bananas and salaks in abundance. The other gastronomic wonder is *udang galah* – giant river prawns which you'll find in the local warungs.

Many *warungs* open in the evening along Jalan Niaga Selatan and in the vicinity of Losmen Hidayah. Try the *Citra Niaga* hawkers' centre, off Jalan Niaga, for good value and variety. The *Sweet Home Bakery* at Jalan Sudirman 8 has the usual pastries. *Depot AC*, behind the Wella Beauty Salon off Jalan Mulawarman, serves delicious and cheap Chinese breakfasts (bubur ayam – porridge of rice or bean with chicken) and rice dishes (nasi bebek, nasi ayam and nasi tahu) in the early morning. For nasi soto or nasi sop, try the *Warung Aida* at the intersection of Jalan Panglima Batur and Jalan Kalimantan.

Getting There & Away

Air Merpati/Garuda is at Jalan Imam Bonjol 4. Bouraq (☎ 21105), Jalan Mulawarman 24, flies to/from Tarakan (125,000 rp), Balikpapan (44,000 rp), Berau (via Bali Air – 105,000 rp) and Banjarmasin (128,000 rp), with connections to Java and Sulawesi from Balikpapan.

Bus The long-distance bus station is at Seberang, on the southern side of the Mahakam River from the main part of town. To get there, take a longboat from the pier at Pasar Pagi on Jalan Gajah Mada for 350 rp. It only takes a few minutes to make the crossing and they also have boats that take motorbikes across. The bus station is immediately behind the boat dock on the other side. From Seberang station, there are many buses to Tenggarong (1800 rp, one hour) and Balikpapan (3000 rp, two hours).

Boat For ships out of Samarinda, try Pelni at Jalan Yos Sudarso 40/56, although the Pelni passenger ships operate through Balikpapan and Tarakan, not Samarinda. Other places to inquire at close by include Terminal Penumpang Kapal Laut Samarinda and Direktorat Jenderal Perhubungan Laut (both on Jalan Yos Sudarso), and the various shipping offices along the same street. It is possible to find boats to Tarakan and to Sulawesi – the KM *Tanjung Slamat* and the KM *Harapanku* sail to Pare Pare three days a week for 42,000 rp.

Boats up the Mahakam River leave from the Sungai Kunjang ferry terminal, southwest of the town centre. Take the green 'taksi A' minibus for 400 rp to the dock. See the following Up the Mahakam River section for further information.

Getting Around

The airport is in the northern suburbs – it costs 8000 rp from the taxi counter into the centre of town. Alternatively, you can just walk out of the terminal down Jalan Pipit to Jalan Serindit and catch a public colt for 300 rp into the city.

TENGGARONG

Situated 39 km west of Samarinda, this little riverside town is noted for its **Sultan's Palace**, built by the Dutch in 1936 and now used as a museum.

Places to Stay

There are two places to stay, both of which are beside the waterfront and right on the boat dock. The *Penginapan Zaranah I* (☎ 148) has rooms for 4000 rp per person. The *Warung & Penginapan Anda* (☎ 78) is slightly more expensive at 5000/9000 rp.

Getting There & Away

Boats go from Samarinda (1000 rp, three hours) and drop you right near the palace, but the colts (2000 rp, one hour) from Samarinda's Seberang bus station are quicker. The colts pulls into the Petugas terminal just outside Tenggarong – it's another 300 rp by another colt into town. It takes about 10 minutes to get from Petugas terminal to Pasar Tepian Pandan, where you get off for the boat dock, palace and tourist office.

UP THE MAHAKAM RIVER

Samarinda is probably the best jumping-off point for visits to the Dayak tribes of East Kalimantan. Some of these are easily reached on the regular longboats that ply the

Mahakam River from Samarinda and Tenggarong all the way to Long Bagun, 523 km upriver. Many of the towns and villages have a budget hotel or two or a longhouse where travellers can stay – the standard price everywhere is 4000 rp per person.

Most people head upriver to **Tanjung Isuy** on the shores of Danau Jempang. The provincial government bought the longhouse there and renovated it as a tourist attraction. The *Penginapan Beringan* provides budget accommodation. Nearby **Mancong** has a longhouse dating from the 1870s, where it is possible to stay. To get to Danau Jempang, take a longboat from Samarinda to Muara Muntai (5000 rp, 13 hours) first and spend the night there before getting a boat to Tanjung Isuy (4000 rp, four hours).

Melak, 325 km from Samrinda, is famous for its 5000-acre Kersid Luwai Orchid Reserve, 16 km from Melak by jeep or ojek charter. The *Rahmat Abadi* is the best place to stay. In nearby **Eheng**, some 200 Banuaq Dayak reside in Eheng's 65-metre longhouse. You can walk there, or rent a jeep or ojek from Melak. Longboats from Samarinda to Melak (8000 rp, 24 hours) leave at 9 am.

Long Iram, 409 km from Samarinda, is the end of the line if the river is low. Long Iram has become a sort of backwater boom town as a result of gold mining, and accommodation is more expensive. From Tering, near Long Iram, it may be possible to hitch to Tanjung Balai and on to Muara Tewah, from where longboats ply the Barito River to Banjarmasin. Long Iram is 33 hours by longboat from Samarinda (12,000 rp).

Further upriver are more longhouses between **Datah Bilang** and **Muara Merak**, including the Bahau, Kenyah and Punan settlements. The end of the line for regular longboat services is **Long Bagun**, or **Long Apari** if the conditions are right.

If you want to start your trip from the top, Asahi flies to **Data Dawai**, an airstrip near Long Lunuk, for 45,000 rp. From there you can work your way downriver back to Samarinda, or trek overland to the Apo-Kayan highlands.

BALIKPAPAN

Apart from the clean, comfortable and highly insulated Pertamina, Union Oil and Total residential areas, Balikpapan consists of grubby backstreets and ravaged footpaths, both overrun by rampaging Hondas and Yamahas. The area north of the oil refinery, bound by Jalan Randan Utara and Jalan Pandanwanyi, is completely built on stilts over the muddy isthmus, and is connected by uneven lurching wooden walkways between the houses. The huge oil refinery dominates the city, and when you fly into the place you'll see stray tankers and offshore oil rigs.

Information

The Bank Negara Indonesia on Jalan Pengeran Antasari and its branch at the airport will change major travellers' cheques and cash currencies.

Places to Stay

There's not much cheap accommodation in Balikpapan and what is available is usually taken over by resident Indonesians. Your best bet is probably the *Penginapan Royal*, close to the Pasar Baru, at the beginning of the road to the airport and near the junction with Jalan Antasari. The rooms cost 5000 rp per person and are basic but clean. Avoid the front rooms facing the main street.

There's a string of places on Jalan Panjaitan including *Hotel Aida* (☎ 21006), which is clean and has rooms from 10,000/14,000 rp. Close by, the *Hotel Murni* is similarly priced but get a room at the back away from the main street. On the same street, the *Penginapan Mama* is cheap with rooms from 6000 rp and it looks OK but always seems to be full.

Other available accommodation is mid-range or upmarket. The *Hotel Gajah Mada* (☎ 21046) at Jalan Gajah Mada 108 has rooms with big beds and bathroom in the 50,000-rp category. *Hotel Sederhana* on Kelandasan Ulu has air-con rooms for 40,000 rp or cheaper rooms in the old section from 15,000 rp.

Places to Eat

One thing that Balikpapan has got to recommend it is good Padang seafood places, although they tend to be expensive. Try *Restaurant Masakan Padang Simpang Raya* next to the Hotel Murni. The *Restaurant Salero Minang* at Jalan Gajah Mada 12B is similarly priced, as is the marginally better *Restaurant Sinar Minang* on Jalan Antasari, which also serves up udang galah (giant river prawns).

More unusual (for decor) is the *Restaurant Roda Baru* near the Penginapan Royal. You eat amidst a rockery featuring a kitsch collection of plaster storks and lit by a chandelier. The cheapest eats can be found, during the evening, at the numerous *warungs* and *food trolleys* along Jalan Dondong near the Hotel Benakutai.

Getting There & Away

Air Merpati (☎ 22380) is at Jalan Ahmad Yani 29, near the Pasar Baru on the road leading out to the airport; Garuda (☎ 22300/1) is at Jalan Ahmad Yani 14. Bouraq (☎ 24766) has its office in the Hotel Budiman at Jalan Ahmad Yani 16, and Sempati (☎ 34555) is in the huge Hotel Benakutai. Direct flights to/from Balikpapan include: Jakarta (277,000 rp), Banjarmasin (84,000 rp), Samarinda (44,000 rp), Tarakan (133,000 rp), Palu (97,000 rp), Manado (231,000 rp) and Ujung Pandang (151,000 rp).

Bus Buses to Samarinda (3000 rp, two hours) depart from the Rapak terminal. Buses to Banjarmasin (20,000 rp, 12 hours) depart from the terminal on the opposite side of the harbour to the city. To get to this terminal take a colt from the Rapak bus station to the pier on Jalan Monginisidi. From here, take a speedboat to the other side. The cost is 1500 rp per person or around 6000 rp to charter, and it takes 10 minutes.

Alternatively, a motorised longboat crosses in half an hour and costs 900 rp. The bus terminal is immediately behind where the boats land.

Boat Pelni (☎ 22187) is on Jalan Yos Sudarso. Pelni's KM *Awu* passes through Balikpapan on its run between Pare Pare (18,000 rp) and Toli-Toli (24,000 rp) in Sulawesi, and it continues on to Tarakan (43,000 rp), Nunukan (47,000 rp) and then returns via the same route. The KM *Kambuna* calls at Balikpapan between Ujung Pandang (24,000 rp) and Pantaloan (18,000 rp) in Sulawesi. The KM *Tidar* runs from Surabaya (43,000 rp) and on to Tarakan. For other ships to Surabaya, try PT Ling Jaya Shipping (☎ 21577) at Jalan Yos Sudarso 40 and PT Sudi Jaya Agung (☎ 21956) at Jalan Pelabuhan 39.

For ships across to Pare Pare in Sulawesi, go to PT Nurlina. Their office is on the pier where you catch speedboats or longboats to the bus terminal on the other side of the harbour. Departures for the 28-hour trip to Pare Pare are just about every day and cost 30,000 rp.

Getting Around

A taxi from Seppingan airport is around 8000 rp, less from town.

Bemos cost 350 rp to anywhere around town. They do circular routes around the main streets from the Rapak terminal at the end of Jalan Panjaitan. Guys with motorbikes also hang around the Rapak terminal and will take you anywhere as a pillion passenger.

BANJARMASIN

Banjarmasin is one of the most stunning cities in Indonesia. It is crisscrossed by canals lined with stilt houses and buildings tacked on top of bundles of lashed, floating logs.

Orientation & Information

Although Banjarmasin is quite a big place, almost everything you'll need is packed into a very small area in the region of the Pasar Baru. Several of the cheaper hotels are found along Jalan Ahmad Yani, on the opposite side of the river.

The South Kalimantan tourist office at Jalan Panjaitan 3, near the Grand Mosque,

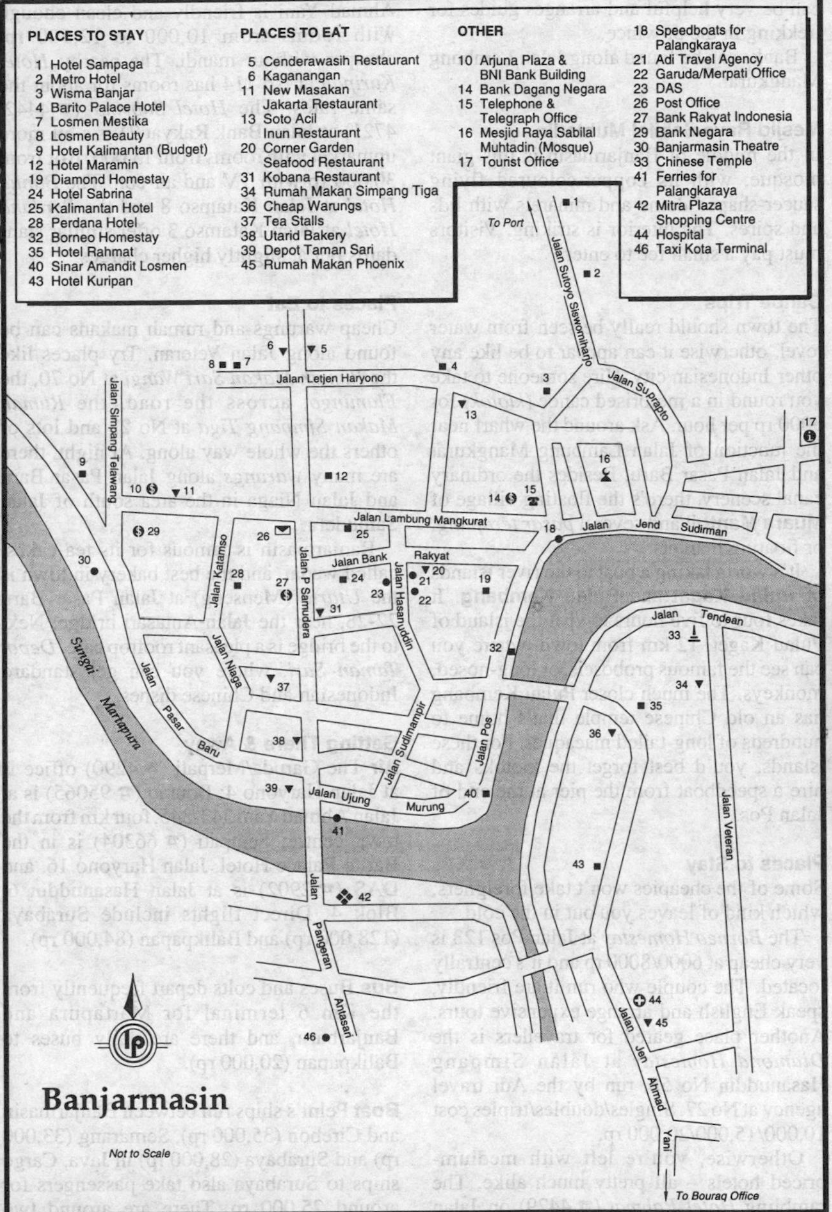
PLACES TO STAY
1 Hotel Sampaga
2 Metro Hotel
3 Wisma Banjar
4 Barito Palace Hotel
7 Losmen Mestika
8 Losmen Beauty
9 Hotel Kalimantan (Budget)
12 Hotel Maramin
19 Diamond Homestay
24 Hotel Sabrina
25 Kalimantan Hotel
28 Perdana Hotel
32 Borneo Homestay
35 Hotel Rahmat
40 Sinar Amandit Losmen
43 Hotel Kuripan
PLACES TO EAT
5 Cenderawasih Restaurant
6 Kaganangan
11 New Masakan Jakarta Restaurant
13 Soto Acil Inun Restaurant
20 Corner Garden Seafood Restaurant
31 Kobana Restaurant
34 Rumah Makan Simpang Tiga
36 Cheap Warungs
37 Tea Stalls
38 Utarid Bakery
39 Depot Taman Sari
45 Rumah Makan Phoenix
OTHER
10 Arjuna Plaza & BNI Bank Building
14 Bank Dagang Negara
15 Telephone & Telegraph Office
16 Mesjid Raya Sabilal Muhtadin (Mosque)
17 Tourist Office
18 Speedboats for Palangkaraya
21 Adi Travel Agency
22 Garuda/Merpati Office
23 DAS
26 Post Office
27 Bank Rakyat Indonesia
29 Bank Negara
30 Banjarmasin Theatre
33 Chinese Temple
41 Ferries for Palangkaraya
42 Mitra Plaza Shopping Centre
44 Hospital
46 Taxi Kota Terminal
To Port
Jalan Sutoyo Siswomiharjo
Jalan Letjen Haryono
Jalan Su prapto
Jalan Simpang Telawang
Jalan Lambung Mangkurat
Jalan Jend Sudirman
Jalan Bank Rakyat
Jalan Katamso
Jalan P Samudera
Jalan Hasanuddin
Jalan Tendean
Jalan Niaga
Jalan Pasar Baru
Sungai Martapura
Jalan Sudimampir
Jalan Pos
Jalan Ujung Murung
Jalan Veteran
Jalan Pangeran Antasari
Jalan Jen Ahmad Yani
To Bouraq Office
Banjarmasin
Not to Scale

can be very helpful and arranges guides for trekking in the province.

Banks can be found along Jalan Lambung Mangkurat.

Mesjid Raya Sabilal Muhtadin

In the middle of Banjarmasin is this giant mosque, with its copper-coloured flying saucer-shaped dome and minarets with lids and spires. The interior is striking. Visitors must pay a small fee to enter.

Canoe Trips

The town should really be seen from water level, otherwise it can appear to be like any other Indonesian city. Hire someone to take you round in a motorised canoe *(klotok)* for 5000 rp per hour. Ask around the wharf near the junction of Jalan Lambung Mangkurat and Jalan Pasar Baru. Besides the ordinary canal scenery, there's the floating village of **Muara Mantuil** and several *pasar terapung*, or floating markets.

It's worth taking a boat to the river islands of **Pulau Kaget** and **Pulau Kembang**. It takes four to five hours to visit the island of Pulau Kaget, 12 km from town, where you can see the famous proboscis, or long-nosed, monkeys. The much closer Pulau Kembang has an old Chinese temple that's home to hundreds of long-tailed macaques. For these islands, you'd best forget the klotoks and hire a speedboat from the pier at the end of Jalan Pos.

INDONESIA

Places to Stay

Some of the cheapies won't take foreigners, which kind of leaves you out in the cold.

The *Borneo Homestay* at Jalan Pos 123 is very cheap at 6000/8000 rp and it's centrally located. The couple who run it are friendly, speak English and arrange expensive tours. Another place geared for travellers is the *Diamond Homestay* at Jalan Simpang Hasanuddin No 58, run by the Adi travel agency at No 27. Singles/doubles/triples cost 10,000/15,000/20,000 rp.

Otherwise, you're left with medium-priced hotels – all pretty much alike. The rambling *Hotel Rahmat* (☎ 4429) on Jalan Ahmad Yani is friendly and clean enough with rooms from 10,000 to 12,500 rp, cheaper without mandi. The nearby *Hotel Kuripan* at No 114 has rooms for about the same rates. The *Hotel Sabrina* (☎ 4442, 4721) at Jalan Bank Rakyat 21 is a bit more upmarket with rooms from 15,000 rp or from 30,000 rp with TV and air-con. The *Banua Hotel* at Jalan Katamso 8 and the *Perdana Hotel* at Jalan Katamso 3 offer similar standards but at slightly higher charges.

Places to Eat

Cheap warungs and rumah makans can be found along Jalan Veteran. Try places like the *Rumah Makan Sari Wangi* at No 70, the *Flamingo*, across the road, the *Rumah Makan Simpang Tiga* at No 22 and lots of others the whole way along. At night, there are many *warungs* along Jalan Pasar Baru and Jalan Niaga in the area south of Jalan Samudera.

Banjarmasin is famous for its tea cakes, called wadai, and the best bakery in town is the *Utarid* (Menseng) at Jalan Pasar Baru 22-28, near the Jalan Antasari bridge. Next to the bridge is a pleasant rooftop cafe, *Depot Taman Sari*, where you can get standard Indonesian and Chinese dishes.

Getting There & Away

Air The Garuda/Merpati (☎ 4290) office is at Jalan Haryono 4; Bouraq (☎ 95065) is at Jalan Ahmad Yani 343-345, four km from the town centre; Sempati (☎ 66304) is in the Barito Palace Hotel, Jalan Haryono 16, and DAS (☎ 2902) is at Jalan Hasanuddin 6, Blok 4. Direct flights include Surabaya (128,000 rp) and Balikpapan (84,000 rp).

Bus Buses and colts depart frequently from the Km 6 terminal for Martapura and Banjarbaru, and there are daily buses to Balikpapan (20,000 rp).

Boat Pelni's ships run between Banjarmasin and Cirebon (35,000 rp), Semarang (33,000 rp) and Surabaya (28,000 rp) in Java. Cargo ships to Surabaya also take passengers for around 25,000 rp. There are around two departures a week. All boats leave from Pelabuhan Trisakti, 300 rp by bemo from Pasar Baru. Agents for all ships are opposite the harbourmaster's office (☎ 4775) on Jalan Barito Hilir, and agents for ships to Surabaya can also be found off Jalan Pasar Baru near the Antasari bridge.

For Pontianak, three or four boats a week go to Pangkalanbun. From there you take another to Ketapang and finally a ferry to Pontianak. The all-up cost for this time-consuming journey is around 40,000 rp.

Bis air (river ferries) go from the Banjar Raya ferry harbour to Palangkaraya (11,000 rp, 18 hours). Speedboats take only six or seven hours to Palangkaraya, cost 21,000 rp and depart from the end of Jalan Pos.

Getting Around

To/From the Airport The airport is 26 km out of town on the road to Banjarbaru. To get there, take a bemo from Jalan Pasar Baru to the Km 6 terminal, and then catch a Martapura-bound colt. Get off at the branch road leading to the airport and walk the short distance to the airport terminal. Alternatively, a taxi all the way to the airport will cost you around 9000 rp.

Local Transport Bemos congregate at the junction of Jalan Samudera and Jalan Pasar Baru and they cost from 300 rp to various destinations around town, including the Km 6 terminal for long-distance buses.

Banjarmasin becak and bajaj drivers ask hefty prices and are hard to bargain with. Guys with motorbikes, who hang around Pasar Baru and Km 6, will take you wherever you want to go.

MARTAPURA

Drop down to Martapura for a look at the market. It's a photographer's paradise on a good day, with lots of colourfully dressed Banjarmasin women. The market is behind the Martapura bus station.

A few minutes' walk diagonally across the nearby playing field is a diamond-polishing factory and shop. Ask for the Penggosokan Intan Tradisional Kayu Tangi. You can get colts to Martapura from the Km 6 terminal in Banjarmasin for 900 rp. The trip takes about 45 minutes along a good surfaced road.

BANJARBARU

This town, on the road from Banjarmasin to Martapura, has an interesting **museum** with a collection of Banjar and Dayak artefacts along with statues excavated from ancient Hindu temples in Kalimantan. The museum is officially open on weekends only but there's usually someone around to let you in on other days. Frequent colts go from Banjarmasin.

CEMPAKA

Cempaka is 43 km south from Banjarmasin. There's a creek here where the people are up to their necks in water panning for gold. Bemos from Martapura are infrequent – inquire at the Km 6 terminal in Banjarmasin if there are any colts going direct to Cempaka. Or, charter a bemo from Martapura bus station for 5000 rp for the round trip which allows a brief stop at the creek.

PONTIANAK

Pontianak, an interesting river city, is only 10 km from the equator, on the confluence of the Landak and Kapuas Kecil rivers. It's a surprisingly large city, with a giant indoor sports stadium and a couple of big girder bridges spanning the river. Like Banjarmasin, it really needs to be seen from the canals, which crisscross the whole city. Or, walk over the Kapuas bridge for a sweeping view of the river and the houses, and the brilliant orange sunsets that make Bali sunsets look ordinary!

This is also the starting point for trips up the **Kapuas River**, Indonesia's longest waterway.

Orientation & Information

The main part of the city is on the southern side of the Kapuas River, in the region around the Kapuas bemo terminal. In this vicinity, you'll find markets, a few hotels, airline offices, the Pelni office, banks etc.

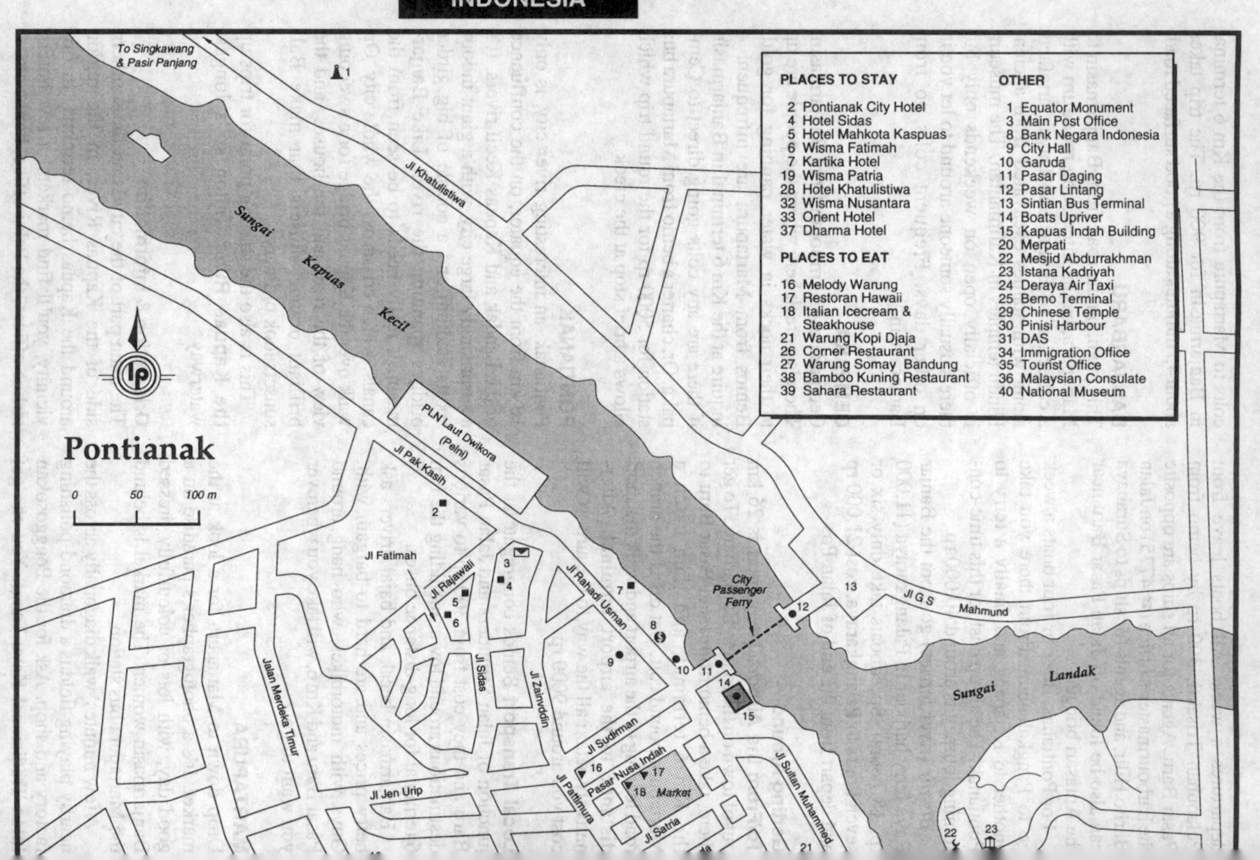

INDONESIA
Pontianak
0
50
100 m
To Singkawang & Pasir Panjang
Sungai Kapuas Kecil
Sungai Landak
Jl Khatulistiwa
PLN Laut Dwikora (Pelni)
Jl Pak Kasih
Jl Fatimah
Jl Rajawali
Jl Sidas
Jl Zainvddin
Jl Rahadi Usman
Jl Sudirman
Pasar Nusa Indah
Market
Jl Satria
Jl Pattimura
Jl Jen Urip
Jalan Merdeka Timur
Jl Sultan Muhammed
Jl G S Mahmund
City Passenger Ferry
PLACES TO STAY
2 Pontianak City Hotel
4 Hotel Sidas
5 Hotel Mahkota Kaspuas
6 Wisma Fatimah
7 Kartika Hotel
19 Wisma Patria
28 Hotel Khatulistiwa
32 Wisma Nusantara
33 Orient Hotel
37 Dharma Hotel
PLACES TO EAT
16 Melody Warung
17 Restoran Hawaii
18 Italian Icecream & Steakhouse
21 Warung Kopi Djaja
26 Corner Restaurant
27 Warung Somay Bandung
38 Bamboo Kuning Restaurant
39 Sahara Restaurant
OTHER
1 Equator Monument
3 Main Post Office
8 Bank Negara Indonesia
9 City Hall
10 Garuda
11 Pasar Daging
12 Pasar Lintang
13 Sintian Bus Terminal
14 Boats Upriver
15 Kapuas Indah Building
20 Merpati
22 Mesjid Abdurrakhman
23 Istana Kadriyah
24 Deraya Air Taxi
25 Bemo Terminal
29 Chinese Temple
30 Pinisi Harbour
31 DAS
34 Immigration Office
35 Tourist Office
36 Malaysian Consulate
40 National Museum

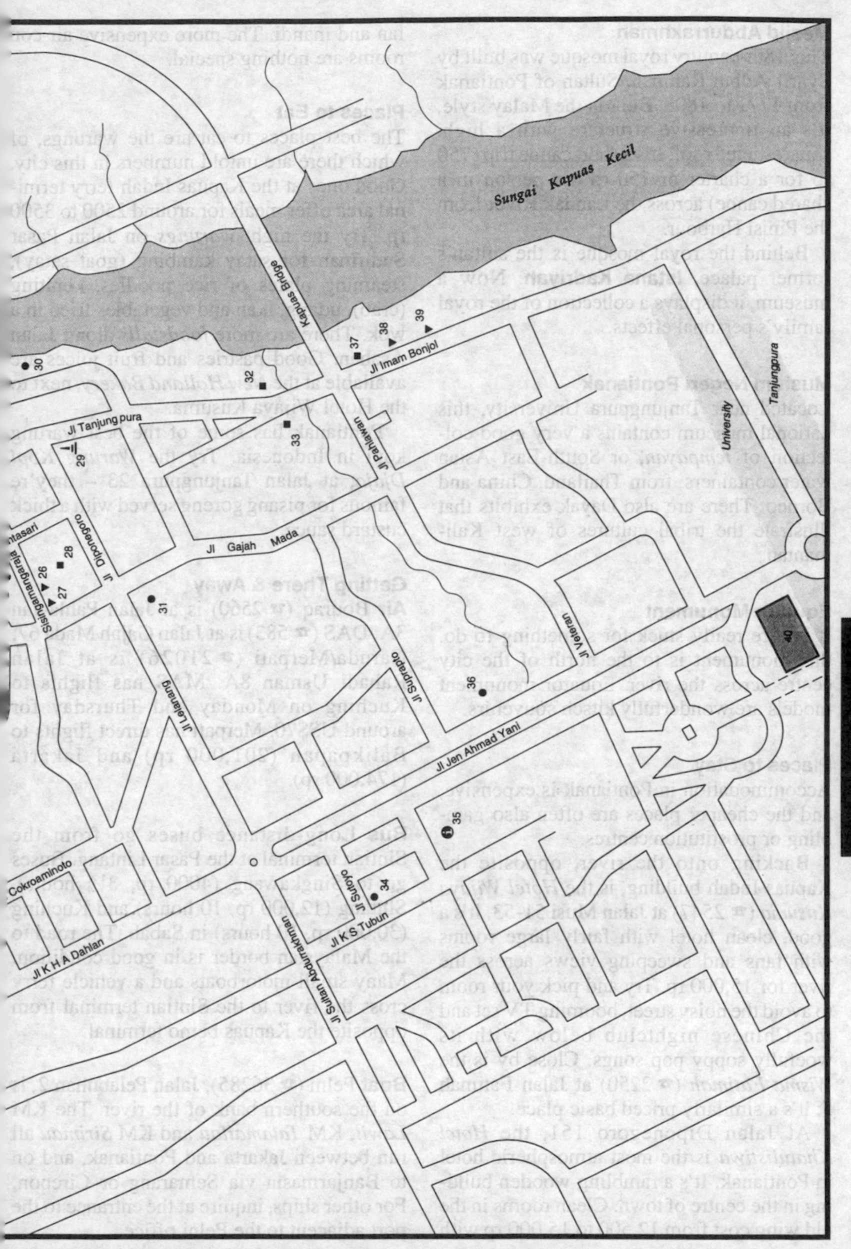
Sungai Kapuas Kecil
Kapuas Bridge
Jl Imam Bonjol
Jl Tanjung pura
Jl Pahlawan
Jl Gajah Mada
Jl Diponegoro
Sisingamangaraja
Jl Suprapto
Jl Veteran
Jl Jen Ahmad Yani
University
Tanjungpura
Cokroaminoto
Jl K H A Dahlan
Jl Sultan Abdurrakhman
Jl Sutoyo
Jl K S Tubun
26
27
28
29
30
31
32
33
34
35
36
37
38
39
40

INDONESIA

Mesjid Abdurrakhman
This 18th-century royal mosque was built by Syarif Adbul Rahman, Sultan of Pontianak from 1771 to 1808. Built in the Malay style, it's an impressive structure with a high, square-tiered roof. It's a short canoe trip (750 rp for a charter or 150 rp per person in a shared canoe) across the Landak River from the Pinisi Harbour.

Behind the royal mosque is the sultan's former palace, **Istana Kadriyah**. Now a museum, it displays a collection of the royal family's personal effects.

Musium Negeri Pontianak
Located near Tanjungpura University, this national museum contains a very good collection of *tempayan*, or South-East Asian water containers, from Thailand, China and Borneo. There are also Dayak exhibits that illustrate the tribal cultures of west Kalimantan.

Equator Monument
If you're really stuck for something to do, this monument is to the north of the city centre across the river. Equator monument models are wonderfully kitsch souvenirs.

Places to Stay
Accommodation in Pontianak is expensive, and the cheaper places are often also gambling or prostitution centres.

Backing onto the river, opposite the Kapuas Indah building, is the *Hotel Wijaya Kusuma* (☎ 2547) at Jalan Musi 51-53. It's a good, clean hotel with fairly large rooms with fans and sweeping views across the river for 15,000 rp. Try and pick your room to avoid the noisy street, booming TV set and the Chinese nightclub below with its woefully soppy pop songs. Close by is the *Wisma Fatimah* (☎ 2250) at Jalan Fatimah 5; it's a similarly priced basic place.

At Jalan Diponegoro 151, the *Hotel Khatulistiwa* is the most atmospheric hotel in Pontianak. It's a rambling wooden building in the centre of town. Clean rooms in the old wing cost from 12,500 to 15,000 rp with fan and mandi. The more expensive air-con rooms are nothing special.

Places to Eat
The best places to eat are the warungs, of which there are untold numbers in this city. Good ones at the Kapuas Indah ferry terminal area offer meals for around 2500 to 3500 rp. Try the night *warungs* on Jalan Pasar Sudirman for satay kambing (goat satay), steaming plates of rice noodles, kepiting (crab), udang, ikan and vegetables fried in a wok. There are more *foodstalls* along Jalan Asahan. Good pastries and fruit juices are available at the *New Holland Bakery*, next to the Hotel Wijaya Kusuma.

Pontianak has some of the best warung kopi in Indonesia. Try the *Warung Kopi Djaja*, at Jalan Tanjungpura 23 – they're famous for pisang goreng served with a thick custard sauce.

Getting There & Away
Air Bouraq (☎ 2560) is at Jalan Pahlawan 3A; DAS (☎ 583) is at Jalan Gajah Mada 67; Garuda/Merpati (☎ 21026) is at Jalan Rahadi Usman 8A. MAS has flights to Kuching on Monday and Thursday for around US$70. Merpati has direct flights to Balikpapan (201,000 rp) and Jakarta (174,000 rp).

Bus Long-distance buses go from the Sintian terminal at the Pasar Lintang. Buses go to Singkawang (4000 rp, 3½ hours), Sintang (12,000 rp, 10 hours) and Kuching (30,000 rp, 10 hours) in Sabah. The road to the Malaysian border is in good condition. Many small motorboats and a vehicle ferry cross the river to the Sintian terminal from opposite the Kapuas bemo terminal.

Boat Pelni (☎ 36285), Jalan Pelabuhan 2, is on the southern bank of the river. The KM *Lawit*, KM *Tatamailau* and KM *Sirimau* all run between Jakarta and Pontianak, and on to Banjarmasin via Semarang or Cirebon. For other ships, inquire at the entrance to the port adjacent to the Pelni office.

River boats up the Kapuas River leave from the Kapuas Indah station near the Hotel Wijaya Kusuma.

Getting Around

To/From the Airport Buy tickets for taxis into town at the airport counter – it costs 10,000 rp for the half-hour drive. Alternatively, walk out of the terminal to the main road in Pontianak and from here you should be able to get a colt.

Local Transport There are two main bemo stations in the middle of the city – the Kapuas terminal near the waterfront and the other on Jalan Sisingamangaraja. Taxis can be found next to the Garuda office.

SINGKAWANG

This predominantly Chinese town's main attraction is nearby **Pasir Panjang**, a beach with clean white sand and calm water, just back from the Pontianak to Singkawang road. Sinkawang has plenty of hotels, and Pasir Panjang has a couple of overpriced places.

Sulawesi

Sulawesi's big attraction is the interesting Tanatoraja area in the south-western leg of this strangely shaped island. Few visitors to Sulawesi get further than the southern area. Travel to the other areas can be difficult or time consuming, although it's getting easier with improvements in the roads and additional air transport.

The Minahasa area of the northern limb of the island is interesting and there are some stunning coral reefs off the coast of Manado, the chief city of the region.

Getting There & Away

Air There are air connections to a number of Sulawesi cities, chiefly to the capital of Ujung Pandang. Garuda, Merpati, Sempati, Mandala and Bouraq all fly to Sulawesi. Many travellers visit Sulawesi as a detour between Java and Bali – Denpasar-Ujung Pandang-Surabaya is the convenient and cheapest way to fly.

Because of its central location, there are all sorts of possibilities available with flights from Ujung Pandang to other parts of Sulawesi and to the other provinces of Indonesia. Sample fares from Ujung Pandang include: Denpasar for 136,000 rp, Surabaya for 183,000 rp, Jakarta for 293,000 rp, Ambon for 200,000 rp, Biak for 362,000 rp, Balikpapan for 151,000 rp, Banjarmasin for 235,000 rp, Manado for 214,000 rp, Palu for 125,000 rp, Samarinda for 195,000 rp, Tarakan for 284,000 rp and Ternate for 297,000 rp.

Boat Ujung Pandang is a major hub on the Pelni network and most Pelni ships stop there, so you can travel to or from Ujung Pandang and most other major centres in the archipelago. A number of other Sulawesi ports are serviced by Pelni. See the Indonesia Getting Around section for route details.

From Surabaya, the main port of Java with connections to Ujung Pandang, it takes less than 24 hours. Then it's a couple of days more around to Bitung (the port for Manado), with several stops in-between. Because road transport in Sulawesi is still poor, the coastal ferries tend to be crowded.

It's also possible to get across from Kalimantan to Sulawesi. Two of the Pelni services operate between Ujung Pandang and Balikpapan and then back to Sulawesi. There are other regular passenger ships from various east Kalimantan ports to Pare Pare, Donggala and Palu. Heading east, Pelni connects to ports in Maluku and Irian Jaya.

When looking for ships in any of the ports, check with the Pelni office first and then check around other shipping agents, and ask around the port. A really interesting trip would be by Makassar schooner – ask at Paotere Harbour in Ujung Pandang or in Java at Surabaya or Jakarta. Travellers occasionally find schooners going to Nusa Tenggara. Fares are totally dependent on negotiation, of course.

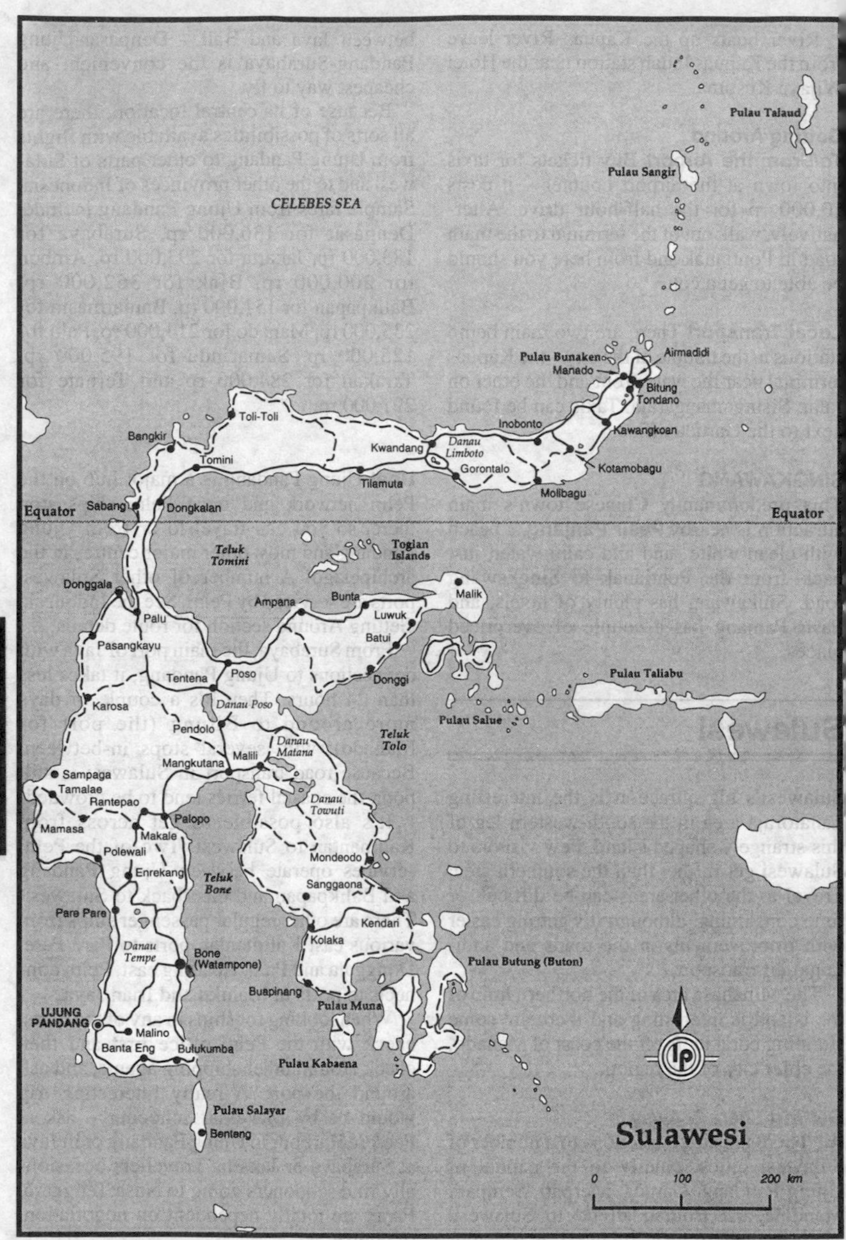

CELEBES SEA
Pulau Talaud
Pulau Sangir
Pulau Bunaken
Manado
Airmadidi
Bitung
Tondano
Inobonto
Kawangkoan
Kotamobagu
Molibagu
Danau Limboto
Gorontalo
Kwandang
Toli-Toli
Bangkir
Tomini
Tilamuta
Sabang
Dongkalan
Equator
Equator
Teluk Tomini
Togian Islands
Donggala
Palu
Ampana
Bunta
Malik
Luwuk
Batui
Pasangkayu
Poso
Tentena
Donggi
Karosa
Danau Poso
Pendolo
Pulau Taliabu
Pulau Salue
Teluk Tolo
Danau Matana
Malili
Mangkutana
Sampaga
Tamalae
Rantepao
Mamasa
Palopo
Makale
Danau Towuti
Polewali
Enrekang
Mondeodo
Teluk Bone
Sanggaona
Pare Pare
Kendari
Kolaka
Danau Tempe
Bone (Watampone)
Pulau Butung (Buton)
Buapinang
Pulau Muna
UJUNG PANDANG
Malino
Banta Eng
Bulukumba
Pulau Kabaena
Pulau Salayar
Benteng
Sulawesi
0
100
200 km

UJUNG PANDANG

The capital of Sulawesi province is also its largest and liveliest city. The Muslim Bugis are now the dominant group in Ujung Pandang and the city is best known as the home of their magnificent perahus that still trade extensively throughout the Indonesian archipelago. In the Dutch era it was known as Makassar.

Information

The main tourist office (☎ 21142) is a long way out of town on Jalan A Pangerang Petta Rani, a street heading south off the airport road.

Fort Rotterdam

Now known as Benteng Ujung Pandang, this fort was originally built in 1634 then rebuilt in typical Dutch style after their takeover in 1667. The buildings gradually fell into disrepair but a major restoration project has renovated the whole complex, apart from a wall or two. The entire fort is shaped like a turtle facing the sea, a symbol of the Makassarese.

The fort contains two museums. The larger one is more interesting and the smaller one has a rather sad and scruffy collection. There are separate admission charges to both museums and they open daily from 8 am to 4 pm.

Perahus

You can see Bugis schooners at Paotere Harbour, a short becak ride north from the city centre. Though they are nowhere near as impressive as the awesome lineup at the Pasar Ikan in Jakarta, if you've never seen them it's worth a look. Elsewhere along the waterfront, you may see *balolang*, large outriggers with sails, or *lepa-lepa*, smaller outrigger canoes.

Tomb of Sultan Hasanuddin

On the outskirts of Ujung Pandang is the tomb of Sultan Hasanuddin, leader of the southern Sulawesi kingdom of Gowa in the middle of the 17th century. Conflicts between Gowa and the Dutch had continued almost incessantly since the early part of that century. This only came to an end in 1660 when a Dutch East Indies fleet attacked Gowa and forced Hasanuddin to accept a peace treaty.

Museum Ballalompoa

In an interesting old wooden palace on stilts, this museum has similar exhibits to those in Fort Rotterdam. It's at Sungguminasa, a half-hour, 300-rp trip from the central bemo station. It opens at various times from Monday to Saturday, or on request.

Clara Bundt Orchid Garden & Shell Collection

This house is at Jalan Mochtar Lufti 15 (☎ 22572), and its compound contains a large collection of seashells, including dozens of giant clams. Behind the house are several blocks of orchids in pots and trays. These are world famous amongst orchid specialists.

Diponegoro Monument

The Yogya Prince Diponegoro was exiled to Makassar after the Dutch double-crossed him. His grave is in a small cemetery on Jalan Diponegoro.

Other Attractions

Other interesting Ujung Pandang peculiarities include the brilliantly ornate **Chinese temples** found along Jalan Sulawesi in the middle of town. Check out **Jalan Sombu Opu** – it has a great collection of jewellery shops. Toko Kerajinam, at No 20, is good for touristy souvenirs and there are lots of people around the streets here selling old coins.

Places to Stay

The *Legend Hostel* (☎ 311922), Jalan Jampea 5G, is far and away the most popular budget place and right on the ball with travel information. Dorm beds cost 5750 rp and rooms are 11,000 rp.

More of a mid-range hotel but the best value for money is the *Ramayana Satrya Hotel* (☎ 442478) on Jalan Gunung Bawa-

Ujung Pandang
Not to Scale
PLACES TO STAY
4 Hotel Murah
5 Hotel Nusantara
14 Hotel Sentral
17 Legend Hostel
24 Marannu Tower Hotel
25 Hotel Purnama
26 Benteng Hotel
28 Losari Beach Inn
29 Makassar Golden Hotel
30 Losari Beach Guesthouse
33 Hotel Victoria & Sempati
35 Hotel Aman
38 Ramayana Satrya Hotel
40 Hotel Marlin
45 Oriental Hotel
PLACES TO EAT
3 Jameson Supermarket
7 Rumah Makan Malabar
8 Rumah Makan Empang
31 Supermarket & KFC
42 Asia Bahru Restaurant
OTHER
1 Schooner Harbour
2 Immigration Office
6 Diponegoro Monument
9 Pelni Office
10 Chinese Temple
11 Main Bemo Station
12 Hasanuddin University
13 Liman Express Head Office
15 Mandala Office
16 Bank Rakyat Indonesia
18 Chinese Temple
19 Garuda Office
20 Entrance to Fort Rotterdam
21 Post Office
22 Police Station
23 Sports Field
27 Cinema
32 Clara Bundt Orchid Garden
34 Big Mosque
36 Harapan Supermarket & Department Store
37 Merpati Office
39 Bemos to Airport
41 Liman Express Office
43 THR Amusement Park
44 Bouraq Office
Paotere Harbour
Panampu Canal
Jalan Sunu
Jalan Andalas
Jalan Tarakan
Jalan Seram Ujung
Jalan Butung
Jalan Irian
Jalan Sarappo
Jalan Banda
Jalan Akademis
Jalan Sangir
Jalan Diponegoro
Jalan Lambeth
Jalan Hasyim
Jalan Timor
Jalan Bali
Jalan Martadinata
Jalan Nusantara
Jalan Sulawesi
Selat Makassar

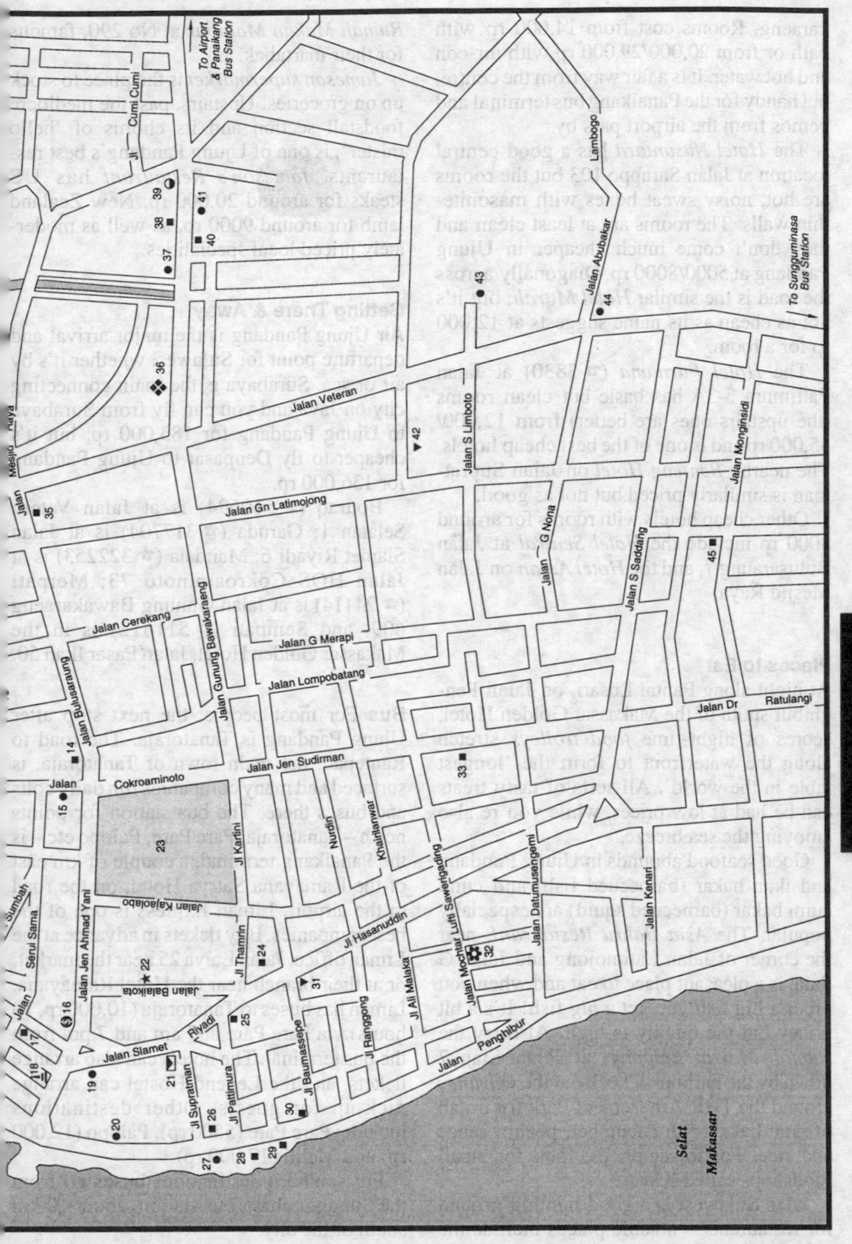
To Airport & Panaikang Bus Station
Jl Cumi Cumi
Lambogo
Jalan Abubakar
To Sungguminasa Bus Station
Jalan Mesjid Raya
Jalan Veteran
Jalan S Limboto
Jalan Monginsidi
Jalan Gn Latimojong
Jalan — G Nona
Jalan S Saddang
Jalan Cerekang
Jalan Gunung Bawakaraeng
Jalan G Merapi
Jalan Lompobatang
Jalan Bulusaraung
Jalan Dr Ratulangi
Jalan Jen Sudirman
Jalan Cokroaminoto
Jl Kartini
Nurdin
Khairilanwar
Jalan Kajaolalido
Jl Hasanuddin
Jalan Mochtar Lufti Sawerigading
Jalan Datumusengemi
Jalan Kenari
Jalan Jen Ahmad Yani
Serui Sama
Sumbah
Jl Thamrin
Jalan Balaikota
Jl Ali Malaka
Jalan Penghibur
Jl Ranggong
Jl Baumassepe
Riyadi
Jalan Slamet
Jl Pattimura
Jl Supratman
Selat Makassar
14
15
16
17
18
19
20
21
22
23
24
25
26
27
28
29
30
31
32
33
35
36
37
38
39
40
41
42
43
44
45

INDONESIA

karaeng. Rooms cost from 14,000 rp with bath or from 20,000/29,000 rp with air-con and hot water. It is a fair way from the centre, but handy for the Panaikang bus terminal and bemos from the airport pass by.

The *Hotel Nusantara* has a good central location at Jalan Sarappo 103 but the rooms are hot, noisy sweat boxes with masonite-thin walls. The rooms are at least clean and they don't come much cheaper in Ujung Pandang at 5000/8000 rp. Diagonally across the road is the similar *Hotel Murah*, but it's not as cheap as its name suggests at 12,000 rp for a room.

The *Hotel Purnama* (☎ 3830) at Jalan Pattimura 3-3A has basic but clean rooms (the upstairs ones are better) from 12,000/15,000 rp and is one of the best cheap hotels. The nearby *Benteng Hotel* on Jalan Supratman is similarly priced but not as good.

Other cheap hotels with rooms for around 8000 rp include the *Hotel Sentral* at Jalan Bulusaraung 7, and the *Hotel Aman* on Jalan Mesjid Raya.

Places to Eat

At night along Pantai Losari, on Jalan Penghibur south of the Makassar Golden Hotel, scores of night-time *food trolleys* stretch along the waterfront to form the 'longest table in the world'. All sorts of tasty treats can be had at low prices, while you're also enjoying the sea breeze.

Good seafood abounds in Ujung Pandang and ikan bakar (barbecued fish) and cumi cumi bakar (barbecued squid) are especially popular. The *Asia Bahru Restaurant*, near the corner of Jalan Latimojong and Jalan G Sala, is a pleasant place to eat and when you order a big fish you get a *big* fish! It's a bit pricey but the quality is high. Also try the *Rumah Makan Empang*, at Jalan Siau 7 down by the harbour. Check out the *warungs* around the THR Amusement Park for a slab of ikan bakar with cucumber, peanut sauce and rice. For lower prices, look for small foodshops called Kios.

Jalan Sulawesi is a good hunting ground for restaurants – notable places include the *Rumah Makan Malabar* at No 290, famous for their martabak.

Jameson supermarket is the place to stock up on groceries. Upstairs, past the mediocre foodstall section and its chorus of 'hello mister', is one of Ujung Pandang's best restaurants. *Jameson's Restaurant* has US steaks for around 20,000 rp, New Zealand lamb for around 9000 rp, as well as moderately priced local specialities.

Getting There & Away

Air Ujung Pandang is the major arrival and departure point for Sulawesi whether it's by air or sea. Surabaya is the main connecting city on Java and you can fly from Surabaya to Ujung Pandang for 183,000 rp, but it's cheaper to fly Denpasar to Ujung Pandang for 136,000 rp.

Bouraq (☎ 510694) is at Jalan Vetern Selatan 1; Garuda (☎ 317704) is at Jalan Slamet Riyadi 6; Mandala (☎ 322253) is at Jalan HOS Cokroaminoto 73; Merpati (☎ 24114) is at Jalan Gunung Bawakaraeng 609; and Sempati (☎ 511612) is in the Makassar Golden Hotel, Jalan Pasar Ikan 50.

Bus For most people, the next stop after Ujung Pandang is Tanatoraja. The road to Rantepao, the main town of Tanatoraja, is surfaced and many companies run daily colts and buses there. The bus station for points north – Tanatoraja, Pare Pare, Palopo etc – is the Panaikang terminal, a couple of km east of the Ramayana Satrya Hotel, on the road to the airport. Liman Express is one of the best companies. Buy tickets in advance at the Liman office, Jalan Laiya 25 near the market, or at their branch near the Hotel Ramayana. Liman has buses to Tanatoraja (10,000 rp, 10 hours) via Pare Pare at 7 am and 7 pm from the bus terminal. The hotels can also arrange tickets, and the Legend Hostel can arrange pick-up for guests. Other destinations include: Pare Pare (5500 rp), Palopo (12,000 rp) and Malili (17,000 rp).

For southern destinations buses go from the Sungguminasa bus station, about 10 km south of the city.

Boat Pelni (☎ 31 7965) is in an unmarked building at Jalan Martadinata 38, down on the waterfront. Ekonomi fares from Ujung Pandang include: Ambon (Maluku) for 41,000 rp, Balikpapan (Kalimantan) for 24,000 rp, Benoa (Bali) for 35,000 rp, Bima (Sumbawa) for 18,000 rp, Lembar (Lombok) for 22,000 rp, Maumere (Flores) for 20,000 rp, Surabaya for 33,000 rp and Jakarta for 54,000 rp.

Getting Around

To/From the Airport Bemos from the main bemo station run past the large intersection just east of the Ramayana Satrya Hotel on their way to Ujung Pandang's Hasanuddin airport (22 km out of town). The airport terminal is off the main road and bemos sometimes detour right to the terminal; otherwise it is a short walk. The fare from the city is 1000 rp.

A taxi coupon from the airport to the town centre (buy your ticket at the taxi counter in the terminal) is 14,300 rp but to the airport by meter should only be about 10,000 rp.

Local Transport The main bemo station is at the northern end of Jalan Cokroaminoto, and bemos run all over town and to outlying districts. Bemos to Panaikang bus terminal cost 350 rp or to Sungguminasa it costs 500 rp.

For short trips there are becaks and taxis – you really need them since Ujung Pandang is too big a place to do much walking. Ujung Pandang has an oversupply of becak drivers who, like their compatriots in Yogya, will never let an *orang turis* pass by without proffering their services. From the Ramayana Satrya Hotel to the waterfront, pay about 1000 rp, and short trips should not be more than 500 rp. Becak drivers tend to ask ridiculous fares, but they bring the price down fast when you walk away. They're fearless drivers, unafraid to put your life on the line. Getting into the traffic or cutting across streets during peak hour is a truly terrifying experience!

Taxis are metered and cheap, but not always easy to find and often not as quick as becaks in downtown traffic.

AROUND UJUNG PANDANG

Bantimurung

This reserve, 41 km from Ujung Pandang, is noted for its waterfall and eroded and overgrown rocky pinnacles and cliffs. There's also a cave with some carvings – scramble along the rocks past the waterfall to the track leading to the cave, a 15-minute walk, and bring a torch. It makes a pleasant day's retreat from Ujung Pandang and is noted for the numerous beautiful butterflies. Admission is 800 rp.

To get to Bantimurung, take a bemo from the central bemo station to the town of Maros (1000 rp, 30 minutes from Ujung Pandang) and then take a bus from there (500 rp, 30 minutes). On Sunday it can be very crowded. There are lots of little shops around here selling soft drinks.

BIRA

Near Bulukumba on the south-eastern tip of South Sulawesi, Bira has fine beaches and is a pleasant retreat from Ujung Pandang for a few days. You can walk around nearby **Lasa Cape** where dolphins are regularly seen.

Places to Stay

Riswan Guest House caters to travellers. Rooms cost 8,500 rp per person including all meals. On the western beach, Riswan has bungalows with attached bath for 13,000/15,000 rp. A more expensive alternative is the *Bira Beach Hotel* with cottages from US$11 to US$15.

Getting There & Away

Direct buses leave Ujung Pandang's Sungguminasa bus station for Bira (6000 rp, four hours) until around 10 am in the morning; otherwise, catch a bus to Bulukumba and then another to Bira.

PARE PARE

Pare Pare is a bustling seaport – a mini Ujung Pandang – but without the obnoxious traffic. For the most part, however, it's just a place

INDONESIA

to hang around in as you await a boat to Kalimantan or northern Sulawesi.

Things to See

One sight of note is the small **Museum of Ethnology** in Bangenge, on the right side of the highway as you enter Pare Pare from Ujung Pandang. On display are wedding ornaments, brassware, ceramics, musical instruments etc.

At the **perahu pier**, or pelabuhan perahu, off Jalan Pinggir Laut, you can check out the local boat scene.

Places to Stay & Eat

The *Hotel Gandaria* (☎ 21093), Jalan Bau Massepe 171, is the best in town and only a five-minute walk from the bus station. Rooms with toilet and shower cost from 12,000/24,000 rp – excellent value.

The *Tanty Hotel* on Jalan Hasanuddin is basic but clean and in a quiet back-street location. Rooms are around 9000 rp. The only sign outside is the one saying 'Office'.

A 15 to 20-minute walk from the bus station, the *Hotel Siswa* (☎ 21374) at Jalan Baso Daeng Patompo 30 is a great rambling, run-down place with grotty rooms for 6000/10,000 rp. *Penginapan Palanro* and *Penginapan AM* (☎ 21801), in the same building on Jalan Bau Massepe, are similar in price and standard.

The *Restaurant Sempurna* on Jalan Bau Massepe is a nice, clean place and good value with its extensive menu featuring seafood. The *Warung Sedap* is an ikan bakar specialist on Jalan Baso Daeng Patompo. Next door, *Restaurant Asia* is a scrupulously clean Chinese restaurant. *Warungs* can be found in the vicinity of the Hotel Siswa.

Getting There & Away

Bus Liman Express and others have buses from Ujung Pandang for 5500 rp. In Pare Pare, the bus companies have their ticket offices at the bus station, with regular buses to Rantepao, Palopo and Bone via Sengkang.

Boat The main reason to come to Pare Pare is to catch a boat to the east coast of Kalimantan. There are daily boats to one port or other. There are also boats to Pantoloan and Toli-Toli in Sulawesi.

Pelni (☎ 21017) is at Jalan Andicami 96. The harbourmaster's office is on the waterfront on Jalan Andicami, and plenty of other agents have their offices here. Pelni fares from Pare Pare include Nunukan from 66,000 rp, Tarakan for 60,000 rp, Balikpapan for 19,000 rp and Toli-Toli for 39,000 rp.

TANATORAJA

The Toraja Land (also known as Tanatoraja or Tator) is about 320 km north of Ujung Pandang. It's a high, mountainous area with beautiful scenery and a fascinating culture. The Torajas are now Christian but they retain strong animist traditions, including complex death rituals.

The first thing that strikes you in Toraja are the traditional houses, shaped like buffalo horns (an animal of great mythic and economic importance to the Torajas) with the roof rearing up at front and rear. The houses are remarkably similar to the Batak houses of Lake Toba in Sumatra and are always aligned north-south with small rice barns facing them.

A number of villages in the region are still composed entirely of these traditional houses but most have corrugated-iron roofs, and some have been built in strategic locations purely for the benefit of foreign tourists. The beams and supports of the Torajan houses are cut so that they all slot together neatly and the whole house is painted (and carved on the older houses) with chicken and buffalo motifs – buffalo skulls are often used as decoration.

The burial customs of the Torajas are unique. Like the Balinese they generally have two funerals – one immediately after the death and then an elaborate second funeral after sufficient time has elapsed to make the complex preparations and raise the necessary cash. Because they believe you can take it with you, the dead generally go well equipped to their graves. Since this led to grave plundering, the Torajas started to secrete their dead in caves (of which there

INDONESIA

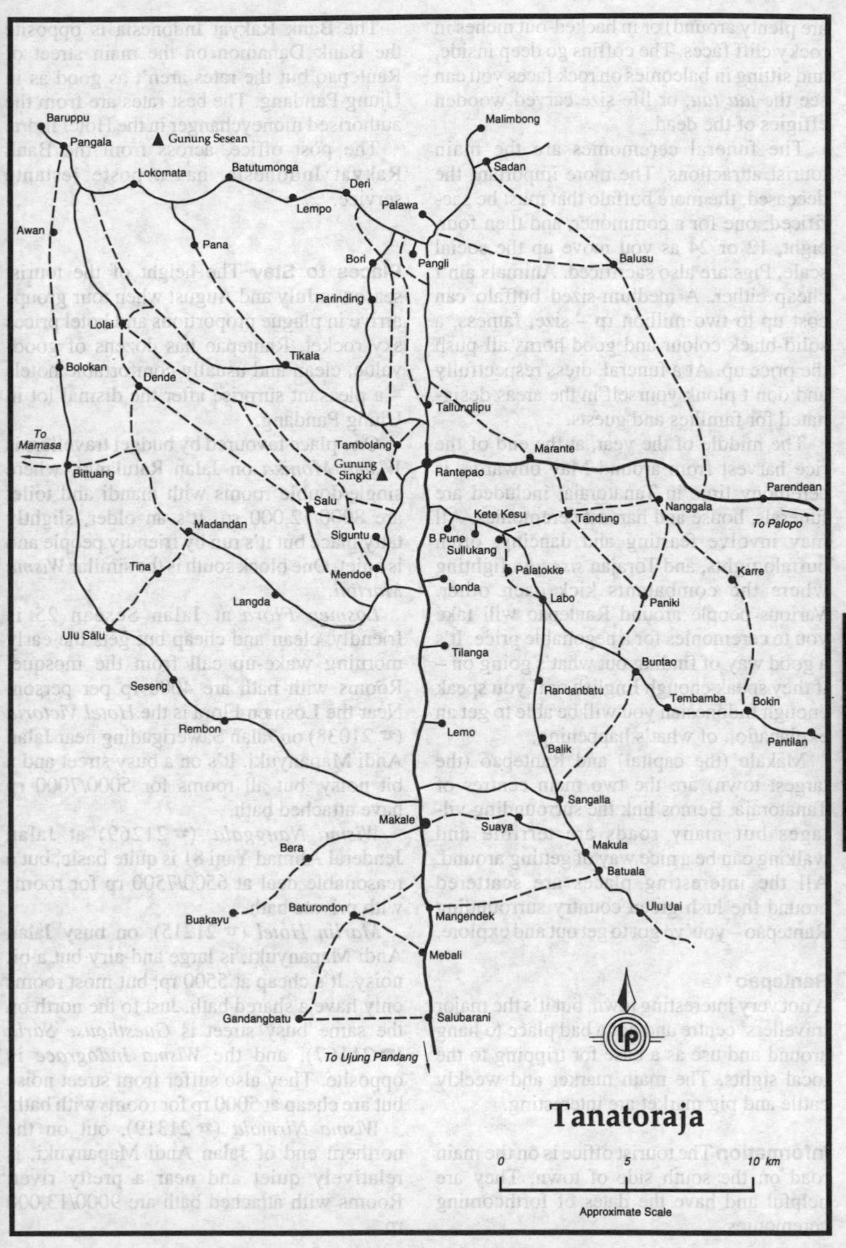
Baruppu
Gunung Sesean
Pangala
Lokomata
Batutumonga
Deri
Lempo
Palawa
Malimbong
Sadan
Awan
Pana
Bori
Pangli
Balusu
Parinding
Lolai
Tikala
Bolokan
Dende
Tallunglipu
To Mamasa
Tambolang
Gunung Singki
Bittuang
Rantepao
Marante
Parendean
Salu
Kete Kesu
Tandung
Nanggala
To Palopo
Madandan
Siguntu
B Pune
Sullukang
Tina
Mendoe
Palatokke
Londa
Karre
Langda
Labo
Paniki
Ulu Salu
Tilanga
Buntao
Seseng
Randanbatu
Tembamba
Bokin
Rembon
Lemo
Pantilan
Balik
Sangalla
Makale
Suaya
Bera
Makula
Batuala
Baturondon
Buakayu
Mangendek
Ulu Uai
Mebali
Gandangbatu
Salubarani
To Ujung Pandang
Tanatoraja
0
5
10 km
Approximate Scale

are plenty around) or in hacked-out niches in rocky cliff faces. The coffins go deep inside, and sitting in balconies on rock faces you can see the *tau tau*, or life-size carved wooden effigies of the dead.

The funeral ceremonies are the main tourist attractions. The more important the deceased, the more buffalo that must be sacrificed: one for a commoner, and then four, eight, 12 or 24 as you move up the social scale. Pigs are also sacrificed. Animals ain't cheap either. A medium-sized buffalo can cost up to two million rp – size, fatness, a solid-black colour and good horns all push the price up. At a funeral, dress respectfully and don't plonk yourself in the areas designated for families and guests.

The middle of the year, at the end of the rice harvest from around May onwards, is ceremony time in Tanatoraja; included are funerals, house and harvest ceremonies. All may involve feasting and dancing, often buffalo fights, and Torajan *sisemba* fighting where the combatants kick each other. Various people around Rantepao will take you to ceremonies for a negotiable price. It's a good way of finding out what's going on – if they speak enough English or if you speak enough Indonesian you will be able to get an explanation of what's happening.

Makale (the capital) and Rantepao (the largest town) are the two main centres of Tanatoraja. Bemos link the surrounding villages but many roads are terrible and walking can be a nice way of getting around. All the interesting places are scattered around the lush green country surrounding Rantepao – you've got to get out and explore.

Rantepao

A not very interesting town, but it's the major travellers' centre and not a bad place to hang around and use as a base for tripping to the local sights. The main market and weekly cattle and pig market are interesting.

Information The tourist office is on the main road on the south side of town. They are helpful and have the dates of forthcoming ceremonies.

The Bank Rakyat Indonesia is opposite the Bank Danamon on the main street of Rantepao but the rates aren't as good as in Ujung Pandang. The best rates are from the authorised moneychanger in the Hotel Indra.

The post office, across from the Bank Rakyat Indonesia, has a poste restante service.

Places to Stay The height of the tourist season is July and August when tour groups arrive in plague proportions and hotel prices sky rocket. Rantepao has dozens of good-value, clean and usually comfortable hotels – a pleasant surprise after the dismal lot in Ujung Pandang.

One place favoured by budget travellers is *Wisma Monika* on Jalan Ratulangi, where single/double rooms with mandi and toilet are 8000/12,000 rp. It's an older, slightly tatty place but it's run by friendly people and is quiet. One block south is the similar *Wisma Martini*.

Losmen Flora at Jalan Sesean 25 is friendly, clean and cheap but gets the early morning wake-up call from the mosque. Rooms with bath are 4000 rp per person. Near the Losmen Flora is the *Hotel Victoria* (☎ 21038) on Jalan Sawerigading near Jalan Andi Mapanyuki. It's on a busy street and a bit noisy, but all rooms for 5000/7000 rp have attached bath.

Wisma Nanggala (☎ 21269) at Jalan Jenderal Ahmad Yani 81 is quite basic, but a reasonable deal at 6500/7500 rp for rooms with private bath.

Marlin Hotel (☎ 21215), on busy Jalan Andi Mapanyuki, is large and airy but a bit noisy. It's cheap at 5500 rp, but most rooms only have a shared bath. Just to the north on the same busy street is *Guesthouse Sarla* (☎ 21167), and the *Wisma Indograce* is opposite. They also suffer from street noise but are cheap at 5000 rp for rooms with bath.

Wisma Nirmala (☎ 21319), out on the northern end of Jalan Andi Mapanyuki, is relatively quiet and near a pretty river. Rooms with attached bath are 9000/13,000 rp.

Further to the north, across the river, *Wisma Rosa* (☎ 21075) has a quiet location and friendly management. Singles/doubles go for 9000/12,000 rp.

Wisma Maria (☎ 21165) at Jalan Ratulangi has a collection of Torajan artefacts in the foyer. Rooms are 7500/12,000 rp with cold-water baths, or 13,000/20,000 rp with hot water. *Wisma Linda* (☎ 21113) is on Jalan Abdul Gani, a quiet back street with lots of greenery. Rooms cost 5000/8000 rp.

Places to Eat Check out the market in the middle of Rantepao for local food, including bamboo tubes full of *tuak* (palm wine). At night, try tuak in the warungs beside the marketplace. Tuak is tapped in the morning, carried into town in long bamboo containers (frothing at the top), left to ferment all day and drunk at night. It comes in a variety of strengths, from the colour of lemonade to the stronger orange or red.

If you tire of the kids asking for candy ('gula gula mister'), indulge your own sweet tooth around the Rantepao Market. Try *wadi bandung*, a sweet rice and grated coconut confection wrapped in paper. Or try *kajang goreng*, an almost oversweet concoction of peanuts and treacle (hard) wrapped in a dry palm leaf. Or try a *baje*, a sticky rice and molasses mixture rolled in a dry palm leaf like a Christmas cracker. Going out to the ceremonies is a good chance to try black rice with pig and buffalo meat roasted in bamboo tubes over an open fire.

There are various restaurants, rumah makan and warungs around Rantepao. *Restaurant Setia Kawan* (☎ 21264) at Jalan Andi Mapanyuki 32 does good Indonesian and Chinese food. Just to the south of the Hotel Indra on Jalan Ratulangi is *Rumah Makan Mambo* which does good Indonesian and Toraja food. *Rumah Makan Sarlota* on the northern end of Jalan Andi Mapanyuki is also popular with travellers.

Restaurant Rachmat on Jalan Abdul Gani at the traffic circle caters mainly to tourist groups. The food is quite expensive, although servings are usually quite large.

Getting There & Away Merpati has flights from Ujung Pandang (73,000 rp) to the airport, 25 km from Rantepao near Makale. The Merpati airport bus costs 8000 rp.

The bus company offices are around Jalan Andi Mapanyuki in the centre of town. Fa Litha, Liman and Alam Indah are the main companies with buses to Ujung Pandang (10,000 rp, 10 hours) at 7 am, 1 pm and 7 pm, and to Pare Pare (5000 rp, five hours).

To the north, Bina Wisata has buses on Tuesday and Saturday to Pendolo (20,000 rp, 10 hours), Tentena (20,000 rp, 11½ hours), Poso (20,000 rp, 13 hours) and Palu (25,000 rp, 20 hours). Pendolo can reached by bemo in 11 hours if done in stages – Rantepao to Palopo (2500 rp) to Mangkutana (3500 rp) to Pendolo (7500 rp). Some bemos go directly from Rantepao to Mangkutana.

Other services include bemos to Palopo (3000 rp, two hours) and buses to Soroako (6000 rp, 10 hours) on Lake Matana.

Bemos run almost continuously from Rantepao to Makale (600 rp, 40 minutes) – you can get off at the signs for Londa or Lemo and walk. Frequent bemos go towards Palopo for the sights in that direction.

Motorcycles can be rented from the Marlin Hotel and groups can think about chartering a bemo or a jeep.

Apart from the roads to Makale, Palopo, Sadan, Kete Kesu and a few other places, most of the roads around Rantepao are terrible. Some are constructed out of compacted boulders – you don't get stuck but your joints get rattled loose. If trekking, bring good footwear, a water bottle, something to eat, a torch in case you end up walking at night, and an umbrella or raincoat, even in the dry season.

Getting Around Central Rantepao is small and easy to walk around, or there are becaks.

Around Rantepao

The following places – the distance in km from Rantepao is shown – are all within fairly easy reach on day trips. If you want to, you can make longer trips and stay overnight in villages as you go. If you do this, don't exploit the Torajan hospitality – make sure you pay your share. Guides aren't necessary but if you want one they're easy to find. Many travellers easily find their way around without a guide – the Torajans are friendly and used to tourists, and it's great to escape on your own into the beautiful countryside around Rantepao.

Karasbik (one km) Karasbik is on the outskirts of Rantepao, just off the road leading to Makale. The traditional-style houses here are arranged in a square. Apparently the complex was erected some years ago for a single funeral.

Singki (one km) You can climb this small hill just outside Rantepao for a panoramic view over the surrounding area.

Kete Kesu (six km) Just off the main road, south of Rantepao, this traditional village is reputed for its wood carving. On the cliff face behind the village are some cave graves and some very old hanging graves – the rotting coffins are suspended from an overhang. The houses at Kete Kesu are decorated with more tourist souvenirs than you've probably ever seen.

Sullukang (seven km) Off to the side of the main road in this village, there's a derelict shack on a rocky outcrop which contains several derelict tau tau, almost buried under the foliage. There's also *rante* here – large stone slabs planted in the ground – one of them about four metres high.

Londa (six km) Two km off the Rantepao to Makale road, this is a very extensive burial cave, with a number of coffins containing bones and skulls. Kids hang around outside renting their oil lamps for 1500 rp (you could try bargaining but they're not very amenable to it) to guide you around. Unless you've got a strong torch, you really do need a guide with a lamp.

Tilanga (nine km) There are several cold and hot springs in the Toraja area, and this natural cold-water pool is very pretty. It's an attractive walk along the muddy trails and through the rice paddies from Lemo to Tilanga – keep asking for directions along the way.

Lemo (11 km) This is probably the most interesting burial area in Tanatoraja. The sheer rock face has a whole series of balconies carved out for tau tau. The biggest balcony has a dozen figures – like spectators at a sports event. One tall tau tau stands on a slightly depressed section of floor so he can fit in. There would be even more if they weren't in such demand by unscrupulous antique dealers.

It's a good idea to go early in the morning so you get the sun on the rows of figures – by 9 am their heads are in the shadows. A bemo from Rantepao will drop you off at the road leading up to Lemo, from where it's a 15-minute walk.

Siguntu (seven km) Siguntu, a traditional village situated on a slight rise off to the west of the main road, is a pleasant walk from Rantepao. The walk from Rantapao via Singki and Siguntu to the main road at Alang Alang near the Londa burial site is pleasant.

Marante (six km) This very fine traditional village is only a few metres off the road east to Palopo.

Nanggala (16 km) In the same direction (and rather further off the Palopo road) is this traditional village with a particularly grandiose traditional house with a whole fleet – 14 in all – of rice barns. Bemos from Rantepao take you straight there for 500 rp, or they might just drop you off on the main road, and then it's a 1½ km walk.

Palawa (nine km) This traditional village a km or two north of Pangli has longkonan houses and rice barns.

Sadan (13 km) Sadan is a weaving centre further to the north. Bemos go there from

Rantepao along a shocking road. The women here have established a tourist market where they sell their weaving.

Batutumonga (23 km) From Batutumonga you can see a large part of Tanatoraja. Bemos go up here occasionally. *Betania Homestay* is a Torajan house with valley views.

Lokomata (26 km) There are more cave graves and more beautiful scenery at Lokomata, just a few km past Batutumonga.

Other Villages At **Pangli** (seven km) are house graves; **Bori** (eight km) is a funeral ceremony site; **Pangala** (35 km) is a traditional village; and **Mt Sesean** (25 km) is the highest point in Tanatoraja. One of the most popular **treks** is from Bittuang (58 km) to Mamasa in the west.

Makale

There's really nothing to Makale, though some people stay here just to be away from tourist-heavy Rantepao. On Sunday, the town echoes with the singing from local churches which seem to be on every nearby hilltop. Makale has the same bus connections to other parts of Sulawesi as Rantepao.

Places to Stay & Eat *Wisma Bungin* (☎ 22255) at Jalan Pongtiku 35 is the best deal in town. Rooms with mandi cost 5000 rp per person. *Losmen Indra* (☎ 22022), Jalan Merdeka 11, on the south side of town, is clean and friendly. Rooms are 10,000 rp, or 15,000 rp with private bath.

Losmen Merry (☎ 22013) is one of the cheaper alternatives, with single rooms for 3500 rp with shared bath. On Jalan Pongtiku, *Losmen Marga* (☎ 22011) looks a bit tattered but has friendly management and rooms with private bath for 5000 rp per person.

One of the disadvantages of Makale is the lack of good restaurants. There are several cheap *noodle shops* on Jalan Merdeka near the mosque.

PENDOLO

A road bears eastwards from Rantepao to Soroako on the shores of Lake Matana in central Sulawesi. Midway along this road is the village of Wotu and, just after Wotu, another road cuts its way due north to the small village of Pendolo on the southern bank of beautiful **Lake Poso**. This former horror-stretch of Sulawesi travel is now a surfaced road.

Pendolo is waiting for a tourist boom. The lake and its lovely beach are the main attractions. You can swim, take boat rides or go for walks. Outriggers will take you across the lake to Tentena on the northern side or there is a ferry at 8 am for 2000 rp.

Places to Stay

The *Victory Hotel* has the best location, overlooking the beach. Rooms with private bath go for a modest 5000 rp per person. *Pondok Wisata Masamba* and *Penginapan Danau Poso* are close to the beach and cost around the same.

TENTENA

On the other side of Lake Matana is Tentena, similar to Pendolo but more developed, noisier and lacking a beach. Having crossed the lake there are regular buses between Tentena and Poso. In Tentena it is possible to organise trips to **Lore Lindu National Park**, but they aren't cheap.

Places to Stay

The *Hotel Wasantara* by the lake is a large and cheery place with economy rooms for 4000 rp per person, standard rooms with bath at 14,000 rp and small bungalows for 18,000 rp. *Losmen Rio* is a dismal edifice that charges 3000 rp – OK for the desperate. Considerably better is *Penginapan Wisata Remaja* where doubles have attached bath and cost from 8000 rp.

Pamona Indah and *Wisma Panorama*, on a hill set back from the lake, are more upmarket

INDONESIA

POSO

Although it's the main town on the northern coast of central Sulawesi there's not much to be said about Poso. It's a fairly dull but pleasant enough place and there are some beaches outside town.

Places to Stay

Hotel Nels on Jalan Yos Sudarso is a good place with rooms for 8000 rp. On Jalan Haji Agus Salim, the *Hotel Kalimantan* is also reasonable and with rooms at 6000 rp, it's cheaper.

A few minutes' walk up the road, at the corner of Jalan Haji Agus Salim and Jalan Imam Bonjol, is the *Penginapan Sulawesi* which has rooms from just 2500 rp. They're very basic little cubicles, but the place is clean and the people friendly.

The *Bambu Jaya Hotel*, Jalan Haji Agus Salim 101, is the top place in town with rooms from 16,000 rp to 70,000 rp.

Getting There & Away

Air Merpati (☎ 21274), Jalan Yos Sudarso 9, fly from Poso to Palu and Luwuk with connections further afield.

Bus Regular buses run from Poso to Tentena on the northern shore of Danau Poso and take 1½ hours. Buses from Palu bound for Rantepao and Palopo come through Poso, but don't count on being able to get on board.

At least eight buses run daily between Poso and Palu (11,000 rp, eight hours), and some run at night.

Boat Ships go to Gorontalo (22,000 rp, two days), on Sulawesi's northern peninsula, on Tuesday, Thursday and Saturday at noon, but expect schedules to change. Buy your ticket at Pos Keamanan Pelabuhan at the port. The ships usually stop at various ports along the coast or in the Togian Islands, including Ampana, Wakai (9000 rp, 12 hours), Dolong and Pagimana.

TOGIAN ISLANDS

These isolated islands have fine beaches and snorkelling. Very few foreigners have made it here but a trickle has started with the opening of the *Togian Islands Hotel* at Wakai on Pulau Batudaka. Basic accommodation starts at 5000 rp per person, and better rooms are 12,500 to 35,000 rp. Wakai is reached on the boats that ply between Poso (see above) and Gorontalo.

PALU

On the western seaboard of Sulawesi, this seaport is rather larger but just as dull as Poso. Palu has a **museum** and a lousy beach.

Places to Stay

The *Hotel Karsam* (☎ 21776), at Jalan Dr Suharso 15 near Pantai Palu, is a good deal with singles/doubles for 8000/15,000 rp, or 12,500/20,000 rp with mandi, but it's about a 15-minute walk from the centre.

Purnama Raya Hotel (☎ 23646) is centrally located at Jalan Dr Wahidin 4, and costs from 8000/12,000 rp for rooms with private bath. It's clean and friendly, though it can be a bit noisy.

Hotel Pasifik, Jalan Gajah Mada 130, is centrally located but astonishingly noisy. However, it's a great place if you're deaf, with rooms starting from 5000 rp with shared bath.

The *New Dely Hotel* (☎ 21037), Jalan Tadulako 17, is a good mid-range hotel near the tourist office, about a 10-minute walk from the centre. Rooms start at 18,000 rp.

Places to Eat

Jalan Hasanuddin II is a busy market street with many places to eat. Here you will find *Milano Ice Cream* with good food and ice cream. The owners organise trekking tours and operate a beachside hotel in Donggala.

Restaurant New Oriental (☎ 23275) is also on Jalan Hasanuddin II, and serves excellent Chinese and Indonesian dishes. *Golden Bakery*, just around the corner on Jalan Dr Wahidin, is excellent for breakfast and midnight snacks.

If you want to self-cater, *Jameson's supermarket* is in the busy Jalan Hasanuddin area.

Getting There & Away

Air Merpati (☎ 21295) is at Jalan Hasanuddin 33. Bouraq (☎ 22563), Jalan W Monginsidi 58, offers the most extensive flight network from Palu with direct flights to Balikpapan (97,000 rp), Gorontalo (92,000 rp), Manado (158,000 rp) and Ujung Pandang (125,000 rp).

Bus Buses to Poso, Palopo, Rantepao, Gorontalo and Manado all leave from the Inpres station. At Masomba station you can get buses to inland cities. Palu to Gorontalo takes 1½ days over a bone-jarring road. Palu to Poso costs 11,000 rp and takes about eight hours.

Boat Larger vessels dock at Pantoloan which is north-east of Palu, and some dock at Donggala which is north-west of Palu. Smaller ships dock at Wani, two km past Pantoloan.

In Palu, the Pelni office is upstairs at Jalan Gajah Mada 86, but their ships dock at Pantoloan, where the Pelni office is opposite the road to the wharf. Two large, modern Pelni liners, the KM *Tidar* and the KM *Kambuna*, stop in at Pantoloan on their way to/from Ujung Pandang, Balikpapan, Tarakan and Toli-Toli. See the Indonesia Getting Around section for route details.

You can avoid the long and winding road through central Sulawesi by taking a ship from Palu to Ujung Pandang or Pare Pare.

Getting Around

Palu's Mutiara airport is seven km from town; it's 1000 rp by bemo or 5000 rp by taxi.

Bemos cost 300 rp anywhere around town. The best place to catch a bemo is along Jalan Gajah Mada. Inpres station has bus and bemo connections to Donggala and other areas around Palu. Karampe station has buses to the harbour at Pantoloan.

DONGGALA

Donggala is a quiet backwater and, though a dull place, excellent **beaches** can be found north of town, where there are opportunities for snorkelling, scuba diving and sailing. From Donggala you can also catch a ship to northern or southern Sulawesi.

Places to Stay & Eat

Milano Beach Cottage attracts a steady stream of travellers. The losmen is run by a German expatriate, Peter Meroniak, and his Indonesian wife, Maureen. They also run the Milano Ice Cream in Palu and arrange transport to the beach. Singles/doubles are 17,500/30,000 rp, including three meals. Donggala also has other cheap losmen.

Getting There & Away

From Palu, you can catch a 'sedan' taxi to Donggala for 1250 rp. Bemos cost 1000 rp and depart from Terminal Inpres. The ride takes 40 minutes. It's another 20 minutes on foot to the beach, or you can take a taxi for 200 rp.

GORONTALO

This quiet town has streets full of Dutch-built villas; fine examples are the Rumah Sakit Umum (Public Hospital) and the Saronde Hotel.

Benteng Otanaha

On a hill at Dembe, overlooking Lake Limbot, are the three towers of this probably Portuguese-built fortress. Take a bendi to the pathway that leads up the hill from Jalan Belibis. Or take an opelet, though these are infrequent on this road. There's a sign at the foot of the pathway pointing the way to the fort.

Places to Stay & Eat

The *Penginapan Teluk Kau* (☎ 21785) at Jalan S Parman 42 used to be one of the most pleasant places to stay in Indonesia but is now run-down, noisy and overpriced at 8000/12,000 rp per person. Other similar crumbling losmen on this same street include *Asia Jaya* and *Asia Baru*.

It's better to spend a little more for accommodation. *Hotel Saronde* (☎ 21735), Jalan Walanda Maramis 17, is the best in town. Rooms cost 14,100/20,000 rp, including breakfast, or big air-con rooms are around

30,000 rp. *Hotel Wisata* (☎ 21736) at Jalan 23 Januari 19 is an excellent place, and is also the location of the Merpati office. Economy rooms start at 10,000 rp and go right up to deluxe for around 40,000 rp.

The *Rumah Makan Padang* is good for Padang food, the *Rumah Makan Dirgahayu* has good satay, or the *Rumah Makan Olympic* has seafood. There are also some very cheap *warungs* in the large Pasar Sentral at the northern end of town.

Getting There & Away

Air The Merpati office (☎ 21736) is in the Hotel Wisata at Jalan 23 Januari 19; Bouraq (☎ 21070) is at Jalan Jenderal Ahmad Yani 34 next to the Bank Negara Indonesia. There are direct flights to Manado (78,000 rp) and Palu (92,000 rp) with connections further afield.

Bus Regular buses to Manado take only 12 hours if the road is dry; if it's wet, good luck. Direct buses to Palu and Poso in central Sulawesi take 1½ days.

Boat Pelni (☎ 21089) is at Jalan 23 Januari 31. Pelni's KM *Awu* stops in Gorontalo on its run around the ports of Sulawesi and Kalimantan, and the KM *Umsini* stops at Kwandang.

Another shipping line, Gapsu (☎ 88173), has an office at Jalan Pertiwi 55 in central Gorontalo, and also at Gorontalo Harbour on Jalan Mayor Dullah (☎ 198). Smaller ships to Poso via the Togian Islands depart on Sunday, Tuesday and Thursday, but the schedule often changes.

Getting Around

A Merpati-Bouraq bus shuttles between the town and the airport (32 km away) for 5000 rp per person.

Bendis cost around 500 rp a trip to anywhere in town. Bemos to Gorontalo Harbour are 250 rp.

AROUND GORONTALO

Fortresses at Kwandang

Near Gorontalo is the port of Kwandang, two hours away to the north by bus. On the outskirts of Kwandang are the remains of two interesting fortresses, possibly Portuguese built. Whilst the town itself is nothing, the fortresses are well worth visiting. The two fortresses are a short walk off the road leading into Kwandang from Gorontalo.

MANADO

Manado is the capital of the province of North Sulawesi, a strongly Christian region that was often referred to as the '12th province of the Netherlands' because of the closeness of its ties to Holland during the colonial days.

Manado is a tidy, prosperous-looking city, and only a half-hour motorboat ride away is the crystal-clear water off Bunaken Island with its brilliant coral reefs. Manado is an interesting place, although the 'sights' are to be found in the surrounding areas.

Orientation

The heart of town is the large market area known as the Pasar 45, near the waterfront. Pasar 45 is also the major opelet station.

Along Jalan Sam Ratulangi, a major artery running north-south, are many of the slightly more upmarket restaurants and more expensive hotels. Slightly further north, the large Pasar Jengki fishmarket backs on to the river which cuts Manado in half.

Information

Tourist Offices The tourist office is at Jalan 17 Augustus off Jalan Eddy Gogola, near the Kantor Imigrasi (immigration office).

Post & Telecommunications The post office is on Jalan Ratulangi 21. International phone calls can be made from the Telkom office on Jalan Ratulangi (near the Hotel Kawanua).

Places to Stay

There's not a great deal of accommodation at the lower end of the price range in Manado – 10,000 rp is cheap here. A popular place with budget travellers is the *Crown Hotel* (☎ 66277), Jalan Hasanuddin 28, across the

INDONESIA

bridge towards Pantai Molas. Rooms are simple but clean and cost 6000 rp. Another good place is *Hotel Kawanua* (☎ 63842), Jalan Sudirman 40 (not the similarly named Kawanua City Hotel, the most expensive place in town). Rooms with shared bath are 12,000 rp and with private bath cost from 16,000 rp.

Ahlan City Hotel (☎ 63454) is in the same neighbourhood at Jalan Sudirman 103. It's basic but clean and rooms are around 11,000 rp, or 16,000 rp with attached bath.

Hotel Jeprinda (☎ 64049) at Jalan Sam Ratulangi 33 is clean and cheery, with singles/doubles for 21,000/25,000 rp. The manager speaks reasonably good English.

Hotel Mini Cakalele (☎ 52842) is at Jalan Korengkeng 40, a street running off Jalan Sam Ratulangi south of the main post office. Doubles are 18,000 rp with fan and 25,000 rp with air-con. It's clean and comfortable.

Hotel Minahasa (☎ 62059) at Jalan Sam Ratulangi 199 is an elegant-looking hotel with an old colonial feel to it. Spotlessly clean rooms with attached bath cost from 20,000 rp, more with air-con.

Places to Eat

Manado is famous for *rintek wuuk* – spicy dog meat, or just plain RW for short. Some other traditional Minahasan delights include *kawaok* which is fried forest rat. Top it off with some *lawa pangang* (stewed bat) and wash it down with *tinutuan* (vegetable porridge).

There's a string of eating houses all the way along Jalan Sam Ratulangi serving up a mixed bag of Chinese and Indonesian food. There's a *KFC* on Jalan Sudirman, right above the *Gelael Supermarket* which itself is well worth a visit for the fine yoghurt. Another outstanding supermarket is *Jumbo* near the Kawanua City Hotel.

Getting There & Away

Air Garuda (☎ 64535) is at Jalan Diponegoro 15; Bouraq (☎ 51459) is at Jalan Sarapung 27; Merpati (☎ 64027) is at Jalan Sam Ratulangi 135; and Sempati (☎ 60221) is in the Kawanua City Hotel. Bouraq has some of the more useful flights. Destinations include: Balikpapan (231,000 rp), Gorontalo (78,000 rp), Jakarta (487,000 rp), Palu (158,000 rp), Ternate (83,000 rp) and Ujung Pandang (214,000 rp). Sempati flies to Balikpapan direct with connections further afield.

Bus From Manado's Gorontalo bus station, buses go daily to Gorontalo (10,000 rp, 12 hours). Flooding can turn this into a 24-hour trip. Daily buses to Palu (27,000 rp) take two days and one night.

Boat Pelni (☎ 62844), Jalan Sam Ratulangi 7, has a number of ships calling into Bitung, North Sulawesi's main port, 48 km from Manado on the eastern tip of the peninsula. Useful connections include: Ternate (14,000 rp) and Ambon (37,000 rp) in Maluku; Sorong (35,000 rp), Manokwari (43,000 rp) and Jayapura (70,000 rp) in Irian Jaya; Gorontalo (12,000 rp) and Ujung Pandang (55,000 rp) in Sulawesi.

From Manado it's easy to take ships along the coast of Sulawesi as far south as Pantoloan (the port of Palu) and Pare Pare, stopping off at various ports on the way, including Kwandang, Paleleh, Leok and Toli-Toli. The *Mauru*, whose Manado office is at the entrance to the harbour terminal, is a regular ship on this run.

For other ships along the northern peninsula, and also for ships to the islands of Tahulandang, Siau and Sangir, inquire at the shipping offices near the port in Manado.

From Manado or Bitung there are ships to Ternate in the Maluku islands for around 20,000 rp. Weekly ships go from Bitung to Poso, in central Sulawesi, via Gorontalo, Pagimana and Ampana.

Getting Around

To/From the Airport Opelets from Sam Ratulangi airport go to Paal2 (or Paal Paal) (400 rp), from where other opelets go to Pasar 45 (300 rp) or elsewhere in the city. A taxi from the airport to the city costs 6000 rp. The airport is 13 km from Manado.

Local Transport Transport around town is by opelet or mikrolet for a flat fare of 300 rp. Destinations are shown on a card in the front windscreen, *not* on the side of the van.

Opelets go to destinations around town and to other parts of northern Sulawesi. Pasar 45 is the central opelet station. From Pasar 45, Wanea and Sario opelets go down Jalan Sam Ratulangi for the Merpati office and the restaurants and hotels along this road. E Gogola opelets go to Jalan Eddy Gogola, for the tourist office, and they also go along Jalan Diponegoro for the telephone office and Garuda.

The other important stations are:

Gorontalo Bus Station – take a Sario opelet from Pasar 45 and tell the driver you want to go to the bus station.

Pasar Paal2 – for the airport, Bitung and Airmadidi. Take a Paal2 opelet from Pasar 45.

Pasar Karombasan – the station for opelets to Tomohon, Tondano and Kawangkoan. Take a Wanea opelet from Pasar 45. Opelets also go from Pasar Karombasan to Langowan, Kotamanbagu, Inobonto, Amurang, Belang and Remboken.

AROUND MANADO

Bunaken Island

The first and foremost attraction of Manado is the stunning coral reefs off nearby Bunaken Island. Boats to Bunaken (1000 rp), depart from the back of the Toko Samudera Jaya in the Kuala Jengki (the large market near the bridge across which Jalan Sisingamangaraja extends).

Once on Bunaken Island, you could ask around for a boat to go to the reefs. Or, walk from the village to the long pier close by and climb down the steps into the water. This lands you right on top of the reef.

To see the reef to best advantage, you really need your own boat. It's probably easiest to charter a boat at Toko Samudera. You'll be looking at about 30,000 rp for them to take you out to the reef in the morning, paddle around for a few hours and take you back to Manado in the afternoon.

Alternatively, the travel agency PT Polita Express (☎ 52231, 52768) at Jalan Ratulangi 74 in Manado organises expensive scuba-diving and glass-bottom boat tours to Bunaken Island. Snorkels and masks (and perhaps fins) can be bought from Toko Akbar Ali in Pasar 45, and possibly from other shops in Manado.

Places to Stay On Bunaken, homestays offer accommodation for 10,000 rp including all meals. Naturally fish features prominently on the menus. *Nelson Homestay* and *Daniel Homestay* are both good, or *Jemy Bastiano* is more upmarket with bungalows on the beach for 25,000 rp. It is also possible to stay on nearby Siladan Island.

Other Attractions

At **Airmadidi**, or Boiling Water, you'll find *warugas*, odd little pre-Christian tombs. Corpses were buried in a squatting position with gold, porcelain and household articles – most have been plundered by now. A group of these tombs are at Sawangan, a 15-minute walk from Airmadidi bemo station.

During the Japanese occupation of Indonesia in WW II, caves were cut into the hills surrounding Manado to act as air-raid shelters, quarters and storage space for supplies. One group of caves is three km out of **Kawangkoan** on the road to Kiawa. More impressive Japanese caves are just outside **Tondano** on the road to Airmadidi.

About five km from Kawangkoan, close to Desa Pinabetengan, **Batu Pinabetengan** is a stone carved with the vague outline of human figures. It is said to be the meeting place for the chiefs of the Minahasan tribes.

BITUNG

Bitung is the port of Manado and you may have to come here to catch a ship. *Penginapan Sansarino* near the main market has rooms for 10,000 rp and a downstairs restaurant. *Penginapan Minang* (☎ 21333) is a dark hovel above a restaurant by the same name at Jalan Sam Ratulangi 34. Rooms go for 15,000 rp with attached mandi. There are many opelets to Bitung from Pasar Paal 2; the trip costs 1200 rp and takes an hour. Pelni (☎ 62 1167) is on Jalan Sumolong 4.

Maluku (Moluccas)

The islands of Maluku are the fabled spice islands of Indonesia and it was mainly for the spices that grew here and nowhere else that foreign traders, including Europeans, came to Indonesia. Maluku Province consists of a scattered series of islands which lie between Sulawesi and Irian Jaya. The largest islands are Halmahera in the north, looking a little like a small-scale version of Sulawesi, and Seram in the south.

Visitors to Maluku usually go to Ambon, the administrative centre, the Banda Islands to the south-east of Ambon, or Ternate and Tidore (two adjacent small islands just off western Halmahera). These days Maluku is noted for fine tropical scenery and for some interesting relics of early European contact. Increasing numbers of foreign visitors are making their way to these interesting islands.

Climate

Timing a visit to Maluku is a bit different from the rest of Indonesia. The dry season in

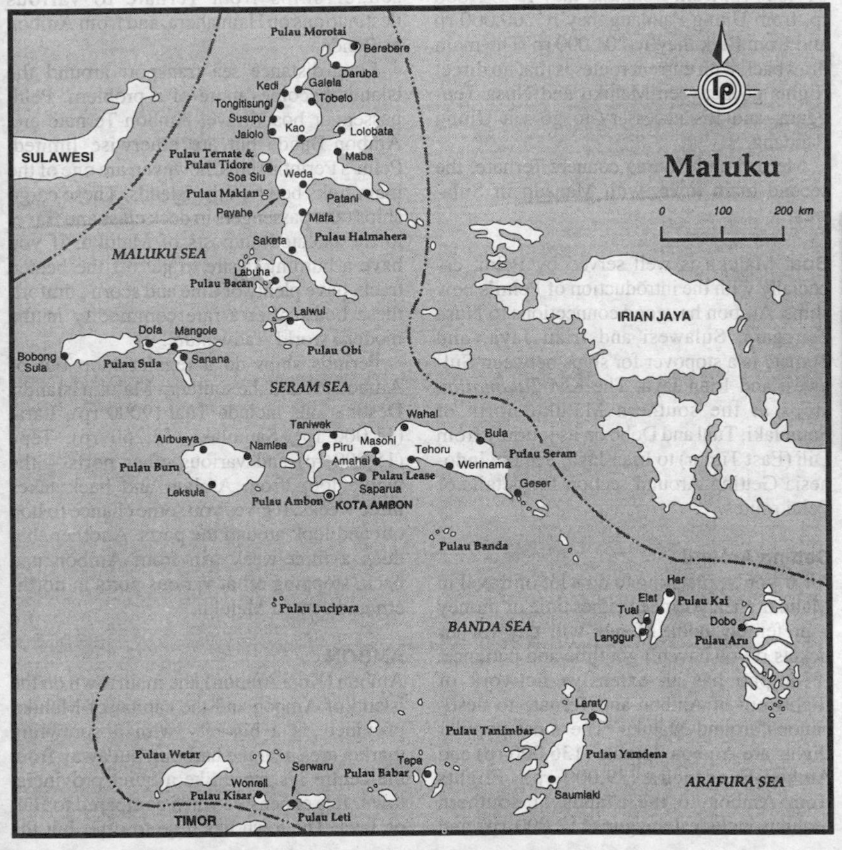

Maluku is from September to March and the wet season is from the beginning of April to the end of August. There's not much point in visiting the region in the wet season as the rain pounds down endlessly. This means the islands are nowhere near their best, and since the seas are rough there's less interisland sea transport.

Getting There & Away

Air The capital of the province – Ambon on Ambon Island – is connected by air to various parts of Indonesia by Merpati, Bouraq, Mandala and Sempati airlines. With Merpati, flights from Jakarta to Ambon are 417,000 rp, from Denpasar they're 291,000 rp, from Ujung Pandang they're 200,000 rp and from Biak they're 201,000 rp. The main drawback with current routes is that no direct flights go between Maluku and Nusa Tenggara, and it's necessary to go via Ujung Pandang.

Merpati and Bouraq connect Ternate, the second main town, with Manado in Sulawesi.

Boat Maluku is well served by Pelni, especially with the introduction of Pelni's new ships. Ambon has good connections to Nusa Tenggara, Sulawesi and Irian Jaya, and Ternate is a stopover for ships between Sulawesi and Irian Jaya. The KM *Tatamailau* stops at the southern Maluku ports of Saumlaki, Tual and Dobo on its journey from Dili (East Timor) to Irian Jaya. See the Indonesia Getting Around section for details of Pelni routes.

Getting Around

Air If you're planning to do a lot of travel in Maluku, then you need either time or money – preferably both. Money will pay for air tickets if you haven't got time and patience.

Merpati has an extensive network of flights out of Ambon and Ternate to destinations around Maluku. The most popular flights are Ambon-Ternate (136,000 rp) and Ambon-Bandaneira (79,000 rp). Flights from Ambon to the islands of southern Maluku include Langgur (152,000 rp) and Saumlaki (161,000 rp). Flights from Ambon to central Maluku include those to Amahai (44,000 rp) on Seram Island and to Namlea (53,000 rp) on Buru. There are flights from Ternate to the islands of central and northern Maluku. Destinations include Morotai (64,000 rp), Galela (55,000 rp) and Kao (45,000 rp).

Boat Transport by sea between adjacent islands is fairly easy. There are regular passenger ferries between Ambon, Saparua and Seram, and frequent motorboats every day make the short hop between Ternate and Tidore. Additionally, there are regular passenger ships from Ternate to various destinations on Halmahera, and from Ambon to Banda.

Long-distance sea transport around the islands becomes more of a problem. Pelni passenger boats travel Ambon-Ternate and Ambon-Banda but are otherwise limited. Pelni's Perintis ships, however, are one of the main links between the islands. These cargo ships take passengers in deck class and travel to the isolated outposts of Maluku. If you have a burning desire to get off the beaten track, have plenty of time and scorn comfort, these boats offer a rare commodity in the modern world – adventure.

Perintis ships do a regular loop out of Ambon around the southern Maluku islands. Destinations include Tual (9000 rp), Larat (11,000 rp), Saumlaki (13,250 rp), Tepa (15,000 rp) and various other ports – the whole loop from Ambon and back takes three weeks. It gives you some chance to hop out and look around the ports. Another ship does a three-week trip from Ambon and back, stopping off at various ports in northern and central Maluku.

AMBON

Ambon (Kota Ambon), the main town on the island of Ambon and the capital of Maluku province, is a big city with a sprawling market area near the harbour, but away from the centre it's more like a quiet provincial town. It is expensive when compared to Bali or Java. The town has little to offer but the island is pretty and has some interesting attractions, which include ruins of European fortifications.

Information

The friendly and helpful tourist office is on the ground floor of Kantor Gubernor, the governor's office. The post office is on Jalan Raya Pattimura. For international calls, a dial-home-direct phone is outside the central Telkom office, on Jalan Tanah Lapang Kecil, to the west of town. Change money before heading to the other islands.

War Cemetery

This WW II cemetery is in the suburb of Tantui, about two km from the centre of Ambon. The cemetery, with its row upon row of marker stones and plaques, is for Australian, Dutch and British servicemen killed in Sulawesi and Maluku. A bemo from the terminal takes you straight to the cemetery.

Fort Victoria

This old Portuguese fortress on Jalan Slamet Riyadi dates back to 1575. The sea walls are still standing but other parts have decayed and have been replaced by new military buildings. You need a permit from the military to visit the fort, which is surrounded by Taman Victoria, a park which always seems to be closed.

Siwalima Museum

This interesting museum is definitely worth a visit. The fine collection includes 'magic' skulls from a cave in northern Buru, model boats made of tortoiseshell, sago palm and cloves, and ancestor statues of south-east Maluku. The museum is in the Taman Makmur Hills, just off the road from Ambon to the village of Amahusu.

Take a bemo from the terminal and tell the driver to drop you at the museum – it's a 10-minute walk from where you get dropped off up to the museum. The museum is closed Monday and Friday.

Places to Stay

Accommodation in Ambon is really expensive, with nothing at the bottom end of the scale and little of even moderate price, but the standards are generally high.

The popular *Penginapan Beta* (☎ 53463) at Jalan Wem Reawaru 114 is a reasonable place in the quieter part of town. It has rooms from 14,000/18,000 rp. Next door at No 115 the *Hotel Transit Rezfanny* (☎ 42300) costs 14,000/22,500 rp and is clean but nothing special. On the other side of the Beta is the *Hotel Hero* (☎ 42978), a spic-and-span mid-range place with all mod-cons, including solar-heated hot water. With rooms starting at 38,500 rp it's no bargain, but discounts are always on offer and breakfast is included.

Nearby, the *Hotel New Silalou* (☎ 53197), at Jalan Sedap Malam 41, is a friendly place and has adequate rooms for 15,000/25,000 rp. The *Hotel Elenoor* (☎ 52834) at Jalan Anthoni Rhebok 30 has rooms for 13,000/20,000 rp and is a pleasant enough place but really quite basic for what you're paying.

More expensive places include the *Hotel Amboina* (☎ 41725) at Jalan Kapitan Ulu Paha 5A. It offers several storeys of comfortable air-con rooms costing from around 25,000 rp.

Places to Eat

Restaurants tend to be expensive and serve Indonesian and Chinese food. *Halim's* on Jalan Sultan Hairun is a popular Chinese place with good food. Next door, the *Tip Top Restaurant* is also good. Try the restaurant in the *Hotel Mutiara* at Jalan Pattimura 90 for a good continental breakfast. A less tourist-oriented place is the *Restaurant & Bakery Amboina* on the main street, Jalan AJ Patty. It's busy, cheap and has a wide choice of Indonesian dishes and baked goods.

Getting There & Away

Air See the Maluku Getting There & Away and Getting Around sections for details on flights to Ambon. Garuda/Merpati (☎ 2481) is on Jalan Ahmad Yani. Mandala (☎ 42551) is at Jalan AJ Patty and Bouraq (☎ 56288) is on Jalan Setia Budi 22.

Bus For road transport around the island, bemos depart from the bemo station at the market east of the city centre, on the waterfront.

Boat The Maluku Getting There & Away and Getting Around sections cover Pelni and Perintis ships; the Pelni office (☎ 53161) is in the main harbour complex.

Smaller boats to destinations all around Maluku leave from a second harbour near the end of Jalan Pala. A board at the harbour shows what's going where and when. There are fewer departures in the wet season. Boats are usually small, slow and crammed with cargo. Half-decent passenger boats, such as the *Waisamar*, go to Bandaneira (19,000 rp, 13 hours) roughly twice a week (currently Monday and Wednesday at 4 pm).

Getting Around

To/From the Airport Pattimura airport is 48 km out of the city on the other side of the bay. A taxi to town costs 20,000 rp, including the vehicle and passenger ferry from just past Galala village (north of Kota Ambon) to the other side of the harbour – thus cutting short the circuitous road route. Beware of rip-offs at the airport – taxi and bemo drivers will ask the earth.

Local Transport There are becaks in profusion around town or you can catch local bemos. Taxis are unmetered and expensive. Bargaining is required, but bear in mind that petrol is expensive in Ambon if you want to charter.

AROUND AMBON

Hila

Hila, a village 42 km from Ambon, is noted for its ruined fortress, originally built of wooden palisades by the Portuguese at the end of the 16th century and later rebuilt by the Dutch and renamed **Fort Amsterdam**. The main tower and fragments of the wall remain (the cannons have gone) and the interior of the tower has been taken over by enormous tree roots. The **church**, a few minutes' walk from the fort, dates from 1780. It is the oldest building in Ambon but has virtually been rebuilt from the stumps up over the years. **Wapauwe** is an old mosque near Hila – the original mosque dated back to the early 15th century.

Bemos go to Hila (1250 rp, 1½ hours) from Ambon.

Pulau Pombo

Pombo is a tiny, attractive island off the north-east coast of Ambon which has a coral garden with good snorkelling. Pulau Pombo has a good beach sheltered by the reef. Take a bemo to the village of Tulehu, from where speedboats can be hired to Pulau Pombo, a 20-minute ride. You could get the boat to drop you off in the morning and pick you up in the afternoon. Bring your own food and water – there's a small derelict shelter on the island.

Latuhalat & Namalatu

The coastline at these southern villages has an extensive reef for snorkelling but much of the coral is dead. Namalatu is just past Latuhalat, 14 km or 45 minutes by bemo from Ambon. Namalatu is a sort of beach littered with concrete tables and chairs, but if you're going there just for the beach don't bother.

Lelisa Beach Resort is a very pleasant but overpriced mid-range resort at Namalatu with rooms for 55,000 rp and 75,000 rp. Villagers rent rooms for around 15,000 rp – ask at the shops. Namalatu has a good dive centre near the resort.

Other Attractions

At **Waai**, 31 km north of Ambon, is a pool which contains a very large 'holy eel'. **Natsepa**, 14 km from Ambon, is a reasonable beach but avoid Sunday when the place gets really crowded. *Miranda Beach Hotel* has rooms for 15,000 to 25,000 rp. **Honimua**, in the north-west of Ambon, has probably the best beach on the island but no accommodation. **Leitimor** is the southern peninsula of the island and **Ema** and **Naku** are interesting villages to walk to along the south coast. There's supposed to be another good coral reef off **Amahusu**, which overlooks Ambon Bay, but there is no beach to speak of. *Tirta Kencana* is another overpriced hotel here with rooms from 65,000 rp.

On your way down to these places, note the old **Japanese blockhouses** dotted along the coast, particularly between Amahusu and Eri.

SERAM

Maluku's second-largest island (17,151 sq km), Seram is wild, mountainous and heavily forested. It engenders wild stories of flying witch doctors, tribal wars, metre-wide butterflies and white crocodiles. Much of the centre is difficult to access and is home to the indigenous Alfuro peoples, some of whom have only relatively recently given up head-hunting. A large chunk of Seram's centre is marked as **Manusela National Park**, where you can trek virtually across the island.

In the south, **Masohi** is the main centre with six *losmen*, and smaller **Amahai** is where the ferry arrives from Tulehu on Ambon. Buses run east from Amahai to Tehoru and motorboats continue on to Saunulu and Hatemete at least three times a week. From Tehoru you can organise treks into Manusela. Tehoru has one losmen, *Losmen Susi*, with rooms for 10,000/15,000 rp.

On the north coast, **Wahai** is the main town and has two *losmen*. The north is reputed to have stunning snorkelling and amazing beaches.

Getting There & Away

Merpati flies from Ambon to Amahai weekly for 44,000 rp, but the flights have a knack of being cancelled.

To reach Seram by boat, take a bemo from Ambon to Tulehu on the east coast. From Tulehu, motorboats to Amahai (8500 rp, three hours) usually leave around 8 am. Otherwise, a passenger and vehicle ferry runs from Ambon to Rumakai on Seram's west coast.

BANDA ISLANDS

The Bandas consists of a group of seven islands to the south-east of Ambon. If you're looking for somewhere quiet then this is it. The residents are friendly, the scenery is beautiful and there's just a handful of motor vehicles. Apart from the scenery, there are several old forts here to scramble around and some coral gardens where you can go snorkelling and diving.

Bandaneira

Bandaneira, on Pulau Neira, is the chief centre of the islands. It was a former Dutch settlement. Today it is a rambling collection of interesting but deteriorating Dutch mansions. Notable buildings include the Dutch church on Jalan Greja. The church dates from 1852 when it replaced an earlier stone building which was destroyed by an earthquake. There's a whole crowd of people buried beneath the floor.

Nutmeg is processed at the government factory and shipped off to Ambon and then exported to other parts of Indonesia as well as overseas.

Information Bandaneira has no bank but the hotels change money at a low rate.

Rumah Budaya Museum Housed in an old Dutch villa, this museum also doubles as a hotel. It includes a small collection of cannon, old coins and modern paintings. One painting depicts the massacre of Bandanese by the Dutch in 1621. It also contains some traditional feathered headdresses and Portuguese helmets.

Forts Built by the Dutch East Indies Company in 1611, **Fort Belgica** stands above Bandaneira. The towers of the fort seem to be held together by a copious quantity of graffiti, but restoration work is being done.

Fort Nassau, below Fort Belgica, was built by the Dutch in 1609 (on the stone foundations laid but eventually abandoned by the Portuguese). It's very overgrown – only three walls and a gateway remain and an old cannon lies rusting on the ground.

Fort Hollandia on Banda Besar (Lontor) was enormous when it was originally constructed by the Dutch in 1621. It was wrecked by an earthquake in 1743 and there's not much left; what's there is derelict and overgrown. A long flight of steps leads up to it. Get to Banda Besar Island by motorboat from Bandaneira Pasar.

Places to Stay & Eat Bandaneira has several horrendously expensive hotels specifically intended for tourists. The three 'budget' places, the *Delfika*, *Selecta* and *Rumah Budaya* all cost 25,000 rp per person including three meals. The Delfika has a pleasant garden and a veranda facing the street, while the Selecta is a bit dingy. They can be persuaded to give a discount if they're not full. You may also be able to get rates with fewer or no meals if you want. Prices usually don't include the 10% tax so it's best to check first.

Going up a step in quality, *Brantz Guest House* is an old Dutch plantation house costing 30,000 rp per person, and worth the extra. Similar but more palatial are the two top-end hotels, the *Laguna Inn* and the *Maulana Inn*, with doubles from 50,000 rp.

There are small rumah makans around, like the very cheap *Rumah Makan Nusantara*, or the big hotels have restaurants. You can improve your diet with fried skewered fish or fruit from the market but you'll generally get a wider variety of food in the port.

Getting There & Away Merpati flies between Ambon and Bandaneira and their office is on Jalan Nusantara. Book well in advance.

As well as Pelni and Perintis ships, regular boats, usually twice a week, make the trip from Ambon to Bandaneira. See under Ambon for details.

Getting Around The town of Bandaneira is very small and easy to walk around. There are few roads and only one on Bandaneira leads to the airport. Trails connect Bandaneira to other places on the island and there are some nice walks.

Take motorboats from the pasar to Banda Besar. There are lots of dugout canoes for rent.

Around Bandaneira

Gunung Api This volcano juts out of the sea directly in front of Bandaneira. The island has some good coral in the shallows approximately opposite Taman Laut and diagonally opposite Bandaneira. It's only a short paddle across to Gunung Api from Bandaneira in a canoe.

Pulau Karaka (Pulau Sareer) This island lies off Gunung Api and has some fine coral reefs. Karaka is close enough to paddle across from Bandaneira in a dugout canoe in about an hour.

Other Attractions There is also a **sea garden** between Bandaneira and Banda Besar. You can take a canoe out there and snorkel around but the coral is nowhere near as attractive as Pulau Karaka. The hotel rents out snorkelling and scuba equipment.

SOUTHERN MALUKU

Probably the most forgotten islands in Indonesia, the islands of southern Maluku are dispersed across the sea between Timor and Irian Jaya. The three main groups, all southeast of Banda, are Kai, Aru and Tanimbar. West of Tanimbar, are the Babar and Leti groups, the islands of Kisar and Wetar, and a northern arc of volcanic, wooded islands (Serua, Nila, Teun, Damar and Romang).

Southern Maluku has some deserted white sandy beaches, good snorkelling and diving, unique flora and fauna, and traditional cultures quite unaffected by tourism. There are *losmen* at Tual in the Kai Islands and at Saumlaki in the Tanimbars. The islands can be reached by Pelni or Perintis, and Merpati flies to Langgur in the Kai Islands and Saumlaki.

TERNATE

This island was one of the first places where the Portuguese and Dutch established themselves in Maluku and the island is littered with the ruins of old European fortifications.

it has a rather slow and placid town, quite a contrast to Ambon. The peace is occasionally broken by the intermittent rumblings of the huge volcano to which the town clings.

Information

The useful tourist information office is hidden inside the Kantor Bupati complex on Jalan Pahlawan Revolusi. The Bank Ekspor Impor, and the Bank Negara Indonesia, on the same street, will both change travellers' cheques and cash.

Kedaton (Palace) of the Sultan of Ternate

This interesting piece of architecture looks more like a European country mansion than a palace and lies just back from Jalan Baballuh, the road leading to the airport. It's now a museum containing a few Portuguese cannon, Dutch helmets and armour. There's not much to see, though the ill-kept building is worth having a look at. To get to the museum, take a bemo from the bemo station on Jalan Pahlawan Revolusi.

Benteng Toloko

This small fort is in better condition than others. To get there, take the road from Ternate out towards the airport. Beyond the Sultan's palace, but before the airport, a path leads off this road to Dufa Dufa and the Benteng Toloko, which is on a rocky hill above the beach.

Fort Orange (Benteng Oranye)

This fort dates from 1637 and is a Dutch construction. It's right in the middle of Ternate, opposite the bemo station. There are forlorn-looking cannons, and overgrown and sadly crumbling walls and buildings. You can get an idea of its importance, however, from its great size. It's an interesting building to walk around.

Benteng Kayuh Merah

At the southern end of Ternate is Pelabuhan Bastion from where you can catch motorboats to Tidore. A km down the road past Pelabuhan Bastion, and just before you get to Desa Kayuh Merah, is Benteng Kayuh Merah. It's a small fort located right on the beach and the waves splash on its walls.

Benteng Kastella

Continuing around the island in a clockwise direction from Benteng Kayuh Merah you come to Benteng Kastella – you'd hardly know it was there. The ring road around Ternate cuts straight through what's left of the fort and it's covered in moss and undergrowth, and grazed by goats. The roots of trees have wrapped themselves around the ruins of the main tower.

Batu Angus (Burnt Corner)

North of Ternate, the Burnt Corner is a volcanic lava flow from the 1737 eruption of Gunung Api Gamalama. What is left today is a massive river of jagged volcanic rocks looking like a landscape from another planet. Take a bemo just past Tarau village to see this.

On the subject of volcanic eruptions, there's a display of photos in the airport restaurant of the eruption of the 1721-metre Gunung Api Gamalama in September 1980.

Danau Tolire

This large volcanic crater, on the northern side of the island, is now filled with deep green water. The lake is just off the road in the vicinity of Takome but bemos don't seem to go up there very often.

Places to Stay

One of the best places to stay in is the *Wisma Alhilal* (☎ 21404) at Jalan Monunutu 2/32. It's quite plain but run by a friendly family and is in a good location. Rooms cost 9000/12,000 rp per person and have a fan, mandi and a toilet. Meals are extra and excellent.

The *Wisma Sejahtera* on Jalan Lawa Mena is a very pleasant place with rooms at 9000/15,000 rp per person – more with meals. On Jalan Pahlawan Revolusi, opposite the harbour entrance, the basic *Penginapan Yamin* has rooms for 7500/15,000 rp. Further up the same road, the

Penginapan Sentosa and *Penginapan Rahmat* are similarly priced.

The *Hotel Nirwana* (☎ 21787), at Jalan Pahlawan Revolusi 58 near the harbour, is a fine place with a few economy doubles for 25,000 rp, or other rooms at 35,000 rp and 45,000 rp. Other pricier places include the *Wisma Chrysant* (☎ 21580) at Jalan Ahmad Yani 131 and the *Hotel Indah* (☎ 21334) at Jalan Bosoiri 3. Almost next door to the Nirwana is the similarly priced *Hotel El Shinta*.

The *Hotel Merdeka* on Jalan Monunutu costs from 15,000/25,000 rp and looks like it must have been built by the Dutch.

Places to Eat

Restaurant Siola is a 10-minute walk west of the town centre and probably has the best food (certainly the best surroundings) in town. In the town centre, the upstairs restaurant in the *Hotel Neraca* has good food and sea views, while the *Restoran Garuda*, also on Jalan Pahlawan Revolusi, comes complete with karaoke in the evenings.

The *Gamalama Restaurant* on Jalan Pahlawan Revolusi is a good cheap place. Further down Jalan Pahlawan Revolusi, the *Rumah Makan Roda Baru* is fairly cheap as Padang food places go. There are more cheap eats at the *Rumah Makan Anugerah* on Jalan Bosoiri, across from the bemo station.

INDONESIA

Getting There & Away

Merpati have a wide variety of connections to Ternate from elsewhere in Maluku and further afield. Their office (☎ 21314, 648/9) is at PT Eterna Raya, Jalan Bosoiri 81. Bouraq (☎ 21487), Jalan Pahlawan Revolusi 58, connects Ternate with northern Sulawesi.

The harbourmaster's office (☎ 21129/206/214) is at Jalan Ahmad Yani 1. Pelni is on Jalan Ahmad Yani, by the harbour.

Getting Around

To/From the Airport The airport is at Tarau, close to Ternate township, and you can get there by chartering a bemo from 3500 rp; or, walk down to the main road from the airport terminal and pick up a bemo for 250 rp.

Local Transport Transport around town and around the island is by bemo, costing a flat 250 rp rate. One way of seeing all the sights quickly in one go would be to charter a bemo – a surfaced road runs in a ring around the island, linking Ternate township with Batu Angus, Lake Tolire (less than a 10-minute walk off the main road), Benteng Kastella, Benteng Kayuh Merah and back to Ternate township. It takes a bit less than two hours to circle the island in a bemo, short breaks included.

TIDORE

This is the island adjacent to Ternate. There's a **fort** above the road as you enter Soa Siu but you need a local to show you the ill-defined track up to it and there's not much to see. The jungle has just about taken over from the fort and you'd really have to be an enthusiast to get worked up about this place. Apparently, there is another **fort** near Rum.

Getting There & Away

To get to Tidore, take a bemo from Ternate township to Bastiong. Boats powered by outboard motors depart frequently from the Pasar Impris at Bastiong for Rum on Tidore. It takes about half an hour and costs 600 rp. From Rum, take a bemo to the main town of Soa Siu (a 45-minute ride).

Irian Jaya

Irian Jaya is the Indonesian side of the island of New Guinea, and it was only acquired from the Dutch in 1963. Since it had no racial or historical connection with the other Indonesian islands, some interesting arm-bending had to be conducted to get the Dutch to hand it over. It was agreed that an 'act of free choice' would later determine if the inhabitants wished to join Indonesia permanently and by choosing a 'representative' selection of voters, a unanimous decision to remain was arrived at! The Indonesians have since moved lots of settlers in from Java or Sulawesi.

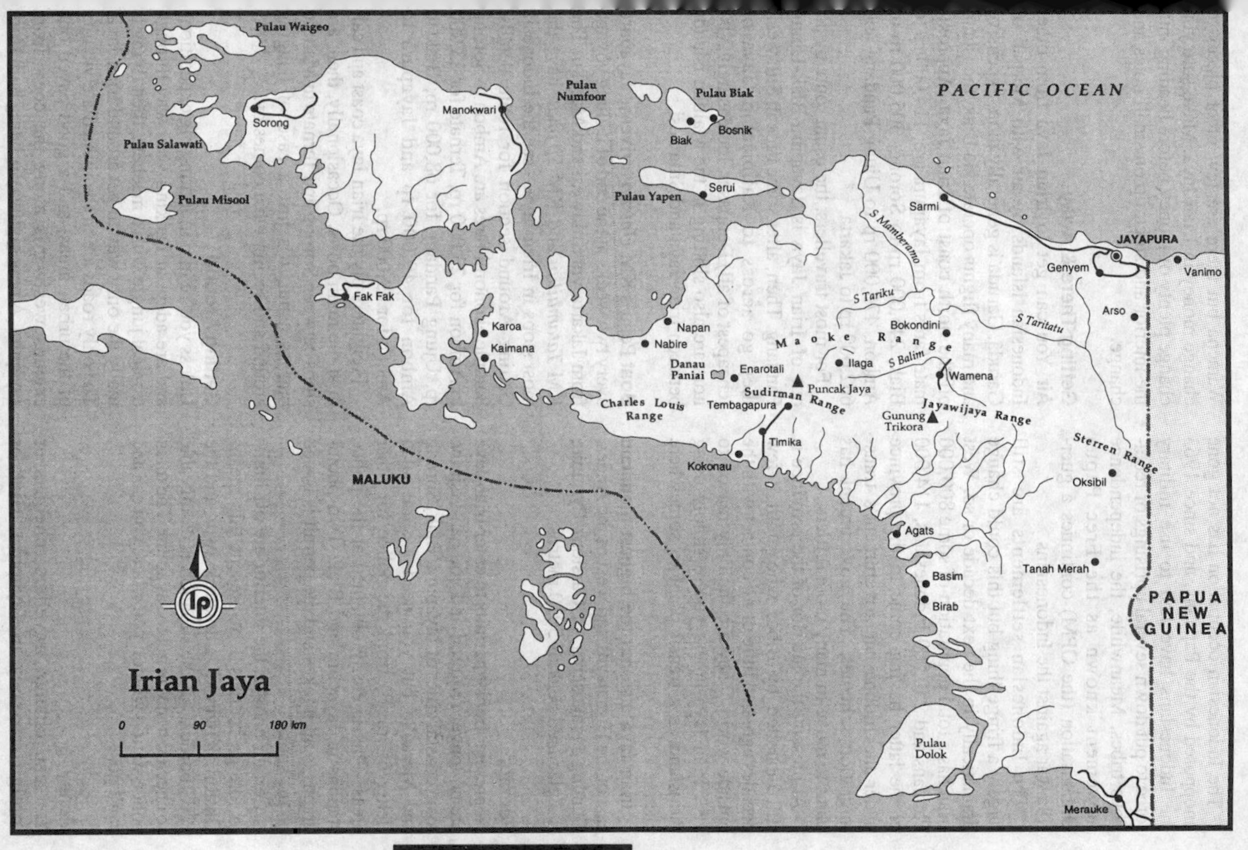

Pulau Waigeo
Pulau Numfoor
Pulau Biak
PACIFIC OCEAN
Sorong
Manokwari
Biak
Bosnik
Pulau Salawati
Pulau Misool
Pulau Yapen
Serui
Sarmi
S Mamberamo
JAYAPURA
Genyem
Vanimo
Fak Fak
S Tariku
S Taritatu
Arso
Karoa
Kaimana
Napan
Nabire
Maoke Range
Bokondini
Danau Paniai
Enarotali
Ilaga
S Balim
Wamena
Puncak Jaya
Sudirman Range
Charles Louis Range
Tembagapura
Jayawijaya Range
Gunung Trikora
Timika
Sterren Range
Kokonau
Oksibil
MALUKU
Agats
Tanah Merah
Basim
Birab
PAPUA NEW GUINEA
Irian Jaya
0
90
180 km
Pulau Dolok
Merauke

INDONESIA

The Indonesian occupation has not gone unopposed by the Papuans, and since 1963 the Indonesians have had to use military force to put down several uprisings of rebellious tribes. Meanwhile, the independence movement known as the Free Papua Organisation (the OPM) continues a guerrilla war against the Indonesians.

The Indonesian settlements are still largely a fringe thing but this could change dramatically in the next decade or so. West Irian has a total population of some 800,000 Papuans and 250,000 Indonesians, 114,000 of the latter having come to the province under the Indonesian government's transmigration schemes. The government has plans to move in many more settlers.

At present, the interior of the province is still inhabited by tribes who, until a few decades ago, had little or no contact with the outside world. They are the only reason to visit Irian Jaya unless you're simply using the island as a transit point to somewhere else.

Irian Jaya also has the highest mountain east of the Himalayas and west of the Andes. Gunung Jayakusema, or Carstenz Pyramid, is a glaciated peak of 5030 metres.

INDONESIA

Permits

At present, transit permits to enter Irian Jaya are no longer required and you can visit the main coastal cities of Jayapura, Biak, Sorong and Merauke but you need a surat jalan (letter of travel) from the police for other areas. This is easily obtained at the police stations in Jayapura and Biak. Two photographs is all it takes and the permit is issued on the spot.

Certain parts of the interior are off limits to foreign tourists – at present this means Oksibil, Kiwirok, Admisibil, Iwur and the PNG border, but the situation is changeable so check when you get to Jayapura. The main police station will tell you where you can and can't go.

Money

You can change travellers' cheques or foreign currency in Jayapura, Biak or Wamena but there are few other places to change money in Irian Jaya. Make sure you change plenty of money before heading into the interior and stock up on small notes and change.

Getting There & Away

Air You can get to Irian Jaya from other Indonesian islands by air with Merpati or Garuda. Garuda is generally more expensive and many flights operate via Biak, the island off the north coast of Irian Jaya. Approximate fares from Jayapura are: 114,000 rp to Biak, 246,000 rp to Sorong, 305,000 rp to Ambon, 476,000 rp to Ujung Pandang and 662,000 rp to Jakarta.

For most travellers, the usual route by air out of Irian Jaya is Jayapura-Biak-Ujung Pandang. Then, after some time in Sulawesi, they go across to Kalimantan, Java or (cheapest of all) Denpasar. Increasingly, visitors are also slotting in the Maluku Islands between Irian Jaya and Sulawesi.

Boat Pelni's KM *Umsini* arrives at Jayapura every two weeks at the end of its long voyage from Jakarta via Sulawesi and Maluku. The KM *Tatamailau* and KM *Sirimau* have the most stops in Irian Jaya – see the Indonesia Getting Around section for route details. Sample ekonomi fares are Ambon to Sorong to Ambon for 23,000 rp, Ternate for 23,000 rp, Ujung Pandang for 68,000 rp, Biak to Ambon for 49,000 rp and Jayapura to Ambon for 89,000 rp.

Freighters ply the Irian Jaya coast and call in at the main ports. Occasionally, there are ships between Sorong and Ternate in Maluku but, as usual, it's just a case of hanging around and seeing what comes by.

Getting Around

Unless you're into mounting big expeditions and are adept at hacking your way through tropical jungle with a machete, then flying is really the only way to get around Irian Jaya. The only roads are in the immediate vicinity of the urban areas, and a good paved one extends westwards along the coast from Jayapura. A new highway is being built from

Jayapura to Merauke via Wamena but when it will be finished is anyone's guess.

Merpati is the main carrier and has flights from Jayapura to Batom, Biak, Lereh, Manokwari, Merauke, Nabire, Sarmi, Senggeh, Serui, Sorong, Tanah Merah and Wamena. There are also numerous flights fanning out from Merauke on the south coast and Nabire on the north coast. Flights from Biak operate to places in the western sector of the province and the 'bird's head'.

Various mission groups are strongly represented in Irian Jaya, and maintain a communication network of airstrips, light aircraft and, occasionally, helicopters. They *will* accept passengers and charters, always subject to their own immediate needs. The air transport organisations of the missions are known by their initials – the MAF (Mission Aviation Fellowship) and the AMA (Associated Missions Aviation). They have set rates for carrying passengers, and both have their offices at Sentani airport, Jayapura, and in Wamena.

It's your own responsibility to get permits for the places you're visiting in the interior, otherwise you'll be flown straight back to Jayapura at your own expense. Book flights on mission planes as far ahead as possible, at least a week.

JAYAPURA & SENTANI

Since the end of its Dutch days as Hollandia, Jayapura, or Victorious City, has really gone through the name changes. First it was Kota Bahru then Sukarnapura (there's one of his Jakarta-style statues in the town square) before its current name was adopted. The hills of Jayapura slope right down to the sea and the town is squeezed onto all available bits of semilevel land. It's a pretty sight from the air at night with the lights of fishing boats twinkling out on the bay.

This is the usual entry point for Irian Jaya from PNG and it is the capital of the province, but it's of no particular interest other than that. It's quite a dull place, and apart from the hills and the Irianese, it looks like any other sizeable Indonesian town. So, there's no real reason to come here unless you're heading inland.

Sentani is a small town on the shores of a magnificent lake near the Jayapura airport, 36 km from Jayapura. It is quieter, less polluted and cooler than Jayapura, so many travellers stay in Sentani, and the Sentani hotels can arrange permits for the interior for about 2000 rp.

Orientation

Just about everything you'll want – most of the hotels, the shops, police headquarters, airline offices, the large IMBI cinema – are all confined to a very small area in the centre of town down near the waterfront. The two main streets are Jalan Ahmad Yani and, running parallel to it, Jalan Percetakan.

Information

Money The Bank Ekspor Impor on Jalan Ahmad Yani will change travellers' cheques and cash. Hotel Dafonsoro and some travel agents also change money at poor rates.

Immigration & Permits The immigration office is on Jalan Percetakan. The head police station, for permits to the interior, is on Jalan Ahmad Yani. The Papua New Guinea consulate is a couple of km from town towards the Numbai Hotel.

Things to See

There's not a great deal to see, although a trip to the suburb of **Hamadi**, a 10 to 15-minute drive by colt from Jayapura, will take you to an interesting market stocked with innumerable varieties of fish. A nearby beach, with rusting barges and Sherman tanks, was the site of an American amphibious landing on 22 April 1944. The site is a military base – you have to leave your passport at the entrance and collect it upon leaving. Bemos to Hamadi (300 rp) leave from opposite the post office or on Jalan Koti.

If you want to while away a few hours then try **Base G**, near the site of an American WW II military base. The beach is pretty dull and the surf can be strong – real dumpers. Colts to Base G go from the terminal at the end of

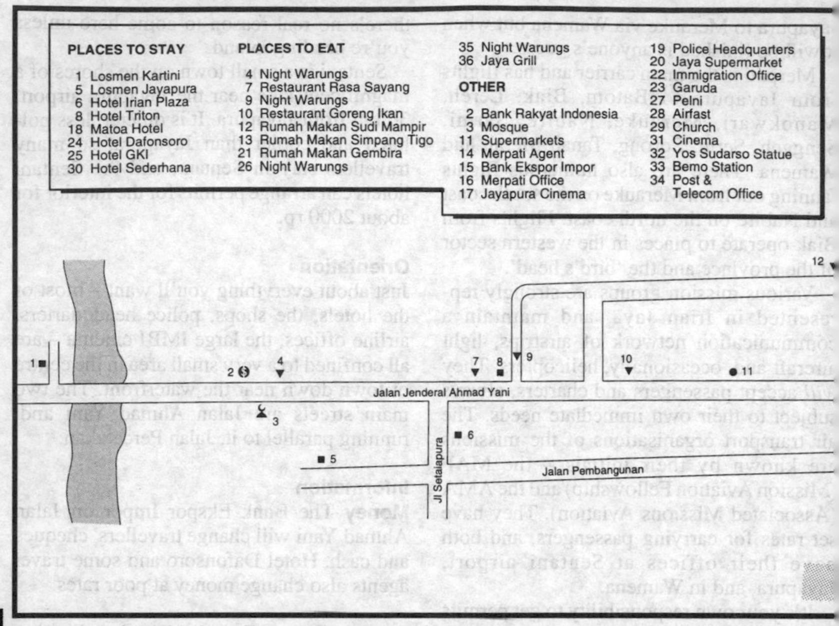

Jalan Percetakan near the IMBI cinema. They drop you off about a 15-minute walk from the beach.

There's also a **university museum** at Abepura, on the road in from the airport, with a lot of interesting but neglected artefacts from all over Irian Jaya.

Places to Stay

Jayapura Hotel prices in Jayapura itself are a black hole for your wallet. The bottom of the price barrel belongs to *Losmen Jayapura* (☎ 21216), a spartan place where singles/doubles, some with attached bath, go for 8800/15,400 rp. *Hotel Sederhana* (☎ 22157) at Jalan Halmahera 2 is good value and centrally located. The rooms are clean enough and cost 11,000/19,800 rp, more with meals, while more expensive rooms with private mandi and air-con cost from 17,600/19,800 rp, plus a 10% tax and service charge.

Hotel GKI (☎ 21574) is a bit of a walk on the northern side of town at Jalan Sam Ratulangi 6. It has a pleasant outdoor sitting area, and costs 15,000/26,000 rp including breakfast. *Losmen Ayu* (☎ 22263) at Jalan Tugu II 101, about 500 metres along Jalan Sam Ratulangi from Jalan Percetakan, has good rooms starting at 20,000 rp.

Sentani Touts from the various hotels in Sentani greet incoming passengers at the airport and many travellers don't bother going into Jayapura at all. The good *Ratna Hotel* (☎ 91435) on Jalan Raya Sentani 7 is new, centrally located and rooms, all with private bath, cost 16,500/28,000 rp, or 28,000/36,000 rp with air-con. Just around the corner is *Hotel Minang Jaya* (☎ 91067) which costs 15,000 rp.

The large and popular *Hotel Mansapur Rani* (☎ 91219) is closer to the airport at Jalan Yabaso 113. Turn right just outside the airport and walk about 400 metres. Rooms with attached mandi and fan are 13,750/ 25,000 rp and air-con pushes the price up to 36,000 rp. Next door is the *Semeru Hotel*.

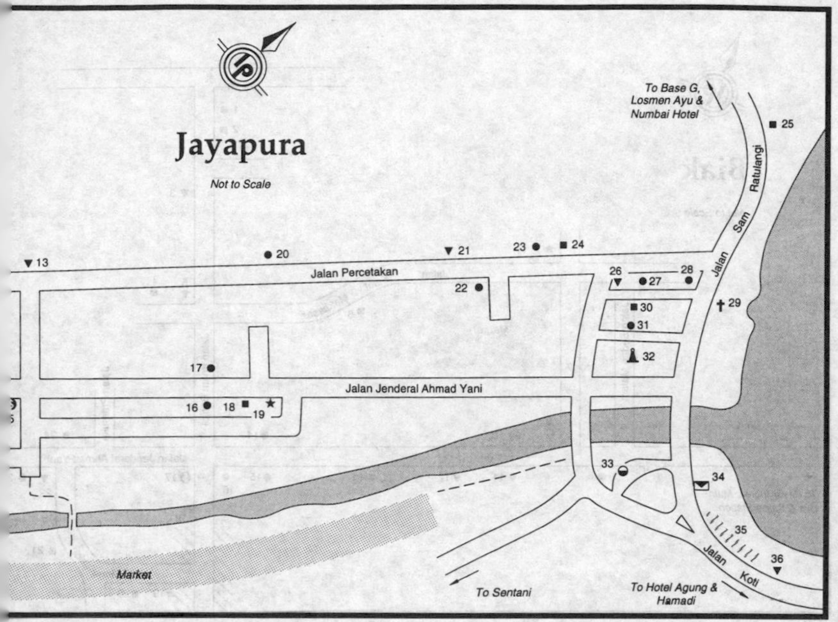

Sentani Inn (☎ 91440), Jalan Raya Sentani, is 1½ km in the Jayapura direction from the airport. Air-con rooms cost 23,500/30,000 rp, and without air-con they are 15,000/24,000 rp, including breakfast.

Places to Eat

The best places to eat in Jayapura are the warungs. Night *foodstalls* in front of the Pelni office serve up gado gado, fried tahu with hot peanut sauce, bubur and many other dishes. There are also many warungs around the mosque on Jalan Ahmad Yani, and along the waterfront on Jalan Koti. Several expensive restaurants can be found along Jalan Percetakan, such as the *Rumah Makan Sudi Mampir* (Indonesian and Chinese) and the *Rumah Makan Simpang Tigo* (Padang).

In Sentani, *Rumah Makan Mickey* is the best place in town.

Getting There & Away

See the Irian Jaya Getting There & Away section for more information on air and sea transport to or from Jayapura.

Merpati (☎ 21220) is at Jalan Ahmad Yani 15 and they also handle Garuda. The MAF office is at Sentani airport while AMA is right next to the MAF terminal. The Pelni office (☎ 21270) is on Jalan Halmahera near the waterfront in the centre of town.

Getting Around

Jayapura's Sentani airport is conveniently located a mere 36 km out of town! It's a hefty 17,500 rp by taxi from the airport to central Jayapura, or walk for 10 minutes into Sentani to the main road and then catch a bemo, first to Abepura for 750 rp and then to Jayapura for 500 rp. Taxis from the airport to Sentani cost a ridiculous 4000 rp.

Bemos around town cost a flat 300 rp.

BIAK

On the island of the same name, off the north coast of Irian Jaya, Biak is not much of a

INDONESIA

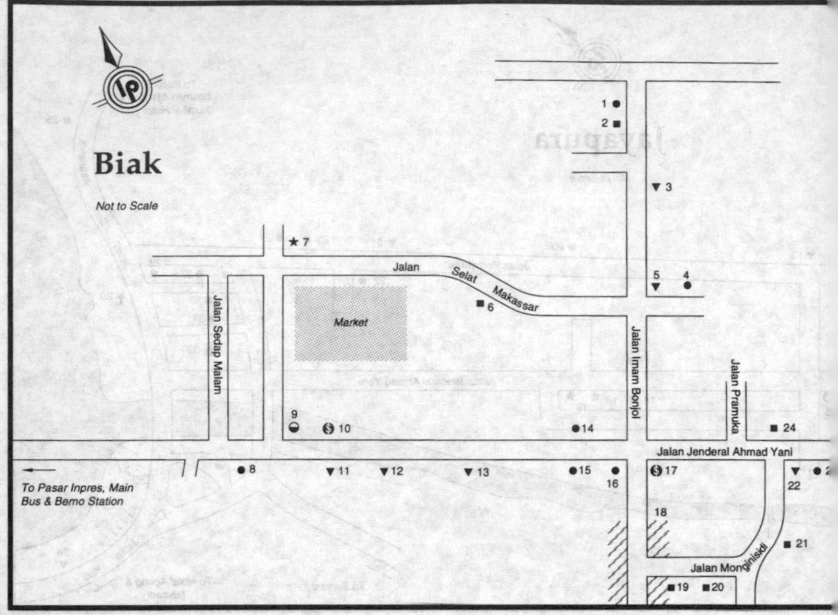

town. It's just somewhere on the way to somewhere else. If you've got to spend a few hours here, the most interesting place is the central **Pasar Panir** (market) where they sometimes sell lorikeets and cockatoos. When a Pelni ship goes through, half the crew seem to buy a bird to sell later in Java. At the end of a flight from Biak to Jakarta, there's the odd sight of birds crammed into cages and boxes being trundled out onto the baggage conveyer belts.

Orientation & Information

Biak is a fairly compact town. Jalan Prof M Yamin runs from the airport and connects with Jalan Ahmad Yani, Biak's main street, along which you will find many of the town's hotels, restaurants, banks and offices. The other main street, Jalan Imam Bonjol, intersects at right angles with Jalan Ahmad Yani.

The Bank Ekspor Impor, at the corner of Jalan Ahmad Yani and Jalan Imam Bonjol, changes foreign currency and travellers' cheques. The post office is on the road coming in from the airport.

The head police station is on Jalan Selat Makassar opposite the Pasar Panir and is a good place for permits into the interior. Permits cost 2000 rp and take 10 minutes. The immigration office is at the corner of Jalan Ahmad Yani and Jalan Imam Bonjol.

Places to Stay

Penginapan Solo (☎ 21397) at Jalan Monginisidi 4 is the cheapest. Singles/doubles are 7700/15,400 rp with shared bath. It's reasonably clean and well run.

Losmen Maju (☎ 21218) at Jalan Imam Bonjol 45 has rooms with fan for 15,750/24,200 rp and air-con rooms for 38,750/55,400 rp. Rooms are basic but clean, with fan and attached mandi.

Hotel Mapia (☎ 21383) on Jalan Ahmad Yani is comfortable but has definitely seen

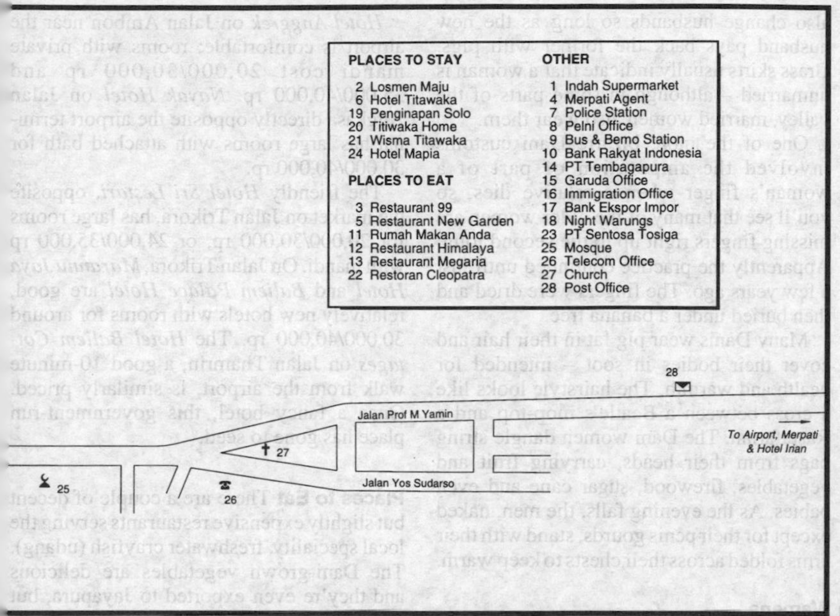

better days. Rooms with fan and attached mandi start at 16,950/23,000 rp; air-con rooms cost 26,650/33,300 rp.

Places to Eat
Biak has several places to eat, but not a great many of note. Probably the best are the evening *foodstalls* in front of the Hotel Mapia, or there are some cheap places along Jalan Ahmad Yani like the *Rumah Makan Anda*, the *Restaurant Megaria* and the *Restaurant Himalaya*.

Getting There & Away
Garuda and Merpati both fly through Biak. Garuda have a twice-weekly Los Angeles-Honolulu-Biak-Denpasar service, a very interesting way of getting to Indonesia from the USA. Garuda (☎ 21416) is at Jalan Sudirman 3.

If you're chasing ships, Pelni (☎ 21065) is at Jalan Sudirman 37.

Getting Around
Much of Biak can be covered easily on foot. You can walk into the city from the airport in 30 minutes if you're feeling energetic. A colt from the airport to the town centre is 300 rp; there's no need to charter one.

BALIM VALLEY
There are a number of places in the interior worth a visit but top of the list is the Balim Valley, where the Dani people were only discovered in 1938. The Danis have adopted many modern conveniences (like steel axes rather than the traditional stone ones) but here you can still see men wearing penis gourds and little else, and some of their other customs have remained intact or have only recently died out.

The Danis maintain their polygamous marriage system – a man may have as many wives as he can afford. Brides have to be paid for in pigs and the man must give five or six pigs to the family of the wife. Women can also change husbands so long as the new husband pays back the former with pigs. Grass skirts usually indicate that a woman is unmarried – although in some parts of the valley, married women also wear them.

One of the more bizarre Dani customs involved the amputation of part of a woman's finger when a relative dies, so you'll see that many of the older women are missing fingers right up to the second joint. Apparently the practice continued until just a few years ago. The fingers were dried and then buried under a banana tree.

Many Danis wear pig fat in their hair and cover their bodies in soot – intended for health and warmth. The hairstyle looks like a cross between a Beatle's mop-top and a Rastafarian. The Dani women dangle string bags from their heads, carrying fruit and vegetables, firewood, sugar cane and even babies. As the evening falls, the men, naked except for their penis gourds, stand with their arms folded across their chests to keep warm.

Wamena

The main town of the Balim Valley, Wamena is a neat and rather spread-out place. It makes a good base, although there's not much in the town itself. The market is a focal point and the villagers come in every day dressed in grass or string skirts or penis gourds. Everything is very expensive compared to the rest of Indonesia but this is understandable as everything has to be flown in.

Information Your permit from Jayapura will probably be stamped at the airport, saving you a trip to the police station, and it must be stamped again on departure. A permit for Wamena is good for surrounding places.

The Bank Rakyat Indonesia and the post office are both near the airport.

Places to Stay *Hotel Syahrial Jaya*, Jalan Gatot Subroto 51, a five-minute walk from the airport, is the cheapest place in town. Rooms start at 10,000 rp, or 15,000 rp with attached mandi, but there have been big arguments over the quoted price and what was finally charged at checking-out time.

Hotel Anggrek on Jalan Ambon near the airport is comfortable; rooms with private mandi cost 20,000/30,000 rp and 35,000/40,000 rp. *Nayak Hotel* on Jalan Angkasa directly opposite the airport terminal has large rooms with attached bath for 30,000/40,000 rp.

The friendly *Hotel Sri Lestari*, opposite the market on Jalan Trikora, has large rooms for 20,000/30,000 rp, or 24,000/35,000 rp with mandi. On Jalan Trikora, *Marannu Jaya Hotel* and *Baliem Palace Hotel* are good, relatively new hotels with rooms for around 30,000/40,000 rp. The *Hotel Baliem Cottages* on Jalan Thamrin, a good 10-minute walk from the airport, is similarly priced. Once a fancy hotel, this government-run place has gone to seed.

Places to Eat There are a couple of decent but slightly expensive restaurants serving the local speciality, freshwater crayfish (udang). The Dani-grown vegetables are delicious and they're even exported to Jayapura, but make sure they're cooked.

The *Hotel Nayak* has its own restaurant serving udang, chicken dishes and the other local speciality, fried goldfish (ikan mas goreng). Almost on a par, the *Cafetaria Sinta Prima* serves similar fare.

On Jalan Trikora, the busy *Rumah Makan Begadang* has nasi meals. Nearby is *Rumah Makan Sari Rasa*, which seems to have very fresh food as well as a friendly manager.

Things to Buy There's quite a good souvenir shop in the market, or you can buy from the Dani in the market or in villages. Items include string bags, intricate bracelets, fibrecoil skirts, necklaces of cowrie shells, penis gourds, stone axes, large black-stone axes and spears. The shop also sells head and arm bands of cowrie shells, feathers and bone, containers made of coconuts, wooden combs and grass skirts.

Some items are cheaper in the market after bargaining. Other things are more expensive. Some of the sellers strike hard bargains so check out prices in both places.

Getting There & Away Merpati has flights several times a day between Jayapura and Wamena (65,000 rp). Flights are in heavy demand – book early and reconfirm often! The MAF and AMA have offices in Wamena and fly to numerous destinations, but again it's a case of waiting around until there's a plane that has space. Be prepared to fly back to Jayapura and back again to some other place in the interior with Merpati. The AMA has a ticket office at the southern end of the airstrip and flights include Wamena to Enarotali or Wamena to Illaga. The MAF has an office next to the airport building.

Another airline worth calling on is Airfast who sometimes has flights from Wamena to Jayapura, Port Moresby and Australia. Inquire at the office of Direktorat Jenderal Pelabuhan at the airport.

Walks in the Balim Valley

While there are dirt and compacted gravel roads leading out of Wamena, essentially the best way to get around is to walk. Trucks sometimes trundle down the roads in the immediate vicinity of Wamena. For places accessible by vehicle, such as Pyramid and Akima, you may be able to charter a bemo or rent a trailbike in town.

This is great hiking country but travel light; trails are muddy and slippery. You have to clamber over stone fences, ford streams or cross trenches and creeks on bridges made of a single rough wooden plank or a slippery log. Rivers are crossed by dugout canoes or rafts made of three logs loosely lashed together and pushed along with a pole.

It can also get bloody cold at night up here, so bring warm clothes. It also rains a lot so bring an umbrella and, if you're camping, a waterproof tent. Besides camping, you could stay with missionaries, but don't count on it; they've been flooded with tourists looking for shelter. Staying in the villages should cost you around 5000 rp per person per night.

Local Dani guides, if you can contact them directly, can cost from 6000 rp per day for younger, inexperienced guides (who really act mostly as porters) to 25,000 rp per day for older, more experienced ones. If you can't find a local guide, then the Cafeteria Sinta Prima can arrange them for 25,000 to 30,000 rp per day – try bargaining! You *don't* need a guide for some walks as many places have obvious tracks and roads leading to them. Sometimes you'll be latched on to by a local who'll show you the way. Possible destinations include the ones listed below.

Akima Akima is a nondescript little village containing the famous (or infamous) smoked mummy. The mummy is completely black, decorated with a string mesh cap and cowrie shell beads and a feather. The penis gourd is still there, though the penis has withered away. The body is bunched up in a sitting position, arms wrapped around knees and clawed fingers draped over feet, with the head tucked down. Bargain with the old men who live in Akima to show you the mummy. Expect to pay 4000 rp. Take a bemo or a two-hour walk to see this tourist mummy.

Sinatma Sinatma is a Protestant mission near Wamena, an hour's walk from Wamena airstrip. You walk there past fields of grazing cows near a raging tributary of the Balim River, crossed by two suspension bridges – frail constructions made of wood and vine and a walkway of thin, rough wooden slats.

Pyramid This hill is named after its shape. A motorable road leads from Sinatma all the way to Pyramid via Elegaima, but if you walk to Pyramid it's quicker to take this route: Wamena-Hom Hom-Musatfak-Miligatmen-Pyramid. There's a dirt road from Wamena to Musatfak, negotiable only by motorbike, and from Musatfak to Pyramid there is a walking-only track.

Hitigima Near the village of Hitigima there are saltwater wells. Banana stems are beaten dry of fluid and then put in a pool to soak up the brine. The stem is then dried and burned, the ashes collected and used as salt. Salt-water wells are also found at Jiwika village.

From Wamena, it's an easy 2½ to three-hour walk to Hitigima past hills with neat chequerboards of stone fences enclosing cultivated fields. From Wamena, just walk straight down Jalan Ahmad Yani, cross the bridge and follow the road. Two hours' walk from the bridge a track branches off the road.

There are actually several tracks, so time your walk and ask people along the way. You can see Hitigima from the road but there's no sign and it's not obvious. The salt wells are past Hitigima, about another two hours' walk. There's a trail; it's not easy to follow but you should find a guide in Hitigima.

OTHER TOWNS

Visiting other towns in Irian Jaya is hardly worth your time and effort. Perhaps you could fly down to Merauke or Tanah Merah, south of the mountain range, or make your way by air or sea to Fak Fak, Manokwari or Sorong on the bird's head, but why bother.

In Sorong, you can stay at *Penginapan Indah* on the main road, where rooms cost 9000 rp, or in the similarly priced *Hotel Bangaria.*

Laos

Laos has been known from antiquity as Lan Xang, or Land of a Million Elephants, and by Indochina War-era journalists as the Land of a Million Irrelevants. It is one of the least developed and most enigmatic countries in Asia. With its 4.3 million inhabitants spread over more than 200,000 sq km, Laos has been spared the population pressures of neighbouring countries.

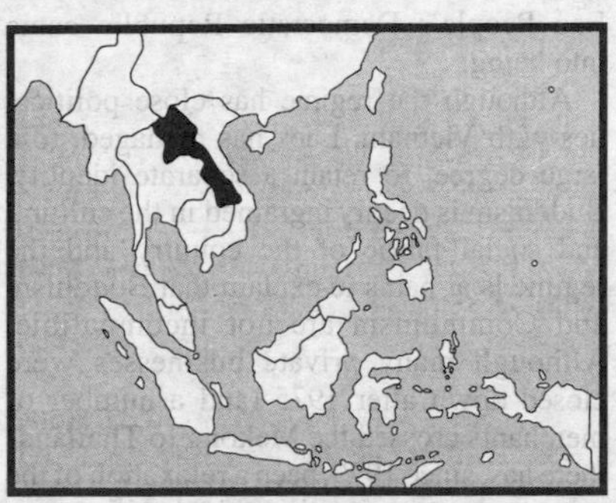

Facts about the Country

HISTORY

The country has long been occupied by migrating Thais (an ethnolinguistic family that includes Shans, Siamese, Lao and many smaller tribes) and by Hmong-Mien hill tribes practising slash-and-burn cultivation (as they do to this day). The first Lao *muang* (districts or principalities), however, were consolidated in the 13th century following the invasion of south-western China by Kublai Khan's Mongol hordes.

In the mid-14th century, a Khmer-sponsored Lao warlord, Fa Ngum, formed his own kingdom, Lan Xang, out of a large coalition of muangs around the town of Luang Phabang. Although the kingdom prospered in the 14th and 15th centuries, it came under increasing pressure from its neighbours and also suffered from internal divisions. In the 17th century, it split up into three warring kingdoms centred around Luang Phabang, Wieng Chan (Vientiane) and Champasak.

By the end of the 18th century, most of Laos came under Thai suzerainty but there was also pressure from the Vietnamese to pay tribute. Unable or unwilling to serve two masters, the country went to war with Siam in the 1820s. After this disastrous challenge, all three kingdoms fell under Thai control. Throughout the 19th century, France was busy establishing French Indochina in the Vietnamese kingdoms of Tonkin and Annam. By 1893, the French and the Siamese had fashioned a series of treaties that put Lao territories under the protection of the French.

During WW II, the Japanese occupied Indochina and a Lao resistance group, Lao Issara, formed to prevent a return to French rule at war's end. The Franco-Laotian Treaty of 1953 granted full independence to Laos but conflict persisted between royalist, neutralist and Communist factions. The American bombing of the Ho Chi Minh Trail in eastern Laos commenced in 1964 and greatly escalated the conflict between the royalist Vientiane government and the Communist Pathet Lao.

Although the ground war in Laos was far less bloody than in Vietnam or Cambodia, the bombing of eastern Laos caused many casualties and, eventually, the displacement of most of the population of the eastern provinces, a process that went on until a ceasefire was negotiated in 1973. By this time, Laos had the dubious distinction of being the most bombed country in the history of warfare (the USA dropped more bombs on Laos between 1964 and 1973, on a per capita basis, than it did worldwide during WW II).

A coalition government was formed but,

with the fall of Saigon in April 1975, it became clear which way the political wind was blowing and most of the rightists went into exile in France. In December 1975, the Lao People's Democratic Republic came into being.

Although the regime has close political ties with Vietnam, Laos has managed, to a large degree, to retain a separate identity. Buddhism is deeply ingrained in the cultural and social fabric of the country and the regime is at pains to explain that Buddhism and Communism are not incompatible. Although many private businesses were closed down after 1975 (and a number of merchants crossed the Mekong to Thailand) there has, since 1979, been a relaxation of the rules and an economic revival with many new shops and restaurants opening.

GEOGRAPHY

Laos covers 235,000 sq km and is bordered by Thailand, Cambodia, Vietnam, China and Myanmar (Burma). Over 70% of the country is mountains and plateaus, and two-thirds is forested.

Most of the population is settled along river valleys. The largest river, the Mekong, or Nam Khong, runs the entire length of the country. It provides fertile floodplains for agriculture and is the main transportation artery.

CLIMATE

The annual Asian monsoon cycle gives Laos two distinct seasons: May to October is wet and November to April is dry.

Average precipitation varies considerably according to latitude and altitude, with southern Laos getting the most rain overall. The peaks of the Annamite Chain receive the heaviest rainfall, over 300 cm annually.

The provinces of Luang Phabang, Sainyabuli and Xieng Khuang, for the most part, receive only 100 to 150 cm a year. Vientiane and Savannakhet get about 150 to 200 cm, as do Phongsali, Luang Nam Tha and Bokeo.

Temperatures vary according to altitude. In the Mekong River Valley (from Bokeo Province to Champasak Province) as in most of Thailand and Myanmar, the highest temperatures occur in March and April (these temperatures approach 38°C, or 100°F) and the lowest occur in December and January (as low as 15°C, or 59°F).

In the mountains of Xieng Khuang, however, December/January temperatures can easily fall to 0°C, or 32°F, at night. In mountainous provinces of lesser elevation, temperatures may be a few degrees higher. During most of the rainy season, daytime temperatures average around 29°C (84°F) in the lowlands, and around 25°C (77°F) in mountain valleys.

GOVERNMENT

Since 1975, the official name of the country has been the Lao People's Democratic Republic (Sathalanalat Pasathipatai Pasason Lao) or LPDR. Informally, it is acceptable to call the country Laos, which in Lao is Pathet Lao – *pathet*, from the Sanskrit *pradesha*, means land or country.

The ruling Lao People's Revolutionary Party (LPRP) is modelled on the Vietnamese Communist Party and is directed by the Party Congress, which meets every four or five years to elect party leaders. In practice, the Political Bureau (Politburo), the Central Committee and the Permanent Secretariat are all dominated by the Prime Minister of the Council of Government (currently Khamtay Siphandone), a position that has enjoyed the full support of the Vietnamese since the 1940s.

Interestingly, the country's constitution, which was only drafted in 1990, contains no reference to socialism with regard to the economy; it formalises private trade and fosters foreign investment.

The country is divided into 16 provinces *(khwaeng)* plus the prefecture of Vientiane. Below the province is the muang, or district, which is comprised of two or more *tasseng* (subdistricts or cantons), which are in turn divided into *ban* (villages).

LAOS

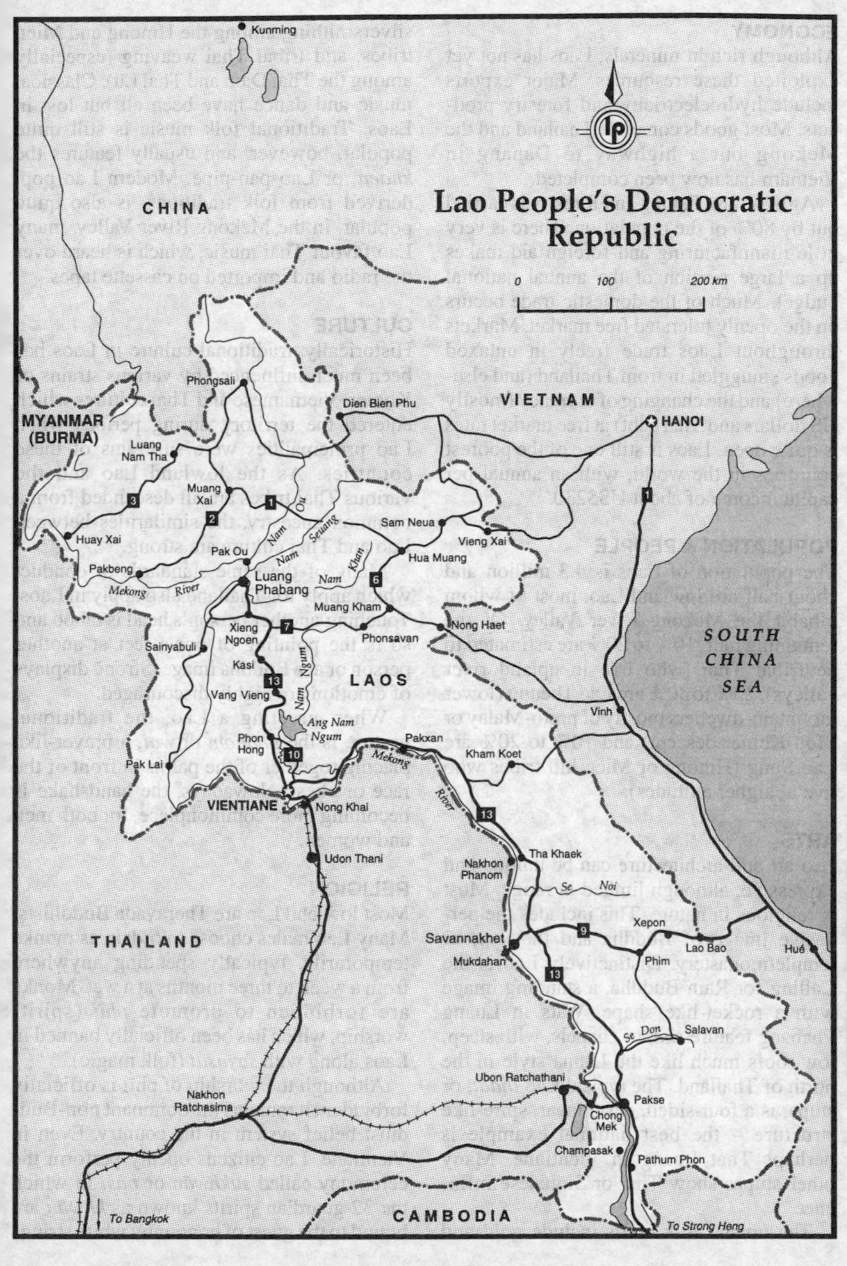
Lao People's Democratic Republic
0
100
200 km
CHINA
Kunming
MYANMAR
(BURMA)
VIETNAM
HANOI
SOUTH
CHINA
SEA
LAOS
THAILAND
CAMBODIA
Phongsali
Dien Bien Phu
Luang
Nam Tha
Muang
Xai
Huay Xai
Pakbeng
Pak Ou
Luang
Phabang
Mekong
River
Nam
Ou
Nam
Seuang
Nam
Khan
Sam Neua
Vieng Xai
Hua Muang
Muang Kham
Phonsavan
Nong Haet
Xieng
Ngoen
Sainyabuli
Kasi
Vang Vieng
Nam
Ngum
Ang Nam
Ngum
Phon
Hong
Pak Lai
VIENTIANE
Nong Khai
Pakxan
Kham Koet
Vinh
Udon Thani
Tha Khaek
Nakhon
Phanom
Se
Noi
Xepon
Savannakhet
Mukdahan
Lao Bao
Phim
Hué
Se
Don
Salavan
Ubon Ratchathani
Pakse
Chong
Mek
Champasak
Pathum Phon
Nakhon
Ratchasima
To Bangkok
To Strong Heng
1
2
3
6
7
9
10
13

LAOS

ECONOMY

Although rich in minerals, Laos has not yet exploited these resources. Major exports include hydroelectricity and forestry products. Most goods come via Thailand and the Mekong but a highway to Danang in Vietnam has now been completed.

Agriculture, fishing and forestry is carried out by 80% of the population. There is very little manufacturing and foreign aid makes up a large portion of the annual national budget. Much of the domestic trade occurs on the openly tolerated free market. Markets throughout Laos trade freely in untaxed goods smuggled in from Thailand (and elsewhere) and the changing of currency (mostly US dollars and Thai baht) at free market rates is quite open. Laos is still one of the poorest countries in the world, with an annual per capita income of about US$230.

POPULATION & PEOPLE

The population of Laos is 4.3 million and about half are lowland Lao, most of whom inhabit the Mekong River Valley. Of the remaining half, 10% to 20% are estimated to be tribal Thai (who live in upland river valleys), 20% to 30% are Lao Theung (lower mountain-dwellers mostly of proto-Malay or Mon-Khmer descent) and 10% to 20% are Lao Sung (Hmong or Mien hill tribes who live at higher altitudes).

ARTS

Lao art and architecture can be unique and expressive, although limited in range. Most is religious in nature. This includes the pervasive image of Buddha and the *wat*, or temple/monastery. Distinctively Lao is the Calling for Rain Buddha, a standing image with a rocket-like shape. Wats in Luang Phabang feature *sim*, or chapels, with steep, low roofs much like the Lanna style in the north of Thailand. The typical Lao *thâat*, or stupa, is a four-sided, curvilinear, spire-like structure – the best national example is perhaps That Luang in Vientiane. Many other stupas show Thai or Sinhalese influence.

The upland folk crafts include gold and silversmithing among the Hmong and Mien tribes, and tribal Thai weaving (especially among the Thai Dam and Thai Lü). Classical music and dance have been all but lost in Laos. Traditional folk music is still quite popular, however, and usually features the *khaen*, or Lao pan-pipe. Modern Lao pop, derived from folk traditions, is also quite popular. In the Mekong River Valley, many Lao favour Thai music, which is heard over the radio and imported on cassette tapes.

CULTURE

Historically, traditional culture in Laos has been much influenced by various strains of Khmer, Vietnamese and Thai cultures which entered the territory during periods when Lao principalities were suzerains of these countries. As the lowland Lao and the various Thai tribes are all descended from a common ancestry, the similarities between Lao and Thai culture are strong.

Many of the same standards of conduct which apply for Thailand also apply in Laos. Touching another person's head is taboo and so is the pointing of one's feet at another person or at a Buddha image. Strong displays of emotion are highly discouraged.

When greeting a Lao, the traditional gesture is the *phanom* or *wai*, a prayer-like placing together of the palms in front of the face or chest. Nowadays, the handshake is becoming more commonplace, for both men and women.

RELIGION

Most lowland Lao are Theravada Buddhists. Many Lao males choose to ordain as monks temporarily, typically spending anywhere from a week to three months at a wat. Monks are forbidden to promote *phīi* (spirit) worship, which has been officially banned in Laos along with *sayasat* (folk magic).

Although the worship of phīi is officially forbidden, it remains the dominant non-Buddhist belief system in the country. Even in Vientiane, Lao citizens openly perform the ceremony called *sukhwān* or *basi* in which the 32 guardian spirits known as *khwān* are bound to the guest of honour by white strings tied around the wrists. Each of the 32 khwãn are thought to be guardians over different organs in a person's body.

Outside the Mekong River Valley, the phĩi cult is particularly strong among tribal Thai, especially the Black Thai (Thai Dam). Priests *(mãw)* who are specially trained in the propitiation and exorcism of spirits preside at important Black Thai festivals and other ceremonies.

The Khamu and Hmong-Mien tribes also practise animism and the latter group combine ancestral worship. During the 1960s some Khamu participated in a 'cargo cult' that believed in the millennial arrival of a messianic figure who would bring them all the trappings of Western civilisation. Some Hmong also follow a Christian version of the cargo cult in which they believe Jesus Christ will arrive in a jeep, dressed in combat fatigues. The Akha, Lisu and other Tibeto-Burman groups mix animism and ancestor cults, except for the Lahu, who worship a supreme deity called Geusha.

LANGUAGE

The official language is Lao, as spoken and written in Vientiane. It's spoken with differing accents and with slightly differing vocabularies as you move from one part of the country to the next, especially in a north to south direction, but the Vientiane dialect is widely understood. Like Thai and Chinese, it's a mostly tonal language with simple grammar. The standard dialect makes use of six separate tones – the word *sao*, for example, can mean 'girl', 'morning', 'pillar' or '20' depending on the tone.

All dialects of Lao are closely related to languages spoken in Thailand, northern Myanmar and pockets of China's Yunnan Province. Standard Lao is close enough to standard Thai (as spoken in central Thailand) that, for native speakers, the two are mutually intelligible. French and English compete for status as the second language, with Russian a distant third. Generally speaking, older Lao will speak some French and younger Lao some English or Russian.

Greetings & Civilities

Greetings
Sa-bãi-dị
How are you?
Sa-bãi-dị baw?
(I'm) fine.
(Khàwy) sa-bãi-dị.
It doesn't matter.
Baw pẹn nyãng.
no (or not)
baw
thank you
khàwp jại

Getting Around

(I) want to go...
...Yàak pại
(I) want a ticket.
Yàak dâi pîi.
Where is...?
...yuu sãi? (subject first)
bus
lot bát or *lot méh*
pedicab
sãam-lâw
boat
heúa
post office
pại-sá-níi
station
sá-thãa-níi

Accommodation

Do you have...?
Míi...baw? (subject goes in the middle)
How much?
thao dại?
bath/shower
àap nâam
hotel
hóhng háem
room
hàwng
toilet
hàwng nâam (rest room)
sùam (commode)

Food

Do you have ...?
Míi .... baw?

(I) don't like it hot and spicy.
Baw mak phét.
(I) only eat vegetarian food.
Khàwy kįn jęh.
market
talàat
restaurant
hâan ąahãan

Numbers

1 *neung*
2 *sãwng*
3 *sãam*
4 *sii*
5 *hâa*
6 *hók*
7 *jét*
8 *páet*
9 *kâo*
10 *síp*
11 *síp-ét*
12 *síp-sąwng*
20 *sáo*
21 *sáo-ét*
30 *sãam-síp*
40 *sii-síp*
50 *hâa-síp*
100 *neung hâwy*
200 *sãwng hâwy*
300 *sãam hâwy*
1000 *neung phán*
10,000 *neung méun*

Emergencies

(I) need a doctor.
Tâwng-kąan mãw.
hospital
hóhng pha-yáa-bąan
doctor
thaan mãw

Facts for the Visitor

VISAS & EMBASSIES

Most travellers to Laos enter on a 14-day tourist visa which, at last report, is usually issued only through travel agencies authorised by the Lao Tourism Authority (LTA).

Lao embassies will occasionally issue tourist visas directly to individuals but the only way to find out is to apply, as their decisions seem to be made on an individual basis (it's never automatic). The embassy in Bangkok is very strict – to get a visa there you have to book a minimum two-day tour through a local agency. No matter how long or short your agency-arranged tour is, you are permitted to remain in Laos for the duration of your 14-day visa. Visas typically cost US$40 to US$100, although the Lao embassy in Yangon, Myanmar, is giving out tourist visas directly for US$15.

Unless you specifically request to enter Laos from Thailand by land, your visa may be stamped 'By Air – Wattay', depending on where you obtain it. Even with such a stamp it's usually no problem crossing by bridge or ferry from Nong Khai.

Thirty-day visas are available in Nong Khai for US$112. It's also possible to obtain a visa in Chiang Khong and cross the Mekong River to Huay Xai in Laos. Travel agencies in Ubon Ratchathani and Nakhon Phanom may be able to arrange visas for entry at Pakse and Tha Khaek respectively.

The transit visa is the easiest visa to get but is the most restricted. It is intended for air stopovers in Vientiane for passengers travelling between two other countries. For example, it's common to request this type of visa when travelling between Hanoi and Bangkok. The visa is granted upon presentation of a confirmed ticket between the two destinations. The maximum length of stay for the transit visa is five days and no extension is allowed. No travel is permitted outside the town of Vientiane on this visa. In Vietnam, the fee for this visa is US$10.

With a sponsor in Laos, persons with a professed investment interest in Laos can easily obtain business visas, valid for 30 days, directly from any Lao embassy.

Lao Embassies Abroad

If you're going to Laos on a tourist visa, you most likely won't deal directly with any Lao embassy, since tour agencies handle all visa arrangements. To apply for a visa on your own, you can try one of these embassies (Vietnam and Cambodia are the best bets):

Thailand
Embassy of the LPDR, 193 Sathon Tai Rd, Bangkok (☎ 286 0010)

Vietnam
LPDR Consular Office, 40 Quang Trung St (on 2nd floor of unmarked building across from offices of the Food & Agriculture Organization), Hanoi (☎ 52588)

Cambodia
LPDR Chancellery, 111 214th St, Phnom Penh (☎ 25 1821)

You can also check with Lao embassies or consulates in other countries which maintain diplomatic relations with Laos, but your chances of getting an individual visa from an embassy or consulate outside Cambodia or Vietnam, except through a tour agency, are somewhat slim (unless you're applying for a business visa).

Visa Extensions

All types of visas except the five-day transit visa may be extended at the discretion of Lao immigration authorities.

The immigration office of the Ministry of the Interior is on Thanon Talaat Sao near Thanon Lan Xang, opposite the Morning Market, in Vientiane (the only Roman-scripted sign reads 'Ministère d'Interieur'). An extension requires the filling out of forms and three passport photos. The application takes about 24 hours to process and you must leave your passport with immigration during this time.

The immigration office is open weekdays from 8 to 11 am and from 2 to 5 pm.

Travel Passes

The government has now basically done away with the provincial travel permit requirement. In theory this means visitors can travel more or less at will around the country. However, a few places may still be off-limits to foreigners, and local permits may still be required in areas where there's considerable undetonated ordnance and in 'sensitive' areas (opium, insurgents). At the time of writing a definitive answer from Vientiane on which areas still require permits was not forthcoming. Some remote areas seem to be run almost like independent fiefdoms by the local police, indicating a conflict between national and local control in parts of the country.

TOURS

All tours in Laos are handled by agencies authorised by the Lao Tourism Authority (LTA). In 1993 there were 20 such agencies operating in Vientiane although word on the grapevine said that the LTA intended to cut this back to a smaller number. For the most part each agency has a standard set of packages, ranging from two nights in Vientiane to 14 days in Vientiane, Luang Phabang, the Plain of Jars (Xieng Khuang), Savannakhet, Salavan and Champasak.

Standard prices vary from company to company but the main differences are linked to the number of people signing up for a package: the per-person rates become less expensive with each person added to the tour. Tour prices typically drop around US$50 to US$100 per person for each person added to the group. If you don't mind travelling with other people, ask if you can join a group already scheduled to depart – some agencies will allow this while some try to keep the groups as small as possible in order to collect the most loot.

It is always cheapest to book a minimum one or two-day package from Thailand or Vietnam and then work directly with Vientiane tour companies for interprovincial travel. It is also possible in some cases to negotiate downward the asking price for a tour. For price, recommended agencies in Vientiane include Lane Xang Travel & Tour, Thanon Pangkham, PO Box 4452 (tel/fax 4320), and Raja Tour, 2nd floor, Anou Hotel, Thanon Heng Boun (☎ 21-3660, fax 21-9378).

In Bangkok, MK Ways (☎ (2) 254 4765, fax 254 5583) at 57/11 Withayu (Wireless) Rd, near the US and Vietnamese embassies, is a reliable and reasonably priced agency for two-day Vientiane packages. In Ho Chi

Minh City, try Ann Tourist (tel/fax (8) 323866), 58 Ton That Tung St, District 1. Tourist visas booked in Vietnam are better than those obtained in Thailand because they generally don't stipulate that you must work with one particular Vientiane agency – this allows you to shop around after your arrival in Vientiane.

MONEY

Currency

The official national currency is the kip. In reality, the Lao use three currencies in day-to-day commerce: kip, Thai baht and US dollars.

Kip notes come in denominations of K1, K5, K10, K20, K50, K100 and K500. Kip coins (aạt) are supposedly available but rarely seen since anything below one kip is virtually worthless.

Exchange Rates

Australia	A$1	=	K519
Canada	C$1	=	K534
New Zealand	NZ$1	=	K427
Britain	UK£1	=	K1089
USA	US$1	=	K720
Japan	Y100	=	K703
Germany	DM1	=	K441
France	FF1	=	K129
Malaysia	M$1	=	K280
Thailand	1B	=	K29.17

Changing Money

In early 1989, US$1 bought K470, but by 1993 you could get K715 per US$1. It seems, however, to be stabilising at that level. A three-tier currency system – baht, US dollars and kip – remains firmly in place. In keeping with the local system, prices in this chapter may be given either in kip, baht or US dollars depending on how they were quoted at the source.

Dollars and baht can be exchanged for kip at the official National Bank rate and the free market rate, which now seem to be about the same. There's no legal requirement that you change money at the bank – moneychangers operate openly in the outdoor markets of Vientiane and most shop owners will also be glad to give you kip in exchange for baht or dollars in cash. In general baht is the most negotiable currency throughout Laos though it's a good idea to have kip available for smaller purchases and US dollars for larger transactions. Cash is much more useful than travellers' cheques, which can be difficult to exchange outside Vientiane.

Laos has no restrictions on the amount of money you're required to exchange at the official rate (as in Myanmar).

By and large the best exchange rates are available at the banks rather than at moneychangers. Travellers' cheques receive a slightly better exchange rate than cash (eg 725 kip per US dollar vs 720). The banks in Vientiane can change British pounds, German marks, Canadian, US and Australian dollars, French francs, Thai baht and Japanese yen. The government bank has a foreign exchange counter in the Wattay airport terminal, but you're better off changing money in town. Outside Vientiane most provincial banks accept only US$ or baht. Kip is often in short supply in provincial banks, however.

Costs

If it weren't for the current tour requirement, Laos would be a very inexpensive country to visit. Locally booked tours to provinces out of Vientiane are actually pretty decent value when you add up everything that's included – though you could do it much more cheaply on your own, especially if you use ground transport rather than air.

In general, food is cheap, hotels are not. The average meal in a Lao restaurant costs less than US$2 per person. A cup of coffee is about US$0.14, and draught beer is only US$0.84 a litre. On the other hand, the Lane Xang Hotel in Vientiane costs US$54 a night for a room that in Thailand would cost half that. The cheapest hotels in Vientiane cost US$5 to US$8.

Estimating a daily cost is difficult since it depends on how much you try to see, which means how many tour packages you purchase at approximately US$100 a day, all-inclusive. In Vientiane, you can get by for about US$10 a day, not counting the cost of the initial package into Vientiane. Towns in southern Laos, like Pakse or Savannakhet, cost about the same, perhaps a bit lower.

Tipping is not customary, even in the tourist hotels.

BUSINESS HOURS

Government offices are generally open from 8 to 11 am and from 2 to 5 pm. Shops and private businesses open and close a bit later and either stay open during lunch or close for just an hour.

HOLIDAYS & FESTIVALS

The Lao Buddhist Era (BD) calendar figures year one as 638 BC (not 543 BC as in Thailand), which means that you must subtract 638 from the Lao calendar year to arrive at the Christian calendar familiar in the West (eg 1990 AD is 2628 BE according to the Lao Buddhist calendar).

Festivals in Lao are mostly linked to agricultural seasons or historic Buddhist holidays. The general word for festival in Lao is *bụn* (or *boun*).

April

Pịi Mai The lunar new year begins in mid-April and practically the entire country comes to a halt and celebrates. Houses are cleaned, people put on new clothes and Buddha images are washed with lustral water. Later the citizens take to the streets and dowse one another with water.

The 15th, 16th, and 17th of April are official public holidays.

May

International Labour Day (1st) Public Holiday.

Visakha Bu-saa (*Visakha Puja*, Full Moon) This falls on the 15th day of the 6th lunar month, which is considered the day of the Buddha's birth, enlightenment and *parinibbana* or passing away. Activities are centred around the wat, with much chanting, sermonising and, at night, beautiful candlelit processions.

Bun Bang Fai (Rocket Festival) This is a pre-Buddhist rain ceremony that is now celebrated alongside Visakha Puja in Laos and north-eastern Thailand. This can be one of the wildest festivals in the country, with plenty of music and dance (especially the irreverent *mãw lám* performances), processions and general merrymaking, culminating in the firing of bamboo rockets into the sky.

July

Khao Phansaa (*Khao Watsa*, Full Moon) This is the beginning of the traditional three-month 'rains retreat', during which Buddhist monks are expected to station themselves in a single monastery. This is also the traditional time of year for men to enter the monkhood temporarily, hence many ordinations take place.

October/November

Awk Phansaa (*Awk Watsa*, Full Moon) This celebrates the end of the three-month rains retreat. Monks are allowed to leave the monasteries to travel and are presented with robes, alms-bowls and other requisites of the renunciative life.

A second festival held in association with Awk Phansaa is the *Bun Nam* (Water Festival). Boat races are commonly held in towns located on rivers, such as Vientiane, Luang Phabang and Savannakhet.

November

That Luang Festival (Full Moon) This takes place at Pha That Luang in Vientiane. Hundreds of monks assemble to receive alms and floral votives early in the morning on the first day of the festival. There is a colourful procession between Pha That Luang and Wat Si Muang. The celebration lasts a week and includes fireworks and music, culminating in a candlelit circumambulation *(wien thien)* of That Luang.

December

Lao National Day (2nd) This celebrates the 1975 victory of the proletariat over the monarchy with parades, speeches etc. It is a public holiday.

February

Magha Puja (*Makkha Bu-saa*, Full Moon) This commemorates a speech given by the Buddha to 1250 enlightened monks who came to hear him without prior summons. Chanting and offerings mark the festival, culminating in the candlelit circumambulation of wats throughout the country.

Vietnamese Tet & Chinese New Year This is celebrated in Vientiane, Pakse and Savannakhet with parties, deafening nonstop fireworks and visits to Vietnamese and Chinese temples. Chinese and Vietnamese-run businesses usually close for three days.

POST & TELECOMMUNICATIONS

Post

Outgoing mail from Vientiane is fairly dependable and inexpensive but incoming mail is unreliable. Forget about mailing things from upcountry Laos. Local residents, and expats who work outside Vientiane, save their mail and pass it on to acquaintances who are going to Vientiane or Thailand.

Telephone

The domestic phone service is inefficient, with phones often unserviceable and lines down, especially in the rainy season.

International calls can be made only from Vientiane. IDD has recently become available at selected locations in Vientiane, including the International Telephone Office.

BOOKS

Lonely Planet's *Laos – a travel survival kit* has more detailed information on Laos and is the only current guide to the country in English.

Some accounts of the country's recent history include *Contemporary Laos: Studies in the Politics & Society of the Lao People's Democratic Republic*, edited by Martin Stuart-Fox, and, by the same author, *Laos: Politics, Economics & Society*, which provides a better overview. More up-to-date is *Laos: Beyond the Revolution* (edited by Joseph Zasloff and Leonard Unger), a collection of essays on political and economic history to 1989. The 1991 *The Ravens: Pilots of the Secret War in Laos* by Christopher Robbins is a highly readable history of the US-directed secret air war.

The Women's International Group, a local expat association, publishes the informative *Vientiane Guide*, which can be purchased at the Lane Xang Hotel gift shop for US$12.

MAPS

The State Geographic Service (SGS) has produced a few adequate maps of Laos and the major provincial capitals. The LPDR tourist map of Vientiane and the administrative map of the whole country (labelled in French only as 'Laos – RDPL Carte Administrative') are available in Vientiane at the Lane Xang Hotel and in some souvenir shops along Thanon Samsenthai and Thanon Pang Kham.

The most detailed maps of Laos available are those that were developed by the US Defence Mapping Agency in the '60s and early '70s. These topographic maps, labelled in English and French, are often seen on the walls of government offices. Since little road travel (there are very few roads!) is permitted in Laos, the more general SGS maps are really sufficient for most travel purposes.

FILM & PHOTOGRAPHY

Colour print film is readily available in larger towns like Vientiane, Savannakhet and Luang Phabang. Ektachrome slide film is available at reasonable prices at a few photo shops along Samsenthai and Khun Bulom Rds in Vientiane. Outside Vientiane, slide film of any kind is rare. For black and white film or other types of slide film bring your own supply. You can get same-day developing and printing done in Vientiane, at Polaroid on Thanon Samsenthai, opposite the Asian Pavilion Hotel.

Military installations, soldiers or airports are not to be photographed. Some hill tribes have strong taboos against having their photos taken, so always ask first.

HEALTH

Opisthorchiasis

Apart from health warnings given in the Facts for the Visitor chapter, travellers in Laos should also be on guard against liver flukes (opisthorchiasis). These are tiny worms that are occasionally present in freshwater fish in Laos. The main risk comes from eating raw or undercooked fish – in particular, avoid eating *pąa dąek* which is fermented fish used as an accompaniment to rice.

A much less common way to contract liver flukes is by swimming in rivers – the only known area where this may happen is the Mekong River around Don Khong (Khong Island) in southern Laos, near the Cambodian border.

Symptoms depend very much on how many of the flukes get into your body. They can range from no symptoms at all to fatigue, a low-grade fever and a swollen or tender liver (or general abdominal pains), along with worms or worm eggs in the faeces.

People suspected of having liver flukes should have a stool sample analysed by a competent doctor or clinic in Vientiane or Bangkok. The usual medication is 750mg of praziquantel (often sold as Biltricide) taken three times daily for a week.

DANGERS & ANNOYANCES

Laos seems to be remarkably free of petty theft, at least in relation to visitors. Ordinary precautions, such as locking your hotel room door and keeping your valuables in a secured place, should of course be followed.

About the only known trouble spot is the area around Kasi on the Vientiane to Luang Phabang road. Anti-government rebels have been known to attack vehicles along this road with small arms, grenades and rocket-launchers. Since 1989, however, no incidents have been reported, and a Lao-Swedish project is currently upgrading the highway in order to facilitate regional security.

ACCOMMODATION

Laos has very few hotels – approximately 25 in Vientiane, four or five each in Savannakhet, Luang Phabang, Phonsavan and Pakse, and two or three in each of the remaining provincial capitals. Facilities vary from comfortable rooms with air-con and hot water in Vientiane to guesthouses (government-run) without running water in the provinces.

In Vientiane and Luang Phabang, the top tourist destinations, it's difficult to find rooms for under US$8 a night but in other provinces prices drop to as low as US$2, *if* you get there on your own. Lao National Tourism would prefer that you pay US$100 a day for a US$10 room, three meals and the services of a guide.

Most hotels, especially those in Vientiane, Luang Phabang and Savannakhet, will require that you fill out a police report *(fiche de police)* when checking in so that your passport and visa numbers on file.

FOOD

Lao cuisine is very similar to Thai in many ways. Like Thai food, almost all dishes are cooked with fresh ingredients, including vegetables *(phák)*, fish *(pąa)*, chicken *(kai)*, duck *(pét)*, pork *(mũu)* and beef *(sìn ngúa)* or water buffalo *(sìn khwái)*. In Luang Phabang, dried water-buffalo skin *(nãng khwái hàeng)* is a popular ingredient in local dishes.

Food is salted with *nâam pąa*, a thin sauce of fermented anchovies (usually imported from Thailand) and *pąa dąek*, a coarser Lao preparation which has fermented freshwater fish, rice husks and rice 'dust' as its main ingredients. Common seasonings include the galingale root *(khaa)*, ground peanuts (more often a condiment), hot chillies *(màak phét)*, tamarind juice *(nâam màak khãam)*, ginger *(khĩng)* and coconut milk *(nâam màak phâo)*. Chillis are sometimes served on the side in hot pepper sauces called *jaew*.

All meals are taken with rice or noodles. Glutinous rice *(khào nĩo)* is the preferred variety although ordinary white rice *(khào jâo)* is also common. Sticky rice is eaten with the hands – the general practice is to grab a small fistful from the woven container that sits on the table, then roll it into a ball and dip it into the various dishes. Khao jao is eaten with a fork and spoon. Noodles may be eaten with fork and spoon or chopsticks. The most common noodles in Laos are *fõe* (flat rice noodles) and *khào pûn* (thin white wheat noodles).

The closest thing to a national dish is *làap*, a spicy beef, duck, fish or chicken salad made with fresh lime juice, mint leaves, onions and lots of chillies. It can be hot or mild depending on the cook.

In Vientiane, Luang Phabang and Savannakhet, French bread is a popular breakfast food. Sometimes it's eaten plain with *kąa-fáe nóm hâwn* (hot coffee with milk), sometimes it's eaten with eggs *(khai)* or in a baguette sandwich that contains Lao-style paté and vegetables. When they're fresh, Lao baguettes are superb. Croissants and other pastries are also available in the bakeries of Vientiane.

Bread *(khào jįi)*
baguette sandwich
khào jįi pá-tê

croissants
kwaa-song
plain bread (usually French-style)
khào jịi

Eggs ***(khai)***
hard-boiled egg
khai tôm
fried egg
khai dạo
plain omelette
khai jẹun
scrambled eggs
khai khùa

Fish ***(pạa)***
crisp-fried fish
jẹun pạa
grilled fish
jịi pạa
steamed fish
nèung pạa
grilled prawns
pîng kûng

Noodles ***(fõe/mii)***
rice noodle soup with vegetables and meat
fõe nâam
same noodles served on plate with gravy
làat nàa
fried noodles with soy sauce
phát sáyûu
yellow wheat noodles in broth, with vegetables and meat
mii nâam
same as mii nâam but without broth
mii hàeng
white flour noodles, served with fish curry sauce
khào pûn

Soups ***(kạeng)***
mild soup with vegetables and pork
kạeng jèut
same as above, with bean curd
kạeng jèut tâo-hûu
fish and lemon grass soup with mushrooms
tôm yám pạa
rice soup with fish/chicken
khào pìak pạa/kai

Miscellaneous
spicy beef salad
làap sìn
grilled chicken
pîng kai
chicken fried with chillies
kai phát màak phét
spicy chicken salad
làap kai
roast duck
óp pét
rice
khào
fried rice
khào phát
spicy green papaya salad
tam-sòm or *sòm màak-hung*
cellophane noodle salad
yám sèn lâwn
stir-fried vegetables
phát phák

DRINKS
drinking water
nâam deum
weak Chinese tea
nâam sáa
hot Lao tea with sugar
sáa dạm hâwn
hot Lao tea with milk and sugar
sáa nóm hâwn
iced Lao tea with milk and sugar
sáa yén
no sugar (command)
baw sai nâam-tạan
hot Lao coffee with sugar
kạa-fáe dạm
hot Lao coffee with milk and sugar
kạa-fáe nóm hâwn
beer
bịa
orange soda
nâam máak kîang
plain milk
nâam nóm
rice whiskey
lào láo
yoghurt
nóm sôm

THINGS TO BUY

Laos is not a big country for shopping. Many of the handicrafts and arts available in Laos are easily obtainable in Thailand. Hill tribe crafts can be less expensive in Laos but only if you bargain. Like elsewhere in South-East Asia, bargaining is a local tradition, first introduced by Arab and Indian traders. Most shops now have fixed prices but you can still bargain for fabrics, carvings, antiques and jewellery.

Getting There & Away

AIR

Vientiane's Wattay airport is the only legal arrival or departure point for all foreign airline passengers. There is a US$5 departure tax.

To/From Thailand

Bangkok to Vientiane flights operate daily. On Monday, Tuesday, Wednesday and Saturday, flights are on Lao Aviation's Boeing 737-200s; the trip takes about an hour. On Thursday, Saturday and Sunday, Thai International flies similar aircraft. In each case the fare is US$100 one way, though specials as low as US$75 are occasionally available.

To/From Vietnam

Vietnam Airlines flies the Hanoi-Vientiane-Hanoi route every Thursday for around US$80 one way. Lao Aviation flies on Tuesday for the same fare.

Lao Aviation connects Vientiane with Ho Chi Minh City (Saigon) via Phnom Penh every Friday for US$152 one way.

To/From Cambodia

Lao Aviation flies from Phnom Penh and Vientiane on Friday. The flight takes about 1½ hours and costs US$122 one way.

To/From China

China Southern Airlines (CSA) flies to Vientiane from Guangzhou (US$280 one way) and Kunming (US$204 one way) every Sunday. Flights take just over an hour from Kunming, about 3½ hours from Guangzhou (including the Kunming stopover). Lao Aviation is the general sales agent for CSA, but CSA reportedly will be opening its own office in the near future.

General Sales Agents

Agents for Lao Aviation within the region include:

Thailand

- Thai Airways International, 89 Vibhavadi Rangsit Rd, Bangkok (☎ 531 0121)
- Lao Aviation, 491/17 Ground Flr, Silom Plaza, Silom Rd, Bangkok (☎ 236 9821)
- Bangkok international airport (☎ 535 3591)

Vietnam

- Vietnam Airlines, 25 Trang Thi St, Hanoi (☎ 53842)

Cambodia

- Kampuchea Airlines, 62 Tou Samouth St, Phnom Penh (☎ 25887)

Hong Kong

- China Travel Air Service, 5/F CTS House, 78-83 Connaught Rd Central (☎ 853 3468, fax 544 6174)

LAND

To/From Thailand

It is now legal for non-Thai foreigners to cross the Mekong into Laos from Thailand at the following points: Nong Khai (near Vientiane), Nakhon Phanom (opposite Tha Khaek), Chiang Khong (opposite Huay Xai) and Mukdahan (opposite Savannakhet).

Nong Khai is the most common crossing point at the moment; the others require advance permission, which is difficult to obtain outside of Laos. Travel agencies in Chiang Khong, Ubon Ratchathani and Nakhon Phanom may be able to arrange visas for entry at Huay Xai, Pakse and Tha Khaek respectively for 1600 to 2000B.

Now that the bridge over the Mekong River from the Nong Khai railway head (Thailand) to Tha Na Leng (19 km from Vientiane) is up, buses and taxis can go straight into Vientiane from Nong Khai. The next step in the plan is to build a parallel railway bridge in order to extend the Bangkok to Nong Khai railway to Vientiane and eventually as far as Xieng Khuang. A second Mekong bridge is tentatively planned to span the river at either Tha Khaek (opposite Thailand's Nakhon Phanom) or Savannakhet (opposite Mukdahan).

Since April 1993 a land crossing from Chong Mek in Thailand's Ubon Ratchathani Province to Champasak has been open for use by foreign visitors. To use this crossing you'll need a visa valid for entry via Chong Mek and Pakse – this must be arranged in advance through a Lao consulate or sponsoring agency.

To/From Other Countries

Laos also shares its land borders with Myanmar, China, Cambodia and Vietnam but, at present, no overland crossing points are usually open for foreigners. There is talk, however, of a Bangkok-Vientiane-Danang (Vietnam) bus service and a Bangkok-based company claims to have the agreement of both the Lao and Vietnamese governments for this operation. Special permission to cross at Lao Bao is sometimes available from the Vietnamese consulate in Savannakhet.

Getting Around

The road system in Laos is undeveloped. Roads around the periphery of Vientiane Prefecture as far as the Nam Ngum Lake are surfaced and adequate for just about any type of vehicle. Elsewhere in the country, rough unsurfaced roads are the rule. Since Laos is 70% mountains, even relatively short road trips take a long time.

The Lao often travel long road distances by arranging rides with trucks carrying cargo from one province to another. Of course, if they can afford it (or the government is paying), they avoid road travel altogether by flying (their fares are often subsidised by the government). The other alternative is river travel which, in many ways, is the most convenient form of transport in Laos.

AIR

You are allowed to book your own flights only if you possess a valid travel pass issued by the Department of Commerce. This usually means booking a tour through a local travel agency. The result is that most shoestringers won't be flying around Laos.

Vientiane is connected by air with Luang Phabang (US$34; daily), Savannakhet (US$54; daily except Thursday), Luang Nam Tha (US$56; four times weekly), Xieng Khuang (US$28; daily), Pakse (US$89; four times weekly), Sainyabuli (US$26; three times weekly) and Salavan (US$86; via Savannakhet Sunday only). Most flights are on the 17-passenger Chinese Y-12 and the 52-passenger Chinese Y-7, both copies of Russian Antonov aircraft.

All departure and arrival times given throughout this chapter are *scheduled* flight times. Flights are often delayed an hour or two due to weather conditions in the mountains (this includes all destinations except Vientiane, Savannakhet and Pakse).

The departure tax for domestic flights is 300 kip.

BUS

Because of road conditions, bus services are usually limited to the areas around provincial capitals while long-distance bus services between towns are rare.

Around Vientiane, buses are mostly crowded, dilapidated affairs but very cheap (less than 700 kip per 50 km). Where the roads are surfaced, they're a very acceptable way to get from one point to another.

TRUCK

Outside of Vientiane Province, there are many Russian, Vietnamese or Japanese trucks that have been converted into passenger carriers by adding two long benches in the back. These passenger trucks are called *thàek-sii* (taxi) – or in some areas *sãwng-thâew*, which means 'two rows' in reference to the benches in the back.

If you're waiting by the side of the road for a ride, it helps to know whether approaching vehicles are likely to take on passengers, since one truck, from a distance, looks like the next. You can identify proprietorship by the colour of the licence tags: black tags indicate that the vehicle is licensed to carry paying passengers; yellow means it's a privately owned vehicle (not very common outside of towns); red is army-owned (not likely to pick up passengers); blue is civil service; and white belongs to embassies or international organisations (who will sometimes pick up foreign passengers).

Trucks may occasionally be stopped and inspected by the Lao army or police. Often, foreigners on a stopped vehicle may be asked to produce travel passes validated for their destination, as it is illegal to board interprovincial transport without a pass.

MOTORBIKE

Small 100cc motorcycles can be rented from some motorcycle dealers in Vientiane as well as in Luang Phabang and Savannakhet. The going rate is US$8 to US$10 a day.

BICYCLE

In Vientiane and Luang Phabang, it is possible to rent bicycles, usually in relatively poor condition, for getting around town. Bicycle rentals in other Lao towns are as yet unknown, however. If you manage to bring your own bicycle into the country, cycling would be an excellent way to see the Mekong River Valley area from Vientiane south, which is mostly flat. For the rest of the country you'd need a sturdy mountain bicycle. You should be able to register it with Lao customs upon entry.

BOAT

Rivers are the true highways and byways of Laos, the main thoroughfares being the Mekong, Nam Ou, Nam Khan, Nam Tha, Nam Ngum and Se Don. The Mekong River is the longest and most important water route and is navigable year-round between Luang Phabang in the north and Savannakhet in the south.

River Ferries

For long distances, large diesel-engine river ferries with overnight accommodation are used. Some of these boats have two decks with sleeping areas and on-board foodstalls. Others have one deck and stop occasionally for food. On overnight trips check if food is available and, if necessary, bring your own.

River ferry facilities are quite basic and passengers sit, eat and sleep on wooden decks. The toilet is an enclosed hole in the deck. The fare for a typical 24-hour river ferry trip is 3000 to 4500 kip. A three-day trip (say upriver from Vientiane to Luang Phabang) is about 9000 kip. As with interprovincial travel by air or road, valid travel passes are required for foreign passengers.

River Taxis

For shorter river trips, such as Luang Phabang to the Pak Ou Caves, it's usually best to hire a river taxi since the large river ferries only ply their routes a couple of times a week. The long-tail boats *(héua hãng nyáo)* with engines gimbal-mounted on the stern are the most typical, though for a really short trip (eg crossing a river) a rowboat *(héua phai)* can be hired. The héua hãng nyáo are not as inexpensive to hire as you might think – figure on around 2800 kip an hour for a boat with an eight to 10-person capacity.

Along the upper Mekong River between Luang Phabang and Huay Xai, Thai-built *héua wái* (speedboats) – shallow, five-metre-long skiffs with 40-hp Toyota outboard engines – are common. These are able to cover a distance in six hours that might take a river ferry two days or more. They're not cheap – charters run about US$20 per hour – but some ply regular routes so that the cost can be shared among several passengers.

LOCAL TRANSPORT

Taxi

Each of the three largest towns – Vientiane, Luang Phabang and Savannakhet – has a handful of car taxis that are used by foreign businesspeople and the occasional tourist. The only place you'll find these are at the airports (arrival times only) and in front of the larger hotels. The cars are usually of Eastern European or Soviet origin (eg Volgas and Ladas) but, occasionally, you'll run across an older American or new Japanese car. These taxis can be hired by the trip, by the hour or by the day. Typical all-day rental costs are from US$15 to US$40. By the trip, you shouldn't pay more than US$0.50 per km.

Three-wheeled motorbike taxis are also common in the larger towns as well as in some smaller ones. This type of vehicle can be called taxi *(thàek-sii)* or samlor *(sãam-lâw)*, meaning 'three-wheels'. The larger ones made in Thailand are called jumbos *(jamboh)* and can hold four to six passengers. Fares are about 200 kip per km per vehicle but you must bargain to get the correct rate. They can go any place a regular taxi can, but they aren't usually hired for distances greater than 20 km.

Pedicabs The bicycle samlor is the mainstay of local transport throughout urban Laos. Samlor fares cost about the same as motorbike taxis but are generally used only for distances less than two km. Bargaining is sometimes necessary to get the correct fare, though pedicab drivers seem to be more honest than the motorbike taxi drivers.

Vientiane

Originally one of the early Lao river-valley fiefdoms (muang) that were consolidated around the time Europe was emerging from the Dark Ages, Vientiane sits on a bend in the Mekong River amidst fertile alluvial plains. At times controlled by the Burmese, Siamese, Vietnamese and Khmers, it was made a capital city by the French in the late 19th century. Throughout the Indochina War years, royalists, neutralists and leftists vied for control of the city and, thereby, the country. Following the Communist takeover of 1975, it continued to serve as the seat of government.

It's one of the three classic Indochinese cities (including Saigon, or Ho Chi Minh City, and Phnom Penh) that conjure up images of exotic Eurasian settings and has remained amazingly laid-back. Vientiane is actually pronounced 'Wieng Chan'.

Orientation

The city curves along a bend in the Mekong River with the central business district at the middle of the bend. Most of the government offices, hotels, restaurants and historic temples are in this district near the river.

Street signs are mostly written in Lao script only, although signs at major street intersections are also written in French. The French designations for street names vary (eg route, rue and avenue) but the Lao script always reads *thanõn* and it's always best just to avoid possible confusion and use the Lao word.

The main streets in the downtown district are Thanon Samsenthai, which is the main shopping area, Thanon Setthathirat, where several of the most famous temples are located, and Thanon Fa Ngum, which runs along the river. Branching off northward is Thanon Lan Xang, Vientiane's widest street.

The main portion of Thanon Lan Xang is a divided boulevard that leads past the Morning Market to the Patuxai, or Victory Gate. After the Patuxai, it splits into two roads, Thanon Phon Kheng and Thanon That Luang. Thanon Phon Kheng leads to the Unknown Soldiers Memorial and the Lao People's Army Museum as well as the Thai Embassy. Thanon That Luang leads to Pha That Luang.

To the north-east of central Vientiane are Pha That Luang and several embassies. To the south-east is the mostly local residential district of Sisattanak and to the west is the similarly residential Sikhottabong.

Information

Tourist Offices The Lao Tourism Authority office is on a hard-to-find side street to the north-east of the Patuxai monument. This road is apparently unnamed, but it runs between Thanon Nehru and Thanon Phonxai Yai and is almost directly across the street from the offices of the Food & Agriculture Organisation.

The only reason to visit Lao Tourism is if

you have questions about official tourism policy (though most travel agencies and tour operators can answer these sorts of questions as well). Some of the staff at LTA speak French and a little English.

Money The Lao Exterior Commerce Bank (La Banque pour le Commerce Exte'rieur Lao) at 1 Thanon Pang Kham (near Lao Aviation and the Lane Xang Hotel), the Joint Development Bank at 31-33 Thanon Lan Xang (opposite the Morning Market) and the Siam Commercial Bank on Thanon Mahasot, north-east of the Morning Market, are the only banks with the facilities to deal with foreigners. The Lao Exterior Commerce Bank has the best exchange rates.

Banking hours are from 8.30 am to 4 pm Monday to Friday. Lao Exterior Commerce Bank is open from 8.30 am to noon on Saturday.

You can change US$ and Thai baht cash at the free market rate in the large sheds at the Morning Market. There is no advantage to doing this other than convenience.

Post The Post, Telephone and Telegraph (PTT) office is on the corner of Thanon Lan Xang and Thanon Khu Vieng, across from the Morning Market. Business hours are from 8 am to 5 pm Monday to Saturday and from 8 am to noon on Sunday.

Telephone The PTT office is only for calls within Laos. Overseas calls can be arranged at the International Telephone Office (Cabines Télécommuniques Internationales) on Thanon Setthathirat. It's open 24 hours a day but lines are sometimes down during heavy rains.

Bookshops Near the fountain on Thanon Pang Kham (next to the Thai International office), Raintree Bookstore (☎ 8113) stocks a selection of mostly used paperbacks, magazines, and other periodicals.

The gift shop at the Lane Xang Hotel has a few books in English and rather expensive maps of Vientiane and Laos.

Police In an emergency, contact the police kiosk on Thanon Setthathirat.

Medical Services Medical facilities in Vientiane are quite limited. The two state hospitals, Setthathirat and Mahasot, operate on levels of skill and hygiene below that available in neighbouring Thailand. Mahasot Hospital operates a Diplomatic Clinic 'especially for foreigners' that is open 24 hours. In reality, few foreigners use this clinic.

The Australian and Swedish embassies in Vientiane maintain clinics that can treat minor problems. Both clinics are behind the Australian Embassy, off Thanon Phonxai Noi. The Swedish Clinic (☎ 4641) is open daily from 8 to 11 am. The Australian Embassy Clinic (☎ 4691, after hours 2183) is open Monday to Friday from 8.30 am to noon and from 2 to 5 pm (except Wednesday when it closes at noon and stays closed the rest of the day). It is on call 24 hours.

These clinics are staffed by registered nurses but aren't equipped to handle major medical emergencies. Both charge small treatment fees. For medical emergencies that can't wait till Bangkok and which can't be treated at one of the embassy clinics, you can arrange to have ambulances summoned from nearby Udon Thani or Khon Kaen in Thailand.

Walking Tour

This walk takes you through the central area and past some of the lesser known wats in a leisurely two to 2½ hours. Start at the fountain on Thanon Pang Kham and walk west on Setthathirat approximately 250 metres to **Wat Mixai** on your left. The sim is built in the Bangkok style, with a veranda that goes all the way round. The heavy gates, flanked by two *nyak*, or guardian giants, are also in Bangkok style.

Another 80 metres west and on the right-hand side of the street is **Wat Hai Sok** with its impressive five-tiered roof (nine if you count the lower terrace roofs). Opposite, and just a bit further on, is **Wat Ong Teu**, and past Thanon Chao Anou on the next block west

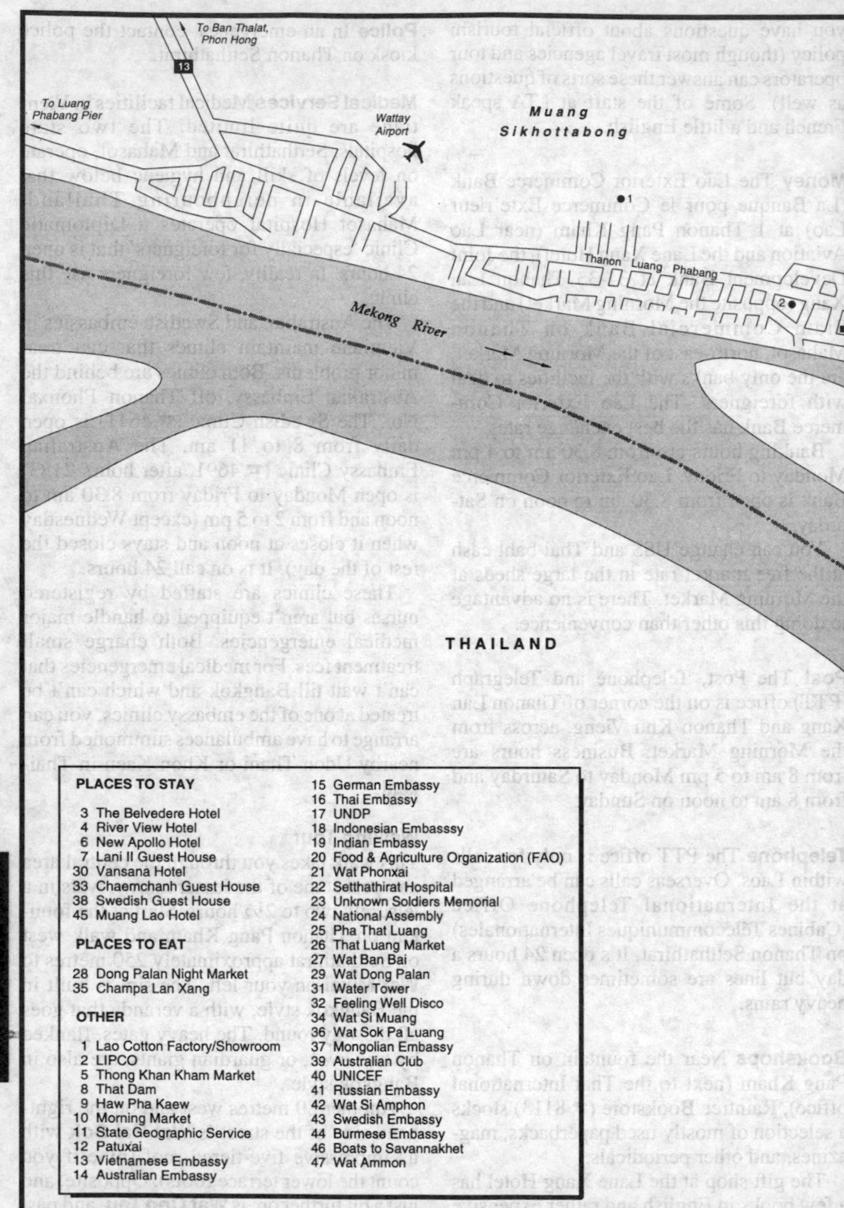
To Ban Thalat, Phon Hong
13
To Luang Phabang Pier
Wattay Airport
Muang Sikhottabong
1
Thanon Luang Phabang
2
Mekong River
THAILAND
PLACES TO STAY
3 The Belvedere Hotel
4 River View Hotel
6 New Apollo Hotel
7 Lani II Guest House
30 Vansana Hotel
33 Chaemchanh Guest House
38 Swedish Guest House
45 Muang Lao Hotel
PLACES TO EAT
28 Dong Palan Night Market
35 Champa Lan Xang
OTHER
1 Lao Cotton Factory/Showroom
2 LIPCO
5 Thong Khan Kham Market
8 That Dam
9 Haw Pha Kaew
10 Morning Market
11 State Geographic Service
12 Patuxai
13 Vietnamese Embassy
14 Australian Embassy
15 German Embassy
16 Thai Embassy
17 UNDP
18 Indonesian Embasssy
19 Indian Embassy
20 Food & Agriculture Organization (FAO)
21 Wat Phonxai
22 Setthathirat Hospital
23 Unknown Soldiers Memorial
24 National Assembly
25 Pha That Luang
26 That Luang Market
27 Wat Ban Bai
29 Wat Dong Palan
31 Water Tower
32 Feeling Well Disco
34 Wat Si Muang
36 Wat Sok Pa Luang
37 Mongolian Embassy
39 Australian Club
40 UNICEF
41 Russian Embassy
42 Wat Si Amphon
43 Swedish Embassy
44 Burmese Embassy
46 Boats to Savannakhet
47 Wat Ammon

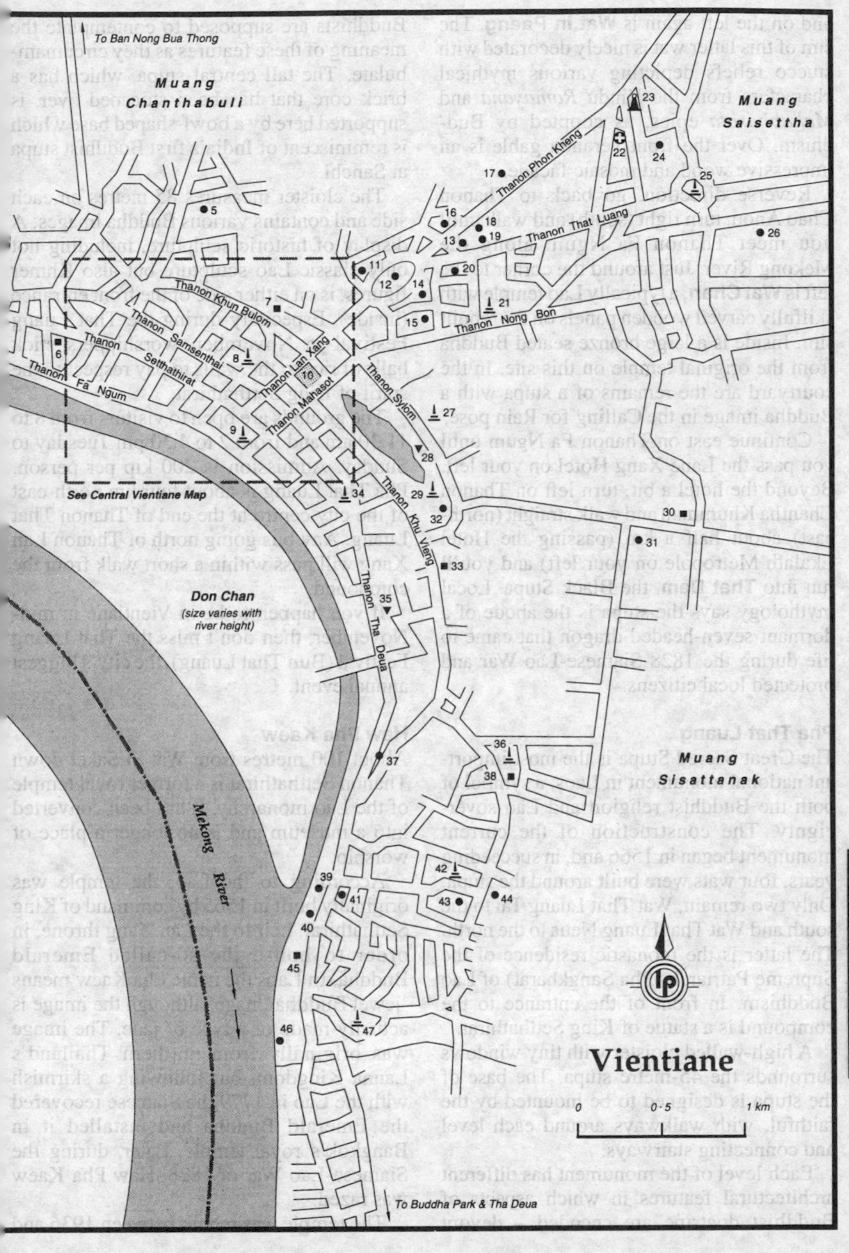
To Ban Nong Bua Thong
Muang Chanthabuli
Muang Saisettha
Thanon Phon Kheng
Thanon That Luang
Thanon Nong Bon
Thanon Khun Bulom
Thanon Samsenthai
Thanon Setthathirat
Thanon Fa Ngum
Thanon Lan Xang
Thanon Mahasot
Thanon Sylom
See Central Vientiane Map
Thanon Khu Vieng
Thanon Tha Deua
Don Chan
(size varies with river height)
Mekong River
Muang Sisattanak
Vientiane
0
0·5
1 km
To Buddha Park & Tha Deua

and on the left again is **Wat In Paeng**. The sim of this latter wat is nicely decorated with stucco reliefs depicting various mythical characters from the Hindu *Ramayana* and *Mahabharata* epics, as coopted by Buddhism. Over the front veranda gable is an impressive wood and mosaic facade.

Reverse direction, go back to Thanon Chao Anou, turn right (south) and walk until you meet Thanon Fa Ngum along the Mekong River. Just around the corner to the left is **Wat Chan**, a typically Lao temple with skilfully carved wooden panels on the rebuilt sim. Inside is a large bronze seated Buddha from the original temple on this site. In the courtyard are the remains of a stupa with a Buddha image in the Calling for Rain pose.

Continue east on Thanon Fa Ngum until you pass the Lane Xang Hotel on your left. Beyond the hotel a bit, turn left on Thanon Chantha Khumman and walk straight (north-east) about half a km (passing the Hotel Ekalath Metropole on your left) and you'll run into **That Dam**, the Black Stupa. Local mythology says the stupa is the abode of a dormant seven-headed dragon that came to life during the 1828 Siamese-Lao War and protected local citizens.

Pha That Luang

The Great Sacred Stupa is the most important national monument in Laos, a symbol of both the Buddhist religion and Lao sovereignty. The construction of the current monument began in 1566 and, in succeeding years, four wats were built around the stupa. Only two remain, Wat That Luang Tai to the south and Wat That Luang Neua to the north. The latter is the monastic residence of the Supreme Patriarch (Pha Sangkharat) of Lao Buddhism. In front of the entrance to the compound is a statue of King Setthathirat.

A high-walled cloister with tiny windows surrounds the 45-metre stupa. The base of the stupa is designed to be mounted by the faithful, with walkways around each level and connecting stairways.

Each level of the monument has different architectural features in which aspects of Buddhist doctrine are encoded – devout Buddhists are supposed to contemplate the meaning of these features as they circumambulate. The tall central stupa, which has a brick core that has been stuccoed over, is supported here by a bowl-shaped base which is reminiscent of India's first Buddhist stupa at Sanchi.

The cloister measures 85 metres on each side and contains various Buddha images. A display of historic sculpture, including not only classic Lao sculpture but also Khmer figures, is on either side of the front entrance (inside). Especially during the That Luang Festival in November, worshippers stick balls of rice to the walls to pay respect to the spirit of King Setthathirat.

The grounds are open to visitors from 8 to 11.30 am and from 2 to 4.30 pm Tuesday to Sunday. Admission is 200 kip per person. Pha That Luang is about four km north-east of the city centre at the end of Thanon That Luang. Any bus going north of Thanon Lan Xang will pass within a short walk from the compound.

If you happen to be in Vientiane in mid-November, then don't miss the That Luang Festival (Bun That Luang), the city's biggest annual event.

Haw Pha Kaew

About 100 metres from Wat Si Saket down Thanon Setthathirat is a former royal temple of the Lao monarchy. It has been converted into a museum and is no longer a place of worship.

According to the Lao, the temple was originally built in 1565 by command of King Setthathirat, heir to the Lan Xang throne, in order to house the so-called Emerald Buddha. In Laos the name Pha Kaew means 'jewel Buddha image' although the image is actually made of a type of jade. The image was originally from northern Thailand's Lanna Kingdom, but following a skirmish with the Lao in 1779 the Siamese recovered the Emerald Buddha and installed it in Bangkok's royal temple. Later, during the Siamese-Lao War of 1828, Haw Pha Kaew was razed.

The temple was rebuilt between 1936 and

1942 in a rather Bangkok-style rococo. Today, the veranda shelters some of the best examples of Buddhist sculpture in Laos. Included are a 6th to 9th-century Dvaravati-style stone Buddha, several bronze standing and sitting Lao-style Buddhas and a collection of inscribed Lao and Mon steles. Various royal requisites are also on display inside, along with some Khmer steles, various wooden carvings (door panels, candlestands, lintels) and palm-leaf manuscripts.

Hours and admission for Haw Pha Kaew are the same as for Pha That Luang.

Wat Si Saket

This temple is located near the Presidential Palace and is at the corner of Thanon Lan Xang and Thanon Setthathirat. Built in 1818, by King Anouvong (Chao Anou), it is the oldest temple in Vientiane – all the others were either built after Wat Si Saket or were rebuilt after destruction by the Siamese in 1828.

In spite of an overall Siamese architectural influence, Wat Si Saket has several unique features. The interior walls of the cloister are riddled with small niches that contain silver and ceramic Buddha images – over 2000 of them. Over 300 seated and standing Buddhas of varying sizes and materials (wood, stone and bronze) rest on long shelves below the niches, and most are sculpted or cast in the characteristic Lao style. Most of the images are from 16th to 19th-century Vientiane but a few hail from 15th to 16th-century Luang Phabang. A Khmer-style Naga Buddha, brought from a Khmer site at nearby Hat Sai Fong, is also on display.

The hours and admission are the same as for Pha That Luang and Wat Pha Kaew. A Lao guide who speaks French and English is usually on hand to describe the temple and answer questions – for free.

Wat Sok Pa Luang

The full name for this forest temple *(wat pąa)* in south Vientiane's Sisattanak district is Mahaphutthawongsa Pa Luang Pa Yai Wat. It's famous for its rustic herbal saunas, which are administered by eight-precept nuns who reside at the temple. After the relaxing sauna, you can take tea while cooling off. Massages are also available. A donation is requested for sauna and massage services.

Wat Sok Pa Luang is also known for its course of instruction in *vipassana*, a type of Buddhist meditation that involves careful mind and body analysis. The abbot and teacher is Ajaan Sali Kantasilo who was born in 1932 in Yasothon, Thailand. He accepts foreign students but only speaks Lao and Thai, so interested persons will have to arrange for an interpreter if they speak neither of these languages.

Taxi, jumbo and samlor drivers all know how to get to Wat Sok Pa Luang. The temple buildings are set back in the woods so all that is visible from the road is the tall ornamental gate.

Wat Xieng Khuan (Buddha Park)

The Spirit City Temple, 24 km south-east of the town centre off the road to Tha Deua, is not a true wat as there are no monks in residence and there never have been. Nor is there any traditional Buddhist architecture. Locals often call it Buddha Park, a more apt description of its collection of Buddhist and Hindu sculpture in a meadow by the side of the Mekong River.

Entry is 100 kip. A few vendors in the park offer fresh young coconuts, soft drinks, beer and Lao food.

Patuxai (Victory Monument)

This large monument, very reminiscent of the Arc de Triomphe in Paris, is known by a variety of names. Ironically, it was built in 1969 with US-purchased cement that was supposed to have been used for the construction of a new airport. Since it commemorates the Lao who had died in prerevolutionary wars, current Lao maps typically label it Old Monument (Ancien Monument in French, or Anusawali Kao in Lao) in order to draw attention to the newer Unknown Soldiers Memorial, erected since the Revolution.

The bas-relief on the sides and the temple-like ornamentation along the top and cornices are typically Lao. Beneath the arch is a small

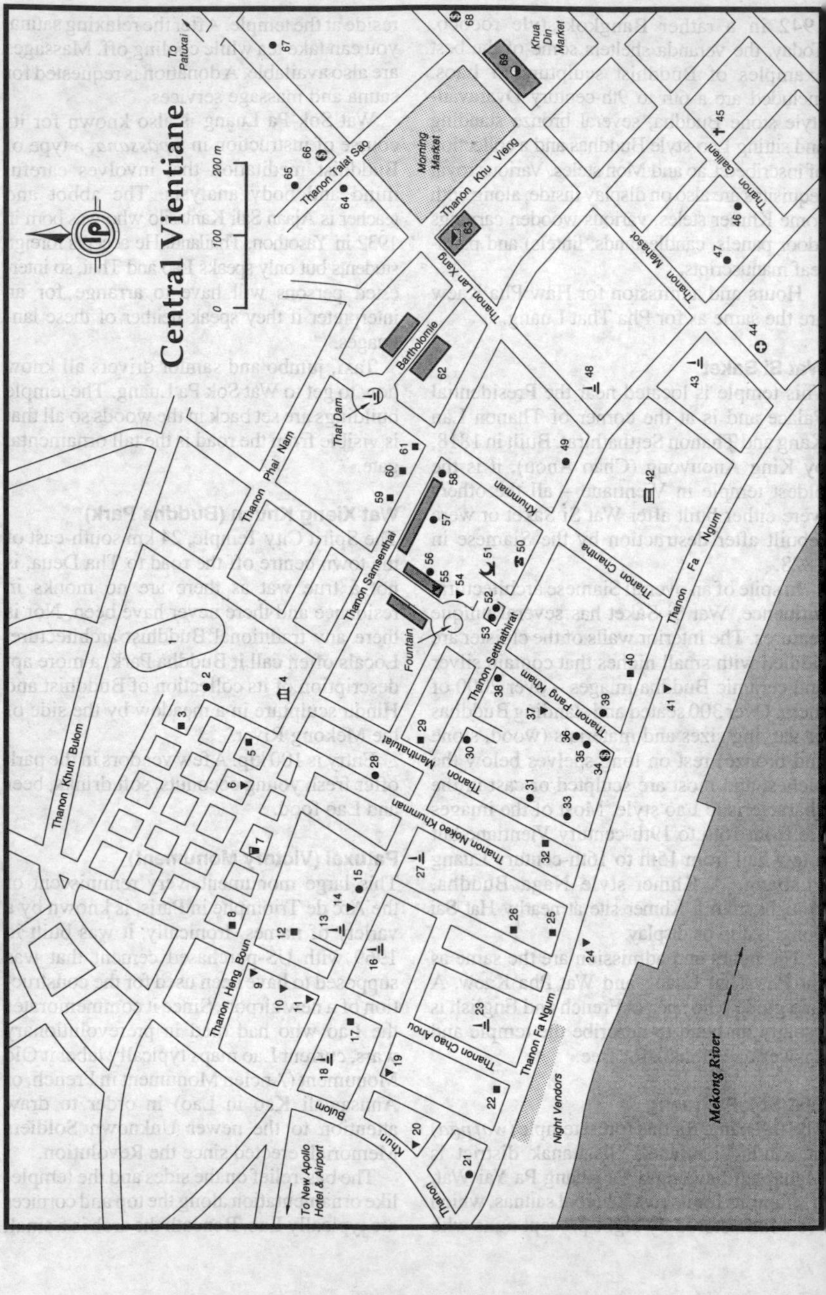

Central Vientiane

0 100 200 m

To Patuxai

Thanon Talat Sao

Morning Market

Khua Din Market

Thanon Khu Vieng

Thanon Lan Xang

Thanon Mahasot

Thanon Gallieni

Bartholomie

That Dam

Thanon Phai Nam

Thanon Samsenthai

Fountain

Khunman

Thanon Chantha

Thanon Fa Ngum

Thanon Setthathirat

Thanon Pang Kham

Manthatulat

Thanon Nokeo Khumman

Thanon Khun Bulom

Thanon Heng Boun

Thanon Chao Anou

Thanon Fa Ngum

Night Vendors

Mekong River

Thanon Khun Bulom

To New Apollo Hotel & Airport

PLACES TO STAY

3 Syri Guest House
5 Santisouk Guest House & Restaurant
8 Anou Hotel
12 Lani I Guest House
17 Saysana Hotel
22 Lao Chaleune Hotel
25 Mixai Guest House
26 Taipan Hotel
29 SECP Guest House
32 Samsenthai Hotel
40 Lane Xang Hotel
59 Hua Guo Guest House
60 Asian Pavilion Hotel
61 Hotel Ekalath Metropole

PLACES TO EAT

6 Thai Food (Phikun) Restaurant
9 Nang Janti
10 Sweet Home & Liang Xiang Bakeries
11 Guangdong Restaurant
14 Le Santal
19 Restaurant Le Vendôme
20 Roast Duck Restaurants
24 Haan Kin Deum Mixai
37 Le Souriya
41 Sukiyaki Bar & Restaurant, Lao Restaurant
54 Nam Phu Restaurant & Government Bookshop
55 The Taj Restaurant

OTHER

1 National Stadium
2 Tennis Club de Vientiane
4 Lao Revolutionary Museum
7 Foster's Modern House Pub
13 Wat Hai Sok
15 Lane Xang Travel
16 Wat Ong Teu
18 Wat In Paeng
21 SODETOUR
23 Wat Chan
27 Wat Mixai
28 Lao Textiles
30 Lao Air Booking
31 Aerocontact Asia
33 The Art of Silk
34 La Banque pour le Commerce Extèrieur Lao
35 Thai International
36 Raintree Bookstore
38 Inter-Lao Tourisme
39 Lao Aviation
42 Presidential Palace
43 Haw Pha Kaew
44 Mahasot Hospital
45 Catholic Church
46 Le Club France
47 French Embassy
48 Wat Si Saket
49 Ministry of Foreign Affairs
50 International Telephone Office
51 Mosque
52 Lao Cotton
53 Diethelm Travel
56 Tailor Shops & Handicrafts
57 Souvenir & Handicraft Shops
58 Phimphone Minimart
62 US Embassy
63 Post, Telephone & Telegraph Office (PTT)
64 Bicycle Rentals
65 Immigration Office
66 Joint Development Bank
67 Vienglaty Mai Disco
68 Siam Commercial Bank
69 Bus Terminal

outdoor cafe with snacks. A stairway leads to the top of the monument, where you can look out over the city (there's a small entry fee to climb the stairs).

Morning Market

The Morning Market (Talàat Sâo) is on the north-east corner of the intersection of Thanon Lan Xang and Thanon Khu Vieng. It actually runs all day, from about 6 am to 6 pm. The sprawling collection of stalls offer fabric, ready-made clothes, hardware, jewellery, electronic goods and just about anything else imaginable. Since the loosening of economic restrictions in 1989, the Morning Market has been expanding.

From about 6 to 8 am, vendors along Khu Vieng in front of the Morning Market sell French bread and the Lao breakfast sandwich (khào jịi pá-têh) – split baguettes filled with a Lao version of paté, a few vegetables and a fish sauce dressing. A few vendors also sell fresh vegetables and fruit during these hours. For the rest of the day you don't see a lot of fresh produce except for the occasional street vendor who may wheel a cart through the market.

Other Markets

South-east of the Morning Market, just across Thanon Mahasot (or Thanon Nong Bon, as it's labelled on some maps) is the **Khua Din Market** (Talaat Khua Din) which offers fresh produce and fresh meats, tobacco and other smoking material, as well as flowers and other assorted goods.

A bigger fresh market is **Thong Khan Kham Market** (Talaat Thong Khan Kham) which is sometimes called the Evening Market since it was originally established to replace the old Evening Market in Ban Nong Duang (which burned down in 1987). Like the Morning Market, it's open all day, but is best in the morning. It's the biggest market in Vientiane and has virtually everything. You'll find it north of the town centre in Ban Thong Khan Kham (Gold Bowl Fields Village), at the intersection of Thanon Khan Kham and Thanon Dong Miang.

The **That Luang Market** is just a little south-east of Pha That Luang on Thanon Talaat That Luang. The speciality here is exotic foods, like bear paws and snakes, that are favoured by the Vietnamese and Chinese.

Festivals

The That Luang Festival takes place at Pha That Luang, on the full moon in November. Hundreds of monks assemble to receive alms and floral votives early in the morning on the first day of the festival.

There is also a colourful procession between Pha That Luang and Wat Si Muang. The celebration lasts a week and includes fireworks, music and other entertainment, culminating in a candlelit walk *(wíen thíen)* around That Luang.

Vietnamese Tet & Chinese New Year (usually centred on a full moon in February) is celebrated with some fervour in Vientiane with parties, fireworks and visits to Vietnamese and Chinese temples. Chinese and Vietnamese-run businesses usually close for three days.

Places to Stay

Vientiane has a choice of over 20 hotels and guesthouses, many of which cost over US$20 per night. Fortunately for budgeteers, during the last two years lower-priced rooms have begun opening up. Foreigners are allowed to stay at any hotel or guesthouse in the city, although if you arrive in Vientiane on a tourist visa you may already have paid for a night or more at a preassigned place. If you plan to extend your stay, you can then seek out a room at your leisure.

The *State Enterprise for Cultural Production (SECP) Guest House*, at the corner of Thanon Manthatulat and Setthathirat, is currently one of the best deals to be found in Vientiane. Large, three-bed rooms with fan cost US$3 to US$6 a night, while two-bed air-con rooms are US$8 to US$10. Rates are payable in kip, baht or dollars.

Lao Chaleune (☎ 2408), on Thanon Chao Anou at the corner of Thanon Fa Ngum and near the river, has singles/doubles with air-con at US$8/10. Formerly the Inter Hotel, it's well located, clean, not so friendly and often full – the restaurant, however, gets high marks.

Samsenthai Hotel (☎ 16-9456, 16-9358), at 15 Thanon Manthatulat near the river, is similar to the Lao Chaleune without the noisy bar/disco. Rooms with fan and shared bath go for US$8, while for US$12 you can get air-con and a private cold-water shower, or for US$20 add hot water.

Hotel Ekalath Metropole (☎ 2881) on the corner of Thanon Samsenthai and Chantha Khumman has undergone at least three incarnations, starting with the pre-1975 Imperial Hotel. The very latest version is basically a middle-class hotel, but a semi-attached annex contains cheap, plain rooms with fan for US$5 to US$6.60 a single and US$8.50 a double with shared cold-water shower, or US$10 a single and US$14 a double with fan and attached cold shower (but shared toilet).

West along Thanon Samsenthai from the Ekalath, the very Chinese *Hua Guo Guest House* (☎ 8633) offers spartan air-con rooms with two beds and little else for US$8 a single, US$10 a double with shared bath, or US$18 for three-bed rooms with private bath.

Santisouk Guest House (☎ 3926), above the Santisouk Restaurant on Thanon Nokeo Khumman, has plain but clean rooms with shared bath for US$10, or US$12 with private bath. The restaurant downstairs is a good breakfast spot.

Anou Hotel (☎ 3571), on Thanon Heng Boun at the corner of Thanon Chao Anou, has rooms in the US$10 to US$18 range for singles, and US$16 to US$25 for doubles. A lot of the cheaper tour packagers in Bangkok use this hotel.

Mekong Guest House (☎ 5975) is at Thanon Tha Deua, Km 4, about 700 metres north-west of the big Mekong Restaurant and about halfway between the city and the Tha Deua ferry crossing. Although it's a bit far from downtown Vientiane, rooms in this guesthouse are only 3000 kip per person.

Places to Eat

Vientiane is good for eating possibilities, with a wide variety of cafes, street vendors, beer halls and restaurants offering everything from rice noodles to filet mignon. Nearly all fit well into a shoestring budget.

Breakfast Most of the hotels in Vientiane offer set 'American' breakfasts (two eggs, toast and ham or bacon) for 1000 to 2800 kip. Or you could get out on the streets and eat where the locals do. A popular breakfast is khào jịi pá-têh, a split French baguette stuffed with Lao-style paté (which is more like English or American luncheon meat than French paté) and various dressings.

Vendors who sell breakfast sandwiches also sell plain baguettes (khào jịi) – there are several regular bread vendors on Thanon Heng Boun and also in front of the Morning Market. The fresh baguettes are usually gone by 8.30 am and what's left will be starting to harden.

At the corner of Thanon Samsenthai and Thanon Chantha Khumman is a little open-air *cafe* that's only open for breakfast and lunch. The family that runs it prepares good egg dishes served with French bread on the side.

Two side-by-side cafes on Thanon Chao Anou, *Liang Xiang Bakery House* and *Sweet Home Bakery*, sell passable croissants and other pastries in the morning, along with strong brewed coffee.

Lao For real Lao meals, try the *Dong Palan Night Market*, off Thanon Ban Fai (marked Thanon Dong Palan on some maps) and behind the Nong Chan ponds near the Lan Thong cinema. Vendors sell all the Lao standards, including làap (spicy salad) and pîng kai (grilled chicken).

The *Haan Kin Deum Mixai*, or Mixai Eat-Drink Shop, is in a wooden building that's open on three sides and overlooks the Mekong River near the intersection of Thanon Fa Ngum and Thanon Nokeo Khumman. The menu is not very extensive, but the làap is very tasty and they have cold draught beer for 600 kip a litre. This is a great spot to watch the sun set over the Mekong River, with the Thai town of Si Chiangmai as the backdrop.

The *Vientiane Department Store* (part of the Morning Market) has a small but excellent food centre with an extensive variety of Thai and Lao dishes for 500 to 1000 kip, plus Lao beer for only 800 kip per large bottle.

Thai With an increasing number of Thais visiting Vientiane for business and pleasure these days, it is no wonder that there are more Thai restaurants. On Thanon Samsenthai, just past the Lao Revolutionary Museum, is the *Phikun* (the English sign reads 'Thai Food') restaurant, which has all the Thai standards, including tôm yam kûng (shrimp and lemon grass soup) and kài phàt bai kàphrao (chicken fried in holy basil). Curries are good here – something you don't see much of in Lao cuisine.

Noodles, Chinese & Vietnamese Noodles of all kinds are very popular in Vientiane, especially along Thanon Heng Boun, the unofficial Chinatown. Basically, you can choose between fõe, a rice noodle that's popular throughout mainland South-East Asia (known as kuaythiaw or kwayteow in Thailand, Malaysia and Singapore), and mee, the traditional Chinese wheat noodle.

Two Chinese-Vietnamese places along Thanon Heng Boun west of Thanon Chao Anou are very popular – *Nang Suli* (also known as Lao Chaloen, or to local expats, Green Hole in the Wall and, next door, *Vieng Sawan* (no English signs for either). Both specialise in khào pùn, Vietnamese spring rolls and barbecue kebabs.

Indian *The Taj* (☎ 2534) on Thanon Pang Kham opposite Nakhonluang Bank (just north of the fountain) has an extensive menu of well-prepared north Indian dishes, including tandoor, curries, vegetarian and many Indian breads. Service is good and the place is very clean, though prices are a bit high by Vientiane standards.

Cheaper Indian food can be found in abundance at a row of vendor stalls opposite the Hotel Phonxai on Thanon Saylom.

European Several commendable French and French-Lao restaurants can be found in Vientiane. Most are costly by local standards but they are definitely better value than Vientiane hotels.

One that is particularly good, as well as inexpensive, is the *Santisouk* (formerly a famous teahouse called La Pagode) on Thanon Nokeo Khumman, under the Santisouk Guest House. The cuisine is of the 'French grill' type and is quite tasty. A filling plate of filet mignon or filleted fish in a mushroom sauce with roast potatoes and veggies costs less than 3500 kip. It's no wonder Santisouk is one of the most popular restaurants in town.

Of the half dozen or so more expensive French and French-Lao restaurants, only two are worth noting. *Nam Phu* (Fountain) is on the Fountain Circle off Thanon Pang Kham and is frequented by diplomats and UN types because it has probably the best European food and service in Vientiane. *Le Santal* on Thanon Setthathirat opposite Wat Ong Teu is a friendly and pleasant air-con restaurant and bar run by a French anthropologist. The menu specialises in pizza and French grill; service is very good and prices are reasonable.

Opposite the Nam Phu Restaurant on the Fountain Circle is the very popular *Girarrosto Ristorante L'Opera*, a branch of a restaurant of the same name in Bangkok. The mostly Italian menu includes a variety of pasta (2600 to 3200 kip), seafood and pizza (2700 to 4000 kip), plus a selection of Italian wines. An attached gelato bar offers takeaway gelato.

Entertainment

Dancing Vientiane has at least six 'discos' with live music. Popular places include the *Vienglaty Mai* on Thanon Lan Xang, a bit north of the Morning Market (and on the same side of the street), along with clubs attached to the *Anou*, *Saysana* and *Lao Chaleune* hotels.

Cinema Lao cinemas generally show, in descending order of frequency, Thai, Chinese, Indian, Bulgarian and Russian films. Prints are often in lousy condition but you can hardly argue with the admission charges – less than 200 kip for the best seats in the house.

The *US Embassy* screens American movies every Wednesday at 7.30 pm for US$2. The theatre is across the street from the main embassy entrance on Thanon Bartholomie.

Le Club France shows French films nightly at the French Embassy, off Thanon Setthathirat. Check with the embassy for schedules – the club issues a monthly bulletin.

Cultural Clubs The *Library Club* is in the garden of the Australian Residence in a building called The Stockade, which is off Thanon Nehru near the Australian Embassy. It's open to members only on Tuesday and Thursday from 4 to 6.30 pm and also on Saturday from 9 am to noon. An annual membership is US$10 (plus a refundable US$10 deposit).

Le Club France features a French library with over 20,000 books and records. They offer French language lessons here and have a bar that's open from 5 to 8 pm.

Things to Buy

Just about anything made in Laos is available for purchase in Vientiane, including hill tribe crafts, jewellery, traditional fabrics and carvings. The main shopping areas are the Morning Market (including shops along Thanon Talaat Sao), west along Thanon Samsenthai (near the Hotel Ekalath Metropole) and on Thanon Pang Kham.

Getting There & Away

Air Vientiane is the only legal port of entry into Laos for international flights. See under the Getting There & Away section at the start of this chapter for details.

Bus The local authorities obviously anticipate bus travel by foreigners since they recently posted intercity and even inter-province fares in English. Sample fares include 700 kip to Vang Vieng (4½ hours) and 5000 kip to Savannakhet (12 hours).

The Thai-Lao Friendship Bridge, which roughly parallels the vehicle ferry route, is now finished. With the bridge in place, bus travel between Vientiane and various points in north-eastern Thailand should be permitted.

Boat Most visitors to Laos, no matter what kind of visa they hold (even if the visa reads 'By Air – Wattay Only'), are permitted to enter and leave via Tha Deua (approximately 22 km south-east of Vientiane). Check the Thai visa regulations if you plan to stay more than 15 days in Thailand.

Boats leave about every five minutes, from 8 am to 12.30 pm and from 1.30 to 4 pm daily (except on Sunday when they don't run at all). The boat ticket is 30B one way.

Car or motorbike taxis from Vientiane to Tha Deua charge a standard 100B for the trip. You can also ride a bus (it departs roughly every half-hour) from the Morning Market out to Tha Deua for 200 kip.

Getting Around

Central Vientiane is entirely accessible on foot. For trips into neighbouring districts, however, you'll need vehicular support.

To/From the Airport Taxis wait in front of the airport for passengers going into town. The going rate for foreigners seems to be 100B, which is overpriced considering it's only a 10 or 15-minute ride to the town centre. If you can catch a motorbike taxi (jumbo), the fare is only 25B or about US$1, but motorbike taxis aren't always available. There are no public buses direct from the airport, but if you walk 100 metres south of the terminal to Thanon Luang Phabang, you can catch a bus into town (turn left) for 200 kip.

To go out to the airport, you can catch a Phon Hong bus from the Morning Market.

Bus There is a city bus system but it's not oriented towards central Chanthabuli where most of the hotels, restaurants, sightseeing and shopping are located. Rather, it's for transport to outlying districts to the north, east and west of Chanthabuli. Fares for any distance within Vientiane Prefecture are low – about 200 kip for a 20-km ride.

Taxi Only a handful of cars operate in Vientiane, and these are stationed in front of the Lane Xang and New Apollo hotels, at the Morning Market (best rates) and at the airport during flight arrival times. For most short trips within town, a pedicab or motorbike is more economical, since cars are usually reserved for longer trips (to Wattay airport or to the Thailand ferry pier in Tha Deua) and for hourly or daily hire. A car and driver for the day costs from US$12 to US$20 if you bargain well.

Motorbike Taxi The standard size holds two or three passengers. The larger jumbos have two short benches in the back and can hold four, five or even six passengers if the passengers are not too large. Hire charges are about the same as for pedicabs but, of course, they're much speedier. A jumbo driver will be glad to take passengers on journeys as short as half a km or as far as 20 km. Although the common asking fare for Europeans seems to be 1000 kip, the standard local fare for a chartered jumbo should be 300 to 500 kip for distances of two km or less; bargaining is mandatory.

Share jumbos which run regular routes around town (eg Thanon Luang Phabang to Thanon Setthathirat, or Thanon Lan Xang to That Luang) cost 100 kip per person; no bargaining is necessary.

Motorbike Vientiane Motor, opposite the fountain on Thanon Setthathirat, rents 100cc motorbikes for US$8 to US$10 per day.

Pedicabs Called *cyclo* in French or *sãam-lâw* (three wheels) in Lao, samlors are one of the most common public conveyances in Vientiane. Charges are about 300 kip per km (but don't hire a samlor for any distance greater than two or three km).

Bicycle Several places rent bikes on a regular basis, including the bicycle shop across from the Immigration Office, near the Morning Market on the south-western corner of Thanon Lan Xang and Thanon Talat Sao. Kanchana Boutique opposite the Hotel Ekalath Metropole on Thanon That Dam also has a few bikes for rent. The going rate is 1400 kip per 24 hours.

AROUND VIENTIANE

Lao Pako

Lao Pako (☎ 4392), a rustic bamboo-thatch village on the Ngum River about 50 km north-east of Vientiane via Ban Somsamai, is a good spot to enjoy the Lao countryside without leaving Vientiane Province. Rates are US$9 in a dormitory and US$21 for private bungalows with bath. All rooms are screened and come with mosquito nets but no electricity. Prices may seem a little high but practically all supplies must be trucked in from Vientiane. Activities include swimming, boating, hiking, Lao-style buffet meals, weekend barbecues and monthly full-moon parties. To get to Lao Pako, take a Pakxap bus from the Morning Market terminal to the end of the line (around an hour, 200 kip), then a long-tail boat along the river to Ban Pako (around 25 minutes; 2000 kip for the whole boat, or as low as 400 kip per person shared).

Ang Nam Ngum (Nam Ngum Reservoir)

Located approximately 90 km north from Vientiane, Ang Nam Ngum is a huge artificial lake that was created by damming the Nam Ngum (Ngum River). A hydroelectric plant here generates most of the power used in the Vientiane Valley as well as the power sold to Thailand via high-power wires over the Mekong River.

The lake is dotted with picturesque islands and a cruise is well worth arranging (7000 kip per hour for boats holding up to 20 persons is the going rate). On the way to the lake you can stop in **Ban Ilai**, in the district of Muang Naxaithong, known for a market with basketry, pottery and other daily utensils. Several other villages can be visited along the way.

Places to Stay Ang Nam Ngum can be visited on a day trip from Vientiane. Nam Ngum Tour Co operates a *floating hotel* with large, clean rooms complete with private hot-water baths and air-con for 10,000 kip per night. The boat is fairly pleasant but rarely leaves the pier except when groups book the entire boat. The dock location is not particularly scenic because of the trashy lumber operations nearby.

Ask around about private accommodation. It's usually around US$2 a night.

Getting There & Away From the Morning Market, you can catch the 7 am bus all the way to Kheuan Nam Ngum (Nam Ngum Dam) for 400 kip. This trip takes three hours and proceeds along Route 13 through Ban Thalat. Taxis in Vientiane charge US$30 return to the lake. If you hire one, ask the driver to take the more scenic Route 10 through Ban Keun; the trip is about the same distance as the trip via Ban Thalat. Or make a circle route to see both areas.

Vang Vieng

Surrounded by scenic karst topography, this small town about 70 km north of Phon Hong (160 km north of Vientiane) via Route 13 nestles in a bend in the Song River. Caverns and tunnels in the limestone are named and play small roles in local mythology – all are said to be inhabited by spirits.

To find these caves, ask an angler or boatman along the river to show you the way – most will be glad to guide you to two or three caves for a few hundred kip. The section of the river where most of the caves are found is within walking distance (about two km south-west) of the town centre. Even if you don't plan on any cave exploration, a walk along the river can be rewarding.

Other than the Chinese-built cement factory just outside of town and a little-used airstrip between Route 13 and the town, Vang Vieng is well removed from modernisation.

Places to Stay Two guesthouses next to the bus terminal and market, *Phou Bane* and *Saynamsong*, offer basic but clean two-bed rooms for 2000 to 3000 kip per night with shared bath. Rumour says a newer, larger hotel will soon be erected.

Getting There & Away You can hire a car or ride a public bus (700 kip, 4½ hours) from Vientiane.

Northern Laos

LUANG PHABANG

The Luang Phabang area was the site of early Thai-Lao muangs that were established in the high river valleys along the Mekong River and its major tributaries, the Nam Khan, the Nam Ou and the Nam Seuang (Xeuang). The first Lao Kingdom, Lan Xang, was consolidated here in 1353 by the Khmer-supported conqueror Fa Ngum. Luang Phabang remained the capital of Lan Xang until King Phothisarat moved the seat of administration to Vientiane in 1545.

Even after the Lan Xang period, Luang Phabang was considered the main source of monarchic power. When Lan Xang broke up following the death of King Suliya Vongsa in 1694, one of Suliya's grandsons established an independent kingdom in Luang Phabang that competed with the other kingdoms in Vientiane and Champasak. From then on, the Luang Phabang monarchy was so weak that it was forced to pay tribute at various times to the Siamese and the Vietnamese, and finally, in the early 20th century, to the French when Laos became a French protectorate.

The French allowed Laos to retain the Luang Phabang monarchy, however, as did the fledgling independent governments that followed, and it wasn't until the Vietnamese-backed Pathet Lao took over in 1975 that the monarchy was finally dissolved.

Today, Luang Phabang is a sleepy town of 16,000 inhabitants with a handful of historic temples and old French mansions in a beautiful mountain setting.

Orientation

The town sits at the confluence of the Mekong River and the Nam Khan. A large hill called Phu Si (sometimes spelt Phousy) dominates the town skyline at the upper end of a peninsula formed by the junction of the two rivers. Most of the historic temples are between Phu Si and the Mekong. The whole town can easily be covered, on foot, in a day or two.

Information

Tours & Tour Operators So far two tour operators have established themselves in Luang Phabang, with a third on its way and others surely to follow since the town is Laos' primary tourist destination after Vientiane. For the most part these agencies service groups who arrive in Luang Phabang on prebooked tours from Vientiane. They are also happy to take walk-ins on excursions around the city or further afield to Kuang Si Falls, the Pak Ou caves and other spots in Luang Phabang province.

Luang Phabang Tourism (☎ 7224) has its office behind the Villa Sisouvannaphoum on Thanon Phothisalat, several blocks south-west of the Phousy Hotel. This agency offers the standard bus and boat tours and is very competent.

Lane Xang Travel (☎ 7225), on Thanon Kitsalat just south-east of the provincial hospital, specialises in trekking as well as the standard city/river tours. Lane Xang's tours tend to be a bit less expensive than those at Luang Phabang Tourism: the former, for example, charges US$50 for one person (or US$18 per person for groups of four or more) going to Pak Ou or Kuang Si (see Around Luang Phabang for details on these destinations) while Luang Phabang Tourism asks US$60 and US$25 respectively for similar trips.

Money It is best to bring enough kip from Vientiane for your stay in Luang Phabang. Lane Xang Bank, 65 Thanon Sisavangvong, will change Thai and US currency only – cash or travellers' cheques – for kip. The bank normally won't change in the other direction – kip for either baht or dollars – because of a claimed shortage of these currencies.

Post & Telecommunications The post office (opposite the Phousy Hotel on Thanon Phothisalat) is notoriously unreliable. Calls to Vientiane can be made from the Mittaphab Hotel. As for international calls, wait until you're back in Vientiane.

Royal Palace Museum

This is a good place to start a tour of Luang Phabang since the displays convey some sense of local history. The palace was originally constructed beside the Mekong River in 1904 as a residence for King Sisavang

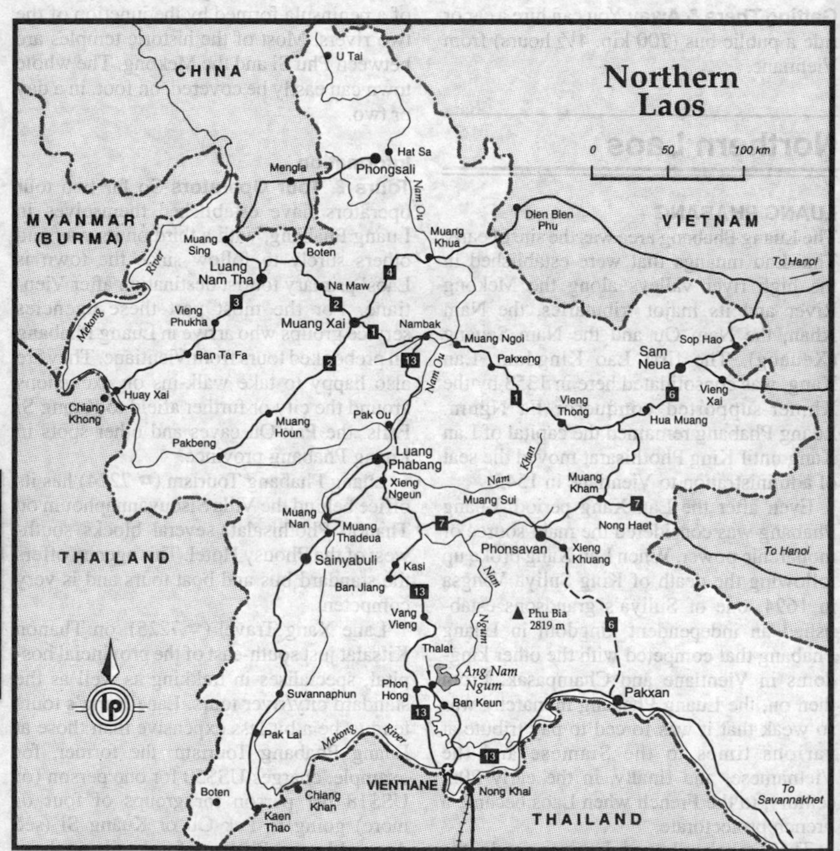

Vong and his family. When the king died in 1959 his son Savang Vattana inherited the throne, but shortly after the 1975 revolution he and his family were exiled to northern Laos (never to be heard from again) and the palace was converted into a museum.

Various royal religious objects are on display in the large entry hall, and as well there is rare Buddhist sculpture from India, Cambodia and Laos. One memorable exhibit is a Luang Phabang-style standing Buddha, which is sculpted from marble and in the Contemplating the Bodhi Tree pose.

The right front corner room of the palace, which opens to the outside, contains the museum's most prized art, including the Pha Bang. This gold standing Buddha is 83 cm tall and is said to weigh either 54 kg or 43 kg, depending on which source you believe.

Also in the same room are large elephant tusks engraved with Buddhas, Luang Phabang-style standing Buddhas, several Khmer-crafted sitting Buddhas, an excellent Lao frieze taken from a local temple and three *saew mâi khán* – beautiful embroidered silk screens with religious imagery that were crafted by the Queen.

In the King's former reception room are busts of the Lao monarchic succession and two large *Ramayana* screens. The murals on the walls depict scenes from traditional Lao life, painted in 1930 by French artist Alix de Fautereau. Each wall is meant to be viewed at a different time of day – according to the light that enters the windows on one side of the room. Other areas of interest include the former throne room and the royal family's residential quarters.

The Royal Palace Museum has posted hours of 8.30 am to 4.30 pm daily except Monday. The museum has been known to close as early as 2 pm on 'slow' days. There is a 200-kip admission charge, but several individual visitors have reported being charged an additional 1000 kip by museum staff.

Wat Xieng Thong

Near the northern tip of the peninsula formed by the Mekong and Nam Khan rivers is Luang Phabang's most magnificent temple, Wat Xieng Thong (Golden City Temple). It was built by King Setthathirat in 1560 and, until 1975, remained under royal patronage. Like the royal palace, Wat Xieng Thong was placed within easy reach of the Mekong.

The sim represents classic Luang Phabang temple architecture, with roofs that sweep low to the ground (the same style is also found in northern Thailand). The rear wall of the sim features an impressive 'tree of life' mosaic set on a red background. Inside, richly decorated wooden columns support a ceiling that's vested with *dhammachakkas* (dharma-wheels).

To one side of the sim, towards the east, are several small chapels and stupa containing Buddha images of the period. Near the compound's eastern gate stands the royal funeral chapel. Inside is an impressive 12-metre-high funeral chariot and various funeral urns for each member of the royal family. Gilt panels on the exterior of the chapel depict erotic episodes from the *Ramayana*.

Wat Wisunalat

This temple, also known as Wat Vixoun, is to the east of the town centre and it was originally constructed in 1513, making it the oldest continually operating temple in Luang Phabang. It was rebuilt in 1898 following a fire two years earlier. The original was made of wood, and in the brick and stucco restoration, the builders attempted to make the balustraded windows of the sim appear to be fashioned from lathed wood (an old south Indian and Khmer contrivance that is uncommon in Lao architecture). Also unique is the front roof which slopes sideways over the terrace.

Inside the high-ceilinged sim is a collection of wooden Calling for Rain Buddhas and 15th to 16th-century Luang Phabang *sima* (ordination stones). In front of the sim is That Pathum (Lotus Stupa) which was built in 1514. It's more commonly called That Mak Mo, or Watermelon Stupa, for its hemispherical shape.

Phu Si

The temples on the slopes of Phu Si are all of rather recent construction, but it's likely that other temples were previously located on this important hill site. None of the temples are that memorable but the top of the hill affords an excellent view of the town.

On the lower slopes of the hill are **Wat Paa Huak** and **Wat Pha Phutthabaat**. At the summit is **That Chomsi**, the starting point for a colourful Lao New Year procession held in mid-April. Behind this temple is a small cave shrine called **Wat Tham Phu Si** or Wat Thammothayaram. On a nearby crest is an old Russian anti-aircraft cannon that children use as a makeshift merry-go-round.

Other Temples

Close to the Phousy Hotel and the GPO is **Wat Mai Suwannaphumaham**, or New Temple, built in 1796 and at one time a residence of the Sangkharat or Supreme Patriarch of the Lao Sangha. The front veranda is remarkable for its decorated columns and for the sumptuous gold relief panels on the doors that recount the legend of Vessantara (Pha Wet), the Buddha's penultimate incarnation, as well as scenes from

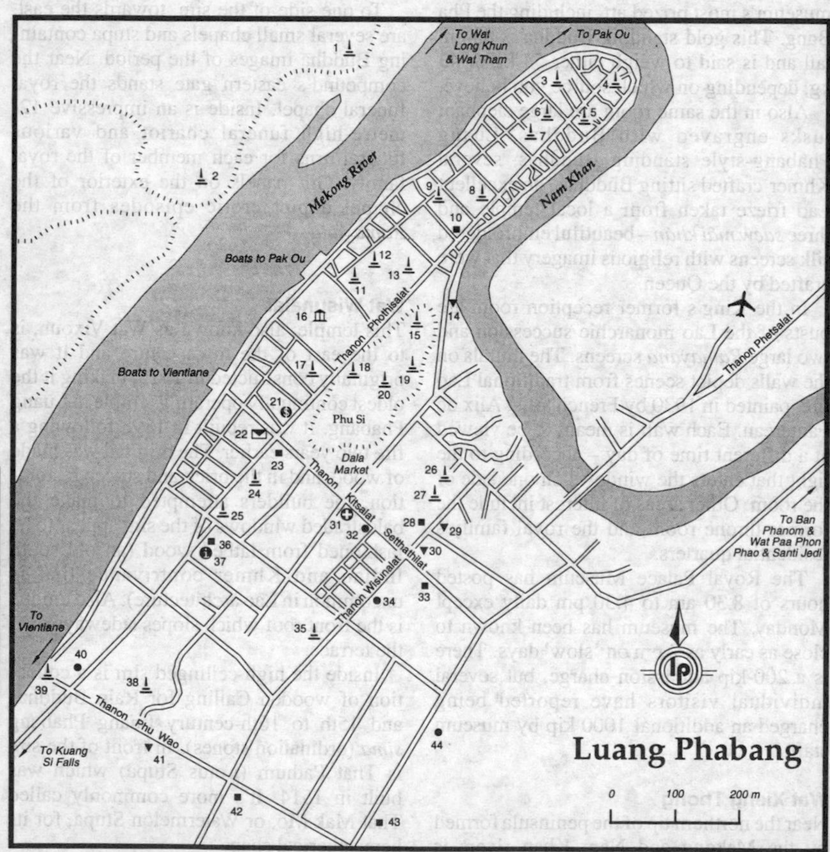

the *Ramayana* and local village life. The Pha Bang, which is usually housed in Luang Phabang's National Museum, is put on public display at Wat Mai Suwannaphumaham during the Lao New Year celebrations.

Across the Mekong River from central Luang Phabang are several temples that aren't remarkable except for the pleasant rural settings. **Wat Tham** is in a limestone cave almost directly across the river from Wat Xieng Thong. Many Buddha images from temples that have burned down or fallen into decay are kept here. Nearby Wat Tham are several other caves that are easily found and explored – bring along a torch (flashlight).

Wat Long Khun is a little to the east of Wat Tham and features a nicely decorated portico of 1937 vintage, plus older sections from the 18th century. When the coronation of a Luang Phabang king was pending, it was customary for him to spend three days in retreat at Wat Long Khun before ascending the throne.

At the top of a hill above the previous two wats is peaceful **Wat Chom Phet**, where one can obtain an undisturbed view of the river.

A few km to the south-east of town is the recently constructed **Santi Jedi**, or Peace Pagoda. This large yellow stupa contains three levels inside plus an outside terrace near the top with a view of the surrounding plains. The interior walls are painted with all manner of Buddhist stories and moral admonitions.

Behind the That Luang market in town is a modern Vietnamese-Lao Buddhist temple, **Wat Pha Baat Tai**.

Markets

The main fresh produce market, **Talaat That Luang**, is at the intersection of Thanon Phothisalat and Thanon Phu Wao near the river, behind Wat That Luang. A big market for dry goods is held daily off Thanon Kitsalat Setthathilat.

Places to Stay

The *Viengkeo Hotel* on Thanon Kitsalat Setthathilat is a funky two-storey house that has seven plain two and three-bed rooms with shared bath for 4200 kip (3000 kip for Lao citizens) per room. An upstairs veranda sitting area overlooks the street.

Around the corner near Wat Wisunalat is the *Rama Hotel* (☎ 7105), where basic doubles with fan and private cold-water bath cost 7000 kip a night. The restaurant downstairs becomes a disco at night – for maximum quiet be sure to request a room at the back and top of the hotel.

For just a bit more you could stay at the new and immaculate guesthouse-style *Muangsua Hotel* (☎ 7056) on Thanon Phu Wao. The Muangsua has 17 modern, two-

PLACES TO STAY

- 10 Villa de la Princesse
- 23 Phousy Hotel
- 28 Rama Hotel
- 33 Viengkeo Hotel
- 36 Villa Sisouvannaphoum
- 42 Muangsua Hotel
- 43 Phu Vao Hotel

PLACES TO EAT

- 14 Khem Karn Food Garden
- 29 Visoun Restaurant
- 30 Young Koun Restaurant
- 41 Maly Restaurant

OTHER

- 1 Wat Chom Phet
- 2 Wat Xieng Maen
- 3 Wat Xieng Thong
- 4 Wat Pakkhan
- 5 Wat Khili
- 6 Wat Si Bun Heuang
- 7 Wat Si Muang Khun
- 8 Wat Saen
- 9 Wat Nong Sikhunmuang
- 11 Wat Chum Thong
- 12 Wat Xieng Muan
- 13 Wat Paa Phai
- 15 Wat Pha Phutthabaat
- 16 Royal Palace Museum
- 17 Wat Mai Suwannaphumaham
- 18 Wat Paa Huak
- 19 Wat Tham Phu Si
- 20 That Chomsi
- 21 Lane Xang Bank
- 22 GPO
- 24 Wat Ho Siang
- 25 Wat That
- 26 Wat Aham
- 27 Wat Wisunalat
- 31 Provincial Hospital
- 32 Lane Xang Travel
- 34 Lao Aviation
- 35 Wat Manolom
- 37 Luang Phabang Tourism
- 38 Wat That Luang
- 39 Wat Pha Baat Tai
- 40 That Luang Market
- 44 New Market

bed rooms with air-con and hot-water baths for US$12, US$15 and US$20 (depending on the room size).

Phousy Hotel is well located at the intersection of Thanon Kitsalat Setthathilat and Thanon Phothisalat (at the site of the former French Commissariat). Rooms with fan and hot-water bath are US$15 a single/double, with air-con it's US$20 a single/double, or it's US$25 for a suite.

Places to Eat

There are numerous small restaurants and cafes along Thanon Phothisarat near the Phousy Hotel, some of which specialise in làap. The *Young Koun Restaurant*, down the street from Wat Wisunalat, has Lao and Chinese food at fairly reasonable prices. Two or three doors up from the Young Koun – and more 'in' these days with visiting development players – is the equally good *Visoun Restaurant*, which serves mostly Chinese food. Both restaurants are open from early in the morning till late at night and have fairly extensive bilingual menus.

Along the Mekong River are several small thatched-roof, open-air restaurants with passable Lao food. Khào pùn (thin wheat noodles topped with curry) is available from early morning till early afternoon at the back of the That Luang Market.

Getting There & Away

Air Lao Aviation has daily flights from Vientiane to Luang Phabang. The flight takes only 40 minutes and the fare is US$35 one way. The Lao Aviation office is on Thanon Wisunalat, around the corner from the Viengkeo Hotel.

Bus & Truck Road travel to/from Luang Phabang has improved a bit during the last few years. The town can be reached via Route 13 from Vientiane (420 km). As soon as the Swedes finish grading and paving the road (estimated end of 1994), foreigners will be permitted to travel this route by bus.

Boat Several times a week river ferries leave Vientiane's Kao Liaw jetty on the Mekong River for the 430-km river trip to Luang Phabang. The duration of the voyage depends on river height but is typically three nights up and two nights down. The fare is 9000 kip per person and on many boats you must bring your own food.

It's also possible to travel by boat along the Mekong River west to Pakbeng (160 km) on the Sainyabuli/Udomxai border (for road trips north to Muang Xai) or all the way to Huay Xai (300 km) in Bokeo Province.

By slow river ferry the trip to Huay Xai takes two days with an overnight in Pakbeng. The passenger fare is 7000 kip one way to Huay Xai and 3500 kip as far as Pakbeng.

Faster and smaller speedboats reach Pakbeng in three hours and get to Huay Xai in six or seven hours. Speedboat charters cost 1500 to 1800 baht (kip or US dollars are also acceptable, but the price is always quoted in baht) to Pakbeng and twice that to Huay Xai, and can carry up to six passengers.

AROUND LUANG PHABANG

Pak Ou Caves

About 25 km by boat from Luang Phabang along the Mekong River, at the mouth of the Nam Ou, are the famous Pak Ou Caves (Pak Ou means Mouth of the Ou). The two caves in the lower part of a limestone cliff are crammed with a variety of Buddha images, most of them classic Luang Phabang standing Buddhas.

On the way to Pak Ou, you can have the boatman stop at small villages on the banks of the Mekong, including one that specialises in the production of *lào láo*, distilled rice liquor.

Getting There & Away You can hire boats from the pier behind the Royal Palace Museum. A long-tail boat should cost about US$25 for the day, including petrol. The trip takes one to 1½ hours one way, depending on the speed of the boat. If you stop at villages along the way, it will naturally take longer.

Kuang Si Falls

This beautiful spot 29 km south of town features a wide, multi-tiered waterfall tumbling over limestone formations into a series of cool, turquoise-green pools. The lower level of the falls has been turned into a public park with shelters and picnic tables. Vendors sell drinks and snacks. A trail ascends through the forest along the left side of the falls to a second tier which is more private (most visitors stay below) and has a pool large enough for swimming and splashing around.

Getting There & Away Guided tours to the falls booked through a local agency cost US$50 to US$60 and include transport and lunch at the falls. Freelance guides in Luang Phabang offer trips by car or motorcycle for US$18 to US$20.

XIENG KHUANG PROVINCE

Along with Hua Phan, Xieng Khuang is one of the northern provinces that was devastated by the war. Virtually every town and village in the province was bombed between 1964 and 1973. Flying into the province, one is struck at first by the awesome beauty of high green mountains, rugged karst formations and verdant valleys. But as the plane begins to descend, you notice how much of the province is pockmarked with bomb craters in which little or no vegetation grows.

The province's population of 170,000 is comprised of lowland Lao, Thai Dam, Hmong and Phuan. The original capital city, Xieng Khuang, was almost totally bombed out, so the capital was moved to nearby Phonsavan (often spelt Phonsavanh) after the 1975 change of government. Not far from Phonsavan is the mysterious Plain of Jars (Thong Hai Hin).

The moderate altitude in central Xieng Khuang, including Phonsavan and the Plain of Jars, means an excellent year-round climate – not too hot in the hot season, not too cold in the cool season and not overly wet in the rainy season.

Phonsavan

There's not much to the new provincial capital – an airfield, a semipaved main street lined with tin-roofed shops, a market and a few government buildings. Local villagers bring war junk, found in their fields or in the forests, to scrap metal warehouses in town. The warehouses buy the scrap (eg bomb shards, parts of Chinese, Russian and American planes), then sell it to larger warehouses in Vientiane, who in turn sell it to the Thais.

Take care when walking in the fields around Phonsavan, as undetonated live bombs are not uncommon. The locals use bomb casings as pillars for new structures and as fenceposts. Muddy areas are sometimes dotted with pineapple bombs or bomblets *(bombi* in Lao), fist-sized explosives that are left over from cluster bombs dropped in the 1970s.

Places to Stay & Eat *Hay Hin Hotel* on the main street near the market has a few basic two-bed rooms with mossie nets and shared cold-water bath for 3000 kip per night. *Muong Phuan Hotel* nearby is a little nicer for 5000 kip a single/double.

The Vietnamese-operated *Mittaphap Hotel*, a bit out from the centre on Route 4, is a larger two-storey affair with concrete rooms (mosquito nets, shared cold-water bath) for 3000/5000 kip a single/double. Guide service is available here. *Phou Phiang Xieng Khuang Hotel*, just outside of town on Route 7, is similar.

About three km from the town centre towards the Plain of Jars is *Hotel Plaine de Jarres*, a two-storey house with four bedrooms, a sitting room and two cold-water showers for 4000/6000 kip a single/double.

Along the road that leads from the airfield are several noodle shops. At night, one of the noodle shops has live music. You can also buy food, including fresh produce, in the market in the centre of town.

Getting There & Away Until late 1990, the only way to get to Xieng Khuang from Vientiane was by Lao Aviation helicopter – quite an experience. A slightly upgraded airfield now handles small planes as well. Hour-long flights are scheduled to leave Vientiane daily (the hour of departure varies). The fare is US$28 one way.

Plain of Jars

A few km south-east of Phonsavan is an area of rolling fields where huge jars of unknown origin are scattered about. The jars weigh an average of 600 kg to one tonne each, though the biggest of them weigh as much as six tonnes. They appear to have been fashioned from solid stone, but there is disagreement on this point.

Various theories (none proved conclusively as yet) have been advanced as to the functions of the stone jars: they were used as sarcophagi, as wine fermenters or for rice storage.

The nearby limestone cave, which has smokeholes in the top, is said to have been a kiln for firing the jars, assuming they're not made of solid stone. Many of the smaller jars have been taken away by collectors, but there are still several hundred or so on the plain.

Tham Piu

In this cave, near the former village of Ban Nameun, nearly 400 villagers, many of them women and children, were killed by a single rocket (most likely from a Nomad T-28 fighter plane manned by a Royal Lao Air Force pilot) in 1969. The cave itself is not much to see, just a large cave in the side of a limestone cliff. It's the journey to Tham Piu that is the real attraction, since it passes several Hmong and Thai Dam villages along the way and involves a bit of hiking in the forest.

The cave is a few km beyond the small town of Muang Kham, which is 33 km east of Phonsavan on Route 7. Also in this area is a hot mineral spring *(baw nâam hâwn)* that feeds into a stream a few hundred metres off the road. You can sit in the stream right where the hot water combines with the cool stream water and 'adjust' the temperature by moving around.

Further east along the same road, 60 km from Phonsavan, is the market town of Nong Haet, only about 25 km short of the Vietnam border.

Getting There & Away To get to Tham Piu, you'd have to take a Nong Haet bus from Phonsavan and ask to be let out at the turn-off for Tham Piu. From the turn-off, start walking towards the limestone cliff north of the road until you're within a km of the cliff. At this point you have to plunge into the woods and make your way along a honeycomb of trails to the bottom of the cliff and then mount a steep, narrow trail that leads up to the mouth of the cave.

It is best to ask for directions from villagers along the way or you're liable to get lost. Better yet, find someone in Phonsavan who knows the way and invite them along for an afternoon hike. You might be able to hire a jeep and driver in town for around US$20 a day.

Old Xieng Khuang (Muang Khun)

Xieng Khuang's ancient capital was so ravaged in the 19th century by Chinese and Vietnamese invaders, then so heavily bombarded during the Indochinese war, that it was almost completely abandoned by 1975. Twenty years after war's end the old capital is once again inhabited, though the original French colonial architecture has been replaced by a long row of plain wooden buildings, with slanted metal roofs, on either side of the dirt road from Phonsavan. Officially the town has been renamed Muang Khun. Many of the local residents are Phuan, Thai Dam or Thai Neua.

Several Buddhist temples built between the 16th and 19th centuries lie in unrestored ruins.

Places to Stay & Eat The town has one funky wooden *hotel* with rooms for 1500 kip. Near the market in the centre of town are a couple of noodle shops. *Raan Khai Foe* (an English sign reads 'Restaurant') opposite the market is the best choice for lunch.

Getting There & Away Four buses a day ply the bumpy, torturous 36-km route between Phonsavan and Xieng Khuang for 450 kip per person. As for anywhere else in the province, you'll most likely need a guide and car to arrange the proper permit to visit; the going rate for permit, guide and car is around

US$60. If permits become unnecessary, you might be able to hire a car and driver for around US$30 for the round trip.

Southern Laos

Only two southern provinces, Savannakhet and Champasak, are regularly travelled by tourists. The Mekong River Valley, including the towns of Savannakhet (also known as Muang Khanthabuli), Salavan and Pakse, is mostly inhabited by lowland Lao. The central highlands are populated by a mixture of Phu Thai, Saek (Sek) and Lao peoples.

SAVANNAKHET PROVINCE

Savannakhet is the country's most populous province (312,000) and is a very active trade junction between Thailand and Vietnam. The rural villages of Savannakhet are among the most typically Lao, especially those near the Vietnam border.

Savannakhet

The provincial capital is Savannakhet, a busy town of 45,000 just across the Mekong River

from Mukdahan, Thailand. Like Vientiane and Luang Phabang, Savannakhet has a number of French colonial and Franco-Chinese buildings, most of which are found in the small downtown business district.

Information The Savannakhet Tourism Co (☎ 7661), housed in the Savanbanhao Hotel on Thanon Saenna, has information on local attractions and can arrange tours to Xepon, the Ho Chi Minh Trail and other spots outside the city.

Places to Stay & Eat Savannakhet's cheaper hotels are clustered in the older part of town towards the ferry piers. The run-down *Santyphab Hotel* on Thanon Tha Dan, two blocks east of the main ferry pier, has basic rooms for 3000 kip with fan or 5000 kip air-con, both with shared bath. Reportedly the Santyphab will be refurbished and upgraded by 1996.

A better choice in this price range is the fairly clean and friendly *Sensabay Hotel*, on a side street opposite the Santyphab. Rooms here cost 3000 to 4000 kip with fan and shared bath or 4000 to 5000 kip with air-con and private bath.

In the downtown area are many small Chinese-Vietnamese restaurants, none of them particularly outstanding.

Getting There & Away Lao Aviation flies Chinese Y-7 turboprops to Savannakhet daily at 7 am. Flights take an hour one way and cost US$54.

One bus per day leaves Vientiane's bus terminal for the 12-hour ride to Savannakhet. The fare is about 5000 kip. From Pakse the bus costs 3000 kip and takes six hours.

A large river ferry leaves Vientiane's south jetty (Tha Heua Lak Si) every few days at 5 am, arriving at 11 am the next day. The fare is 5000 kip per person; food is not always available on board so bring your own.

Catch a ferry to get to Mukdahan in Thailand. They cross the Mekong River between Savannakhet and Mukdahan frequently between 8.30 am and 5 pm weekdays, and 8.30 am to 12.30 pm Saturday. The cost is 30 baht each way.

It's now legal for foreigners to enter and exit the country via Savannakhet. To enter you must have a visa that's endorsed for Savannakhet entry; your sponsoring agency should be able to arrange this.

Getting Around Samlor fares are comparable with those in Vientiane, around 200 kip per km.

That Ing Hang

Thought to have been built in the mid-16th century (about the same time as Vientiane's Pha That Luang and north-eastern Thailand's That Phanom), this well-proportioned, nine-metre thâat is the holiest religious edifice in southern Laos. The monument features three terraced bases topped by a traditional Lao stupa and a gold umbrella weighing 40 *baht* (450 grams). A hollow chamber in the lower section contains an undistinguished collection of Buddha images (by religious custom, women are not permitted to enter the chamber).

On the full moon of February or March is the big That Ing Hang Festival featuring processions and fireworks.

Getting There & Away That Ing Hang is 12 km north of Savannakhet via Route 13, then three km east on a dirt road. Any north-bound bus passes this turn-off.

Xepon & the Ho Chi Minh Trail

The infamous Ho Chi Minh Trail – actually a complex network of dirt paths and gravel roads – runs parallel to the Lao-Vietnamese border beginning at a point directly east from Savannakhet.

Though mostly associated with the 1963-74 Indochinese War, the road network was originally used by the Viet Minh against the French in the 1950s as an infiltration route to the south. The Trail's heaviest use occurred between 1966 and 1971 when over 600,000 NVA troops – along with 100 tonnes of provisions and a half-million tonnes of trucks, tanks, weapons and ordnance –

passed along the route. At any one time around 25,000 NVA troops guarded the Trail, which was honeycombed with underground barracks, fuel and motor repair depots and anti-aircraft emplacements.

The nearest town to the Ho Chi Minh Trail is Xepon (pop 5000), approximately 170 km east of Savannakhet via Route 9. Xepon was destroyed during the war and is now just another of the many makeshift wooden towns that mark the long-term bombing legacy of eastern Laos. From here the outer edges of the Ho Chi Minh Trail are another 15 to 20 km.

A short distance north or south along the Trail, parts of downed helicopters and fighter planes, along with tonnes of other war junk, can be seen. Because of the area's remoteness from scrap metal markets, much of the debris lies untouched. Eastern Savannakhet Province (along with Salavan, Sekong and Attapeu further south) is also one of the primary areas where joint Lao-American teams – under the direction of a US colonel based in Vientiane – are searching for the remains of American MIAs.

Places to Stay Rustic accommodation is available in Xepon although visitors who

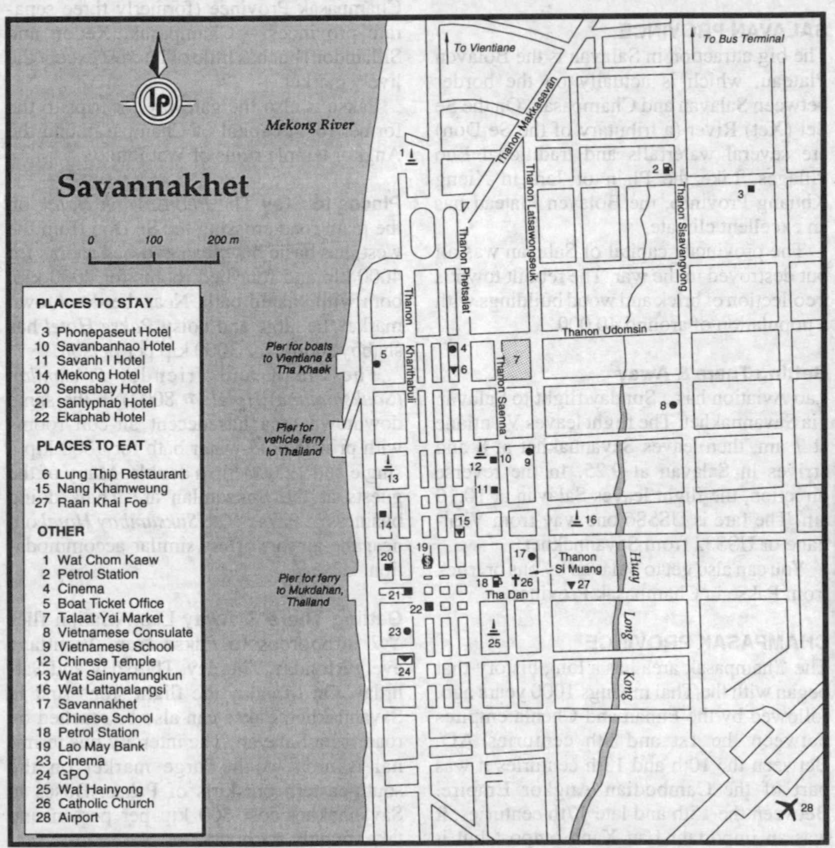

LAOS

travel out to the Ho Chi Minh Trail typically make it an out-and-back trip from Savannakhet.

Getting There & Away Travel to Xepon and the Ho Chi Minh Trail requires a permit valid for travel outside the Savannakhet municipality. Savannakhet Tourism at the Savanbanhao Hotel can arrange permits plus car and driver for up to five passengers for around US$200. If permits become unnecessary, the cost of a car and driver will probably drop to around US$120. Road travel can be very difficult during the rainy season, June to October.

SALAVAN PROVINCE

The big attraction in Salavan is the Bolaven Plateau, which is actually on the border between Salavan and Champasak. On the Se Set (Xet) River (a tributary of the Se Don) are several waterfalls and traditional Lao villages. Like the Plain of Jars in Xieng Khuang Province, the Bolaven Plateau has an excellent climate.

The provincial capital of Salavan was all but destroyed in the war. The rebuilt town is a collection of brick and wood buildings with a population of around 40,000.

Getting There & Away

Lao Aviation has a Sunday flight to Salavan via Savannakhet. The flight leaves Vientiane at 7 am, then leaves Savannakhet at 8 and arrives in Salavan at 9.25. In the reverse direction, the flight leaves Salavan at 10.10 am. The fare is US$86 one way from Vientiane or US$32 from Savannakhet.

You can also get to Salavan by bus or truck from Pakse in Champasak Province.

CHAMPASAK PROVINCE

The Champasak area has a long history that began with the Thai muangs 1000 years ago, followed by the Funan and Chenla empires between the 1st and 9th centuries AD. Between the 10th and 13th centuries it was part of the Cambodian Angkor Empire. Between the 15th and late 17th centuries, it was an important Lan Xang outpost but it later became an independent Lao Kingdom when the Lan Xang Empire disintegrated at the beginning of the 18th century.

Champasak Province has a population of around 160,000 that includes lowland Lao, Khmer, Phu Thai and various Mon-Khmer groups. The province is well known for *matmii*, silks and cottons that are hand-woven of tie-dyed threads.

Pakse

Pakse is a relatively new town at the confluence of the Mekong and the Se Don that was founded in 1905 by the French as an administrative outpost. It is now the capital of Champasak Province (formerly three separate provinces – Champasak, Xedon and Sithandon) but has little of interest except the lively market.

Pakse is also the gateway for trips to the former royal capital of Champasak and the Angkor temple ruins of Wat Phu.

Places to Stay The *Phonsavanh Hotel*, on the main road crossing the Se Don from the west, has basic but clean two-bed rooms for 4000 kip and four-bed rooms for 8000 kip, both with shared bath. Near the downtown market the large and noisy *Pakse Hotel* has shabby rooms for 3000 kip per person.

The clean and friendly *Suksamlan (Souksamlane) Hotel* (☎ 8002) in the same downtown area has decent air-con rooms with private cold-water bath for 9000 kip a single and 12,000 kip a double. Many of the guests at the Suksamlan are Thais doing business in Pakse. The *Suksambay Hotel* out near the airport offers similar accommodation.

Getting There & Away Lao Aviation flies Y-7 turboprops to Pakse from Vientiane every Monday, Tuesday, Thursday and Saturday. On Monday the flight stops first in Savannakhet. Pakse can also be reached by road from Salavan. The intercity bus terminal is next to the large market on the south-eastern outskirts of Pakse. Buses to Savannakhet cost 300 kip per person and take roughly six hours.

To/From Chong Mek, Thailand Ferries run back and forth between the pier at the junction of the Don and Mekong Rivers and Ban Muang Kao on the west bank of the Mekong throughout the day. The regular ferry costs 100 kip per person or you can charter a boat across for 2000 kip.

To get from Ban Muang Kao to the Lao-Thai border you can queue up for a share taxi that carries six passengers for 1000 kip each or hire a whole taxi for 6000 kip (or 200 baht). The 40-km journey to the Lao side of the border takes about 45 minutes. At the border you simply check out through Lao immigration, walk across the line and check in on the Thai side. Passenger trucks on the other side are waiting to take passengers onward to Ubon Ratchathani via Phibun Mangsahan.

To enter Laos from the Thai side you must be carrying a Lao visa endorsed for entry at Pakse.

Bolaven Plateau

Centred in north-eastern Champasak province, the fertile Bolaven Plateau (sometimes spelt Bolovens and known in Lao as Phu Phieng Bolaven) wasn't farmed intensively until the French planted coffee, rubber and bananas here in the early 20th century. Today the Lao have revived the cultivation of coffee beans throughout the region; soft world coffee prices have, however, kept production low and small-scale. Other local agricultural products include fruits, cardamom and rattan.

The plateau is a centre for several Mon-Khmer ethnic groups, including the Alak, Suay, Katu and Bru. The Alak arrange their palm-and-thatch houses in a circle and are well known in Laos for a water buffalo sacrifice which they perform yearly (usually on a full moon in March). The number of buffalos sacrificed – typically one to four animals – depends on availability and the bounty of the previous year's agricultural harvest. During the ceremony, the men of the village don wooden masks, hoist spears and dance around the buffalos in the centre of the circle formed by their houses.

Places to Stay *Tadlo Resort*, next to the Tat Lo waterfall on the Bolaven Plateau, is a modest complex of thatched bungalows of which several are owned by the government while a few are privately owned and used by SODETOUR (☎ 8056), a tour operator in Pakse. Simple 3rd-class rooms with shared cold-water bath cost 5000 kip, while 2nd-class rooms provide a private cold-water bath for 10,000 kip.

Getting There & Away Infrequent passenger trucks between Pakse and Paksong (passing the entrance to Tadlo Resort) cost 1000 kip per person and take about three hours. There are also one or two trucks a day between Salavan and Paksong; these take up to five hours and cost 1500 kip.

Champasak

This small town of less than 20,000 on the west bank of the Mekong is a ghost of its former colonial self. An ambitious fountain circle in the middle of the red-dirt main street looks almost absurd, while either side of the street is lined with French colonial homes in various states of disrepair, along with a couple of noodle shops and a morning market.

The town's single hotel is in such a state of disrepair that travellers are urged to stay in nearby Pakse rather than in Champasak.

Getting There & Away Ferries from Ban Muang on the eastern side of the Mekong River to Ban Phaphin on the western side (five km north of Champasak) run regularly throughout daylight hours for 100 kip per person.

Wat Phu

This Angkor-period (10th to 13th centuries) Khmer temple site is on the lower slopes of Phu Pasak, about eight km south-west of the town of Champasak.

The site is divided into lower and upper parts joined by a stairway. The lower part consists of two ruined palace buildings at the edge of a pond used for ritual ablutions. The upper section is the temple sanctuary itself, which once enclosed a large Shiva phallus. Some time later it was converted into a Buddhist temple but the original Hindu sculpture remains in the lintels, which feature various forms of Vishnu and Shiva as well as Kala, the Hindu god of time and death. The *naga* (dragon) stairway leading to the sanctuary is lined with *dok jampa* (plumeria) which is the Lao national tree. The upper platform affords a good view of the valley below.

Festivals Near Wat Phu is a large crocodile stone that may have been the site of the purported Chenla sacrifices. Each year, in June, the locals perform a ritual water buffalo sacrifice to the ruling earth spirit for Champasak, Chao Tengkham. The blood of the buffalo is offered to a local shaman who serves as a trance medium for the appearance of Chao Tengkham.

Another important local festival is Bun Wat Phu, when pilgrims from throughout southern Laos come to worship at Wat Phu in its Buddhist incarnation. The festival lasts three days and features Thai boxing matches, cockfights, music and dancing. It's held as part of Magha Puja (Makkha Bu-saa) at the full moon in February.

Getting There & Away Wat Phu is 46 km south from Pakse but only eight km from Champasak. When you're hiring a taxi from Champasak, ask for Múang Kao (Old City). Champasak can be reached by road or ferry boat (along the Mekong River) from Pakse; the cost round-trip cost is 5000 to 6000 kip.

Si Phan Don (Four Thousand Islands)
During the rainy season this very scenic 50-km section of the Mekong River just north of the Cambodian border reaches a breadth of 14 km, the river's widest girth along its entire 4350-km journey from the Tibetan Plateau to the South China Sea. During the dry months between monsoons the river recedes to reveal hundreds (or thousands if you count every sandbar) of river islands and islets. The largest of the permanent islands are inhabited year round and offer fascinating glimpses of tranquil river-oriented village life.

The French left behind a defunct short-line railway (the only railway ever built in Laos), a couple of river piers and a few colonial villas on the islands of Don Khong, Don Det and Don Khon. Other attractions include some impressive rapids and waterfalls where the Mekong riverbed suddenly drops in elevation at the Cambodian border, and a rare species of freshwater dolphin.

Places to Stay & Eat The *Auberge Sala Done Khong* in Muang Khong on Don Khong, the largest island, offers simple, spacious, clean rooms in an old teak house. Costs are 9000 kip per night for a standard two-bed room with shared bath, 12,000 kip for a standard three-bed room and 18,000 kip for a 1st-class double with air-con and private bath.

Near the Muang Khong pier are a couple of adequate *hâan kịn dẹum* (eat-drink shops). The dining room at the Sala Done Khong is good.

Getting There & Away From Pakse there are one or two buses per day to Hat Xai Khun, directly opposite Muang Khong on the east mainland shore of the Mekong River. The 1000-kip fare includes the short vehicle ferry ride across to Muang Khong.

There is some talk that an old airstrip on Don Khong may be renovated and used by charter tourist flights from Vientiane.

Macau

Sixty km west of Hong Kong, on the other side of the Pearl River's mouth, is the oldest European settlement in the East – the tiny Portuguese territory of Macau. The lure of Macau's casino gaming tables has been so actively promoted that its other attractions are almost forgotten.

Macau is a fascinating blend – steeped in history and Old World elegance, but prosperous and changing fast. It has a very different look and feel from Hong Kong, and is well worth the one-hour boat trip to get there. Better yet, spend at least one night – this is a place to enjoy and relax.

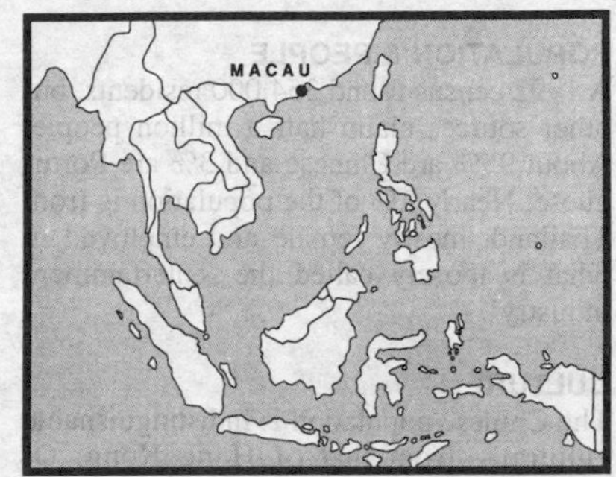

Facts about the Country

HISTORY

Portuguese galleons visited Macau in the early 1500s, and in 1557, as a reward for clearing out a few pirates, China ceded the tiny enclave to the Portuguese.

For centuries, it was the principal meeting point for trade with China. In the 19th century, European and American traders could operate in Canton, now called Guangzhou (just up the Pearl River), only during the trading season. They would then retreat to Macau during the off season.

When the Opium Wars erupted between the Chinese and the British, the Portuguese stood diplomatically to one side and Macau soon found itself the poor relation of the more dynamic Hong Kong.

Macau's current prosperity is given a big boost from the Chinese gambling urge which sends hordes of Hong Kongers shuttling off to the casinos every weekend. Not mentioned in the glossy tourist brochures is the thriving massage, sauna and brothel business. In recent years, Macau's economy has been helped by the high wages and rents in Hong Kong, which have caused a migration of light manufacturing industries to Macau.

Macau is slated to be handed back to China in 1999, two years after Hong Kong. It's said the Portuguese wanted to last out 500 years, which would have taken them well into the next century. They finally settled for any date which put them one up on Hong Kong.

GEOGRAPHY

Macau's 16 sq km consists of the city itself, which is part of the Chinese mainland, and the islands of Taipa and Coloane, which are joined together by a causeway and linked to Macau city by two bridges.

CLIMATE

The weather is almost identical to that of Hong Kong, with short, occasionally chilly winters, and long, hot and humid summers. November is usually the best month, with mild temperatures and dry weather. Typhoons are most common from June to October.

GOVERNMENT

Officially, Macau is not considered a colony. Instead, the Portuguese government regards Macau as a piece of Chinese territory under Portuguese administration. The colony-cum-Chinese territory has a governor who is appointed by Portugal's president, but in theory the main governing body is the 23-

member Legislative Assembly of which eight members are elected by direct vote while the remainder are appointed by the Governor and 'economic interest groups'.

POPULATION & PEOPLE

A 1992 census found 354,000 residents, but other sources claim half a million people. About 95% are Chinese and 3% are Portuguese. Nearly 1% of the population is from Thailand, mostly female and employed in what is loosely called the 'entertainment industry'.

CULTURE

The Chinese population is indistinguishable culturally from that of Hong Kong. Of course, the Portuguese minority has a vastly different culture, which they have kept largely intact. Although mixed marriages are not uncommon in Macau, there has been little cultural assimilation between the two ethnic groups – most Portuguese cannot speak Chinese and vice versa.

RELIGION

For the Chinese majority, Buddhism and Taoism are the dominant religions, but Portuguese influence has definitely had an impact and Catholicism is very strong in Macau. Many Chinese have been converted and you are likely to see Chinese nuns.

LANGUAGE

Portuguese may be the official language but Cantonese is the real one. However, you will have little trouble communicating in English, especially in hotels. Mandarin Chinese *(putonghua)* is spoken by about half the population. See the Hong Kong chapter for a few Cantonese phrases.

Facts for the Visitor

VISAS & EMBASSIES

For most visitors, all that's needed to enter Macau is a passport. Everyone gets a 20-day stay on arrival. Visas are not required for the following nationalities: Australia, Austria, Belgium, Brazil, Canada, Denmark, Finland, France, Germany, Greece, Hong Kong, India, Ireland, Italy, Japan, Luxembourg, Malaysia, Netherlands, New Zealand, Norway, Philippines, Singapore, South Africa, South Korea, Spain, Sweden, Switzerland, Thailand, UK and USA.

All other nationalities must have a visa, which can be obtained on arrival in Macau. Visas cost M$175 for individuals, M$350 for married couples and families, and M$88 per person in a bona fide tour group (usually 10 persons minimum). People holding passports from countries which do not have diplomatic relations with Portugal must obtain visas from an overseas Portuguese Consulate before entering Macau. An exception is made for Taiwanese, who can get visas on arrival despite their lack of diplomatic relations. The Portuguese Consulate (☎ 5225488) in Hong Kong is on the 10th floor, Tower Two, Exchange Square, Central.

MONEY

Currency

The pataca (M$) is divided into 100 avos and is worth about 4% less than the HK$. HK$ are accepted everywhere, which is just as well because there's nowhere to change currency on arrival. So make sure you have some HK$ or you'll have difficulty getting from the Jetfoil Pier into town!

Although Hong Kong coins are acceptable in Macau, you'll need pataca coins to make calls at public telephones. Get rid of your patacas before departing Macau – they are hard to dispose of in Hong Kong, though you can change them at the Hang Seng Bank.

Exchange Rates

Australia	A$1	=	M$7.64
Canada	C$1	=	M$7.87
New Zealand	NZ$1	=	M$6.29
Britain	UK£1	=	M$16.04
USA	US$1	=	M$10.60
Japan	¥100	=	M$10.35
Germany	DM1	=	M$6.50
France	FF1	=	M$1.90

Costs
As long as you don't go crazy at the roulette wheel or slot machines, Macau is cheaper than Hong Kong. To help keep costs down, avoid visiting on weekends.

Tipping
Classy hotels and restaurants automatically hit you with a 10% service charge, a mandatory tip. Just how much of this money actually goes to the employees is a matter for speculation.

You can follow your own conscience, but tipping is not customary among the Chinese. Of course, porters at expensive hotels have become accustomed to hand-outs from well-heeled tourists.

Bargaining
Most stores have fixed prices, but if you buy clothing, trinkets and other tourist junk from the street markets, there is some scope for bargaining. On the other hand, if you buy from the pawnshops, bargain ruthlessly. Pawnbrokers are more than happy to charge whatever they can get away with – charging five times the going price for second-hand cameras and other goods is not unusual!

TOURIST OFFICES
Local Tourist Offices
The Macau Government Tourist Office (☎ 315566), or MGTO, is well-organised and extremely helpful. It's at Largo do Senado, Edificio Ritz No 9, across from the Leal Senado building in the square in the centre of Macau.

Tourist Offices Abroad
On Hong Kong Island, there's a small but useful branch of the MGTO (☎ 5408180) at Room 3704, Shun Tak Centre, 200 Connaught Rd, next to the Macau Ferry Pier.

BUSINESS HOURS & HOLIDAYS
The operating hours for most government offices in Macau are weekdays from 8.40 am to 1 pm and from 3 to 5 pm, and Saturday until 1 pm. Private businesses keep longer hours and some casinos are open 24 hours a day.

Banks are normally open on weekdays from 9 am to 4 pm, and on Saturday until noon.

The Chinese in Macau celebrate the same religious festivals as their counterparts in Hong Kong but there are also a number of Catholic festivals and some Portuguese national holidays. Most important is the Feast of Our Lady of Fatima when the Fatima image is removed from St Dominic's Church and taken in procession around the city.

Macau's main festival time is November when the Grand Prix is held – it's not a good time to go unless you're a racing fan as the place is packed and prices skyrocket. As in Monte Carlo, the actual streets of the town make up the raceway. There are in fact two races, one for cars and one for motorbikes, plus various support races. The six-km circuit attracts contestants from all over the world.

CULTURAL EVENTS
Find out about cultural events, concerts, art exhibitions and other such activities from the tourist newspaper *Macau Travel Talk*. Free copies are available from the tourist office.

The Dragon Boat Festival is a Chinese holiday well known for its exciting dragon boat races. Similar races are held in Hong Kong and Taiwan. The Dragon Boat Festival, scheduled according to the lunar calendar, usually takes place during June.

The International Music Festival is held during the third week of October.

POST & TELECOMMUNICATIONS
Postal Rates
Domestic letters cost M$1 for up to 20 grams. As for international mail, Macau divides the world into zones. Zone 1 is east Asia, including Korea, Taiwan etc; Zone 2 is everywhere else. There are special rates for China and Portugal.

The GPO on Largo do Senado is open from 9 am to 8 pm Monday to Saturday. It has an efficient poste restante service and English-speaking postal clerks. Large hotels like the Lisboa also sell stamps.

Rua D Belchior Carneiro
Calcada de S Paulo
L da Companhia
Rua Colonos
C Botelho
Rua Santo Antonio
Rua S Paulo
Rua dos Faitioes
R Nossa Senhora do Amparo
Rua de Cinco Outubro
Rua do Teatro
T Armazem Velho
Rua Nova do Comercio
Rua Visconde Paco de Arcos
Rua das Estalagens
Rua Palha
Rua de S Domingos
Largo da Se
Rua do Pagode
Rua Camilo Pessanha
T do Soriano
Rua Mercadores
Largo do Senado
Travessa Pagode
Rua da Madeira
Avenida de Almeida Ribeiro
Rua Caldeira
Travessa Caldeira
Travessa Auto Novo
T da Felicidade
Rua Felicidade
T Aterro Novo
Rua Cules
Calcada Tronco Velho
Rua Central
Macau-Guangzhou Ferry Wharf
Rua das Lorchas
Rua do Bocage
Rua Gamboa
Rua Alfandega
Praca Ponte e Horta
Patio Francisco Antonio
Santo
Rua de S Lourenco
Rua do Seminario
Rua Prata
Travessa Chan Loc
Rua do Barao
Travessa
Travessa

1 2 3 26 27 28 29 30 31 32 33 34 35 36 37 38 39 40 41 42 43 44 66 67 68 69 70 71 72 73 74 75 76 77 78

MACAU

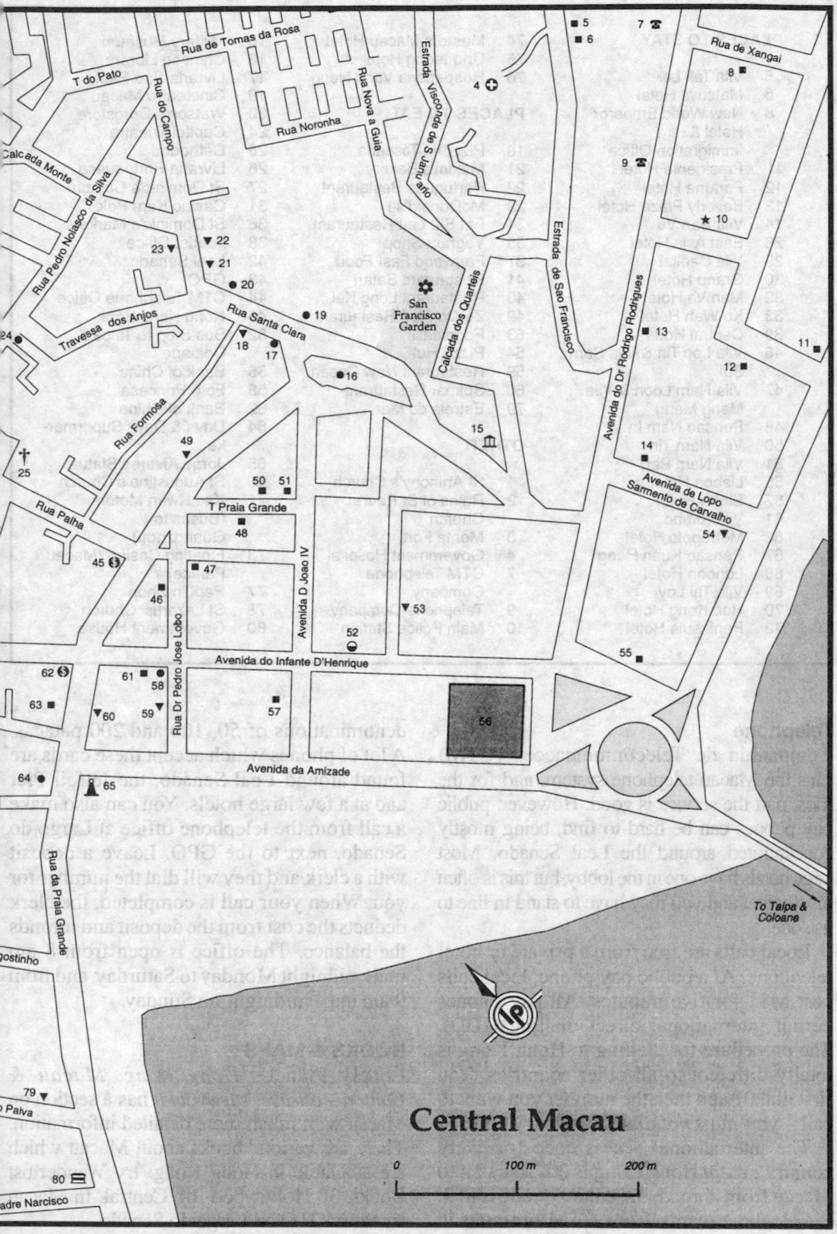

Central Macau

0 100 m 200 m

Rua de Tomas da Rosa
T do Pato
Rua do Campo
Rua Noronha
Rua Nova a Guia
Estrada Visconde de S Januario
Rua de Xangai
Calcada Monte
Rua Pedro Nolasco da Silva
Estrada de Sao Francisco
Avenida do Dr Rodrigo Rodrigues
Calcada dos Quarteis
San Francisco Garden
Travessa dos Anjos
Rua Santa Clara
Rua Formosa
T Praia Grande
Avenida de Lopo Sarmento de Carvalho
Rua Palha
Avenida D Joao IV
Rua Dr Pedro Jose Lobo
Avenida do Infante D'Henrique
Avenida da Amizade
Rua da Praia Grande
gostinho
o Paiva
Padre Narcisco
To Taipa & Coloane

PLACES TO STAY

5 Vila Tak Lei
6 Matsuya Hotel
8 New World Emperor Hotel & Immigration Office
11 Presidente Hotel
12 Fortuna Hotel
13 Beverly Plaza Hotel
14 Vila San Vu
28 East Asia Hotel
29 Vila Capital
30 Grand Hotel
32 Man Va Hotel
33 Ko Wah Hotel
39 Central Hotel
46 Vila Loc Tin & Vila Sam Sui
47 Vila Nam Loon & Vila Meng Meng
48 Pensao Nam In
50 Vila Nam Tin
51 Vila Nam Pan
55 Lisboa Hotel
57 Sintra Hotel
61 Vila Kimbo
63 Metropole Hotel
67 Pensao Kuan Heng
68 London Hotel
69 Vila Tai Loy
70 Hou Kong Hotel
72 Peninsula Hotel
74 Masters Macau Hotel
75 Ung Ieong Hotel
76 Hospedaria Vong Hong

PLACES TO EAT

18 Pizzeria Toscana
21 Maxim's Bakery
22 Portugués Restaurant
23 McDonald's I
34 Fat Siu Lau Restaurant
35 Yoghurt Shop
37 Fairwood Fast Food
41 Restaurant Safari
40 Restaurant Long Kei
49 Ze Do Pipo Restaurant
53 Foodstalls
54 Pizza Hut
59 Restaurant New Ocean
60 Solmar Restaurant
79 Estrela do Mar

OTHER

1 St Anthony's Church
2 Ruins of St Paul's Church
3 Monte Fort
4 Government Hospital
7 CTM Telephone Company
9 Telephone Company
10 Main Police Station
15 Military Museum
16 Chinese Library
17 Livraria Sao Paulo
19 Cineteatro Macau
20 Watson's Drugstore
24 Capitol Theatre
25 Cathedral
26 Livraria Portuguesa
27 St Dominic's Church
31 Casino Kam Pek
36 St Dominic's Market
38 Tourist Office
42 Leal Senado
43 GPO
44 CTM Telephone Office
45 Hong Kong Bank
52 Bus Stop to Taipa & Coloane
56 Bank of China
58 Foto Princesa
62 Bank of China
64 Days & Days Supermarket
65 Jorge Alvares Statue
66 St Augustine's Church
71 Kee Kwan Motors (Buses to Guangzhou)
73 Floating Casino (Macau Palace)
77 Park 'n Shop
78 St Lazarus' Church
80 Government House

Telephone

Companhia de Telecomunicacoes (CTM) runs the Macau telephone system, and for the most part the service is good. However, public pay phones can be hard to find, being mostly concentrated around the Leal Senado. Most large hotels have one in the lobby, but this is often insufficient and you may have to stand in line to use one.

Local calls are free from a private or hotel telephone. At a public pay phone, local calls cost M$1 for five minutes. All pay phones permit international direct dialling (IDD). The procedure for dialling to Hong Kong is totally different to all other countries. You first dial 01 and then the number you want to call – you must *not* dial the country code.

The international access code for every country *except* Hong Kong is 00. To call into Macau from abroad, the country code is 853.

Telephone cards from CTM are sold in denominations of 50, 100 and 200 patacas. A lot of phones which accept these cards are found around Leal Senado, the Jetfoil Pier and at a few large hotels. You can also make a call from the telephone office at Largo do Senado, next to the GPO. Leave a deposit with a clerk and they will dial the number for you. When your call is completed, the clerk deducts the cost from the deposit and refunds the balance. The office is open from 8 am until midnight Monday to Saturday, and from 9 am until midnight on Sunday.

BOOKS & MAPS

Lonely Planet's *Hong Kong, Macau & Canton – a travel survival kit* has a section on Macau with much more detailed information. There are various books about Macau which are available in Hong Kong: try Wanderlust Books, 30 Hollywood Rd, Central. In Macau try the MGTO on Largo do Senado.

Macau's best bookshop for English-language publications is Livraria Sao Paulo (☎ 323957) on the Rua do Campo (near McDonald's). For Portuguese-language publications, check out Livraria Portuguesa (☎ 566442), 18-20 Rua de S Domingos.

MEDIA

Newspapers & Magazines

Other than the monthly tourist newspaper *Macau Travel Talk*, there is no English-language newspaper published in Macau. However, both the *South China Morning Post* and *Hong Kong Standard* are readily available. It's also easy to buy foreign news magazines.

Radio & TV

Macau has three radio stations, two of which broadcast in Cantonese and one in Portuguese. There are no local English-language radio stations, but you should be able to pick up Hong Kong stations.

Teledifusao de Macau (TdM) is a government-run station which broadcasts on two channels. The shows are mainly in English and Portuguese, but with some Cantonese programmes. It's easy to pick up Hong Kong stations in Macau (but not vice versa) and you can also receive stations from China. Hong Kong newspapers list Macau TV programmes.

Hong Kong's famous satellite TV system, STAR TV, is readily available in Macau at any hotel with a cable or satellite dish hookup.

FILM & PHOTOGRAPHY

You can find most types of film, cameras and accessories in Macau, and photoprocessing is of a high standard. The best store in town for all photographic services is Foto Princesa (☎ 555959), 55-59 Avenida do Infante D'Henrique, one block east of Rua da Praia Grande. This is also the best place for visa photos.

HEALTH

The water, purified and chlorinated, is OK to drink. Nevertheless, the Chinese always boil it (more out of custom than necessity). Hotel rooms are always supplied with a thermos filled with hot water.

EMERGENCY

The emergency telephone number for fire, the police and ambulance is ☎ 999. Medical treatment is available at the Government Hospital (☎ 514499, 313731).

DANGERS & ANNOYANCES

In terms of violent crime, Macau is pretty safe, though not as safe as it used to be. Residential burglaries and pickpocketing are problems. Most hotels are well guarded, and if you take reasonable care with your valuables you should have no trouble. Security at casinos is particularly heavy – there are metal detectors and body searches of 'suspicious' people.

Traffic is congested and quite a few tourists have been hit while jaywalking. Cars are supposed to stop for pedestrians in crosswalks – you can rest assured that they won't stop for pedestrians anyplace else. Macau police are quite tough with traffic violators – foreigners also get fined for jaywalking.

Cheating at gambling is a serious criminal offence, so don't even think about it.

ACTIVITIES

Windsurfing is possible at Hac Sa Beach on Coloane Island, and rental equipment is readily available. Two good swimming beaches can be found on Coloane – Hac Sa and Cheoc Van. Cheoc Van Beach also has a yacht club. Horses can be hired for riding near the beach at Hac Sa. There are hiking trails in the hills of Coloane Island. Bicycles are available for hire on both Taipa and Coloane.

Getting There & Away

AIR

Helicopter

For people in a hurry to lose their money, East Asia Airlines runs a helicopter service between Hong Kong and Macau. Flying time from Hong Kong is 20 minutes at a cost of HK$1086 on weekdays, M$1189 on weekends – quite an expense just to save the extra 30 minutes required by boat. There are at least 12 flights daily in each direction, and departures are from the ferry piers in both Hong Kong and Macau. You can get the tickets in Hong Kong (☎ 8593359) at Shun Tak Centre, 200 Connaught Rd, Sheung Wan, Hong Kong Island. In Macau, you can book at the Jetfoil Pier (☎ 572983, 550777).

Macau's new airport is planned for completion in 1995. When it finally opens, expect major changes – not only to transport, but to Macau's character.

LAND

Macau is an important gateway into China. You simply take a bus to the border and walk across. Bus No 3 runs between the Jetfoil Pier and the Barrier Gate at the Macau-China border. You can also catch a bus directly from Macau to Guangzhou. Tickets are sold at Kee Kwan Motors, across the street from the Floating Casino.

SEA

Although Macau is separated from Hong Kong by 65 km of water, the journey can be made in as little as one hour. There are frequent departures throughout the day from 7 am to 9.30 pm.

You have a wide selection of boats to choose from. There are jetfoils, hoverferries, jumbocats (jet-powered large catamarans) and high-speed ferries. The fastest and most popular of the boats are the jetfoils and jumbocats.

For reasons only understood by the geniuses of marketing management, the jumbocat has now been renamed the 'super-shuttle'. The jumbocats are marginally more comfortable than the jetfoils, but neither this nor the catchy 'super-shuttle' slogan has been able to increase market share. The jetfoils remain far more popular with the Hong Kongers apparently because of the big 10 minutes they save. Perhaps the management of the super-shuttle should try another marketing gimmick, like a karaoke lounge or on-board casino.

Smoking is prohibited on the jetcats and super-shuttles. Most of the boats depart from the huge Macau Ferry Pier next to Shun Tak Centre at 200 Connaught Rd, Sheung Wan, Hong Kong Island. This is easily reached by MTR to the Sheung Wan Station.

Hoverferries depart from the China Hong Kong City ferry pier in Tsimshatsui. However, these are far less numerous than jetfoils.

Luggage space on the jetfoils is limited to what you can carry. You'll be OK just carrying a backpack or one suitcase, but no way will they let you on with a trunk or something requiring two people to move it.

If you have to return to Hong Kong the same day as departure, you'd be wise to book your return ticket in advance because the boats are sometimes full, especially on weekends and holidays. Even Monday mornings can be difficult for getting seats back to Hong Kong. If you can't get on the jetfoil or super-shuttle, you might have a chance with the hi-speed ferries which have a lot more room.

Jetfoil tickets can be purchased up to 28 days in advance in Hong Kong at the pier and at Ticketmate offices in some MTR stations, or booked by phone (☎ 8595696) if you have a credit card. Super-shuttle bookings

Vessel	*Travel Time*	*Weekday*	*Weekend*	*Night*
Hi-Speed Ferry	95 minutes	HK$59/78/93	HK$81/101/116	–
Hoverferry	80 minutes	HK$9	HK$11	HK$125
Jetfoil	55 minutes	HK$111/126	HK$119/134	HK$138/158
Super-Shuttle	65 minutes	HK$11	HK$129	–

(☎ 5599255) can be made 35 days in advance by telephone if you pay with plastic.

There are three different classes on the hi-speed ferries: economy, tourist and first. The jetfoils have two classes: economy and first. All other boats have only one class. The Hong Kong government charges HK$26 departure tax which is included in the price of your ticket. Macau charges M$20, also included in the ticket price. See the table on the previous page for Hong Kong prices.

Getting Around

Macau is fairly compact and it's relatively easy to walk almost everywhere, but you'll definitely need motorised transport to visit the islands of Taipa and Coloane. The pedicabs are essentially for touristy sightseeing. They have to be bargained for and it's hardly worth the effort – if there are two of you make sure the fare covers both.

BUS

There are minibuses and large buses, and both offer air-con and frequent service. They operate from 7 am until midnight.

You'll find it easier to deal with the bus system if you buy a good map of Macau showing all the routes.

Buses on the Macau peninsula cost M$1.80. The major routes are as follows:

No 3 – Jetfoil Pier, Beverly Plaza Hotel, Lisboa Hotel, San Francisco Garden, Avenida Almeida Ribeiro, GPO, Grand Hotel, Avenida do Almirante Lacerda, Lin Fong Miu (Lotus Temple), Barrier Gate

No 3A – Jetfoil Pier, Beverly Plaza Hotel, Lisboa Hotel, San Francisco Garden, Avenida Almeida Ribeiro, GPO, Floating Casino, Praca Ponte e Horta

No 9 – (loop route) Barra Fortress, A-Ma Temple, Floating Casino, GPO, Rua do Campo, Lou Lim Ieoc Garden, Avenida Horta e Costa, Barrier Gate, Lin Fong Miu (Lotus Temple), Canidrome, Avenida do Almirante Lacerda, Avenida do Ouvidor Arriaga, Flora Garden, Sun Yatsen Memorial Home, St Dominic's Church, GPO, Avenida Almeida Ribeiro, Rua da Praia Grande, Government House, Avenida da Republica, Barra Fortress

No 10 – Barra Fortress, Floating Casino, Grand Hotel, Avenida Almeida Ribeiro, GPO, Metropole Hotel, Sintra Hotel, Lisboa Hotel, Presidente Hotel, Macau Forum, Outer Harbour, Barrier Gate

No 12 – Jetfoil Pier, Beverly Plaza Hotel, Lisboa Hotel, Rua do Campo, Lou Lim Ieoc Garden, Mondial Hotel, Avenida Horta e Costa, Avenida Coronel Mesquita, Kun Iam Temple, Bairro da Areia Preta

No 18 – Barra Fortress, Floating Casino, Avenida Almeida Ribeiro, Camoes Gardens, Rua da Barca, Rua Francisco Xavier Pereira, Avenida Coronel Mesquita, Montanha Russa Garden, Areia Preta, Avenida Coronel Mesquita, Jun Iam Temple, Lou Lim Ieoc Garden, Avenida Sidonio Pais, Rua do Campo, Government House, St Lazarus Church, Barra Fortress

No 28C – Jetfoil Pier, Beverly Plaza Hotel, Lisboa Hotel, Estrada de Sao Francisco, Matsuya Hotel, Guia Hotel, Royal Hotel, Lou Lim Ieoc Gardens, Mondial Hotel, Avenida Horta e Costa, Avenida Coronel Mesquita, Kun Iam Temple, Bairro da Areia Preta, Barrier Gate

Buses to the island of Taipa cost M$2.30, while buses to Coloane are M$3.30. The complete bus routes to the islands are as follows:

No 11 – Barra Fortress, Floating Casino, Avenida Almeida Ribeiro, GPO, Lisboa Hotel, bridge, Hyatt Regency Hotel (Taipa), University of Macau, Taipa Village, Macau Jockey Club

No 14 – Taipa Village, causeway, Coloane Park, Coloane Village, Pousada de Coloane, Hac Sa Beach

No 15 – Coloane Village, Ka Ho

No 21 – Barra Fortress, Praca Ponte E Horta, Floating Casino, Avenida Almeida Ribeiro, GPO, Lisboa Hotel, bridge, Hyatt Regency Hotel (Taipa), Coloane Park, Coloane Village

No 21A – Barra Fortress, Praca Ponte E Horta, Floating Casino, Avenida Almeida Ribeiro, GPO, Lisboa Hotel, bridge, Hyatt Regency Hotel (Taipa), Taipa Village, Coloane Park, Coloane Village, Cheoc Van Beach, Hac Sa Beach

No 28A – Jetfoil Pier, Beverly Plaza Hotel, Lisboa Hotel, bridge, Hyatt Regency Hotel (Taipa), Macau University, Taipa Village

No 33 – Fai Chi Kei, Lin Fong Miu (Lotus Temple), Avenida Almeida Ribeiro, Lisboa Hotel, Hyatt Regency Hotel (Taipa), Macau University, Taipa Village, Macau Jockey Club

No 38 S– pecial bus running from the city centre to the Macau Jockey Club one hour before the races

TAXI

Macau taxis are black with cream roofs. They all have meters and drivers are required to use them. Flagfall is M$6.50 for the first 1.5 km, thereafter it's 80 avos every 250 metres. There is a M$5 surcharge to go to Taipa, and M$10 to go to Coloane, but there is no surcharge if you're heading the other way back to Macau. There is also an additional M$1 service charge for each piece of luggage carried in the boot (trunk). Taxis can be dispatched by radio if you ring up ☎ 519519. Not many taxi drivers speak English, so it would be helpful to have a map with both Chinese and English or Portuguese.

CAR

The mere thought of renting a car in Macau is ridiculous but between a group it might make sense for exploring on Taipa and Coloane. On Macau Peninsula, horrendous traffic and the lack of parking space makes driving more of a burden than a pleasure.

As in Hong Kong, driving is on the left-hand side of the road. Another local driving rule is that motor vehicles must always stop for pedestrians at a crosswalk if there is no traffic light. It's illegal to beep the horn.

Macau Mokes (☎ 378851) is Macau's rent-a-car pioneer. They are on Avenida Marciano Baptist, just across from the Jetfoil Pier in Macau. There is a Hong Kong office (☎ 5434190) at 806 Kai Tak Commercial Building, 317-321 Des Voeux Rd, Sheung Wan, near Macau Ferry Terminal on Hong Kong Island. A moke costs M$280 on weekdays and M$310 on weekends and holidays.

You can also rent mokes from Avis Rent A Car (☎ 336789, 567888 ext 3004) which is located at the Mandarin Oriental Hotel. It's probably not necessary on weekdays, but you can book in advance at the Avis Hong Kong office (☎ 5412011).

BICYCLE

You can hire bicycles out on the islands of Taipa and Coloane. On the peninsula, there are no places to hire bikes, and it wouldn't be pleasant riding anyway with the insane traffic.

TOURS

A typical city tour (booked in Macau) of the peninsula takes three to four hours and costs about M$70 per person, often including lunch. Bus tours out to the islands run from about M$20 per person. You can also book a one-day bus tour across the border into Zhuhai in China, which usually includes a trip to the former home of Dr Sun Yat-sen in Zhongshan County. There are large numbers of tour operators.

Around Macau

THINGS TO SEE

There's far more of historical interest to be seen in Macau than Hong Kong. Simply wandering around is a delight – the streets are winding and always full of interest. Old hands say it's now getting speedy like Hong Kong but it has a way to go.

Macau Peninsula

The **ruins of St Paul's Church** are the symbol of Macau – the facade and majestic stairway are all that remain of the old church. It was designed by an Italian Jesuit and built in 1602 by Japanese refugees who had fled anti-Christian persecution in Nagasaki. In 1853 the church was totally burned down during a catastrophic typhoon.

The **Monte Fort** overlooks the ruins of St Paul's Church and almost all of Macau from its high and central position. It was built by the Jesuits. In 1622, a cannonball fired from the fort conveniently landed in a Dutch gunpowder carrier during an attempted Dutch invasion, demolishing most of their fleet.

The **Kun Iam Temple** is the city's most historic. In the temple study are 18 wise men in a glass case – the one with the big nose is said to be Marco Polo. The 400-year-old temple is dedicated to Kun Iam, the queen of heaven and goddess of mercy.

The **Old Protestant Cemetery** is a fasci-ating place to wander around. Lord 'hurchill (one of Winston's ancestors) and he English artist George Chinnery are uried here, but far more interesting are the 'arious graves of missionaries and their fam-ies, traders, and seamen, and the often etailed accounts of their lives and deaths. One JS ship seems to have had half its crew 'fall rom aloft' while in port.

Next door to the cemetery is the fine little **.uis de Camoes Museum** which has items rom China and a fine collection of paintings, rints and engravings showing Macau in the ast two centuries. The **Barrier Gate** used to e of interest because you could stand 100 netres from it and claim that you'd seen into China. Now you can stand on the other side nd claim you've seen Macau.

The **Leal Senado** (Loyal Senate) looks out over the main town square and is the main administrative body for municipal affairs. At one time it was offered (and turned down) a monopoly on Chinese trade! The building also houses the **National Library**.

The highest point in Macau is the **Guía Fortress** with a 17th-century chapel and lighthouse built on it. The lighthouse is the oldest on the China coast, first lit up in 1865.

One of the most beautiful churches in Macau is **St Dominic's Church**, a 17th-century building which has an impressive tiered altar. There is a small museum at the back, full of church regalia, images and paintings.

The peaceful **Lou Lim Ioc Gardens** with its ornate mansion (now the Pui Ching School) is a mixture of Chinese and European influences with huge shady trees, lotus ponds, pavilions, bamboo groves, grottos and odd-shaped doorways.

Macau means the City of God and takes its name from A-Ma-Gau, the Bay of A-Ma. The **A-Ma Temple** (Ma Kok Miu), which dates from the Ming Dynasty, stands at the base of Penha Hill on Barra Point. According to legend, A-Ma, goddess of seafarers, was supposed to have been a beautiful young woman whose presence on a Guangzhou-bound ship saved it from disaster. All the other ships of the fleet, whose rich owners had refused to give her passage, were destroyed in a storm. The boat people of Macau come here on a pilgrimage each year in April or May.

A restored colonial-style building beside the A-Ma Temple houses the **Macau Maritime Museum**. Across the road on the waterfront there are a number of boats, including a tug, a dragon boat and a *lorcha*, a type of sailing cargo-vessel used on the Pearl River.

The Islands

Directly south of the mainland peninsula are the islands of Taipa and Coloane. Two bridges connect Taipa Island to the mainland, and a causeway connects Taipa and Coloane.

Taipa This island seems to have become one big construction site with the Hyatt Regency Hotel and Macau University just the first of a number of projects. Taipa village is pleasant and there are some fine little restaurants to sample. You can rent a bicycle to explore the village and farther afield. There's an old church, a couple of temples and the **Taipa House Museum**.

Coloane This island also has a pretty village where you can see junks under construction. Bicycles can also be rented there. Situated in a muddy river mouth, Macau is hardly likely to be blessed with wonderful beaches but Coloane has a couple that are really not bad. **Hac Sa Beach** is a long but not particularly inspiring stretch of sand but tiny **Cheoc Van Beach** is quite pretty.

PLACES TO STAY

Weekends are a bad time to visit Macau; try to make your trip on a weekday. During the quieter midweek time, it's worth bargaining a little. Cheap hotels usually call themselves *vila*, but often they are called *hospedaria* or *pensao*.

Places to Stay – bottom end

The street in front of the Floating Casino is Rua das Lorchas, and one block east is an

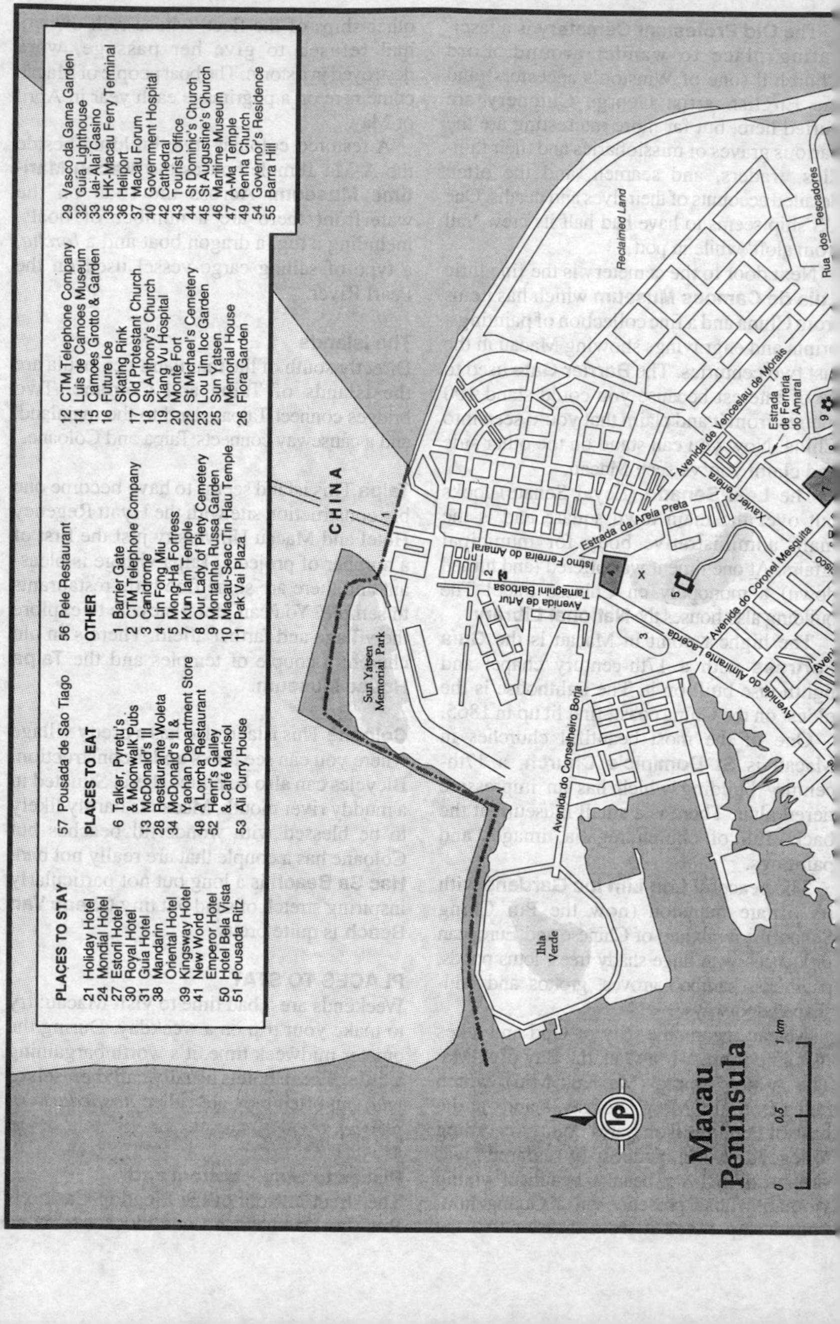

Macau Peninsula

0 0.5 1 km

PLACES TO STAY

21 Holiday Hotel
24 Mondial Hotel
27 Estoril Hotel
30 Royal Hotel
31 Guia Hotel
38 Mandarin Oriental Hotel
39 Kingsway Hotel
41 New World Emperor Hotel
50 Hotel Bela Vista
51 Pousada Ritz
57 Pousada de Sao Tiago

PLACES TO EAT

6 Talker, Pyretu's & Moonwalk Pubs
13 McDonald's III
28 Restaurante Woleta
34 McDonald's II & Yaohan Department Store
48 A Lorcha Restaurant
52 Henri's Galley & Café Marisol
53 Ali Curry House
56 Pele Restaurant

OTHER

1 Barrier Gate
2 CTM Telephone Company
3 Canidrome
4 Lin Fong Miu
5 Mong-Ha Fortress
7 Kun Iam Temple
8 Our Lady of Piety Cemetery
9 Montanha Russa Garden
10 Macau-Seac Tin Hau Temple
11 Pak Vai Plaza
12 CTM Telephone Company
14 Luis de Camoes Museum
15 Camoes Grotto & Garden
16 Future Ice Skating Rink
17 Old Protestant Church
18 St Anthony's Church
19 Kiang Vu Hospital
20 Monte Fort
22 St Michael's Cemetery
23 Lou Lim Ioc Garden
25 Sun Yatsen Memorial House
26 Flora Garden
29 Vasco da Gama Garden
32 Guia Lighthouse
33 Jai-Alai Casino
35 HK-Macau Ferry Terminal
36 Heliport
37 Macau Forum
40 Government Hospital
42 Cathedral
43 Tourist Office
44 St Dominic's Church
45 St Augustine's Church
46 Maritime Museum
47 A-Ma Temple
49 Penha Church
54 Governor's Residence
55 Barra Hill

CHINA
Sun Yatsen Memorial Park
Ilha Verde
Reclaimed Land
Avenida do Conselheiro Borja
Istmo Ferreira do Amaral
Avenida de Artur Tamagnini Barbosa
Estrada da Areia Preta
Avenida do Almirante Lacerda
Avenida do Coronel Mesquita
Xavier Pereira
Avenida de Venceslau de Morais
Estrada de Ferreira do Amaral
Rua dos Pescadores

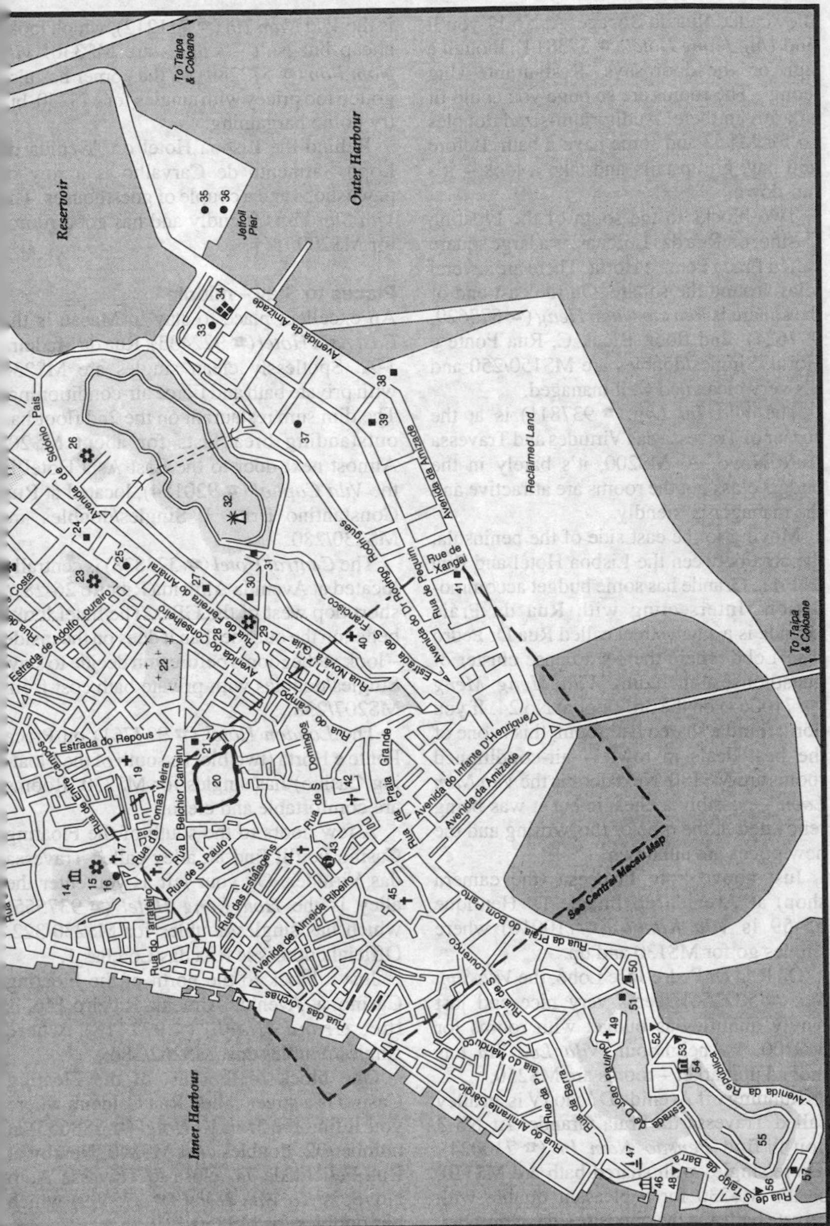
Reservoir
Outer Harbour
Inner Harbour
To Taipa & Coloane
Jetfoil Pier
Reclaimed Land
See Central Macau Map
Avenida da Amizade
Avenida do Infante D'Henrique
Avenida do Dr Rodrigo Rodrigues
Rua de Pequim
Rue de Xangai
Estrada de S Francisco
Rua Nova à Guia
Avenida do Conselheiro
Rua de Ferreira do Amaral
Estrada de Adolfo Loureiro
Avenida de Sidónio Pais
Estrada do Repous
Rua de Entre Campos
Rua de Tomás Vieira
Rua D Belchior Carneiro
Rua do Campo
Rua de S Domingos
Rua da Praia Grande
Rua de S Paulo
Rua das Estalagens
Rua do Tarrafeiro
Avenida de Almeida Ribeiro
Rua das Lorchas
Rua da Praia do Bom Parto
Rua de S Lourenço
Rua da Praia do Manduco
Rua do Almirante Sérgio
Rue de D João Paulino
Rua da Barra
Estrada da Barra
Avenida da Republica
Rua de S Tiago da Barra
14
15
16
17
18
19
20
21
22
23
24
25
26
27
28
29
30
31
32
33
34
35
36
37
38
39
40
41
42
43
44
45
46
47
48
49
50
51
52
53
54
55
56
57

MACAU

alley called Rua do Bocage. At No 17 you'll find *Ung Ieong Hotel* (☎ 573814), though a sign on the door says 'Restaurante Ung Ieong'. The rooms are so huge you could fit an army in there! Auditorium-sized doubles go for M$52 and some have a bath. Before you pay, go upstairs and take a look – it's run-down.

Two blocks to the south of the Floating Casino, on Rua das Lorchas, is a large square called Praca Ponte e Horta. There are several vilas around the square. On the east end of the square is *Pensao Kuan Heng* (☎ 573629, 937624), 2nd floor, Block C, Rua Ponte e Horta. Singles/doubles are M$150/250 and it's very clean and well managed.

The *Vila Tai Loy* (☎ 937811) is at the corner of Travessa das Virtudes and Travessa Auto Novo. At M$200, it's barely in the budget class but the rooms are attractive and the manager is friendly.

Moving to the east side of the peninsula, the area between the Lisboa Hotel and Rua da Praia Grande has some budget accommodation. Intersecting with Rua da Praia Grande is a small street called Rua Dr Pedro Jose Lobo where there's a dense cluster of guesthouses, including *Vila Meng Meng* (☎ 710064) on the 3rd floor at No 24. If you don't mind a shared bathroom, this is one of the best deals in town – air-conditioned rooms are M$130. Next door is the *Vila Nam Loon* – possibly a cheapie but it was being renovated at the time of this writing and the new prices are unknown.

Just above Foto Princesa (the camera shop) at Avenida do Infante D' Henrique 55-59 is *Vila Kimbo* (☎ 710010) where singles go for M$130 and up.

On Rua Dr Pedro Jose Lobo, the *Vila Sam Sui* (☎ 572256) seems very nice and just barely qualifies as budget with rooms for M$200. Its neighbour, *Vila Loc Tin* has moved upmarket – rooms are M$250.

Running off Avenida D Joao IV is an alley called Travessa da Praia Grande. At No 3 you'll find *Pensao Nam In* (☎ 710024), where singles with shared bath are M$110, or it's M$230 for a pleasant double with private bath. On the opposite side of the alley is the *Vila Nam Tin* (☎ 711212), which looks cheap but isn't – singles are M$330! *Vila Nam Pan* (☎ 572289) on the corner has also gotten too pricey with singles for M$250, but try polite bargaining.

Behind the Lisboa Hotel on Avenida de Lopo Sarmento de Carvalho is a row of pawnshops and a couple of guesthouses. The *Vila San Vu* is friendly and has good rooms for M$200.

Places to Stay – middle

An excellent place to stay in Macau is the *East Asia Hotel* (☎ 922433), Rua da Madeira 1-A. Spotlessly clean singles are M$230 with private bath and fierce air-conditioning. The dim sum restaurant on the 2nd floor has outstanding breakfasts for about M$20. Almost next door to the East Asia Hotel is the *Vila Capital* (☎ 920154), located at Rua Constantino Brito 3. Singles/doubles are M$230/280.

The *Central Hotel* (☎ 373838) is centrally located at Avenida Almeida Ribeiro 26-28, a short hop west of the GPO. The hotel looks better on the outside than it does on the inside – look at the rooms before you decide to stay. Singles/doubles with private bath cost from M$207/238.

The *London Hotel* (☎ 937761) on Praca Ponte e Horta (two blocks south of the Floating Casino) has singles for M$230. Rooms are comfortable and clean.

A few doors to the south of the Floating Casino you'll find an alley called Travessa das Virtudes. On your left as you enter the alley is the *Hou Kong Hotel* (☎ 937555) which has singles/doubles for M$230/322. Official address is Rua das Lorchas 1.

Just a block to the north of the Floating Casino, at Avenida Almeida Ribeiro 146, is the *Grand Hotel* (☎ 922418), where singles/doubles cost M$262/386.

One block to the east of the Floating Casino is a street called Rua Caldeira where you'll find the *Man Va Hotel* (☎ 388655) at number 32; doubles cost M$340. Nearby at Rua Felicidade 71, close to Travessa Auto Novo, is *Ko Wah Hotel* (☎ 375599) which has doubles for M$250.

Just on the north side of the Floating asino on Rua das Lorchas is the *Peninsula 'otel)* (☎ 318899). Singles/twins are 1$300/350. This hotel is large, clean and opular.

One more place to look around is the area orth of the Lisboa Hotel on a street called strada Sao Francisco. You have to climb a eep hill to get up this street. Up here you'll nd the fancy *Matsuya Hotel* (☎ 577000, fax 68080) where the doubles/twins cost 1$330/390 and suites are M$650.

Next to the Matsuya Hotel at Estrada Sao rancisco 2A is *Vila Tak Lei* (☎ 577484), here doubles go for M$300. However, bar-aining is possible in this place.

'LACES TO EAT

lacau Peninsula

)ne of the most conveniently located street arkets dishing up cheap food is Rua da scola Commercial, a tiny lane one block est of the Lisboa Hotel, just next to a sports eld. For economy snacks, try the *Yoghurt hop* at 65 Avenida Almeida Ribeiro – oghurt is served Chinese-style in a rice owl.

A long, lazy Portuguese meal with a carafe f red to wash it down with is one of the most leasant parts of a Macau visit. The menus re often in Portuguese, so a few useful vords are cozido (stew), cabrito (kid), ordeiro (lamb), carreiro (mutton), galinha chicken), caraguejos (crabs), carne de vaca beef) and peixe (fish). Apart from carafe vine you can also get Mateus Rosé. For conomy-minded wine lovers, Macau is the ne of the best bargains around. You can ring a litre of wine or spirits back to Hong Kong, where it's more expensive.

Another Macau pleasure is to sit back in ne of the many little cake shops *pastelarias)* with a glass of cha de limao lemon tea) and a plate of cakes – very genteel! These places are good for a cheap reakfast. People eat early in Macau – you an find the chairs being put away and that he chef has gone home around 9 pm.

Henri's Galley (☎ 556251) is on the vaterfront at 4 Avenida da República, on the south end of the Macau Peninsula. Also known as Maxims (not the Hong Kong fast-food chain), Henri's Galley is known for its African chicken, spicy prawns, prawn fondue and Chinese food.

Next door is the excellent *Cafe Marisol*. They set up outdoor tables so you can take in the view across to the islands.

Also adjacent to Henri's Galley is the *Ali Curry House*, which also has outdoor tables and a wide menu of curry dishes and steaks with a Portuguese flavour.

For Portuguese and Macanese food which is both good and cheap, the *Estrela do Mar* (☎ 81270) at 11 Travessa do Paiva, off the Rua da Praia Grande, is the place to go. So is the *Solmar* (☎ 74391) at 11 Rua da Praia Grande. Both places are famous for African chicken and seafood.

Fat Siu Lau (☎ 73580) serves Portuguese and Chinese food. It's at 64 Rua Felicidade, once the old red-light Street of Happiness. The speciality is roast pigeon.

Another place known for good Portuguese food is *Portugués* (☎ 75445) at 16 Rua do Campo. One place known for its good food and fine Spanish decor is *Algarve Sol* (☎ 89007) at 41-43 Rua Comandante Mata e Oliveira, two blocks west of the Lisboa Hotel between Rua da Praia Grande and Avenida D Joao IV.

An excellent place is *Restaurant Safari* (☎ 574313) at 14 Pateo do Cotovelo, a tiny square off Avenida de Almeida Ribeiro across from the Central Hotel. It has good coffee-shop dishes as well as spicy chicken, steak and fried noodles. For a good pizza, try *Pizzeria Toscana*, Rua Formosa 28B.

Taipa

Lots of people hop over to Taipa village for the excellent restaurants found there, but it's no longer cheap. One place to try is *Pinocchio's*. Other popular Taipa village restaurants include the very Portuguese *Restaurante Panda*, the Italian (despite the name) *Restaurante Leong Un*, the cheaper *Casa de Pasto Tai Tung*, the *Kung Kai, Cozinha Ricardo's Kitchen* and the pleasant sidewalk-café-like *Cafe Tai Lei Lai Kei* opposite the Tin Hau Temple.

Coloane

At Hac Sa Beach on Coloane Island, *Fernando's* deserves honourable mention for some of the best food in Macau. Fernando recommends the clams.

ENTERTAINMENT

Gambling

Even if gambling holds no interest for you, it's fun to wander the casinos at night. There are three main arenas for losing money. Largest is the *Lisboa Hotel* with all the usual games, a special private room for the really high rollers, and row upon row of 'hungry tigers', also known as slot machines. It is gambling Chinese-style though, none of the dinner jacket swank of Monte Carlo or the neon gloss of Vegas – at Macau you put your money down, take your chances and to hell with the surroundings. For M$200, you can also watch about 10 graduates of the Crazy Horse in Paris cavort around the stage of Lisboa Hotel attired in outfits ranging from very little to nothing at all. It's called the Crazy Paris Show.

At the other end of the main street is *Macau Palace*, usually referred to as the 'Floating Casino', and midway between is the Chinese casino (the Casino Kam Pek) where they play games like Dai-Siu (big an small). You can also bet on the games at th *Jai-Alai Casino* near the ferry terminal.

There's also *horse racing* on Taipa Islan and *dog racing* at the 'Canidrome' (yes, the really call it that).

Discos

The most popular with the locals is th *Mondial Disco* at the Mondial Hotel, Rua d Antonio Basto. There is no cover charge, bu you are obligated to buy two drinks fo M$80.

The Presidente Hotel is home to the *Sky light Disco*. There is no cover charge her but you must buy one drink for M$80.

THINGS TO BUY

Pawnshops are ubiquitous in Macau, and is possible to get good deals on cameras watches and jewellery, but you must be pre pared to bargain without mercy. In Macau a least, the nasty reputation of pawnbrokers i well deserved!

The MGTO has a number of good souve nir items for sale at bargain prices. Some o the items to consider are Macau T-shirts poster-size 'antigue maps of Macau', sets o postcards, umbrellas and raincoats.

St Dominic Market, in the alley behind th Central Hotel, is a good place to pick u cheap clothing.

Malaysia

Malaysia is a country known more for its beautiful scenery than its points of historical or cultural interest. Travel is easy and comfortable, and the people are exceptionally friendly. Apart from its superb beaches, mountains and national parks, it is one of the most developed and prosperous countries in the region.

Malaysia's fascinating mixture of people range from Peninsular Malays and the commercially minded Chinese to the diverse tribespeople of Sabah and Sarawak in East Malaysia.

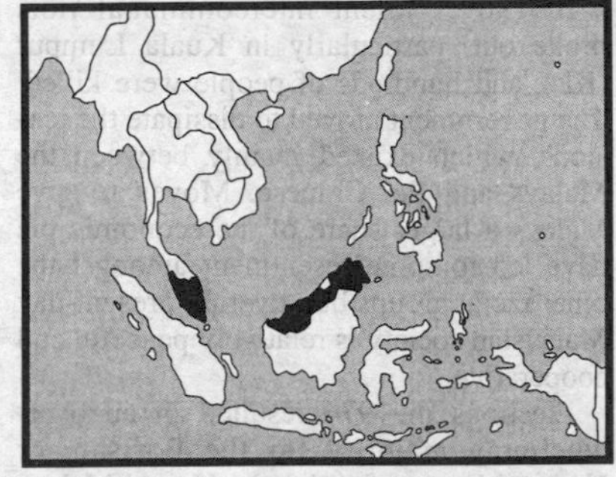

Facts about the Country

HISTORY

Little is known about prehistoric Malaysia, but around 10,000 years ago the aboriginal Malays – the Orang Asli – began to move down the peninsula from a probable starting point in south-western China.

In the early centuries of the Christian era, Malaya was known as far away as Europe. Ptolemy showed it on his early map with the label 'Golden Chersonese'. It spelt gold not only to the Romans but to others as well, for it wasn't long before Indian and Chinese traders arrived in search of that most valuable metal and Hindu ministates sprung up along the great Malay rivers.

The Malay people were ethnically similar to the people of Sumatra, Java and even the Philippines, and from time to time various South-East Asian empires exerted control over all or parts of the Malay Peninsula.

In 1405, the Chinese Admiral Cheng Ho arrived in Melaka with greetings from the Son of Heaven (the emperor) and, more importantly, the promise of protection from the encroaching Siamese to the north. With this support from China, the power of Melaka extended to include most of the Malay Peninsula.

At about the same time, Islam arrived in Melaka and soon spread through Malaya. Melaka's wealth and prosperity soon attracted European interest, and it was the Portuguese who first took over in 1511, followed by the Dutch in 1641 and, finally, the British in 1795.

For years, the British were only interested in Malaya for its seaports and to protect their trade routes, but the discovery of tin prompted them to move inland and take over the whole peninsula. Meanwhile, Charles Brooke, the White Rajah, and the North Borneo Company made similar British takeovers of Sarawak and Sabah respectively. The British, as was their custom, also brought in Chinese and Indians, an action which radically changed the country's racial mix.

Malaya achieved *merdeka* (independence) in 1957 but there followed a period of instability due to an internal Communist uprising and the external 'confrontation' with neighbouring Indonesia. In 1963, the north Borneo states of Sabah and Sarawak, along with Singapore, joined Malaya to create Malaysia.

Relations with Singapore soured almost immediately and, only two years later, Singapore withdrew from the Malaysian confederation. Sukarno's demise ended the disputes with Indonesia and the Communist threat has simply withered away to become a total anachronism in modern Malaysia.

In 1969, violent intercommunal riots broke out, particularly in Kuala Lumpur (KL), and hundreds of people were killed. The government moved to dissipate the tensions, which existed mainly between the Malays and the Chinese. Moves to give Malays a larger share of the economic pie have led to some resentment amongst the other racial groups but, overall, present-day Malaysian society is relatively peaceful and cooperative.

Elections in 1974 resulted in an overwhelming majority for the Barisan, or National Front, of which the United Malays National Organisation (UMNO) is the key party. All elections since then have seen power remain with the UMNO. Prime Minister Dr Mahathir Mohammed presides over an economically booming Malaysia and is keen to exert his influence on the world stage as a pan-Asian leader.

Internationally, the country has a very high standing as one of the most rapidly advancing countries of Asia, although it has come under intense pressure to stop exporting tropical timber from its rapidly diminishing rainforests. Regionally, it is an important member of the Association of South-East Asian Nations (ASEAN). Dr Mahathir's favourite hobby horse is the East Asian Economic Caucus (EAEC), a proposal for an all-Asian economic zone that excludes the Western countries such as the USA, Canada, Australia and New Zealand, all of which are pushing for a Pacific rim economic zone.

GEOGRAPHY

Malaysia consists of two distinct parts. Peninsular Malaysia is the long finger of land extending down from Asia, as if pointing towards Indonesia and Australia, and it accounts for about 40% of the country's area. Although most of the forests have been cleared over the years to make way for plantations of rubber trees and oil palms, there are still stands of virgin forest remaining largely in the national park of Taman Negara.

The balance of the land area is made up of the states of Sabah and Sarawak, which occupy the northern segment of the island of Borneo. Here too, the forests have been cleared for agriculture and timber export and the tracts of virgin rainforest are still rapidly diminishing. Mt Kinabalu in Sabah is the highest peak in South-East Asia.

CLIMATE

Malaysia has a typically tropical climate – it's hot and humid year-round. The temperature rarely drops below 20°C (68°F), even at night, and usually climbs to 30°C (86°F) or more during the day.

The west coast of Peninsular Malaysia gets heavier rainfall from September to December. On the east coast, and also in Sarawak and Sabah, October to February is the wet season. Throughout the region the humidity tends to hover around the 90% mark, but on the peninsula you can escape from the heat and humidity by retreating to the delightfully cool hill stations.

GOVERNMENT

Malaysia is a confederation of 13 states and the capital district of Kuala Lumpur. Nine of the peninsular states have sultans and every five years an election is held to determine which one will become the Yang di-Pertuan Agong, or 'King' of Malaysia.

The states of Sabah and Sarawak in East Malaysia are rather different from those of Peninsular Malaysia since they were separate colonies, not parts of Malaya, prior to independence. They still retain a greater degree of local administrative autonomy than the peninsular states.

ECONOMY

Malaysia is a prosperous and progressive country and one of the world's major suppliers of tin, natural rubber and palm oil. Indeed, rubber plantations, interspersed with oil palm plantations, seem to cover a large part of the peninsula. In East Malaysia the economy is based on timber and, in Sarawak oil and pepper are major exports. A great deal of effort is being made to industrialise Malaysia and jump onto the hi-tech bandwagon which has proven to be so successful for other regional states.

POPULATION & PEOPLE

Malaysia's population is currently around 19 million. The people of Malaysia come from a number of different ethnic groups – Malays, Chinese, Indians, the indigenous Orang Asli of the peninsula and the various tribes of Sarawak and Sabah.

It's reasonable to say that the Malays control the government while the Chinese have their fingers on the economic pulse. Approximately 85% of the population lives in Peninsular Malaysia and the remaining 15% in the much more lightly populated states of Sabah and Sarawak.

There are still small scattered groups of Orang Asli, or Original People, in Peninsular Malaysia. Although most have given up their nomadic or shifting-agriculture techniques and have been absorbed into modern Malay society, a few groups of Orang Asli still live in the forests.

Dayak is the term used for the non-Muslim people of Borneo. These people migrated to Borneo at times, and along routes, which are not clearly defined. It is estimated that there are more than 200 Dayak tribes in Borneo, the most important being the Iban and Bidayuh in Sarawak and the Kadazan in Sabah. Other smaller groups include the Kenyah, Kayan and Punan, whose lifestyle and habitat is under siege due to the logging activities in Sarawak.

ARTS

It's along the east coast, the predominantly Malay part of Malaysia, that you'll find Malay games, culture and crafts at their liveliest and most widely practised.

Top-spinning, or *main gasing*, and kite-flying are two popular activities, while *sepak raga*, the national ball game, is played with a lightweight ball woven from strips of rotan. *Silat*, a traditional martial art, is today a highly refined and stylised activity.

The *wayang kulit* is similar to the shadow puppet performances of other South-East Asian countries, in particular Java in Indonesia, and retells the tales from the Hindu epic, the *Ramayana*. As in other parts of the region, Malay music is principally percussion based.

Although originally an Indonesian craft, batik has made itself equally at home in Malaysia. You'll find it in Penang on the west coast, although Kelantan is its true home. *Kain songket* is a handwoven fabric from Kelantan, the main feature of which is the silver and gold thread. Kelantan is also famed for its silversmiths who work in a variety of ways and specialise in filigree and repousse work. In Kuala Terengganu, brasswork is an equally traditional skill.

CULTURE

As many Muslim countries have in the last decade, Malaysia has been going through a period of increasing concentration on religion and religious activity. It's certainly a world away from the sort of fundamentalism found in other parts of the world, but you still need to be aware of local sensibilities so as not to offend.

It's wise to be appropriately discreet in dress and behaviour, particularly on the stricter Muslim east coast of the peninsula. For women, topless bathing is definitely not acceptable and away from the beaches you should cover up as much as possible. For men, shorts are considered low class away from the beach, and bare torsos are not acceptable in the villages and towns.

RELIGION

The variety of religions found in Malaysia is a direct reflection of the diversity of races living there. Although Islam is the state religion of Malaysia, freedom of religion is guaranteed. The Malays are almost all Muslims and there are also some Indian Muslims. The Chinese are predominantly followers of Taoism and Buddhism, though some are Christians. The majority of the region's Indian population come from the south of India and are Hindu.

Although Christianity has made no great inroads into Peninsular Malaysia, it has had a much greater impact upon East Malaysia where many of the indigenous people have converted to Christianity, although others still follow their animist traditions.

LANGUAGE

The official language is Bahasa Malaysia, or Bahasa Melayu, language of the Malays. You can get along quite happily with English throughout Malaysia and, although it is not the official language, it is often still the linking language between the various ethnic groups, especially the middle class.

Other everyday languages include Chinese dialects like Hakka or Hokkien. The majority of the region's Indians speak Tamil, although there are also groups who speak Malayalam, Hindi or other Indian languages.

Bahasa Malaysia is virtually the same as Indonesian. See Lonely Planet's *Indonesia Phrasebook* and the Language section in the Indonesia chapter for an introduction to the language.

Facts for the Visitor

VISAS & EMBASSIES

Commonwealth citizens (except those from India, Bangladesh, Sri Lanka and Pakistan) and citizens of the Republic of Ireland, Singapore, Switzerland, the Netherlands and Brunei do not require a visa to visit Malaysia. Citizens of the USA, Germany, France, Italy, Norway, Sweden, Denmark, Belgium and Finland do not require a visa for a visit not exceeding three months.

Normally you get a 30-day or 60-day stay permit on arrival, depending on your expected length of stay. This is extendible for up to three months. Note that Sabah and Sarawak are treated in some ways like separate countries. Your passport will be checked again on arrival in each state and a new stay permit issued, usually for 30 days.

Even though Sarawak is a part of Malaysia, it has its own immigration controls which are designed, in theory, to protect the indigenous tribal people from being swamped by migrants from the peninsula and elsewhere. On arrival, most nationalities will be granted a one-month stay. In theory, it can be extended for another month in Kuching or Miri, but in practice this is very difficult. The Sarawak government is touchy about unannounced researchers, journalists, photographers and the like so remember: you're a tourist, nothing more.

Like Sarawak, Sabah is semi-autonomous and has its own immigration controls. On arrival, you are likely to be given a month's stay permit and it's rare to be asked to show money or onward tickets. Permits can be renewed at an immigration office, which can be found at most points of arrival.

Malaysian Embassies Abroad

Malaysian embassies in other countries of the region include:

Brunei
: 473 Kampung Pelambayan, Jalan Kota Baru, Bandar Seri Begawan (☎ 228410)

Hong Kong
: 24th floor, Malaysia Building, 50 Gloucester Rd, Wanchai (☎ (5) 270921)

Indonesia
: 17 Jalan Imam Bonjol, Jakarta 10310 (☎ 336438)

Thailand
: 35 South Sathorn Rd, Bangkok 10500 (☎ 286-1390)

Vietnam
: Block A-3 Van Phuc, Hanoi (☎ 53371)

Visas for Other Countries

You can get Thai visas from the embassy in KL or the consulates in Penang, Kota Bharu or Kota Kinabalu. The consulates are quick and convenient.

For information on the visa requirements for Brunei, see the Facts for the Visitor section of the Brunei chapter.

Most citizens of Western countries do not require a visa to enter Indonesia through the recognised entry/exit ports. A visa is required to travel overland from Kuching in Sarawak to Pontianak, or by sea from Tawau in Sabah to Tarakan or Melaka to Dumai.

Foreign Embassies

Countries with diplomatic representation in Malaysia include:

Australia
: 6 Jalan Yap Kwan Sweng, Kuala Lumpur (☎ 03-2423122)

Brunei
: MBF Plaza, 172 Jalan Ampang, Kuala Lumpur (☎ 03-2612800)

India
: 20th Floor West Block, Wisma Selangor Dredging, 142-C Jalan Ampang (☎ 03-2617095)

Indonesia
: 233 Jalan Tun Razak, Kuala Lumpur (☎ 03-9842011)
: 467 Jalan Burma, Penang (☎ 04-374686)
: 5A Pisang Rd, Kuching, Sarawak (☎ 082-241734)
: Jalan Karamunsing, Kota Kinabalu, Sabah (☎ 088-219578)
: Jalan Apas, Tawau, Sabah (☎ 089-765930)

Myanmar
: 5 Jalan Taman U Thant, Kuala Lumpur (☎ 03-2424085)

Philippines
: 1 Changkat Kia Peng, Kuala Lumpur (☎ 03-2484233)

Singapore
: 209 Jalan Tun Razak, Kuala Lumpur (☎ 03-2616277)

Thailand
: 206 Jalan Ampang, Kuala Lumpur (☎ 03-2488222)
: 1 Jalan Tunku Abdul Rahman, Penang (☎ 04-23352)
: 4426 Jalan Pengkalan Chepa, Kota Bharu (☎ 09-782545)
: Hong Kong & Shanghai Bank Building, Kota Kinabalu, Sabah (☎ 088-212622)

Vietnam
: Vietnam House, 4 Persiaran Stonor, Kuala Lumpur (☎ 03-2484036)

MONEY

Currency

The Malaysian ringgit (RM), sometimes called the Malaysian dollar, is divided into 100 sen. Notes in circulation are RM1, RM5, RM10, RM20, RM50, RM100, RM500 and RM1000; the coins in use are 1, 5, 10, 20 and 50 sen, and RM1.

Banks are efficient and there are also plenty of moneychangers to be found in the main centres. Credit cards are widely accepted at major hotels, restaurants and craft shops. Cash advances on credit cards can be obtained over the counter at many banks, and through any automatic teller machine (ATM) that displays credit card symbols. The Hong Kong & Shanghai Bank provides Visa and MasterCard cash advances and has branches in most major cities in Malaysia.

Exchange Rates

Australia	A$1	=	M$1.85
Canada	C$1	=	M$1.90
New Zealand	NZ$1	=	M$1.53
Britain	UK£1	=	M$3.88
USA	US$1	=	M$2.56
Japan	¥100	=	M$2.5
Germany	DM1	=	M$1.57
France	FF1	=	M$0.46
Thailand	1B	=	M$0.10

Costs

Malaysia is more expensive than other South-East Asian nations, although less so than Singapore. You get pretty much what you pay for – there are lots of hotels where a couple can get a quite decent room for around US$5, food is refreshingly cheap and the transport is also reasonable and efficient.

TOURIST OFFICES

Malaysia has an efficient national tourist body, Tourism Malaysia. It produces a huge variety of glossy brochures and other literature, most of it fairly useful. There are also quite a number of local tourist promotion organisations, such as the Penang Tourist Association, who back up the activities of Tourism Malaysia.

BUSINESS HOURS

Government offices are usually open Monday to Friday from around 8 am to 12.45 pm, and then again from 2 to 4.15 pm. On Friday the lunch break usually lasts from 11.30 am to 2.30 pm. On Saturday morning the offices are open from 8 am to 12.45 pm. These hours vary slightly from state to state;

on the east coast of the peninsula most government offices are closed on Friday.

Shop hours are also somewhat variable, although from 9.30 am to 7 pm is a good rule of thumb. Major department stores, Chinese emporiums and some stores catering particularly to tourists are open until 9 or 10 pm seven days a week.

HOLIDAYS

Although some public holidays have a fixed date each year, the Hindus, Muslims and Chinese all follow a lunar calendar which means the dates for many events vary each year.

National public holidays are New Year's Day (1 January), Chinese New Year (January or February), Hari Raya Puasa (March), Labour Day (1 May), Wesak Day (April or May), Hari Raya Haji (June), King's Birthday (5 June), Awal Muharam (May or June), Birthday of the Prophet (July or August), National Day (31 August), Deepavali (November) and Christmas Day (25 December). In addition, each state has its own public holidays to celebrate the birthdays of the sultans or other state-specific events, such as the Dayak harvest festivals in Sabah and Sarawak.

During school holidays, Hari Raya Puasa (the end of the fasting month) and Chinese New Year, accommodation may be difficult to obtain and transport can be fully booked.

CULTURAL EVENTS

With so many cultures and religions there is quite an amazing number of occasions to celebrate in Malaysia. The most important and colourful are described here, and Tourism Malaysia puts out a *Calendar of Events* booklet with specific dates and venues of various festivals and parades.

The major Muslim annual events are connected with Ramadan, the 30 days during which Muslims cannot eat or drink from sunrise to sunset. Hari Raya Puasa marks the end of the month-long fast with three days of joyful celebration. This is the major holiday of the Muslim calendar.

Chinese New Year is the most important celebration for the Chinese community. Dragon dances and pedestrian parades mark the start of the new year. Families hold open house, unmarried relatives (especially children) receive *ang pows*, or money in red packets, businesses traditionally clear their debts and everybody wishes you a 'kong hee fatt choy' (a happy and prosperous new year). The Moon Cake Festival around September celebrates the overthrow of the Mongol warlords in ancient China with the eating of moon cakes and the lighting of colourful paper lanterns. The Festival of the Nine Emperor Gods involves nine days of Chinese operas, processions and other events honouring the nine emperor gods. In KL and Penang, in October or November, fire-walking ceremonies are held on the evening of the ninth day. The Dragon Boat Festival is celebrated around June with boat races in Penang.

Thaipusam is one of the most dramatic Hindu festivals, in which devotees honour Lord Subramaniam with acts of amazing masochism. Self-mutilating worshippers make the procession to the Batu Caves outside Kuala Lumpur, usually in January or February. The festival of Deepavali celebrates Rama's victory over the demon King Rawana with the Festival of Lights, where tiny oil lamps are lit outside Hindu homes. It is held in October.

If you are in Sarawak from 1 to 2 June, don't miss Gawai Dayak, the festival of the Dayaks to mark the end of the rice season. War dances, cockfights and blowpipe events all take place. National Day, 31 August, is celebrated throughout the country with parades and special events.

POST & TELECOMMUNICATIONS

Post

Malaysia has an efficient postal system with a reliable poste restante service at the major post offices. Post offices are generally open from 8 am to 5 pm Monday to Friday and until noon Saturday.

Aerogrammes and postcards cost 50 sen to any destination.

Telephone
There are good telephone communications throughout the country. You can direct dial long-distance calls between all major towns in Malaysia. Local calls cost 10 sen for three minutes.

Convenient card phones, Kadfon, are found all over the country and take plastic cards, though two telephone systems – Telekom and Uniphone – operate using different cards. Credit card phones are also available. International calls can be direct dialled from public phone booths and from most Telekom offices. Reverse charge international calls can easily be made from any phone by dialling the Home Country Direct numbers that are to be found listed in the telephone book. Calls to Singapore are long-distance calls rather than being international calls.

BOOKS
There are a wide variety of books available in Malaysia and a number of good bookshops in which to find them. The main chains are MPH and Berita.

Kampong Boy and the more recently published *Town Boy* by Malaysian cartoonist Lat (Straits Times Publishing) provide a delightful introduction to Malay life. They are a humorous autobiographical cartoon series on growing up in a village and then moving to the town of Ipoh.

Culture Shock, by JoAnn Craig, attempts to explain the customs, cultures and lifestyles of Malaysia and Singapore's polyglot population to expats who work there.

For more detail on the history of Malaysia, a good source is *A Short History of Malaysia, Singapore & Brunei* by C Mary Turnbull. The 'White Rajahs' in North Borneo have also been well documented and *Nineteenth Century Borneo – A Study in Diplomatic Rivalry* by Graham Irwin is the best book on the fascinating history of Sarawak, Sabah and Brunei.

Vanishing World, the Ibans of Borneo by Leigh Wright has some beautiful colour photographs. Redmond O'Hanlon's *Into the Heart of Borneo* is a wonderfully funny tale of a jaunt through the jungles of north Borneo. For Bornean wildlife, *A Field Guide to the Mammals of Borneo* by Junaidi Payne, Charles M Francis and Karen Phillipps is a must.

Malaysia has provided a fertile setting for novelists and Joseph Conrad's *The Shadow Line* and *Lord Jim* both use the region as a setting. Somerset Maugham also set many of his classic short stories in Malaya – look for the *Borneo Stories*. Paul Theroux's *The Consul's File* is based in the small town of Ayer Hitam. Another excellent read is *Turtle Beach* by Blanche d'Alpuget, which gives an insight into the Vietnamese boat people, the impact of their arrival in Malaysia and the racial tension those events engendered – with flashbacks to the horrors of 1969.

MAPS
You can get good road maps from petrol stations. Probably the best map is that produced by Shell, which has a larger scale as it is two-sided. However, the Mobil map also shows relief.

The Nelles Verlag *Malaysia* map is excellent for the peninsula and East Malaysia. It also has a number of city maps. It has a scale of 1:1.5 million and is widely available in Malaysia.

MEDIA
Malaysia has newspapers in English, Malay, Chinese and Tamil. The *New Straits Times* is the main offering in English.

Malaysia has two government TV channels and one commercial TV station. Programmes range from local productions in the various languages to imports from the USA and UK.

HEALTH
Malaysia enjoys good standards of health and cleanliness. The usual rules for healthy living in a tropical environment apply. The main problem to look out for is malaria in East Malaysia, so take those tablets or carry a net, or both.

For more information, see the Health

section in the Facts for the Visitor chapter at the beginning of this book.

DRUGS

In Malaysia, the answer is simple – don't. Drug trafficking carries a mandatory death penalty and the list of Malaysian drug executions is quite a long one and includes Westerners. In almost every village in Malaysia, you will see anti-'dadah' (drugs) signs portraying a skull and crossbones and a noose. No one can say they haven't been warned!

ACCOMMODATION

For the budget traveller, the best places to track down are traditional Chinese hotels, which are found in great numbers all over Malaysia. They're the mainstay of budget travellers and backpackers, and in Malaysia you can generally find a good room from RM10 to RM16. Chinese hotels are generally spartan – bare floors and just a bed, a couple of chairs, a table, a wardrobe and a sink. A gently swishing ceiling fan completes the picture.

Couples can sometimes economise by asking for a single, since in Chinese hotel language single means one double bed and double means two beds. Don't think this is being tight, as in Chinese hotels you can pack as many into one room as you wish.

The main catch with these hotels is that they can sometimes be terribly noisy. Part of the noise comes from the street, as the hotels are often on main roads, but there's also the traditional dawn chorus of coughing, hacking and spitting which has to be experienced to be believed. It's worst in the oldest hotels where the walls don't quite reach the ceiling but are meshed in at the top for ventilation.

Malaysia also has a variety of cheap local accommodation, usually at beach centres. These may be huts on the beach or guesthouses (private homes or rented houses divided by partition walls into a number of rooms). A dorm bed costs from RM5 to RM8 and rooms range from RM8 to RM20.

FOOD

While travel in some parts of Asia can be as good as a session with Weight Watchers, Malaysia is quite the opposite. The food is simply terrific, the variety unbeatable and the costs pleasantly low. Whether you're looking for Chinese, Malay, Indian or Indonesian food, or even a Big Mac, you'll find happiness!

Chinese Food

You'll find the full range of Chinese cuisine in Malaysia. If you're kicking round the backwoods of Sabah or Sarawak, however, Chinese food is likely to consist of little more than rice and vegetables.

Indian Food

Indian food is one of the region's greatest delights. Indeed, it's easier to find good Indian food in Malaysia than in India! You can roughly divide Indian food into southern, Muslim and northern: food from southern India tends to be hotter with the emphasis on vegetarian dishes, while Muslim food tends to be more subtle in its spicing and uses more meat. The rich Moghul dishes of northern India are not so common and are generally only found in more expensive restaurants.

A favourite Indian Muslim dish which is cheap, easy to find and of excellent standard is *biryani*. Served with a chicken or mutton curry the dish takes its name from the saffron-coloured rice it is served with.

Malay, Indonesian & Nonya Food

Surprisingly, Malay food is not as easily found in Malaysia as Chinese or Indian food, although many Malay dishes, like *satay*, are everywhere.

Nonya cooking is a local variation on Chinese and Malay food. It uses Chinese ingredients, but employs local spices like chillies and coconut cream. Nonya cooking is essentially a home skill rather than a restaurant one – there are few places where you can find Nonya food. *Laksa*, a spicy coconut-based soup, is a classic Nonya dish that has been adopted by all Malaysians.

Other Cuisine

Western fast-food addicts will find that Ronald McDonald, the Colonel from Kentucky and A&W have all made inroads into the regional eating scene.

Tropical Fruit

Once you've tried rambutans, mangosteens, jackfruit and durians, how can you ever go back to boring old apples and oranges? Refer to the Food section in the Facts about the Region chapter at the beginning of this book for all the info on these delights.

DRINKS

Life can be thirsty in Malaysia, so you'll be relieved to hear that drinks are excellent, economical and readily available. For a start, water can be drunk straight from the tap in most larger Malaysian cities.

Fruit juices are popular and very good. With the aid of a blender and crushed ice, delicious concoctions like watermelon juice can be whipped up in seconds. Old-fashioned sugar cane crushers, which look like grandma's old washing mangle, can still be seen in operation.

Halfway between a drink and a dessert are *es kacang* and *cendol*. An es or ais (ice) kacang is rather like an old-fashioned snocone, but the shaved ice is topped with syrups and condensed milk and it's all piled on top of a foundation of beans and jellies. It sounds gross and looks lurid but tastes terrific! Cendol consists of coconut milk with brown sugar syrup and greenish noodle-like things topped with shaved ice.

Other oddities? Well, the milky white drink in clear plastic bins sold by street drink sellers is soybean milk which is also sold in a yoghurty form. Soybean milk is also available in soft drink bottles. Medicinal teas are a big deal with the health-minded Chinese.

Beer drinkers will probably find Anchor Beer or Tiger Beer to their taste, although the minimum price for a bottle of beer is at least RM3. Locally brewed Carlsberg and Guinness are also popular.

Getting There & Away

AIR

The usual gateway to Malaysia is KL, although Penang also has international connections. Singapore is also a handy arrival point as it's just a short trip across the causeway from Johor Bahru.

Penang is a major centre for cheap airline tickets. These days the better agents are usually OK, but beware of places which ask for big advance payments before they issue you with the tickets. Typical one-way fares being quoted out of Penang include Madras in India for RM630, Phuket for RM170, Bangkok for RM310 and Hong Kong for RM760. Other fares may involve flying from KL or even Bangkok.

To/From Thailand

MAS and Thai International fly between Penang and Hat Yai, Phuket and Bangkok. You can fly from Penang to Bangkok for about RM290, more from KL. From Penang to Phuket it's RM170 – flying from Penang to Phuket can save a lot of time wasted in crossing the border by land.

To/From Indonesia

There are several interesting variations from Indonesia to Malaysia. The short hop from Medan in Sumatra to Penang costs around US$60; from Penang it's RM149 (MAS) or RM140 (Sempati). There are also twice-weekly MAS flights (on Monday and Thursday) between Kuching in Sarawak and Pontianak in Kalimantan, the Indonesian part of the island of Borneo, for RM177. An Indonesian visa is not required to enter Pontianak by air. MAS and Bouraq, the Indonesian feeder airline, have international flights from Tawau in Sabah to Tarakan in Kalimantan (Indonesia) for around RM180. See the Kota Kinabalu (Sabah) Getting There & Away section for details of airline offices in that city.

To/From Brunei
MAS has flights from Kota Kinabalu in Sabah to Bandar Seri Begawan in Brunei for RM83.

To/From Singapore
It is much cheaper to fly from Malaysia to Singapore than in the reverse direction. See the Singapore chapter for details on flights to and from Singapore.

To/From Other Places in Asia
Although Indonesia and Thailand are the two usual places to travel to or from Malaysia, there are plenty of other possibilities including Sri Lanka, India and Myanmar. MAS and Cathay Pacific fly between Kota Kinabalu and Hong Kong for around RM650, but you will probably find cheaper tickets on Philippine Airlines. Cathay Pacific also have direct flights from Penang to Hong Kong.

MAS has direct flights from Kota Kinabalu in Sabah to Tokyo and Seoul. MAS flies from Kota Kinabalu to Manila five times a week. Philippine Airlines also operates on this route – the fare is around US$200 and flight time is just under two hours. See the Kota Kinabalu (Sabah) Getting There & Away section for details of airline offices in that city.

LAND

To/From Thailand
You can cross into Thailand from Malaysia by land at Changlun (road), Padang Besar (road or rail) or Keroh (road) in the west, or at Rantau Panjang (road) in the east. An alternative route into Thailand is via the river ferry at Pengkalan Kubor on the east coast, but few travellers go this way.

Road – West Coast The majority of travellers go from Changlun to Sadao in Thailand, then on to Hat Yai. From Georgetown (on Penang) Thai taxis and buses go straight through to Hat Yai, and from Hat Yai there are plenty of buses and trains to Phuket, Surat Thani, Bangkok or other places.

It is difficult to cross the border in stages. You can easily get a bus or taxi up to Changlun on the Malaysian side and on from Sadao to Hat Yai on the Thai side, but between the two is a long stretch of neutral territory.

The alternative is to cross at Padang Besar, where the railway also crosses and where the border is an easy walk across. There is another border point at Keroh, but this is the least convenient crossing.

Road – East Coast The Thai border is at Rantau Panjang (Sungai Kolok on the Thai side), 1½ hours by bus from Kota Bharu. From Rantau Panjang you walk across the border and then it's about one km to the station or a trishaw costs RM3. Malaysian currency is accepted in Sungai Kolok. From Sungai Kolok there are trains to Surat Thani at 6 am, one to Bangkok at 10.05 am and an express train to Bangkok at 10.55 am. All trains stop at Hat Yai and Surat Thani.

Train The Butterworth-Alor Setar-Hat Yai rail route crosses into Thailand at Padang Besar. You can take the International Express from Butterworth all the way to Bangkok with connections from Singapore and KL. Once in Hat Yai, there are frequent train and bus connections to other parts of Thailand.

Fares from Butterworth to Hat Yai are RM14.80 in 2nd class. Travelling to Bangkok on the International Express, the fare is RM42.30 in 2nd class and the additional cost for berths ranges from RM9 to RM22.60. The International Express leaves Butterworth at 2 pm, arriving in Hat Yai at 6.10 pm and Bangkok at 9.50 am the next day.

To/From Indonesia
A daily express bus runs between Kuching in Sarawak and Pontianak in Kalimantan for RM35. An Indonesian visa is required for the land border crossing at Tebedu/Entikong. See the Kuching Getting There & Away section for more details.

To/From Brunei
The Miri Belait Transport Company at the main bus stand in Miri, Sarawak, has buses

at 7, 9, 10.30 am and 1 and 3 pm to Kuala Belait, the first town in Brunei. The fare is RM11.50 and the trip takes about 2½ hours. Buses depart Kuala Belait for Seria frequently throughout the day; they cost B$1 and take about 30 minutes. There are several buses from Seria to Bandar Seri Begawan (B$4; two hours) until 2.30 pm.

The alternative to all this bus hopping is take one of the private minibus services which go all the way to Bandar Seri Begawan for RM30. Miri-Sibu Express (☎ 085-33898) at the bus station has minibuses leaving Miri at 11 am and 2 pm.

To/From Singapore

Most travellers enter or exit Singapore by the causeway connecting Johor Bahru and Singapore Island. Frequent buses do the short run, and a number of long-distance buses operate from the regional centres in Malaysia direct to Singapore city. The Malaysian rail system also terminates in Singapore.

SEA

To/From Thailand

There are several yachts operating between Langkawi, 30 km off the coast from Kuala Perlis in the north-west of Peninsular Malaysia, and Phuket in Thailand. Typically, they sail the Langkawi-Ko Phi Phi-Krabi-Phuket route and cost US$200 per person. The Kuala Perlis-Langkawi Ferry Service also had a Penang-Langkawi-Phuket express ferry service, but at the time of writing the service had stopped and its future was uncertain. It may start up again if there is enough demand in peak tourist seasons.

Cheaper and more frequent are the small boats that skip across the border from Kuala Perlis through to Satun in Thailand. There are customs and immigration posts here so you can cross quite legally, although it's an unusual and rarely used entry or exit point. Make sure you get your passport stamped on entry.

To/From Indonesia

To/From Sumatra & Java The most popular way to reach Sumatra is to travel from Penang to Medan by high-speed ferry. It is also possible to reach Medan from Lumut (the departure point for Pulau Pangkor) or Port Kelang (near KL). Ferries also operate to Dumai in Sumatra from Port Kelang and Melaka but you need a visa to enter or leave Indonesia through Dumai.

From Penang, two companies, both near the local tourist office, operate boats to Medan and between them there is a departure every day except Friday and Sunday. The journey takes 4½ hours and costs RM110/90 in 1st/2nd class. The boats land in Belawan (the port of Medan) and the 26-km journey to Medan is completed by bus (45 minutes, included in the price). Kuala Perlis Langkawi Ferry Service (☎ 04-625630) has ferries on Tuesday, Thursday and Saturday at 9 am. Ekspres Bahagia (☎ 04-631943) has departures from Penang on Monday (noon), Wednesday (9 am), Thursday (noon) and Saturday (10 am).

Ferries from Lumut go to Belawan (RM110/90, 3½ hours) on Wednesday, Friday and Sunday at 9 am.

From Port Kelang the most useful service is to Belawan (RM120, six hours) at 10 am on Sunday. Ferries also leave for Dumai at 10 am on Tuesday (RM180, four hours).

There's also a ferry service daily (except Sunday) between Melaka and Dumai (RM80, 2½ hours).

From Pasir Gudang, about 30 km from Johor Bahru, boats go to Batam (RM30, 1½ hours) and Bintang (RM 50, three hours) in Sumatra's Riau Archipelago, and to Surabaya in Java (RM200, 60 hours). See under Johor Bahru for more details.

To/From Kalimantan In Borneo, the *K M Samudra Express* operates between Tawau in Sabah and Nunukan and then continues to Tarakan in Kalimantan. It leaves from the customs wharf around the back of the large supermarket at 8.30 am on weekdays. The cost to Nunukan is RM25 and to Tarakan costs RM60. Other boats that operate only to Nunukan are the *K M Samudrah Indah* and the *K M Harapan Mulia*. From Nunukan other boats go to Tarakan. Schedules are haphazard on the Tawau-Nunukan run and constantly subject to change, but there is usually a boat every day.

If you are travelling to Nunukan or Tarakan, it's worth noting that visas cannot be issued on arrival and you must get one before crossing into Indonesia.

To/From Brunei

The most popular way to reach Brunei from Sabah is to take a ferry from Kota Kinabalu or Merapok to Labuan Island, which is off the coast of south-western Sabah, and then another ferry to Bandar Seri Begawan in Brunei. Boats to Brunei (RM24) depart at 8 am, noon and either 2 or 3 pm. Buy tickets at the small kiosk outside the ferry terminal building at least half an hour before the departure, or book through agents in town. From Brunei you can travel overland to Sarawak.

There are frequent boats daily to Bandar Seri Begawan, which is the capital of Brunei, from Limbang in Sarawak. The trip takes about 30 minutes and the cost is RM10. Another boat for Brunei leaves from Lawas in Sarawak at 7.30 and costs RM20.

To/From Singapore

Ferries operate between Changi in Singapore and Pengerang and Tanjung Belungkor in the state of Johor (see under the Singapore Getting There & Away section for more details). The ferries mostly service the popular Malaysian weekend resort of Desaru.

A high-speed ferry also runs between Tioman Island and Singapore's World Trade Centre (see Tioman Island in the Peninsula Malaysia – East Coast section for details).

Getting Around

AIR

The Malaysian Airline System (MAS) is the country's main domestic operator and has an extensive network linking the major regional centres on the peninsula, Sabah and Sarawak, and the offshore islands of Tioman and Langkawi. Pelangi Air is a small regional airline that has useful services to Tioman, Langkawi, Pangkor and Melaka, among other destinations. The airfares chart below details

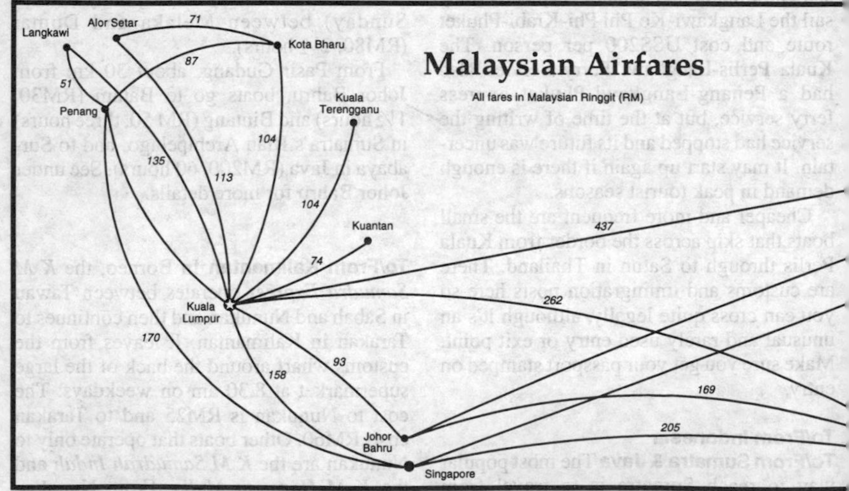

some of the main regional routes and their fares in Malaysian dollars.

The main reason to catch flights within Malaysia is to travel between the peninsula and East Malaysia. You can save quite a few dollars if flying to Sarawak or Sabah by flying from Johor Bahru rather than Kuala Lumpur or Singapore. The regular economy fare is RM169 from Johor Bahru to Kuching against RM262 from KL and RM205 from Singapore. To Kota Kinabalu, the respective fares are RM347, RM437 and RM418. MAS has many other regional routes in Sarawak and Sabah.

MAS also has a number of special night flights and advance purchase fares. The 14-day advance purchase tickets are available for the following one-way flights:

Route	*Fare*
Johor Bahru to Kuching	RM144
Johor Bahru to Kota Kinabalu	RM295
Johor Bahru to Penang	RM150
Kuala Lumpur to Kuching	RM227
Kuala Lumpur to Kota Kinabalu	RM372
Kuala Lumpur to Pulau Labuan	RM372

BUS

Malaysia has an excellent bus system. There are public buses on local runs and a variety of privately operated buses on the longer trips. In larger towns there may be a number of bus stops – a main station or two, plus some of the private companies may operate directly from their own offices.

Buses are fast, economical and reasonably comfortable, and seats can be reserved. Many routes use air-con buses which usually cost just a few ringgit more than regular buses. They make midday travel a sweat-free activity, but beware – as one traveller put it, 'Malaysian air-conditioned buses are really meat lockers on wheels with just two settings: cold and suspended animation'.

TRAIN

Malaysia has a modern, comfortable and economical railway service, although there are basically only two railway lines. One runs from Singapore to Butterworth and continues on into Thailand. The other branches from this line at Gemas, south of KL, and runs through Kuala Lipis up to the north-east corner of the country near Kota Bharu.

Malaysia basically has two types of rail service – express and ordinary trains – and there are a number of variations of each.

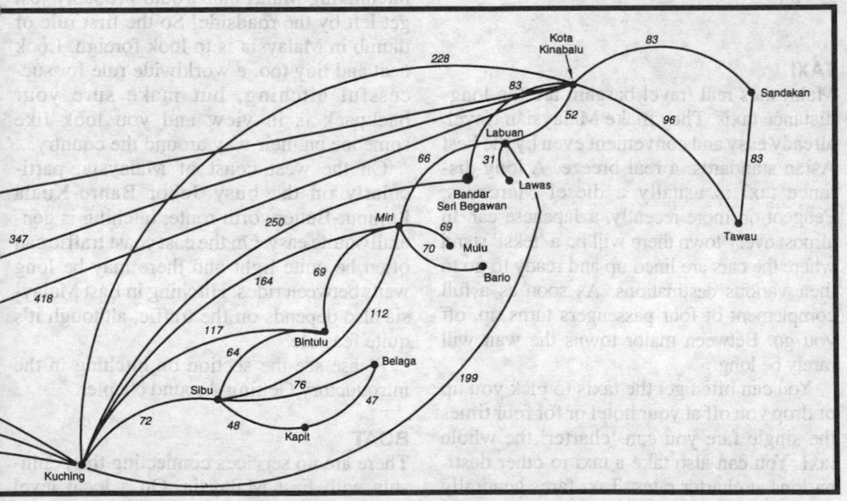

Express trains are air-con and night trains have a choice of sleepers or seats. They are generally 1st and 2nd class only, though 3rd class is sometimes available. Ordinary trains are usually 3rd class non-air-con only, but some also have 1st and 2nd-class carriages. Express trains cost about 20% more than ordinary trains, are faster, only stop at main stations and in most respects are the ones to take. Book as far in advance as possible for the express trains.

The recently privatised national railway company Keretapi Tanah Melayu (KTM) offers a Railpass to students and anyone under 30 for 21 days for US$54, 14 days for US$43 and seven days for US$32. It is valid for all classes on the trains.

In Sabah there's also a small narrow-gauge line which can take you through the Padas River gorge from Tenom to Beaufort. It's a great trip and is well worth doing.

Fares (RM) from Kuala Lumpur

Destination	*Express*		*Ordinary*	
	2nd	3rd	2nd	3rd
Padang Besar	44	24	35.10	20.00
Butterworth	34	19	25.40	14.40
Ipoh	22	112	13.70	7.80
Johor Bahru	33	118	24.10	13.70
Singapore	34	19	26.00	14.80

TAXI

Malaysia's real travel bargain are the long-distance taxis. They make Malaysian travel, already easy and convenient even by the best Asian standards, a real breeze. A long-distance taxi is usually a diesel Mercedes, Peugeot or, more recently, a Japanese car. In almost every town there will be a 'teksi' stand where the cars are lined up and ready to go to their various destinations. As soon as a full complement of four passengers turns up, off you go. Between major towns the wait will rarely be long.

You can often get the taxis to pick you up or drop you off at your hotel or for four times the single fare you can 'charter' the whole taxi. You can also take a taxi to other destinations at charter rates. Taxi fares generally work out at about twice the comparable bus fares.

CAR

Rent-a-car operations are well established in Malaysia. Basically, driving in Malaysia follows much the same rules as in Britain or Australia – cars are right-hand drive and you drive on the left side of the road. The roads are good and most drivers in Malaysia are relatively sane, safe and slow though a fair few specialise in overtaking on blind corners and otherwise trusting in divine intervention.

Petrol costs are around RM1.13 a litre; diesel fuel costs RM0.65 per litre. Major rental operators in Malaysia include Avis, Budget, Hertz, National and Thrifty, although there are numerous local operators. Unlimited distance rates for a Proton Saga, the most popular car in Malaysia, start at around RM800 per week, including insurance and collision damage waiver.

HITCHING

Malaysia has long had a reputation for being an excellent place for hitchhiking and it's generally still true. You'll get picked up by expats and by Malaysians and Singaporeans, but it's strictly an activity for foreigners – a hitchhiking Malaysian would probably just get left by the roadside! So the first rule of thumb in Malaysia is to look foreign. Look neat and tidy too, a worldwide rule for successful hitching, but make sure your backpack is in view and you look like someone on their way around the country.

On the west coast of Malaysia, particularly on the busy Johor Bahru-Kuala Lumpur-Butterworth route, hitching is generally quite easy. On the east coast traffic can often be quite light and there may be long waits between rides. Hitching in East Malaysia also depends on the traffic, although it's quite feasible.

Please see the section on hitching in the introductory Getting Around chapter.

BOAT

There are no services connecting the peninsula with East Malaysia. On a local level there are boats between the peninsula and offshore islands, and along the rivers of Sabah and Sarawak – see the relevant sections for full details.

LOCAL TRANSPORT

Local transport varies widely from place to place. Almost everywhere there are taxis and in most cases these are metered. In major cities there are buses – in Kuala Lumpur the government buses are backed up by private operators.

In many towns there are also bicycle rickshaws – while they are dying out in Kuala Lumpur and have become principally a tourist gimmick in many Malaysian cities they are still a viable form of transport. Indeed in places like Georgetown, with its convoluted and narrow streets, a bicycle rickshaw is probably the best way of getting around.

Peninsular Malaysia – West Coast

The peninsula is a long finger of land stretching down from the Thai border to Singapore, the tip of which is only 137 km north of the equator. It comprises 11 of the 13 states that make up Malaysia. On the western side of the peninsula, you'll find the major cities – oriental Penang, the bustling, modern capital of Kuala Lumpur, historic Melaka – and the restful hill stations.

The shining beaches of the east coast, Taman Negara National Park and the wild central mountains are covered in the Peninsular Malaysia – East Coast section later in this chapter. The following description starts with the capital, Kuala Lumpur, but otherwise follows the route from Johor Bahru, just across the causeway from Singapore, and moves up the west coast to the Thai border.

KUALA LUMPUR

Malaysia's capital city is a curious blend of the old and the new. It's a modern and fast-moving city although the
on the nightmare proportions
has gleaming high-rise office blo
multilane highways, but the old co
architecture still manages to stand
proudly.

It's also a blend of cultures – the Malay capital with a vibrant Chinatown, an Indian quarter and a playing field in the middle of the city where the crack of cricket bat on ball can still be heard.

KL, as it's almost always called, started in the 1860s when a band of prospectors in search of tin landed at the meeting point of the Kelang and Gombak rivers and named it Kuala Lumpur, or Muddy Estuary.

Orientation

The real heart of KL is Merdeka Square, not far from the confluence of the two muddy rivers from which KL takes its name. Just to the south-east of this square is the modern business centre of KL and the older Chinatown. Heading east is Jalan Tun Perak, a major trunk road which leads to the Puduraya bus and taxi station on the eastern edge of the central district.

Running north from Merdeka Square is Jalan Tuanku Abdul Rahman (henceforth also known as Jalan TAR) with a number of KL's popular cheaper hotels and more modern buildings. Jalan Raja Laut runs parallel to Jalan TAR and takes the northbound traffic.

The GPO is just to the south of Merdeka Square and a little further on is the Masjid Negara (National Mosque) and the KL railway station. Beyond them, to the west, is KL's green belt where you can find the Lake Gardens, the Muzium Negara (National Museum) and the National Monument, and the Malaysian Parliament.

Information

Tourist Offices The Tourism Malaysia tourist information counter (☎ 03-4411295) is on level two of the Putra World Trade Centre on Jalan Tun Ismail in the north-western section of KL. It is open Monday to

Peninsular Malaysia

0 50 100 km

SOUTH CHINA SEA

STRAITS OF MELAKA

SUMATRA (INDONESIA)

KEDAH

PENANG

PERAK

KELANTAN

TERENGGANU

PAHANG

SELANGOR

KUALA LUMPUR

NEGERI SEMBILAN

MELAKA

JOHOR

SINGAPORE

Yala

Kuala Perlis

Changlun

Alor Setar

Tumpat

Kota Bharu

Sungai Kolok

Rantau Panjang

Pasir Puteh

Kuala Besut

Pulau Perhentian Kecil

Pulau Perhentian Besar

Pulau Redang

Betong

Keroh

Georgetown

Pulau Pinang

Kulim

Butterworth

Grik

Kuala Krai

Kuala Terengganu

Marang

Taiping

Gua Musang

Rantau Abang

Kuala Kangsar

Ipoh

Kuala Dungun

Taman Negara

Batu Gajah

Cameron Highlands

Kemasik

Tapah

Kemaman

Chukai

Pulau Pangkor

Lumut

Kuala Lipis

Bidor

Cherating

Selim River

Jerantut

Beserah

Kuantan

Gambang

Kuala Kubu Bahru

Maran

Mentakab

Temerloh

Pekan

Genting Highlands

Triang

Port Kelang

Serdang

Ayer Hitam

Pulau Tioman

Banting

Morib

Seremban

Kuala Rompin

Gemas

Endau

Port Dickson

Segamat

Mersing

Labis

Melaka

Jemaluang

Yong Peng

Kluang

Muar

Batu Pahat

Ayer Hitam

Kota Tinggi

Pontian Kecil

Johor Bahru

Kukup

Vietnam

Philippines

Thailand

Peninsular Malaysia

Brunei

East Malaysia

Sumatra (Indonesia)

Singapore

Kalimantan (Indonesia)

Friday from 8.30 am to 4.45 pm and on Saturday from 8 am to 12.45 pm.

More convenient is the KL Visitors Centre (☎ 03-2936661), near the junction of Jalan Raja Laut and Jalan Tun Perak in the centre of KL. Tourism Malaysia also have offices at the railway station and at the airport.

To complete the picture there is also the Malaysia Tourist Information Centre (☎ 03-2423929) on Jalan Ampang, north-east of the city centre. As well as a tourist information counter, there's a moneychanger (9 am to 9 pm daily), MAS counter, Expres Nasional bus booking counter, a Taman Negara information counter and a Telekom office (open office hours only). The centre also has audio-visual shows, dance performances and an expensive restaurant and souvenir shop.

Money There are plenty of banks throughout the central area of KL. For moneychangers try Jalan Sultan near the Kelang bus station or Jalan Ampang.

The American Express office (☎ 03-2613000) is in the MAS Building on Jalan Sultan Ismail.

Post & Telecommunications The huge GPO building is across the Kelang River from the central district. It is open Monday to Saturday from 9 am to 6 pm. Poste restante mail is held at the information desk, and there's a credit card fax machine.

For international calls during business hours the best place to head for is the Malaysia Tourist Information Centre. At other times the Telekom office just off Jalan Raja Chulan close to the centre is open 24 hours a day. There's also a Home Country Direct phone at the railway station.

Immigration Office The Immigration Office (☎ 03-2555077) is located at Block 1, Jalan Damansutra, about one km west of the Lake Gardens. Take a Sri Jaya bus No 250 from the Jalan Sultan Mohammed bus stand.

Travel Agencies STA Travel (☎ 03-2305720) has an office in the Asia Hotel in Chow Kit. This is a reliable company and they often have some interesting deals on offer.

Chinatown

Just south of the Masjid Jame are the teeming streets of KL's Chinatown. Bounded by Jalan Sultan, Jalan Cheng Lock and Jalan Sultan Mohammed, this crowded, colourful area is the usual melange of signs, shops, activity and noise. At night, the central section of Jalan Petaling is closed to traffic to become a brightly lit and frantically busy *pasar malam*, or **night market**.

Masjid Negara

Sited in seven hectares of landscaped gardens, the modernistic National Mosque is one of the largest in South-East Asia. A 73-metre-high minaret stands in the centre of a pool and the main dome of the mosque is in the form of an 18-pointed star which represents the 13 states of Malaysia and the five pillars of Islam.

Historic Buildings

If the National Mosque is altogether too modern for you, then you have only to cross the road to find a building full of Eastern promise – KL's magnificent **railway station**. Built in 1911, this delightful example of British colonial humour is a Moorish fantasy of spires, minarets, towers, cupolas and arches.

Across from this superb railway station is the equally wonderful **Malayan Railway Administration Building**. Almost directly across from the station stands the shell of the once-gracious colonial Majestic Hotel.

Designed by the British architect A C Norman and built between 1894 and 1897, the **Sultan Abdul Samad Building**, formerly known as the Secretariat Building, and the adjoining old **GPO** and **City Hall** are in a Moorish style similar to that of the railway station. The Sultan Abdul Samad Building is topped by a 43-metre-high clocktower.

The **Masjid Jame**, or Friday Mosque, is built at the confluence of the Kelang and Gombak rivers and overlooks Merdeka Square. This was the place where KL's

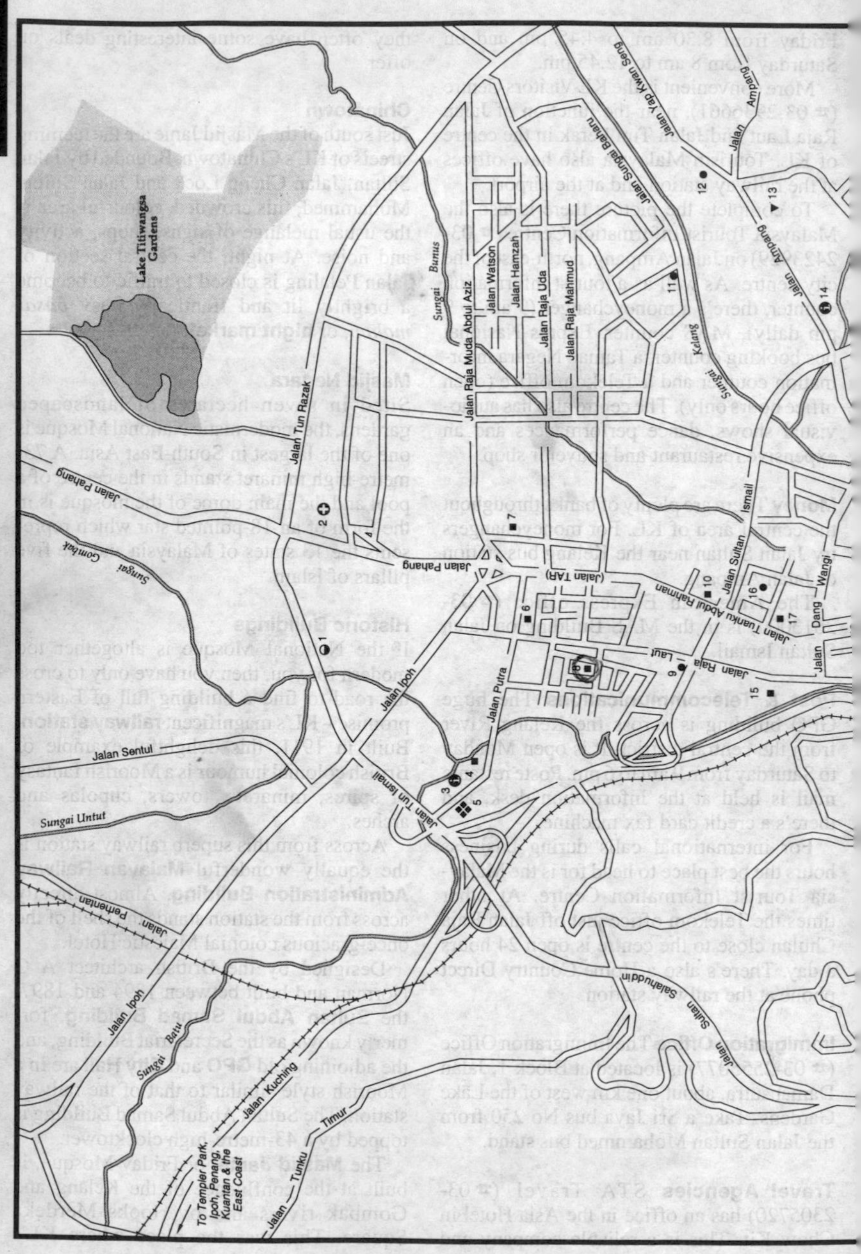
Lake Titiwangsa Gardens
Jalan Tun Razak
Jalan Pahang
Sungai Gombak
Sungai Bunus
Jalan Raja Muda Abdul Aziz
Jalan Watson
Jalan Hamzah
Jalan Raja Uda
Jalan Raja Mahmud
Jalan Sungai Baharu
Jalan Yap Kwan Seng
Jalan Ampang
Sungai Kelang
Jalan Sultan Ismail
Jalan Pahang
(Jalan TAR)
Jalan Tuanku Abdul Rahman
Jalan Dang Wangi
Jalan Raja Laut
Jalan Putra
Jalan Ipoh
Jalan Sentul
Jalan Tun Ismail
Sungai Untut
Jalan Perhentian
Jalan Ipoh
Sungai Batu
Jalan Kuching
Jalan Tunku Timur
Jalan Sultan Salahuddin
To Templer Park, Ipoh, Penang, Kuantan & the East Coast
1
2
3
4
5
6
7
8
9
10
11
12
13
14
15
16
17

Kuala Lumpur
0
250
500 m
To Petaling Jaya
Jalan Damansara
Lake Gardens
Jalan Parlimen
Jalan Kuching
Jalan Raja Laut
Jalan Tun Perak
Jalan Cheng Lock
Jalan Sultan
Jalan Kinabalu
See Central Kuala Lumpur Map
Jalan Maharajalela
Jalan Stadium
Jalan Hang Jebat
Jalan Hang Tuah
Jalan Pudu
Jalan Bukit Bintang
Jalan Imbi
Jalan Sultan Ismail
Jalan P Ramlee
Jalan Raja Chulan
Jalan Ampang
Cangkat Tambi Dollah
To Pudu Market, Melaka & Singapore
Jalan Sungai Besi
Jalan San Peng
Jalan Loke Yew
Jalan Lapangan Terbang
Jalan Istana
Jalan Syed Putra
To Airport
Jalan Tun Sambanthan
Jalan Travers

PLACES TO STAY

4 Pan Pacific Hotel
6 Transit Villa
7 Asia Hotel
8 Ben Soo Homestay
10 Paradise Hotel
15 City Point Holiday Inn
17 Shiraz Hotel & Restaurant
18 Kowloon Hotel
19 Concorde Hotel
20 Shangri La Hotel
22 Holiday Inn on the Park
23 Equatorial Hotel
29 Kuala Lumpur Hilton
30 The Lodge Hotel
34 Istana Hotel
37 Regent Hotel
39 Apollo Hotel
42 Bintang Bed & Breakfast
43 Malaysia Hotel
45 Parkroyal Hotel
48 Swiss Garden Hotel
50 YMCA

PLACES TO EAT

13 Le Coq D'Or Restaurant
27 Food Centre
47 Ramadan Restaurant

OTHER

1 Pekeleling Bus Station
2 General Hospital
3 Tourism Malaysia
5 The Mall Shopping Centre
9 National Library
11 Pasar Minggu
12 Australian High Commission
14 Malaysia Tourist Information Centre
16 Wisma Loke
21 Life Centre
24 Pernas International Building
25 MAS
26 AIA Building
28 Wisma Stephens
31 The Weld Shopping Centre
32 Parliament Building
33 National Monument
35 National Handicrafts Museum
36 Karyaneka Handicraft Centre
38 KL Plaza
40 Lot 10 Shopping Centre
41 Bukit Bintang Plaza
44 Sungei Wang Plaza
46 Imbi Plaza
49 Muzium Negara
51 International Buddhist Pagoda
52 Istana Negara

founders first set foot in the town and where supplies were landed for the tin mines.

Jalan Ampang

Lined with impressive mansions, Jalan Ampang, proceeding north-east from the city centre, was built up by the early tin millionaires. Today, many of the fine buildings have become embassies and consulates so that the street is KL's Ambassador's Row.

Museums & Galleries

At the southern end of the Lake Gardens and less than a km along Jalan Damansara from the railway station is the **Muzium Negara** (National Museum). It's full of unusual exhibits, such as the skull of an elephant which derailed a train!

Another strange sight is an 'amok catcher', an ugly barbed device used to catch and hold a man who has run amok. Admission to the museum is free and it is open daily from 9 am to 6 pm except Friday when it closes between noon and 2.45 pm.

At the **National Art Gallery**, the exhibits change regularly and include art, often modern, from around the world. The art gallery is housed in the former Majestic Hotel, opposite the railway station.

Lake Gardens

The 60-hectare gardens form the green belt of KL. You can rent boats on Tasik Perdana for RM4 per hour.

Markets

KL has a number of markets which are worth investigating. The **Central Market** in Chinatown was previously the city's produce market but has now been refurbished to become the focus for handicraft and art sales. At night, Jalan Petaling in Chinatown becomes an incredibly busy pasar malam.

The Kampung Bahru area north-east of the city centre is the site each Saturday night for KL's **Pasar Minggu** (Sunday Market), so called, possibly, because it continues into Sunday morning. It's a food and produce market, a handicrafts market and a place to sample a wide variety of Malay foods. The **Pudu Market** is a huge wet (produce) market, on Jalan Pudu about three km south-east of the city centre, near the intersection of Jalan Pudu and Jalan Tun Razak.

Places to Stay

Hostels KL has a number of good hostels which cater almost exclusively for the budget traveller. Most shoestring travellers find these places ideal. They all offer similar services: dorm beds as well as rooms, cooking and washing facilities, a fridge and a notice board.

A very popular place on the edge of Chinatown and only a few minutes from the Puduraya bus station is the *Travellers' Moon Lodge* (☎ 03-2306601) at 36C Jalan Silang. Dorm beds cost RM8.50 and double rooms are RM20 with fan, including breakfast. A few doors along, and run by the same people, is the *Travellers Home* (☎ 03-2306601) at 46C Jalan Silang, with similar prices and facilities. Both offer good value for money, although the walls are basically only hardboard partitions and many rooms lack a window.

Also in Chinatown, at 60 Jalan Sultan, the *Backpackers Travellers Inn* (☎ 03-2382473) is another popular hostel, and consequently gets pretty cramped. The rooms are typically small and windowless. Dorm beds cost RM8, or RM10 with air-con. Singles/doubles cost RM23/25, or RM40/50 with air-con.

Close by at Wisma BWT, 103 Jalan Petaling, is the *Chinatown Guest House* (☎ 03-2320417). Dorm beds cost RM9, or RM10 with a light breakfast. Rooms are RM15/22, or RM17/24 with breakfast.

The *Sunrise Travellers Lodge* (☎ 03-2308878), 89-B Jalan Pudu Lama, near the Puduraya bus station, is very similar to the Travellers' Moon Lodge and almost as popular. Dorm beds cost RM10, or rooms cost from RM20 to RM35 with fan; all include a light breakfast.

The *KL City Lodge* (☎ 03-2305275) at 16A Jalan Pudu, opposite the bus station, is much more a regular hotel. Dorm beds cost RM8.50 or RM10 with air-con, while rooms are RM25 for a double or RM20/30 with air-con. In the same area, the *Kawana Tourist Inn* (☎ 03-2386714), 68 Jalan Pudu Lama, has tiny rooms, a very crowded dorm and lacks atmosphere.

North of the centre, just off Jalan Raja Laut at 61-B Jalan Tiong Nam, is the very friendly, family-run *Ben Soo Homestay* (☎ 03-2718096). Dorm beds are RM8 and double rooms with fan are RM25; all include breakfast. Ring ☎ 010-327013 to be picked up from the bus or railway station.

Further north, between Jalan Raja Laut and Jalan Tuanku Abdul Rahman, is another good place, the *Transit Villa* (☎ 03-4410443) at 36-2 Jalan Chow Kit, near the 7-Eleven. Dorm beds cost RM8.50, while double rooms cost RM26, or RM32 with air-con. Also in this area is the *Paradise Bed & Breakfast* but it's not great value.

The *Riverside Lodge* (☎ 02-2011210) is in a quiet area at 80A Jalan Rotan, just south of Chinatown. It's a friendly little place with dorm beds for RM8.50 and rooms for RM20/25.

At the top of the hostel range is the *Bintang Bed & Breakfast* (☎ 03-2448053) at 72 Jalan Bukit Bintang, east of the city centre. This place offers a bit more space than the Chinatown hostels, and costs RM18 for a dorm bed (RM25 with air-con), or rooms cost RM30/45 or RM37/55 with air-con.

Over the river, just off Jalan Masjid India at 20 Lorong Bunus Enam, is the *TI Lodge* (☎ 03-2930261), with dorm beds for RM11.50. Double rooms are RM30, RM36 with air-con or RM46 with air-con and attached bath.

KL also has a couple of youth hostels. The *Meridian International Youth Hostel* (☎ 03-2321428) is right in the centre of Chinatown, tucked away at 36 Jalan Hang Kasturi, very close to the Central Market. It is a typical friendly youth hostel with dorm beds for RM6.50 for members and RM7.50 for non-members, or RM8/10 with air-con. The hostel has a curfew.

The *KL International Youth Hostel* (☎ 03-2306870) is at 21 Jalan Kampung Attap, about five minutes walk south of Chinatown. Beds cost RM12 for the first night and RM8 on subsequent nights. It is fully air-conditioned and is within walking distance of the railway station. The *Wisma Belia* (☎ 03-

2744833) at 40 Jalan Syed Putra is a government-run affiliated hostel. It has air-con rooms for RM35, less 20% discount. It's some way south of the town centre but bus No 52 takes you there.

Finally there are the Ys. The *YMCA* (☎ 03-2741439), 95 Jalan Padang Belia, is a long way out. Dorm beds go for RM24, or rooms are RM20/30. Take a minibus No 12 and ask for the Lido Cinema. The *YWCA* (☎ 03-283225) is much more central at 12 Jalan Hang Jebat. It has rooms at RM25/35 for women and takes couples for RM45. Family rooms cost RM60 – a good deal.

Hotels – Jalan Tuanku Abdul Rahman Moving up Jalan TAR from its junction with Jalan Tun Perak there's the *Coliseum Hotel* (☎ 03-2926270) at No 100 with its famous old-planter's restaurant and very popular bar downstairs. Good-value rooms cost RM20/22 with fan and RM30 for a double with air-con. The rooms are large, clean and quiet and the location is very good.

At No 134 the *Tivoli Hotel* (☎ 03-2924108) is a reasonable Chinese cheapie which charges RM20/25 for rooms with fan and common bath. The *Rex Hotel* at No 134 is similar.

The *Shiraz Hotel* (☎ 03-2922625) at 1 Jalan Medan Tuanku, on the corner of Jalan TAR, is an unremarkable place at the top of this range, and has rooms for RM40 with air-con and bath.

For a mid-range hotel, the *Kowloon Hotel* at 142 Jalan Tuanku Abdul Rahman (☎ 03-2934246) is both very modern and clean. Singles/doubles start at RM80/98. Near the top end of Jalan Tuanku Abdul Rahman is the *Asia Hotel* (☎ 03-2926077) at 69 Jalan Haji Hussein. This long-running place is quite popular and costs RM140 for standard rooms and from RM190 for deluxe rooms.

Hotels – Chinatown Cheapest of the Chinese cheapies is the *Leng Nam Hotel* (☎ 03-2301489) at 165 Jalan Tun HS Lee. Basic rooms with fan cost RM20. Another

PLACES TO STAY		PLACES TO EAT			
1	TI Lodge	6	Jai Hind Restaurant	17	Infokraf Handicrafts Centre
2	Coliseum Hotel	7	Bilal Restaurant	24	Puduraya Bus & Taxi Station
18	Kawana Tourist Inn	23	Shakey's Pizza & Satay Ria	25	British Council
19	Sunrise Travellers Lodge	29	KFC	26	Central Market
20	KL City Lodge	35	Angel Cake House	28	Standard Chartered Bank
21	Travellers Home	37	Food Centre	30	Rex Cinema
22	Travellers' Moon Lodge	48	McDonald's	31	Dayabumi Complex
27	Meridian International Youth Hostel	54	Food Stalls	32	GPO
33	Hotel Malaya	OTHER		38	Sri Mahamariamman Temple
34	Hotel Furama			39	Jalan Sultan Mohammed Bus Station (Airport Buses)
36	Backpackers Travellers Inn	3	Little India Night Market		
		4	Masjid Little India		
40	Starlight Hotel	5	Kuala Lumpur Visitors Centre	49	UDA Ocean Plaza
41	Leng Nam Hotel			50	Kelang Bus Station
42	Mandarin Hotel	8	City Hall	51	Swimming Pool
43	Wan Kow Hotel	9	St Mary's Church	52	Masjid Negara
44	Chinatown Guest House	10	High Court	53	Islamic Centre
45	YWCA	11	Selangor Club	55	Chan See Shu Yuen Temple
46	Hotel Lok Ann	12	Masjid Jame		
47	Hotel City Inn	13	Sultan Abdul Samad Building	56	Stadium Merdeka
61	Riverside Lodge			57	Khoon Yam Temple
62	KL International Youth Hostel	14	HongkongBank	58	Railway Station
		15	Telekom Building	59	National Art Gallery
		16	Standard Chartered Bank	60	UMBC Building

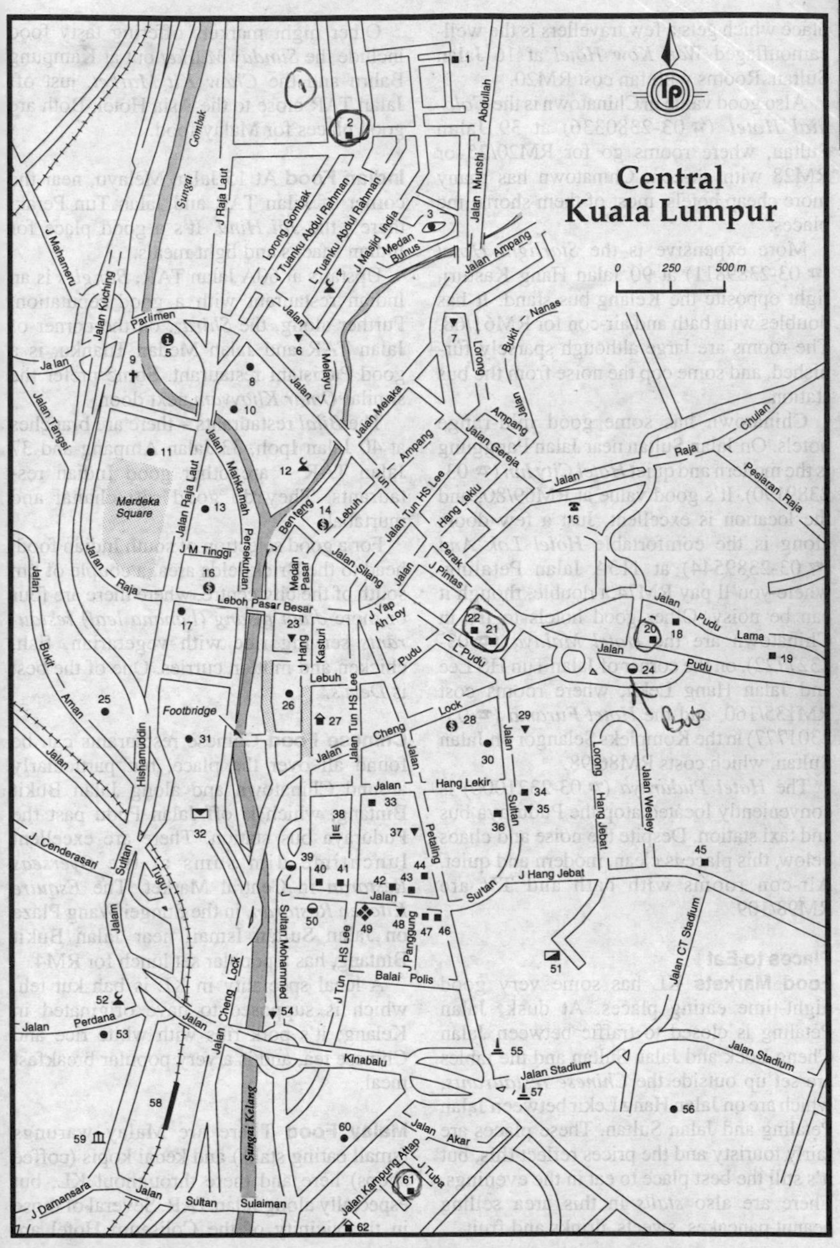
Central
Kuala Lumpur
0
250
500 m
Sungai Gombak
J Raja Laut
Lorong Gombak
J Tuanku Abdul Rahman
L Tuanku Abdul Rahman
J Masjid India
Medan Bunus
Jalan Munshi Abdullah
Jalan Ampang
Bukit Nanas
Lorong Ampang
Jalan Melayu
Jalan Melaka
Jalan Parlimen
Jalan Kuching
J Maharneru
Jalan Tangsi
Jalan Mahkamah Persekutuan
Jalan Raja Laut
Merdeka Square
Tun Perak
J Benteng
Lebuh Ampang
Jalan Tun HS Lee
Jalan Gereja
Hang Lekiu
Jalan Raja Chulan
Pesiaran Raja
J M Tinggi
Jalan Raja
Leboh Pasar Besar
Medan Pasar
Jalan Silang
Jalan Perak
J Pintas
J Yap Ah Loy
Jalan Pudu
L Pudu
Pudu Lama
Bukit Aman
J Hang Kasturi
Lebuh Pudu
Footbridge
Jalan Cheng Lock
Hishamuddin
Jalan Hang Lekir
Jalan Sultan
Lorong Hang Jebat
Jalan Wesley
J Hang Jebat
Jalan Petaling
J Cenderasari
Jalan Sultan
Tugu
J Sultan Mohammed
J Tun HS Lee
J Panggung
Balai Polis
Jalan CT Stadium
Jalan Stadium
Jalan Perdana
Jalan Cheng Lock
Kinabalu
Sungai Kelang
Jalan Akar
J Tuba
Jalan Kampung Attap
J Damansara
Jalan Sultan Sulaiman

place which gets a few travellers is the well-camouflaged *Wan Kow Hotel* at 16 Jalan Sultan. Rooms with fan cost RM20.

Also good value in Chinatown is the *Colonial Hotel* (☎ 03-2380336) at 39 Jalan Sultan, where rooms go for RM20/25 or RM28 with air-con. Chinatown has many more cheap hotels, most of them short-time places.

More expensive is the *Starlight Hotel* (☎ 03-2389811) at 90 Jalan Hang Kasturi, right opposite the Kelang bus stand. It has doubles with bath and air-con for RM61/68. The rooms are large although sparsely furnished, and some cop the noise from the bus station.

Chinatown has some good mid-range hotels. On Jalan Sultan near Jalan Panggung is the modern and quiet *Hotel City Inn* (☎ 03-2389190). It's good value at RM69/80, and the location is excellent. Just a few doors along is the comfortable *Hotel Lok Ann* (☎ 03-2389544) at 113A Jalan Petaling, where you'll pay RM74 a double, though it can be noisy. Other good hotels to try in Chinatown are the *Hotel Malaya* (☎ 03-2327722), on the corner of Jalan Tun HS Lee and Jalan Hang Lekir, where rooms cost RM135/160, and the *Hotel Furama* (☎ 03-2301777) in the Kompleks Selangor on Jalan Sultan, which costs RM86/98.

The *Hotel Puduraya* (☎ 03-2321000) is conveniently located atop the Puduraya bus and taxi station. Despite the noise and chaos below, this place is clean, modern and quiet. Air-con rooms with bath and TV are RM98/109.

Places to Eat

Food Markets KL has some very good night-time eating places. At dusk, Jalan Petaling is closed to traffic between Jalan Cheng Lock and Jalan Sultan and the tables are set up outside the *Chinese restaurants*, which are on Jalan Hang Lekir between Jalan Petaling and Jalan Sultan. These places are fairly touristy and the prices reflect this, but it's still the best place to eat in the evenings. There are also *stalls* in this area selling peanut pancakes, sweets, drinks and fruit.

Other night markets offering tasty food include the *Sunday Market* out at Kampung Bahru and the *Chow Kit Market*, just off Jalan TAR close to the Asia Hotel. Both are good places for Malay food.

Indian Food At 15 Jalan Melayu, near the corner of Jalan TAR and Jalan Tun Perak, there's the *Jai Hind*. It's a good place for Indian snacks and light meals.

Upstairs at 60A Jalan TAR, *Bangles* is an Indian restaurant with a good reputation. Further along, the *Shiraz*, on the corner of Jalan TAR and Jalan Medan Tuanku, is a good Pakistani restaurant. Some prefer the similar *Omar Khayyam* next door.

The *Bilal* restaurants – there are branches at 40 Jalan Ipoh, 33 Jalan Ampang and 37 Jalan TAR – are other good Indian restaurants. They do good roti chanai and murtabak.

For a good selection of south Indian food, head to the Brickfields area, a couple of km south of the city centre, where there are four or more *daun pisang (banana leaf) restaurants* serving rice with vegetarian, fish, chicken and mutton curries. One of the best is *Devi's*.

Chinese Food Chinese restaurants can be found all over the place, but particularly around Chinatown and along Jalan Bukit Bintang, which is off Jalan Pudu past the Puduraya bus station. There are excellent lunchtime dim sums at the *Overseas Restoran* in Central Market. The *Esquire Kitchen Restoran*, in the Sungei Wang Plaza on Jalan Sultan Ismail near Jalan Bukit Bintang, has a popular set lunch for RM4.

A local speciality in KL is bah kut teh, which is supposed to have originated in Kelang; it's pork ribs with white rice and Chinese tea, and is a very popular breakfast meal.

Malay Food There are Malay warungs (small eating stalls) and kedai kopis (coffee shops) here and there throughout KL, but especially along Jalan TAR. Several of those in the vicinity of the Coliseum Hotel are excellent and cheap. Look for the nasi lemak in the early mornings – coconut rice topped with dried fish, boiled egg, peanuts and curry. The *Restoran Imaf* is a good bet and just down from the Minerva Bookshop. The area around Stadium Merdeka is also renowned for its Malay warungs.

Western Food KL has a surprising variety of Western restaurants including, at the bottom of Jalan TAR, *Kentucky Fried Chicken* and *A&W* takeaways. There are several American-style hamburger joints around the Kelang bus station including *Wendy's* and *McDonald's*.

Not to be missed is the restaurant in the *Coliseum Hotel* on Jalan TAR which serves excellent steaks at around RM20. The place is quite a colonial experience and has hardly changed over the years.

There are lots of restaurants along Jalan Bukit Bintang, including many of the fast-food chains, and various bakeries and Indian and Chinese restaurants.

In Chinatown, don't miss the *Angel Cake House* on Jalan Sultan. They offer all kinds of buns and rolls stuffed with chicken curry or cheeses – fresh from the oven. Also available are pizza, macaroni, fruit tarts and chocolate cakes.

Entertainment

KL has plenty of discos, bars and the dreaded karaoke lounges. The hottest spot in town is currently the *Hard Rock Cafe* in the Concorde Hotel on Jalan Sultan Ismail, near Jalan P Ramlee. A first-drink cover charge applies. KL's sweet young things head for the *Voodoo* disco at 76 Jalan Ampang. It's a huge place with four bars open until 3 am and there's also a one-drink cover charge (RM12).

For other discos, try *Machine One* or *Winston's* in the Life Centre on Jalan Sultan Ismail or *Betelnut* on Jalan Penang behind the Holiday Inn on the Park.

For something a little more sedate, the *Blues Cafe* in the Lot 10 shopping centre on the corner of Jalan Sultan Ismail and Jalan Bukit Bintang features local jazz musicians on Sunday evening. In the same building you'll find *Jimmy Dean's*. Jazz music is also featured at the pleasant *Riverbank* bar in the Central Market.

For a drink in a bar, try the *Bull's Head* in the Central Market, or step back in time to the bar at the *Coliseum Hotel* on Jalan TAR.

Things to Buy

Karyaneka Handicraft Centre, out past the Hilton on Jalan Raja Chulan, displays a wide variety of local craftwork in quasi-traditional settings. Hours are 9 am to 6 pm except for Friday when they close at 6.30 pm.

The night market along Jalan Petaling is a good place to shop for cheap clothes. 'Genuine' Lacoste shirts sell for around RM10, while copy jeans and designer T-shirts are also very cheap and virtually indistinguishable from the real McCoy.

The Central Market complex, housed in a cavernous art-deco building (formerly a wet market) between the GPO and Chinatown, offers an ever-changing selection of Malaysian art, clothes, souvenirs and more.

Getting There & Away

Air KL is well served by many international airlines and there are flights to and from Australia, Singapore, Indonesia, Thailand, India, Philippines, Vietnam, Hong Kong and various destinations in Europe.

On the domestic network, KL is the hub of MAS services and there are flights to most major towns and cities on the peninsula and in East Malaysia. MAS (☎ 03-2610555, 03-7463000 for 24-hour reservations) is in the MAS Building, Jalan Sultan Ismail.

Bus Most buses operate from the busy Puduraya bus and taxi station on Jalan Pudu, just east of Chinatown. There are departures to most places throughout the day, and at night to main towns. Check at the ticket offices inside the bus station or outside on Jalan Pudu. The bus station has a left luggage office. Typical fares from KL are RM17.70 to Singapore, RM17 to Johor Bahru, RM6.75 to Melaka, RM15 to Lumut, RM10 to the

Cameron Highlands, RM19 to Butterworth and RM12.10 to Kuantan.

Buses to Kelang and Port Kelang (No 793) and Shah Alam (No 337, 338) leave from the Kelang bus station at the end of Jalan Hang Kasturi in Chinatown.

Buses for Jerantut (for Taman Negara) and Kuala Lipis operate from the Pekeleling bus station in the north of the city, just off Jalan Tun Razak. To Jerantut (RM9, 3½ hours) there are six daily and to Kuala Lipis there are at least four departures daily (RM8, four hours).

Train KL is also the hub of the railway system. There are daily departures (express trains are marked *) for Butterworth (7.20*, 9 am, 3.10*, 8*, 8.35 and 10* pm) and Singapore (7.10*, 8.30 am, 2.25*, 8.45 and 10* pm). For the east-coast line to Jerantut (for Taman Negara) and Kota Bharu, you first have to take a south-bound train to Gemas and then get another connection – forget it and take a bus.

Taxi Taxis depart from upstairs in the Puduraya bus and taxi station, although there are also some taxi offices along Jalan Pudu near the bus station. There are lots of taxis, and fares include Melaka (RM15/17) normal/air-con, Johor Bahru (RM33/38), Ipoh (RM18/21), Kuala Lipis (RM13/17), Lumut (RM24.50/30), Cameron Highlands (RM25/30), Taiping (RM24/29), Butterworth (RM30/36), Genting Highlands (RM8), Kuantan (RM20/ 25), Kuala Terengganu (RM35/45), Kota Bharu (RM35/45) and Singapore (RM36/42).

Getting Around

To/From the Airport Taxis from the KL International Airport operate on a coupon system costing RM22 from the booth to the right outside the terminal. Avoid the non-registered drivers who ask you for exorbitant amounts. To travel by metered taxi to the airport, count on around RM30.

The Sri Jaya bus No 47 goes to the airport every 20 minutes from 6.30 am to 10.30 pm from the Jalan Sultan Mohammed bus stand, opposite the Kelang bus station, and costs RM1.60. The trip takes 45 minutes but allow more time since traffic can be bad.

Bus The government has called for a tender to take over the services run by a myriad of bus companies, but until then KL's bus system remains chaotic. City bus companies include Sri Jaya, Len Seng, Len, Foh Hup and Toong Foong. Fares start at 20 sen for the first km and go up 5 sen each two km. As well as the buses, the faster pink minibuses operate on a fixed fare of 60 sen for anywhere along their route. Whenever possible have correct change ready when boarding the buses, particularly during rush hours.

Taxi There are plenty of taxis and fares are quite reasonable. They start at RM1.50 for the first two km and then it's an additional 10 sen for each 200 metres. If you arrive at the railway station, taxis are only available from outside platform 4 (the river side of the station) and they operate on a coupon system.

Car All the major car-rental companies have offices at the airport and in the city. These companies are Avis (☎ 03-2423500), Budget (☎ 03-2425006), Hertz (☎ 03-2421014) and National (☎ 03-2480522).

AROUND KUALA LUMPUR

Batu Caves

The huge Batu Caves are the best known attraction in the vicinity of KL. They are just 13 km north of the capital, a short distance off the Ipoh road. The caves are in a towering limestone formation and were little known until about 100 years ago. Later, a small Hindu shrine was built in the major cave and it became a pilgrimage centre during the annual **Thaipusam Festival**.

The major cave, a vast open space known as the **Cathedral Cave**, is reached by a straight flight of 272 steps. Also reached by the same flight of steps is the long and winding **Dark Cave**, but this has been closed for some time because quarrying in the limestone outcrop has made the cave unsafe. There are a number of other caves in the same formation, including a small cave at the base of the outcrop which has been made into a museum with figures of the various Hindu gods – admission is 50 sen.

Getting There & Away Take minibus No 11 (60 sen, 45 minutes) from Central Market and tell the driver that you are going all the way to the caves. During the Thaipusam Festival, you can take a train to the caves – No 140 leaves the KL station at 9 am and No 141 leaves Batu Caves at 11.30 am.

National Zoo & Aquarium

East of KL, on the road to Ulu Kelang and about 13 km out, is the 62-hectare site of the National Zoo and Aquarium. Laid out around a central lake, the zoo collection emphasises Malaysian wildlife. There are elephant rides and other amusements for children.

The zoo is open daily from 9 am to 6 pm and admission is RM4, plus RM1 if you want to use your camera. To get there, take Len Seng bus No 170 or minibus No 17 from Lebuh Ampang.

Orang Asli Museum

About 19 km from KL, on the Genting Highlands road, is this very informative museum which gives some good insights into the life and culture of Peninsular Malaysia's 70,000 indigenous inhabitants. It's well worth a look.

Templer Park

Beside the Ipoh road, 22 km north of KL, Templer Park was established during the colonial period by the British High Commissioner Sir Gerald Templer. The 1200-hectare park is intended to be a tract of jungle, preserved within easy reach of the city. There are a number of marked jungle paths, swimming lagoons and several waterfalls within the park boundaries.

To get there, take bus No 66, 72, 81 or 83 from the Puduraya bus station.

JOHOR BAHRU

The state of Johor comprises the entire southern tip of the peninsula. It's capital is Johor Bahru, the southern gateway to Peninsular Malaysia as it is connected to Singapore by a 1038-metre-long causeway.

Johor Bahru's history goes back to the mid-19th century when Melaka fell to the Portuguese and the sultans fled and then re-established their capital in this area.

Few people stop for long in Johor Bahru as both Singapore and Melaka offer better prospects. However, if you do stop, it's worth exploring the **Istana Besar**, the former palace of the Johor royal family and now an impressive museum.

Places to Stay

The best place to stay is the friendly *Footloose Homestay* (☎ 07-242881) at 4H Jalan Ismail, about 10 minutes walk from the bus station, just off Jalan Gertak Merah. There's one double room for RM24, or just six dorm beds for RM12 per person, all including breakfast.

There're a number of typical Chinese hotels right in the centre of town, but they're neither particularly good or cheap. The *Hotel Chuan Seng Baru*, at 35 Jalan Meldrum, is a very basic Chinese cheapie costing RM20/25.

For something better, the best value is the *Hotel JB* (☎ 07-234788) at 80A Jalan Wong Ah Fook. The rooms here are fairly clean, not as box-like as some other places, and cost RM33.60, RM42 with bath and RM50 with air-con and bath.

Places to Eat

For good Malay food, try the *Restoran Medina* on the corner of Jalan Meldrum and Jalan Siew Niam. They serve excellent murtabak and other curries. There's also a food centre opposite the railway station on Jalan Tun Abdul Razak.

Getting There & Away

Air Johor Bahru is well served by MAS flights and, as an incentive to fly from Johor Bahru rather than Singapore, fares from here to other places in Malaysia are much cheaper than from Singapore.

Pelangi Air (☎ 07-220888) has twice-

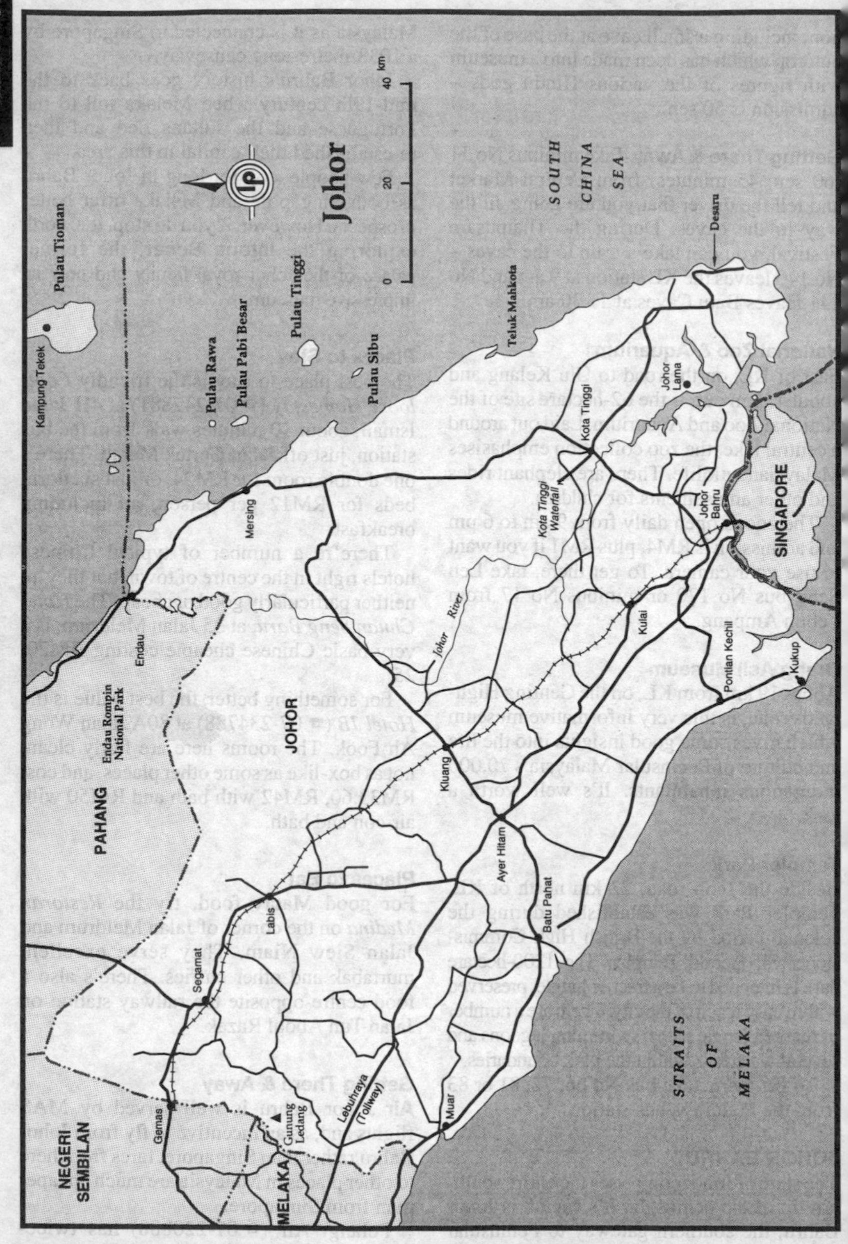
Johor
0
20
40 km
SOUTH CHINA SEA
STRAITS OF MELAKA
PAHANG
NEGERI SEMBILAN
MELAKA
JOHOR
SINGAPORE
Pulau Tioman
Kampung Tekek
Pulau Rawa
Pulau Pabi Besar
Pulau Tinggi
Pulau Sibu
Teluk Mahkota
Desaru
Johor Lama
Kota Tinggi
Kota Tinggi Waterfall
Johor Bahru
Kulai
Pontian Kechil
Kukup
Johor River
Kluang
Ayer Hitam
Batu Pahat
Muar
Lebuhraya (Tollway)
Gunung Ledang
Gemas
Segamat
Labis
Mersing
Endau
Endau Rompin National Park

weekly flights to Medan in Sumatra for RM306 (US$109 from Medan).

Bus & Taxi With Singapore so close, travel connections are important. Due to the hassles that are involved in crossing the causeway – customs, immigration and so on – there's a much wider selection of buses and long-distance taxis to other towns in Peninsular Malaysia from Johor Bahru than there are in Singapore.

Regular buses go from Johor Bahru to Melaka (RM10), to KL (RM17) and to Butterworth (RM35). On the east coast buses service Kota Tinggi (RM2), Mersing (RM8) and Kuantan (RM16). From the Johor Bahru taxi station, there are regular taxis to Mersing (RM12), Kuantan (RM30), Kota Tinggi (RM4), Melaka (RM25) and KL (RM38).

Bus No 170 goes every 15 minutes to Singapore and costs RM1, or the air-con bus costs RM1.80.

Train There are daily trains from Johor Bahru to KL and Butterworth for west-coast destinations and an 8.30 am direct east-coast train for Taman Negara and Kota Bharu. There are also connections to Singapore, although a bus or taxi is quicker.

Boat Boats operate from Pasir Gudang, about 30 km from Johor Bahru, direct to Batam and Bintang islands in Indonesia's Riau Archipelago, and to Surabaya in Java. SS Holidays (☎ 07-511577), Level 3, 12-13, Kompleks Pusat Bandar, Pasir Gudang, have daily boats to Batam (1½ hours, RM30) at 10 am and 3 pm, and an 11 am boat to Bintang (three hours, RM 50). The boat to Surabaya leaves at 5 pm on Saturday and takes 60 hours. Fares range from RM200 in an eight-berth economy cabin to RM280 in a two-berth cabin. A taxi to the harbour at Pasir Gudang costs around RM25, or take the red bus No 224 to Pusat Bandar for RM1.20 and then a taxi to the harbour.

MELAKA

Melaka (Malacca), Malaysia's most historically interesting city, has [...] some dramatic events over th[...] complete series of European incursions [...] Malaysia – Portuguese, Dutch and English – occurred here. Yet this was an important trading port long before the first Portuguese adventurers set foot in the city.

In 1405, Admiral Cheng Ho, the 'three-jewelled eunuch prince', arrived in Melaka bearing gifts from the Ming Emperor, the promise of protection from arch-enemies (the Siamese) and, surprisingly, the Muslim religion. Despite internal squabbles and intrigues, Melaka grew to be a powerful trading state and successfully repulsed Siamese attacks.

In 1511, Alfonso d'Albuquerque took the city for the Portuguese and the fortress of A'Famosa was constructed. Finally, the Dutch attacked the city and in 1641 it passed into their hands after a siege lasting eight months.

In 1795, the French occupied Holland so the British, allies of the Dutch, temporarily took over administration of the Dutch colonies. In 1824, Melaka was ceded to the British in exchange for the Sumatran port of Bencoolen (Bengkulu today).

Today, Melaka is a sleepy backwater and no longer of any major commercial influence. It's a place of intriguing Chinese streets, antique shops, old Chinese temples and cemeteries, and nostalgic reminders of former European colonial powers.

Information

The Melaka tourist office, facing the Christ Church in the heart of the city, is open every day. The GPO is about three km north of the town centre and bus No 19 will get you there from the bus station.

Stadthuys

The most imposing relic of the Dutch period is the massive pink town hall which was built between 1641 and 1660. It is believed to be the oldest Dutch building in the East and, today, is used for government offices. It displays all the typical features of Dutch colonial architecture, including substantial solid doors and louvred windows.

Christ Church

Between the Stadthuys and the old GPO building, facing one end of the square, is the bright red Christ Church. The pink bricks were brought out from Zeeland in Holland and faced with local red laterite when the church was constructed in 1753.

St Paul's Church

Bukit St Paul (St Paul's Hill) rises up above the Stadthuys and, on top, stand the ruins of St Paul's Church. Originally built by the Portuguese in 1571 as the small Our Lady of the Hill chapel, it was regularly visited by Francis Xavier.

Following his death in China, the saint's body was brought here and buried for nine months before being transferred to Goa in India where it is to this day.

The church has been in ruins now for 150 years, but the setting is beautiful, the walls imposing and fine old Dutch tombstones stand around the interior.

Porta de Santiago

This is the sole surviving relic of the old fort that was originally constructed by Alfonso d'Albuquerque. This was part of the fort which the Dutch reconstructed in 1670 following their takeover and it bears the Dutch East India Company's coat of arms.

There is a sound and light show at the gate each evening (conducted in Malay at 8.15 pm and in English at 10 pm) and the cost is RM5.

Museums

Just south-east of St Paul's Hill and housed in a typical Dutch house dating from 1660, the small **Proclamation of Independence Hall** has historical displays on the events leading up to independence in 1957.

On the other side of St Paul's Hill is a wooden replica of a Melaka sultan's palace which contains the **Muzium Budaya**, or Cultural Museum (entry RM1.50). At 48-50 Jalan Tun Tan Cheng Lock, in the old part of the city, is a traditional Peranakan (Straits-born Chinese) townhouse which has been made into the small **Baba-Nonya Heritage Museum**.

Old Melaka

A walk through the old part of Melaka can be fascinating. Although Melaka has long lost its importance as a port, ancient-looking junks still sail up the river and moor at the banks. River-boat trips, leaving from behind the tourist office, operate several times daily, take 45 minutes and cost RM6.

You may still find some of the treasures of the East in the antique shops scattered along Jalan Hang Jebat, formerly known as Jonkers St. The **Sri Pogyatha Vinoyagar Moorthi Temple**, dating from 1781, and the Sumatran-style **Kampung Kling Mosque** are both in this area. The fascinating **Cheng Hoon Teng Temple** on Jalan Tokong Emas is the oldest Chinese temple in Malaysia and has an inscription commemorating Cheng Ho's epochal visit to Melaka.

Beaches

The main beaches nearby are **Tanjung Kling** and, a little further out, **Pantai Kundor** but the Straits of Melaka have become increasingly polluted over the years and it's worst around Melaka itself. There are a few cheap places to stay, but few travellers bother these days.

Places to Stay

Guesthouses Melaka has plenty of traveller-oriented guesthouses, offering very similar facilities. Most of them are in the area known as Taman Melaka Raya, the reclaimed land just south of Jalan Merdeka. Almost all have dorm beds and charge standard rates of RM6 in the dorm and RM12/16 for singles/doubles.

Located in the street directly south of the roundabout, at 214B, is the popular *Travellers' Lodge*. It's a friendly place with a nicely decorated common room. The long-running *Trilogy Guest House* (☎ 06-245319) at 223B is run by a friendly couple. On the other side of the road is the similar *Shirah's Guest House*. *Amy Home Stay* at 244B is another popular place with a good atmosphere.

In the next street from the roundabout are a few more choices. One of the most popular is *Robin's Nest Guest House* at 247B. The *Samudra Inn* (☎ 06-227441) at 250B has just five rooms for RM12/16. *Sunny's Inn* (☎ 06-237990) at 253B has good travel information while the *SD Rest House* (☎ 06-247080) at 258B offers alcoholic drinks, an international phone call service and some air-con rooms for RM20 to RM35.

On the main thoroughfare in this area is the *Malacca Town Holiday Lodge* (☎ 06-248830) at 148B. Although it doesn't have a dorm or the decorated common room of many of the other hostels, it is squeaky clean and well run.

Away from Taman Melaka Raya there are a number of other guesthouses. The pick of them is probably the well-located *Eastern Heritage Guest House* (☎ 06-233026), 8 Jalan Bukit China, housed in a typical old Melaka building.

Another good place is the *Kancil Guest House* at 177 Jalan Bandar Hilir. It's a bit of a walk from the centre or take bus Nos 17 from the local bus station. Also close to the Cheng Hoan Teng Temple is *My Place Guest House*, a scruffy but friendly place at 205 Jalan Parameswara. They also have more expensive but good value air-con rooms for RM25 across the road.

The *Paradise Hostel* (☎ 06-230821), 4 Jalan Tengkera, is close to Chinatown. Apart from the usual, some rooms have attached bath. Also north of the river, the *Malacca Town Holiday Lodge 2* (☎ 06-246905) at 52 Jalan Kampung Empat has rooms for RM15 or large rooms with carpet, air-con and attached bath for RM30/36.

Hotels Melaka is also well endowed with hotels in all price ranges.

Of the cheapies, the *Ng Fook* (☎ 06-228055) at 154 Jalan Bunga Raya is basic, but one of the better ones, with double rooms from RM18.40 up to RM32.20 with a[illegible] and bath. The *Hong Kong Hotel* (☎ 06-223392) is slightly cheaper. Cheaper still is the well-located *Central Hotel* (☎ 06-222984) at 31 Jalan Bendahara. The rooms are a bit shabby, but hard to beat for the price – RM11/15.

The rambling old *Majestic Hotel* (☎ 06-222367) at 188 Jalan Bunga Raya has high ceilings, and swishing fans add to the cool, lazy atmosphere. It's in need of a good scrub and a coat of paint, but is still not bad value at RM27 with fan or RM37 with air-con.

In the old part of town the *Chong Hoe Hotel* (☎ 06-226102) at 26 Jalan Tukung Emas is well located and good value with rooms for RM16 up to RM24/32 with air-con and bath.

A good place in the mid-range is the *May Chiang Hotel* (☎ 06-222101) at 52 Jalan Munshi Abdullah. Rooms in this very friendly and immaculately clean place cost RM35/40 with air-con and bath. At the top of this range is the small *Hotel Accordian* (☎ 06-221911) on Jalan Munshi Abdullah. Rooms start at RM65/75 for standard rooms and go up to RM120 for 'executive' doubles, plus taxes.

Places to Eat

Melaka has no shortage of places to eat. On Jalan Taman, on what used to be the waterfront, the permanent stalls serve all the usual food-centre specialities. Try the *Bunga Raya Restaurant* at No 40 which has excellent steamed crabs.

On Jalan Laksamana, right in the centre of town, the *Restaurant Kim Swee Huat* at No 38 is a cheap restaurant that is good for Chinese food and Western breakfasts.

The *Tai Chong Hygienic Ice Cafe* at 39/72 Jalan Bunga Raya has a wide variety of ice-cream treats, and the *UE Tea House*, 20 Lorong Bukit China, is a great place for a dim sum breakfast with prices from 50 sen per plate.

In the city centre, the *Sri Lakshmi Vilas* and the *Sri Krishna Bavan* next door are good south Indian restaurants. Around the [illegible] menggong, the *Restoran* [illegible]ian place for a roti chanai [illegible] the new travellers' guesthouses at Taman Melaka Raya, the *Restoran Kerala* and the *Restoran Curry House* are good for cheap daun pisang Indian meals and masala dosas. For Western food, such as steak and chips, the *Restoran Odeon Istimewa* is very popular.

In the heart of the old town on Jalan Hang Jebat, the *Jonkers Melaka Restoran* is in a traditional Peranakan house and serves both Western and Nonya dishes. The set menu of four Nonya dishes for RM16 is a good deal.

At Medan Portugis (Portuguese Square), you can sample Malay-Portuguese cuisine at tables facing the sea. They serve excellent seafood, and for around RM20 per person you can eat very well.

Getting There & Away

Air Pelangi Air has flights to Singapore (RM110) and Ipoh (RM125).

Bus Most bus companies have their offices near the express bus stand. To or from KL there are 10 daily Jebat Express air-con buses for RM6.75. Melaka-Singapore Express buses leave hourly from 8 am to 6 pm, and the fare is RM11. There are also regular buses to Lumut (RM21), Johor Bahru (RM10) and Butterworth (RM21.40). Buses to the east coast are less frequent and usually run at night.

Taxi Taxis leave from the taxi station just opposite the local bus station. Sample fares are: Port Dickson (RM10), Johor Bahru (RM25), KL (RM13) and Mersing (RM12).

Boat The Madai Ferry Service (☎ 06-240671), 321-A Jalan Tun Ali, has daily (except Sunday) ferries to Dumai in Sumatra, but you need an Indonesian visa to enter or leave via Dumai. The fare is RM80 one way and takes 2½ hours. Backpackers' guesthouses can arrange Indonesian visas.

Getting Around

A bicycle rickshaw is the ideal way of getting around compact and slow-moving Melaka. By the hour, they should cost about RM7, or RM2 for any one-way trip within the town, but you'll have to bargain.

You can easily walk around the central sights or rent a bike from one of the hostels for RM5 a day.

PORT DICKSON

Port Dickson itself has nothing of great interest, but south of the town, a beach stretches for 16 km to **Cape Rachado**, and it's almost clean enough to swim in – the best part of the beach starts from around the Km 8 peg. There are a number of places to stay along the beach and it's an interesting walk along the coast to the cape.

Places to Stay

The *Port Dickson Youth Hostel* is above the road 6½ km out of Port Dickson along the way to Cape Rachado. It attracts few visitors although it costs just RM8 per night and has freshly painted dorms.

At Km 13, the Chinese *Kong Ming Hotel* (☎ 06-40 5683) is right by the beach. It's nothing special but is reasonably priced at RM35 for a double. Also here is the *Lido Hotel* (☎ 06-40 5273) which is set in spacious grounds. Rooms cost RM35 for a double or RM40 with air-con.

Getting There & Away

By bus, Port Dickson is RM3.30 from Melaka and RM4 from KL. A taxi is about RM10 from either town. From Port Dickson town, there are buses which will drop you off anywhere along the beach.

SEREMBAN

Seremban, the capital of Negeri Sembilan, is the centre of the Malaysian Minangkabau area – closely related to the Minangkabau area of Sumatra. The small **State Museum**, in the lake area overlooking the town centre, is a good example of the Minangkabau style of architecture. Seremban has the usual assortment of cheap Chinese hotels.

GENTING HIGHLANDS

The Genting Highlands is a thoroughly modern hill station – casinos are the attraction here rather than the jungle walks. Accommodation is relatively expensive.

It's about 50 km north from KL and buses and taxis go there from the Puduraya bus station.

FRASER'S HILL

Fraser's Hill, set at a cool altitude of 1524 metres, is quiet and relatively undeveloped – possibly because it's not the easiest hill station to get to. Very few foreign travellers stay here and it's mostly a middle-class Malaysian resort. The *Corona Nursery Youth Hostel* (☎ 09-38 2225) and the *Gap Rest House* are reasonably priced places, but hard to get to.

Getting There & Away

Fraser's Hill is 103 km north of KL and 240 km from Kuantan on the east coast. The twice-daily bus service from Kuala Kubu Bahru costs RM2.50 and departs at 8 am and noon, or a charter taxi is RM35. A bus from KL's Puduraya bus station to Kuala Kubu Bahru is RM3.50; a share-taxi costs RM8.

CAMERON HIGHLANDS

Situated about 60 km north from Tapah, off the KL-Ipoh road, this is the best known and most extensive hill station. The Highlands stand at 1500 metres and the weather is pleasantly cool, not cold. Jungle walks are the thing to do here and, in the shops in Tanah Rata, you can buy somewhat inaccurate maps of the main walks. Most consist of a stroll of an hour or two but some take quite a bit longer and can be tough going.

The only wildlife you are likely to see is the fantastic variety of butterflies. It was here that the American Thai silk entrepreneur, Jim Thompson, mysteriously disappeared in 1967 – he was never found. The hills around the Highlands are dotted with tea plantations, some of which are open for inspection.

Orientation

From the turn-off at Tapah it's 46 km up to Ringlet, the first village of the Highlands. About 14 km past Ringlet you reach Tanah Rata, the main town of the Highlands, where you'll find most of the hotels, as well as the bus and taxi stations. Continue on, and at around the 65 km peg you reach the other main Highland town, Brinchang, where there are a few more restaurants and cheap hotels.

The road continues up beyond Brinchang to smaller villages and the Blue Valley Tea Estate (90 km from Tapah) off to the north-east, or to the top of Gunung Brinchang (80 km from Tapah) to the north-west.

Things to See

The **Sam Poh Temple**, just below Brinchang and about one km off the road, is a typically Chinese kaleidoscope of colours with Buddha statues, stone lions and incense burners. **Mardi** is an agricultural research station in Tanah Rata and visits must be arranged in advance.

There are a number of **flower nurseries** and vegetable and strawberry **farms** in the Highlands. There is also an Orang Asli settlement near Brinchang but there's little reason to visit it.

About 10 km beyond Brinchang is the **Butterfly Garden** where there are over 300 varieties fluttering around. It's worth a visit if you can hitch or if you have your own vehicle.

Places to Stay

Bookings are advisable in the peak holiday periods around April, August and December. Most cheap hotels are in Tanah Rata. Brinchang has a couple of places but there's little reason to stay there.

The *Twin Pines Chalet* (☎ 05-902169), just a short walk from the centre of Tanah Rata, is popular with travellers. This congenial place is quite new and very clean. Dorm beds cost RM7, or doubles/triples are RM20/26. You can get breakfast and drinks here.

Equally good is the *Cameronian Holiday Inn* (☎ 05-901327), also a short walk from

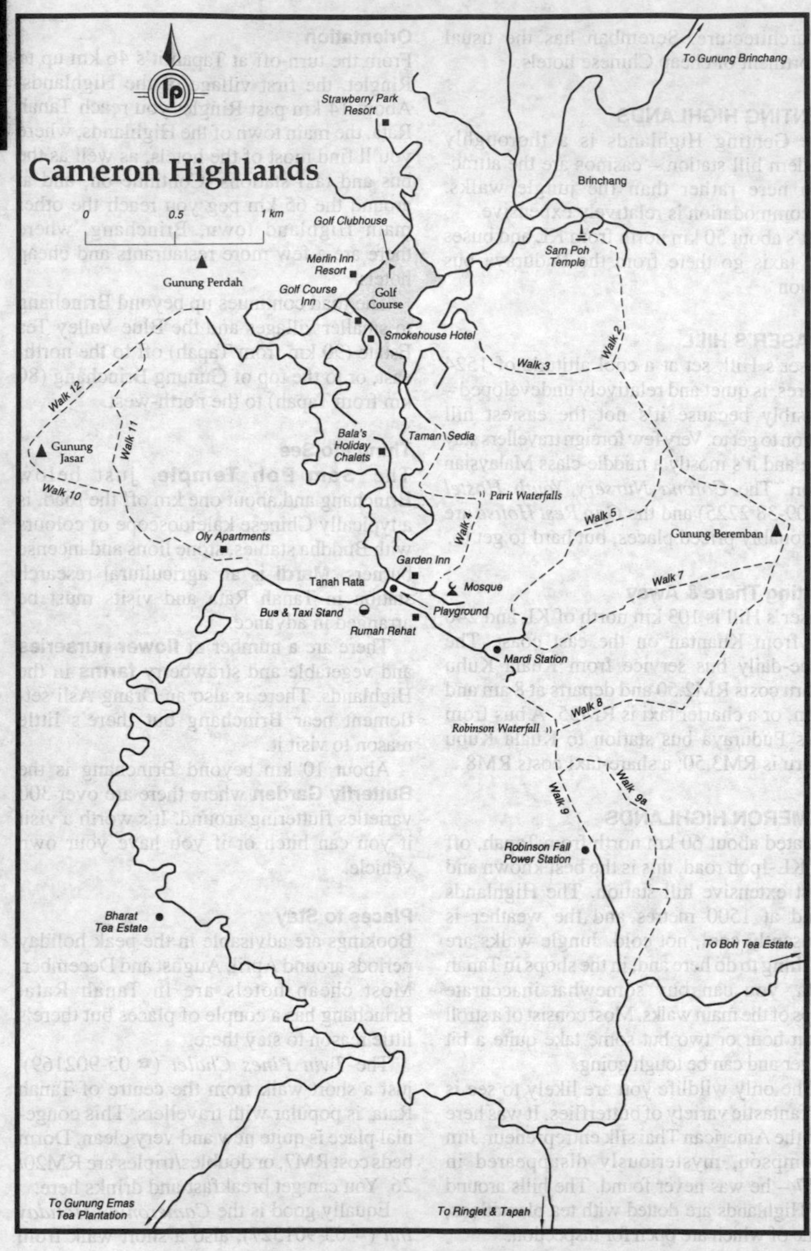
Cameron Highlands
0
0.5
1 km
To Gunung Brinchang
Strawberry Park Resort
Brinchang
Golf Clubhouse
Merlin Inn Resort
Sam Poh Temple
Gunung Perdah
Golf Course Inn
Golf Course
Smokehouse Hotel
Walk 2
Walk 3
Walk 12
Walk 11
Gunung Jasar
Walk 10
Bala's Holiday Chalets
Taman Sedia
Parit Waterfalls
Walk 5
Walk 4
Gunung Beremban
Oly Apartments
Garden Inn
Walk 7
Tanah Rata
Mosque
Bus & Taxi Stand
Playground
Rumah Rehat
Mardi Station
Walk 8
Robinson Waterfall
Walk 9
Walk 9a
Robinson Fall Power Station
Bharat Tea Estate
To Boh Tea Estate
To Gunung Emas Tea Plantation
To Ringlet & Tapah

town. Facilities are similar to the Twin Pines, although the rooms are bigger and carpeted and some have attached bath for RM26 – very good value. As at the Twin Pines, breakfast and drinks are available.

Father's Guest House is signposted off the main road, next to the bridge about 50 metres from the tourist office. It's a friendly place with dorm beds for RM6, or rooms in the main building for RM20. There's a communal kitchen as well as the usual facilities.

About two km from town along the road to Brinchang is the quiet *Bala's Holiday Chalets* (☎ 05-941660). Dorm beds go for RM6 and RM7, and rooms, some with attached bath, cost RM35 to RM50. Reasonable meals are available and there are good views from the lawn. The distance from the centre is the only drawback.

Of the regular hotels in Tanah Rata, the best value is the friendly *Seah Meng Hotel* (☎ 05-941618) at 39 Main Rd. Singles with common bath cost RM18 or singles/doubles with attached bath are RM30/35. The *Highlands Lodge* (☎ 05-941922), 4 Main Rd, is a bit seedy but cheap at RM20, and the *Federal Hotel* (☎ 05-941777), located at 44 Main Rd, has rooms for RM25 or doubles with bath for RM45.

The *Garden Inn* (☎ 05-941911) has large rooms with polished wooden floors, attached bath and hot water for RM69, but only RM50 in quiet periods. For something salubrious, *The Smokehouse Hotel* (☎ 05-901214) is an English country pub in the Malaysian highlands and costs RM110/180, including a full English breakfast.

Places to Eat

The cheapest food in Tanah Rata is to be found at the row of Malay foodstalls along the main street. One stall, the *Excellent Food Centre*, has an extensive menu with good food and on Saturday nights it has cheap steaks. The adjoining *Fresh Milk Corner* sells fresh pasteurised milk, yoghurt and lassis.

On the other side of the road there are a number of restaurants in the row of shops. The *Restaurant Kumar* and the adjacent *Restoran Thanam* both serve good Malay and Indian food. The *Restoran No 14* next to the Malayan Bank also does good Indian food, including the popular masala dosa.

Steamboat, a sort of Oriental variation of a Swiss fondue, is the Highlands' real taste treat. You can try it at the *Oriental Restaurant* in the main street for RM10 per person (minimum of two people).

Further along Main Rd is the *Jasmine Restaurant* which has a set four-course Chinese meal for RM10 per person. The *Roselane Coffee House* serves good breakfasts for RM5 and set meals for RM6.80.

In addition to these places, all the middle and top-end hotels have their own expensive restaurants.

Getting There & Away

Bus Bus No 153 runs approximately every hour, 8 am to 5 pm, from Tapah to Tanah Rata (RM3, two hours). All the bus drivers on this route seem to be frustrated racing-car drivers and the way they drive can be fairly hair-raising.

Long-distance buses can be booked at any of the backpackers' places, or at CS Travel & Tours on the main street in Tanah Rata. Destinations include Singapore (RM36), Butterworth (RM26) and KL (RM10).

From Tapah there's a much greater range of buses to places including Lumut, Kuantan and Melaka.

Taxi There are regular taxis from the taxi stand (☎ 05-941555) on the main street in Tanah Rata. Things are much busier in the mornings. The fares are RM6 to Tapah, RM13 to Ipoh and RM25/30 to KL.

IPOH

The 'city of millionaires', 219 km north of Kuala Lumpur and 173 km south of Butterworth, made its fortune from tin mining. It is a thriving Chinese town with some of the best Chinese food in Malaysia. Interesting cave-temples on the outskirts of the town are the **Perak Tong Temple**, the most important temple, about six km north of town, and the **Sam Poh Temple**, a few km south of town. Both are right on the main road and easy to get to.

Ipoh is also the best take-off point for Lumut and the island of Pangkor.

Places to Stay

The *New South Eastern Hotel* (☎ 05-548709) at 48 Jalan Lahat is a Chinese cheapie of the most basic variety. The rooms are noisy as it's right on a busy intersection but it is very handy for transport connections. Rooms with fan cost RM15.

The main hotel area, however, is around the Jalan Chamberlain area. The *Beauty Hotel* on Jalan Yang Kalsom is reasonably clean and is cheap at RM16 for rooms with fan and common bath. A better bet is the nearby *Cathay Hotel* (☎ 05-513322) which charges RM18.70 for rooms with fan or RM20.70 with air-con and bath.

Of a slightly better standard, the *Embassy Hotel* (☎ 05-549496) at 35 Jalan Chamberlain has rooms with fan and bath for RM25 or RM29 for an air-con double with bath.

Better still is the *Win Wah (Winner) Hotel* (☎ 05-515177) on Jalan Ali Pitchay, a spotless Chinese hotel with large rooms with bath and hot water for RM23 or RM37 with air-con – a definite winner.

Places to Eat

Ipoh has plenty of restaurants, and the rice noodle dish known as kway teow is reputed to be better in Ipoh than anywhere else in Malaysia. The most well-known place for kway teow is *Kedai Kopi Kong Heng* on Jalan Leech, between Jalan Pasar (Market) and Jalan Station, although these days it seems to have become a small food centre. Kong Heng is one of the oldest Chinese restaurants in the city but there are several others like it on and off Jalan Leech.

There's a good food centre on Jalan Raja Musa Aziz just south of Jalan Sultan Iskandar serving all the usual items, but not beer.

For Malay food the *Rahman Restaurant* on Jalan Chamberlain is very clean and has a wide range of dishes, and an air-con room upstairs. Near the bus station, the *Krishna Bhavan Restaurant* on Jalan Lahat serves curries.

The huge *Central Market* has a wide range of fruit and vegies for putting your own meals together. On the street which runs along the northern edge of the market the *Lido Cake & Hot Bread Shop* has good breads and pastries.

Finally, for something more familiar, *McDonald's* is on Jalan Clare near Central Market.

Getting There & Away

Air Pelangi Air (☎ 05-204770) flies to Singapore (RM209), Kuala Lumpur (RM71), Penang (RM77) and to Hat Yai in Thailand (RM120; 1995B from Thailand).

Bus The bus station is in the south-east corner of the city centre, a taxi ride from the main hotel area. Numerous companies have departures at varying times, though most departures to places outside the immediate Ipoh area leave at night. Tickets should be booked in advance. Destinations and fares include Butterworth (RM8), KL (RM10), Melaka (RM15.80) and Johor Bahru (RM25.90). Buses to Lumut (RM3.50) leave from the service station across Jalan Kidd from the bus station.

Taxi Long-distance taxis leave from beside the bus station. Destinations include Taiping (RM7), Butterworth (RM15/20 non-air-con/air-con), Lumut (RM7) and KL (RM18/21).

LUMUT

The Malaysian navy has its principal base in this small river port, but Lumut is little more than a departure point for nearby Pangkor Island or Medan in Indonesia. If you get marooned in Lumut there is a reasonable choice of Chinese hotels.

Getting There & Away

Bus & Taxi Lumut is 101 km from Ipoh, the usual place for Lumut bus connections. Buses to other destinations include Johor Bahru (RM29), Kota Bharu (RM21), Kuala

Lumpur (RM15), Melaka (RM21) and Kuantan (RM25). Long-distance taxis go to Butterworth (RM18), Ipoh (RM7) and KL (RM25).

Boat Kuala Perlis Langkawi Ferry Service has a high-speed service from Lumut to Belawan in Sumatra (RM110/90, 3½ hours) on Wednesday, Friday and Sunday at 9 am, and from Belawan on the same days at 1 pm. The fare includes the 45-minute bus ride between Belawan and Medan. The booking office at Lumut (☎ 05-934258) is in the small park just back from the ferry jetty.

For ferries to Pangkor see the following Pulau Pangkor section.

PULAU PANGKOR

The island of Pangkor is close to the coast, off Lumut, and easily accessible via Ipoh. It's a popular resort island known for its fine and, often, quite isolated beaches, many of which can be walked to along an interesting 'around the island' route. A visit to the island is principally a 'laze on the beach' operation.

Ferries from Lumut stop on the eastern side of the island at Sungai Pinang Kecil and then Pangkor village, where there are banks, restaurants and shops. The main beaches are on the west of the island. **Pasir Bogak** is the most developed beach, and the next bay to the north, **Teluk Nipah**, has the budget accommodation beach. Golden Sands Beach (Teluk Belanga) at the northern end of the island is the preserve of the Pan-Pacific Pangkor Resort. Between these beaches are a number of virtually deserted beaches, the best being **Coral Bay**.

Emerald Bay on nearby Pulau Pangkor Laut is a beautiful little horseshoe-shaped bay but the entire island has been taken over by a French hotel-restaurant conglomerate.

Pangkor's one bit of history, a **Dutch fort** dating from 1670, is three km south of Pangkor village at Teluk Gedong.

Places to Stay & Eat

Teluk Nipah The current favourite is *Joe Fisherman's Village* (☎ 05-952389) with basic A-frames costing RM20 for two people; slightly more substantial cottages cost RM25. Dorm beds should be available by now. Basic meals are available, and motorbikes and bicycles can be rented.

Right next door is the *Coral Beach Camp*, offering the same facilities as Joe's, but it lacks atmosphere. An A-frame hut costs RM20 or rooms are RM20 to RM30.

Behind Joe's is the *Nazri Nipah Camp*, also offering A-frame accommodation and meals. The owners are friendly, but their lack of English makes communication difficult.

More upmarket places are the *Nipah Bay Villa* (☎ 05-952198) and the *Sukasuka Beach Resort* (☎ 05-952494), which costs RM85 or RM95 on weekends for full-board.

Pasir Bogak Pasir Bogak used to be the best beach to stay at but recent development has seen it become cramped. Most accommodation is mainly aimed at the upper end of the market.

The best place to stay for any reasonable price is the *Pangkor Anchor*. Small and somewhat ageing A-frame huts rent for RM11.50/18.40 and for this you get a mattress on the floor. Children are not made especially welcome and there's a bit of the 'lights out' mentality of a youth hostel.

All the hotels have restaurants, and there are two small food centres. The *Pangkor Restaurant* is a cheap seafood and Chinese food restaurant, and the restaurant in the *Hotel Sea View* has mediocre food but it's an excellent place to watch the sunset.

Getting There & Away

Air Pelangi Air have started daily flights to Singapore (RM209, S$190 from Singapore), and twice-daily flights to Kuala Lumpur (RM125).

Boat Frequent ferries from Lumut to Pangkor village go throughout the day and cost RM4 return. From Lumut four ferries a day also go to the northern end of the island, across the isthmus from the Pan-Pacific Resort. Another ferry service connects Lumut with the Pansea Resort on Pulau

Pangkor Laut, from where ferries also go to and from Pasir Bogak.

Getting Around

Buses run every half hour or so from Pangkor village across the island to the far end of the beach at Pasir Bogak and back again, but they don't go to Teluk Nipah. Pangkor also has plenty of minibus taxis costing RM3 from Pangkor to Pasir Bogak, and RM10 to Teluk Nipah.

Motorcycles can be rented for RM30 per day and bicycles for RM8 per day.

KUALA KANGSAR

The royal town of Perak state has the fine **Ubadiah Mosque**, with its onion dome and the minarets squeezed up against it as if seen in a distorting mirror. This is the place where rubber trees were first grown in Malaysia.

TAIPING

The 'town of everlasting peace' was once a raucous mining town. It has a beautiful **lake** and **zoo** and the oldest **museum** in the country. Above the town is **Maxwell Hill**, Malaysia's smallest and oldest hill station. To get there, you have to take a government Land Rover from the station (☎ 05-827243) at the foot of the hill for RM3.

Places to Stay & Eat

Taiping has plenty of cheap Chinese hotels. The *Hong Kong Hotel* (☎ 05-823824) at 79 Jalan Barrack (shown on street signs as Jalan Lim Tee Hooi) is a bargain at RM15/20 for a huge room with air-con and bath attached. It's two blocks from the main street, Jalan Kota. Up the scale a notch is the *Hotel Meridien* (☎ 05-831133) at 2 Jalan Simpang. Rooms start from RM42, also with air-con and bath.

Better still is the *New Rest House (Rumah Rehat Baru)* (☎ 05-822044), overlooking the beautiful Lake Gardens, about a km from the town centre. It's clean, secure and very good value at RM30 for large doubles or RM35 with air-con.

Taiping's large night market has many open-air eating stalls and satay is one of the city's specialities.

Getting There & Away

Taiping is several km off the main KL-Butterworth road. If you're heading south from Butterworth to Lumut for Pangkor Island and miss the direct bus it's straightforward to take a Butterworth-Taiping bus and another bus on from Taiping to Lumut. Buses direct to KL cost RM13.20.

Taxis to KL cost RM24, or to Butterworth RM9.

PENANG

The oldest British settlement in Malaysia, predating both Singapore and Melaka, is also one of Malaysia's major tourist attractions. This is hardly surprising as the 285-sq-km island of Penang has popular beach resorts and an intriguing and historically interesting town, Georgetown, which is also noted for its superb food.

Captain Francis Light sailed up and took over the virtually uninhabited island in 1786. Encouraged by free-trade policies, Georgetown became a prosperous centre as well as a local mecca for dreamers, dissidents, intellectuals and artists.

Sun Yat-Sen planned the 1911 Canton uprising in Georgetown, probably in one of the local Hainanese coffee shops. Unmistakably Chinese, it's one of the most likeable cities in South-East Asia. With easy-going *kampungs* (villages), sandy beaches, warm water, good food and plenty of things to see, who wouldn't like Penang?

Orientation

Penang's major town, Georgetown, is often referred to as Penang, although correctly that is the name of the island (the actual Malay spelling is Pinang and it means betel nut). Georgetown is in the north-east of the island, where the straits between the island and the mainland are at their narrowest.

A vehicle and passenger ferry service operates 24 hours a day across the three-km-wide channel between Georgetown and Butterworth on the mainland. South of the ferry crossing is the Penang Bridge – the longest in South-East Asia – which links the island with Malaysia's north-south highway.

Georgetown is a compact city and most places can easily be reached on foot or by bicycle rickshaw. Two important streets to remember are Lebuh Chulia and Lebuh Campbell. You'll find most of Georgetown's popular cheap hotels along Lebuh Chulia or close to it, while Lebuh Campbell is one of the town's main shopping streets. Jalan Penang is another popular shopping street and in this area you'll find a number of the more expensive hotels including, at the waterfront end of Jalan Pe able Eastern & Oriental Hot

If you follow Jalan Penang so pass the modern, multistorey blot o skyline known as the Kompleks Tun Abdul Razak (Komtar).

Information

Tourist Offices The Penang Tourist Association (☎ 04-366665) is on Jalan Tun Syed Sheh Barakbah, close to Fort Cornwallis. They are a useful source of information and the office is open normal business hours. Tourism Malaysia (☎ 04-620066) has an

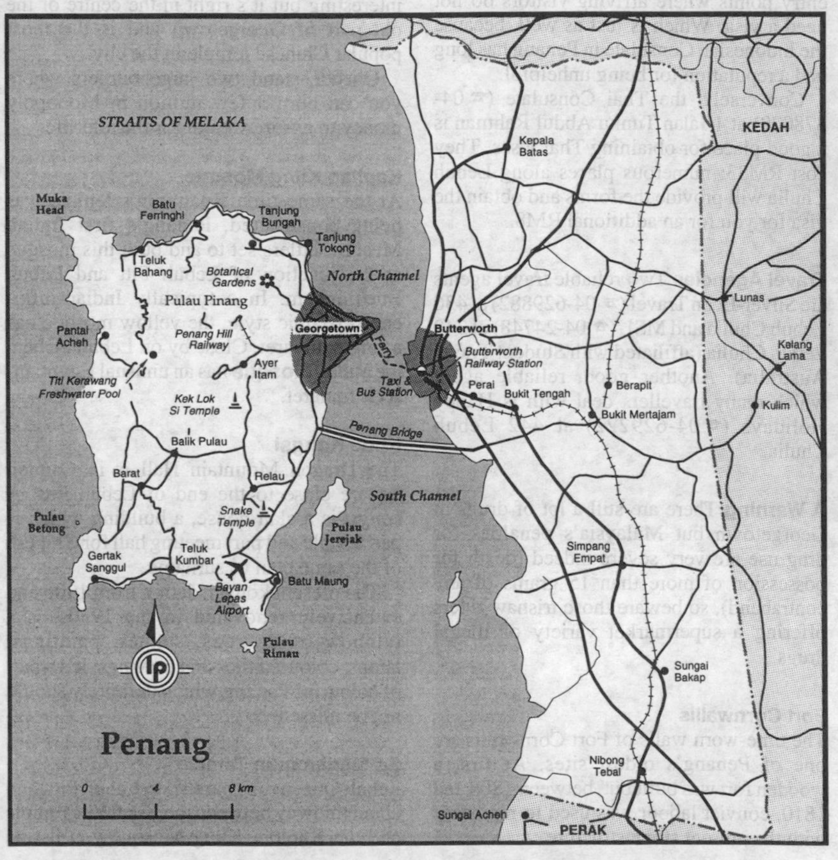

…ce a few doors along in the same building.

The Penang Tourist Guides Association office (☎ 04-614461), on the 3rd floor of the Komtar, is open daily from 9.30 am to 6.30 pm and is staffed by volunteer guides who really know their stuff.

Post The poste restante facility at the GPO is efficient and popular.

Foreign Embassies Medan, the entry point from Penang to the Indonesian island of Sumatra, is counted as one of the 'usual' entry points where arriving visitors do not need a visa. Which is just as well, because the Indonesian Consulate in Penang has long had a reputation for being unhelpful.

Conversely, the Thai Consulate (☎ 04-378029) at 1 Jalan Tunku Abdul Rahman is a good place for obtaining Thai visas. They cost RM33; numerous places along Lebuh Chulia will provide the forms and obtain the visa for you for an additional RM8.

Travel Agencies Two reliable travel agents are Silver-Econ Travel (☎ 04-629882) at 436 Lebuh Chulia and MSL (☎ 04-24748) at 340 Lebuh Chulia (affiliated with Student Travel Australia). Another good, reliable agent which many travellers deal with is Happy Holidays (☎ 04-629222) at 442 Lebuh Chulia.

A Warning There are still a lot of drugs in Georgetown but Malaysia's penalties for drug use are very severe indeed (death for possession of more than 15 grams of any contraband), so beware those trishaw riders offering a supermarket variety of illegal drugs.

Fort Cornwallis

The time-worn walls of Fort Cornwallis are one of Penang's oldest sites. At first a wooden fort was built but, between 1808 and 1810, convict labour was used to replace it with the present stone structure.

Penang Museum & Art Gallery

This little museum has gory details of Chinese secret society squabbles. There is also an art gallery which has a statue of Francis Light outside. Opening hours are from 9 am to 5 pm daily, except Friday when it is closed from noon to 2.45 pm. Admission is free.

Kuan Yin Teng Temple

Just round the corner from the museum, on Lebuh Pitt, is the temple of Kuan Yin, the Goddess of Mercy. The temple was built in the 1800s by the first Chinese settlers in Penang. It's neither terribly impressive or interesting but it's right in the centre of the old part of Georgetown and is the most popular Chinese temple in the city.

Outside stand two large burners where you can burn a few million in Monopoly money to ensure wealth for the afterlife.

Kapitan Kling Mosque

At the same time Kuan Yin's temple was being constructed, Penang's first Indian Muslim settlers set to and built this mosque at the junction of Lebuh Pitt and Lebuh Buckingham. In a typically Indian-influenced Islamic style, the yellow mosque has a single minaret. Close by on Lebuh Acheh, the **Malay Mosque** has an unusual Egyptian-style minaret.

Khoo Kongsi

The Dragon Mountain Hall is in Cannon Square close to the end of Lebuh Pitt. A *kongsi* is a clan house, a building which is part temple and part meeting hall for Chinese of the same clan or surname.

The present kongsi, dating from 1906 and extensively renovated in the 1950s, is a rainbow of dragons, statues, paintings, lamps, coloured tiles and carvings. It's a part of colourful Penang which definitely should not be missed.

Sri Mariamman Temple

Lebuh Queen runs parallel to Lebuh Pitt, and about midway between the Kuan Yin Temple and the Kapitan Kling Mosque you'll find another example of Penang's religious diversity. The Sri Mariamman Temple is a typical south Indian temple with its elaborately sculptured and painted *gopuram*, or pyramidal gateway tower, soaring over the entrance.

Wat Chayamangkalaram

Located at Burma Lane, just off the road to Batu Ferringhi, is a major Thai temple – the Temple of the Reclining Buddha. This brightly painted temple houses a 32-metre-long reclining Buddha, loudly proclaimed in Penang as the third longest in the world. Take that claim with a pinch of salt; there's at least one other in Malaysia that's larger, plus one in Thailand (at least) and two in Myanmar.

Penang Hill

Rising 830 metres above Georgetown, the top of Penang Hill provides a cool retreat from the sticky heat below as it's generally about 5°C cooler than at sea level. From the summit, you've got a spectacular view over the island and across to the mainland. There are pleasant gardens, a small cafe and a hotel as well as a Hindu temple and a Muslim mosque on the top. Penang Hill is particularly pleasant at dusk as Georgetown, far below, starts to light up.

Getting There & Away Take bus No 1 from Pengkalan Weld Quay to Ayer Itam (every five minutes), then bus No 8 to the funicular station. The ascent of the hill costs RM3 for the round trip. There are departures from the bottom every 30 minutes from 6.30 am to 9.30 pm, and up until 9.15 pm from the top. There are later departures until midnight on Wednesday and Saturday. The queues here are often horrendous and waits of half an hour and more are not uncommon.

The energetic can get to the top by an interesting eight-km hike which starts from the Moon Gate at the Botanical Gardens. The hike takes nearly three hours so be sure to bring a water bottle.

Kek Lok Si Temple

On a hilltop at Ayer Itam, close to the funicular station for Penang Hill, stands the largest Buddhist temple in Malaysia. The construction commenced in 1890 and took more than 20 years to complete.

The entrance is reached through arcades of souvenir stalls. Go past a tightly packed turtle pond and murky fish ponds until you reach the Ban Po Thar, or Ten Thousand Buddhas Pagoda.

A 'voluntary' contribution is the price to climb to the top of the seven-tier, 30-metre-high tower which is said to be Burmese at the top, Chinese at the bottom and Thai in-between.

Snake Temple

The Snake Temple, at Km 15 on the road to the airport, is reached by bus No 66 or 78 from Lebuh Chulia. Live snakes, suitably doped on the incense smoke, are photogenically draped over you. There's no admission fee but 'donations' are requested. The number of snakes varies throughout the year.

Beaches

Penang's beaches are not as spectacular or as clean as the tourist brochures would have you believe and they suffer from pollution, but they make a pleasant enough day trip from Georgetown and have accommodation for longer stays. They are mainly along the north coast. **Tanjung Bungah** is the first real beach, but it's not attractive for swimming. **Batu Ferringhi** (Foreigner's Rock) is the resort strip but the beach is somewhat of a disappointment compared to other beaches in Malaysia. **Teluk Bahang** is less developed and is still principally a small fishing village.

Places to Stay

Hostels Georgetown has a well-situated, but extremely anonymous, *Youth Hostel* (Asrama Belia) on Lebuh Farquhar. Dorm beds will cost you RM5, although non-YHA members pay an extra RM2 on the first night. The front door closes at midnight.

The *YMCA* (☎ 04-362211), 211 Jalan Macalister, has singles/doubles for RM30/32 or RM35/37 with air-con, all with attached shower. The RM2 temporary membership

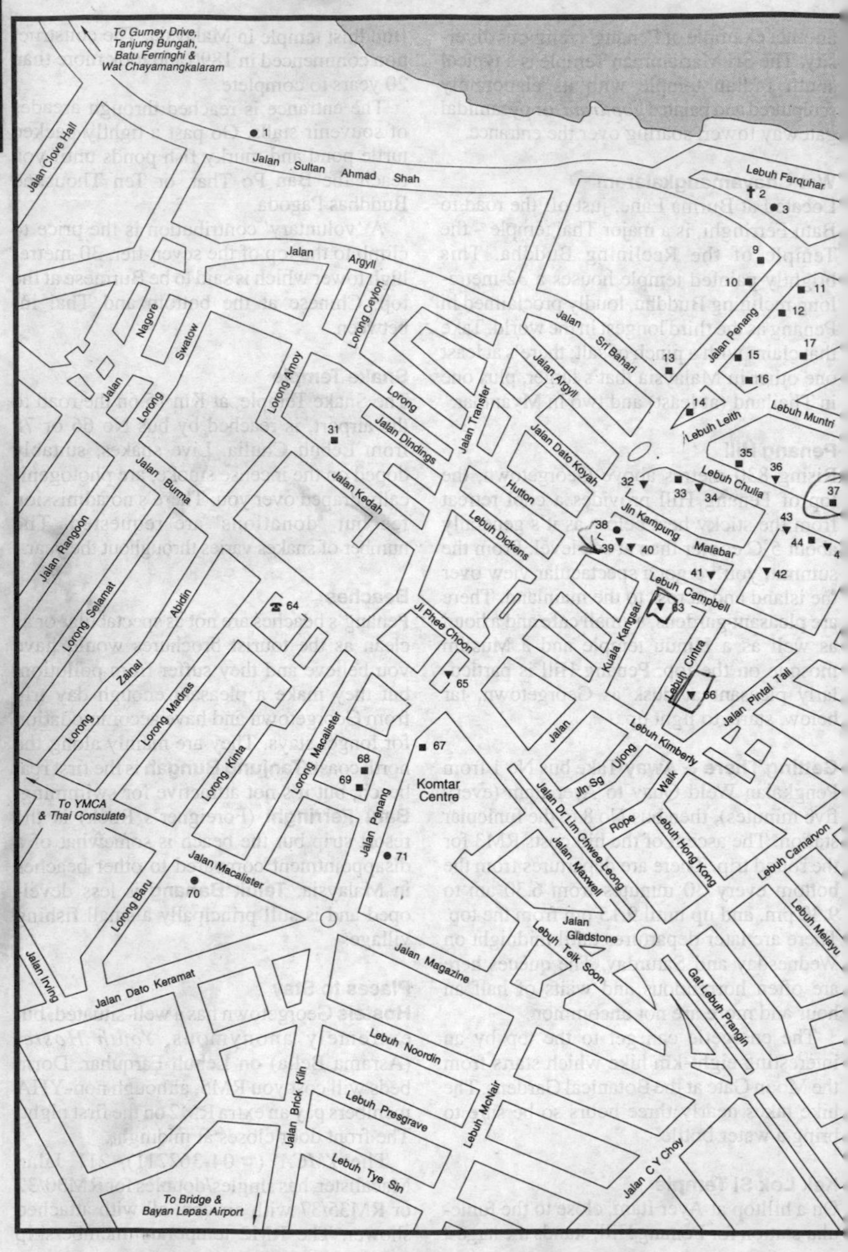
To Gurney Drive, Tanjung Bungah, Batu Ferringhi & Wat Chayamangkalaram
Jalan Clove Hall
1
Jalan Sultan Ahmad Shah
Lebuh Farquhar
2
3
Jalan Argyll
9
10
11
12
Nagore
Swatow
Lorong Ceylon
Jalan Penang
Jalan Sri Bahari
13
15
16
17
Jalan
Lorong
Lorong Amoy
Lorong
Jalan Argyll
Jalan Transfer
14
Lebuh Leith
Lebuh Muntri
31
Jalan Dindings
Jalan Dato Koyah
35
36
Jalan Burma
Jalan Kedah
Hutton
32
33
34
Lebuh Chulia
37
Jln Kampung Malabar
38
39
40
43
44
4
Jalan Rangoon
Lebuh Dickens
Abidin
41
42
Lebuh Campbell
64
63
Jl Phee Choon
Kuala Kangsar
Lorong Selamat
Zainal
Lebuh Cintra
66
65
Jalan Pintal Tali
Lorong
Lorong Madras
Lorong Kinta
Lorong Macalister
Jalan
Lebuh Kimberly
67
68
69
Komtar Centre
Jln Sg Ujong
Rope Walk
To YMCA & Thai Consulate
Jalan Penang
Jalan Dr Lim Chwee Leong
Jalan Maxwell
Lebuh Hong Kong
Lebuh Carnarvon
71
Jalan Macalister
70
Lorong Baru
Jalan Gladstone
Lebuh Melayu
Lebuh Teik Soon
Jalan Irving
Jalan Magazine
Jalan Dato Keramat
Gat Lebuh Prangin
Lebuh Noordin
Jalan Brick Kiln
Lebuh Presgrave
Lebuh McNair
Jalan C Y Choy
Lebuh Tye Sin
To Bridge & Bayan Lepas Airport

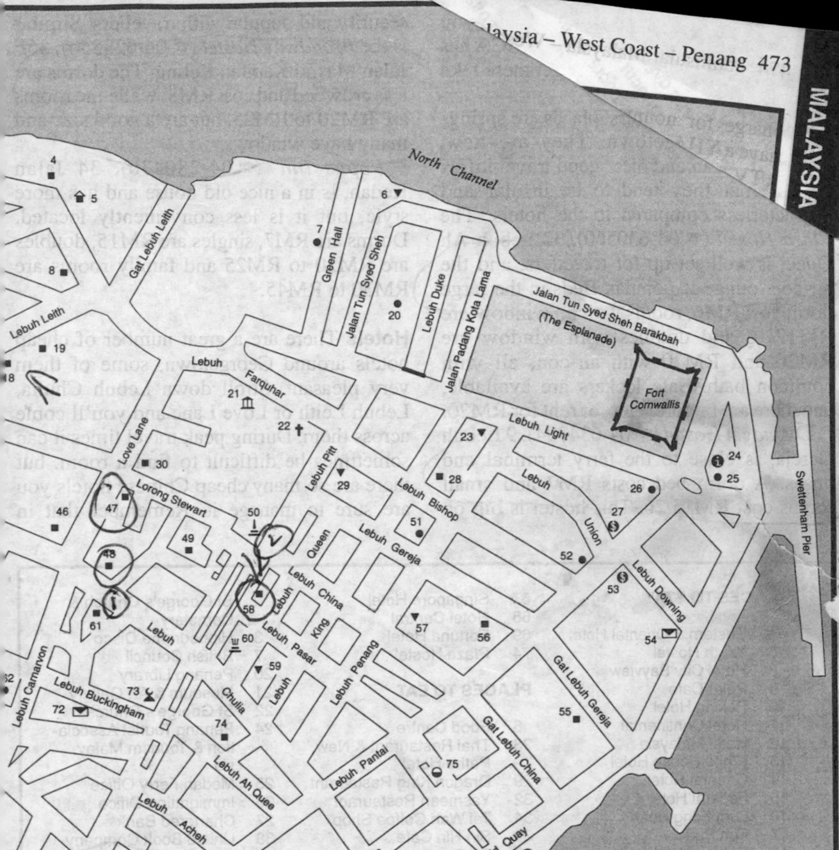

Georgetown

0 150 300 m

North Channel

South Channel

Jalan Tun Syed Sheh Barakbah (The Esplanade)

Fort Cornwallis

Swettenham Pier

Gat Lebuh Leith

Lebuh Leith

Green Hall

Jalan Tun Syed Sheh

Lebuh Duke

Jalan Padang Kota Lama

Lebuh Farquhar

Love Lane

Lorong Stewart

Lebuh Pitt

Lebuh Light

Lebuh Bishop

Lebuh Union

Lebuh Gereja

Lebuh Queen

Lebuh China

Lebuh King

Lebuh Downing

Gat Lebuh Gereja

Gat Lebuh China

Lebuh Pasar

Lebuh Penang

Lebuh Chulia

Lebuh Carnarvon

Lebuh Buckingham

Lebuh Ah Quee

Lebuh Pantai

Lebuh Acheh

Lebuh Victoria

Pengkalan Weld Quay

Lebuh Armenian

Gat Lebuh Acheh

Lorong Carnarvon

Gat

Lebuh Melayu

…aived if you … The YMCA has … cafeteria. To get there take …

…ber of travellers' places are springing up in Georgetown. They are new, spotlessly clean and offer good travel information, but they tend to be insular and characterless compared to the hotels. The *Plaza Hostel* (☎ 04-630560), 32 Lebuh Ah Quee, is well set up for travellers, and the air-con lounge is popular. Beds in the large dorm cost RM6, rooms with no window are RM12/16 and doubles with window are RM20 and RM30 with air-con, all with common bath. Safe lockers are available, and there are motorcycles for rent for RM20.

D'Budget Hostel (☎ 04-634794), 9 Lebuh Gereja, is close to the ferry terminal and buses. A dorm bed costs RM7 and small rooms cost RM15/26. This hostel is big on security and popular with travellers. Similar is the *Broadway Hostel* (☎ 04-628550), 35F Jalan Masjid Kapitan Keling. The dorms are less crowded and cost RM8, while the rooms are RM20 to RM25, but are a good size and many have windows.

Popus Inn (☎ 04-280436), 34 Jalan Kedah, is in a nice old house and has more style, but it is less conveniently located. Dorms are RM7, singles are RM15, doubles are RM20 to RM25 and family rooms are RM30 to RM45.

Hotels There are a great number of cheap hotels around Georgetown, some of them very pleasant. Stroll down Lebuh Chulia, Lebuh Leith or Love Lane and you'll come across them. During peak travel times it can sometimes be difficult to find a room, but there are so many cheap Chinese hotels you are sure to manage it. Remember that in

PLACES TO STAY

4 Eastern & Oriental Hotel
5 Youth Hostel
8 Hotel City Bayview
9 Polar Cafe
10 Peking Hotel
11 Hotel Continental
12 Hotel Malaysia
13 White House Hotel
14 Oriental Hotel
15 Federal Hotel
16 Lum Fong Hotel
17 Fun Pub
18 Cathay Hotel
19 Waldorf Hotel
23 New Pathe Hotel & Thai Restaurant
28 Hotel Rio
30 Tiong Wah Hotel
31 Popus Inn
33 Eastern Hotel
35 Lum Thean Hotel
37 Eng Aun Hotel
44 Swiss Hotel
46 Pin Seng Hotel
47 Wan Hai Hotel
48 Tye Ann Hotel
49 Hotel Noble
55 D'Budget Lodge
56 D'Budget Hostel
58 Broadway Hostel
61 Honpin Hotel
67 Singapore Hotel
68 Hotel Central
69 Fortuna Hotel
74 Plaza Hostel

PLACES TO EAT

6 Food Centre
23 Thai Restaurant & New Pathe Hotel
29 Dragon King Restaurant
32 Yasmeen Restaurant
34 Tai Wah Coffee Shop
36 Sin Hin Cafe
39 Taj Restaurant
40 Hameediyah Restaurant
41 Everlight Cafe
42 Hong Kong Restaurant
43 Sin Kuan Hwa Cafe
45 Eng Thai Cafe
57 Kaliaman Restaurant
59 Dawood Restaurant
63 Diners Bakery
65 Restoran Loke Thye Kee
66 Green Planet Restaurant

OTHER

1 Citibank Building & Singapore Airlines
2 St George's Church & Cemetery
3 Hippodrome Disco
7 British Council
20 Penang Library
21 Museum & Art Gallery
22 St George's Church
24 Penang Tourist Association & Tourism Malaysia
25 Medan Ferry Office
26 Immigration Office
27 Chartered Bank
38 United Book Company
50 Kuan Yin Teng Temple
51 Cathay Pacific
52 MS Alley
53 Hong Kong & Shanghai Bank
54 GPO
60 Sri Mariamman Temple
62 Market
64 Telekom Office
70 Thai International
71 MAS Office
72 Post Office
73 Kapitan Kling Mosque
75 City Bus Terminal
76 Khoo Kongsi
77 Malay Mosque
78 Round Island Buses
79 Railway Booking Office

virtually all the places listed here, two people can share a bed and just take a single room.

Two popular places are the *Swiss Hotel* (☎ 04-620133) at 431-F Lebuh Chulia and the *Eng Aun* (☎ 04-612333), directly across the road at 380 Lebuh Chulia. The Swiss Hotel has singles/doubles with fan and common bath at RM16.50/19.80, but the service these days is not what it might be – how about a smile once in a while, guys? The much friendlier Eng Aun charges RM16/20 for large rooms with common facilities. Both of these hotels attract a steady stream of travellers.

At 282 Lebuh Chulia the *Tye Ann Hotel* (☎ 04-614875) is very popular, particularly for its breakfasts downstairs in the restaurant section. Rooms cost RM16 per single or double and there are also dorm beds for RM6.

At 35 Love Lane the *Wan Hai Hotel* (☎ 04-616853) is a good Chinese cheapie with beds in a nine-bed dorm for RM6 and rooms for RM16/20. It's a quiet place with a small roof terrace. The *Tiong Wah Hotel* (☎ 04-622057), close by at 23 Love Lane, is a typical older-style Chinese place in a very quiet area. Rooms go for RM16/20.

Another popular place is the *White House Hotel* (☎ 04-632385) at 72 Jalan Penang, although the entrance is in the side street. Large rooms with air-con, attached bath and hot water cost RM28/33, or RM18/24 with the air-con switched off.

At 36 Lorong Pasar, just one small block in from Lebuh Chulia, the *Hotel Noble* (☎ 04-612372) is a quiet place with rooms for RM14/18 with common bath.

Back on Lebuh Chulia near the junction with Jalan Penang, similar cheap hotels are the *Eastern Hotel* (☎ 04-614597) at No 509, the *Hang Chow Hotel* (☎ 04-610810) at No 511 and the *Lum Thean Hotel* (☎ 04-614117) at No 422.

The *Polar Cafe* (☎ 04-622054), 48A Jalan Penang, is a bed & breakfast place and has a good cafe downstairs. Double rooms are RM20, or RM40 to RM50 with air-con, attached bath and hot water, all including breakfast.

More expensive hotels with style include the wonderful-looking *Cathay Hotel* (☎ 04-626271) at 22 Lebuh Leith. This hotel has a cavernous lobby and huge spotless rooms for RM46 with fan and bath, or RM58 with air-con and bath. Grandest (and oldest) is the fine old *Eastern & Oriental* (E&O) Hotel (☎ 04-630630), one of those superb old establishments in the Raffles manner – indeed it was built by the Sarkies Brothers who also constructed the Raffles in Singapore and the Strand in Yangon. It features in several Somerset Maugham stories. Rooms cost from RM118/128 and suites start at RM270, plus taxes. There's also a good bookshop here.

Beach Accommodation Few travellers seem to stay out at the Penang beaches these days though there are some budget places at Tanjung Bungah, Batu Ferringhi and Teluk Bahang.

The best offering at Tanjung Bungah is the *Lost Paradise*, at the western end of town, just past the Marvista Resort. It's run by the same people who own the Green Planet restaurant in Georgetown. It's right on the beach and consists of a few traditional Penang bungalows. Rooms range from RM15 to RM60 and are good value. Meals are available and the lush garden setting is very attractive.

Batu Ferringhi has plenty of big hotels and some budget guesthouses. Best of them is *Shalini's Guest House* (☎ 04-811859, right on the waterfront. This very clean and modern family-run place has good rooms for RM30 or RM45 with air-con. Meals are available and the balcony is a nice place to relax. Right next door is the long-running *Ali's Guest House* (☎ 04-811316), although it's not that great these days. Dorm beds are RM12, while rooms cost from RM35. On the other side of Shalini's is the *Baba Guest House* (☎ 04-811686), but it also lacks atmosphere and is not great value at RM25 or RM42 with air-con.

At Teluk Bahang is the well-kept *Rama's* (☎ 04-811179) with beds for RM6, or rooms for RM12 with discounts for longer stays. It's run by a Hindu family and is well kept.

Miss Loh has a guesthouse off the main road towards the butterfly farm – ask at the Kwong Tuck Hing shop opposite the Kassim Brothers Restaurant. The guesthouse is very comfortable and set in a large garden. Dorm beds are RM7 and doubles cost RM15 to RM30.

Places to Eat

Penang is another of the region's delightful food trips with a wide variety of restaurants and many local specialities to tempt you. For a start, there are two types of laksa, or soup, that are particularly associated with Penang. *Laksa assam* is a fish soup with a sour taste from the tamarind or assam paste and it is served with special white laksa noodles. Originally a Thai dish, *laksa lemak* has been adopted by Penang. It's basically similar to laksa assam with coconut milk being substituted for the tamarind.

Seafood, of course, is very popular in Penang and there are many restaurants that specialise in fresh fish, crabs and prawns – particularly along the northern beach fringe.

Despite its Chinese character, Penang also has a strong Indian presence and there are some popular specialities to savour. Curry kapitan is a Penang chicken curry which supposedly takes its name from a Dutch sea captain asking his Indonesian mess boy what was on that night. The answer was 'curry kapitan' and it's been on the menu ever since.

Murtabak, a thin roti chanai pastry stuffed with egg, vegetables and meat, while not actually a Penang speciality, is done with particular flair on the island.

Night Markets Georgetown has a wide selection of *street stalls* with nightly gatherings at places like Gurney Drive or along the Esplanade. The latter is particularly good for trying local Penang specialities.

The big pasar malam changes venue every two weeks, so check at the tourist office for its current location. It's mainly for clothes and other household goods but there are a few hawkers' stalls. It doesn't really get going until around 8 pm.

Medicated tea is a popular item and one Georgetown tea stall has a sign announcing that it will cure everything from 'headache, stomachache and kidney trouble' to 'malaria, cholera and (wait for it) fartulence'.

Indian Food Amongst the more popular Indian restaurants is *Dawood* at 63 Lebuh Queen, opposite the Sri Mariamman Temple. Curry kapitan is just one of the many curry dishes at this reasonably priced restaurant. On Lebuh Campbell, the *Taj* at No 166 and the *Hameediyah* at No 164A both have good curries and delicious murtabak.

The *Yasmeen Restaurant* at 177 Jalan Penang, near the corner of Lebuh Chulia, is another place for murtabak, but this is also an excellent place for a quick snack of roti chanai with dhal dip – a cheap meal at any time of the day.

A good little place for masala dosa and lunchtime thalis is the *Shan Vilas* restaurant next to the Plaza Hostel on Lebuh Ah Quee. All food is served on banana leaves and is eaten with the fingers.

Penang has a 'little India' along Lebuh Pasar between Lebuh Penang and Lebuh Pitt and along the side streets between. Several *small restaurants* and *stalls* in this area offer cheap north (Muslim) and south Indian food.

For something a bit more upmarket, try the *Kaliaman Restaurant* on Lebuh Penang. This air-con place has banana-leaf curries at lunchtime for RM3 (or RM4 for nonvegetarian) and does excellent north Indian food in the evenings.

Chinese Food There are so many Chinese restaurants in Penang that specific recommendations are probably redundant.

At 29 Lebuh Cintra, the *Hong Kong Restaurant* is good, cheap and varied, and has a menu in English. At night, this brightly lit restaurant is a real travellers' centre. A number of places around Georgetown provide excellent Hainanese chicken rice. The *Sin Kuan Hwa Cafe*, on the corner of Lebuh Chulia and Lebuh Cintra, is one that specialises in this.

More good Chinese food can be found at the fancier *Dragon King*, on the corner of

Lebuh Bishop and Lebuh Pitt, which specialises in traditional Nonya wedding cuisine and is definitely worth a try. Expect to pay around RM20 for two.

One of the most popular outdoor Chinese places is *Hsiang Yang Cafe*, across the street from the Tye Ann Hotel on Lebuh Chulia. It's really a hawkers' centre with a cheap and good Chinese buffet (rice with three or four side dishes for RM2.50), plus noodle, satay and popiah vendors.

The *Tzechu-lin* at 229-C Jalan Burmah is a Buddhist vegetarian restaurant which has excellent food. Expect to spend around RM20 for two.

Breakfast & Western Food At breakfast time, the popular travellers' hang-out is the *Tye Ann Hotel* on Lebuh Chulia. People visit this friendly little establishment for its excellent porridge, toast and marmalade and other breakfast favourites.

Western breakfasts are also available at the *New China, Eng Aun, Swiss* and *Cathay Hotels*, and opposite the Wan Hai Hotel. Another morning hang-out is the tiny *Eng Thai Cafe* at 417B Lebuh Chulia, not far from the Eng Aun and Swiss hotels. There are other small Chinese cafes with Western breakfast menus like the popular little *Sin Hin Cafe* at 402 Lebuh Chulia. The *Tai Wah Coffee Shop* at 487 Lebuh Chulia is a very busy little place, buzzing with activity until late at night.

Another cheap cafe is the *Everlight Cafe* on Lebuh Cintra, not far from Lebuh Campbell. Further along the same street is the *Green Planet* restaurant. While it's certainly not the cheapest place in town, it has a varied menu of Western dishes, the music is good and the atmosphere relaxed. To kill a bit of time while waiting for your meal you can read (and add to) the travel-tips notebooks. Most travellers make it here at least once.

At the supermarket located in the Komtar complex you can find all the usual supermarket goodies, and on floors one to three you'll find *Kentucky Fried Chicken, McDonald's, Shakey's, White Castle, Pizza Hut, A&W* and *Satay Ria*. On the 5th floor there's a pleasant hawkers' centre with all the usual Chinese and local dishes.

Getting There & Away

Air The MAS office (☎ 04-620011) in the Komtar building is open Monday to Saturday from 8.30 am to 6 pm and Sunday until 1 pm.

See the Getting There & Away section at the start of this chapter for details of flights to other countries in the region.

Bus The bus terminal is beside the ferry terminal in Butterworth. Some travel agents in Georgetown (several are near the Eng Aun and Swiss hotels for example) offer good bargains on bus tickets. The long-distance buses which these places deal with often leave from somewhere in Georgetown rather than Butterworth. Typical bus fares include Ipoh for RM8, KL for RM19, Kota Bharu for RM20, Melaka for RM24 and Singapore for RM35.

There are also bus services to Thailand: Hat Yai (RM20), Phuket (RM35), Surat Thani (RM40) and Bangkok (RM65). Any of the hotels or travel agents can arrange tickets.

Train The railway station is, like the bus and taxi stations, right by the ferry terminal at Butterworth. Trains to KL (* denotes express) depart at 7.30*, 8.30 am, 3.20*, 8.30, 9.50* and 10.30*pm. The 7.30 am train continues on to Singapore; it arrives at 10.35 pm and costs RM60/34 in 2nd/3rd class.

The International Express to Hat Yai and Bangkok in Thailand departs at 2 pm (see the Getting There & Away section at the start of this chapter for full details). A train to the border town of Padang Besar leaves at 6.05 am and costs RM11.10/6.30 in 2nd/3rd class.

You can make reservations at the station (☎ 04-347962) or at the railway booking office (☎ 04-610290) at the ferry terminal, Pengkalan Weld Quay, Georgetown. There's a good left-luggage facility at the station costing RM1 per item per day.

Taxi Yes, the long-distance taxis also operate from a depot beside the Butterworth ferry terminal. It's also possible to book them at some of the hotspot backpacker hotels or directly with drivers. Typical fares include Ipoh for RM15, KL for RM38, Kota Bharu for RM38 and Tapah for RM22.

There are Thai taxis and minibuses operating to Hat Yai – a convenient way of getting across the border. You'll find them at the popular cheap hotels in Georgetown – the fare is around RM20.

Boat Kuala Perlis Langkawi Ferry Service has a ferry every day at 8 am to the island of Langkawi to the north. The fare is RM45/35 in 1st class/economy.

There are several yachts operating between Penang and Phuket in Thailand. Typical trips sail Penang-Langkawi-Ko Phi Phi-Krabi-Phuket and cost US$200 per person.

See the Getting There & Away section at the start of this chapter for details of boats to Indonesia.

Getting Around

To/From the Airport Penang's Bayan Lepas airport, with its Minangkabau-style terminal, is 18 km south of Georgetown. A coupon system operates for taxis from the airport. The fare to Georgetown is RM18, or RM21 for an air-con taxi.

You can get a yellow bus No 83 to the airport from Pengkalan Weld or Lebuh China – they operate on this route from 6 am to 10 pm. Taxis take about 30 minutes from the centre of town, the bus an hour.

Bus There are three main bus departure points in Georgetown and five bus companies. The city buses (MPPP Buses) all depart from the terminal at Lebuh Victoria which is directly in front of the ferry terminal. Most of these buses also go along Lebuh Chulia, so you can pick them up at the stops along that street.

The other main stand is at Pengkalan Weld, next to the ferry terminal, where the other bus companies operate from – Yellow Bus, Hin Bus, Sri Negara Transport and Lim Seng Bus Co.

For the beaches take Hin Bus No 93 from Lebuh Chulia, and for the Thai Consulate take Sri Negara Transport bus No 136 or 137, also from Lebuh Chulia.

Around the Island For around RM5 you can make the circuit of the island in one day by public transport. Start with a Yellow Bus No 66 and hop off at the Snake Temple. This Yellow Bus No 66 will then take you all the way to Balik Pulau from where you have to change to another Yellow Bus, No 76, for Teluk Bahang. There are only half a dozen of these each day and the last one leaves around mid-afternoon so it's wise to leave Georgetown early and check the departure times when you reach Balik Pulau. At Teluk Bahang you're on the northern beach strip and you simply take a blue Hin Bus No 93 to Georgetown, via Batu Ferringhi and Tanjung Bungah.

Taxi Penang's taxis are all metered but getting the drivers to use the meters is virtually impossible, so negotiate the fare before you set off. Some sample fares from Georgetown are: Batu Ferringhi for RM18, Botanical Gardens for RM12, Penang Hill/ Kek Lok Si for RM14 and the Snake Temple for RM18.

Trishaw Bicycle rickshaws are ideal on Georgetown's relatively uncrowded streets and cost around RM1 per km, but as with the taxis, agree on the fare before departure. If you come across from Butterworth on the ferry, grab a trishaw to the Lebuh Chulia cheap hotels area for RM3, although you can walk there in five or 10 minutes. For touring, the rate is around RM10 an hour.

Bicycle & Motorbike Most of the hotels catering to travellers have bicycles for hire for RM8, as do the shops along Lebuh Chulia. Motorbikes cost from RM15 to RM25.

Boat There's a 24-hour ferry service between Georgetown and Butterworth on the mainland. Passenger ferries and ferries for cars and trucks operate from adjacent terminals. Ferries operate every 20 minutes from 6 am to midnight and then every hour after midnight. The vehicular ferries operate only slightly less frequently, but do not operate at all between 10 pm (10.20 pm from Penang) and 6.30 am, except on Saturday, Sunday and public holidays when they continue to 1.30 am.

Fares are only charged from Butterworth to Penang; the other direction is free. The adult fare is 60 sen; motorcycles cost RM1.60 and cars RM7.

ALOR SETAR

The capital of Kedah state is on the mainland north of Penang on the main road to the Thai border and it's also the turn-off point for Kuala Perlis, from where ferries run to Langkawi Island. Few people stay very long in Alor Setar but it does have a few places of interest.

The large open town square has a number of interesting buildings around its perimeter. The **Balai Besar**, or Big Hall, was built in 1898 and is still used by the Sultan of Kedah for ceremonial functions. The **Balai Nobat**, an octagonal building topped by an onion-shaped dome, houses the *nobat*, or royal orchestra.

Places to Stay

There are a number of cheap hotels around the bus and taxi stations in the centre of town. The *Station Hotel* (☎ 04-723786) at 74 Jalan Langgar is one of the cheapest in town with rooms from RM14. The *Regent Hotel* (☎ 04-721291) at 1536 Jalan Sultan Badlishah is a step up the scale with air-con rooms for RM36/42.

Places to Eat

On Jalan Tunku Ibrahim, the *Restoran Empire* is a hawkers' centre in a restored wet market with a good selection of fruit juices, chicken rice, rojak, appam balik and curry sambal rice. Mee jawa is a local speciality – spicy noodles in a sauce of bean curd, squid, potatoes, peanuts, bean sprouts and appam chips.

Getting There & Away

Alor Setar is 91 km north of Butterworth. By bus it's RM3 to Kuala Perlis, RM5 to Butterworth, RM15 to Ipoh, RM35 to KL and RM45 to Singapore. A taxi costs RM4 per person to Kuala Perlis and RM9 to Butterworth.

There are also buses to Hat Yai in Thailand for RM10 – go to the Tunjang Ekspres office at the bus station. See the Getting There & Away section at the start of this chapter for more details.

KUALA PERLIS

This small port town in the extreme north-west of the peninsula is visited mainly as the departure point for Langkawi. You can also use Kuala Perlis as an unusual gateway into Thailand.

Places to Stay

On the main street, the *Pens Hotel* (☎ 04-754122) opposite the taxi stand will cost you RM35.

Getting There & Away

Direct buses from Butterworth (RM6) connect, more or less, with ferry departures to Langkawi. A taxi between Butterworth and Kuala Perlis costs RM12.50.

Buses depart from Kuala Perlis for Padang Besar (for Thailand) for RM2 (taxi RM4) and to KL for RM25. The short taxi ride into Kangar costs RM2.

LANGKAWI

The 104 islands of the Langkawi group are 30 km off the coast from Kuala Perlis, at the northern end of Peninsular Malaysia. They're accessible by boat from Kuala Perlis, Kuala Kedah and Georgetown (Penang) or by air from Penang, 112 km south, and KL.

It is quite a pleasant place to visit but Langkawi doesn't have the atmosphere (or the beaches) of the islands on the east coast, or even Pangkor further south on the west coast. Langkawi has seen a lot of government-promoted tourist development but it is not yet totally spoiled.

During school holidays, and at the peak time from November to February, Langkawi gets very crowded, but at other times of the year supply far exceeds demand and the prices come down considerably.

There's not a great deal to see apart from waterfalls (**Telaga Tujuh**), a rather pathetic **hot spring**, a legendary **tomb** and a freshwater **lake** on an adjacent island. The best known beaches are the west coast beaches of **Pantai Cenang** and **Pantai Kok**, on the opposite side of the island from the main town, Kuah.

Places to Stay & Eat

Kuah The only real budget hotel is about a km past the hospital. The *Malaysia Hotel & Restaurant* (☎ 04-788298) costs from RM10 for a small single up to RM35 for a double with air-con. There's an Indian restaurant downstairs and they also hire taxis, boats, motorbikes and bicycles at lower rates than just about anyone else on the island.

Pantai Cenang Accommodation at Pantai Cenang ranges from basic chalet places to the international standard Pelangi Beach Resort. The water tends to be somewhat murky year-round so Pantai Kok is a better choice.

Lowest costs are at the *Delta Motel* (☎ 04-911307), the last place before the headland. It's one of the older places and has A-frame chalets for RM25/30 or RM55/60 with air-con.

Towards the north is the *Sura* (☎ 04-911232) and *Samila*, two basic and cramped places with fairly unattractive chalets for RM35 with bath. Right across the road is the *Sri Inai* (☎ 04-911269) with rooms for RM35 and a restaurant.

The *AB Motel* (☎ 04-911300) is about the best value here, with big chalets around a lawn for RM30 to RM35, all with bath, and there's a decent restaurant. Next door is the *Sandy Beach Motel* (☎ 04-911308). It is a popular place but suffers from inept management, overcrowding and a horrendously smelly drain by the road. The A-frame chalets cost RM25 and RM35 with bath. There's also an ugly new block of air-con rooms.

Many of the hotels at Pantai Cenang have restaurants. The one at the *Sandy Beach* is cheap and popular with good food but rather slow service. Next door, the somewhat pricey *Semarak* serves good food.

Pantai Kok Pantai Kok, the best beach on the island, has a few places spread out along about 500 metres of beach. The best place is the *Last Resort* (☎ 04-740545), run by an expatriate Englishman and his Malay wife. Longhouse rooms are RM35 while chalets with attached bath are RM40. The restaurant serves good seafood and other local dishes.

The *Country Beach Motel* (☎ 04-411447) next door is in a pleasant spot and the front chalets are well located. Overall, it's good value at RM15 for rooms with common bath, RM25 for double chalets with fan and bath and RM60 with bath and air-con. The restaurant here serves good food and they have motorbikes and bikes for rent.

Getting There & Away

Air MAS have flights each day between Langkawi and KL (RM112), Penang (RM42) and Singapore (RM180).

Boat Kuala Perlis-Langkawi Ferry Service (☎ 04-917688) operate a high-speed ferry daily between Penang and Langkawi. The fare is RM45/35 in 1st class/economy.

Ferries between Kuala Perlis and Langkawi leave hourly in either direction between 8 am and 6 pm, and the trip takes around one hour. Fares depend on demand. If there are plenty of passengers you pay the full fare (RM10 to RM12) but if things are slack they discount it to RM5. There are also regular ferries between Langkawi and the small port town of Kuala Kedah, not far from Alor Setar, for RM12.

Yachts operate from Pantai Kok from mid-November to March. They cost US$250 for six days, all inclusive.

Smaller ferries operate to Satun on the

Thai coast a few times a day, except during the monsoon season.

Getting Around

To/From the Airport The only means of transport to or from the airport is taxi; they charge a fixed rate of RM12 to Pantai Kok, Teluk Ewa, Pantai Rhu or the Langkawi Island Resort, and RM10 to Pantai Cenang or Kuah.

Bus The bus station is opposite the hospital, in the centre of Kuah. The problem with the buses is that services are not that frequent and are limited in scope. Buses run from Kuah to Pantai Cenang (RM1.20), Pantai Kok (RM1.60) and Teluk Ewa.

Bicycle & Motorbike The easiest way to get around is to hire a motorbike (usually a Honda 70 step-thru) for RM25 per day or a mountain bike for RM12.

Peninsular Malaysia – East Coast

The east coast is lazy, easy-going, relaxing and fun. The people are very hospitable and hitching is relatively easy, although the traffic is light. Beaches and turtles are the main attractions, plus there's a sprinkling of truly delightful tropical islands off the coast. In contrast to the west coast, with its Chinese-dominated cities, the east coast is much more Malay in character.

This section follows the east coast northwards from Johor Bahru to Kota Bharu.

JOHOR BAHRU TO MERSING

Most travellers head direct to Mersing from Johor Bahru, though there are a few points of interest en route, mostly weekend retreats popular with Singaporeans.

Outside **Kota Tinggi**, 42 km from Johor Bahru, are the **waterfalls** at Lumbong, 15 km north-west of the town. Accommodation is available at the falls and Kota Tinggi town also has a few basic hotels.

Johor Lama was the seat of the sultanate following Melaka's fall to the Portuguese. Today, the old fort of Kota Batu, overlooking the river, has been restored. Johor Lama is about 30 km down the Johor River from Kota Tinggi and getting there entails arranging a boat.

The south-east coast has some beach resorts popular with Singaporeans fleeing the lion city for sun and sand, but they hold little interest for foreign visitors. The sheltered waters of quiet **Jason's Bay** are 37 km from Kota Tinggi.

Desaru is the big beach resort with large, mediocre hotels and chalet resorts. The cheapest accommodation is at the *Desaru Holiday Resort* (☎ 07-229422) where the 21-bed dorm costs RM12 per person or unattractive chalets are RM31/62 to RM200. Buses (RM3.50) and taxis go to Desaru from Kota Tinggi, and Desaru can be reached from Singapore by the ferries that run to nearby Pengerang and Tanjung Belungkor (see the Singapore Getting There & Away section for details).

MERSING

Mersing is a small fishing village on the east coast. It's the departure point for Tioman Island and the other beautiful islands lying just off the coast in the South China Sea.

Places to Stay

Sheikh Tourist Agency (☎ 07-793767), 1B Jalan Abu Bakar, is the travellers' place with dorm beds for RM5; the travel agency downstairs provides good information. It's opposite the post office and a few hundred metres before the boat dock. Right next door is *Omar's Backpackers Hostel* which offers identical accommodation at RM6 or RM14 for a double room.

There are a couple of Chinese cheapies on Jalan Abu Bakar. The *East Coast Hotel* (☎ 07-791337) at 43A Jalan Abu Bakar has clean, large rooms from RM12. Next door at 44A is the *Syuan Koong Hotel* (☎ 07-791498) with rooms from RM14.

Up the scale a bit is the popular *Hotel Embassy* (☎ 07-791301), on Jalan Ismail near the roundabout, where clean, comfortable rooms with attached bath, hot water and fan cost RM21 or RM31 with air-con. For something a little more salubrious there's the *Country Hotel* (☎ 07-791799) right at the bus station. Rooms in this recently renovated hotel cost RM45/50 with air-con and bath.

Places to Eat

For a roti telur and coffee breakfast, try the *Restoran Keluarga* on Jalan Ismail, or there's the *E&W Cafe* just around the corner from the Hotel Embassy. The *Plaza R&R* centre down by the jetty has foodstalls, and the ais kacang (ABC Special) at stall No 6 is sensational.

Mersing has plenty of cheap *Chinese cafes*, or for Indian food try the *Restoran Zam Zam* on Jalan Abu Bakar and the *Sri Laxmi Restoran* at 30 Jalan Dato Mohammed Ali. The Chinese *Golden Dragon Restaurant* in the Hotel Embassy has good seafood, or you can try curried wild-boar meat here.

Getting There & Away

Mersing is 133 km north of Johor Bahru and 189 km south of Kuantan. The local bus and taxi station is opposite the Country Hotel on Jalan Sulaiman near the river. Long-distance buses stop at the Restoran Malaysia opposite the roundabout, but as the buses only pass through Mersing on their way to/from Kuantan or Singapore, it can be difficult to get a seat, especially on weekends.

There are many travel agents around town and all advertise boat and bus tickets. Destinations served from Mersing by bus include: Johor Bahru (RM8, three daily), Kota Tinggi (RM3.95, hourly), Kuantan (RM11, four daily), Kuala Terengganu (RM18, two daily), Kota Bharu (RM24, one daily) and Kuala Lumpur (RM18, two daily). Taxi destinations include: Johor Bahru (RM12), Kota Tinggi (RM8), Melaka (RM25), Kuantan (RM15) and Pekan (RM12).

At the new Plaza R&R centre by the ferry jetty is the office of the Mersing Tourist Boat Hire Association (☎ 07-791222), which is the best place to find out the complete story about what boats are going when.

See the Tioman Island Getting There & Away section for details of how to get to the island.

TIOMAN ISLAND

The largest and most spectacular of the east-coast islands, Tioman is 39-km long and 12-km wide. It has beautiful beaches, clear water and coral for snorkelling or diving enthusiasts, but its major attraction has to be the contrasts and diversity it offers – high mountains and dense jungle are only a short walk away from the coast.

Tioman has abundant natural beauty, but many of the beaches suffer from over-crowding. The popular beaches for foreign backpackers are Air Batang, Salang, Juara and Tekek, while the southern beaches, Genting and Paya – and also Tekek – are popular with Malaysians and Singaporeans during holiday periods. It's also possible to walk across the island from Tekek to Juara.

Places to Stay & Eat

Accommodation is mostly in wooden chalets. Cheapest are the old A-frame huts, which cost from RM7 to RM15 (no bath, no fan, no net, no light), while more comfortable but often cramped chalets with attached bath cost from RM15 to RM50, depending on size and facilities. It's worth bargaining for accommodation, especially for longer stays.

Resort The *Berjaya Imperial Island Resort* (☎ 09-445445) is the only international-standard hotel on the island. It costs from RM245 to RM500, with discounts of up to 25% from November to February. It has an impressive array of facilities and the beach here is probably the best on the island.

Kampung Tekek Tekek is the largest village on the island and is the administrative centre. Tekek's beach is good, though the string of cheap places to stay north of the jetty are something of a blight on the landscape.

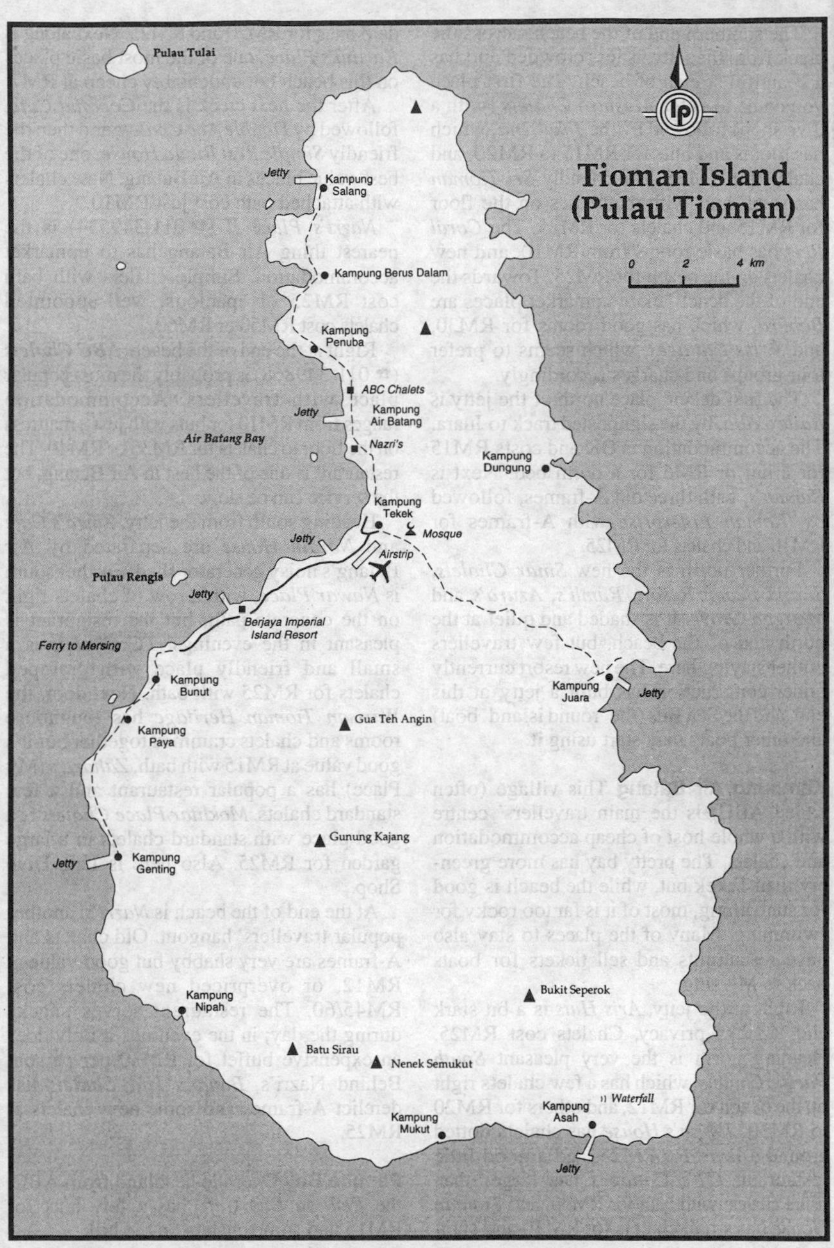

Tioman Island
(Pulau Tioman)
0
2
4 km
Pulau Tulai
Jetty
Kampung Salang
Kampung Berus Dalam
Kampung Penuba
ABC Chalets
Jetty
Kampung Air Batang
Air Batang Bay
Nazri's
Kampung Dungung
Kampung Tekek
Mosque
Jetty
Airstrip
Pulau Rengis
Jetty
Berjaya Imperial Island Resort
Ferry to Mersing
Kampung Bunut
Kampung Juara
Jetty
Gua Teh Angin
Kampung Paya
Gunung Kajang
Jetty
Kampung Genting
Bukit Seperok
Kampung Nipah
Batu Sirau
Nenek Semukut
Waterfall
Kampung Asah
Kampung Mukut
Jetty

The southern end of the beach, across the creek from the jetty, is less crowded and has a beautiful stretch of beach. The first place you come to is the *Mastura Chalets* (with a dive shop) followed by the *Tekek Inn*, which has rooms and huts for RM15 to RM20, and chalets for RM25. The friendly *Sri Tioman* has small huts with mattresses on the floor for RM15 and chalets for RM25. The *Coral Reef* has basic rooms from RM10, and new chalets on the beach for RM25. Towards the end of the beach, more upmarket places are *Babura*, which has good rooms for RM30, and *Swiss Cottages*, which seems to prefer tour groups and charges accordingly.

The first decent place north of the jetty is *Railey Villa*, by the signposted track to Juara. The accommodation is OK and costs RM15 for a hut or RM6 for a dorm bed. Next is *Raman's*, with three old A-frames, followed by *Tioman Enterprise* with A-frames for RM10 and chalets for RM25.

Further north is the new *Sinar Chalets*, *Saroja Beach Resort*, *Ramli's*, *Azura's* and *Manggo Grove*. It is shaded and quiet at the north end of the beach, but few travellers bother staying here. The new resort currently under construction has built a jetty at this end, and the Sea Bus (the 'round island' boat) and other boats may start using it.

Kampung Air Batang This village (often called ABC) is the main travellers' centre with a whole host of cheap accommodation and chalets. The pretty bay has more greenery than Tekek but, while the beach is good for sunbathing, most of it is far too rocky for swimming. Many of the places to stay also have restaurants and sell tickets for boats back to Mersing.

Right at the jetty, *Aris Huts* is a bit stark and it lacks privacy. Chalets cost RM25. Heading north is the very pleasant *South Pacific Chalets*, which has a few chalets right on the beach for RM12, and others for RM20 to RM30. *Johan's House* has chalets dotted around a lawn for RM25, and a good little restaurant. *CT's Cottages* has larger than usual chalets with bath for RM30, and *Tioman House* has small chalets for RM10 and standard ones for RM20 and RM25. Next along is *Kartini's Place*, one of the most basic places on this beach but undeniably cheap at RM7.

After the next creek is the *Coconut Cafe*, followed by *Double Ace Chalets* and then the friendly *Simple Rest Rinda House*, one of the best-value places in Air Batang. New chalets with attached bath cost just RM10.

Nazri's Place II (☎ 011-349534) is the nearest thing Air Batang has to upmarket accommodation. Simple chalets with bath cost RM25 or spacious, well-appointed chalets cost RM50 or RM60.

Right at the end of the beach, *ABC Chalets* (☎ 011-349868) is probably the most popular place with travellers. Accommodation ranges from RM10 for huts with just a mattress on the floor to chalets for RM35 or RM40. The restaurant is one of the best in Air Batang, but the service can be slow.

Heading south from the jetty, *Zinza's Cafe* and *Nordin House* are separated by Air Batang's noisy generator shed. Further south is *Nawar Place*, with a row of chalets right on the concrete path, but the restaurant is pleasant in the evenings. *TC Chalets* is a small and friendly place with cramped chalets for RM25 with bath. Next door, the *Warisan Tioman Heritage* has longhouse rooms and chalets crammed together but it's good value at RM15 with bath. *Zahara's* (My Place) has a popular restaurant and a few standard chalets. *Mokhtar Place Chalets* is a good place with standard chalets in a large garden for RM25. Also here is Ianz Dive Shop.

At the end of the beach is *Nazri's*, another popular travellers' hangout. Old chalets and A-frames are very shabby but good value at RM12, or overpriced new chalets cost RM45/60. The restaurant serves snacks during the day; in the evenings it only does an expensive buffet for RM30 per person. Behind Nazri's, *Banana Hut Chalets* has derelict A-frames and some new chalets at RM25.

Penuba Bay Over the headland from ABC, the *Penuba Bay Cafe* has a few huts for RM15 and some chalets on the hill.

Kampung Salang The small bay at Salang is one of the most beautiful on Tioman but accommodation is limited and often full. Salang is popular with divers, as is Ben's Diving Centre.

South of the jetty, *Salang Pusaka* (Khalid's Place) (☎ 011-953421) has dorm beds for RM10 and chalets for RM25 up to RM80 with air-con. It's set back from the beach and has a nice garden, although it does get a bit of noise from the generator shed.

Nora's Chalets has its reception and restaurant on the beach, but the chalets are back across the creek. Next along is the *Salang Inn* with a row of rooms right along the path for RM25 with attached bath. *Zaid's* is popular with travellers and has dorm beds in large A-frame chalets, as well as longhouse rooms and some old A-frames.

The *Indah Salang* (☎ 011-730230), north of the jetty, sprawls along the beach and has a big restaurant, bar and shop. Dorm beds cost RM6, basic bungalows are RM20 to RM30, and four-bed chalets cost RM30 up to RM120 with air-con.

The *Salang Beach Resort* (☎ 07-793123) has a fiercely expensive restaurant and overpriced chalets at RM40 and RM80. Next along, *Ella's Place* has new chalets in a garden setting for RM25 and a tiny cafe. Right at the end of the beach, *Salang Huts* has nice views around the bay. It's very rocky here, but it's still very pleasant and much quieter than the southern end of the beach.

Kampung Juara Accommodation is plentiful and slightly cheaper than the other beaches, but because of its isolation Juara doesn't get as crowded. The beach is excellent, but the sea is very rough in the monsoon season. You can also arrange river trips and excursions to the nearby rubber plantation.

Juara's accommodation is cheaper, in old A-frames right on the beach, while new chalets are behind. A-frames generally cost RM7/10, while chalets with bath, fan and mosquito net are RM15/25.

Happy Cafe, right by the jetty, is a clean and tidy little establishment with A-frames and chalets. The cafe is good and there is a library for guests. *Atan's Cafe* is similar, while the *Juara Mutiara Cafe* has some old longhouse rooms as well as chalets. Further south are older places such as *Din's*, *Sunrise Place* and *Rainbow Chalet*, the last of these being purely old A-frames, some with psychedelic paint jobs.

Paradise Point just north of the jetty is another good place with a restaurant, old A-frames and new chalets.

Kampung Nipah This superb beach has good snorkelling but is very isolated. *Desa Nipah* has chalets with attached bathrooms from RM25 to RM70 and dormitory accommodation is available for RM10.

Kampung Genting Genting is the second-largest village on the island and more traditional than the other beaches. Genting is easily reached from Mersing, but there are no regular boats to other parts of the island.

There's a string of cheap places with rooms from RM8 to RM10. *Shmaimunah House* is on the best part of the beach while the *Genting Damai Resort* (☎ 07-713032) is the top place, with a good restaurant and comfortable chalets for RM35/40.

Kampung Paya Paya is a few km south of the Berjaya Resort. The beach is OK but nothing special. The *Paya Beach Resort* (☎ 07-791432) has air-con rooms for RM90/110. A much cheaper option is the *Paya Holiday Resort* with rooms from RM25.

Getting There & Away

Air Silk Air and Pelangi Air have daily flights to/from Singapore for RM132 (S$99). Pelangi also flies daily to KL (four daily, RM125) and to Kuantan (daily, RM77). Berjaya is another small feeder airline with daily flights to KL for the same price. The booking office for all air tickets is in the Berjaya Resort.

Boat A variety of boats make the 56-km trip from Mersing to Tioman. The fast boats, such as the *Madai Express*, take about 1½ hours and cost RM25 one way. They normally stop at Genting, Paya, the resort, Tekek, Air Batang and Salang. Slower boats take about 2½ hours and cost RM20. Return tickets costing RM5 less than the full one-way prices are possible. Because of silting at the mouth of the Mersing River, the large boats can only leave and arrive at high tide.

The daily catamaran service between Singapore and Tioman departs Singapore daily at 7.50 am, and from the Berjaya Resort jetty at 1.30 pm. The trip takes 4½ hours and costs RM142. Bookings can be made at the desk in the lobby of the Berjaya Resort.

Getting Around

The excellent Sea Bus service operates regular boats between the resort, Tekek, Air Batang and Salang. They also have a 'round island' boat stopping in Juara. It's also possible to charter boats for RM200 per day.

OTHER EAST-COAST ISLANDS

Although Tioman is the largest and best known of the islands off Mersing, there are

PLACES TO STAY

4 Hotel Makmur
5 Hotel Pacific
6 Hotel New Meriah
11 New Capitol Hotel
15 Suraya Hotel
16 Hotel Embassy
21 Min Heng Hotel
22 Samudra River View Hotel
23 Tong Nam Ah Hotel
25 Hotel Baru Raya

PLACES TO EAT

3 Central Market
7 Restoran Parvathy
8 Restoran Biryani
10 Grandy's Restaurant
19 Tiki's Restoran
24 Outdoor Foodstalls

OTHER

1 Stadium
2 Hindu Temple
9 MAS
12 Immigration
13 Post Office
14 Malayan Banking
17 Standard Chartered Bank
18 Mosque Sultan Ahmed I
20 Local Bus Station
26 Long-Distance Bus Station
27 Taxi Station
28 Tourist Office
29 Kampung Tanjung Lumpur

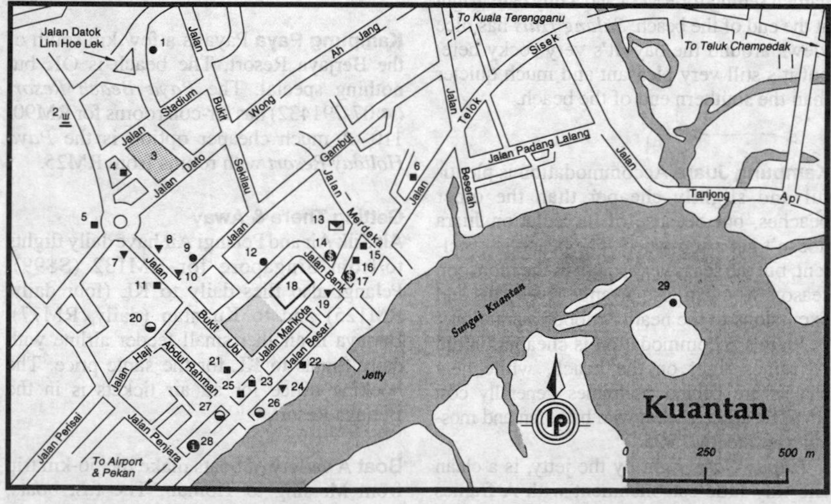

many others with beautiful white sandy beaches and crystal-clear waters. Accommodation is mostly mid-range chalets, and the prices are higher than Tioman.

Pulau Rawa

Pulau Rawa is a tiny island 16 km from Mersing. *Rawa Safaris Island Resort* (☎ 07-791204) has simple but comfortable thatched bungalows for RM60.

Pulau Sibu

Sibu is one of the largest and most popular islands, with good snorkelling and jungle walks across the island. Of the five places to stay, *O&H Kampung Huts* is the cheapest with budget chalets for RM25. The 2½ hour trip to Sibu from Mersing costs RM25 return.

Pulau Babi Besar

Pulau Babi Besar is one of the islands closest to the peninsula. A variety of accommodation is available here. *Radhin Chalets* (☎ 07-793124) is one of the cheapest at RM25 for an A-frame chalet. Boats from Mersing take one hour and cost RM15 one way.

Pulau Tengah

Near Pulau Babi Besar is Pulau Tengah, 16 km off the coast. It takes 1½ hours to get there by boat (costing RM15 one way). Once a Vietnamese refugee camp, it is now gazetted as a marine park and leatherback turtles come here to lay their eggs in July. The *Pirate Bay Island Resort* (☎ 07-241911) is the only resort, and chalets cost from RM125.

Pulau Tinggi

This is probably the most impressive island when seen from a distance as it's an extinct volcano. The *Tinggi Island Resort* (☎ 07-794451) and the *Koperasi Felda Chalets* (☎ 07-223432) have mid-range chalets. Boats from Mersing take two hours and cost RM30.

KUANTAN

Located about midway up the east coast of Peninsula Malaysia, Kuantan is the capital of the state of Pahang and the start of the east-coast beach strip which extends all the way to Kota Bharu.

It is a well-organised, bustling city and is a major stopover point when you are travelling north, south or across the peninsula.

Teluk Chempedak

Kuantan's major attraction is Teluk Chempedak Beach, about four km from the town. The beach, bound by rocky headlands at each end, is quite pleasant but there are better beaches on the peninsula. There are a number of walking tracks in the park area on the promontory.

Places to Stay

On Jalan Mahkota near the taxi station, the *Min Heng Hotel* (☎ 09-524885) is the cheapest place in town costing RM12/14 for singles/doubles – it's a classic, very basic Chinese cheapie.

The *Tong Nam Ah Hotel* (☎ 09-521204) located on Jalan Besar near the long-distance bus station is a good, cheap hotel with rooms for around RM15. The *Hotel Baru Raya* (☎ 09-522344), which is in-between the taxi and bus stations, is better but overpriced at RM26/32.

On Jalan Telok Sisek, between Jalan Merdeka and Jalan Bank, are a number of cheap places to stay. The *Hotel Moonlight* (☎ 09-524277), 50-52 Jalan Telok Sisek, has good rooms with balcony for RM15 and more expensive rooms with bath and air-con. A few doors along, the *Mei Lai Hotel* is noisy but clean and a good buy at RM10/12. On the corner of Jalan Merdeka is the *Hotel Embassy*, which costs RM23/28 for a room with bath.

Also for a room with bath, the *New Capitol Hotel* (☎ 09-505222), 55 Jalan Bukit Ubi, has spotless rooms for RM20.

You can also stay at Teluk Chempedak Beach, but it has mostly overpriced mid-range hotels or large resorts like the Hyatt and Merlin. The only budget possibilities are in the street behind the Hotel Hillview. *Sri Pantai Bungalows* (☎ 09-525250) at No 19 has good, clean, carpeted rooms with fans for

RM20/30. Plenty of other places in this street charge from RM20 for a room, but some are in a dire state – just ask at a 'room to let' sign.

Places to Eat

The small Muslim *foodstalls* dotted along the riverbank, behind the long-distance bus station, are a great place to sit and watch the boats pass by. The seafood is particularly good and the prawns are huge.

In the evenings, *foodstalls* are set up near the central market and there are a few interesting serve-yourself nasi padang places and good Chinese seafood satay – select what you want and cook it in the vats of boiling water.

For breakfast, try *Tiki's Restoran*, up the far end of Jalan Mahkota. It's only open during the day and the two ever-busy brothers who run this place really welcome travellers. There are plenty of good *bakeries* around, including the one under the Min Heng Hotel and the *Terantum Bakery & Cafe* in the Kompleks Terantum, which is opposite the tourist office.

Not far from Tiki's Restoran is the popular *Restoran Cheun Kee* which serves good Chinese food for around RM3. There are good Indian restaurants on Jalan Bukit Ubi, north of Jalan Gambut.

Teluk Chempedak has a good selection of flash restaurants. On the foreshore, *Pataya* and *Restoran Massafalah* are pleasant, open-air places specialising in seafood, though the air-con places on the main road are generally better value.

Getting There & Away

Air MAS (☎ 09-521218) has direct flights from Kuantan to Singapore (RM120) and KL (RM61), and handles bookings for Pelangi Air flights to Tioman.

Bus Buses to KL cost RM11, to Mersing RM11, to Johor Bahru RM15 and to Singapore RM16. To Kuala Terengganu, it's RM8, to Kota Bharu RM15, to Melaka RM13 and to Penang RM4.50. For Taman Negara there are direct buses to Jerantut (RM7.70).

Taxi Taxis cost RM4 to Pekan, RM15 to Mersing and RM5 to Kemaman. To Kuala Terengganu it's RM17, and RM25 to Kota Bharu. Across the peninsula, it's RM9 to Temerloh, RM13 to Jerantut, RM18 to Raub and RM20 to KL.

Getting Around

Bus No 39 will take you from town to Teluk Chempedak for 50 sen. You can catch it at the local bus station or, more conveniently, at the M3 bus stand on Jalan Mahkota, near the mosque. For Cherating, take the 'Kemaman' bus No 27 from the long-distance bus station for RM2.20.

AROUND KUANTAN

The coast north from Kuantan has passable beaches and mostly mid-range accommodation scattered along the road to Cherating. At **Beserah**, a small fishing village 10 km north of Kuantan, is *Jaafar's Place*, a kampung house with very basic accommodation for RM6 a night or RM12, including all meals. Buses to Kemaman (No 27), Balok (No 30) or Sungai Karang (No 28) all pass through Beserah.

Gua Charas is a limestone outcrop containing the Charas caves with Thai Buddhist statuary. The caves are 26 km north of Kuantan – take bus No 48 to Panching and then it's a four-km walk or you can hitch.

TASIK CHINI

Tasik Chini is a series of 12 lakes, about 60 km west of Kuantan, and around its shores live the Jakun people, an Orang Asli tribe. It's a beautiful area and you can walk for miles in jungle territory and stay at the Orang Asli village of **Kampung Gumum**.

Places to Stay & Eat

The low-key *Lake Cini Resort*, on the southern shore of the lake system, has good cabins with attached bathroom for RM58/68 for singles/doubles or dormitory accommodation for RM15, plus a 10% service charge. Camping facilities are also available and the resort has a restaurant.

A much cheaper option is *Rajan Jones*

Guest House in the Orang Asli settlement of Kampung Gumum, a two-minute boat ride from the resort or a 30-minute walk. Accommodation is extremely basic – no electricity or running water – but it's a rare opportunity to stay near the jungle. The cost is RM15 including meals.

Getting There & Away

Getting to Tasik Chini is not easy. From Kuantan catch a bus to Maran and get off at the Tasik Chini turn-off, 56 km away. Irregular buses from Maran go via the turn-off to Belimbing, 12 km away. From Belimbing a boat to Tasik Chini costs RM40 per boat for the beautiful two-hour trip.

The alternative to this is to take a bus to Kampung Chini, south of the lake, from Kuantan (RM5.50, two hours) and then hire a motorcycle (about RM5) or a taxi to take you the 11 km to the lake.

A taxi from Kuantan costs RM50.

CHERATING

This is one of the most popular travellers' centres on the east coast. Cherating, meaning Sand Crab, is actually divided into two parts – the main village and, two km further north, Pantai Cherating, which is the travellers' centre. Cherating's beach won't win any awards but there's a host of good, cheap accommodation and restaurants.

Cherating is also a good base to explore the surrounding area. You can arrange minitreks and river trips, and most of the places to stay can organise tours to Tasik Chini (RM35), Gua Charas, Sungai Lembing (and Pandan Falls) (RM30) and Pulau Ular.

Information

There's no bank in Cherating, but you can change money (at a poor rate) and also make international phone calls at the Connection Cherating shop on the beach road.

Places to Stay

Accommodation ranges from basic A-frame huts for around RM10 to more comfortable 'chalets' with bathroom for RM15 to RM50.

On the main road are two of the longest-running homestays – *Mak Long Teh's* and *Mak De's*. Both places charge RM12 per person for accommodation, breakfast and dinner.

The very relaxed *Matahari Chalets* is on the road to the beachfront. Large rooms with balcony, fridge and mosquito net but no fan are a bargain at RM9/12. You can do batik courses here.

On the beach road is a group of three places, all with similar facilities and all good. The *Coconut Inn* has basic A-frame chalets for RM8/12 and RM15/20 with bath. Next door is the well-kept *Tanjung Inn*, with attractive although quite small chalets for RM25 and RM35 with bath. The third place is the *Kampung Inn* (☎ 09-439344), set in a pretty coconut grove. Chalets cost RM15 or RM20 and RM30 with bath.

Across the road from these three, the *Restaurant Sayang* has a few very basic chalets. Right on the bank of the river is the cosy and rustic *Green Leaves Inn*. The chalets are very small and the facilities quite basic, but it's still popular. The *Payung Cafe*, also on the riverbank, has a few chalets around a large lawn for RM10. It's also popular.

Other reasonable places are the *Cherating Indah*, with chalets for RM20, and the *Cherating Inn Beach Resort*, which has ugly but quite large chalets for RM15/20 with bath. Cherating also has some good mid-range options such as the *Duyong Beach Resort* and *Cherating Bayview Resort*.

Places to Eat

Most of the places to stay have their own restaurants and you can easily spend a few days in Cherating and not sample them all. The *Sayang* restaurant does good Indian food, and *Mimi's*, at the opposite end of the beach, is a popular place. In the evenings, the *Payung Cafe* is a good place for spaghetti and goulash, and *foodstalls* are set up opposite. For Chinese and Malay food there's the *Moonlight Lagoon* and the *Blue Lagoon*.

Getting There & Away

Catch one of the hourly 'Kemaman' buses from the main bus station in Kuantan

(RM2.50, one hour). From Cherating to Kuantan, wave down a Kuantan bus from the bus stop outside Mak Long Teh's.

RANTAU ABANG

This is the principal turtle beach and the prime area for spotting the great leatherback turtles during the laying season. The long, sandy beach is good for extended, lonely walks. Swimming is possible but the undertow can be savage.

The **Turtle Information Centre**, near the main budget accommodation area, has good displays and shows films six times a day. The centre is open every day during the turtle-watching season but otherwise it is closed on Friday and public holidays. Note that the nearest bank is at Kuala Dungun, 22 km south.

August is the peak laying season, when you have an excellent chance of seeing turtles, but you may also be lucky in June and July. Full moon and high-tide nights are said to be best.

Unfortunately, the east coast's primary tourist attraction has resulted in a decline in turtle numbers, but the government is making a concerted effort to preserve the turtles and their egg-laying habitat. The beach is now divided into three sections during the season – prohibited, semi-public (where you have to buy tickets) and free access – in an attempt to control the 'hey gang, the turtles are up' mentality.

Places to Stay & Eat

Right on the beach in front of the Turtle Information Centre are two travellers' places. *Awang's* (☎ 09-843500) gets most of the travellers and has a good restaurant. Rooms with bath go for RM5/10, or on the beachfront it's RM12/15. The *Ismail Beach Resort* (☎ 09-841054), next door, has similar rooms for RM10 a double, RM20 with bath and RM30 for a large double room with bath.

Dahimah's Guest House (☎ 010-934500), about one km south towards Kuala Dungun, is less convenient but very good. Dorm beds cost RM5 and rooms are RM10, RM30 with bath and RM48 with air-con and bath. They have a good restaurant and arrange trips in the area.

The more upmarket *Rantau Abang Tanjung Jara Visitor Centre*, one km north of Awang's, has very good four-bed chalets for RM70 to RM120, depending on the season.

Getting There & Away

Rantau Abang is 80 km south of Kuala Terengganu and 138 km north of Kuantan. Kuala Dungun-Kuala Terengganu buses run in both directions every hour. Rantau Abang to Kuala Terengganu costs RM4 and to Kuala Dungun costs RM1.50. Heading south, you can try to hail down a long-distance bus, or take the bus to Dungun from where hourly buses go to Kuantan, as well as Mersing, Singapore and KL.

MARANG

Marang, a large fishing village at the mouth of the Marang River, is very picturesque. It's a popular travellers' centre, a beautiful place to relax and is also the departure point for Pulau Kapas.

Marang is a conservative village, however, especially in the area across the river from the main town. Reserve in dress and behaviour is recommended.

Places to Stay & Eat

The *Marang Inn* (☎ 09-681878), on the main street near the bus station, costs RM4 for a dorm and RM10 for a room. It's popular and has a good restaurant.

Most of the guesthouses close to town are on the lagoon, a stone's throw from the beach. *Kamal's Guest House* is the longest running and one of the best. Dorm beds are RM4, rooms are RM10 and chalets are RM12. The *Island View Resort* (☎ 09-682006) is also good, has free bicycles for guests and charges the same as Kamal's. On the hill behind Kamal's is the *Marang Guest House*. It's a notch up from the other guesthouses and has its own restaurant, but it's a bit dull. A dorm bed is RM5, and rooms are RM12 and RM15 with bath and mosquito nets.

Apart from the restaurants at the *Marang*

Inn and *Marang Guest House*, there are good *foodstalls* near the market and some grotty *restaurants* on the main street.

Two km south of the river, around the 20-km marker, *Angullia Beach House* (☎ 09-682403) is the top place in town. It's very welcoming but overpriced – most chalets are RM40 to RM50.

Getting There & Away

Marang is about 45 minutes south of Kuala Terengganu and regular buses run to and from there (RM1) and Dungun.

PULAU KAPAS

Six km offshore from Marang is the beautiful little island of Kapas. There are walks and snorkelling to keep you busy, but the island is best avoided during holidays and long weekends when it is overrun by day-trippers.

Places to Stay & Eat

The *Kapas Garden Resort* has A-frames for RM 15 and rooms with bath for RM45 and RM55. *Mak Cik Gemuk Chalets* is similarly priced. *Zaki Beach Chalet* is the cheapest place with rooms for RM10/15, RM20 with bath or RM30 for chalets. A short walk around the headland brings you to the upmarket *Primula Beach Resort* and the overpriced *Sri Kapas Lodge*.

Getting There & Away

Boats shuttle back and forth between Marang and Kapas throughout the day and cost RM7.50 one way.

KUALA TERENGGANU

Standing on a promontory formed by the South China Sea on one side and the wide Terengganu River on the other side, Kuala Terengganu is the capital of Terengganu state and the seat of the sultan. Despite a lot of recent oil-based development, the town still has a quiet backwater feel once you get away from the main streets and there's enough to amuse you during a short stay.

Things to See

Most of Kuala Terengganu's colourful atmosphere can be appreciated along Jalan Bandar, Kuala Terengganu's Chinatown. The **Central Market** is also colourful and active, and the floor above the fish section has a fabulous collection of batik and songket. Past the market is the **Istana Maziah**, the sultan's palace, and the gleaming new **Zainal Abidin Mosque**.

Pantai Batu Buruk is the city beach and a popular place to stroll in the evening when the foodstalls open up. Across the road, the **Cultural Centre** sometimes stages pencak silat and wayang shows on Friday between 5 and 6.30 pm.

The jetty behind the taxi station is the place for a 40-sen ferry ride to the boat-building island of **Pulau Duyung**. It's the largest island in the estuary and worth exploring.

Places to Stay

Ping Anchorage (☎ 09-620851), upstairs at 77A Jalan Dato Isaac, is the number one travellers' place. Dorm beds are RM5 and rooms range from RM10 to RM12, or RM18 with bath. The rooms are good, but most have wire-topped walls and can be noisy.

Awi's Yellow House is a unique guesthouse built on stilts over the river. It's on Pulau Duyung, a 15-minute ferry ride across the river. A bed with mosquito net costs RM5 per night in the open dorm or small thatched rooms are RM14. It's a beautiful, relaxed place, and highly recommended.

The *Rex Hotel*, opposite the local bus station on Jalan Masjid, has good clean rooms with bath from RM15/16. A few doors down the street, the *Hotel Evergreen* (☎ 09-622505) has rooms without bath for RM14/ 16.

The *Seri Pantai Hostel* (☎ 09-635766), 35 Jalan Sultan Zainal Abidin, costs RM8 in large dorms or RM15 for doubles overlooking the sea. It's quiet unless a school group arrives.

In the mid-price bracket, the *Kenangan Hotel* (☎ 09-622688) was once a top hotel but has seen better days. It is fully air-conditioned, and costs RM44/67. Next door, the *Meriah Hotel* (☎ 09-627983), 67 Jalan

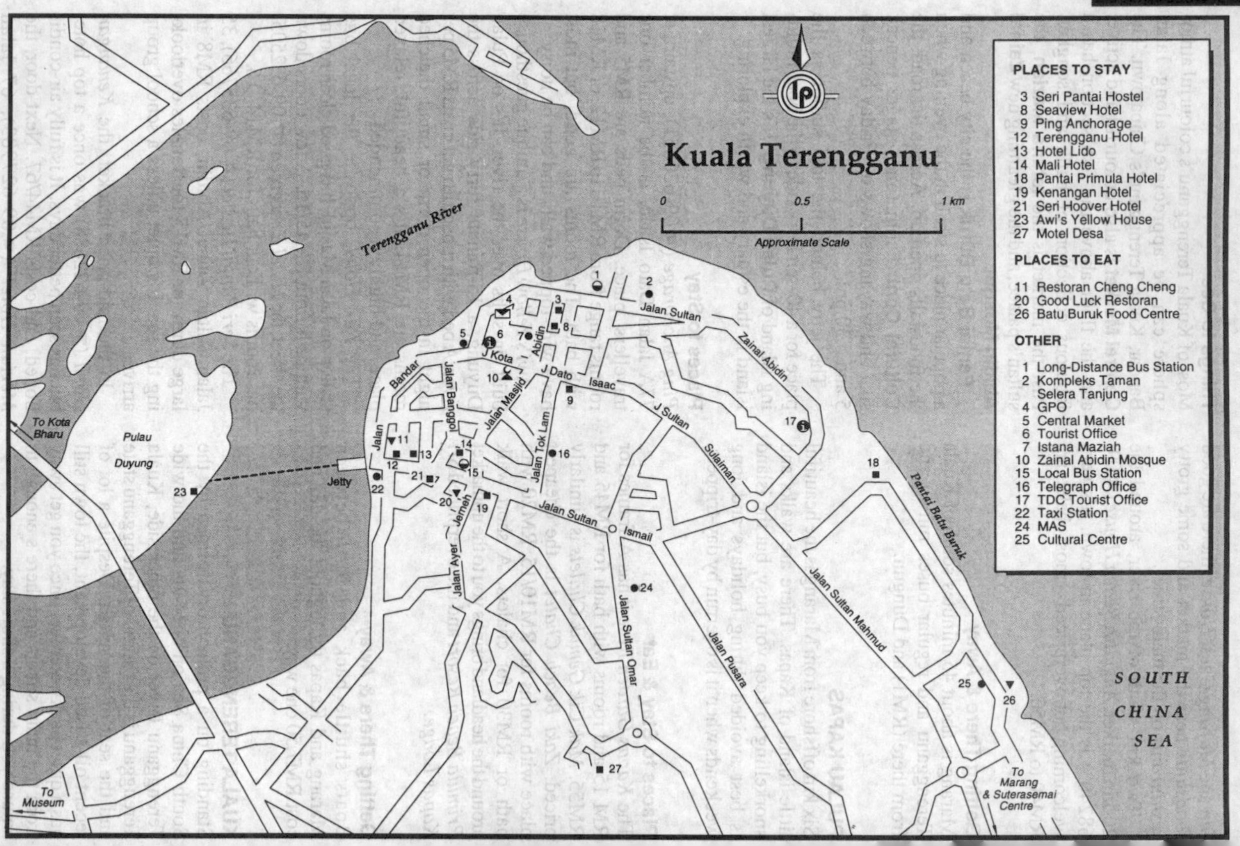
Kuala Terengganu
0
0.5
1 km
Approximate Scale
PLACES TO STAY
3 Seri Pantai Hostel
8 Seaview Hotel
9 Ping Anchorage
12 Terengganu Hotel
13 Hotel Lido
14 Mali Hotel
18 Pantai Primula Hotel
19 Kenangan Hotel
21 Seri Hoover Hotel
23 Awi's Yellow House
27 Motel Desa
PLACES TO EAT
11 Restoran Cheng Cheng
20 Good Luck Restoran
26 Batu Buruk Food Centre
OTHER
1 Long-Distance Bus Station
2 Kompleks Taman Selera Tanjung
4 GPO
5 Central Market
6 Tourist Office
7 Istana Maziah
10 Zainal Abidin Mosque
15 Local Bus Station
16 Telegraph Office
17 TDC Tourist Office
22 Taxi Station
24 MAS
25 Cultural Centre
SOUTH CHINA SEA
Pantai Batu Buruk
Terengganu River
Jalan Sultan Mahmud
Jalan Pusara
Jalan Sultan Omar
Jalan Sultan Ismail
Jalan Sultan Zainal Abidin
J Sultan Sulaiman
J Kota
Abidin
J Dato Isaac
Jalan Bandar
Jalan Banggol
Jalan Masjid
Jalan Tok Lam
Jalan Ayer Jerneh
Jetty
Pulau Duyung
To Kota Bharu
To Museum
To Marang & Suterasemai Centre

Sultan Ismail, has rooms with fan and bath for RM21/29 and large air-conditioned rooms for RM29/52.

Places to Eat

You can find *foodstalls* on Jalan Tok Lam near the telegraph office and at the Batu Buruk food centre on the beach front. The 2nd floor of the new Kompleks Taman Selera Tanjung is devoted to *foodstalls*. For Indian food, *Taufiq*, 18-C Jalan Masjid, is cheap and one of the best in town.

If you have trouble deciphering Chinese menus, then the *Restoran Cheng Cheng* at 224 Jalan Bandar is a good place to head for. It's buffet style – you get a plate of rice or noodles and help yourself to the display of vegetable and meat dishes. The staff will price your meal using their colour-coded peg system – when you've finished eating take the plate with peg to the counter and pay.

One of the best areas for Chinese food is at the southern end of Jalan Banggol around the Plaza Perdana.

Things to Buy

Kuala Terengganu is a good place to buy batik and songket, the intricate weaving using gold and silver threads. You can see silk-weaving at the Suterasemai Centre, a few km from town on the road to Marang. The handicraft centre is 10 km from town at Rhusila, not far from Marang, but the best place to buy handicrafts is upstairs at the Central Market.

Getting There & Away

Air MAS (☎ 09-621415) has direct flights to and from KL for RM104.

Bus The long-distance bus station is on Jalan Sultan Zainal Abidin, near the waterfront. The local bus station (for Merang, Penarik and Marang) is on Jalan Masjid. There are regular buses to Marang (RM1), Rantau Abang (RM4), Kuantan (RM9), Mersing (RM18), Johor Bahru (RM23), Singapore (RM25), Kota Bharu (RM7.50) KL (RM21.50) and Butterworth (RM24).

Taxi The main taxi station is at the bottom of Jalan Sultan Ismail, right at the waterfront. It costs RM2.50 to Marang, RM8 to Jerteh (for Kuala Besut), RM6 to Rantau Abang, RM12 to Kota Bharu, RM15 to Kuantan and RM35 to KL.

Getting Around

A taxi to the airport costs around RM15.

Kuala Terengganu is famous for its trishaws, and although numbers have dwindled slightly, they are still found in profusion at the Central Market. Around town, the trishaws cost around RM1 per km, or there are taxis.

MERANG

The sleepy little fishing village of Merang (not to be confused with Marang) is 14 km north of Kuala Terengganu. There's nothing to do here, but the beautiful beach is lined with coconut palms and lapped by clear water. Merang is also the place to get boats to Pulau Redang and other nearby islands.

Places to Stay & Eat

The easygoing *Naughty Dragon's Green Planet Homestay*, right in the centre of the village, is run by a friendly German-Malay couple. Accommodation is basic but comfortable and costs RM15 for a double, or a very economical RM13 per person for full board.

For traditional hospitality go try *Man's Homestay*, half a km from the village on the Penarik road. Facilities are basic and the cost is RM10 per night including all meals. Another option is *Razak's Kampung House*, also in the centre of the village. Here the cost is RM15 per person.

The other place to stay is the *Merang Beach Resort*, overpriced at RM25 or RM45 for a chalet with bath, but it's on a great stretch of beach.

Getting There & Away

From Kuala Terengganu, take a Penarik bus and get off at Merang.

KUALA BESUT

Kuala Besut, on the coast south of Kota Bharu, has a reasonably pleasant beach and is an interesting, though grubby, fishing village. A visit to this town is usually just a preliminary to a trip to the Perhentian Islands.

Places to Stay

The *Primula Beach Resort*, which costs RM100/120 and up, is the only accommodation. If you want budget accommodation in Kuala Besut, ask around in the shops on the main street next to the river.

Getting There & Away

From the south, take a bus to Jerteh on the main highway. From there, buses go every 40 minutes to Kuala Besut. From Kota Bharu, it's easier to get off at Pasir Puteh and take a bus from there. A share taxi from Jerteh or Pasir Puteh to Kuala Besut costs RM1.50.

PERHENTIAN ISLANDS

A two-hour boat trip from Kuala Besut takes you to the two beautiful islands of Perhentian Besar and Perhentian Kecil, just 21 km off the coast. As far as things to 'see and do' go, it's a simple case of lazing around watching coconuts fall. The beaches are arguably the best in Malaysia and there is excellent snorkelling.

Places to Stay & Eat

Pulau Perhentian Besar Apart from the resort, accommodation is in beach huts with washing from wells. The *Perhentian Island Resort* (☎ 011-333910) is a mid-range resort on a good beach with chalets for RM40 and roomy bungalows with attached bath for RM110.

The budget accommodation beach faces the mainland and is just across the strait from the village on Perhentian Kecil. It's a 20-minute clamber over two headlands from the resort.

At the northern end of the beach is *Coral View*, with a number of closely bunched chalets, each with attached bath, which cost RM40. Next along is *Cozy*, with chalets for RM20. *Coco Hut* and *Samudin* are unremarkable, while next south is *ABC* which is well set up with cheap basic huts right on the beach under the trees. *Abdul's Chalets* is one of the quietest and rooms with big verandas cost RM15.

Over the headland, next to the resthouse, is *Isabella Coffee Shop* which has good food and great squid. A track behind the restaurant leads to the next bay, Flora Bay, where the *Flora Bay Chalets* cost from RM20 up to RM70 for a two-room chalet with attached bath.

Pulau Perhentian Kecil This is the place to stay. Unless otherwise stated, all places charge RM10/12 for a basic chalet with two beds, mosquito net and washing from a well.

The best range of accommodation is found at Long Beach. At the southern end is *Chempaka Chalets*, a very laid-back place with well-spaced chalets and facilities to do your own cooking. *Cottage Hut* is popular, largely because of its restaurant right on the beach. The chalets are quite OK but cramped together and not as good as others. *Matahari Chalets* is set back from the beach and has a popular restaurant. Right at the northern end of the beach is the *Moonlight Chalets*, with just a few chalets tucked into the corner of the bay. It's well set up and a good place to stay.

Other small bays around the west of the island, each with just one set of chalets, are ideal if you really want to get away from it all. Access is by boat. *D Lagoon* on Teluk Kerma has a few chalets and a small restaurant. *Coral Bay Chalets* has a good atmosphere and afternoon monitor lizard feeding sessions. It is a short walk across the 'waist' of the island to Long Beach. Further south on the west coast, *Mira Chalets* is another beautiful little beach with only a handful of chalets.

On the south coast at Pasir Petani, *Pleasure Chalets* has a few chalets by the beach, or the more upmarket *Pasir Petani Village* has very pleasant chalets with attached bath for RM45.

Getting There & Away

The one-way trip from Kuala Besut to Perhentian costs RM15. Most boats leave Perhentian early in the morning and return late morning and throughout the afternoon. The boats will drop you off at any of the beaches. It's a good idea to let the owner of your chalets know the day before you want to leave. Small boats ply between the two islands for RM3 per person.

KOTA BHARU

In the north-eastern corner of the peninsula, Kota Bharu is the termination point of the east-coast road and a gateway to Thailand. It is the capital of the state of Kelantan, the centre for Malay culture, crafts and religion. The present state government is strongly Islamic – keen on banning alcohol and public dance performances and enforcing other party-pooping restrictions.

Kota Bharu is a bustling city set on the banks of a wide river. Many travellers stop here overnight on their way to or from Thailand, but end up staying much longer.

Information

The Kota Bharu tourist office (☎ 09-785534) is on Jalan Sultan Ibrahim, just south of the clocktower.

In Kelantan, state public offices and banks are closed Thursday afternoon and Friday, but open on Saturday and Sunday.

For Thai visas, the Thai consulate (☎ 09-72 2545) on Jalan Pengkalan Chepa is open from 9 am to 12.30 pm and 2.30 to 4 pm, Sunday to Thursday.

Things to See

The central **Padang Merdeka** (Independence Square) was built as a memorial following WW I. At the eastern end of the square is the **Istana Balai Besar**, or Palace of the Large Audience Hall, built in 1844. The adjacent **Royal Museum**, housed in the Istana Jahar which dates from 1887, is a wonderful mixture of traditional architecture and Victoriana. Other old buildings on the square are the **State Mosque** and the **Religious Council Building**.

Further along is the **Karyaneka Handicraft Centre**. The handicrafts and prices are not that stunning but the small art gallery upstairs has good exhibitions of traditional arts.

On the river, **raft houses** still exist in defiance of modern amenities. Nearby on Jalan Post Office Lama, a neglected but picturesque street, is an interesting **antique shop**.

The **Central Market** is one of the most colourful and active in Malaysia. Near the market is the **Buluh Kubu Bazaar**, a good place to buy handicrafts.

One of the best things about Kota Bharu is the chance to see performances of top-spinning, wayang kulit and other traditional activities not yet banned. They're at **Gelanggang Seni** cultural centre from February to October, except during Ramadan. Check with the tourist office.

Kota Bharu is also a centre for Malay crafts. Batik, songket, silverware, woodcarving and kite-making factories and shops are dotted around town, especially on the road to Pantai Cahaya Bulan, Kota Bharu's best known beach.

Places to Stay

Kota Bharu is overrun with good cheap guesthouses catering to travellers. Competition is fierce and, unless otherwise stated, all charge RM6 for a dorm bed and RM8/10 for singles/doubles. Most have cooking facilities, bicycles, free tea and coffee.

Quite close to the centre, the *KB Inn* (☎ 09-741786) and *Yee Guest House* (☎ 09-741944) are a couple of doors from each other on Jalan Padang Garong, not far from the central bus station. Both are friendly, though not as nice as some of the accommodation in private houses. Further out on Jalan Pengkalan Chepa, the ever-popular *Town Guest House* (☎ 09-785192) is similar. The big plus is the rooftop restaurant with good cheap food. If you ring they will pick you up from the bus station.

One of the best is the *Ideal Travellers' Guest House* (☎ 09-7442246), in a private house down an alley off Jalan Pintu Pong.

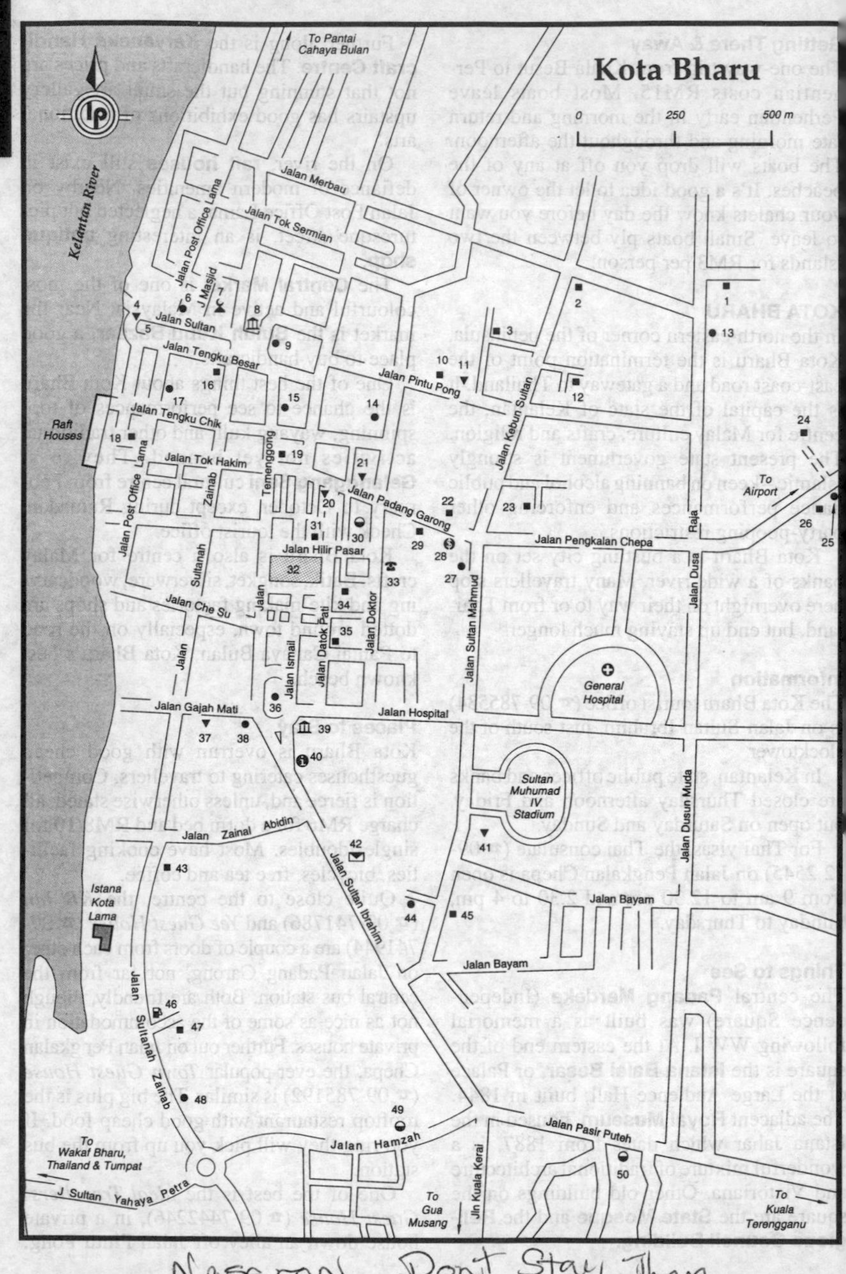

Nassron Dont Stay There.

It's quiet, central and has a pleasant garden, but is often full. Apart from the standard rates, they have rooms with attached bath for RM12. They also run the *Friendly Guest House*, a few hundred metres away, just off Jalan Kebun Sultan. It's not as attractive, but is also quiet and has good rooms, most with attached bath for RM10/12.

Another good place, although it's a bit of a walk from the centre along Jalan Dusa Raja, is the quiet *Johnty's Guest House* (☎ 09-748866). It has a good garden, the occasional evening barbecue and a basic breakfast is included.

Located at 3338-D Jalan Sultanah Zainab, *Menora Guest House* (☎ 09-781669) has a variety of accommodation ranging from dorm beds for RM5 up to large doubles for RM18. Although on a busy road, it's fairly quiet and the rooftop terrace is popular.

On Jalan Pengkalan Chepa near the Thai consulate is the *Rainbow Inn Guest House* (☎ 09-742708). This house has a pleasant garden and some great artwork on the walls, courtesy of inspired travellers. Across the road and up an alley is the popular *Mummy's Hitec Hostel* in a funky old house with a large garden. Mummy is a real character and enjoys a night out with the boys.

The *Rebana Hostel*, up an alleyway off Jalan Sultan Zainab, is a long way from the town centre but it's a lovely house, decorated Malay-style with lots of artwork around. Rooms range from the RM6 dorm and pokey RM8 singles, to some beautiful old rooms and chalets in the garden for RM10 to RM15.

Of course there are also plenty of cheap Chinese hotels. A basic but interesting old hotel is the *Thye Ann Hotel* (☎ 09-785907), on Jalan Hilir Pasar opposite the old Central Market, with huge rooms for RM10/15. Other possibilities, where you can get a room for around RM12, are on Jalan Padang Garong/Jalan Tok Hakim.

The excellent *Star Hostel*, just off Jalan Kebun Sultan, has small but good air-con rooms with bath and TV for just RM25. It's a brand new hotel with a very pleasant open lounge area. The *Hotel Tokyo Baru* (☎ 09-749488) on Jalan Tok Hakim has large, very clean rooms that are good value at RM26 for a double with bath and RM35/45 with air-con.

Places to Eat

The best and cheapest Malay food in Kota Bharu is found at the *night market*, opposite the central bus station. The foodstalls are set

PLACES TO STAY

1 Johnty's Guest House
2 Star Hostel
3 Ideal Travellers' Guest House
10 City Guest House
12 Hostel Pantai
16 Indah Hotel
18 Hotel North Malaysia & Restoran Donald Duck
19 Temenggong Hotel
22 Kencana Inn
23 Friendly Guest House
24 Mummy's Hitec Hostel
26 Rainbow Inn Guest House
29 Yee Guest House
31 Thye Ann Hotel
34 Hitect Hostel
35 Hotel Murni
43 Menora Guest House
45 Hotel Perdana
47 Rebana Hostel

PLACES TO EAT

4 Food Stalls
11 KFC
20 Razak Restoran
21 Night Market Food Stalls
37 Meena Curry House
41 Food Stalls

OTHER

5 Padang Merdeka
6 Karyaneka Handicraft Centre
7 State Mosque
8 Royal Museum
9 Istana Balai Besar
13 Bird-Singing Place
14 Central Market
15 Buluh Kubu Bazaar
17 Antique Shop
25 Thai Consulate
27 Maybank
28 Hongkong Bank
30 Central Bus & Taxi Station
32 Old Central Market
33 Telekom Office
36 Clocktower
38 MAS Office
39 State Museum
40 Tourist Information Centre
42 Post Office
44 Gelanggang Seni
46 Caltex Station
48 Silversmith
49 Jalan Hamzah External Bus Station
50 Langgar Bus Station

up in the evenings and there's a wide variety of delicious, cheap Malay food. The local specialities include ayam percik (marinated chicken enclosed between bamboo skewers) and nasi kerabu (rice with coconut, fish and spices).

There are more good *foodstalls* next to the river (opposite the Padang Merdeka) and at the stadium where a number of stalls sell ABC (air batu kacang – the shaved-ice dessert).

There are plenty of Chinese restaurants around town, including good chicken rice places on Jalan Padang Garong near the Kencana Inn. The *Restoran Vegetarian*, on Jalan Post Office Lama opposite the antique shop, has good Chinese vegetarian food.

The *Razak Restoran*, on the corner of Jalan Datok Pati and Jalan Padang Garong, is cheap and has excellent Indian Muslim food.

Getting There & Away

Air MAS (☎ 09-747000) has direct flights to Penang (RM87), Alor Setar (RM71) and KL (RM104).

Bus The state-run SKMK is the largest bus company and runs all the city and regional buses as well as most of the long-distance buses. They operate from the central bus station (city and regional buses) and the Langgar bus station (long-distance buses). All the other long-distance bus companies operate from the Jalan Hamzah external bus station.

SKMK are the easiest to deal with as they have ticket offices at all the bus stations. Long-distance departures are from the Langgar station but, just to make things confusing, a few evening buses also go from the central bus station.

Regular buses go to Kuantan (RM16), Kuala Terengganu (RM7.50), Johor Bahru (RM24), Singapore (RM25), KL (RM21), Butterworth (RM20), Jerantut (RM18) and Melaka (RM 22.40). Book as far ahead as possible, especially for the Butterworth (Penang) buses.

The Thai border is at Rantau Panjang (Sungai Golok on the Thai side), 1½ hours by bus from Kota Bharu. Bus No 29 from the central bus station costs RM2.60. From Rantau Panjang, walk across the border and then it's about one km to the station (a trishaw costs RM3). Malaysian money is accepted in Sungai Kolok.

Pengkalan Kubor is the immigration checkpoint for a back route into Thailand. During the day a large car ferry crosses the river to busy Tak Bai in Thailand. From Kota Bharu take bus No 27, 27A or 43.

Train The nearest station to Kota Bharu for the jungle railway is at Wakaf Bahru, a 50 sen trip on bus No 19 or 27. See the following Kota Bharu to Kuala Lumpur section for more details of this railway.

Taxi The taxi station is on the southern side of the bus station. Main destinations are Kuala Terengganu (RM12), Kuantan (RM25), KL (RM35), Butterworth (RM38) and Kuala Lipis (RM35).

Share taxis from Kota Bharu to Rantau Panjang cost RM3.50.

Getting Around

The airport is eight km from town – take bus No 9 from the old Central Market. A taxi costs around RM10.

To Pantai Cahaya Bulan take bus No 10 for 90 sen; it leaves from the Balah Kubu Bazaar or you can catch it at the bus stand in front of the Kencana Inn.

AROUND KOTA BHARU

Beaches

There are a number of beaches on the coast around Kota Bharu. None of them are anything special. Only 30 minutes from Kota Bharu, **Pantai Cahaya Bulan** used to be Pantai Cinta Berahi, the Beach of Passionate Love, until the local fanatics thought the name too raunchy and changed it. It's a pleasant enough day trip, but the only real thing of interest was the name. Other beaches are **Pantai Irama**, or Beach of Melody, at Bachok and **Pantai Dasar Sabak**, 13 km from Kota Bharu, where the Japanese landed in December 1941 during WW II – 1½ hours before they arrived at Pearl Harbor.

Other

Also in the Kota Bharu vicinity are **waterfalls** (Pasir Puteh area), a number of Thai temples, including **Wat Phothivihan** at Kampung Jambu with its 40-metre reclining Buddha. There are also a number of interesting river trips you can make. At **Kuala Krai**, 65 km south of Kota Bharu, there's a small zoo specialising in local wildlife. The *Hotel Kuala Krai* is OK for a night.

EAST-WEST HIGHWAY

The east-west road starts near Kota Bharu and runs roughly parallel to the Thai border, eventually meeting a little-used road (running north from Kuala Kangsar to Keroh on the Thai border) at Grik. The views from the highway are often superb.

The east-west road was a massive undertaking. Hitching is fairly easy along this stretch if you're on the road early.

Kota Bharu to Kuala Lumpur

THE JUNGLE RAILWAY

The central railway line goes largely through aboriginal territory. It's an area of dense jungle and offers magnificent views.

Commencing near Kota Bharu, the line runs through Kuala Krai, Gua Musang, Kuala Lipis, Jerantut (access point for the Taman Negara) and eventually meets the Singapore-KL railway line at Gemas. Unless you have managed to book a sleeping berth right through, you'll probably find yourself sharing a seat with vast quantities of agricultural produce, babies and people moving their entire homes. Expect the train to run at least a couple of hours late (even the express).

The line's days are probably numbered as roads are rapidly being pushed through. The road now goes all the way from Singapore, through Kuala Lipis, to Kota Bharu. The train is a lot slower but definitely more interesting.

KUALA LIPIS

The road from Fraser's Hill through Raub meets the railway line at this town. Kuala Lipis is a well-maintained pretty town with fine rows of colonial shops down the main street. There's not much to do in Kuala Lipis, but you can arrange jungle treks to **Kenong Rimba Park**. We have had good reports about some treks organised out of Kuala Lipis but female travellers should avoid those organised by Johnny Tan Bok.

Places to Stay

The *Gin Loke Hotel* (☎ 09-311388) at 64 Main St has cheap plywood-partitioned rooms and a friendly atmosphere. The cost is RM10/12 with fan and common bath. Other cheap places include the *Hotel Paris*, the quirky *Hotel Central* and the *Hotel Tiong Kok*, which costs RM14. The *Hotel Jelai* is a very clean Chinese hotel with rooms for RM17 or RM38 with air-con. The old *Rest House* (the Rumah Persinggahan) (☎ 09-312599), overlooking the town, has the best rooms around and costs RM40.

Getting There & Away

There is an express train to Singapore (eight hours) at 12.30 pm, and to Kota Bharu (five hours) at 3.35 pm.

There are also buses and taxis to Kota Bharu (RM35 by taxi), KL (RM8 by bus, RM13/17 by taxi) and Kuantan.

JERANTUT

Jerantut is the gateway to Taman Negara National Park. Most visitors to the park spend at least one night here, but the town itself has no real attractions.

Places to Stay & Eat

The dismal *Hotel Tong Heng* has rooms for RM10 while the slightly better *Hotel Wah Hing* has rooms from RM9 to RM14. The

Hotel Jerantut, with rooms from RM15 to RM25, is definitely worth the extra money.

Right opposite the bus station, the new *Hotel Chett Fatt* is a friendly place that welcomes travellers. The rooms are spotless, but a little featureless. It is good value at RM15, RM20 with air-con or RM35 with air-con and bath. The top place in town is the *Jerantut Resthouse*, with motel-style rooms with bath for RM20 or RM44 with air-con.

There are *foodstalls* near the bus station and plenty of cheap *coffee shops* along the main road. The liveliest area at night is on the road to Taman Negara past the emporium, where you can find plenty of *Chinese restaurants*, such as the good *Restaurant Liang Fong*, and a couple of *karaoke bars*.

You can stock up on supplies in Jerantut at the emporium on the main road towards Temerloh.

Getting There & Away

Bus Buses from Jerantut to Kuantan leave every hour until 4 pm and cost RM8.50. A bus to Kota Bharu leaves at 9.30 am and costs RM21. To KL there are at least two buses daily and the fare is RM13.

Buses to Kuala Tembeling, for Taman Negara, depart at 8.15 and 11 am and 1.30 and 5.15 pm, and they will drop you at the jetty, 500 metres past the township.

Train There's a daily express train to Singapore at 1.30 pm and an ordinary train at 9.10 pm. To get to Tumpat (for Kota Bharu) there's an express at 2.40 pm and an ordinary train at 5.20 am.

Taxi Taxis cost RM3 to Kuala Tembeling, RM5 to Temerloh and RM15 to KL and Kuantan.

TAMAN NEGARA

Peninsular Malaysia's great national park covers 4343 sq km and sprawls across the states of Pahang, Kelantan and Terengganu. The part of the park most visited, however, is all in Pahang. Reactions to the park depend totally on the individual's experience. Some people see lots of wildlife and come away happy, others see little more than leeches. The chances of seeing game are greatest if you do an extended trek away from the more frequented parts of the park, but even a short visit is worth it to experience the pristine primary rainforest.

Orientation & Information

The park headquarters is at the Taman Negara Resort at Kuala Tahan. There's a Wildlife Department office, restaurant, cafeteria, hostel, some chalets and a shop selling provisions at inflated prices. You can rent camping, hiking and fishing gear. Every night at 8.45 pm there is a free slide show during which a free map of Taman Negara and its trails is handed out. Arrange a guide for trekking or a stay in a hide at the Wildlife Department office. At the resort you can also change money (lousy rate) and make phone calls (expensive).

Although everyday clothes are quite suitable around Kuala Tahan, you will need heavy-duty gear if you're heading further afield. River travel in the early morning hours can be surprisingly cold. If overnighting in a hide, you'll need a powerful torch (flashlight).

Mosquitos can be annoying but you can buy repellent at the park shop. Leeches are generally not a major problem, although they can be a real nuisance after heavy rain.

The kampung of Kuala Tahan, right across the Tembeling River from the park headquarters, also has a couple of basic shops, cafes and two small lodges.

Entrance to the park costs RM1 and a camera permit is RM5. You get these at the office at the Kuala Tembeling jetty. If you are driving there's a free undercover car park here too.

Hides & Salt Licks

There are several accessible hides and salt licks in the park. A number of them are close to Kuala Tahan and Kuala Trenggan, but your chances of seeing wildlife will increase if you head for the hides furthest from park headquarters. All hides are built overlooking salt licks and grassy clearings.

For overnight stays, take food and your own sleeping bag or sheets from Kuala Tahan (lent free of charge) – you won't need blankets. Each hide costs RM5 per person per night. Even if you're not lucky enough to see any wildlife, the fantastic sounds of the jungle are well worth the time and effort taken to reach the hides. The 'symphony' is at its best at dusk and dawn.

Bumbun Tahan is an artificial salt lick less than five-minutes walk from the reception building. It is often packed with noisy locals who find the hide a convenient venue for all-night parties – no chance of seeing any animals here!

Better hides within one to 1½ hours walk from the park HQ are **Bumbun Blau** (you can go and visit Gua Telinga along the way), **Bumbun Tabing** and **Bumbun Cegar Anjing**. **Bumbun Yong**, on the Yong River, is about 1½ hours past Blau. **Bumbun Kumbang** is about seven hours from Kuala Tahan or take the 10 am boat (around RM10) up the Tembeling River to Kuala Trenggan. All these hides have sleeping facilities for six to eight people and nearby fresh water.

Mountains & Walks

Trails around the park headquarters are well marked, though some of the paths are hard going. Trails are signposted and have approximate walking times marked clearly along the way.

There are daily walking tours conducted by park officials, including a visit to an Orang Asli village, costing from RM5 to RM15 per person; they are well worth doing.

There's a well-marked **trail** along the bank of the Tembeling River for nine km to Kuala Trenggan. You need to set out early; allow five hours.

Gua Telinga is a cave south-west of the park HQ, and it takes about 1½ hours to walk there, after first crossing the Tahan River. There is a stream through the cave and a rope to guide you for the 80 metres (bring a torch). It's a strenuous half-hour walk – and crawl – through the cave. You can return to the main path through the cave, or take the path around the rocky outcrop at the far end of the cave. Once back at the main path, it's a further 15 minutes walk to the Bumbun Blau hide, where you can spend the night or walk directly back to Kuala Tahan.

If you stay at Nusa Camp, you can walk to **Abai Waterfall** (one hour) or **Gunung Warisan**.

The trek for the really adventurous is the ascent of **Gunung Tahan** (at 2187 metres, the highest mountain in Peninsular Malaysia), which is 55 km from the park HQ. It takes nine days, but can be done in seven with a faster descent. A guide is compulsory and costs RM400 per week and RM50 for each extra day.

A shorter three-day walk is **Rentis Tenor** (Tenor Trail). It's quite popular and can be done without a guide.

Places to Stay & Eat

Kuala Tahan *Camping* at the park HQ with your own tent costs RM1 per person per night, or you can hire a tent for RM5. Beyond the park HQ, you can camp anywhere in Taman Negara.

The hostel part of the *resort* has nine rooms, each clean and comfortable with four bunk beds, overhead fans and personal lockers. Men and women share the dormitory rooms but there are separate toilets and showers. The hostel costs RM11 per person.

There's a range of comfortable chalets from RM60 up to RM210 with air-con and other mod cons. The resort has one expensive restaurant, and a much cheaper self-service cafeteria. Bookings can be made at the resort's head office in KL at Suite 505-A, Pernas International Building, Jalan Sultan Ismail (☎ 03-2634434).

Across the river from the park HQ in Kuala Tahan village, *Tembeling Camp* has a row of basic longhouse rooms for RM10 per person, and a small restaurant. Nearby is *Rumah Sabri* with tin-roofed bamboo huts perched high on the riverbank for RM8 per person. The small *eating places* on the sandbar (more a rockbar) opposite the park HQ are only a couple of minutes walk away, and the *Restaurant Terapong* is a small floating barge moored to the sandbar. All places sell basic mee and rice meals.

Nusa Camp *Nusa Camp*, 15 minutes up the Tembeling River from Kuala Tahan, is probably the best place to stay. There are A-frame huts for RM25, slightly more sophisticated cottages with attached bath for RM40 and 40 dorm beds for RM7. It's much more of a 'jungle camp' than anything at Kuala Tahan. The restaurant serves good but unexciting food. You can make advance bookings in KL at the Nusa Camp desk at the tourist centre on Jalan Ampang (☎ 03-2423929, ext 112), or in Jerantut at 16 LKNP Building, New Town (☎ 09-262369).

Kuala Trenggan Located about 35 minutes upstream from Kuala Tahan is the *Trenggan Lodge*, run by the same people who have the resort at the park HQ. There are 10 chalets with attached bath at RM90, or you can camp for RM1.

Getting There & Away

Air Pelangi Air operate flights three times a week from KL to Kuala Tiang, about halfway between Kuala Tembeling and Kuala Tahan. Boats from the resort meet all planes (RM10).

Boat Boats to the park leave from Kuala Tembeling jetty, 18 km from Jerantut, at 9 am and 2 pm only. There's no need to book in advance, except perhaps during holiday periods. Make reservations with the Nusa Camp office in KL or Jerantut, or with the resort's office in KL. The 2½ to three-hour trip to Kuala Tahan costs RM30 return.

Leaving the park, boats also leave at 9 am and 2 pm and take two to 2½ hours. Direct boats also go from the jetty to Nusa camp for RM17.

Kuala Tembeling is most easily reached from Jerantut. Kuala Tembeling can also be reached by train, though it is less convenient. Tembeling Halt, 2½ km from the jetty, is the station between Jerantut and Kuala Lipis and you must arrange in advance for the train to stop there.

Getting Around

Within the park, boats go from Kuala Tahan to Nusa Camp (RM5, RM1.50 for Nusa Camp guests) at 10 am, 12.30 and 6 pm, and in the reverse direction at 8.15 and 11 am and 4 pm. The boat to Kuala Trenggan (RM10) goes via Nusa Camp at 10 am, returning at 11 am. Another boat goes from Nusa Camp (RM5) at 3.15 pm and returns at 3.30 pm.

The only other services are from Kuala Tahan to Bumbun Blau and Bumbun Yong at 8.30 am and 5.30 pm.

Sarawak

Sarawak's history reads much more like Victorian melodrama than hard fact. In 1838, James Brooke, a British adventurer, arrived in Borneo with his armed sloop, *Royalist*, to find the Brunei sultanate facing rebellion from the dissatisfied inland tribes. He quelled the unrest and in gratitude was given power over part of what is today Sarawak.

Appointing himself Rajah Brooke, he successfully cooled down the warring tribes and suppressed head-hunting, eliminated the dreaded Borneo pirates and founded a dynasty that lasted until after WW II. The Brooke family of White Rajahs continued to bring increasing amounts of Borneo under their power until the arrival of the Japanese in WW II.

Today, Sarawak is an economically important part of Malaysia with major oil exports plus timber, pepper, rubber and palm-oil production. Although Sarawak suffered even more than Peninsular Malaysia from Communist guerrilla activity, things are peaceful today.

The biggest attractions for the visitor to Sarawak are the excellent national parks, longhouses and villages of the diverse Dayak tribes and the amazing rainforests (see them while you can).

Visas & Permits

See under Visas and Embassies in the Facts for the Visitor section at the start of this

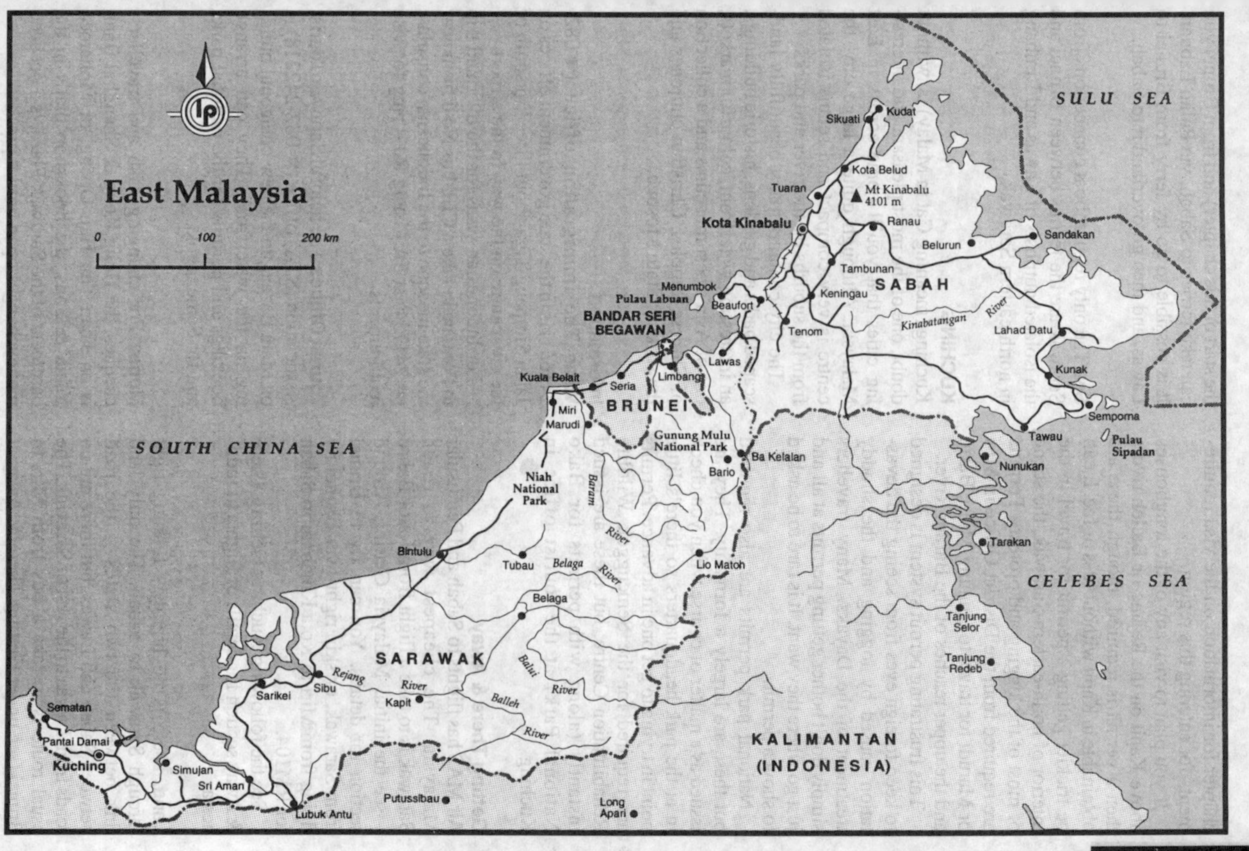
East Malaysia
0
100
200 km
SULU SEA
CELEBES SEA
SOUTH CHINA SEA
SABAH
SARAWAK
BRUNEI
KALIMANTAN
(INDONESIA)
Kudat
Sikuati
Kota Belud
Mt Kinabalu
4101 m
Ranau
Tambunan
Keningau
Tuaran
Kota Kinabalu
Tenom
Beaufort
Menumbok
Pulau Labuan
Lawas
Limbang
BANDAR SERI
BEGAWAN
Seria
Kuala Belait
Miri
Marudi
Baram
River
Gunung Mulu
National Park
Bario
Ba Kelalan
Lio Matoh
Long
Apari
Belaga
River
Belaga
Balui
River
Balleh
River
Niah
National
Park
Tubau
Bintulu
Rejang
River
Kapit
Putussibau
Sibu
Sarikei
Lubuk Antu
Sri Aman
Simujan
Sematan
Pantai Damai
Kuching
Sandakan
Belurun
Kinabatangan
River
Lahad Datu
Kunak
Semporna
Pulau
Sipadan
Tawau
Nunukan
Tarakan
Tanjung
Selor
Tanjung
Redeb

chapter for information on the visa requirements for entering this region.

If you plan to visit any of the longhouses above Kapit on the Rejang or Balleh rivers then a permit is required, though these are obtainable in Kapit without fuss or fee. It can be trickier getting a permit for travel in the interior of north-eastern Sarawak, the scene of most of the logging and protests. Permits are required from the District Office in Miri or Marudi for travel to Gunung Mulu, Bario and the upper reaches of the Baram River.

This frustrating permit system is designed to keep foreign eyes from seeing the devastation caused by logging and the shoddy treatment of the Dayaks. Many travellers simply don't bother getting permits at all and just go where they want. It is rare to be asked to show a permit.

National park permits are also required but these are largely a formality. They are issued as a matter of course when you check in at the park headquarters so there's little point in trying to get one in advance. Permits are required for the Semenggok Wildlife Rehabilitation Centre, but these are issued instantly (along with permits for Bako National Park) at the tourist office in Kuching.

Getting There & Away

Air MAS has flights to Sabah and Peninsular Malaysia. The cheapest way to reach Sarawak is to take a flight from Johor Bahru – see the initial Malaysia Getting Around section for details. You can fly to Brunei from Sarawak, or skip right over Brunei by flying from Miri to Kota Kinabalu in Sabah for RM104.

See the following Kuching Getting There & Away section for details of flights to Indonesia.

Land There is no highway running right through Sarawak to Sabah. The only land link between the two states is the road between Sabah and Lawas, but there are no roads from Lawas to the rest of Sarawak. The usual route is to take a bus from Miri to Brunei (see under Getting There & Away at the start of this chapter) and from Brunei you can take ferries to Sabah, via Pulau Labuan. It is possible to go by ferry from Brunei to Lawas, and then go overland into Sabah.

Sea The only regular boat connections from Sarawak are the ferries between Brunei and the isolated outposts of Lawas and Limbang in north-eastern Sarawak.

KUCHING

Kuching (meaning Cat in Malay) is, without doubt, one of the most pleasant and interesting cities that you'll come across in East Malaysia. Although quite a large city, the centre is very compact and seems isolated from the suburbs by the river and parks.

The city contains many beautifully landscaped parks and gardens, historic buildings, an interesting waterfront, colourful markets, one of Asia's best museums and a collection of Chinese temples, Christian churches and the striking State Mosque.

Information

Visas The immigration office (☎ 082-245661) is in the state government offices on Jalan Simpang Tiga about three km south of the city centre on the way to the airport.

For Indonesian visas for the overland trip to Pontianak, take a CLL bus No 6 from near thc state mosque to the Indonesian consulate (☎ 241734) at 5A Pisang Rd – ring for visa requirements.

Tourist Offices The helpful Sarawak Tourist Association (STA) office (☎ 082-242218) is on Main Bazaar, in the new octagonal building on the waterfront. They can arrange bookings and permits for the national parks and for Semenggok.

Money For changing cash and travellers' cheques, the Hong Kong & Shanghai Bank is on Jalan Tun Haji Openg, or Mohamed Yahia & Sons, the bookshop that's in the basement of the Sarawak Plaza, is a licenced moneychanger open until 9 pm.

Post The GPO is right in the centre on Jalan Tun Haji Openg.

Fort Margherita

Built by Charles Brooke in the mid-19th century and named after his wife, Margaret, the fort was designed to guard the entrance to Kuching in the days when piracy was commonplace. It is now an interesting Police Museum (Muzium Polis). To get there take one of the small *tambangs* (ferry boats) which ply back and forth between the landing stage behind the Square Tower and the bus stop below the fort.

Nearby, on the same side of the river, is the impressive **Istana**, built by Rajah Brooke. It is now the Governor of Sarawak's residence.

Sarawak Museum

This is one of the best museums in Asia and should not be missed. It consists of two segments, the old and new, connected by a footbridge over Jalan Tun Haji Openg. Built in the style of a Normandy townhouse, the old part was opened in 1891 and was strongly influenced by the anthropologist Sir Alfred Russell Wallace, a contemporary of Darwin, who spent two years there at the invitation of Charles Brooke. The original section was expanded in 1911. Next to the new section is **Muzium Islam Sarawak**, just to show that not all Sarawak is pagan.

You can easily spend a few hours there and to top it all, it's free. The museum is open every day from 9 am to 6 pm.

Temples, Mosques & Churches

The most interesting of these are the Chinese temples, and the best of these is perhaps the **Hong San** at the junction of Jalan Carpenter and Jalan Wayang at the back of the Rex cinema (Jalan Carpenter is Kuching's Chinatown and always worth a look). Other temples include the **Kuan Yin Temple** on Jalan Tabuan, built in honour of the goddess of mercy.

The **Masjid Negeri** (State Mosque), completed in 1968, is visually impressive but otherwise uninteresting.

Of the Christian churches perhaps the most interesting is the futuristic, single-roofed **Roman Catholic Cathedral** past the Sarawak Museum on Jalan Tun Haji Openg.

Places to Stay

One of the popular places is the *Anglican Cathedral Hostel* (☎ 082-414027) on the hill at the back of St Thomas's church. A 'donation' of RM20/25 for a single/double gets you a large, spotlessly clean room with fan, polished wooden floors, comfortable beds, cane chairs, clean toilets, showers and good views. It fills up quickly.

Best of the cheap hotels is the friendly *Kuching Hotel* (☎ 082-413985), opposite the Rex cinema on Jalan Temple. Spartan but clean rooms are RM17/18 and RM22/23 for larger rooms, all equipped with fan and sink. The *Ban Hua Hin* (☎ 082-242351), 36 Jalan Padungan, is similar. Fan rooms cost RM20 and air-con rooms are RM25 and RM28.

On Jalan Green Hill there's a whole group of mid-range 'lodging houses', many of which cater to long-term residents. They all have good rooms with bath, air-con and TV, and cost roughly the same. The best of these are the *Orchid Inn* (☎ 082-411417) at No 2 and the *Goodwood Inn* (☎ 082-244862) at No 16, which both have rooms between RM35 and RM45. The *Green Mountain Lodging House* (☎ 082-246952) at No 1 has rooms for RM35 and RM38, and the *Mandarin Lodging House* (☎ 082-418269) at No 6 has rooms from RM35 to RM40.

Places to Eat

The best food you'll come across in Sarawak is in Kuching, so make the most of it. For tasty Indian food, head for Jalan India. The *Jubilee, Madinah* and *Malaya* restaurants are next to each other. Not far away, on Jalan Carpenter, the *National Islamic Cafe* also serves excellent rotis and murtabak.

For cheap Chinese food, close to the Anglican hostel and budget hotels, try the small *hawker's centre* on Jalan Wayang opposite the end of Jalan Carpenter, or the *Green Hill Corner* and *Tiger Garden* further along. *Suan Chicken Rice*, next to the Pizza

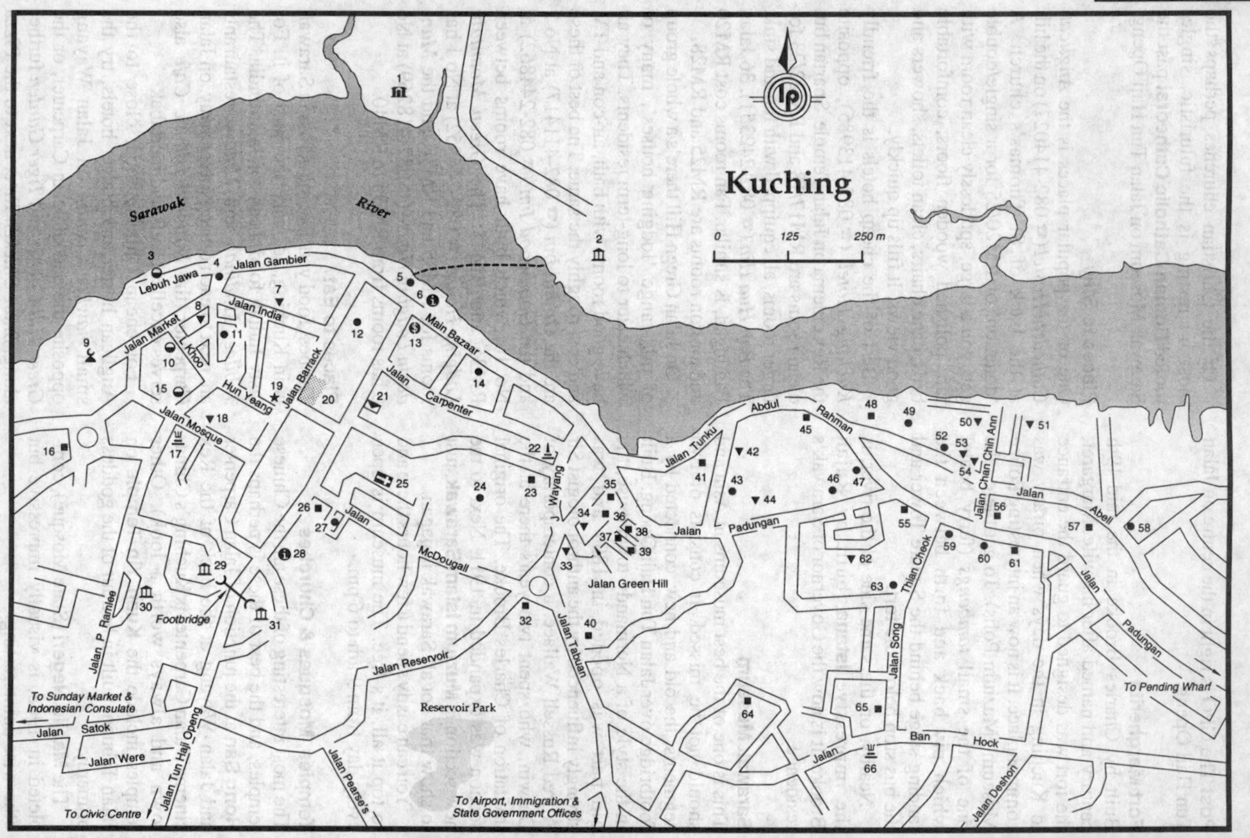
Kuching
0
125
250 m
Sarawak
River
Jalan Gambier
Lebuh Jawa
Jalan India
Jalan Market
Khoo
Hun Yeang
Jalan Barrack
Main Bazaar
Jalan Carpenter
Jalan Mosque
J. Wayang
Jalan Tunku
Abdul
Rahman
Jalan Chan Chin Ann
Jalan
Abell
Padungan
Jalan Padungan
Thian Cheok
Jalan Song
Jalan Green Hill
McDougall
Jalan
Jalan Tabuan
Jalan Reservoir
Reservoir Park
Footbridge
Jalan P. Ramlee
Jalan Satok
Jalan Were
Jalan Tun Haji Openg
Jalan Pearse's
Jalan Ban Hock
Jalan Deshon
Jalan Padungan
To Pending Wharf
To Sunday Market & Indonesian Consulate
To Civic Centre
To Airport, Immigration & State Government Offices

Hut, does a great chicken rice with the best sauces.

Take the lift to the 5th floor of the Saujana car park for Malay hawker food with a view. Beef rendang pizza is available here! The *Permata Food Centre*, on Jalan Padungan behind the MAS building, is a popular food stall centre that specialises in seafood, but you can also get steak and other dishes. The *Kuching Food Centre* is a restaurant that sets up tables on the waterfront in the evening and you can dine under the stars next to the Sarawak River. The seafood here is moderately priced, or you can get cheaper dishes.

Things to Buy

Kuching is one of the best centres in Sarawak for buying tribal artefacts. Shops selling arts and crafts are scattered around the city but be warned that prices are outrageously high.

The best area is along Main Bazaar at the Jalan Wayang end. Shops with a good selection include Unika Sarawak at No 78 and Native Arts at No 92.

Getting There & Away

Air MAS (☎ 082-24 4144), Jalan Song Thian Cheok, have flights to Johor Bahru (RM169), Sibu (RM72), Bintulu (RM117), Miri (RM164), Kota Kinabalu (RM228) and other destinations. MAS flights to Pontianak (RM177) in Indonesia leave on Monday and Thursday.

Bus The main bus station area is near the market. Green and yellow Sarawak Transport Company (STC) buses leave from Lebuh Jawa and service south-western Sarawak, including Sarikei and Sri Aman. Petra Jaya buses (yellow with red and black stripes) leave from Lebuh Khoo Hun Yeang near Electra House and go to Bako National Park (No 6) and Damai/Santubong (No 2B).

Other long-distance buses leave from Jalan Penrissen, five km from town, but most have ticket offices near the Petra Jaya bus station. For Bintulu and Miri, it is necessary to go via Sarikei or Sibu, which are quicker and easier to reach by boat.

PLACES TO STAY

16 Arif Hotel
23 Anglican Cathedral Hostel
26 Aurora Hotel
32 Fata Hotel
35 Kuching Hotel
36 Metropole Inn Hotel & Concorde Office
37 Mandarin Lodging House
38 Goodwood Inn
39 Orchid Inn
40 Borneo Hotel
41 Hilton Hotel
45 Riverside Majestic
48 Holiday Inn
55 Ban Hua Hin
56 Kapit Hotel
57 Longhouse Hotel
61 Ching Hin Hotel
64 Telang Usan Hotel
65 Liwah Hotel

PLACES TO EAT

7 Jubilee Restaurant
8 Food Centre
18 Saujana Food Centre
33 Tiger Garden
34 Green Hill Corner
42 Koreana
44 Stamang BBQ
50 Kuching Food Centre
51 KTS Seafoods Canteen
53 Suan Chicken Rice
54 Pizza Hut
62 Permata Food Centre

OTHER

1 Istana
2 Fort Margherita
3 STC Buses
4 Taxi Station
5 Square Tower
6 Sarawak Tourist Association Office
9 Masjid Negeri
10 Petra Jaya Buses
11 Electra House
12 Courthouse
13 Hong Kong & Shanghai Bank
14 Star Bookshop
15 Chin Lian Long Buses
17 Sikh Temple
19 Central Police Station
20 Night Market
21 GPO
22 Hong San Temple
24 Bishop's House
25 Anglican Cathedral
27 Kuching Plaza
28 Tourism Malaysia
29 Sarawak Museum
30 Muzium Islam Sarawak
31 Sarawak Museum (Old Building)
43 Mahana Rent-a-Car
46 Borneo Excursion Travel
47 Singapore Airlines
49 Sarawak Plaza
52 Eeze Trading
58 British Council
59 Ekspres Bahagia
60 Tan Brothers
63 MAS
66 Hindu Temple

Biaramas Express (☎ 082-452139), 3½ mile, Penrissen Rd, has a bus to Pontianak in Indonesia leaving at 10 am and arriving at 6 pm. The cost is RM35. An Indonesian visa is required for the land border crossing at Tebedu/Entikong.

Boat The quickest and easiest way to reach Sibu, from where you can head up the Rejang River or continue north to Niah National Park, is to take an express boat. They take four hours, and a change of boat (from a sea-going boat to a smaller river boat) is required at Sarikei. Boats leave from the wharfs in Pending, about six km east of the city centre (take bus No 17 or 19, or a taxi costs RM8).

Bookings should be at least the day before departure. The addresses of boat operators, departure times and one-way fares from Kuching are:

Ekspres Pertama (☎ 082-414735), 196 Jalan Padungan; 8.30 am, RM29
Concòrde Marine, Metropole Inn Hotel (☎ 082-412551), Jalan Green Hill; 8.30 am, RM29
Ekspres Bahagia (☎ 082-421948), 50 Padungan Rd; 1 pm, RM33

Getting Around

To/From the Airport A taxi between Kuching airport and the city centre costs RM12, 50% more after midnight. STC bus No 12A operates every 40 minutes between the airport and the city centre for about 80 sen.

Bus The blue and white Chin Lian Long Company buses leave from Lebuh Gartak near the mosque for the Indonesian consulate (No 6) and the ekspres boat wharf (No 17 or 19).

Taxi Taxis wait around the market and also at the area where long-distance buses drop passengers.

AROUND KUCHING

Semenggok Wildlife Rehabilitation Centre

The Semenggok sanctuary, 32 km south of Kuching, is a rehabilitation centre for orang-utans, monkeys, honey bears and hornbills which have either been orphaned or kept illegally. The sanctuary is interesting, but the Sepilok sanctuary in Sabah is better.

The centre is reached from the Forest Department Nursery along a plankwalk through the forest – a very agreeable walk. A permit is required in order to visit the sanctuary and these can be arranged, free of charge, at the tourist office in Kuching.

Getting There & Away Take an STC Penrissen bus No 6 from Kuching (40 minutes, RM1.40).

Bako National Park

This park is at the mouth of the Bako River, north of Kuching, and contains some 27 sq km of unspoilt tropical rainforest, beaches, rocky headlands and some beautiful marked walking trails – well worth a visit. A permit is needed to visit the park and this, along with accommodation bookings, must be made in advance at the National Parks & Wildlife office in Kuching.

Places to Stay There are resthouses, hostels and a camp site at the park. It costs RM3 per person in the hostel and the standards are very good. It costs RM60 per resthouse or RM30 per double room in the new resthouse, and RM50 and RM25 in the old resthouse. Cooking facilities and utensils are provided.

Places to Eat The park canteen sells cheap meals – fried rice and fried noodles – and has a variety of goods for sale (mainly tinned food); there is also fresh bread and vegetables.

Getting There & Away The park is 37 km from Kuching and can be reached by a Kampung Bako bus No 6 (RM1.90, 45 minutes), followed by a 30-minute boat trip from Kampung Bako to the park HQ. Boats cost RM3 per person on a share basis for more than 10 people.

Santubong & Damai

North of Kuching on the coast, Santubong is a small fishing village with a so-so beach.

Near Santubong, the **Holiday Inn Damai Beach Resort** has made its own beach at Damai. The main attraction, however, is the **Sarawak Cultural Village** (☎ 082-422411), a traditionally styled theme park with longhouses, and there are also craft and cultural demonstrations from the different peoples of the interior. It is all very touristy as you would expect, and expensive at RM45, but well done.

UP THE REJANG RIVER

The Rejang is the main 'highway' of central and southern Sarawak, and most of the trade in the interior is carried out along it. It is also the way the logs from the forests in the upper reaches of the Rejang (and its tributaries the Balleh, Belaga and Balui rivers) are brought down to Sibu for processing and export. The number of log-laden barges on the river is astounding but equally depressing.

If you wish to travel up the Rejang, the best time is in late May and early June, as this is the time of the Iban harvest festival, Gawai, so there is plenty of movement on the rivers and the longhouses welcome visitors. There're also plenty of celebrations, which usually involve the consumption of copious quantities of *arak* and *tuak* (rice wine).

On the river above Sibu, there is hotel accommodation in Song, Kanowit, Kapit and Belaga.

Visiting a Longhouse

A longhouse is a traditional home divided by partition walls into a number of rooms. If you intend to visit a longhouse then you need plenty of time. The best place to head for is Kapit, a small administrative town upriver, where you should be able to find someone to take you to a longhouse – ask around and make yourself known. Before heading upriver from Kapit, you need to get a permit from the state office. It only takes a few minutes but they're not available on Saturday afternoon or Sunday.

Many travellers head for the stretch of the Rejang River between Kapit and Belaga (see under Getting There & Away in the following Sibu section for information on getting to Kapit). This area is easily accessible as there are express boats operating between the two towns, in the wet season at least. Perhaps a more interesting river is the Balleh River, which branches off to the east a short distance upstream from Kapit.

At Belaga, the Balui and Belaga rivers merge and become the Rejang River. To travel up either of these rivers from Belaga requires permission from the Resident's office in Belaga, and this is generally not given. The Katibas River joins the Rejang at Song (between Sibu and Kapit), this is also a good river to explore and no permits are required.

Having found someone to take you, you'll need to stock up on gifts with which to 'pay' for your visit. Alcohol, cigarettes and sweets are the most appreciated.

On arrival at the longhouse, ask for the *tuai rumah* (headman). You'll then probably be offered a place to stay for the night, and you'll be invited to join them for a meal.

What to Take

Apart from gifts, other indispensable items include a torch, mosquito repellent, a medical kit with plenty of aspirin and Panadol, and some Lomotil, Imodium or other antidiarrhoeal.

SIBU

Sibu is the main port city on the Rejang River and will probably be your first river stopover. There's not a lot to do in Sibu so most travellers only stay overnight and head off up the Rejang the next day. It's worth climbing the tower of the **Chinese temple** as there are great views over the river.

Places to Stay

By far the best budget place to stay is the Methodist guesthouse, *Hoover House*, next to the church on Jalan Pulau. It's excellent value at RM10 per person but the only problem is that it's often full.

The *Hoover Lodging House* (☎ 084-334490), not to be confused with the Methodist guesthouse, is a cheap long-term place. It's at 34 Jalan Tan Sri, just a few minutes walk from the bus station. Depressing, windowless boxes with fan are RM8/10 for singles/doubles, but what can you expect for the price? Nearby, facing the waterfront, is the reasonable *Mehung Hotel* (☎ 084-324852), 17 Maju Rd. Small rooms cost from RM10, and decent rooms with a tiny bathroom cost from RM18 or RM28 with air-con.

Close to the waterfront, along Jalan Channel, *Hotel Ria* is more upmarket with good air-con rooms for RM30 with bath and TV. The *Hotel Sadang* is right in the action next to the market, but is noisy. Fan rooms with bath go for RM20 or air-con rooms cost RM28.

The *Sibu Hotel* (☎ 084-330784) on Jalan Marshidi Sidek is good for the price with rooms for RM15, RM20 with bath or RM25 with air-con, bath and TV. Right beside the bus station, the friendly *River View Hotel* (☎ 084-325241), 65 Mission Rd, has comfortable, mid-range rooms with TV and attached bathroom for RM32/36.

Places to Eat

The best cheap food in Sibu is found at the various hawker centres and foodstalls. The small two-storey *food centre* at the end of Market Rd, at the rear of the Palace Cinema, has stalls selling Malay curries, roti and laksa, as well as Chinese food and ais kacang. There are also foodstalls on the 2nd floor of the *market*.

Rex Food Court is a small air-con food centre with a selection of Chinese and Western food, including the Good Morning Sibu breakfast stall which does a reasonable job at Western breakfasts.

In the late afternoon *stalls* set up near the market, mainly outside the Miramar Hotel, and these are great for picking up snack foods such as pau (steamed dumplings), barbecued chicken wings and all manner of sweets.

For Western fast food, *Sugar Bun* and *McDonald's* are on Jalan Kampung Nyabor, and there's a *Kentucky Fried Chicken* on Jalan Wong Nai Siong.

Getting There & Away

Air There are flights from Sibu to Kapit (RM48), Belaga (RM76), Marudi (RM100), Kuching (RM72), Bintulu (RM64), Miri (RM112), Kota Kinabalu and Sabah (RM180).

Bus Lanang Bus Company has seven buses daily to Bintulu (RM14.80, four hours). Syarikat Bus Express has air-con buses to Bintulu (RM18) and Miri (RM35).

Boat All express boats to Sarikei and Kuching (change at Sarikei) leave from the Sarikei Wharf in front of the Chinese temple. Three companies operate boats to Kuching and the trip takes around four hours and costs RM29 to RM33 depending on the company.

Getting to Kapit is the first leg of the journey up the Rejang River. The newest express launches cost RM15 and cover the 130 km or so from Sibu to Kapit in a shade over two hours! When the river is high, an early morning boat goes all the way to Belaga.

KAPIT

This small town on the eastern bank of the Rejang River dates from the days of the White Rajahs and still sports an old wooden **fort** built by Charles Brooke.

Information

If you are looking for a lift and introduction to a longhouse, ask at the Petronas or Shell fuel barges.

For permits for travel beyond Kapit, go to the Pejabat Am office on the 1st floor of the state government complex. It takes about 15 minutes but, remember, the office is only open business hours.

Places to Stay

Head for the *Rejang Hotel* (☎ 084-796709), which has cheap (and hot) rooms on the top floor for RM15/18 or rooms with bath and air-con for RM20/24 – good value. Cheap, but seedy and not recommended, are the *Hiap Chiong* and the *Kapit Longhouse*.

The *New Rejang Inn* (☎ 084-796600) is an immaculate place with good rooms for RM40. For a bit of luxury at bargain prices, the *Greenland Inn* (☎ 084-796009) has excellent rooms for RM45, RM50 and RM55.

Places to Eat

Foodstalls set up in the evening at the night market. The *River View Restaurant* (Ming Hock) on the top floor of the market building is good.

Kapit has a number of good Chinese coffee shops. The *Hua Sin Cafe* serves some reasonably priced food, as well as more expensive seafood. The popular *Kah Ping Cafe* on the main square has good pork dishes.

Vikings restaurant has fried chicken and other Western fast food, while the *Frosty Boy* under the Greenland Hotel has pizzas and ice cream.

Getting There & Away

Air MAS fly Sibu-Kapit-Belaga and back on Thursday and Sunday. The fare to Belaga is RM47 and to Sibu RM48.

Boat There are frequent express launch departures to Sibu from 8 am until around 3 pm for RM15. During the wet season, express launches leave for Belaga daily from the main jetty. The trip takes up to six hours and costs RM20. During the dry season, when the river is low, the express boats can't get through the Pelagus Rapids about an hour upstream of Kapit. Small cargo boats still do the run, however. They are slow and uncomfortable, take around eight hours and charge RM50.

There are also cargo boats heading up the Balleh River on a daily basis as far as Interwau – ask at the fuel barges in Kapit.

BELAGA

Belaga is just a small village and government administration centre on the upper reaches of the Rejang where the river divides into the Belaga and Balui rivers. Many Kayan and Kenyah longhouses are further upriver.

Permits

Permits are required for travel upriver from Belaga, though these may be restricted to travel as far as the Bakun Rapids, one hour upstream. There's no need to have a permit to travel on the logging route to Tubau and Bintulu.

Places to Stay

The *Belaga Hotel* (☎ 084-461244) is the most popular with rooms at RM15 with bath or RM25 to RM30 with air-con. The *Bee Lian Hotel* (☎ 084-461416) is similar and charges RM25 with air-con, or the basic *Huan Kilah Lodging House* (☎ 084-461259) has rooms for RM15.

Getting There & Away

Express boats go from Belaga upriver as far as Long Pangai.

In the dry season, it's possible to travel from Belaga to Bintulu. The journey is not easy or cheap unless you get the right connections at the right time. It can be done in one day, but allow two in case you get stuck along the way. First take a boat up the Belaga River to the logging camp just past Long Mitik. An express boat goes from Belaga for RM5 when there is enough demand, otherwise hire a longboat for RM90. From the camp, a regular Landcruiser does the run to Tubau for RM150 (RM25 per person between six people). The best time to get a Landcruiser is around 8 am, when there are likely to be more people to share the cost. It is three hours to Tubau, from where express boats go to Bintulu (RM14, 3½ hours) until noon. If you are stuck in Tubau, there is accommodation for RM10.

BINTULU

Bintulu is a modern, air-conditioned boom town which is best passed through as quickly as possible, unless you want holes burned in every pocket. There's nothing of interest in the town.

Places to Stay

You don't get much for your money in Bintulu. The *Capital Hotel* (☎ 086-34667) on Keppel Rd is a big anonymous place with a few scruffy rooms for RM15, and a variety of air-con rooms with bath for RM20 to RM45.

Two better places are near the big Plaza Hotel. The *Duong Hing* (☎ 086-336698) is at 20 New Commercial Centre just around the corner from Jalan Abang Galau, the main street. Rooms with bath are quite good for RM20 or air-con rooms cost RM25/28. The *Dragon Inn* (☎ 086-334223) nearby mostly has air-con rooms with bath and TV for RM30 or some cheaper fan rooms with bath for RM20.

Going up in quality and price, the *AA Inn* (☎ 086-335733), 113 Jalan Masjid, has air-con rooms with bath and TV for RM32/39. Bintulu also has a host of good mid-range hotels, such as the *Ung Ping Inn* (☎ 086-337373), 127 Jalan Masjid, which costs RM40.

Places to Eat

The top floor of the new market has dozens of *foodstalls* and you can sit and look across the river. The *night market* at the bus station is good for take-away snacks such as satay, grilled chicken and fish. By the waterfont, the *Seaview Restoran* has standard Chinese tucker, or for Indian food, the *Islamik Restoran* on the main street has good roti and murtabak and a wide selection of curries to dip them in.

Getting There & Away

Air MAS has daily flights from Bintulu to Sibu (RM64), Kuching (RM117), Miri (RM69) and Kota Kinabalu (RM127). The airport is smack in the middle of town.

Bus There are eight daily buses direct to Batu Niah (RM9, two hours) from Bintulu: non-air-con buses go at 7.30, 9, 10.30 am, 1 and 3 pm and air-con buses at 6.45 am and noon. To Miri there are 10 buses daily and the journey takes at least four hours. Departures are between 6 am and 2 pm, and also at 6 pm. The cost is RM15.40 non-air-con or RM18 air-con. To Sibu, buses depart between 6 am and 2 pm and cost RM14.80, or RM18 with air-con. There are also buses to Sarikei and these link up with buses to Kuching.

Boat For Belaga, launches go up the Kemena River as far as Tubau between 9 am and noon.

NIAH NATIONAL PARK & NIAH CAVES

A visit to the Niah Caves is one of the most memorable experiences in East Malaysia. The **Great Cave**, one of the largest in the world, is in the centre of the Niah National Park. The park is dominated by the 394-metre-high limestone massif of **Gunung Subis**, visible from far away. In the 1950s, a human skull, estimated to be 35,000 years old, was found. There were also signs that the caves were inhabited up until the 15th century.

The caves are a source for that most famous Chinese dish, bird's nest soup. Countless tiny swifts build their nests in crevices in the walls and ceilings of the cave, constructing them out of hardened sticky saliva. Collecting the nests is a dangerous occupation, as you'll see once inside the caves. To increase the swift population, the government has placed a temporary moratorium on the collection of birds' nests.

Guano (bird and bat excrement) is also collected from the cave floors for use as fertiliser. It's quite a sight each evening as the vast population of swifts flock in from the dayshift while the bats leave on the night-shift.

The park HQ is four km from the village of Batu Niah and the caves themselves are a further three km along a plankwalk – an interesting one-hour walk. The plankwalk continues inside the caves, so it's impossible to get lost, although a torch is essential.

Places to Stay & Eat

The *Visitors' Hostel* at the park headquarters is a great place to stay. Cooking facilities are provided and a bed costs RM3 per night in crowded 12-bed dorms. The park has a good canteen and there is a store nearby for basic, slightly expensive provisions. On the opposite side of the river are comfortable two-bedroom *resthouses* which are completely self-contained. The charge is RM30 for a double room or RM60 for the whole resthouse.

The town of Batu Niah has a few hotels. *Niah Caves Hotel* (☎ 086-737726) is clean and reasonably cheap at RM26 for doubles; it has good basic food in the restaurant downstairs.

Getting There & Away

Whether you come from Bintulu or Miri, you will end up at Batu Niah. From there, the best way to get to the park HQ is to take a private boat up the river for RM2 per person for five or more people, or RM10 if you have to charter a whole boat. Private cars also double as taxis but unless you can bargain them down to under RM10, the boat trip is much more pleasant.

From Batu Niah, buses to Miri (RM9, two hours) depart at 6.45, 7.45, 8 and 11 am, 1 and 3 pm. Buses to Bintulu (RM9, 2½ hours) depart at 6, 7 and 10 am, noon, 1.30 and 3 pm.

LAMBIR HILLS NATIONAL PARK

This national park, encompassing a chain of sandstone hills, covers an area of 6952 hectares and at one point is only 20 km from Miri. While it doesn't have the spectacular scenery of Niah and Mulu, or the diversity of Bako, Lambir Hills is an excellent park for short jungle walks through rich rainforest containing many species of flora and fauna.

Lambir Hills is a good day trip from Miri, though best avoided on weekends when Miri residents come by the carload to the visit the waterfalls near the park HQ. With the building of accommodation, visitors can now

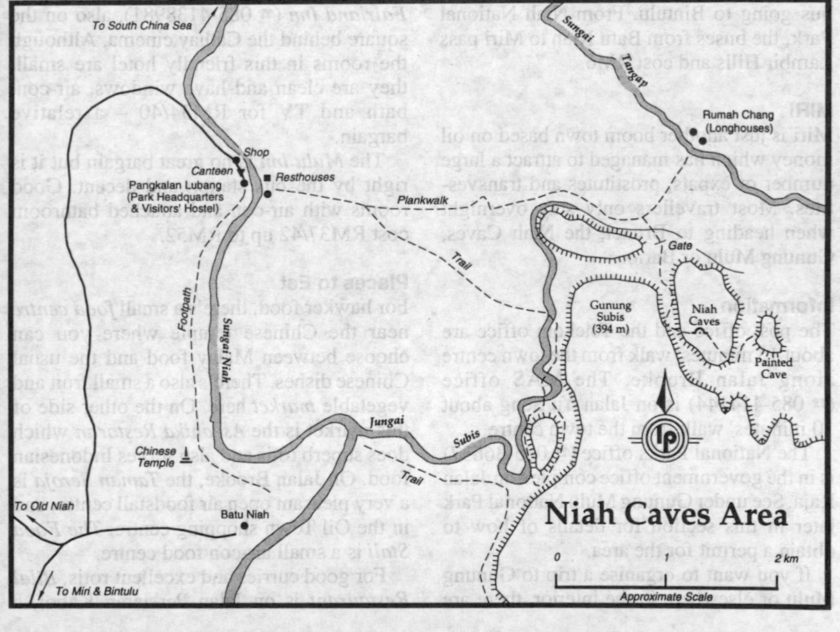

enjoy the forest and explore the longer walks without having to hurry.

The park HQ is 32 km south of Miri. Here you'll find the park office (☎ 085-36637) and information centre, a canteen and the chalets.

Places to Stay & Eat

Accommodation is very comfortable. Bookings can be made at the national parks office in Miri, or at Niah National Park.

The *hostel* costs RM3 per person in a six-bed room. Standard *resthouses* cost RM20 per room or RM40 for the whole chalet, while the deluxe resthouses cost RM30 per room or RM60 per chalet. The canteen serves basic fried rice meals. The hostel and resthouses have their own cooking facilities – the canteen sells some provisions for self-catering but it is best to bring fresh food.

Getting There & Away

Park HQ is on the main highway and easily reached by bus from Miri. Take the Batu Niah bus for RM2.40, or any non-express bus going to Bintulu. From Niah National Park, the buses from Batu Niah to Miri pass Lambir Hills and cost RM6.

MIRI

Miri is just another boom town based on oil money which has managed to attract a large number of expats, prostitutes and transvestites. Most travellers only stay overnight when heading to Brunei, the Niah Caves, Gunung Mulu or Bario.

Information

The post office and the Telekom office are about 15 minutes' walk from the town centre along Jalan Brooke. The MAS office (☎ 085-414144) is on Jalan Yu Seng about 10 minutes' walk from the town centre.

The National Parks office (☎ 085-36637) is in the government office complex on Jalan Raja. See under Gunung Mulu National Park later in this section for details of how to obtain a permit for the area.

If you want to organise a trip to Gunung Mulu or elsewhere in the interior, there are plenty of travel agents in Miri. Tropical Adventure (☎ 085-419337), 228 Jalan Maju near the MAS office, is one of the largest agencies with an interesting but expensive range of tours.

Places to Stay

Miri is a fairly lively town, not only because of the oil and development, but also because Bruneians in search of a bit of action flock here on weekends.

Finding a cheap room is almost impossible. Everything is air-conditioned – even the brothels – and expensive. The only remotely cheap options are the dorms in a couple of the Chinese hotels, although these have little privacy and no security. The *Tai Tong Lodging House* (☎ 085-34072) at 26 Jalan China is about the best deal with dorm beds for RM8 or rooms for RM27/35 with fan and common bath. Another place with dorm beds (RM7) is the *South East Asia Lodging House* (☎ 085-416921), on the square behind the Cathay cinema.

For a private room, your best bet is the *Fairland Inn* (☎ 085-4138981), also on the square behind the Cathay cinema. Although the rooms in this friendly hotel are small, they are clean and have windows, air-con, bath and TV for RM34/40 – a relative bargain.

The *Mulu Inn* is no great bargain but it is right by the bus station and decent. Good rooms with air-con and attached bathroom cost RM37/42 up to RM52.

Places to Eat

For hawker food, there's a small *food centre* near the Chinese temple where you can choose between Malay food and the usual Chinese dishes. There's also a small fruit and vegetable *market* here. On the other side of this market is the *Aseanika Restoran* which does superb rotis and also serves Indonesian food. On Jalan Brooke, the *Taman Seroja* is a very pleasant open air foodstall centre, and in the Oil Town shopping centre, *The Food Stall* is a small air-con food centre.

For good curries and excellent rotis, *Bilal Restaurant* is on Jalan Persiaran Kabor, a pedestrian mall, and in the evenings the restaurant sets up tables on the pavement.

Entertainment

Miri has a surprisingly good live entertainment scene in the evenings – discos, live bands and the inevitable karaoke lounges. Most places, such as *The Cottage* and the *Pub*, are along Jalan Yu Seng.

Getting There & Away

Air MAS has services from Miri to Marudi (RM29), Mulu (RM69), Bario (RM70), Long Lellang (RM66), Limbang (RM57), Lawas (RM59), Labuan (RM57), Bintulu (RM69), Kota Kinabalu (RM104), Kuching (RM164) and Sibu (RM112).

Bus Syarikat Bas Suria operates nine daily buses between 6.30 am and 2 pm to Bintulu (RM15.40, 4½ hours). There are buses direct to Batu Niah (RM9, two hours) at 6.45, 7.45, 8 and 11 am, 1 and 3 pm. Three daily air-con buses go all the way to Sibu, taking eight hours at a cost of RM29 or RM35 air-con.

See the Getting There & Away section at the start of this chapter for details of bus services to Brunei.

MARUDI

Marudi is devoid of attractions but you may find yourself coming through here on your way to or from the interior. Unless you fly from Miri to Bario, you need to get a permit from the District Office here to head further upstream or to Gunung Mulu.

Places to Stay

The popular *Grand Hotel* (☎ 085-755712), Marudi Bazaar, is a good place four or five blocks from where the express launches dock. The cheapest room is RM14.70, but most are air-con and cost RM31.50 to RM52. The *Alisan* (☎ 085-755911) has rooms from RM17/35 and the *Hotel Zola* has air-con rooms from RM36 to RM58.

Getting There & Away

Air MAS operates flights from Marudi to Miri (RM29), Bario (RM55), Sibu (RM100), Long Lellang (RM46) and Gunung Mulu (RM40).

Bus The express boats from Kuala Baram to Marudi operate hourly and cost RM15. If heading upriver, there is an express boat to Kuala Apoh or Long Terrawan (depending on water level) daily at noon (RM18, 3½ hours).

GUNUNG MULU NATIONAL PARK

Gunung Mulu National Park is one of the most popular travel destinations in Sarawak. Unfortunately, it's also one of the most expensive places to visit, and recent moves to discourage individual travellers means that it is largely the preserve of tour groups, which come to Gunung Mulu in big numbers. Reports from travellers vary and some feel the expense worthwhile whereas others don't.

Gunung Mulu is Sarawak's largest national park, covering 529 sq km of peat swamp, sandstone, limestone and montane forests. The two major mountains are **Gunung Mulu**, a four-day trek, and **Gunung Api** with its spectacular limestone **Pinnacles**, a three-day trek. Trekking is hard going, but is the highlight of a trip to the park if you are fit and can afford it.

The park is noted for its many underground caves. Cave explorers recently discovered the largest cave chamber in the world, the **Sarawak Chamber**, and the 51-km-long **Clearwater Cave**, one of the longest in the world. The **Deer Cave** and adjoining **Lang's Cave** are an easy three-km walk from the park HQ along a plankwalk. The more spectacular Clearwater and **Wind** Caves can only be reached by boat.

Information

Permits for Gunung Mulu National Park must be obtained at the National Parks office (☎ 085-36637) in Miri. When you front up there, the first response may well be that you have to take a tour. 'Independent' is something of a dirty word at Gunung Mulu but it can be done. First you have to get a permit from the Resident's Office in Miri and then take it to the police station for clearance (both are on Jalan Raja in the centre of town). Don't mention the Penan or logging and say you are a carpenter if you have a suspect occupation like 'journalist' or 'environmental scientist'. After you have obtained the Resident's Office permit, you can then get a national park permit and book accommodation.

Unfortunately, you cannot go anywhere in the park without taking a guide. Guides' fees cost RM20 for each cave and RM35 per day for trekking. Boat hire costs RM85 for a visit to the Clearwater and Wind Caves, and RM350 for the Pinnacles trek. Unless you have a group of five or more, costs are prohibitive.

Places to Stay & Eat

A bed in one of the park's four six-bed *dorms* costs RM3. A room in the *chalets* costs RM30 or a whole chalet is RM60. There is also a VIP *resthouse* (RM60), accommodation at the bat *observatory* outside the Deer Cave (RM5 per bed) and *mountain huts* (RM2) for trekking. You can cook your own food as there are gas cookers and you can use the cutlery, crockery, pots and pans. There is a canteen at park headquarters and a small store selling basic tinned foods, bread, milk, eggs and margarine.

Private accommodation outside the park includes the excellent *Melinau Canteen* (☎ 011-291641) on the other side of the river from the park HQ. It costs RM6 per person and hearty meals are provided for RM6. If you arrive without a permit this is the place to head for.

Getting There & Away

Air It costs almost the same to fly from Miri (RM69) as it is to go by boat. There are also flights from Gunung Mulu to Marudi (RM40) and Limbang (RM40). The airstrip is a few minutes upstream from the park HQ – RM5 by boat.

Bus & Boat When coming from Miri by bus and river, take the 6 am bus to Kuala Baram if you want to get there in one day. From Kuala Baram, you can take an express launch up the Baram River to Marudi (RM12, three hours). Take the daily noon express boat from Marudi to Long Terrawan (if the river is high) for RM18, or to Kuala Apoh (if there's less water) for RM10, from where you can get another launch to Long Terrawan for RM8.

From Long Terrawan, a longboat meets the noon boat from Marudi and leaves for Gunung Mulu around 3.30 pm, arriving at around 5 pm. The cost is set at RM35 per person if there are more than four people, or RM150 for the whole boat for four or less people.

KELABIT HIGHLANDS

If you're heading out for a long trek into the interior to places such as Bario, Lio Matoh and Long Lellang, the first step is to get a permit from the Resident in Miri. You can also get these permits from the District Officer in Marudi. Bario is the place to arrange treks, and if you do a long trek to Ba Kelalan or Long Semado, you can then fly out to Lawas. Long Lellang is connected by flights to Miri.

Bario

Bario sits on a beautiful high valley floor in the Kelabit Highlands, close to the Indonesian border, and it makes an ideal base for treks into the highlands. Bario has shops where you can stock up on supplies and gifts to take to the longhouses, as does Ba Kelalan.

There are interesting treks around Bario to places such as Pa Lungan, Ba Kelalan, Long Semado and Lio Matoh. You need to be well prepared and hire local guides.

Places to Stay *Tarawe's* is the place to head for. It costs RM25 per person and they can provide details on treks in the area.

Getting There & Away MAS flies Twin Otters from Bario to Miri (RM70), usually via Marudi (RM55). The flights are very much dependent on the weather and it's not uncommon for flights to be cancelled, so make sure your schedule is not too tight.

Getting There & Away

The easiest way to reach the highlands is by air, but you can also travel along the mighty Baram River. The Baram region has been the scene of disputes between logging interests and the local Dayaks and conservationists, so permits are hard to get. There are a few regular boats from Marudi to Long Lama. From Long Lama to Long Akah is a full day's journey, and from there to Lio Matoh about the same. Normal boats sometimes do this trip, but you may have to charter a boat – count on at least RM100 per day.

LIMBANG

This town is the divisional headquarters of the Limbang District, sandwiched between Brunei and Sabah. You may well find yourself coming through on the way to or from Brunei or Gunung Mulu.

Places to Stay

If you have to spend the night, the *Muhibbah Hotel* is about the cheapest non-brothel with some rooms for RM34/40, or the *Kingstar Inn* has better rooms.

Getting There & Away

Air MAS has flights to Miri (RM45), Gunung Mulu (RM40), Labuan (RM30), Lawas (RM25) and Kota Kinabalu (RM60).

Boat An express boat goes to Lawas (RM15) at 8 am. There are frequent boats daily to Bandar Seri Begawan (RM10; 30 minutes), the capital of Brunei.

LAWAS

Like Limbang, Lawas is essentially a transit town and you may find yourself here either en route to or from Brunei or Sabah, on your way up to the Kelabit Highlands, or in order to take the short flight to Miri, skipping clean over Brunei.

Places to Stay

The friendly *Hup Guan Lodging House* (☎ 085-85362), above a pool hall opposite the town park, has large but hot rooms for RM15/20. All other hotels are air-conditioned and expensive. The *Soon Seng* (☎ 085-85871) is the pick of these with good rooms for RM45.

Getting There & Away

Air There are flights to Kota Kinabalu (RM47), Miri (RM59), Limbang (RM25), Ba Kelalan (RM46), Long Semado (RM40), Labuan (RM31) and Long Pasia (RM30).

Bus The bus to Kota Kinabalu, via Sipitang and Beaufort, leaves at 7.30 am and costs RM20. Otherwise catch a bus to Merapok, in-between Lawas and Beaufort on the Sarawak/Sabah border, for RM5 and then wait for a bus to Sipitang. At the border you have to go through immigration formalities for both states.

Boat One boat a day goes to Labuan at 7.30 am for RM20. The boat to Limbang goes at 9 am and costs RM15. To get to Brunei there is only one boat; it goes at 7.30 am and costs RM20.

Sabah

Once part of the great Brunei Empire, Sabah eventually came under the influence of the North Borneo Company after centuries of being avoided due to its unpleasant pirates. At one time, Kota Kinabalu was known as Api Api (Fire, Fire), from the pirates' tiresome habit of repeatedly burning it down. Eventually, in 1888, North Borneo, along with Brunei and the Brooke family's Sarawak, came under British protection.

Today, Sabah is an integral part of Malaysia and its economy is based chiefly on oil, timber and agriculture. The road network is good, apart from a few short horror stretches, and the eccentric little railway, which runs from Beaufort to Tenom in the south-west of the state, is a delightful jungle trip.

The principal attractions for the visitor are

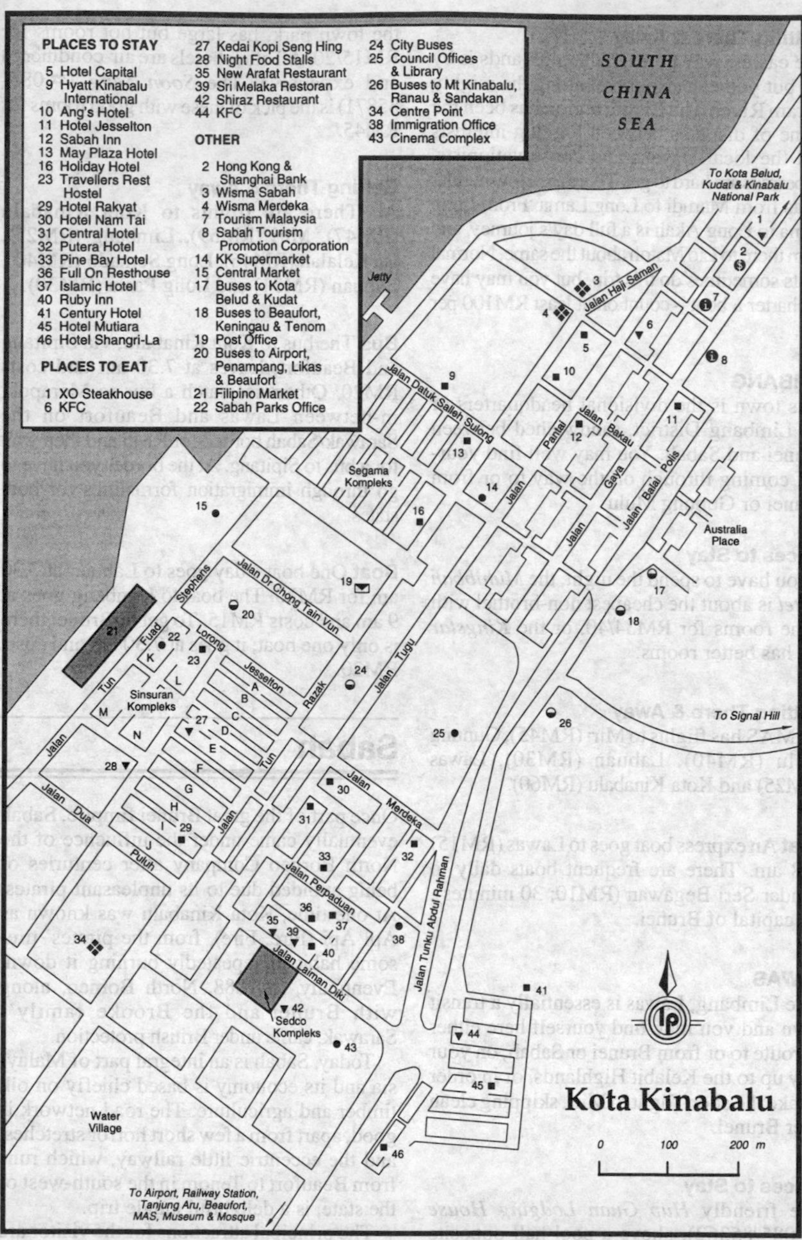
PLACES TO STAY
5 Hotel Capital
9 Hyatt Kinabalu International
10 Ang's Hotel
11 Hotel Jesselton
12 Sabah Inn
13 May Plaza Hotel
16 Holiday Hotel
23 Travellers Rest Hostel
29 Hotel Rakyat
30 Hotel Nam Tai
31 Central Hotel
32 Putera Hotel
33 Pine Bay Hotel
36 Full On Resthouse
37 Islamic Hotel
40 Ruby Inn
41 Century Hotel
45 Hotel Mutiara
46 Hotel Shangri-La
PLACES TO EAT
1 XO Steakhouse
6 KFC
27 Kedai Kopi Seng Hing
28 Night Food Stalls
35 New Arafat Restaurant
39 Sri Melaka Restoran
42 Shiraz Restaurant
44 KFC
OTHER
2 Hong Kong & Shanghai Bank
3 Wisma Sabah
4 Wisma Merdeka
7 Tourism Malaysia
8 Sabah Tourism Promotion Corporation
14 KK Supermarket
15 Central Market
17 Buses to Kota Belud & Kudat
18 Buses to Beaufort, Keningau & Tenom
19 Post Office
20 Buses to Airport, Penampang, Likas & Beaufort
21 Filipino Market
22 Sabah Parks Office
24 City Buses
25 Council Offices & Library
26 Buses to Mt Kinabalu, Ranau & Sandakan
34 Centre Point
38 Immigration Office
43 Cinema Complex
SOUTH CHINA SEA
To Kota Belud, Kudat & Kinabalu National Park
Jetty
Jalan Haji Saman
Jalan Datuk Salleh Sulong
Jalan Pantai
Jalan Bakau
Jalan Gaya
Jalan Balai Polis
Segama Kompleks
Australia Place
Jalan Dr Chong Tain Vun
Jalan Tun Fuad Stephens
Lorong Jesselton
Jalan Tun Razak
Jalan Tugu
Sinsuran Kompleks
To Signal Hill
Jalan Merdeka
Jalan Dua Puluh
Jalan Pepaduan
Jalan Laiman Diki
Jalan Tunku Abdul Rahman
Sedco Kompleks
Water Village
Kota Kinabalu
0 100 200 m
To Airport, Railway Station, Tanjung Aru, Beaufort, MAS, Museum & Mosque

the scenery and the wildlife. Mt Kinabalu is the highest mountain in South-East Asia and is well worth the trek. Other highlights include the Sepilok Orang-utan Rehabilitation centre in Sandakan, the Kinabatangan River and national parks such as Turtle Islands and Tunku Abdul Rahman, which has the best beaches in Sabah.

Unfortunately, Sabah is quite expensive. Only at Kinabalu National Park, Poring Hot Springs and Sandakan will you find accommodation that could be classed as 'budget'. Elsewhere, it's the familiar story of at least RM20 per night and often much more. But with planning it's possible to keep the costs down.

Visas & Permits

For details of the visa requirements of this region, please see the Facts for the Visitor section at the start of this chapter.

Getting There & Away

Air MAS has direct flights from Kota Kinabalu to KL and Johor Bahru in Peninsula Malaysia – see the Getting Around section at the start of this chapter for details. MAS also flies direct to Miri (RM104), Bintulu (RM127) and Kuching (RM228) in Sarawak, and to Labuan (RM52).

See the Getting There & Away section at the start of this chapter for details of flights to other countries in the region.

Land The only way to leave Sabah by land is to cross the border into Sarawak and head to Lawas, but there are no road connections from Lawas to the rest of Sarawak.

Sea From Lawas one ferry per day goes to Labuan, but few travellers bother with this route.

See the Getting There & Away section at the start of this chapter for details of boats to Brunei and Indonesia.

KOTA KINABALU

Known as Jesselton until 1963, Kota Kinabalu was razed during WW II to prevent the Japanese using it as a base. Now it's just a modern city with wide avenues and tall buildings without any of the historical charm of Kuching. All the same, KK, as the locals call it, is a pleasant city, well landscaped in parts, and its coastal location gives it an equable climate.

Orientation

The city sprawls for many km along the coast, from the international airport at Tanjung Aru to the new developments at Tanjung Lita. The centre, however, is quite small and most places are within easy walking distance.

Information

Tourist Offices Kota Kinabalu has two excellent tourist offices. Tourism Malaysia (☎ 088-211732) is on the ground floor of the Wing Onn Life Building on Jalan Segunting at the northern end of the city centre. The Sabah Tourism Promotion Corporation (☎ 088-218620) is housed in an historic building nearby at 51 Jalan Gaya.

Other Offices The Sabah Parks office (☎ 088-211585) is very conveniently situated in Block K of the Sinsuran Kompleks on Jalan Tun Fuad Stephens. This is the place to make reservations for accommodation at Mt Kinabalu, Tunku Abdul Rahman National Park, Poring Hot Springs or Pulau Tiga.

The immigration office is on the 4th floor of the tall government building, near Jalan Tunku Abdul Rahman and around the corner from the Diamond Inn.

Post & Telecommunications The GPO is right in the centre of town and has an efficient poste restante counter. For international calls, the Telekom office, in Block B of the Kompleks Kuwara, is about a 15-minute walk south of the town centre.

Foreign Embassies To find the Indonesian consulate (☎ 088-54100) go to Jalan Karamunsing, south of the city centre. This office reportedly issues one-month visas without any fuss.

Things to See

As an example of contemporary Islamic architecture at its best, the **State Mosque** is well worth a visit. It's on the outskirts of town and you'll see it if you're on your way to or from the airport.

The **Sabah Museum** is next to the State Legislative Assembly Hall on Jalan Tunku Abdul Rahman. If you'd like a view over the city, go for a stroll up **Signal Hill** at the eastern edge of the city centre above the former GPO.

There is also the **market** which is in two sections – the waterfront area, for fish, and an area in front of the harbour for fruit and vegetables. Next to the central market on the waterfront is a market known locally as the **Filipino Market**. This is mainly because all the stalls are owned by Filipinos and they sell a wide variety of handicrafts made in the Philippines.

Places to Stay

The *Travellers Rest Hostel* (☎ 088-216926) is centrally located on the 3rd floor, Block L of the Sinsuran Kompleks. It can get crowded but dorm beds at RM16, including breakfast, are not bad value.

Jack's Bed & Breakfast (☎ 088-232367), 17 Block B, 1st Floor, Jalan Karamunsing, is further out but spotlessly clean and well run. It costs RM18 for a dorm bed and breakfast. Jack's is a couple of blocks behind the Kompleks Kuwasa, out towards the state mosque, about one km past the cinema complex on Jalan Tunku Abdul Rahman.

Farida's Bed & Breakfast (☎ 088-35733), 413 Jalan Saga in Likas, is six km north of the centre of town, but is set in a large, quiet, suburban house. It costs RM12 per person in a double room, RM18 including breakfast.

The *Seaside Travellers Inn* (☎ 088-750313), H 30 Gaya Park, Jalan Penampang, is 20 km from town past the airport towards Papar. It is inconvenient for exploring KK, but it's on the beach. Good accommodation ranges from a dormitory bed that costs RM20, to single/double rooms for RM35/50 up to bungalows from RM80 to RM90.

The regular hotels include the friendly *Hotel Mutiara* (☎ 088-54544), 16 Bandaran Berjaya, not far from the Hotel Shangri-La. Clean, quiet rooms cost RM25, or RM32 to RM37 with air-con and bath. The *Islamic Hotel* (☎ 088-54325), above the restaurant of the same name at 8 Jalan Perpaduan, is also good value for KK with rooms for RM25.

For just a little more the *Hotel Rakyat* (☎ 088-211536), Block I of the Sinsuran Kompleks, is very good value and costs RM30/35 with bath and RM35 to RM55 with air-con and bath.

The *Full Hua* (☎ 088-234950) at 14 Jalan Tugu near the Central Hotel is one of the best buys in the mid-range; rooms with air-con, attached bath and TV cost RM52/62.

Places to Eat

For the variety of restaurants and the quality of food available, KK is probably the best city in Borneo. There are Chinese, Indian, Malay, Indonesian, Spanish, Filipino, Japanese, Korean and Western restaurants right in the centre of town.

For hawkers' food, there's a lively *night market* which sets up in the evenings in the vacant lot at the southern end of the Sinsuran Kompleks, which is opposite the Filipino Market. You can even get that Indonesian delicacy coto makassar (buffalo-gut soup) if you're feeling adventurous.

Centre Point has a whole collection of moderately priced eating places in the basement serving Malay and Chinese food as well as Western fast food. On the 2nd floor of the Yaohan department store are some slightly expensive *foodstalls* in squeaky clean, air-con surroundings.

Wisma Merdeka has a small, good *food centre* on the 2nd floor overlooking the sea.

For Indian food try *New Arafat Restaurant* in Block I of the Sinsuran Kompleks. This 24-hour place is run by very friendly Indians and serves excellent curries, rotis and murtabak.

In the evenings is when the mostly mid-range *restaurants* in the Sedco Kompleks, opposite the Ruby Inn, set up tables outside and hawkers' food can also be had. The *Sri Melaka*, 9 Jalan Laiman Diki, has excellent local dishes for around RM6 to RM8 for mains.

Getting There & Away

Air In Sabah and Sarawak, MAS has regular flights to Brunei (RM83), Bintulu (RM127), Kuching (RM228), Labuan (RM52), Lahad Datu (RM106), Limbang (RM60), Lawas (RM47), Kudat (RM50), Miri (RM104), Sandakan (RM83) and Tawau (RM96).

MAS (☎ 088-213555) and Philippine Airlines (☎ 088-239600) are in the Kompleks Karamunsing, about five minutes' walk south of the Hotel Shangri-La along Jalan Tunku Abdul Rahman. On the other side of Jalan Tunku Abdul Rahman is the Kompleks Kuwasa, which also contains a number of airline offices including:

Cathay Pacific (☎ 088-54733)
Royal Brunei Airlines (☎ 088-242193)
Singapore Airlines (☎ 088-55444)
Thai Airways (☎ 088-232896)

Bus There is no main bus station in KK; instead, there are a few places from where buses, minibuses and taxis depart. Most of the long-distance buses leave from the open area south-east of the council offices along Jalan Tunku Abdul Rahman.

All minibuses leave when full and there are frequent early morning departures. There are fewer departures later in the day, and don't count on departures for long-haul destinations in the afternoon. Some examples of minibus fares from KK are:

Beaufort (90 km) – regular departures up to about 3 pm, two hours on a very good road, RM5
Keningau (128 km) – regular departures to about 1 pm, about 2½ hours on a road which is surfaced all the way, RM10
Kota Belud (77 km) – departures until 3 pm, two hours, RM5
Kudat (122 km) – departures to about 1 pm, three hours, RM12
Lawas (195 km) – buses depart at 7.30 am and 2 pm, five hours on a paved road except for the 47-km stretch between Beaufort and Sipitang, RM20
Ranau (156 km) – early morning departures, the last bus leaves at 12.30 pm and takes about two hours. All buses pass Kinabalu National Park, RM10
Sandakan (386 km) – minibus departures early morning only, about six hours for RM35. The big air-con buses, operated by Mizume Enterprise and Lim Sim Siau, depart at 7.30 am and 1.30 pm. A recent discount war has had the price as low as RM20. The road is sealed all the way.
Tenom (154 km) – regular departures on a good sealed road, RM25 by taxi, RM20 by minibus

For Kinabalu National Park (RM10, 1½ hours), take the minibus for Ranau or Sandakan and get off at the park headquarters, which is right by the side of the road.

Train The railway station is five km south of the city centre at Tanjung Aru, close to the airport. There are daily trains to Beaufort and Tenom at 8 and 11 am; the trip takes four hours to Beaufort, seven hours to Tenom. Minibuses are quicker and easier.

Taxi Besides the minibuses, there are share taxis to most places. They also go when full and their fares are at least 25% higher than the minibuses. Their big advantage is that they are faster and more comfortable.

Boat There are twice-daily boats to Labuan (RM28 in economy, RM33 in 1st class) from the jetty behind the Hyatt Hotel. The *Duta Muhibbah* leaves at 8 am, *Labuan Express* at 1 pm and the *Express Kinabalu* (☎ 088-219810) at 10 am. Discounting has seen the price as low as RM15.

Getting Around

To/From the Airport To get to the airport take a 15-minute taxi ride for RM10, or a red 'Putatan' bus for 65 sen from Jalan Tunku Abdul Rahman and ask to be dropped at the airport.

Taxis operate on a coupon system and prices are listed at the airport desk.

Taxi Local taxis are plentiful in the extreme. They are not metered so it's a matter of negotiating the fare before you set off. Taxi stands are all over town, but most can be found in the large area between the council offices and the GPO.

AROUND KOTA KINABALU

Tunku Abdul Rahman National Park

The park has a total area of 4929 hectares and is made up of the offshore islands of Gaya, Mamutik, Manukan, Sapi and Sulug. Only a short boat ride from the city centre, they offer good beaches, crystal-clear waters and a wealth of tropical corals and marine life. If you want beaches in Sabah, the islands have some of the best and they are certainly the most accessible.

Places to Stay & Eat Very good chalets, ranging from RM112 to RM200 per night, are available on Manukan and Mamutik – book at the Sabah Parks office. Most budget travellers day trip from KK. The park headquarters and the most developed facilities, including a restaurant, are on Manukan.

Getting There & Away Coral Island Tours have boats from behind the Hyatt Hotel to the islands at 10 am, returning at 3.30 pm, from Monday to Friday. On the weekend boats leave at 9, 10 and 11 am and return at 2 and 4 pm. It costs RM16 return to any of the islands.

Sea Quest (☎ 088-230943), B207 Wisma Merdeka, also has ferries to Manukan, Sapi, Mamutik and Gaya for RM15, or to Police Bay on Gaya for RM20.

RAFFLESIA FOREST RESERVE

The highway from Kota Kinabalu to Tambunan and the central valley region crosses the forested Crocker Range, and near the top is the Rafflesia Forest Reserve, devoted to the world's largest flower. The Rafflesia is a parasitic plant that is hidden within its host, the stems of jungle vines, until it bursts into bloom and grows up to one metre in diameter. The Rafflesia Information Centre, on the highway 59 km from Kota Kinabalu, has interesting displays and information. From the centre, trails lead into the forest where the rafflesias can be found in season.

Places to Stay

Gunung Emas Highlands Resort (☎ 011-811562), 52 km down the KK-Tambunan road, is perched on the side of a mountain only seven km from the information centre. The views are superb and the climate refreshingly mild, if not downright cold. This mid-range resort has a variety of simple accommodation for RM40 per double, or four-bed bunk rooms are RM20 per person. Hilltop cabins built around tree trunks are RM60. The restaurant is overrun with day trippers on weekends.

Getting There & Away

From KK take a Tambunan or Keningau minibus to the reserve or the resort for RM8.

TAMBUNAN

Tambunan is an agricultural service town about 90 km from KK. This was the stamping ground of Mat Salleh, who rebelled against the British late last century.

Tambunan can be used as a base to climb **Mt Trus Madi**, Sabah's 2nd-highest peak and a much more difficult proposition than Mt Kinabalu.

Places to Stay

The rundown *Tambunan Village Resort Centre* charges RM25 for a double room in the longhouse and also has chalets for RM35 and motel rooms for RM30. The *Government Rest House* costs RM40 per person.

Getting There & Away

There are regular minbuses plying between Tambunan and KK, Ranau, Keningau and Tenom.

BEAUFORT

Beaufort is a quiet little provincial town on the Padas River with a fair amount of charm, but the only reason to come here is to catch the train to Tenom.

From Beaufort you can continue on to Menumbok where frequent ferries go to Labuan. Going south to Lawas in Sarawak, you pass through Sipitang, which has cheap accommodation and early morning boats to

Labuan, and Merapok on the Sabah/Sarawak border.

Places to Stay

The three hotels in town are of the same standard and have air-con rooms with TV and attached bathrooms. They show a surprising lack of competitive spirit and all charge RM30/36 for singles/doubles. The *Hotel Beaufort* (☎ 087-211911) and the *Beaufort Inn* are near each other in town, while the *Mandarin Inn* (☎ 087-212798) is over the bridge across the river. The Hotel Beaufort wins by a nose for position.

Getting There & Away

Bus There are frequent minibus departures for KK (RM5, two hours) and along a dirt road to Menumbok (RM8, one hour) until early afternoon. Buses to Lawas from KK pass through Beaufort, or if you miss them, minibuses go along the bone-crunching road to Sipitang (RM5, 1½ hours), and from there infrequent buses go to Merapok.

Train It's a spectacular railway trip between Beaufort and Tenom, where the line follows the Padas River through steamy jungle. At times the dense jungle forms a bridge over the narrow track. The railcar is quicker and more comfortable and costs RM8.35, while the diesel train costs RM2.75. Book as soon as you arrive in Beaufort, or at the Tanjung Aru station (☎ 088-52536, 54611) in KK. Departures are listed in the table below.

PULAU LABUAN

Off the coast from Menumbok, Labuan is one of the departure points for the trip to Brunei. Labuan is a Federal Territory and is governed directly from KL. The island acts as a duty-free centre and as such attracts many day-tripping Bruneians, as well as Malaysians, for quick shopping and sin sprees.

Places to Stay

The *Pantai View Hotel* (☎ 087-411339) on Jalan Bunga is a decent hotel and large RM25 rooms on the top floor are the best value around. Otherwise air-con rooms with attached bath and TV cost RM40 to RM50.

Around the corner on Jalan OKK Awang Besar, *Hotel Sri Villa* (☎ 087-416369) has large rooms for RM35 or smaller rooms for RM30. Air-con rooms range from RM40 to RM56 with attached bath and TV. The *Melati Inn* (☎ 087-416307) has small air-con rooms with common bathroom for RM35, but most rooms have attached bathroom and cost RM43 to RM48.

Getting There & Away

Air There are flights to Kota Kinabalu (RM52), KL (RM372), Kuching (RM199), Miri (RM66), Lawas (RM31) and Limbang (RM30).

Boat Boats to Kota Kinabalu depart at 8.30 am, 1 and 3 pm. The normal fare is RM28 but discounting may apply. The car ferry to

Beaufort-Tenom

Day	*Time*				
Mon-Sat	8.25 (R)	10.50 am (D)	noon (G)	1.55 (D)	3.50 pm (R)
Sun	6.45 (D)	10.50 am (D)	2.30 (D)	4.05 pm (R)	

Tenom-Beaufort

Day	*Time*				
Mon-Sat	6.40 (R)	7.30 (D)	8 am (G)	1.40 (D)	4 pm (R)
Sun	7.20 (R)	7.55 am (D)	12.10 (D)	3.05 pm (D)	

R = Railcar, D = Diesel, G = Goods Train

Menumbok (RM5 for passengers, 1½ hours) leaves at 8 am and 1 pm. Frequent small launches also go to Menumbok (RM10, 30 minutes) between 7.30 am and 5 pm. From Menumbok, minibuses go to Beaufort and Kota Kinabalu (RM15, two hours).

From Labuan you can also get ferries to Sipitang (RM20), Limbang (RM20) and Lawas (RM20).

See the Getting There & Away section at the start of this chapter for details of boats to Brunei.

TENOM

Tenom is the home of the friendly Murut people, most of whom are farmers. It's a very pleasant rural town, and is also the railhead on the line from Tanjung Aru (KK).

Despite the peaceful setting, there's absolutely nothing to do in the town itself. Just outside of town, the **Tenom Agricultural Research Station** makes an interesting diversion, and the train ride to Beaufort is highly recommended.

Places to Stay

The cheapest hotel in town is the *Hotel Syn Nam Tai* on the main street. It's a basic Chinese cheapie and has rooms for RM15/20 with common bath. The Indian-run *Sabah Hotel* is a definite step up and rooms costs RM20 or RM34 with air-con. The *Hotel Kim San* (☎ 087-735485), set back from the main road, has rundown air-con rooms for RM25 a double. Right across the road is the *Hotel Tenom* (☎ 087-735567), which has large, airy, carpeted rooms with air-con, bath and TV for RM30 a double.

Places to Eat

As usual there are plenty of Chinese kedai kopis all over town selling basic Chinese food.

For good Indian food, rotis and murtabak try the *Bismillah Restaurant* in the Sabah Hotel or the *Restoran Istimewa*, which sets up tables outside in the evening.

Getting There & Away

There are plenty of minibuses from Tenom to Keningau (RM5) and fewer to KK and Tomani. Taxis also make the run to Keningau (RM5) and on to KK (RM25). The 46-km train journey to Beaufort is recommended.

KOTA BELUD

The town is the venue of Sabah's largest and most colourful **tamu**. Tamus are local markets that attract villagers from the surrounding area. The tamu takes place every Sunday – get there as early as possible.

Places to Stay

The only hotel in town is the *Hotel Kota Belud* (☎ 088-976576), which costs about RM30/36 with common bathroom – no bargain. The only other accommodation, and the best place to stay, is the small *Government Rest House* (☎ -67532), one km from the bus station. It costs RM40 per person.

Getting There & Away

Minibuses go to KK (RM5, 2 hours) and Kudat (RM5, 2 hours).

KUDAT

Kudat is right at the north-eastern tip of Sabah and gets very few tourists. Some good beaches can be found outside of Kudat, but there are no facilities and you have to hire a taxi to reach them. There are Rungus longhouses at and around **Matunggung** on the way to Kudat.

Places to Stay & Eat

The cheapest is the *Restoran dan Hotel Islamik*. Large, clean rooms with fan cost RM15/20 for singles/doubles. The management is quite friendly and the restaurant downstairs does decent roti and murtabak. All the other hotels are air-con mid-range places. The *Hotel Sunrise* (☎ 088-61517) has rooms for RM28 or RM40 with bath and TV, and the *Hotel Kudat* (☎ 088-61379) is similar. A better buy is the newer *Hotel Kinabalu* (☎ 088-62493) in the new section of town near the golf course.

Getting There & Away

Several minibuses a day make the four-hour trip from KK for RM12.

MT KINABALU

Sabah's number-one attraction is the highest mountain in South-East Asia with views from the top which can stretch all the way to the north coast, Kalimantan to the south and the islands of the Philippines to the north-east. Getting to the top of the 4101-metre peak is not so much a climb as a steep and stiff walk. It's well worth it with fantastic views and some very interesting plant life.

The climb to the top requires an overnight halt on the way, so bring plenty of warm clothes – you can also hire sleeping bags. A RM10 climbing permit is required for Mt Kinabalu; it's RM2 for students. Hiring a guide is compulsory and the guide's fee is RM25 per day for one to three people, RM28 for four to six people and RM30 for seven to eight (the maximum). Attach yourself to a group to save costs.

On the first day, you get to within about 700 metres of the summit and there are numerous huts. In the morning, you leave well before dawn to be at the top before the clouds roll in around mid-morning. The trip back down to the park HQ takes the rest of the day.

It's well worth spending a day or more exploring the well-marked trails around park HQ's. At 11.15 am each day, there is a guided walk which starts from the administration building and lasts for one to two hours. It's well worth taking and follows an easy path.

At the administration building, a slide and video show is presented from Friday to Monday at 7.30 pm and gives an excellent introduction to the mountain.

Places to Stay & Eat

Park Headquarters The accommodation and catering at the park headquarters is excellent and well organised. It's in a beautiful setting with a magnificent view of Mt Kinabalu when the clouds are not obscuring the slopes and summits. You should make advance reservations for accommodation at the Sabah Parks office in KK.

Dormitory accommodation costs RM10, or RM5 for students with official ID, at the *Old Hostel* or the *New Hostel*. Both hostels are clean and comfortable, and have cooking facilities and a dining area with an open fireplace. Blankets and pillows are provided free of charge. The rest of the accommodation at park headquarters is in quite luxurious, expensive chalets ranging from RM50 up to RM360.

The cheaper and more popular of the two restaurants is known as *Kinabalu Dalsam*. It's down below reception and offers Malay, Chinese and Western food at reasonable prices. There's also a small shop which sells a limited range of tinned foods, chocolate, beer, spirits, cigarettes, T-shirts, bread, eggs and margarine.

The other *restaurant* is in the main administration building, just past the hostels. It's more expensive than the Dalsam though the food is quite good. Both restaurants are open from 7 am to 9 pm.

On the Mountain On your way up to the summit, you will have to stay overnight at one of the mountain huts or the 54-bed *Laban Rata Rest House* at Panar Laban, which costs RM25 per person in four-bed rooms. It has electricity, hot water and a restaurant.

The mountain huts are equipped with wooden bunks and mattresses, gas stoves, cooking facilities and some cooking utensils. Get sleeping bags from the resthouse. Take a torch and your own toilet paper. Don't expect a warm Swiss-type chalet with a blazing fire at these huts. They're just tin sheds with the absolute minimum of facilities.

There are three huts at 3300 metres: the 12-bed *Waras* and *Panar Laban* huts and the 44-bed *Guntin Lagadan Hut*. There's also the 10-bed *Sayat-Sayat Hut* at 3750 metres. A bed in any of these huts costs RM10 per person, RM5 for students.

The huts at 3300 metres are the most popular as it's as far as most people can comfortably get in one day. There's a canteen in the nearby Laban Rata Rest House which is not only open for regular meals but also opens from 2 to 3 am so you can grab some breakfast before attempting the summit. It's *very* cold in the early mornings (around 0°C, or 32°F!), so take warm clothing with you.

Getting There & Away

There are several minibuses daily from KK to Ranau which depart up to about 1 pm. The 85-km trip as far as park headquarters takes about 1½ to two hours and the fare is around RM10. If you're heading back towards KK, minibuses pass the park HQ's until the afternoon but the best time to catch them is between about 8 am and noon.

There is a large bus to Sandakan (RM25, four hours) which passes park headquarters around 9 am. There are also other minibuses which pass Kinabalu National Park on their way to Ranau (RM3) and Sandakan, but the last one goes by before 2 pm.

RANAU

Ranau is just a small provincial town halfway between KK and Sandakan, and 22 km from Kinabalu National Park. Nothing much ever happens but it has a friendly population.

Few travellers stay overnight here as the big attraction is Poring Hot Springs, about 19 km north of the town.

Places to Stay

The *Hotel Ranau* (☎ 088-875531), opposite the petrol stations, is the first place you see when entering the town. Rooms start at RM30/45 with fan. *Hotel Kinabalu* is similar.

Getting There & Away

Minibuses and taxis depart for Kota Kinabalu daily up to about 4 pm, cost RM10 and take about 2½ hours. Air-con buses leave for Sandakan (RM20, four hours) from around 7.30 am until noon. Minibuses also go to Sandakan, but can take a long time to fill up in the afternoon.

PORING HOT SPRINGS

The Poring Hot Springs are also part of the Kinabalu National Park but are 43 km away from the park HQ's and 19 km north of Ranau.

There are tubs for soaking in, walking trails for a bit of exercise and an excellent jungle canopy walkway for a monkey's-eye view of the forest.

Places to Stay & Eat

You should make advance reservations for accommodation at Poring Hot Springs at the Sabah Parks office in KK.

The 24-bed *Poring Hostel* costs RM10 per person (RM5 for students); blankets and pillows are provided free of charge. There's a camping ground which costs RM2 per night where pillows and blankets can be hired for 50 sen each. There are also more expensive cabins from RM60 to RM100.

There are cooking facilities at Poring but you should take your own food from Ranau, or there are small inexpensive eating places just outside the park gate.

Getting There & Away

There are share taxis to Poring Hot Springs, for RM3 on weekends. On weekdays, you may have to hitch (difficult) or charter a taxi (RM15) as there are fewer minibuses. It is easier to arrange something when leaving – ask the rangers or ask at the shops opposite the park.

SANDAKAN

The former capital city of Sabah, Sandakan is today a major commercial centre where the products of the interior – rattan, timber, rubber, copra, palm oil and even birds' nests from the **Gomantong Caves**, which are on the other side of the bay from Sandakan and about 20 km inland – are brought to be loaded onto boats for export.

The main attractions, however, are well outside the city. At **Sepilok** is one of the world's three orang-utan sanctuaries and it's well worth a visit. Offshore, there's one of the world's few **turtle sanctuaries** where giant turtles come to lay their eggs.

Information

The Sabah Parks office (☎ 089-273453) is on the 9th floor of Wisma Khoo Siak Chew at the end of Lebuh Tiga. This is where you need to come to make a reservation to visit the Turtle Islands National Park.

Places to Stay

Most travellers head straight for *Uncle Tan's* (☎ 089-531639) out at Batu 17½, Labuk Rd, 29 km from town on the main highway. It is only a few km from Sepilok and buses can drop you off there. The accommodation is simple but the atmosphere is very friendly and it's a great place to stay. It costs RM15 for a dorm bed, which includes a huge breakfast, or RM20 including all meals. As a sideline Tan runs very low-key (and cheap) trips to the Turtle Islands, a jungle camp he has on the lower Kinabatangan River, and to Tanjung Aru fishing village.

Borneo Bed & Breakfast (☎ 089-216381), 2nd Floor, Lot 12, Block E, Bandar Kim Fung, Mile 4, Jalan Labuk, is closer to the town though not close enough to be convenient. It is good value at RM15 per person, or a double for a couple is RM25. Breakfast is RM5 per person. It is behind the big Capital Supermarket on the main road, seven km from town.

All the other so-called cheap accommodation is in the centre of town and is no great bargain. The *Hotel Hung Wing* (☎ 089-218895) located on Jalan Tiga is a middle-range hotel with some cheaper rooms for RM25/30. Other air-con rooms range from RM44 to RM65. The *Merlin Hotel* (☎ 089-213903) is a friendly hotel and has some cheaper, rundown rooms with attached bath for RM25/40. The *Mayfair Hotel* (☎ 089-219855) at 24 Jalan Pryer is the best bet for an air-con room with attached bath, costing RM32/40.

Places to Eat

For good Malay food, try the *Habeeb Restoran* on Jalan Pryer. They do excellent murtabak and also have an air-con room upstairs. There are a couple of similar places close by including the *Cita Rasa* and *Restoran Gane*.

For a Western breakfast or snack, there are a few choices. The best is probably *Fat Cat* on Jalan Tiga. Another possibility is the *Apple Fast Food* restaurant on the ground floor of the Hotel Nak on Jalan Edinburgh.

Getting There & Away

Air Sandakan is on the MAS domestic network and there are regular flights to KK (RM83), Lahad Datu (RM48) and Tawau (RM61).

Bus All long-distance minibuses leave from the area next to the footbridge over Jalan Tiga; local minibuses leave from the area next to the old Port Authority building. There are buses to KK which cost RM35 and take six hours. You can take the same transport to Kinabalu National Park headquarters for RM25.

Minibuses to Ranau cost RM20. There is one large Bungaraya Co bus for Lahad Datu and Tawau daily at 5.30 am, but there are also many minibuses which leave throughout the morning to Lahad Datu, some going on to Tawau. The trip to Lahad Datu takes about three hours and costs RM15.

Getting Around

If you're arriving or leaving by air, the airport is about 11 km from the city. To get to the airport from the town centre take a Batu 7 airport minibus, which stops on the road outside the terminal. A taxi to or from the airport costs RM15.

AROUND SANDAKAN

Sepilok Orang-utan Rehabilitation Centre

This is one of only three orang-utan sanctuaries in the world, and it is one of Sabah's main tourist attractions. Apes are brought to Sepilok to be rehabilitated to forest life. About 20 still return regularly to be fed but it's unlikely you'll see anywhere near this number at feeding time – three or four is a more likely number.

The apes are fed from two platforms, one

in the middle of the forest (platform B) about 30-minutes walk from the centre, and the other close to the headquarters (platform A). The latter platform is for the juvenile orang-utans and they are fed daily at 10 am and 2 pm. At platform B, the adolescent apes which have been returned to the forest are fed daily at 11 am. For this feeding, the rangers leave from in front of the Nature Education Centre at 10.30 am daily.

In addition to the orang-utans, there are a couple of Sumatran rhinos at the centre and some fine walks through the forest. The visiting hours at the centre are Saturday to Thursday from 9 am to noon and 2 to 4 pm, and on Friday from 9 to 11.30 am and 2 to 4 pm. Admission is RM10 (RM1 for Malaysians).

Some find the crowded, camera-snapping sessions at platform A a bit too much like a zoo, but Sepilok is well worth a visit.

Getting There & Away Sepilok is 25 km from central Sandakan. Take the blue Labuk bus marked 'Sepilok Batu 14' from the local bus stand next to the Central Market on the waterfront (RM1.50, 45 minutes).

Turtle Islands National Park

The Taman Pulau Penyu comprises three small islands 32 km north of Sandakan. Pulau Selingan, Pulau Bakungan Kecil and Pulau Gulisan are visited by marine turtles which come ashore to lay their eggs, mostly between the months of August and October each year.

Places to Stay It's not possible to visit the islands on a day trip, so any excursion involves staying overnight. The only accommodation is at *Sabah Parks Chalet* on Pulau Selingan, which costs RM30 per person per night. Bookings must be made in advance at the Sabah Parks office in Sandakan as facilities are limited.

Getting There & Away The Sabah Parks office can arrange transport to the islands and will try to put individuals in with a group to share the cost of the boat – RM350 or RM85 per person.

Uncle Tan (see the earlier Sandakan Places to Stay section) organises trips out to the islands for RM80 for transport, and he's as cheap as you'll find.

KINABATANGAN RIVER

The Kinabatangan River is one of the main rivers in Sabah and flows generally north-east to enter the sea east of Sandakan. Although logging is widespread along the upper reaches of the river, below the Sandakan-Lahad Datu road the jungle is relatively untouched. It is an ideal place to observe the wildlife of Borneo and sightings of the native proboscis monkeys are common along the banks in the morning and evening.

This area is virtually inaccessible but Uncle Tan (see the Sandakan Places to Stay section) has a jungle camp about an hour downstream from the Sandakan-Lahad Datu road. While it is extremely basic, it does give the traveller the opportunity to get out of the towns and stay in the jungle. He charges RM15 per person per day for accommodation and meals – it's not the Hilton but is perfectly adequate – and RM130 for return transport from Sandakan, so obviously it's better if you have a few days to spare. Many travellers come to the camp with the intention of staying a couple of days, but stay much longer.

LAHAD DATU

Lahad Datu is a busy little plantation and timber service town of 20,000 people. There are very few tourists and the only reason for visiting is if you are going to or from the excellent Danum Valley Field Centre.

The town is full of Filipino and Indonesian migrants and refugees, and the streets are full of women trying to make a few ringgit selling cigarettes.

Places to Stay

The cheapest place that isn't a brothel is the *Rumah Tumpangan Malaysia* (☎ 089-83358), in the side street opposite the Esso station in the centre of town. It is seedy but clean enough with rooms for RM20 to RM30. The *Ocean Hotel* (☎ 089-81700) on the main street opposite the Hap Seng building is much better with good-sized rooms for RM38/48 with air-con and attached bath.

Getting There & Away

Air MAS operate services between Lahad Datu and KK (RM106), Sandakan (RM48) and Tawau (RM40).

Bus The long-distance minibuses leave from the vacant lot near the waterfront. There are frequent departures for Sandakan (RM15, 3½ hours), Semporna (RM8, 2½ hours) and Tawau (RM8, 2½ hours).

DANUM VALLEY FIELD CENTRE

On the Segama River, 85 km west of Lahad Datu, this field centre has been set up by the Sabah Foundation and a number of private companies, many of them logging companies, to provide facilities for research, education and recreation in an untouched rainforest area. Most of Borneo's mammals can be found at the field centre and there are more than 50 km of walking trails through the jungle.

Information

It's necessary to get a permit (RM25) and to make bookings in advance with the Innoprise Corporation office (☎ 088-243245), Sadong Jaya, in KK; failing that, book at the Innoprise office (☎ 089-81092) on the 2nd floor of the Hap Seng building on the main street in Lahad Datu.

Places to Stay & Eat

Lahad Datu may be put beyond the reach of budget travellers with the building of a new luxury resort, away from the field centre. There are plans to then make the field centre off limits, but until then the 30-bed *hostel* costs RM36 and the *resthouse* costs RM60/110 (student discounts are available). Meals are provided for RM36 per day.

Getting There & Away

A Sabah Foundation vehicle leaves the centre on Monday, Wednesday and Friday at 9 am and returns from Lahad Datu on the same days at around 3 pm – the one-way cost is RM30.

SEMPORNA

Semporna, between Lahad Datu and Tawau, has a hotel/restaurant **stilt village** and there's a cultured **pearl farm** off the coast.

About the only time you're likely to come through here is if you are on a diving trip to **Sipadan Island**, off the coast to the south-east. Sipadan is billed as one of the world's great diving spots. It is also the centre of a dispute between Malaysia and Indonesia, which both claim the island. Sipadan has three diving resorts – all very expensive.

Places to Stay

The main hotel in Semporna is the very nice *Dragon Inn Hotel* with thatched rooms built out over the water for RM68/78. The *Hotel Semporna* is cheaper but poor value with rooms at RM45 and RM55.

Getting There & Away

There are plenty of minibuses between Semporna and Lahad Datu for RM8 (2½ hours, 160 km) and between Semporna and Tawau for RM4 (1½ hours, 110 km).

TAWAU

A mini boom town on the south-eastern corner of Sabah close to the Indonesian border, Tawau is a provincial capital and the centre for export of the products of the interior – timber, rubber, Manila hemp, cocoa, copra and tobacco.

There's precious little to do or see in Tawau – it's just a town you pass through on the way to or from Tarakan in Kalimantan.

Information

The MAS office (☎ 089-765533) is in the Wisma SASCO, close to the centre of town. Bouraq, the Indonesian feeder airline, uses Merdeka Travel (☎ 089-771927) at 41 Jalan Dunlop as its agent. The Indonesian consulate (☎ 089-765930) is on Jalan Apas, some distance from the centre on the main road coming into town.

Places to Stay

For rock-bottom accommodation, the *Penginapan Kinabalu*, an older-style, seedy lodging house, costs RM15/20 with a bit of bargaining. The *Hotel Malaysia* is similar and bare but clean rooms with fan cost RM20 and air-con rooms cost RM30.

Much better is the very clean, well-run *Hotel Soon Yee* (☎ 089-772447). A fan room will cost you RM20 and air-con rooms with bath start at RM30. The *Loong Hotel* (☎ 089-765308), 3868 Jalan Wing Lok, is the best bet for good mid-range facilities. Spotlessly clean air-con rooms with attached bathroom and TV are RM35/45.

Places to Eat

For good Malay food, try the *Restoran Sinar Murni* – good chicken curry here.

For hawker food, there are the *stalls* in the Central Market and at night, the *foodstalls* along the road near the waterfront get going and are definitely the best places to eat.

For a bit of a splurge, the restaurant in the *Hotel Emas* has a steamboat buffet in the evening and the coffee shop in the *Marco Polo Hotel* has a breakfast buffet for RM14.

Getting There & Away

Air MAS has flights between Tawau and KK (RM96), Sandakan (RM74) and Lahad Datu (RM40).

See the Getting There & Away section at the start of this chapter for details of flights to Indonesia.

Bus There are frequent minibuses to Semporna (RM4) and Lahad Datu (RM15). There's also a large bus daily at 5.30 am which goes all the way to Sandakan.

Boat See the Getting There & Away section at the start of this chapter for details of boats to Indonesia.

Myanmar

Myanmar, formerly Burma, is one of the world's least Western-influenced countries – even China has Coca-Cola today. For the visitor Myanmar is a fascinating glimpse of a culturally unique country which exists in a social, political and economic time warp. It is virtually sealed off from the outside world save for a steady stream of black market commodities and a trickle of visitors.

Although a visit to Myanmar involves a fair bit of red tape and initial expense, the good news is that 30-day tourist visas are now being issued. For many, the effort is well worthwhile; this is a country with which nearly every visitor becomes enthralled.

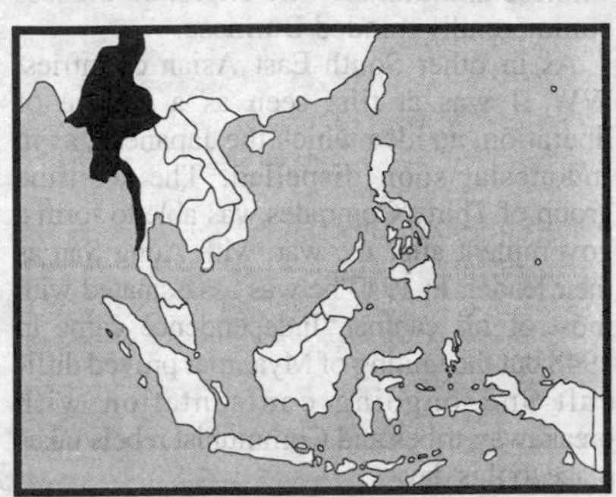

Should You Visit Myanmar?

Anyone contemplating visiting Myanmar should bear in mind any small contribution they make to the nation's economy may allow Myanmar's repressive, inept government to stay in power that little bit longer.

If you'd like to find out more about what's really happening in Myanmar, write to the Burmese Relief Centre, PO Box 48, Chiang Mai University, Chiang Mai, Thailand.

On the other hand, keeping the Burmese isolated from international witnesses to the internal oppression may also help to cement government control over the Burmese people. This is why the Ne Win government restricted tourism in the first place. It's your choice!

Facts about the Country

HISTORY

The Mons were the first people known to have lived in the area and their influence extended into what is now Thailand. The Mons were pushed back when the Burmese, who now comprise two-thirds of the total population, arrived from the north.

King Anawrahta came to the throne of Pagan (now called Bagan) in 1044, and, with his conquest of the kingdom of Thaton in 1057, inaugurated the golden age of Burmese history. The spoils he brought back took Pagan to fabled heights and he also introduced Buddhism and the Burmese alphabet. Today, Myanmar is 90% Buddhist, although belief in *nats*, or animal spirits, still persists.

Despite Anawrahta's efforts, Myanmar had entered a period of decline by the 13th century, helped on its way by the vast amounts of money and effort squandered on making Pagan such an incredible monument to man's vanity. Kublai Khan hastened the decline by ransacking Pagan in 1287, at that time said to contain 13,000 pagodas. In the following centuries, the pattern of Burmese history was basically one of conflicts with kingdoms in neighbouring Siam and a series of petty tribal wars.

The coming of Europeans to the East had little influence on the Burmese, who were too busy fighting to be interested in trade. Unfortunately for the Burmese, their squabbles eventually encroached on the Raj in neighbouring Bengal and the British moved in to keep their borders quiet. In three moves in 1824, 1852 and 1883, the British took over all of Myanmar. They built railroads, made

Myanmar the world's greatest rice exporter and developed large teak markets. Less commendably, they brought in large numbers of Chinese and Indians who exploited the less commercially minded Burmese.

As in other South-East Asian countries, WW II was at first seen as a chance of liberation, an idea which the Japanese, as in Indonesia, soon dispelled. The wartime group of Thirty Comrades was able to form a government after the war, with Aung San as their leader. In 1947 he was assassinated with most of his cabinet. Independence came in 1948 but the uniting of Myanmar proved difficult and ongoing confrontation with breakaway tribes and Communist rebels takes place to this day.

U Nu led the country during the early years of independence, attempting to establish a Buddhist socialism whose objective was 'Social Nibbana'. In 1962, General Ne Win led that most unusual event, a left-wing army takeover. After throwing out U Nu's government and imprisoning U Nu for four years, Ne Win set the country on the 'Burmese Way to Socialism'. The path was all downhill. He nationalised everything in sight, including retail shops, and quickly crippled the country. The Burmese saw their naturally well-endowed economy stumble as exports of everything plummeted.

It has been said that the three major Burmese industries are rice, teak and smuggling but for a few years, in the early '80s, the economy did improve slightly. Then world commodity prices slumped and Myanmar's already crumbling economy slid even faster downhill.

Finally, in 1987 and 1988, after a long period of suffering, the Burmese people had had enough of their incompetent, arrogant government. They packed the streets in huge demonstrations, insisting that Ne Win had to go. He finally did go in July 1988 but in the following month massive confrontations between pro-democracy demonstrators and the military contributed to an estimated 3000 deaths over a six-week period.

Ne Win's National Unity Party (formerly the Burmese Socialist Programme Party) was far from ready to give up control and the public protests continued as two wholly unacceptable Ne Win stooges followed him. The third Ne Win successor came to power after a military coup in September 1988 which, it is generally believed, was organised by Ne Win.

The new State Law & Order Restoration Council (SLORC) established martial law under the leadership of General Saw Maung, Commander-in-Chief of the armed forces, and promised to hold democratic National Assembly elections in May 1989.

The opposition quickly formed a coalition party and called it the National League for Democracy (NLD) and in the following months it campaigned tirelessly.

The long-suppressed Burmese population rallied around the charismatic NLD spokesperson Aung San Suu Kyi, daughter of national hero Aung San. Nervous, the SLORC tried to appease the masses with new roads and paint jobs in Yangon (Rangoon), and then attempted to interfere in the electoral process by shifting villages from one part of the country to another.

In spite of all preventive measures, the National Unity Party lost the May National Assembly elections to the NLD. However, the military refused to allow the opposition to assume their parliamentary seats and arrested most of the party leadership, including Aung San Suu Kyi, who was awarded the Nobel Prize in 1991.

Martial law continues and all signs indicate that the current government will never hand over the reins of power peacefully. Whether or not the majority of Burmese can mount an effective opposition to their military rulers remains to be seen.

GEOGRAPHY

Myanmar covers an area of 671,000 sq km. It is sandwiched between Thailand and Bangladesh, with India and China bordering to the north. The centre of the country is marked by wide rivers and expansive plains, and mountains rise to the east along the Thai border and to the north, where you find the easternmost end of the Himalayas.

Myanmar possesses huge stands of teak

and other hardwoods but, if timber smuggling to China, Thailand and other countries continues at current rates, mass deforestation will be inevitable. Even if the central government had the means to curb the illegal timber trade (they don't, since most of the forests lie in ethnic rebel territory), they would probably sell it off quickly anyway to increase or maintain the Tatmadaw, or military strength, as they are doing with oil and other resources.

One of the cursory changes instituted by the government since the 1988 uprising has been a long list of geographic name changes in an effort to further purge the country of its colonial past. The official name of the country has been changed from the Socialist Republic of the Union of Burma to the Union of Myanmar.

According to the government, 'Myanmar' doesn't identify the nation with the Burman (Bamar) ethnic group. 'Burma' is said to be an English corruption of the Burmese term for that ethnic group. Inexplicably, the domestic Burma Airways is now Myanma Airways, with no 'r', while the international branch is called Myanmar Airways International. In all other cases, the new Romanised versions are phonetically closer to the everyday Burmese pronunciation.

Old Name	New Name
Akyab	Sittwe
Burma	Myanmar
Bassein	Pathein
Irrawaddy River	Ayeyarwady River
Mandalay	no change
Maymyo	Pyin Oo Lwin
Moulmein	Mawlamyine
Myohaung	Mrauk-U
Pagan	Bagan
Pegu	Bago
Prome	Pyi
Rangoon	Yangon
Salween River	Thanlwin River
Sittang River	Sittoung River

CLIMATE

The rainy season lasts from mid-May until mid-October. For the next few months, the weather is quite reasonable. In fact, it is actually cool in Mandalay at night and near freezing in Kalaw. From February, it gets very hot until the rains arrive once more. The Burmese New Year in April, at the peak of the hot season, means much fun and throwing water at all concerned. November to February are the best months to visit. In late December it can be quite difficult to travel as the number of visitors to the country can exceed the transport and accommodation capacity.

GOVERNMENT

The Tatmadaw (armed forces) and their political junta, the SLORC, currently rule Myanmar with an iron fist. The only political party with any actual power is Ne Win's National Unity Party (originally called the Burmese Socialist Programme Party). General Saw Maung, a borderline lunatic who was known to ramble on in political speeches about Jesus Christ's sojourn in Tibet, led this party from 1988 until his nervous breakdown in 1992; the party is now led by another Ne Win appointee, General Than Shwe.

Burmese citizens have relative economic freedom in all but state-owned trade spheres (naturally these are the big ones, like timber and oil), but their political freedom is strictly curtailed by continued martial law.

Peaceful political assembly is banned and citizens are forbidden to discuss politics with foreigners. All government workers in Myanmar, regardless of level and status of their occupation, must sign a pledge not to discuss the government among themselves or risk losing their jobs.

The opposition movement that began in 1988 appears to be quelled now, with all leaders and spokespersons under arrest or having fled the country and the SLORC firmly in control. Amnesty International reports state that the junta has effectively silenced the democracy movement through the systematic use of terror and torture.

The streets in Yangon are festooned with huge red banners bearing slogans: 'Crush All Destructive Elements', 'The Strength of the

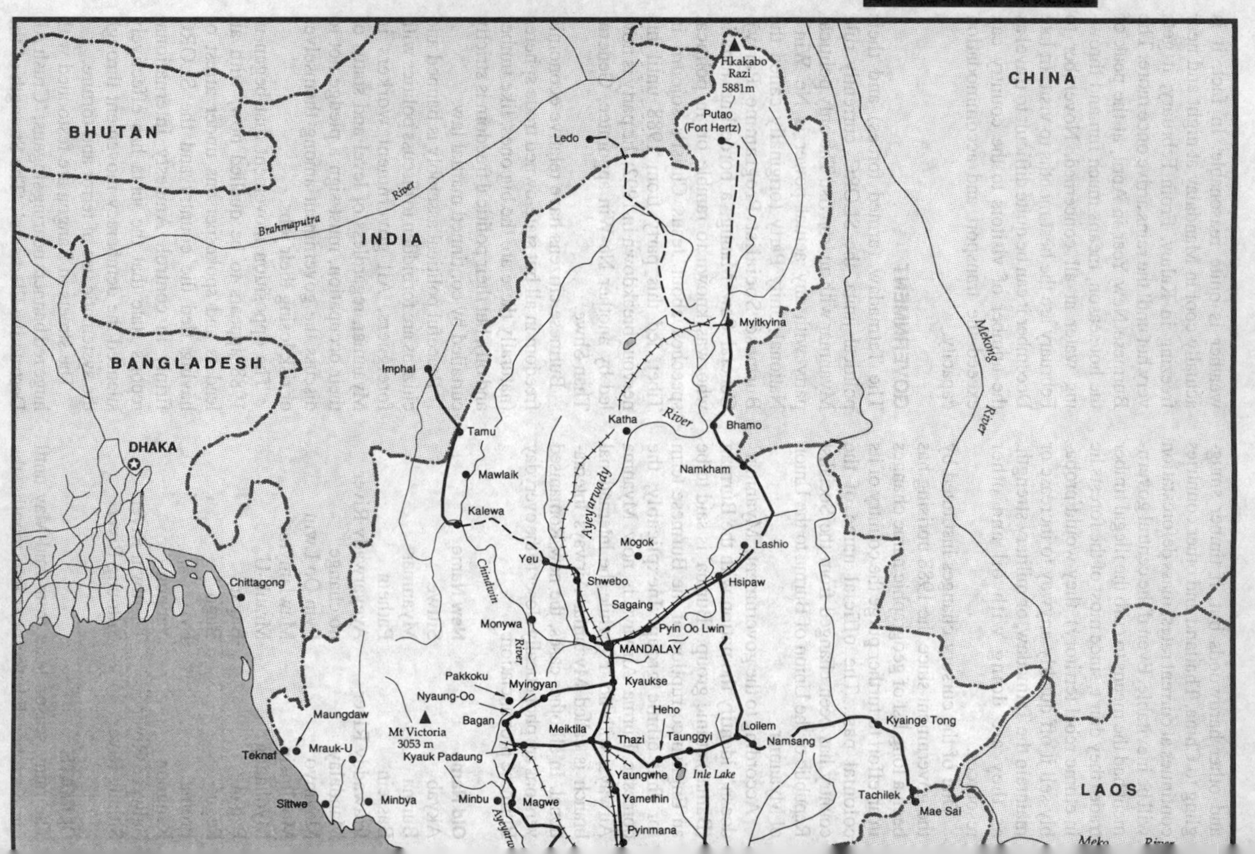
BHUTAN
CHINA
INDIA
BANGLADESH
LAOS
DHAKA
Chittagong
Brahmaputra River
Mekong River
Hkakabo Razi 5881m
Putao (Fort Hertz)
Ledo
Myitkyina
Imphal
Katha
River
Bhamo
Tamu
Namkham
Mawlaik
Kalewa
Ayeyarwady
Mogok
Lashio
Yeu
Chindwin
Shwebo
Hsipaw
Sagaing
Monywa
Pyin Oo Lwin
MANDALAY
River
Pakkoku
Myingyan
Kyaukse
Nyaung-Oo
Heho
Maungdaw
Bagan
Loilem
Kyainge Tong
Mt Victoria 3053 m
Meiktila
Thazi
Taunggyi
Namsang
Teknaf
Mrauk-U
Kyauk Padaung
Yaungwhe
Inle Lake
Yamethin
Tachilek
Sittwe
Minbya
Minbu
Magwe
Mae Sai
Pyinmana

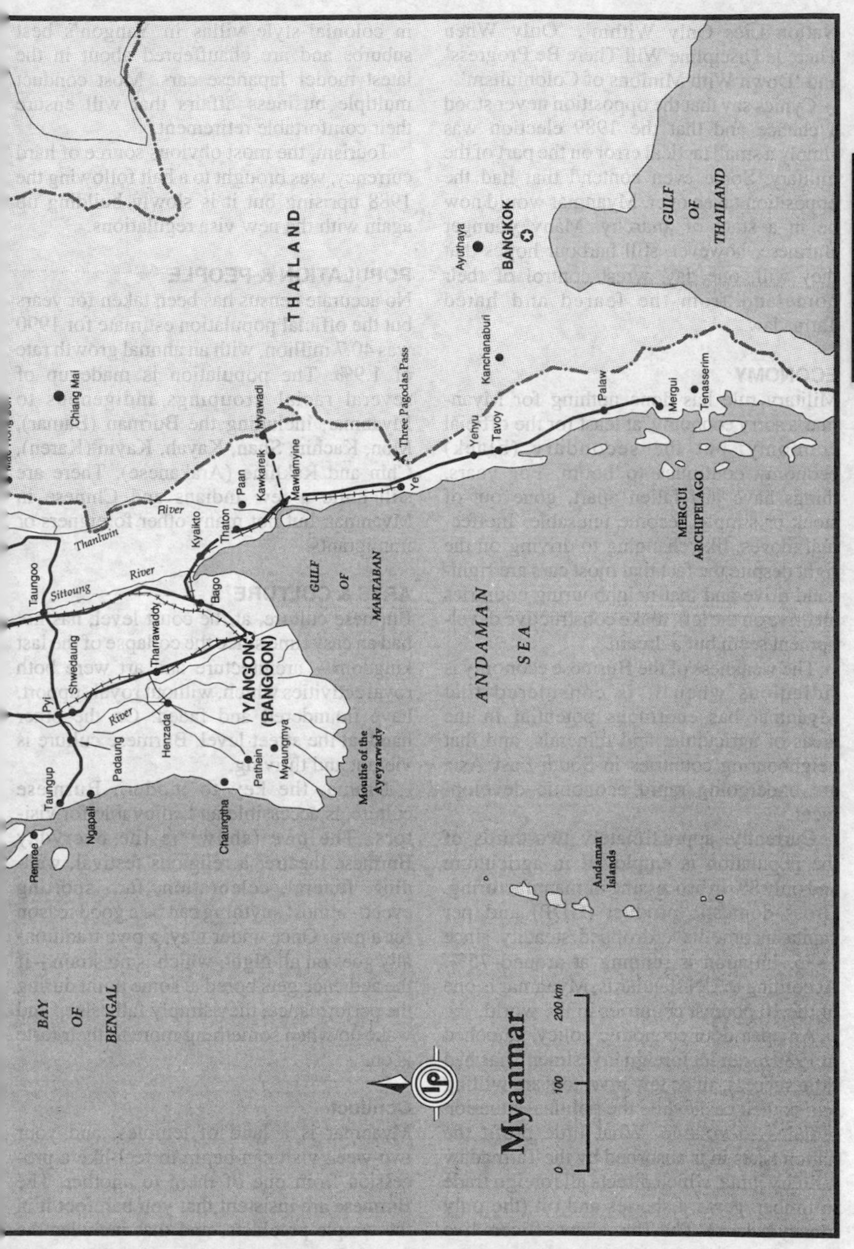
Myanmar
0
100
200 km
BAY OF BENGAL
ANDAMAN SEA
GULF OF MARTABAN
GULF OF THAILAND
THAILAND
MERGUI ARCHIPELAGO
Andaman Islands
Mouths of the Ayeyarwady
YANGON (RANGOON)
BANGKOK
Ayuthaya
Kanchanaburi
Three Pagodas Pass
Chiang Mai
Remree
Ngapali
Taungup
Chaungtha
Padaung
Pyi
Shwedaung
Pathein
Myaungmya
Henzada
Tharrawaddy
River
Taungoo
Sittoung
River
Thanlwin
River
Bago
Kyaikto
Thaton
Paan
Kawkareik
Myawadi
Mawlamyine
Ye
Yehyu
Tavoy
Palaw
Mergui
Tenasserim

Nation Lies Only Within', 'Only When There Is Discipline Will There Be Progress' and 'Down With Minions of Colonialism'.

Cynics say that the opposition never stood a chance and that the 1989 election was simply a small tactical error on the part of the military. Some even contend that had the opposition taken over, Myanmar would now be in a state of anarchy. Many younger Burmese, however, still harbour hopes that they will, one day, wrest control of their homeland from the feared and hated Tatmadaw.

ECONOMY

Military rule has done nothing for Myanmar's sorry economy, at least for the official economy, but the secondary (black) economy continues to boom. For years, things have just fallen apart, gone out of stock or simply become unusable. Ineffectual moves, like changing to driving on the right despite the fact that most cars are right-hand drive and that neighbouring countries all drive on the left, make constructive development seem but a dream.

The weakness of the Burmese economy is ridiculous when it is considered that Myanmar has enormous potential in the areas of agriculture and minerals, and that neighbouring countries in South-East Asia are undergoing rapid economic development.

Currently, approximately two-thirds of the population is employed in agriculture and only 8% in processing or manufacturing. Gross domestic product (GDP) and per capita income have dropped steadily since 1985. Inflation is running at around 75%. According to UN standards, Myanmar is one of the 10 poorest countries in the world.

An open-door economic policy, launched in 1989 to attract foreign investment, has had little success, since few investors are willing to risk their cash while the political situation remains so volatile. What little profit the nation takes in is absorbed by the Tatmadaw military junta, which directs all foreign trade in timber, gems, fisheries and oil (the only moneymakers). The Tatmadaw officers live in colonial-style villas in Yangon's best suburbs and are chauffeured about in the latest model Japanese cars. Most conduct multiple business affairs that will ensure their comfortable retirement.

Tourism, the most obvious source of hard currency, was brought to a halt following the 1988 uprising but it is slowly building up again with the new visa regulations.

POPULATION & PEOPLE

No accurate census has been taken for years but the official population estimate for 1990 was 40.7 million, with an annual growth rate of 1.9%. The population is made up of several racial groupings indigenous to Myanmar, including the Burman (Bamar), Mon, Kachin, Shan, Kayah, Kayin (Karen), Chin and Rakhine (Arakanese). There are still quite a few Indians and Chinese in Myanmar, but not many other foreigners or immigrants.

ARTS & CULTURE

Burmese culture, at the court level, has not had an easy time since the collapse of the last kingdom – architecture and art were both royal activities which, without royal support, have floundered and faded. On the other hand, at the street level, Burmese culture is vibrant and thriving.

Drama, the key to modern Burmese culture, is accessible and enjoyable for visitors. The *pwe* (show) is the everyday Burmese theatre; a religious festival, wedding, funeral, celebration, fair, sporting event – almost anything can be a good reason for a pwe. Once under way, a pwe traditionally goes on all night, which is no strain – if the audience gets bored at some point during the performance, they simply fall asleep and wake up when something more to their taste is on.

Conduct

Myanmar is a land of temples, and your two-week visit can begin to feel like a procession from one of them to another. The Burmese are insistent that you barefoot it in the temple precincts, and that includes the steps from the very bottom of Mandalay Hill, the shop-lined arcades to the Shwedagon Pagoda and even the ruins of Bagan. Carry your shoes and socks with you.

RELIGION

Myanmar is Theravada Buddhist from top to bottom, but there is also a strong belief in nats, the animist spirits of the land. Many of the hill tribes are Christian.

LANGUAGE

There is a wide variety of languages spoken in Myanmar – fortunately, English is widely spoken. The Burmese alphabet is most unusual and looks like a collection of interlocked circles. If you would like to tackle Burmese (the main language), look for Lonely Planet's handy *Burmese Phrasebook.*

Following are some useful Burmese words and phrases.

Greetings & Civilities

excuse me
kwin pyu baa
good morning/afternoon/evening
min ga la baa
goodbye (I'm going)
pyan dor mai
How are you?
Mah yeh laa?
I'm well.
Maa bah day.
please
chay-zoo tin-baa day
thank you
chay zoo tin baa dai

Other Useful Words & Phrases

Do you understand?
Kin byar har lai tha laa?
How much?
Bah lout lai?
too much
myar dai
I do not understand.
Chun note nar ma lai boo.
Where is...?
...beh mah lai?
no
ma hoke boo
yes
hoke ket

Numbers

1	*tit*
2	*nit*
3	*thone*
4	*lay*
5	*ngar*
6	*howk*
7	*kun nit*
8	*sit*
9	*co*
10	*ta sei*
11	*sair tit*
12	*sair nit*
20	*na sei*
30	*thone sei*
100	*ta yar*
500	*gar yar*

Facts for the Visitor

VISAS & EMBASSIES

The tourist visa situation in Myanmar has been in a state of flux since the upheavals in mid-1988 when the country was briefly closed to all visitors, then reopened under more strict regulations.

By early 1994, 30-day tourist visas were being issued with regularity at Burmese embassies abroad; it is no longer necessary to book a package tour in advance.

This new 30-day tourist visa is a vast improvement over the old seven-day visa which compelled many travellers to rush around Myanmar in a frenzy. Once in Yangon, you're free to plan your own itinerary and go where you like – within the confines of the officially designated tourist destinations, as in previous years.

The cost of the visa itself is only 400B (around US$16). Unfortunately, the new fly in the ointment is that you are required to exchange US$300 into Foreign Exchange Certificates (FECs) at the artificially high official rate (see the following Money section) – very similar to the system formerly used in China. Basically, this policy is a way of ensuring that the government gets a stash of your hard currency at the official rate before you tool around the country.

Myanmar Embassies Abroad

Malaysia
: 5 Jalan Taman U Thant, Kuala Lumpur (☎ 03-2424085)

Singapore
: 15 St Martin's Drive (☎ 737 8566)

Thailand
: 132 Sathon Neua Rd, Bangkok (☎ 233 2237)

Visa Extensions

The government currently allows no routine extensions of the 30-day visa. If, however, you show up at the Yangon Airport a day or two late due to unavoidable transport difficulties, there's usually little hassle if immigration authorities can verify your story. If not, be prepared to part with some baksheesh (a tip).

Foreign Embassies

Yangon is usually a good place to get visas for other countries. You can pay for them with your whisky kyats (see the Money section) so they're very cheap and because the embassy officials know your time is limited they issue them very quickly. You may be able to get Nepalese visas here in as little as 15 minutes.

Travel Restrictions

The xenophobic government does try to keep tabs on you while you are in Myanmar, more so since the events of August 1988. They don't want you wandering off into touchy regions and that's part of the reason for the 30-day visa. Also, with so much difference between the official exchange rate and the real one, the government obviously wants to stop you from spending 'black' money. The further you get from Myanmar Tours & Travel (MTT)-approved destinations, the less likely you'll have to pay official rates.

Most visitors do not wander off the Yangon-Mandalay-Bagan-Inle Lake circuit apart from short detours to Bago, Syriam, Pyin Oo Lwin or the deserted cities around Mandalay. If you ask about going to other places, you'll probably receive a firm 'no'. But if you simply set out to go there it's quite possible you'll manage it.

Of course, there are really touchy areas (the north-east towards the Golden Triangle and north of Mandalay towards the China border) which are absolutely no go. Lots of people manage, however, to get to Kyaikto to see the balancing pagoda (of Kyaiktiyo) and even further to Thaton. A few have even managed Mrauk-U, while Pathein and Pyi are quite easy to get to. If only we all had more time!

MONEY

Currency

The kyat (say 'chat') is divided into 100 pyas with a collection of confusing coins which are now rarely seen since the tremendous decrease in the value of the kyat over the last few years. Generally, it's easier to change money at MTT offices, which have longer opening hours than the banks.

The government has a nasty habit of demonetising large denomination notes from time to time. The theory is that anybody who has some large denomination notes sitting around must have obtained them by less than legal means. So the government simply declares that (say) all even-numbered denominations are no longer legal tender.

This does not tend to inspire much confidence in the currency, particularly if you happen to have a stash of now worthless kyat notes under the mattress. You can be sure that government officials get advance notice of which denominations are going to be invalidated so that they can cash in before it's too late.

At present, only these paper denominations are in use: K1, K5, K10, K15, K45, K90 and K200. Don't accept any other denominations (say 50s or 100s) when changing money since you won't be able to use them in any transactions.

Exchange Rates

Australia	A$1	=	K3.67
Canada	C$1	=	K3.78
New Zealand	NZ$1	=	K3.02
Britain	UK£1	=	K7.70
USA	US$1	=	K5.09
Japan	¥100	=	K5
Germany	DM1	=	K3.12
France	FF1	=	K0.91
Malaysia	M$1	=	K1.98
Thailand	1B	=	K0.21

The official exchange rates for travellers' cheques and cash (travellers' cheques are worth more than cash) bear little relation to reality. Unofficially, cash is worth far more than the official rates above. You can buy kyats in Singapore, Penang or Bangkok and illegally bring them in with you. Or you can illegally change US$ or FECs on the black market – Yangon is the best place and you can expect to get around K120 for US$1. Larger denomination US$ notes are preferred. There is also a good market for Thai baht and Singapore dollars, at their equivalent rates.

Either of these procedures has some element of risk but it's part of the Myanmar government's often benevolent incompetence that there is a delightfully simple way round this. At the airport, when you depart for Yangon, invest in some duty-free goods. A couple of cartons of 555 cigarettes and two bottles of Johnny Walker Red Label whisky (that's the current duty-free limit) will cost you around US$15. If you can't get the preferred brands move downmarket rather than up.

No sooner have you left customs at Yangon airport than people will leap forward offering to take them off your hands. It's better to wait until you're in town for a day or two before you sell them, however, so you can find out from other foreigners what the going rate is.

For one carton of 555s and one 750 ml bottle of whiskey, around K1500 (K1000 for the whisky, K500 for the cigarettes) seems to be the norm although the price varies from week to week. You've now changed your US$15 at a rate of K100 for US$1. Obviously cash earns the better exchange rate these days. If you run low, there's a place in Yangon called the Tourist Department Store (formerly the Diplomatic Store) just north of Sule Pagoda where the Burmese government has set up further opportunities for visitors to indulge in small-scale capitalism, supply and demand etc. It's a good practice to carry a few packets of 555s with you through Myanmar as payment for the occasional bureaucratic favour.

Foreign Exchange Certificates

As soon as you exit the immigration check at Yangon international airport you must stop at a counter and exchange US$300 for an envelope full of Foreign Exchange Certificates (FECs). Printed in China, these Monopoly-like notes are issued by the Central Bank of Myanmar 'for the convenience of tourists visiting Myanmar' in denominations of US$10, US$5 and US$1. Payment is accepted *only* in US dollars or British pound sterling, in the form of cash, travellers' cheques or credit cards (Visa only).

Along with the FECs you'll also receive a Foreign Exchange Certificate Voucher which you'll only need to save if you plan to convert more than US$300 at the official rate. Reconversion of kyat to dollars or pound sterling is possible only for conversions in excess of US$300 and only when accompanied by the FEC Voucher.

The required US$300 purchase of FECs is not a complete waste as you'll need them to pay for officially approved hotel rooms. If you run out of FECs while on the road, the MTT-sponsored hotels are quite happy to accept dollars or pound sterling in cash – at the official rate of course. FECs may also be purchased at the Central Bank of Myanmar in Yangon and at state-owned hotels.

Costs

Whether or not you think Myanmar is cheap or expensive depends on how you look at it. Using the official exchange rate with FECs changed through MTT make it appear to be quite expensive. With free market kyats it is a great deal cheaper, but that initial 'entry fee' removes it from the traveller's list of dirt-cheap places.

If you exclude the fixed rates for visas (400B), airport taxes (200B out of Bangkok, US$6 out of Yangon) and the round-trip airfare (around US$234), this means that your minimum expenditure is US$14 a day for 14 days. Even then, you will have to contend with the official rates set for MTT-designated hotels throughout the country, which now average around US$18 to US$35 per night.

When it's possible to pay these rates with unofficial kyats, this works out to only US$1.12 to US$2.17 a night, cheap by any standards. In order to get around paying with FECs, you'll have to convince the hotel staff to accept ordinary kyats, which is highly unlikely in MTT-controlled areas.

Certain kinds of transport also officially require FEC payment, like the Yangon to Mandalay Express train, the Mandalay to Bagan boat and Myanma Airways flights. Here again, you'll have to deal with MTT – usually directly. Other train, bus and boat fares can be paid with unofficial kyats, however, as can the costs of all meals (even at the official tourist hotels), drinks, souvenirs and so on. Those so inclined might even consider it a moral duty to divert as much of their spending money away from the government as they possibly can.

Tipping

There is no tradition of tipping in Myanmar, even in the tourist hotels, unless the common practice of bribery is viewed as a form of tipping. MTT guides will usually ask for 'something for the driver' at the end of a guided tour – this actually means something for both the guide *and* the driver, so giving is left to your discretion.

Bargaining

Prices are always negotiable, except in government establishments (MTT craft shops, hotels etc).

TOURIST OFFICES

The main tourist information office is on Sule Pagoda Rd in Yangon, close to the central Sule Pagoda. The information it has to hand out is sparse and uninteresting, but the officials are friendly and helpful. Anything to do with timetables and costs in places you are 'officially' permitted to visit they will have right on hand. There are MTT offices in all the main centres, but they sometimes give the feeling that their purpose is to hinder rather than to be useful.

POST & TELECOMMUNICATIONS

Consider yourself incommunicado while in Myanmar, as post and telephone services are notoriously unreliable.

Aerogrammes have a better chance of getting through than either letters or postcards. Parcels – forget it, unless you have a friend at your embassy or foreign office in Yangon.

BOOKS & MAPS

For more information about travelling in Myanmar look for Lonely Planet's *Myanmar – a travel survival kit*. Apa Productions have the informative *Insight Guide Burma* in their series of glossy coffee-table guidebooks. In Yangon, before you head upcountry, or in Bagan itself, get a copy of *Pictorial Guide to Pagan*, an invaluable introduction to the many temples, pagodas and ruins.

The most comprehensive sociopolitical account of pre-1988 Myanmar is *Burma: A Socialist Nation of Southeast Asia* by David Steinberg (Westview Press, Boulder, Colorado, 1982).

George Orwell's *Burmese Days* is the book to read in order to get a feel for the country under the British Raj. *Golden Earth* by Norman Lewis (Eland Books) is a reprint of a classic account of a visit to Burma soon after WW II.

Yangon has quite a few bookshops, most along Bogyoke Aung San St opposite the Bogyoke Market, where you can find some really interesting books. Also check the Pagan Bookshop at 100, 37th St, quite close to The Strand Hotel. You never know what will turn up in this little shop that specialises in

English-language material – much of it is vintage stuff.

The Tourist Department Store on Sule Pagoda Rd has a selection of tourist-oriented books on Myanmar as well as recent political treatises like *The Conspiracy of the Treasonous Minions within the Myanmar Naing-Ngan (Nation) and Traitorous Cohorts Abroad*. Photographic evidence of collusion between foreign powers and the Burmese 'minions' includes pictures of ordinary Burmese citizens walking in and out of foreign embassies or the local residences of foreigners. In xenophobic Myanmar, even walking into a foreign enclave is a potential act of treason.

Outrage: Burma's Struggle for Democracy by journalist Bertil Lintner (White Lotus, London and Bangkok, 1990) chronicles the violent suppression of Myanmar's pro-democracy movement from 1987 to 1990, with particular focus on the events of 1988. It is a somewhat polemic, one-sided look at the student uprisings, but basically it's very informative. *Freedom from Fear & Other Writings* by Aung San Suu Kyi (Viking, London and New York, 1991) is a collection of essays by and about the Nobel Peace Prize winner.

MEDIA

Newspapers & Magazines

The only English-language newspaper readily available in Myanmar is the unintentionally humorous *New Light Of Myanmar*, a thin, state-owned daily that's chock full of Orwellian propaganda of the 'War is Peace' or 'Freedom is Slavery' nature.

Recent issues of international magazines like *Time*, *Newsweek* or the *Economist* are quite often available at The Strand Hotel in Yangon. Whenever a feature about Myanmar appears in one of these magazines, however, that issue mysteriously fails to appear. Older issues are sold on the street by sidewalk vendors.

Radio & TV

All legal radio and television broadcasts are state-controlled. Voice of Myanmar radio broadcasts only 2½ hours per day. TV Myanmar broadcasts nightly from 7 to 9.35 pm. Regular features include military songs and marching performances, 'Songs of Yesteryear', locally produced news and weather reports and a sports presentation.

Educated Burmese generally listen to shortwave BBC and VOA broadcasts for news from the world outside. On Friday evening, the American Center on Merchant St packs them in for the 4.30 pm broadcast of the *ABC World News*.

FILM & PHOTOGRAPHY

Bring a sufficient film supply with you to Myanmar as brand-name film is unavailable. The Burmese don't seem to mind having their photos taken, but you should always ask first as a gesture of courtesy.

Photographing airports, train stations, bridges or military installations is prohibited by law. If anything political starts happening, you will risk having your camera confiscated if you try to take any photos. Government observers (or their informers) may also accuse you of being a foreign journalist and arrange for your immediate detention. SLORC are at war with foreign journalists, including photographers.

HEALTH

Myanmar doesn't have the highest of sanitation standards, but then you can't expect very much from one of the world's 10 poorest countries. Frankly, it pays to be very careful with food and drink throughout this country. Only eat food that is cooked, or if eating raw fruits or vegetables, ensure they are of the peelable type and peel them yourself. All water should be boiled or otherwise treated before consumption, and safe bottled water is available at most tourist destinations.

Dysentery of various types is quite common and you should stock up on appropriate medicines for the prevention and treatment of both the bacillic and amoebic forms (consult a doctor in advance). A supply of diarrhoeal suppressants like Lomotil or Imodium is a must unless you're unusually stoic. If you eat only in the hotels, you'll probably be OK but you'll have to put up with bland, uninspired cooking (The Strand Hotel in Yangon is one exception).

Malaria is not a problem in the areas most frequented by foreign travellers.

DANGERS & ANNOYANCES

Theft from tourists seems quite rare in Myanmar, but don't tempt fate by leaving valuables lying around. The common presence of Tatmadaw troops, especially in Yangon and Mandalay, can be unsettling but unless you get caught up in a pro-democracy demonstration, you have little to worry about.

ACCOMMODATION

Hotel rooms in Myanmar are very poor value at the official exchange rate, but they are bargains at the free market rate. Facilities are often in a state of disrepair, but otherwise they're quite adequate as places to sleep and shower.

The official selection is quite slim, although a few places have been added to the approved list since 1993. They range in price from a low of US$11 for a single at the YMCA in Yangon to a high of US$200 for a room at The Strand – newly refurbished – in Yangon.

These are official rates at the exchange rate of K5.09 to the US$. If you can manage to pay for accommodation with free market kyats, these same rates range from less than a dollar a night! The higher-end places quote prices in US$. In reality, if you travel all over Myanmar, you'll probably find that you'll have to pay with FECs about half the time and free market kyats the other half.

FOOD & DRINKS

Food in Myanmar is basically curry and rice. You normally get two kinds of rather mild curry and a side plate of salad. Unlimited quantities of soup and Chinese tea will be included in the price. It's straightforward, unexciting but quite good food. You will probably also see some less appetising Burmese cuisine. A popular favourite on the trains are crunchy grasshopper kebabs! Indian and Chinese food are also generally available. In fact, you're far more likely to find restaurants run by Indians or Chinese than by Burmese.

Burmese soft drinks, usually around K10, are fairly safe and not too bad, particularly if you dilute them with soda water or ice. A bottle of Mandalay Beer from the People's Brewery & Distillery will cost around K50. It's a bit watery but not bad – cheap at the free market rate of exchange. In 1987 there were a couple of months when none of this beer was brewed because Myanmar ran out of bottle caps. See why it is considered a ramshackle economy?

Burmese tea is usually mixed with other herbs and stains your tongue a lurid orange colour, though some people grow to like it. Ice cream, in the more hygienic-looking ice cream parlours in Yangon and Mandalay, seems to be OK, and I managed to drink a lot of crushed sugar cane during one hot-season visit without any ill effects, but be careful.

Some useful words relating to food and drinks include:

bread
  pow mohn
butter
  taw but
chicken
  kyet (chet) *tar*
coffee
  kaw pee
drinking water
  tao ye
egg (boiled)
  chet u byok
egg (fried)
  chet u chor
fish
  ngar
hot
  ah poo
mutton
  seik tar
noodles
  kaw swe
restaurant
  sar tao syne

rice (cooked)
ta min
soup
hin jo
sugar
ta jar
tea
la bet ye
tea shop
la bet yea syne
toast
pow moh gin

THINGS TO BUY

There is nice lacquerware available, particularly at Bagan. The black and gold items probably aren't as good quality as in Chiang Mai in Thailand, but coloured items are much more vibrant. Look for flexibility in bowls or dishes and clarity of design. Opium weights are cheaper than in Thailand. Beautiful shoulder bags are made by the Shan tribes. *Kalagas*, tapestries embroidered with silver thread, sequins and colourful glass beads, are a good buy.

Be very careful if you decide to buy gems. Many foolish travellers buy fake gemstones. It's another of those fields to dabble in only if you really know what is and what isn't. However, I must admit I bought what looked like a ruby on one trip and it turned out to actually be one.

If you want to sell things, virtually any Western goods from radio batteries to cheap make-up are in amazing demand in Myanmar but they have to be name brands, not any old rubbish.

Getting There & Away

Myanmar is purely fly in, fly out. Tourists are not permitted to arrive by ship and all roads are closed at the borders except for day trips from Thailand at Three Pagodas Pass, Mae Sot and Mae Sai. Myanmar Airways International's (MAI's) Boeing 757s fly to and from Bangkok every day of the week (US$234 return) and also connect to Calcutta and Kathmandu. They also have flights to/from Hong Kong twice a week and Singapore three times per week. MAI's ticketing office (☎ 89772) in Yangon is at 123 Sule Pagoda Rd.

Thai International also fly from Bangkok to Yangon three times weekly. Bangladesh Biman fly Bangkok-Yangon-Dhaka once a week and Air China (the old CAAC) fly from Yangon to Kunming once a week. Singapore International's offshoot Silk Air (formerly Tradewinds), a subsidiary of Singapore Airlines, recently started flying between Singapore and Yangon twice weekly.

Fares are a bit of a mix-up due to the keen fare-cutting in Bangkok. Shopping around, with a student card handy, should enable you to fly Bangkok-Yangon-Bangkok for around US$200. Bangkok-Yangon-Calcutta or Bangkok-Yangon-Kathmandu costs around US$250. Some travel agents in Bangkok will do an all-in deal getting you your tickets and your visa.

Aeroflot fly twice a week from Vietnam and Laos to Yangon, then on to Bombay and Moscow, although not many travellers are likely to use that route. Some people have been entering Myanmar from Kunming in China with Air China (one flight per week). If you're travelling around China, this makes a very interesting way of continuing on to South-East Asia, rather than going back to Hong Kong and flying on from there.

If you're counting on getting out on the last day that your visa is valid, be sure to reconfirm your departure before leaving the airport when you first arrive – all the airlines tend to overbook flights leaving Myanmar, especially from December to February.

Getting Around

Travel in Myanmar is not that easy – it's uncertain and often uncomfortable by whatever means of travel you choose.

AIR

Because of the short visa period, travellers to Myanmar sometimes fly where normally they would be quite happy to travel by land, although with the new 30-day visa things are significantly more relaxed. Flying can save a lot of time and effort but all tickets must be bought through MTT with FECs. Once in a long while we hear of someone buying an air ticket on the black market, but this seems to be rare.

The problem with flying Myanma Airways (MA), apart from the airline's terrible safety record on internal flights, is that you never know if flights will leave or not. Schedules are fixed from day to day and you'll find it virtually impossible to be certain of any reservation. The officials tell you to arrive at the airport at noon for a 2 pm flight which may not leave until 4 or 5 pm or who knows when – very frustrating when time is limited.

There are only four planes currently in operation, all Fokker F-27 props. They fly only one daily, clockwise route: Yangon-Bagan-Mandalay-Heho (Inle Lake). You can't, therefore, fly from Bagan to Yangon, for example, without going through the rest of the loop.

For a while, there was a 'tourists only' service around the loop but this still wasted a lot of time and involved a lot of uncertainty before you actually got up in the air. The shortage of aircraft, due to the lack of foreign exchange to buy spare parts (and because of all the crashes), has made flight schedules even worse. If it's any consolation, when it comes to a fight for seats, foreigners have priority over Burmese! But then a foreigner travelling independently will get bumped off a flight by a foreigner on a package tour. And you'll all get bumped off for a government official!

Fares range from US$35, for the Bagan to Mandalay and Mandalay to Heho legs, to US$98 for Yangon to Mandalay.

BUS & TRUCK

Not much travelling is done by road for longer trips. The exceptions would be between Inle Lake and Mandalay, Mandalay and Bagan or Bagan-Thazi-Inle Lake. Burmese buses tend to be extremely crowded, with people hanging out the sides, sitting on the roof and occupying every possible space inside.

In recent years, however, small Japanese pick-up trucks have started to appear on Burmese roads in increasing numbers. With a couple of benches down each side they operate just like Indonesian *bemos* or Thai *songthaews*. They can be uncomfortable when crowded but groups of people can sometimes charter them through MTT, such as for trips between Bagan and Inle Lake or even further afield.

In the mid-1980s, this could be done through private arrangement but this method of transport became so popular that the government clamped down on it (of course). It's been further complicated by the fuel shortage – yes, the country has oil reserves but this is Myanmar, remember! The 'official' price of petrol is only about US$1 a gallon but it's rationed (only four gallons per month per vehicle) and it's said that black market fuel can cost as much as US$20 a gallon.

TRAIN

Apart from the daily Yangon to Mandalay special express, the ordinary-class trains are better forgotten – they are dirty, slow, unreliable and very dark at night due to a national shortage of light bulbs! Upper-class (equivalent to 1st class) and 1st-class (equivalent to 2nd class) travel are generally better.

Except for the main tourist routes, you may find it impossible to buy railway tickets through MTT and the station is not supposed to sell tickets to foreigners, who should get them from MTT! The answer is to ask somebody at the station to buy them for you although I've bought tickets at several points not watched over by MTT and had no trouble whatsoever.

BOAT

The boat trip downriver from Mandalay to Bagan is popular and you can also make other, shorter trips from Mandalay or Yangon. If you had the time you could continue the boat trip from Bagan right down the river to Yangon

– you'd be devoting an entire week to just that one trip.

LOCAL TRANSPORT

The impossibly crowded and delightfully ancient buses in Yangon and Mandalay are very cheap and convenient although you may well end up hanging out the side or off the back. Trishaws, in which the passengers sit back to back, are also economic but always negotiate the fare beforehand.

Taxi-trucks are becoming more readily available throughout Myanmar. Some of them operate fixed routes, others can be hired like a taxi. There are also taxis in Yangon and smaller three-wheelers like an Indian *autorickshaw* or Thai *samlor*. Mandalay also has horse carts *(tongas)* which are somewhat more expensive than trishaws. You can hire bicycles in Bagan.

Yangon (Rangoon)

The capital of Myanmar for less than 100 years, Yangon (formerly called Rangoon) is 30 km upriver from the sea and has an air of seedy decay along with a great pagoda that is one of the real wonders of South-East Asia. A city of wide streets and spacious architecture, it looks run-down, worn-out and thoroughly neglected, although with the roadwork and new coats of paint ordered by the SLORC, your initial impression will probably be favourable. The streets are lively at night with hordes of stalls selling delicious-looking food, piles of huge cigars and those Western cigarettes you've just unloaded. Look for the tape-recorder studios where young Burmese entertain themselves by adding Burmese words to Western pop music. Recently, electronic games have also become a Yangon craze. Watch out for rats late at night!

Orientation & Information

The MTT office is right by the Sule Pagoda at the junction of Sule Pagoda Rd and Mahabandoola St. In central Yangon, it's relatively easy to find your way around. The centre is quite compact, the streets are laid out in a grid pattern and walking is no problem. The GPO is a short stroll east of The Strand Hotel on Strand Road.

Shwedagon Pagoda

Dominating the entire city from its hilltop site, this is the most sacred Buddhist temple in Myanmar. Nearly 100 metres high, it is clearly visible from the air as you fly in or out of Yangon. I saw it once as a tiny golden dot while flying over Myanmar to Kathmandu – magic! Visit it in the early morning or evening when the gold spire gleams in the sun and the temperature is cooler. Or see its shimmering reflection from across the Kandawgyi Lake at night. In 1587, a European visitor wrote of its 'wonderful bignesse' and that it was 'all gilded from foote to the toppe'. The Shwedagon has an equally impressive appearance at night when it glows gold against a velvet backdrop.

A few facts and figures: the site is over 2500 years old (the current stupa dates to the 18th century); there are over 8000 gold plates covering the pagoda; the top of the spire is encrusted with more than 5000 diamonds and 2000 other precious or semiprecious stones; and the compound around the pagoda has 82 other buildings – it is this sheer mass of buildings that gives the place its awesome appeal.

In the pagoda's north-western corner is a huge bell which the butter-fingered British managed to drop into the Yangon River while carrying it off. Unable to recover it, they gave the bell back to the Burmese who refloated it by tying a vast number of bamboo lengths to it.

The official admission fee for the pagoda is now US$5, which includes an elevator ride to the raised platform of the stupa. There are separate elevators for Burmese and foreigners. If you come before 7 am, you can get in for free.

Sule Pagoda

Also over 2000 years old and right in the centre of town, the Sule Pagoda makes a fine

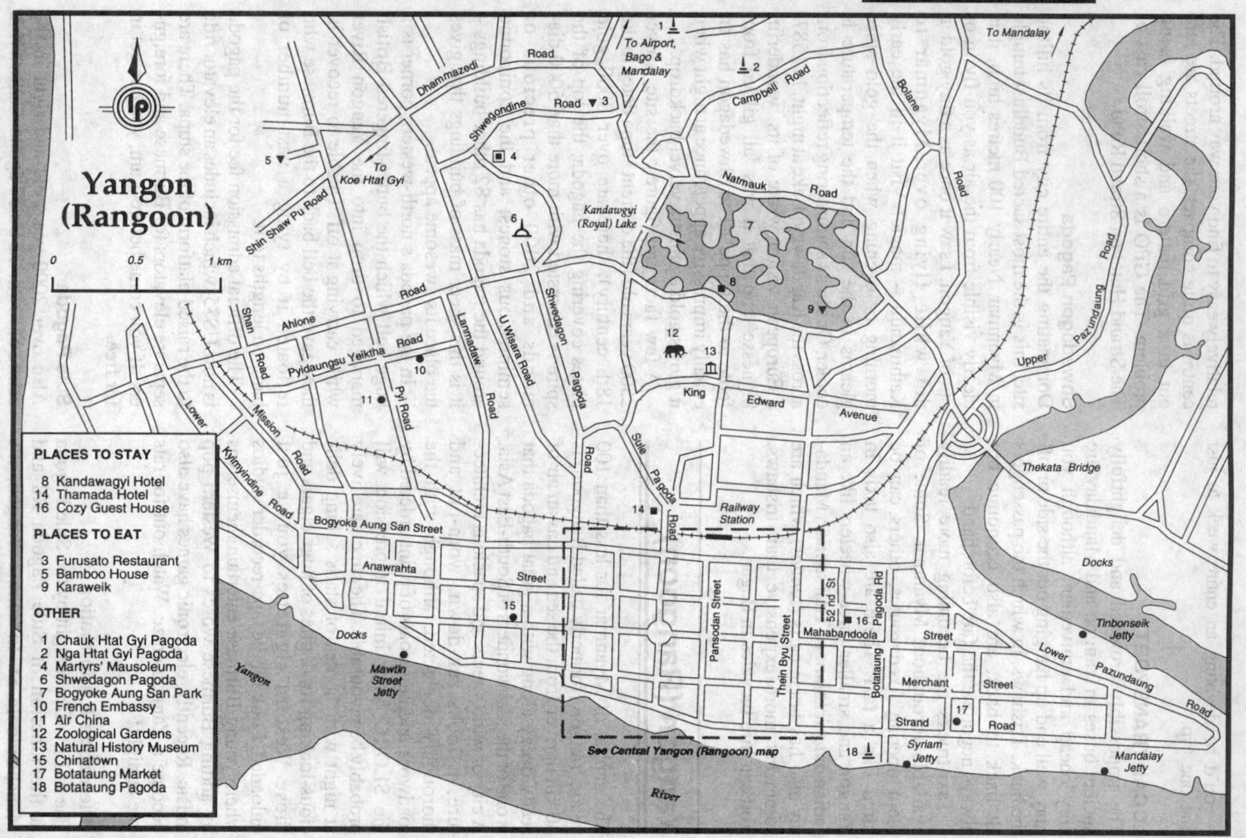
Yangon (Rangoon)
0
0.5
1 km
PLACES TO STAY
8 Kandawagyi Hotel
14 Thamada Hotel
16 Cozy Guest House
PLACES TO EAT
3 Furusato Restaurant
5 Bamboo House
9 Karaweik
OTHER
1 Chauk Htat Gyi Pagoda
2 Nga Htat Gyi Pagoda
4 Martyrs' Mausoleum
6 Shwedagon Pagoda
7 Bogyoke Aung San Park
10 French Embassy
11 Air China
12 Zoological Gardens
13 Natural History Museum
15 Chinatown
17 Botataung Market
18 Botataung Pagoda
To Airport, Bago & Mandalay
Dhammazedi Road
Shwegondine Road
Campbell Road
Bolane Road
To Mandalay
To Koe Htat Gyi
Shin Shaw Pu Road
Natmauk Road
Kandawgyi (Royal) Lake
Upper Pazundaung Road
Ahlone Road
Shan Road
Pyidaungsu Yeiktha Road
Pyi Road
Lanmadaw Road
U Wisara Road
Shwedagon Pagoda Road
King Edward Avenue
Lower Mission Road
Kyimyindine Road
Sule Pagoda Road
Railway Station
Thekata Bridge
Bogyoke Aung San Street
Anawrahta Street
Docks
Pansodan Street
Thein Byu Street
52 nd St
Botataung Pagoda Rd
Mahabandoola Street
Merchant Street
Strand Road
Lower Pazundaung Road
Tinbonseik Jetty
Yangon River
Mawtin Street Jetty
See Central Yangon (Rangoon) map
Syriam Jetty
Mandalay Jetty

spectacle at night and the inside of the complex is all lit by pulsating neon.

National Museum

The museum, which is on Pansodan (Phayre) St (around the corner from The Strand Hotel), houses nothing spectacular, but if you have time to kill in Yangon you could do worse.

There are three floors – the stairs to the upper floors are a bit difficult to find. The bottom floor contains jewellery and royal relics and the upper floors feature art and archaeology. Admission is US$4 and it's open from 10 am to 3 pm from Monday to Thursday and 1 to 3 pm on Saturday. It is closed on Sunday and on 'government gazetted holidays'. If you plan to use a camera you must pay an additional K5 for a photography permit.

Other

There's a mirror maze in the stupa of **Botataung Pagoda**. Yangon has a fine **open-air market** and the extensive **Bogyoke Aung San Market** is always worth a wander. It's a very pleasant stroll around **Kandawgyi Lake** where you can visit the huge Karaweik nonfloating restaurant. The Karaweik, a local attraction in its own right, is a reinforced concrete reproduction of a Royal Barge. Yangon has a **zoo** with a collection of Burmese animals, and on Sunday there is a snake charmer and an elephant performance.

The **Kaba Aye** (or World Peace) pagoda is about 11 km north of the city, and was built in the mid-1950s for the 2500th anniversary of Buddhism. The **Martyrs' Mausoleum**, dedicated to Aung San and his comrades, is close to the Shwedagon Pagoda; admission is US$1. The huge reclining Buddha at **Chauk Htat Gyi Pagoda** is also close by and there are a couple of other gigantic Buddha figures in Yangon.

An interesting excursion from Yangon can be made across the river to Syriam, where you can take a bus to **Kyauktan** with its small island pagoda or take a longer river trip to **Twante**, two or three hours away.

About 45 minutes from Yangon on the road to Pyi is the recently established **Hlawa Park** on the banks of a large reservoir. A joint operation of the ministries of forestry and agriculture, the park features an impressive animal reserve, boat rides, elephant rides and picnic areas.

Places to Stay

All of the MTT-approved hotels are well overpriced (by Burmese or Asian standards) at the official exchange rate, and it's unlikely than any will allow you to pay without stamping your currency form. For shoestringers, the only solution is to spend as few days as possible in Yangon in the hope that you'll have better luck upcountry.

The Strand Hotel, one of Asia's most historic hotels, has recently undergone a monumental renovation – after the fashion of Bangkok's Oriental or Singapore's Raffles – under the guidance of Hong Kong's New World Hotels International. It's worth a visit even if you can't afford the US$200 price tag for a standard room. There are still a few unrestored 'economy' rooms that go for US$46 – eventually these will be brought up to the US$200 standard.

Least expensive is the *YMCA* which is tatty but relatively central and bearable. The dormitory no longer exists, or if it does it's not open to foreigners. Rooms are now US$11 per single with shared bath, and US$20/30 for a single/double with fan and private bath and US$30/40 for rooms with air-con and fridge. Both sexes may stay at this Y, although couples are supposed to be married if they share double rooms, a quaint custom for Asia.

On our first visit to Myanmar, we were plagued by mosquitos here. They subsequently installed mosquito nets, then took them out again and put wire mesh on the windows, which keeps the air out and lets the insects in once the inevitable holes appear. They do have fans, however, and the toilets work.

Tony Wheeler

The *YWCA* is open to women only. It's at 119 Brooking St and has just two singles and two doubles. Rates are approximately the same as for the YMCA.

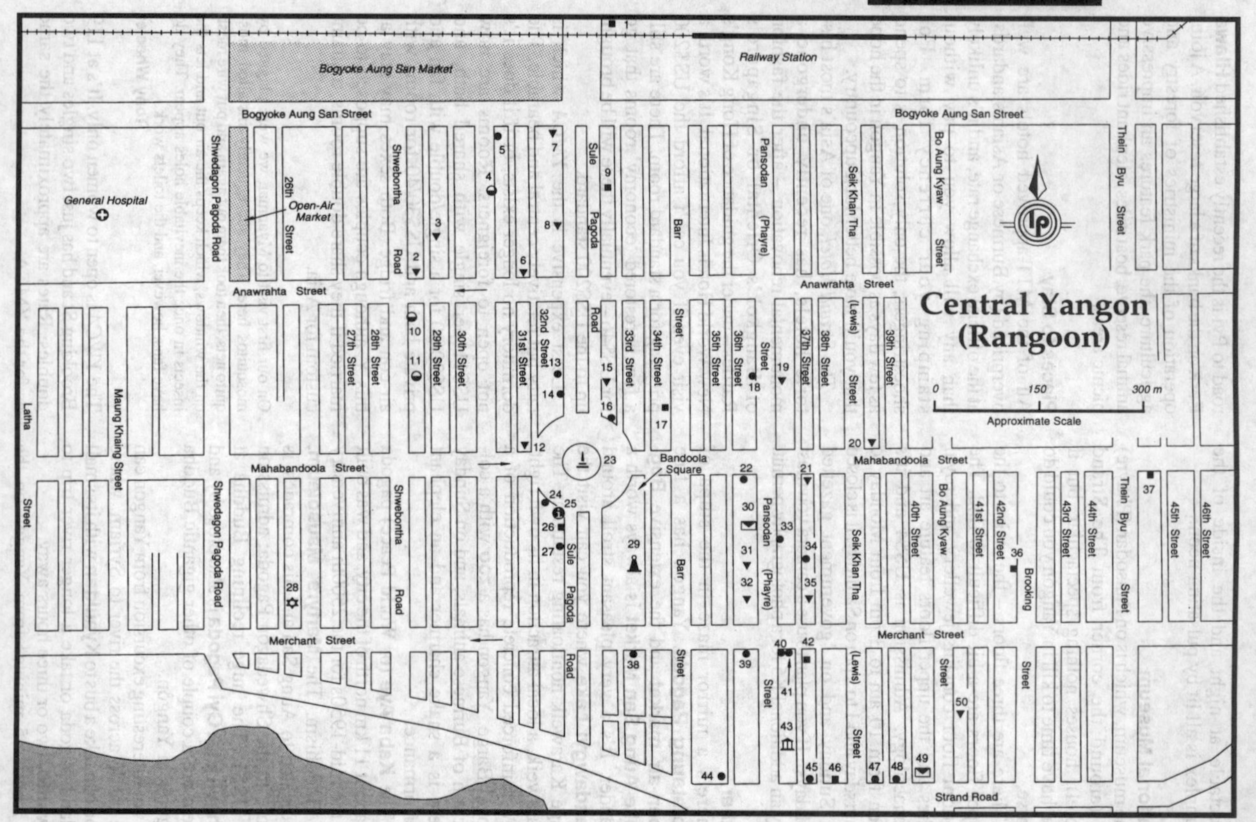
Central Yangon (Rangoon)
Approximate Scale
0
150
300 m
Railway Station
Bogyoke Aung San Market
Open-Air Market
General Hospital
Bandoola Square
Bogyoke Aung San Street
Anawrahta Street
Mahabandoola Street
Merchant Street
Strand Road
46th Street
45th Street
Thein Byu Street
44th Street
43rd Street
Brooking Street
42nd Street
41st Street
Bo Aung Kyaw Street
40th Street
39th Street
Seik Khan Tha (Lewis) Street
38th Street
37th Street
Pansodan (Phayre) Street
36th Street
35th Street
Barr Street
34th Street
33rd Street
Sule Pagoda Road
32nd Street
31st Street
30th Street
29th Street
Shwebontha Road
28th Street
27th Street
26th Street
Shwedagon Pagoda Road
Maung Khaing Street
Latha Street

If the Ys are full, as they occasionally are, there are a number of alternatives. The old Orient Hotel at 256/260 Sule Pagoda Rd is now named the *Dagon* (☎ 89354) and is a fairly pleasant place to stay except that the rooms at the front are very noisy. There are nice views from the balcony, there's good food in the restaurant downstairs (upstairs from the street) and it's a fine place for a beer. Rooms are US$15 per single and US$20 to US$25 for a double.

Right next door to the MTT office on Sule Pagoda Rd is the *Garden Hotel*. It's a slightly more modern establishment than either Y and is kept fairly clean. Quoted rates for economy rooms are US$18/24 for singles/doubles with private bath. Superior rooms – a bit larger – cost US$30/36.

Perhaps Yangon's best buy is the old travellers' standby of *Pyin Oo Lwin* (☎ 74005) at 183 Barr (Mahabandoola Garden) St, two blocks east of the Sule Pagoda. Reopened to foreigners in 1993, tidy rooms with fan here cost US$15 per single and US$20 to US$25 per double.

There are dozens of other pleasant-looking guesthouses in central Yangon but few are officially approved for foreigners. A new one open to the world at large is the *Zar Chi Win Guest House* at 59, 37th St, where clean air-con rooms are US$30 per single and US$40 per double, including breakfast.

A string of others with similar US$30 to US$40 rates are open in Bahan township north-west of the lake, including *Beauty Land Hotel* (☎ 51525, 9 Bo Cho Rd), *Diamond Inn* (☎ 53865, 182 Shwegondine Rd), *Arnanda Inn* (☎ 31251, Aungzeya Lane, off University Ave), and *Asia Villa 1* (☎ 33536, 55 Inyamaing Rd).

Well east of downtown at 126, 52nd St (between Mahabandoola and Anawrahta Sts) in the Pazundaung township, the new *Cozy Guest House* (☎ 91623) has decent rooms with private bath for US$20/30 per single/double.

Places to Eat

There are numerous Indian restaurants around, particularly along Anawrahta St going west from Sule Pagoda Rd. The *New Delhi Restaurant* between 29th St and Shwebontha Rd serves a wide selection of north and south Indian dishes and is quite good. Some of the smaller Indian places specialise in biryani (which is spiced rice

PLACES TO STAY

- 1 Sakhantha Hotel
- 9 Dagon Hotel
- 17 Pyin Oo Lwin Guest-house
- 26 Garden Hotel
- 36 YWCA
- 37 YMCA
- 42 Zar Chi Win Guest House
- 46 The Strand Hotel

PLACES TO EAT

- 2 New Delhi Restaurant
- 3 Burmese Restaurants
- 6 Nila Briyane Shop
- 7 Myanmar Patisserie
- 8 Gold Cup Café
- 12 Yatha Tea Shop
- 15 Lombani Tea House
- 19 Great Wall Restaurant
- 20 Bharat Restaurant
- 21 Nilar Win's Cold Drink Shop
- 31 Nan Yu Restaurant
- 32 Mya Sabe Café
- 35 Palace Restaurant
- 50 Cheap Burmese Foodstalls

OTHER

- 4 Meiktila Buses (Road & Transport Co)
- 5 Bookstalls
- 10 Mawlamyine Buses
- 11 Pyi Buses
- 13 Tourist Department Store
- 14 Myanmar Airways International (MIA)
- 16 City Hall & Library
- 18 Ava Tailoring
- 22 Central Telegraph Office
- 23 Sule Pagoda
- 24 Thai International
- 25 Myanmar Travels & Tours (MTT)
- 27 Air France
- 28 Synagogue
- 29 Independence Monument
- 30 Post Office
- 33 Bangladesh Biman Airways
- 34 Pagan Bookshop
- 38 US Embassy
- 39 Indian Embassy
- 40 Silk Air
- 41 Sarpay Beikman Library
- 43 National Museum
- 44 Customs House
- 45 Myanma Airways
- 47 Australian Embassy
- 48 British Embassy
- 49 GPO

with chicken). Try the *Nila Briyane Shop* between 31st and 32nd Sts. It's crowded but the service is snappy. On Mahabandoola St, at the corner of Seik Khan Tha (Lewis) St, is the dependable and cheap *Bharat*, which is similar to the New Delhi.

The fancier restaurants sprinkled throughout Yangon are mostly Chinese. At 84, 37th St, the *Palace* has a reputation for serving the best Chinese food in Yangon but has become a little grotty in recent times. Some argue that the *Nan Yu* at 81 Pansodan St and the *Ruby* at 50 Bo Aung Gyaw St (round the corner from the GPO) are better.

There are lots of places for tea, a quick snack or a cold beer. The *Lombani Tea House* on Sule Pagoda Rd is a good place to try Burmese tea and the snacks served along with it. The large *Myanmar Patisserie* at the northern end of Sule Pagoda Rd near the Bogyoke Aung San Market is a government-run teahouse with low, subsidised prices. You can get yoghurt or lassi (a delicious yoghurt drink) at *Nilar Win's Cold Drink Shop* at 377 Mahabandoola St, about midway between the YMCA and the Sule Pagoda. Before 1988, it was quite a travellers' meeting spot and the proprietors have been keeping the premises well scrubbed in preparation for the travellers' return. *Yatha*, a white-fronted building within sight of the tourist office, is a good place for drinks and ice cream as well as tea and snacks. The friendly owner speaks excellent English.

Try the genuine Burmese food in the *Hla Myanma Rice House* at 27, 5th St, behind the Shwedagon Pagoda. It's popularly called the Shwe Ba because the famous Burmese actor of the same name had his house nearby. It's a plain and straightforward restaurant, but the food is very good and they also have Chinese and Indian dishes. Prices are quite reasonable – count on around K70 to K80 per person.

There are dozens of Burmese *foodstalls* along 41st St between Strand Rd and Merchant St.

Getting There & Away

See the Myanmar Getting There & Away section or sections on the relevant destinations for transport details to and from Yangon.

Getting Around

To/From the Airport The fixed fare for a taxi between the airport and Yangon is US$6 or 6 FECs. You pay the fare at the MTT counter in the airport and four passengers may share one vehicle. You can also walk out to the road and pay K350 to K450 for a taxi (assuming you have kyats to spend or whisky/cigarettes to trade) or take a local bus, although the latter entails getting out to the main road, about a km away, first. On departure, MAI provides a bus for its passengers but it departs so long before flight time that you may prefer to sleep in and get a taxi for an early morning departure. All international departures are levied a US$6 airport tax.

Local Transport You can get around Yangon on the fairly comprehensive bus service or by trishaws, taxis or the small Mazda taxi-trucks. Some of these operate just like taxis (though they're cheaper) while others seem to run their own little bus routes with fares of a few kyats or so. A trishaw ride within the city centre should be around K30 to K40. Government taxis from The Strand and Thamada hotels charge around K30 per hour for long-term hire. Since you can pay in black market kyat this is extremely reasonable.

An interesting way of seeing the city, suburbs and surrounding countryside is to take the 'circle line' train from Yangon station. It's crowded with commuters on weekdays but on Saturday morning you can make a 2½ hour loop, allowing you to see the outskirts of the city and surrounding villages.

Around Yangon

BAGO (Pegu)

Bago is 80 km north-east from Yangon on the Mandalay railway line. This city used to be a major seaport until the river changed course. This event, coupled with Bago's destruction by a rival Burmese king in 1757, was the city's downfall.

Shwemawdaw Pagoda

The Great Golden God Pagoda was rebuilt after an earthquake in 1930 and is nearly as high as the Shwedagon Pagoda in Yangon. Murals tell the sad story of the quake. Note the large chunk of the *hti* (the umbrella or decorated top of a pagoda), which was toppled by a quake in 1917, embedded in the north-eastern corner of the pagoda.

Shwethalyaung

This huge reclining Buddha image is over five metres longer than the one in Bangkok and claimed to be extremely life-like. A terrific signboard gives the dimensions of the figure's big toe and other vital statistics.

Other

Bago has other attractions. Beyond the Shwemawdaw is the **Hintha Gone**, a hilltop shrine guarded by mythical swans. On the Yangon side of town, the **Kyaik Pun** has three back-to-back sitting Buddhas – a fourth one has fallen down. Just before the Shwethalyaung is the **Maha Kalyani Sima**, or Hall of Ordination, and a curious quartet of standing Buddha figures.

Carry on beyond the Shwethalyaung and you soon come to the **Mahazedi Pagoda**, where you can climb to the top for a fine view of the surrounding country. The **Shwegugale Pagoda**, with 64 seated Buddha images, is a little beyond the Mahazedi.

Places to Stay & Eat

The official MTT-approved hotel is the *Shwewatan* with single/double rooms for US$25/35. There are a number of foodstalls around the marketplace and some snack bars and restaurants near the railway station. The *Three Five Restaurant* between the railway bridge and the river (left side as you walk from the station) has good, cheap Chinese food; the house speciality is 'goat fighting balls' (goat testicles).

Getting There & Away

There are plenty of buses and trains between Yangon and Bago. If you plan to disembark at Bago from the Mandalay to Yangon special express, you can only officially do so on the day train. On one trip to Myanmar, however, I took the night train from Thazi and it went through the station so slowly that I simply hopped off the moving train.

Don't try to visit Bago on the way north to Mandalay; you may have trouble getting a seat on another northbound train. Coming south, it's only another hour or two into Yangon by train or bus. In Yangon, train tickets to Bago must be purchased from MTT for US$8 one way. Coming back, you may be able to buy a ticket at the Bago station with free market kyats.

Buses to Bago cost around K20 from the bus terminal on the northern outskirts of Yangon; they start from Yangon as early as 5 or 6 am. City bus No 34 goes from the intersection of Barr St and Anawrahta St in central Yangon to the bus terminal for K2. Avoid Bago on weekends when it is very crowded with Burmese – the excursion there from Yangon is a popular one. If you want to splash out a bit, get a group together and hire a huge old American taxi from near The Strand Hotel and ride there like Al Capone. Count on around US$15 to US$20 for the whole day.

Getting Around

The easiest way to explore Bago is to hire a trishaw by the station and negotiate a rate to visit all the Bago attractions. Or if you've hired a car from Yangon, ask the driver to take you around to all the sights.

Mandalay Region

MANDALAY

Mandalay was the last capital of Myanmar to fall before the British took over, and for this reason it still has great importance as a

MYANMAR

PLACES TO STAY

11 Inwa Inn
12 Mandalay Hotel/MTT
13 Mya Mandala Hotel
15 Manmyo Hotel

PLACES TO EAT

14 La Shu Restaurant

OTHER

1 Golf Course
2 Military Cemetery
3 Kuthodaw Pagoda
4 Kyauktawgyi Pagoda
5 Sandamani Pagoda
6 Shwenandaw Kyaung
7 Atumashi Kyaung
8 Royal Palace
9 GPO
10 Independence Monument
16 Bus to Bagan
17 Shwe In Bin Monastery
18 Shwegon Pagoda
19 Goldleaf Workshop
20 Kin Wun Monastery
21 Buddha Image Makers
22 Mahamuni Pagoda
23 Royal Garden

cultural centre. It is Myanmar's second city with a population around 500,000 and was founded, comparatively recently, in 1857. Dry and dusty in the hot season, Mandalay is a sprawling town of dirt streets, trishaws and horse carts.

In 1981, a disastrous fire destroyed a great number of buildings along the riverside but did not affect any of Mandalay's sights. Although Mandalay is itself of some interest, the 'deserted cities' around it are probably even more worthwhile.

Orientation & Information

Mandalay is laid out on an extremely straightforward grid pattern but it is a sprawling place – distances in Mandalay are quite vast. The MTT office is in the Mandalay Hotel, a very long walk from the main part of town where most of the cheap hotels are located.

Royal Palace

Once complete within the enormous palace walls and moat, this amazing example of wooden architecture was completely burnt out during the closing days of WW II. Some foundations and a model can be seen. You must get permission to enter from the sentry at the south gate.

Mandalay Hill

An easy half-hour's barefoot climb up the sheltered steps brings you to a wide view over the palace, Mandalay and the pagoda-studded countryside.

Kuthodaw Pagoda

This pagoda's 729 small temples each shelter a marble slab inscribed with Buddhist scriptures. The central pagoda makes it 730. Built by King Mindon around 1860, it is the world's biggest book. Don't confuse it with the **Sandamuni Pagoda** which is right in front of it and which also has a large collection of inscribed slabs. The ruins of the **Atumashi Kyaung**, or Incomparable Monastery, are also close to the foot of Mandalay Hill.

Shwenandaw Kyaung

Once a part of King Mindon's palace, this wooden building was moved to its present site and converted into a monastery after his death. This is the finest remaining example of traditional wooden Burmese architecture since all the other palace buildings were destroyed during WW II. Admission is US$3.

Kyauktawgyi Pagoda

This pagoda at the base of Mandalay Hill was another King Mindon construction. The marble Buddha is said to have taken 10,000 men 13 days to install in the temple.

Mahamuni Pagoda

The 'Arakan Pagoda' stands to the south of town. It's noted for its venerated Buddha image which is thickly covered in goldleaf. Around the main pagoda are rooms containing a huge five-tonne gong and Khmer-style bronze figures. Rubbing parts of the figures is supposed to cure afflictions on the corresponding parts of your own body. Outside

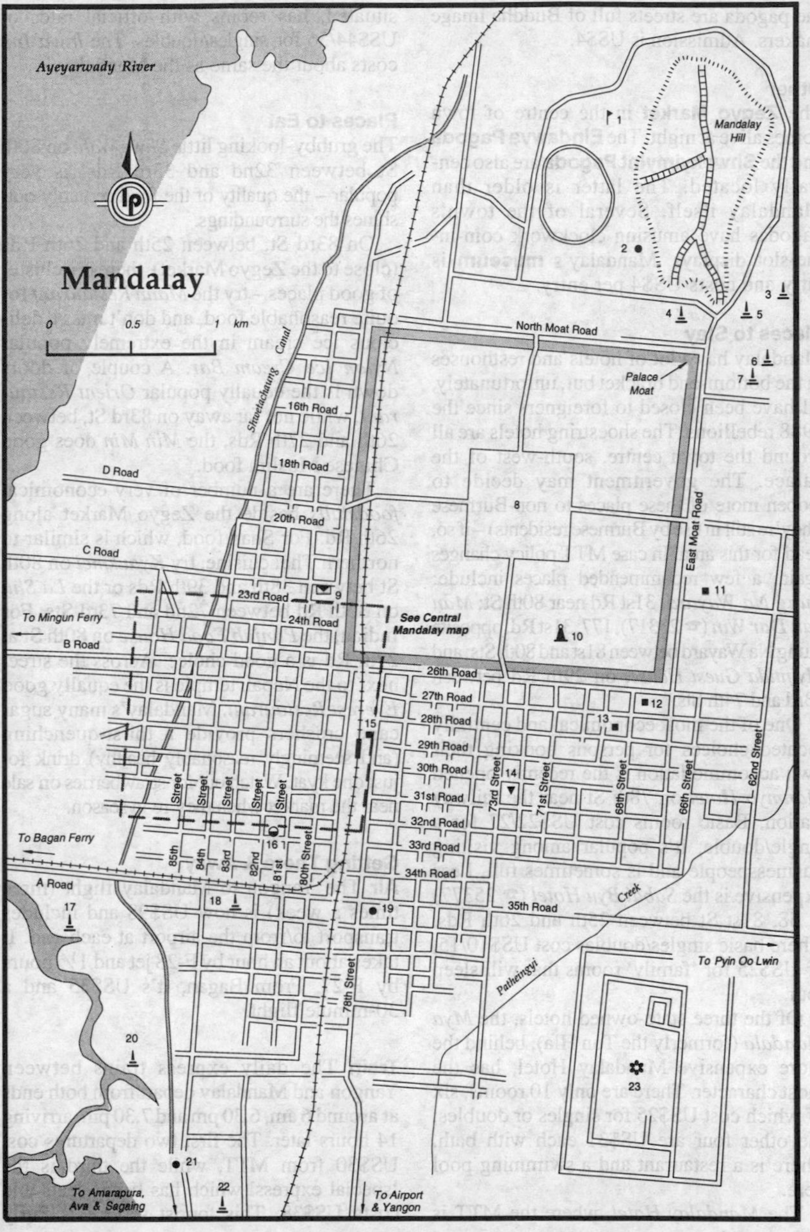
Mandalay
Ayeyarwady River
0
0.5
1 km
Mandalay Hill
1
2
3
4
5
6
7
North Moat Road
Palace Moat
16th Road
Shwetachaung Canal
18th Road
D Road
8
20th Road
East Moat Road
C Road
23rd Road
9
11
To Mingun Ferry
24th Road
See Central Mandalay map
B Road
10
26th Road
27th Road
12
28th Road
13
15
29th Road
30th Road
14
73rd Street
71st Street
68th Street
66th Street
62nd Street
31st Road
32nd Road
Street
Street
Street
Street
Street
To Bagan Ferry
16
33rd Road
85th
84th
83rd
82nd
81st
80th Street
34th Road
Creek
A Road
17
18
19
35th Road
78th Street
To Pyin Oo Lwin
Patheingyi
20
23
21
22
To Amarapura, Ava & Sagaing
To Airport & Yangon

the pagoda are streets full of Buddha image makers. Admission is US$4.

Other

The **Zegyo Market** in the centre of town comes alive at night. The **Eindawya Pagoda** and the **Shwekyimyint Pagoda** are also centrally located. The latter is older than Mandalay itself. Several of the town's pagodas have amusing clockwork coin-in-the-slot displays. Mandalay's **museum** is tatty and costs US$4 per entry.

Places to Stay

Mandalay has a lot of hotels and resthouses in the bottom-end bracket but, unfortunately, all have been closed to foreigners since the 1988 rebellions. The shoestring hotels are all around the town centre, south-west of the palace. The government may decide to reopen more of these places to non-Burmese (they're still in use by Burmese residents) – if so, head for this area. In case MTT policy changes again, a few recommended places include: *Aung Na Wayard*, 31st Rd near 80th St; *Man San Dar Win* (☎ 23317), 177, 31st Rd, opposite Aung Na Wayard between 81st and 80th Sts; and *Myintida Guest House*, on 29th Rd between 73rd and 74th Sts.

One of the most economical and centrally located choices for persons booking their own accommodation is the recently opened *Manmyo Hotel* on 78th St near the railway station. Basic rooms cost US$22/27 for a single/double; it's popular among visiting businesspeople and is sometimes full. Less expensive is the *Sabai Byu Hotel* (☎ 25377) at 58, 81st St between 25th and 26th Rds, where basic singles/doubles cost US$10/15, or US$25 for 'family' rooms that will sleep four.

Of the three state-owned hotels, the *Mya Mandala* (formerly the Tun Hla), behind the more expensive Mandalay Hotel, has the most character. There are only 10 rooms, six of which cost US$25 for singles or doubles; the other four are US$31 each with bath. There is a restaurant and a swimming pool here.

The *Mandalay Hotel*, where the MTT is situated, has rooms with official rates of US$44/56 for singles/doubles. The *Inwa Inn* costs about the same as the Mandalay.

Places to Eat

The grubby-looking little *Shwe Wah*, on 80th St between 32nd and 33rd Rds, is very popular – the quality of the food certainly outshines the surroundings.

On 83rd St, between 25th and 26th Rds (close to the Zegyo Market), there is a cluster of good places – try the *Mann Restaurant* for quite reasonable food, and don't miss a delicious ice cream in the extremely popular *Nylon Ice Cream Bar*. A couple of doors down is the equally popular *Orient Restaurant*, while not far away on 83rd St, between 26th and 27th Rds, the *Min Min* does good Chinese Muslim food.

There are a number of very economical *foodstalls* beside the Zegyo Market along 26th Rd. For Shan food, which is similar to northern Thai cuisine, try *Kyaukmei* on 80th St between 38th and 39th Rds or the *La Shu* on 30th Rd between 72nd and 73rd Sts. For Indian, the *Punjab Food House* on 80th St at 27th Rd is a good choice. Across the street next to the Nepali temple is the equally good *Everest Restaurant*. Mandalay's many sugar cane crushers provide a thirst-quenching (and seemingly reasonably healthy) drink for just one kyat. Watch out for strawberries on sale near the market when they're in season.

Getting There & Away

Air The Yangon to Mandalay flight (three times a week) is now US$98 and includes transport to/from the airport at each end. It takes about an hour by F-28 jet and 1½ hours by F-27. From Bagan, it's US$35 and a 30-minute flight.

Train The daily express trains between Yangon and Mandalay depart from both ends at around 6 am, 6.30 pm and 7.30 pm, arriving 14 hours later. The first two departures cost US$30 from MTT, while the third is the 'special express' which has better seats and costs US$38. This tourist service is fairly

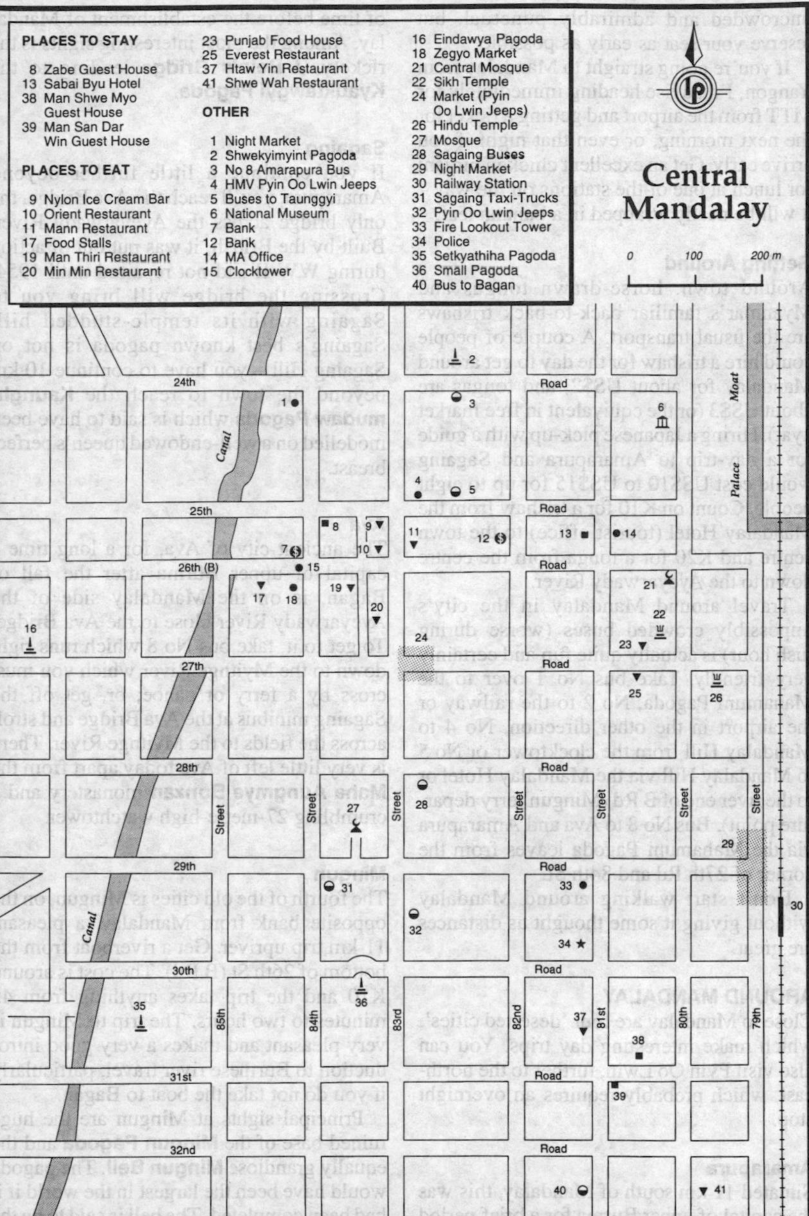
Central Mandalay
PLACES TO STAY
8 Zabe Guest House
13 Sabai Byu Hotel
38 Man Shwe Myo Guest House
39 Man San Dar Win Guest House
PLACES TO EAT
9 Nylon Ice Cream Bar
10 Orient Restaurant
11 Mann Restaurant
17 Food Stalls
19 Man Thiri Restaurant
20 Min Min Restaurant
23 Punjab Food House
25 Everest Restaurant
37 Htaw Yin Restaurant
41 Shwe Wah Restaurant
OTHER
1 Night Market
2 Shwekyimyint Pagoda
3 No 8 Amarapura Bus
4 HMV Pyin Oo Lwin Jeeps
5 Buses to Taunggyi
6 National Museum
7 Bank
12 Bank
14 MA Office
15 Clocktower
16 Eindawya Pagoda
18 Zegyo Market
21 Central Mosque
22 Sikh Temple
24 Market (Pyin Oo Lwin Jeeps)
26 Hindu Temple
27 Mosque
28 Sagaing Buses
29 Night Market
30 Railway Station
31 Sagaing Taxi-Trucks
32 Pyin Oo Lwin Jeeps
33 Fire Lookout Tower
34 Police
35 Setkyathiha Pagoda
36 Small Pagoda
40 Bus to Bagan
0
100
200 m
24th
25th
26th (B)
27th
28th
29th
30th
31st
32nd
Road
Street
85th
84th
83rd
82nd
81st
80th
79th
Canal
Moat
Palace
MYANMAR

uncrowded and admirably punctual, but reserve your seat as early as possible.

If you're going straight to Mandalay from Yangon, I'd advise heading immediately for MTT from the airport and getting a ticket for the next morning, or even that night if you arrive early. Get an excellent chicken biryani for lunch at one of the stations on the way – it will be neatly wrapped in a banana leaf.

Getting Around

Around town, horse-drawn tongas and Myanmar's familiar back-to-back trishaws are the usual transport. A couple of people could hire a trishaw for the day to get around Mandalay for about US$2, and tongas are about US$3 (or the equivalent in free market kyat). Hiring a Japanese pick-up with a guide for a day-trip to Amarapura and Sagaing would cost US$10 to US$15 for up to eight people. Count on K10 for a trishaw from the Mandalay Hotel (tourist office) to the town centre and K20 for a tonga from the centre down to the Ayeyarwady River.

Travel around Mandalay in the city's impossibly crowded buses (worse during rush hour) is actually quite fun and certainly very friendly. Take bus No 1 over to the Mahamuni Pagoda, No 2 to the railway or the airport in the other direction, No 4 to Mandalay Hill from the clocktower or No 5 to Mandalay Hill via the Mandalay Hotel or to the river end of B Rd (Mingun ferry departure point). Bus No 8 to Ava and Amarapura via the Mahamuni Pagoda leaves from the corner of 27th Rd and 84th St.

Don't start walking around Mandalay without giving it some thought as distances are great.

AROUND MANDALAY

Close to Mandalay are four 'deserted cities', which make interesting day trips. You can also visit Pyin Oo Lwin, further to the north-east, which probably requires an overnight stop.

Amarapura

Situated 11 km south of Mandalay, this was the capital of upper Burma for a brief period of time before the establishment of Mandalay. Among the most interesting sights is the rickety **U Bein's Bridge** leading to the **Kyauktawgyi Pagoda**.

Sagaing

If you continue a little further beyond Amarapura, you'll reach the Ava Bridge, the only bridge across the Ayeyarwady River. Built by the British, it was put out of action during WW II and not repaired until 1954. Crossing the bridge will bring you to Sagaing with its temple-studded hill. Sagaing's best known pagoda is not on Sagaing Hill – you have to continue 10 km beyond the town to reach the **Kaunghmudaw Pagoda** which is said to have been modelled on a well-endowed queen's perfect breast.

Ava

The ancient city of Ava, for a long time a capital of upper Burma after the fall of Bagan, is on the Mandalay side of the Ayeyarwady River close to the Ava Bridge. To get to it, take bus No 8 which runs right down to the Myitnge River which you must cross by a ferry or canoe; or, get off the Sagaing minibus at the Ava Bridge and stroll across the fields to the Myitnge River. There is very little left of Ava today apart from the **Maha Aungmye Bonzan** monastery and a crumbling 27-metre-high watchtower.

Mingun

The fourth of the old cities is Mingun, on the opposite bank from Mandalay, a pleasant 11-km trip upriver. Get a riverboat from the bottom of 26th St (B Rd). The cost is around K10 and the trip takes anything from 45 minutes to two hours. The trip to Mingun is very pleasant and makes a very good introduction to Burmese river travel, particularly if you do not take the boat to Bagan.

Principal sights at Mingun are the huge ruined base of the **Mingun Pagoda** and the equally grandiose **Mingun Bell**. The pagoda would have been the largest in the world if it had been completed. The bell is said to be the largest uncracked bell in the world – there is a bigger one in Russia but it is badly cracked.

Monywa

The **Thanboddhay Pagoda** here is one of the largest in Myanmar and there are said to be 582,357 Buddha images ensconced thereon. The town of Monywa, a trade centre for the Chindwin Valley, is 135 km northwest of Mandalay. Buses leave for Monywa regularly from the corner of 84th St and 30th Rd in Mandalay, cost around K45 and take about three hours. You can also take a Ye-U train from Mandalay for only K15, but this trip takes four to five hours.

The state-owned *Monywa Hotel* has rooms for US$25 to US$36.

Pyin Oo Lwin (Maymyo)

If you haven't time to head downriver to Bagan, then Pyin Oo Lwin may make an interesting substitute. It's an old British hill station, formerly called Maymyo after the British Colonel May. It's just 60 km northeast of Mandalay and about 800 metres higher.

The chief pleasure of Pyin Oo Lwin is a stay at the old British bachelor's quarters of Candacraig. You can read a delightful description of it in Paul Theroux's *Great Railway Bazaar*.

Places to Stay & Eat Candacraig, officially known as the *Pyin Oo Lwin Government Rest House*, was once the bachelor quarters of the Bombay Burma Trading Company. It was run by the late Mr Bernard until around his 90th birthday and was maintained in the exact state it was in during the British era.

It has lost some of its colonial splendour but it is still pleasant, with rooms costing US$25/31 (official rate) for singles/doubles. A roaring fire, a cold bottle of Mandalay beer and the English dinner all add to the atmosphere. You can hire bicycles here to explore Pyin Oo Lwin. You might inquire first at MTT in Mandalay to make sure it is open, as in recent times it has occasionally been closed for repairs.

The *Nan Myaing*, on your left as you enter town from Mandalay, has standard singles/doubles at US$40 or larger 'superior' rooms for US$69. Actually, Candacraig is officially an annex to the Nan Myaing; MTT will try to send you there first.

Other places to stay in town include the *Thiri Myaing* on Anawrahta Rd and the *Yuzana Myaing* on Aing Daw Rd, both with basic rooms in the US$20 to US$30 range. Cheapies *Thin Sabai*, *Shwe Yema* and *Ububahan* are near the entrance of town but are presently closed to foreigners – but who knows what the future will hold. The *YMCA* might allow foreigners in for US$11 a room.

There are a variety of restaurants around the town centre, including a couple of Chinese places reputed to have some of the best Chinese food in Myanmar.

Getting There & Away From Mandalay, you can take a jeep to Pyin Oo Lwin for K35 per person. Jeeps depart from several places around the centre of Mandalay (there are frequent departures from some markets – see the map) from 5 am until about 3 pm and the trip takes about two to 2½ hours up, one to 1½ down. Chartering a whole jeep costs K250 to K300. There is also a daily train but it's more for railway enthusiasts as it takes four to five hours to negotiate the many switchbacks.

Bagan Region

BAGAN (Pagan)

One of the true wonders of Asia, Bagan (formerly Pagan) is a bewildering, deserted city of fabulous pagodas and temples on the banks of the Ayeyarwady, to the south-west of Mandalay. Bagan's period of grandeur started in 1057 when King Anawrahta conquered Thaton and brought back artists, craftsmen, monks and 30 elephant-loads of Buddhist scriptures.

Over the next two centuries, an enormous number of magnificent buildings were erected, but after Kublai Khan sacked the city in 1287 it was never rebuilt. A major earthquake in 1975 caused enormous damage but everything of importance has now been restored or reconstructed. Unhappily, the plunderers who visit places like Bagan to scavenge for Western art collectors have also done damage but it is definitely the place in Myanmar not to be missed.

Orientation & Information

As a place of human habitation, Bagan is once again as deserted as it was after Kublai Khan passed through centuries ago. Following the 1988 uprising, the government forced the tiny Bagan village to move some four km away, supposedly so they could undertake archaeological digs (which so far haven't occurred). The numerous shops, houses, small guesthouses and restaurants that once lined the dirt road have all been demolished.

The largest nearby settlement is Nyaung-Oo. Buses depart from here and it's also where the Mandalay ferry docks. Bagan airport is also near Nyaung-Oo. MTT has an office in the main street of Bagan.

Without fail, you should get a copy of the *Glimpses of Glorious Pagan* (or its previous edition, *Pictorial Guide to Pagan*) as an aid to exploring the ruins. A newer photographic guide simply entitled *Pagan* is also quite good but very expensive.

The entry fee into the 'Archaeological Zone' is US$10 per day for the first two days, US$2 per day thereafter.

Things to See

The following section describes just a handful of the more interesting of Bagan's 5000-plus temples.

Ananda This huge white temple was built in 1091 and houses four standing Buddhas and two sacred Buddha footprints. It's close to the Bagan village and is one of the most important temples. In 1989 the tower was regilded and the niches filled with Buddha images.

Thatbyinnyu This is the highest temple in Bagan, with Buddha images in the upper storey and magnificent views from the top. Bagan has to be seen from above for proper appreciation.

Gawdawpalin Also close to the village of Bagan, Gawdawpalin looks like a slightly smaller Thatbyinnyu. Built between 1174 and 1211, this is the best place to watch the sunset over the Ayeyarwady. This temple was probably the most extensively damaged in the 1975 quake but has been completely restored.

Mingalazedi One of the last temples completed before Kublai Khan sacked the city. Fine terracotta tiles can be seen around the base of the huge bell-shaped stupa.

Shwesandaw A cylindrical stupa on top of five ultra-steep terraces with good views from the top. In the shed beside the stupa is a 20-metre reclining Buddha.

Shwezigon This traditionally shaped gold pagoda was started by King Anawrahta and stands close to the village of Nyaung-Oo. The view of the magnificent lions guarding the entrances is ruined by the arcades built between them.

Manuha This temple was built by King Manuha, the 'captive king', in the village of Myinkaba. The Buddhas are impossibly squeezed in their enclosures – an allegorical representation of the king's own discomfort with captivity. Excellent lacquerware workshops can be visited in Myinkaba.

Other The **Htilominlo**, or Blessing of Three Worlds, was built in 1211 and has fine Buddhas on the ground and upper levels. It's beside the road from Bagan to Nyaung-Oo.

In Bagan village, the **Pitakat Taik** is the library built in 1058 to house those 30 elephant-loads of scriptures. Down towards the Ayeyarwady, the **Mahâbodhi** is modelled on Indian-style temples. There is a **museum** (admission US$4) near the Gawdawpalin Temple which houses Bagan artefacts.

Further out from the centre, the massive and brooding **Dhammayangyi** has superb

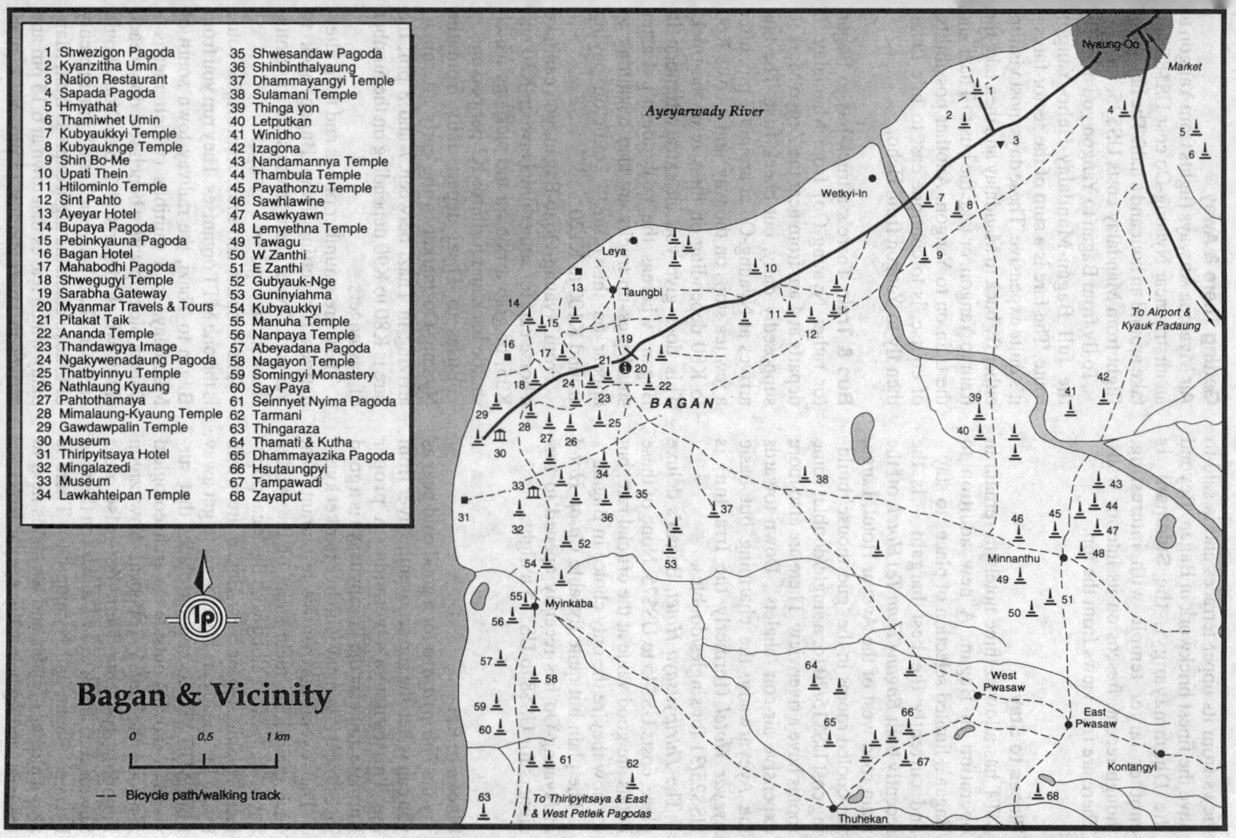
Bagan & Vicinity
0
0.5
1 km
Bicycle path/walking track
1 Shwezigon Pagoda
2 Kyanzittha Umin
3 Nation Restaurant
4 Sapada Pagoda
5 Hmyathat
6 Thamiwhet Umin
7 Kubyaukkyi Temple
8 Kubyauknge Temple
9 Shin Bo-Me
10 Upati Thein
11 Htilominlo Temple
12 Sint Pahto
13 Ayeyar Hotel
14 Bupaya Pagoda
15 Pebinkyauna Pagoda
16 Bagan Hotel
17 Mahabodhi Pagoda
18 Shwegugyi Temple
19 Sarabha Gateway
20 Myanmar Travels & Tours
21 Pitakat Taik
22 Ananda Temple
23 Thandawgya Image
24 Ngakywenadaung Pagoda
25 Thatbyinnyu Temple
26 Nathlaung Kyaung
27 Pahtothamaya
28 Mimalaung-Kyaung Temple
29 Gawdawpalin Temple
30 Museum
31 Thiripyitsaya Hotel
32 Mingalazedi
33 Museum
34 Lawkahteipan Temple
35 Shwesandaw Pagoda
36 Shinbinthalyaung
37 Dhammayangyi Temple
38 Sulamani Temple
39 Thinga yon
40 Letputkan
41 Winidho
42 Izagona
43 Nandamannya Temple
44 Thambula Temple
45 Payathonzu Temple
46 Sawhlawine
47 Asawkyawn
48 Lemyethna Temple
49 Tawagu
50 W Zanthi
51 E Zanthi
52 Gubyauk-Nge
53 Guninyiahma
54 Kubyaukkyi
55 Manuha Temple
56 Nanpaya Temple
57 Abeyadana Pagoda
58 Nagayon Temple
59 Somingyi Monastery
60 Say Paya
61 Seinnyet Nyima Pagoda
62 Tarmani
63 Thingaraza
64 Thamati & Kutha
65 Dhammayazika Pagoda
66 Hsutaunggpy
67 Tampawadi
68 Zayaput
Ayeyarwady River
Nyaung-Oo
Market
To Airport & Kyauk Padaung
Wetkyi-In
Taungbi
Leya
BAGAN
Minnanthu
West Pwasaw
East Pwasaw
Kontangyi
Myinkaba
Thuhekan
To Thiripyitsaya & East & West Petleik Pagodas

views from its upper terraces and is said to have the finest brickwork in Bagan. Beyond the Dhammayangyi, the **Sulamani** is another larger temple with interesting, though recent, frescos on its interior walls. There are fine views from the top.

Places to Stay

MTT has allowed three hotels to remain in operation in Bagan. A new addition to Bagan's limited selection of places to stay – and currently the best bargain – is the recently built *Bagan (Than Te) Hotel*, off the main road west of the Ayeyar Hotel. Large, fan-cooled rooms in the 'guesthouse' building cost US$15/20 for a single/double; some rooms have a river view. There are also more expensive air-con 'chalets'. Down towards the Ayeyarwady, the charming but basic *Ayeyar Hotel* (formerly the Irra Inn) is US$25/31 for singles/doubles.

The *Thiripyitsaya Hotel*, Bagan's deluxe place, costs US$45 to US$75. None of these hotels are good value at the official rate, but for now they're the only choice in Bagan.

The plain but quite liveable *Co-op Hotel* in Nyaung-Oo has recently opened to foreigners for US$8 to US$15 a night.

Places to Eat

Try the *Thiripyitsaya* for a good cold beer as you can watch the sun set over the river from the Thiripyitsaya's veranda. A proper Burmese dinner at the Thiripyitsaya is a good investment if you pay with free market kyats.

The several inexpensive restaurants that once graced the main street of the village have disappeared along with the local populace. Nyaung-Oo or New Bagan are worth trying for cheap eats if you want to get away from MTT. Three popular places that survived by moving outside the archaeological zone are the *Nation* (opposite Shwezigon Pagoda), *Aye Yike Thar Yar* (also near Shwezigon) and *Mya Ya Da Nar* (on the road between Bagan and Nyaung-Oo). There is also a cluster of cafes and tea shops next to the boat landing below the Ayeyar Hotel.

Getting There & Away

Air Myanma Airways flights from Yangon to an airstrip near Nyaung-Oo cost US$85 and take around an hour and a half. The half-hour flight from Mandalay costs US$35.

To fly from Bagan to Yangon you must fly the full Bagan-Mandalay-Heho-Yangon route. The fare is a sum of the sector fares – it's quite expensive. These days most visitors either fly back to Mandalay and then take the train to Yangon, or take the bus to Thazi and the train on to Yangon. Another possibility, of course, is to continue east to Inle Lake, then fly to Yangon from Heho.

Bus & Train There's a truck-bus to Bagan (or rather Nyaung-Oo) from Mandalay. It departs at 4 am from near the Zegyo Market, supposedly daily, but check first. The bus arrives at Nyaung-Oo at around 2 pm, after a few tea stops on the way, and it costs K60 to K80 depending on the size of the truck. This does give you an extra afternoon in Bagan, whereas the boat doesn't. Faster small pick-up trucks are also beginning to appear on this route – count on paying around K100 to K120.

From Nyaung-Oo to Bagan, you can take a horse cart for something between K30 and K35, or grab a ride on the pick-ups which shuttle back and forth for K2 per person.

Buses to Thazi depart daily from the Nyaung-Oo market in the early afternoon, arriving in Thazi between 7 and 8 pm; the fare is K80 to K90 depending on the number of passengers.

There are a number of bus and train alternatives for getting from Bagan back to Yangon. One of them rates as the most miserable train trip I've ever made.

The simplest and most comfortable route is the one MTT organises. They run you from Bagan to Thazi, the railway town south of Mandalay, in a minibus (which means a Datsun pick-up with a bench seat down each side!) which departs at 2 pm. You should arrive in Thazi between 7 and 8 pm, in plenty of time to catch the night express from Mandalay which leaves that town at 6.15 pm and arrives in Thazi about 9.15 pm. MTT guarantee you a seat on the train if you take their truck, but you must book ahead in Bagan or Mandalay. If there are enough to fill a truck, the cost is only around US$10 per person. If not, the fare is prorated upward for the number of passengers.

Another bus and train alternative is a do-it-yourself version of the above. First of all, get into Nyaung-Oo from Bagan, then take a bus-truck (ie a truck with benches in the back) to Kyauk Padaung, a ride of a couple of hours. Follow this with another bus to Meiktila, about three hours away, then a short half-hour ride to Thazi. Total fare will be about K60 but there is no way you can do this in time for the morning train. There's a catch to this method too. It's quite possible that when the comfortable Mandalay to Yangon train rolls in it will be completely full and the alternative will be a dirty, slow, crowded, miserable local train that rolls in many hours later (and many hours late).

There are two solutions to this problem – one is to book a Mandalay to Yangon ticket before you leave Mandalay. The fare from Thazi is a few kyats less than from Mandalay so it's not very wasteful and much more comfortable. The other solution is just to ignore the fact that the fast train is full and you're not allowed on. Just get on anyway – you'll find the floor of the deluxe train much more comfortable than that of the slow train and you'll get there faster.

The final bus-train alternative is the one to be avoided at all costs. Stage one is to take the same bus-truck to Kyauk Padaung, which is the railhead nearest Bagan. At somewhere between 2 and 5 pm an absolute horror of a train crawls off to Yangon, arriving something like 24 hours later. The fare is virtually the same as from Thazi and it's a dirty, uncomfortable, unlit, slow, crowded, tedious and unpleasant train. Avoid it.

Boat A new fast boat to Nyaung-Oo leaves Mandalay every Sunday and Thursday at 4 am, arriving in Nyaung-Oo at around 6 pm. MTT would prefer you pay US$10 for a spot on the 1st-class deck – a section of well-spaced sling chairs with good river views. You can also sit with the masses in adjacent 2nd class for K50. Foreigners aren't allowed to ride in steerage on the deck below, which is even cheaper. There is also a more expensive 1st-class cabin area with eight two-berth rooms usually reserved for tour groups. Many travellers sleep on the boat the night before departure to save on hotel rooms – it also means not having to get up in the middle of the night for a 4 am departure.

A slower, much cheaper ferry does the same route every day, leaving at 5 am and taking roughly 38 hours to reach Nyaung-Oo. This boat is off-limits to foreigners, though some travellers have managed to board and ride all the way to Nyaung-Oo with no hassle. The slower boat stops for the night a little north of Bagan and on the opposite bank of the river at a town called Pakkoku, where there are several places to stay including the yayatanar Inn at 2288 Main Road at around US$4 a night. From Nyaung-Oo the slow ferries continue on downriver to Pyi, where you could change boats and continue all the way to Yangon.

Getting Around

The ruins are fairly widespread, and this is particularly a problem when you want to get to some of the more remote ones. You can hire a horse cart for around K20 to K30 an hour or a jeep for around K60 an hour. Both are less by the day or half-day of course. You can also hire bicycles from the Ayeyar Hotel for around K50 for a day. They're a very pleasant way of getting around Bagan but check that the brakes and other vital equipment are operating.

AROUND BAGAN

Mt Popa

Near Kyauk Padaung, the monastery-topped hill of Mt Popa can be visited as a day trip from Bagan. If you get a group together to charter a taxi-truck to Thazi or Inle Lake, a detour can be made to visit it. It takes 20 minutes or so to make the stiff climb to the top of the hill. This is a centre for worship of the nats.

PAKKOKU

Pakkoku is a stopover for boats travelling from Mandalay to Bagan. You may be able to leave your boat for the night and stay in the pleasant *Myayatanar Inn*, 2288 Main Rd. Pakkoku also has some good restaurants, even a cinema! Don't forget that the boat will leave at 5 am the next morning (don't worry if you miss it – there are other boats later in the morning).

THAZI

Thazi is really nothing more than a place people find themselves in when travelling to or from Bagan or Inle Lake.

In Thazi you're now officially allowed to stay at the *Moon-Light Rest House* for US$5 per person. On the main road, just before the railway line, there's the *Wonderful* restaurant with good Chinese food and the *Red Star* with excellent Indian food.

The Thazi to Yangon train fare is US$27 in upper (tourist) class and US$33 for the special express. There are also two trucks a day from Thazi to Inle Lake for K125 per person.

Inle Lake Region

INLE LAKE

Inle Lake and nearby Taunggyi are the only other destinations in the Shan states, besides Pyin Oo Lwin, that are open to foreigners. The lake itself is extraordinarily beautiful and famous for its leg rowers, who propel their boats by standing at the stern on one leg and wrapping the other leg around the oar. This strange technique has arisen because of all the floating vegetation – it's necessary to stand up to plot a path around all the obstacles.

Taunggyi is the centre for official and black market trade in the region. To enter the Inle Lake zone, tourists are required to pay a US$10 entry fee.

To get out on the lake, you must charter an MTT boat – K45 to K50 per person or K400 to K500 for an entire boat with a mandatory guide. The boat tour takes about half a day and includes visits to the floating village of **Ywama**, **Phaungdaw Oo Pagoda**, a floating market (best on Ywama market days, otherwise it's just souvenir-oriented) and to the MTT souvenir shop.

You are not allowed to take ordinary water taxis around the lake like the Burmese do. MTT has, however, in the past tolerated a few entrepreneurs who arrange canoe rides along the canals that run off the lake in the town of Yaunghwe – check around. In Yaunghwe, the **Yatamamanaung Temple** is worth a quick visit.

Orientation

There are four place names to remember in the lake area. First, there's Heho, where the airport is located. Continue east from there and you reach Shwenyaung where the railway terminates and where you turn south off the road to get to the lake. Continue further east and you reach Taunggyi, the main town in the area. At the northern end of the lake is Yaunghwe.

Places to Stay

At Yaunghwe, right by the lake, several tourist lodges have been reopened to foreigners. At US$10 for a single and US$15 per double (for a room with shared bath), the *Inle Inn* (formerly the Bamboo Lodge) is the most economical place to stay. The *Inle Hotel* has singles/doubles at US$25/31 and doubles/triples with softer beds and attached bath at US$31/38. A reader has recommended the new *Golden Express*, a simple but clean and friendly place with singles and doubles for US$10/15.

In Taunggyi the *Taunggyi Hotel* now costs US$30 to US$60. The rooms are modern with bathrooms and it's very pleasant, if overpriced at the official exchange rate.

Places to Eat

Shwe Inlay, near the Yaunghwe town entrance, is good for Shan-style meals. The impecunious can find cheaper food in the market. Best for Chinese food is the clean *Hu*

Pin. The *Inle Hotel* has a dining room with the usual bland but edible tourist fare.

There's excellent food at the *Lyan You*, in the hotel of the same name on the main street of Taunggyi. You can't stay here, however, as it's not on the approved list. The *Academy Cafe*, close to the San Pya, is a friendly place for breakfast. *Shan You Ma*, in the open market at the northern end of town, is renowned for good Shan and Chinese food. The best teahouse in town is the government-run *Shwe Kai Nai Yi* on the main street, featuring favourite Burmese snacks like nam-bya (flatbread) and palata with pots of free tea.

Getting There & Away

Air The Mandalay to Heho airfare is US$35 and Bagan to Heho is US$70 (via Mandalay only). Myanma Airways provides free transport from Heho to Taunggyi. Heho to Yangon is US$98. All Yangon to Heho flights entail stops in Bagan and Mandalay and the total fare is the sum of the sectors.

Bus You can reach Yaunghwe and Taunggyi by bus from Bagan, Mandalay and Thazi. Buses and taxi-trucks leave Mandalay every morning from 25th Rd for K75 per person. The buses leave around 4.30 or 5 am – the trip takes 10 to 12 hours. The Datsun taxi-trucks depart around 6 am and are rather faster. Costs range from around K100 to K150.

It is now fairly feasible to combine Inle Lake with Bagan because chartered minivans holding up to 10 persons operate between Nyaung-Oo and Yaunghwe for US$125. These typically leave from either end at around 5.30 am and arrive at their destination at around 5.30 pm. It's a long and fairly gruelling one-day trip from Nyaung-Oo to the lake – an overnight in Meiktila, Thazi or Kalaw is recommended. A short detour to Mt Popa can also be arranged.

Train From Yangon, you may take the regular Mandalay train and disembark at Thazi, only an hour or so before Mandalay. From there, you can take another train to Shwenyaung, near the lake. This is rather time-consuming though and it's better to take a jeep from Thazi for K100, which only takes six to eight hours, or a bus (Japanese pick-up), which costs considerably less than a jeep but takes longer. If you're heading back to Yangon by this method note the possible problems in getting a seat on the train from Thazi if you haven't prebooked it.

KALAW & PINDAYA

There are several excursions you can make en route to the lake. The Thazi to Taunggyi road passes through Kalaw, once a popular British hill station. There is only one MTT-operated resthouse in Kalaw, the rambling *Kalaw Hotel*, where rooms with shared facilities cost US$10/15 per single/double or US$30/35 for singles/doubles with private bath.

At Aungban, you can turn off the main road and travel north to Pindaya where the **Pindaya Caves** are packed with countless Buddha images, gathered there over the centuries. The *Pindaya Hotel*, the only official choice here, has singles/doubles for US$20/US$25 or US$25/US$30 depending on the size of the room.

Other Places

For a while, it seemed to be getting easier to visit some of the supposedly 'off-limits' places. Following the crackdown of 1989, however, the government has become more xenophobic about foreigners travelling around without permission.

The **Sandoway Beach Resort** (which includes Ngapali Beach) on the Bay of Bengal is now officially open and a standard room at the *Ngapali Beach Hotel* costs US$25 to US$30, US$40 to US$45 for a deluxe. The less expensive *Shwewargyaing Hotel* has rooms for US$15 to US$20. Scheduled flights from Yangon operate only between November and March and cost US$35 on an F-27 turboprop and US$40 on an F-28 jet. The flights are often overbooked. Ngapali can be approached by road from the south-east via Pathein or from the north-east via Pyi.

It is now possible to make it to the **balancing pagoda** at Kyaiktiyo, near the town of Kyaikto beyond Bago. Buses depart regularly from Bago since this is a popular pilgrimage spot. However, having got there you have a 10-km walk where you ascend about 1000 metres. It's not possible to get back to Bago (or Yangon) in the same day so come prepared to camp out. The *Kyaikto Hotel* offers basic but adequate rooms for US$15/20 per single/double, or US$20/25 with private bath.

Pathein, **Sittwe** and **Mrauk-U** can be reached by road and river from Yangon but this leg would consume an entire two-weeks of your visa. Each of these towns has a tourist hotel in the US$18-32 range.

Kyainge Tong (also spelt Chiang Tung and Kengtung), in the remote north-eastern corner of the Shan State near the Chinese border, was opened to tourists in 1993. At the moment foreigners are only permitted to visit this scenic Khün capital by road from Mae Sai, Thailand. See the Thailand chapter for more details.

You can probably also visit **Pyi** (formerly Prome) without too much trouble. The scattered ruins of the ancient city of **Sri-Kshetra** are nearby and definitely worth exploring. For all these places, ignore MTT and simply go!

The Philippines

The Philippines are the forgotten islands of this book. Because they're off the regular overland route they've never attracted the travelling hordes in great numbers. So, if you make the effort to get there, you're in for a pleasant surprise. The food's pretty good, accommodation is easy to find, and you've got over 7000 remarkably diverse islands to choose from; and if island-hopping attracts you, the Philippines are the place to go. There are cheap flights and boats go everywhere – they are very frequent, remarkably cheap and reasonably comfortable, although not always that safe.

Add ease of travel to islands of very friendly people, many of whom speak English, and it's hard not to have a good time. In fact, many travellers reckon the Philippines is their favourite country in the whole region. Despite the continuing post-Marcos instability, most of the Philippines is still a safe and pleasant place to visit.

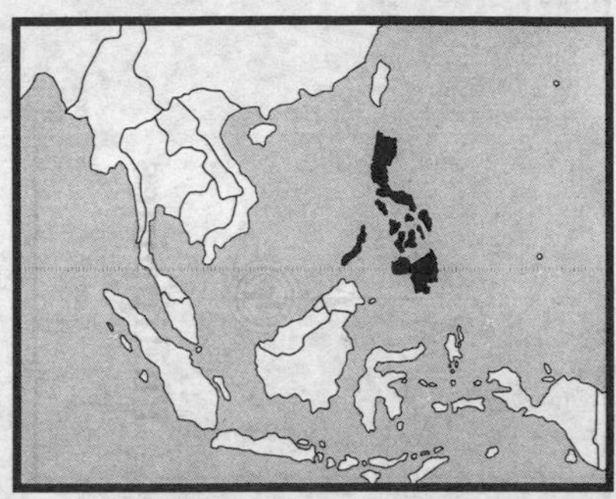

Facts about the Country

HISTORY

The Philippines is unique among the countries of South-East Asia, both for the variety of its colonisers and for its energetic attempts to cast off the colonial yoke. The Filipinos are a Malay people, closely related to the people of Indonesia and Malaysia. Little is known about their precolonial society, as the Spaniards – who ruled the country for over 300 years – energetically eradicated every trace of what they felt was 'pagan' in the culture.

Ferdinand Magellan, a Portuguese who had switched sides to arch-rival Spain, set off from Europe in 1519, with instructions to sail round the world, claim anything worth claiming for Spain and to bring back some spices (a very valuable commodity in Europe). Finding a way round the southern tip of South America took nearly a year but, finally, the small fleet (two of the original four ships) reached the Philippines in 1521.

At the island of Cebu, Magellan claimed the lot for Spain and managed to make a few Christian conversions to boot. Unfortunately, he then decided to display Spanish military might to his newly converted flock by dealing with an unruly tribe on the nearby island of Mactan. Chief Lapu-Lapu managed to kill Magellan. The Cebuanos decided their visitors were not so special after all and the survivors scuttled back to Spain, after collecting a cargo of spices on the way. They arrived in the sole remaining ship in 1522.

The Philippines, named after King Philip II of Spain, was more or less left alone from then until 1565 when Miguel de Legaspi stormed the no-longer-friendly island of Cebu and made the first permanent Spanish settlement. In 1571, Spanish HQ was moved to Manila and from here Spain gradually took control of the entire region – or more correctly converted the region, since Spanish colonial rule was very much tied up with taking the cross to the heathen.

The Spanish were far from alone in the area: other European powers and the Japanese and Chinese also made forays into the Philippines and, throughout the Spanish period, the strongly Muslim regions of Min-

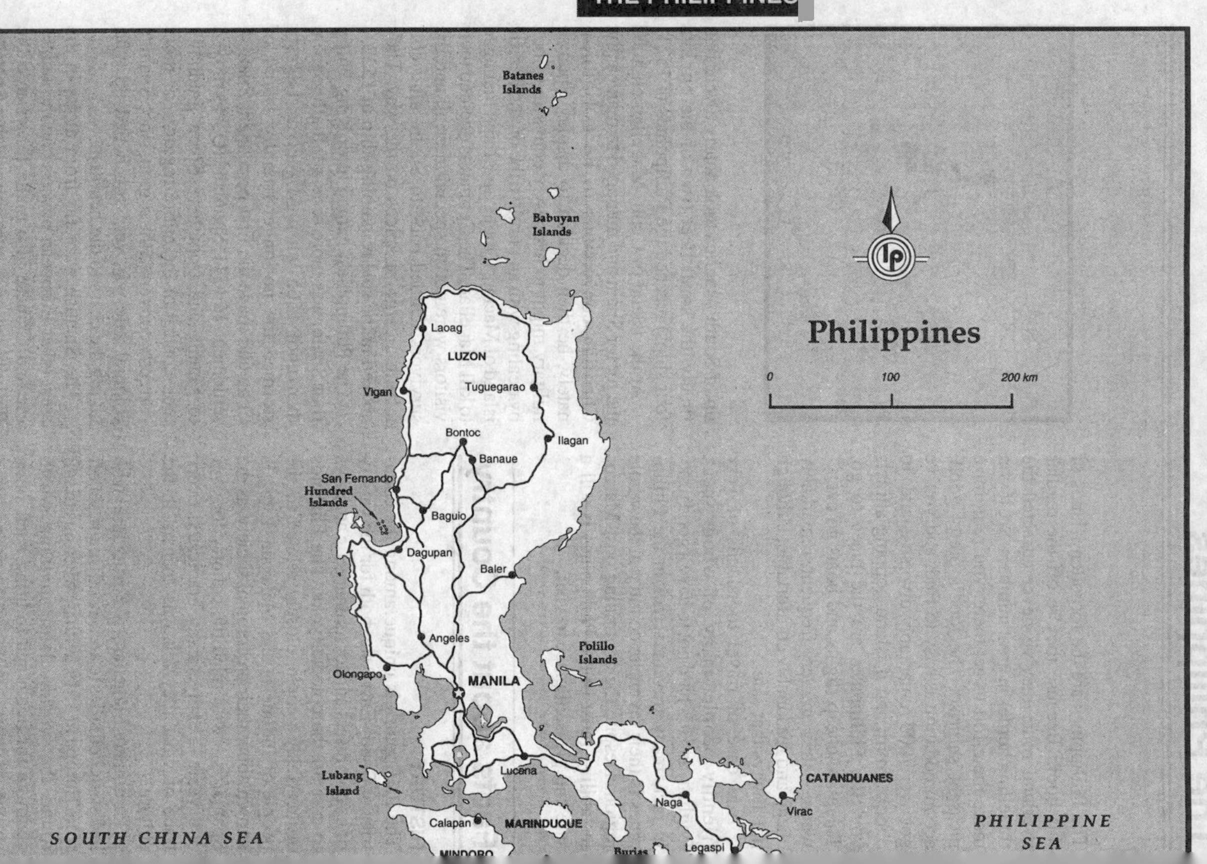
Philippines
0
100
200 km
Batanes Islands
Babuyan Islands
Laoag
LUZON
Vigan
Tuguegarao
Bontoc
Ilagan
Banaue
San Fernando
Hundred Islands
Baguio
Dagupan
Baler
Angeles
Polillo Islands
Olongapo
MANILA
Lucena
Lubang Island
CATANDUANES
Naga
Virac
Calapan
MARINDUQUE
SOUTH CHINA SEA
PHILIPPINE SEA
MINDORO
Burias
Legaspi

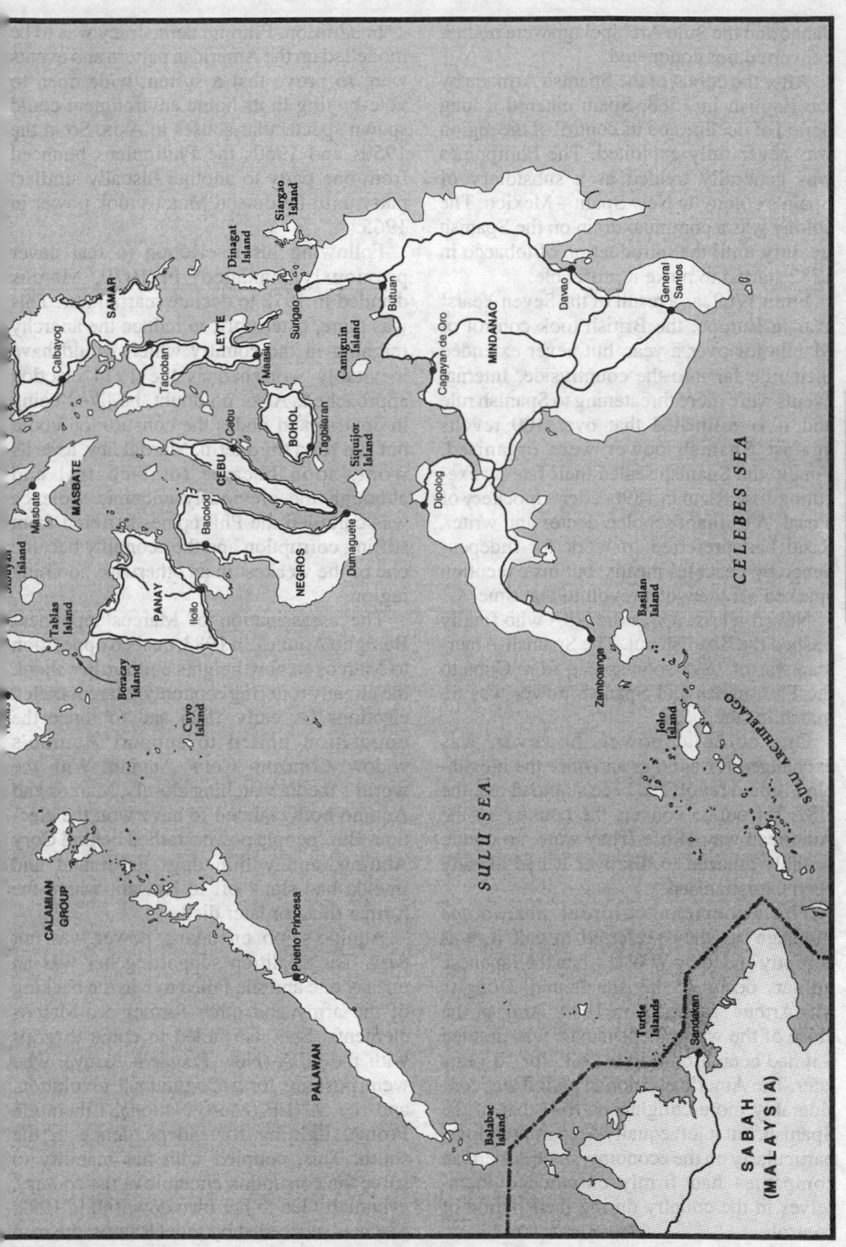
CALAMIAN GROUP
PALAWAN
Puerto Princesa
Balabac Island
SABAH (MALAYSIA)
Sandakan
Turtle Islands
SULU SEA
SULU ARCHIPELAGO
Jolo Island
Zamboanga
Basilan Island
CELEBES SEA
Dipolog
Cagayan de Oro
MINDANAO
General Santos
Davao
Butuan
Surigao
Siargao Island
Dinagat Island
Camiguin Island
Maasin
LEYTE
Tacloban
SAMAR
Calbayog
BOHOL
Tagbilaran
Siquijor Island
Cebu
CEBU
Dumaguete
NEGROS
Bacolod
MASBATE
Masbate
PANAY
Iloilo
Tablas Island
Boracay Island
Cuyo Island

danao and the Sulu Archipelago were neither converted nor conquered.

After the defeat of the Spanish Armada by the English in 1588, Spain entered a long period of decline and its control of the region was never fully exploited. The Philippines was generally treated as a subsidiary of Spain's colony in New Spain – Mexico. The colony was a continual drain on the Spanish treasury until the introduction of tobacco in 1782 started to make it profitable.

From 1762, as a result of the Seven Years' War in Europe, the British took control of Manila for over a year, but never extended their rule far into the countryside. Internal events were more threatening to Spanish rule and it is estimated that over 100 revolts against Spanish power were organised. Finally the Spanish sealed their fate by executing Jose Rizal in 1896, after a mockery of a trial. A brilliant scholar, doctor and writer, Rizal had preferred to work for independence by peaceful means, but his execution sparked off the worst revolt to that time.

Nevertheless, it was the USA who finally pushed the Spanish out. The Spanish-American war of 1898 soon spread from Cuba to the Philippines and Spanish power was no match for the USA.

One colonial power, however, was exchanged for another and once the inevitable Filipino revolt had been stamped out, the USA set out to convert the country to the American way of life. They were, no doubt, suitably amazed to discover it had already been Christianised.

The American colonial period, or 'tutelage' as they preferred to call it, was abruptly ended by WW II when the Japanese military occupied the islands until Douglas MacArthur 'returned' in 1944. And, at the close of the war, independence was granted – it had been promised in 1935 for 10 years later. The American colonial period was considerably more enlightened than that of the Spanish, but it left equally deep impressions, particularly on the economy, since American companies had firmly entrenched themselves in the country during their period of control.

In addition, Filipino democracy was to be modelled on the American pattern and events were to prove that a system wide open to vote-buying in its home environment could spawn spectacular abuses in Asia. So in the 1950s and 1960s the Philippines bounced from one party to another (usually similar) party until Ferdinand Marcos took power in 1965.

Following his re-election (a feat never previously managed) in 1970, Marcos decided in 1972 to declare martial law. This was done, ostensibly, to reduce the anarchy reigning in the country which would have inevitably worsened as the 1974 election approached. Also, no doubt, he liked being in control and under the constitution could not run for a third term. Martial law, as is its wont, soon became total control and although the previously endemic violence was curtailed the Philippines suffered from stifling corruption and the economy became one of the weakest in an otherwise booming region.

The assassination of Marcos' opponent Benigno Aquino, in 1983, pushed opposition to Marcos to new heights and further shook the already tottering economy. Marcos called elections for early 1986 and for once the opposition united to support Aquino's widow, Corazon 'Cory' Aquino. With the world's media watching closely, Marcos and Aquino both claimed to have won the election. But 'people power' rallied behind Cory Aquino, and within days Ferdinand and Imelda had slunk off to Hawaii, where the former dictator later died.

Aquino's job on taking power was not easy. The coalition supporting her was an uneasy one and she failed to win the backing of the army and other former pro-Marcos elements. She also failed to come to grips with the NPA (New People's Army), who were pushing for a Communist revolution, and the MNLF (Moro National Liberation Front), fighting for independence in the south. This, coupled with her inability to solve the corruption endemic in the country, eventually led to her own downfall in 1992. She was succeeded by Fidel Ramos, the man whose support had maintained her in power and helped her survive seven attempted coups.

The Protestant Fidel Ramos won the election in 1992 without the support of the Catholic Church and immediately appointed a government clearly intending to fight against corruption, revitalize the economy, create jobs and reduce the enormous foreign debt. Equipped with sweeping new powers, he has since moved to secure the ailing energy sector, encourage foreign investment and, in a surprise move, has even lifted the ban on the Communist Party in an attempt to end the guerilla war draining the resources of the country.

GEOGRAPHY

The official statistics state that the Philippines is comprised of over 7000 islands – but what is an island and what is a rock that occasionally appears above water level? Together, they make a land area of about 299,000 sq km, 94% of which is on the 11 largest islands.

The Philippines can be conveniently divided into four areas:

- Luzon, the largest island (site of the capital, Manila), and the nearby island of Mindoro.
- The Visayas, the scattered group of several islands south of Luzon.
- Mindanao, the Muslim trouble-centre in the south and the second-largest island in the country, along with the string of islands in the Sulu Archipelago, like stepping stones to Borneo.
- Palawan Island, nearly 400 km long but averaging a width of only 40 km.

CLIMATE

The Philippines is typically tropical – hot and humid year round. The climate can be roughly divided into a January-June dry and a July-December wet. January, February and March are probably the best months for a visit as it starts to get hotter after March, peaking in May. In some places it seems to rain year round and, in others, it rarely rains at all. From May to November there may be typhoons.

ECONOMY

The economy is principally agricultural. Like several other countries in the region, the Philippines is potentially self-sufficient in rice and other important foods but, due to poor yields and the continued evils of absentee landlordism in a peasant society, it generally ends up having to import rice along with fish and meat. All of these could conceivably be produced locally. Slow or nonexistent progress towards much-needed land reform has been a problem in the Philippines ever since independence.

Copra, sugar and *abaca* (a fibre from a relative of the banana plant), tobacco, bananas and pineapples are the principal agricultural exports. Some gold and silver mining are other important economic activities. There is some industry and it has been growing in recent years. Endemic corruption and inefficiency have meant that the boom conditions of other South-East Asian nations have failed to rub off on the Philippines.

POPULATION & PEOPLE

The population of the Philippines is estimated to be about 60 million and still growing too fast for comfort. The people are mainly of the Malay race although there is the usual Chinese minority and a fair number of *mestizos* – Filipino-Spanish or Filipino-American. There are still some remote pockets of pre-Malay people living in the hills, including the stone-age Tasaday who were discovered in a remote Mindanao valley as recently as 1972.

ARTS & CULTURE

The Philippines has developed a mixed culture from the historical blending of foreign influences with indigenous elements. Today, the Muslims and some of the isolated tribes are the only people whose culture remains unadulterated by Spanish and American influences. The ability of the Filipinos to improvise and copy is very apparent: you need only consider how the army jeeps left by the Americans were converted into colourful, shining-chrome taxis through painstaking detailed work before Filipinos began to produce these vehicles themselves.

The ideas of the New Society propagated by Marcos really caught the national consciousness of the Filipinos in the 1970s, just as People Power did in the 1980s. People recollected their cultural heritage and began to care about their traditional arts and crafts.

Consequently, the national language is strongly used today in theatre, and literature and *kundimans* – romantic and sentimental love songs – are popular again. The good old folk dances, foremost among them the national dance *tinikling*, have become a new tourist attraction.

RELIGION

The Philippines is unique for being the only Christian country in Asia – over 90% of the population claims to be Christian and over 80% are Roman Catholic. The Spanish did a thorough job! Largest of the minority religions are the Muslims who live chiefly on the island of Mindanao and in the Sulu Archipelago.

When the Spanish arrived, toting the cross, the Muslims were just establishing toeholds in the region. In the northern islands the toehold was only a small one and easily displaced, but in the south the people had been firmly converted and Christianity was never able to make strong inroads.

LANGUAGE

As in Indonesia there is one nominally national language and a large number of local languages and dialects. It takes 10 languages to cover 90% of the population! English and Spanish are still official languages, although the use of Spanish is now quite rare. English is also not as widespread as in the American days, although the English-speaking visitor will not have any trouble communicating – it remains the language of secondary school education and to say someone 'doesn't even speak English' means they've not gone beyond primary school.

Tagalog, or Pilipino, the local language of Manila and parts of Luzon, is now being pushed as the national language. It sounds remarkably like Indonesian. Listen to them roll their rrrrs. Lonely Planet's *Pilipino Phrasebook* has the full story. The following words are in Pilipino:

Greetings & Civilities

good morning
magandáng umága
goodbye
paálam
good evening
magandáng gabí
hello
haló
welcome/farewell
mabúhay

Food & Drinks

beer
serbésa
coffee
kapé
food
pagkaín
milk
gátas
restaurant
restorán
sugar
asúkal
water
túbig

Other Useful Words & Phrases

How many?
Ilán?
How much?
Magkáno?
that one
iyón
too expensive
mahál
Where is?
Saán ang?

yes
oó
no
hindí
good
mabúti
bad
masamá
bank
bangko
boat
sakayán
cheap hotel
múrang hotél
price
halagá
train station
estasyón ng tren

Numbers

1	isá
2	dalawá
3	tatló
4	apát
5	limá
6	ánim
7	pitó
8	waló
9	siyám
10	sampú

Facts for the Visitor

VISAS

Visa regulations vary with your intended length of stay. The simplest procedure is to simply arrive without a visa, in which case you will be permitted to stay for up to 21 days. If you obtain a visa overseas it will usually allow a 59-day stay. This will normally be granted for about US$35. If you already have a visa on arrival make sure the immigration officers know this or your passport will still be stamped for just 21 days.

To extend the 21-day stay period to 59 days apply with your passport and the relevant documents to the immigration office in Manila, Cebu City or Angeles. The Manila office is at the Department of Immigration & Deportation, Magallanes Drive, Intramuros, Manila. The extension costs P500 for the Visa Waiver plus P10 for a Legal Research Fee. If you want the four-hour Express Service it costs an additional P250. You must be neatly dressed if you apply in person at the office – rubber thongs/flip flops will ensure an instant refusal. A number of travel agencies will handle the extension application for a P100 to P200 fee.

After 59 days it gets really complicated although it's possible to keep on extending for about a year. Further extensions cost P200 per month for the Extension Fee but you have to add in Alien Head Tax (P200), Alien Certificate of Registration (P400), Emigration Clearance Certificate (P500), plus a whole series of Legal Research fees.

Staying beyond six months also involves a Certificate of Temporary Residence (P700) and after one year there's a travel tax (P1620).

MONEY

Currency

The unit of currency is the peso (P, correctly spelt piso), divided into 100 centavos (c). Throughout this section when it says 'c' it means centavos not cents of another currency. The only foreign currency to have in the Philippines is US dollars – it's no longer true to say that nothing else is considered to exist but the US dollar certainly exists more than most.

Furthermore, American Express travellers' cheques are more easily exchanged than other varieties. There are no particular hassles with the peso although you'll need an exchange receipt if you want to convert any back on departure.

The main problem is that changing travellers' cheques can be slow, particularly away from Manila. Of the banks, the Philippines Commercial International Bank (PCI Bank) is said to offer the best rates for travellers' cheques but Interbank or American Express are faster. Around Ermita, along Mabini St in particular, there are a great number of moneychangers who are much faster than the banks and give a better rate for cash. The rate varies with the size of the bill – US$100 and US$50 bills are best, US$1 bills are hardly wanted at all.

Rates tend to vary from one changer to another so shop around. Some of the moneychangers will change travellers' cheques as well, but at a worse rate. Even at banks cash tends to get a better rate than cheques, unlike in many other countries.

You are only permitted to take P1000 out of the country with you but try not to take any as they're difficult to exchange abroad.

There is said to be a small black market but the rate is only minimally better and it's not worth the risk. The risk is real – there are a lot of money rip-off scams in Manila and any offer of a spectacular exchange rate is bound to be a set-up. There is a wide and interesting variety of tricks involving sleight of hand and other subterfuges.

Exchange Rates

Australia	A$1	=	P18.77
Canada	C$1	=	P19.33
New Zealand	NZ$1	=	P15.46
Britain	UK£1	=	P39.40
USA	US$1	=	P26.03
Japan	¥100	=	P25.40
Germany	DM1	=	P15.98
France	FF1	=	P4.66
Malaysia	M$1	=	P10.14

Credit Cards & ATMs

Well-known international cards such as American Express, Diner's Club, MasterCard and Visa are accepted by many hotels, restaurants and businesses in the Philippines. With your Visa and MasterCard you can withdraw cash in pesos at any branch of the Equitable Bank (almost every big city has a branch).

ATM withdrawals are possible on savings account cards, but you must open an account with a Philippine bank first. With your Visa card you can withdraw as much as P40,000 (debited from your account back home) per day from any PCI Bank ATM. Several branch offices have been equipped with ATMs throughout the country.

Costs

Despite high inflation, prices remain lower in the Philippines than in most other countries in the region. Some things seem amazingly cheap – local transport and beer are two good examples. Airfares within the Philippines are also good value but not as comparatively cheap as in past years. The reduced flow of visitors to the Philippines also works in your favour as there's more competition for your custom which keeps prices down.

TOURIST OFFICES

The vast Department of Tourism (DOT) office in Manila could be more aptly called the Temple of Tourism. The smaller regional DOT offices can be quite different – the staff are often very knowledgeable, have all the facts at their fingertips and, best of all, are ready at hand with useful information sheets on their localities.

Philippine Airlines (PAL) may also have some useful information.

BUSINESS HOURS

Businesses first open their doors in the morning between 8 and 10 am. Offices, banks and public authorities have a five-day week. Some offices are also open on Saturday morning. Banks open at 9 am and close at 3 pm. Embassies and consulates are open to the public mainly from 9 am to 1 pm.

Offices and public authorities close at 5 pm. Large businesses like department stores and supermarkets continue until 7 pm, and smaller shops often open until 10 pm.

POST & TELECOMMUNICATIONS

Post

The Philippine postal service is generally quite efficient. You can get mail sent to you at poste restantes at the GPO in all the major towns. Opening hours in Philippine post offices are not the same everywhere. Many close at noon, others shut on Saturday as well. The following hours can usually be relied upon: Monday to Friday from 8 am to noon, and from 1 to 5 pm.

Telephone

You do not find telephones everywhere in the Philippines; in an emergency try the nearest police station, which in many areas will have the only telephone. Telephone numbers are always changing so obtain a local directory before calling.

In contrast to overseas calls, local calls in the Philippines are full of problems. It can take a ridiculously long time to be connected and the lines over long distances are bad. International calls are simple in comparison.

International telephone calls can be made from many hotels (operator or direct dialling; it depends on their equipment) or from any PLDT (Philippine Long Distance Telephone Company) office.

BOOKS & MAPS

If you want more information on travelling in the Philippines, then look for Lonely Planet's *The Philippines – a travel survival kit.*

There has been a spate of books about Cory Aquino and the downfall of Marcos. You'll see them in every bookshop in Manila and, no doubt, more will be along in the next few years. Manila has a good selection of bookshops.

The Nelles Verlag *Philippines* map is an excellent map of the islands at a scale of 1:1,500,000. *The Philippine Motorists' Road Guide* is available in bookshops.

MEDIA

After 20 years of press censorship under Marcos, the change of government brought a flood of new national and local newspapers and magazines indulging in a marvellous journalistic free-for-all; many are in English.

Radio and TV operate on a commercial basis, and there are 22 TV channels. Seven of these broadcast from Manila, sometimes in English and sometimes in Tagalog.

DANGERS & ANNOYANCES

The Philippines has rip-offs like anywhere else, but in recent years it has had more of them. New tricks pop up every year so it's always wise to be on your toes.

Beware of people who claim to have met you before. 'I was the immigration officer at the airport when you came through' is one often-used line. Manila has lots of fake immigration officers ready to dupe the unwary. There are also fake police officers and a favourite scam is to ask to check your money for counterfeit notes. When they return it the money may well be fake, or some of it may be missing.

Don't accept invitations to parties or meals from people who accost you in the street. Drugged coffee is a favourite with these folk and when you wake up your valuables will be long gone. Baguio is a popular place for unexpected invitations.

Beware of pickpockets in crowded areas of Manila or on tightly packed jeepneys or buses. Favourite places are around Ermita, especially in the crowded PAL office and in Rizal Park. Sleight-of-hand scams by street moneychangers are another speciality. Invitations to card games are another good way to lose money.

ACCOMMODATION

Finding cheap hotels is no problem. The exception may be Manila, but even there you'll find a wide selection of reasonably priced guesthouses and medium-priced hotels. Even the biggest hotels will offer attractive discounts.

There are quite a few youth hostels or YH-associated places around the country, so a IYHA card (student cards are also generally acceptable) is worth having. Even in Manila you can get dorm-style accommodation for P70 to P100 and away from the big cities rooms often cost P60 or less. In the Mountain Province, and at some of the beach resorts, the places will be pretty basic – no electricity, for example.

Maintenance in many hotels is a little lackadaisical so it's worth checking if the electricity and water are working before you sign in. Places in North Luzon tend to be cheaper than in the southern islands or elsewhere. Beware of fires in cheap hotels – Filipino hotels don't close down, they burn down. Check fire escapes and make sure windows will open. Finally, it's often worth asking for a discount, or bargaining a little on prices as they'll often come down.

FOOD

The Filipinos have taken on US fast foods wholeheartedly, so there are plenty of hamburgers and hot dogs. Chinese food is also widely available and in Chinese restaurants there is actually one of the few reminders of Spain – a lot of the menus are in a mixture of Spanish and English. Local Filipino food, usually called 'native' food, is a bit like Indonesian *nasi padang* in that all the food is laid out on view – and to Western palates it would often taste a lot better if it were hot. It's worth a splurge to try really good authentic Filipino food as it can be really delicious. Some popular dishes include:

Adobo – stewed chicken and pork pieces.
Arroz caldo – boiled rice with chicken, garlic, ginger and onions.
Balut – a popular street-side snack, boiled duck egg containing a partially formed duck embryo – yuck!
Bangus – milkfish, lightly grilled, stuffed and baked.
Crispy pata – crispy fried pig skin, another delicacy or feast dish.
Gulay – vegetable dish, sometimes simmered in coconut milk, particularly gabi leaves.
Inihaw – grilled fish or meat.
Lechon – a feast dish, roast baby pig with liver sauce.
Lumpia – spring rolls filled with meat or vegetables. Lumpia Shanghai are small fried spring rolls filled with meat.
Mami – noodle soup, like mee soup in Malaysia or Indonesia.
Menudo – stew with vegetables and small liver pieces or chopped pork.
Mongos – chick peas, similar to Lebanese humus.
Pancit – noodle dish, either Pancit Canton (thick noodles) or Pancit Guisado (thin noodles).
Pinangat – Bicol vegetable dish laced with very hot peppers – 'the Bicol express'.

DRINKS

There are also a number of Filipino drinks worth sampling (apart from Coke, which they must consume faster than any country apart from the USA):

Halo-Halo – a crushed ice, flavouring and fruit dessert. It means 'all mixed together' and is similar to an *es kacang* in Malaysia.
Iced buko – buko is young coconut.
Kalamansi – the tiny lemons known as kalamansi are served as lemon juice or with black tea. They are thought to have amazing curative effects.
San Mig – San Miguel beer must be the cheapest beer in the world and it's also very good.
Tuba – coconut wine, can be very strong.

THINGS TO BUY

There are a wide variety of handicrafts available in the Philippines and you will find examples of most crafts on sale in Manila. Clothing, cane and basket work, woodcarving and all manner of regional specialities can be found. See the various Manila, Luzon and islands sections for more details.

Getting There & Away

AIR

Apart from occasional boats from Hong Kong or Taiwan and illegal smuggling routes from Sabah (Malaysia) through the Sulu Archipelago, the best way to get to the Philippines is to fly. Although Cebu and Davao now have international airports, Manila is virtually the only international gateway, so, for probably 99% of visitors to the Philippines, Manila is their first experience of the country.

Hong Kong is the regional gateway to the Philippines. Fares from Hong Kong to Manila with Air France, British Airways or Philippine Airlines cost around US$162 one way and US$234 return. You can also look for cheap fares from Singapore or Bangkok. Singapore to Manila with Singapore Airlines costs US$292 one way and US$418 return, while from Bangkok to Manila can cost you around US$141 to US$165 one way and around US$236 to US$271 return. From Sabah (Malaysia) you can fly from Kota Kinabalu or alternatively from Bandar Seri Begawan (Brunei) to Manila – Kota Kinabalu to Manila on Malaysia Airlines costs M$492 one way and M$986 return. You can also fly to Manila from Kuala Lumpur for US$281 one way or US$490 return. Manila

THE PHILIPPINES

is not a great bargain centre for cheap tickets elsewhere.

There are very few alternatives to Manila as an entry point to the Philippines. However, there are regular flights now twice a week with the Indonesian airline Bouraq Airlines between Davao in the south of Mindanao and Manado in the north of Sulawesi in Indonesia – the fare is US$150 one way and US$262 return.

Airport departure tax is P500.

Getting Around

AIR

Philippine Airlines (PAL) runs a frequent and often economical service to most parts of the country (see the chart on the following page). The only thing that can really be said against it is that there are often flights from Manila to town A, B or C but rarely flights between towns A, B and C. They're pretty security conscious so expect to be thoroughly frisked.

Student-card holders, under 26 years of age, are eligible for a 15% discount on round-trip domestic flights. PAL also offers a Golden Age Discount of 15% for passengers over 60 years of age.

PAL flights are often heavily booked and crowded so, unless you can book ahead, you may find it necessary to join the wait list which, fortunately, is quite efficient in Manila. The wait list is started each day at the stroke of midnight and as soon as you put your name on the list, you're given a wait-list number.

When a flight is called they announce down to what number on the list can be carried. You're wait-listed for a destination, not a flight, so if there are several flights during the day your chances improve with each flight. At midnight the day's wait list is scrubbed and a new list starts for the next day. The period from 15 December to 4 January is totally hopeless for flights anywhere in the Philippines.

To make reservations or inquire about the wait list, ring PAL at the following numbers in Manila: ☎ 818 6757 or 817 1509.

PAL no longer monopolises all domestic services. There are now a number of smaller operators like Aerolift and Pacific Airways and they've become popular since the spate of late-1980s shipping disasters.

BUS

There are an enormous number of bus services running all over the Philippines and they are generally very economical. As a rule of thumb on a regular bus you cover about 2½ km per peso and average about 50 km an hour. Thus a 100-km journey will cost about P40 and take about two hours. Air-con buses will be more expensive and trips on gravel roads are more expensive than on sealed roads.

Departures are very frequent although buses sometimes leave early if they're full – take care if there's only one bus a day! People like to travel early when it's cool so there will probably be more buses going early in the day. Note that on Luzon all roads lead to Manila and so do all bus routes. If you're heading from South Luzon to North Luzon you'll have to take one bus into Manila and another out. The main companies include Dangwa Tranco, Victory Liner and Philippine Rabbit.

As well as the regular buses there are more expensive air-con buses (and even more expensive tour buses) operated by companies like Sarkies Tours. Typical fares from Manila for ordinary buses include: Alaminos (237 km, P98), Baguio (250 km, P91), Batangas (110 km, P38), Olongapo (126 km, P50) or Legaspi (544 km, P254).

TRAIN

There were once only three passenger rail services in the Philippines and that has now shrunk to one, which looks unlikely to last long. The only route left is south from Manila to Naga in the Bicol region of South Luzon. The service is so slow and unreliable that everyone recommends the bus. The service north from Manila to San Fernando and the route on the island of Panay have both closed down.

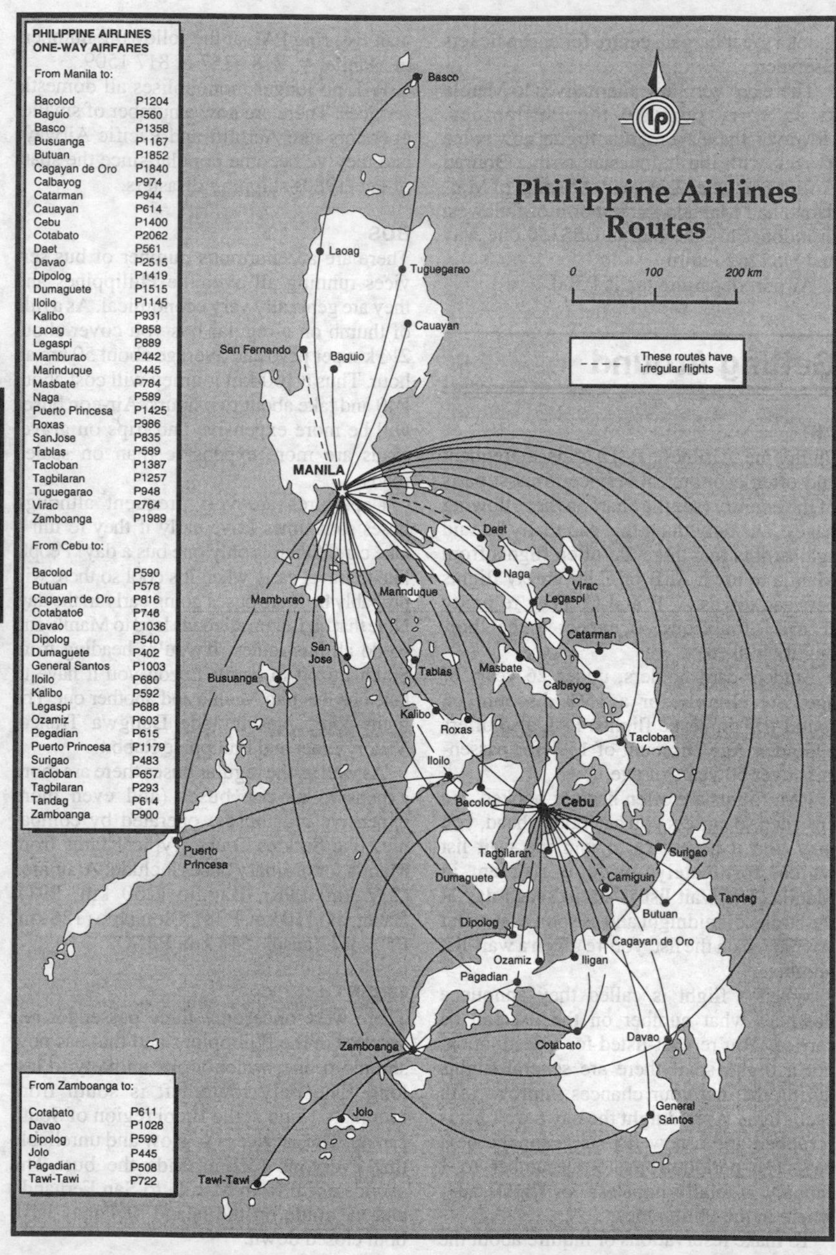

PHILIPPINE AIRLINES ONE-WAY AIRFARES

From Manila to:

Bacolod	P1204
Baguio	P560
Basco	P1358
Busuanga	P1167
Butuan	P1852
Cagayan de Oro	P1840
Calbayog	P974
Catarman	P944
Cauayan	P614
Cebu	P1400
Cotabato	P2062
Daet	P561
Davao	P2515
Dipolog	P1419
Dumaguete	P1515
Iloilo	P1145
Kalibo	P931
Laoag	P858
Legaspi	P889
Mamburao	P442
Marinduque	P445
Masbate	P784
Naga	P589
Puerto Princesa	P1425
Roxas	P986
SanJose	P835
Tablas	P589
Tacloban	P1387
Tagbilaran	P1257
Tuguegarao	P948
Virac	P764
Zamboanga	P1989

From Cebu to:

Bacolod	P590
Butuan	P578
Cagayan de Oro	P816
Cotabato6	P746
Davao	P1036
Dipolog	P540
Dumaguete	P402
General Santos	P1003
Iloilo	P680
Kalibo	P592
Legaspi	P688
Ozamiz	P603
Pegadian	P615
Puerto Princesa	P1179
Surigao	P483
Tacloban	P657
Tagbilaran	P293
Tandag	P614
Zamboanga	P900

From Zamboanga to:

Cotabato	P611
Davao	P1028
Dipolog	P599
Jolo	P445
Pagadian	P508
Tawi-Tawi	P722

BOAT

Getting around by boat is much easier than in Indonesia – it's not a matter of 'will there be a boat this week?' but 'will there be a boat this day?'; and the answer is often 'this morning'. And the boats are cheap, usually comfortable and pretty fast. The Philippines' mass of islands are very tightly packed which makes all the difference.

The real hub of the shipping services is Cebu – everything seems to run through here, and there are many shipping companies. Apart from the major interisland ships there are also many ferries shuttling back and forth between nearby islands.

The main booking offices will often tell you that the economy tickets are sold out when, if you ask at the pier, you'll find they are still available. Also inquire about student discounts; some shipping lines give 20% or 30%. Fares differ markedly from company to company. See the fares table below for some base fares from Manila to other popular destinations in the Philippines.

Ship travel has its disadvantages. The first is that standards do vary and some of the boats are dirty, badly kept and overcrowded. A rough voyage with plenty of seasick fellow passengers can be a real trial. The more serious problem is safety. A disastrous collision just before Christmas 1987 where a Sulpicio Lines ship went down, with something like 2000 deaths and only 24 survivors, focused international attention on something Filipinos have been all too aware of for some time.

The small local boats are often the worst as they may be grossly overloaded and safety equipment is simply nonexistent. Even the very short trips can be risky – there have been some unhappy incidents at Boracay (no deaths but people have lost all their gear), and the Roxas (Mindoro) to Tablas (Romblon) boats are particularly bad.

Drinks are usually available on board but, on longer trips, it's not a bad idea to bring some food supplies. Be prepared for long unscheduled stops at ports along the way. It's important to allow for a flexible schedule if travelling by ship.

Boat Fares

Destination	*Fare (P) deck class*
Bacolod	323
Cagayan de Oro	495
Cebu City	385
Coron	300
Davao	701
Dumaguete	425
Iloilo City	334
Kalibo	260
Puerto Princesa	357
Roxas	260
Surigao	451
Tacloban	366
Zamboanga	503

LOCAL TRANSPORT

Jeepneys

The true Filipino local transport is the jeepney. The recipe for a jeepney is: take one ex-US-Army jeep, put two benches in the back with enough space for about 12 people, paint it every colour of the rainbow, add tassles, badges, horns, lights, aerials, about a dozen rearview mirrors, a tape deck with a selection of Filipino rock music, a chrome horse (or better a whole herd of them) and anything else you can think of. Then stuff 20 passengers on those benches for 12, add four more in front and drive like a maniac. But they're cheap and you'll find them in cities and doing shorter runs between centres.

At one time it was thought the jeepney was a threatened species, disappearing to be replaced by the new locally manufactured South-East Asian utility vehicles. But now it seems that the Filipinos are simply making brand new ex-US-Army-style jeeps. They're stretched so you can get more passengers in but otherwise they're just like jeepneys have always been.

The usual jeepney fare is P1.50 for up to the first four km and then 50c (sometimes only 25c) a km. You pay on getting out, or anywhere along the way if you prefer and know what it's going to be. To stop a jeepney (when you want to get off) you can rap on

THE PHILIPPINES

the roof, hiss or use the correct term which is *'pará'* or *'báyad'*, Tagalog for 'payment'.

For longer journeys in the country, it's wise to find out what the fare should be before you set off. Beware of 'Special Rides' where you charter the whole vehicle. Try not to be the first person to get into an empty jeepney, because if the driver suddenly takes off you may find you've chartered it. Take care also if several men suddenly get into a jeepney and all try to sit near you. Chances are you're being set up to be pickpocketed – get off and find another vehicle.

Taxis

Taxis are all metered in Manila and they are almost the cheapest in the world. Insist that the meter is used and make sure you have plenty of small change – the driver certainly won't if it's to his advantage. In smaller towns, taxis may not be metered and you will have to negotiate your fare beforehand – tricycles are cheaper. PU-Cabs, found in some larger towns but not in Manila, are unmetered taxis.

Other Local Transport

The other local transport, mainly found in smaller towns, are tricycles, which are small Japanese motorbikes with a crudely made sidecar. Normal passenger load should be two or three but six and seven are not unknown! Fares generally start at P1.50 to P2 per person – longer distances are by negotiation. You will also see some bicycle trishaws. *Calesas* are two-wheeled horse carriages found in Manila's Chinatown, in Vigan in North Luzon and in Cebu City where they are known as *tartanillas*.

Manila

The capital of the Philippines and by far the largest city, Metro Manila has a population of over 10 million. Although it sprawls for a great distance along Manila Bay the main places of interest are fairly central. Manila is not a city of great interest in itself; it's really just an arrival and departure point for the rest of the Philippines. Once you've seen the Spanish remains in Intramuros you've pretty much seen all Manila has to offer in an historical sense.

The other Manila attraction, however, is entertainment – there are countless reasonably priced restaurants, pubs, folk music clubs, girlie bars, pick-up joints and anything else you could care to ask for.

Orientation

Manila is quite a sprawling town but the main places of interest and/or importance to the visitor are concentrated just south of the Pasig River. Immediately south of the river is Intramuros, the old Spanish town, where many of Manila's historic buildings are. South of that is the long rectangle of Rizal Park (the Luneta), the lungs of the central area.

Further south again is Ermita, the so-called tourist belt with its numerous hotels, restaurants and travel agencies. However, it is not worth the visitor's trouble any more to look for the equally numerous bars and nightclubs that once made Ermita famous, for Manila's mayor, General Lim, kept his election promise to rule with an iron fist and lead the battle against corruption, crime, prostitution and dirt in the City of Manila. All bars and nightclubs had to be closed down by mid-1993. And closed they are.

You'll find not only the big international hotels but many of the medium and low-priced places in Ermita. Although the Ermita area is the visitor's downtown Manila, the businessperson's downtown is Makati, which is several km away.

Information

Tourist Offices The Department of Tourism's grand office (☎ 59 9031, 50 1928) is in Ermita at the Taft Ave end of Rizal Park. The actual TIC is on the ground floor. The staff are friendly and hand out lots of useful brochures and a good Manila map. There are smaller counters just behind customs at the airport and at the nearby Nayong Pilipino complex.

The DOT also maintains a 24-hour tourist assistance hotline (☎ 50 1660/728) for 'travel information, emergency assistance, lost & found and language problems'.

Post Offices The main GPO for poste restante mail is near the river in Intramuros. There's a small office at the harbour end of Rizal Park, near the Manila Hotel, which is generally not so busy.

Bookshops The National Book Store at 701 Rizal Ave in Santa Cruz is the largest bookstore in the Philippines and has a number of other branches in the Metro Manila area. The Solidaridad Book Shop on Padre Faura is particularly good for political books.

For maps go to Namria, formerly the Bureau of Coast & Geodetic Survey, on Barraca St in San Nicolas.

Other Information There's a laundromat in R Salas St, Ermita, between Mabini and Adriatico Sts. The Laundryette Britania in Santa Monica St, Ermita, between Mabini and M H del Pilar Sts, can also be recommended. Mayer Photo in Carlos Palanca St, Quiapo, has cheap film. There are more camera shops around the corner in Hidalgo St. There's a convenient 7-Eleven on the corner of Padre Faura and Adriatico St in Ermita.

Dangers & Annoyances Beware of over-friendly Filipinos in Manila. Unwary tourists are often picked up around Luneta or simply pickpocketed while wandering the park. Beware of the Manila slum areas too. It is here that 'a mad scramble to pick your pockets ensues', one visitor commented!

Intramuros

The bitter fighting at the end of WW II did a pretty good job of flattening Manila but there are still some places of interest in Intramuros, the oldest part of the city.

The first Chinese settlement at the site of Manila was destroyed almost immediately by Limahong, an unfriendly Chinese pirate, who dropped by in 1574. The Spanish rebuilt this centre as a fort. In 1590 the wooden fort was replaced by stone and it was gradually extended until it became a walled city which they called Intramuros. The walls were three km long, 13 metres thick and six metres high. Seven main gates entered the city, in which there were 15 churches and six monasteries – and lots of Spanish who kept the Filipinos at arm's length.

The walls are just about all that was left after WW II finished off what MacArthur had started. During the 1930s he had his HQ there and 'modernised' the place by knocking down lots of old buildings and widening those nasty narrow streets.

San Agustin The church and monastery of San Agustin is one of the few buildings left from the earliest construction. It was here in 1898 that the last Spanish governor of Manila surrendered to the Filipinos. There is a museum inside which is open daily from 8 am to noon and 1 to 5 pm. Admission is P20.

Cathedral The Roman Catholic Cathedral is also in Intramuros and has a history that reads like that of a lot of Spanish-built churches in the Philippines: built 1581, damaged (typhoon) 1582, destroyed (fire) 1583, rebuilt 1592, partially destroyed (earthquake) 1600, rebuilt 1614, destroyed (earthquake) 1645, rebuilt 1654-71, destroyed (earthquake) 1863, rebuilt 1870-79, destroyed (WW II) 1945, rebuilt 1954-58. On that average an earthquake should knock it down again in 2006.

Fort Santiago The ruins of the old Spanish fort, at one time connected to Intramuros, stand just north of the cathedral. They are now used as a pleasant park – you can see the collection of the Presidents' cars (rusting) and climb up top for the view over the Pasig River. The most interesting part of the fort is the **Rizal Shrine Museum** with many items used or made by the Filipino martyr. The room in which he was imprisoned before his execution can be seen. The shrine is open daily except on Saturday and public holidays

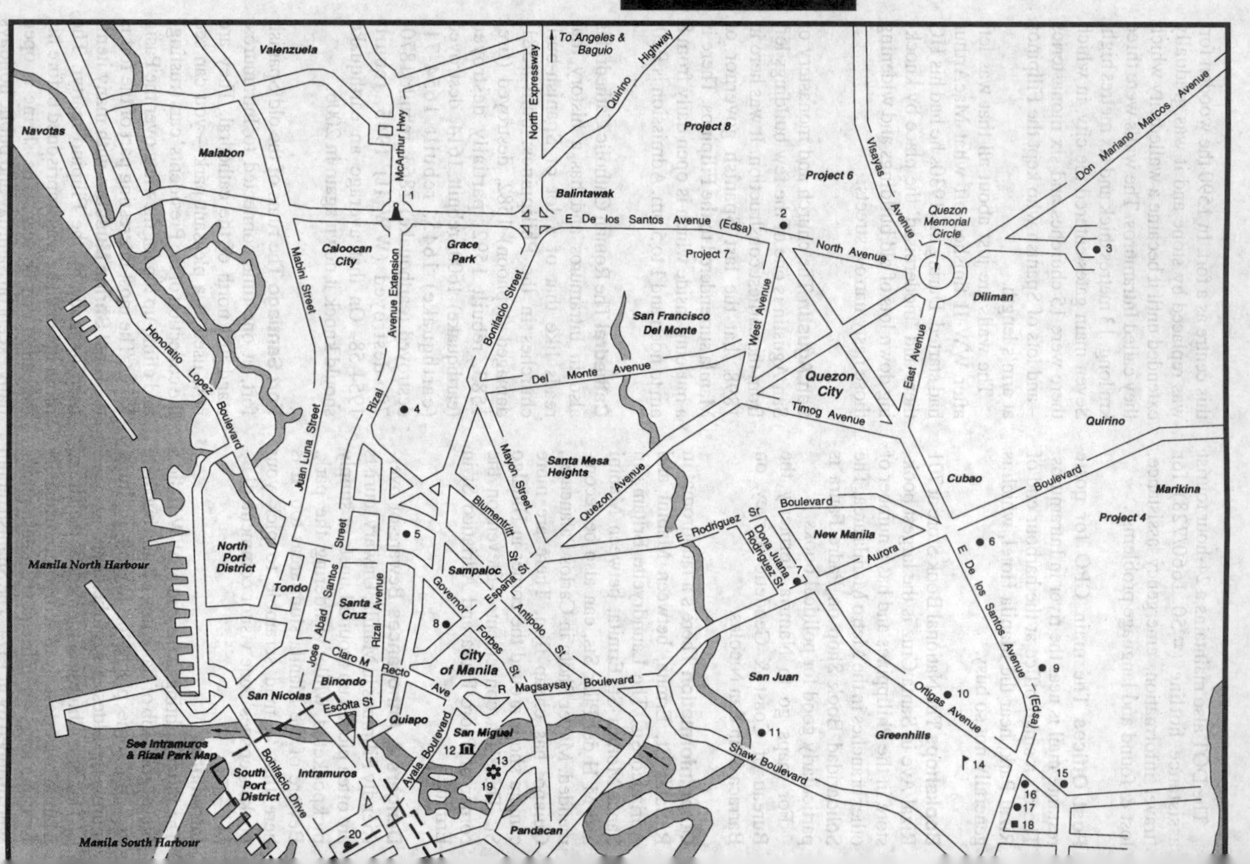
Valenzuela
To Angeles & Baguio
Quirino Highway
North Expressway
Navotas
Malabon
McArthur Hwy
Project 8
Project 6
Balintawak
Visayas Avenue
Don Mariano Marcos Avenue
Quezon Memorial Circle
E De los Santos Avenue (Edsa)
North Avenue
Caloocan City
Grace Park
Project 7
Mabini Street
Rizal Avenue Extension
Bonifacio Street
Diliman
San Francisco Del Monte
West Avenue
Honoratio Lopez Boulevard
Del Monte Avenue
East Avenue
Quezon City
Timog Avenue
Quirino
Juan Luna Street
Mayon Street
Santa Mesa Heights
Cubao
Boulevard
Marikina
Quezon Avenue
Blumentritt St
Project 4
E Rodriguez Sr
New Manila
Dona Juana Rodriguez St
Aurora
E De los Santos Avenue (Edsa)
North Port District
Manila North Harbour
Tondo
Jose Abad Santos Street
Santa Cruz
Rizal Avenue
Sampaloc
España St
Governor Forbes St
Antipolo St
City of Manila
Claro M Recto Ave
Binondo
San Nicolas
R Magsaysay Boulevard
San Juan
Ortigas Avenue
Escolta St
Quiapo
Ayala Boulevard
San Miguel
Greenhills
See Intramuros & Rizal Park Map
Shaw Boulevard
South Port District
Bonifacio Drive
Intramuros
Pandacan
Manila South Harbour

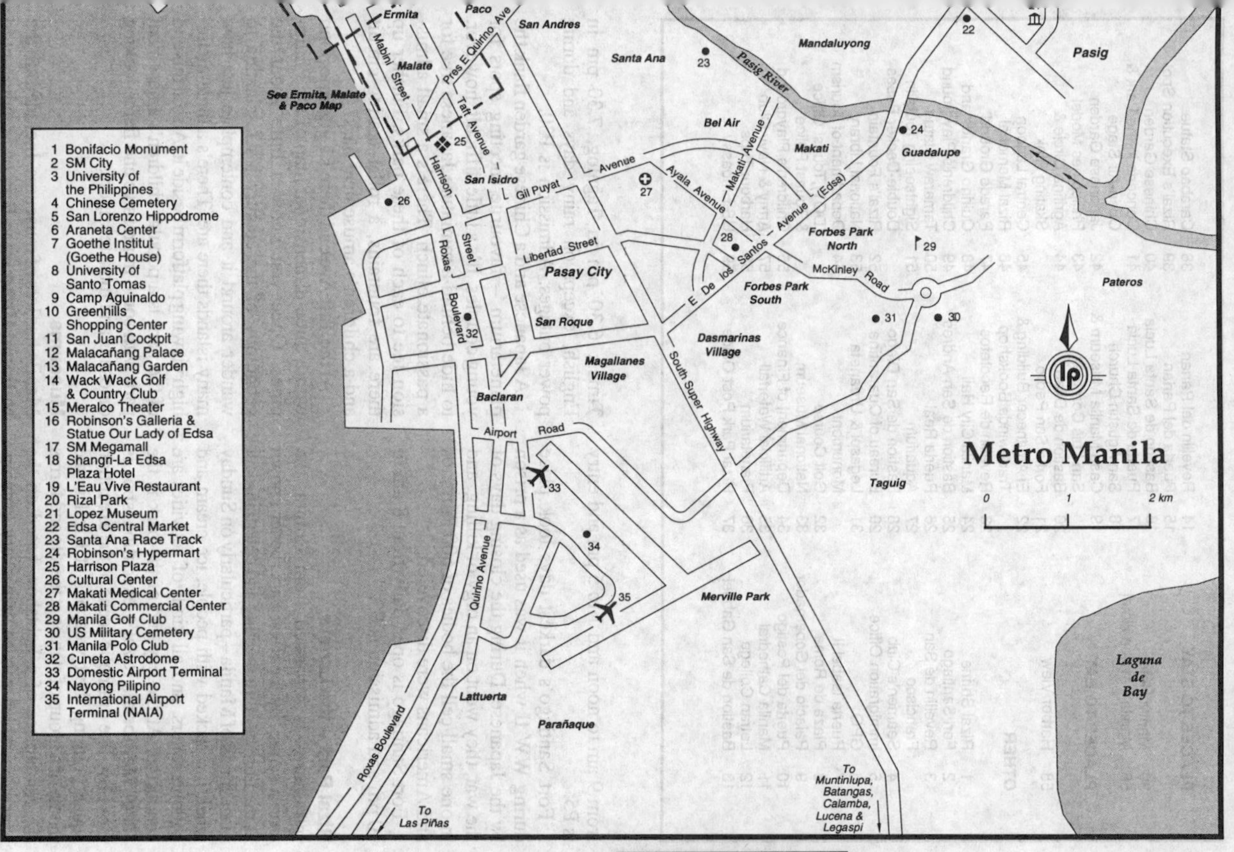
Metro Manila
0
1
2 km
See Ermita, Malate & Paco Map
1 Bonifacio Monument
2 SM City
3 University of the Philippines
4 Chinese Cemetery
5 San Lorenzo Hippodrome
6 Araneta Center
7 Goethe Institut (Goethe House)
8 University of Santo Tomas
9 Camp Aguinaldo
10 Greenhills Shopping Center
11 San Juan Cockpit
12 Malacañang Palace
13 Malacañang Garden
14 Wack Wack Golf & Country Club
15 Meralco Theater
16 Robinson's Galleria & Statue Our Lady of Edsa
17 SM Megamall
18 Shangri-La Edsa Plaza Hotel
19 L'Eau Vive Restaurant
20 Rizal Park
21 Lopez Museum
22 Edsa Central Market
23 Santa Ana Race Track
24 Robinson's Hypermart
25 Harrison Plaza
26 Cultural Center
27 Makati Medical Center
28 Makati Commercial Center
29 Manila Golf Club
30 US Military Cemetery
31 Manila Polo Club
32 Cuneta Astrodome
33 Domestic Airport Terminal
34 Nayong Pilipino
35 International Airport Terminal (NAIA)
Ermita
Malate
Paco
Mabini Street
Taft Avenue
Pres E Quirino Ave
San Isidro
San Andres
Santa Ana
Harrison
Roxas
Boulevard
Street
Gil Puyat
Avenue
Libertad Street
Pasay City
San Roque
Baclaran
Airport
Road
Magallanes Village
Ayala Avenue
Makati Avenue
Bel Air
Makati
Pasig River
Mandaluyong
Guadalupe
Pasig
Pateros
Forbes Park North
Forbes Park South
E De los Santos Avenue (Edsa)
McKinley Road
Dasmarinas Village
South Super Highway
Taguig
Merville Park
Quirino Avenue
Roxas Boulevard
Lattuerta
Parañaque
To Las Piñas
To Muntinlupa, Batangas, Calamba, Lucena & Legaspi
Laguna de Bay

PLACES TO STAY

30 Manila Hotel
56 Manila Pavilion Hotel

PLACES TO EAT

58 Harbor View

OTHER

1 Rizal Shrine
2 Fort Santiago
3 Revellin de San Francisco
4 Seamen's Club
5 Immigration Office
6 GPO
7 Puerta Isabel II
8 Plaza de Roma
9 Palacio del Gobernador
10 Puerta del Postigo
11 Manila Cathedral
12 Letran College
13 Bastion de San Gabriel
14 Revellin del Parian
15 Puerta del Parian
16 Bastion de Santa Lucia
17 Puerta de Santa Lucia
18 San Agustin Church
19 Casa Manila Museum & San Luis Complex
20 Bastion de Dilao
21 Fortin San Pedro
22 El Amanecer Building & Tradewinds Bookshop
23 Revellin de Recoletos
24 Manila City Hall
25 Bastion de San Andres
26 Puerta Real
27 Aquarium
28 Bastion de San Diego
29 Bureau of Quarantine
31 Legaspi & Urdaneta Monument
32 Golf Course
33 National Museum
34 Department of Finance
35 Artificial Waterfall
36 Planetarium
37 Rizal Park Post Office
38 Carabao Statue
39 Rizal's Execution Spot
40 Chinese Garden
41 Concerts in the Park & Open-Air Stage
42 Japanese Garden
43 Philippines Model
44 Agrifina Circle & Skating Rink
45 Central Lagoon
46 Rizal Memorial
47 Parade Ground
48 Quirino Grandstand
49 Children's Playground
50 Tamaraw Statue
51 Sightseeing Tours in Double-Decker Buses
52 Rizal's Fountain
53 National Library
54 Department of Tourism (DOT),Tourist Office & Tourist Police
55 Children's Playground
57 Army & Navy Club
58 Harbour Trips
59 US Embassy

from 9 am to noon and 1 to 5 pm and entry is P5.

Fort Santiago's darkest days took place during WW II when it was used as a prison by the Japanese. During the closing days of the war, they went on an orgy of killing, and in one small cell the bodies of 600 Filipinos and Americans were discovered.

Fort Santiago is open daily from 8 am to 10 pm and admission is P5.

Rizal Park – the Luneta

Intramuros is separated from Ermita, the tourist centre, by the Rizal Park, better known as the Luneta. It's a meeting and entertainment place for all of Manila – particularly on Sunday when it's packed with people, ice cream and balloon sellers, and all kinds of activities are conducted. At the bay end of the park is the **Rizal Memorial**. Rizal's execution spot is close by. The dramatic scene of the execution squad pointing their weapons at Rizal is the theme of a group of statues at the site and forms the centrepiece of a lightshow based on the execution which can be seen every evening. Times: 6.30 pm in Tagalog, 7.30 pm in English, except on rainy days and during power outages. Admission is P30.

A Japanese and a Chinese garden flank the planetarium – favourite meeting spots for young couples. It's a little difficult, however, to hide behind a miniature Japanese tree for a passionate clinch. There's a small admission fee to each of these parks. Further up there are fountains, a roller-skating circuit and a children's amusement park.

At the Taft Ave end there's a gigantic pond with a three-dimensional map of the Philippines. Once you know a little about the geography of the country it's fascinating to wander around it and contemplate just how many islands there are. There's a three-metre-high viewing platform beside it. Also at this end of the park is a popular children's amusement park with some impressive and fierce-looking dinosaur and monster figures.

Museums

Manila has lots of museums. Included are the **National Museum** in Burgos St, adjacent to

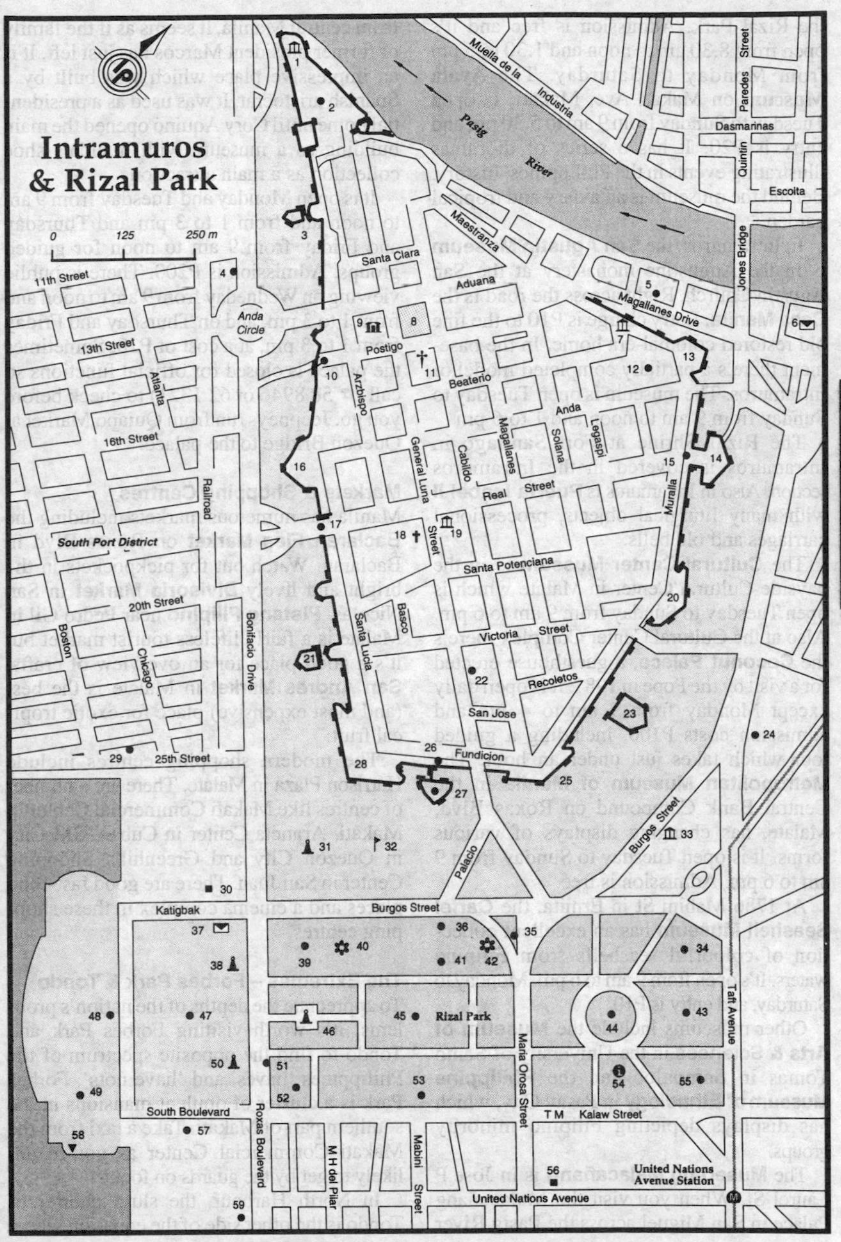

THE PHILIPPINES

the Rizal Park. Admission is free and it's open from 8.30 am to noon and 1.30 to 5 pm from Monday to Saturday. The **Ayala Museum** on Makati Ave, Makati, is open Tuesday to Sunday from 9 am to 5.30 pm and entry is P20. It has a series of dioramas illustrating events in the Philippines' history. Behind the museum is an aviary and tropical garden.

In Intramuros, the **San Agustin Museum** is in the Augustine monastery at the San Agustin Church. Right across the road is the **Casa Manila**. Entry charge is P10 to the fine old restored colonial-era home. In the basement there's a partially completed model of Intramuros. The museum is open Tuesday to Sunday from 9 am to noon and 1 to 6 pm .

The Rizal Shrine at Fort Santiago in Intramuros is covered in the Intramuros section. Also in Intramuros is **Puerta Isabel II** with many liturgical objects, processional carriages and old bells.

The **Cultural Center Museum** is in the bayside Cultural Center in Malate which is open Tuesday to Sunday from 9 am to 6 pm. Also at the Cultural Center Complex there's the **Coconut Palace**, a guesthouse erected for a visit by the Pope in 1981. It is open daily except Monday from 9 am to 4 pm and admission costs P100, including a guided tour which takes just under an hour. The **Metropolitan Museum of Manila** in the Central Bank Compound on Roxas Blvd, Malate, has changing displays of various forms. It is open Tuesday to Sunday from 9 am to 6 pm. Admission is free.

At 1786 Mabini St in Ermita, the **Carfel Seashell Museum** has an excellent collection of colourful seashells from Filipino waters. It's open from 9 am to 6 pm, Monday to Saturday, and entry is P10.

Other museums include the **Museum of Arts & Sciences** in the University of Santo Tomas in Sampaloc and the **Philippine Museum of Ethnology** in Pasay City, which has displays depicting Filipino minority groups.

The **Museo ng Malacañang** is in Jose P Laurel St. When you visit the Malacañang Palace in San Miguel across the Pasig River from central Manila, it seems as if the family of former president Marcos has just left. It is an impressive place which was built by a Spanish aristocrat. It was used as a presidential home until Cory Aquino opened the main building as a museum with Imelda's shoe collection as a main attraction.

It is open Monday and Tuesday from 9 am to noon and from 1 to 3 pm and Thursday and Friday from 9 am to noon for guided groups. Admission is P200. There is public viewing on Wedneday from 9 am to noon and from 1 to 3 pm, and on Thursday and Friday from 1 to 3 pm, at a cost of P20. Sometimes the palace is closed for official functions so call (☎ 58 8946 or 62 1321) to check before you go. Jeepneys run from Quiapo Market at Quezon Bridge to the palace.

Markets & Shopping Centres

Manila has numerous markets including the **Baclaran Flea Market** on Roxas Blvd in Baclaran. Watch out for pickpockets in the bright and lively **Divisoria Market** in San Nicolas. **Pistang Pilipino** near Pedro Gil in Malate is a fairly lifeless tourist market but it's a good place for an overview of crafts. **San Andres Market** in Malate is the best (and most expensive) place for exotic tropical fruit.

The modern shopping centres include Harrison Plaza in Malate. There are a number of centres like Makati Commercial Center in Makati, Araneta Center in Cubao, SM City in Quezon City and Greenhills Shopping Center in San Juan. There are good fast-food places and a cinema complex in these shopping centres.

The Extremes – Forbes Park & Tondo

To appreciate the depths of the nation's problems, it's worth visiting Forbes Park and Tondo to find the opposite spectrum of the Philippines 'haves' and 'have nots'. Forbes Park is a cluster of opulent mansions in the southern part of Makati. Take a taxi from the Makati Commercial Center as you're unlikely to get by the guards on foot.

In North Harbour, the slum quarter of Tondo is the other side of the equation where about 180,000 Filipinos live in 17,000 huts in just 1½ sq km.

Other Attractions

Across the river, **Chinatown** is interesting to wander through, and the luxurious **Chinese Cemetery**, about two km north of Chinatown near the Abad Santos Metrorail Station, is a bizarre attraction. A tricycle from the station to the South Gate will be about P5. It's in the north of Santa Cruz, just where Rizal Ave becomes Rizal Ave Extension.

Quiapo, an older and more traditional part of Manila, has the Quiapo Church by Quezon Bridge. The **wooden statue of Christ** known as the Black Nazarene can be seen here.

Nayong Pilipino is the Filipino edition of 'the whole country in miniature'. It's out by the international airport and it has lots of handicraft shops as well as a good little folk museum with some incredible photographs of the forgotten Tasaday tribe. Entry is P85 for foreigners and P15 for Filipinos, and it's open 9 am to 6 pm weekdays and to 7 pm on Saturday and Sunday.

Places to Stay

There is a wide variety of accommodation possibilities in Manila, many of them close to the central Ermita area. Cheapest are the hostels and Ys but there are also many cheap hotels and pensions.

Hostels & Guesthouses Many of the cheaper guesthouses and pensions offer dormitory accommodation. There are numerous small places around Ermita ranging from rock bottom upwards in standards and price. Some of the streets in Ermita can be very noisy so check where the room is if you're going to stay in a guesthouse on a busy street.

At times a lot of the cheaper places are full. If you've just arrived in Manila, it might be a good idea to check the DOT information desk at the airport, where there's an exhaustive list of just about everything available in the city. Many of the guesthouses can be booked through the tourist office desk at the airport – a few phone calls could save you a lot of walking.

Manila International Youth Hostel (☎ 832 0680; fax 818 7948) at 4227 Tomas Claudio St, Parañaque, has dorm beds for P95 (YHA members P70). It's a good clean place with a garden and it is also the office for YSTAPHIL, the Youth & Student Travel Association of the Philippines. It is next to the Excelsior Building, on the corner of Roxas Blvd (asking for the Excelsior will make taxi trips easier).

The *Town House* (☎ 833 1939; fax 804 0161) at the Villa Carolina Townhouse, 201 Roxas Blvd, Unit 31, Parañaque, has dorm beds with fan for P80, singles/doubles with fan for P200 and P250, with fan and bath for P300 and P350 and with air-con and bath for P500 and P550. Weekly rates can be arranged. It is pleasant with a friendly atmosphere created by Bill and Laura, who like travelling themselves. It's in a small side street called Sunset Drive and is only about five minutes away by taxi from the Domestic Airport and the Ninoy Aquino International Airport. They offer airport service for P50 (one or two persons).

The *Malate Pensionne* (☎ 59 5489; fax 59 3489) at 1771 Adriatico St, Malate, is off the main road and therefore is quiet. This friendly and helpful place has a restaurant area downstairs and is probably the most popular travellers' centre in Manila. A dorm bed costs P95 with fan and P110 with air-con. Rooms cost P295 and P360 with fan, P400 with fan and bath, P500 and P600 with air-con and bath and, lastly, P750 with air-con, TV, kitchen and bath. Lockers can be rented and luggage left without charge for up to two weeks. Prostitutes are not encouraged.

Santos Pension House (☎ 59 5628) at 1540 Mabini St, Ermita, also has a pleasant atmosphere. Doubles with fan are P230, with fan and bathroom P280 and with air-con and bathroom P430. The rooms vary in quality but they're clean and there's a restaurant.

In the central Ermita area, the well-run *White House Tourist Inn* (☎ 522 1535; fax 522 4451) is at 465 Pedro Gil, on the corner of M H del Pilar St. A single/double with fan

Ermita, Malate & Paco
Rizal Park
T M Kalaw Street
United Nations Avenue
United Nations Avenue Station
A Flores St
Arquiza Street
Ermita
Padre Faura Street
Padre Faura
Santa Monica Street
R Salas St
Pedro Gil Street
Pedro Gil Station
J Quintos St
Gen Miguel Malvar Street
Alonzo St
Julio M Napkil St
Remedios Street
Remedios Circle
Malate
San Andres St
Aldecoa St
Quirino Avenue
Quirino Avenue Station
Roxas Boulevard
Alhambra Street
M H del Pilar Street
Cortada St
Mabini Street
Jorge C Bocobo Street
Grey St
Maria Orosa Street
Adriatico Street
Luis M Guerrero St
Antonio De Vasques Street
Indiana Street
Taft Avenue
General Luna Street
San Marcelino Street
Romualdez Street
Paco Park
Galicano Apacible Street
Leon Guinto St
Felipe Agoncillo St
Josefa L Escoda Street
Leon Guinto Street
Singalong St
0
100
200 m

PLACES TO STAY

8 Mabini Mansion
9 San Carlos Mansion
11 Manila Pavilion Hotel & Budget Rent-a-Car
23 Hotel Soriente
24 Swagman Hotel
26 P M Apartelle
29 Birdwatcher's Inn & Bar
30 City Garden Hotel
31 Richmond Pension
33 Pension Filipina & Ralph Anthony Suites
35 Doña Petronila Mall
36 Tadel Pension House & Yasmin Pension
37 Hotel La Corona
40 Aurelio Hotel
42 Sandico Apartel
43 Iseya Hotel/ Restaurant & Rooftop Restaurant
44 Royal Palm Hotel
45 Midtown Inn
46 Jetset Executive Mansion
47 Tower Hotel & PT&T Telegram
53 Manila Tourist Inn
54 Mabini Pension
55 Midland Plaza
56 Cherry Lodge Apartelle
57 Robinson's Apartelle
58 Hotel Swiss & Park Hotel
61 Casa Blanca I
62 Sundowner Hotel
63 Hotel Roma
64 Villa Ermita Travel Lodge
65 Boulevard Mansion
69 Ermita Tourist Inn
70 Santos Pension House
71 White House Tourist Inn
72 Manila Midtown Hotel
73 The Gateway Hotel
74 Rothman Inn Hotel
75 Palm Plaza Hotel
76 Alexandria Pension Inn & Las Palmas Hotel
78 Manila Diamond Hotel
79 Pension Natividad
80 Tropicana Apartment Hotel
82 Dakota Mansion
83 Pearl Garden Apartel
84 Adriatico Arms Hotel
85 APP Mayfair Hotel
86 Victoria Mansion
88 New Solanie Hotel
90 Remedios Pension House
91 Malate Pensionne & Shoshana Pension House
96 Grand Boulevard Hotel
97 Euro-Nippon Mansion
98 Winner Lodge
99 Marabella Aparments
100 Ambassador Hotel
101 Carolina Pension
102 Hotel Royal Co-Co & Interbank
104 Admiral Hotel
105 Aloha Hotel
106 Lucen's Pension House
107 True Home
108 Victoria Court Motel

PLACES TO EAT

6 Maxim's Tea House
7 Hong Kong Tea House
10 Kentucky Fried Chicken
13 McDonald's
14 Diamond Tea House
15 Yakiniku Sakura Restaurant
22 Max's
27 Myrna's
32 Bulwagang Pilipino
34 Barrio Fiesta
38 Hang's 'N'
39 Emerald Garden Restaurant
41 The Pool
48 Mrs Wong Tea House
50 Lili Marleen
51 Guernica's
52 Aida's
66 Rosie's Diner
68 Fischfang
87 Sala-Thai
92 Erieze Seafood Restaurant
93 Shakey's Pizza
94 Aristocrat

OTHER

1 Tourist Office
2 Tabacalera
3 Avis Rent-a-Car
4 Singapore Airlines
5 Pakistan International Airways
12 Manila Doctors Hospital
16 Hidden Valley Springs Office & Grande Island Office
17 Alemar's
18 Equitable Bank
19 American Express
20 Western Police Station
21 Manila Medical Centre
22 Hertz Rent-a-Car
23 International Supermarket
25 US Embassy
28 Ermita Church
33 Sabena Belgian Airlines
41 The Pool
49 Avis Rent-a-Car, Broadway Travel & Interisland Travel & Tours
59 Philippine General Hospital
60 Robinson's
67 PAL
69 Scenic View Travel Inc
71 Sunshine Run Office
77 Pistang Pilipino
81 PLDT (PhilippineLong Distance Telephone Company)
89 Sarkies Tours
95 Malate Church
103 My Father's Moustache
109 Manila Zoological & Botanical Gardens

is P270, or with air-con P400 and P480. There's a restaurant in this quite reasonable place.

The *Richmond Pension* (☎ 58 5277) is tucked away at 1165 Grey St, Ermita, and has small rooms with fan for P185/315 and rooms with air-con for P435/465. *Pension Filipina* (☎ 521 1488) is at 542 Arkansas St, Ermita, close to the corner of Maria Orosa St. It's pleasant and has rooms with fan for P225/280 and air-con rooms for P300/350.

The *Alexandria Pension Inn* (☎ 536 1336) at 1620 Mabini St, Malate, has unpretentious rooms with fan for P225 and fairly small but pleasant and clean rooms with TV, air-con and bath for P595. They have a coffee shop and are located directly next to the Las Palmas Hotel across from the Fiesta Filipinas.

The *Mabini Pension* (☎ 59 4853, 50 5404; fax 59 5219) at 1337 Mabini St, Ermita, just by the post office, has singles/doubles with fan and bath for P380/450 or with air-con and bath for P650. The rooms are tidy and are all differently furnished and the people there are friendly and helpful. They will take care of tickets for Aerolift flights, visa extensions and will look after left luggage.

The *Midtown Inn* (☎ 58 2882) located at 551 Padre Faura, Ermita, has passable, clean rooms with fan and bath from P400 to P500 and with TV, air-con and bath for P635 and P675. All rooms facing the street are very noisy.

The *Pension Natividad* (☎ 521 0524; fax 522 3759) at 1601 M H del Pilar St, Malate, has dorm beds with fan for P120. Doubles with fan and bath are P500 and with air-con and bath P700. There's a pleasant atmosphere in this well-run place. They have a coffee shop and will look after left luggage.

Hotels & Apartments Manila has a number of mid-range hotels, which are slightly more expensive than the pensions and guesthouses. In this same bracket there are numerous apartments, usually with cooking facilities. Although they are usually intended for longer term visitors it is possible to stay at some on a short-term basis.

The *Sandico Apartel* (☎ 59 2036) in M H del Pilar St, Ermita, has good rooms with air-con and bath, fridge and TV for P495/530. At 1549 Mabini St, the *Ermita Tourist Inn* (☎ 521 8770/72; fax 521 8773) is a pleasant and fairly clean place with air-con rooms with bath from P530 to P600. They have a restaurant.

Directly above the International Supermarket, the *Hotel Soriente* (☎ 59 9133) is at 595 A Flores St, Ermita, on the corner of J Bocobo St, and has well-kept air-con rooms with bath at P730.

The *Iseya Hotel* (☎ 59 2016/18; fax 522 4451) at 1241 M H del Pilar St, on the corner of Padre Faura, Ermita, has a restaurant, and quite comfortable singles/doubles with TV, fridge, air-con and bath for P750. The rooms facing M H del Pilar St are, however, quite noisy.

The *Rothman Inn Hotel* (☎ 521 9251/60; fax 522 2606) at 1633-1635 Adriatico St, Malate, has air-con rooms with TV at a variety of prices from P800 to P950. The more expensive rooms have fridges. There is also a restaurant.

The *APP Mayfair Hotel* (☎ 50 3850, 50 4440; fax 521 3039) in 1767 Mabini St, Malate, has quite comfortable rooms with TV, air-con and bath for P720 and P800. A fridge is P50 extra. The rooms in the back building are bigger and quieter than on the Mabini St side.

The *City Garden Hotel* (☎ 521 8841; fax 50 4844) at 1158 Mabini St, Ermita, has rooms with TV, fridge, air-con and bath for P900 and P1200. The rooms are nice and in good shape; they are often fully booked. There is a restaurant.

Other places in the middle bracket include the central and convenient *Sundowner Hotel* (☎ 521 2751/61; fax 521 5331) at 1430 Mabini St, Ermita. It has an attractive lobby and is a departure point for tour buses to various locations around Manila including Puerto Galera. Air-con rooms with fridge and TV are P1640 and P2000. The *Swagman Hotel* (☎ 59 9881/85; fax 521 9731) at 411 A Flores St, Ermita, is a clean and well-kept place with rooms with TV, fridge, air-con and bath at P1300. There is a restaurant and airport service.

Places to Eat

Manila is full of places to eat – with all types of food and all types of prices. The tourist ghetto of Ermita is a good hunting ground. Although you'll pay more here than in other parts of the Philippines, you'll still find good, reasonably priced food of all types. Apart from Filipino food and a variety of other Asian cuisines there are also Western fast-food operators and a choice of fixed-price buffets at the best hotels.

The recommendations that follow are essentially in Ermita and Malate because most visitors will be staying there. There are plenty of other restaurants in Makati, Binondo, Santa Cruz and in other parts of Manila.

Filipino Food On busy M H del Pilar St, Ermita, *Myrna's* is a popular and often crowded little place appealing essentially to local people rather than the tourist crowds. A meal typically costs about P80; it's closed on Sunday.

The *Aristocrat*, on the corner of Roxas Blvd and San Andres St, Malate, is good value despite the name. This big Filipino restaurant is the most popular of the six Aristocrats in Manila. Try lapu lapu fish (expensive) or the fish soup here – a meal costs about P150.

Further down Roxas Blvd, in Pasay City, *Josephine's* has superb seafood and live music in the evenings. A meal in this well-known restaurant costs about P150.

Definitely more expensive but probably worth it is the *Kamayan* on Padre Faura St in Ermita, near the corner with Mabini St. The name means Bare Hands because that's what you eat with; knives and forks aren't used. The food, however, is not only authentic but it's also delicious – tasty, well prepared but relatively expensive. Across the back of the restaurant is a line of tapped water jars for you to wash your hands before and after eating. A meal costs about P200.

Barrio Fiesta at J Bocobo St, Ermita, is a popular place for real Filipino food and is usually full of people really tucking in. Try crispy pata or kare-kare in this bright, cheerful and busy place. The menu is extensive but the prices are a little more expensive than ordinary restaurants, about P200 for a meal.

Other Asian Restaurants You can try plenty of other regional and Western cuisines in Manila. The *Sea Food Market* at J Bocobo St, Ermita, right across the road from Barrio Fiesta, positively bounces. You select your fish or other seafood from a display area on one side and it's cooked up by a squad of short-order cooks lined up along an open window on the street side. They're all frantically stirring woks, scooping pots and juggling frying pans while flames leap high. An even larger squad of waiters and waitresses jostle near the counter on the other side. It's wonderful entertainment for passersby. A meal here will cost about P300 and you can round it off with coffee and cakes in the *Café Alps* next door.

Manila has a great number of Japanese and Chinese restaurants. For simple and economical Chinese food try *Mrs Wong Tea House* on the corner of Padre Faura and M H del Pilar Sts, Ermita. A meal will cost from P75 to P100.

Other good Chinese restaurants include the *Hong Kong Tea House* on M H del Pilar St, Ermita, and *Maxim's Tea House* on Roxas Blvd, Ermita. There are even more Chinese restaurants across the river in Chinatown and Binondo.

Next to the Kamayan Restaurant on Padre Faura there's good north Indian food at *Kashmir* – about P200 for a meal. For Japanese food, the *Iseya Restaurant* on Padre Faura St in Ermita is good value with a P100 business lunch and regular meals at around P175. There are a number of Thai restaurants in Makati including the *Sukhothai* on Makati Ave where you can eat for about P150.

Western Restaurants There are plenty of Western restaurants like the very pleasant *Café Adriatico,* at 1790 Adriatico St. This is a good place for a drink or a meal; there are tables outside and others, upstairs, overlook the Remedios Circle street scene. The food ranges from burgers to pasta. It's not cheap but it is a very relaxed, stylish place to dine.

Popular German and Swiss restaurants include the *München Grill Pub* on Mabini St, Ermita, with Bavarian dishes, and the *Old Swiss Restaurant* in the Hotel Swiss on Belen St, Paco, the place to go for Swiss specialities. They have good meals of the day for about P200.

On the corner of Adriatico St and Pedro Gil, Ermita, *El Comedor* offers traditional Spanish food at around P250. There's live music in the pleasant and slightly cheaper *Guernica's* on M H del Pilar St, Ermita.

Other international possibilities include Australian-style food and beer at the *Rooftop Restaurant* on top of the Iseya Hotel at the corner of Padre Faura and M H del Pilar Sts, Ermita. There's a good view over the bay and an Aussie barbecue on Sunday. Mexican food can be found at *Tia Maria's* in Remedios St, on the corner of Carolina St, Malate. *Max's* on Maria Orosa St, Ermita, is one of 10 branches around the city and offers a variety of chicken dishes at about P150.

Buffets All-you-can-eat breakfast buffets typically cost P150 to P200 at the big hotels in Manila. The *Sundowner Hotel* on Mabini St, Ermita, offers one at P170.

At the big tourist hotels, lunch buffets typically cost P200 to P300, plus 25% government tax and service. Dinner at one of these places would be P250 to P350 and is often accompanied by cultural entertainment or a fashion show.

Fast Food & Cheap Eats Manila has lots of fast-food places including a selection of *McDonald's, Kentucky Frieds, Pizza Huts* and *Shakey's Pizzas*. Shakeys are quite a Philippines institution and they do pretty good pizza – you'll find one at the corner of Mabini and Arquiza and another on Remedios near Roxas Blvd. The Harrison Plaza shopping centre, beside the Century Park Sheraton Hotel, has a *Pizza Hut, McDonald's* and *Kentucky Fried* all together. Doughnut specialists are also popular and 7-Elevens are also appearing in the Philippines. *Jollibee* is a local burger chain with numerous branches: there's one on Padre Faura, Ermita. *Rosie's Diner* in M H del Pilar St, Ermita, is comfortable and always fairly full, in the style of a US snack-bar of the 1950s – all that's missing is the Wurlitzer. It is open all day, every day and a meal costs around P100.

There are lots of reasonably priced small foodstalls in J Bocobo St, between Padre Faura and Robinson's, Ermita, that sell Filipino snacks and meals for around P50.

Entertainment

There is plenty to do after hours in Manila. Although Mayor Lim's campaign to clean up Ermita has meant most of the lights going out there, this doesn't mean the entertainment business isn't flourishing in other areas of Metro Manila where other mayors have their say.

Music The folk clubs often have amazing 'replicas' of Dylan, Simon & Garfunkel, James Taylor or other Western pop stars. Try the popular *Hobbit House* at 1801 Mabini St, Malate. After 8.30 pm there's a P60 minimum charge and waiters here are indeed all hobbit-sized as it's entirely staffed by dwarfs. Mexican dishes are a speciality. Admission is P50, except when Freddie Aguilar is performing, when it is P120. The most popular singer in the Philippines, he performs his songs of social criticism here about twice a week, usually Tuesday and Saturday. Further along from Ermita, in Malate, *My Father's Moustache*, at 2144 M H del Pilar St, also has good folk music.

Jazz can be heard in several of the international hotels. Every Sunday from 10 am to 1 pm well-known musicians play at the Jazz Brunch in *The Lobby* in the Manila Peninsula Hotel, Ayala Ave, on the corner of Makati Ave, Makati.

Bars There are plenty of pubs and nightclubs in Makati and Pasay City. Among the best known bars in Makati are the *Danish Con-*

nection, *Papillion* and *Jool's*, all in Burgos St. In Pasay City, the nightlife has taken root in the International Karaoke Complex on Roxas Blvd, across from the Cultural Center.

Bistros & Music Lounges Places for a drink and a snack have become very popular. The *Café Adriatico* at 1790 Adriatico St, Malate, near the Remedios Circle started the craze and is still a favourite. Next door is the *Hard Rock Café*, with an aeroplane crashing into the roof and rock music videos.

Also on Remedios Circle is *Moviola* with a piano bar and restaurant, while nearby on Remedios St is the lively *Penguin Café Gallery*. In Makati the *Bistro RJ* in the Olympia Building, Makati Ave, features live '50s and '60s music with admission costs varying from P75 to P100 (depending on the night).

Discos Manila is very much disco-land with popular places like *Faces* on Makati Ave, Makati. Entry is P140. *Equinox* on Pasay Rd, Makati, is so far the newest disco in Manila and entry is P100 or P150 (depending on the night).

Others include *Stargazer* in the Silahis Hotel, Roxas Blvd, Malate, and *Club Valentino* in the Manila Midtown Hotel, on the corner of Pedro Gil and Adriatico Sts, Ermita. *Lost Horizon* is in the Philippine Plaza Hotel, Cultural Center complex, Malate, while *Euphoria* in the Hotel Inter-Continental, Ayala Ave, Makati, is a modern disco that's very popular with the Filipino trendies.

Other Casinos are established in the *Grand Boulevard Hotel* on Roxas Blvd, Malate, and in the *Manila Pavilion Hotel* on United Nations Ave, Ermita. Cockfights are a popular local activity and there are cockpits at various places which operate on Sunday. Films are advertised in the daily press.

Zamboanga Restaurant on Adriatico St, Malate, has nightly Filipino and Polynesian dancing.

In the idyllic Paco Park, San Marcelino St, *Paco Park Presents* puts on free chamber music at 6 pm on Friday. The free *Concert at the Park* takes place every Sunday at 5 pm in Rizal Park.

Things to Buy

The Philippines is a great handicraft centre and you can find all sorts of interesting things around Manila but, not surprisingly, you'll find them even cheaper out in the country. There are many handicraft shops and centres around Manila – check out the Pistang Pilipino between M H del Pilar St and Mabini St and the variety of handicraft places at the Nayong Pilipino (demonstrations there on Monday). The Shoemart department store at the Makati Commercial Center is good for souvenirs if you can't get around the country. Prices are fixed and competitive.

In Intramuros, the El Amanecer Building at 744 General Luna St, has Silahis for art and crafts, Chang Rong for antiques and Galeria de las Islas for paintings and sculptures on its three floors. Further up General Luna, opposite San Agustin, is the beautiful Casa Manila complex.

Good buys include canework, carvings, hanging-lamps of shell, and clothes.

Bargaining is not done as much in the Philippines as in other South-East Asian countries but you should still haggle a little.

Getting There & Away

Manila is virtually the only entry point to the Philippines. See the Philippines Getting There & Away section for details on flying to the Philippines. Manila is the centre for bus travel to the north and south and for ships from Luzon to the other islands of the Philippines. What little remains of Luzon's railway system also runs from Manila.

Air See the Philippines Getting Around section for details of PAL operations. International departure tax is P500.

Bus The Philippines has a great number of bus companies and they operate from many bus stations in Manila. To further complicate matters, some individual companies will have more than one terminal – there might be a southern terminal for southbound services and a northern one for northbound services, for example. There is no single central long-distance bus station in Manila. Several terminals, including those on E de los Santos Ave (Edsa) in south Manila, can be reached by Metrorail.

Coming in to Manila from other centres, buses will generally be signed for their terminal rather than for Manila. The sign may simply announce that the bus is heading for 'Avenida', 'Cubao' or 'Pasay' and it's assumed you know that these are destinations within Manila.

Baliwag Transit (☎ 990132) at 33 Edsa, Cubao, Quezon City, has buses going north to Aparri, Bulacan Province, Baliwag, San Jose and Tuguegarao.

BLTB (Batangas-Laguna-Tayabas Bus Company) (☎ 833 5501) is at Edsa, Pasay City (near Victory and Philtranco lines). Buses operate to Nasugbu, Calamba, Batangas, Santa Cruz (for Pagsanjan), Lucena, Naga and Legaspi.

Philippine Rabbit (☎ 711 5819) is at 819 Oroquieta, Santa Cruz (entrance in Rizal Ave). Get a jeepney towards Monumento from Mabini St or Metrorail to D Jose station. This terminal is known as 'Avenida', and if you're coming from the north take a Philippine Rabbit bus marked 'Avenida via Dau'. It takes the Dau Expressway from Angeles and is much faster. Avoid 'Avenida via Caloocan' buses. Buses operate to various destinations in south-west and central Luzon including Angeles, Baguio, Balanga, Laoag, Mariveles, San Fernando (Pampanga & La Union), Tarlac and Vigan.

Philtranco (☎ 833 5061) is at Edsa, Pasay City. Get a jeepney towards Baclaran from Taft Avenue or M H del Pilar St or Metrorail to Edsa station. Buses from here run to Daet, Naga, Tabaco, Legaspi, Sorsogon, Samar, Leyte and Mindanao.

Victory Liner (☎ 361 1514) is at 713 Rizal Avenue Extension, Caloocan City. Jeepneys towards Monumento from Mabini St or Metrorail go to the North terminal. Buses go to Alaminos, Dagupan, Iba, Olongapo and Mariveles from the North terminal.

The second Victory Liner terminal (☎ 833 5019) is at Edsa, Pasay City. Jeepneys and buses heading for Baclaran leave from Taft Ave or M H del Pilar St – change in Baclaran or before, or take the Metrorail to the Edsa station. Buses from this terminal run to Olongapo, Zambales, Baguio and Dagupan.

Train The Philippines' shrinking rail operation has contracted to just the one route south from Manila to the Bicol region (Naga), and it is much slower and less reliable than the bus services. You are not recommended to use it.

Boat The shipping companies generally advertise departures in the Manila English-language dailies. Cebu, in the Visayas, is the main hub of Filipino shipping, but there are plenty of departures from Manila. Scenic View Travel Inc. (☎ 522 3495; fax 521 8773), beside the Ermita Tourist Inn on the corner of Mabini and Soldado Sts, Ermita, sells tickets for Aboitiz Lines, saving a trip to the wharves.

Nearly all interisland departures are made from North Harbour in Manila. If you have trouble finding it ask a coastguard opposite Pier 8. A taxi from Ermita to North Harbour should cost about P40. In the other direction, travelling to Ermita from the harbour after a ship arrival, is likely to be more expensive. Nobody's meter seems to work properly and the fare is likely to be P70 to P100. The jeepney route between the harbour and Ermita is circuitous and slow.

Shipping company offices in Manila are:

Aboitiz Lines
Pier 4, North Harbour, Tondo (☎ 21 7581, 27 6332, 50 1816)
Destinations: Panay, Romblon

Asuncion Shipping Lines
3038 Jose Abad Santos St, Sampaloc, Santa Mesa (☎ 711 3743)
Pier 2, North Harbor, Tondo (☎ 20 4024)
Destinations: Lubang/Mindoro, Palawan (Coron, Culion, Dumaran, El Nido)

Carlos Gothong Lines
Pier 10, North Harbor, Tondo (☎ 21 3611, 21 4121)
Destinations: Cebu, Mindanao, Panay

Negros Navigation Lines
Negros Navigation Building, 849 Pasay Rd, Makati (☎ 818 3804, 816 3481)
Pier 2, North Harbor, Tondo (☎ 21 5741, 21 2691)
Destinations: Negros, Panay, Romblon

Sulpicio Lines
415 San Fernando St, San Nicolas (☎ 47 9621, 47 5346)

Pier 12, North Harbour, Tondo (☎ 20 1781)
Destinations: Cebu, Leyte, Masbate, Mindanao, Negros, Palawan, Panay, Samar

William Lines
1508 Rizal Ave Extension, Caloocan City (☎ 361 0764)
Pier 14, North Harbour, Tondo (☎ 21 9821, 40 5458)
Destinations: Cebu, Leyte, Mindanao, Palawan, Panay, Romblon, Samar

Getting Around

To/From the Airport If Manila is your first stop on a first visit to Asia then hold your breath as it's pure chaos out there. For some reason the Filipinos seem totally unable to make the airport work, a complete contrast to efficient, smooth operations like Hong Kong, Bangkok or Singapore. In fact, when things do work (like the efficient Golden Cabs, now history) they're immediately banned!

Domestic and international flights go from the same airport but the terminals are some distance apart. Manila International Airport (MIA) has officially been renamed Ninoy Aquino International Airport (NAIA).

Metrorail An economic alternative is a taxi trip from NAIA to the Metrorail South Terminal in Baclaran for about P30 (providing, that is, one will take you for this short distance). From there you can ride the train to Pedro Gil or United Nations Ave station for P6. The Baclaran Terminus is only two km from the airport.

Taxi At present, only air-con taxis with set fares are allowed to service the airport (eg P220 to Pasay, P300 to Ermita, P300 to Makati and P380 to Quezon City). If you don't want to put up with the hassle, then you can take the stairs up to the departure level, where you can wait for a taxi that has just dropped off passengers and would otherwise have to head back to town empty. Mind you, lots of sneaky taxi drivers have hit on this trick and now wait for victims at the departure level with bargain 'deals'.

It's only 12 km from the city centre and since taxi fares are very low it should be pretty cheap to get between the airport and the centre. On the meter the fare between the airport and Ermita should be about P60 to P70 but the drivers will try for at least P150 or much more if they can get it.

When going out to the airport you can take any taxi. You will probably have better luck at getting a properly working meter.

Other Other alternatives include free or relatively cheap hotel limousine services, usually provided if you book a room with one of the hotels represented at the accommodation counters near the main exit in the arrivals hall.

Taxis heading into town will usually travel along the coast on Roxas Blvd. If you do find yourself on a Metrorail you will come into the tourist area along Taft Avenue. Ermita will appear to your left with a cluster of high buildings before you pass Rizal Park and the imposing buildings of the Department of Tourism and the National Museum.

PAL have a shuttle bus to the domestic terminal, ostensibly only for their own passengers but a polite request will normally get you on board.

Bus There's a comprehensive bus system around Manila but it's a little difficult to find your way around until you've got some idea of Manila's geography and can recognise the destination names. There are many different bus companies. Metro Manila buses are modern, blue in colour and easy to get around on. Fares are from P1.50 on regular buses. The air-con Love Buses cost a flat P10.

Buses, like jeepneys, generally display their destinations on a board in front. This might be a large complex like NAIA, a street name like Ayala (Ayala Ave, Makati) or a whole suburb like Quiapo. The Escolta-Ayala/Medical Center service is a Love Bus route which runs along M H del Pilar St through Ermita to Makati (the embassies) and the Makati Commercial Center, then returns along Mabini St to Ermita.

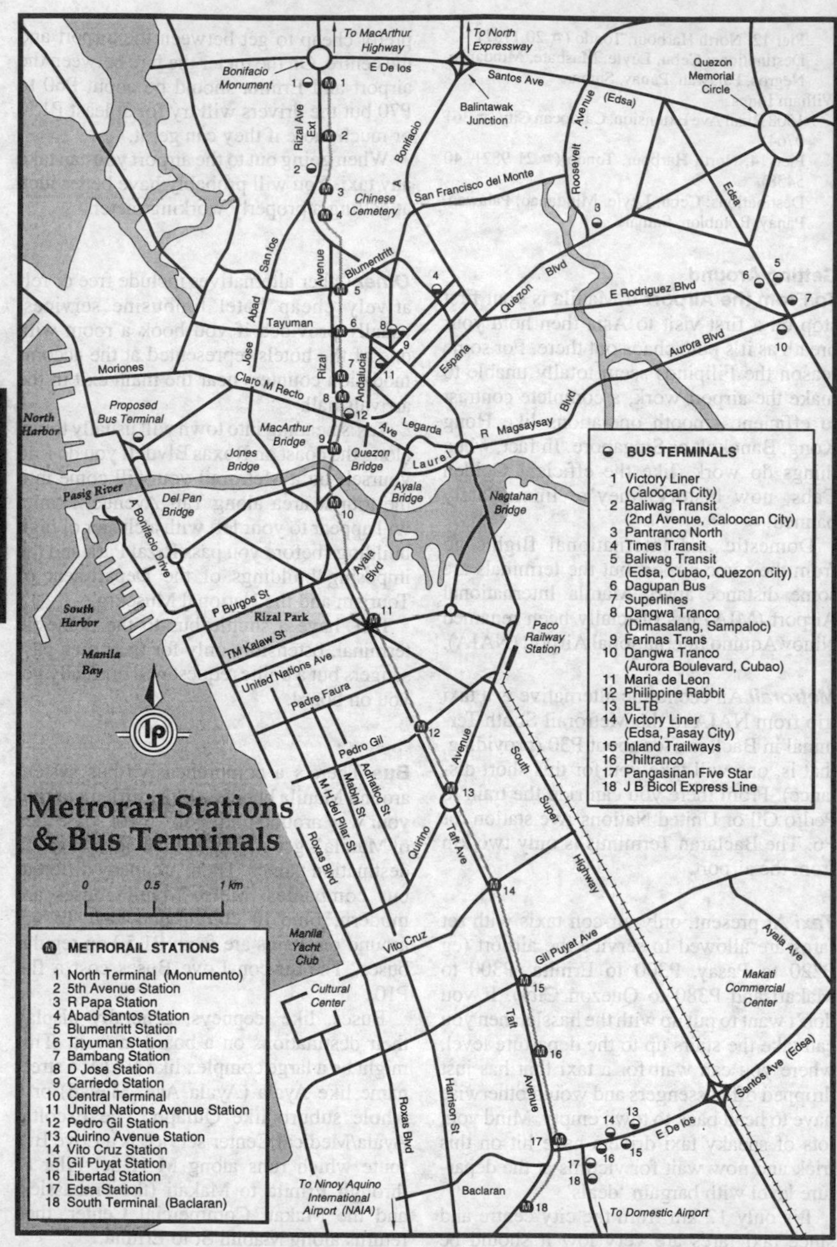
Metrorail Stations & Bus Terminals
To MacArthur Highway
To North Expressway
Bonifacio Monument
E De los
Santos Ave
Balintawak Junction
Quezon Memorial Circle
Avenue (Edsa)
Roosevelt
Edsa
Rizal Ave Ext
Bonifacio
San Francisco del Monte
Chinese Cemetery
San los
Abad
Jose
Avenue
Blumentritt
Tayuman
Rizal
Andalucia
Quezon Blvd
E Rodriguez Blvd
Aurora Blvd
Espana
Moriones
Claro M Recto
Legarda
Ave
R Magsaysay Blvd
Laurel
Proposed Bus Terminal
North Harbor
MacArthur Bridge
Jones Bridge
Quezon Bridge
Ayala Bridge
Nagtahan Bridge
Pasig River
Del Pan Bridge
A Bonifacio Drive
Ayala Blvd
P Burgos St
Rizal Park
TM Kalaw St
South Harbor
Manila Bay
Paco Railway Station
United Nations Ave
Padre Faura
Pedro Gil
M H del Pilar St
Mabini St
Adriatico St
Roxas Blvd
Quirino
Avenue
Taft Ave
South Super Highway
0 0.5 1 km
Manila Yacht Club
Vito Cruz
Gil Puyat Ave
Ayala Ave
Makati Commercial Center
Cultural Center
Harrison St
Taft Avenue
Santos Ave (Edsa)
E De los
Baclaran
To Ninoy Aquino International Airport (NAIA)
To Domestic Airport
BUS TERMINALS
1 Victory Liner (Caloocan City)
2 Baliwag Transit (2nd Avenue, Caloocan City)
3 Pantranco North
4 Times Transit
5 Baliwag Transit (Edsa, Cubao, Quezon City)
6 Dagupan Bus
7 Superlines
8 Dangwa Tranco (Dimasalang, Sampaloc)
9 Farinas Trans
10 Dangwa Tranco (Aurora Boulevard, Cubao)
11 Maria de Leon
12 Philippine Rabbit
13 BLTB
14 Victory Liner (Edsa, Pasay City)
15 Inland Trailways
16 Philtranco
17 Pangasinan Five Star
18 J B Bicol Express Line
METRORAIL STATIONS
1 North Terminal (Monumento)
2 5th Avenue Station
3 R Papa Station
4 Abad Santos Station
5 Blumentritt Station
6 Tayuman Station
7 Bambang Station
8 D Jose Station
9 Carriedo Station
10 Central Terminal
11 United Nations Avenue Station
12 Pedro Gil Station
13 Quirino Avenue Station
14 Vito Cruz Station
15 Gil Puyat Station
16 Libertad Station
17 Edsa Station
18 South Terminal (Baclaran)

Metrorail The quick and convenient Metrorail or Light Rail Transit trains run on an elevated line which runs right along Taft Ave beside Ermita. It extends as far as the Bonifacio Monument (Monumento) at Caloocan in the north and south to Baclaran (Pasay), quite close to Manila airport.

It's very convenient for getting to the Philtranco/Victory Liner (Edsa) terminals in the south and the Philippine Rabbit and Victory Liner bus terminals in the north. It is also an alternative way of getting to the airport. When traffic is really clogged up you'd probably get to the airport faster (and cheaper) by taking the Metrorail to the South terminal and then taking a taxi from there. The fare is a flat P6.

Taxi There are countless metered taxis (make sure the meter is on) and it's generally held that the white Fil-Nipon taxis and City taxis are much better than the more prolific yellow ones. Meters in these cabs are said to 'work better' and the drivers are less inclined to argue about the fares. Always ensure you have plenty of spare change before starting out. Ordinary taxis (those not equipped with air-conditioning) have a flag-down charge of P10 which includes the first 500 metres; thereafter they charge P1 for every further 250 metres. However, almost all of the meters still show the old flag-down charge of P2.50, so there will be a surcharge of P7.50. Air-con taxis begin with P16 (the old flag-down charge of P3.50 plus P12.50 surcharge).

Jeepney Jeepneys are very reasonably priced with fares from P1.50. As with the buses, it can be a little difficult to find your way around but they're so cheap it's no great loss to get on the wrong one. Most jeepneys pass by the city hall, north of Rizal Park. Heading north, they usually split there and either head north-west to Tondo, straight north to Monumento and Caloocan or north-east to Quezon City or Cubao or various other destinations in that direction.

Heading south, the routes from north of the river converge at City Hall then split to either go down Taft Ave or M H del Pilar St.

Around Manila

Luzon is the largest island in the Philippines and has a lot to offer apart from Manila. The places in this Around Manila section can all be visited as day trips from the capital although a number are worth overnight stops, or can be combined with visits to places further afield. The attractions around Manila include Mt Pinatubo north of Manila and the WW II battle site of Corregidor at the entrance to Manila Bay. South of Manila, prime attractions include beach resorts, the Pagsanjan rapids and the Taal Lake volcano. These can be visited en route to South Luzon or to the island of Mindoro.

OLONGAPO & SUBIC

North-west of Manila, on the Bataan Peninsula, Olongapo used to be where the US Navy was stationed. In 1991 the Philippine Senate made the decision not to extend the MBA (Military Bases Agreement) which had regulated the lease of the bases since the end of WW II.

From Olongapo you can easily do a day trip to Mt Samat on the Bataan Peninsula. What's more, Olongapo is a good starting point for trips to the Mt Pinatubo area or along the Zambales coastline. There are also some so-so beaches around Subic, but San Miguel, slightly north of Subic Bay, is better than any of the beaches between Olongapo and Subic.

Places to Stay

At 765 Rizal Ave in Olongapo the *Ram's Inn* has quite comfortable rooms with fan for P150 and with air-con for P175.

Along the coast, from Olongapo to Barrio Barretto and Subic, there are several resorts with rooms from P250 or so.

Getting There & Away
It's a two to three-hour bus ride from the Victory Liner station in Manila. From Baguio buses depart hourly and the trip takes six hours. It's only 12 km from Olongapo to Subic but watch out for pickpockets on the jeepneys.

ANGELES
Angeles has noticeably recovered from the close-down of Clark Air Base and the eruption of Mt Pinatubo, at least as far as tourism is concerned. The hotels are busier than ever before. Restaurants, bars and nightclubs are experiencing an unprecedented boom, and the demand for tours of Pinatubo is still rising. There's no doubt that Manila's Mayor Lim and his campaign to clean up the entertainment business in his city has given Angeles a big boost at just the right time.

Places to Stay
Thanks to the former American base, Angeles has a large selection of comfortable hotels with restaurants and swimming pools. The *Liberty Inn* (☎ 4588) on MacArthur Highway, Balibago, has rooms with fan and bath for P160 and with air-con and bath from P250. The *Southern Star Hotel*, on Sampaguita St, Clarkview, has rooms with TV, fan and bath for P200 and with air-con and bath for P300. The *Bonanza Hotel* (☎ 27321) on San Pablo St, Mountain View, has rooms with TV, air-con and bath from P300 to P380. The *Endeavour Lord Hotel* (☎ 51210) on Malabanas Rd, Plaridel I, has comfortable rooms with TV, air-con and bath for P360.

Getting There & Away
There are several Philippine Rabbit buses daily from Manila. They take about 1½ hours but make sure the bus is marked 'Expressway/Dau'. Alternatively, there are many bus services operating to North Luzon via Dau, from where you are able to catch a jeepney or tricycle the short distance back to Angeles.

There are several daily air-con buses from Manila. One leaves from the Swagman Hotel on A Flores St, Ermita, at 10.30 am and another from the La Corona Hotel, M H del Pilar St, Ermita, at noon and 9 pm.

There are hourly Victory Liner services from Olongapo which take two hours. Victory Liner also have hourly buses from Baguio. They're marked 'Olongapo' and take four hours. Many of the services between Manila and North Luzon go via Dau, a short tricycle ride from Angeles.

Bus services from Manila or Baguio to Olongapo usually go through San Fernando.

AROUND ANGELES
Mt Pinatubo
For many of those involved, the unprecedentedly violent eruption of Mt Pinatubo on 15 June 1991 was like a bad dream. The clouds of steam and detritus produced by the eruption shot up to 40 km into the stratosphere, darkening the sky. Unbelievable amounts of ash and sand settled in wide areas around the volcano. To the west of Angeles the grey mass of coagulated material can reach heights of up to 20 metres. The impressive terrain is criss-crossed with bizarre ravines, through which you can wander for hours. Other areas can be better explored with a vehicle. Several hotels in Angeles offer tours to Pinatubo and will arrange guides who know their way around. For safety reasons, car tours and hikes should only be attempted in the dry season, the best months being February, March and April.

San Fernando
Not to be confused with San Fernando La Union north-west of Baguio, this town is between Manila and Angeles and is notorious for its Easter celebrations when at least one local religious fanatic has himself nailed to a cross.

CORREGIDOR
This small island, at the mouth of Manila Bay, was the US-Filipino last stand after the Japanese invaded. It certainly wasn't as impregnable as planned but it did hold out for a long time. Now it's a national shrine and you can have a look around the underground

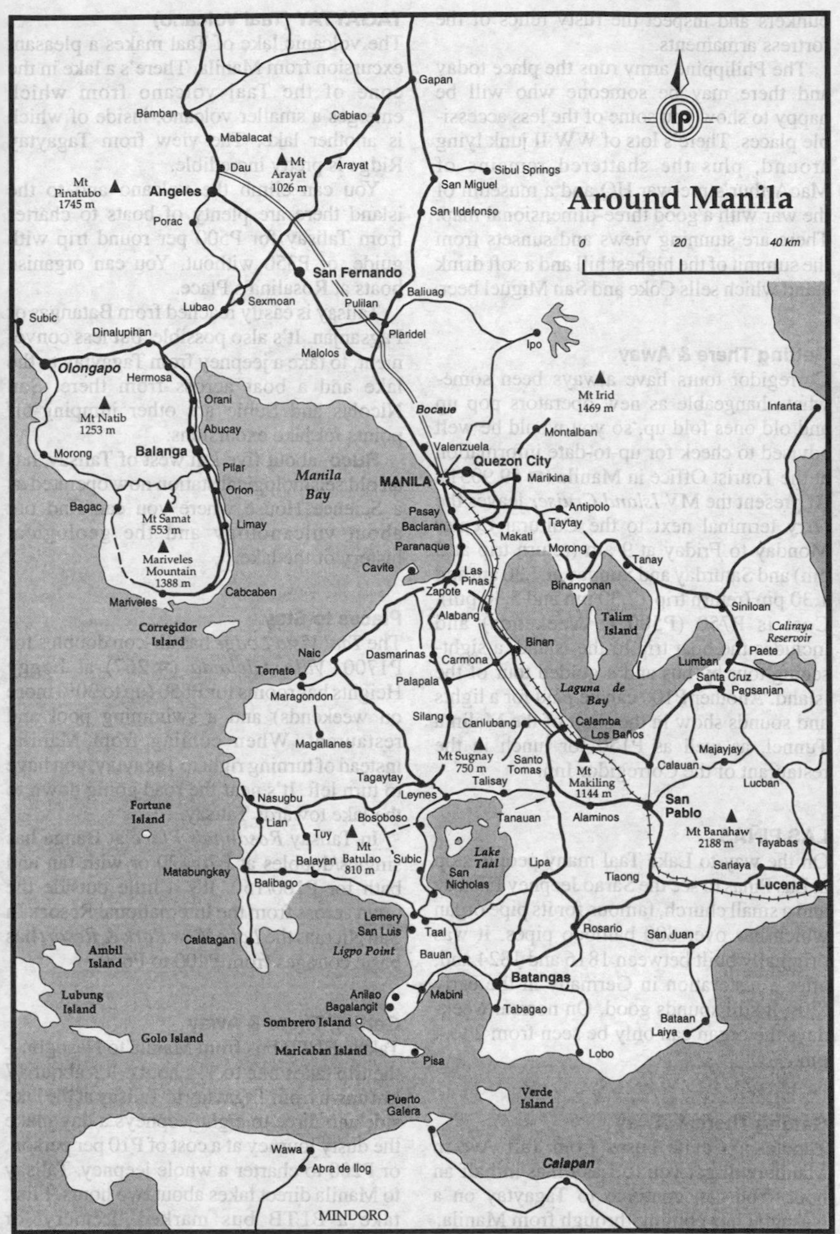

THE PHILIPPINES

bunkers and inspect the rusty relics of the fortress armaments.

The Philippine army runs the place today and there may be someone who will be happy to show you some of the less accessible places. There's lots of WW II junk lying around, plus the shattered remains of MacArthur's pre-war HQ and a museum of the war with a good three-dimensional map. There are stunning views and sunsets from the summit of the highest hill and a soft drink stand which sells Coke and San Miguel beer.

Getting There & Away

Corregidor tours have always been somewhat changeable as new operators pop up and old ones fold up, so you would be well advised to check for up-to-date information at the Tourist Office in Manila (☎ 59 9031). At present the MV *Island Cruiser* leaves the ferry terminal next to the Cultural Center Monday to Friday at 9 am (return trip at 3 pm) and Saturday and Sunday at 7.30 am and 1.30 pm (return trip 12.30 pm and 5.30 pm). Cost is P750 (P500 at weekends) and includes the boat trip to the island, a sightseeing tour by bus and a guided tour of the island. Another P100 can be paid for a lights and sounds show in the shaft of the Malinta Tunnel, as well as P150 for lunch in the restaurant of the Corregidor Inn.

LAS PIÑAS

On the way to Lake Taal many people stop at Las Piñas to see the Sarao Jeepney Factory and a small church, famous for its pipe organ which has over 800 bamboo pipes. It was originally built between 1816 and 1824 and, after a restoration in Germany in the early '70s, it still sounds good. On normal weekdays the organ can only be seen from 2 to 4 pm.

Getting There & Away

Zapote or Cavite buses from Taft Ave in Manila will get you to Las Piñas in half an hour. You can continue to Tagaytay on a Nasugbu bus coming through from Manila.

TAGAYTAY (Taal Volcano)

The volcanic lake of Taal makes a pleasant excursion from Manila. There's a lake in the cone of the Taal volcano from which emerges a smaller volcano, inside of which is another lake. The view from Tagaytay Ridge is pretty incredible.

You can climb the volcano and to the island there are plenty of boats to charter from Talisay for P500 per round trip with guide, or P350 without. You can organise boats at Rosalina's Place.

Talisay is easily reached from Batangas or Pagsanjan. It's also possible, but less convenient, to take a jeepney from Tagaytay to the lake and a boat across from there. San Nicolas and Subic are other jumping-off points for lake excursions.

Buco, about five km west of Talisay, has an old seismological station now operated as a Science House where you can find out about vulcanology and the geological history of the lake.

Places to Stay

The *Taal Vista Lodge* has air-con doubles for P1700. *Villa Adelaida* (☎ 267) at Foggy Heights has rooms for P850 (up to 20% more on weekends) and a swimming pool and restaurant. When coming from Manila, instead of turning right to Tagaytay, you have to turn left. It's near the road going down to the lake towards Talisay.

In Talisay *Rosalina's Place* at Banga has singles/doubles at P70/120 or with fan and bath for P100/150. It's a little outside the town across from the International Resort. In San Nicolas the *Lake View Park & Resort* has basic cottages from P400 to P600.

Getting There & Away

Take a BLTB bus from Manila to Nasugbu – the trip takes one to 1½ hours. It's about 17 km down from Tagaytay to Talisay at the lake side and three to eight jeepneys a day make the dusty journey at a cost of P10 per person, or P200 to charter a whole jeepney. Talisay to Manila direct takes about two hours. First, take a BLTB bus marked 'Lemery' or

THE PHILIPPINES

'Batangas' as far as Tanauan, then a jeepney from the public market to Talisay.

You can reach Talisay from Pagsanjan by first taking a jeepney to Santa Cruz. From there take a Manila-bound bus as far as the Calamba junction, where you catch a jeepney to Tanauan, walk to the far side of the market (about half a km) and, finally, take another jeepney to Talisay. It sounds complicated but in actual fact it's quite fast and simple.

To get to Tagaytay take a jeepney from the Calamba junction through Binan to Palapala and a bus from there to Tagaytay. Or continue past Calamba to Alabang, get a jeepney from there to Zapote and catch a bus coming from Manila through Zapote to Tagaytay.

The easiest way from Batangas to Talisay is to take a Manila bus as far as Tanauan and a jeepney from there down to Talisay. Total travel time is about two hours.

There's also an interesting back-roads route from Batangas to Lake Taal. Take a jeepney from Batangas to Lemery, a dusty 1½-hour ride. From there, take a jeepney to San Nicolas on the south-western shore of the lake.

NASUGBU & MATABUNGKAY

Matabungkay is the most popular beach in the neighbourhood of Manila and is busy on weekends. Nasugbu has better beaches, including **White Sands**, three or four km north of the town. You can get there by tricycle or outrigger.

Places to Stay & Eat

The *Swiss House Hotel* in Matabungkay has rooms with fan and bath for P400 or there's the *Coral Beach Club* at P600 for a double with fan and bath. Nasugbu is more expensive.

Getting There & Away

BLTB buses for Nasugbu take about two hours from Manila and leave almost hourly. For Matabungkay get off the bus at Lian and travel the last few km by jeepney. It takes three or four stages by jeepney between Matabungkay and Batangas.

BATANGAS

Batangas can make a good base for visiting Lake Taal, Los Baños and sites along the coast, but the main reason for coming here is to take the ferry service across to the island of Mindoro. If you don't leave Manila early enough you won't arrive in Batangas in time to get a boat across to Mindoro that day.

Places to Stay & Eat

Located on the outskirts of town *Alpa Hotel* (☎ 2213) has rooms with fan for P100/200, with air-con for P260/300 and with air-con and bath from P400 to P600. There's also a restaurant and a swimming pool.

The *Guesthaus* (☎ 1609) at 224 Diego Silang St, on the corner of M H del Pilar St, has rooms with fan and bath for P200/250. On Rizal Ave Extension you'll find *Macsor Hotel* (☎ 3063) which has singles/doubles with fan and bath for P300 or with air-con and bath for P400/600. It is on the outskirts, towards the harbour.

Getting There & Away

Always ask for Batangas City to avoid confusion with the general Batangas area, and try to get a Batangas Pier bus, otherwise you'll have to take a jeepney for the final stretch. Several buses leave the BLTB Terminal in Manila daily for Batangas. The 2½-hour trip costs about P40. BLTB air-con buses are only a few pesos more expensive but not all of them go to the pier.

Try to get to Batangas reasonably early if you want to get the Puerto Galera boat at 11.30 am or 12.30 pm. Beware of pickpockets on these buses. They often operate in groups of three.

The Si-Kat Ferry Inc. has a daily air-con bus and ship service which departs Manila from Sundowner Hotel in Mabini St, Ermita, at 9 am.

To get to Batangas from Pagsanjan, take a jeepney to Santa Cruz, a Manila-bound bus from there to the Calamba junction and, from there, either a jeepney direct to Batangas or a jeepney to Tanauan. In Tanauan wait for a Batangas-bound bus coming through from Manila and take that.

THE PHILIPPINES

LOS BAÑOS & CALAMBA

The **Los Baños Botanical Gardens** has a big swimming pool and the town is noted for its **hot springs** (most resorts are outside of town, along the highway as far as Calamba). Los Baños is also the location of the **International Rice Research Institute** where the rice varieties that prompted the Asian 'green revolution' were developed.

Just before Los Baños is Calamba, where national hero Jose Rizal was born. **Rizal House** is now a memorial and museum.

Getting There & Away

Buses from Manila for Los Baños or Santa Cruz will get you to both towns. Calamba is the junction town if you're travelling down to Batangas or to Lake Taal.

SAN PABLO & ALAMINOS

There is a wide variety of hikes around San Pablo. There's an easy hour's stroll around **Sampaloc Lake** in an extinct volcanic cone. Alternatively, make the longer half-day trip to the twin lakes of **Pandin** and **Yambo**.

Near here at Alaminos, **Hidden Valley** is a private park with lush vegetation, natural springs, a swimming pool and a hefty admission charge of about P1000, which includes a drink on arrival, a buffet lunch and use of the facilities such as the swimming pool.

The 1144-metre-high **Mt Makiling** is best reached from Alaminos or Los Baños, while from San Pablo you can climb 2188-metre-high **Mt Banahaw**.

Places to Stay

The *Sampaloc Lake Youth Hostel* (☎ 4448) has dorm beds for P90 and singles with fan and bath for P120. A tricycle from the church or plaza in San Pablo will only cost a few pesos. The very simple *City Inn Agahan* at 126 Colago Ave has rooms for P50/100.

More expensive San Pablo possibilities include the *San Rafael Swimming Pool Resort* with singles/doubles at P300/450 (and two swimming pools).

At Alaminos you can stay at *Hidden Valley Springs* for about P4500 which includes a breakfast and the resort entry charge. Reservations are made in Manila (☎ 50 9903).

Getting There & Away

Buses going from Manila to Lucena, Daet, Naga and Legaspi in South Luzon, or San Pablo direct buses, all run via Alaminos en route to San Pablo (about two hours). It's about five km from Alaminos to Hidden Springs and tricycles will firmly demand P100 for this short trip.

From Pagsanjan take a jeepney to Santa Cruz and another from there to San Pablo.

PAGSANJAN

Situated 70 km south-east of Manila in the Laguna province, this is where you can shoot the rapids by canoe. The standard charge for a canoe is P400 for one or two people, including the entry fee. You are paddled upriver to the falls (good place for a swim) by two *banqueros* and then come rushing down the rapids – getting kind of wet on the way. At the last major waterfall you can ride on a bamboo raft for an extra P20.

You'll probably get hassled for extra money since plenty of rich tourists come here and toss pesos around. It's reported that if you're unwilling to give in to demands for increased payment, you will not enjoy the rest of the trip. Some boatman aggressively demand P500 or even P1000 as a tip. So you have been warned! Banqueros organised by the Youth Hostel, Pagsanjan Falls Lodge or the Willy Flores Lodge are reported to be more reasonable, but you're certainly expected to at least tip the boatmen.

The final scenes of *Apocalypse Now* were shot along the river but, despite all the tourist hype, this is no nail-biting white-water maelstrom, more a gentle downriver cruise most of the time. The water level is highest, and the rapids are at their best, in August and September. The best time to go is early in the morning before the tourist hordes arrive, so spend the night in Pagsanjan. The various hotels are all willing to arrange boats for you, no doubt taking a cut of the proceeds. On weekends it's terribly crowded.

Places to Stay
Avoid the accommodation 'guides' at Pagsanjan as their commission will cost you extra. There is plenty of accommodation, particularly along Garcia St, the road which runs along the river, doubling back from beside the post office. On the main road into town the clean and neat *Camino Real Hotel* (☎ 2086) at 39 Rizal St has rooms from P300 to P750, depending on whether they have fan, air-con and/or bathroom.

The *Willy Flores Lodge* at 821 Garcia St has rooms for P60 and with fan for P90/120. It's a simple, clean place with a homely atmosphere and they'll help you organise boat trips. Miss Estella y Umale's *Riverside Bungalow* (☎ 2465) is nearby at 792 Garcia St. There are two bungalows at P220/380 with fan and P500/600 with air-con. Miss Estella is a good cook. Also along Garcia St, the *Pagsanjan Village Hotel* (☎ 2116) has singles/doubles with fan at P550, with air-con at P600 and with air-con and bath for P700.

Places to Eat
There are plenty of good eating places in Pagsanjan. Right on the plaza in town is the pleasant *D'Plaza* which serves great sauteed chicharo with cauliflower. Turn left from the square and you soon come to the *Dura-Fe Restaurant* on General Jaina St. Or turn right, cross the river, and you'll find the very pleasant *Maulawin Bistro* with excellent food. Finally, just before the Pagsanjan Falls Lodge, and thus some distance out of town, there's the *D&C Luncheonette*.

Getting There & Away
Several BLTB buses leave Manila daily for Santa Cruz from where jeepneys run the last few km to Pagsanjan.

See the Batangas and Tagaytay sections for transport details from Pagsanjan. Several changes of jeepney or bus are required en route but the process sounds more complex than it actually is.

As an alternative route back to Manila from Pagsanjan, you can follow the lesser-used route on the north side of Laguna de Bay back to Manila. It's more scenic, the roads are paved and buses and jeepneys operate on this route – it's only slightly further.

From Santa Cruz, you can continue south through Lucena to the Bicol region in the south or take the ferry from Lucena to the island of Marinduque. Lucban, en route to Lucena, is an interesting little town which looks much like it must have under Spanish rule.

North Luzon

After a spell on the beaches at Hundred Islands, most travellers continue north to the famed rice terraces in the Mountain Province. The Ifugao villages around Banaue and their superb rice terraces have been dubbed the 'eighth wonder of the world'. North Luzon also has the popular summer capital of Baguio and the interesting old town of Vigan with its many reminders of the Spanish period.

Things to Buy
In North Luzon look for wood carvings by the Ifugao tribespeople and also for interesting hand-woven fabrics. The cottons are produced in such limited quantities that they rarely even reach Manila. They're much cheaper in Bontoc or Banaue than in Baguio. The baskets and wooden salad bowls are remarkably cheap, but a little bulky to carry home.

ZAMBALES COAST
The Zambales coast stretches north from Olongapo to Hundred Islands but, although there are some good stretches of beach, few travellers come this way. **San Antonio**, about an hour north of Olongapo, is a pleasant little town with a market. From nearby Pundaquit, you can arrange trips out to **Camera** and **Capones** islands. **Iba** is the capital of the province and has several beach resorts, most of them rather run-down. **Masinloc**, further north towards Santa Cruz,

also has some places to stay and diving possibilities. Buses run up the Zambales coast from Manila via Olongapo.

HUNDRED ISLANDS, LUCAP & ALAMINOS

The most popular of the west-coast resort areas is Hundred Islands, with the nearby towns of Lucap and Alaminos. Actually there are more than 100 islands and if swimming or just lazing around and sunbathing are your thing then this is a good place.

Unfortunately, the snorkelling and diving isn't as good as it once was due to long-term use of dynamite for fishing, and because the water is less than crystal clear. Lucap, just three km from Alaminos, is the main accommodation centre for the islands and, from here, you can hire boats to get out to them. There are no beaches on the coast and only a few of the islands have beaches. There are, however, plenty of hidden coves, caves and coral reefs.

There is a tourist office on the Lucap Pier which has a map of the islands and arranges boats. **Quezon**, the largest island, is being developed as a tourist resort. Other popular islands for snorkelling include **Cathedral**, **Parde** and **Panaca**.

Hundred Islands is still remarkably untouristic so be prepared to fend for yourself. November and May are the best beach months. If you haven't got snorkelling equipment you can rent it at Lucap.

Places to Stay

Prices vary considerably with the season, jumping up at Easter week and April and May weekends. Most of the accommodation is in Lucap.

The *Kilometre One Tourist Lodge* has dorm beds for P85 and rooms with fan for P130/180. It is clean, simple, has a restaurant and also functions as a youth hostel. It's a km from town, as the name indicates. *Gloria's Cottages* have rooms with fan and bath for P150. Opposite is the *Ocean View Lodge & Restaurant* which is clean and has a good restaurant. Rooms start from P150 with fan, P200 with fan and bath and P450/550 with air-con and bath.

The *Hundred Islands View Lodge* (☎ 552 7203) has rooms with fan and bath at P350 and with air-con and bath for P450. *Maxime by the Sea* has a beautiful terrace and rooms from P395 with fan and bath or P495 with air-con and bath.

In Alaminos, the *Alaminos Hotel* (☎ 552 7241) on Quezon Ave has rooms with fan at P100, with fan and bath for P150 and with air-con and bath for P400.

If you want to camp out on the islands, there's a P10 fee on Quezon, Governor's and Children's islands. Quezon has a *pavilion* for P600, a *cottage* with rooms for six costs P1000 on Governor's while on Children's there are *huts* for two for P350 and P900. Bring your own food.

Places to Eat

The wharfside canteens are a good place for cheap eats. The *Ocean View Restaurant* is one of the lodge restaurants with good inexpensive food. The *Last Resort Restaurant* is one of the few places which doesn't close down early in the evening. Lucap is a quiet place at night. If you need a beer, catch a tricycle to nearby Alaminos where the *Plaza Restaurant* usually has a folk singer, or there's the *Imperial Restaurant*.

Getting There & Away

Dagupan Bus buses run hourly from Manila to Alaminos, taking about five hours. You can also catch these buses at Dau, near Angeles. Victory Liner have several buses daily for the six-hour trip from Olongapo to Alaminos. A few Dagupan and Byron buses operate to Alaminos from Baguio, taking about four hours.

Getting Around

From Alaminos, it's just a short tricycle ride to Lucap at P20 to P25 for up to four passengers.

An outrigger from Lucap to the Hundred Islands costs about P250 for up to six people plus a P5 entry fee per person. For about P100 you can be dropped off and picked up later. Four or five hours is enough for most people, especially where there is no shade. Quezon is the most popular island and you can get drinks at the kiosk there.

BOLINAO

Bolinao is a small town at the north-west point of Lingayen Gulf . There are unfortunately no acceptable beaches in the area, so you have to drive a few km to get to them. There's a **museum** on the outskirts of town and an **historic fortress church** dating from 1609.

Places to Stay & Eat

The *A&E Garden Inn*, in the centre, has rooms with fan for P80/150, with fan and bath for P150/200 and with air-con and bath for P300/350. By the sea the *Celeste Sea Breeze Resort* is P200/250. You can hire outrigger sailing boats here. Both places have restaurants.

Getting There & Away

There are regular buses, minibuses and jeepneys to Bolinao from Alaminos. Manila is six hours away and there are several buses daily.

LINGAYEN, DAGUPAN & SAN FABIAN

Dagupan is mainly a transport hub but there are also some beaches in the vicinity, none of them particularly memorable. Between Lingayen and Dagupan you could try **Lingayen Beach** (15 km from Dagupan) and **Blue Beach** (three km away at Bonuan), while **White Beach** is 15 km north-east at San Fabian. White Beach is really brownish-grey.

Places to Stay & Eat

Lingayen The *Viscount Hotel* (☎ 137) on Maramba Blvd has rooms with fan and bath for P200 and with air-con and bath for P350. On Lingayen Beach, the *The Lion's Den Resort* (☎ 198) costs P350 and *Letty & Betty Cottages* cost P200/300.

Dagupan The *Vicar Hotel* (☎ 2616) on A B Fernandez Ave has rooms with fan at P100/150, with fan and bath at P180/240 or with air-con and bath at P320.

The *Hotel Victoria* (☎ 2081), also on A B Fernandez Ave, has clean and spacious rooms with fan and bath for P285/325 and with air-con and bath for P345/395. On Blue Beach at Bonuan, which is about three km out of Dagupan, the *Tondaligan Fiesta Cottages* (☎ 2593/5) has air-con rooms with bath for P540/720.

San Fabian The *Holiday Village & Beach Resort* is not very clean but it does have a restaurant. There are singles/doubles with fan for P120/180, doubles with air-con and bath for P350 and cottages with fan and bath for P250.

The *Lazy A Resort* (☎ 4726) has cottages with fan and bath from P600 and rooms with air-con and bath from P700. The *Sierra Vista Beach Resort* (☎ 7668; fax 7532) is a nice little hotel with pleasantly furnished rooms with air-con and bath for P1120/1900. There is a restaurant, a swimming pool, windsurfing and diving.

The *Windsurf Beach Resort* in Alacan, five km north-east of San Fabian, has spacious cottages with fan and bath for P400.

Getting There & Away

Frequent Victory Liner and Dagupan Bus services operate from Manila and take about five hours. The best way to get from Manila or Angeles to San Fabian is to take a bus heading for San Fernando (La Union), Vigan or Laoag, get out at Damortis and cover the remaining 15 km to San Fabian via Alacan and Bolasi by minibus.

There are a few Dagupan Bus and Byron buses between Baguio and Dagupan each day, also taking about two hours. Buses from Baguio go via San Fabian to Dagupan. Between the two towns, you can take a Baguio bus or a local minibus service.

AGOO & ARINGAY

Between San Fabian and Bauang is Agoo, which has a **basilica** rebuilt after an 1892 earthquake. Aringay has the small **Don Lorenzo Museum** opposite the old church.

THE PHILIPPINES

BAUANG

Further north on the coast, Bauang has a long stretch of beach with many resort hotels. There are better beaches in the Philippines, but Bauang is only an hour or two's travel from Baguio in the hills and this probably accounts for its popularity. San Fernando (La Union) is just six km north of Bauang and the beach area is between the two – about two km north of Bauang and four km south of San Fernando. Lots of jeepneys shuttle back and forth.

Places to Stay

Bauang's hotels are mainly along the long grey-sand beach between Baccuit and Paringao. Prices at these places are often negotiable.

The *Jac Corpuz Cottages*, between the Leo Mar and Lourdes resorts at Baccuit, have rooms with bath from P200. The *Lourdes Beach Homes* have large cottages with fan and bath for P200 but they've definitely seen better days. At the *Leo Mar Beach Resort* simple but well-kept rooms with fan and bath cost from P350. Also at the southern end of the beach you'll find the *Hide Away Beach Resort*, a large house with rooms from P280 to P600.

The *China Sea Beach Resort* (☎ 41 4821) in Paringao has rooms with fan and bath for P650 and with air-con and bath for P750, a restaurant and a swimming pool. Similar in price, and in Paringao, are *Coconut Grove Resort*, *Bali Hai Resort*, *Cabana Beach Resort*, *Fisherman's Wharf Beach Club* and *Southern Palms Beach Resort*. These hotels offer boat rentals, windsurfing as well as other entertainment possibilities.

Places to Eat

Food in the resort hotels tends to be expensive so, for cheaper meals, go into Bauang or San Fernando. The *Anchorage, Fisherman's Wharf* and *Bali Hai* are all pretty good. The *Ihaw-Ihaw Restaurant*, next to the Sir William Disco on the highway, serves grills.

Getting There & Away

The many buses from Manila to Bauang take over five hours and some continue north to Vigan and Laoag. It takes over an hour from Baguio on Philippine Rabbit or Marcitas Liner and slightly less by jeepney. It's a nice trip down the winding road to the coast but try to sit on the left side for the best views. Jeepneys take about 30 minutes to get to San Fernando.

SAN FERNANDO (LA UNION)

The 'city of the seven hills' is the capital of the La Union Province, and the **Museo de La Union** next to the Provincial Capitol Building gives a cultural overview of the region.

Places to Stay

The *Plaza Hotel* (☎ 41 2996) on Quezon Ave (which becomes the main highway) has rooms with fan and bath from P280 and with air-con and bath from P460.

There are several resorts three km southwest along the beach at Poro. The *Ocean Deep Resort* (☎ 41 4440; fax 41 4439) has rooms with fan and bath for P200/300. *The Driftwood Beach Resort* (☎ 41 3411; fax 41 4525) is a big building with six rooms with air-con and bath for P550.

Three km north of San Fernando, the *Shalom Beach Cottages* on Santo Niño Road in Lingsat has spacious rooms with cooking facilities, fridge, fan and bath for P350. There is a nice garden and they offer weekly and monthly rates.

Places to Eat

The *Mandarin Restaurant* has reasonably priced food and there are lots of cheap snack places around, a number of which offer complete fixed-price meals. Places to try include the *New Society Restaurant*, opposite the market in Burgos St, the *Crown Restaurant* and the *Garden Food Center*.

Getting There & Away

There are numerous daily buses from Manila which take six hours. See Bauang for other transport information.

BAGUIO

Located at an altitude of about 1500 metres, Baguio is much cooler than Manila and for this reason it once served as a summer capital. It's still popular as an escape from the lowland heat. It's a laid-back place with plenty of parks and an interesting market. It's also good for buying handicrafts (although you have to bargain aggressively in order to get a good price).

Baguio is also famed for its 'faith healers' to whom many people flock each year. To most travellers, however, the town's main role is as a gateway to the Mountain Province and the amazing rice terraces.

On 16 July 1990, Baguio was struck by a disastrous earthquake which caused a great deal of damage. Since then most places have either been repaired or demolished and rebuilt, so that visitors will hardly notice any of the damage done by this natural catastrophe.

Things to See

The **City Market** has local produce and crafts including basketware, textiles, woodcarvings and jewellery. There's a small **Mountain Provinces Museum** in Camp John Hay, a recreation area in the south-eastern suburbs of town. **Burnham Park** is in the town and the **Baguio Botanical Gardens** are a km out. There are scenic views over the surrounding countryside from the **Statue of Our Lady of Lourdes**.

In **La Trinidad**, the provincial capital just to the north of the city, visit the governor's offices and see the Kabayan mummies. These remarkably well-preserved mummified bodies were brought from burial caves in the north.

Places to Stay

The *Highland Lodge* (☎ 7086) at 48 General Luna Rd has friendly staff and rather small rooms at P100/150 or with bath at P230/250. The basic *Travelers Inn* (☎ 5444) at 60 Lakadula Rd has rooms for P100/200. The simple but well-kept *Baguio Goodwill Lodge* (☎ 6634) at 58 Session Rd has rooms for P140/220 or P270/340 with bath. The *Benguet Pine Tourist Inn* (☎ 7325), at 82 Chanum St on the corner of Otek St, is a clean and quiet place and has dorm beds for P100, singles/doubles from P200 to P300 and with bath from P350 to P450.

For P120 you can get a bed in the clean dorm at the *Baden Powell Inn* (☎ 5836) on 26 Governor Pack Rd. Quiet, very clean rooms go for P400 to P800.

The *Casa Vallejo* (☎ 3045, 4601) at 111 Session Rd Extension costs P200/300 or P300/400 with bath. It's a rustic house with a pleasant atmosphere. The *Mountain Lodge* (☎ 4544) on 27 Leonard Wood Rd has singles/doubles with bath for P450/500 and doubles with a fireplace for P650. This pleasant, friendly hotel is cosy, comfortable and good value for the money.

Places to Eat

The *Dangwa Tranco Bus Terminal* has a good and cheap basic restaurant. The so-called *Slaughterhouse Restaurants* near the Times Transit Bus Terminal on Balayadia St are also simply furnished but offer excellent meat dishes at good prices. At both the *Ganza Steak & Chicken House* and the *Solibao* in Burnham Park you can eat outside.

There are various other restaurants along Session Rd, Baguio's main street, like the *Sizzling Plate*, a good place for a proper breakfast, and the *Bread of Life*, where you can get good cheese and European sausages as well as coffee and bread. If you like to try out traditional Cordillera cooking and drinks, then the *Café by the Ruins* opposite the city hall is the place to go.

Entertainment

There are a number of good music places in town. Jazz freaks meet at the *Songs Music Gallery* in Session Rd. The *Music Box Pizza House* in Zandueta St has folk music, whereas the *Orange County* in Abanao St specializes in country and western and rock music. By far the most popular disco is called *Spirits* and is in a magnificent building in Otek St.

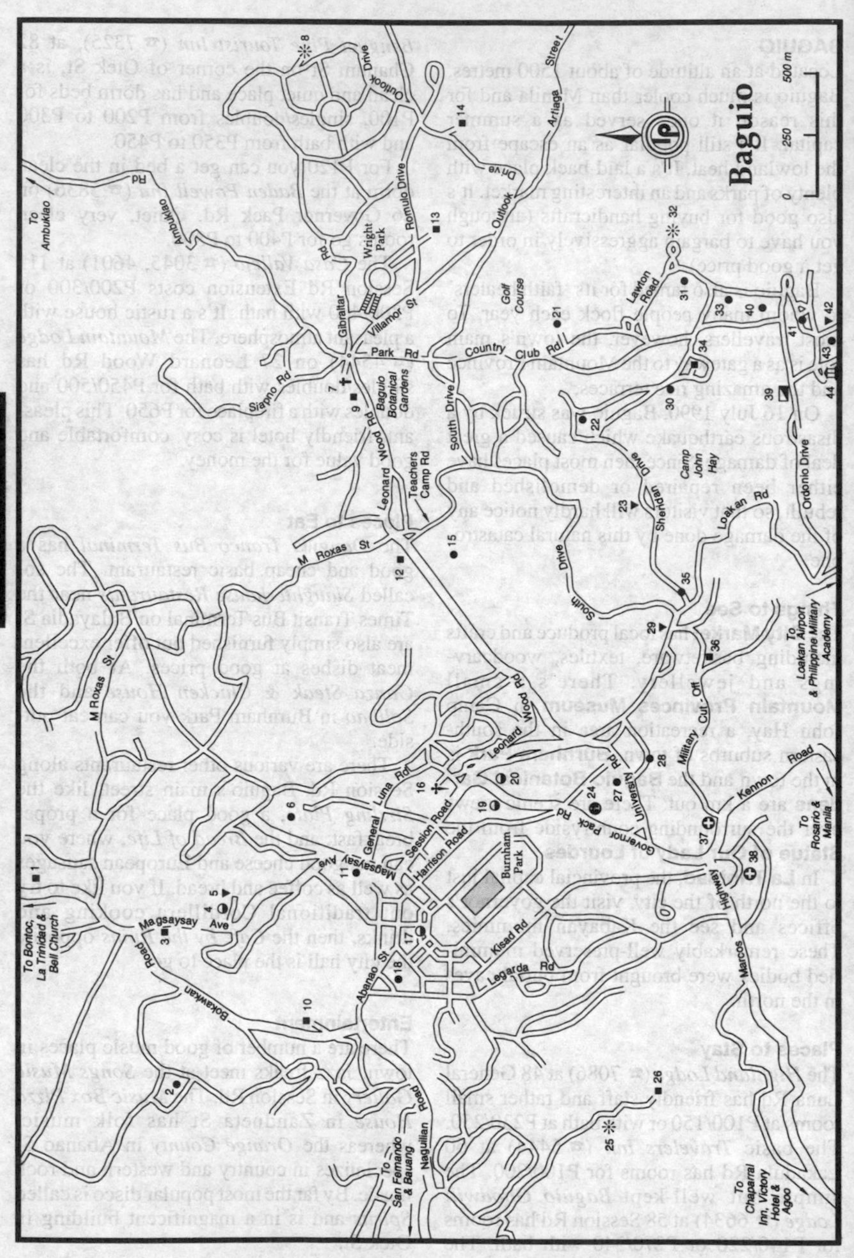

THE PHILIPPINES

PLACES TO STAY

1 Hotel Supreme
3 Baguio Village Inn
9 Vacation Hotel Baguio
10 Skyview Lodge
12 Mountain Lodge
13 Mansion House
14 Villa La Maya Inn
26 Diplomat Hotel & Dominican Hill
34 Igorot Lodge
36 Woods Place Inn

PLACES TO EAT

5 Slaughterhouse Restaurants
23 Halfway House
29 Uncle's Music Lounge & Restaurant,Session Bistro Music Lounge & Restaurant
42 Lone Star Steak House & Mexican Restaurant

OTHER

2 Easter School of Weaving
4 Times Transit Bus Terminal
6 St Louis University
7 St Joseph Church
8 Mines View Park
11 City Market
15 Teacher's Camp
16 Cathedral
17 Marcitas Liner Bus Terminal
18 City Hall
19 Dagupan Bus Terminal, Pantranco Bus Terminal & Philippine Rabbit Bus Terminal
20 Victory Liner Bus Terminal
21 Baguio Country Club
22 Mile-Hi Recreational Center
24 Tourist Office
25 Lourdes Grotto
27 University of the Philippines (UP)
28 Convention Center
30 Snider Hall
31 Tennis Courts
32 MacArthur Park View Point
33 19th Tee Patio
35 Camp John Hay Main Gate
37 Baguio Medical Center
38 Baguio General Hospital
39 Swimming Pool & Tennis Courts
40 Main Club
41 Cemetery of Negativism & Liberty Park
43 Tennis Courts
44 Mountain Provinces Museum

Getting There & Away

Air PAL has 50-minute flights from Manila to Baguio five times a week. Jeepneys to the airport leave from Mabini Rd, between Session and Harrison Rds.

Bus Philippine Rabbit, Victory Liner, Dangwa Tranco and Dagupan Bus all operate from Manila to Baguio daily and take about six hours (Victory Liner has the most extensive schedule and comfortable buses). Fares are P90 for ordinary buses and P125 for air-con. It takes about half an hour less from Baguio to Manila since it's downhill at first. You can also catch these buses from Dau, near Angeles.

There are hourly Victory Liner buses from Olongapo to Baguio (six hours), a few Dagupan Bus and Byron buses from Dagupan (two hours) and several Philippine Rabbit and Marcitas Liner buses from San Fernando (two hours).

Dangwa Tranco have two daily bus services to Banaue, which depart early in the morning and take nine hours. Dangwa Tranco departures to Bontoc are also in the morning and take eight hours. Dangwa Tranco is also the operator to Sagada, with a daily early morning bus, which takes about seven hours.

MOUNTAIN PROVINCE

Mountain Province starts 100 km north-east of Baguio and is famed for interesting tribes and spectacular rice terraces. If you've spent much time in South-East Asia, deliberately going to a place just to see more rice terraces seems a little weird, but these are definitely special.

Some 2000 to 3000 years ago the Ifugao tribespeople carved terraces out of the mountainsides around Banaue which are as perfect today as they were then. They run like stepping stones to the sky – up to 1500 metres high – and if stretched end to end would extend over 20,000 km. The Ifugao people, in the more remote areas, still practice traditional ways – this no longer includes head-hunting.

Getting There & Away

You can approach Mountain Province from two directions. The more spectacular route is by the rough, winding mountain road that climbs up from Baguio to Bontoc, the main town in the region. The trip takes about eight hours and from there you can make a variety of side trips to places like Sagada or continue on to Banaue, the main town for rice terraces and another three or four-hour trip.

The faster alternative route is direct from Manila via the Nueva Viscaya Province – on good roads the bus trip only takes seven to eight hours. The Baguio-Bontoc-Banaue road is often cut off during the wet season, but it's far more interesting so you should try to make the trip in at least one direction by this route.

July to August is the wettest period. The road reaches a height of 2000 metres and is the highest road in the Philippines. Dangwa Tranco is the main operator for bus services north of Baguio.

BONTOC

Bontoc is the first major town you come to from Baguio and the main town of the area. It's possible to walk from here to the villages of the Igorot people – they build their rice terraces with stone dykes, unlike the earth terraces of Banaue. Take food and water for yourself and dried fish or other gifts for the villagers.

The village of **Malegcong** is a two or three-hour walk into the mountains. You have to follow a narrow creek for about 200 metres before you reach the footpath leading to the village. It's not a bad idea to take a guide with you. Always ask permission before taking photographs of the people here.

The excellent **Bontoc Museum** is run by the local Catholic mission and includes head-hunting relics, Chinese vases and photos from the mountain tribes; admission is P15. Bontoc is a good place to buy locally woven materials, woodcarvings and other handicrafts of Mountain Province.

Places to Stay & Eat

The *Mountain Hotel* (☎ 3018) has small, basic rooms for P50/90 and a restaurant. Near the bus stop, the simple but well-kept *Bontoc Hotel* has rooms for P50 per person and good food. The popular *Happy Home Inn* (☎ 3021), opposite the bus stop, has fairly good accommodation at P50/100 for singles/doubles plus larger rooms with attached bathroom for P160. The *Chico Terrace* (☎ 3099) has rooms with bath for P60/110.

The cosy *Village Inn* has singles for P60 and doubles for P110. The *Vista Pension* behind the town hall is a small hotel with a pleasant atmosphere. Rooms are clean and cost P70/140 or P420 for a double with bath. The *Pines Kitchenette & Inn* is a fairly good place with rooms for P70/140 or P25/300 for a double with bath. It's about five minutes' walk from the bus stop and there's also a good, although somewhat pricey, restaurant.

Food is pretty good in Bontoc – try the great cinnamon rolls in the local bakery. Bontoc is also a centre for the Filipino passion for dog meat – about which there has been much controversy in the West of late. 'Cheap and not bad', reported one obviously dog-loving traveller.

Getting There & Away

There are five Dangwa Tranco buses daily between Baguio and Bontoc, generally departing in the early morning. Some start from La Trinidad, a couple of km north of Baguio.

The 150-km trip takes about eight hours. On from Bontoc to Banaue there is usually a daily jeepney at 6.30 to 7.30 am and a daily (except Sunday) bus at 7.30 to 8 am. As elsewhere in Mountain Province, transport is somewhat unreliable. If you can't find regular transport you can charter a jeepney.

You can cross over from the coast to Bontoc or Sagada by taking a jeepney from near Tagudin, north of San Fernando, to Cervantes and another jeepney or bus from there towards Baguio. Get off at Abatan and catch a Baguio to Bontoc bus. This is a lengthy, time-consuming and rough trip.

SAGADA

Only 18 km from Bontoc, the village of Sagada is famed for its **burial caves**. The people are friendly and it's a good place to buy local weaving. The cliff-face burial caves here are somewhat similar to those of the Toraja people of Sulawesi in Indonesia. You'll probably need a local guide and some sort of light to explore the more extensive caves.

Near Sagada is the **Bokong Waterfall** with a natural swimming pool. A little further towards Bontoc is the **Eduardo Masferré Studio** with photographs of life in Mountain Province from the '30s to the '50s.

Places to Stay & Eat

The places to stay in this popular little town all seem to follow a standard charging policy of around P50 per person.

Masferrés Inn is very popular – 'quaint, charming, cosy and rustic' was how one traveller described it and many others have given similar reports. Other places include the *St Joseph Resthouse*, across from the hospital where the bus stops. It's also friendly and well kept and the food is superb value. The *Mapiyaaw Pensione*, about a km up the hill from Sagada itself, is clean and has hot water. Or there's the *Sagada Guesthouse* which once again is a pleasant place and does good meals, particularly breakfasts.

You can also eat at the *convent*, close to the church. The *Shamrock Café* and the *Moonhouse Café* are other good places. The food at the latter is very good and the bar is the 'in' place to spend the evening. Banana cake is a Sagada speciality and is served in all of these places.

Getting There & Away

There are daily Dangwa Tranco, Skyland Express and Lizardo Trans buses from Baguio in the early morning. The trip takes about seven hours. The Dangwa Tranco buses may possibly start from La Trinidad, a few km north of Baguio. In this case it's wise to take a jeepney to the La Trinidad bus terminal well before departure to ensure a seat.

A jeepney from Bontoc to Sagada only takes an hour but there are only three or four a day, usually leaving early in the morning or in the afternoon.

BANAUE

From Bontoc the road turns south and runs through incredibly spectacular countryside to Banaue, the heart of the terrace scenery. It's a narrow, rough road and travel is slow – but what a view. Take the right side of the bus to appreciate it best.

There are many hiking trails in the vicinity of Banaue. **Batad** is one of the best viewpoints and takes two hours to walk to after a 12-km jeepney ride from the town. There are a number of small places to stay in Batad. Near Batad, there's a delightful waterfall with good swimming. The **Ifugao villages** and the **handicraft centres** in Banaue are also worth visiting.

Information

There is no bank in Banaue but, if you're really stuck, you can probably change money at the Banaue Hotel (at a bad rate). The information office has a good P6 map of Banaue's surroundings.

Places to Stay

Banaue There are plenty of small places to stay here, mainly at around P50 to P75 per person. The *Jericho Guest House* is simple, clean and has rooms for P40/80, or try the *Brookside Inn* or *Traveler's Inn* (☎ 4020) at P45/90. The popular *Wonder Lodge* (☎ 4017) has singles/doubles for P60/100, as does the *Half Way Lodge*.

The pleasant *Stairway Lodge* (☎ 4030) is a good, clean place with a restaurant. Singles/doubles are P75/150 and doubles with bath are P250. The *People's Lodge* (☎ 4014) is a friendly place with a bakery and restaurant. Rooms are basic, clean and good and cost P75/100 and with bath P350. The *J&L Lodge* (☎ 4035) has rooms at P150/250 but it's slightly out of Banaue on the way to the Banaue Hotel.

At the *Terrace Ville Inn* clean and comfortable rooms with bath are P350. *Sanafe Lodge* (☎ 4085) has dorm beds for P75 or really comfortable rooms with bath for P470/600.

Finally, the expensive Banaue Hotel administers the *Banaue Youth Hostel* where dorm beds are P150. You can use the hotel swimming pool.

Batad Places in Batad are spartan but the atmosphere is friendly and it's worth staying here, rather than just day-tripping from Banaue. The *Hillside Inn, Mountain View Inn, Batad Pensione, Cristina's Guest House, Foreigner's Inn* or *Simon's Inn* cost around P50 per person.

In Cambulo, *Lydia Domanlig* offers overnight accommodation for P30 per person.

Places to Eat

Most hotels have small restaurants or offer meals – the *Stairway, Half Way, Cool Winds* and *Las Vegas* restaurants are all good and cheap.

The restaurant at the *Banaue Hotel* is excellent and, if there are enough guests, Ifugao dances are held at night. Entry is P10. The *Patina Bar Folkden* also has live music and you can get a beer or snacks until late.

Getting There & Away

You can reach Banaue from either direction but, while the Bayombong route is faster, the Bontoc route is much more interesting.

From Baguio, there are two daily Dangwa Tranco buses via Bayombong. They leave early in the morning and take about nine hours. At busy times these buses will leave an hour early if they're full.

Also from Baguio, via Bontoc, you have to overnight in Bontoc en route. From Bontoc it takes about three hours on the bus which departs daily (except Sunday) early in the morning. Arrive very early for a good seat. There's also a daily jeepney.

From Manila, the daily Dangwa Tranco bus leaves early in the morning and takes nine hours up but only eight hours back to Manila. If you miss the direct bus take a Baliwag Transit bus to Solano, just before the Banaue turn-off. From there, jeepneys run to Lagawe and then to Banaue, and take another two or three hours.

Getting Around

You can get transport 12 km of the way to Batad from Banaue but the rest of the way you have to walk. A chartered jeepney for that first stretch will cost P500 and carry up to 14. The driver will either wait at the turn-off or come back for you at a prearranged time. It takes about two hours along the signposted path from between Dalican and Bangaan. Beware of self-appointed, but expensive, 'guides'. Walking all the way would take about five hours.

VIGAN

North of San Fernando, this interesting old town was second only to Manila during the Spanish era and today is the best preserved Spanish town in the country. If you're interested in old Spanish architecture and ancient-looking churches this region of Ilocos is a prime hunting ground.

It's fascinating just wandering around the town, taking in the narrow streets, listening to the clip-clop of horse-drawn calesas. 'Vigan', according to one traveller, 'is the only town in the Philippines with a population of 10,000 or more without a single disco. Local teenagers sit around the cathedral and discuss theology'.

Things to See

The house where Jose Burgos was born now houses the **Ayala Museum**. He was executed by the Spanish in 1872. The museum is behind the Capitol Building, has lots of antiques, old paintings and photographs and the curator is delighted to tell tourists the history of the area. Ferdinand Marcos was also from this region and the **National Museum** on Liberation Blvd is partly used as a showcase for the Marcos era. It also gives a good idea of life during the Spanish rule. The **Cathedral of St Paul** dates from 1641 and is one of the oldest and largest churches in the country.

Places to Stay

At 1 Bonifacio St, *Grandpa's Inn* (☎ 2118) is a basic place run by friendly people. Rooms with fan are P130, with fan and bath

P200 or with air-con and bath P350. The *Vigan Hotel* (☎ 2588) on Burgos St has rooms with fan for P200/300 and with air-con and bath for P400/500. The *Cordillera Inn* (☎ 2526; fax 2840), at 29 Mena Crisologo St on the corner of General Luna St, has comfortable, tastefully furnished rooms with fan for P340, with fan and bath for P550 and with air-con and bath from P730 to P840.

Places to Eat

There's great ice cream and good sandwiches at the *Vigan Plaza Restaurant* in Florentino St. The *Tower Café*, on Burgos St (corner of the main plaza, opposite the cathedral), and the *Unique Café*, also on Burgos St, offer barbecues and beer.

The *Victory Restaurant* on Quezon Ave offers different menus each day. The *Cool Spot Restaurant* is a lovely half-open-air place, not far from the Vigan Hotel and known for its good Ilocano cooking. You can get coffee and cake at *Mr Donut* in Quezon Ave.

Getting There & Away

From Manila, the trip takes over seven hours with Philippine Rabbit, Times Transit, Farina Trans or Maria de Leon. Some buses continuing north to Laoag bypass the town, in which case you will have to take a tricycle from the highway. Buses also connect from San Fernando, Aparri and Laoag. You can reach Vigan from Baguio via San Fernando or by the coast from Hundred Islands and Dagupan, again via San Fernando.

It's about two hours beyond Vigan to Laoag and you can continue right around the north of Luzon to Claveria, Aparri, Tuguegarao and back down to Manila.

LAOAG

There are many old Spanish churches in the Ilocos Norte Province and Laoag, the capital of the province, has **St William's Cathedral**, built between 1650 and 1700. Near Laoag, in **Bacarra**, the town's church has a massive and earthquake-damaged belltower. Salt is produced at Seksi Beach, four km from Pasuquin which, in turn, is 10 km from Laoag.

South-east of the town is **Sarrat**, birthplace of the former president, Ferdinand Marcos. In the center of town is the restored Sarrat Curch & Convent, built in 1779 by Augustinian monks. Marcos memorabilia can be found at the so-called **Malacañang del Norte** in Batac, south of Laoag. A few km south-west of Batac is the fortress-like **Paoay Church** in a style referred to as 'earthquake baroque'.

Places to Stay & Eat

At the popular *City Lodging House* on General Antonio Luna St, rooms with fan are P80/160 and there's a restaurant. The *Modern Hotel,* on Nolasco St, has rooms with fan for P80/160 and with fan and bath for P260. The *Texicano Hotel* (☎ 22 0606/290) on Rizal St has rooms in the old building with fan for P100/140, with fan and bath for P130/150 and with air-con and bath for P330/400. In the new building air-con rooms are P420/520.

Casa Llanes Pension (☎ 22 1125) on Primo Lazaro Ave has spacious rooms with fan and bath for P140 and with air-con and bath for P240. The *Pichay Lodging House* (☎ 22 1267), in Primo Lazaro Ave, has singles/doubles with fan and bath for P120/180 and with air-con and bath for P270/300. This may be the best place in town.

The *City Lunch & Snack Bar*, on the corner of General Antonio Luna and Nolasco Sts, has good cheap Chinese and Filipino dishes and reasonably priced breakfasts. The *Magic Bunny* and the *Dohan Food & Bake Shop* on Rizal St are also worth trying. *Peppermint Brickside Café* on Don Severo Hernando Ave is good although meals are more expensive.

McBurgee, as the name suggests, is a fast-food place, and *Colonial Fast Food* is an air-con restaurant which serves tasty Filipino food; both are on F R Castro Ave.

Getting There & Away

There are three weekly flights between

Manila and Laoag. Buses from Manila take 10 hours and from Vigan three hours. Less frequent buses travel around the north coast to Claveria (four hours) and Aparri (eight hours).

LAOAG TO APARRI

At **Pagudpud**, 60 km north of Laoag, there is one of the best beaches in North Luzon. There are Ita tribespeople living south of Claveria and you can also make trips from here to the **Babuyan Islands**. Aparri's only real interest is for deep-sea fishing.

Places to Stay & Eat

In Pagudpud, the *Villa del Mar* has basic rooms from P80 to P200 and cottages with two rooms and a kitchen for about P500.

The *Pipo Hotel* at 37 Macanaya St has rooms with fan for P100/200 or with fan and bath for P200/350.

The *Ryan Mall Hotel* (☎ 22369) has good rooms with fan and bath for P250 and with air-con and bath from P375 to P500. The Ryan Mall also has a pool and a good restaurant; otherwise the only decent place to eat is the *Magnolia Restaurant* near the river.

Getting There & Away

It takes two hours from Laoag to Pagudpud, two more hours to Claveria and another four from there to Aparri. There are regular buses between Manila and Aparri, running up the eastern side of Luzon and taking about 11 hours.

TUGUEGARAO

The **Callao Caves** are near Peñablanca, about 25 km east of Tuguegarao. There are some good walks in the **Sierra Madre**.

Places to Stay

The *LB Lodging House* on Luna St has simple rooms at P60 per person. *Hotel Leonor* (☎ 1806) on Rizal St has clean rooms for P80/150, with fan for P100/180 and with air-con for P200/250, or there's the *Olympia Hotel* (☎ 1805) on Washington St where rooms with fan and bath are P130/180 and with air-con and bath P220/300.

Georgie's Inn (☎ 1434) on Aguinaldo St has rooms with fan and bath for P140/180 or with air-con and bath for P240/280. The *Pensione Abraham* (☎ 1793) on Bonifacio St is slightly cheaper but not so good.

On Gonzaga St, *Hotel Delfino* (☎ 1952/3) has rooms with air-con and bath from P280 to P400. The best accommodation in town is *Pensione Roma* (☎ 1057, 1282) on the corner of Luna and Bonifacio Sts. Rooms with fan and bath are P200 and with air-con and bath P500/550.

At Peñablanca you can stay in the *Callao Caves Resort* (☎ 1801, 1087) where rooms cost P120 to P300, or there are cottages for P400 to P600.

Places to Eat

Opposite Pensione Abraham, the *Pampanguena Restaurant* changes its menu daily and has a surprisingly large choice of cakes. Other possibilities include the *Olympia Hotel* and the restaurants at *LB Lodging House* and *Georgie's Inn*. *Apollo Restaurant* is an Ihaw-Ihaw restaurant near the Pantranco bus terminal.

Getting There & Away

PAL flies between Manila and Tuguegarao three times a week. Baliwag Transit buses from Manila take nine hours and depart hourly. There's a daily bus to Bontoc, via Banaue, taking 10 hours.

BALER & EAST LUZON

Much of *Apocalypse Now* was shot near Baler on the wild east coast of North Luzon. The town itself is not very interesting but you can visit the surrounding country and the coast. In December, the strong surf should attract surfers.

Places to Stay & Eat

The *Amihan Hotel* on Bitong St has rooms with fan for P120/140 and with fan and bath for P150/200. There are various places along the beach in Sabang like *Baler Guest House* where rooms are P120 to P200, *Ocean View Lodge* with rooms at P170/220 or *MIA Surf*

& Sports Resort with rooms with fan at P120/180 and with fan and bath at P220/280.

Getting There & Away
It takes 2½ hours to get from Manila to Cabanatuan and another four hours from there to Baler. If coming south from Tuguegarao you also change buses at Cabanatuan.

South Luzon

The South Luzon Bicol region is composed of four provinces and two islands (Catanduanes and Masbate). Plenty of buses (and the odd train) run there from Manila or you can fly. The major attraction of the Bicol region is the majestic Mayon volcano, claimed to be the most perfectly symmetrical volcano cone in the world.

Things to Buy
In South Luzon, abaca products are the main craft. Abaca is a fibre produced from a relative of the banana tree. It's best known end-product was the rope known as Manila hemp (as opposed to Indian hemp, produced from the fibre of the marijuana plant!) but today it's made into all manner of woven products including bags or place mats. *Pili* nuts are a popular favourite of the Bicol region.

Around Daraga you can find oddities like marble eggs from Romblon or whole suites of furniture made from used car tyres! Some interesting pottery can be found in Tiwi.

Getting There & Away
You can get south to the Bicol region from Manila by bus or rail. Buses to Legaspi all pass through Naga. BLTB, Inland Trailways, Philtranco and JB Bicol Express buses depart from their terminals on Edsa in Pasay City and the trip takes nine to 11 hours. There are also air-con buses at night, which leave at 7 and 8 pm. The fare to Legaspi ranges from P220, depending on the bus. The train service south is no longer worth considering.

LUCENA
The capital of Quezon Province, Lucena is a departure point for boats to Marinduque and Romblon. They leave either from Dalahican or from the river harbour of Cotta Port, just outside the town. Take along water and food if you intend to go hiking in the **Quezon National Park**, one of the largest wildlife reserves in Luzon.

Places to Stay & Eat
Cheap hotels are mainly in the Barrio Iyam area – get there on a jeepney or tricycle. They include the *Tourist Hotel* (☎ 71 4456), which has a restaurant and singles with fan at P90, singles/doubles with fan and bath for P110/150 or with air-con and bath at P200/250.

The *Lucena Fresh Air Hotel & Resort* (☎ 71 2424, 71 3031) is in the Isabang district at the edge of town as you enter from Manila. Rooms with fan cost P135/155, with fan and bath P200 to P265 and with air-con and bath P385/440. There's also a restaurant and pool.

The *Casa Arias Garden Restaurant*, in the centre near the BLTB bus station, is good.

Getting There & Away
Philtranco, Inland Trailways, Superlines and BLTB buses operate to Lucena from Manila, taking about 2½ hours. Some services continue south to Daet, Naga, Legaspi or Matnog.

Supreme Lines buses from Santa Cruz/Pagsanjan to Lucena take three hours but it may be faster to take a jeepney from Santa Cruz to Lucban and another from there to Lucena City.

SAN MIGUEL BAY
San Miguel Bay, with its beaches and islands, is an interesting detour on the route south. **Daet** is a good overnight stop en route to the bay. **Mercedes**, a small coastal village about 10 km north-east of Daet, has a 6 to 8 am fish market and from here you can reach **Apuao Grande Island** in San Miguel Bay with its white sand beach.

Places to Stay & Eat
In Daet, on the outskirts on Vinzons Ave, the *Mines Hotel* (☎ 2483) has basic rooms with fan and bath for P60/90 and with air-con and bath for P125/160. The centrally located *Karilagan Hotel* (☎ 2265) has clean and quite good rooms with fan and bath for P130/165 and with air-con and bath for P295/350.

A few streets away from the Karilagan Hotel, the *Golden House Restaurant* has good food, as does the *Sampaguita Restaurant* upstairs in the Sampaguita Department Store.

Getting There & Away
Pacific Airways has flights to Daet from Manila two times a week.

Buses from Manila take about seven hours to Daet, some continuing to centres further south. It's about three hours further south to Legaspi, via Naga. Jeepneys go to Mercedes, the jumping-off point for the San Miguel Bay islands.

NAGA
This friendly and noticeably clean town has the **Peñafrancia Festival** (late September) which includes a huge and colourful procession.

Places to Stay
The *Fiesta Hotel* (☎ 2760) on Padian St has quite clean rooms for P90/120 with fan, P180/220 with fan and bath and P280/350 with air-con and bath. It's a good place and has a restaurant and disco on the roof. The friendly and fairly good *Sampaguita Tourist Inn* (☎ 21 4810, 21 2712) on Panganiban Drive has singles with fan and bath for P145 (good value), singles with air-con and bath for P235 and doubles with air-con and bath for P325 and P450.

The *Aristocrat Hotel* (☎ 21 5230, 21 3422) on Elias Angeles St has reasonably comfortable rooms with fan for P245, with fan and bath for P310 and P365, and with air-con and bath for P430 and P555. The clean and good *Moraville Hotel* (☎ 33584, 21 3513) on Dinaga St has singles with air-con and bath for P350 and doubles with air-con and bath for P400. The rooms are quiet, comfortably furnished and have TV.

Places to Eat
The *Ming Chun Foodhouse* on Peñafrancia Ave serves good Filipino and Chinese dishes. The *New China Restaurant* on General Luna St offers daily specials, and *Carl's Diner* at Plaza Rizal is a clean, inexpensive and popular '50s-style fast-food restaurant.

Getting There & Away
PAL has a daily flight from Manila which takes one hour. Buses take 8½ hours from Manila and there are also buses from Daet (1½ hours) and Legaspi (two hours).

IRIGA & LAKE BUHI
About midway between Naga and Legaspi, Iraga is the jumping-off point for visits to **Lake Buhi** where the smallest edible fish in the world are netted (with tiny mesh nets!). You can see the fish in the aquarium in the Municipal Building. Boat trips from the market building are expensive but there's a much cheaper ferry which crosses the lake.

Places to Stay & Eat
Just as you come into town from Naga, the *Lemar's Lodge* (☎ 594) on San Nicolas St has singles/doubles with fan for P70/90, with fan and bath for P120/140 or doubles with air-con and bath for P180.

Bayanihan Hotel (☎ 556/8), on Governor Felix Alfelor St and close to the railway line, has singles at P75 or rooms with air-con and bath at P160/195.

The *Ibalon Hotel* (☎ 352/3), on San Francisco St and below the grotto on the hill, is small and elegant and has rooms at P360/420. It's the best hotel in town.

Getting There & Away
Jeepneys to Lake Buhi leave from outside the Bayanihan Hotel.

LEGASPI

The main city of the Bicol region hugs the waterfront in the shadow of the Mayon volcano. The 'headless monument' in front of the post office to those who died at the hands of the Japanese in WW II is sadly neglected. In the **St Rafael Church**, on Aguinaldo St and across from the Rex Hotel, the altar is a 10-tonne volcanic rock from Mayon.

Legaspi is actually divided into two parts. Inland from the port area is the Albay area of the town. Here you will find the tourist office beside Peñaranda Park, near the cathedral. The two areas are linked by Rizal Ave.

Places to Stay

There are plenty of cheap hotels around Legaspi but none of them will win any prizes for high accommodation standards.

On Magallanes St, close to the centre of town, the basic *Peking Lodge* (☎ 3198) has rooms with fan for P50/70, with fan and bath for P100/120, and with air-con and bath for P150/170.

There is quite a choice along Peñaranda St, parallel to the waterfront. *Catalina's Lodging House* (☎ 3593) is a friendly place with simple rooms with fan at P60/90 and with fan and bath for P100/30. On the same street the *Shirman Lodge* (☎ 23031) has fairly clean rooms with fan for P90/130. *Hotel Xandra* (☎ 2688) has rooms with fan for P70/90, with fan and bath for P150/170 or with air-con and bath for P180/250.

Tanchuling International House (☎ 2788, 3494) on Jasmine St has clean and spacious rooms and is only a few minutes' walk from the town centre. Rooms with fan are P120/150, with air-con and bath P250/300.

More expensive places include the *Legaspi Plaza Hotel* (☎ 3344) on Lapu-Lapu St with rooms with fan and bath for P355/340 and with air-con and bath for P490/590. The *Hotel Casablanca* (☎ 3130, 3131) on Peñaranda St has air-con rooms with bath for P625 and P700.

Places to Eat

Legaspi offers a wide choice of places to eat – like the *Peking House Restaurant* and the *Shangrila Restaurant*, both on Peñaranda St, and the *New Legaspi Restaurant* on Lapu-Lapu St, where the special meal is to be recommended. The food is basically Chinese with some Filipino dishes. Try the New Legaspi's pineapple pie for a special treat.

The *Waway Restaurant* on Peñaranda St Extension in the north of town has a local reputation for Filipino food. Watch out for the 'Bicol express' here – dishes with red-hot peppers that get you running for relief at express speed.

The *Mamalola Bakery & Snack House* on Peñaranda St will surprise you not only with its plucky Karaoke singers but also with its excellent cooking. The *Legaspi Ice Cream House* in Magellanes St makes wonderful ice cream.

Getting There & Away

Air PAL have daily fights from Manila which take 50 minutes.

Bus It's 10 to 12 hours by bus from Manila to Legaspi. Buses to Tabaco take about 45 minutes. Direct buses to Matnog generally come through from Manila and may well be full. It's probably easier to take local services to Sorsogon or Irosin and change there.

AROUND LEGASPI

Santo Domingo

This long black-sand beach is 15 km north-east of Legaspi and sometimes has quite high surf. Jeepneys run from Legaspi to Santo Domingo and tricycles run from there to the resorts along the beach.

Daraga & Cagsawa

The eruption of Mayon in 1814 totally destroyed the villages of Camalig, Cagsawa and Budiao on the southern side of Mayon. The **Cagsawa Church** was rebuilt in an ornate baroque style at nearby Daraga. It's just a short jeepney ride from Legaspi. The **Cagsawa ruins** are a short distance west of Daraga. There are also some ruins at **Budiao**, about two km from Cagsawa, but they are not so interesting.

Camalig

The interesting **Hoyop-Hoyopan Caves** are about 10 km from Camalig – hire a tricycle there and back or take a jeepney. In Camalig, the church has artefacts that were excavated from the caves in 1972. Camalig is about 14 km from Legaspi and is reached by jeepneys and buses. Tricycles operate from Camalig to the caves.

MAYON

Derived from the word 'beautiful' in the local dialect, Mayon is claimed to be the world's most perfect volcano cone. You can best appreciate it from the ruins of Cagsawa church. In 1814, Mayon erupted violently, killing 1200 people including those who took shelter in the church. To get to Cagsawa, take a jeepney bound for Camalig and alight at the Cagsawa sign, from where it's a few minutes' walk.

Mayon is said to erupt every 10 years and recently it's been doing even better than that. The spectacular eruption in 1968 was followed by another in 1978 and then another in late 1984. The last serious eruption was in February 1993. Seventy people died and a further 50,000 had to be evacuated.

If you want to appreciate Mayon from closer up, you can climb it in a couple of days – the tourist office in Legaspi will fix you up. The usual cost for two people is US$50, including a guide, a porter and a tent. Provisions are extra. Count on P300 per person for food and for a second porter if you don't want to carry your own food and gear.

You take a jeepney to Buyuhan (extra cost) and then climb 2½ hours to Camp 1 (Camp Amporo) at about 800 metres. If you start late you spend the night in the simple hut there. Another four hours takes you to Camp 2 (Camp Pepito), at about 1800 metres. Here you have to use a tent as there is no hut. The night can be fairly cold and from here it's a four-hour climb to the summit.

The last 250 metres is a scramble over loose stones and steep rocks; it's advisable to be roped. Going down takes three hours from the crater to Camp 2, two hours to Camp 1 and two hours to the road.

Take warm clothing, a sleeping bag and provisions for two days. You can try hiring a guide and porter in Buyuhan for about P500 a day. To try the ascent without a guide is reckless and irresponsible as many of the harmless-looking canyons turn out to be dead ends with sheer drops.

The *Mayon Vista Lodge* (formerly known as the Mayon Resthouse) is a good viewpoint, 800 metres up the 2450-metre volcano. To get there, take a Ligao-bound jeepney from Tabaco to the turn-off, from where it's an eight-km walk (or hitch) to the lodge. Alternatively, hire a jeepney from Tabaco or, more economically, persuade the regular Ligao jeepney, for a consideration, to make the detour to the lodge. The Tourist Office will be able to say whether it is possible in the meantime to stay overnight in the Mayon Vista Lodge. They advise people not to climb the north slope of the volcano as it is apparently too dangerous.

TABACO

Tabaco is just a departure point for the Catanduanes ferry.

Places to Stay & Eat

Tony's Hotel on Riosa St near the market has rooms with fan and bath for P90/130 and with air-con and bath for P170/220. The *EF-Palace Restaurant* is in the same building or try the very clean *Royal Crown Canteen* opposite the Municipal Hall.

Getting There & Away

Buses go direct to Tabaco from Manila or it's just 45 minutes from Legaspi and another half-hour on to Tiwi.

TIWI

The hot springs at Tiwi are a real disappointment. They've been commercialised in very bad taste and the development of geothermal power plants in the area has pretty well dried them up. The hostel is still a pleasant place to stay while you explore the area. There are beaches, bubbling pools of hot mud, steam issuing from the ground, the geothermal plant and some interesting old church ruins in the town of Tiwi.

Places to Stay

About three km beyond the town of Tiwi you'll find the *Baño Manantial de Tiwi Youth Hostel and Mendoza's Resort* at the hot springs. There's a swimming pool outside and thermal baths in the basement. Rooms are P350/400 with fan and bath or P500/600 with air-con and bath.

Getting There & Away

Jeepneys from Peñaranda St in Legaspi run directly to Tiwi or you can go via Tabaco. It's a three-km tricycle ride from Tiwi to the hot springs. There are two daily Philtranco buses from Manila to Tiwi.

CATANDUANES

There are some excellent beaches and pleasant waterfalls on this island, but few tourists come here. The main town and accommodation centre is **Virac**. **Puraran**, 30 km north-east, has a wonderful long white beach.

Places to Stay

In the main town on Catanduanes Island you can stay at the *Cherry Don* (☎ 516) on San Pedro St, where singles/doubles are P60/100 with fan. *Sandy's Pension House* (☎ 617) at Piersite has basic rooms with fan for P85/170. The more expensive *Catanduanes Hotel* (☎ 280) on San Jose St has rooms with fan and bath for P200/275. It is unpretentious but quite cosy and has a good restaurant on the roof. All three places are located within walking distance of the pier.

Getting There & Away

PAL fly daily to Virac from Manila and from Legaspi. The ferry to Virac, on Catanduanes, departs Tabaco daily and takes three or more hours.

SORSOGON, GUBAT & BULAN

Sorsogon, the capital of the southernmost province of Luzon, is really just a transit region to the Visayas. The **Rizal Beach** is at nearby Gubat, but it's nothing to write home about. Ferries cross to Masbate from Bulan.

Places to Stay

The *Dalisay Hotel* (☎ 6926), 182 V L Peralta St, Sorsogon, is simple and fairly clean with rooms at P60/100 with fan and P90/130 with fan and bath.

At the *Rizal Beach Resort Hotel*, at Gubat, rooms are P200/300 with fan and bath and P400 for an air-con double with bath.

Mari-El's Lodging House (☎ 721) by the pier in Bulan is a straightforward place with rooms for P35/70 and with fan for P50/100.

Getting There & Away

Buses to Sorsogon, from Legaspi, leave every half hour and take 1½ hours. It's 3½ hours from Legaspi to Bulan.

BULUSAN & IROSIN

Mt Bulusan is the 1560-metre volcano at the centre of the Juban-Bulusan-Irosin triangle. Nearby is a small crater lake of the same name, a pleasant six-km walk from Bulusan.

Places to Stay

The *Bulusan Lodging House* behind the town hall has clean rooms at P60/120 with fan. The pleasant *Villa Luisa Celeste Resort* in Dancalan, Bulusan, has clean and spacious rooms with fan and bath for P250/300 and with air-con and bath for P450. They have a restaurant and a swimming pool. At the *Mateo Hot & Cold Springs Resort* in Irosin rooms are P100/200.

Getting There & Away

Buses from Legaspi go to Irosin or to Bulan via Irosin in about 2½ hours.

MATNOG

Right at the southern tip of Luzon, this is the departure point for boats to Allen on Samar.

Places to Stay

Mely's Snack House costs P30 per person. It's a basic place and the only one left in Matnog. If they miss the last ferry, most

Filipinos prefer to sleep in the big waiting room at the pier.

Getting There & Away

Buses run to Irosin from Legaspi, from where you continue by jeepney. You can do the trip with all connections in 3½ hours. There are also direct Philtranco buses, but the bus comes straight through from Manila and it can be difficult to get a seat. Coming from Allen there are usually jeepneys waiting to meet the ferry.

Other Islands

Although Luzon is the main island of the Philippines and offers a lot of things to see and do, it is only the start – there are still nearly 7000 islands left to explore. The majority of these 'other islands' are in the group known as the Visayas. This tightly packed scattering of islands lies between Luzon to the north and Mindanao to the south. The main Visayan islands are Samar, Leyte, Bohol, Cebu, Negros, Panay and Romblon. It is in these islands that you can really come to grips with Filipino island-hopping. With so many islands, so many ferries and boats and such relatively short distances to travel between them, the possibilities are immense.

Cebu, the central Visayan island, is the travel centre of the group, and its capital, Cebu City, is one of the most historic and interesting cities in the Philippines, as well as being third in size to Manila and Davao. It was here that Magellan landed on his epic circumnavigation of the world and here that the Spanish first claimed the Philippines.

At the extreme south of the Philippines is the large island of Mindanao. This is the second largest of the Philippine islands and the centre for much of the unrest in the country. The predominantly Muslim Mindanaoans have campaigned long and hard for separation from the rest of the country. There is also Palawan, the long, narrow island that almost looks like a bridge

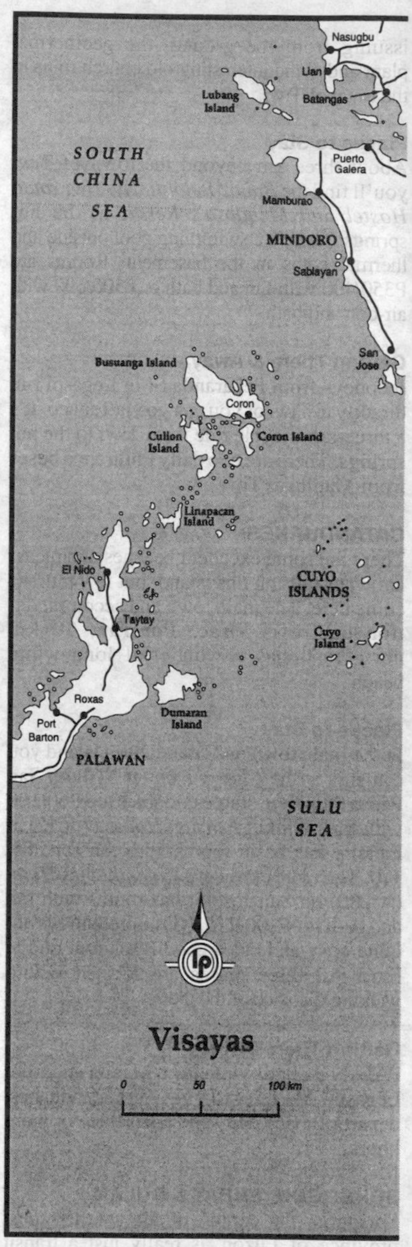

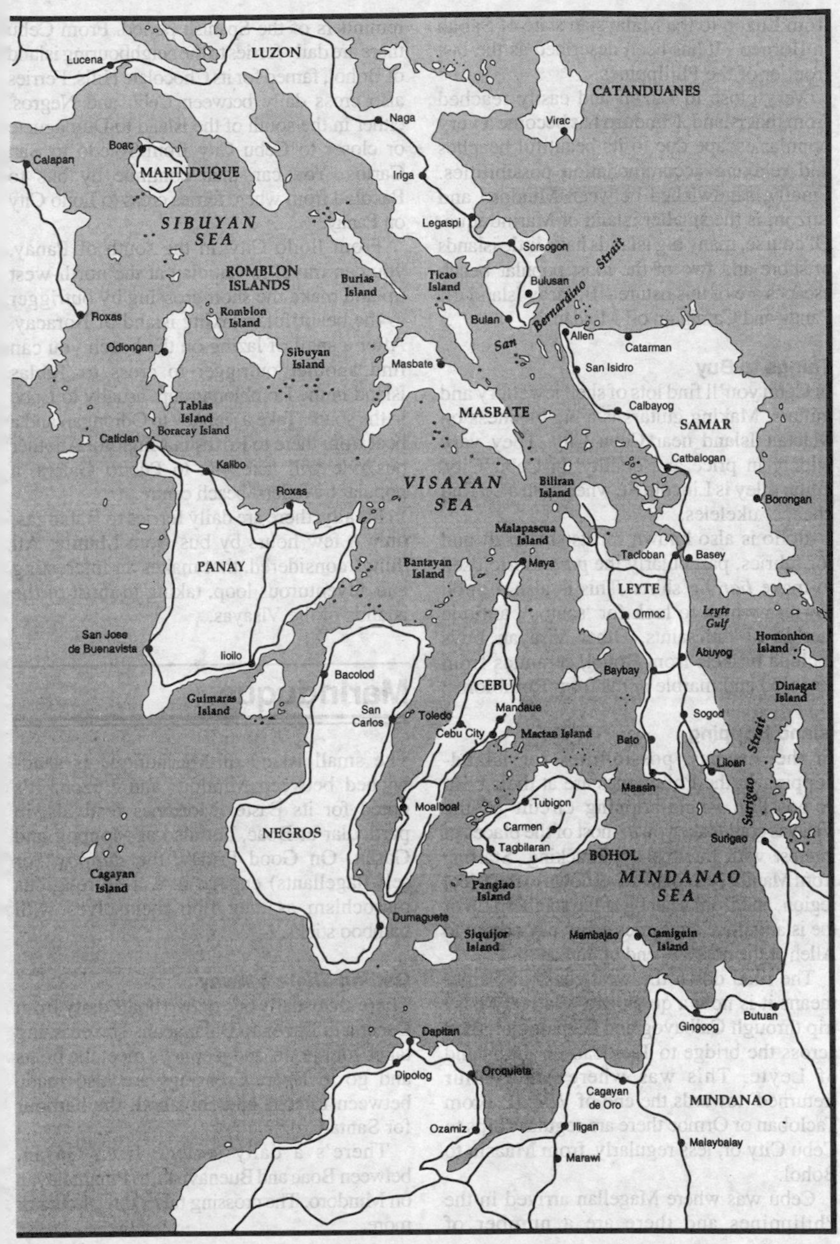

THE PHILIPPINES

from Luzon to the Malaysian state of Sabah in Borneo. It has been described as the last frontier of the Philippines.

Very close to Luzon and easily reached from that island, Mindoro has become a very popular escape due to its beautiful beaches and relaxing accommodation possibilities. Finally, sandwiched between Mindoro and Luzon, is the smaller island of Marinduque. Of course, many big islands have little islands offshore and two of the most popular beach escapes are of this nature – Boracay Island off Panay and Camiguin off Mindanao.

Things to Buy

In Cebu you'll find lots of shell jewellery and guitars. Making guitars is a big business on Mactan Island near Cebu City. They vary widely in price and quality. In Cebu City, guitar alley is Lincoln St, where you also find cheaper ukeleles.

Iloilo is also known for its shellcraft and for fabrics, particularly the *pina* fabric used to make *barong* shirts. This is also a good town in which to look for 'santos', antique statues of the saints. Other Visayan buys include baskets from Bohol, ceramics from Bacolod and marble items from Romblon.

Island Hopping

In the Visayas, possibilities for island-hopping in the Philippines are at their best. A possible island-hopping circuit of the Visayas could take you to most of the places of interest with minimal backtracking. Starting from Manila you could travel down to the Bicol region, and from Matnog at the southern tip of the island there are ferries every day across to Allen at the northern end of Samar.

The road down the west coast of Samar means it is now a quick and relatively easy trip through Calbayog and Catbalogan, then across the bridge to Tacloban on the island of Leyte. This was where MacArthur 'returned' towards the end of WW II. From Tacloban or Ormoc there are regular ships to Cebu City or, less regularly, from Maasin to Bohol.

Cebu was where Magellan arrived in the Philippines and there are a number of reminders of the Spanish period. From Cebu there are daily ferries to the neighbouring island of Bohol, famed for its Chocolate Hills. Ferries also cross daily between Cebu and Negros, either in the south of the island to Dumaguete or closer to Cebu City from Toledo to San Carlos. You can then continue by bus to Bacolod from where ferries cross to Iloilo City on Panay.

From Iloilo City, in the south of Panay, you can travel to Caticlan at the north-west tip and make the short crossing by outrigger to the beautiful, relaxing island of Boracay. After a spell of lazing on the beach you can find another outrigger to cross to Tablas Island in the Romblon group, usually to Looc in the south. Take a jeepney to Odiongan and a boat from there to Roxas in Mindoro. Another bus ride will take you to Puerto Galera, a popular travellers' beach centre.

Finally, there are daily ferries to Batangas, only a few hours by bus from Manila. All things considered, that makes an interesting and adventurous loop, taking in most of the islands of the Visayas.

Marinduque

The small island of Marinduque is sandwiched between Mindoro and Luzon. It's noted for its Easter Moriones festivals, in particular at Boac, but also at Mogpog and Gasan. On Good Friday, the *antipos*, (or self-flagellants) engage in a little religious masochism as they flog themselves with bamboo sticks.

Getting There & Away

There are usually one or two boats daily from Lucena in Luzon to Balanacan. The crossing takes four hours and jeepneys meet the boats and go to Boac. Crossings are also made between Lucena and Buyabod, the harbour for Santa Cruz.

There's a daily service from Gasan, between Boac and Buenavista, to Pinamalayan on Mindoro. The crossing takes three hours or more.

BOAC

On Easter Sunday at Boac, one of the most colourful religious ceremonies in the Philippines takes place. Dressed as Roman centurions wearing large carved masks, the participants capture Longinus, the centurion who was converted after he had stabbed Christ in the side with his spear. The festival ends with a *pugutan* (mock beheading) of the hapless Longinus.

Places to Stay

Cely's Lodging House (☎ 1519) on 10 de Octobre St has rooms with fan for P150. On Nepomuceno St, the *Boac Hotel* has simple singles with fan for P100/120 or rooms with fan and bath for P160.

On the beach at Caganhao, between Boac and Cawit, is the *Pyramid Beach Resort* with rooms at P200/250. The pebbly beach also has the *Aussie-Pom Guest House* with spacious rooms at P200, and the *Cassandra Beach Resort* with rooms for P150 and cottages with fan and bath for P175. A short way out of Boac, towards Mogpog, is *Swing Beach Resort* (☎ 1252) on Deogratias St. Rooms here are P200 per person.

The *Sunraft Beach Hotel* in Cawit, eight km from Boac, has rooms from P120, or there's the *Seaview Hotel* where rooms with fan and bath are P240/300.

SANTA CRUZ

Boac is the capital, but Santa Cruz is the largest town and has an impressive church dating from 1714. Diving trips can be made from Santa Cruz.

Places to Stay & Eat

The *Park View Lodge* near the town hall has simple rooms at P200. On the corner of Palomares and Pag-asa Sts the *Tita Amie Restaurant* is the best place to eat.

OTHER PLACES

From Buenavista, on the south coast, you can climb **Mt Malindig**, a 1157-metre dormant volcano. The weekend **Buenavista Market** is worth seeing. The **Tres Reyes Islands** are 30 minutes by outrigger from Buenavista – **Gaspar Island** has a small village and a nice coral beach. **White Beach**, near Torrijos, is probably the best beach on Marinduque. The town of **Gasan** is also heavily involved in the Easter passion play.

Mindoro

The relatively undeveloped island of Mindoro is the nearest 'last frontier' to Manila – the Philippines have quite a few last frontiers. Because you can get there very easily from Manila many travellers make the trip to try the beautiful beaches.

Puerto Galera vies with Boracay as the best place in the Philippines for simply lazing on the beach, although it's well on its way to becoming a victim of its own popularity. Mindoro's population is concentrated along the coastal strip and the inland is mainly dense jungle and mountains.

Getting There & Away

To/From Luzon The usual route to Mindoro is from the Luzon port of Batangas City to Calapan or Puerto Galera. You can get buses directly to Batangas City from the BLTB bus terminal in Manila for P40 (regular) to P50 (air-con) but beware of pickpockets who work overtime on this route. You have to leave Manila as early as possible in the morning in order to get to Puerto Galera the same day. The earliest bus leaves about 5 am.

The ferry crossing takes about two hours; there are eight Batangas to Calapan services and at least three Batangas to Puerto Galera services. The services to Puerto Galera are at 11.30 am, noon or 12.30 and 4 pm, and sometimes at 1.30 pm (depending on time of year and weather conditions). The fare is P40 to P65. The services to Calapan are between 6 and 10.30 am and between 2 and 6.30 pm, so you would possibly have to stay overnight in Calapan before continuing to Puerto Galera.

From the Sundowner Hotel on Mabini St, Ermita, a daily Si-kat Ferry Inc. air-con bus departs at 9 am to connect with the

THE PHILIPPINES

company's noon Si-kat ferry from Batangas which arrives at Puerto Galera at around 2.30 pm. The through trip costs P260.

To/From Other Islands From Pinamayalan on Mindoro you can continue on to Marinduque, and from Roxas on to Boracay (Panay) or Romblon. It's becoming quite a popular route from Mindoro to Boracay, thus combining the two very popular beach destinations of Puerto Galera and Boracay. You can either go there via Tablas Island in the Romblon group of islands, by way of Bongabong or Roxas, or direct to Boracay from Roxas. Be careful, as some of the boats on this route are leaky buckets and are often dangerously overloaded.

There's a big outrigger from Roxas to Boracay on Monday and Thursday which takes five hours. From December to May it can even leave as often as every other day. If it has to go via Looc in Romblon it takes at least 10 hours. The fare is about P200. There's a big outrigger from Bongabong to San Agustin on Tablas on Sunday at 2 pm for about P80. It takes about six hours and continues from San Agustin to the town of Romblon on Romblon. Another big outrigger operates from Roxas to Odiongan, on Tablas, on Tuesday, Wednesday, Friday and Sunday at 10 am, and takes three hours.

PUERTO GALERA

The fine beaches and excellent snorkelling around Puerto Galera have been attracting travellers for some time. There are also some pleasant walks, but the whole area is starting to become very popular, especially with Germans (at White Beach) and Australians (at Sabang).

There are many places to stay at the various beaches which include **La Laguna**, **Sabang Beach**, **White Beach** at San Isidro (seven km out of town), **Aninuan Beach**, **Talipanan Beach** and **Balete Beach**.

Information

The Rural Bank in Puerto Galera changes cash and may also change travellers' cheques. The Margarita Shopping Centre changes both.

Places to Stay

In Town Rooms in Puerto Galera generally cost from around P100 in low season to P200 in high season, although there are still a few cheaper places. The simple *Melxa's Greenhill Nipa Hut* has rooms with fan for P60/120. *Bahay Pilipino* has rooms with fan for P100/150, as does the friendly *Malou's Hilltop Inn*.

Christine's Place is on the edge of town, at quiet Balete Beach, and has rooms for P150/180. Just out of town on the road to Sabang, *Apple's Hut's* has basic cottages for P100/120. It's a nicely laid-out place.

Right at the wharf, the *El Cañonero Marivelis Hotel* has rooms with fan and bath for P200/250 and there is a restaurant. The *Villa Margarita Bamboo House* has rooms with fan and bath for P250 or there's the *Villa Margarita White House* with singles with fan and bath for P250/350. Villa Margarita also runs the *Holiday Garden Apartelle* where doubles with fan and bath are P350 and apartments are P750.

The *Fishermen's Cove Beach House* is on a quiet bay about a km out of town towards White Beach, and has rooms with fan and bath for P300. *Cathy's Travellers Inn* is the same price and also has cottages with bath for P450. It's about two km out of town towards Halige and Boquete Beaches.

About 1½ km out of town, towards Sabang, the *Encenada Beach Resort* has rooms or cottages with fan and bath for P700. The *Tanawin Lodge*, near Encenada Beach, has small fully furnished two-storey houses with living rooms and bedrooms for P700 to P1800. There is a swimming pool.

At the Beaches Out on the beaches there are lots of cottages with fan and bath from around P250 to as much as P600 a day. The places that follow are just a small selection of the numerous possibilities.

The beaches include Sabang Beach, Big and Small La Laguna beaches, White Beach (San Isidro), Aninuan Beach and Talipanan Beach. An outrigger from Puerto Galera to

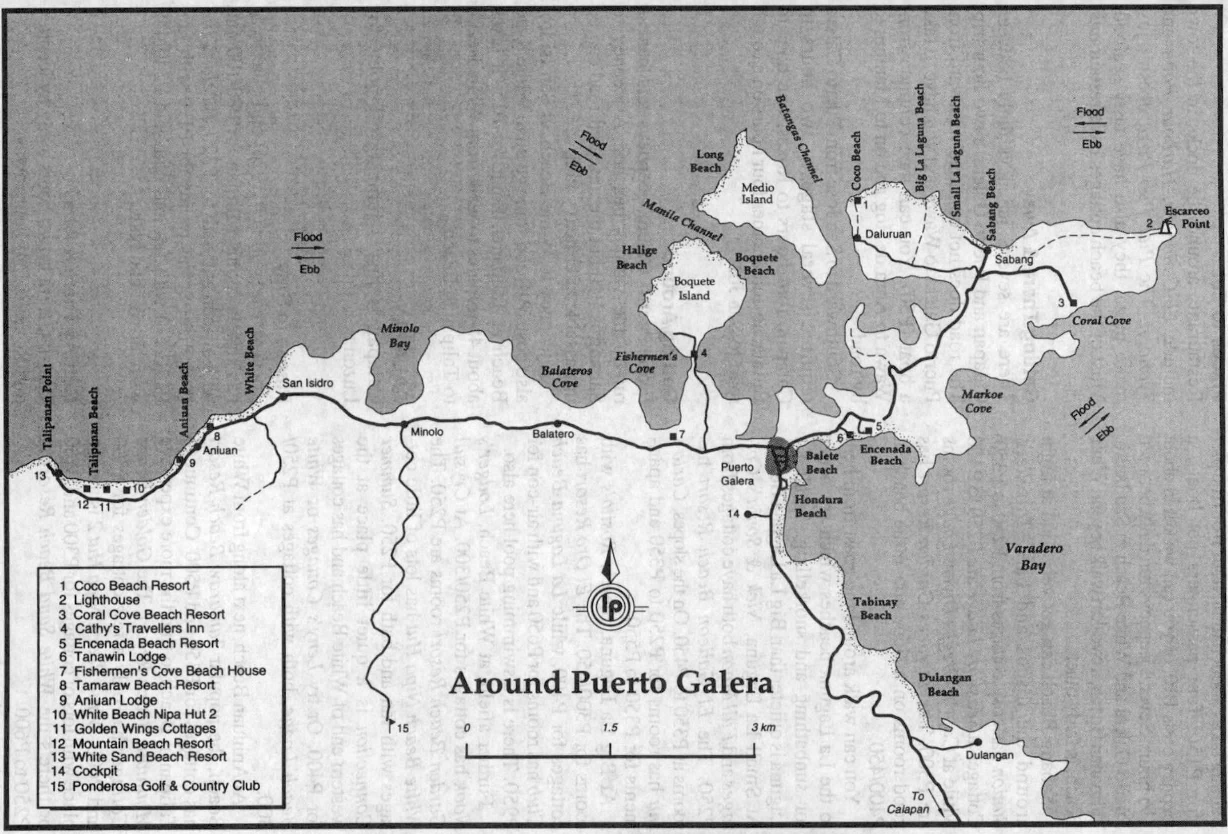
Around Puerto Galera
0
1.5
3 km
1 Coco Beach Resort
2 Lighthouse
3 Coral Cove Beach Resort
4 Cathy's Travellers Inn
5 Encenada Beach Resort
6 Tanawin Lodge
7 Fishermen's Cove Beach House
8 Tamaraw Beach Resort
9 Aniuan Lodge
10 White Beach Nipa Hut 2
11 Golden Wings Cottages
12 Mountain Beach Resort
13 White Sand Beach Resort
14 Cockpit
15 Ponderosa Golf & Country Club
Escarceo Point
Coral Cove
Sabang
Sabang Beach
Small La Laguna Beach
Big La Laguna Beach
Daluruan
Coco Beach
Batangas Channel
Medio Island
Long Beach
Boquete Beach
Boquete Island
Manila Channel
Halige Beach
Fishermen's Cove
Balateros Cove
Balatero
Puerto Galera
Balete Beach
Encenada Beach
Hondura Beach
Markoe Cove
Varadero Bay
Tabinay Beach
Dulangan Beach
Dulangan
To Calapan
Minolo
Minolo Bay
San Isidro
White Beach
Aniuan
Aniuan Beach
Talipanan Beach
Talipanan Point
Flood
Ebb

Sabang takes about half an hour from the pier (for P150; four passengers per boat), a jeepney costs P10, or you can walk it in about 1½ hours. Several jeepneys run daily between Puerto Galera and White Beach in San Isidro. Talipanan Beach, a two-km walk beyond White Beach, is fairly quiet.

Sabang Beach can get very loud at night around the discos and bars. *Travellers' Station* has cosy cottages from P250 to P350. Cottages at *Seashore Lodge* are P250 to P400 while at *Capt'n Greggs Divers Lodge* rooms are P300. The *Terraces Garden Resort* has good rooms on a slope above the beach at P400/450.

You can walk around the coast from here to the La Laguna beaches which are better for sunbathing and snorkelling. Small La Laguna is quieter than Big La Laguna Beach. At Small La Laguna, *Nick & Sonia's Cottages* and *Full Moon* both have cottages from P250. The *El Galleon Beach Resort* has rooms at P350 to P450. On the slopes, *Carlo's Inn* has rooms for P250 to P350 and apartments for P350 to P550.

At Big La Laguna, there's *Rosita's* with rooms for P300/450. The *El Oro Resort* has cottages for P400, while *La Laguna Beach Club* has rooms for P650 and with air-con for P950. There is a swimming pool here also.

Further afield, at White Beach, *Lodger's Nook* has cottages for P250/300. At *Crystal Garden Beach Resort* rooms are P250. The *White Beach Nipa Hut* has lots of little cottages with fan and bath for P250. *Summer Connection* is a quiet little place at the western end of White Beach and has cottages for P400. Or try *Leny's Cottages* or *White Beach Lodge*, both with cottages at P250/300.

At Aninuan Beach, next along from White Beach, the popular *Tamaraw Beach Resort* has cottages for P350 and P500. Continue to Talipanan Beach to find the more expensive *Mountain Beach Resort*. The *Golden Wings Cottages* has only a few cottages for P300 and P600. *White Beach Nipa Hut 2* is a large place with lots of cottages for P300 and P400 or there's the *White Sand Beach Resort* at P250 to P600.

Places to Eat

Restaurants around the docks in the town include *El Cañonero*, *Harbour Point* and *Typhoon*. The *Pier Pub Pizza* doesn't just make pizza, they also have tasty seafood. Most of the beach cottages have restaurants.

Getting There & Away

There are several jeepneys daily between Calapan and Puerto Galera, a two-hour trip. The road does not continue westward from Puerto Galera to Wawa and you have to take a boat (P50). You can then continue from Wawa to Abra de Ilog and on to Mamburao by road.

Southward to San Jose from Puerto Galera requires several stages – two hours to Calapan, four hours to Roxas, one hour to Bulalacao and another four hours on a rough road to San Jose.

Getting Around

From Puerto Galera, jeepneys and bancas run to the various beaches. A jeepney to Sabang is P10 but the unsealed road can be impassable after heavy rain.

A jeepney to White Beach, at San Isidro, also costs P10 and some go on to White Sand Beach at Talipanan Point for P15. It takes about 45 minutes to walk from White Beach to Talipanan Beach.

CALAPAN

Calapan is just a jumping-off point for Luzon.

Places to Stay

The *Travellers' Inn* (☎ 1926) on Leuterio St has simple rooms with fan for P80/100 and with air-con and bath for P320. *Riceland Inn I* on Rizal St has rooms for P110 with fan, P120/270 with fan and bath and P340/440 with air-con and bath.

Getting There & Away

Puerto Galera is two hours away by jeepney and Roxas is four hours away.

BONGABONG, ROXAS & MANSALAY

You can get boats for Romblon from Bongabong or Roxas and, for Boracay, from Roxas. From Mansalay, further south from Roxas, you can walk to the villages of the Mangyan tribes.

Places to Stay

In Bongabong, the basic *Mabuhay Lodging House* is cheap at P50/100. Roxas has the *Santo Nino Lodging House* with rooms for P50 per person and a good restaurant. The *Catalina Beach Resort* at Lodpond has simple rooms for P50/100. It's 1½ km from Roxas. An alternative to staying in Roxas is to stay at the *Melco Beach Lodge*, along the beach a little way at Dangay. The beach is nothing special but it's OK as a place to wait for a boat and has cottages from P65 to P150. It's a P15 tricycle ride from town.

Getting There & Away

See the introductory Getting There & Away section of the Mindoro section for boat information. From Calapan buses take three hours to Bongabong and four hours to Roxas.

SAN JOSE

From San Jose, it may be possible to visit the Mangyan tribes or you can rent a boat to **Ambulong** or **Ilin Island** for swimming and snorkelling. **Apo Reef**, a popular diving spot well offshore, can be reached from San Jose or Sablayan.

Places to Stay & Eat

The *Jolo Hotel* (☎ 618) on Rizal St has cheap rooms from around P60/80 for the simplest rooms. Rooms with fan and bath cost P100. The *Sikatuna Town Hotel* (☎ 697) on Sikatuna St is a simple, clean and fairly good place. They have rooms with fan for P70/100, with fan and bath for P145 and with air-con and bath for P410.

San Jose has only a few acceptable places to eat. You could try the *Emmanuel Panciteria* on Rizal St and *Nice & Spice* on Sikatuna St, where they serve pizzas.

Getting There & Away

It usually takes several stages to round the southern end of Mindoro between Roxas and San Jose and the road is often none too good. To go on to Mamburao, via Sablayan, is tough going and takes six hours by bus.

SABLAYAN & NORTH PANDAN ISLAND

From this friendly, clean little coastal town you can cross over to one of the offshore islands in Pandan Bay in about 30 minutes.

North Pandan Island is a gorgeous spot and has a beautiful white-sand beach.

Places to Stay

The *Emely Hotel* in Sablayan has simple but clean rooms for P60/120. On North Pandan Island, the pleasant *Pandan Island Resort* has rooms for P180 and cottages with fan and bath for P300.

MAMBURAO

Few travellers get this far up the west coast of Mindoro. But it's a fair bet that it will not be long before the northern stretch of the coastline from Mamburao to Sablayan becomes a centre of tourism.

Places to Stay

The *Traveller's Lodge* in Mamburao has rooms with fan for P80/150 or with fan and bath for P150/250.

Four km north-west from Mamburao, the *Tayamaan Palm Beach Club* has cottages with fan and bath for P450. About 12 km south of Mamburao, the *La Dolce Vita Garden Resort*, at Fatima, has cottages with fan and bath from P250 to P450. They have a swimming pool and you can hire a motorbike.

Getting There & Away

There are flights between Mamburao and Manila. See the Puerto Galera section for travel between Mamburao and the west coast.

THE PHILIPPINES

Romblon

This scattering of small islands is in the middle of the area bordered by South Luzon, Masbate, Panay and Mindoro. It's noted for its marble. Marble carving is carried out and an extensive range of souvenirs is produced. There are some good beaches and the town of Romblon has a notable cathedral. The three main islands of the group are Romblon and the two larger islands, Sibuyan and Tablas.

Romblon is useful as a stepping stone from the beach resort of Puerto Galera on Mindoro to the resort island of Boracay, just off Panay and directly south of Tablas.

Getting There & Away

PAL flies daily, except Sunday, between Manila and Tugdan on Tablas Island.

Regular boats operate between Lucena on Luzon and Magdiwang on Sibuyan Island and between Lucena and Romblon town on Romblon Island. There are also services between Manila and various Romblon ports. Other boats, some of them large outriggers, operate between Romblon ports and Masbate, Mindoro, Palawan and Panay.

See the Mindoro and Boracay sections for details of Mindoro to Tablas and Tablas to Boracay travel, used by some intrepid travellers as a route between the two popular beach centres of Puerto Galera and Boracay.

ROMBLON ISLAND

The small port of **Romblon** on Romblon Island is the capital of the province. **San Andres** and **Santiago Hill forts** were built by the Spanish in 1640, while the **San Joseph's Cathedral** dates from 1726 and houses a collection of antiques. There are good views from the **Sabang** and **Apunan lighthouses**. **Lugbon Island** shelters the bay and has a beautiful white beach.

Places to Stay & Eat

The *Moreno Seaside Lodge*, by the harbour, has rooms for P60/120. The *Feast-Inn Lodge* near the church is slightly more expensive at P70/140. Also by the harbour is the *Kawilihan Food House* but the *Tica Inn* is probably the best restaurant in town.

You can stay in the *Selangga Tree House* at Agnay, six km from Romblon town, for P75 per person. *D'Marble Beach Cottages* in San Pedro is a well looked-after place with neat cottages for P170 and P220.

Getting There & Away

Boats go about four times weekly between Romblon town and Sibuyan Island in two hours. There are daily outriggers to San Agustin on Tablas Island taking 45 minutes.

TABLAS ISLAND

Tablas is the largest island in the Romblon group. The main towns are San Agustin, Odiongan, Looc and Santa Fe.

Places to Stay

The *S&L Lodge* in San Agustin is cheap at P40/80. In Odiongan, the *Shellborne Hotel* costs P70/140 with fan and bath. In Looc, the *Plaza Inn* is P90/180 with fan and bath. The *Tablas Pension House* is P100/200. Tugdan has the *Monte Carlo Lodging* and the *Airport Pension House*, both for P50/100.

Getting There & Away

Flights to Tugdan from Manila are almost always heavily booked. Jeepneys meet the plane and go to San Agustin (one hour), Santa Fe (one hour) and Looc (45 minutes).

San Agustin is the port for boats to Romblon town. Odiongan's small harbour is just outside the town and, from here, boats go to Batangas on Luzon and Roxas on Mindoro. Looc is the port for boats to Boracay. They cost P50 per person (although they ask P80) and there's a connecting jeepney service from the airport in Tugdan. There's also a daily boat from Santa Fe to Carabao (the island between Tablas and Boracay), Boracay and Caticlan on Panay. The two-hour trip to Boracay costs P70.

SIBUYAN ISLAND

Sibuyan is more mountainous and less developed than the other islands. There are several

waterfalls and the 2050-metre **Mt Guiting-Guiting**.

Masbate

The small island of Masbate is between Luzon and the main Visayan group. It's noted for its large cattle herds but very few travellers come here.

Getting There & Away

There are a couple of ships a week from Cebu (11 hours) and a daily boat making the four-hour trip from Bulan in South Luzon. Boats go from Mandaon on Masbate to Sibuyan Island in Romblon Province. There are flights and boats between Masbate and Manila, and flights between Masbate and Legaspi.

MASBATE TOWN

Masbate is also the main town on the island. **Bitu-on Beach**, a few km south-east, has some cottages which make a good alternative to staying in town.

Places to Stay & Eat

The *St Anthony Hotel* (☎ 180) on Quezon St has simple rooms with fan for P110/150, with fan and bath for P200/250 and with air-con and bath for P300/350. It's the only halfway decent hotel in town.

Try *Peking House,* in the port area, for good food or the *Petit Restaurant* opposite the St Anthony Hotel in Quezon St.

Panay

The large, triangular Visayan island of Panay has a number of decaying forts and watchtowers – relics from the days of the Moro pirates – plus some interesting Spanish churches. The south coast, which stretches from Iloilo around the southern promontory at Anini-y to San Jose de Buenavista, has many beaches and resorts. The Ati-Atihan Festival in January, in Kalibo, is one of the most popular in the Philippines. Last, but far from least, off the north-western tip of the island is the delightful little island of Boracay, one of the Philippines' major travellers' centres.

Getting There & Away

There are a variety of flights and shipping services to Panay from Manila, Cebu City and other major centres. PAL fly from Manila to Iloilo, Kalibo and Roxas and from Cebu City to Kalibo, while Aerolift and Pacific Airways fly from Manila to Caticlan. Travellers bound for Boracay head for Kalibo or Caticlan, but the Kalibo flights are often heavily booked.

You can reach Panay by boat from Cebu, Leyte, Luzon, Mindanao, Mindoro, Negros, Palawan and Romblon. The shortest crossing is the two to 2½-hour trip from Bacolod in Negros to Iloilo City. There are several boats daily.

It's possible (with some difficulty) to travel from Mindoro to Boracay via Tablas in Romblon Province but this can be a dangerous trip as the outrigger boats are often not a match for severe conditions in the Tablas Strait.

ILOILO CITY

Iloilo City is the capital of Iloilo province and the main city on Panang. It is a large town which was very important during the Spanish era. There's the small but interesting **Window on the Past museum** in the city plus the coral **Molo Church**. Iloilo City is noted for its *jusi* (raw silk) and *piña* (pineapple-fibre) weaving. Today, Sinamay Dealer on Osmeña St has the only remaining loom.

Places to Stay

The *Iloilo Lodging House* (☎ 72384) on Aldeguer St has rooms with fan for P130/180, with fan and bath for P160/230 and with air-con and bath for P230/310. The rooms are small and bathrooms are shared between two rooms. The *Eros Travellers Pensionne* (☎ 76183) on General Luna St has basic rooms with fan and bath for P120/190 and with air-con and bath for

P200/270. The popular *Family Pension House* (☎ 27070, 79208), also on General Luna St, has clean rooms with fan and bath for P150/175 or air-con doubles with bath from P275 to P600.

The *Original River Queen Hotel* (☎ 27 0176; fax 20 0854) on Bonifacio Drive has rooms with fan and bath for P185/260 and with air-con and bath for P360/460. Other middle-bracket places include *Madia-as Hotel* (☎ 72756/59), hidden away in a lane off Aldeguer St. Rooms with fan and bath are P240/270 or with air-con and bath are P350/400. It's clean and comfortable and has a restaurant.

Centrally situated in a lane between J M Basa and Iznart Sts, *Centercon Hotel* (☎ 73431/3) has rooms with fan for P150 (noisy) and with air-con and bath for P220/280.

Places to Eat

You can get good Chinese and Filipino meals in J M Basa St, upstairs in the *Mansion House Restaurant* and in *The Summer House*, which also serves a proper Western breakfast.

Batchoy is a speciality of the western Visayas and consists of beef, pork and liver in noodle soup; the *Oak Barrel* on Valeria St is one of the best of the batchoy restaurants. *The Tavern Pub*, on the corner of Quezon and Delgado Sts, is air-con, well kept and cosy although prices are slightly higher than the usual. You can eat Filipino food with your fingers at *Nena's Manokan* restaurant in General Luna St. However, the most popular, and probably the best, local restaurant is called *Tatoy's Manokan & Seafood* and is located at Villa Beach on the western edge of town, about eight km from the city centre.

The airy *Tree House Restaurant*, of the Family Pension House, has a pleasant atmosphere while the *Golden Salakot*, in the Hotel Del Rio, serves fairly cheap buffet lunches and dinners. The *Aldous Snack Bar* keeps long hours.

If you have a sweet tooth, don't miss the *S'Table Restaurant & Snack Bar* in J M Basa St, which probably has the best selection of cakes in Iloilo. For snacks and ice cream, try the *Magnolia Ice Cream & Pancake House* in Iznart St.

Getting There & Away

Buses from Iloilo City to Kalibo and Caticlan (where boats run to Boracay) leave from 'Tanza' on the corner of Rizal and Ledesma Sts. There are a variety of flights to Iloilo City.

Getting Around

The airport is about seven km out and a PU-Cab there costs P40.

GUIMARAS ISLAND

Guimaras Island, between Panay and Negros, makes a pleasant day-trip from nearby Iloilo City. There is a fairly good swimming beach about a 45-minute walk from Nueva Valencia. The Isla Naburot beach resort, south-west of San Miguel, is beautiful and the walk to the Daliran Cave from Buenavista is pleasant, although the cave is not that memorable.

Places to Stay

The *Colmenaras Hotel & Beach Resort* has rooms with fan and bath for P120 or cottages for P100/200 but there's no swimming beach here although there is a pool. The *Isla Naburot Resort* is lovely but, at P2000 per person, including meals, it's also expensive as are other resorts on the island.

Getting There & Away

Small ferries cross from Iloilo City to the island almost hourly and take less than half an hour.

SOUTH COAST

The south coast, from Iloilo City to Anini-y on the southern tip of Panay and around to San Jose de Buenavista on the opposite coast, is full of interest. At **Guimbal**, 28 km west of Iloilo City, is an old Spanish watchtower – from this cone-shaped, now moss-covered building smoke signals were once sent up to warn of pirate attacks.

The 1787 **Miagao Church** is 11 km

further on. It was originally built as a fort, as well as a religious centre, hence the two sturdy sandstone towers. Look for the relief sculpture of St Christopher surrounded by coconut and papaya trees.

The **Church of San Joaquin**, 15 km further again, was built of white coral in 1869 and its facade is carved as a sculpture of the Spanish victory at the battle of Tetuan in Morocco, 10 years earlier.

All along the coast, between Arevalo and San Joaquin, there are beach resorts with cottages available to rent but the beaches are unexceptional. It's a very attractive coastal road and, at Anini-y and San Jose de Buenavista, there are good sites for diving.

Getting There & Away

Buses depart every two hours from Iloilo City to San Jose de Buenavista – a two-hour trip barring breakdowns. Only one bus a day makes the excursion down the peninsula, at the south-western end of the island, to Anini-y.

SAN JOSE DE BUENAVISTA

This town is known to Filipinos as San Jose Antique, since it's the capital of Antique Province.

Places to Stay

The basic *Susana Guest House*, across from the Seventy Six Bus Terminal, has rooms at P50/100 and a restaurant. The *Annavic Hotel* (☎ 558) is P170/225 with fan and P400/450 with air-con.

Getting There & Away

Although there are regular buses from Iloilo City, transport further north is difficult. It takes four hours on a bad road to Culasi and another three to Pandan. From Culasi you can visit Mararison Island.

ROXAS

Roxas is nothing special, just a stop on the way to or from Manila, Romblon or Boracay. The **Halaran Festival** takes place in October.

Places to Stay

The *Beehive Inn* (☎ 418) on Roxas Ave has rooms with fan for P75/100, with fan and bath for P100/170 and with air-con and bath for P260. The pleasant *Halaran Avenue Pension* (☎ 675) on Roxas Ave has rooms with fan for P130/160, with fan and bath for P160/200 and with air-con and bath for P280/330. *Halaran Plaza* (☎ 649), on Rizal St and opposite the city hall, is also quite good with rooms with fan and bath for P180/230 or with air-con and bath for P275/330.

Well located on Baybay Beach, between the airport and the harbour, is *Marc's Beach Resort* (☎ 103) with rooms for P300 with fan and bath and P400 with air-con and bath.

Places to Eat

Of the few restaurants in Roxas, *John's Fast Foods* on Roxas Ave, opposite Halaran Avenue Pension, is remarkably cheap and has a large selection of Filipino and Chinese dishes. *Halaran Restaurant* serves comida or well-priced meals of the day, but not beer.

Getting There & Away

Ceres Liner buses operate several times daily from Iloilo City to Roxas and take over four hours. Several buses a day go from Roxas to Kalibo, departing between 5 am and noon and taking over three hours.

KALIBO

The only real item of interest here is the annual **Ati-Atihan Festival** in January, the Mardi Gras of the Philippines. Similar festivals are held elsewhere in the country but this one is the most popular.

Places to Stay

Gervy's Lodge (☎ 3081) on R Pastrada St has simple, clean rooms for P60/120. In the same street the *RB Lodge* (☎ 2604) has rooms with fan for P75/120 or doubles with air-con and bath for P250. The *LM Plaza Lodge* on Martyrs St has basic, clean and fairly good rooms with fan for P100/140, with fan and bath for P150/200 and with air-con and bath for P300/400.

The *Green Mansions* (☎ 2244) on M Laserna St has dorm beds with fan for P60, rooms with fan for P100/150 and with fan and bath for P160/220.

There are a couple of passable hotels on S Martelino St. The *Glowmoon Hotel* (☎ 3193) has clean and fairly good rooms with fan for P200/300, with fan and bath for P350/550 and rooms with air-con and bath for P500/600. The *Casa Alba Hotel* (☎ 3146) has slightly overpriced rooms with fan for P300/400 and with air-con and bath for P700/800.

A little outside of town is the pleasant *Hibiscus Garden Club* in Andagao, about 10 minutes away from Kalibo (a tricycle costs P20). It has quite comfortable rooms with fan for P300/400 and with fan and bath for P600/700. There is a restaurant and a swimming pool here.

During the Ati-Atihan Festival, prices in Kalibo may triple and it can be almost impossible to find a hotel room.

Places to Eat

The *Peking House Restaurant*, on Martyrs St, and the *Bistro*, next to the Casa Alba Hotel on S Martelino St, have good Chinese food. The *Glowmoon Hotel* also has a restaurant with excellent, if not that cheap, food.

Getting There & Away

PAL flights between Manila and Kalibo are very heavily booked so make reservations well ahead of time and reconfirm as early as possible. PAL also flies between Cebu City and Kalibo.

Ceres Liner buses operate Iloilo City to Kalibo daily and take five hours. From Kalibo the buses leave from the service station on the south-eastern edge of town.

Buses from C Laserna St in Kalibo to Roxas take over three hours and there are also minibuses.

From Kalibo to Caticlan, where boats cross to Boracay, takes about two hours by jeepney from Roxas Ave (P30). If you arrive by plane from Manila in the early afternoon you might be able to get to Boracay before sunset. After the flight from Manila arrives, jeepneys and comfortable air-con buses leave the airport for Caticlan. The trip takes about 1½ hours. The fares are: air-con bus P150 (including the boat transfer which costs P12.50); jeepney P50.

IBAJAY

Located between Kalibo and Caticlan, this small village claims to have the original Ati-Atihan Festival. You can stay in the *RLA Hotel* opposite the service station for P125/225.

CATICLAN

Outrigger boats cross from Caticlan to Boracay and there's also a small airport for the increasingly popular flights from Manila. Sunday, market day, merits a trip from Boracay.

Places to Stay

The *Twin Pagoda Inn*, near the pier, has rooms for P150/250.

Getting There & Away

Jeepneys from Kalibo take two or more hours and leave several times daily. There are direct buses from Iloilo City to Caticlan but it takes seven hours – five to Kalibo and two more to Caticlan.

BORACAY

This superb little island, off the north-western tip of Panay, has beautiful clear water and splendid beaches. It is seven km long, only a km wide and you can walk across it in just 15 minutes.

Beach and water activities, general lazing and watching the sunset are daily attractions at Boracay. Although electricity has arrived at Boracay it's still a good idea to bring along a torch (flashlight).

Information

The Department of Tourism runs a small office in Mangayad, at about the middle of White Beach. The Allied Bank next to the PAL office in Angol will change travellers' cheques.

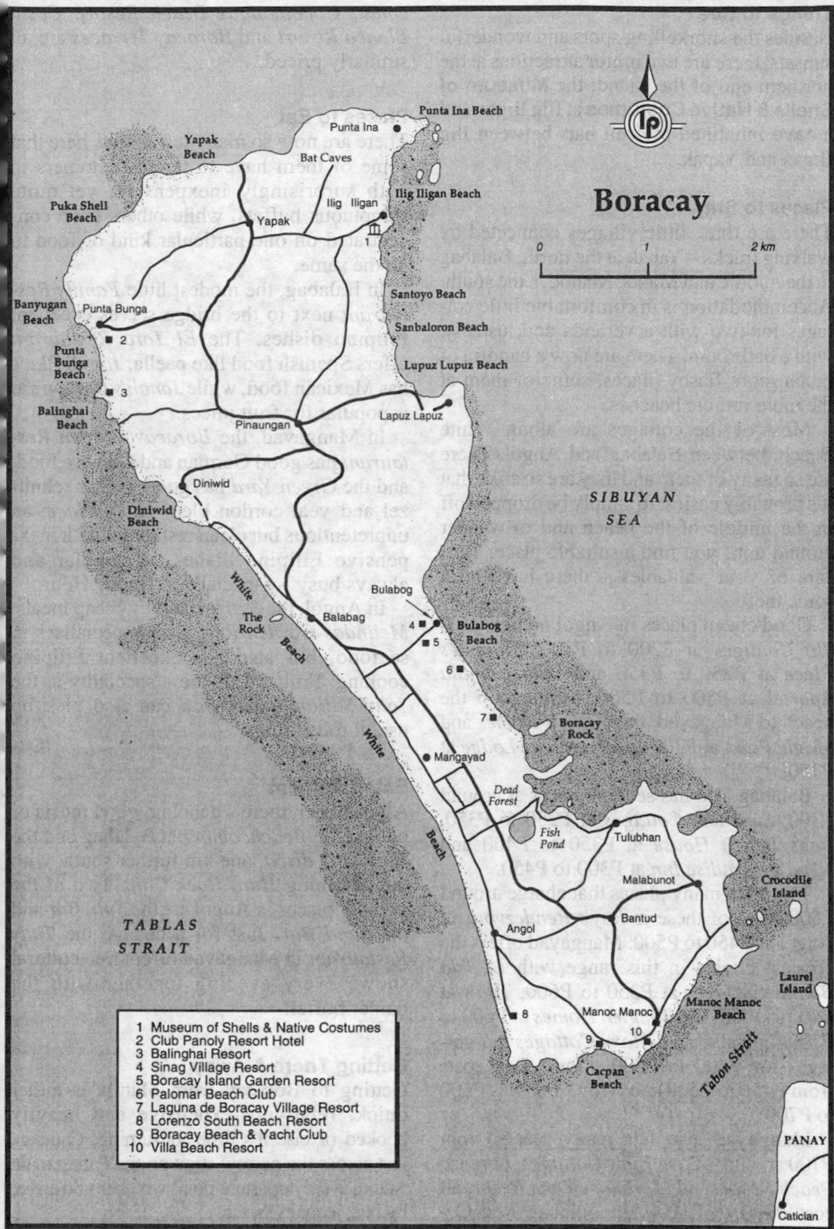
Boracay
0
1
2 km
Punta Ina Beach
Punta Ina
Yapak Beach
Bat Caves
Ilig Iligan
Ilig Iligan Beach
Puka Shell Beach
Yapak
1
Santoyo Beach
Sanbaloron Beach
Banyugan Beach
Punta Bunga
2
Punta Bunga Beach
Lupuz Lupuz Beach
3
Balinghai Beach
Lapuz Lapuz
Pinaungan
Diniwid
Diniwid Beach
SIBUYAN SEA
White Beach
Bulabog
The Rock
Balabag
4
5
Bulabog Beach
6
7
Boracay Rock
White
Mangayad
Dead Forest
Fish Pond
Tulubhan
Beach
Malabunot
Crocodile Island
Bantud
Angol
TABLAS STRAIT
Laurel Island
8
Manoc Manoc
Manoc Manoc Beach
9
10
Cacpan Beach
Tabon Strait
PANAY
Caticlan
1 Museum of Shells & Native Costumes
2 Club Panoly Resort Hotel
3 Balinghai Resort
4 Sinag Village Resort
5 Boracay Island Garden Resort
6 Palomar Beach Club
7 Laguna de Boracay Village Resort
8 Lorenzo South Beach Resort
9 Boracay Beach & Yacht Club
10 Villa Beach Resort

Things to See

Besides the snorkelling spots and wonderful sunsets, there are two minor attractions at the northern end of the island: the **Museum of Shells & Native Costumes** at Ilig Iligan and a **cave** inhabited by fruit bats between Ilig Iligan and Yapak.

Places to Stay

There are three little villages connected by walking tracks – Yapak at the north, Balabag in the middle and Manoc Manoc in the south. Accommodation is in comfortable little cottages for two with a veranda and, usually, with a bathroom. There are now a handful of much more flashy places, some of them at the more remote beaches.

Most of the cottages are along White Beach, between Balabag and Angol. There are so many of them and they are so alike that it's probably easiest to simply be dropped off in the middle of the beach and to wander around until you find a suitable place. Take care of your valuables – there have been some thefts.

Good cheap places in Angol include *Heidio Cottages* at P200 to P300, *Moreno's Place* at P250 to P350 and *Villa Camilla Apartel* at P300 to P500. Moving up the beach to Mangayad, there's *Lea Homes* and *Magic Palm* at P300 and *Trafalgar Lodge* at P350.

Balabag also has several places at around P300: *Sunshine Cottages* at P250 to P350, *Bans Beach House* at P350 to P400 and *Nena's Paradise Inn* at P300 to P450.

There are many places that charge around P600. One of these is *Roy's Rendezvous* in Angol at P450 to P500. Mangayad offers the greatest choice in this range with *La Isla Bonita Cottages* at P350 to P600, *Tito's* at P400 to P500 and *Tonglen Homes* at P600 to P700. In Balabag, *Galaxy Cottages* has cottages for P400 to P500, *Lion's Den* costs from P450 to P600 and *Willy's Place* is P500 to P700.

Mangayad also has many places from P700 and up – *Casa Pilar Cottages, Lorenzo Beach Resort* and *Morimar Beach Resort* all cost P700 to P1000. In Balabag *Red Coconut, Cocomangas Beach Resort, Costa Blanca Resort* and *Boracay Terraces* are all similarly priced.

Places to Eat

There are now so many restaurants here that some of them have to tempt customers in with surprisingly inexpensive, yet quite sumptuous buffets, while others have concentrated on one particular kind of food to do the same.

In Balabag, the modest little *Family Restaurant* next to the bridge serves excellent Filipino dishes. The *El Toro Restaurant* offers Spanish food like paella, *Jony's Place* has Mexican food, while *Jonah's Restaurant* is popular for fruit juices.

In Mangayad, the *Boracay Garden Restaurant* has good German and Chinese food, and the *Green Yard* has good wiener schnitzel and veal cordon bleu. *Tito's Place*, an unpretentious but clean restaurant with inexpensive Filipino dishes, is popular and always busy – especially at Happy Hour.

In Angol, the *Starfire* serves cheap meals. *Melindas Garden Restaurant* specialises in seafood, but also has excellent Filipino cooking. Fruit salads are a speciality at the *Jolly Sailor*, where you can also pick up useful travel hints.

Entertainment

After dinner, there's dancing, good music or pool at the *Beachcomber* at Balabag and the *Bazura D disco*, one km further south, with the adjoining *Hard Rock Café*. Two of the popular places in Angol are the *Sulu Bar* and the *Sand Bar*. Just for a change the *Titay Restaurant* in Mangayad offers free cultural shows every evening together with the dinner buffet.

Getting There & Away

Getting to Boracay from Manila is either quick, relatively expensive and heavily booked or else it's time-consuming. Caticlan, just across the narrow strait on the Panay main island, is the departure point whether you arrive by bus, jeepney or air.

Air The quickest (and most expensive) way to Boracay from Manila is to fly to Caticlan with Aerolift or Pacific Airways (P1700). PAL fly to Kalibo from where it's two hours by road to Caticlan; fares are less than half of what you must pay for the Aerolift or Pacific Airways flights. PAL also fly to Tugdan on Tablas Island in the province of Romblon but the sea crossing from there to Boracay via Santa Fe is not always easy. You can also fly from Manila to Iloilo City but it's a long bus ride from there to Caticlan.

There are air connections to some other islands as well, including Kalibo to Cebu City and Iloilo City to Cebu City on Cebu with PAL.

The PAL office is at the South Seas Resort, Aerolift is at Lorenzo Resort and Red Coconut, and Pacific Airways is at Dublin Resthouse and Red Coconut.

Boat Outriggers shuttle back and forth between Caticlan and Boracay. From June to November, during the south-western monsoons, the sea on the west side of Boracay can get too rough for outriggers. They then have to tie up on the east coast, at or near Bulabog. The crossing takes only 15 minutes but they're inclined to grossly overload the boats and more than one traveller has lost gear from a capsize.

There's a big outrigger between Boracay and Looc, on Tablas, twice a week, which takes about two hours in good conditions. There's also a daily one to Santa Fe on Tablas, taking one to two hours. There are jeepneys from Santa Fe and Looc to Tugdan, the airport on Tablas. The boat departs from Tablas when passengers arrive from the airport.

There are also several ports in north Panay, including Dumaguit and New Washington, both near Kalibo.

Negros

Sandwiched in-between Cebu and Panay, and well connected by ferry services in both directions, is the sugar island of the Philippines. Kanlaon Volcano may, it is hoped, become a similar tourist attraction to the famous Mayon Volcano in South Luzon. The east and south-east coasts can offer Spanish-style charm – perhaps a reason why foreigners often spend a few days in the pleasant little town of Dumaguete.

Getting There & Away

There are two ferry departures daily (except Sunday, when there is only one) between Toledo in Cebu and San Carlos in Negros. The crossing takes two hours. Other regular services across the comparatively narrow waters between the two islands are from Tampi to Bato, San Jose to Talisay and Sibuyan to Liloan in the far south; Tangil to Guihulngan in the centre; and Hagnaya via Bantayan Island to Cadiz in the north. Ships also operate between Cebu City and Dumaguete.

The next island north is Panay and the popular route from Negros to Panay is the Bacolod to Iloilo City boat service, but you can also go via Guimaras Island. The Bacolod to Iloilo City ferry operates two or three times daily and takes two hours. Allow an hour to get by jeepney from Bacolod to the Banago wharf. Other Negros to Panay connections include the daily boats from Victorias to Culasi and Malayu-an, both near Ajuy, on the east coast of Panay.

There are less frequent shipping connections between Negros and other islands including Siquijor, Luzon (a 24-hour trip) and Mindanao. PAL flies to Bacolod and Dumaguete from Cebu City and from Manila.

Getting Around

It's 313 km between Bacolod and Dumaguete, which are at opposite ends of the island. The trip takes 7½ hours and it's wise to take an express bus as it avoids the many small village stops. Bacolod to San Carlos takes four hours.

BACOLOD

Bacolod is a typical Filipino city of no great interest. You can visit the huge **Victoria Milling Company Central**, one of the world's largest sugar refineries, 35 km north of the city.

THE PHILIPPINES

Bacolod is also one of the major ceramics centres of the Philippines.

Places to Stay

Although it's some distance out of town, the *Family Pension House* (☎ 81211) at 123 Locsin St Extension is reasonably clean and comfortable and has a quiet city edge location. Dorm beds in fan-cooled rooms are P75, rooms with bathroom cost P150 with fan and P200 with air-con. The small, well-managed *Ester Pension* (☎ 23526) in Araneta St has rooms with fan and bath from P120 to P200 and with air-con and bath from P270.

The *Sea Breeze Hotel* (☎ 24571/5) on San Juan St is a fairly clean and good place with rooms with air-con and bath at P350/400. Finally, the *Bascon Hotel* (☎ 23141/3) on Gonzaga St is neat and clean and has air-con rooms at P450/540 and a restaurant.

Places to Eat

Reming's & Sons Restaurant in the city plaza serves good Filipino fast food as does the air-con *Gaisano Food Plaza* on Luzuriaga St. Next door to the Best Inn on Bonifacio St the *Kong Kee Diners & Bakery* does economically priced Chinese and Filipino dishes. The *Ang Sinugba Restaurant* on San Sebastian St is clean, well kept and does good native food while *Mira's Café* on Locsin St serves native coffee. Try the cosy *Cactus Room Restaurant* in the Family Pension House for a good choice of steaks. Nearby is *Alavar's Sea Foods House* with excellent Zamboanga-style dishes.

You can get barbecues and beer at the many all-night restaurants at the *Manokan Country* in the Reclamation Area.

Getting There & Away

There are a number of Ceres Liner buses daily between Bacolod and Dumaguete – a nine-hour trip. It's about four hours, again by Ceres Liner, between San Carlos and Bacolod. Jeepneys run to Mambucal, Ma-ao, Silay and Victorias.

Getting Around

A PU-Cab from the airport to the centre shouldn't cost more than P30 or you can stop a passing jeepney, as they all go to the city plaza. Banago Wharf is about seven km north, say P7 by jeepney or P40 by PU-Cab. The Northern bus terminal is a P2 trip on a jeepney labelled 'Libertad' or 'Shopping'.

AROUND BACOLOD

Sugar Plantations

Old steam locomotives used on the sugar cane fields, until recently, can be seen at the **MSC** (Ma-ao Sugar Central). Ma-ao is an hour by jeepney from Bacolod. The **Hawaiian-Philippine Sugar Company** in Silay has a 180-km rail network and some excellent steam engines. Silay is only half an hour from Bacolod.

Guided tours of the **Vicmico** (Victorias Milling Company) plant are operated daily from the porter's lodge. Again, there are some fine old steam locomotives but Victorias also has the St Joseph the Worker Chapel with its famous mural of the Angry Christ. Victorias is an hour by bus or jeepney from Bacolod and it's a further 15 minutes to the Vicmico sugar mill.

DUMAGUETE

Dumaguete is a very pleasant little town, centred around the large Silliman University campus. There's a small **anthropological museum** here and a cheap cafeteria. There are some passable beaches south of Dumaguete. **Silliman Beach**, close to the town, is not very good. **Camp Lookout**, 14 km west of the city, provides fine views over Dumaguete and across to Cebu and Bohol.

Places to Stay

Jo's Lodging (☎ 2160) on Silliman Ave is basic and has rooms with fan for P40/80. The fairly comfortable *Opena's Hotel* (☎ 3462) on Katada St has singles with fan at P150 and rooms with bath at P180/230 or P350/450 with air-con. The *O K Pensionne House* (☎ 2133, 2755) on Santa

Rosa St has simple but clean rooms with fan and bath for P180/ 230 and with air-con and bath for P350/450.

On Real St, the pleasant *Hotel El Oriente* (☎ 3486, 2539) starts at P250 and follows the same upward path to P520/840 for the better rooms with air-con and bathroom. The *Insular Flintlock Hotel* (☎ 3495, 4255) on Silliman Ave is a quite good place near the university with rooms from around P400 to P600.

The *Panorama Haus & Beach Resort* (☎ 2640) is an attractive large house at Cangmating Beach, Sibulan, about six km to the north. It has singles/doubles with fan and bath for P450.

Places to Eat

You can eat well and cheaply at *Opena's Restaurant* in Opena's Hotel, or at the *Rosante Restaurant* on Percides St. There's excellent food at the Chinese *Chin Loong Restaurant* on Rizal Blvd. *N's Pizza Plaza* on Percides St is a student hang-out with fruit juices, cakes and pizzas. The roof-garden restaurant *Aldea* on the corner of Percides and San Juan Sts is extremely pleasant and offers good Filipino and Chinese food.

Getting There & Away

Ceres Liner buses from Bacolod, via San Carlos, take nine hours and from San Carlos five hours. There are less frequent Bacolod to Dumaguete buses round the southern end of the island via Hinoba-an. This longer and rougher trip takes 12 hours.

MAMBUCAL

Mambucal, a pleasant resort town with hot springs, is just an hour from Bacolod. It takes three or four days to climb the **Kanlaon Volcano** from here. A local guide plus equipment (tent and cooker) will cost at least P2000.

You can stay in the simple *Pagoda Inn* for P70 or in the *Mambucal Health Resort* for even less. Mambucal is just a one-hour jeepney ride from Libertad St in Bacolod. The morning trip back can be much longer because of frequent stops.

SAN CARLOS

San Carlos, jumping-off point for Cebu, is nothing special but outriggers cross to nearby Sipaway Island for only a few pesos. It's a pleasant and quiet place with some good beaches but bring your own food and water.

Cheap places to stay include *Van's Lodging House* near the pier (P40/80) or the more expensive *Coco Grove Hotel* on Ylagan St (P150 to P750).

MALUAY (MALATAPAY) & ZAMBOANGUITA

Right at the southern end of the island, this is the best area near Dumaguete for beaches and snorkelling. You can charter a boat from here to get to popular offshore Apo Island. A day trip will cost about P300.

Two km beyond Zamboanguita, if coming from Dumaguete, is the friendly and well-maintained *Salawaki Beach Resort* with dorm beds for P150 and cottages with fan and bath for P300 and P500.

HINOBA-AN

Most visitors take the shorter route round the north coast of the island but you can also take the much longer and rougher southern route via Hinoba-an, site of a gold rush in 1982. The *Gloria Mata Lodging House* and *Mesajon Lodging House* are both simple and very cheap. Bacolod to Dumaguete, via Hinoba-an, takes about 12 hours.

Cebu

The most visited of the Visayan islands, Cebu is also the shipping hub of the Philippines. The number of shipping companies and agents in Cebu City and the number of ships at the dock is quite incredible. This is also the place where Magellan marked the beginning of Christianity in the Philippines with the erection of a cross and where he was killed in the battle of Mactan Island on 27 April 1521.

THE PHILIPPINES

Getting There & Away

Shipping company addresses in Cebu City include:

Aboitiz Lines
183 Osmeña Blvd (☎ 611157)
Carlos Gothong Lines
Quezon Blvd (☎ 72511, 211181)
Cokaliong Shipping Lines
46 Jakosalem St (☎ 212262)
George & Peter Lines
Jakosalem St (☎ 75914, 74098)
Sulpicio Lines
Reclamation Area (☎ 73839, 99723)
Trans-Asia Shipping Lines
Cuenco Ave (☎ 96909, 73101)
William Lines
Briones St (☎ 73619, 71233)

To/From Bohol There are several departures daily between Cebu City and Tagbilaran and Tubigon on Bohol. The crossing takes 2½ hours to Tubigon (P60) and four hours to Tagbilaran (P60 to P95 depending on class). PAL also flies from Cebu City to Tagbilaran. There is plenty of transport from Tagbilaran or Tubigon to the Chocolate Hills so there's no reason to prefer one route over the other.

To/From Camiguin The usual route is Cebu City to Cagayan de Oro or Butuan in Mindanao by air or ship, then a bus to Balingoan from where ferries run across to Benoni three times daily.

To/From Leyte A variety of ships operate between Cebu City and Baybay, Maasin, Ormoc, Tacloban and other ports on Leyte. There are flights with PAL between Cebu City and Tacloban.

To/From Luzon You can fly between Cebu City and Manila or Legaspi. Lots of ships operate between Cebu and Manila and the trip takes about 20 to 24 hours.

To/From Mindanao There are an enormous number of ships operating between Cebu and Mindanao. It takes 10 to 12 hours between Cebu City and Butuan, Cagayan de Oro, Dipolog, Iligan, Ozamiz or Surigao. Zamboanga is about 16 hours away and Davao about 24 hours. There is an equally wide variety of flights between Cebu City and major towns on Mindanao.

To/From Negros There are two departures daily (one on Sunday) between Toledo on Cebu and San Carlos on Negros; the trip takes two hours. There are connecting buses between San Carlos and Bacolod. Other less regular routes between these narrowly separated islands include Bato to Tampi, Talisay to San Jose and Liloan to Sibuyan in the far south; from Guihulngan to Tangil in the centre; and from Cadiz via Bantayan Island to Hagnaya in the north. Ships also operate between Dumaguete and Cebu City.

To/From Other Places There are also connections between Cebu and Palawan, Panay, Samar and Siquijor.

Getting Around

Buses run from Cebu City's Southern bus terminal to Toledo and the other west-coast departure points from Cebu for the neighbouring island of Negros.

CEBU CITY

Cebu City is the capital and main city on the island of Cebu, and Colon St is claimed to be the oldest street in the Philippines. The city is currently undergoing considerable redevelopment and modernisation. It's an easy-going city with plenty of places to stay and eat.

Orientation & Information

Colon St is the main street in the town and where you will find most of the restaurants, department stores and travel agencies. The tourist office is next to the Fort San Pedro.

The Philippine National Bank, near Cebu City Hall, and Interbank, on Fuente Osmeña, are good places to change money.

If you are arriving or leaving by ship take great care with your valuables – pickpockets are notorious around the Cebu City dock area and it's easy to lose things in the crush. They also work the Colon St and Osmeña Blvd area, particularly in the late afternoon and evening.

Fort San Pedro

This is the oldest Spanish fort in the country. It was originally built in 1565 by Legaspi to keep out the marauding pirates with whom the Spanish were having more than a little trouble. Today, it is gradually being restored and the main entrance is very impressive. Entry is P7.50.

Magellan's Cross

A small circular building, opposite the town hall, houses a cross which is said to contain fragments of the actual cross brought here by Magellan and used in the first conversions.

Basilica Minore del Santo Niño

Opposite the Magellan kiosk is the only basilica in the Far East. The *Santo Niño*, an image of Jesus as a child, was said to have been given to Queen Juana by Magellan on the queen's baptism in 1521. It's the oldest religious relic in the country.

Other

There's an interesting **small museum** in the University of San Carlos. Overlooking the town, in the ritzy Beverley Hills residential area, is a gaudy **Taoist temple**. To get to the temple take a Lahug jeepney and ask to stop at Beverley Hills – you've then got a 1½-km walk uphill. Alternatively, take a taxi for about P30.

Colon St in Cebu is said to be the oldest street in the Philippines but you'd never know it. The interesting **Carbon Market** sells produce and handicrafts, and is south of Magellanes St. In the downtown Parian district, the **Casa Gorordo Museum** is a restored and period-furnished home dating from the turn of the century.

Places to Stay

At 61 Osmeña Blvd, about halfway from Fuenta Osmeña (the airport bus stops here) to the city centre, the *YMCA* (☎ 21 4057) has good dormitory accommodation at P10, rooms with fan for P150/300 and with air-con and bath for P240/480. Couples are accepted and there's a charge for short-term membership. Opposite the YMCA at 24 K Uytengsu Rd (off Osmeña Blvd) is the clean, quiet *Jovel Pension House* (☎ 21 5242) with singles/doubles for P245/300 with fan or P375/425 with air-con.

The *Ruftan Pensione* (☎ 79138) in Legaspi St, is much closer to the centre. It's a good, clean place and has simple rooms with fan at P180 and with fan and bath for P250/350. The *McSherry Pension House* (☎ 52749, 96772) in Pelaez St has rooms with fan and bath for P210/280 and with air-con and bath for P320/430. It's a pleasant central place in a quiet lane off Pelaez St, next to the Hotel de Mercedes.

The *Elicon House* (☎ 21 0367; fax 73507), on the corner of P del Rosario and General Junquera Sts, has fan rooms for P120/190, and with air-con and bath from P260 to P390. It's a good, clean place and the Elicon Café is right downstairs.

The peaceful *Mayflower Pension House* (☎ 72948) on East Capitol Site has rooms with fan for P135/185, with fan and bath for P215/265 and with air-con and bath from P275 to P455.

The *Kukuk's Nest Pension House* (☎ 31 2310) at 157 Gorordo Ave is a pleasant house with clean, cosily furnished rooms with fan for P300/350 and with fan and bath for P450, including breakfast.

At the better quality places in Cebu City, it's worth asking if they've got rooms without air-con, if you're looking for cheaper accommodation. They'll always try to steer you towards air-con first of all.

Places to Eat

There are lots of places to eat at in Cebu City, many of them along Colon St – you can, of course, eat much more cheaply off this beaten track. The *Snow Sheen Restaurant* is near the corner of Osmeña Blvd and Colon St and has very good and low-priced Chinese and Filipino food. There is another *Snow Sheen* around the corner in Colon St. *Pete's Kitchen,* on Pelaez St, also has keenly priced Chinese and Filipino food. Nearby is *Pete's*

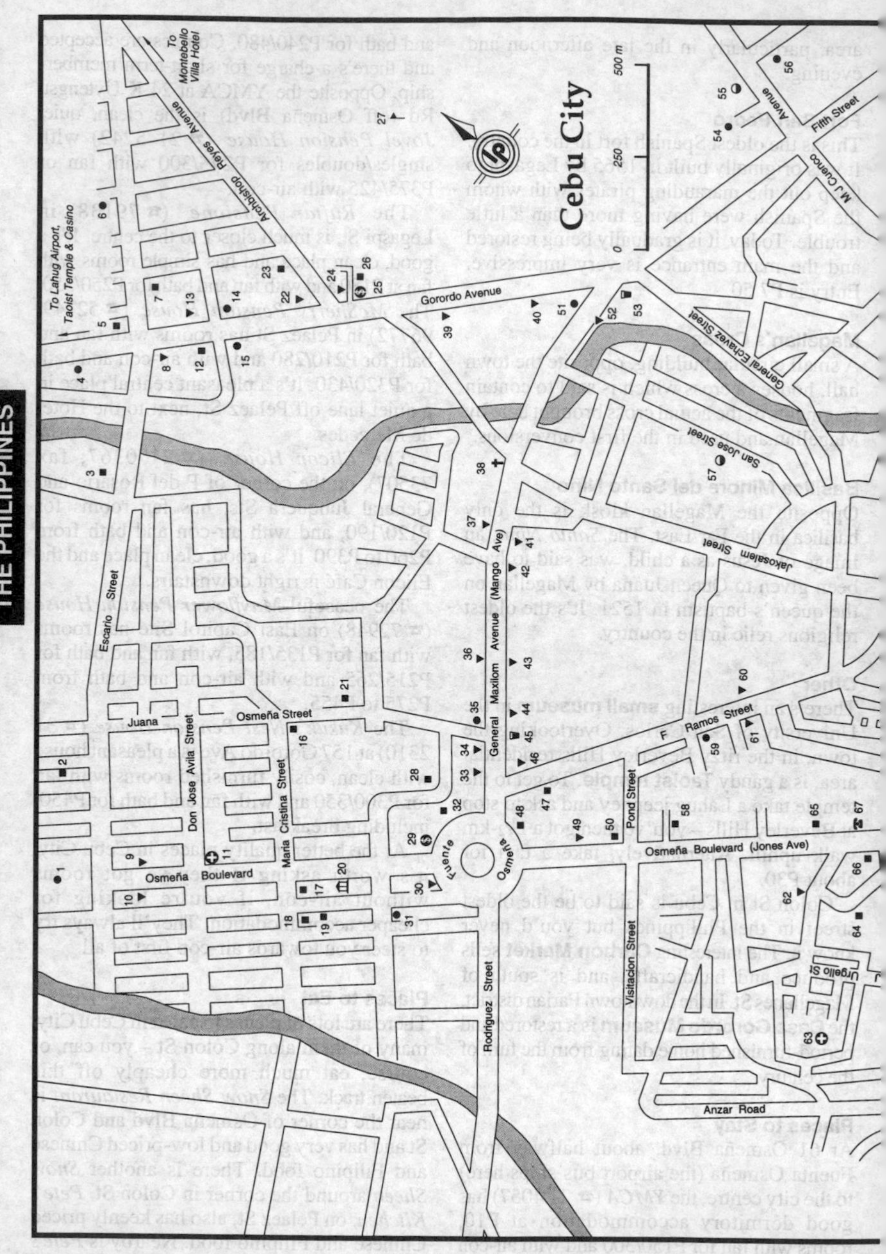
Cebu City
0
250
500 m
To Lahug Airport, Taoist Temple & Casino
To Montebello Villa Hotel
Archbishop Reyes Avenue
Gorordo Avenue
Escario Street
Juana
Osmeña Street
Don Jose Avila Street
Osmeña Boulevard
Maria Cristina Street
General Maxilom Avenue (Mango Ave)
Fuente Osmeña
Rodriguez Street
Visitacion Street
Pond Street
F Ramos Street
Osmeña Boulevard (Jones Ave)
Jakosalem Street
San Jose Street
General Echavez Street
M J Cuenco Avenue
Fifth Street
Urgello St
Anzar Road

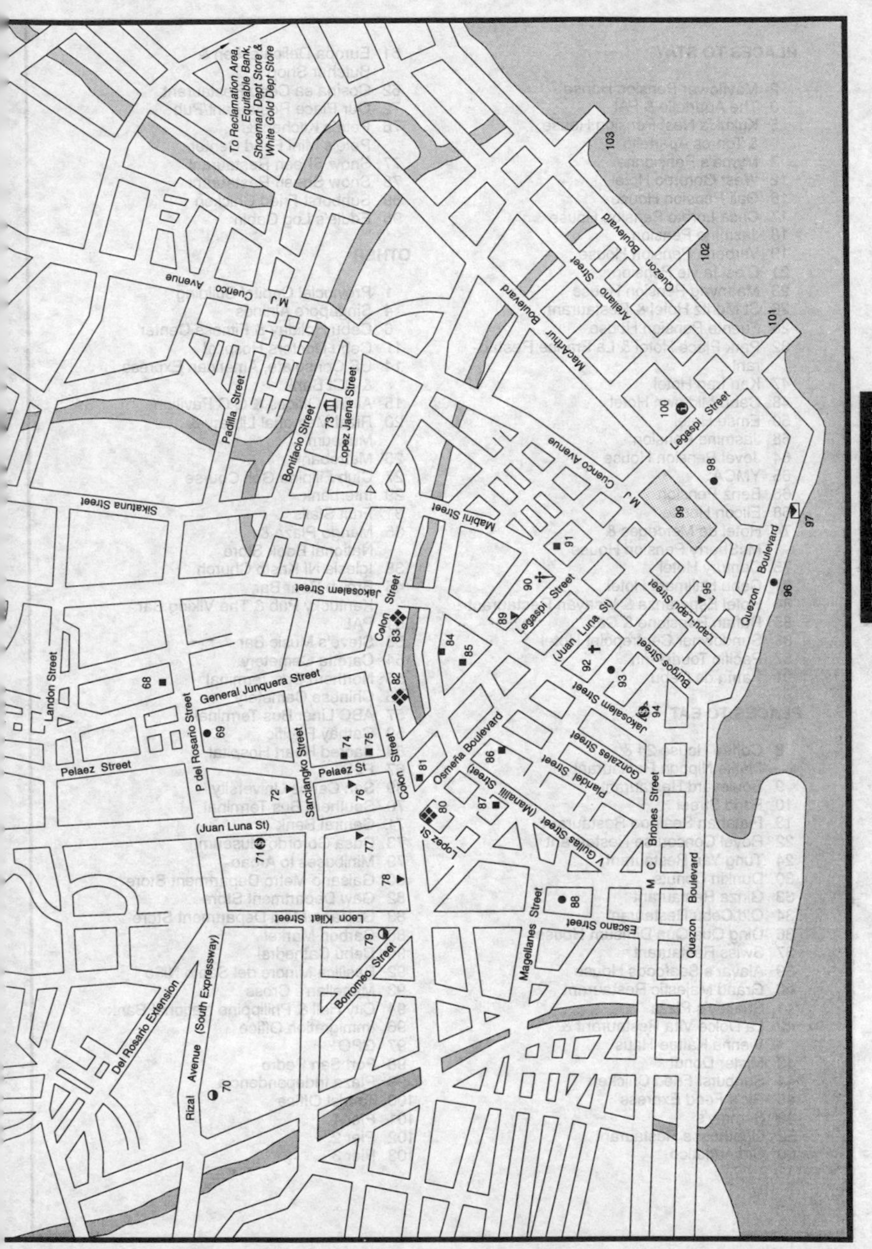
To Reclamation Area, Equitable Bank, Shoemart Dept Store & White Gold Dept Store
M J Cuenco Avenue
Padilla Street
Bonifacio Street
Lopez Jaena Street
Sikatuna Street
Jakosalem Street
Colon Street
Landon Street
General Junquera Street
P del Rosario Street
Pelaez Street
Sanciangko Street
Pelaez St
(Juan Luna St)
Leon Kilat Street
Borromeo Street
Rizal Avenue (South Expressway)
Del Rosario Extension
Lopez St
Osmeña Boulevard
V Gullas Street
(Manalili Street)
Mabini Street
MacArthur Boulevard
Arellano Street
Quezon Boulevard
M J Cuenco Avenue
Legaspi Street
Legaspi Street
(Juan Luna St)
Lapu-Lapu Street
Burgos Street
Jakosalem Street
Gonzales Street
Plaridel Street
M C Briones Street
Magallanes Street
Escaño Street
Quezon Boulevard
Quezon Boulevard
68
69
70
71
72
73
74
75
76
77
78
79
80
81
82
83
84
85
86
87
88
89
90
91
92
93
94
95
96
97
98
99
100
101
102
103

PLACES TO STAY

2 Mayflower Pension House
3 The Apartelle & PAL
5 Kukuk's Nest Pension House, & Tonros Apartelle
7 Myrna's Pensionne
12 West Gorordo Hotel
16 Gali Pension House
17 Casa Loreto Pension House
18 Jasmine Pension
19 Verbena Pension House
21 C'est la vie Pension
23 Maanyag Pension House
26 St Moritz Hotel & Restaurant
28 Fuente Pension House
32 Park Place Hotel & La France Restaurant
47 Kan Irag Hotel
48 Cebu Midtown Hotel
50 Emsu Hotel
58 Jasmine Pension
64 Jovel Pension House
65 YMCA
66 Benz Pension
68 Elicon House
74 Hotel de Mercedes & McSherry Pension House
75 Century Hotel
81 Cebu Hallmark Hotel
84 Hotel Esperanza & Visayan Restaurant
85 Ruftan Pensione & Caf
86 Sundowner Centrepoint Hotel
87 Pacific Tourist Inn
91 Patria de Cebu

PLACES TO EAT

8 Coffee House 24 & Maiko Nippon Restaurant
9 Boulevard Restaurant
10 Food Street
13 Pistahan Seafood Restaurant
22 Royal Concourse Restaurant
24 Tung Yan Restaurant
30 Dunkin Donuts
33 Ginza Restaurant
34 Old Cebu Restaurant
36 Ding Qua Qua Dimsum House
37 Swiss Restaurant
39 Alavar's Seafoods House
40 Grand Majestic Restaurant
41 Shakey's Pizza
42 La Dolce Vita Restaurant & Vienna Kaffee-Haus
43 Mister Donut
44 Sunburst Fried Chicken
46 Ric's Food Express
49 Sammy's
52 Lighthouse Restaurant
60 Caf Adriatico
61 Europa Delicatessen & Butcher Shop
62 Cosina sa Cebu Restaurant
72 Our Place Restaurant/Pub
76 Pete's Kitchen & Pete's Mini Food Center
77 Snow Sheen Restaurant
78 Snow Sheen Restaurant
89 Sunburst Fried Chicken
95 Eddie's Log Cabin

OTHER

1 Provincial Capitol Building
4 Singapore Airlines
6 Cebu Holiday & Fitness Center
11 Cebu Doctors Hospital
14 US Consulate, American Express & PCI Bank
15 Airline Offices & Q C Pavilion
20 Rizal Memorial Library & Museum
25 Metrobank
27 Club Filipino Golf Course
29 Interbank
31 Fruit Stalls
35 Mango Plaza & National Book Store
38 Iglesia Ni Kristo Church
45 Brown Bear Bar, Kentucky Pub & The Viking Bar
51 PAL
53 Steve's Music Bar
54 Caretta Cemetery
55 Northern Bus Terminal
56 Chinese Cemetery
57 ABC Liner Bus Terminal
59 Cathay Pacific
63 Sacred Heart Hospital
67 PLDT
69 San Carlos University
70 Southern Bus Terminal
71 Central Bank
73 Casa Gorordo Museum
79 Minibuses to Argao
80 Gaisano Metro Department Store
82 Gaw Department Store
83 Gaisano Main Department Store
88 Carbon Market
90 Cebu Cathedral
92 Basilica Minore del Santo Ni$o
93 Magellan's Cross
94 City Hall & Philippine National Bank
96 Immigration Office
97 GPO
98 Fort San Pedro
99 Plaza Independencia
100 Tourist Office
101 Pier 1
102 Pier 2
103 Pier 3

Mini Food Center, a big, partly open-air restaurant.

The *Visayan Restaurant* in V Gullas St is notable for its excellent, inexpensive food, big portions and friendly service. The *Ruftan Café* on Legaspi St is good for breakfast, as is the cheap *YMCA Restaurant* on Osmeña Blvd.

General Maxilom Ave (it used to be called Mango Ave) has lots of places to eat including a *Shakey's Pizza*, the *Lighthouse* for Filipino food and the *Swiss Restaurant* with excellent European food.

The *Royal Concourse* on Gorordo Ave is a big, very clean self-service restaurant with inexpensive Filipino and Japanese dishes. For fresh seafood, try the *Pistahan Seafood Restaurant* on this same street.

Entertainment

Cebu City is nearly as active as Manila when it comes to entertainment. Try *Our Place* in Pealez St for cheap beer and good food, or have a drink in the friendly *Kentucky Pub* in General Maxilom Ave. There are plenty of discos, nightclubs and go-go joints or there's the *Casino Filipino*, in Lahug, if you really feel like throwing money around.

Getting There & Away

Cebu is the major travel hub in the southern islands of the Philippines with flights and shipping services radiating out in all directions. There are frequent flights and ships between Manila and Cebu City, in particular.

There are several buses daily from the Southern bus terminal for the 1½-hour trip from Cebu City to Toledo on the other coast. You also find buses at the Southern bus terminal for Santander and Moalboal, other departure points for Negros. If you want to travel to northern Cebu (eg Hagnaya for Bantayan Island or Maya for Malapascua Island), Cebu City's Northern bus terminal is the place to get on the bus.

Getting Around

To/From the Airport There's a shuttle bus to the city which costs P30. They stop at the Park Place Hotel at Fuente Osmeña. Alternatively, you can take a taxi for about P100 to P150 or take a tricycle from near the terminal to the Mactan Bridge (P10) and a jeepney into the city (P4.50) from there.

Local Transport Jeepneys around Cebu City cost P1.50. There are also lots of taxis, which cost P10 (air-con taxis cost P16) for the first 500 metres, thereafter P1 for every further 200 metres. The Southern bus terminal is on Rizal Ave and the Northern bus terminal is on Cuenco Ave. The boat piers are not far from the centre.

AROUND CEBU

Mactan Island

The island where Magellan met Lapu-Lapu (and lost) is now the site for Cebu's airport and is joined to Cebu by a bridge. On the island there is a monument to Lapu-Lapu. This is also the place where guitars, one of the big industries in Cebu, are manufactured. Magellan also rates a monument. Around the island there are now a number of fine, expensive beach resorts.

On the road from Lapu-Lapu to Marigongon, therefore not directly on the beach, the *Hawaiian Village Inn* has cottages with fan and bath for P400.

Bantayan Island

Off the north-west coast of Cebu, on the south coast of Bantayan Island, there are some good beaches. The island can also be used as a stepping stone to Negros.

Places to Stay The *Santa Fe Beach Club* in Talisay, just north of Santa Fe, has cottages with fan and bath for P300 and nice rooms with air-con and bath for P900. Just south of Santa Fe is the *Kota Beach Resort* with cottages with fan and bath for P500 while the *Saint Josef Lodge* and the *Admiral Lodging House* are cheaper places in Bantayan.

Getting There & Away Buses run from Cebu City's Northern bus terminal to San Remigio and Hagnaya, taking about three hours. There are boats twice daily from Hagnaya to

THE PHILIPPINES

Santa Fe, taking two hours. A daily boat connects Bantayan with Cadiz on Negros.

Malapascua Island

Beautiful little Malapascua Island is about eight km north-east of Cebu and 25 km west of Leyte. The blindingly white Bounty Beach on the west coast is a gorgeous bathing beach, and the coral reefs offshore in crystal-clear water offer loads of variety for snorkelling.

At *Cocobaba Beach Resort* cottages with bath cost P500, and in the off season from May to November they cost P300. You can sleep in a tent for P200.

Getting There & Away Buses leave from Cebu City's Northern bus terminal for Maya early in the morning, taking 3½ hours. Outrigger boats leave Maya for Malapascua between 10.30 and 11.30 am. There is a boat connection between Maya and San Isidro on Leyte.

Toledo

Toledo is the jumping-off point for boats to San Carlos on Negros Island. It is about 1½ hours by bus from Cebu City.

Places to Stay If you have to stay here inquire about the *Lodging House* at the *Vizcayno Restaurant*.

Moalboal

There's good, reasonably priced scuba diving at **Pescador Island**, near Moalboal, and a number of beach resorts near the town along Panagsama Beach.

Places to Stay & Eat You can stay in town but it's better to rent a cottage on the beach for P80 to P400 depending on the facilities. Try *Pacita's Nipa Hut, Eve's Kiosk, Norma's Travellers Resthouse, Pacifico's Cottages* and Cora's Palm Court. They are all at the lower end of the price scale.

The beach discos can be very loud, so try for a place as far from them as possible if you want some peace and quiet. There's good food at most of these places, or slightly more expensive, but delicious, dishes at *Hannah's Place*.

Getting There & Away Numerous buses make the daily 90-km, two-hour trip from Cebu City for about P30. A friendly bus driver may even take you right down to the beach, so it's worth asking. Otherwise take a tricycle from Moalboal for about P20.

Transport between Moalboal and Toledo is tricky and may require several changes.

Buses run regularly to San Sebastian, at the southern end of the island, from where ships make the short crossing to Negros.

Bohol

It's a short ferry trip from Cebu City to the island of Bohol. Its 'Chocolate Hills' are strangely rounded and look rather like chocolate drops when the vegetation turns brown in the dry season. They are about 60 km from Tagbilaran, the main town. Bohol is an easy-going, quiet sort of place with some fine beaches, relatively untouched forests and interesting old churches.

Getting There & Away

Most people get to Bohol via Cebu. There are PAL flights daily from Cebu City to Tagbilaran plus a couple of daily ferries to Tagbilaran (three to four hours), a number of daily ferries to Tubigon (three hours) and a couple to Talibon (four hours).

PAL has daily flights from Manila to Tagbilaran. There are a couple of ships weekly to Leyte, a weekly ship to Manila and a number of services to ports in Mindanao and Negros.

TAGBILARAN

There's not much in Tagbilaran, the capital and main port, but you can make worthwhile day trips from the city. The old **Punta Cruz pirate watchtower** is 15 km north near Maribojoc. **Loon**, a few km north-west of Maribojoc, has a beautiful old church dating from 1753. **Antequera**, about 10 km north-east of Maribojoc, has a Sunday market where basketware is sold.

At **Bool**, three km east of Tagbilaran, there's a monument recalling the blood compact between Legaspi and Rajah Sikatuna. **Baclayon**, four km east of Bool, is the oldest town in Bohol and has one of the oldest churches in the Philippines, dating from 1595. Boats go from there to nearby Pamilacan Island.

Loay has an old church. Outrigger boats go up the Loboc River. The large **San Pedro Church** in Loboc dates from 1602 and there is a remarkable naive painting on its ceiling.

Places to Stay

On Lesage St, the *Vista Lodge* (☎ 3072) is fairly good with rooms from P75/95, with fan and bath for P100/120 and with air-con and bath for P250/275. The *Nisa Travellers Inn* (☎ 3731) on Carlos P Garcia Ave has rooms with fan at P120/150, with fan and bath at P150/180 or with air-con and bath at P300/450. The *Executive Inn* (☎ 3254) on J S Torralba St has simple rooms with fan for P80/100, with fan and bath for P130/240 and with air-con and bath for P290/390.

The *Charisma Lodge* (☎ 3094) on Carlos P Garcia Ave has passable, clean rooms with fan for P100/150, with fan and bath for P175/200 and with air-con and bath for P330/350. Also on Carlos P Garcia Ave, the *LTS Lodge* (☎ 3082, 3310) has good rooms with fan for P100/160 and with air-con and bath for P300/420.

The *Gie Garden Hotel* (☎ 2021, 3182) on M H del Pilar St has rooms with air-con and bath for P330/480. The *Hotel La Roca* (☎ 3179) is on Graham Ave, on the northern edge of town towards the airport, and has rooms with fan and bath for P250/380 and with air-con and bath for P460/600. There is a swimming pool as well. Near Hotel La Roca, the *Bohol Tropics Resort Club* (☎ 2134, 3510/14; fax 3019) is the best hotel in town. Rooms with TV, air-con and bath cost from P980 to P1450. They have a restaurant and a swimming pool.

Places to Eat

The restaurant at the *Gie Garden Hotel* has good and economically priced food as does the reasonable *JJ's Food Stream* on Carlos P Garcia Ave. The *Garden Café* is a pleasant place next to the church.

PANGLAO ISLAND

Two bridges connect Bohol to Panglao Island where there are now several beach resorts. **Alona Beach** is popular but the bathing, unfortunately, is spoilt a bit by the seagrass which is inhabited by sea urchins, so care is required. **Doljo Beach** is also good although the water is very shallow. **Hinagdanan Cave** at Bingag in the north-east of the island is interesting to look at, but resist the urge to swim in its cool but possibly diseased waters.

Places to Stay

Alonaville, operated by Tagbilaran's Executive Inn, has rooms for P100/150 and cottages with fan and bath for P250/300. *Playa Blanca* has cottages with fan and bath for P250/300. There's a restaurant and they will arrange excursions by boat and jeep. The *Samira Pyramid Resort* has rooms with fan for P200 and cottages with fan and bath for P350 and P400; the latter are spacious, two-storey cottages with a balcony. *Alona Tropical* has cottages with fan and bath for P250 as well as a very good, popular restaurant.

Alona Kew White Beach has rooms with fan for P250/300, cottages with fan and bath from P400 to P600 and a fine, big restaurant. They also arrange excursions. The *Bohol Divers Lodge* (☎ 61949; fax 21 6993) has cottages from P400 to P600.

Getting There & Away

JG Express buses go several times a day from Tagbilaran to the island, leaving on the corner of Noli Me Tangere and F Rocha Sts. Those marked 'Panglao' go right across the island to Panglao town near Doljo Beach. Those marked 'Panglao-Tauala' go along the southern coast and detour to Alona Beach. It takes 1½ hours to Panglao town or Alona

THE PHILIPPINES

Beach and costs about P10. By tricycle it costs P100 and takes an hour.

OTHER ISLANDS

There's some superb diving around Bohol. **Balicasag Island**, just 10 km south-west of Panglao Island, is surrounded by a coral reef. **Pamilacan** is a beautiful little island, 20 km south-east, but it gets very few visitors. **Cabilao Island**, 30 km north-west of Tagbilaran, has excellent diving and snorkelling.

CHOCOLATE HILLS

Legends relate that the Chocolate Hills are either the teardrops of a heartbroken giant or the debris from a battle between two giants, but the scientific explanations for these curious, similarly shaped hills are more mundane. Some scientists think the hills are the result of volcanic eruptions at the time when this area was submerged. Others think that this is nonsense, believing that the hills are the result of special weathering of a marine limestone formation over impermeable claystone.

The hills (there are more than 1000 of them) are around 30 metres high, and hiking in the area is best in the December to May dry season. At this time they are also most 'chocolate-like' since the vegetation has turned brown.

Places to Stay

The *Hostel Chocolate Hills* is right in amongst the hills, about 53 km from Tagbilaran. It's a km off the main road on the top of the highest hill. Dorm beds are P80 and double rooms with bath and balcony (beautiful view) are P200. There's also a restaurant and a swimming pool (which is unusable most of the time).

Getting There & Away

Carmen, the town for the Chocolate Hills, is 58 km from Tagbilaran. As you have to get out four km before Carmen, don't forget to tell the driver. It is about a 500-metre walk from the main road to the Chocolate Hills Complex. There are several St Jude Bus and Arples Line buses a day from Tagbilaran to Carmen. The trip takes two hours. It's about two hours by bus between the Chocolate Hills and Tubigon.

OTHER PLACES

Tubigon is a small town from where ships operate to and arrive from Cebu. **Talibon** also has shipping services to Cebu and is the jumping-off point for nearby Jao Island. From **Ubay**, on the east coast, boats run to Leyte.

Places to Stay

The *Cosare Lodging House* in Tubigon has simple but clean rooms with fan for P60/120. The *Lapyahan Lodge* in Talibon has rooms with fan and bath for P50/100. In Ubay, you can stay in the *Royal Orchid Pension House* where rooms with fan are P120/180.

Getting There & Away

From Tubigon, buses to Carmen take two hours, and to Tagbilaran, 1½ hours. Buses from Tagbilaran to Talibon take four hours and go via Carmen and the Chocolate Hills at the midpoint of the trip. Tagbilaran to Ubay buses also go via Carmen.

Leyte

As is the case with Samar, few Westerners get to Leyte, so you can expect to be stared at a lot. Although there are some outstanding national parks and an impressive mountain region there is little tourist development on Leyte. It's notable for being the island where MacArthur fulfilled his promise to return to the Philippines. Towards the end of WW II Allied forces landed here and started to push the Japanese out.

Getting There & Away

You can fly daily between Leyte and Cebu, from Tacloban to Cebu City, with PAL. Ships operate between Cebu City and a variety of ports around Leyte. It takes about six hours from Ormoc (daily), six hours from Hilongos (six days a week) or Maasin (four days a week). Outriggers take about four hours between Carmen on Cebu and Isabel on Leyte and operate daily. Another outrigger leaves Maya in northern Cebu for San Isidro daily, taking two hours.

There are also daily outriggers connecting Ubay on Bohol with Bato and Maasin. The trip takes about four hours to either port. To Mindanao, buses run from Tacloban to Liloan in the south of the island, from where a ferry takes you across to Lipata, 10 km north-west of Surigao, and from there buses continue to Cagayan de Oro or Davao. The ferry crossing takes three hours. There are also daily ships from Maasin to Surigao.

The San Juanico Bridge connects Leyte with neighbouring Samar. There are daily buses from Tacloban via Catbalogan and Calbayog in Samar and right on through Luzon to Manila, a 28-hour trip in total. PAL has daily flights between Tacloban and Manila.

Getting Around

Buses go hourly between Tacloban and Ormoc – the trip takes four to five hours. Ormoc to Baybay and Tacloban-Baybay-Maasin also have regular bus services.

TACLOBAN

The small port of Tacloban is the main city of Leyte and home town of the great shoe collector, Mrs Marcos. There are a variety of shops along Justice Romualdez St which sell local handicrafts. Seven km out of town, **Red Beach** (it isn't red, as that was just a WW II codename) is the exact place where Douglas MacArthur fulfilled his famous 'I shall return' pledge in October 1944. There's a memorial statue showing MacArthur wading ashore. Take a jeepney there but return by getting another jeepney in the same direction; it loops back via Palo.

For a short period Tacloban served as the capital of the Philippines until Manila was liberated from the Japanese.

Viewpoint

There are great views over the town and its busy port from the base of the Christ statue, reached from the market along Torres St.

Places to Stay

Tacloban offers a wide variety of places to stay. *San Juanico Travel Lodge* at 104 Justice Romualdez St has singles/doubles with fan at P80/100 or with fan and bath at P100/120. It gets mixed reports – 'clean and friendly' report some travellers, 'a dump' say others.

Manabó Lodge (☎ 3727) on Zamora St has fairly good rooms from P160/250. *Cecilia's Lodge* (☎ 2815) at 178 Paterno St is simple but reasonably good value from around P100 but more expensive with bathroom or air-con. *Leyte State College House* (☎ 3175) on Paterno St is also known as the LSC House, and it's pricier with rooms from around P180 to P320.

More expensive places include the *Tacloban Plaza Hotel* (☎ 2444) on Justice Romualdez St, the *Tacloban Village Inn* (☎ 2926) on Imelda Ave, and the *Manhattan Inn* (☎ 4170) on Rixal Ave. All three are good clean places with comfortable, similarly priced air-con rooms for P300 to P600.

Places to Eat

You can start the day at the *Good Morning Restaurant* with its adjoining bakery on Zamora St. *Sunburst Fried Chicken* on Burgos St has good chicken and Filipino dishes. The *Asiatic Restaurant* and the *Rovic House*, both on Zamora St, have good Chinese and Filipino food.

In Justice Romualdez St, *Mandawe Fast Food* serves inexpensive Filipino food, as does the clean and popular *Dahil Sa Iyo Fastfood* on the corner of Burgos and Real Sts.

ORMOC

Ormoc is just the jumping-off point for boats to Cebu. Near Ormoc is the start of the 50-km **Leyte Nature Trail**, which crosses right over the island from Lake Danao to Lake Mahagnao. Because of the chance of NPA guerilla activities in this area, the Tacloban Tourist Office at present advises against a stay in the Leyte National Park.

Places to Stay & Eat

The *Hotel Don Felipe* (☎ 2460; fax 2160) on Bonifacio St has rooms with fan and bath for

THE PHILIPPINES

P130/200. The more expensive rooms with air-con are the best you'll find in Ormoc. On the same street the *Pongos Hotel* (☎ 2211, 2482) has clean rooms with fan and bath for P150/280 and with air-con and bath for P250/360.

The *Don Felipe* has a good restaurant or try the *Magnolia Sizzler*, on the corner of Bonifacio and Lopez Jeana Sts.

OTHER PLACES

You can soak in the **Tungonan Hot Springs**, just north of Ormoc, but the area has been desecrated by a geothermal project.

Biliran Island can be reached by taking a bus from Tacloban to Naval. At Naval, you can stay at the *Rosevic Executive Lodge* on Vicentillo St. This area is undeveloped and has great snorkelling. A few km north of Almeria is the pleasant little *Agta Beach Resort*, located on a pretty bay, with basic rooms from P75/150 or with air-con and bath for P350.

THE PHILIPPINES

Samar

The large Visayan island of Samar acts as a stepping stone from Luzon to Leyte. There is a regular ferry service from Matnog, at the southern end of Luzon, to Allen and San Isidro at the northern end of Samar. From there, the Pan-Philippine Highway runs along the coast and a bridge connects Samar with Leyte.

This recently constructed road has made transport through Samar much easier but elsewhere the island is fairly undeveloped so finding transport can be hard going. Samar also experiences guerrilla activity so check the situation before venturing there. The northern part of Samar and the west coast are usually OK. The Sohoton National Park, near Basey in southern Samar, is the island's outstanding attraction.

Getting There & Away

There are a number of ferries daily between Matnog and Allen, and between Matnog and San Isidro. The crossing takes 1½ to two hours. Buses between Catbalogan and Tacloban, in Leyte, take two hours.

ALLEN

This is simply a port town for the ferry service to Luzon.

Several buses daily operate between Allen and Catbalogan via Calbayog, taking over three hours all the way.

CALBAYOG

Calbayog is just another 'through' town, although the road there from Allen runs along the coast almost the entire way. The views are especially fine around **Viriato**, between Allen and Calbayog. The **Blanca Aurora Falls** are about 50 km south-east of Calbayog. They're reached by riverboat to Buenavista (one hour) from near the village of Gandara. Check first to find out if the NPA is active in the area.

Places to Stay

At the *Calbayog Hotel* basic rooms with fan are P60/120 and there's a restaurant. The *San Joaquin Inn* (☎ 387) on the corner of Nijaga and Orquin Sts costs P90/180 for rooms with fan and P140/280 with fan and bath.

The best hotel in Calbayog is the *Seaside Drive Inn* (☎ 234), in Rawis, with rooms at P80/160, with fan and bath for P200 or with air-con and bath for P350.

Getting There & Away

There are a couple of daily Philippine Eagle buses and several jeepneys between Catarman and Calbayog, via Allen. Several buses a day go from Catbalogan to Calbayog (two hours). There are some slower jeepneys.

CATBALOGAN

There are beaches around Catbalogan, but it's really just a stepping stone to Tacloban on Leyte. Buses go across to the east coast from here.

Places to Stay & Eat

Hotel Saint Bartholomew on San Bartolome St has simple but fairly good rooms with fan for P100/190, with fan and bath for P150/260 and with air-con and bath for P350.

The *Fortune Hotel* (☎ 680) on Del Rosario St has rooms with fan for P100/160, with fan and bath for P220 and with air-con and bath for P350. On the same street, *Tony's Hotel* has rooms with fan for P100/180 and with air-con for P180/250.

You can get good meals in the *Fortune Restaurant* in the hotel of the same name. *Tony's Kitchen* is another cheap restaurant where you can eat well.

Getting There & Away

Several buses and jeepneys run daily from Catarman to Catbalogan, via Allen and Calbayog. Going to Catbalogan, the trip takes five hours from Catarman, four hours from Allen and two hours from Calbayog.

Camiguin

Located off the north coast of Mindanao, this is an idyllic, small, get-away-from-it-all sort of place. The tiny island actually has seven volcanos, best known of which is Hibok-Hibok which last erupted in 1951. The beaches are nothing special, but the people are great.

Getting There & Away

There may be occasional ships from other islands, but the usual route is from Balingoan in Mindanao to Benoni on Camiguin. A ferry crosses three or more times daily and the trip takes an hour or more.

If you leave Cebu City in the evening you can reach Cagayan de Oro on Mindanao in 10 hours, make the 1½-hour bus trip to Balingoan and then ferry across to Camiguin, arriving by mid-afternoon.

From Cagayan de Oro, you can also take a boat leaving at 7 or 8 am for Guinsiliban on the southern tip of Camiguin, taking three hours.

Getting Around

The 65-km circuit of the island takes about three hours actual travelling time. While it is possible to travel around the island on jeepneys and tricycles, there are not many vehicles between Yumbing and Catarman. You are more independent of public transport with a hired motorbike. Many resorts will arrange motorbikes on request for P250 or P300 a day.

MAMBAJAO

Mambajao is the capital and main town of Camiguin. Here you'll find tourist information in the Provincial Capitol Building and a bank where you can change travellers' cheques.

Places to Stay

The *Tia's Pension House*, near the Town Hall, has rooms with fan for P100/150. There are also *Tia's Beach Cottages,* just a few minutes from the centre in Tapon, with cottages with bath for P250.

Just about one km north-west from the town proper, right on the seafront, at Bolok-Bolok, there is the *Tree House* with rooms with bath for P150/200 and tree houses for P250.

Between Kuguita and Bug-ong there are several beach bungalows.

AROUND THE ISLAND

Starting from Mambajao, and travelling anti-clockwise, at **Kuguita** there's a beach and some coral where you can snorkel. The *Turtles Nest Beach Cottages* costs P225/300 with bath. Another four km takes you to **Agoho** where the *Caves Resort* is a beautiful place near the beach with rooms from P100 to P350. The food here is also good value. Some other possibilities are the *Camiguin Seaside Lodge* and the *Morning Glory Cottages*, both with dorm beds, rooms and cottages. In Bug-ong, the pleasant *Jasmine by the Sea* has cottages with bath for P250 and P350.

Continuing beyond Yumbing, **Bonbon** has some interesting church ruins and a cemetery which is submerged in the sea. Near

Catarman, a track leads to the **Tuwasan Falls**. Down at the southern end of the island, there's a 300-year-old **Moro watchtower** at Guinsiliban.

Benoni is near the artificial Tanguine Lagoon where the peaceful *Travel Lodge Lagoon* has rooms with fan and bath for P300 and with air-con and bath for P450. The rather run-down *Mychellin Beach Resort* is opposite Mantigue (Magsaysay) Island in Mahinog and has rooms for P150.

Hibok-Hibok Volcano

The 1320-metre Hibok-Hibok volcano can be climbed in the dry season – inquire at the tourist department in the Provincial Capitol Building, Mambajao. A guide is useful as the weather on the mountain is changeable and you can easily get lost. The volcano erupted disastrously in 1951 and it's now monitored from the Comvol station. You can have a look around, and this is also a good place to stay on the way up or down.

Katibawasan Waterfall

The waterfall, with good swimming, is three km from Pandan, which in turn is only two km from Mambajao. Near here is the Ardent Hot Spring, a favourite for weekend outings with a beautifully designed swimming pool.

White Island

Three km off Agoho, this small island is just a sand bar. There is no shade but there is good swimming and snorkelling. Count on P200 to rent a boat for the round trip but arrange a definite time to be picked up.

Mindanao

The island of Mindanao, second largest in the country, is the Philippines' biggest trouble spot. Mindanao has a large Muslim population and they have long chafed at Christian rule. Armed at one time by Libya's fervent (and oil-rich) Gaddafi, the Mindanao guerrilla force (the Moro National Liberation Front or MNLF) has staged a long-running battle with the government forces. It is wise to inquire carefully and think twice before travelling through troubled areas.

Mindanao certainly isn't a new trouble spot. This was the one area of the Philippines where the Muslim religion had gained a toehold by the time the Spanish arrived, and throughout the Spanish era, the situation varied from outright rebellion to uneasy truce.

Things to Buy

In Mindanao, *Badjao* sea gypsies bob up and down in their outriggers beside the Lantaka Hotel in Zamboanga. They sell shells, coral and ship models. The Rocan shell shop is worth a look if you like shells. In Davao, once you've checked out the brassware, jewellery and handicrafts, devote your time to sampling the amazing variety of fruits – durians are the Davao speciality. Cagayan de Oro and Marawi are centres for Muslim arts and crafts.

Getting There & Away

You can fly to Mindanao from Cebu City or Manila. There are flights to a number of major cities in Mindanao including Zamboanga, Davao, Cagayan de Oro and Surigao. There are several ships weekly from Cebu City to various Mindanao ports and also from Leyte, Negros and Panay. From Manila there are a couple of ships each week to Zamboanga, taking about 32 hours.

There are also regular weekly ships to neighbouring Bohol while Leyte is connected by the Liloan to Lipata (10 km north-west of Surigao) ferry service with through buses to and from Tacloban. Balingoan on Mindanao is the departure point for visits to Camiguin Island.

Getting Around

It is wise to be careful when travelling by bus in Mindanao – guerrilla shoot-ups do occur and bus travel is none too safe in any case. The tourist office will advise you on which routes are safe and which ones to forget.

From Zamboanga, there are buses to Pagadian and Dipolog. From Pagadian, you can continue to Iligan from where another bus ride will take you to Cagayan de Oro. Buses continue from Cagayan de Oro to Surigao from where you cross to Leyte. If you're feeling adventurous, you can head south from Iligan to Marawi. Davao can be reached from Cagayan de Oro or Surigao. There are also shipping services around the coast.

SURIGAO

There are a number of beautiful small islands around Surigao, which is located on the north-eastern tip of Mindanao. They can be reached from General Luna on the island of Siargao. The five to six-hour trip out to the island from Surigao passes through beautiful scenery with many small islands. You can stay in Dapa but the smaller town of General Luna, on the south-east coast of Siargao Island, is where foreigners usually head for.

Places to Stay

The *Flourish Lodge* on Borromeo St, Port Area, has simple but reasonably good rooms for P60/100. At 306 San Nicolas St, the *Dexters Pension* has basic but clean rooms with fan for P50 to P150 and with air-con and bath for P250/300. On the same street, the *Garcia Hotel* (☎ 658) is a good place with a variety of rooms from P60/120. Back on Borromeo St, the *Tavern Hotel* (☎ 293) starts at P60/90 for the simplest fan-cooled rooms and goes up to around P600 for an air-con double with bath. It's a pleasant place with a seaside restaurant.

Places to Eat

The *Tavern Hotel* has a pleasant open-air restaurant. The *Cherry Blossom Restaurant*, on the corner of San Nicolas and Vasques Sts, is worth trying for good food and live music.

Getting There & Away

It's about six hours to Cagayan de Oro by bus and eight hours to Davao.

From Surigao, you can travel by bus, taking the ferry across to Leyte, and on through Leyte, Samar and right through Luzon to Manila.

Getting Around

A tricycle between the airport and town is about P10. Most boats use the wharf south of town but the ferries to and from Leyte operate from the Lipata wharf, about 10 km north-west. A regular tricycle trip should be less than P5 per person (P50 for a 'special ride') but there are also buses.

BUTUAN

Butuan is just a junction town two hours south of Surigao by bus. It's thought that this might be the oldest settlement in the Philippines.

Places to Stay

Near the bus terminal on Langihan Rd, the *A&Z Lowcost Lodging House I* is very cheap with rooms from P30/60, more with fan. There's another *A&Z (No II)* on the corner of Burgos and San Francisco Sts.

The simple and straightforward *Elite Hotel* (☎ 3133), on the corner of San Jose and Concepcion Sts, costs from P60/80 with prices stepping up as you add fan, air-con or a bathroom. The *Imperial Hotel* (☎ 2199) on San Francisco St has rooms from P85, again with more expensive rooms with fan and bath or air-con and bath.

The pricier *Embassy Hotel* (☎ 3737) on Montilla Blvd has clean and good air-con rooms with bath for P300/400. The service is friendly, and they have a good restaurant.

Getting There & Away

Butuan is about two hours by bus from Surigao with onward connections to Davao (six hours), Cagayan de Oro (three hours plus) and Iligan.

BALINGOAN

Situated midway between Butuan and Cagayan de Oro, this is the port for ferries to nearby Camiguin Island. You can stay in *Ligaya's Restaurant & Cold Spot* for just P40/80 or there's a similar place opposite.

THE PHILIPPINES

CAGAYAN DE ORO

On the north coast, Cagayan de Oro is an industrial town and the centre of the Philippines' pineapple industry. The **Xavier University Folk Museum** (Museo de Oro) is worth a visit but, otherwise, there's not much to see here.

Places to Stay

The *Mabini Lodge* (☎ 3539), at 113 Mabini St on the corner of Velez St, has clean and fairly good rooms from P150 to P300 and has a restaurant. The *Parkview Lodge* (☎ 5869) is located in a quiet area next to the Golden Friendship Park. Rooms cost P110/140 with fan, P185 with fan and bath, and P290 with air-con and bath.

The *Nature's Pensionne* (☎ 723718; fax 726033) on T Chavez St is more expensive with clean rooms with air-con and bath from P460 to P790.

Places to Eat

You can get big, cheap meals at the *Bagong Lipunan Restaurant* on Don A Velez St. About 100 metres south of there you will find the *Persimmon Fastfoods & Bakeshoppe*, an inexpensive self-service restaurant with good, standard Filipino dishes. The *Singkil Restaurant & Coffee Shop* in the VIP Hotel is pretty good value and is open 24 hours. A little further north is the air-con *Caprice Steak House* and the small *Salt & Pepper Restaurant* which has cheap beer. Cagayan de Oro has plenty of discos and bars.

Getting There & Away

There are almost hourly buses to Butuan via Balingoan, taking three hours plus. Davao is eight to 10 hours away and Iligan only an hour. Zamboanga is a 16-hour bus trip; buses depart when full.

Getting Around

The airport is 10 km from town and P50 by PU-Cab if you bargain hard. The main bus terminal is on the edge of town beside the Agora Market and jeepneys run between there and the town centre. Look out for a Divisoria jeepney from the station or a Gusa Cugman jeepney from the town. The wharf is five km out. Beware of pickpockets on local transport.

ILIGAN

Iligan is a major industrial city but there is not much of interest here apart from the **Maria Cristina Falls**, nine km from the city. Iligan is the jumping-off point for visits to Marawi and the Lake Lanao area, 33 km south. This is a centre of guerrilla activity so make inquiries first before setting out.

The **Aga Khan Museum** in Marawi is noted for its exhibits of the Mindanao Muslim culture. You can find some local handicrafts here too.

Places to Stay

The *Iligan Star Inn* (☎ 20601) on Quezon Ave has basic rooms from P140/175 – those facing the road are noisy. *MC Tourist Inn* (☎ 5194) is on Tibanga Highway on Baslayan Creek, some distance out from the centre. Rooms start at P150.

The *Maria Cristina Hotel* (☎ 20645), on the corner of Aguinaldo and Mabini Sts, is the best central hotel with air-con rooms from P500/650.

At Marawi you can stay in the comfortable and pleasantly furnished *Marawi Resort Hotel*. Cottages with bath are P350/450.

Places to Eat

Iligan has a surprising variety of restaurants, but they tend to close early. The *Canton Restaurant* does Chinese food, while mid-price range places with Filipino dishes include the *Iceberg Café & Restaurant* and the *Bahayan Restaurant*. The *Bar-B-Q Inn*, on the plaza, is good for an evening meal, or try the clean and friendly *Enrico's* next to the PAL office.

Getting There & Away

Iligan is only about an hour from Cagayan de Oro and there are jeepneys and minibuses as well as regular buses. Buses to Zamboanga usually start in Cagayan de Oro and come via

Iligan. Jeepneys and shared taxis operate between Iligan and Marawi.

DIPOLOG & DAPITAN

Close to the city of Dipolog, Dapitan is the site of Jose Rizal's period of exile from 1892 to 1896. The city waterworks and a grass-covered relief map of Mindanao, in the town square, were made by Rizal. A few km away from the city is the place he stayed in, which has a dam he built to create a swimming pool. Other attractions include a fruit-bat roosting place and some good swimming and diving areas.

Places to Stay

Ranillo's Pension House (☎ 3030) on Bonifacio St in Dipolog has quite good rooms with fan for P80/100, more with bathroom or air-con. On Magsaysay St, the *Ramos Hotel* (☎ 3299) costs from P120/240 for the simplest rooms with fan.

More expensive places include the *CL Inn* (☎ 3491) on Rizal Ave, which has comfortable rooms with air-con and bath from P300/450. The *Village Hotel* (☎ 56154) at Sicayab, about three km outside of Dipolog towards Dapitan, has clean rooms of various sizes with fan and bath for P200 and with air-con and bath for P400.

Getting There & Away

PAL fly between Dipolog and Zamboanga. Buses take about 13 hours via Pagadian where you may have to change buses.

ZAMBOANGA

The most visited city in Mindanao is Zamboanga, which acts as the gateway to the Sulu Archipelago.

Information

The tourist office is in the Lantaka Hotel, east of the town centre towards Fort Pilar and Rio Hondo.

Fort Pilar & Rio Hondo

Fort Pilar is an old Spanish fort on the waterfront south of the city. Some restoration is going on and there's now a **Marine Life Museum**. From the fort battlements, you get a good view to Rio Hondo, the Muslim village on stilts a little further down the coast.

Markets & Shops

The colourful **Fish Market** at the docks is busy in the late afternoon. In the alleys of the public markets next door there are lots of little shops – flea-market style.

Parks

The **Pasonanca Park** is a large park in the hills, a little beyond the airport – the main attraction here is the famous tree house. Nearby is **Climaco Freedom Park**, named after a murdered mayor of Zamboanga.

Islands

Ten minutes across the bay by *banca* (outrigger) is the island of **Santa Cruz**, with good swimming, snorkelling and a beautiful beach. It costs around P200 to rent a boat for the round trip. You can rent snorkelling equipment at the waterfront Lantaka Hotel. The island of **Basilan**, about a two-hour boat ride away, is the centre for the colourful Yakan tribespeople.

Places to Stay

The *Unique Hotel* (☎ 3598), on Corcuera St near the wharf, is straightforward and quite noisy, with rooms from P75. The *Atilano's Pension House* (☎ 4225) on Mayor Climaco Ave is a comfortable place with big rooms from P100 to P250. The food is good, too.

The *New Pasonanca Hotel* (☎ 4579), on the corner of Almonte and Tomas Claudio Sts, has clean but small rooms from P190 with fan and bathroom. The *Mag-V Royal Hotel* (☎ 4614), on the corner of San Jose Rd and Don Basilio Navarro St, is a bit out of town but it's clean, well kept and the rooms are spacious, although not all of them have windows. Prices vary from around P100 to P350.

The centrally located and well-kept *Hotel Paradise* (☎ 2936) on R Reyes St has air-con rooms with bathroom for P360/450. *Paradise Pensionhouse* (☎ 3005/8) is similarly

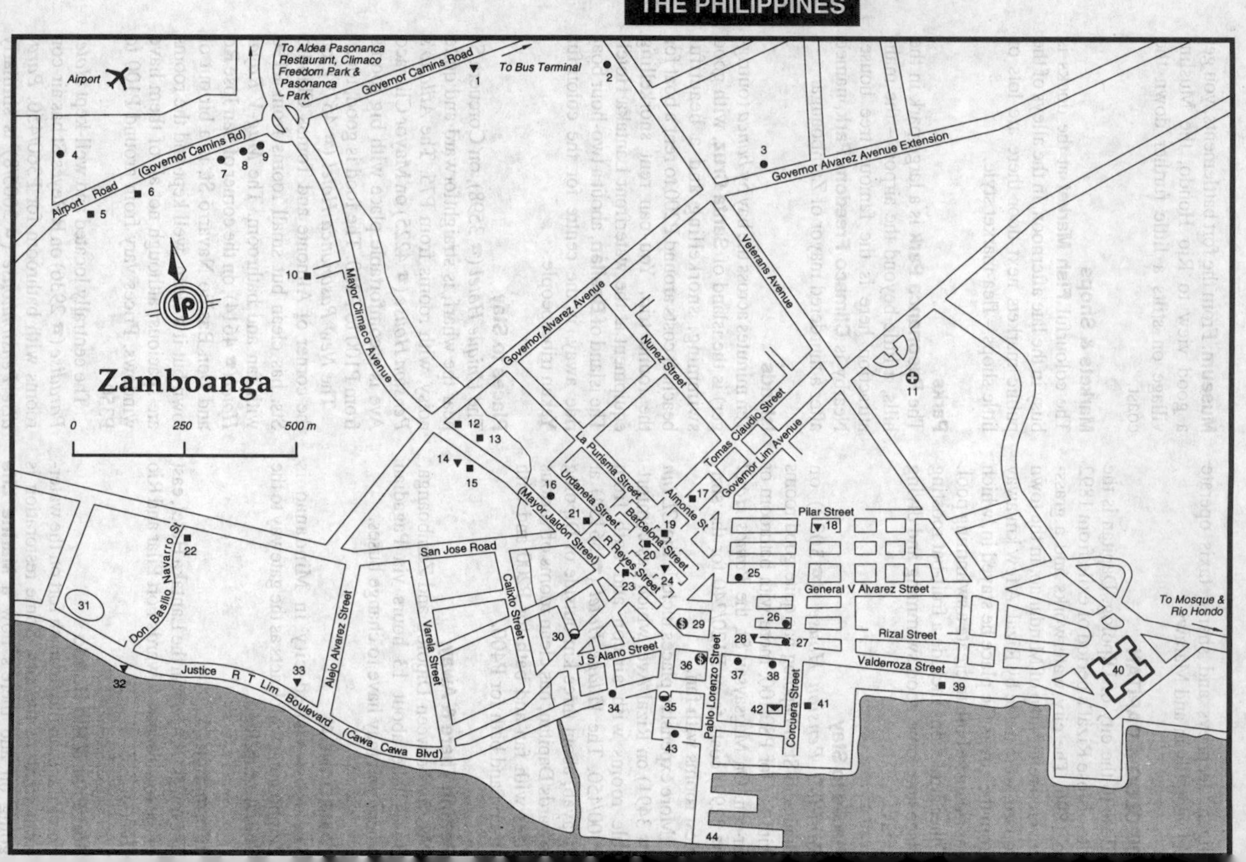
Zamboanga
0
250
500 m
Airport
Airport Road
Governor Camins Road
(Governor Camins Rd)
To Aldea Pasonanca Restaurant, Climaco Freedom Park & Pasonanca Park
To Bus Terminal
Governor Alvarez Avenue Extension
Veterans Avenue
Nunez Street
Governor Alvarez Avenue
Mayor Climaco Avenue
Tomas Claudio Street
Governor Lim Avenue
La Purisima Street
Almonte St
Pilar Street
General V Alvarez Street
Rizal Street
Valderroza Street
Corcuera Street
Pablo Lorenzo Street
Barcelona Street
Urdaneta Street
R Reyes Street
(Mayor Jaldon Street)
J S Alano Street
Calixto Street
San Jose Road
Varela Street
Alejo Alvarez Street
Justice R T Lim Boulevard
(Cawa Cawa Blvd)
Don Basilio Navarro St
To Mosque & Rio Hondo
1
2
3
4
5
6
7
8
9
10
11
12
13
14
15
16
17
18
19
20
21
22
23
24
25
26
27
28
29
30
31
32
33
34
35
36
37
38
39
40
41
42
43
44

›riced and is also centrally located on the :orner of Barcelona and Tomas Claudio Sts. The *New Astoria Hotel* (☎ 2075/7) on Mayor Climaco Ave has reasonable rooms with fan ınd bath for P280 and with air-con for ?380/470.

Places to Eat

There are lots of places to eat around the :entre of Zamboanga. Right next to the George & Peter Lines office on Valderroza St is the cheap *Flavorite Restaurant* and, nearby, there's the *Sunflower Luncheonette*.

The *Food Paradise* on Tomas Claudio St is a popular meeting spot with a fast-food outlet on the ground floor and a Chinese restaurant upstairs. The *Café Blanca*, on the ground floor of the Platinum 21 Pension House on Barcelona St, is open day and night and offers good food at reasonable prices.

The *Abalone Restaurant*, beside the New Astoria Hotel, has good seafood while *Alavar's House of Seafoods* is also good but somewhat more expensive.

The *Lantaka's* pleasant waterfront Talisay Bar is a good place for a beer; a reasonably priced buffet dinner is served and it's also a good spot for breakfast.

Entertainment

The best nightspots are found outside the city. Some on Governor Camins Rd kick on to late in the night. Good cheerful places for a beer include *Lutong Pinoy*, *Village Zamboanga*, *Latin Quarter* and *Love City Disco*, all near the airport.

Getting There & Away

PAL flights connect Zamboanga with other towns in Mindanao and further afield in the Philippines. There are also numerous shipping services to and from Zamboanga. There are several buses daily to Cagayan de Oro, taking about 15 hours. To Iligan is 13 hours and to Dipolog is 15 hours.

Getting Around

Although the airport is only two km from the city you will probably have to pay P20 for a tricycle. Jeepneys should only cost P1.50 and there are lots of them to places around Zamboanga. A taxi to or from the airport might demand P60.

DAVAO

This cosmopolitan city on the south coast of Mindanao has the second fastest growth in

PLACES TO STAY

5 Garden Orchid Hotel & Village Zamboanga
6 Hotel Marcian Garden
10 Atilano's Pension House
12 Zamboanga Hermosa Hotel
13 Hotel Preciosa
15 New Astoria Hotel
17 New Pasonanca Hotel
19 Platinum 21 Pension House & Caf Blanca
20 Paradise Pensionhouse
21 Imperial Hotel
22 Mag-V Royal Hotel
23 Hotel Paradise & Food Paradise
39 Lantaka Hotel & Tourist Office
41 Unique Hotel

PLACES TO EAT

1 Quostaw Restaurant
14 Abalone Restaurant
18 Sunburst Fried Chicken
24 Dunkin Donut & Shakey's Pizza
28 Sunflower Luncheonette
32 Boulevard Restaurant by the Sea
33 Alavar's House of Seafoods

OTHER

2 Santa Cruz Market
3 Alta Mall Building
4 Airlanes Disco & Lutong Pinoy
7 Love City Disco
8 Yagbulls Disco
9 Latin Quarter Disco
11 Zamboanga General Hospital
16 Fire Department
25 Sulpicio Lines
26 S K T Shipping Lines
27 Immigration Office & George & Peter Lines
29 Interbank
30 Buses to San Ramon
31 Athletic Field
34 Public Market
35 Jeepneys to Pasonanca Park & Taluksangay
36 Philippine National Bank
37 City Hall
38 Basilan Shipping Lines
40 Fort Pilar
42 Post Office
43 Fish Market
44 Wharf

population in the Philippines after Manila. Settlers have come here from all over the country and the population is approaching one million.

Orientation & Information

San Pedro St and Claro M Recto Ave are the two main streets of Davao. There is a tourist office (☎ 74861, 71534) in the Apo View Hotel on J Camus St.

Around Town

Davao has a large **Buddhist temple** with the 'Buddha with 1000 hands', a **Chinatown**, the **Shrine of the Holy Infant Jesus of Prague** and some pleasant parks. The city is renowned for its wide variety of tropical fruits – particularly the durian, for which there is even a durian monument! The fruit stalls are colourful and offer tasty treats; there are lots of them along Ponciono Reyes St.

Beaches

There are a variety of black beaches around the city, like **Talomo** (eight km south), **Santa Cruz** (41 km south) and **Digos** (59 km south), but probably the best one is the white **Paradise Island Beach** on Samal Island. **Samal Island** is only a short banca ride away (outriggers leave near Sasa Bridge shortly before Lanang towards the airport).

Mt Apo

The highest mountain in the Philippines overlooks Davao and can be climbed in four to five days. On your way to the top you'll pass waterfalls, hot springs, pools of boiling mud and you might even spot the rare Philippine eagle. No special equipment is needed for the climb. March to May are the driest (hence best) climbing months and the tourist office can offer advice and arrange guides.

Places to Stay

The *El Gusto Family Lodge* (☎ 73662) at 51 A Pichon St has rooms with fan from P100/180 up to around P390 for an air-con room with bath. *Le Mirage Family Lodge* (☎ 63811) on San Pedro St is a good place with very similar prices.

Men Seng Hotel (☎ 75185; fax 64994) on San Pedro St is basic. The rooms, which vary in standard and cleanliness, have big beds and cost from P175/240 or more with air con. *Trader's Inn* (☎ 73578; fax 64976) on Juan Dela Cruz St has singles with fan and bath for P200 and air-con rooms with bath for P280/380. The *Royale House* (☎ 73630) at 34 Claro M Recto Ave starts at P150/240 with fan and goes up to P320/460 for air-con doubles.

More expensive places include the *B S Inn* (☎ 2213980/89; fax 2210740) on the corner of Monteverde and Gempesaw Sts with clean rooms with air-con and bath from P450 to P585, and the *Hotel Maguindanao* (☎ 78401; fax 2212894) at 86 Claro M Recto Ave, opposite the cathedral. Rooms with TV, air-con and bath are P810 to P1190.

Places to Eat

Dencia's Kitchenette on Legaspi St, the *Shanghai Restaurant* on Magsaysay Ave and the *Men Seng Restaurant*, in the Men Seng Hotel on San Pedro St, all have good cheap Chinese food.

San Pedro St also has the *Kusina Dabaw* for Chinese and Filipino dishes and the *Merco Restaurant* where the ice cream is excellent. Try the *Sunburst Fried Chicken* on Anda St for fried chicken. On Florentino Torres St, the *Harana* and the *Sarung Banggi* are both good for barbecues while at the Muslim fishing village near Magsaysay Park anything that swims is likely to end up on the grill.

Davao's fruit stalls are famous and they are interesting places so don't forget to sample a durian if they're in season. PAL ban durians from their aircraft.

Getting There & Away

PAL fly from Cagayan de Oro, Zamboanga and further afield. There's at least one weekly ship between Zamboanga and Davao. Buses take about six hours from Butuan, 10 from Cagayan de Oro, four from

General Santos and more than eight from Surigao.

Getting Around

The airport is 12 km north-east of the centre, say P50 by taxi or P1 by a tricycle to the main road, from where you can get a jeepney for P2.50. To town, take the jeepney 'San Pedro'; from town to the airport junction, take the 'Sasa' jeepney.

GENERAL SANTOS (DADIANGAS)

There's not a great deal of interest in this city in the south-west of Mindanao. It's in a major fruit-producing area.

Places to Stay

The unpretentious *Concrete Lodge* (☎ 4876) on Pioneer Ave has rooms with fan and bath for P130/160. The *South Sea Lodge I* (☎ 5146) on Pioneer Ave is very similarly priced. There's also a *South Sea Lodge II* on Salazar St, on the corner of Magsaysay Ave.

The *Pioneer Hotel* (☎ 2422) on Pioneer Ave has rooms with fan and bath for P280/300 and with air-con and bath for P320/350. On P Acharon Blvd, the clean *Matutum Hotel* (☎ 4901) costs from P150/240 and has a good restaurant.

Getting There & Away

Buses take four hours to Davao or an hour to Koronadel (Marbel).

Sulu Archipelago

The string of islands that dribble from Zamboanga to Sabah in north Borneo are home for some of the most fervently Muslim people in the country. The Spanish and Americans never dominated them and even now things still aren't under total control.

Jolo is the main town and island, and the old walled city, with its gate and watchtowers, is worth seeing. The people of the archipelago are great seafarers – many, particularly the Badjao, or 'sea gypsies', live on houseboats or in houses built on stilts over the water. Smuggling and piracy occur in the area and some of the practitioners are reputed to be very well equipped and armed.

Palawan

Off to the west of the Visayas, Palawan is the long thin island stretching down to the Malaysian north Borneo state of Sabah. Things to do and see here are mainly natural – islands, scuba diving and caves with underground rivers and wildlife.

Getting There & Away

There are a variety of shipping services which ply a variety of routes between Manila and ports on Palawan. Alternatively, there are daily PAL flights between Manila and Puerto Princesa, plus services with Aerolift and Pacific Airways from Manila to other centres on the island. You can also reach Palawan from Cebu, Panay, Romblon and other islands.

Getting Around

Puerto Princesa, the capital, is roughly halfway down the island. Buses and jeepneys run up and down the island, as far as Brooke's Point (four to five hours' drive south) or to El Nido, Taytay and Port Barton to the north.

PUERTO PRINCESA

The remarkably clean capital of the island is a relatively small town with a population of about 100,000. It's simply a place to use as a base for excursions to elsewhere on the island. Palawan is popular for scuba diving and there are several diving outfits in town.

Information

There's an information counter at the airport, a City Tourist Office on Rizal Ave near the corner of Roxas St, and a Provincial Tourist Office in the Provincial Capitol Building, Rizal Ave, at the corner of Fernandez St.

THE PHILIPPINES

Places to Stay

The pleasant *Duchess Pension House* (☎ 2873) on Valencia St has clean fan-cooled rooms for P75/120 and more expensive doubles with bathrooms.

Abelardo's Pension (☎ 2049), 63 Manga St, has reasonably good rooms with fan for P100/150 or with fan and bath for P175. *Yayen's Pension* (☎ 2261) on Manalo St Extension is a pleasant place with a coffee shop and a garden. Rooms start at P75/120 and P175 with bathroom. The tastefully designed *Puerto Pension* on 35 Malvar St has rooms with fan for P135/165 and with fan and bath for P200.

Sonne Gasthaus, a quiet place at 366 Manalo St Extension, has clean rooms with fan at P170/200 and cottages with fan and bath at P280. On 263 Manalo St Extension, the *International Guest House* (☎ 2540) has good rooms with fan for P150/180.

More expensive places include the *Badjao Inn* (☎ 2761) on 350 Rizal Ave. It is a clean, well-kept place with comfortable rooms from P260 to P600. The *Casa Linda* (☎ 2006) on Trinidad Rd has rooms with fan and bath for P300/350 and with air-con and bath for P440/500. This is a pleasant place with a nice garden. It's in a quiet area, about 80 metres off Rizal Ave.

Places to Eat

There's a cosmopolitan selection of restaurants along Rizal Ave. Try the attractive *Café Puerto* for French food or the *Roadside Pizza Inn & Folkhouse* for Italian. The *Pink Lace* prepares everything from Filipino, Chinese, Indian and Mexican to Vietnamese! At the *Kamayan Folkhouse & Restaurant*, you can try Filipino dishes and you get the choice of sitting on the terrace or in a tree house.

Head to *Zum Kleinen Anker* for a cold beer and the charmingly rustic *Kalui Restaurant* for fresh seafood. At the entrance to the Vietnamese refugee camp, two km out of town behind the airport, the *Pho Dac Biet Restaurant* has cheap Vietnamese food and French-style bread.

The pleasant and busy *Swiss Bistro Valencia* in Valencia St has excellent steaks and European dishes, together with what must be the best music in town.

Entertainment

Café Nostalgia offers golden oldies while the *Kamayan Folkhouse & Restaurant* has folk singers. There are also several discos around town.

Getting Around

There are plenty of tricycles for getting around town and they will take you out to the airport for P15 to P20.

CENTRAL PALAWAN

There are various places within day-trip distance of Puerto Princesa, such as **Irawan** with its Irawan Crocodile Farming Institute and **Iwahig** with the Iwahig Penal Colony.

Sabang is famed for St Paul Subterranean National Park with its long **Underground River**. To get there, take a jeepney between 8 and 10 am from Puerto Princesa. From Sabang, you can either take a boat for P300 or walk to the mouth of the river – it takes about three hours. There are even a few cottages in Sabang where you can stay for P150.

There's good diving in **Honda Bay**, off Tagburos (Santa Lourdes Pier), only 10 km from Puerto Princesa. There are many small islands in the bay. White **Nagtabon Beach** lies on a beautiful calm bay on Palawan's west coast and is another interesting swimming spot.

SOUTH PALAWAN

At **Quezon**, halfway from Puerto Princesa to the southern end of the island, is the jumping-off point for the **Tabon Caves**. There's a small **National Museum** in Quezon and the caves have yielded some interesting stone-age finds. It takes three hours to reach Quezon and from there half an hour by boat to the caves. You can stay at the *New Bayside Lodging House* for P70 per person. *Tabon Village Resort* at Tabon Beach, about four km north-east of Quezon, has rooms at P90/110 and cottages with bath for P220/310.

Brooke's Point, further south, is the jumping-off point for **Ursula Island**, but the island's interest to bird-watchers has been drastically reduced by bird hunters.

NORTH PALAWAN

From **San Rafael**, you can visit the villages of the Bataks. You can stay at the peaceful *Duchess Beachside Cottages* for P150.

There's good diving off **Roxas**, three to four hours further north from San Rafael. On the opposite coast, **Port Barton** on Pagdanan Bay is something of a travellers' hang-out. There are a number of fine islands in the bay, some beautiful beaches and good snorkelling. You can stay at *Elsa's Place* in rooms (P100/150) or cottages with bath (P250/300) or at the similarly priced *Swissippini Cottages*. The *Paradiso Beach Resort* has dorm beds for P70. Rooms and cottages are also available.

Right up in the north-west of Palawan, there's more fine diving in the islands of the **Bacuit Archipelago**. El Nido, on the mainland, can be reached by road during the dry season when there are several jeepneys daily from Taytay and even one from Puerto Princesa. There is a wide choice of accommodation in El Nido and on offshore islands.

The northernmost part of Palawan consists of the **Calamian Group**, whose main islands are Busuanga, Culion and Coron. The improvements made to the travel links with other islands and towns, together with the expansion in overnight accommodation, have brought about a modest upsurge in tourism in this beautiful island world. There are several guesthouses in **Coron**, the main town on Busuanga.

Singapore

Singapore is a small island at the tip of the Malay Peninsula. It thrives on trade and, through a combination of hard work and efficient if at times repressive government, has become the most affluent country in Asia after Japan. It's a crossroads for travellers but also offers a wide variety of places to visit, things to buy and some of the best food in Asia.

Singapore, with its preoccupation with cleanliness and orderliness, can be a pleasant break from the more hectic travelling you find elsewhere in the region. But it's also tending to become more and more antiseptic and dull – just another big city with numerous huge hotels and air-conditioned shopping centres.

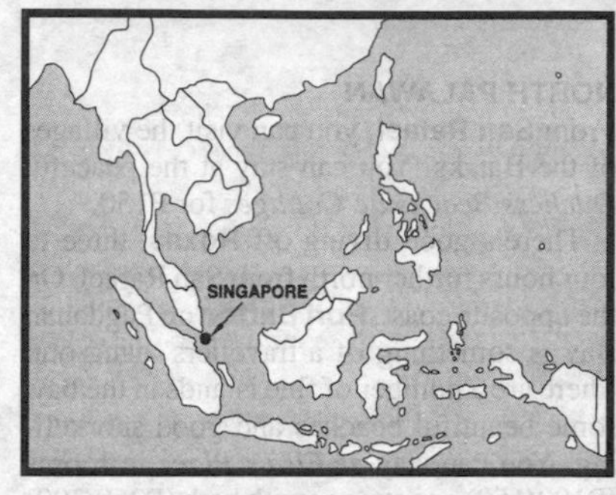

Facts about the Country

HISTORY

Singapore's improbable name, which means Lion City, came from a Sumatran prince who thought he saw a lion when he landed on the island – it was much more likely a tiger. Singapore would have drifted on as a quiet fishing village if Sir Stamford Raffles had not decided, in 1819, that it was just the port he needed. Under the British it became a great trading city and a military and naval base, but that didn't save it from the Japanese in 1942.

In 1959, Singapore became internally self-governing, in 1963 it joined Malaysia and, in 1965, this federation was in tatters and Singapore became independent. The reason behind this was a basic conflict of interest between 'Malaysia for the Malays' and Singapore's predominantly Chinese population. Under Prime Minister Lee Kuan Yew, Singapore made the best of its independence. Trade, tourism and industrialisation soon made up for the loss of British military bases.

Mr Lee's somewhat iron-fisted government also turned Singapore into a green, tidy garden city where no one dares to litter the streets, or even carelessly drop cigarette ash. The economy is dynamic, the water from the taps is drinkable, smoking in public places is forbidden, cars are heavily taxed and all drivers are discouraged from venturing into the city centre during rush hour.

Singapore's progressive attitudes have another side: criticism of the government is not a recommended activity, the press is tightly controlled and the minuscule elected opposition has always had a hard time. It has even been loudly mooted as to whether the country actually needs any opposition to the People's Action Party. Lee Kuan Yew finally stepped down from the leadership in 1990 and handed over the reigns to Goh Chok Tong, though Lee is still Special Minister and exerts a major influence.

Complaints about the Communist threat have a somewhat hollow ring in Singapore these days. One commentator noted that anybody planning a Marxist revolution would have to ensure they provided plenty of parking spaces for the downtrodden masses' BMWs, Mercedes and late-model Japanese cars.

GEOGRAPHY

The population squeezes itself into a low-lying 616-sq-km island at the tip of the Malay Peninsula, not much more than 100 km north of the equator. A km-long causeway connects Singapore with Johor Bahru in Malaysia.

CLIMATE

Singapore is hot and humid all year round as it is situated so close to the equator. It does get better at night, however, and the weather never seems to be quite as sticky as Bangkok, 1500 km to the north. November to January tend to be the wettest months, and May to July the driest, but the difference between these two periods is not dramatic and Singapore gets an abundance of rainfall in every month.

ECONOMY

The economy is based on trade, shipping, banking, tourism and light industry (often hi-tech). Shipbuilding and maintenance and oil refining are also important industries. Along with Hong Kong, Taiwan and South Korea, Singapore is one of East Asia's economically booming 'mini-dragons'.

POPULATION & PEOPLE

Singapore's polyglot population of 2.7 million is made up of 78% Chinese, 14% Malay, 7% Indian and the remaining 1% of any and every nationality you can imagine. Curiously, after years of promoting birth control, the government has decided they've been too successful and the joys of the three-child family are now extolled. Of course, it has a Singapore twist to it – there are extra incentives to having children if the parents have university degrees.

ARTS

In the liberalised environment under Goh Chok Tong, Singapore contemporary arts, especially literature and theatre, are starting to flourish, but the more traditional forms of music and dance can still be seen.

Chinese opera or *wayang* is a colourful mixture of dialogue, music, song and dance. The acting is heavy and stylized, and the music can be searing to Western ears, but a performance is well worthwhile if you should chance upon one. Street performances are held during important festivals such as Chinese New Year, Festival of the Hungry Ghosts or the Festival of the Nine Emperor Gods.

The Lion Dance is a spectacular, acrobatic dance accompanied by musicians who bash cymbals and drums to invoke the spirits. The intricate papier-mâché lion's head is worn by the lead performer while another dancer takes the part of the body. It is usually performed during Chinese festivals to gain the blessings of the gods.

CULTURE

Growing Westernisation and the pace of modern life has seen changes in the traditional customs in Singapore. While some traditional customs are given less importance or have been streamlined, the strength of traditional religious values and the practice of time-honoured ways remain.

For the Chinese, the moment of birth is strictly recorded as it is essential for astrological consultations that are important in later life. Funerals are traditional, colourful and expensive affairs. Paper houses, cars, television sets and even paper servants are offered and burnt so that the deceased can enjoy all these material benefits in the next life. The importance of the grave and its upkeep remains and most Chinese will pay their respects to the elders on All Souls Day. The major Chinese celebration is Chinese New Year.

Islam provides the focus for Malays, but *adat* or customary law guides the important ceremonies and events in life such as birth, circumcision and marriage. Many aspects of adat exhibit Hindu and even pre-Hindu influences. The most important festival for Malays is Hari Raya Puasa, the end of the fasting month.

Most Singaporean Indians come from southern India and so the customs and festivals that are more important in the south, especially Madras, are the most popular in

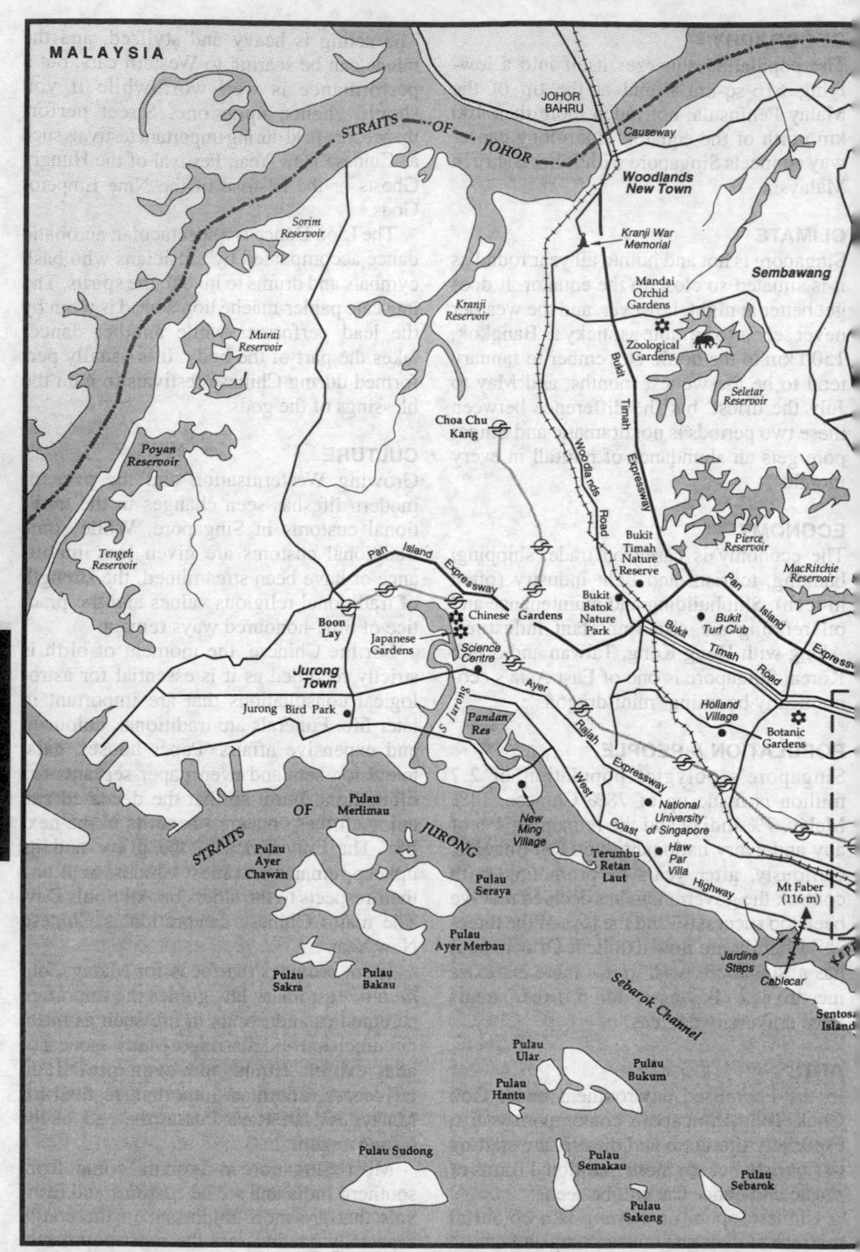
MALAYSIA
STRAITS OF JOHOR
JOHOR BAHRU
Causeway
Woodlands New Town
Kranji War Memorial
Sembawang
Sorim Reservoir
Kranji Reservoir
Murai Reservoir
Mandai Orchid Gardens
Zoological Gardens
Seletar Reservoir
Bukit Timah Expressway
Woodlands Road
Choa Chu Kang
Poyan Reservoir
Tengeh Reservoir
Pan Island Expressway
Bukit Timah Nature Reserve
Pierce Reservoir
MacRitchie Reservoir
Bukit Batok Nature Park
Boon Lay
Chinese Gardens
Japanese Gardens
Science Centre
Bukit Turf Club
Bukit Timah Road
Jurong Town
Ayer Rajah Expressway
S Jurong
Jurong Bird Park
Pandan Res
Holland Village
Botanic Gardens
West Coast Highway
New Ming Village
National University of Singapore
Pulau Merlimau
STRAITS OF JURONG
Pulau Ayer Chawan
Terumbu Retan Laut
Haw Par Villa
Pulau Seraya
Mt Faber (116 m)
Pulau Ayer Merbau
Jardine Steps
Cablecar
Pulau Sakra
Pulau Bakau
Sebarok Channel
Sentosa Island
Pulau Ular
Pulau Bukum
Pulau Hantu
Pulau Sudong
Pulau Semakau
Pulau Sebarok
Pulau Sakeng

SINGAPORE

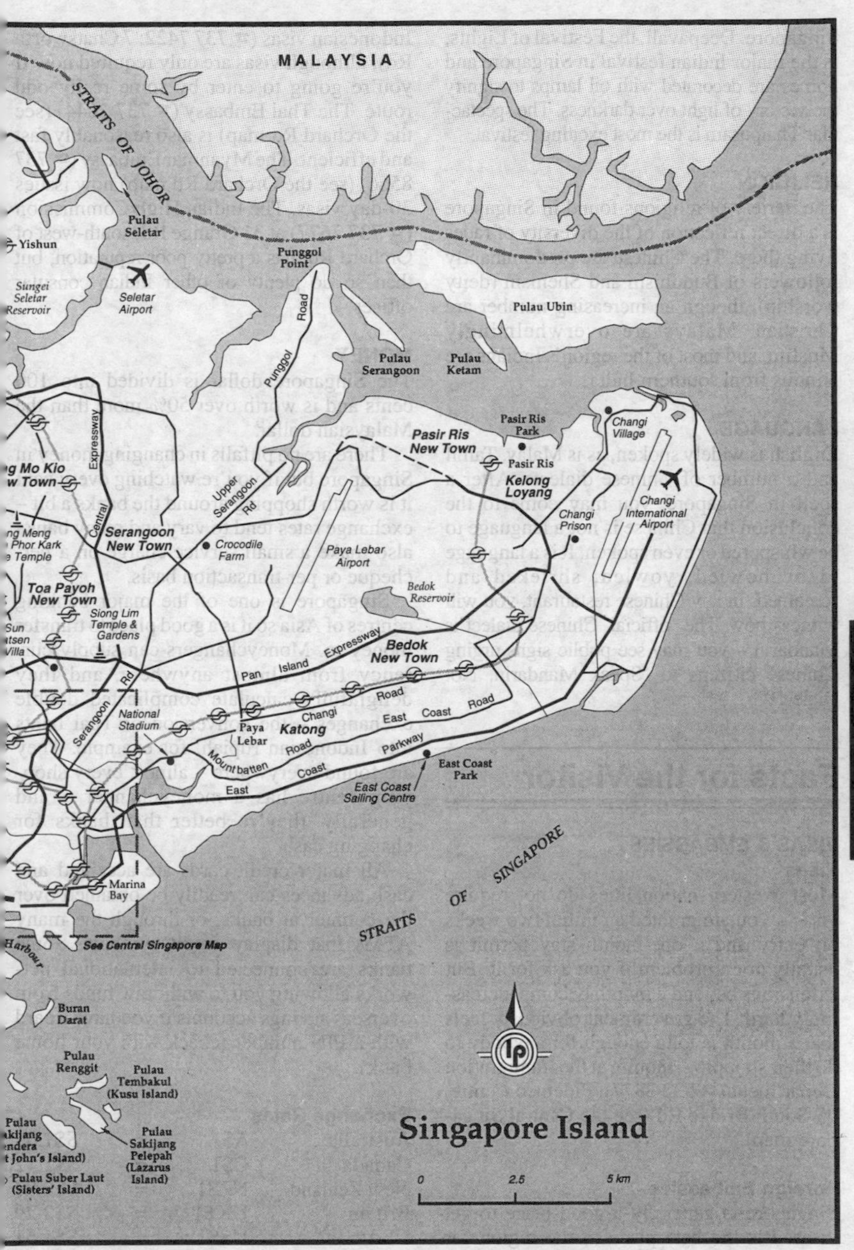
MALAYSIA
STRAITS OF JOHOR
Pulau Seletar
Yishun
Sungei Seletar Reservoir
Seletar Airport
Punggol Point
Punggol Road
Pulau Ubin
Pulau Serangoon
Pulau Ketam
Pasir Ris Park
Changi Village
Pasir Ris New Town
Pasir Ris
Kelong Loyang
Changi Prison
Changi International Airport
Central Expressway
Upper Serangoon Rd
Serangoon New Town
Crocodile Farm
Paya Lebar Airport
Bedok Reservoir
Toa Payoh New Town
Siong Lim Temple & Gardens
Pan Island Expressway
Bedok New Town
Serangoon Rd
National Stadium
Paya Lebar
Changi Road
East Coast Road
Katong
Mountbatten Road
East Coast Parkway
East Coast Park
East Coast Sailing Centre
Marina Bay
Harbour
See Central Singapore Map
STRAITS OF SINGAPORE
Buran Darat
Pulau Renggit
Pulau Tembakul (Kusu Island)
Pulau Sakijang Pelepah (Lazarus Island)
Pulau Suber Laut (Sisters' Island)
Singapore Island
0
2.5
5 km

SINGAPORE

Singapore. Deepavali, the Festival of Lights, is the major Indian festival in Singapore and homes are decorated with oil lamps to signify the victory of light over darkness. The spectacular Thaipusam is the most exciting festival.

RELIGION

The variety of religions found in Singapore is a direct reflection of the diversity of races living there. The Chinese are predominantly followers of Buddhism and Shenism (deity worship), though an increasing number are Christian. Malays are overwhelmingly Muslim, and most of the region's Indians are Hindus from southern India.

LANGUAGE

English is widely spoken, as is Malay, Tamil and a number of Chinese dialects. After a spell in Singapore, you may come to the conclusion that Chinese is not a language to be whispered or even spoken. It is a language to be howled, yowled, shrieked and screamed. In any Chinese restaurant, you will witness how. The 'official' Chinese dialect is Mandarin – you may see public signs urging Chinese citizens to 'Speak Mandarin, Not Dialect!'.

Facts for the Visitor

VISAS & EMBASSIES

Visas

Most Western nationalities do not require visas – you are granted an initial two weeks on entry and a one-month stay permit is usually not a problem if you ask for it. But extensions beyond a month become increasingly hard. The government obviously feels that a month is long enough for anybody to do their shopping. Inquire at the Immigration Department (☎ 532 2877), Pidemco Centre, 95 South Bridge Rd (see the Central Singapore map).

Foreign Embassies

Singapore is generally a good place to get visas. It's the best place in the region for Indonesian visas (☎ 737 7422; 7 Chatsworth Rd), although visas are only required now if you're going to enter by some really odd route. The Thai Embassy (☎ 737 2644) (see the Orchard Rd map) is also reasonably fast and efficient. The Myanmar Embassy (☎ 737 8566) (see the Orchard Rd map) now issues 30-day visas. The Indian High Commission (☎ 737 7677) at 31 Grange Rd, south-west of Orchard Rd, has a pretty poor reputation, but then so do plenty of other Indian consular offices.

MONEY

The Singapore dollar is divided into 100 cents and is worth over 50% more than the Malaysian dollar.

There are no pitfalls in changing money in Singapore but if you're watching every cent it is worth shopping around the banks a bit – exchange rates tend to vary and many banks also make a small service charge on a per-cheque or per-transaction basis.

Singapore is one of the major banking centres of Asia so it is a good place to transfer money to. Moneychangers can supply currency from almost anywhere, and they delightfully calculate complicated double exchanges – the conversion of Thai bahts into Indonesian rupiah, for example. They are found everywhere – almost every shopping centre has a moneychanger – and generally, they're better than banks for changing cash.

All major credit cards are accepted and cash advances can readily be obtained over the counter at banks, or through the many ATMs that display credit symbols. Some banks are connected to international networks allowing you to withdraw funds from overseas savings accounts if you have a card with a PIN number (check with your home bank).

Exchange Rates

Australia	A$1	=	S$1.09
Canada	C$1	=	S$1.12
New Zealand	NZ$1	=	S$0.90
Britain	UK£1	=	S$2.29
USA	US$1	=	S$1.51

Japan	¥100	=	S$1.48
Germany	DM1	=	S$0.93
France	FF1	=	S$0.27
Malaysia	M$1	=	S$0.59

Costs

Singapore is much more expensive than other South-East Asian countries, especially with the continuing strength of the Singapore dollar. The only cheap accommodation is the guesthouse dormitory, which will cost around US$4, but a private room starts at around US$15. Singapore has plenty of cheap dining possibilities, public transport is cheap and many attractions are free. It is possible to stay in Singapore for around US$15 per day, but be prepared to spend a lot more if you want to indulge in some of the luxuries you may have craved in less developed countries.

Taxes & Service Charge

A 10% service charge and a 4% government tax are added to the more expensive hotel and restaurant bills, but this is usually absorbed into the price in the cheaper places. Singapore is also introducing a 3% goods and services tax.

TOURIST OFFICES

There is a Tourist Information Centre upstairs in the Raffles Hotel shopping arcade, 02-34 Raffles Hotel Arcade (☎ 1-800-334 1335) in the colonial district. It is open daily from 9 am to 8 pm. The other office is in the Orchard Rd area at 02-02 Scotts Shopping Centre (☎ 738 3778) on Scotts Rd and is open from 9.30 am to 9.30 pm.

These offices gives out a variety of leaflets, brochures and useful information, much of which you can also pick up at the airport on arrival or at the big hotels. Pick up a copy of the excellent *Singapore Official Guide*, which is updated every month.

BUSINESS HOURS & HOLIDAYS

In Singapore, government offices are usually open from Monday to Friday and on Saturday morning. Hours vary, starting from around 7.30 to 9.30 am and closing between 4 and 6 pm (on Saturday, closing times are between 11.30 am and 1 pm). Shop hours are also variable, although Monday to Saturday from 9 am to 8 or 9 pm is a good rule of thumb.

The following days are public holidays. For those not based on the Western calendar, the months they are likely to fall in are given: New Year's Day (1 January), Chinese New Year (January or February), Hari Raya Puasa (February or March), Good Friday (April), Vesak Day (April or May), Labour Day (1 May), Hari Raya Haji (May or June), National Day (9 August), Deepavali (November), Christmas Day (25 December).

FESTIVALS

Singapore's polyglot population celebrates an amazing number of festivals and events. Most are also celebrated in Malaysia (see the Malaysia chapter for details) but Chinese New Year is the major festival, and even Chinese who profess no religion will clear out the old and bring in the new. The house is given a spring clean and all business affairs and debts brought up to date before the new year. It falls in late January or early February, goes on for a week and can be quite a hassle for travellers. It's more a stay-at-home holiday than one offering lots of attractions, and hotels will be packed out, taxis scarce, restaurants often closed and prices temporarily higher, including those of many of the cheaper Chinese hotels.

POST & TELECOMMUNICATIONS

The GPO is on Fullerton Rd, close to the Singapore River, and is open 24 hours for basic postal services. The GPO's efficient poste restante service is open from 8 am to 6 pm Monday to Friday and 8 am to 2 pm on Saturday. There are also 24-hour post offices at Changi Airport and in the Comcentre, 31 Exeter Rd, near the Somerset MRT station on Orchard Rd.

Singapore is a good place for international phone calls. There are several telecom centres, like the one in the GPO, and at 15 Hill St (in the colonial district) or 71 Robinson Rd (south-west of Marina Bay – see the Central Singapore map) where you can make calls charged by the actual time used, not in three-minute blocks. The phone centres also have Direct Home phone (press a country button for direct connection with your home country operator and then reverse the charges) and credit-card phones. International calls can also be dialled from public payphones but it's easier with a stored-value phonecard. They cost from S$2 and are available in phone centres and retail outlets.

BOOKS & MAPS

The Lonely Planet *Singapore City Guide* is a detailed and compact guidebook to the busy city-state and includes many colour maps.

Singapore has experienced something of a literary boom, especially after Goh Chok Tong's relaxation of censorship laws, and bookshops are packed with Singaporean titles. For a novel contrasting the differences between the modern and the traditional, the old and the young in modern Singapore, try Suchen Christine Lim's *Fistful of Colours*.

Singapore probably has the best bookshops in South-East Asia. The main MPH shop on Stamford Rd, in the colonial district, is excellent, but there are numerous other good bookshops around the city including other MPH branches, Times Bookshops and Kinokuniya Bookshops. Centrepoint shopping complex on Orchard Rd has branches of Times and MPH.

Excellent free maps are available at the airport, big hotels and some shopping centres.

HEALTH

Health worries are not so much of a problem in Singapore. It possesses the best medical facilities in the region and many people come here from neighbouring countries if they need medical attention. If you need to renew vaccinations, try the Vaccination Centre (☎ 222 7711), Block 1, Level 5, 226 Outram Rd, on the corner of Chin Swee Rd (a half km west of Pearl's Centre – see the Central Singapore map). It is open from 8 am to 1 pm and from 2 to 4.30 pm weekdays, and on Saturday from 8 am to 12.30 pm. It is closed on Sunday and public holidays.

Many of the shopping centres have a floor dedicated to medical services. Try the 3rd floor of the Peace Centre on Selegie Rd in the colonial district. There are several doctor's surgeries here where you can get vaccinations, and the 3rd-floor pharmacy has antimalarials, cholera vaccine and gamma-globulin.

A visit to a doctor costs from S$20 to S$40. A consultation with a senior nurse costs S$30 at the Singapore General Hospital on Outram Rd, near Chinatown and the Outram Park MRT station.

ACCOMMODATION

Singapore's hotels run the full range from dormitories in travellers' guesthouses to five-star high-rises and old world luxury at the Raffles. See Places to Stay for a rundown on budget and mid-range accommodation, but if you want to splash out and stay in luxury, Singapore has scores of international standard hotels, and Orchard Rd has the biggest concentration. When competition hots up, the big hotels offer large discounts – if you arrive by air check out the latest rates at the airport.

THINGS TO BUY

Shopping is a big attraction in Singapore. There are plenty of bargains to be had although a few ground rules should be followed if you want to get your money's worth. First of all, don't buy anything unless you really want it and, secondly, don't buy anything unless you know the savings are worth the hassles of carting it back home.

There are lots of discount houses in the West whose prices for many items may be competitive with those of Singapore.

Prices & Bargaining

When buying you have to bargain (except in big department stores) and to do so with a measure of success you need some idea of the value of what you want. The prices in big department stores will provide a good guide.

After all, it's no feat to knock $160 down to $140 if a fixed-price place has it for $120 all along. Maintain a lack of interest when bargaining (there are plenty of other shops) but remember, when you've made an offer, you're committed.

Guarantees & Compatibility

Make sure a guarantee is an international one. It's no good having to bring something back to Singapore for repair. Check that electronic goods are compatible with your home country – voltages vary, and TVs and VCRs made for Japan and the USA operate on a different system to most other countries.

Where to Shop

Almost anywhere. Some good places include the People's Park Complex and the People's Park Centre, huge shopping centres in Chinatown where you'll find clothes, watches, electronic gear, cameras and so on. There are many ultramodern centres, particularly down Orchard Rd and its periphery. For modern consumer goods, the fixed-price shops at Changi airport offer surprisingly competitive rates compared to the shops in town.

For oddities, try Arab St (just south of the Sultan Mosque – see the Colonial District map), Serangoon Rd or Chinatown. For luxury goods, it's Orchard Rd again.

What to Buy

Almost anything – Levis or other brand-name jeans at reasonable prices, cameras and film (cheaper by the dozen, although Singapore is no longer a real bargain basement for film), tape recorders, prerecorded tapes, radios, typewriters, calculators, watches (expensive ones for India if you're planning to resell them) and even Persian carpets.

Chinese emporiums and some night markets have good money belts. All sorts of Chinese crafts can be found at emporiums. Sim Lim Square on Bencoolen St (see the Colonial District map) has inexpensive computer peripherals and software.

Getting There & Away

AIR

Singapore is a major travel hub and flights operate in and out of Changi airport at all hours. There are direct flights to all the capital cities in South-East Asia, and to regional centres such as Phuket and Hat Yai in Thailand, Cebu in the Philippines, and many destinations in Malaysia and Indonesia.

Singapore is a very good place to look for cheap airline tickets although Penang, Bangkok and Hong Kong are other equally competitive centres. Some typical rock-bottom discount fares being quoted in Singapore include South-East Asian destinations like Bangkok from S$180 one way. It is also possible to fly to Delhi for S$430 one way or S$860 return and Kathmandu for S$410 or S$740 return.

Long-running, reliable agents are Airpower Travel (☎ 294 5664), 26 Sultan Gate, near Arab St (see the Central Singapore map), and Airmaster Travel (☎ 338 3942), 46 Bencoolen St (see the Colonial District map). STA Travel (☎ 734 5681) in the Orchard Parade Hotel is also worth trying. Many others advertise in the classified columns of the *Straits Times*.

Fares vary according to when you want to fly and who you want to fly with. The cheapest fares are likely to be with the least loved airlines (various Eastern European ones, Bangladesh Biman etc), via inconvenient routes (you're forced to make stopovers on the way) at awkward times (they only fly every other Tuesday at 3 am).

Airport departure tax is S$15.

To/From Malaysia

Singapore International Airlines (SIA) and Malaysian Airlines System (MAS) have flights between Singapore and Kuala Lumpur (S$147, RM159), Kuantan (S$136, RM146), Langkawi (S$204, RM218), Penang (S$170, RM182), Kuching (S$193, RM205) and Kota Kinabalu (S$391,

SINGAPORE

RM418). Pelangi Air and Silk Air have flights to other destinations including Melaka, Ipoh, Tioman Island (S$99, RM132) and Pangkor Island (S$190, RM209).

There is no discounting on flights between Malaysia and Singapore, but note that it's much cheaper to fly from Malaysia to Singapore than Singapore to Malaysia – the Malaysian ringgit is worth around 50% less than the mighty Singapore dollar.

It's also much cheaper to fly to Malaysian destinations from Johor Bahru, just across the causeway from Singapore, than directly from Singapore. MAS operate a connecting bus service for S$10 from the Novotel Orchid, 214 Dunearn Rd (see the Central Singapore map), to the Johor Bahru airport.

To/From Indonesia

The most popular flight is from Singapore to Jakarta. Many airlines do this route and discounting has seen the price as low as S$120 one way, S$200 return. Sempati often have the lowest fares. There are also direct flights between Singapore and Medan, Padang, Palembang, Pekanbaru, Pontianak, Surabaya and Ujung Pandang. Garuda is the main carrier.

SINGAPORE

Singapore Airport

Singapore's ultramodern Changi airport is vast, efficient, organised and was built in record time. It has banking and money-changing facilities, a post office and telephone facilities (open 24 hours), hotel reservation counters (no charge) open from 7 am to 11.30 pm, left-luggage facilities, nearly 100 shops, day rooms, a fitness centre and a business centre. There are free films, audiovisual shows, bars with entertainment, hairdressers, medical facilities, a mini Science Discovery Museum, and if you're in transit for a long time you can even take a free two-hour tour of the city. Kids are catered for with an imaginative play area.

Changi is divided into Terminal I and Terminal 2, each in themselves international airports to match the world's best, connected in less than two minutes by the Changi Skytrain.

There are plenty of eating places at the airport (this is Singapore after all, food capital of South-East Asia), and if you are one of the many air travellers fed up with overpriced and terrible food at airports, then Changi airport has a myriad of excellent restaurants with food at normal prices. Even better, take the elevator beside McDonald's on the arrival level of Terminal 1 and press the button for the basement 1 Food Centre. There you'll find a complete Singapore hawkers' centre with Chinese and Malay food. It's essentially the airport staff cafeteria but the public can eat there.

LAND

To/From Malaysia

Bus Although there are plenty of buses operating from Singapore into Malaysia, the choice is much greater and the fares cheaper in Johor Bahru, where there is also a wide variety of taxi services. To get to Johor Bahru, take bus No 170 for 90c from the Ban San terminal at the corner of Queen and Arab Sts (see the Colonial District map), or take the Singapore-Johor Express buses (S$1.80, departing every 10 minutes from the same terminal). The Ban San terminal is very convenient for the Bencoolen St and Beach Rd backpackers' places.

Buses stop at the Singapore checkpoint, but don't worry if yours leaves while you clear immigration – keep your ticket and you can just hop on the next one that comes along.

In Singapore, most of the long-distance buses to Malaysia leave from the bus terminal at the corner of Lavender St and Kallang Bahru, near the top end of Jalan Besar (the continuation of Bencoolen St). The Lavender MRT station is a half-km walk away or take bus No 5 or 61. Pan Malaysia Express (☎ 294 7034) has buses to Kuala Lumpur (S$17.80), Mersing (S$11.10), Kuantan (S$16.50) and Kota Bharu (S$30.10). Hasry-Ekoba (☎ 292 6243) has buses to Kuala Lumpur, Ipoh (S$24), Taiping, Penang (S$30) and Melaka. Malacca-Singapore

Express (☎ 293 5915) has eight buses a day to Melaka (S$11) and the trip takes six hours. Many travel agents also sell bus tickets to Malaysia.

Morning Star Travel (☎ 299 2221) is another agent right at the Lavender MRT station with buses to Kuala Lumpur, Penang, Alor Setar and Melaka. Kuala Lumpur-Singapore Express (☎ 292 8254), at the Ban San Terminal, also have buses to Kuala Lumpur at 9 am and 10 pm for S$17.30. For Butterworth, you can also take one of the Hat Yai (Thailand) buses from the terminal at the Golden Mile Complex, 5001 Beach Rd (see the Central Singapore map), the main terminal for Thailand buses.

Train Singapore is the southern termination point for the Malaysian railway system. When you leave Singapore you clear immigration and customs at the station so there is no further delay at the causeway when crossing into Malaysia.

Five trains go every day to Kuala Lumpur. Fares range from S$19 in 3rd class to S$68 in 1st class on the express trains, and from S$14.80 to S$60 on the ordinary trains. The Ekspres Rakyat leaves at 7.30 am (arrives 2.50 pm), the mail train at 8.30 am (arrives 5.45 pm), the Ekspres Sinaran Pagi at 3.30 pm (arrives 10.45 pm), a limited express train at 8 pm (arrives 6.15 am) and the Sinandung Malam leaves at 10.35 pm (arrives 7.05 am). The Ekspres Rakyat continues on to Butterworth, arriving at 10.20 pm. There is also a train to Tumpat (in the very north-east of Malaysia) at 8.10 am, which passes Jerantut and Kuala Lipis for Taman Negara National Park in the afternoon. Phone the Singapore railway station (☎ 222 5165) for full schedule and fare information.

Taxi Taxis to Johor Bahru go from the Ban San terminal for S$4 per person or S$16 for the whole taxi. If you're not Singaporean or Malaysian, you may have to pay more as you will take longer at the border. At busy times and weekends, the bus will probably be faster than a taxi since they can use the special bus lanes.

For long-distance taxis to other Malaysian destinations, it is best to catch them from Johor Bahru but the Kuala Lumpur Taxi Service (☎ 223 1889), 191 New Bridge Rd, has taxis to Kuala Lumpur for S$40 per person.

SEA

To/From Malaysia

The overwhelming majority of travellers going to or coming from Malaysia will either be coming through Changi airport or crossing the causeway by road or rail.

Take bus No 2 from central Singapore out to Changi village, near Changi airport, and for S$5 you can take a ferry across to Pengerang in Malaysia. This interesting back-door service into Malaysia operates from 7 am to 4 pm.

A car ferry also operates from north Changi (take a taxi from Changi Village) to Tanjung Belungkor, east of Johor Bahru. The 11-km journey takes 45 minutes and costs S$15/24 (RM15/27) one way/return. From the Tanjung Belungkor jetty two bus services operate to Desaru, and a Kota Tinggi service is planned.

To Tioman Island, Resort Cruises Pty Ltd (☎ 278 4677), 02-03 Shing Loong Building, 337 Telok Blangah Rd, is the agent for the high-speed catamaran that does the trip in 4½ hours. Departures are at 7.50 am from the World Trade Centre.

To/From Indonesia

Curiously, there are no direct shipping services between any of the major towns of Indonesia and its near neighbour, Singapore. You can, however, travel by sea between the two countries via the Riau Archipelago, the Indonesian islands to the south of Singapore.

Batam and Bintan, the two major islands closest to Singapore, are undergoing extensive Singapore-financed development and there are numerous high-speed ferry services shuttling across from the World Trade Centre, opposite Sentosa Island. Nearly 100 ferries per day do the half-hour run to

Sekupang on Batam Island at a cost of S$16 one way. High-speed ferries go from Sekupang to Pekanbaru and other destinations in Sumatra. This is now a popular travellers' route to Indonesia. Batam is also a hub for flights to other parts of Indonesia.

For Bintan, Dino Shipping has ferries to Tanjung Pinang at 10 am and 3 pm for S$51. From Bintan the only real option is to catch the Pelni boat that calls in every two weeks on its way to Jakarta or Sumatra.

You don't require a visa to enter Indonesia via Batam or Bintan. For full details of this interesting and economical entry route into Indonesia see under Sumatra in the Indonesia chapter.

Getting Around

TO/FROM THE AIRPORT

Singapore's Changi international airport is at the extreme eastern end of the island, about 20 km from the city. An expressway runs on reclaimed land to the city, and with fast bus services it is no problem getting into town.

For the public buses follow the signs in the airport terminal to the basement bus stop. The air-con bus No 390 stops on Stamford Rd for the Bencoolen St-Beach Rd cheap accommodation enclave and continues on to Orchard Rd where many of the expensive hotels are located. The fare is a flat S$1.20 and you are supposed to have the correct change so get some when you change money on arrival. If you are going to the airport, catch the bus on Orchard or Bras Basah Rds. The bus operates every 8 to 12 minutes from 6 am to midnight, and takes about half an hour.

Taxis from (but not to) the airport are subject to a S$3 supplementary charge on top of the metered fare, which will probably be from S$12 to S$15 to most places.

BUS

Singapore has a comprehensive bus network with frequent buses. You rarely have to wait more than a few minutes for a bus and they will get you almost anywhere you want to go. If you intend to do a lot of travelling by public transport in Singapore, a copy of the *Transitlink Guide*, listing all bus and MRT services, is an essential investment.

Fares start from 50c (60c for air-con buses) and go up in 10c increments to a maximum of 90c (S$1.20 for air-con). Drop the exact fare into the change box on boarding – change is not given.

Singapore Explorer bus passes cost S$5 for one day or S$12 for three days of unlimited travel, but you have to do a lot of bus travelling to get your money's worth.

MRT

Singapore's ultramodern Mass Rapid Transit (MRT) system is the easiest, fastest and most comfortable way of getting around the city. The Somerset, Orchard and Newton MRT stations are all close to Orchard Rd. Dhoby Ghaut station is closest to Bencoolen St. Bugis and City Hall stations straddle Beach Rd.

Fares vary from 60c to S$1.50. You check the fare from a fare map, press the appropriate button on the ticket vending machine for the fare you want, and insert money. The machine gives you your ticket and change, and you then use the ticket to enter and exit at the stations. You can also buy Transitlink stored-value tickets for S$10 (plus S$2 deposit); the exit machine electronically deducts fares from the encoded card and returns the card to you until its full value has been utilised. The cards can also be used in some buses that have validator machines.

Trains run from around 6 am to midnight and operate every four to eight minutes.

TAXI

Singapore has plenty of taxis, all air-con, metered, neat and clean, with drivers who know their way round and have been taught to be polite, believe it or not!

Flag fall is S$2.20 for the first 1½ km then 10c for each additional 250 metres. From midnight to 6 am, there is a 50% surcharge over the metered fare. NTUC (☎ 452 5555) is one of the biggest companies.

Cars entering Singapore's Central Business District (CBD) between 7.30 and 10.15 am, Monday to Saturday, have to purchase a special CBD licence, so you will have to pay the S$3 fee for a taxi if no else has already done so. A S$1 surcharge also applies for trips from the CBD in afternoon peak times.

OTHER TRANSPORT

You still see a few bicycle rickshaws in Chinatown and in the other older sections of town. Always agree on the fare beforehand if you try one. Rickshaw tours are also available.

You can easily rent cars in Singapore from S$90 per day, although it is rather pointless when you consider parking costs, CBD licences and the excellent public transport which is available. Expensive surcharges apply if you take a rental car into Malaysia, where rental rates are cheaper anyway.

Check the following Things to See section for details on the ferries out to various islands.

Bicycling in Singapore may not have too much appeal but if you want a bicycle to ride further afield, then Singapore could be a good place to buy it. Check the yellow pages of the phone directory.

Around Singapore

THINGS TO SEE

Singapore offers an accessible selection of varied Asian flavours in a small package. There's a modern central business district, a nearby but fast-disappearing old Chinatown and relics of a British colonial past, as well as colourful Little India and Arab St.

River & Central Business District

The river is no longer the city-state's commercial artery but it's still in the heart of Singapore, flanked by the business district, Chinatown and colonial Singapore.

Start at Raffles Place, the trading centre of a city that thrives on trade. The banks, offices and shipping companies are clustered around here. Located at the southern end of the business district, **Lau Pa Sat** (see the Central Singapore map) is a 'festival market', with souvenir shops and a host of foodstalls, housed in the restored Telok Ayer Centre, a fine old cast-iron Victorian marketplace. From **Clifford Pier**, you can get a good view over the teeming harbour or take a harbour boat tour. From there, walk along what used to be the waterfront to **Merlion Park**, where Singapore's Merlion symbol spouts water over the Singapore River.

The Singapore River has been comprehensively cleaned up and is now a recreational stretch of colonial restoration and photo opportunities. The old **Empress Place** building is now a museum with rotating exhibits from China. Nearby is **Raffles' Statue**, standing imperiously by the water. On the south bank, **Boat Quay** is a picturesque area of restored old shops housing restaurants and bars, with soaring office buildings right behind them. North Boat Quay leads upriver to **Clarke Quay**, where the restored old godowns (warehouses) and shopfronts house a variety of shops and restaurants. One of the best ways to see the river is to take a **river boat tour** (S$6) from in front of the Hill St Centre, near Clarke Quay.

Colonial District

The centre of colonial Singapore is north of the river. Near Empress Place is the **Victoria Concert Hall & Theatre**, home of the Singapore Symphony Orchestra. **Parliament House** has had a varied history as a mansion, courthouse, colonial government centre and, now, the seat of independent Singapore's parliament.

North of Empress Place, cricket matches still take place on the open expanse of the **Padang**, overlooked by the **Supreme Court** and **City Hall**. On Beach Rd, north of the Padang, **Raffles Hotel** is another symbol of colonial Singapore. Despite extensive restoration, it continues to ooze tradition, and a Singapore Sling in the Long Bar (the drink was concocted there in 1915) is a part of the Singapore experience. The museum on the

SINGAPORE

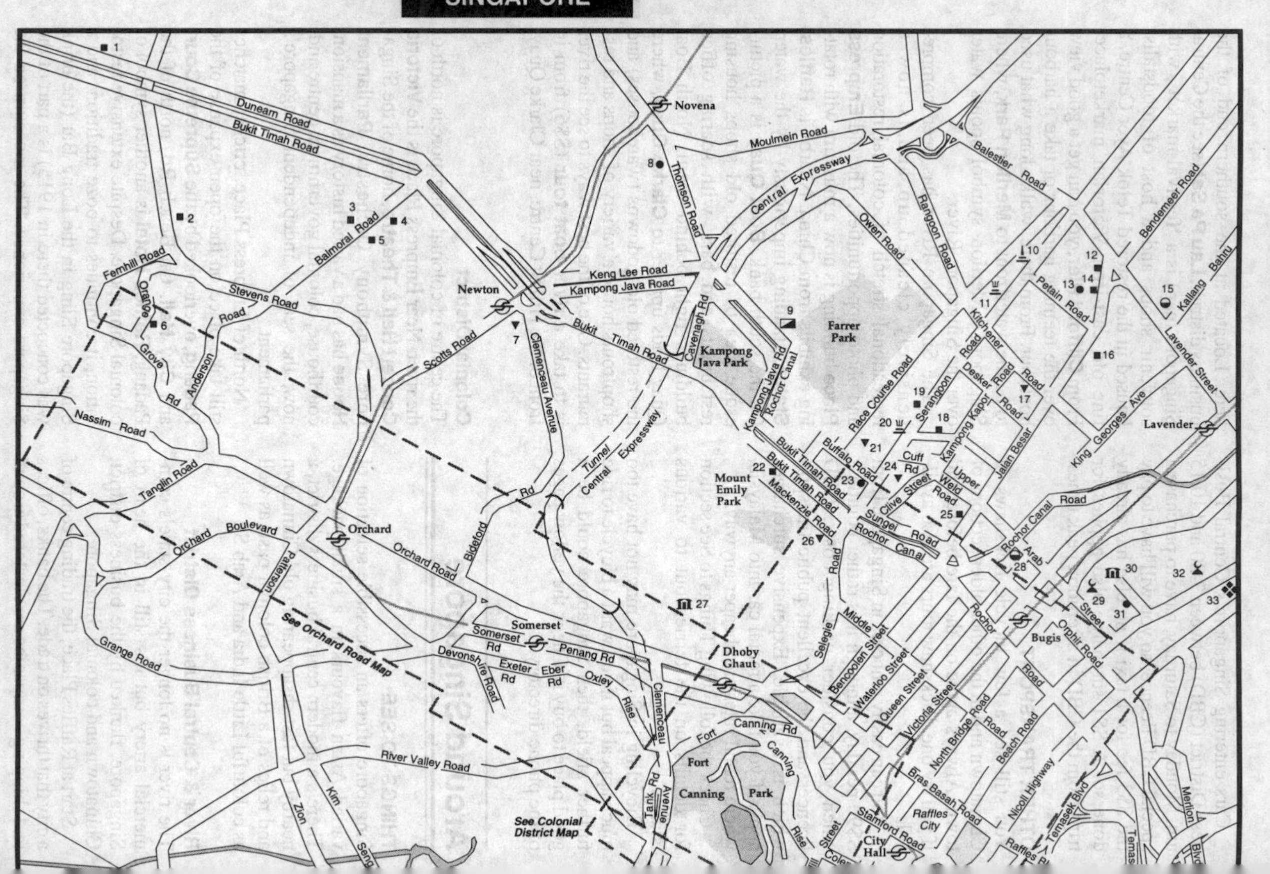

Duneam Road
Bukit Timah Road
Novena
Moulmein Road
Balestier Road
Bendemeer Road
Kallang Bahru
Thomson Road
Central Expressway
Owen Road
Rangoon Road
Petain Road
Lavender Street
Balmoral Road
Fernhill Road
Orange Grove Rd
Stevens Road
Anderson Road
Newton
Keng Lee Road
Kampong Java Road
Bukit Timah Road
Cavenagh Rd
Kampong Java Park
Kampong Java Rd
Rochor Canal
Farrer Park
Race Course Road
Serangoon Road
Kitchener Road
Desker Road
Kampong Kapor Road
Jalan Besar
King Georges Ave
Lavender
Scotts Road
Clemenceau Avenue
Nassim Road
Tunnel
Central Expressway
Buffalo Road
Bukit Timah Road
Mackenzie Road
Mount Emily Park
Cuff Rd
Upper Weld Road
Clive Street
Sungei Road
Rochor Canal
Rochor Canal Road
Arab
Tanglin Road
Orchard Boulevard
Orchard
Orchard Road
Bideford Rd
Patterson
Selegie Road
Middle
Rochor
Bugis
Street
Ophir Road
See Orchard Road Map
Grange Road
Somerset
Somerset Rd
Penang Rd
Devonshire Road
Exeter Rd
Eber Rd
Oxley Rise
Dhoby Ghaut
Bencoolen Street
Waterloo Street
Queen Street
Victoria Street
North Bridge Road
Beach Road
Clemenceau Avenue
Fort Canning Rd
Canning Rise
Fort Canning Park
Tank Rd
River Valley Road
Kim Seng
Zion
See Colonial District Map
Bras Basah Road
Raffles City
Stamford Road
City Hall
Nicoll Highway
Temasek Blvd
Raffles Bl
Merlion
Temas
Blvd

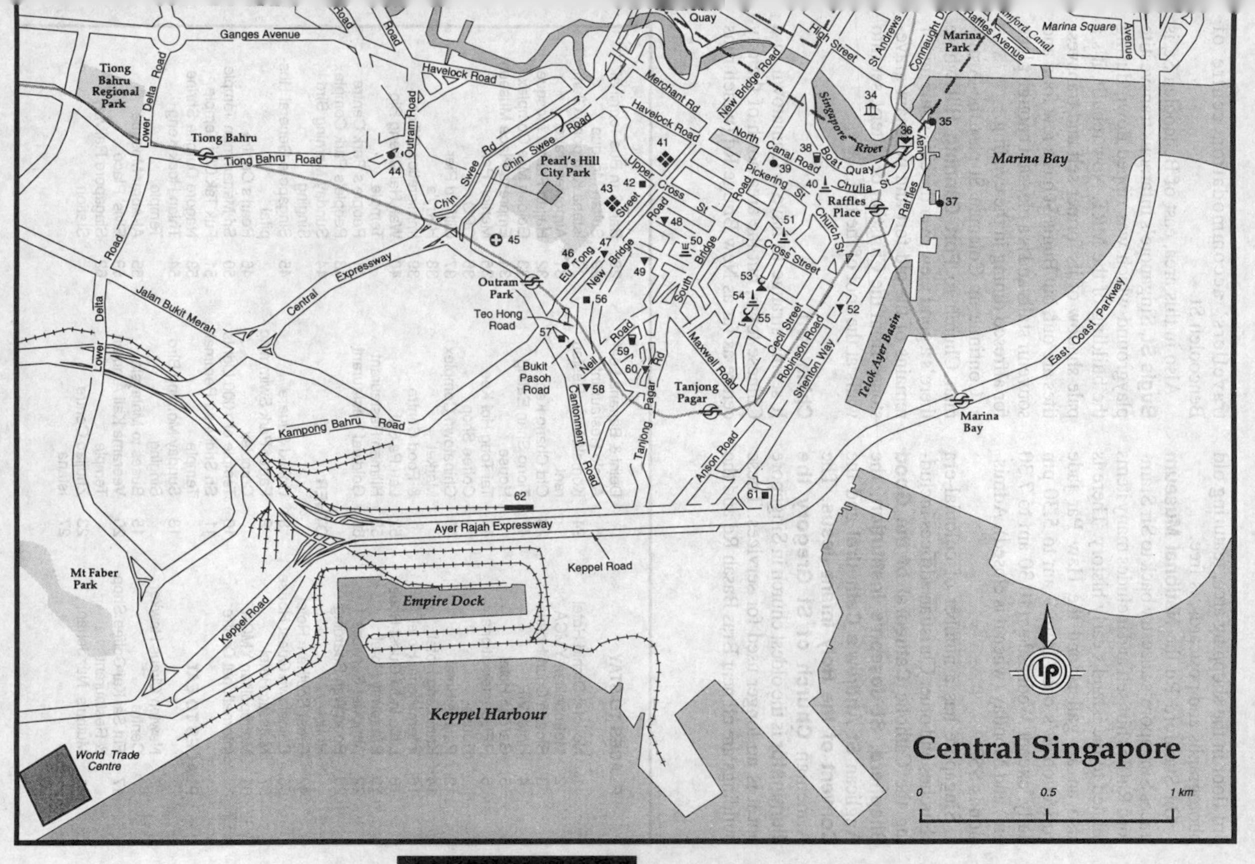
Central Singapore
0
0.5
1 km
Marina Bay
Marina Square
Marina Park
Raffles Avenue
Avenue
Connaught Dr
St Andrews
High Street
Singapore River
Boat Quay
Quay
Raffles
Raffles Place
Chulia St
Church St
Telok Ayer Basin
East Coast Parkway
Shenton Way
Robinson Road
Cecil Street
Cross Street
North Canal Road
Pickering St
New Bridge Road
Merchant Rd
Havelock Road
Upper Cross St
Street
South Bridge
Maxwell Road
Tanjong Pagar
Tanjong Pagar Rd
Anson Road
Neil Road
Cantonment Road
Eu Tong
New Bridge
Pearl's Hill City Park
Chin Swee Rd
Chin Swee Road
Outram Park
Outram Road
Teo Hong Road
Bukit Pasoh Road
Kampong Bahru Road
Keppel Road
Ayer Rajah Expressway
Central Expressway
Tiong Bahru Road
Tiong Bahru
Tiong Bahru Regional Park
Ganges Avenue
Lower Delta Road
Lower Delta
Jalan Bukit Merah
Empire Dock
Keppel Harbour
Mt Faber Park
World Trade Centre
34
35
36
37
38
39
40
41
42
43
44
45
46
47
48
49
50
51
52
53
54
55
56
57
58
59
60
61
62
SINGAPORE

3rd floor in the shopping area, featuring old photographs and postcards, is free.

On Stamford Rd the **National Museum** traces Singapore's ancestry back to Sir Stamford Raffles himself and includes many items related to the island's early history. There is also an art gallery and the Haw Par jade collection. It's open from 9 am to 5.30 pm daily, except Wednesday (10.30 am to 7.30 pm) and Monday (when it is closed). Admission is S$2.

Singapore has a number of colonial-era churches and other Christian edifices including the Catholic **Cathedral of the Good Shepherd**, **St Joseph's Institution**, the Anglican **St Andrew's Cathedral** and the **Convent of the Holy Infant Jesus**. The Armenian **Church of St Gregory the Illuminator** is the oldest church in Singapore but it is no longer used for services. These buildings are all near Bras Basah Rd and the travellers' accommodation centre of Bencoolen St.

Also in this area, east of Bencoolen St, is **Bugis St**, Singapore's infamous transvestite playground which was ripped down during the building of the MRT. Now rebuilt, it's a pale shadow of its former self and transvestites are out, but Bugis St has a few food and souvenir stalls and is a pleasant enough place for alfresco dining in the evening.

Continue up Coleman St past the Armenian Church to **Fort Canning Hill** where there's a good view over the city, some minor remains of the old fort and poignant gravestones from the Christian cemetery, set into walls at the foot of the hill.

Chinatown

It seems strange to have a Chinatown in a Chinese town, but the area north of the city centre as far as New Bridge Rd (which runs

PLACES TO STAY

1 Novotel Orchid Hotel
2 Metropolitan YMCA
3 Sloane Court Hotel
4 Hotel VIP
5 Garden Hotel
6 RELC International House
12 Palace Hotel
14 Kam Leng Hotel
16 International Hotel
18 Little India Guest House
19 Broadway Hotel
22 Airpower Services
25 Boon Wah Boarding House
42 Great Southern Hotel
56 Chinatown Guest House
57 Majestic Hotel
61 Metropolitan YMCA International Centre

PLACES TO EAT

7 Newton Circus Hawker Centre
17 Fut Sai Kai Coffee Shop & Restaurant
21 Muthu's, Nur Jehan, Delhi & Banana Leaf Apolo Restaurants
24 Komala Vilas Restaurant
26 Old Chang Kee
47 Tiong Shan Eating House
48 Tai Tong Hoi Kee Coffee Shop
49 Chinatown Complex Market & Food Centre
52 Lau Pa Sat
58 Hillman Restaurant
60 Goldleaf Restaurant

OTHER

8 United Square
9 Farrer Park Swimming Complex
10 Temple of 1000 Lights
11 Sri Srinivasa Perumal Temple
13 Sunday Morning Bird Singing
15 Buses to Malaysia
20 Veerama Kali Amman Temple
23 Zhujiao Centre
27 Istana
28 Ban San Bus Terminal
29 Sultan Mosque
30 Istana Kampong Glam
31 Airpower Travel
32 Hajjah Fatima Mosque
33 Golden Mile Complex
34 Empress Place Museum
35 Merlion Park
36 GPO
37 Clifford Pier
38 Harry's
39 Immigration Office
40 Wak Hai Cheng Bio Temple
41 People's Park Centre
43 People's Park Complex
44 Sunday Morning Bird Singing
45 Singapore General Hospital
46 Pearl's Centre
50 Sri Mariamman Temple
51 Fuk Tak Ch'i Temple
53 Nagore Durgha Shrine
54 Thian Hock Keng Temple
55 Al-Abrar Mosque
59 Elvis' Place
62 Singapore Railway Station

south-west from the Singapore River) is just that. It's a maze of streets, shops and stalls with overhanging windows from which poke flagpoles of laundry.

Much of this area, one of the most picturesque in Singapore, was ploughed under for development and cleaned up at the same time. There are still some small pockets of interest and, somewhat belatedly, some measures have been made to preserve and restore part of the old Singapore. In a fashion characteristic of Singapore, it's been done neatly, cleanly and antiseptically.

There's a whole dictionary of religions in Singapore, so you'll find a lot of temples. A walk around Chinatown (see the Central Singapore map) will take you to the **Wak Hai Cheng Bio** and **Fuk Tak Ch'i** temples, the **Nagore Durgha Shrine**, the **Thian Hock Keng Temple**, dating from 1840 and one of the most colourful in Singapore, and the **Al-Abrar Mosque**. Also in this intriguing area is the Malaysia Mariamman Temple on South Bridge Rd, a technicolour Hindu shrine with brilliant statuary on the tower over the entrance. Originally built in 1827, its present form dates from 1862. Several times a year there are fire-walking ceremonies inside – the firewalkers start at a slow ceremonial pace but soon break into a sprint!

There's always something interesting to see as you wander the convoluted 'five-foot ways' of Chinatown. A five-foot way, which takes its name from the fact that it is roughly five feet wide, is a walkway at the front of the traditional Chinese shophouses which is enclosed, veranda-like, in the front of the building. The difficulty with them is that every shop's walkway is individual – one may well be higher or lower, or closer to or further from the street, than the next.

The **Tanjong Pagar** conservation area, the first major restoration project in Chinatown (wedged between Neil and Tanjong Pagar Rds) is the showpiece of restored Chinatown.

Little India

Although Singapore is predominantly Chinese, there's a colourful Indian district around Serangoon Rd, just north of the colonial district. The smell of spices and curries wafting through the area is as much a part of the district's flavour as the colours and noises.

Attractions in Little India include the **Zhujiao Centre** market, the backstreets off Serangoon Rd with their exotic little shops and the temples, including the **Veerama Kali Amman** and **Sri Srinivasa Perumal** temples. The **Temple of 1000 Lights** on Race Course Rd at the northern edge of Little India has a fine 15-metre-high seated Buddha, illuminated, for a small fee, by the promised 1000 lights. There is also a mother-of-pearl replica of the Buddha's footprint.

To the east of Little India is Jalan Besar where you can find bird-singing meets on Sunday morning around Petain Rd, and an active red-light district any night of the week.

Arab St

Located to the south-east of Little India is Arab St, the Muslim centre, especially along North Bridge Rd. Here you'll find old shops with Malaysian and Indonesian goods and the **Sultan Mosque** on North Bridge Rd, the biggest mosque in Singapore. It was originally built in 1825 but was totally replaced a century later. The **Istana Kampong Glam** was the centre for Malay royalty which predated Raffles' arrival.

It's always interesting to wander around the picturesque streets, with picturesque names like Baghdad St, Kandahar St and Haji Lane. Bussorah St is newly renovated and it comes to life during Ramadan, when foodstalls set up after dark for the faithful who fast during the day.

Orchard Rd

This area is a corridor of big hotels and busy shopping centres. Beyond Orchard Rd are the fine old colonial homes where the wealthy elite of Singapore still live. Holland Village is an expat enclave out on the western continuation of Orchard Rd.

Peranakan Place, at Orchard and Emerald Hill Rds, is one old-fashioned exception to the glass and chrome gloss of

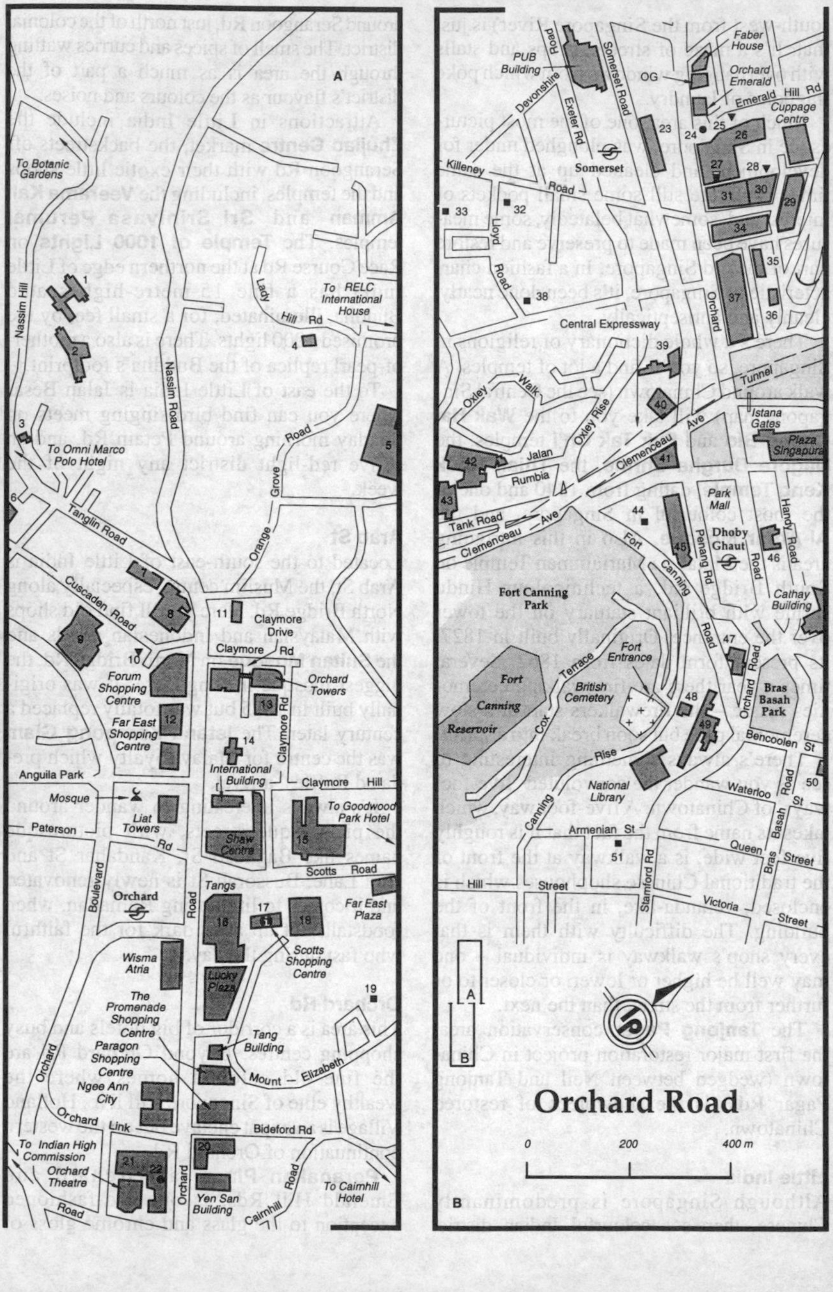

Orchard Road

0 200 400 m

A

B

To Botanic Gardens
Nassim Hill
Nassim Road
Lady Hill Rd
To RELC International House
Orange Grove Road
To Omni Marco Polo Hotel
Tanglin Road
Cuscaden Road
Claymore Drive
Claymore Rd
Orchard Towers
Claymore Rd
Forum Shopping Centre
Far East Shopping Centre
International Building
Claymore Hill
Anguilla Park
Mosque
Liat Towers
Paterson Rd
To Goodwood Park Hotel
Shaw Centre
Scotts Road
Orchard
Boulevard
Orchard Road
Tangs
Far East Plaza
Scotts Shopping Centre
Wisma Atria
Lucky Plaza
The Promenade Shopping Centre
Paragon Shopping Centre
Tang Building
Mount Elizabeth
Ngee Ann City
Orchard Link
Bideford Rd
To Indian High Commission
Orchard Theatre
Orchard Road
Yen San Building
Cairnhill Road
To Cairnhill Hotel

PUB Building
Devonshire Road
Exeter Rd
Somerset Road
Faber House
OG
Orchard Emerald
Emerald Hill Rd
Cuppage Centre
Somerset
Killeney Road
Lloyd Road
Orchard
Central Expressway
Oxley Walk
Oxley Rise
Tunnel
Istana Gates
Plaza Singapura
Clemenceau Ave
Jalan Rumbia
Park Mall
Tank Road
Clemenceau Ave
Fort Canning
Penang Rd
Dhoby Ghaut
Handy Road
Fort Canning Park
Cathay Building
Fort Entrance
Terrace
British Cemetery
Fort Canning Reservoir
Cox
Orchard Road
Bras Basah Park
Rise
Bencoolen St
National Library
Canning
Waterloo St
Bras Basah Road
Armenian St
Queen Street
Hill Street
Stamford Rd
Victoria Street

SINGAPORE

PLACES TO STAY

1 Hotel Premier
2 ANA Hotel
4 Ladyhill Hotel
5 Shangri La Hotel
6 Regent Hotel
8 Orchard Parade Hotel
9 Boulevard Hotel
11 Orchard Hotel
12 Hilton International Hotel
13 Hotel Negara
15 Royal Holiday Inn Crown Plaza
16 Dynasty Hotel
18 Hyatt Regency Hotel
19 York Hotel
20 Crown Prince Hotel
21 Mandarin Hotel
23 Hotel Phoenix
29 Holiday Inn Park View
32 Mario-Ville Boarding House
33 Mitre Hotel
35 Hotel Grand Central
36 Supreme Hotel
37 Le Meridien Hotel
38 Lloyd's Inn
39 Cockpit Hotel
42 Imperial Hotel
44 YWCA Hostel
47 YMCA International House
50 Bayview Inn
51 Mayfair City Hotel

PLACES TO EAT

10 Hard Rock Cafe
25 Azizas Restaurant
28 Cuppage Thai Food Restaurant

OTHER

3 Myanmar Embassy
7 Tanglin Shopping Centre
14 Thai Embassy
17 STPB Tourist Office
22 Singapore Airlines
24 Peranakan Place
26 Centrepoint
27 Saxophone Bar & Grill
30 Cuppage Plaza
31 Orchard Point
34 Orchard Plaza
40 House of Tan Yeok Nee
41 Singapore Shopping Centre
43 Chettiar Hindu Temple
45 Supreme House
46 MacDonald House
48 Drama Centre
49 National Museum & Art Gallery

Orchard Rd. In recent times, there has been a resurgence of interest in Peranakan culture in Singapore. *Peranakan* is the term for Straits-born Chinese, also called *nonyas* (women) and *babas* (men). Traditionally, the Straits-born Chinese have spoken a Malay dialect and practiced their own customs, a hybrid of Chinese and Malay. This is probably the nearest Singapore comes to having a cultural identity. Peranakan Place is a lane of restored shophouses, one of which is a small, interesting museum (entry S$4).

The **Istana** (president's palace) is open to the public on selected public holidays such as New Year's Day. The recently rebuilt **Chettiar Hindu Temple** is on Tank Rd near the intersection of Clemenceau Ave and River Valley Rd. It's a short walk from Orchard Rd and most active during the spectacular Thaipusam festival.

Jurong

Jurong Town, west of the city centre, is a huge industrial complex but it also has a few tourist attractions.

On the way out to Jurong is **Haw Par Villa** (formerly the Tiger Balm Gardens), originally built with the fortune amassed from the Haw Par brothers' miracle medicament. It has recently had a major overhaul. Much of the gory and crazy charm of the old gardens has disappeared and it's now much more of a tame fun park with an emphasis on Chinese mythology and fun rides. Entry is an overpriced S$16 – skip it.

Out at Jurong, there are the adjoining **Chinese Gardens** and **Japanese Gardens**, right by the Chinese Garden MRT station.

The **Jurong Bird Park** is interesting, even if you're not a feathered-friend freak. There's even a two-hectare walk-in aviary which alone contains 3000 birds. The bird park is open from 9 am to 6 pm during the week and 8 am to 6 pm on weekends. Admission is S$5. Get there on bus No 251, 253 or 255 from the Boon Lay MRT station. Right opposite the bird park is **Jurong Crocodile Paradise**, open from 9 am to 6 pm and costing S$4.50.

The **Singapore Science Centre**, on Science Centre Rd in Jurong, has handles to crank, buttons to push and levers to pull – all in the interest of making science come alive. It's open from 10 am to 6 pm Tuesday to Sunday, and admission is S$2. The 3D Omnitheatre costs an extra S$9. To get there take the MRT to Jurong East and walk a half km or take bus No 336. Alternatively, take bus

No 197 from North Bridge Rd in the colonial district.

Tang Dynasty City, about two km south of the Chinese and Japanese gardens, is a huge theme park recreation of old Chang'an, China's Tang Dynasty capital from the 6th to 8th centuries AD. Silk Road camel rides, craft demonstrations and shops are part of this artificial recreation. Admission is a hefty S$15.

East Coast & Changi

The East Coast district, out towards the airport, has a popular beach with recreational and dining facilities along the foreshore. **East Coast Park** has swimming, windsurfing and bicycle rental.

If you want to find the Malay influence within Singapore head inland from East Coast Park to the **Katong** district. Along East Coast Rd you'll find old terraces, excellent nonya restaurants and antique shops.

Nearby **Geylang Serai**, a Malay residential area, is easily accessed by the Paya Lebar MRT station. On Geylang Rd is the Malay Cultural Centre, a new complex of Malay-style houses, and next door, the interesting, old-fashioned Geylang Serai market.

At the far eastern end of the island is **Changi**, the village from which the airport takes its name, which makes an interesting excursion. There's a reasonable beach and at Changi Prison there's a fascinating little museum about the prisoner-of-war camp operated by the Japanese during WW II. It's open from 9.30 am to 12.30 pm and from 2 to 4.30 pm Monday to Saturday. Bus No 2 runs to Changi from the Bencoolen St and Raffles City area.

Islands, Beaches & Watersports

Singapore's sprinkling of islands to the south have undergone a lot of development over the past few years. **Sentosa** has been the most developed – it's rather plastic, although very popular as a local weekend escape. Entry to the island is S$4 and the ferry trip from the World Trade Centre costs 80c or there are buses. Alternatively, you can take the cable car to the island from Mt Faber or the World Trade Centre for S$5. The views are the best part of a Sentosa visit.

Most attractions on the island cost extra but monorail and bus transport on the island is included in the entry cost. Attractions here include the Pioneers of Singapore exhibit and the Surrender Chamber, with waxworks figures showing the formal surrender of Japanese forces in 1945. Underwater World is a spectacular aquarium where the marine life swims around and over you while you move along an acrylic tunnel. Entry is S$10. Then there's Butterfly Park, the Mystery Maze, the Rare Stone Museum and much more of a similar nature. There are also sports facilities and beaches.

Other islands are not as developed as Sentosa. There are ferry trips several times a day (much more frequently on weekends) to **St John's Island**, also known as Pulau Sakijang Bendera, and **Kusu Island**, also known as Pulau Tembakul. Tiny Kusu has a Chinese temple and a Malay shrine. Both islands are good places for a quiet swim. The round-trip ferry ticket costs S$6. The islands are crowded on weekends.

There are other islands both to the north and south. Boats to the other islands of the southern group can be arranged from Jardine Steps, or you can hire bumboats from there or Clifford Pier. To go to the northern islands, boats can be hired from Sembawang or from Punggol Boatel at Punggol Point. **Pulau Ubin** and **Pulau Tekong** can be easily reached from Changi village. These islands have some quiet beaches and popular seafood restaurants.

Of course, you don't have to leave the main island of Singapore to find watersports. There's the huge **East Coast Lagoon** at the East Coast Park and the **CN West Leisure Park** at Jurong. You'll find pools, water-slides and other attractions at **Big Splash** at East Coast Park.

The **Farrer Park Swimming Complex** (see the Central Singapore map) is the nearest public swimming pool to the Bencoolen St area. Head to the **East Coast Sailing Centre** for windsurfing or sailing. Scuba-diving trips are made to the islands south of Singapore.

Other Attractions

There are numerous parks and gardens in Singapore including the fine **Botanic Gardens** on Cluny and Holland Rds, not far from Tanglin Rd (west of the city centre – see the Singapore Island map). Or, you can climb **Mt Faber** (west of the city centre), or **Bukit Timah** (north-west of the gardens), about as high as you can get in Singapore. The nature reserve at Bukit Timah has the only large area of primary rainforest left in Singapore and some good walking trails traverse the jungle.

The **Zoological Gardens** are at 80 Mandai Lake Rd in the north of the island. The orang-utan colony and the Komodo dragons are major attractions. This world-class zoo is open from 8.30 am to 6 pm, and entry is S$7. Take bus No 171 from Stamford and Orchard Rds. The big, new attraction at the zoo is the night safari park, open from 7.30 pm until midnight. The **Mandai Orchard Gardens** are beside the zoo.

Sunday morning **bird-singing** sessions are one of Singapore's real pleasures. Bird lovers get together to let their caged birds have a communal sing-song while they have a cup of coffee. The main centre is at the junction of Tiong Bahru and Seng Poh Rds, near the Havelock Rd hotel enclave (just west of the city centre – see the Central Singapore map). It's a half-km walk from the Tiong Bahru MRT station or a number of buses run there. Another bird-singing session takes place just off Jalan Besar, near the Palace Hotel (see the Central Singapore map). It's all very organised – tall pointy birds go in tall pointy cages and little fat ones in little fat cages.

PLACES TO STAY

If you're looking for mid-range places, it is worth checking out the top-end places – some big discounts have been on offer recently. If you arrive by air, the Singapore Hotels Association (☎ 542 6955) stall at Changi airport keeps a list of available rooms and you will be quoted the current discount rates, which are usually a much better deal than the walk-in rates. STA Travel (☎ 734 5681) in the Orchard Parade Hotel (see the Orchard Rd map) can also make bookings at discounted rates for a selection of cheaper luxury hotels.

Places to Stay – bottom end

The budget accommodation is to be found in the cheap Chinese hotels and the guesthouses or 'crash pads' as they have been known as for years by travellers.

New guesthouses are constantly opening up, and they offer the only really cheap accommodation in Singapore, with dormitory beds and cheap rooms (often small spartan boxes with a fan). Free tea and coffee are standard offerings and a basic breakfast is usually thrown in. They are the best places to meet other travellers.

Most of the cheap hotels have seen better days, but they do have more character than the guesthouses. Rooms range from around S$25 to S$60. This will get you a fairly spartan room with a bare floor, a few pieces of furniture, a sink and a fan. Couples should always ask for a single room – a single usually means just one double bed, whereas a double has two.

The main area for budget accommodation is in the part of the colonial district bounded by Bras Basah, Rochor, Beach and Selegie Rds. Bencoolen St has traditionally been the backpackers' centre in Singapore, and while it still has a number of guesthouses, most of the old buildings and Chinese hotels have fallen to the wrecker's ball. Many backpackers' places have relocated to the Beach Rd area, which is the other major centre for budget accommodation. Other cheap possibilities are found further north in Little India and nearby Jalan Besar, and in Chinatown (south of the Singapore River).

Camping The best place for camping is at Sentosa Island where pre-erected four-person tents with camp beds cost S$15 per night. They cater primarily for groups, but individuals can stay by booking in advance through the Sentosa Information Centre (☎ 270 7888).

Bencoolen St Area Located at 46-52 Bencoolen St, near Airmaster Travel, you'll

SINGAPORE

find an entire building devoted to guesthouses. Go around the back and take the lift. The biggest here is the *Lee Traveller's Club* (☎ 338 3149). Reception is at room 52 on the 7th floor but they have rooms on most of the floors. A bed in an air-con dorm costs S$7 or S$8. Good, hotel-style rooms with air-con and bath cost S$40 to S$45 and air-con rooms without bath cost S$35 to S$40. *Peony Mansions* (☎ 338 5638), one of the original crash pads, is on the 4th floor. Dormitory beds cost S$7 and rooms go for S$30 to S$45. The dorms aren't great but the rooms are reasonable.

On the other side of Bencoolen St, at No 27, between the Strand and Bencoolen hotels, is the well-managed *Bencoolen House* (☎ 338 1206). The reception area is on the 7th floor. Dorm beds cost S$6 and most rooms cost from S$25, ranging up to S$45 for a very good air-con room.

Why Not Homestay (☎ 338 0162), 127 Bencoolen St, has a popular restaurant-cum-travellers' meeting place downstairs. It's a rabbit-warren with plenty of rooms upstairs and in the adjoining buildings. Most rooms are small and windowless and cost from S$26 with fan or from S$30 with air-con. The dormitories are better – the cost is S$10 in a four-bed, air-con dorm.

At 171 Bencoolen St is another centre for guesthouses. *Goh's Homestay* (☎ 339 6561), up a long flight of stairs on the 4th floor, has a good eating/meeting area where you can get breakfast, snacks and drinks. The rooms are very clean but small and without windows. They cost S$28 or a dorm bed costs S$12. *Hawaii Hostel* (☎ 338 4187) on the 2nd floor at 171-B has reasonable air-con singles/doubles for S$25/35.

Of the hotels, the *San Wah* (☎ 336 2428) at 36 Bencoolen St is a little better than the cheapest Chinese hotels and it has a pleasant courtyard area. Doubles cost S$40 or S$45 with air-con. At 260-262 Middle Rd, near the corner of Selegie Rd, is the good, spotlessly clean *Sun Sun Hotel* (☎ 338 4911). Singles/doubles cost S$36/42, or air-con doubles cost S$48.

The *Victoria Hotel* (☎ 338 2381), next to the Allson Hotel at 87 Victoria Street, is a more modern hotel with clean, comfortable rooms. Doubles without bath are S$50 or S$60 with bath. The *South-East Asia Hotel* (☎ 338 2394), 190 Waterloo St, is also good and well located. All rooms are air-con with attached bathroom and cost S$62.75.

Beach Rd Area Another *Lee Traveller's Club* (☎ 339 5490) is on the 6th floor of the Fu Yeun Building at 75 Beach Rd and they have more rooms on the 4th floor. It is a large place and popular; it can get crowded. It costs S$6 for a dorm bed, S$8 in an air-con dorm, S$15/25 for singles/doubles with fan or S$35/40 with air-con. *Willy's* (☎ 337 0916) is a smaller, homelier place in the same building on the 4th floor. They have a few rooms for around S$25 and dorms beds for S$6 in the common room (a common fault with guesthouses).

Willy's have two other good places, charging the same prices: the second *Willy's* (☎ 338 8826) is on the 3rd floor at 101 Beach Rd and *Raffles Home Stay* (☎ 334 1608) is on the 3rd floor, 490 North Bridge Rd.

The *New Backpackers Lodge* (☎ 334 8042), 18A Liang Seah St, is spotlessly clean and has a little more character than most. A dorm bed costs S$7 and most rooms go for S$25. The *Das Travellers' Inn* (☎ 294 9740) on the 2nd floor at 87 Beach Rd is a long-running place that has been running a little too long. A bed in the large common dorm costs S$6, or S$8 in an air-con eight-bed dorm. Rooms cost from S$15 to S$40 with air-con and shower.

The Beach Rd area has some classic old Chinese hotels. At 54 Middle Rd, the *Lido* (☎ 337 1872) costs S$22/24. The rooms are large and good value. The *Shang Onn* (☎ 338 4153) at 37 Beach Rd, on the corner of Purvis St, has character but not much else. Singles/doubles/triples cost S$30/34/45. At the corner of Liang Seah St and North Bridge Rd is the *Ah Chew Hotel* (☎ 336 3563), a very traditional old Chinese Hotel with rooms for S$25. 'It's nothing to sneeze at,' reported a guest.

SINGAPORE

Little India & Jalan Besar The *Friendly Rest House* (☎ 294 0847) is at 357A Serangoon Rd, just past Kitchener Rd. This guesthouse is not very popular with travellers but it is close to Little India. The rooms are better than average and good value at S$15 and S$20.

The new and well-appointed *Little India Guest House* (☎ 294 2866) is just off Serangoon Rd in the heart of Little India at 3 Veerasamy Rd. It is more of a hotel and small rooms will cost you S$38/50/62 for singles/doubles/triples.

Jalan Besar has a number of cheap hotels. The friendly *Boon Wah Boarding House* (☎ 299 1466), at 43A Jalan Besar on the corner of Upper Dickson Rd, has renovated rooms with air-con, TV and attached bathroom for S$60/70. The *International* (☎ 293 9238) at 290A, on the corner of Allenby Rd, costs S$35/40 or doubles with bath cost S$45. The rooms are large, well kept and most have balconies. Right opposite Bugis Square Food Centre at 383 Jalan Besar is the *Kam Leng* (☎ 298 2289) with rooms for S$26 or S$32 with air-con.

At the northern end of Jalan Besar at 407A-B, near the Lavender St bus station, is the spotlessly clean *Palace Hotel* (☎ 298 3108), which is exceptionally good for the price. Large, double rooms with balcony cost S$22.

Chinatown The *Chinatown Guest House* (☎ 220 0671), 5th floor, 325D New Bridge Rd, opposite Pearl's Centre, has dorm beds for S$8 and a few rooms for S$30. There are better guesthouses in Singapore, but this is the only cheap option if you want to stay in Chinatown.

The *Great Southern Hotel* (☎ 533 3223) at the corner of Eu Tong Sen and Upper Cross Sts is right in the heart of Chinatown and the rooms are reasonable, but it gets a lot of traffic noise. Rooms with fan start at S$35 and air-con singles/doubles with attached bath are S$50/60.

The well-kept *Majestic Hotel* (☎ 222 3377), 31 Bukit Pasoh Rd, is an excellent hotel. It's on a quiet street in an interesting, traditional area, right near the Outram Park MRT station. Air-con rooms are S$45/59 without bath, S$57/69 with bath.

Other Areas *Airpower Services* (☎ 334 3496), 124-B Mackenzie Rd, is a quiet, relaxed guesthouse with a good atmosphere. It is near Little India but is otherwise a little inconvenient. Dormitories cost S$7 or S$8 for air-con. There are a few rooms for S$20 to S$35.

Orchard Rd has a number of guesthouses that come and go, and private apartments occasionally take in travellers. It is worth keeping an eye out for these places as they can often offer a better class of guesthouse accommodation.

The *Mayfair City Hotel* (☎ 337 4542) is at 40-44 Armenian St near Orchard Rd, behind the National Museum. Good rooms with air-con, shower and TV cost from S$52 to S$74.

A couple of cheap hotels are near Orchard Rd. The *Mitre Hotel* (☎ 737 3811), 145 Killeney Rd, would have to be the most dilapidated flea pit in Singapore, but lovers of the seedy might find it interesting. It is an old villa with large grounds, and the dingy bar is frequented by the oil-rig workers who stay here. Rooms range from S$23 for a rough single with fan to S$36 for a passable double with air-con and bath. Just around the corner is the *Mario-Ville Boarding House* (☎ 734 5342), 64 Lloyd Rd, also in a crumbling old villa but in much better condition than the Mitre. Windowless singles cost S$45 or better doubles with windows are S$50 or S$60 with bath.

The Ys Singapore has a number of 'Ys' – all of the YMCAs in Singapore take men, women and couples. They are very good value and very popular, so advance bookings in writing with a one-night deposit are essential.

The *YMCA International House* (☎ 336 6000, fax 337 3140) is at 1 Orchard Rd. It is more like a mid-range hotel and costs S$60/70 for singles/doubles, S$80 for a family room and S$90 for a superior room, plus a 10% service charge. All rooms have air-con, TV, telephone and attached bathroom. A bed in the large dorm costs S$20. The facilities at this YMCA are exceptionally good and include a fitness centre, rooftop swimming pool, squash and badminton courts, and a billiards room.

The other YMCAs also have good facilities and rooms. The *Metropolitan YMCA* (☎ 737 7755, fax 235 5528), 60 Stevens Rd, is a good 15-minute walk north of Orchard and Tanglin Rds. Singles/doubles/triples with bathroom, TV and air-con range from S$55/65/75 to S$80/90/100. The *Metropolitan YMCA International Centre* (☎ 222 4666, fax 222 6467) is at 70 Palmer Rd, near the railway station and the Tanjong Pagar MRT station (see the Central Singapore map). It costs S$15 in the dorm, and singles for men only are S$24, but other rooms with shower are S$37/40 and open to women and couples. Add a 5% service charge to the prices for both these places.

The *YWCA Hostel* (☎ 336 1212) at 6-8 Fort Canning Rd is quite close to the Orchard Rd YMCA. A double room with air-con and shower costs S$45. Nice dorm rooms are available for S$15; they only take women or couples. This place has been recommended by solo women travellers as a safe and secure place.

SINGAPORE

Places to Stay – Middle

While Singapore has dozens of high-rise, luxury hotels with all mod-cons, mid-range hotels are in short supply. Most rooms in these hotels will have air-con, TV, telephone and a bathroom attached. In the major hotels, a 4% government tax and a 10% service charge is added to your bill but many mid-range hotels, like those in the bottom end, include this in the price.

The *New 7th Storey Hotel* (☎ 337 0251) at 229 Rochor Rd, at the northern end of the colonial district, is an upmarket cheapie. Good budget rooms go for S$59 or S$75 with attached bathroom.

Smaller modern hotels include the *Bencoolen Hotel* (☎ 336 0822), 47 Bencoolen St. The rooms are cheaply put together and cost S$85/93.50. A notch up in quality and with better facilities is the *Strand Hotel* (☎ 338 1866), 25 Bencoolen St, with rooms for S$95. The *Metropole Hotel* (☎ 336 3611), on Seah St behind Raffles, is a former three-star place that has lost its shine. It costs S$85/100 plus 14%.

The *Broadway Hotel* (☎ 292 4661), 195 Serangoon Rd, is one of the few hotels in Little India, and has a good, cheap Indian restaurant, but the rooms are musty and need maintenance. Singles/doubles cost S$80/90 and S$90/100, plus 4% tax.

You can find a few reasonably priced hotels around Orchard Rd. Located at Kramat Rd, one block north of Orchard Rd, the *Supreme Hotel* (☎ 737 8333) is central and a good deal for the position. Doubles cost S$85. *Lloyd's Inn* (☎ 737 7309), 2 Lloyd Rd, is a small, attractive hotel less than a 10-minute walk from Orchard Rd in a quiet street among the old villas of Singapore. Lee Kuan Yew is a neighbour. Well-appointed doubles cost S$80 a double or S$90 with fridge.

In the quiet residential area to the north of Orchard and Tanglin Rds you'll find the *Sloane Court* (☎ 2353311), 17 Balmoral Rd, a Tudor-style hotel in a garden setting with an English pub. The rooms are comfortable but nothing special for S$80/90. A few hundred metres away is the *Hotel VIP* (☎ 235 4277), 5 Balmoral Crescent, which has a swimming pool. The rooms are a grade above the Sloane Court and cost S$99. The *RELC International House* (☎ 737 9044), 30 Orange Grove Rd, is a quality hotel edging into the top-end category. Large doubles with balcony and fridge are S$102 to S$110.

PLACES TO EAT

Singapore is far and away the food capital of Asia. When it comes to superb Chinese food, Hong Kong may actually be a step ahead but it's Singapore's sheer variety and low prices which make it so good. Equally important, Singapore's food is so accessible – you don't have to search out obscure places, you don't face communication problems and you don't need a lot of money.

CLOSE TO : Banks, G.P.O., Public [illegible] Market, Hawkers food stalls, Money Changers, Travel Agents, Cinemas, 7-ELEVEN, 24 HRS Coffee House, Fast Food Chains, Hospital, Pharmacy (ALL within 500 M) And other places of interest.

SERVICES : Reservation for Taman Negara transfer, accommodation and boat, Reservation for sightseeing tours, Bus Tickets, Airport Taxi, Van Hire, Refreshments, Lockers, Left Luggage, Fax, Typewriting, and LAUNDRY.

FEATURES : Air-Con Lounge with colour TV, Video, Tourist Information, Book Exchange, Indoor Games and Public Phone.

ROOMS : Choice of Non Air-Con Single, Double, Triple, Quad Room, with or without showers (RM25-RM40) Air-Con (RM50-RM70). DORM (RM8 only) Weekly rate available.

BACKPACKERS

TRAVELLERS INN

No 60 (2nd Floor)
Jalan Sultan
50000 Kuala Lumpur
Malaysia
(Opposite Furama Hotel)
Tel : (603) 2382473, 2021855

BACKPACKERS
TRAVELLERS LODGE

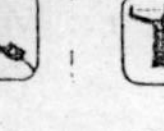

NO 158 (1st Floor)
Jalan Tun H. S. Lee
50000 KUALA LUMPUR
MALAYSIA
(Opposite Malaya Hotel)
Tel : (03) 2010889
Fax : (03) 2381128

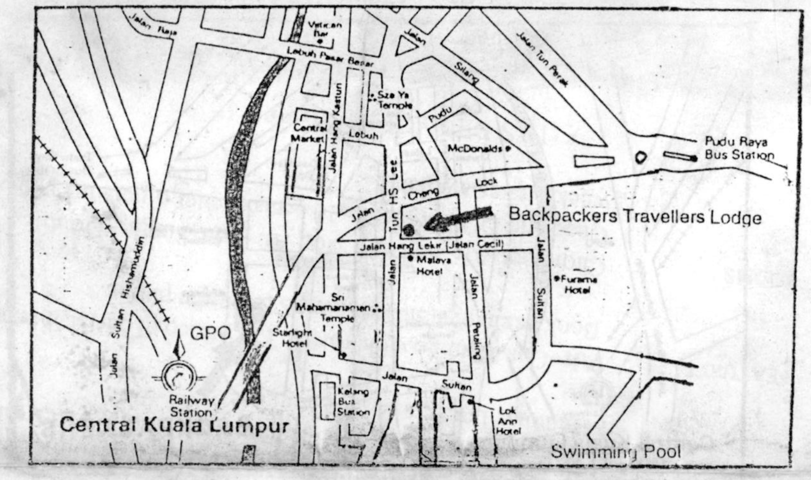

LOCATION : In the heart of Chinatown
5 Min walk from Puduraya Bus Station (Exit Pintu 6)
2 Min walk from Airport Bus Station
6 Min walk from Railway Station (Exit Platform 4)

... Pool, Chinatown Night

Hawkers' Food

Traditionally, hawkers had mobile foodstalls (pushcarts), set up their tables and stools around them and sold their food right on the streets. Real, mobile, on-the-street hawkers have now been replaced by hawkers' centres where a large number of stationary hawkers can be found under the one roof. These centres are the baseline for Singapore food, where the prices are lowest and the eating is possibly the most interesting.

Scattered amongst the hawkers are tables and stools, and you can sit and eat in any area you choose – none of them belong to a specific stall. A group of you can sit at one table and all eat from different stalls and purchase drinks from another.

One of the wonders of food-centre eating is how the various operators keep track of their plates and utensils – and how they manage to chase you up with the bill. The real joy of these food centres is the sheer variety; while you're having Chinese food, your companion can be eating a biryani and across the table somebody else can be trying the satay. As a rough guide, most one-dish meals cost from S$1.50 to S$3; the price is higher for more elaborate dishes.

City Centre In the business centre, *Empress Place*, beside the Singapore River, is a pleasant place to sit and have a meal, but is very busy at lunchtime.

Near the waterfront is the trendy *Lau Pa Sat*, on Raffles Quay near the Raffles Place MRT station. Hawkers inside serve nonya, Korean and Western food, as well as more usual fare. Quasi-mobile hawkers set up in the evenings on Boon Tat St.

Orchard Rd Area *Newton Circus Hawker Centre*, on Scotts Rd right near the Newton MRT station (see the Central Singapore map), is very popular with tourists and therefore tends to be a little more expensive, but it is lively and open until the early hours of the morning.

The *Scotts Picnic Food Court* in the Scotts Shopping Centre on Scotts Rd, just off Orchard Rd by the Hyatt Hotel, is quite a different sort of food centre. It's glossier and more restaurant-like than the general run of food centres, and the stalls around the dining area are international. Similar food centres are the *Orchard Emerald Food Court* in the basement of the Orchard Emerald shopping centre (just north-west of Peranakan Place – see the Orchard Rd map) and the foodstalls downstairs in *Orchard Towers* (next to the Hotel Negara). The busy centre on the 6th floor of *Lucky Plaza* (near the Orchard MRT station) has a good range of cheap hawkers' favourites.

Colonial District The *Albert Centre*, on Albert Rd between Waterloo and Queen Sts, is an extremely good, busy and very popular centre which has all types of food at low prices. On the corner of Bencoolen St and Albert St, in the basement of the Sim Lim Square complex, is the *Tenco Food Centre*, a very clean establishment.

Victoria St Food Court, next to the Victoria Hotel, has an air-con section at the back and a bar with draught beer. The *Tropical Makan Palace* in the basement of the Beach Centre, 15 Beach Rd, is close to Raffles Hotel. It has foodstalls in the air-con section or you can eat outside.

The famous *Satay Club*, by the waterfront at the foot of Stamford Rd near Raffles Hotel, is a colourful place to dine. The satay here is the best in Singapore, just make sure you specify how many sticks (30c a time) you want or they'll assume your appetite is much larger than it is. It's only open in the evening.

Chinatown The Chinatown area has a number of excellent food centres. The *People's Park Complex* has a good, large food centre, and the *Maxwell Food Centre* is an old-fashioned centre on the corner of South Bridge and Maxwell Rds (near the Tanjong Pagar MRT station – see the Central Singapore map).

Some of the best Chinese foodstalls in town are on the 2nd floor at the *Chinatown Complex* on the corner of Sago and Trengganu Sts, where there is also a market. Try the *Fu Ji Crayfish*, stall No 02-221,

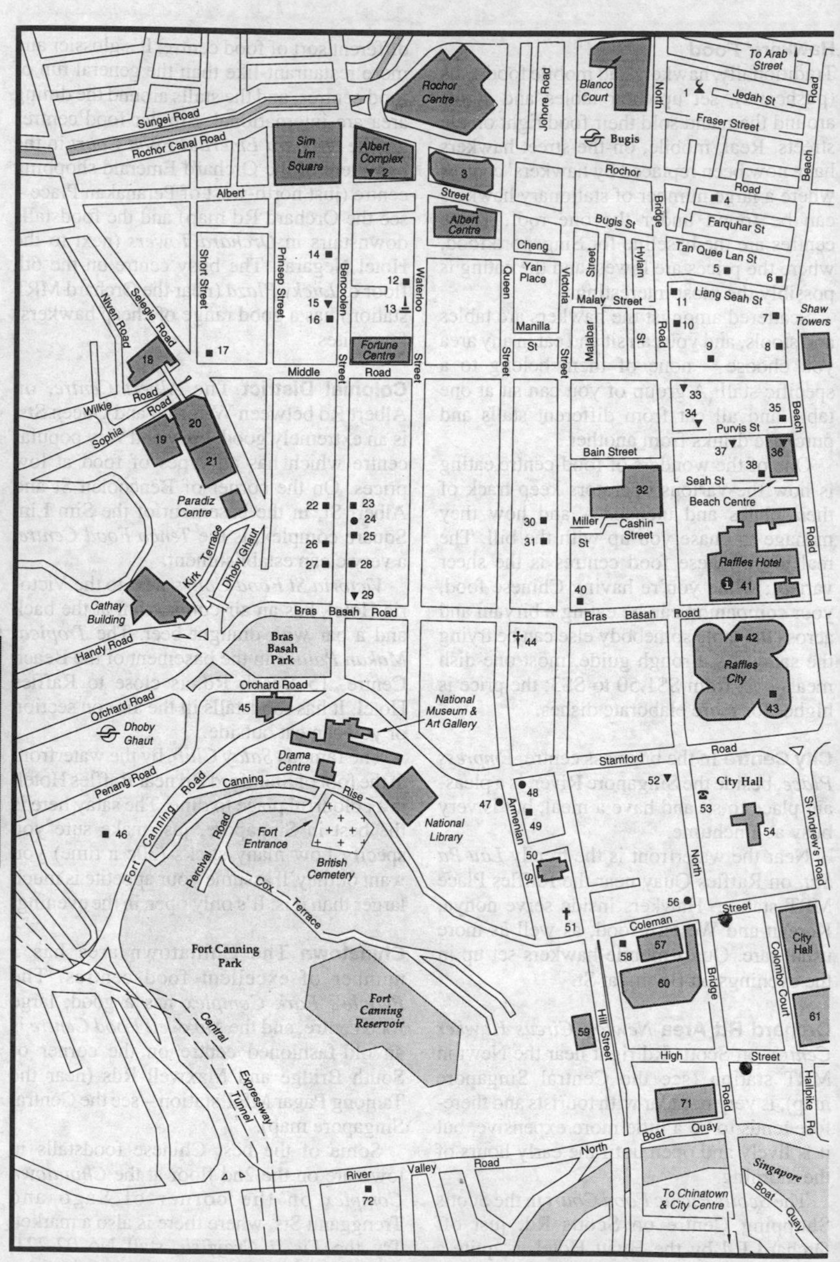

SINGAPORE

Cozy Lodge

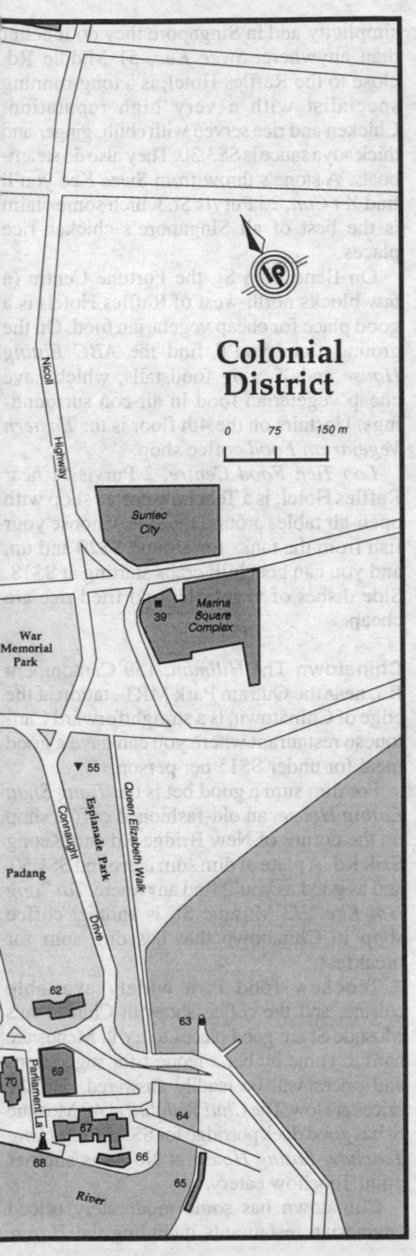

PLACES TO STAY

4 New 7th Storey Hotel
5 New Backpackers Lodge
6 Willy's (2) Guest House
7 Das Travellers' Inn
8 Lee Traveller's Club & Willy's Guest House
9 Lido Hotel
10 Raffles Home Stay
11 Ah Chew Hotel
12 South-East Asia Hotel
14 Goh's Homestay & Hawaii Hostel
16 Why Not Homestay
17 Sun Sun Hotel
22 Bencoolen Hotel
23 Lee Traveller's Club, Peony Mansions & Latin House
25 San Wah Hotel
26 Bencoolen House
27 Strand Hotel
28 Bayview Inn
30 Allson Hotel
31 Victoria Hotel
35 Shang Onn Hotel
38 Metropole Hotel
39 Marina Mandarin Hotel
40 Carlton Hotel
42 Westin Plaza Hotel
43 Westin Stamford Hotel
45 YMCA International House
46 YWCA Hostel
49 Mayfair City Hotel
57 Peninsula Hotel
58 Excelsior Hotel
72 New Otani Hotel

PLACES TO EAT

2 Fatty's Wing Seong Restaurant
15 Sahib Restaurant
29 Regency Palace
33 Swee Kee Restaurant
34 Loo Tien Food Centre
36 Tropical Makan Palace Food Stalls
37 Yet Con Restaurant
52 Third Man
55 Satay Club
59 Hill Street Food Centre
65 Food Centre
66 Empress Place Food Centre

OTHER

1 Mosque
3 Fu Lou Shou Complex
13 Kuan Yin Temple
18 Selegie Complex
19 Peace Mission
20 Peace Centre
21 Parklane Shopping Mall
24 Airmaster Travel
32 Bras Basah Complex
41 STPB Tourist Office
44 Cathedral of the Good Shepherd

47	Substation
48	MPH Bookstore
50	US Embassy
51	Church of St Gregory the Illuminator
53	Telecom Office
54	St Andrew's Cathedral
56	Peninsula Plaza
60	Funan Centre
61	Supreme Court
62	Singapore Cricket Club
63	Merlion Park
64	Cavenagh Bridge
67	Empress Place Building & Museum
68	Raffles' Statue
69	Victoria Concert Hall & Theatre
70	Parliament House
71	High Street Centre

where a superb crayfish or prawn claypot with vegetables and rice costs around S$5.

The *Fountain Food Court* at 51 Craig Rd is a different type of food centre in keeping with the new Chinatown. You can dine in air-con comfort, and the nouveau decor includes sandblasted and bag-painted walls. They have satay and other Malay food, popiah and kueh, and good congee.

Chinese Food

Singapore has plenty of restaurants serving everything from a south Indian rice plate to an all-American hamburger, but naturally it's Chinese restaurants that predominate.

Colonial District The famous *Fatty's Wing Seong Restaurant*, at 01-33 Albert Complex on Albert St near the corner of Bencoolen St, has an extensive menu that unfortunately lacks prices but the food is consistently good and moderately priced. Most dishes cost around S$5 to S$8, and go up to S$20 or more for crab.

The *Esquire Kitchen* (☎ 336 1802), 02-01 Bras Basah Complex, is another moderately priced place with air-con, Chinese decor and good food. Most small mains cost from S$6 to S$10, and ice creams and spiders are a speciality.

Chicken rice is a common and popular dish all over town. Originally from Hainan in China, chicken rice is a dish of elegant simplicity and in Singapore they do it better than anywhere. *Swee Kee*, 51 Middle Rd, close to the Raffles Hotel, is a long-running specialist with a very high reputation. Chicken and rice served with chilli, ginger and thick soya sauce is S$3.30. They also do steamboats. A stone's throw from Swee Kee you'll find *Yet Con*, 25 Purvis St, which some claim is the best of all Singapore's chicken-rice places.

On Bencoolen St, the Fortune Centre (a few blocks north-west of Raffles Hotel) is a good place for cheap vegetarian food. On the ground floor you'll find the *ABC Eating House* and *Yi Song* foodstalls, which have cheap vegetarian food in air-con surroundings. Upstairs on the 4th floor is the *Eastern Vegetarian Food* coffee shop.

Loo Tien Food Centre, 2 Purvis St near Raffles Hotel, is a Teochow coffee shop with open-air tables around the side. Choose your fish from the tanks for around S$20 and up, and you can get chilli crabs starting at S$18. Side dishes of vegetables and fried rice are cheap.

Chinatown The *Hillman*, 159 Cantonment Rd, near the Outram Park MRT station at the edge of Chinatown, is a straightforward Cantonese restaurant where you can have a good meal for under S$15 per person.

For dim sum a good bet is the *Tiong Shan Eating House*, an old-fashioned coffee shop on the corner of New Bridge Rd and Keong Saik Rd. A plate of dim sum is around S$1.50, and as good as you'll find anywhere. *Tai Tong Hoi Kee*, 2/3 Mosque St, is another coffee shop in Chinatown that has dim sum for breakfast.

Teochew food is a widely available cuisine, and the coffee shops in Chinatown's Mosque St are good places to try it. Menus are hard to come by but a request for suggestions and prices will be readily answered, and the prices are low. The *Chui Wah Lin* at 49 Mosque St has good duck porridge for S$3. *Liang Heng Teochow Eating House* at No 48 is another good Teochow eatery.

Chinatown has some moderately priced vegetarian restaurants including the *Happy*

Realm on the 3rd floor of Pearl's Centre on Eu Tong St (see the Central Singapore map), one of the best around. Mains cost around S$5 to S$6 and they have good claypot dishes.

Coast Singapore has another local variation on Chinese food which is worth making the effort to try. Seafood in Singapore is simply superb, whether it's prawns or abalone, fish-head curry or chilli crabs. Seafood isn't cheap, and a whole fish, crab or prawns start at just under S$20 per dish. Many of the seafood places don't have set prices but base it on 'market price' and the size of the fish. Make sure you check the price first.

The *UDMC Seafood Centre*, at the beach on East Coast Parkway (several km east of the city centre), has a number of seafood restaurants and is very popular in the evenings. The food and the setting are good, but they tend to hustle a bit at some of these places, so definitely check the prices first. Another Singapore seafood institution is Punggol Point on the north-eastern coast, where you'll find some of the best and cheapest seafood.

Indian Food

To sample eat-with-your-fingers south Indian vegetarian food, the place to go is the Little India district off Serangoon Rd (just north of the colonial district – see the Central Singapore map). The famous and very popular *Komala Vilas*, 76 Serangoon Rd, has an open downstairs area where you can have masala dosa (S$1.50) and other snacks. The upstairs section is air-conditioned and you can have their all-you-can-eat rice meal for S$4.50. Remember that it is customary to wash your hands before you start, use your right hand and ask for eating utensils only if you really have to!

Another main contender in the local competition for the best southern Indian food is the *Madras New Woodlands Cafe*, at 14 Upper Dickson Rd off Serangoon Rd, around the corner from Komala Vilas. A branch of the well-known Woodlands chain in India, New Woodlands serves freshly prepared vegetarian food in very clean air-conditioned rooms. Prices are about the same as at Komala Vilas.

Race Course Rd, a block north-west from Serangoon Rd, is the best area in Singapore for nonvegetarian curry. Try the *Banana Leaf Apolo* at 56 Race Course Rd for superb nonvegetarian Indian food, including Singapore's classic fish-head curry, or the very popular *Muthu's Curry Restaurant* at No 78. *Delhi Restaurant* (☎ 296 4585) at No 60 is an excellent north Indian restaurant, with tandoori food and curries from S$7 to S$10. Expect to pay S$15 to S$20 per person with bread and side dishes. Similar places on Race Course Rd are *Nur Jehan* at No 66 and *Maharajahs's Tandoor* at No 70.

For Indian Muslim food (chicken biryani for S$3.50, as well as murtabak and fish-head curry), there are a string of venerable establishments on North Bridge Rd, near the corner of Arab St, opposite the Sultan Mosque. They are great places for biryani and other Indian dishes at very low prices. The *Victory* and *Zam Zam* are two of the most well known.

Sahib Restaurant at 129 Bencoolen St, near Middle Rd (see the Colonial District map), is a small, basic Indian restaurant with very good food, including fish-head curry. Meals are around S$4 and they are open 24 hours. At the other end of the scale, *Maharani* (☎ 235 8840) is on the 5th floor of the Far East Plaza, 14 Scotts Rd (near the Hyatt Hotel – see the Orchard Rd map). The northern Indian food and the service are good in this casual restaurant. You can eat well for S$20 per person.

Malay, Indonesian & Nonya Food

The Orchard Rd area has a number of good restaurants. *Bintang Timur* (☎ 235 4539), 02-Far East Plaza, 14 Scotts Rd, has excellent Malay food and you can try a good range of dishes and eat your fill for under S$20. *Tambuah Mas* (☎ 733 3333), 04-10/13 Tanglin Shopping Centre, 19 Tanglin Rd (near the Orchard Parade Hotel), is a moderately priced Indonesian restaurant with a good selection of seafood dishes and

Indonesian favourites such as rendang, gado gado and cendol. If you like the fiery food of northern Sumatra, a good nasi padang specialist is *Rendezvouz*, 02-19 in the Raffles City Shopping Centre on Bras Basah Rd (see the Colonial District map).

Nonya & Baba Restaurant (☎ 734 1382) is one of the best restaurants to try nonya food at reasonable prices. Most mains cost around S$6 for small claypots and up to S$15 for large serves. A variety of snacks and sweets are also available. It is at 262-264 River Valley Rd, near the corner of Tank Rd and directly behind the Imperial Hotel (see the Orchard Rd map). The Dhoby Ghaut MRT station at the start of Orchard Rd is a 15-minute walk away.

East Coast Rd in Katong is also a great place to try nonya food. The *Peranakan Inn & Lounge*, 210 East Coast Rd, is one of the cheapest places in Singapore to eat nonya food in an air-con setting. Most dishes cost S$4 to S$6, or more expensive seafood dishes cost S$12 to S$18. During the day, try the nonya kueh (cakes) and curry puffs at the *Katong Bakery & Confectionary*, 75 East Coast Rd. This wonderful old-fashioned cake shop is a throwback to the Singapore of yesterday. The best bus for East Coast Rd is No 14, which goes along Orchard Rd and Bras Basah Rd in the colonial district.

SINGAPORE

Other Asian Food

The Golden Mile Complex at 5001 Beach Rd (see the Central Singapore map) is a modern shopping centre catering to Singapore's Thai community where you'll find a number of small coffee shops serving Thai food and Singha beer. You can get a good meal for S$4, but there are no menus in English. Also here is the *Pornping Thai Seafood Restaurant*, which has a wide variety of good Thai food including Isarn dishes. In Orchard Rd, *Parkway Thai* (☎ 737 8080) in Centrepoint, 176 Orchard Rd, has an extensive menu – small mains range from S$6 up to S$15 for seafood.

Singapore has experienced a Japanese restaurant boom, and while you can still spend a small fortune at a Japanese restaurant, you can sample Japanese food at moderate prices. *Restaurant Hoshigaoka* is a chain of Japanese restaurants, with branches at 03-45 Centrepoint and 04-02 Wisma Atria (south of the Orchard MRT station) on Orchard Rd.

Or there's Taiwanese food. Try the reasonably priced *Goldleaf* at 24-24A Tanjong Pagar Rd in Chinatown. A speciality is chicken covered in fried whole chillies. You can eat very well for less than S$20.

If you are hankering after spicy Asian food but can't decide what type of cuisine, try *Spice Express* (☎ 734 8835), B1-20/21 Forum shopping centre, 583 Orchard Rd (next to the Hard Rock Cafe). Indian, Thai, Malay, Chinese and Vietnamese dishes are all on offer and the lunch buffet for S$18.50 or the buffet dinner on Friday and Saturday for S$22.50 are good value.

Western Food

Yes, you can get Western food in Singapore too. There are nearly 40 *McDonald's*, found all over town, as well as *A&W Restaurants, Kentucky Fried Chicken, Burger King, Dunkin' Donuts, Dennys, Pizza Hut, Baskin Robbins* and *Swensen's Ice Cream* outlets.

The *Hard Rock Cafe*, 50 Cuscaden Rd, near the corner of Orchard and Tanglin Rds, is one of the most popular places for American-style steaks, BBQ grills and ribs. Main meals cost around S$20, and snacks such as burgers cost around S$8. The *Third Man*, 11 Stamford Rd near Raffles City (see the Colonial District map), is a pub-style place that does changing set lunches and dinners for around S$15. Home-sick Brits can get Bass on tap.

In Bencoolen St, the *Golden Dragon Inn* is a Chinese coffee shop on the 2nd floor of the Fortune Centre that does a reasonable job of Western grills. You can get steak or prawns with chips and eggs served on a sizzler for only S$6, or if you crave cholesterol for breakfast, ham and eggs costs S$3.

El Felipes Cantina (☎ 733 3551), 02-09 International Building, 360 Orchard Rd (north of the Orchard MRT station), is an old favourite that has large serves and moderate prices.

Breakfast, Snacks & Delis

The big international hotels have their large international breakfast buffets of course (around S$18 to S$20) but there are still a few old coffee shops which do cheap Chinese and Indian breakfasts – take your pick of dosa and curry or yu-tiao and hot soy milk.

Many places do a fixed-price breakfast – continental or American. Try the *Silver Spoon Coffee House* in Supreme House (see the Orchard Rd map) on Penang Rd off Orchard Rd, or the *Chameleon* on the ground floor of Orchard Plaza. *Arcadia Cafe*, 01-42 Lucky Plaza in Orchard Rd (near the Orchard MRT station), is a Chinese/Western greasy spoon with breakfast for S$3.50; at other times steaks cost S$8 and fish and chips are S$5. One of the nicest breakfasts is undoubtedly *Breakfast with the Birds* (☎ 265 0022) at Jurong Bird Park (west of the city centre – see the Singapore Island map). The buffet breakfast costs S$12 (admission is extra), the waffles are great and the birds will tell your fortune for free.

Old Chang Kee is a chain that specialises in that old favourite – curry puffs. There is one at Lau Pa Sat (see the Central Singapore map), but the best is at the corner of MacKenzie and Niven Rds, near Selegie Rd in the colonial district. Try their range, washed down with coffee in an old-style kopi tiam (coffee shop). *Sweet Secrets*, at the back of Centrepoint in Orchard Rd, is a Western-style coffee shop with a magnificent array of cakes.

Singapore has plenty of delis that cater for lunching office workers and snacking shoppers in the central business district and Orchard Rd. Try cakes, cookies, yoghurt and muesli in *Steeple's Deli*, 02-25 Tanglin Shopping Centre on Tanglin Rd (next to the Orchard Parade Hotel – see the Orchard Rd map). This is one of Singapore's original delis and they do great deli-style sandwiches from S$8 to S$10.

ENTERTAINMENT

At night, eating out is one of the favourite Singaporean occupations and it takes place at the hundreds of restaurants and countless food-centre stalls. Chinese street-operas still take place around the city – it's all fantastic costumes and (to Western ears) a horrible noise. There are a number of 'instant Asia' style cultural shows performed in and around Singapore, including Instant Asia (at the Singa Inn Seafood Restaurant, 920 East Coast Parkway), ASEAN Night (at the Mandarin Hotel on Orchard Rd), and the Lion City Revue (at The Cockpit Hotel – see the Orchard Rd map).

Modern live music is often middle-of-the-road but thriving, with many Filipino musicians working the Orchard Rd hotels and nightspots. Cover charges are typically S$15 to S$25. A glass of beer will cost around S$8. The free tourist magazines have gig guides, or check the Thursday edition of *Straits Times* for what's on and where.

The Orchard Rd area is the main centre for live music, and one of the biggest places is *Fire* in Orchard Plaza, 150 Orchard Rd. The interesting resident band, Energy, live up to their name and there are other lounges in the three-floor complex. The *Hard Rock Cafe*, 50 Cuscaden Rd, has the usual rock memorabilia, good atmosphere and better bands than most venues.

Some good places don't usually have a cover charge. *Club 392* in Orchard Towers (next to the Hotel Negara) has good jazz bands and an interesting, slightly seedy atmosphere. *Anywhere* in the Tanglin Shopping Centre, 19 Tanglin Rd (near the Orchard Parade Hotel), is a long-running rock 'n' roll place. The music is nothing to write home about but the atmosphere is casual and convivial. The *Saxophone Bar & Grill*, 3 Cuppage Terrace near the corner of Orchard Rd, is a small place – so small that the band has to play on a platform behind the bar – with blues and jazz music. *Brannigans* in the Hyatt Regency, 10-12 Scotts Rd (see the Orchard Rd map), is a popular pick-up spot for expat and Singaporean professionals. This is more of an intimate pub and the music is jazz.

Singapore has plenty of bars, and no restoration project is complete without a few. Most bars have happy hours from around 5 to 8 pm, and sometimes offer all-you-can-drink extended happy hours, which makes Singapore's high alcohol prices more palatable. A good place for a pub crawl is the Tanjong Pagar area, near the Singapore railway station. Tanjong Pagar Rd, Duxton Rd and Duxton Hill all have a number of bars. *Elvis' Place*, 1A Duxton Hill (see the Central Singapore map), is lined with Elvis memorabilia and plays the King's hits and '50s music non-stop. The *Flag & Whistle*, 10 Duxton Hill, is a pub nearby.

The renovated Boat Quay is another good area to look for bars. *Harry's*, 28 Boat Quay (see the Central Singapore map), is very popular and sometimes has bands. Of course you can have a drink at *Raffles* (see the Colonial District map), at the Long Bar or in the Bar & Billiard Room where that infamous tiger was supposedly shot. For English pub ambience, try the cosy *Third Man*, in the Capitol Building, 11 Stamford Rd near Raffles City. They have English Bass on tap.

Risque nightlife is not on in Singapore. The famous transvestite scene in Bugis St is gone. Singapore does have a highly active red-light district, stretching from Jalan Besar to Serangoon Rd and parallel to Desker Rd, but Singaporeans in search of sex and sin usually head across the border to Malaysia or to nearby Batam Island in the Riau Archipelago of Indonesia.

SINGAPORE

Thailand

There is probably more visible historical evidence of past cultures in Thailand than in any other South-East Asian country. If you've got the slightest interest in ruins, deserted cities and Buddhas, Thailand is the place to go. It's a remarkably fertile country, a major agricultural exporter and very much one big city and a lot of countryside – Nakhon Ratchasima, the second-largest city, is a small town compared to Bangkok.

Easy travel, excellent and economic accommodation, some fine beach centres and an interesting (but very hot!) cuisine make Thailand a very good country to visit. Thailand's economic boom of the last few years has been accompanied by an equally spectacular tourist boom; it's a very popular country.

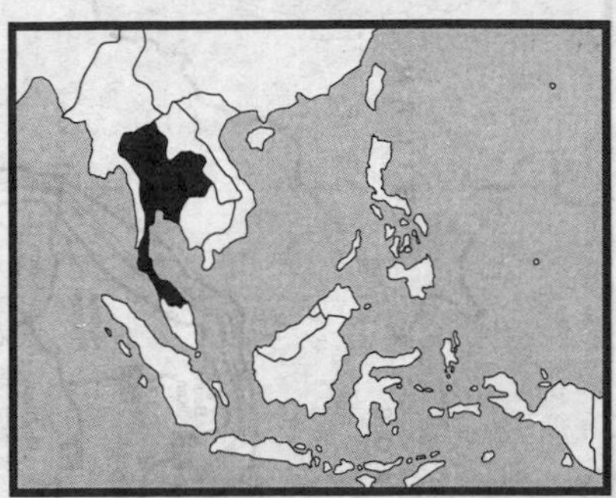

Facts about the Country

HISTORY

Thailand's history often seems very complex – so many different peoples, kings, kingdoms and cultures have had a hand in it. The earliest civilisation in Thailand was probably that of the Mons who brought a Buddhist culture from the Indian subcontinent. The rise of the Davaravati kingdoms in central Thailand was ended by the westward movement of the energetic Khmers whose influence can be seen in Thailand at Phimai and Lopburi. At the same time, the Sumatran-based Srivijaya Empire extended up through Malaya and into southern Thailand.

Kublai Khan's expansionist movements in China speeded up the southern migration of the Thai people and, in 1220, Thai princes took over Sukhothai, their first Siamese capital. Other Thai peoples migrated to Laos and the Shan states of Burma. Another Thai kingdom called Lanna Thai (Million Thai Rice-Fields), under King Mengrai, formed in Chiang Rai in northern Thailand and later moved to Chiang Mai. In 1350, the Prince of U Thong founded still another Thai capital in Ayuthaya which eventually overshadowed Sukhothai. For two centuries, Ayuthaya was unsurpassed, pushing the Khmers right out of Siam, and the Khmer capital of Angkor was abandoned to the jungles, which hid it almost to this century.

In the 16th century, the Burmese – arch-rivals of the Thais – who had become disunited after Kublai Khan's sacking of Pagan, regrouped and wrought havoc in Thailand. Chiang Mai, which Ayuthaya had never absorbed, was captured by the Burmese in 1556, and in 1569 Ayuthaya also fell to them. Their success, however, was short lived and, in 1595, the Thais recaptured Chiang Mai. During the next century, European influences first appeared in Thailand, but the execution of Constantine Phaulkon, Greek emissary of the French, ended that little episode.

In the 18th century, the Burmese attacked again and in 1767, after a prolonged siege, took and utterly destroyed Ayuthaya. The Siamese soon regrouped and expelled the Burmese, but Ayuthaya was never reconstructed. In 1782, the new capital at Thonburi was moved across the river to its present site at Bangkok, and the still-ruling

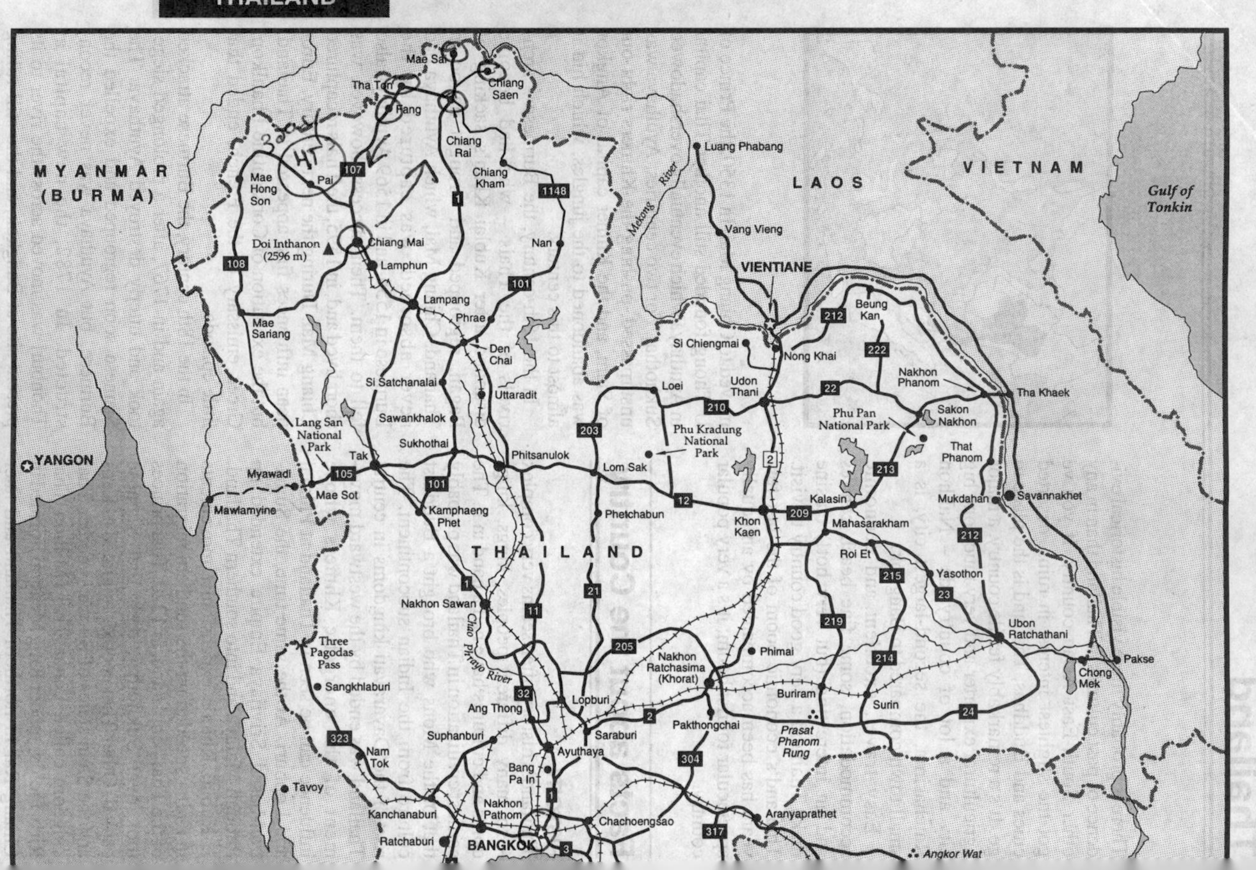
THAILAND
MYANMAR (BURMA)
LAOS
VIETNAM
Gulf of Tonkin
YANGON
Mae Sai
Tha Ton
Chiang Saen
Fang
Chiang Rai
Chiang Kham
Mae Hong Son
Pai
Doi Inthanon (2596 m)
Chiang Mai
Lamphun
Nan
Lampang
Phrae
Den Chai
Mae Sariang
Si Satchanalai
Uttaradit
Sawankhalok
Sukhothai
Lang San National Park
Tak
Phitsanulok
Myawadi
Mae Sot
Mawlamyine
Kamphaeng Phet
THAILAND
Nakhon Sawan
Chao Phrayo River
Three Pagodas Pass
Sangkhlaburi
Ang Thong
Suphanburi
Nam Tok
Tavoy
Kanchanaburi
Ratchaburi
Nakhon Pathom
BANGKOK
Bang Pa In
Ayuthaya
Lopburi
Saraburi
Chachoengsao
Aranyaprathet
Angkor Wat
Mekong River
Luang Phabang
Vang Vieng
VIENTIANE
Si Chiengmai
Nong Khai
Beung Kan
Loei
Udon Thani
Phu Kradung National Park
Lom Sak
Phetchabun
Khon Kaen
Kalasin
Mahasarakham
Roi Et
Phu Pan National Park
Nakhon Phanom
Tha Khaek
Sakon Nakhon
That Phanom
Mukdahan
Savannakhet
Yasothon
Ubon Ratchathani
Pakse
Chong Mek
Nakhon Ratchasima (Khorat)
Phimai
Buriram
Surin
Pakthongchai
Prasat Phanom Rung

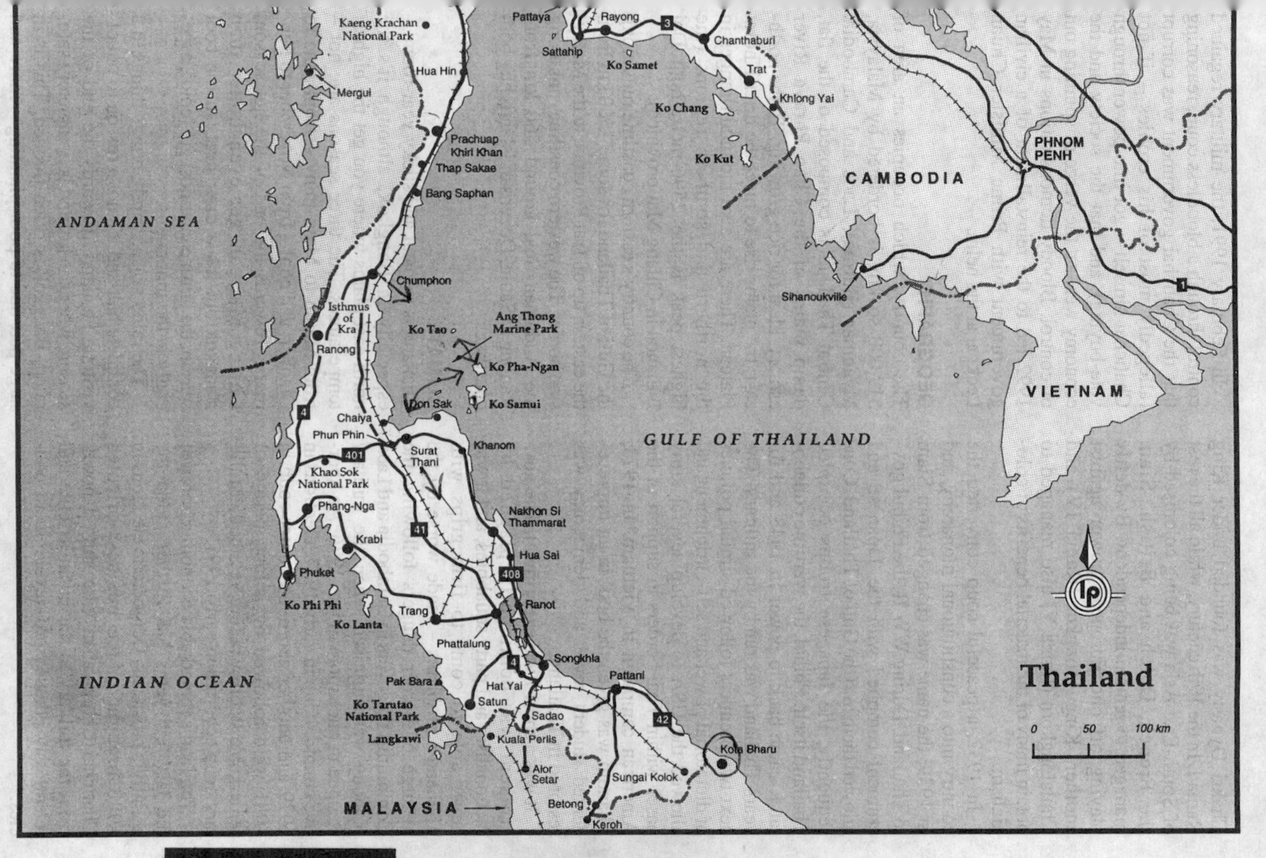
Kaeng Krachan National Park
Pattaya
Rayong
Sattahip
Ko Samet
Chanthaburi
Trat
Khlong Yai
Ko Chang
Ko Kut
PHNOM PENH
CAMBODIA
Sihanoukville
VIETNAM
Hua Hin
Mergui
Prachuap Khiri Khan
Thap Sakae
Bang Saphan
ANDAMAN SEA
Chumphon
Isthmus of Kra
Ranong
Ko Tao
Ang Thong Marine Park
Ko Pha-Ngan
Ko Samui
Don Sak
Chaiya
Phun Phin
Surat Thani
Khanom
GULF OF THAILAND
Khao Sok National Park
Phang-Nga
Krabi
Nakhon Si Thammarat
Hua Sai
Phuket
Ko Phi Phi
Ko Lanta
Trang
Ranot
Phattalung
Songkhla
Pattani
INDIAN OCEAN
Pak Bara
Hat Yai
Satun
Ko Tarutao National Park
Sadao
Langkawi
Kuala Perlis
Kota Bharu
Alor Setar
Sungai Kolok
MALAYSIA
Betong
Keroh
Thailand
0 50 100 km
1
3
4
41
42
401
408

THAILAND

Chakri Dynasty was founded under King Rama I. In the 19th century, while all the rest of South-East Asia was being colonised by the French, Dutch and British, Siam managed to remain independent. By deftly playing off one European power against another, King Mongkut (Rama IV) and Chulalongkorn (Rama V) also managed to obtain many of the material benefits of colonialism.

In 1932, a peaceful coup converted the country into a constitutional monarchy, and in 1939, the name was changed from Siam to Thailand. During WW II, the Phibul government complied with the Japanese and allowed them into the Gulf of Thailand. Consequently, the Japanese troops occupied Thailand itself. Phibul, the wartime collaborator, came back to power in 1948 and for years Thailand was run by the military. The next two premiers followed similar policies of dictatorial power and self-enrichment and allowed the USA to develop several army bases within Thai borders in support of the American campaign in Vietnam. In 1973, Thanom was given the boot in an unprecedented student revolt and democracy was restored in Thailand.

It was a short-lived experiment. The government was continually plagued by factionalism and party squabbles, and it was never able to come to firm grips with Thailand's problems – made worse by the upsurge of border dangers following the Communist takeovers in Cambodia and Laos. Nobody was surprised when the military stepped in once more in late 1976. An abortive counter-coup in early 1977, elections in 1979 and another abortive counter-coup in 1981 were followed by a long period of remarkable stability before yet another military coup occurred in early 1991.

Thailand's remarkable economic boom of the last few years has further aided the country's prospects. Democratic elections in 1988 brought in the business-oriented Chatichai Choonvahan who shifted power from the military to the business elite and relentlessly pursued pro-development policies.

In February 1991, the military regained control through a bloodless coup, reasoning that the Chatichai government was corrupt (allegedly most of his cronies – if not Chatichai himself – got into power through vote-buying), and that the society and the economy were on the verge of spinning out of control. Bloody demonstrations in May 1992 led to the reinstallment of a civilian government with Prime Minister Chuan Leekpai at the helm.

GEOGRAPHY

The country, which occupies an area of 517,000 sq km, is bordered by Malaysia, Myanmar (Burma), Laos and Cambodia. Central Thailand is composed of the flat, damp plains of the Chao Phraya River estuary, ideal for rice growing. To the north-east, the plains rise to meet the drier Khorat Plateau. There are also mountain ranges in the northern and southern regions (the highest peak is the 2596-metre-high Doi Inthanon in Chiang Mai province).

The country's eastern coastline runs along the Gulf of Thailand for some 1500 km from the eastern tip of Trat Province to the Malaysian border. The western coastline runs along the Andaman Sea, around 560 km from Ranong to Satun. Dozens of islands hug both coastlines.

CLIMATE

Thailand is tropical and sticky year-round – especially in Bangkok, although it's the north-east plains where you get the highest temperatures. The three seasons are: hot – from March to May; rainy – from June to October; and cool – from November to February. Towards the end of the hot season, Chiang Mai can get even hotter than Bangkok but it's a drier heat. In the cool season, the north can almost get 'cold', especially in the mountains.

The rainy season rarely brings things to a complete halt and it's not a reason to put off visiting Thailand. Towards the end of the season, when the ground is completely saturated, Bangkok is often flooded. This is in large part due to poor planning – more and more canals are being filled in and wells are drilled indiscriminately, thus lowering the water table, and the whole place is sinking anyway!

ECONOMY

Rice is the mainstay of the Thai economy and is widely exported to surrounding countries. Other major export products are tapioca, maize, sugar, rubber, tin, cement, pineapple, tuna and textiles.

Many economists are painting a bright economic future for Thailand, saying that it will join the ranks of the NICs (Newly Industrialised Countries) like Korea and Taiwan within five to 10 years. Others say that the infrastructure is far from ready to handle the current rate of growth (about 8% per annum) and change. Average annual per capita income is about US$1650 but there is a wide gap between affluent Bangkok and the much less affluent countryside.

POPULATION & PEOPLE

Thailand's population is about 54 million. Although basically homogeneous, there are many hill tribes in the northern area and some Malays in the south, as well as numbers of Mon, Khmer, Phuan and other common South-East Asian ethnic groups. About 10% of the population is Chinese, but they're so well assimilated that almost no one bothers to note the difference. There are also a large number of refugees from Myanmar, Laos and Cambodia in festering camps in the border areas, and Thailand has also been affected by the Vietnamese refugee problem.

CULTURE

Conduct

Monarchy and religion are the two sacred cows in Thailand. Thais are tolerant of most kinds of behaviour as long as it doesn't insult one of these.

Monarchy The monarchy is held in considerable respect in Thailand and visitors should be respectful too – avoid disparaging remarks about the king, queen or anyone in the royal family. One of Thailand's leading intellectuals, Sulak Sivarak, was arrested in the early '80s because of a passing reference to the king's fondness for sailing when he called him 'the skipper'.

While it's OK to criticise the Thai government and even Thai culture openly, it's considered a grave insult to Thai nationhood as well as to the monarchy not to stand when you hear the national anthem (composed by the king, incidentally).

Religion Correct behaviour in temples entails several guidelines, the most important of which is to dress neatly (no shorts or tank tops) and to take your shoes off when you enter any building that contains a Buddha image. Buddha images are sacred objects, so don't pose in front of them for pictures and definitely do not clamber upon them.

Monks are not supposed to touch or be touched by women. If a woman wants to hand something to a monk, the object should be placed within reach of the monk and not handed directly to him.

When sitting in a religious edifice, keep your feet pointed away from any Buddha images. The usual way to do this is to sit in the 'mermaid' pose in which your legs are folded to the side, with the feet pointing backwards.

Social Gestures

Traditionally, Thais greet each other not with a handshake but with a prayer-like palms-together gesture known as a *wai*. If someone wais you, you should wai back (unless wai-ed by a child).

The feet are the lowest part of the body (spiritually as well as physically) so don't point your feet at people or point at things with your feet. In the same context, the head is regarded as the highest part of the body, so don't touch Thais on the head.

Thais are often addressed by their first name with the honorific *Khun* or a title preceding it. Friends often use nicknames or kinship terms like *phii* (elder sibling) or *nong* (younger sibling).

Dress & Attitude

Beach attire is not considered appropriate for trips into town and is especially counter-productive if worn to government offices (eg when applying for a visa extension). As in most parts of Asia, anger and emotions are rarely displayed and generally get you nowhere. In any argument or dispute, remember the paramount rule is to keep your cool.

RELIGION

Buddhism is the dominant religion for about 95% of the population. Orange-robed monks, and gold, marble, and stone Buddhas sitting, standing or reclining are common sights. The prevalent form of Buddhism practised is the Theravada (Council of the Elders) school. Also known as Hinayana, it is the same as that found in Sri Lanka, Myanmar, Laos and Cambodia. Theravada Buddhism emphasises the potential of the individual to attain Nibbana (Nirvana) without the aid of saints or gurus.

In Thailand's four southernmost provinces – Yala, Narathiwat, Pattani and Satun – there's a large Muslim minority.

LANGUAGE

Although Thai is a rather complicated language with its own unique alphabet, it's fun to try at least a few words. The *Thai Phrasebook* by Lonely Planet gives a handy basic introduction to the language and contains many helpful words and phrases.

The main complication with Thai is that it is tonal; the same word could be pronounced with a rising, falling, high, low or level tone and could theoretically have five meanings!

There are several different words that can be used to mean 'I' but the safest are *phóm* for men and *díichán* for women. You can also omit the pronoun altogether and say, for example, *mâi khâo jai* (do not understand). *Mâi pen rai* is a very useful phrase although it actually has far more meanings than simply 'it doesn't matter'. It can mean 'don't bother', 'forget it', 'leave it alone', 'take no notice', or even 'that's enough'.

The 'ph' in a Thai word is always pronounced like an English 'p', not as an 'f'.

Greetings & Civilities

hello
sawàt dii
How are you?
Pen yangai?
I'm fine.
Sabàay dii.
excuse me
khãw thôht
please
kaa-ru-naa or *pròht*
thank you
khàwp khun

Getting Around

I want to go to...
Yàak pai
Where is the ...?
...Yùu thîi nãi?
bus
rót meh
train
rót fai
hotel
rohng raem
post office
praisanii
station
sathaanii
beach
ao
island
ko
house or village
ban
How far?
Klai thâo rai?
here/there
thîi-nîi/thîi-nûun
near/far
klâi/klai
left/right
sái/khwaa
straight ahead
trong pai

Time & Dates
When?
Mêu-arai?
What time?
Kìi mohng?
leave/arrive
àwk/the\ung
today
wan níi
tomorrow
phrûng níi
yesterday
mêua waan

Other Useful Words & Phrases
foreigner of European descent
farang
yes (female)
khâ
yes (male)
khráp
no
mâi
How much?
Thâo rai?
too expensive
phaeng pai
It doesn't matter (or never mind.)
Mâi pen rai.
I do not understand.
Mâi khâo jai.
What is this in Thai?
Níi phãasãa thai riâk wâa arai?
toilet
hâwng sûam

Numbers

1	*nèung*
2	*sãwng*
3	*sãam*
4	*sìi*
5	*hâa*
6	*hòk*
7	*jèt*
8	*pàet*
9	*kâo*
10	*sìp*
11	*sìp èt*
20	*yîi sìp*
21	*yîi sìp èt*
30	*sãam sìp*
100	*nèung roi*
200	*sãwng roi*
1000	*nèung phan*

Emergencies
Help!
Chûay dûay!
Go away.
Pai láew.
doctor
mãw
police
tam-ruat

Facts for the Visitor

VISAS & EMBASSIES

You've got a variety of choices in the visa game for Thailand. First of all, you can enter Thailand without any visa and be granted a 15-day stay permit. Officially, you must have an outward ticket but in practice this does not always seem to be rigidly enforced. The major catch with the 15-day permit is that no extension is possible – 15 days is your lot.

In 1993 the Thai government considered a proposal to issue 30-day transit visas on arrival for citizens of 55 countries (including most Western nations). Most likely the proposed policy will be approved and put into effect by the end of 1994.

Visa fees have recently been raised. The pre-arranged one-month transit visa costs around US$15 and (like the 15-day permit) cannot be extended. From the traveller's point of view, the best deal is a two-month tourist visa which costs approximately US$20. They are issued quickly and without fuss. Singapore, Penang, Kota Bharu and Kathmandu are all good places to get Thai visas. Those from Sweden, Denmark, New Zealand, and South Korea take note: you can travel in Thailand for up to 90 days without a visa.

A one-month extension of your tourist visa is possible but costs 500B. You'll need two photos and photocopies of the photo and visa pages of your passport.

If you are leaving Thailand and then returning (for example, going to Myanmar for a week), you can get a re-entry visa, but this is double the cost of a single-entry visa so there are no savings. The immigration office in Bangkok for these visas is on Soi Suan Phlu. If you can provide a good reason for getting one (business for example), non-immigrant visas are also available – these cost US$20 and are valid for 90 days.

Thai Embassies Abroad

Laos
    Thanon Phon Kheng (☎ 2508, 2765)
Malaysia
    206 Jalan Ampang, Kuala Lumpur (☎ 03-2488222)
Singapore
    370 Orchard Rd (☎ 737 2644)

Other Visas

Bangkok is a popular place for getting visas for onward travel, particularly for people heading on to West Asia.

Following the upheavals in the Punjab, visas are now required for most nationalities visiting India. The Indian Embassy (☎ 258 0300) in Bangkok is at 46 Soi Prasanmit (Soi 23), off Sukhumvit Rd. This embassy can be slow in issuing visas. In Chiang Mai, however, there is an efficient Indian Consulate and visas are no problem at all.

Visas are not required in advance for Nepal. They can be obtained on arrival at the airport or at the land borders. This 'on arrival' visa is only valid for seven days, however, and extending it is such a time-consuming hassle that it's worthwhile obtaining a visa in advance if you have the time. The Nepalese Embassy (☎ 391 7240) is at 189 Soi Phuengsuk (Soi 71), a long way down Sukhumvit Rd.

Visas for Bangladesh are required for some nationalities and the embassy (☎ 391-070) is at 8 Soi Charoenmit (Soi 63), Sukhumvit Rd. Travellers heading for China usually get their visas in Hong Kong but they can be obtained in Bangkok for around 500 or 600B; again, the Khao San Rd agents will have the news.

All nationalities require visas for entry into Myanmar, Laos and Vietnam. For Laos and Vietnam they are only issued to tourists through approved travel agencies. A number of agencies in the Khao San Rd area can make these arrangements. Typically, the cost is around 2000 to 2500B for a Vietnam visa which takes five days to issue. Visas for Laos are similarly priced. Burmese visas may now be obtained in just a few hours through the Myanmar Embassy (☎ 233 2237) at 132 Sathon Neua Rd.

If you're returning to Thailand from Laos and plan to stay there beyond 15 days, you'll need a Thai visa. You can apply for one at the Thai Embassy in Vientiane, which is on Thanon Phon Kheng, a couple of hundred metres north-east of the Patuxai Monument. The embassy is open from 8.30 am to 11 am and 2 to 4 pm weekdays. A 60-day tourist visa costs 300 baht, payable only in Thai currency. The application process requires three passport photos and takes one to three days to come through (three is normal but one if you can convince them it's urgent). The visa fee is currently under review and may be increased by the end of 1994. There is also a proposal to allow a visa-free 30-day stay in Thailand for visitors from 55 countries (including most European countries, the USA, Australia and New Zealand).

If you'll be exiting Laos by air or via the river ferry to Nong Khai, and will be in Thailand less than 15 days, you don't need to get a visa in advance. The Thai Embassy in Vientiane may claim it's necessary, but Nong Khai immigration says it isn't. Our experience is that they automatically issue a 15-day transit visa on arrival at the Tha Sadet Pier.

Visas for Cambodia are now available on arrival at Phnom Penh International Airport for US$10.

Most travellers doing the Indochina circuit start by flying to Saigon (Ho Chi Minh City) in Vietnam. There they apply for their Cambodian visa and make a Saigon-Cambodia-Saigon sidetrip. They can then travel up to Hanoi where they apply for a Lao visa and travel Hanoi-Vientiane-Bangkok. Numerous agents around Bangkok handle visas for Vietnam – try MK Ways (☎ 254 5583) at 57/11 Wireless Rd, or 18/4 Soi Saint Louis 3, Sathon Tai Rd.

MONEY

Currency

The baht (B) is divided into 100 satang, although 25 and 50 satang are the smallest coins you'll see. Coins come in 1B (three sizes), 5B (two sizes) and 10B denominations. Notes are in 10B (brown), 20B (green), 50B (blue), 100B (red) and 500B (purple) denominations of varying shades and sizes. Changing a note larger than 100B can be difficult in small towns and villages.

In upcountry markets, you may hear prices referred to in saleng – a saleng is equal to 25 satang.

Exchange Rates

Australia	A$1	=	17.79B
Canada	C$1	=	18.32B
New Zealand	NZ$1	=	14.70B
Britain	UK£1	=	37.34B
USA	US$1	=	24.67B
Japan	¥100	=	24B
Germany	DM1	=	15.14B
France	FF1	=	4.42B
Malaysia	M$1	=	9.6B

The baht is aligned with the US$, and the US$-baht rate fluctuates only slightly from day to day. Baht rates against other currencies will, of course, fluctuate relative to the US$.

Banks give the best exchange rates and are generally open from 8.30 am to 3.30 pm Monday to Friday. Avoid hotels, which give the worst rates. In the larger towns and tourist destinations, there are also foreign exchange kiosks that are open longer hours, usually from around 8 am to 8 pm. All banks deduct a 7 to 10B service charge per cheque – thus you can save money by using larger denomination travellers' cheques (eg cashing a US$100 cheque will cost you seven to 10B while cashing five US$20 cheques will cost 35 to 50B).

There is no black market for US$ but Bangkok is a good centre for buying Asian currencies, particularly those of neighbouring countries where black-market moneychanging flourishes (eg Laos and Myanmar) – try the moneychangers on New (Charoen Krung) Rd for these.

Credit cards are becoming widely accepted at hotels, restaurants and other business establishments. Visa and MasterCard are the most commonly accepted, followed by American Express and Diners Club. Cash advances are available on Visa and MasterCard at many banks and exchange booths.

Costs

Thailand is an economical country to visit and it offers excellent value for your money. Transport is reasonably priced, comfortable and reliable. Finding a place to stay is rarely difficult, although the tourist boom has created some problems in the on seasons (from December to January and from July to August). Costs are low and you get good value for your money. So long as you can stand a little spice, the food is also very good and cheap.

Bangkok is, of course, more expensive than elsewhere in the country. In part, that's because there are lots of luxuries available in Bangkok which you simply won't be tempted with upcountry, but so many cheap guesthouses have sprung up in the Banglamphu area of the city that accommodation needn't necessarily be more expensive than elsewhere in the country. Of course, the Bangkok hassles – noise and pollution being the main ones – also drive you to look for extra comfort, and air-conditioning can be very nice.

One good way to save money is to travel in the off seasons, which in Thailand means from April to June or from September to October. During these periods, tourist destinations are less crowded and prices for accommodation are generally lower. In the remainder of the year, hotels and guesthouses often raise their prices to whatever the traffic will bear.

Tipping

Tipping is not customary except in the big tourist hotels of Bangkok, Pattaya, Phuket and Chiang Mai. Even here, if a service charge is added to the bill, tipping isn't necessary.

Bargaining

Bargaining is mandatory in almost all situations. Arab and Indian traders brought bargaining to Thailand early in the millennium and the Thais have developed it into an art. Nowhere in South-East Asia is it more necessary not to accept the first price, whether dealing with Bangkok taxi drivers or village weavers. While bargaining, it helps to stay relaxed and friendly – gritting your teeth and raising your voice is almost always counterproductive.

TOURIST OFFICES

The Tourist Authority of Thailand (TAT) has an office at the airport in Bangkok, another in central Bangkok and quite a few in regional centres around the country (see the regional sections for addresses). They have a lot of useful brochures, booklets and maps and will probably have an information sheet on almost any Thai subject that interests you. The TAT is probably the best tourist office in South-East Asia for the production of useful information sheets rather than (often useless) pretty colour brochures.

Each regional office also puts out accommodation guides that include cheap places to stay. In Bangkok, they sell the invaluable bus map which lists all the Bangkok bus routes. The flip side of the bus map has a pretty good map of Thailand with Thai script as well. Make sure any map you get has names on it in Thai as well as English.

TAT also has offices in Hong Kong, Malaysia, Singapore and several Western countries.

THAILAND

BUSINESS HOURS & HOLIDAYS

Most businesses are open from Monday to Friday. Many retail establishments and travel agencies are also open on Saturday. Government offices are open from 8.30 am to 4.30 pm and some close, from noon to 1 pm, for lunch.

National Holidays

There's always a festival happening somewhere in Thailand. Many are keyed to Buddhist or Brahmanic rituals and follow a lunar calendar. Thus they fall on different dates (by the Western solar calendar) each year, depending on the phases of the moon.

Such festivals are usually centred around the *wats* (Thai Buddhist temple-monasteries) and include: Makkha Bucha (full moon in February – commemorating the gathering, without prior summons, of 500 monks to hear the Buddha speak); Wisakha Bucha (full moon in May – commemorating the birth, enlightenment and death of the Buddha); Asanha Bucha (full moon in July – commemorating the Buddha's first public discourse); and Khao Phansaa (full moon in July – celebrating the beginning of the Buddhist Rains Retreat). For other holidays, the Thai government has assigned official dates that don't vary from year to year, as follows:

1 January
: *New Year's Day*

6 April
: *Chakri Memorial Day*

12-14 April
: *Songkran Festival (Thai New Year)*

1 May
: *National Labour Day*

5 May
: *Coronation Day*

12 August
: *Queen's Birthday*

23 October
: *Chulalongkorn Day*

5 December
: *King's Birthday*

10 December
: *Constitution Day*

31 December
: *New Year's Eve*

On the above dates, government offices and banks will be closed. Some businesses will also choose to close on these days. As in any country, the days before and after a national holiday are marked by heavy air and road traffic as well as full hotels.

Regional Holidays

Many provinces hold annual festivals or fairs to promote their specialities, eg Chiang Mai's Flower Festival, Kamphaeng Phet's Banana Festival, Yala's Barred Ground Dove Festival and so on. A complete, up-to-date schedule of events around the country is available from TAT offices in each province or from the central Bangkok TAT office.

POST & TELECOMMUNICATIONS

The Thai postal system is relatively efficient and few travellers complain about undelivered mail or lost parcels. Poste restante mail can be received at any town in the country that has a post office. In addition, most hotels and guesthouses will be glad to hold mail for guests as long as the envelopes are so marked.

The telephone system is also fairly modern and efficient – larger *amphoe muang* (provincial capitals) are connected with the IDD system. The central post office in any amphoe muang will house or be located next to the international telephone office. There is usually someone at this office who speaks English. In any case, the forms are always bilingual.

BOOKS

Bangkok has some of the best bookshops in South-East Asia. See under Bookshops in the Bangkok section later in this chapter for details.

Travel Guides

Lonely Planet's *Thailand – a travel survival kit* provides much more detail on the country than can be squeezed into this chapter. *Discovering Thailand* (Oxford University Press) by Clarac & Smithies is good for architectural and archaeological points of interest, even if it's dated. The *Insight Guide Thailand*, another Apa coffee-table guidebook, is rich in photos and background information.

Arts

Several books on Thai arts have appeared over the years. Perhaps the easiest to find (but not necessarily the most accurate) is *Arts of Thailand* (hardback) by Bangkok's dynamic duo, writer Steve Van Beek and photographer Luca Invernizzi Tettoni. William Warren and Tettoni have authored a worthy book on Thai design called *Thai Style* (hardback).

Culture

Denis Segaller's *Thai Ways* and *More Thai Ways* (both paperbacks) are readable collections of cultural vignettes relating to Thai culture and folklore. *Mai Pen Rai* by Carol Hollinger (paperback) is often suggested as an introduction to Thai culture but is more a cultural snapshot of Thailand in the 1960s. More useful as a cultural primer is Robert & Nanthapa Cooper's *Culture Shock! Thailand & How to Survive It*, part of a series that attempts to educate tourists and business travellers in local customs.

Hill Tribes

The Hill Tribes of Northern Thailand by Gordon Young (Monograph No 1, The Siam Society, paperback) covers 16 tribes, including descriptions, photographs, tables and maps. Young was born of third-generation Christian missionaries among Lahu tribespeople, speaks several tribal dialects and is an honorary Lahu chieftain. *From the Hands of the Hills* by Margaret Campbell (hardback) has beautiful pictures of hill tribe handicrafts. *Peoples of the Golden Triangle* by Elaine & Paul Lewis (hardback) is also good, very photo-oriented and expensive.

History & Politics

The Indianized States of South-East Asia (paperback) by George Coedes, *The Thai Peoples* by Erik Seidenfaden (hardback, out of print), *Siam in Crisis* (paperback) by Sulak Sivarak and *Political Conflict in Thailand: Reform, Reaction, Revolution* (hardback) by David Morrell & Chai-anan Samudavanija are all worth reading. Two of the best modern histories are David Wyatt's *Thailand: A Short History* (paperback) and *The Balancing Act: A History of Modern Thailand* (paperback) by Joseph Wright Jr.

MAPS

Bangkok Thailand Tour'n Guide Map has the most up-to-date bus map of Bangkok on one side and a fair map of Thailand on the other – it is usually priced around 40B. The bus side is quite necessary if you plan to spend time in Bangkok and want to use the very economical bus system. It is available at most bookstores in Bangkok which carry English-language materials. A better map of the country is published by Nelles Verlag. It costs around US$7 and is also available at many Bangkok bookstores, as well as overseas.

Look for Lonely Planet's new *Thailand Travel Atlas*, which is a comprehensive, full-colour map of the country in handy book form. It was checked for accuracy on the road by the authors of our Thailand book.

Another source is a 48-page bilingual road atlas called *Thailand Highway Map*, published by the Roads Association of Thailand, that includes detailed highway department maps, dozens of city maps, driving distances, and lots of travel and sightseeing information. The cost is around 120B.

There are also Nancy Chandler's very useful and detailed city maps of Bangkok and Chiang Mai.

MEDIA

Two English-language newspapers are published daily in Thailand and distributed in most provincial capitals. They are the *Bangkok Post* (morning) and the *Nation* (afternoon). The *Post* is the better of the two for regional and international news and is in fact regarded by many journalists as the best English daily in South-East Asia.

FILM & PHOTOGRAPHY

Print film is inexpensive and widely available throughout Thailand. Slide film is also inexpensive but it can be hard to find outside of Bangkok and Chiang Mai – be sure to stock up before heading upcountry. Film processing is generally quite good in Thailand's larger cities and also quite inexpensive. Kodachrome must be sent out of the country for processing which can take up to two weeks.

Pack some silica gel with your camera equipment to prevent mould growing on the inside of your lenses. Keep an eye on your camera – they're very expensive in Thailand and are thus tempting to thieves.

Hill tribespeople in some of the more visited areas expect money if you photograph them, while certain Karen and Akha flee a pointed camera. Use discretion when photographing villagers anywhere in Thailand as a camera can be a very intimidating instrument. You may feel better leaving your camera behind when visiting certain areas.

HEALTH

Refer to the Health section of the Facts about the Region chapter for general health information relevant to South-East Asia.

Malaria

Malaria is mostly restricted to a few rural areas in Thailand, most notably the islands of the eastern seaboard (Chonburi to Trat), and the provinces (but not the capitals) of Chaiyaphum, Phetchabun, Mae Hong Son and Tak. Virtually all strains of malaria in Thailand are resistant to chloroquine and thus it's advisable to take an alternative.

Thailand's Malaria Control Centre recommends avoiding contact with mosquitos from dusk to dawn (when they bite) by making liberal use of repellents, mosquito nets and proper clothing (long-sleeved shirts and long pants). The less you're bitten, the less chance you have of contracting the disease.

Japanese Encephalitis

A few years ago, this viral disease was practically unheard of. Although long endemic to tropical Asia (as well as China, Korea, Japan and eastern Russia), there have been recent

THAILAND

rainy season epidemics in northern Thailand and Vietnam which increase the risk for travellers. Mosquitos are the carriers for JE and the risk is said to be greatest in rural zones near areas where pigs are raised or rice is grown, since pigs and certain wild birds, whose habitat may include rice fields, serve as reservoirs for the virus.

People who may be at risk of contracting JE in Thailand are those who will be spending long periods of time in rural areas during the rainy season (July to October). If you belong to this group, you may want to get a JE vaccination. Check with the government health service in your home country to see if it's available before you leave. If not, arrange to be vaccinated in Bangkok, Hong Kong or Singapore, where the vaccine is easy to find.

Timing is important in taking the vaccine, however; you must receive at least two doses, seven to 10 days apart. The USA Center for Disease Control recommends a third dose 21 to 30 days after the first for improved immunity. Immunity lasts about a year after which it's necessary to get a booster shot, then it's every four years after that.

The symptoms of JE are sudden fever, chills and headache, followed by vomiting and delirium, a strong aversion to bright light, and sore joints and muscles. Advanced cases may result in convulsions and coma. Estimates of the fatality rate for JE range from 5% to 60%.

As with other mosquito-borne diseases, the best way to prevent JE (apart from vaccination) is to avoid mosquito bites.

AIDS

As of September 1993, the Ministry of Health estimated Thailand had around 300,000 HIV-positive individuals, including roughly a thousand cases of full-blown AIDS. In spite of rumours to the contrary, the Thai government keeps all AIDS-related records open to public scrutiny and is trying to educate the general public about AIDS prevention.

In Thailand, the disease is most commonly associated with intravenous heroin use but is also known to be transmitted through sexual contact, both heterosexual and homosexual. If you're going to have sex in Thailand, use condoms.

WOMEN TRAVELLERS

Foreign women have been known to be attacked while travelling alone in remote areas. Everyday incidents of sexual harassment are much less common in Thailand than in India, Indonesia or Malaysia and this may lull women who have recently travelled in these countries into thinking that Thailand travel is safer than it is. If you're a woman travelling alone, try to pair up with other travellers when travelling at night or in remote areas. Urban areas seem relatively safe; the exception is Chiang Mai, where there have been several reports of harassment. Make sure hotel and guesthouse rooms are secure at night – if they're not, demand another room or go somewhere else.

DANGERS & ANNOYANCES

There's always a lot of talk about safety in Thailand – guerrilla forces along three international borders, muggings, robberies and who-knows-what get wide publicity. Communist insurgency in the north and north-east was wiped out in the early 1980s, and in the south it came to an official end in 1989. The remaining danger areas are along the Burmese (drug-smuggling and ethnic insurgents) and Cambodian (Khmer Rouge) border areas. Take extra care when travelling in these areas and avoid travelling at night.

Robberies and hold-ups, despite their publicity, are relatively infrequent. If there is a rule of thumb, however, it's that the hold-up gangs seem to concentrate more on tour buses than on the ordinary buses or the trains, probably assuming that the pickings will be richer.

Precautions

Theft in Thailand is still usually a matter of stealth rather than strength. You're more likely to be pickpocketed than mugged. Take care of your valuables, don't carry too much cash around with you, and watch out for razor artists (they slit bags open in crowded quarters) and the snatch-and-run experts in Bangkok. Don't trust hotel rooms, particularly in the beach-hut places like Ko Samui and Ko Pha-Ngan. Try not to have your bag on the roof of buses or in the underfloor luggage compartments.

Also, take care when leaving valuables in hotel safes. Many travellers have reported unpleasant experiences after having left valuables in Chiang Mai guesthouses. On their return home, they received huge credit card bills for purchases (usually jewellery) charged to their cards in Bangkok. The cards had, supposedly, been secure in the hotel or guesthouse safe while the guests were out trekking!

Women in particular, but men also, should ensure their rooms are securely locked and bolted at night. Inspect cheap rooms with thin walls for strategic peepholes.

Thais are a friendly lot and their friendliness is usually genuine. Nevertheless, on trains and buses, particularly in the south, beware of strangers offering cigarettes, drinks or chocolates. Several travellers have reported waking up with a headache sometime later to find their valuables have disappeared. Travellers have also encountered drugged food or drink from friendly strangers in bars and from prostitutes in their own hotel rooms.

Keep zippered luggage secured with small locks, especially while travelling on buses and trains. This will not only keep out most sneak thieves, but prevent con artists posing as police from planting contraband drugs in your luggage. That may sound paranoid, but it happens.

Armed robbery appears to be on the increase in remote areas of Thailand but the risk of armed robbery should still be considered fairly low. The safest practice in remote areas, however, is not to go out alone at night and, if trekking in north Thailand, always walk in groups.

THAILAND

Scams

Over the years, LP has received dozens of letters from victims who've been cheated out of large sums of money by con men posing as 'friendly Thais'. All of the reports have come from Bangkok and Chiang Mai, and they always describe invitations to buy gems at a special price or participate in a card game. The usual practice is for the con artists to strike up an easy friendship on the street (often near Wat Phra Kaew), then invite the foreigner along to observe a gem purchase or card game in which the friendly stranger will participate. After explaining how easy it is to make heaps of money in the gem or card scheme, the foreigner is invited to invest. It may seem hard to believe, but lots of visitor fall for these schemes, which always end in huge financial losses.

If you become involved in one of these scams, the police (including the tourist police) are usually of little help. It's not illegal for gem stores to sell gems at outrageously high prices. In the case of the card game, everyone's usually gone by the time you come back with the police. Some gem outlets to treat with caution include H Thai Gems Centre, Pinklao Gems, Vimarn Gems, Ploy and Phayathai Gem Centre.

Remember gems and card games are this year's scam so, no doubt, some totally new and highly original scheme will pop up next year. The contact men are usually young, friendly, personable, smooth talking 'students'. They prey on younger travellers – if you're in your 20s you're a prime target. We've even heard of combining the old drugging games with the new selling ones – 'I never thought of buying gems until I drank that soft drink they gave me'.

Tuk-Tuks

Any *tuk-tuk* (three-wheeled motorcycle taxi) driver in Bangkok that offers you a ride for only 10B or 20B is a tout who will undoubtedly drag you to one or more 'factory' showrooms selling gems, clothes or handicrafts – no matter that you've already agreed on another destination in advance! To avoid this extremely frustrating situation, avoid tuk-tuks in Bangkok and use metered taxis instead – they're just as cheap.

Drugs
Penalties for drug offences are stiff: if you're caught using marijuana, you face a fine and/or up to one year in prison, while for heroin, the penalty for use can be anywhere from six months to 10 years' imprisonment, or worse. Remember that it is illegal to buy, sell or possess opium, heroin or marijuana in any quantity (the exception is opium, possession of which is legal for consumption, but not for sale, among hill tribes).

ACCOMMODATION
For consistently good value, the cheap Thai hotels are amongst the best in the region. Almost anywhere in Thailand, even Bangkok, you can get a double for 120B or less. In fact, Bangkok has had such a proliferation of small guesthouses that it's become easier to find rooms in the rock-bottom price category.

There can often be an amazing variance in prices in the same hotel. You'll find fancy air-con rooms at over 400B and straightforward fan-cooled rooms at a third of that price. Even the smallest towns will have a choice of hotels, although 'hotel' will often be the only word on them in English script. Finding a specific place in some smaller towns can be a problem if you don't speak Thai.

A typical Thai 120B room is plain and spartan but will include a toilet, a shower and a ceiling fan. Rooms with a common toilet can cost from 60 to 100B. The Banglamphu places in Bangkok are likely to be a little more basic and not have bathrooms. At the less touristic beach centres of southern Thailand, you'll find pleasant individual beach cottages for 100B and less.

As in Malaysia, many of the hotels are Chinese-run and couples can often save money by asking for a single – a single means one double bed, a double means two.

FOOD
Thai food is like Chinese with a sting – it can be fiery. Eating Thai style involves knowing what to get, how to get it and, finally, how to get it for a reasonable price. Outside of the tourist areas, few places have a menu in English, and as for having prices on a menu... To make matters worse, your mangled attempts at asking for something in Thai are unlikely to be understood. Make the effort for there are some delicious foods to be tried. *Eating in Thailand*, a useful leaflet available from the tourist office, has English descriptions and the equivalent Thai script.

Khâo phàt is the daily national dish – a close cousin to Chinese fried rice or Indonesian nasi goreng. It usually comes with sliced cucumber, a fried egg on top and some super hot peppers to catch the unwary. When you don't know what else to order, this will almost always be available. *Kài phàt bai ka-phrao*, a fiery stir-fry of chopped chicken, chillies, garlic, and fresh basil, is another Thai favourite.

A Thai dish I developed a real liking for is sour hot beef, *yam néua*, a very spicy and hot concoction of shredded beef with salad. *Phàt thai* is fried noodles, beansprouts, peanuts, eggs, chillies and often prawns – good value at any street stall.

Many Thai restaurants are actually Chinese serving a few of the main Thai dishes amongst the Chinese, or some Thai-influenced Chinese ones. In the south, look for delicious seafood, and in the north and north-east there are various local specialities centred around 'sticky rice' *(khâo niaw)*.

Other examples of Thai food include:

fried rice
khâo phàt
with chicken
khâo phàt kài
with pork
khâo phàt muu
with prawns
khâo phàt kûng
pork, chicken or prawn soup
kaeng jèut
spicy lemon soup
tôm yam
Indian-style curry
kaeng kari
Thai curry
kaeng phèt

curried chicken
kaeng kài
thin rice noodles with tofu, vegetables & egg
phàt thai
stir fried vegetables
phàt phàk ruam mít
beef in oyster sauce
néua phàt nám-man hãwy
chicken with vegetables & peanut sauce
phrá raam long sõng kài
fried prawns
kûng thâwt
grilled fish
plaa phão
clear fine noodle salad
yam wún sên
fried eggs
khài dao
scrambled eggs
khài kuan
omelette
khài jii oh

DRINKS

Nonalcoholic Drinks

Soft drinks are cheaper than almost anywhere in South-East Asia, which is just as well since the Thais brew tea and coffee in a very non-Western way. Some say they taste like the two have been mixed together and left to stew for a month. Others grow to like them strong, milky and sweet. Thais also have a penchant for putting salt in fruit drinks. More dairy products are available in Thailand than anywhere else in Asia – including very good yoghurt.

black coffee
kafae dam ráwn
white coffee
kafae ráwn
black tea
chaa dam ráwn
white tea
chaa ráwn

Alcohol

Beer is good but fairly expensive. Singha is the most popular brand – 25 to 35B for a small bottle and 45 to 60B for a large. There are a variety of local firewaters including the famous Mekong whisky, which is about half the strength of Scotch and drunk in enormous quantities.

Getting There & Away

Except for people coming from Malaysia, almost all visitors arrive by air. There are plenty of land crossing points between Thailand and Myanmar, Laos or Cambodia, but very few border crossings are made – officially, at least! By air, however, Bangkok is a major arrival point for flights from all over the world.

AIR

See the introductory Getting There & Away chapter for fares between Bangkok and Europe, Australia and North America. You can also fly to Bangkok from various other Asian cities such as Hong Kong, Manila, Singapore, Kuala Lumpur, Penang, Colombo, Yangon (Rangoon), Dhaka, Calcutta and Kathmandu. Bangkok is a major access point for Myanmar, Nepal, Vietnam, Laos and Cambodia. Although Bangkok is the main entry point for Thailand, you can also fly into Chiang Mai from Hong Kong, Mandalay (Myanmar) and Kunming (China), and to Hat Yai from Penang (Malaysia).

Bangkok is a popular place for buying airline tickets, although it's no longer the number-one bargain centre of the region. Some typical one-way fares available from Bangkok include: Hong Kong US$110 to US$160, Manila US$240, Penang US$104, Singapore US$100 to US$140, Taipei US$240, Yangon US$100 and Vientiane US$80. Interesting multi-stop routes are also available - eg Tokyo via Manila for US$375, New York via Bombay and Paris for US$650, Denpasar via Singapore US$280, and Bangkok-Yangon-Dhaka-Kathmandu for US$220.

Over the years, we have had a lot of letters complaining about various travel agencies in Bangkok – and a few saying what a good deal they got. Remember nothing is free, so if you get quoted a price way below other agencies, be suspicious. In smaller agencies, insist on getting the ticket before handing over your cash. Don't sign anything either.

A favourite game of some agents has been getting clients to sign a disclaimer saying that they will not request a refund under any circumstances. Then, when the client picks their ticket up, they find it is only valid for one week or something similar – not very good when you're not planning to leave for a month or two. Alternatively, the ticket may only be valid within certain dates, or other limitations may be placed upon it.

Another catch is you may be told that the ticket is confirmed (OK) only to find on closer inspection that it is only on request (RQ) or merely open. Or even worse, the ticket actually has OK on it when in actual fact no reservation has been made at all. So read everything carefully and remember – *caveat emptor*, buyer beware. STA Travel (☎ 281 5314/5), the Student Travel Australia outlet, is friendly, knowledgeable and reliable. They're at the Thai Hotel, 78 Prachatipatai Rd, quite close to the Khao San Rd travellers' enclave.

LAND

To/From Malaysia

West Coast The basic land route between Penang and Hat Yai is by taxi. It is fast, convenient and, for around RM30 or 260B, not expensive. The taxis that operate this route are generally big old Chevrolets, all Thai-registered. From Penang, you'll find the taxis at the various travellers' hotels around Georgetown. In Hat Yai, they'll be at the railway station or along Niphat Uthit 2. Magic Tour, downstairs from the Cathay Guest House in Hat Yai, has buses for only 220B which leave twice daily and take five hours. This is the fastest way of travelling by land between the two countries and you cross the border with the minimum of fuss.

It's a different story with local transport. On the map, it looks pretty easy to travel between Malaysia and Thailand by local transport, but in actual fact the long stretch of no-man's land between Changlun, the Malaysian border post, and Sadao, the Thai equivalent, makes crossing the border rather difficult. It's quite easy to get to either side by local bus or taxi but there is no local bus or taxi service across the border. I've hitched across on three occasions, once getting a ride on a Thai fish truck and arriving at the other end smelling a little odd! However, there is not exactly a steady flow of vehicles across the border and they're unwilling to pick up hitchhikers.

If, however, you go a few km west to Padang Besar, where the railway line crosses the border, you can easily just walk across the border. Buses run there from either side, and there's also a train from Butterworth to the border.

The International Express train will take you from Padang Besar to Hat Yai and Bangkok without a change of trains. There are also connecting services to or from Singapore and Kuala Lumpur. The train, which only has 1st and 2nd-class tickets, now operates every day and, it appears, without the border delays which used to be a problem on the train services.

The International Express departs Bangkok at 3.15 pm daily, arrives in Hat Yai at 7.04 am the next day and in Padang Besar at 8 am that afternoon. From Malaysia, it leaves Padang Besar at 5 pm, arrives in Hat Yai at 6.10 pm and in Bangkok at 9.50 am the next day. Fares from Padang Besar to Hat Yai are 13B for 2nd class and 30B for 1st. From Padang Besar to Bangkok is 326B and 694B respectively. There is no longer a direct Bangkok-Butterworth train; the line ends in Padang Besar.

There is an additional express surcharge on the International Express of 50B. Berth charges on the International Express are 100B for a 2nd-class upper berth, 150B for a 2nd-class lower berth and 250B for 1st class. You can travel between Bangkok and Hat Yai on other trains in 3rd class.

East Coast From Kota Bharu (Malaysia), you can take a share taxi to Rantau Panjang – 45 km for about RM6. It's then just a half-a-km (maybe nearer one km) stroll across the border to the town of Sungai Kolok. From here, trains run to Hat Yai and Bangkok. The actual border used to be very inconspicuous and it was easy to miss the immigration authorities as you entered Malaysia, which caused lots of problems when you came to extend your stay or to depart. It's now much more visible but is still only open from 6 am to 6 pm.

To/From Laos

Official Thai-Lao border crossings that are open to foreigners include Chong Mek (near Pakse), Mukdahan (opposite Savannakhet), Nakhon Phanom (opposite Tha Khaek), Nong Khai (near Vientiane) and Chiang Khong (opposite Huay Xai). Exits from Laos into Thailand at any of these crossings can be arranged in Vientiane, but only the Nong Khai-Vientiane crossing is regularly used to enter Laos from Thailand. See the Laos chapter for more information on entry/exit restrictions.

To/From Cambodia

At the moment no land or sea crossings between Cambodia and Thailand are officially allowed. Sometimes special permission to enter Cambodia from Aranyaprathet, Thailand (opposite Poipet, Cambodia) is granted by Thailand's Interior Ministry. Eventually – if and when Cambodia stabilises – this may become a common way to reach Phnom Penh from Thailand. A railway line links Poipet with the Cambodian capital.

Please see the Getting There & Away section of the Cambodia chapter for other details.

To/From Myanmar

Day trips into Myanmar are allowed from Three Pagodas Pass (for Payathonzu), Mae Sot (for Myawaddy) and Mae Sai (for Thachilek and Chiangtung). At present overland travel to Yangon from Thailand is not permitted.

SEA

To/From Malaysia

There are also some unusual routes between Malaysia and Thailand. One of the oddest is to go to Kuala Perlis (the jumping-off point for Langkawi Island) and take a long-tail boat for about RM5 to Satun (or Satul), just across the border in Thailand. These are legal entry and exit points, with immigration and customs posts. On arrival in Satun, it costs about 10B for the three-km ride from the docks to immigration. You can then bus into Hat Yai. Again, make sure you get your passport properly stamped.

You may also be able to get a boat to Satun via Langkawi, a large Malaysian island on the Thai-Malaysian marine border. When they're running, boats to Langkawi leave Satun about every one or 1½ hours and cost from RM10 to RM15. Though it's cheaper to go straight to Satun from Kuala Perlis, Langkawi is worth a stop if you have the time.

Another possibility is to take a yacht between Penang and Phuket. From time to time, there have been people running yachts back and forth on a regular basis.

LEAVING THAILAND

Reconfirmation

Flights in and out of Thailand are often overbooked these days so it's imperative that you reconfirm any return or ongoing flights you have as soon as you arrive in Thailand. If you don't, there's a very good chance you'll be bumped from your flight at the airport. It never hurts to reconfirm more than once.

Departure Tax

The departure tax on international flights is 200B. You're exempted from paying it if you're only in transit and have not left the transit area. Domestic departure tax is 20B.

Getting Around

AIR

Thai International (THAI) operates both international and domestic routes. They have a useful flight network around Thailand – the Airfares in Thailand chart shows the main routes and fares. It's not much used by budget travellers because ground-level transport is generally so good. Domestic flights use turboprop, Boeing 737 and Airbus aircraft.

The internal fares are generally firmly fixed but it's quite possible that you'll be able to find cheaper tickets for the international sectors such as Bangkok to Penang. On some sectors, there are operations by propjet and jet aircraft. In these cases, fares will be lower on the prop aircraft than the jets. The fares shown on the airfares chart are all for jet travel.

A company called Bangkok Airways has been flying selected routes (Ko Samui, Phuket) since 1989. The company is trying to get rights to fly to other destinations in Thailand not served by THAI, including several cities in the south and north-east.

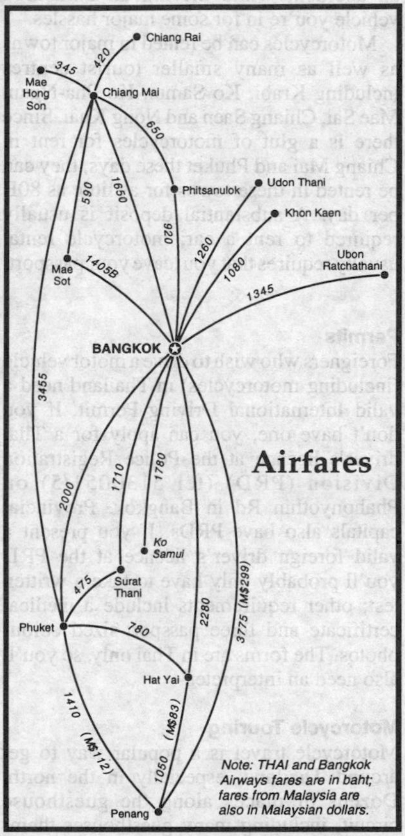

Airfares

Note: THAI and Bangkok Airways fares are in baht; fares from Malaysia are also in Malaysian dollars.

BUS

The Thai bus service is widespread and phenomenally fast – terrifyingly so much of the time. Nothing would get me to sit in the front seats of a Thai bus as some drivers have a definite kamikaze streak. There are usually air-con buses as well as the normal ones, and on major routes there are also private, air-con tour buses. The air-con buses are so cold that blankets are handed out as a matter of routine and the service is so good it's embarrassing. You often get free drinks, pillows, free meals and even 'in-flight movies' on some routes! There are often a number of bus stations in a town – usually public and private stations.

Warning

Beware the low-priced 'VIP' buses and minivans that leave from the Khao San Rd area. Rarely do these bus lines provide the services promised in advance; Khao San Rd buses have even left passengers stranded alongside the highway halfway between Bangkok and the supposed destination. The government buses from the official bus terminals are generally safer and more reliable.

TRAIN

The government-operated trains in Thailand are comfortable, frequent, punctual, moderately priced and rather slow. On comparable routes, the buses can often be twice as fast, but the relatively low speed of the train means you can often leave at a convenient hour in the evening and arrive at your destination at a pleasant hour in the morning.

Train fares plus sleeping-berth charges make train travel appear a bit more expensive than bus travel. However, with a sleeping berth you may save over the cost of the bus fare plus one night's hotel costs. The trains have a further advantage over the buses in that they're far safer and there's more room to move around. All in all, Thailand's railways are a fine way to travel. One caveat: food served on trains is rather expensive by

Thai standards; you'll save considerable baht by bringing your own food on board.

There are four main railway lines plus a few minor side routes. The main ones are: the northern line to Chiang Mai; the southern line to Hat Yai (where the line splits to enter Malaysia on the west coast via Padang Besar and to terminate near the east coast at Sungai Kolok); the eastern line to Ubon Ratchathani; and the north-eastern line to Nong Khai.

Very useful condensed railway timetables are available in English at the Hualamphong railway station in Bangkok. These contain schedules and fares for all rapid and express trains as well as a few ordinary trains.

Bookings

Unfortunately, the trains are often heavily booked, so it's wise to book ahead. At the Hualamphong station in Bangkok, you can book trains on any route in Thailand. The advance booking office is open from 8.30 am to 6 pm Monday to Friday, and from 8.30 am to noon on Saturday, Sunday and holidays. Seats, berths or cabins may be booked up to 90 days in advance.

Charges

There is a 30B surcharge for express trains and a 20B surcharge for rapid trains – the greater speed is gained mainly through fewer stops. Some 2nd and 3rd-class services are air-con in which case there is a 50B surcharge (note that there are no 3rd-class cars on either rapid or express trains).

Sleeping berths also cost extra. In 2nd class, upper berths are 70B, lower berths are 100B or both an extra 100B if the sleeping berths are air-con. The lower berths are cooler since they have a window whereas upper do not. In 1st class, the berths cost 250B per person in two-berth cabins and 350B in single-berth cabins. Sleepers are only available in 1st and 2nd class, but apart from that, 3rd class is not too bad.

Fares are roughly double for 2nd class over 3rd and double again for 1st class over 2nd. Count on around 180B for a 500-km trip in 2nd class. You can break a trip for two days for each 200 km travelled but the ticket must be endorsed by the stationmaster, which costs 1B.

CAR & MOTORBIKE

Cars, jeeps or vans can be rented in Bangkok and large provincial capitals. The best deals are usually on 4WD Suzuki Caribians (sic), which can be rented for as low as 700 to 800B per day for long-term rentals or during low seasons. Check with travel agencies or large hotels for rental locations. Always verify that a vehicle is insured for liability before signing a rental contract and ask to see the dated insurance documents. If you have an accident while driving an uninsured vehicle you're in for some major hassles.

Motorcycles can be rented in major towns as well as many smaller tourist centres including Krabi, Ko Samui, Ko Pha-Ngan, Mae Sai, Chiang Saen and Nong Khai. Since there is a glut of motorcycles for rent in Chiang Mai and Phuket these days, they can be rented in these towns for as little as 80B per day. A substantial deposit is usually required to rent a car; motorcycle rental usually requires that you leave your passport.

Permits

Foreigners who wish to drive a motor vehicle (including motorcycles) in Thailand need a valid International Driving Permit. If you don't have one, you can apply for a Thai driver's licence at the Police Registration Division (PRD) (tel 5130051/5) on Phahonyothin Rd in Bangkok. Provincial capitals also have PRDs. If you present a valid foreign driver's licence at the PRD you'll probably only have to take a written test; other requirements include a medical certificate and three passport-sized colour photos. The forms are in Thai only, so you'll also need an interpreter.

Motorcycle Touring

Motorcycle travel is a popular way to get around Thailand, especially in the north. Dozens of places along the guesthouse circuit, including many guesthouses themselves, have set up shop with no more than a couple of motorbikes for rent. It is also possible to buy a new or used motorbike and sell it before you leave the country – a good used 125cc bike costs around 20,000B. Daily rentals range from 80B a day for an 80cc or 100cc step-through (eg Honda Dream, Suzuki Crystal) to 500B a day for a good 250cc dirt bike.

The legal maximum size for motorcycle manufacture in Thailand is 150cc, though in reality few bikes on the road exceed 125cc. Anything over 150cc must be imported, which means an addition of up to 600% in import duties. The odd rental shop specialises in bigger motorbikes (average 200 to 500cc) – some were imported by foreign residents and later sold on the local market but most came into the country as 'parts' and were discreetly assembled, and licensed under the table.

While motorcycle touring is undoubtedly one of the best ways to see Thailand

it is also undoubtedly one of the easiest ways to cut your travels short, permanently. You can also run up very large repair and/or hospital bills in the blink of an eye. However, with proper safety precautions and driving conduct adapted to local standards, you can see parts of Thailand inaccessible by other modes of transport and still make it home in one piece. Some guidelines to keep in mind:

1. If you've never driven a motorcycle before, stick to the smaller 80 to 100cc step-through bikes with automatic clutches. If you're an experienced rider but have never done off-the-road driving, take it slow the first few days.
2. Always check a machine over thoroughly before you take it out. Look at the tyres to see if they still have tread, look for oil leaks, test the brakes. You may be held liable for any problems that weren't duly noted before your departure. Newer bikes cost more than clunkers, but are generally safer and more reliable. Street bikes are more comfortable and ride more smoothly on paved roads than dirt bikes; it's silly to rent an expensive dirt bike if most of your riding is going to be along decent roads. A two-stroke bike suitable for off-roading generally uses twice the fuel of a four-stroke bike with the same engine size, thus lowering your cruising range in areas where roadside pumps are scarce (eg the 125cc Honda Wing gives you about 300 km per tank while a 125cc Honda MTX gets about half that).
3. Wear protective clothing and a helmet (most rental places will provide a helmet with the bike if asked). Without a helmet, a minor slide on gravel can leave you with concussion, cuts or bruises. Long pants, long-sleeved shirts and shoes are highly recommended as protection against sunburn and as a second skin if you fall. If your helmet doesn't have a visor, then wear goggles, glasses or sunglasses to keep bugs, dust and other debris out of your eyes. It is practically suicidal to ride on Thailand's highways without taking these minimum precautions for protecting your body. Gloves are also a good idea – to prevent blisters from holding on to the twist-grips for long periods of time.
4. For distances of over 100 km or so, take along an extra supply of motor oil and, if riding a two-stroke machine, carry two-stroke engine oil. On long trips, oil burns fast.
5. You should never ride alone in remote areas, especially at night. There have been incidents where farang bikers have been shot or harassed while riding alone, mostly in remote rural areas. When riding in pairs or groups, stay spread out so you'll have room to manoeuvre or brake suddenly if necessary.
6. In Thailand the de facto right of way is determined by the size of the vehicle, which puts the motorcycle pretty low in the pecking order. Don't fight it and keep clear of trucks and buses.
7. Distribute whatever weight you're carrying on the bike as evenly as possible across the frame. Too much weight at the back of the bike makes the front end less easy to control and prone to rising up suddenly on bumps and inclines.
8. Get insurance with the motorcycle if at all possible. The more reputable motorcycle rental places insure all their bikes; some will do it for an extra charge. Without insurance you're responsible for anything that happens to the bike. If an accident results in a total loss, or if the bike is somehow lost or stolen, you can be out 25,000B plus. To be absolutely clear about your liability, ask for a written estimate of the replacement cost for a similar bike – take photos as a guarantee. Some agencies will only accept the replacement cost of a new bike.

Health insurance is also a good idea – get it before you leave home and check the conditions in regard to motorcycle riding.

HITCHING

Although hitching is not the relatively easy proposition it is in Malaysia, it is possible to hitch through Thailand. In places, traffic will be relatively light and the wait for a ride can be quite long, but it is certainly done (please see the section on hitching in the introductory Getting Around chapter).

BOAT

There are lots of opportunities to travel by river or sea in Thailand. You can take boats out to many offshore islands and there are many riverboats operating on Thailand's large number of waterways. The traditional Thai runabout for these river trips is the long-tail boat, so called because the engine operates the propeller via a long open tail-shaft. The engines are often regular car engines with the whole thing mounted on gimbals – the engine is swivelled to steer the boat.

LOCAL TRANSPORT

There is a wide variety of local transport available in Thailand. In the big cities, you'll find taxis, which are never metered except in Bangkok. Always negotiate your fare before departure. Then there are *samlors*, Thai for three-wheels. There are regular bicycle samlors (cycle rickshaws) and also motorised samlors which are usually known as tuk-tuks because of the nasty put-put noise their woefully silenced two-stroke engines make. You'll find bicycle samlors in all the smaller towns throughout Thailand. Tuk-tuks will be found in all the larger towns as well as in Bangkok. In Bangkok they are notoriously unreliable – either they can't find the destination you want or they make time-consuming detours to shops where they are hoping for commissions. Samlors and tuk-tuks require bargaining and agreement on a fare before departure, but in many towns there is a more-or-less fixed fare anywhere in town.

Songthaew literally means 'two-rows' and these small pick-ups with a row of seats down each side also serve a purpose rather like tuk-tuks or minibuses. In some cities, certain routes are run on a regular basis by songthaews or minibuses.

Finally, there are regular bus services in certain big cities. Usually in Thailand, fares are fixed for any route up to a certain length – in Bangkok up to 10 km. Of course, there are all sorts of unusual means of getting around – horse-drawn carriages in some smaller towns, and ferries and riverboats in many places. In some of the more touristic centres, you can also rent motorbikes or bicycles at very economical rates.

Bangkok

Thailand's coronary-inducing capital is surprisingly full of quiet escapes if you make your way out of the busy streets. Before you get out, you will have to put up with some of the worst traffic jams in Asia, noise, pollution, annual floods and sticky weather. It's hardly surprising that many people develop an instant dislike for the place, but beneath the surface Bangkok has plenty to offer, including cheap accommodation and some excellent food. There are lots of sights – step out of the street noise and into the calm of a wat, for example. The Chao Phraya River is refreshing compared to the anarchy of the streets and a visit to Jim Thompson's house will show you how delightful the *khlongs* (canals) were and, occasionally, still are.

Bangkok, or Krung Thep as it is known to the Thais, became the capital of Thailand after the Burmese sacked Ayuthaya in 1767. At first, the Siamese capital was shifted to Thonburi, across the river from Bangkok, but in 1782 it was moved to its present site.

Orientation

The Chao Phraya River divides Bangkok from Thonburi. Almost the only reason to cross to Thonburi (apart from the Southern bus terminals or the Bangkok Noi railway station) is to see Wat Aran (Temple of the Dawn).

The main Bangkok railway line virtually encloses a loop of the river and within that loop is the older part of the city, including most of the interesting temples and the Chinatown area. The popular travellers' centre of Banglamphu is also in this area.

THAILAND

East of the railway line is the new area of the city where most of the modern hotels are located. One of the most important roads is Rama IV Rd which runs right in front of the Hualamphong railway station and eventually gets you to the Malaysia Hotel area. A little to the north, and approximately parallel to Rama IV, is Rama I which passes Siam Square and eventually becomes Sukhumvit Rd, with many popular hotels, restaurants and entertainment spots.

Small streets or lanes are called *sois*.

Information

Tourist Offices There are tourist offices at the airport and in Bangkok – the Thai tourist office is very good for detailed leaflets and information sheets. You'll find the city office of the Tourist Authority of Thailand (TAT) (☎ 226 0060) at 327 Bamrung Muang Rd. It's open from 8.30 am to 4.30 pm every day.

One thing to buy from them (or elsewhere) as quickly as possible is a Bangkok bus map (35 to 40B). It's very easy to follow and an absolute necessity for coping with Bangkok's frenetic bus system. *Nancy Chandler's Map of Bangkok* is a colourful map of Bangkok's unusual attractions. It has all the Chao Phraya Express river-taxi stops in Thai script and costs 70B.

Money Thai banks have currency exchange kiosks in many areas of Bangkok, heavily concentrated in the Sukhumvit Rd, Khao San Rd, Siam Square and Silom Rd areas. Hours vary from location to location but they tend to be open from 8 am to 8 pm daily.

Close to the GPO are a number of moneychangers along Charoen Krung (New) Rd, good if you want to buy another Asian currency such as Burmese kyats.

Post & Telecommunications The GPO is on Charoen Krung (New) Rd and has a very efficient poste restante service open from 8 am to 8 pm on weekdays and from 9 am to 1 pm on weekends and holidays. Every single letter is recorded in a large book and you're charged 1B for each one. They also have a packing service here if you want to send parcels home.

After the GPO is shut, you can send letters from the adjacent central telegraph office which is open 24 hours. This is also a place where you can make international telephone calls at any time of the day or night. Hotels and guesthouses usually make service charges on every call, whether they are collect or not.

At the airport and in some post offices and shopping centres, special telephones with Home Direct service are available. On these you simply push a button for a direct connection with long-distance operators in 20 countries, including Australia, Canada, Denmark, Germany, Hong Kong, Italy, Japan, New Zealand, the UK and the USA.

Travel Agencies Bangkok is packed with travel agents of every manner and description but if you're looking for cheap airline tickets it's wise to be cautious. Ask other travellers for advice about agents. The really bad ones change their names frequently so saying this week that J Travel, for example, is not to be recommended is useless when they're called something else next week. Wherever possible, try to see the tickets before you hand over the money.

The STA Travel agent in Bangkok is Tour Center (☎ 281 5314) at the Thai Hotel, 78 Prachatipatai Rd. They sell discount air tickets and seem reliable. We have yet to receive a negative report about them.

Three agents that are permitted to do Thai railway bookings at regular SRT fares are Airland (☎ 252 5557), 866 Ploenchit Rd; Songserm Travel Center (☎ 250 0768, 252 5190), 121/7 Soi Chalermnit, Phayathai Rd; and Viang Travel (☎ 280 1385), Viengtai Hotel, Tanee Rd. Other agencies can arrange rail bookings but will slap on a surcharge of 50B or more per ticket. The TAT Head Office has the addresses of all the different sales agencies.

Bookshops Bangkok has some of the best bookshops in South-East Asia. Asia Books at Soi 15-17, Sukhumvit Rd, has an excellent

To Saraburi
To Suphanburi
PAK KRET
BANG BUA THONG
Choeng Wattana Road
Tiwanon Road
Khlong Bang Talat
Vibhavadi Rangsit Hwy
Nonthaburi Sanam Binnam Rd
Outer Ring Road
Khlong Om
BANG YAI
NONTHABURI
Ngam Wongwan Road
Phahonyothin Road
Khlong Bangkok Noi
BANG SON
LAT PHRAO
Khlong Bang Luang
BANG SEU
Weekend Market
BANG KRUAY
Khlong Maha Sawat
To Nakhon Pathom
BANGPHAT
SRIYAN
TALING CHAN
Charan Sanitwong Road
Chao Phraya River
Ratwithi Rd
Phahonyothin Rd
Vibhavadi Rangsit Rd
HUAY KHWANG
BANGKOK NOI
BANGLAMPHU
Khlong Saen Saep
Phetburi Rd
Rama I Rd
New Phetburi Road
Khlong Bangkok Noi
THONBURI
CHINA-TOWN
Expressway
KHLONG TAN
Rama IV Rd
Sukhumvit Rd
KHLONG TOEY
To Nakhon Pathom
Phetkasem Rd
THUNG MAHAMEK
See Central Bangkok Map
Khlong Phasi Charoen
Khlong Dao Khanong
DAO KHANONG
TROK CHAN
PORT
PHRA KHANONG
Taksin Rd
THANON TOK
Expressway
PHASI CHAROEN
BANG KHUN THIAN
Ratchadaphisek Road
K. Sanam Chai
Outer Ring Road
RAT BURANA
Suksawat Rd
Floating Market
Chao Phraya River
BANG NA
To Samut Sakhon
PHRA PRADAENG
To Samut Prakan
3099
3110
3110
306
302
304
3125
301
340
31
306
338
303
35
3
4
1
2
3
4
5
6
7
8
9
10
11
12

THAILAND

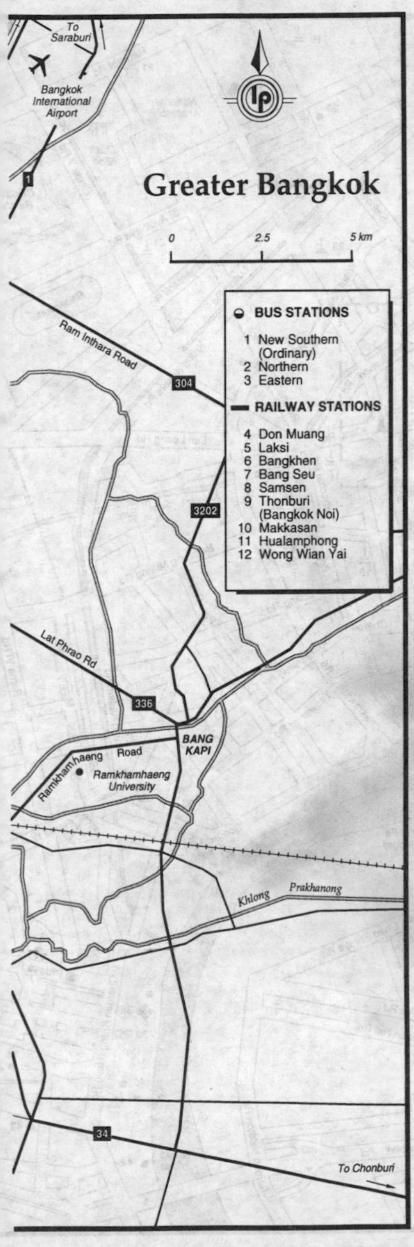

selection of English-language books. There are also branches in the Landmark Hotel on Sukhumvit Rd, opposite Soi 5, and in the Peninsula Plaza. Duang Kamol (DK) Books, with branches in Siam Square, the Mahboonkrong Center, Patpong Rd and Soi 8, Sukhumvit Rd, also has a wide selection.

On Patpong Rd, The Bookseller is another good place for browsing. You can also find decent book departments in various branches of the Central department store (306 Silom Rd, Ploenchit Rd and Wang Burapha) and in many of the better hotels.

Medical Services There are several good hospitals in Bangkok:

Bangkok Adventist Hospital
430 Phitsanulok Rd (☎ 281 1422)
Bangkok Christian Hospital
124 Silom Rd (☎ 233-6981/9)
Samitivej General Hospital
133 Soi 49, Sukhumvit Rd (☎ 392 0010/9)
Samrong General Hospital
Soi 78, Sukhumvit Rd (☎ 393 2131/5)

Tourist Police The tourist police are a separate force established to deal with problems encountered by tourists. In Bangkok there are over 500 English-speaking officers stationed in tourist areas – their kiosks, cars and uniforms are clearly marked. If you have any problems relating to criminal activity, contact the tourist police first; they can act as a bilingual liaison with the regular police if this is necessary. The tourist police headquarters (☎ 221 6206) are at the Crime Suppression Division, 509 Worachak Rd, near the intersection of Worachak and Charoen Krung Rds at the north-eastern edge of Chinatown.

Temples

Bangkok has about 400 wats, or Buddhist temple-monasteries, and those described in this section are just some of the most interesting. Remember to take your shoes off before entering the *bot* (the central sanctuary or chapel in a Thai temple). Dress and behave soberly in the wats as the Thais take Buddhism seriously.

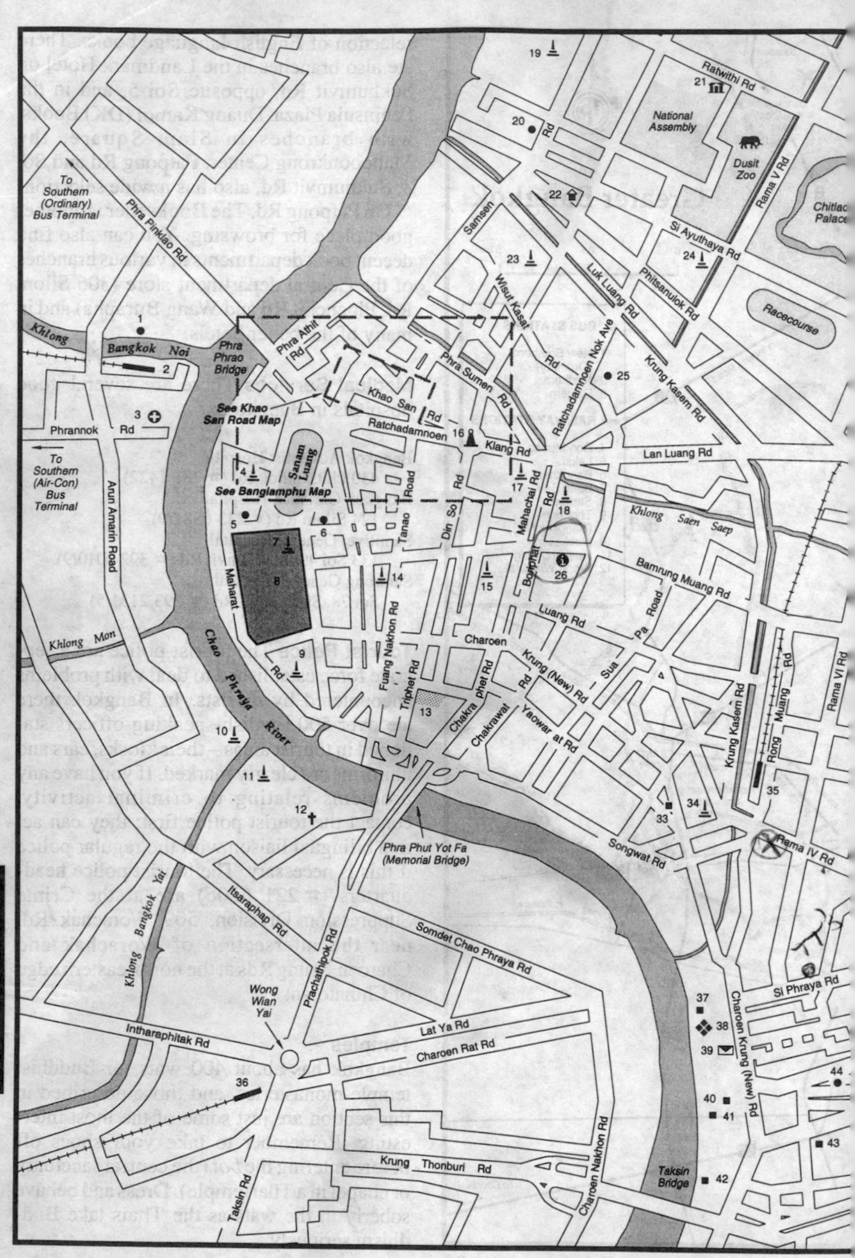
To Southern (Ordinary) Bus Terminal
Phra Pinklao Rd
Khlong Bangkok Noi
Phra Phrao Bridge
Phrannok Rd
To Southern (Air-Con) Bus Terminal
Arun Amarin Road
See Khao San Road Map
See Banglamphu Map
Phra Athit Rd
Khao San Rd
Ratchadamnoen Klang Rd
Sanam Luang
Tanao Road
Din So Rd
Mahachai Rd
Maharat Rd
Khlong Mon
Chao Phraya River
Fuang Nakhon Rd
Triphet Rd
Chakra phet Rd
Chakrawat Rd
Charoen Krung (New) Rd
Yaowar at Rd
Phra Phut Yot Fa (Memorial Bridge)
Itsaraphap Rd
Khlong Bangkok Yai
Somdet Chao Phraya Rd
Prachathipok Rd
Wong Wian Yai
Intharaphitak Rd
Lat Ya Rd
Charoen Rat Rd
Krung Thonburi Rd
Taksin Rd
Charoen Nakhon Rd
Taksin Bridge
Samsen Rd
Wisut Kasat Rd
Phra Sumen Rd
Ratchadamnoen Nok Ave
Luk Luang Rd
Phitsanulok Rd
Krung Kasem Rd
Si Ayuthaya Rd
Ratwithi Rd
National Assembly
Dusit Zoo
Rama V Rd
Chitlada Palace
Racecourse
Lan Luang Rd
Khlong Saen Saep
Bamrung Muang Rd
Bori phat Rd
Luang Rd
Sua Pa Road
Rong Muang Rd
Rama VI Rd
Songwat Rd
Rama IV Rd
Si Phraya Rd
Charoen Krung (New) Rd
1 2 3 4 5 6 7 8 9 10 11 12 13 14 15 16 17 18 19 20 21 22 23 24 25 26 33 34 35 36 37 38 39 40 41 42 43 44

THAILAND

Central Bangkok
0
0.5
1 km
To Bangkok International Airport (Don Muang Airport)
To Northern Bus Terminal & Weekend Market
Victory Monument
Sukhothai Rd
Sawankhalok Rd
Ratwithi Rd
Rama VI Rd
Phahonyothin Rd
Vibhavadi Rangsit Rd
Yothi Rd
Si Ayuthaya Rd
Din Daeng Rd
Phetburi Rd
Makkasan Rd
Ratchaprarop Rd
New Phetburi Road
Rama I Rd
Siam Square
Ploenchit Rd
Royal Bangkok Sports Club
Chulalongkorn University
Phayathai Rd
Henri Dunant Rd
Ratchadamri Rd
Soi Lang Suan
Withayu (Wireless) Rd
Soi Ruam Rudi
Soi Nana Tai (Soi 4)
Soi 1
Expressway
Sukhumvit Rd
Soi Asoke
To Eastern Bus Terminal
Soi 10
Ratchadaphisek Rd
Sarasin Rd
Lumphini Park
Rama IV Rd
Sala Daeng
Patpong
Surawong Rd
Convent Rd
Road
Silom Rd
Sathon Neua (North) Rd
Sathon Tai (South) Rd
Soi Suan Phlu
Soi Ngam Duphli
Soi Si Bamphen
27
28
29
30
31
32
45
46
47
48
49
50
51
52
53
54
55
56
57
58
59
60
61
62
63
64
65
66
67
68
69
70
71
THAILAND

PLACES TO STAY

22 Bangkok International Youth Hostel
30 Muangphol Building
31 National Scout Hostel
33 New Empire Hotel
37 Royal Orchid Sheraton
40 Swan Hotel
41 Oriental Hotel
42 Shangri-La Hotel
43 Holiday Inn Crowne Plaza
46 Narai Hotel
50 Mandarin Hotel
52 Montien Hotel
55 Dusit Thani Hotel
58 YMCA
59 YWCA
61 Malaysia Hotel
64 Grand Hyatt Erawan
69 Atlanta Hotel
70 Landmark Hotel

OTHER

1 Royal Barges
2 Thonburi (Bangkok Noi) Railway Station
3 Sirirat Hospital
4 Wat Mahathat
5 Silpakorn University
6 Lak Muang (City Pillar)
7 Wat Phra Kaew
8 Grand Palace
9 Wat Pho
10 Wat Arun
11 Wat Kalayanamit
12 Santa Cruz Church (Wat Kuti Jiin)
13 Pahurat Market
14 Wat Ratchabophit
15 Wat Suthat
16 Democracy Monument
17 Wat Ratchanatda
18 Wat Saket
19 Wat Ratchathiwat
20 National Library
21 Vimanmek Teak Mansion
23 Wat Intharawihan
24 Wat Benchamabophit
25 Ratchadamnoen Boxing Stadium
26 TAT Office
27 Samsen Railway Station
28 Phra Mongkutklao Hospital
29 Jim Thompson's House
32 National Stadium
34 Wat Traimit
35 Hualamphong Railway Station
36 Wong Wian Yai Railway Station
38 River City Shopping Complex
39 GPO
44 Neilson Hays Library & British Club
45 Maha Uma Devi Temple
47 THAI Office
48 Lao Embassy
49 Singapore Embassy
51 Saovabha Institute (Snake Farm)
53 Chulalongkorn Hospital
54 Bangkok Christian Hospital
56 Australian Embassy
57 Malaysian Embassy
60 Immigration Office
62 Lumphini Boxing Stadium
63 AUA Language Center
65 Pratunam Market
66 New Zealand Embassy
67 US Embassy
68 Makkasan Railway Station
71 Siam Society (Ban Kamthieng)

Wat Phra Kaew & the Grand Palace Consecrated in 1782, the so-called Temple of the Emerald Buddha is the royal temple within the palace complex. It has a variety of buildings and frescoes of the *Ramakien* (the Thai *Ramayana)* around the outer walls. In the main chapel stands the Emerald Buddha (made of jasper). The image was originally discovered at Chiang Rai inside a stucco Buddha. It was later moved to Lampang and then Chiang Mai before being carried off to Luang Prabang and Vientiane by the Lao, from where it was later recaptured by the Thais.

Admission is 125B which includes entry into the Royal Thai Decorations and Coin Pavilion (on the same grounds) as well as Vimanmek, 'the world's largest golden teak mansion' near the Dusit Zoo (next to the National Assembly). Opening hours are from 8.30 to 11.30 am and from 1 to 3.30 pm. Wat Phra Kaew's strict dress code requires long pants or skirts, covered shoulders and shoes with enclosed heels.

Wat Pho The Temple of the Reclining Buddha (the name actually means Temple of the Bodhi Tree) has an extensive collection of panels, bas reliefs, *chedis* (stupas) and statuary to view, apart from the celebrated 46-metre reclining Buddha, which looks like a beached whale with mother-of-pearl feet. This is the oldest and largest wat in Bangkok, and it's from here that all those Thai temple rubbings come. Admission is 10B and the reclining Buddha can be seen from 8 am to 5 pm daily.

Wat Traimit A large stucco Buddha was moved here from an old temple and stored in a temporary shelter for 20 years. When moving it to a permanent chapel, a crane dropped it, revealing over five tons of solid-gold Buddha under the stucco. The stucco covering was probably intended to hide it from the Burmese during one of their invasions. The wat is now known as the Temple of the Golden Buddha. Admission is 10B and the golden image can be seen from 9 am to 5 pm daily. It's a short walk from the Hualamphong railway station.

Wat Arun The Temple of the Dawn stands on the Thonburi side of the Chao Phraya River. It's seen at its best from across the river, especially at night when the 82-metre-high *prang* (Khmer-style tower), decorated with ceramics and porcelain, is lit by spotlights. You can climb halfway up the tower and admission is 5B. To get there, hop on a ferry from the pier at the end of Na Phra Lan Rd (near Wat Phra Kaew) or at Thai Wang Rd (near Wat Pho).

Wat Benchamabophit The Marble Temple is relatively new (built by Rama V in 1899) and has a huge collection of Buddha images from all periods of Thai Buddhist art. There is a pond full of turtles beside the temple – admission is 10B.

Wat Saket The Golden Mount is a most ugly lump of masonry atop an artificial hill. As Bangkok is pancake flat, it provides a fine view from the top. Admission is free, but it costs 5B to get to the top terrace.

Other Temples Across Mahachai Rd from Wat Saket is **Wat Ratchanatda**, the site of a popular market selling Buddha images, amulets and charms. **Wat Bowonniwet** (Bovornives) on Phra Sumen Rd is the headquarters of the minority Thammayut monastic sect. **Wat Suthat**, just north of Banglamphu on Wisut Kasat Rd (near the junction with Samsen Rd), has an enormous standing Buddha image. The 'giant swing', **Sao Ching Cha**, used to be the centre for a spectacular festival which is no longer held.

A small Hindu temple, **Sri Mariamman**, sits on the corner of Pan and Silom Rds. The three main deities contained therein are Khanthakumara, Ganesh and Uma Devi, although a whole pantheon of Hindu and Buddhist statuary lines one wall.

National Museum

Supposedly the largest museum in South-East Asia, this is a good place for an overview of Thai art and culture before you start exploring the former Thai capitals. All the periods and styles of Thai history and art are shown here. Located on Na Phrathat Rd, the museum is open from 8.30 am to 4 pm, but is closed on Monday and Tuesday – admission is 20B. There are free tours of the museum, conducted in English, on Tuesday (Thai culture), Wednesday (Buddhism) and Thursday (Thai art) – all begin at 9.30 am.

Jim Thompson's House

Located on Soi Kasem San 2, Rama I Rd, this is the beautiful house of the American Thai silk entrepreneur Jim Thompson, who disappeared without trace back in 1967 in the Cameron Highlands in Malaysia. His house, built from parts of a number of traditional wooden Thai houses and furnished with a superb collection of Thai art and furnishings, is simply delightful. Pleasantly sited on a small khlong, the house is open daily from 8 am to 5 pm. Admission is 40B for anyone under 25 and 100B for everyone else.

Floating Markets

The Wat Sai floating market in Thonburi is really a tourist trap – although there are still a few market boats, there are even more tourist boats. The trip to the market is picturesque but with all the tourist shops, snake farms and the like it all looks very artificial. We recommend skipping the Wat Sai market for the less touristic floating market at Khlong Damnoen Saduak, beyond Nakhon Pathom. See under Nakhon Pathom in the Bangkok Region section later in this chapter for details.

Other Attractions

An interesting **river tour** in Bangkok can be made by taking a Chao Phraya River taxi from Wat Ratchasingkhon pier (lots of buses go there) as far north as Nonthaburi. This is a three-hour, 15B trip with plenty to see along the way. The Klong Bangkok Noi canal taxi route from Tha Phra Chan, next to Thammasat University, only costs 10B and takes you along a colourful 45-minute route, seemingly far from Bangkok.

All sorts of oddities can be found at the enormous **Weekend Market** which takes place opposite the Northern bus terminal. Take an air-con bus No 2, 3, 9, 10 or 13. It's open all day Saturday and Sunday, and you can find almost anything there from opium pipes to unusual posters. It also has lots of other activities to watch. There are a number of other interesting markets around Bangkok. Bangkok also has a **Chinatown** with a thieves' market and an Indian district on its periphery. This area is around Chakrawat Rd, midway between the Grand Palace and the Hualamphong train station.

At the **Saovabha Institute (Snake Farm)** on Rama IV Rd, snakes are milked of their venom every day at 11 am and 2 pm (11 am only on weekends and holidays) – admission is 70B.

The **Oriental Hotel** is an attraction in its own right. It's the Raffles of Bangkok and is consistently voted the best hotel in Asia.

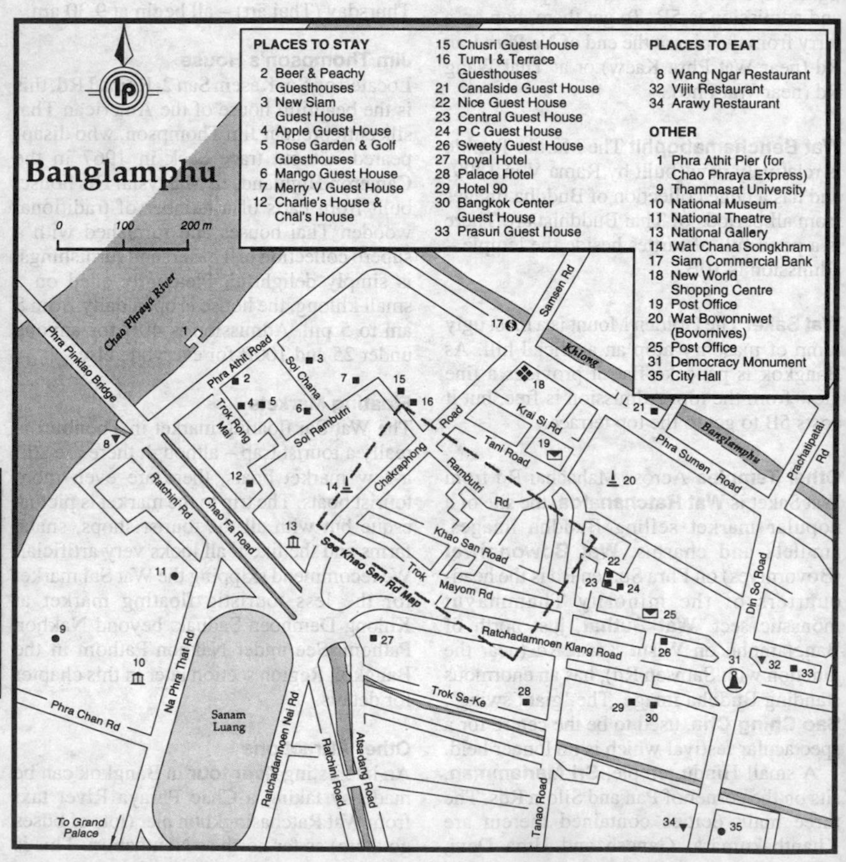

Somerset Maugham and Joseph Conrad are among the Oriental's historic guests (commemorated in the hotel's Authors' Wing). Be sure to dress nicely or you may be barred from entering the lobby.

Lumphini Park, situated at Rama IV and Ratchadamri Rd, offers a shady respite from the city's noise and traffic. Likewise for the **Dusit Zoo** on Rama V Rd, which is open from 8 am to 6 pm daily; admission is 20B.

One of Bangkok's more unusual sights is the **shrine** outside the Grand Hyatt Erawan Hotel, where people come to seek help for some wish they want granted – like their girlfriend to marry them. The person promises that if the grant is made they will pay for something to be done – a favourite promise is to pay for 20 minutes dancing by the Thai dancers who are always ready and waiting for such commissions.

Another hotel shrine worth seeing is the **lingam (phallus) shrine** behind the Hilton International in Nai Loet Park off Withayu (Wireless) Rd. Clusters of carved stone and wooden lingam surround a spirit house and shrine built by a millionaire businessman to honour Jao Mae Thapthim, a female deity thought to reside in the old banyan tree on the site.

Places to Stay

There are all sorts of places to stay in Bangkok with a wide range of prices, mainly concentrated in certain distinct areas.

Banglamphu is the number one travellers' centre with a simply amazing number of budget-priced guesthouses, together with restaurants, snack bars, travel agents and all the other back-up facilities. A big advantage of Banglamphu is that it's central to many of Bangkok's major tourist attractions.

Soi Ngam Duphli, at one time the main travellers' centre, is quieter and slightly more expensive but still attracts many visitors. Then there's the Sukhumvit Rd area with some travellers' hotels amongst the more expensive places. Much more central are the noisy Hualamphong station, Chinatown and Siam Square areas.

Competition in the Banglamphu area is so fierce that you can still get a room in Bangkok for scarcely more than it was 10 years ago. The cheapest rooms start from 80B for a single or 100B for a double in the Banglamphu and Hualamphong areas. The air-con places in Soi Ngam Duphli and along Sukhumvit Rd are now from 400 to 500B. Some hotels give student discounts if you ask.

If you have to stay near the airport, there's the expensive *Amari Airport Hotel* or the rather dismal *Bamboo Guest House*, several hundred metres north of the terminal on the Don Muang side. Right across the road from the airport terminal (take the Airport Hotel pedestrian bridge), there's the Don Muang town area with lots of little shops, a market, many small restaurants and foodstalls, and even a wat.

There's a hotel booking desk at the airport which can book you into many of the cheaper (but not rock-bottom) hotels. Thailand continues to experience a tourist boom and as a result finding a room can sometimes be quite difficult, particularly if you arrive late at night.

Banglamphu Also known as the Khao San Rd area, Banglamphu is over towards the river, near the Democracy Monument and on the route towards the airport.

The Banglamphu area is central, particularly for the various wats and the National Museum. Most of the Banglamphu guesthouses are basic but they can be excellent value. The standard Banglamphu price is around 70B or 80B for a single, and from 100 to 120B for a double. Some very basic guesthouses are even cheaper in the off seasons, so it doesn't hurt to try bargaining.

It's quite difficult to recommend any of them since names and management change periodically. Check your room first because, in some cases, a 'room' is just a tiny cubicle, virtually partitioned off with cardboard. Like losmen at Kuta Beach on Bali, there are so many places around Khao San Rd that it's just a case of wandering about until you find one that suits. The map shows many, but not all of them.

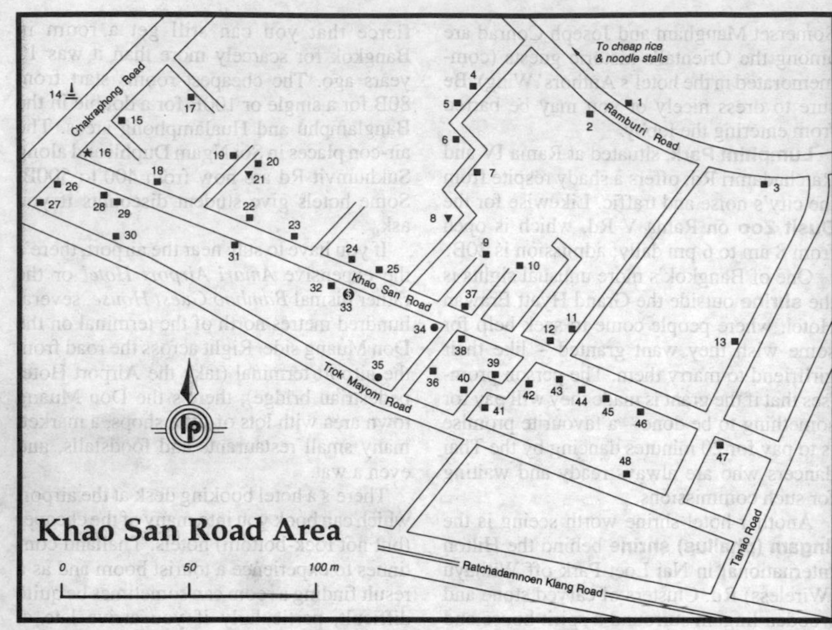

PLACES TO STAY

1 Viengtai Hotel
2 ST Guest House
3 Panee Guest House
4 Green House
5 AT Guest House
6 Suneeporn Guest House
7 Dolls Guest House & Others
9 Khao San Palace Hotel
10 New Nith Jaroen Hotel
11 Best Guest House & Restaurant
12 Nat Guest House
13 Ham, VS & Nisa Guesthouses
15 Siam Guest House
17 Chuanpis Guest House
18 Sitdhi Guest House
19 Paradise Guest House
20 Chart Guest House
22 Hello Guest House & Restaurant
23 Mam's Guest House
24 Lek Guest House
25 Buddy Guest House
26 Ploy Guest House
27 J Guest House
28 Thai Guest House
29 NS Guest House
30 Joe Guest House
31 Chart Guest House
32 PB Guest House
36 Bonny & Top Guesthouses
37 Grand Guest House
38 Dior Guest House
39 Good Luck Guest House
40 Marco Polo (160 Guest House)
41 Tong Guest House
42 VIP Guest House
43 Ice Guest House
44 Nana Plaza Inn
45 Siri Guest House
46 CH Guest House
47 Chada Guest House
48 7-Holder Guest House

PLACES TO EAT

8 Buddy Beer & Sonic Restaurants
21 Royal India Restaurant

OTHER

14 Wat Chana Songkhram
16 Chana Songkhram Police Station
33 Krung Thai Bank
34 Shops
35 School

Popular places along Khao San Rd or on the alleys just off it include the *Bonny* (☎ 281 9877), *Top* (☎ 281 9954), *Hello* (☎ 281 8579), *Lek* (☎ 281 2775), *Marco Polo (160) Guesthouse*, *VIP* (☎ 282 5090), *Good Luck, Chada, Nat* and many others, all very similar.

There are a couple of places along Khao San Rd which are not in the usual guesthouse mould. The *Khao San Palace Hotel* (☎ 282 0578) at 139 Khao San Rd is Chinese-owned and costs from 150B for a room with a fan and a bath. Next door is the popular *New Nith Jaroen Hotel* (☎ 281 9872) which has similar rooms and rates but slightly better service.

On the soi parallel and just south of Khao San Rd, which connects with Chakraphong Rd via Trok Mayom, you'll find the *Joe, J, 7-Holder* and, by now, probably several other guesthouses.

There's a small soi east off Tanao Rd (at the end of Khao San) that offers several more cheapies, including the plain and basic *Central* (☎ 282 0667), *Nice, PC, Sweety* (☎ 281 6756), *Chart II* and *Nat II* guesthouses, all at the usual Khao San rates. This network of alleys is fairly quiet since it's off the main road.

Another relatively quiet area is the network of sois and alleys between Chakraphong Rd and Phra Athit Rd to the west of Khao San Rd, including Soi Rambutri, Soi Chana and Trok Rong Mai. Good choices include the *New Siam* (Soi Chana (☎ 282 4554), *Merry V* (Soi Rambutri), *Mango* (Soi Rambutri), *Tum 1* (Soi Rambutri), *Apple* (Soi Rambutri), *Rose Garden* (Trok Rong Mai; (☎ 281 8366) and the *Golf* (Trok Rong Mai). On Phra Athit Rd, near the river, are the *Beer, Peachy* (☎ 281 6471) and *New Merry V* guesthouses, which are slightly up-market for Banglamphu with rates from 120 to 350B.

The guesthouses along Chakrapong Rd tend to be a bit noisy as it's a fairly major thoroughfare.

Khao San Rd is an amazingly cosmopolitan place these days. Back in the old Asia overland days of the early 1970s, there were the three Ks – travellers' 'bottlenecks' where you were bound to meet up with anybody travelling trans-Asia. These days you could substitute Khao San for Kabul to make it three with Kuta and Kathmandu.

All along the road are the little signs indicating it's a travellers' hang-out – countless small guesthouses and restaurants with fruit salad and muesli on the menu. At night, they spill out first across the sidewalk and then right into the street. Loud rock music booms out from the cassette sellers; clothes are sold from shops and sidewalk stalls; books are bought and traded; travel agents offer cheap tickets and fake student cards; and there are places to store your baggage or wash your clothes.

Buses and taxis seem to come and go constantly, disgorging one band of backpackers and picking up another who are patiently waiting with their packs by the roadside. This one block of intense activity is definitely the travellers' centre of Bangkok.

Around Banglamphu More guesthouses have started to pop up around the Banglamphu area. Go up Chakrapong Rd and then Samsen Rd (it changes names) north from Banglamphu and after about a km, just before the National Library, Phitsanulok Rd dead-ends on Samsen Rd and Si Ayuthaya Rd crosses it.

On two parallel sois off Si Ayuthaya Rd toward the river (west from Samsen) are five guesthouses run by various members of the same extended family: *Tavee Guest House* (☎ 282 5983), *Sawatdee Guest House* (☎ 282 5349), *Backpacker's Lodge*, *Shanti Lodge* (☎ 281 2497) and the latest addition, *Paradise Guest House* (☎ 282 4094/8673). All are clean, well kept, fairly quiet and cost 40 to 50B for a dorm bed, and from 80/110B for singles/doubles. Watch your bill at the Paradise as some travellers have reported overcharging. There's a lot of friendly family competition between these places. One alley back, at No 83, the *Tavee Guest House* (☎ 280 1447) costs 110B for doubles and has a 50B dorm. This area has the distinct advantage of being a short walk from Tha Thewet, a Chao Phraya River Express pier; from the pier you walk east along Krung Kasem Rd to Samsen Rd, turn left, cross the canal and then take another left into Si Ayuthaya Rd.

Close by here is the *Bangkok International Youth Hostel* (☎ 282 0950) at 25/2 Phitsanulok Rd. It has a 60B dorm and air-

THAILAND

con singles/doubles with toilet and shower at 250/300B if you have a youth hostel card. Nonmembers can purchase a temporary membership for 50B or a full annual membership for 300B. Several readers have written to say that the Hostel staff can be quite rude to guests.

Chinatown-Hualamphong Station This is one of the cheapest areas in Bangkok but also one of the noisiest. The traffic along Rama IV Rd has to be heard to be believed. There are several hotels right alongside the station but these station-area cheapies are no bargain compared to the even cheaper places over in Banglamphu, and it's nowhere near as pleasant a place to stay.

The *Sri Hualamphong Hotel* (☎ 214 2610) at 445 Rong Muang Rd is one of the better ones with rooms at around 100B with fan. The *Sahakit (Shakij) Hotel* is a few doors down towards Rama IV Rd, while between the two is the rather basic *Jeep Seng* (☎ 214 2808) and the equally forgettable *Toonkee*. There are numerous good, cheap eating places right around the station but take care here – some of Bangkok's best pickpockets and razor artists work the station area.

Across Rama IV near Wat Traimit, the *New Empire Hotel* (☎ 234 6990) at 572 Yaowarat Rd has air-con doubles from 440B up to 700B. It is kind of noisy but in a good Chinatown location near the intersection of Yaowarat and Charoen Krung (New) Rds. The *Burapha* (☎ 221 3545/9), at the intersection of Chakraphet and Charoen Krung (New) Rds and on the edge of Chinatown, is similar. There are a number of other Chinatown hotels around, but most don't have signs in English.

The *TT II Guest House* (☎ 236 2946), about a 10-minute walk south from the station at 516-518 Soi Samang, Si Phraya Rd, is near the junction with Mahanakhon Rd. It's a short walk from the GPO and river. From the station, turn left and walk a block along Rama IV Rd then turn right (south) down Mahanakhon Rd. There will be signs close to Si Phaya Rd. It's worth the effort to find this comparatively large, well-kept and popular place. Single/double rooms cost 180B; there's a strict midnight curfew.

Siam Square Near the National Stadium, on Rama I Rd, there are more places including the *National Scout Hostel* (Sala Vajiravut) which is one of the cheapest places in Bangkok (at the time of writing this hostel was closed for renovations). You'll find it on the 4th floor of the National Scout Executive Committee Building near the National Stadium. There are five dorms, each with 12 beds at 30B each. Women can stay and there's no need to be a Boy Scout but the dorms are gender-segregated. It's not a bad place, although the traffic is a little noisy. Bring a padlock for your cupboard. Bus No 15, 25, 40, 48, 54, 73 or 204 will get you there. The No 29 airport bus goes near this area, stopping at the Rama I and Phayathai Rds intersection.

Nearby Soi Kasem San 1, off Rama I Rd opposite the National Stadium, has several places which are good value. Right on the corner of this Soi and Rama I Rd is the *Muangphol Building* (☎ 215 3056/0033) which offers decent air-con singles/doubles for 450/550B and has a restaurant downstairs. The *Pranee Building* next door has 400B rooms but no restaurant.

More home-like are the family-run *A-One Inn* (☎ 215 3029) and the *Bed & Breakfast Inn* (☎ 215 3004), both of which are at the end of Soi Kasem San 1 and cost 350/450B for air-con rooms; the A-One also has some 300B rooms. Both have small dining areas on the ground floor. Rates at the Bed & Breakfast Inn include breakfast but rooms are a bit larger at the A-One. The newer *Wendy House* and *White Lodge* opposite the A-One Inn offer clean, modern rooms in the 400 to 500B range. Avoid the *Reno* and *Star* hotels on this soi; both are overpriced and rather unfriendly.

Soi Ngam Duphli Just off Rama IV Rd, this was for many years the travellers' centre of Bangkok but the places are no longer the best value to be found. Get there on an ordinary bus No 4, 13, 14, 22, 27, 46, 47 or 74, or a

No 7 air-con bus, getting off just after the roundabout on Rama IV Rd.

Once, the prime attraction here was the *Malaysia Hotel* (☎ 286 3582) at 54 Soi Ngam Duphli – back in the Vietnam War days this was one of the hotels quickly thrown together for the R&R trade. It is multistorey and has air-con, a swimming pool and all that sort of thing. When the war ended they decided to cut prices to the bone and fill it with the travellers who were invading the region at that time. For a while the Malaysia was a sort of working test on how long a building could hang together with much abuse and no care.

Now the Malaysia has been cleaned up and is just another mid-range hotel. There are 120 rooms, all with air-con and bathroom costing 496B for a standard single or double, 546B with a TV and small fridge, or 700B with a TV, larger fridge and carpet.

Right across the road is the *Tungmahamek*, or Privacy Hotel (☎ 286 8811), which acts as an overflow centre for the Malaysia Hotel. It's probably a bit quieter, and the rooms, all air-con, are 350B for a double. The nearby *LA Hotel* (the English sign just says 'Hotel') is a bit better value if you don't need air-con but it's on the 'short-time' circuit – large rooms with bath and fan are 180B, air-con rooms 500B.

Today, there are also many smaller guesthouses around Soi Ngam Duphli – in that respect, it's becoming a quieter version of Khao San Rd. They include the *Anna Guest House* at 21/30 Soi Ngam Duphli and the *Lee Guest House* at 21/38, each with rooms starting at 80B. At the northern end of Soi Ngam Duphli near Rama IV Rd is *ETC Guest House* (☎ 286 9424, 287 1478), an efficiently run, multistorey place with a travel agency downstairs. Rooms are small but clean; rates are 120B with shared bath, 160/200B for singles/doubles with private bath. All room rates include a light breakfast.

There are four on-again, off-again *Freddy Guest Houses* in the area with rooms from 80 to 100B. None are particularly clean. Better places to stay include *Kenny, Turkh, Madam, Sala Thai Daily Mansion* (☎ 287 1436) and *Kit's Youth Center*. Apart from the hotels there are also lots of travel agencies, restaurants, bars and all manner of 'services' in the area.

The *YWCA* (☎ 286 1936) is close to the Soi Ngam Duphli area at 13 Sathon Tai (South) Rd. Rooms have air-con and baths, and cost from around 300B. There's also a 100B dormitory. This Y takes only women guests and has a restaurant, swimming pool and other facilities. At 27 Sathon Tai Rd is the more expensive *YMCA* (☎ 286 5134), where rooms start at 960B – both men and women can stay here.

Sukhumvit Rd North of Rama IV Rd and running out from the centre, much like Rama IV Rd, this is a major tourist centre. Take an ordinary bus No 2, 25, 40 or 48 or an air-con bus No 1, 8, 11 or 13. The hotels here are not Bangkok's top-notch places, although most of them are out of the budget traveller's price range. There are a few worthwhile places scattered in amongst them, however. All the small lanes running off Sukhumvit Rd are called Soi, and then a number – so the bigger the number, the further up (east) Sukhumvit Rd it is. All even numbers are to the south and odd to the north.

Starting at the Rama I end (Rama I changes into Sukhumvit Rd), you'll find the *Atlanta Hotel* at 78 Soi 2. It was an old standby from the '70s, before the Malaysia rose to the top, and is still reasonably popular. Simple but well-kept rooms cost from 150/200B with fan but shared bath, and up to 300/350/400B with air-con. Facilities include a small coffeeshop and swimming pool. The heavily annotated coffeeshop menu offers a crash course in Thai cuisine that could prove very useful upcountry.

Further up at Soi 13, the *Miami Hotel* (☎ 253 5611/3) is one of the cheaper tourist hotels. Rooms with fan are 180B, or around 550B with air-con. After taking a long, slow dive through the '80s, the Miami is looking a bit better – the pool is even clean enough to swim in again! Still, ask to see a room first and get a reduction if it's not up to par.

The *Crown* (☎ 258 0318) at Soi 29 was once a mid-range R&R joint in the same class as the old Miami but standards here have also been slipping. Rooms start at around 220B and all have air-con. The *Golden Palace Hotel* at 15 Soi 1 is better and costs from 400 to 500B. There are many other hotels tucked here and there along the Sukhumvit sois.

Guesthouses are also beginning to appear on Sukhumvit Rd, just like everywhere else in Bangkok. Try the *Disra House* (☎ 258 5102) between Soi 33 and Soi 33/1 (off the access street to the Villa cinema). Clean, comfortable rooms range from 80 to 150B. Of similar standard is the *SV Guest House* (☎ 253 0606) at 19/35-36 Sukhumvit Rd, Soi 19.

Places to Eat

Banglamphu & Around There are lots of cheap eating places around Banglamphu including several on the ground floors of Khao San Rd guesthouses. For the most part, these places serve Western food and Thai food prepared for Western palates. Popular places include the two *Hello Restaurants* and the *Buddy Beer Restaurant*. For more authentic fare, try the many Thai places along Rambutri Rd, just north of Khao San Rd. Of outstanding value and selection is the 8th-floor food mall in the *New World Shopping Centre*, three blocks north of Khao San Rd.

The *Yok Yor* on Samphraya Pier has good seafood, a menu in English and main dishes costing from around 40B. The Yok Yor also operates a dinner-cruise boat that offers the same menu with a reasonable 50B surcharge for boat service. Nearby is the similar *Chawn Ngoen*; it has no English sign, but there is an English menu.

Phra Athit Rd, over towards the river where you find the Trok Rong Mai guesthouses, has some inexpensive restaurants and foodstalls.

Hualamphong Lots of good cheap restaurants, mostly Chinese, can be found along Rong Muang Rd by the station.

Pahurat The *Royal India* at 392/1 Chakraphet Rd in Pahurat is one of the better places in the Pahurat district. The *ATM Shopping Centre*, on Chakraphet Rd and opposite the Royal India, has an Indian food centre on the top floor. The alley alongside the centre features cheap Indian foodstalls as well.

Siam Square The Siam Square sois have plenty of good places in varying price ranges. Try the big noodle restaurant *Coca* on Henri Dunant Rd, close to Rama I Rd. At 93/3 Soi Lang Suan, Ploenchit Rd, is the *Whole Earth Restaurant* which does good if somewhat expensive Thai and Indian vegetarian food. The Whole Earth has a second branch on Soi 26, Sukhumvit Rd.

Directly opposite the Siam Center on Rama I Rd, there's a *Kentucky Fried Chicken*, a *Dunkin' Donuts* and a string of other American-style fast-food eateries. *Uncle Ray's* has some of the best ice cream in Bangkok.

The 6th floor of the *MBK*, or *Mahboonkrong Center* (on the south-west corner of Rama I and Phayathai Rds), has a good Singapore-style food centre with everything from steak and salad to Thai vegetarian fare. It's open from 10 am to 9 pm daily. On the 4th floor of the same building are a number of other food vendors as well as several slightly up-market restaurants serving Western or Japanese food. At street level there are a host of fast-food places.

At the intersection of Soi Kasem San I and Rama I Rd is the excellent, inexpensive *Thai Sa-Nguan* restaurant, where curry and rice is 10 to 15B a plate. Good kway teow (rice noodles) and khao man kai (chicken rice) are also available here.

Silom & Surawong Rds At 30/37 Patpong 2, the *Thai Room* has reasonable Thai-Chinese-Mexican food. Try the *Bobby's Arms* on Patpong Rd for a good Aussie-Brit pub. Silom and Surawong Rds are south-west of Lumphini Park.

Opposite the Silom Rd entrance to Patpong Rd, in the CP Tower building, are a cluster of air-con American and Japanese-style fast-food places: *McDonald's, Pizza Hut, Chester's Grilled Chicken, Suzuki Coffee House* and *Toplight Coffee House*. Several are open late to catch the night-time Patpong traffic.

Halfway down Silom Rd, across from the Narai Hotel, you can get good Indian snacks near the Tamil temple. For south Indian food, try the *Simla Cafe* at 382-384 Soi 34 off Silom Rd, which serves idlis, dosas and a few other south Indian snacks along with a wide selection of north Indian dishes. There are several other interesting possibilities along Silom Rd like the reliable and moderately priced *Maria Bakery* at 1170-72, which serves all manner of Thai and Vietnamese dishes as well as pizza and pastries. The *Silom Village* shopping complex has a couple of good Thai restaurants.

Sukhumvit Rd The *Yong Lee Restaurant* at 211 Sukhumvit Rd, near Soi 15 and Asia Books, does standard Thai and Chinese food. *Laikhram*, down Soi 49 with several twists and turns, has superb Thai food at not too outrageous prices. It's so far down Soi 49 you may want to take a motorcycle taxi from Sukhumvit Rd. A second branch has opened on Soi 33 and there's also one at Thaniya Plaza, Silom Rd.

The ground floor of the *Ambassador Hotel* between Sois 11 and 13 has a good food centre. It offers several varieties of Thai, Chinese, Vietnamese, Japanese, Muslim and vegetarian food at 20 to 40B per dish using the coupon system.

On Soi 12, *Cabbages & Condoms*, famous for its name alone, is run by Thai's hyperactive family planning association. By Soi 17, there's the fancy *Robinson's Department Store* with a branch of *McDonald's* at street level and a basement supermarket and food centre, featuring everything from *Dunkin' Donuts* to frozen yoghurt, ice cream, noodles and a variety of Thai food stands.

Entertainment

Thai Classical Dance The *National Theatre* periodically hosts classical Thai dance performances – call ☎ 224 1342 weekdays between 8.30 am and 4.30 pm for the current schedule. Special exhibition performances by the Chulalongkorn University Dance Club are offered once a month – ask at TAT for the latest schedule.

To see some Thai classical dance for free, hang out at the *Lak Muang Shrine* near Sanam Luang, or the *Erawan Shrine*. Another good venue is the *Center for Traditional Performing Arts* on the 4th floor of the Bangkok Bank, just off Ratchadamnoen Rd in Bangkok. Free public performances are given every Friday at 5 pm – arrive at least an hour early for a seat.

Several Bangkok restaurants sponsor dinner performances that feature a mix of dance and martial arts, all very touristy (the food is usually nothing special), for around 250 to 500B. At 11 am on Thursday and Sunday, there's a dance and martial arts performance (the Kodak Siam show) at the historic *Oriental Hotel* for 100B.

Live Music Along Soi Lang Suan and Soi Sarasin between Rama IV and Ploenchit Rds are has several bars that feature live Western pop, folk, blues, and jazz played by Thai bands. Among the most popular (and better) music bars are the *Brown Sugar* and *Old West*. Opposite the Asia Hotel on Phayathai Rd is the *Rock Pub*, a hangout for Thai metalheads. Bangkok has its own *Hard Rock Cafe*, with live music nightly, at Siam Square Soi 11. The three-storey *Saxophone Pub Restaurant*, south-east of the Victory Monument circle at 3/8 Victory Monument, Phayathai Rd, has become a Bangkok institution for musicians of several genres.

Thai Boxing This sport, where they kick as well as punch, is quite a scene. There are two stadiums: *Lumphini*, at Rama IV Rd near Soi Ngam Duphli, and *Ratchadamnoen*, on Ratchadamnoen Nok Ave. Admission prices start from around 180B and go up to 800B for ringside seats. The out-of-the-ring activity is sometimes even more frenzied and entertaining than that within the ring.

Massage & Go-Go Bars Bangkok is, of course, known as the Oriental sin-city extraordinaire (though Manila and Taipei each have more sex workers per capita) and hordes of (male) package tourists descend upon the city simply to sample its free-wheeling delights. Patpong Rd, just off Silom Rd, is the centre for the city's spectator sports, while massage parlours are found at many hotels and in the tourist ghettos like Sukhumvit Rd or, of course, on Patpong Rd.

In Thailand, a 'body massage' means the masseuse's, not yours. Avoid Bangkok's large massage parlours along Phetburi Tat Mai Rd, which cost as much as US$40 for a lukewarm bath and massage. Go-go bar ghettos include infamous Patpong Rd I and II (between Silom and Surawong Rds), the Nana Plaza group on Soi 4, Sukhumvit Rd, and the alley known as Soi Cowboy, parallel to Sukhumvit Rd between Sois 21 and 23. Alongside the railway tracks, opposite Soi 1, there's a collection of very rustic open-air bars. Or, there are the coffee-bar pick-up joints like the infamous *Thermae Coffee House* on Ploenchit Rd.

Many Bangkok visitors find that indulgence in the pleasures of sin-city can easily lead to social diseases or worse. In addition to all the usual STDs such as gonorrhoea and syphilis, Thailand also has a serious AIDS problem (see Health in the Thailand Facts for the Visitor section), so the use of condoms – or total abstinence – really is imperative. Less physical problems also occasionally befall Bangkok revellers – wallets have disappeared while people's pants were down, and hookers have been known to spike patrons' drinks with knockout drugs.

Of course, Bangkok also has plenty of straightforward nightspots. Not every bar is a pick-up joint and even in the ones that are you can have just a drink, if that's all you want.

THAILAND

Things to Buy

Anything you can buy out in the country you can also get in Bangkok – sometimes the prices may even be lower. Silom Rd and Charoen Krung (New) Rd are two good shopping areas that cater to tourists.

Better deals are available in Bangkok's large open-air markets at Chatuchak Park (Weekend Market), Yaowarat (Chinatown), Pratunam and Pahurat. Things to look for include:

Cotton & Silk Lengths of cotton and the beautifully coloured and textured Thai silk can be made into clothes or household articles. There are some good shops along Silom Rd but the fabric stalls in the Indian district of Pahurat are cheaper.

Temple Rubbings Charcoal on rice paper or coloured on cotton, these rubbings used to be made from temple bas reliefs. Today, they're made from moulds taken from the temple reliefs. Wat Pho is a favourite place with a very wide choice, but check prices at shops in town before buying at Wat Pho as they often ask too much.

Clothes The Thais are very fashion-conscious and you can get stylish clothes ready made or made to measure at attractive prices. The Mahboonkrong Shopping Centre near Siam Square and New World Centre in Banglamphu are two of the best places to shop for inexpensive clothes – also check the Siam Square alleys.

Gems Buyer beware. Unless you know stones, Bangkok is no place to seek out 'the big score'. *Never* accept an invitation from a tout or friendly stranger to visit a gem store, as the visit will soon turn into a confidence game in which you're the pigeon. See Dangers & Annoyances in the Thailand Facts for the Visitor section for more details on gem scams.

If you want to learn about gemstones before having a look around (a very sensible idea), visit the Asian Institute of Gemological Sciences (☎ 513 2112; fax 236 7803) at 484 Rachadaphisek Rd in the Huay Khwang district north-east of Bangkok. The institute offers reputable, reasonably priced gemology courses of varying lengths. The staff can also assess the authenticity and quality of stones (but not their value) that are brought to them.

Other Silver, bronze and nielloware (silver inlaid with black enamel) items include a variety of jewellery, plates, bowls and ornaments. Antiques are widely available but you'd better know what you're looking for. Temple bells and carved wooden cow bells are nice souvenirs. There is a string of art galleries along Charoen Krung (New) Rd from the GPO where you will find those attractive little leaf paintings – nicely framed and small enough to make handy little presents.

The Weekend Market, opposite the Northern bus terminal is, of course, a great place to look for almost any oddity. Behind the Chalerm Thai Theatre at Wat Ratchanatta, there's an amulet market where you can buy an amulet to protect you against almost anything.

Getting There & Away

Bangkok is the travel focus of Thailand. Unless you enter by crossing the border in the south from Malaysia, this is the place where you're most likely to arrive in Thailand. It's also the centre from where travel routes fan out across the country.

Air Bangkok is a major centre for international ticket discounting. It's also the centre for Thai International's domestic flight schedules. Check the Thailand Getting There & Away section for various warnings about discounted tickets and further information.

Bus The Bangkok bus terminals are:

North

Northern Route Terminal, Phahonyothin Rd (☎ 279 4484). The Northern terminal is on the road out to the airport. Go there for buses to Ayuthaya, Sukhothai, Chiang Mai and Chiang Rai, plus the towns in the north-east.

East

Eastern Route Terminal, Soi 40 (Ekamai), Sukhumvit Rd (☎ 392 3310). The Eastern terminal out along Sukhumvit Rd has buses for Pattaya and Ancient City.

South

New Southern Route Terminal, Highway 338 and Phra Pinklao Rd (☎ 434 5557). The Southern terminal is where you can get buses for Nakhon Pathom, Kanchanaburi, Hua Hin, Surat Thani, Phuket and Hat Yai.

All terminals have good left-luggage facilities.

Train There are two main railway stations. The big Hualamphong station on Rama IV Rd handles services to the north, north-east and some of the services to the south. The Thonburi, or Bangkok Noi, station handles some services to the south. If you're heading south ascertain from which station your train departs.

Getting Around

To/From the Airport Bangkok Airport is 25 km north of the city centre, and there are a variety of ways of getting to/from there.

Bus Just a few steps outside the airport there's a highway that leads straight into the city. You can get an air-con public bus (No 4) into the city for just 16B. It's less if you get off in northern Bangkok but you've got to sort this out before you pay. Bus No 4 goes down Vibhavadi Rangsit Rd to Ratchaprarop/Ratchadamri Rd, crosses Phetburi, Rama I, Ploenchit and Rama IV Rds, then goes down Silom Rd, turns left on Charoen Krung (New) Rd and continues across the river to Thonburi.

Alternatively, bus No 13 from the airport goes down Phahonyothin Rd, turns left at the Victory Monument to Ratchaprarop Rd then travels south to Ploenchit Rd and east on Sukhumvit Rd all the way to Bang Na. Air-con bus No 29 also goes by the airport and runs to Siam Square and Hualamphong. These air-con buses stop running at 8 pm.

If money is all-important, you can take the regular bus No 29 which follows a similar route to the No 13 but continues beyond Sukhumvit Rd to Rama IV Rd (get off there for the Soi Ngam Duphli hotels) and then turns right to the Hualamphong station area. The No 59 bus goes straight to the Democracy Monument area, which is handy if you're going to Banglamphu/Khao San Rd. Fares for these are just 3.50B and they operate 24 hours a day. Note that if a bus is crowded you may have trouble getting your gear on board.

There is a Thai International minibus which goes to most major hotels (and some minor ones, if the driver's in the mood) for 100B per person. It seems to depart erratically. There are air-con buses direct to Pattaya from the airport at 9 am, noon and 7 pm for 180B.

Minibuses depart regularly for the airport from the Khao San Rd accommodation enclave. They charge 50B.

Train The railway into Bangkok runs right by the airport. You can get a train straight to Hualamphong station for 5B in 3rd class. Walk over the pedestrian bridge from the international terminal to the Airport Hotel. The railway station is right in front of the hotel. The departure times aren't always that convenient, however. It's timed for commuters to or from work, not for passengers to or from the airport.

Taxi Greedy Thai International touts try to steer all arriving passengers toward one of their expensive limousine services, which are just glorified air-con taxi services costing a flat 350B – a definite rip-off. Just ignore them and head straight for the city taxi counter. Metered taxis from the airport are around 150B, or 200B if you buy a ticket at the city taxi counter tucked away at the far end of the arrival hall. Between three or more people, it's as cheap as the airport bus and rather more convenient.

If it's your first time in Bangkok, I'd suggest the 200B taxi fare, particularly if there are several of you to split the cost.

Bus The Bangkok bus service is frequent and frantic – a bus map is an absolute necessity. Get one from the tourist office or from bookshops and newsstands for 35 to 40B. The buses are all numbered and the bus map is remarkably easy to follow. Don't expect it to be 100% correct though – routes change regularly. Fares for ordinary buses vary according to the type of bus, from 2.50B (green or blue buses) to 3.50B (red buses) for any journey under 10 km; over 10 km it jumps to as high as 5B – out to the airport for example. The No 17 bus does a useful circuit of the city attractions and terminates near the National Museum and Emerald Buddha.

There are also a number of public air-con buses with numbers that may cause confusion with the regular buses. They start at 6B but jump to 16B on the long trips. Take care when hopping on a bus that it's not the air-con one if you're economising. Apart from the cool comfort, the air-con buses are uncrowded, especially in comparison to the mayhem on the regular buses.

At peak hours, an unofficial and mildly illegal shadow service of private songthaews operates on the same routes and with the same numbers as the public buses for 2B per person. They're necessary, which is why no attempt is made to control them.

Taxi & Samlor You must fix fares in advance for other taxis or the hideously noisy little three-wheeled samlors. The samlors must be one of the prime causes of Bangkok's pollution. Samlors (also known as tuk-tuks) are really only useful for shorter trips. When the distances get longer they often become more expensive than regular taxis. Often, you need real endurance to withstand a long samlor trip and, half the time, the drivers don't know their way around Bangkok anyway.

Bangkok recently instituted a metered taxi service, a welcome change from the days when curbside haggling added to the stress of moving around crowded streets. Around central Bangkok, metered taxi fares should generally be from 50 to 75B (35B at flagfall, plus 2B for each additional time/distance increment). Some drivers try to pad fares by driving around in circles, so keep an eye on a map to make sure your driver is proceeding in the right direction (some detours may be necessary to avoid traffic snarls, however).

Bicycle Cycling in Bangkok sounds like a recipe for disaster but, out in the country, it can be fine. Larnluang Trading at 355 Luang Rd between Worachak and Suapa Rds in Chinatown has been recommended for bicycles. There are also other bicycle shops along this road.

Boat River travel through and around Bangkok is not only much more interesting and peaceful than fighting your way through town in a bus or taxi, it is also much faster. There are a number of regular services along the Chao Phraya River through Bangkok and on the associated khlongs. Boats also buzz back and forth across the river from numerous points.

Easiest to use and understand is the Chao Phraya Express that runs up and down the river, although it only stops at certain landing stages, like the Oriental Hotel. This river-bus service costs 4B, 6B or 8B depending on the distance you travel. You buy your ticket on the boat. The Chao Phraya Express is a big, long boat with a number on the roof.

Bangkok still has quite a few khlongs but it's no longer the 'Venice of the East'. More and more of the canals are being filled in to become roads to ease Bangkok's ever-growing traffic jams. Periodic flooding in the city is in part due to the loss of the drainage the canals used to provide.

Places you can still go to include the khlong between the Democracy Monument area and the Ramkhamhaeng University area, along which long-tailed boats run. The boat from Banglamphu to the Ramkhamhaeng University area costs 10B and takes only 20 minutes. A bus would take nearly an hour under normal traffic conditions.

Bangkok Region

There are a number of interesting places within day-trip distance of Bangkok – some also make interesting stepping stones on your way north, east or south. You can stop at Ayuthaya on your way north, for example, or Nakhon Pathom on your way south.

The **Ancient City** (Muang Boran) is an artificial tourist attraction 33 km out of Bangkok which spreads over 80 hectares. Admission has been reduced to a reasonable 50B and you can get there by taking bus No 25 from Sukhumvit Rd to Pak Nam and then taking a small local bus.

There is also a **Crocodile Farm** in the same area and the **Rose Garden Country Resort** south of Bangkok. About 15 km out of the city, there's an excellent swimming pool complex at **Siam Park**. Bus No 27 gets you there, although not every No 27 goes to Siam Park. Entry is 60B, which ensures it is not very crowded.

AYUTHAYA

Until its destruction by the Burmese in 1767, this was the capital of Thailand. It is 86 km north of Bangkok. Built at the junction of three rivers, an artificial channel has converted the town into an island. To find your way around, get a copy of the excellent guidebook and map available from the Chan Kasem Museum here or in Bangkok.

During the 10 days leading to the Songkran Festival in mid-April, there is a sound-and-light show with fireworks over the ruins. This is a great time to visit Ayuthaya, but you might want to take refuge in a smaller town during the final water-throwing days of Songkran itself – unless you fancy staying wet for the day! Loi Krathong – when tiny votive boats are floated in rivers and ponds as tribute to the River Goddess – is another good time to be in Ayuthaya.

On the Island

Places to see are either 'on the island' or 'off the island'. There's a 10 to 20B admission charge to some of the ruins between 8 am and 4.30 pm. The best way to see the ruins is by bicycle. These can be rented at the guesthouses. Tuk-tuk tours cost from 200 to 300B for a day's sightseeing.

The **Chao Sam Phraya National Museum** is open from 9 am to noon and from

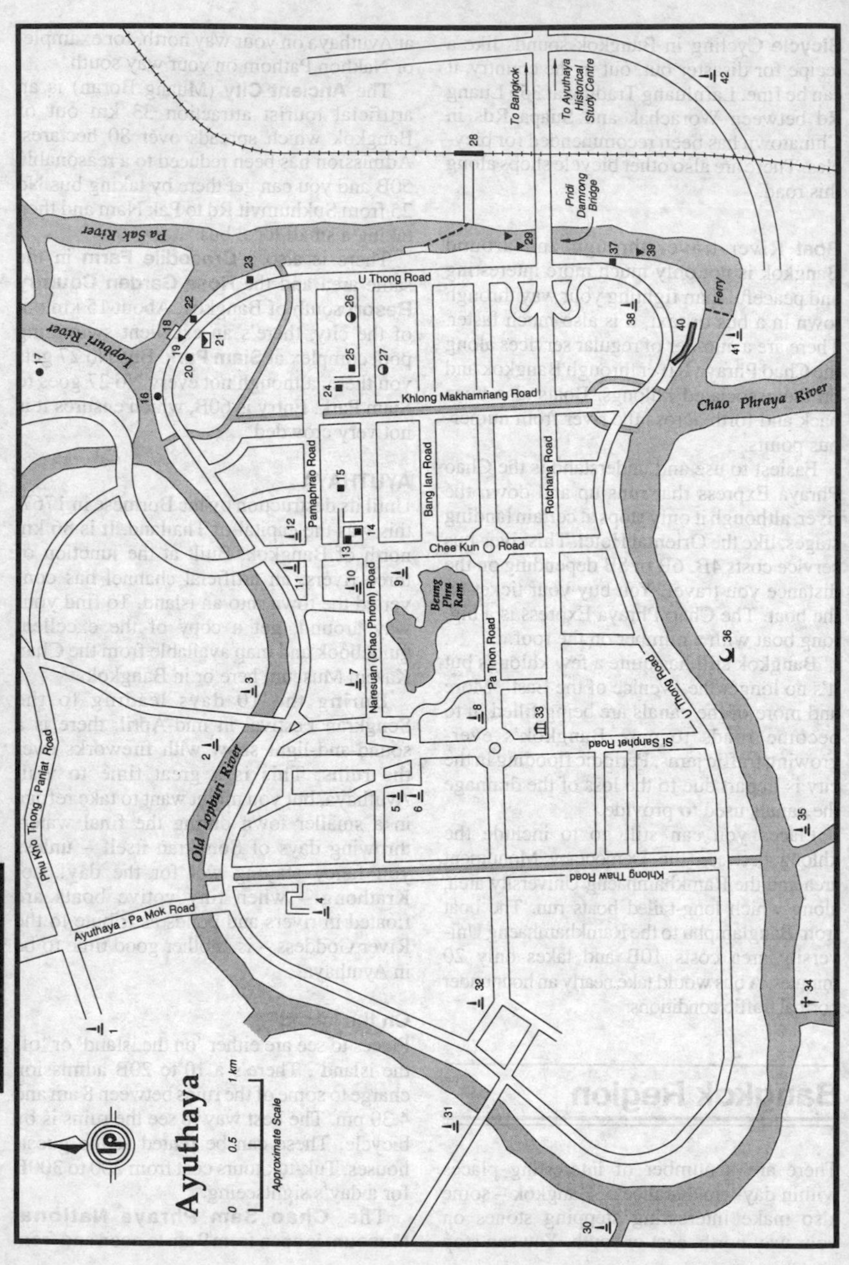
Ayuthaya
0
0.5
1 km
Approximate Scale
Phu Kho Thong - Paniat Road
Ayuthaya - Pa Mok Road
Old Lopburi River
Naresuan (Chao Phrom) Road
Pamaphrao Road
Bang Ian Road
Pa Thon Road
Rotchana Road
U Thong Road
Khlong Makhamriang Road
Chee Kun Road
Si Sanphet Road
Khlong Thaw Road
Beung Phra Ram
Lopburi River
Pa Sak River
Chao Phraya River
Pridi Damrong Bridge
To Bangkok
To Ayuthaya Historical Study Centre
Ferry

THAILAND

PLACES TO STAY		OTHER			
13	Thongchai Guest House	1	Phu Khao Thong Temple (Golden Mount Chedi)	20	Chan Kasem Palace
14	New BJ Guest House	2	Wat Na Phra Men (Meru)	21	Post Office
15	Thai Thai Hotel	3	Wat Kuti Thong	26	Air-con Minivans to Bangkok
22	U Thong Hotel	4	Wat Lokaya Sutha	27	Bus Terminal
23	Cathay Hotel	5	Wat Phra Si Sanphet	28	Railway Station
24	Ayuthaya & Old BJ Guesthouses	6	Wat Mongkhon Bophit	30	Wat Chai Wattanaram
25	Si Samai Hotel	7	Wat Thammikarat	31	Wat Kasatthirat
37	Pai Thong Guest House	8	Wat Phra Ram	32	Queen Suriyothai Memorial Pagoda
PLACES TO EAT		9	Wat Phra Mahatat	33	Chao Sam Phraya Museum
19	Night Market	10	Wat Ratburana	34	St Joseph's Cathedral
29	Floating Restaurants	11	Wat Suwannarat	35	Wat Phutthaisawan
39	Phae Krung Kao	12	Chinese Shrine	36	Mosque
		16	Hua Raw Market	38	Wat Suwan Dararam
		17	Elephant Kraal	40	Phet Fortress
		18	Pier (Boat Landing)	41	Wat Phra Phanan Choeng
				42	Wat Yai Chai Mongkhon

1 to 4 pm, Wednesday to Sunday. Admission is 10B on weekdays and it's free on weekends. There's a second national museum at the **Chan Kasem Palace**, and the opening hours are the same.

The **Wat Phra Si Sanphet** is the old royal temple with its three restored chedis. Adjoining it is **Wihaan Phra Mongkhon Bophit**, housing a huge bronze seated Buddha. **Wat Thammikarat** is particularly appealing for its overgrown, deserted feeling and the stone lions which guard a toppling chedi.

Wat Suwannarat was built towards the close of the Ayuthaya period and has been completely and very colourfully restored. **Wat Ratburana** and **Wat Phra Mahathat** are both extensively ruined but majestic.

Off the Island

The **Wat Phra Chao Phanan Choeng** was a favourite of Chinese traders and has a big seated Buddha. **Wat Chai Wattanaram** used to be one of Ayuthaya's most overgrown, evocative-of-a-lost-city type of ruin with stately lines of disintegrating Buddhas. Today, some hard restoration work (and the wonders of modern cement) has produced a row of lookalike brand new Buddhas! It's still a lovely wat with nice gardens.

The **Golden Mount** to the north of the city has a wide view over the flat country. Also to the north is the **elephant kraal** – the last of its kind in Thailand. **Wat Yai Chai Mongkon** to the south-east has a massive ruined chedi which contrasts with surrounding contemporary Buddha statues.

For a historical overview of the Ayuthaya period, check out the **Ayuthaya Historical Study Centre** near Wat Yai Chai Mongkon. Japanese-funded, this ambitious facility houses hi-tech displays that cover not only art and archaeology but also the social and political history of the period.

Wat Na Phra Men (Meru), opposite the old royal palace *(wang luang)* grounds via a bridge, is notable because it escaped destruction in 1767. The main *bot* (chapel) was built in 1546 and features fortress-like walls and pillars.

Places to Stay

Guesthouses The family-run *Ayuthaya Guest House* (☎ 25 1468) is down a soi off Naresuan Rd, near the bus terminal and the Si Samai Hotel. Rates are 50B per single and 80B per double. Next door a branch of the same family runs the *Old BJ Guest House* (☎ 25 1526) at the same rates. Both offer food service and bike rentals (30B a day).

The *New BJ Guest House* (☎ 25 1512) at 19/29 Naresuan Rd has clean rooms for 80 to 100B and a nice eating area in front. The newly established *Ayuthaya Youth Hostel (Reuan Doem)* (☎ 24 1978), an old house close to the railway station at 46/2 U Thong Rd, has tastefully decorated rooms for 150B single/double.

Hotels At 13/1 Naresuan Rd, the *Thai Thai* (☎ 25 1505) has comfortable rooms with bath from 120B up to 230B with air-con. The *U Thong Hotel* (☎ 24 2618), on U Thong Rd near the boat landing and the Chan Kasem Palace, is noisy but otherwise tolerable with rooms for 150B with fan or 300B with air-con. A few shops down, the *Cathay* (☎ 25 1562) is a better choice at 100/150B with fan. Also good is the slightly upmarket *Si Samai* at 12/19 Naresuan Rd near the Thai Thai, which costs 300B for a room with fan and bath, and 400B with air-con.

Places to Eat

There are lots of places to eat in Ayuthaya, including the night market opposite the Chan Kasem Palace. The *Chainam* opposite Chan Kasem Palace next to the Cathay Hotel has tables on the river, a bilingual menu and friendly service; it's also open for breakfast.

There are a couple of floating restaurants on the river near the Pridi Damrong Bridge, worth considering for a splurge. The *Phae Krung Kao* has a good local reputation – it's on the south side of the bridge on the west bank.

Getting There & Away

Bus There are buses to Ayuthaya from the Northern bus terminal in Bangkok every 10 minutes; the 1½ hour trip costs 22B. The first bus is at 5 am and the last at 7 pm.

Train From the Hualamphong station, there are frequent trains and the travel time is the same as the buses. The 3rd-class fare is 15B but the Ayuthaya station is some distance from the town centre. On the other hand, at the Bangkok end, it saves you trekking out to the Northern bus terminal.

Boat You can also get to Ayuthaya by boat but the only really regular service is the expensive tour boat from the Oriental Hotel in Bangkok (around US$30). Doing it by a local boat isn't easy. You could try chartering a long-tail boat which costs around 1200B for a return trip from Bangkok to Ayuthaya.

Getting Around

The cheapest way to see the town is by rented bicycle – 50 to 60B per day from the Ayuthaya or New BJ guesthouses. You can also hire a taxi or samlor by the hour (60B) or by the day (from 200 to 300B) to explore the ruins. Or, get a group of people together and hire a boat from the Palace Pier to do a circular tour of the island and see some of the less accessible ruins. Figure on about 200B per hour with a maximum of eight passengers. During the Songkran Festival in April, the local government runs daily boat tours from the U Thong Pier for a bargain 50B per person.

A minibus from the Ayuthaya railway station into town will cost from 5 to 10B.

BANG PA IN

The **Royal Palace** in Bang Pa In has a strange collection of baroque buildings in Chinese, Italian and Gothic style, and a Thai-style pavilion in a small lake. It's not all that interesting, but makes a pleasant riverboat trip from Ayuthaya, which is 20 km to the north. Admission is 10B but note that the palace is closed on Monday. Across the river from the palace is an unusual church-like wat reached by a trolley-cum-cable-car across the river – the crossing is free.

Getting There & Away

There are minibuses (or large songthaew trucks) between Bang Pa In and Ayuthaya every 15 minutes. The short trip costs 7B.

From Bangkok, there are buses to Bang Pa In every half-hour from 6 am to 6 pm; the fare is 20B.

LOPBURI

Situated 154 km north of Bangkok, this former capital of the Khmer Lavo period (10th century) shows strong Hindu and

THAILAND

Khmer influences in its temple and palace ruins.

Phra Narai Ratchaniwet

This former palace of King Narai is a good place to begin a tour of Lopburi. Built between 1665 and 1677, the palace was designed by French and Khmer architects – an unusual blend that works quite well. The main gate into the palace is off Sorasak Rd, opposite the Asia Lopburi Hotel. Inside the grounds are the remains of the royal elephant stables, a water reservoir, a reception hall, various pavilions and residence halls, and the **Lopburi National Museum**.

The museum is housed in three separate buildings which contain an excellent collection of Lopburi period sculpture, as well as an assortment of Khmer, Dvaravati, U Thong and Ayuthaya art, traditional farm implements and dioramas of farm life. It's open Wednesday to Sunday from 8.30 am to noon and from 1 to 4 pm. Admission into the palace grounds is free and museum entry is 10B.

Other Ruins

Most important is the **Prang Sam Yot**, or Sacred Three Spires, which was originally built as a Hindu shrine and is reckoned to be the finest Khmer structure in the region. **Prang Khaek** and **Wat Phra Si Ratana Mahathat** are also notable.

Phaulkon's House, the home of the Greek adviser to Ayuthaya during its heyday, is also in Lopburi. Phaulkon was beheaded by the king's ministers when he began courting French influence in the area. You can get a good map of Lopburi from the tourist office.

Places to Stay & Eat

You can do a day trip to Lopburi from Ayuthaya but if you want to stay, the *Thai Sawat* on Na Kala Rd, close to the railway station, is about the cheapest around at 60B. Also on Na Kala Rd, opposite Wat Nakhon Kosa, the *Indra* costs 70B for passable rooms with fan and bath. On the same road, but closer to the railway station, is the *Julathip* which doesn't have an English sign. Rooms with fan and bath are also 70B, but ask to see them first.

Still on Na Kala Rd, the *Suparaphong* is not far from Wat Phra Sri Ratana Mahathat and the railway station. It's similar in price and standard to the Julathip and the Indra. Overlooking King Narai's palace, the *Asia Lopburi* (☎ 41 1892) is on the corner of Sorasak and Phra Yam Jamkat Rds. It's clean and comfortable and has two Chinese restaurants downstairs. Rooms with fan and bath are 120B. *Muang Thong* (☎ 41 1036), across from Prang Sam Yot, has noisy but adequate rooms for 100B with fan and bath plus some cheaper rooms without bath for 80B.

There are several *Chinese restaurants* along Na Kala Rd, parallel to the railway line, but they tend to be a bit pricey. The places on the side streets of Ratchadamnoen and Phra Yam Jamkat Rds are better value.

Getting There & Away

Bus Ordinary buses leave about every 10 minutes from Ayuthaya or every 20 minutes from Bangkok – the three-hour trip costs 39B. From Kanchanaburi, you can get to Lopburi via Suphanburi and Singhburi on a series of public buses or share taxis.

Train You can reach Lopburi from Bangkok by train for 28B in 3rd class, and 57B in 2nd. One way of visiting Lopburi on the way north is to take the train from Ayuthaya (or Bangkok) early in the morning, leave your gear at the station for the day while you look around and then continue north on the night train.

Getting Around

Samlors go anywhere in Lopburi for 10B.

SARABURI

There's nothing of interest in Saraburi itself, but between here and Lopburi you can turn off to the **Phra Phutthabat**. This small, delicate and beautiful shrine houses a revered Buddha footprint. Like all genuine Buddha footprints, it is massive and identified by its 108 auspicious distinguishing marks. In February and March, there are pilgrimage festivals at the shrine.

Places to Stay

Try the *Thanin* or *Suk San* at Amphoe Phra Phutthabat – both cost 100 to 120B. In town, the *Kiaw An* (☎ 21 1656) on Phahonyothin Rd also has rooms from 100B. Other hotels include the slightly cheaper *Saraburi* (☎ 21 1646, 21 1500) opposite the bus stand.

SUPHANBURI

This very old Thai city has some noteworthy Ayuthaya-period chedis and one Khmer prang. **Wat Phra Si Ratana Mahathat** (is there a more popular name for a wat in Thailand?) is set back off Malimaen Rd close to the city centre. A staircase inside its Lopburi-style Khmer prang leads right to the top.

About seven km west of Suphan town (about seven km) is **Don Chedi**, a pagoda that commemorates the 16th-century mounted elephant duel between Thailand's King Naresuan and the Prince of Burma. Naresuan won, thus freeing Ayuthaya from Pegu's rule. During the week of 25 January, there's an annual **Don Chedi Monument Fair** in which the elephant battle is re-enacted in full costume.

Places to Stay

The *King Pho Sai* (☎ 51 1412) at 678 Nane Kaew Rd has rooms from 100B. The *KAT* (☎ 51 1619/39) at 433 Phra Phanwasa and the *Suk San* (☎ 51 1668) at 1145 Nang Pim Rd are similarly priced.

NAKHON PATHOM

At 127 metres, the gigantic orange-tiled **Phra Pathom Chedi** is the tallest Buddhist monument in the world. It was begun in 1853 to cover the original chedi of the same name. Nakhon Pathom is regarded as the oldest city in Thailand – it was conquered by Angkor in the early 11th century and in 1057 was sacked by Anawrahta of Pagan (Burma). There is a museum near the chedi and outside the town is the pleasant park of **Sanam Chan** – the grounds of the palace of Rama VI. In November, there's a **Phra Pathom Chedi Fair** that packs in everyone from fruit vendors to fortune tellers.

From Nakhon Pathom, you can make an excursion to the **floating market** at Klong Damnoen Saduak. This has become a popular, less-touristic alternative to the over-commercialised Bangkok floating market. All you have to do to get there is hop on a bus bound for Samut Songkhram to the south and ask to be let off in Damnoen Saduak or *talaat nam* (floating market). Go early in the morning (around 6 or 7 am is best) to avoid the tourist hordes from Bangkok.

Places to Stay & Eat

On Lungphra Rd, near the railway station, the *Mitsamphan Hotel* (☎ 24 2422) has rooms from 80B with fan and bath, and more with air-con. The *Mitrthaworn (Mittaowan)*, on the right as you walk towards the chedi from the train station, has rooms at 130/150B with fan and bath, 180B for air-con.

The *Mitphaisan* (its English sign says 'Mitr Paisal') is further down the alley to the right from the Mittaowan and has rooms from 150B. All three 'Mit' hotels are owned by the same family. The Mittaowan is probably the best.

There's an excellent *fruit market* along the road between the train station and the Phra Pathom Chedi. The excellent *Ha Seng* Chinese restaurant is on the south side of the road which intersects the road from the train station to the chedi. Turn right if walking from the chedi and walk about 20 metres.

Getting There & Away

Nakhon Pathom is 56 km west of Bangkok. Every weekend, there's a special rail trip to Nakhon Pathom and on to Kanchanaburi. Otherwise, you can get there by bus from the Southern bus terminal in Bangkok or by rail. Buses leave every 10 minutes and cost 16B for the one-hour trip. The rail fare is 14B in 3rd class.

RATCHABURI

This unexciting town is on the way south from Nakhon Pathom, well before you get to the coast and Hua Hin. The *Zin Zin Hotel* on Railway Rd is cheap.

KANCHANABURI

Kanchanaburi (pronounced Kan-cha-NA-buri) is often referred to as Kan. During WW II, the infamous bridge over the River Kwai was built here, 130 km west of Bangkok. The bridge that stands today is not the one constructed during the war – that was destroyed by Allied air raids – though the curved portions of the structure are original. The graves of thousands of Allied soldiers can be seen in Kanchanaburi or you can take a train across the bridge and continue further west where there are caves, waterfalls and a neolithic burial site.

The town was originally founded by Rama I as protection against Burmese invasion over the Three Pagodas Pass, which is still a major smuggling route into Myanmar.

Information

There's a good TAT office near the bus station.

Death Railway Bridge

The bridge made famous by the film *Bridge Over the River Kwai* spans the Khwae Yai River, a tributary of the Mae Klong River, a couple of km north of town. The bridge was only a small but strategic part of the Death Railway to Burma and was in use for 20 months before the Allies bombed it in 1945.

Every year, during the first week of December, there's a nightly light and sound show at the bridge. It's a pretty impressive scene with the sounds of bombers and explosions, and fantastic bursts of light. The town gets a lot of tourists during this week, so book early if you want to attend.

Get to the bridge from town by catching a songthaew (2B) along Pak Phraek Rd (parallel to Saengchuto Rd, close to the river) heading north.

JEATH War Museum

This interesting little outdoor museum is run by monks. It's set up just like a POW camp on the actual spot where there was a camp during the war. Entry is 20B and it's worth seeing. It's estimated that 16,000 Western POWs died in the construction of the Death Railway to Burma but the figures for labourers, many forcibly conscripted from Thailand, Burma, Indonesia and Malaysia, were even worse. As many as 100,000 to 150,000 may have died in this area during WW II.

Other Attractions

There are two Allied **war cemeteries** near Kanchanaburi, one just north of town off Saengchuto Rd near the railway station, and the other across the river west of town, a few km down the Khwae Noi tributary. The town also has an interesting **Lak Muang**, or city pillar shrine on Lak Muang Rd, two blocks north-west of the tourist office.

Wat Tham Mongkon Thong is well known for its famous 'Floating Nun' who meditates while floating in a pool of water, an attraction that draws daily busloads of Thai and Chinese tourists. This cave temple is some distance west of town.

Places to Stay

Guesthouses You can stay on the river in a raft house (or over the river in the case of bungalows built on piers) from 30 to 50B per person depending on the raft. At the junction of the Khwae Yai and Khwae Noi rivers is the well-run *Nita Raft House* (☎ 51 4521), where singles/doubles with mosquito net are 40/60B. Two other popular places of this sort are the *River* and *VN* guesthouses where small, basic rooms are 40/80B, more with private bath. Both are on the river, not far from the railway station. One drawback to these places, especially on weekends and holidays, is the presence of floating disco rafts that ply up and down the river blasting pop music nearly all night long.

North of the VN and River guesthouses is the very popular *Jolly Frog Backpacker's* – it costs 70B for a double with veranda, mossie screens and shared bath. Other places come and go but they're all pretty similar. In the floating restaurant area is the well-run

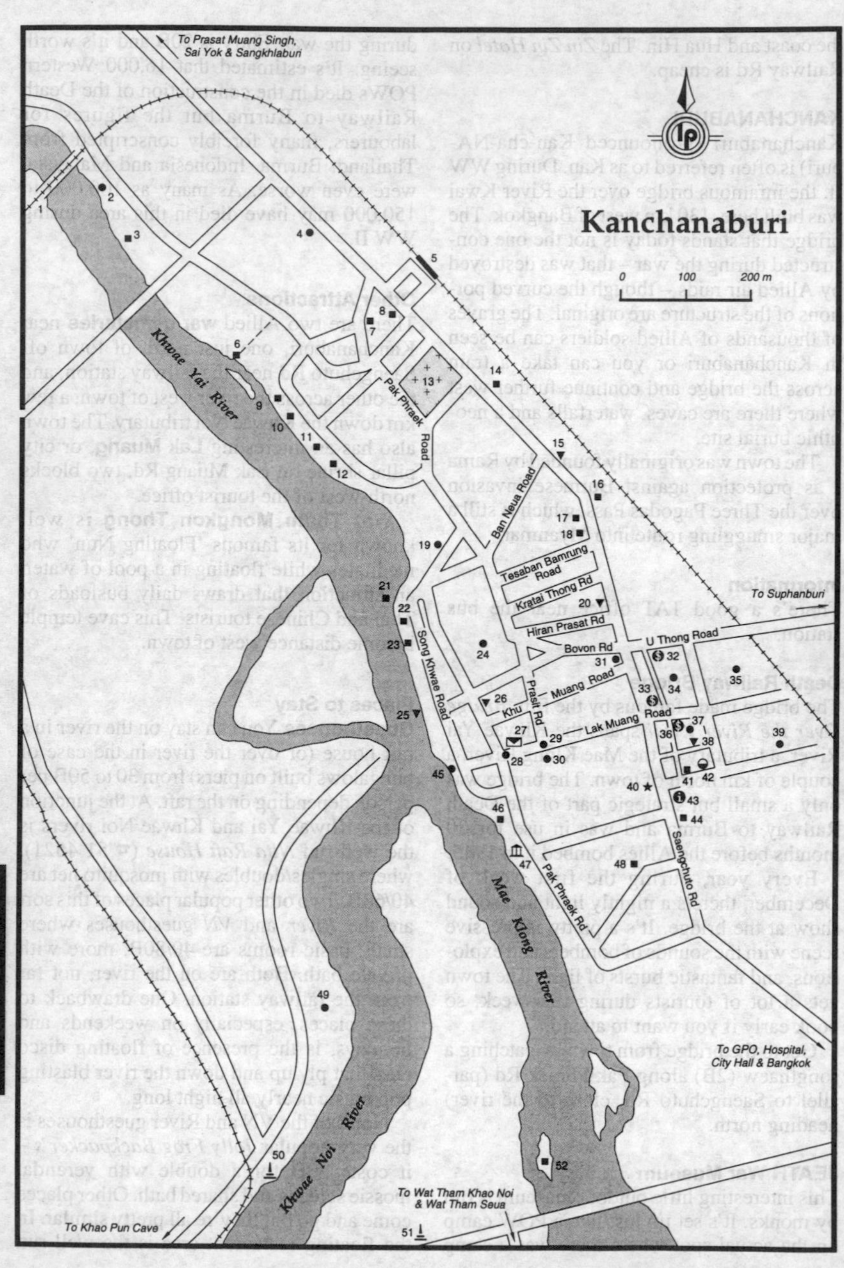
Kanchanaburi
0
100
200 m
To Prasat Muang Singh, Sai Yok & Sangkhlaburi
Khwae Yai River
Pak Phraek Road
Ban Neua Road
Tesaban Bamrung Road
Kratai Thong Rd
Hiran Prasat Rd
Bovon Rd
U Thong Road
To Suphanburi
Muang Road
Khu Prasit Rd
Lak Muang Road
Song Khwae Road
Saengchuto Rd
Pak Phraek Rd
Mae Klong River
Khwae Noi River
To GPO, Hospital, City Hall & Bangkok
To Wat Tham Khao Noi & Wat Tham Seua
To Khao Pun Cave

PLACES TO STAY

- 3 Bamboo Guest House
- 6 Jolly Frog Backpacker's
- 7 Si Muang Kan Hotel
- 8 Rung Rung Bungalows
- 9 PS Guest House
- 10 Rick's Lodge
- 11 VN Guest House
- 12 River Guest House
- 14 Luxury Hotel
- 16 River Kwai Hotel
- 17 Prasopsuk Hotel
- 18 VL Guest House
- 21 Nitaya Raft House
- 22 Sam's Place
- 23 Supakornchai Raft House
- 41 BT Travel
- 44 Thai Seri Hotel
- 46 Nita Raft House
- 48 Thipvaree Bungalow
- 52 Kasem Island Resort

PLACES TO EAT

- 15 Sabai-jit Restaurant
- 20 Isaan Restaurant
- 25 Floating Restaurants
- 26 Aree Bakery
- 38 Si Fa Bakery

OTHER

- 1 Death Railway Bridge
- 2 Japanese War Memorial
- 4 Army Post
- 5 Railway Station
- 13 Kanchanaburi Allied War Cemetery
- 19 Songthaews to Khwae River Bridge
- 24 Markets
- 27 Lak Muang Rd Post Office
- 28 Town Gate of Kanchanaburi
- 29 Lak Muang
- 30 Municipal Office
- 31 Taxi Stand
- 32 Bangkok Bank
- 33 Thai Military Bank
- 34 Market
- 35 Cinema
- 36 Thai Farmers Bank
- 37 Market
- 39 Cinema
- 40 Police Station
- 42 Bus Station
- 43 TAT Office
- 45 Ferry Pier
- 47 JEATH War Museum
- 49 Chung Kai Allied War Cemetery
- 50 Wat Tham Kao Pun
- 51 Wat Tham Mongkon Thong

Sam's Place, where rooms with shared bath start at 70B.

If you want to stay out near the bridge, the *Bamboo Guest House* (☎ 51 2532) at 3-5 Soi Vietnam, on the river about a km before the Japanese War Memorial, has double rooms for 100B.

A bit more expensive but good value is the *VL Guest House*, in town across the street from the River Kwai hotel. Clean, spacious rooms with fan and bath are 100B for singles or doubles. Larger rooms which hold four to eight persons cost 50B per person. The VL has a small dining area downstairs and they rent bicycles and motorbikes.

Hotels The *Prasopsuk Hotel* (☎ 51 1777) at 277 Saengchuto Rd has good 110B bungalows – if you don't mind the horizontal mirrors next to the beds. The *Luxury Hotel* (☎ 51 1168) is a couple of blocks north of the River Kwai Hotel and offers clean rooms from 70B.

Places to Eat

There are plenty of places to eat along the northern end of Saengchuto Rd near the River Kwai Hotel. The quality generally relates to the crowds! Good, inexpensive eating can also be found in the *markets* along Prasit Rd and between U Thong and Lak Muang Rds east of Saengchuto Rd.

The *Sabai-jit* restaurant, just north of the River Kwai Hotel, has an English menu and consistently good food. The *Isaan*, on Saengchuto Rd between Hiran Prasat and Krathai Thong Rds, serves great kài yâang (whole spicy grilled chicken) and other north-eastern Thai specialities.

Down on the river, there are several large *floating restaurants* where the quality of the food varies but it's hard not to enjoy the atmosphere. Across from the floating restaurants along the road are several smaller, cheaper foodstalls which open in the evenings.

The *Aree Bakery* has excellent baked goods, ice cream, coffee, tea and sandwiches. There are tables and chairs for a sit-down.

Getting There & Away

Bus Regular buses leave Bangkok every 20 minutes daily for Kanchanaburi from the Southern bus terminal in Thonburi. The trip takes about three hours and costs 34B. Air-

THAILAND

con buses leave every 15 minutes and cost 62B. The last bus back to Bangkok leaves Kan around 10 pm.

Train The regular train costs 28B for 3rd class. There are only two a day and they both leave from the Bangkok Noi station in Thonburi, not from Hualamphong.

Share Taxi & Minivan You can take a share taxi from Saengchuto Rd to Bangkok for 50B per person. Taxis leave throughout the day whenever five passengers accumulate at the taxi stand. These taxis will make drops at Khao San Rd or in the Pahurat district. Kanchanaburi guesthouses also arrange daily minivans to Bangkok for 80B per person, with drop-offs at Khao San Rd.

Getting Around

You can hire motorbikes from the Suzuki dealer near the bus station. The cost is 150B per day and they are a good way of getting to the rather scattered attractions around Kanchanaburi.

Samlors within the city are 10 to 15B a trip. Regular songthaews in town are 2B but be careful you don't 'charter' one or it'll be a lot more.

AROUND KANCHANABURI

There are numerous interesting excursions to be made from Kanchanaburi.

Waterfalls

The **Erawan Falls** are an interesting bus trip (1½ to two hours) beyond Kanchanaburi. Take an early morning bus from the station. It costs 19B to the end of the line from where you have to walk a couple of km to the start of the waterfall trail.

For the lazy or those with the money, minibuses cruise by the river guesthouses around 9 am daily and take passengers right into Erawan Park for 60B per person – they return around 3.30 pm. There's a 5B admission charge to the two-km footpath which goes along the river and past seven waterfalls. There are plenty of good plunge pools so take along your swimming gear, but make an early start since the last bus back is at 4 pm.

Other waterfalls are generally too far from Kanchanaburi for a day trip. For overnighters, the **Huay Khamin** falls are one of the most interesting.

Other Attractions

There are a few places of interest along the road to Sangkhlaburi. From Kanchanaburi, take the Nam Tok Sai Yok road. A few km past the river you can visit the **Phu Phra Cave**. Another pause can be made at the **Prasat Muang Sing Temple**, a western outpost of the Khmer Empire. The **Sai Yok Falls** are 60 km out (overnight raft trips head down the Khwae Noi River from here) and another 44 km takes you past the **Sai Yok Yai National Park**. Around 107 km out, there's the **Hin Dat Hot Springs**. Remember to dress discreetly if you decide to try them out – don't swim in the nude.

SANGKHLABURI & THREE PAGODAS PASS

These days it's relatively easy to travel up to the pass (Chedi Sam Ong in Thai) and have a peek into Myanmar. Getting there requires an overnight pause in Sangkhlaburi, 223 km north from Kan. The village on the Myanmar side of the pass has been the scene of firefights between the Mon and Karen insurgents – both armies want to control the collection of 'taxes' levied on border smuggling.

In March 1990, the Burmese government regained control of the area, rebuilt the bamboo village in wood and concrete and renamed it Payathonzu. A row of tourist shops have been built and tourists are allowed over the border for day trips; there is an entrance fee of 130B. There is talk of reopening the road all the way to Mawlamyine. The three pagodas themselves are rather inconspicuous, small and whitewashed monuments.

Places to Stay

At Thong Pha Phum, the last town before Sangkhlaburi, there are several places to stay for around 80B a night.

In Sangkhlaburi, the *Sri Daeng Hotel* is on the first street to the left when you enter town and has rooms for 130B. Two km east of the bus station, near the lake, is the *Burmese Inn*, with lakeview rooms for 60B single, 80B double. The similar *P Guest House* a bit farther on has less expensive rooms for 40 to 50B.

There's a resort with bungalows for 300B at the Three Pagodas Pass.

Getting There & Away

Four buses a day go to Sangkhlaburi from Kanchanaburi between 6 am and 1 pm for 70B; the ride takes 4½ hours. More expensive, faster air-con minivans are also available. You can also get to Sangkhlaburi by a rented motorbike from Kan. This is not a road for the inexperienced motorcyclist – it has lots of dangerous curves, steep grades and long stretches without available assistance. If you go by motorbike, refuel in Thong Pha Phum, 150 km north of Kan – there isn't another fuel stop before Sangkhlaburi, another 70 km away. From

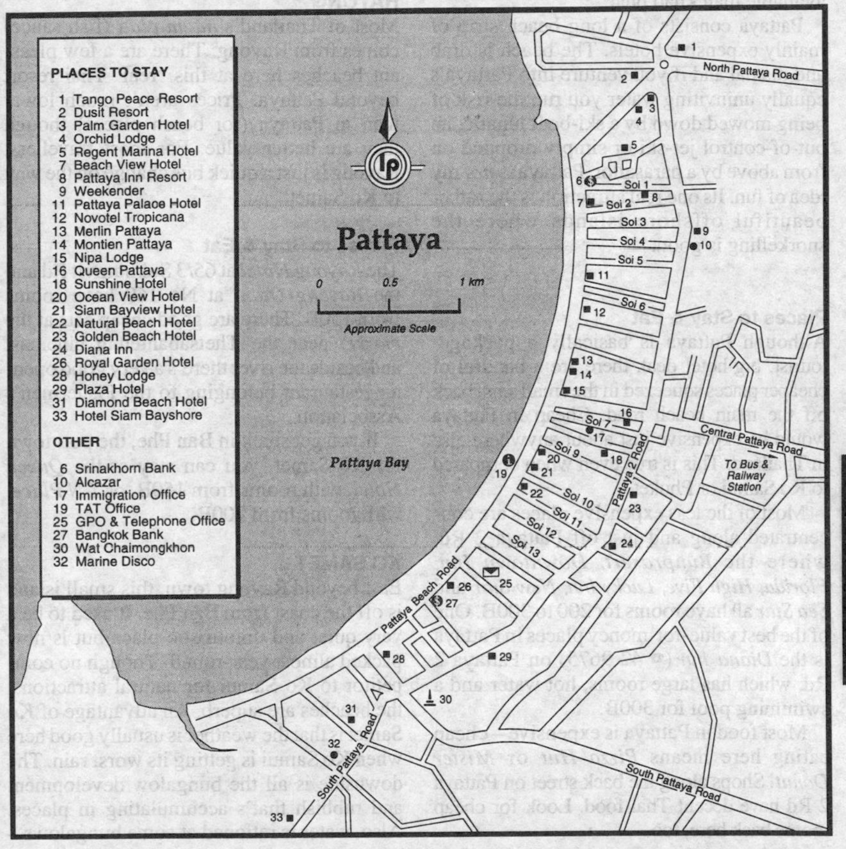

Sangkhlaburi, there are hourly songthaews (30B, 40 minutes) to Three Pagodas Pass all day long.

PATTAYA

Thailand's biggest and once most popular beach resort is a long way from being its nicest. Situated 154 km south of Bangkok, a fourth 'S' (for sex) can be added to Sun, Sea & Sand in this gaudy and raucous resort. Pattaya is designed mainly to appeal to European package tourists, and there are plenty of snack bars along the beach strip proclaiming that 'bratwurst mit brot' is more readily available than khao phat.

Pattaya consists of a long beach strip of mainly expensive hotels. The beach is drab and dismal and if you venture into Pattaya's equally uninviting water you run the risk of being mowed down by a ski-boat lunatic, an out-of-control jet-ski or simply dropped on from above by a parasailor. Pattaya is *not* my idea of fun. Its one real attraction is the rather beautiful offshore islands where the snorkelling is good.

Places to Stay & Eat

Although Pattaya is basically a package-tourist, big-hotel deal, there are a handful of cheaper places squeezed in the small sois, back off the main beach road. Cheap in Pattaya would be expensive just about anywhere else in Thailand. This is true even when compared to Ko Samui or Phuket.

Most of the less expensive places are concentrated along and just off Pattaya 2 Rd, where the *Bunprasert, Downtown Inn, Florida, High Five, Lucky Inn, New Star* and *Sea Star* all have rooms for 200 to 300B. One of the best value-for-money places in Pattaya is the *Diana Inn* (☎ 42 9675) on Pattaya 2 Rd, which has large rooms, hot water and a swimming pool for 300B.

Most food in Pattaya is expensive – cheap eating here means *Pizza Hut* or *Mister Donut*! Shops along the back street on Pattaya 2 Rd have decent Thai food. Look for cheap rooms back here, too.

Getting There & Away

There are departures every half-hour from the Eastern bus terminal in Bangkok for the two-hour, 37B trip to Pattaya. Air-con buses are 66B. There are also all sorts of air-con tour buses to Pattaya run by a number of tour companies. At 9 am, noon and 7 pm, there are buses direct from Bangkok International Airport for 250B one way.

Getting Around

Songthaews cruise Pattaya Beach and Pattaya 2 Rds for 5B per person. Don't ask the fare first or drivers will think you want a charter.

RAYONG

Most of Thailand's *náam plaa* (fish sauce) comes from Rayong. There are a few pleasant beaches here at this 'real' Thai resort beyond Pattaya. Prices aren't much lower than in Pattaya (for beach places) though they are better value. For most travellers, Rayong is just a quick bus change on the way to Ko Samet.

Places to Stay & Eat

The *Rayong Hotel* at 65/3 Sukhumvit Rd and the *Rayong Otani* at No 169 have rooms from 150B. There are good cheap eats at the *market* near the Thetsabanteung cinemas, and beside the river there's a very good open-air restaurant belonging to the Fishermen's Association.

If you get stuck in Ban Phe, the port town for Ko Samet, you can stay at the *Queen Hotel*, with rooms from 150B, or *T N Place*, with rooms from 200B.

KO SAMET

East beyond Rayong town, this small island is off the coast from Ban Phe. It used to be a very quiet and untouristic place but is now packed almost year-round. Though no competitor to Ko Samui for natural attractions, the beaches are superb. An advantage of Ko Samet is that the weather is usually good here when Ko Samui is getting its worst rain. The downside is all the bungalow development and rubbish that's accumulating in places. Also, water is rationed at some bungalows –

a reasonable policy given the scarcity of water on the island.

There are rumours that the National Park Service may step in soon and order most of the bungalows to close down to preserve the environment. This could make Ko Samet a far more pleasant place to visit. At the moment there is a moratorium on building new accommodation and a 50B park entry fee for non-Thais.

Places to Stay

Beach accommodation costs from 60 to 250B and is mainly concentrated along the north-east coast. *Naga Bungalows*, between Ao Tubtim and Hat Sai Kaew near the concrete mermaid, is recommended, as are *Little Hut* and *Tubtim*. There are plenty of others to choose from, even a couple of places on Ao Phrao (Coconut Bay) on the western side of the island. Avoid Ao Wong Deuan on the central east coast – it's crowded and overpriced. Another warning: during Thai national holidays all of Ko Samet can get quite crowded.

Getting There & Away

It's a three-hour, 47B (85B air-con) bus ride from the Eastern bus terminal in Bangkok to Rayong, then a 10B bus to Ban Phe (the touts will find you). For 90B you can get a direct air-con bus from Bangkok to Ban Phe, so why bother with Rayong? From Ban Phe, a fishing boat will take you out to Na Dan on the north end of Ko Samet for 30B. Other boats go to Ao Wong Deuan or Ao Thian on the central east coast for the same price. A boat to Ao Wai will cost 40B.

Many Khao San Rd agencies in Bangkok organise round-trip transport to Ko Samet including the boat fare for around 260B one way. Not only is this twice as expensive as doing it on your own, you won't have a choice of which boat to take or where it stops.

Getting Around

Taxi trucks on the island cost from 10 to 30B per person depending on how far you're going. There are trails all the way to the southern tip of the island, and a few cross-island trails as well.

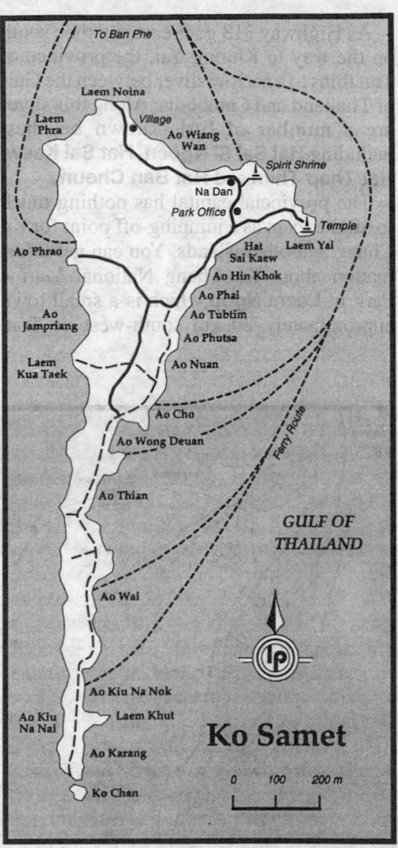

TRAT PROVINCE

Located about 400 km south-east from Bangkok, the province of Trat borders Cambodia. Gem-mining and smuggling are the most important occupations, though tourism at Ko Chang National Marine Park is becoming popular. You'll find gem markets at the Hua Thung and Khlong Yo markets in Bo Rai district, about 40 km north of Trat town. You can make good buys if (and only if) you know what you're buying.

As Highway 318 goes east and then south on the way to Khlong Yai, the province of Trat thins to a narrow sliver between the Gulf of Thailand and Cambodia. Along this sliver are a number of little-known beaches, including **Hat Sai Si Ngoen**, **Hat Sai Kaew**, **Hat Thap Thim** and **Hat Ban Cheun**.

The provincial capital has nothing much to offer except as a jumping-off point for Ko Chang and other islands. You can get information about Ko Chang National Marine Park in **Laem Ngop**, which is a small town approximately 20 km south-west of Trat. You can also get boats from Laem Ngop to Ko Chang.

Places to Stay

Trat The *Trat Inn* (☎ 51 1028) at 66-71 Sukhumvit Rd and *Thai Roong Roj (Rung Rot)* (☎ 51 1141) at 196 Sukhumvit Rd have rooms from around 80 to 200B. The *Max & Tick Guest House* (☎ 520799), in a lane which is a continuation of Tat Mai Rd, behind the Municipal Market, is new and clean and costs 80B per person or 120B per person in a triple. Rumour says they may be

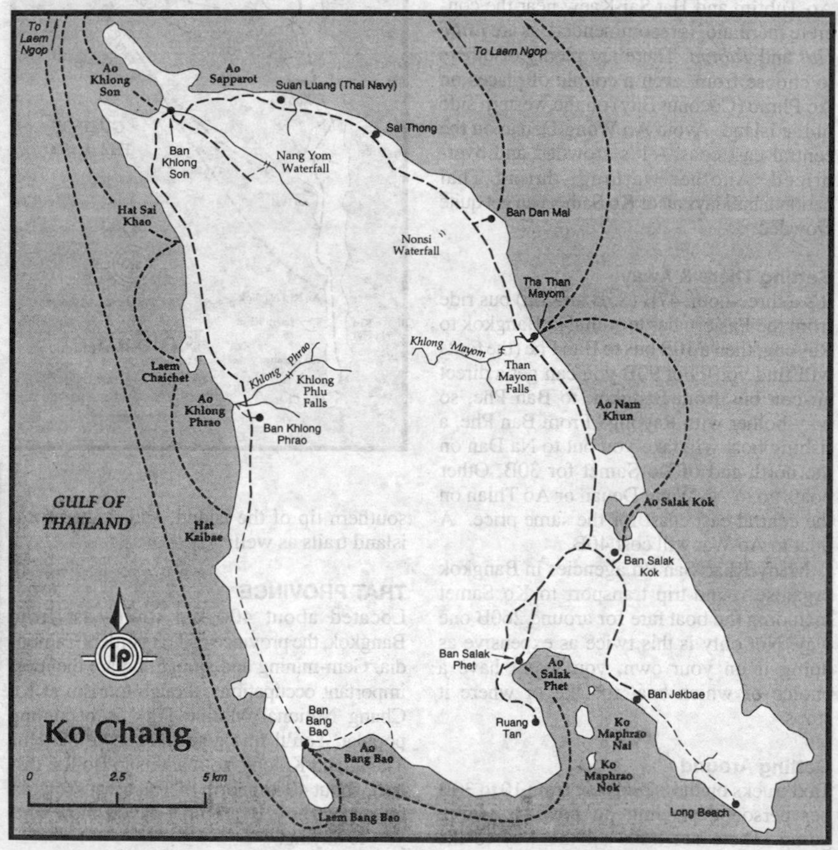

moving to a new location in the near future. Also good is the *Foremost Guest House* (☎ 51 1923) at 49 Thana Charoen Rd, towards the canal. Rooms here are 30B per person in a dorm, or 50/70/90B for single/double/triple rooms. The same family runs the *Windy Guest House* across the road on the canal.

Laem Ngop There's really no reason to stay here since most boats to Ko Chang leave in the afternoon and it's only 20 km from Trat, but the cosy *Chut Kaew Guest House* has rooms from 60/100B.

Places to Eat

The municipal *market* in the centre of town will satisfy your nutritional needs cheaply, day or night. On the Trat River, north-east of town, is a smaller *night market* which sells seafood.

Getting There & Away

Regular buses from Bangkok's Eastern terminal to Trat cost 80B and take seven to eight hours. By air-con bus, it's 140B and takes about five hours.

Getting Around

Samlors around town cost from 5 to 10B per person, while Mazda taxi trucks are 5B and motorbike taxis are 10B. A door-to-door minibus from Trat to Bo Rai is 30B.

KO CHANG NATIONAL MARINE PARK

Ko Chang is the second largest island in Thailand after Phuket; the park actually covers 47 of the islands off Trat's coastline. The main island has a few small villages supported by coconuts, fishing and smuggling but increasing numbers of tourists are attracted to the small bays and beaches, especially along the western side of the island. In the interior are a series of scenic waterfalls called **Than Mayom Falls** or Thara Mayom.

Places to Stay

Ko Chang Starting at the northern tip of the island near the pier at Ao Khlong Son, the *Manee* has very basic huts from 50 to 70B a night, bath outside. A bit further down at pretty Hat Sai Khao are the much better *Sunsai* and *Cookie*; they have huts from 100B. On Ao Khlong Phrao, you'll find huts at the *Chaichet Resort, Magic* and several others.

Down along the south coast at Ao Bang Bao is the *Bang Bao Beach Resort* (☎ 51 604) at 100B for average bungalows. You may also be able to rent rooms cheaply in nearby Ban Bang Bao. At Than Mayom National Park, on the east coast, there are a few park bungalows at the usual national park rates. A couple of private places, *Thanmayom* and *Maeo*, also rent huts from 60 to 100B a night.

Other Nearby islands with bungalow accommodation include Ko Kut, Ko Kradat, Ko Lao-Ya and Ko Mak.

Getting There & Away

To/From Ko Chang Take a songthaew (10B) from Trat south-west to Laem Ngop on the coast, then a ferry to Ko Chang. Ferry fares differ according to the beach destination: 30B to Ao Khlong Son, 60B to White Sand (Hat Sai Khao), 70B to Ao Khlong Phrao and so on. Ferries to the beachless east coast are less expensive: Ban Dan Mai costs 10B and Than Mayom 20B. Departures are once daily, usually in the afternoon.

For the unadventurous, air-con minibuses leave daily from Khao San Rd in Bangkok and go direct to Laem Ngop for 250B. The fare includes a ferry ride to Ao Khlong Son.

To/From Other Islands Two or three fishing boats a week go to Ko Kut from the Tha Chaloemphon Pier on the Trat River towards the eastern side of Trat town. The fare is 50B per person. Coconut boats go to Ko Kut once or twice a month from a pier on the canal.

Coconut boats go to Ko Mak from the Canal Pier once or twice a week – the trip takes five hours and costs 50B per person.

Getting Around

At Ko Chang there is a daily boat service between Than Mayom and Ao Salak Kok further south along the east coast for 20B per person. Between Ao Salak Kok and Ao Salak Phet, a daily jeep service costs 10B per person. Motorcycle taxis or pick-ups go from Klong Son to Hat Sai Khao (40B), Khlong Phrao (50B) and Hat Kaibae (60B).

Northern Thailand

The northern area was where early Thai kingdoms (Lanna Thai, Hariphunchai and Sukhothai) first developed, so it's full of interesting ruins. Most visitors tend to cluster around the northern capital of Chiang Mai, while the more adventurous head for the somewhat more remote provinces of Chiang Rai, Mae Hong Son, Nan and Phrae. From here, you can make treks through the area inhabited by Thailand's many hill tribes. This too is the region of the infamous Golden Triangle where Thailand, Laos and Myanmar meet and from where much of the world's opium comes.

Hill Tribe Treks

One of the most popular activities from Chiang Mai, Chiang Rai or Mae Hong Son is to take a trek through the tribal areas in the hills in the north. There are six major tribes in the north and they are one of the most interesting facets of the area. Tribal groups are also found across the border in Myanmar and Laos and, to them, political lines on the maps have little meaning. Although pressure is being applied to turn them to more acceptable types of agriculture, opium is still a favourite crop up here and ganja grows wild.

The best known tribes are the Hmong (Meo) with their bright costumes and jewellery, the Karen, the Lisu, the Lahu (Musoe), the Mien (Yao) and the Akha.

Unfortunately, the treks have really become a bit too popular over the last decade or so and a little care is needed to ensure a good experience. Some areas are simply overtrekked. A constant stream of camera-waving visitors, often accompanied by guides who cannot speak English let alone the hill-tribe languages, is hardly a ticket to an interesting trip.

Finding a good tour guide is probably the key to having a good trek, but it's also important to check out your fellow trekkers. Try to organise a meeting before departure. The best guides will be conversant with the tribes and their languages and have good contacts and easy relations with them. The best way of finding a good operator is simply to ask other travellers in Chiang Mai. People just back from a trek will be able to give you the low-down on how their trek went.

For an up-to-date list of trekking operators, visit the TAT office. Making a recommendation here would be meaningless since guides often change companies and operators open and close with alarming frequency.

Treks normally last four days and three nights, and the usual cost is around 1000B, although longer treks are also available. Bring a water bottle, medicines and money for lunch on the first and last day and for odd purchases. Don't bring too much money or other valuables with you – it seems that every year some parties get 'held up' by local bandits. You can leave your gear behind in Chiang Mai with your hotel or the trek operator. A useful checklist of questions to ask would be:

1. How many people in the group? 'Six is a good maximum,' reported one traveller, although others have said that 10 is equally OK.
2. Can they guarantee no other tourists will visit the same village on the same day, especially overnight?
3. Can the guide speak the language of each village to be visited? Can he speak English too?
4. Exactly when does the tour begin and end? The three-day treks of some companies turn out to be less than 48 hours.
5. Do they provide transport before and after the trek or is it just by public bus, which can involve long waits?

You can also just head off on your own or hire a guide or porter by yourself, but the treks are not that expensive and there are some areas where it is unwise to go. If you've got to bring gifts for the villagers, make it Band-aids and disinfectant rather than ciga-

THAILAND

rettes and candy. It may be more for show but it doesn't do any harm. 'Toothpaste and soap,' suggested another clean-minded traveller.

Most people who go on these treks have a thoroughly good time and reckon they're great value. Comments included 'the best experience of my life...I hope we left the villages as we found them', and 'the area we covered was only recently opened for trekking and the guides were some of the nicest people I have ever met'.

Note, however, that there have been a number of hold-ups and robberies over the years. This area of Thailand is relatively unpoliced, with a 'wild west' feel. Ask around that everything is OK before setting blithely off into the wilds. People who run into trouble often discover afterwards that their guide didn't really know where they were going, or went into areas they should have known were not safe.

Hill Tribe Directory

The term hill tribe refers to ethnic minorities living in the mountainous regions of northern and western Thailand. The Thais refer to them as *chao khao*, literally meaning mountain people. Each hill tribe has its own language, customs, mode of dress and spiritual beliefs.

Most are of seminomadic origins, having migrated to Thailand from Tibet, Burma, China and Laos during the past 200 years or so, although some groups may have been in Thailand much longer.

The Tribal Research Institute in Chiang Mai recognises 10 different hill tribes but there may be up to 20 in Thailand. The institute's 1993 estimate of the total hill tribe population was 550,000.

The following descriptions cover the largest tribes, which are also the groups most likely to be encountered on treks. Linguistically, the tribes can be divided into three main groups: the Tibeto-Burman (Lisu, Lahu, Akha); the Karenic (Karen, Kayah); and the Austro-Thai (Hmong, Mien). Comments on ethnic dress refer mostly to the female members of each group as hill tribe men tend to dress like rural Thais. Population figures are 1986 estimates.

The Shan *(Thai Yai)* are not included as they are not a hill tribe group per se; they live in permanent locations, practice Theravada Buddhism and speak a language very similar to Thai.

Lonely Planet's *Thai Hill Tribes Phrasebook* gives a handy, basic introduction to the culture and languages of a number of the tribes.

Akha (Thai: *I-kaw)*

Population: 33,600
Origin: Tibet
Present locations: Thailand, Laos, Myanmar, Yunnan (China)
Economy: rice, corn, opium
Belief system: animism, with an emphasis on ancestor worship.
Distinctive characteristics: head dresses of beads, feathers and dangling silver ornaments. Villages are along mountain ridges or on steep slopes from 1000 to 1400 metres in altitude. The Akha are amongst the poorest of Thailand's ethnic minorities and tend to resist assimilation into the Thai mainstream. Like the Lahu, they often cultivate opium for their own consumption.

Hmong (Thai: *Meo* or *Maew)*

Population: 80,000
Origin: southern China
Present locations: southern China, Thailand, Laos, Vietnam
Economy: rice, corn, opium
Belief system: animism
Distinctive characteristics: simple black jackets and indigo trousers with striped borders or indigo skirts, and silver jewellery. Most women wear their hair in a large bun. They usually live on mountain peaks or plateaus. Kinship is patrilineal and polygamy is permitted. They are Thailand's second-largest hill tribe group and are especially numerous in Chiang Mai Province.

Karen (Thai: *Yang* or *Kariang)*

Population: 265,600
Origin: Burma
Present locations: Thailand, Myanmar
Economy: rice, vegetables, livestock
Belief system: animism, Buddhism, Christianity – depending on the group.
Distinctive characteristics: thickly woven V-neck tunics of various colours (unmarried women wear white). Kinship is matrilineal and marriage is endogamous. They tend to live in lowland valleys and

practice crop rotation rather than swidden (slash and burn) agriculture. There are four distinct Karen groups – the White Karen (Skaw Karen), Pwo Karen, Black Karen (Pa-o) and Kayah. These groups combined are the largest hill tribe in Thailand, numbering a quarter of a million people or about half of all hill tribe people. Many Karen continue to migrate into Thailand from Myanmar, fleeing Burmese government persecution.

Lahu (Thai: *Musoe)*
Population: 58,700
Origin: Tibet
Present locations: southern China, Thailand, Myanmar
Economy: rice, corn, opium
Belief system: theistic animism (supreme deity is Geusha) and some groups are Christian.
Distinctive characteristics: black and red jackets with narrow skirts for women. They live in mountainous areas at about 1000 metres. Their intricately woven shoulder bags *(yaam)* are prized by collectors. There are four main groups – Red Lahu, Black Lahu, Yellow Lahu and Lahu Sheleh.

Lisu (Thai: *Lisaw)*
Population: 24,000
Origin: Tibet
Present locations: Thailand, Yunnan (China)
Economy: rice, opium, corn, livestock
Belief system: animism with ancestor worship and spirit possession.
Distinctive characteristics: the women wear long multi-coloured tunics over trousers and sometimes black turbans with tassels. Men wear baggy green or blue pants pegged in at the ankles. They wear lots of bright colours. Premarital sex is said to be common, along with freedom in choosing marital partners. Patrilineal clans have pan-tribal jurisdiction, which makes the Lisu unique among hill tribe groups (most tribes have power centred at the village level with either the shaman or a village headman). Their villages are usually in the mountains at about 1000 metres.

Mien (Thai: *Yao)*
Population: 35,500
Origin: central China
Present locations: Thailand, southern China, Laos, Myanmar, Vietnam
Economy: rice, corn, opium
Belief system: animism with ancestor worship and Taoism.
Distinctive characteristics: women wear black jackets and trousers decorated with intricately embroidered patches and red fur-like collars, along with large dark blue or black turbans. They have been heavily influenced by Chinese traditions and use Chinese characters to write the Mien language. They tend to settle near mountain springs at between 1000 and 1200 metres. Kinship is patrilineal and marriage is polygamous.

Getting There & Away

The straightforward way of getting to the north is simply to head directly from Bangkok to Chiang Mai either by bus, train or air. From Bangkok, you can visit the ancient capitals of Ayuthaya, Lopburi and Sukhothai on your way to Chiang Mai. If you visit these ancient cities southbound rather than northbound, you'll hit them in chronological order. Or, you could take a longer and less 'off-the-beaten-track' route by first heading west to Nakhon Pathom and Kanchanaburi and then back-tracking and travelling north-east by bus to Suphanburi and Lopburi.

From Chiang Mai, you can head north to Fang and take the daily riverboat down the Kok River (a tributary of the Mekong) to Chiang Rai. From there, you can head back towards Chiang Mai, get off at Lampang and either catch a bus via Tak to Sukhothai or take the train to Phitsanulok. From Phitsanulok, you can bus it to Lom Sak and then Loei and Udon Thani. There is also a road between Lom Sak and Khon Kaen. Udon Thani and Khon Kaen are both on the rail and bus routes back to Bangkok but there are a number of other places worth exploring in the north-east before heading back to the capital (see the North-Eastern Thailand section later in this chapter).

CHIANG MAI

Thailand's second-largest city is a bit of a tourist trap – full of noisy motorbikes and souvenir shops – but it offers interesting contrasts with the rest of the country and there is plenty to see. It's also a useful base for trips further afield.

At one time, Chiang Mai was part of the independent Lanna Thai (Million Thai Rice-Fields) Kingdom, much given to warring with kingdoms in Burma and Laos, as well as Sukhothai to the south. You can still see the moat that encircled the city at that time, but the remaining fragments of the city wall are mainly reconstructions. Originally founded in 1296, Chiang Mai fell to the Burmese in 1556, but was recaptured in 1775.

Orientation

The old city of Chiang Mai is a neat square bound by moats. Moon Muang Rd, along the east moat, is one of the main centres for cheap accommodation and places to eat. Tha Phae Rd runs east from the middle of this side and crosses the Ping River where it changes name to Charoen Muang Rd. The railway station and the GPO are both further down Charoen Muang Rd, a fair distance from the centre.

Information

Tourist Office The TAT (☎ 24 8604/07) is in an office (not shown on some Chiang Mai maps) on Chiang Mai-Lamphun Rd, a couple of hundred metres south of the Nawarat Bridge. They have piles of useful hand-outs on everything from guesthouse accommodation to trekking.

Post & Telecommunications The main post office in Chiang Mai is on Charoen Muang Rd near the railway station. It is open Monday to Friday from 8.30 am to 4.30 pm, Saturday and Sunday from 9 am to 1 pm. Overseas calls, telexes, faxes and telegrams can be arranged here 24 hours a day.

Bookshops & Libraries The best bookshops in Chiang Mai are the DK Book House on Tha Phae Rd and the Suriwong Book Centre on Si Donchai Rd. Check Suriwong's 2nd floor for books on Thailand and South-East Asia, along with various other English-language selections.

The USIS/AUA library on Ratchadamnoen Rd inside the east gate has a selection of English-language newspapers and magazines. The Library Service is a small bookshop-cum-cafe with used paperbacks for sale or trade at 21/1 Ratchamankha Soi 2, not far from Tha Phae Gate. You can also pick up a copy here of the useful *Pocket Guide for Motorcycle Touring in North Thailand*, written by the Australian, David Unkovich, who runs the shop.

Maps Finding your way around Chiang Mai is fairly simple. A copy of Nancy Chandler's *Map Guide to Chiang Mai* is worth its 70B price. If you're planning to get around by city bus, you ought also to have a copy of P&P's *Tourist Map of Chiang Mai: Rose of the North*, which has a good bus map on one side and a very detailed highway map of northern Thailand on the other.

Medical Services The McCormick Hospital (☎ 24 1107) on Kaew Nawarat Rd is the traveller's best bet. A consultation and treatment for something simple costs about 250B.

Tourist Police The Tourist Police can be reached in Chiang Mai by dialling ☎ 24 8974 from 6 am to midnight or ☎ 49 1420 after hours. Their office is attached to the TAT office on Chiang Mai-Lamphun Rd.

Warning Beware of drug busts in Chiang Mai. Some guesthouses and samlor drivers have been known to supply you with dope and then turn you in. Also take care with valuables stored at guesthouses while out trekking. A few years ago, Thailand was swept by a range of credit-card scams and a favourite method was borrowing credit cards from trekkers' baggage while they were away. Months later, back in their home country, they would discover enormous bills run up during the period they were trekking.

Wat Chiang Man

This is the oldest wat within the city walls and was erected by King Mengrai, Chiang Mai's founder, in 1296. Two famous Buddha images are kept here in the *wihan* (smaller chapel) to the right of the main bot. One is the Buddha Sila and the other is the Crystal Buddha which, like Bangkok's Emerald Buddha, was once shuttled back and forth between Siam and Laos.

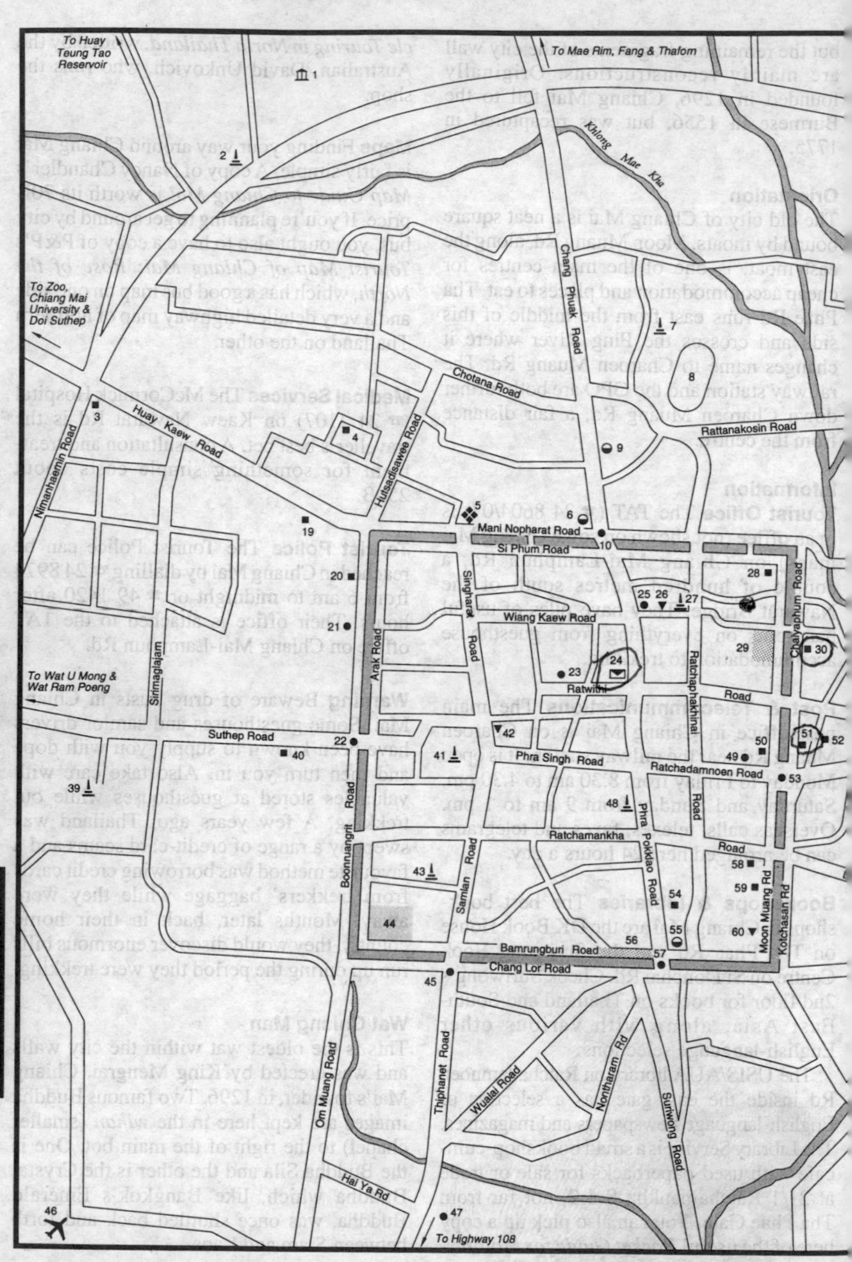
To Huay Teung Tao Reservoir
To Mae Rim, Fang & Thafom
Khlong Mae Kha
To Zoo, Chiang Mai University & Doi Suthep
Chang Phuak Road
Chotana Road
Rattanakosin Road
Huay Kaew Road
Nimanhaemin Road
Hutsadisawee Road
Mani Nopharat Road
Si Phum Road
Singharat Road
Wiang Kaew Road
Chaiyaphum Road
Ratchaphakhinai Road
Ratwithi
Road
Arak Road
Sirimaglajarn
To Wat U Mong & Wat Ram Poeng
Suthep Road
Phra Singh Road
Ratchadamnoen Road
Ratchamankha
Road
Phra Pokklao Road
Boonruangrit Road
Samlan Road
Moon Muang Rd
Kotchasan Rd
Bamrungburi Road
Chang Lor Road
Thiphanet Road
Nontharam Rd
Wualai Road
Suriwong Road
Om Muang Road
Hai Ya Rd
To Highway 108

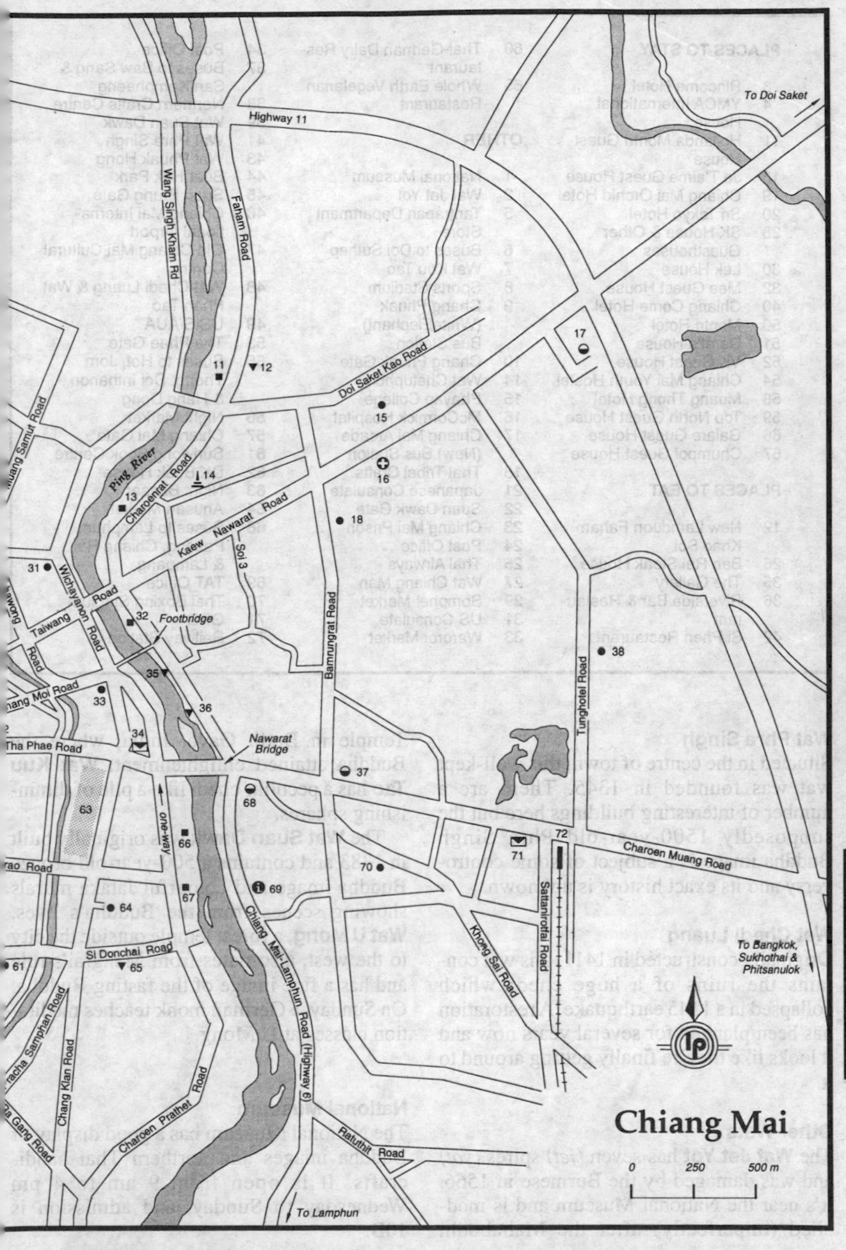
To Doi Saket
Highway 11
Wang Singh Kham Rd
Faham Road
Doi Saket Kao Road
Muang Samut Road
Ping River
Charoenrat Road
Kaew Nawarat Road
Soi 3
Wichayanon Road
Taiwang Road
Footbridge
Bamrungrat Road
Tunghotel Road
Nawarat Bridge
Tha Phae Road
one-way
Charoen Muang Road
Sattanrotfai Road
Khong Sai Road
Si Donchai Road
Chiang Mai-Lamphun Road (Highway 6)
Charoen Prathet Road
Chang Klan Road
Ratuthit Road
To Lamphun
To Bangkok, Sukhothai & Phitsanulok
Chiang Mai
0
250
500 m
11
12
13
14
15
16
17
18
31
32
33
34
35
36
37
38
61
63
64
65
66
67
68
69
70
71
72

THAILAND

PLACES TO STAY

3 Rincome Hotel
4 YMCA International House
11 Hollanda Montri Guest House
13 Je T'aime Guest House
19 Chiang Mai Orchid Hotel
20 Sri Tokyo Hotel
28 SK House & Other Guesthouses
30 Lek House
32 Mee Guest House
40 Chiang Come Hotel
50 Montri Hotel
51 Daret's House
52 VK Guest House
54 Chiang Mai Youth Hostel
58 Muang Thong Hotel
59 Top North Guest House
66 Galare Guest House
67 Chumpol Guest House

PLACES TO EAT

12 New Lamduon Faham Khao Soi
26 Ban Rai Steak House
35 The Gallery
36 Riverside Bar & Restaurant
42 Si Phen Restaurant
60 Thai-German Dairy Restaurant
65 Whole Earth Vegetarian Restaurant

OTHER

1 National Museum
2 Wat Jet Yot
5 Tantrapan Department Store
6 Buses to Doi Suthep
7 Wat Kuu Tao
8 Sports Stadium
9 Chang Phuak (WhiteElephant) Bus Station
10 Chang Phuak Gate
14 Wat Chetuphon
15 Phayap College
16 McCormick Hospital
17 Chiang Mai Arcade (New) Bus Station
18 Thai Tribal Crafts
21 Japanese Consulate
22 Suan Dawk Gate
23 Chiang Mai Prison
24 Post Office
25 Thai Airways
27 Wat Chiang Man
29 Somphet Market
31 US Consulate
33 Warorot Market
34 Post Office
37 Buses to Baw Sang & San Kamphaeng
38 Northern Crafts Centre
39 Wat Suan Dawk
41 Wat Phra Singh
43 Wat Phuak Hong
44 Buat Hak Park
45 Suan Prung Gate
46 Chiang Mai International Airport
47 Old Chiang Mai Cultural Centre
48 Wat Chedi Luang & Wat Phan Tao
49 USIS/AUA
53 Tha Phae Gate
55 Buses to Hot, Jom Thong, Doi Inthanon & Hang Dong
56 Night Market
57 Chiang Mai Gate
61 Suriwong Book Centre
62 DK Book House
63 Night Bazaar
64 Anusan Market
68 Buses to Lamphun, Pasang, Chiang Rai & Lampang
69 TAT Office
70 Thai Boxing Stadium
71 GPO
72 Railway Station

Wat Phra Singh

Situated in the centre of town, this well-kept wat was founded in 1345. There are a number of interesting buildings here but the supposedly 1500-year-old Phra Singh Buddha image is a subject of some controversy and its exact history is unknown.

Wat Chedi Luang

Originally constructed in 1411, this wat contains the ruins of a huge chedi which collapsed in a 1545 earthquake. A restoration has been planned for several years now and it looks like they're finally getting around to it.

Other Wats

The **Wat Jet Yot** has seven *(jet)* spires *(yot)* and was damaged by the Burmese in 1566. It's near the National Museum and is modelled (imperfectly) after the Mahabodhi Temple in Bodh Gaya, India, where the Buddha attained enlightenment. **Wat Kuu Tao** has a peculiar chedi like a pile of diminishing spheres.

The **Wat Suan Dawk** was originally built in 1383 and contains a 500-year-old bronze Buddha image and colourful Jataka murals showing scenes from the Buddha's lives. **Wat U Mong**, a forest temple outside the city to the west, also dates from Mengrai's rule and has a fine image of the fasting Buddha. On Sunday, a German monk teaches meditation classes at U Mong.

National Museum

The National Museum has a good display of Buddha images and northern Thai handicrafts. It is open from 9 am to 4 pm Wednesday to Sunday, and admission is 10B.

Other Attractions

The **Tribal Research Centre** at Chiang Mai University has a small but good museum of hill tribe artefacts. Head out west from the city centre – it's two blocks north once you get to the university. **Old Chiang Mai** is a touristy 'instant hill tribes' centre. There are Thai and hill tribe dance performances here every night.

You'll often see local hill tribespeople in Chiang Mai – check the night bazaar just off Tha Phae Rd. There are lots of handicrafts on sale in Chiang Mai. In the centre of town, Chiang Mai's jail has a large, resident foreigner population, most of them from drug busts.

Festivals

The annual dry-season **Songkran** (Water Festival) takes place, with particular fervour, in mid-April in Chiang Mai. The late-December to early-January **Winter Fair** is also a great scene with all sorts of activities and lots of interesting visitors from the hills. The biggest festival of them all is the **Flower Festival**, held during the first week of February. This festival features parades in which the various *amphoes*, or districts, throughout Chiang Mai Province compete for the best flower-bedecked float and enter their most beautiful young women in the Queen of the Flower Festival contest.

Places to Stay

Guesthouses In Chiang Mai, travellers' accommodation is usually in guesthouses. There are plenty of them with prices mainly in the 50 to 100B bracket. The guesthouse definition is a rather loose one, as some cheap hotels have changed their name in English to 'guesthouse' while retaining the word 'hotel' in Thai. It's simply a convenient buzz word. Many of the guesthouses are along Moon Muang Rd and on the other side of the east moat. Others can be found along Charoenrat Rd, on the east side of the Ping River, or on Charoen Prathet Rd, on the west side of the river. The latter streets are some distance from the city centre, but convenient for the railway station and Chiang Rai buses.

TAT lists over 100 guesthouses at last count – so if you don't like one, move. During peak periods (from December to March and from July to August), it may be best to go to the TAT office first, pick up a free copy of the guesthouse list, and make a few calls to find out where rooms are available. All guesthouses have phones these days. Costs are typically 70 to 80B for a double room.

Popular places include the *Lek House* at 22 Chaiyaphum Rd, near the Chang Moi Rd intersection. It's quiet and has a nice garden. Single/double rooms with fan and bath are 80/100B downstairs and 100/120B upstairs (larger, newer rooms). There's a good restaurant and breakfast is inexpensive. Nearby at 9 Chang Moi Kao Rd, the *Pao Come Guest House* has similar facilities and cheaper rooms (50/70B), should you find Lek House full.

The *Chang Moi Guest House* (☎ 25 1839) at 29 Chang Moi Rd is behind the New Chiang Mai Hotel and has rooms for 50/60/70B plus a triple for 100B. Avoid the two small annexed rooms in front which can be noisy. Nearby is the popular *Happy House* at 11 Chang Moi Rd, with big, clean rooms for 100B/180B. Also on Chang Moi Rd is the comfortable *Eagle House* (☎ 23 5387) at 80/100B, or 30B in a dorm. The long-standing *VK Guest House*, down an alley off Chang Moi Rd near Tha Phae Rd, is quiet and friendly – it costs 50/70B for basic but clean rooms; a triple with bath costs 35B per person.

On Chaiyaphum Rd, in the same area, is the extremely popular *Daret House*. Rooms cost 70/100B and it's almost always full – simply because it's so visible. Farther north inside the moat along Soi 9 are a number of decent places with rooms for 80/100B with shared bath, 150/180B with private bath: *Libra, SK House, Supreme House, Dear House, Racha* and *Peter*.

The *Top North Guest House* at 15 Soi 2, Moon Muang Rd, is an efficiently run place costing 200B for a double with fan, 300B with air-con. Up from the original Youth Hostel at 7 Soi 6, Phra Pokklao Rd, is the *Nat Guest House*, a comfortable place with rooms from 80B.

The *Chiang Mai Youth Hostel* (☎ 27 2169) at 31 Phra Pokklao Rd (Soi 3) has a dorm at 40B per person, singles from 60B and doubles from 100B with a student or YHA card, 10B more without. There is another branch on Changklan Rd with more mid-range rates – 250B for a room with fan and bath and 300B with air-con.

The *Je T'aime Guest House* (☎ 24 1912) at 247 Charoenrat Rd is a long-running favourite in a peaceful and relaxed garden-like setting. It's rather far from the city centre, but that doesn't seem to bother people. The rooms all have a fan and shower, and cost 60 to 150B. They'll arrange to pick you up from the bus or train station if you phone.

Two pleasant places along Charoenrat Rd next to the Ping River are the *Gold Riverside* at 282/3 and the *Mee Guest House* at 193/1. Both have rooms in the 60 to 80B range. There are lots of others tucked away throughout Chiang Mai.

Hotels Apart from the guesthouses, there are also plenty of hotels, in all price ranges. The *Roong Ruang Hotel* (☎ 23 2017/18) at 398 Tha Phae Rd, near the east side of the moat, has a good location and clean rooms at 180/200B.

The *YMCA International House* (☎ 22 1819, 22 2366) is at 2/4 Mengrai-Rasni Rd, above the north-west corner of the moat. After recent renovations, it's gone upmarket – 250/300B for all air-con rooms. *Sri Rajawongse* (☎ 23 5864) is at 103 Ratchawong Rd, between the east moat and the river, and costs from 70B for a fan-cooled room with bath. The funky *Muang Thong* (☎ 23 6438) at 5 Ratchamankha Rd costs 100/150B, and the *Nakhorn Ping* (☎ 23 6024), 43 Taiwang Rd between the east moat and the river, costs 90B.

Moon Muang Golden Court (☎ 21 2779), off the street at 95/1 Moon Muang, is good value for 100/150B with fan and private bath. Hot water showers are also available.

THAILAND

Places to Eat

Thai South of Tha Phrae Rd, on the moat, is the big open air *Aroon Rai* which specialises in northern Thai food and is a great place to try sticky rice and other northern specialities. Get a group together in order to try the maximum number of dishes – some of them are *very* hot and spicy. Nearby on Chaiyaphum Rd, just up from Tha Phae Gate, the *Thanam Restaurant* is smaller but even better for local food. It's very clean and no alcohol is served.

The *Riverside Bar & Restaurant* on Charoenrat Rd, on the banks of the Ping River, features home-style Thai cooking and country/folk music. On weekend nights it's quite the scene.

Along Kotchasan Rd, just south of the Loi Kroa Rd intersection, are several *restaurants* serving cheap and tasty north-eastern food including grilled chicken and sticky rice.

Chiang Mai is famed for its fine noodles. *Koliang*, on the corner of Moon Muang and Ratchamankha Rds, does great 'boat noodles'. Khao soi, a concoction of spicy curried chicken with flat wheat noodles, is the true Chiang Mai speciality. *New Lamduon Faham Khao Soi* (formerly Khao Soi Lam Duang) on Charoenrat Rd, across from Hollanda Montri Guest House, is particularly good and their noodles cost just 8B a bowl. Even the king has tried them! More towards the centre of town is a noodle shop opposite Tha Phae Gate, on Chaiyaphum Rd (near the entrance to the Times Square Guest House), where khao soi is also the speciality.

Western-Thai Along either side of the east moat near Tha Phae Gate are a number of places that pack in the travellers attracted to Western food and fruit drinks. The long-running *Daret's House* does some great drinks and Westernised Thai food but service can be slow when it's crowded.

The *JJ Bakery* under the Montri Hotel has a good menu of Thai, Chinese and Western food at very reasonable prices, especially considering how clean the place is and the fact that it has air-con.

The popular *Ban Rai Steak House* is next to Wat Chiang Man, behind the Thai Airways office. It's just the place for people in dire need of an infusion of steak and potatoes or a shish-kebab with potatoes and vegetables. It's the 'nearest thing to home in Asia', reported one happy traveller. *Lek House* at 22 Chaiyaphum Rd still draws raves for its buffalo steak and other French grill items. The friendly *Dara Steak Shop*, next to Queen Bee Car Rental, at the corner of Moon Muang and Ratchamankha Rds, has a very good and reasonably priced Thai and Western menu.

Chinese Chiang Mai has a small Chinatown in an area centred around Ratchawong Rd north of Chang Moi Kao Rd. Here you'll find a whole string of Chinese rice and noodle shops, most of them offering variations on Tae Jiu (Chao Zhou) or Yunnanese cooking.

Vegetarian Chiang Mai has several vegetarian places. Try *Whole Earth*, which is run by the local Transcendental Meditation (TM) folk and is a quite a bit more expensive. It's on Si Donchai Rd, past the Chang Klan Rd intersection, and has Thai and Indian vegetarian fare. There's also a traveller-oriented vegetarian place on Moon Muang Rd called *AUM Vegetarian Restaurant*. Reports are mixed on this one – we liked it but some people think the food's not so great.

Behind the mosque, on Charoenrat Rd (Soi 1), are several inexpensive Thai-Muslim restaurants which serve a few vegetarian dishes.

Markets There is a very large *night bazaar* just west of Chiang Mai Gate on Bamrungburi Rd, a great place to make an evening of eating and drinking. The *Warorot Market*, at the intersection of Chang Moi and Changklam Rds, is open from 6 am to 5 pm daily. Upstairs, inside the market, are vendors who serve excellent and very cheap Chinese rice and noodle dishes.

Things to Buy

There are a lot of things to attract your money in the northern capital of Chiang Mai, but basically the city is a very commercial and touristy place and a lot of junk is churned out for the undiscerning – so buy carefully. The night bazaar in Chiang Mai, near the expensive hotels, is a good place to look for almost anything, but you have to bargain hard.

For ceramics, Thai Celadon, about six km north of Chiang Mai, turns out ceramic-ware modelled on the Sawankhalok pottery that used to be made at Sukhothai and exported all over the region hundreds of years ago. Other ceramics can be seen close to Old Chiang Mai Cultural Centre.

All sorts of wood carvings and lacquerware are available, and you'll see lots of antiques around, including opium weights – the little animal-shaped weights used to measure out opium in the Golden Triangle.

There are a number of silverwork shops close to the South Moat Gate. The hill tribe jewellery – heavy chunky stuff – is very nice. Plain and embroidered clothes are available at low prices but check the quality carefully.

Getting There & Away

Air There are flights to Chiang Mai three or four times daily from Bangkok. The flight takes an hour and the normal fare is 1650B – a special night fare is less. There are also flights between Chiang Mai and other towns in the north including Chiang Rai. You can enter Thailand at Chiang Mai since there is a regular Thai International connection with Hong Kong.

Bus Regular buses from Bangkok take 10 or 11 hours to reach Chiang Mai and cost from 161 to 164B (depending on the route); air-con buses cost around 300B and take about nine to 10 hours. There are lots of buses from the Northern bus terminal in Bangkok, starting at 5.30 am and finishing at around 10 pm. The fare depends on the routing. A variety of more expensive tour buses also make the trip from Bangkok to Chiang Mai – a 'VIP' bus with 30 reclining seats is 370 to 400B.

Several travel agencies on Bangkok's

Khao San Rd offer air-con bus tickets from 200B which include a free night's accommodation in Chiang Mai. Some of these trips work out OK. Others are rip-offs in which the Chiang Mai guesthouse charges bathroom and electricity fees in lieu of a room charge. The only real advantage to these trips is that they depart from Khao San Rd, saving you a trip to the Northern bus terminal. But the entire bus will be loaded with foreigners – not a very cultural experience.

If you're intending to hop from town to town on your way north, Chiang Mai buses operate via Phitsanulok, Sukhothai, Uttaradit and Lampang.

Train The trains to Chiang Mai from Bangkok are rather slower than buses, although this is no problem on the overnight service since it gives you a night's sleep if you have a sleeper. There are express trains at 6 and 7.40 pm, which arrive at 7.25 and 8.05 am respectively, plus a rapid train at 3 pm which arrives at 5.15 am. On the express, you can get 2nd-class tickets for 285B plus the sleeper cost. Third-class tickets are only available on the rapid trains and cost 141B. Whether travelling by bus or train, you should book in advance if possible.

Getting Around

To/From the Airport A taxi from the airport costs 60B, door-to-door minibuses are 40B and a songthaew will be five to 10B. The airport is only two or three km south-west of the city centre.

Local Transport You can rent bicycles (from 20 to 25B a day) or motorbikes (from 150 to 250B) to explore around Chiang Mai – check with your guesthouse or the 65 Motorcycle Rental Service on Moon Muang Rd near the Tha Phae Gate. There are plenty of songthaews around the city with standard fares of 5B, and city buses cost 2B.

Hordes of songthaew jockeys meet incoming buses and trains at Chiang Mai – they wave signs for the various guesthouses and if the one you want pops up you can have a free ride.

AROUND CHIANG MAI

Doi Suthep

From the hill-top temple of **Wat Phra That Doi Suthep**, 16 km west of Chiang Mai, there are superb views over Chiang Mai. Choose a clear day to make the hairpinned ascent to the temple. A long flight of steps, lined by ceramic-tailed *nagas* (dragons) leads up to the temple from the car park.

The **Phu Ping Palace** is five km beyond the temple – you can wander the gardens on Friday, Saturday and Sunday. Just before the palace car park, a turn to the left will lead you to a **Meo village**, four km away. It's very touristic since it's so near to Chiang Mai, but the opium 'museum' is worth a visit if you're in the vicinity.

Getting There & Away Minibuses to Doi Suthep leave from the west end of Huay Kaew Rd and cost 40B – downhill it's 30B. For another 5B, you can take a bicycle up with you and zoom back downhill.

Baw Sang & San Kamphaeng

The 'umbrella village' of Baw Sang is nine km east of Chiang Mai. It's a picturesque though touristy spot where the townspeople engage in just about every type of northern Thai handicraft. Beautiful paper umbrellas are hand painted. A huge garden one is around 500B, but postage and packing can add a fair bit more. Attractive leaf paintings – framed – are also made here. Four or five km further down highway 1006 is San Kamphaeng, which specialises in cotton and silk weaving. Pasang, however, is probably better for cotton.

Getting There & Away Buses to Baw Sang (sometimes spelled Bo Sang or Bor Sang) leave from the north side of Charoen Muang Rd in Chiang Mai, between the river and the GPO, every 15 minutes. The fare is 5B to Baw Sang and 5B to San Kamphaeng.

Elephants

A daily 'elephants at work' show takes place near the Km 58 marker on the Fang road north of Chiang Mai. Arrive around 9 am or earlier to see bath-time in the river. It's really just a tourist trap, but probably worth the admission price. Once the spectators have gone, the logs are all put back in place for tomorrow's show!

It's a good idea to have a picture of an elephant to show the bus conductor, or 'elephant' may be interpreted as 'Fang', the town further north. There's a northern Thailand elephant meeting in November each year – hotel and food prices go up at that time.

Another place to see elephants is the **Young Elephant Training Centre** at Thung Kwian on the road from Chiang Mai to Lampang. The place is set up for tourists and has seats and even toilets, but nobody seems to know about it. When the trainer feels like it, sometime between 8 am and noon, the show begins and you'll see the elephants put through their paces. The elephants appreciate a few pieces of fruit – 'it feels like feeding a vacuum cleaner with a wet nozzle,' reported one visitor. Any bus on the main road south-east will take you on to Lampang.

Doi Inthanon

Thailand's highest peak, Doi Inthanon (2595 metres), can be visited as a day trip from Chiang Mai. There are some impressive waterfalls and pleasant picnic spots here. Between Chiang Mai and Doi Inthanon, the small town of Chom Thong has a fine Burmese-style temple, **Wat Phra That Si Chom Thong**.

Getting There & Away Buses run regularly from Chiang Mai to Chom Thong for 15B. From there, you take a songthaew the few km to Mae Klang for about 15B and another to Doi Inthanon for 35B.

Lamphun

This town, only 26 km south of Chiang Mai, has several interesting wats. **Wat Phra That Haripunchai** has a small museum and a very old chedi, variously dated at 897 or 1157 AD. There are some other fine buildings in the compound. **Wat Chama Thevi**, popularly known as Wat Kukut, has an unusual chedi with 60 Buddha images set in niches. Another Haripunchai-era wat in the town, **Wat Mahawan**, is a source of highly reputable Buddhist amulets.

Places to Stay *Si Lamphun* (☎ 511 1760) on the town's main street, Inthayongyot Rd, has rather grotty rooms for 100/120B. *Suan Kaew Bungalows* at Km 6 on the highway from Lamphun to Lampang has rooms from 80B.

Getting There & Away Buses depart Chiang Mai regularly from the south side of Nawarat Bridge on Lamphun Rd. The fare is 6B, or 8B by minibus. A minibus straight through to Pasang will cost 10B.

Lampang

South-east of Chiang Mai, this town was another former home for the Emerald Buddha. The old town's fine wats include **Wat Phra Saeng** and **Wat Phra Kaew** on the banks of the Wang River to the north of the town. In the village of Koh Kha, 20 km south-west of Lampang, **Wat Lampang Luang** was originally constructed in the Haripunchai period and restored in the 16th century. It's an amazing temple with walls like a huge medieval castle. Getting there is a little difficult, so start out early in the day.

Places to Stay & Eat The friendly *Si Sa-Nga* (☎ 21 7070) at 213-215 Boonyawat Rd has large rooms with fan and bathroom for 80B up. There are a number of other hotels along Boonyawat Rd, most with rooms starting at 70 to 100B. *Jakrin*, beneath the Sri Sangar Hotel opposite the Kim Hotel, is a popular, inexpensive Thai-Chinese place with all the standard dishes. There are several other good rice and noodle shops along Boonyawat Rd.

Getting There & Away There are regular buses between Lampang and Chiang Mai, Chiang Rai, Phitsanulok or Bangkok. The bus station in Lampang is some way out of town. It's a few baht by samlor, more if you arrive late at night. You can also get air-con buses to Bangkok or Chiang Mai from Lampang. An air-con bus can be taken from town and then you don't have to go out to the bus station.

Pasang

Only a short songthaew ride south of Lamphun, Pasang is a centre for cotton-weaving. The Nantha Khwang shop has fine locally made cotton goods.

PHITSANULOK

There's not a great deal of interest in this town, which is mainly used as a stepping stone to other places. It's on the rail line between Bangkok and Chiang Mai, and it's here you get off for Sukhothai. **Wat Phra Si Ratana Mahathat** (known locally as Wat Yai) is an interesting old wat, however, and it contains one of the most revered Buddha images in Thailand.

Places to Stay & Eat

If you come straight out of the railway station and turn left by the expensive *Amarin Nakhon Hotel*, on the corner of the first and second right turns you'll find some cheaper hotels. The rather grubby *Haw Fah* at 73 Phayalithai Rd and the *Unachak* both have rooms from 80B. The *Phitsanulok* at 82 Naresuan Rd is a bit better at 150B.

For a more relaxed atmosphere, consider the *Phitsanulok Youth Hostel* (☎ 24 2060) at 38 Sanam Bin Rd (take bus No 3 from the railway station). Large, rustic wooden rooms cost 90B a single or 50B per person in two, three and four-bed rooms; dorm beds are 40B. A Hostelling International membership is a prerequisite for staying here. The hostel has a modest restaurant and there are several cheap eateries in the vicinity.

At any of the *flying vegetable* restaurants in town, cooks fling fried morning glory vine through the air from wok to plate, held by a waiter who has climbed onto the shoulders of two colleagues (or onto a truck in the night market)! *Floating restaurants* along the river are also popular.

Getting There & Away

Buses for Sukhothai go from the town centre, but the stations for buses to the east or north are on the other (east) side of the railway tracks, on the outskirts of town. From Chiang Mai or Bangkok, you can reach Phitsanulok by bus or rail. Buses from Bangkok cost 88B, or 161B with air-con. You can also fly here from Bangkok.

Getting Around

Grey buses run between the town centre and the airport or bus station for 2B. The big hotels also run free buses to and from the airport, or a songthaew costs 5B.

SUKHOTHAI

Sukhothai was Thailand's first capital but its period of glory was short. From its foundation as a capital in 1257, it only lasted a little over 100 years to 1379 before being superseded by Ayuthaya. Nevertheless, its achievements in art, literature, language and law, apart from the more visible evidence of great buildings, were enormous. In many ways, the ruins visible today at Sukhothai and the other cities of the kingdom, like Kamphaeng Phet and Si Satchanalai, are more appealing than Ayuthaya because they are less commercial and more off the beaten track.

Orientation & Information

Old Sukhothai, known as Muang Kao, is spread over quite an area but bicycles can be hired. New Sukhothai has a good market but otherwise it's an uninteresting place, 12 km from the old town. Sukhothai is 55 km east of the Bangkok to Chiang Mai road from Tak. A map, available at the old town entrance, is essential for exploring the scattered ruins. The ruins are divided into five zones and there is a 20B admission fee into each zone.

Ramkhamhaeng National Museum

This museum offers an introductory look at Sukhothai history and culture, and is a good place to begin your explorations. They also sell guides to the ruins here. It's open

Wednesday to Sunday from 9 am to 4 pm and admission is 20B.

Wat Mahathat

This vast assemblage, the largest in the city, once contained 198 chedis – apart from various chapels and sanctuaries. Some of the original Buddha images still remain, including a big one amongst the broken columns. The large ornamented pond provides fine reflections.

Wat Si Chum

A massive seated Buddha figure is tightly squeezed into this open, walled building. A narrow tunnel inside the wall leads to views over the Buddha's shoulders and on to the top. Candle-clutching kids used to guide you up and point out the 'Buddha foot' on the way. However, in recent years the tunnel has been closed to visitors.

Other Attractions

The **Wat Si Sawai**, with three prangs and a moat, was originally intended to be a Hindu temple. It's just south of Wat Mahathat. **Wat Sa Si** is a classically simple Sukhothai-style wat set on an island. **Wat Trapang Thong,**

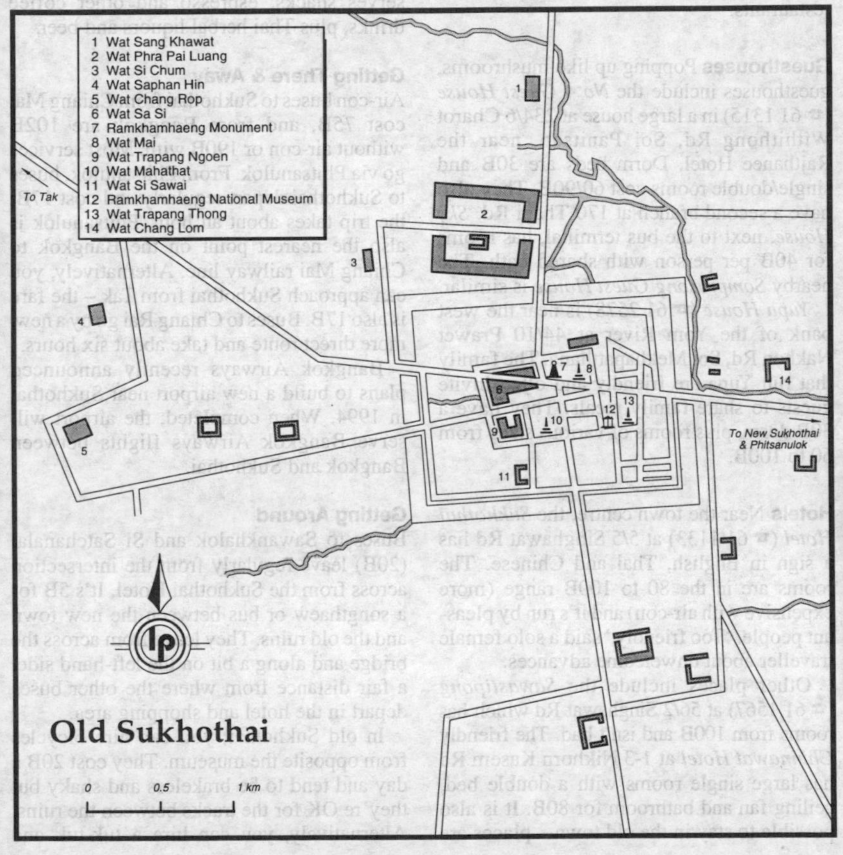

THAILAND

next to the museum, is reached by the footbridge crossing the large lotus-filled pond which surrounds it. It is still in use. Somewhat isolated to the north of the city, **Wat Phra Pai Luang** is similar in style to Wat Si Sawai. **Wat Chang Lom** is to the east; the chedi is surrounded by 36 elephants. **Wat Saphan Hin** is a couple of km west of the old city walls on a hillside and features a large standing Buddha looking back to Sukhothai.

Places to Stay

New Sukhothai is a clinical and dull town, although there are some good hotels and restaurants.

Guesthouses Popping up like mushrooms, guesthouses include the *No 4 Guest House* (☎ 61 1315) in a large house at 234/6 Charot Withithong Rd, Soi Panitsan, near the Rajthanee Hotel. Dorm beds are 30B and single/double rooms cost 60/90B. They also have a second branch at 170 Thani Rd. *Sky House*, next to the bus terminal, has rooms for 40B per person with shared bath. The nearby *Somprasong Guest House* is similar.

Yupa House (☎ 61 2578) is near the west bank of the Yom River at 44/10 Prawet Nakhon Rd, Soi Mekhapatthana. The family that run Yupa are friendly and often invite guests to share family meals. They have a 30B dorm, plus rooms of various sizes from 60 to 100B.

Hotels Near the town centre, the *Sukhothai Hotel* (☎ 61 1133) at 5/5 Singhawat Rd has a sign in English, Thai and Chinese. The rooms are in the 80 to 100B range (more expensive with air-con) and it's run by pleasant people. 'Too friendly,' said a solo female traveller about unwelcome advances.

Other places include the *Sawastipong* (☎ 61 1567) at 56/2 Singhawat Rd which has rooms from 100B and isn't bad. The friendly *Chinnawat Hotel* at 1-3 Nikhorn Kasem Rd has large single rooms with a double bed, ceiling fan and bathroom for 80B. It is also possible to stay in the old town – places are available opposite the museum in the small village where the bus stops.

Places to Eat

Both the *night market* and the *municipal market* near the town centre are good and cheap places to eat. The *Sukhothai* and *Chinnawat* hotel restaurants are also good. Across from Win Tour is the *Rainbow Restaurant & Ice Cream*, owned by the same family that runs the Chinnawat Hotel. They serve a variety of noodle dishes, Thai curries, sandwiches, Western breakfasts and ice cream at very reasonable prices. On the same side of the street is *Dream Café*, an air-con cafe that serves snacks, espresso and other coffee drinks, plus Thai herbal liquors and beer.

Getting There & Away

Air-con buses to Sukhothai from Chiang Mai cost 75B, and from Bangkok are 102B without air-con or 190B with. Most services go via Phitsanulok. From Phitsanulok, buses to Sukhothai depart regularly and cost 17B; the trip takes about an hour. Phitsanulok is also the nearest point on the Bangkok to Chiang Mai railway line. Alternatively, you can approach Sukhothai from Tak – the fare is also 17B. Buses to Chiang Rai go by a new, more direct route and take about six hours.

Bangkok Airways recently announced plans to build a new airport near Sukhothai in 1994. When completed, the airport will serve Bangkok Airways flights between Bangkok and Sukhothai.

Getting Around

Buses to Sawankhalok and Si Satchanalai (20B) leave regularly from the intersection across from the Sukhothai Hotel. It's 5B for a songthaew or bus between the new town and the old ruins. They leave from across the bridge and along a bit on the left-hand side, a fair distance from where the other buses depart in the hotel and shopping area.

In old Sukhothai, you can hire bicycles from opposite the museum. They cost 20B a day and tend to be brakeless and shaky but they're OK for the tracks between the ruins. Alternatively, you can hire a tuk-tuk and driver by the hour from 40 to 50B if you want to save your feet. Motorbikes are only 80 to 100B a day.

AROUND SUKHOTHAI

Si Satchanalai

More isolated and less touristic than the Sukhothai ruins, these stand 56 km to the north of new Sukhothai. Climb to the top of the Golden Mountain for a view over the city and river. **Wat Chedi Jet Thaew** has a group of stupas in classic Sukhothai style. **Wat Chang Lom** has a chedi surrounded by Buddha statues in niches and guarded by the fine remains of elephant buttresses. Walk along the riverside for two km or go back down the main road and cross the river to **Wat Phra Si Ratana Mahathat**, a very impressive temple with a well-preserved prang and a variety of seated and standing Buddhas.

Sawankhalok Pottery Sukhothai was famous for its beautiful pottery, much of which was exported. Fine specimens can be seen in the National Museum in Jakarta, a legacy of the Indonesians who, at that time, were keen collectors. Much of the pottery was made in Si Satchanalai. Rejects – buried in the fields – are still being found. Misfired, broken, warped and fused pieces can be found in shops at Sukhothai and Si Satchanalai. The ceramic-ware from Thai Celadon, near Chiang Mai, is a modern interpretation of the old craft.

Places to Stay In Sawankhalok, the *Muang In* (☎ 64 2622) at 21 Kasemrat Rd has rooms from 120B. Just outside Si Satchanalai is the *59 Bungalow* with similar rates. There are some newer, more expensive *bungalows* next to the Si Satch ruins – it's not really worth staying there overnight but it's not a bad place for food and drink.

Getting There & Away Take a bus to Sawankhalok and then change to a Si Satchanalai bus. The ruins are 11 km before the new town – tell the bus conductor 'muang kao' (old city) and look for a big corn cob-shaped prang. The river is less than a km off the road and there is now a suspension bridge across it. The last bus back leaves around 4 pm.

TAK

This is just a junction town from Sukhothai on the way north to Chiang Mai. It's pronounced 'Tahk' not 'Tack'. From here, you can visit the Lang San National Park and you have to pass through Tak to get to Mae Sot.

Places to Stay & Eat

If you have to stay here, then try the *Tak* (☎ 51 1234) at 18/10 Mahadtai Bamrung Rd (the main street) or the *Thavisak* at No 561, on the same road; rooms at either start at 80B. The *Sanguan Thai* (☎ 51 1265) at 619 Taksin Rd has rooms from 120B, or from 150B with air-con. A traveller who made a lengthy pause here, and liked the place, recommended the *Mae Ping* (☎ 51 1807) opposite the food market on Mahadtai Bamrung Rd. Rooms here are 80B and there is a good coffee bar downstairs.

KAMPHAENG PHET

This town is only a couple of km off the road from Bangkok to Chiang Mai. There are a number of relics within the old city and the very fine remains of the long city wall. Outside the wall is **Wat Phra Si Ariyabot** with the shattered remains of standing, sitting, walking and reclining Buddha images. **Wat Chang Rop**, or 'temple surrounded by elephants', is just that – a temple with an elephant-buttressed wall.

Places to Stay

It can be a little difficult to find places here since few signs are in English script. *Nitaya Prapha* (☎ 71 1381) at 49 Thesa Rd is a little squalid and has rooms from 60B. It's on the main road leading to the river bridge. There are foodstalls opposite at night and the main ruins are beyond these, further down the road away from the bridge towards Sukhothai.

At 114 Ratchadamnoen Rd, the *Ratchadamnoen*, in the newer part of the city, has rooms for 100B as well as more expensive air-con ones. One of the friendlier places is the *Gor Choke Chai (Kaw Chokchai) Hotel* (☎ 71 1247) at 7-31 Ratchadamnoen Rd (Soi 6) – fan-cooled rooms cost 150 to 250B.

Getting There & Away

The bus fare from Bangkok is 84B, or 157B with air-con. Most visitors come here from Sukhothai (22B), Phitsanulok (30B) or Tak (15B).

MAE SOT

This outpost sits on Thailand's border facing the Burmese town of Myawaddy and, as such, is a big centre for smuggling between the two countries. The area used to be a hotbed of Communist guerrilla activity in the 1960s and 1970s, but is now merely a relay point for the highly profitable trade in guns, narcotics, teak and gems. The local population is an interesting mixture of Thais, Chinese, Indians, Burmese and Karen tribespeople.

Songthaews can take you right to the Moei River border from Mae Sot for 5B. If the border is open you may be permitted to cross the footbridge to Myawaddy for the day. The Pan-Asian Highway (Asia Route 1) continues on from here all the way to Istanbul, if only you were allowed to follow it.

Highway 1085 runs north from Mae Sot to Mae Hong Son province and makes an interesting trip.

Places to Stay & Eat

At the west end of town towards the river, the *Mae Sot Guest House* at 736 Intharakhiri Rd has dorm beds for 30B and single/double rooms for 60/80B. They also hand out helpful area maps. The *No 4 Guest House*, a large house well off the road at 736 Intharakhiri Rd, has the same rates as the Mae Sot Guest House.

The very basic *Mae Moei Hotel*, on Intharakhiri Rd near the post and police offices, has noisy rooms from 40 to 50B. On the next street over is the *Siam Hotel* (☎ 53 1376) with fairly clean rooms for 120 to 150B.

There is a good food centre next door to the Siam Hotel. The market also has good takeaway food.

Getting There & Away

Air THAI flies to Mae Sot from Bangkok (1405B) four times a week via Phitsanulok (495B) and Tak (300B).

Bus Air-con minibuses (28B) and share taxis (50B) to Mae Sot leave hourly, 6 am until 6 pm, from the Tak bus station. The trip takes 1½ hours. There is a daily air-con bus to Mae Sot from Bangkok's Northern bus terminal that leaves at 10.15 pm for 224B.

MAE HONG SON

North-west of Chiang Mai – 368 km away by road and close to the Burmese border – this is a crossroads for Burmese visitors, opium traders, local hill tribes and tourists seeking out the 'high north'. There are several Shan-built wats in the area and a fine view from the hill by the town. It's a peaceful little place that's fast becoming a travellers' centre. Treks booked out of this town are generally less expensive than out of Chiang Mai or Chiang Rai.

Places to Stay

All the hotels are on the two main streets, Khunlum Praphat and Singhanat Bamrung Rds. *Siam* (☎ 61 1148) and *Methi (Mae Tee)* (☎ 61 1121), both on Khunlum Praphat Rd, are pretty good at 100 to 150B for a room with fan and bath.

There is also a plethora of inexpensive guesthouses scattered around Mae Hong Son. About a km north-west of town is the new location of the long-running *Mae Hong Son Guest House*, along with the secluded *Sang Tong Huts* with its panoramic views. Rates are typical of all guesthouses in Mae Hong Son, from 50 to 70B for basic accommodation. As tourism develops, look for new bungalow operations to be built in this neighbourhood since there's plenty of space.

In the area of Jong Kham Lake are several very pleasant guesthouses, including *Jong Kham*, *Holiday House* and *Johnnie House*. All are friendly little places with rates starting at 50 to 80B.

Places to Eat

Many guesthouses cook Western-style meals and, as well, offer northern Thai food. *Khai Muk* and *Fai Khum* are good restaurants on Khunlum Praphat Rd. A little more expensive, but also very good, is *Ban Buatong*, across from the Siam Hotel.

Getting There & Away

Air Mae Hong Son must be getting more popular – there are now daily flights from Chiang Mai. There are also daily flights between Mae Hong Son and Chiang Mai for 345B.

Bus By bus, it's nine hours from Chiang Mai to Mae Hong Son via Mae Sariang. There are about five departures a day, and the trip costs 100B, or 180B in an air-con bus. Coming back, you can take the shorter route through Pai and Mae Taeng on Route 1095. Although this route is slow and windy, recent road improvements mean the trip can take as little as seven hours (don't count on it to be on time, however). The scenery is quite spectacular in parts and you can break the trip by staying overnight in Pai.

PAI

This little town between Chiang Mai and Mae Hong Son is an interesting, somewhat remote kind of place and is a good base for exploring the surrounding country. It is becoming increasingly popular for trekking. For a view of the town, climb the hill to nearby **Wat Phra That Mae Yen**.

Places to Stay

Guesthouses line the two main streets in Pai. Across from the bus terminal is the *Duang Guest House* where clean rooms with hot showers cost 60B single/double. At the far western end of Chaisongkhram Rd, past the hospital, is the *Kim Guest House*. It's a bit isolated but quiet, and rooms cost from 30 to 50B per person.

On the main road through town are *Charlie's, Tao* and *Nunya's*, with rooms from 60 to 120B with fan.

Spacious rooms are available at the *Wiang Pai Hotel*, a traditional wooden hotel with rooms from 50 to 100B. On the south edge of town, off the road a bit, is the *Shan Guest House*, run by a Shan who tries hard to please. Bungalows with bath are 60/80B and there are also single/double rooms in the main building for 40/60B.

There are several bungalow operations along the Pai River east of town, including the *Riverside, Pai River Lodge* and *Pai Guest House*, all with accommodation in the 40 to 80B range.

Places to Eat

Most of the eating places in Pai line the main north-south and east-west roads. Many serve farang-oriented food like falafel, hummus and tacos. The *Thai Yai* does a good farang breakfast, plus a few Thai and Shan dishes. For authentic local food, try the *Muslim Restaurant* for noodle and rice dishes, or the *Khun Nu* which has a variety of Thai dishes. The *Nong Beer* restaurant is also quite good. All of the guesthouses in Pai serve food as well.

Getting There & Away

The Chiang Mai to Pai road is now completely paved. It takes just four hours to travel between the towns – the bus fare is 50B.

FANG & THA TON

Fang was founded by King Mengrai in 1268 but there is little of interest today apart from the earth ramparts of his old city. Fang is, however, a good base for hill tribe visits or for the downriver ride to Chiang Rai. It's 152 km north of Chiang Mai and there are some points of interest along the way apart from the elephant camp mentioned in the previous Around Chiang Mai section.

Places to Stay

Fang If you must stay in Fang, then the *Fang Hotel* has rooms from 80B. Alternatives are the friendly *Wiang Kaew Hotel*, behind the Fang Hotel, and the *Ueng Khum (Euang Kham) Hotel* around the corner on Thaw Phae Rd, both with rooms in the 80 to 120B range.

Tha Ton It's probably better not to stay in Fang itself but at Tha Ton, from where the boats run downriver to Chiang Rai. *Thip's Travellers Guest House* continues to get good reports and costs 40/80B for singles/doubles with shared bath, 80/100B with private shower. Further on the road nearest the pier is the *Chan Kasem Guest House* with rooms from 60B.

Getting There & Away

It takes three hours from Chiang Mai to Fang. The fare is 35B by regular bus and 40B by minibus – the buses go from the new bus station north of White Elephant (Chang Phuak) Gate. It's 8B from Fang to Tha Ton.

AROUND FANG & THA TON

Trekking

Trekking in the immediate vicinity of Fang isn't all that interesting as most of the villages are either Shan or Chinese (not hill tribe at all) or Lahu, and in this area the Lahu no longer wear their traditional costume.

Further north, towards the Burmese border, there are some interesting trekking areas with fewer tourists where you will find Karen, Lisu and Akha villages. Across the river from Tha Ton, you can get taxis east to the villages. Go at least to **Ban Mai**, a quiet, neat, untouristic Shan village on the river. Another four or five km takes you to **Muang Ngam**, a Karen village. Accommodation may be available in Sulithai, a Kuomintang Chinese village to the east, and in Laota, a Lisu village.

River Trip to Chiang Rai

The downriver trip from Fang to Chiang Rai is a bit of a tourist trap these days – the villages along the way sell Coke and there are lots of TV aerials. But it's still fun. The

PLACES TO STAY

- 4 Dusit Island Resort
- 6 Chat House
- 8 Mae Kok Villa
- 12 Ruang Nakhon Hotel
- 13 Siriwattana Hotel
- 16 Bow Ling Guest House
- 17 Mae Hong Son Guest House
- 18 Pintamorn Guest House
- 19 Joke House
- 21 Chiangrai Inn
- 25 Chiang Rai Guest House
- 26 Lek House
- 27 Head Guest House
- 28 Ben Guest House
- 30 Paowattana Hotel
- 31 Rama Hotel
- 34 Saenphu Hotel
- 38 Chiang Rai (Chiengrai) Hotel
- 40 Sukniran Hotel
- 41 Krung Thong Hotel
- 42 New Boonyoung Guest House
- 43 Boonbundan Guest House
- 45 Tourist Inn
- 47 Wiang Come Hotel
- 48 Siam Hotel
- 51 Golden Triangle Inn
- 58 Wiang Inn Hotel
- 60 Jira Garden Guest House
- 61 Seegerd Guest House

PLACES TO EAT

- 29 Mae Ui Khiaw Restaurant
- 36 Phetburi Restaurant
- 46 La Cantina Restaurant
- 49 Nakhon Pathom Restaurant
- 53 Napoli Pizza

OTHER

- 1 Wat Doi Thong
- 2 Wat Ngam Muang
- 3 Kok River Pier
- 5 Government Office & Town Hall
- 7 Wat Phra Kaew
- 9 TAT Office
- 10 Hospital
- 11 Wat Phra Singh
- 14 Post Office
- 15 Police Station
- 20 Wat
- 22 Hilltribe Education Centre
- 23 Telephone Office
- 24 King Mengrai Monument
- 32 Market
- 33 Wat Ming Muang
- 35 Mosque
- 37 Bangkok Bank
- 39 Clocktower
- 44 Wat Jet Yot
- 50 Church
- 52 Alliance Franaise & La Terrase Restaurant
- 54 THAI Office
- 55 Rama I Cinema
- 56 Bus Station
- 57 Rama II Theatre
- 59 KM Car Rent
- 62 Wat Si Koet

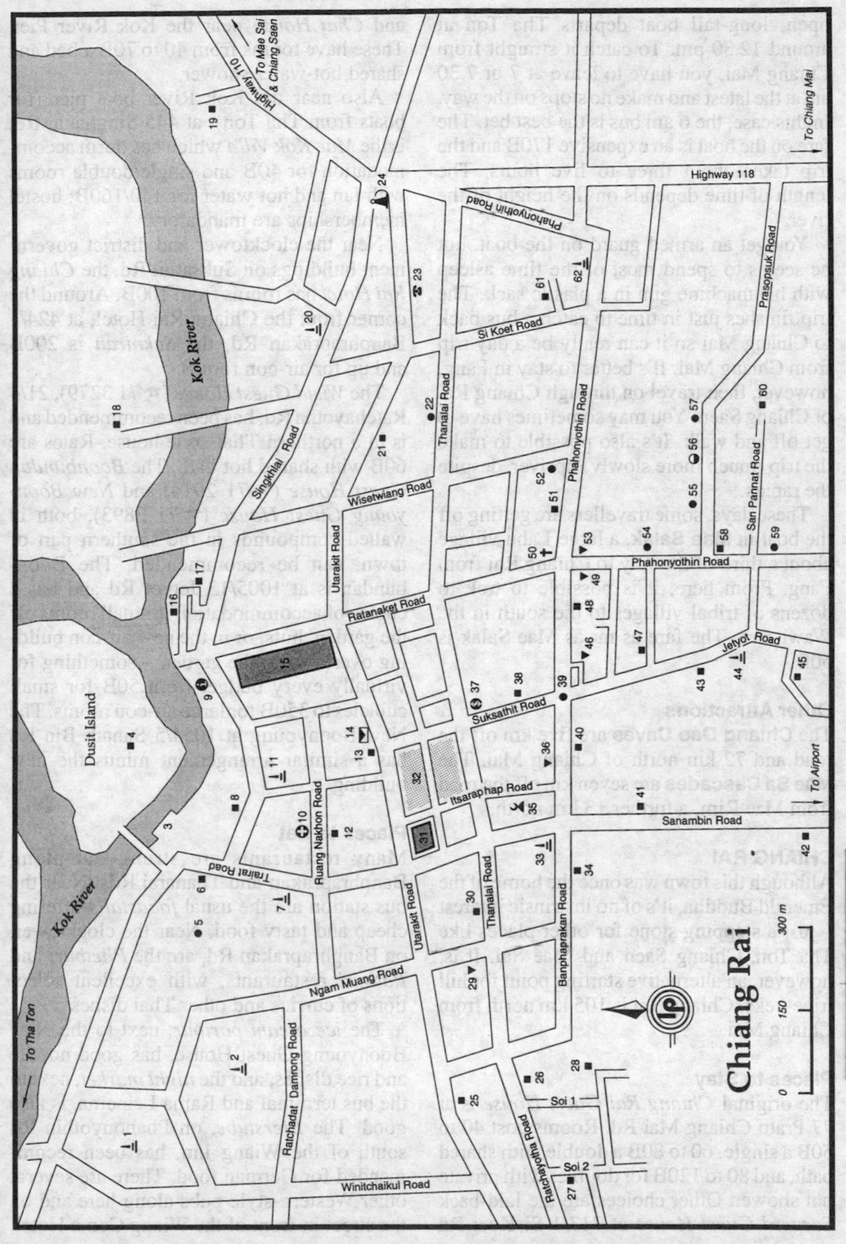
Chiang Rai
0
150
300 m
Kok River
Kok River
Dusit Island
To Mae Sai & Chiang Saen
Highway 110
To Chiang Mai
Highway 118
To Airport
To Tha Ton
Phahonyothin Road
Si Koet Road
Prasopsuk Road
Thanalai Road
Phahonyothin Road
San Pannat Road
Singkhlai Road
Wisetwiang Road
Utarakit Road
Ratanaket Road
Phahonyothin Road
Jetyot Road
Suksathit Road
Itsaraphap Road
Sanambin Road
Ruang Nakhon Road
Trairat Road
Thanalai Road
Banphaprakan Road
Utarakit Road
Ngam Muang Road
Ratchadat Damrong Road
Soi 1
Soi 2
Ratchayotha Road
Winitchaikul Road

open, long-tail boat departs Tha Ton at around 12.30 pm. To catch it straight from Chiang Mai, you have to leave at 7 or 7.30 am at the latest and make no stops on the way. In this case, the 6 am bus is the best bet. The fare on the boat is an expensive 170B and the trip takes about three to five hours. The length of time depends on the height of the river.

You get an armed guard on the boat, but he seems to spend most of the time asleep with his machine gun in a plastic sack. The trip finishes just in time to catch a bus back to Chiang Mai so it can really be a day trip from Chiang Mai. It's better to stay in Fang, however, then travel on through Chiang Rai or Chiang Saen. You may sometimes have to get off and walk. It's also possible to make the trip (much more slowly) upriver, despite the rapids.

These days, some travellers are getting off the boat in **Mae Salak**, a large Lahu village about a third of the way to Chiang Rai from Fang. From here, it is possible to trek to dozens of tribal villages to the south in the Wawi area. The fare as far as Mae Salak is 50B.

Other Attractions

The **Chiang Dao Caves** are five km off the road and 72 km north of Chiang Mai. The **Mae Sa Cascades** are seven km off the road from Mae Rim, a further 13 km north.

CHIANG RAI

Although this town was once the home of the Emerald Buddha, it's of no instrinsic interest – just a stepping stone for other places like Tha Ton, Chiang Saen and Mae Sai. It is, however, an alternative starting point for hill tribe treks. Chiang Rai is 105 km north from Chiang Mai.

Places to Stay

The original *Chiang Rai Guest House* is at 77 Pratu Chiang Mai Rd. Rooms cost 40 to 50B a single, 60 to 80B a double with shared bath, and 80 to 120B for doubles with private hot shower. Other choices are the laid-back *Seegerd Guest House* at 717/1 Si Koet Rd and *Chat House* near the Kok River Pier. These have rooms from 40 to 70B a bed and shared hot-water shower.

Also near the Kok River boat pier (for boats from Tha Ton), at 445 Singhakai Rd, is the *Mae Kok Villa* which has dorm accommodation for 40B and single/double rooms with fan and hot water for 140/160B; hostel memberships are mandatory.

Near the clocktower and district government buildings on Suksathit Rd, the *Chiang Rai Hotel* has rooms from 100B. Around the corner from the Chiang Rai Hotel, at 424/1 Banphraprakan Rd, the *Sukniran* is 200B and up for air-con rooms.

The *Wisid Guest House* (☎ 71 3279), 21/4 Ratchayotha Rd, has been recommended and is in a northern Thai-style house. Rates are 60B with shared hot bath. The *Boonbundan Guest House* (☎ 71 2914) and *New Boonyoung Guest House* (☎ 71 2893), both in walled compounds in the southern part of town, can be recommended. The Boonbundan is at 1005/13 Jetyot Rd and has a choice of accommodation in small rooms off the garden, huts, or in the new air-con building overlooking the garden – something for virtually every budget from 50B for small cubicles to 350B for large air-con rooms. The New Boonyoung at 1054/5 Sanam Bin Rd has a similar arrangement minus the new building.

Places to Eat

Many restaurants are strung out along Banphraprakan and Thanarai Rds. Near the bus station are the usual *foodstalls* offering cheap and tasty food. Near the clocktower, on Banphraprakan Rd, are the *Phetburi* and *Ratburi* restaurants, with excellent selections of curries and other Thai dishes.

The *ice cream parlour*, next to the New Boonyoung Guest House, has good noodle and rice dishes, and the *night market*, next to the bus terminal and Rama I cinema, is also good. The *Bierstube*, on Phahonyothin Rd south of the Wiang Inn, has been recommended for German food. There are several other Western-style pubs along here and on the street in front of the Wiang Come Hotel.

La Cantina (☎ 71 6808), operated by an Italian expat and situated on a small soi called Clocktower Plaza (also Sapkaset Plaza), offers an extensive selection of pizza, pasta, Italian regional specialities and wines.

Getting There & Away

The new Chiang Rai international airport, about 10 km north of town, fields daily flights from Bangkok. THAI hopes to establish routes between Chiang Rai and other Asian capitals – possibly Luang Prabang (Laos) and Kunming (China) – over the next few years.

Buses between Chiang Mai and Chiang Rai are 50B (regular), 70B (air-con) or 90B (with air-con and video). Be sure to get the *sãi mài* (new route) buses which only take four hours. By the old road (via Lampang) the trip takes seven hours.

CHIANG SAEN

Only 61 km north of Chiang Rai, this interesting little town on the banks of the Mekong River has numerous ruins of temples, chedis, city walls and other remains from the Chiang Saen period. There is also a small museum. Across the river from Chiang Saen is Laos, while further north is the official apex of the Golden Triangle at Sop Ruak (at the point where the Sop Ruak River meets the Mekong), where Myanmar, Laos and Thailand meet. The area has become very touristy in recent years; even Chiang Saen is beginning to sacrifice its charms to riverside construction.

Places to Stay

The *Chiang Saen Guest House* is on the Sop Ruak Rd in Chiang Saen and costs 40/60B for singles/doubles right on the river. A bit further along this road, on the same side, is the newer *Siam Guest House*, which has huts for 50B/60B, or 70/80B with bath.

Back in town, there's the bright blue *Poonsuk Hotel*, a decrepit looking place towards the river end of Chiang Saen's main street. The only sign in English says 'hotel', but singles/doubles are 40/70B.

Behind the post office is the new *JS Guest House* with rooms for 100B. The couple that run this guesthouse also hire out bicycles and provide vegetarian meals.

Getting There & Away

By bus it's a 40 minute to two-hour (very variable!) trip from Chiang Rai to Chiang Saen for 17B. A bus up to Mae Sai from Chiang Saen is 15B. Returning to Chiang Mai from Chiang Saen is faster (4½ hours versus nine) if you don't take the direct Chiang Mai bus. Instead, go back to Chiang Rai first and take a Chiang Mai bus from there. The Chiang Saen to Chiang Mai buses take a roundabout route over poor roads.

AROUND CHIANG SAEN

Sop Ruak

Nowadays Sop Ruak, 14 km north of Chiang Saen, is besieged daily by bus loads of package tourists who want their pictures taken in front of the 'Welcome to the Golden Triangle' sign. One place worth a visit is the **House of Opium**, a small museum with historical displays pertaining to opium culture.

Places to Stay Taking advantage of the Golden Triangle myth, development here is reaching absurd proportions. *Golden Central Guest House*, opposite the Golden Triangle Resort Hotel, has singles/doubles with shared hot bath at 80/100B.

Phukham Guest House, next to the House of Opium, has thatched bungalows for 80B a single or double. The 150-room *Golden Triangle Resort Hotel*, built on a hillside overlooking the river, is a 1st-class place with rooms from 2000B – the wave of the future here.

Getting There & Away There's a bus a day from Chiang Saen to Sop Ruak in the early morning, but you can also hitch.

MAE SAI-MAE SALONG AREA

Mae Sai is the northernmost point in Thailand, right across the Sai River from the Burmese trading post of Takhilek. The bridge crossing the river has recently been opened to foreigners for day trips. Although the town of Takhilek is not very exciting, Mae Sai makes a good base from which to explore mountain areas like Doi Tung and Mae Salong, infamous for opium cultivation, and is a good place to shop for gems (only if you know what you're doing), lacquerware from Myanmar and other crafts.

Cross-Border Trips to Takhilek & Kyainge Tong

Foreigners may cross the bridge over the Sai River into Takhilek (also spelt Tachilek) upon payment of a US$10 fee and the deposit of their passports at the immigration post on the Thai side. Besides shopping for Shan and Burmese handicrafts (which are about the same price as on the Thai side) and eating Shan/Burmese food, there's little to do on the Burmese side.

Three-night, four-day excursions 163 km north to the town of Kyainge Tong (usually spelt Chiang Tung by the Thais) may be arranged through any Mae Sai guesthouse or travel agency or you can do it on your own by paying US$18 for a three-night permit at the border, plus a mandatory exchange of US$100 for Myanmar's Foreign Exchange Certificates (FECs). These FECs can be spent on hotel rooms or exchanged on the black market for real kyat (the Burmese currency – see the Myanmar chapter for details on the money system).

Kyainge Tong is a sleepy but historic capital for the Shan State's Khün culture – the Khün speak a Northern Thai language related to Shan and Thai Lü and call their town 'Kengtung'. It's a bit more than halfway between the Thai and Chinese borders – eventually the road will be open all the way to China but for now Kyainge Tong is the limit.

There's even less to do in Kyainge Tong than in Takhilek but it's a scenic town dotted with Buddhist temples around a small lake. The road trip allows glimpses of small Shan, Akha, Wa and Lahu villages along the way. The *Noi Yee Hotel* costs US$10 per person per night in multi-bed rooms. Myanmar Tours & Travel tries to steer tourists toward the more expensive, government-run *Kyainge Tong Hotel*, where rooms range from US$30 to US$42.

As with the Takhilek day trips, you must leave your passport at the border. You can rent a jeep on either side of the border, but Thai vehicles are charged a flat rate of US$50 for vehicles with a capacity of five or fewer passengers and US$100 for vehicles with a capacity of over five. Burmese vehicle hire is more expensive and requires the use of a driver. The cheapest form of transport to Kyainge Tong is via the 44B songthaews that leave each morning from Takhilek. Whatever form of transport, count on at least six to ten gruelling hours (depending on road conditions) to cover the 163-km stretch between Takhilek and Kyainge Tong.

Places to Stay & Eat

Mae Sai Near the town entrance is the *Chad Guest House*, which is run by a friendly Shan family and has rooms for 70B and a dorm for 30B per person. They also have a good kitchen. The *Mae Sai Guest House* is right on the Sai River, a couple of km from the bridge. Bungalows cost from 40B a single to 120B for a newer double, but recent reports are unanimous in condemning the rude, surly staff. Much better is the nearby *Mae Sai Plaza Guest House*, with a variety of rooms from 50 to 200B. Also on the river are the *Northern Guest House* and *Sai Riverside*, with secure, comfortable rooms for 100 to 200B.

Other budget places include the *Sin Wattana* and *Mae Sai* hotels along the main street which have rooms from 100 to 150B.

Mae Salong Area In Mae Salong, the *Mae Salong Guest House* at the end of the road leading into town has rooms from 80 to 100B. The old wooden *Shin Sane (Sin Sae) Hotel* just around the corner has rooms from 50B. East of Mae Salong near Ban Klang, in the Lisu village of Ban That (just off the highway to Ban Basang), *Nid's Guest House*

THAILAND

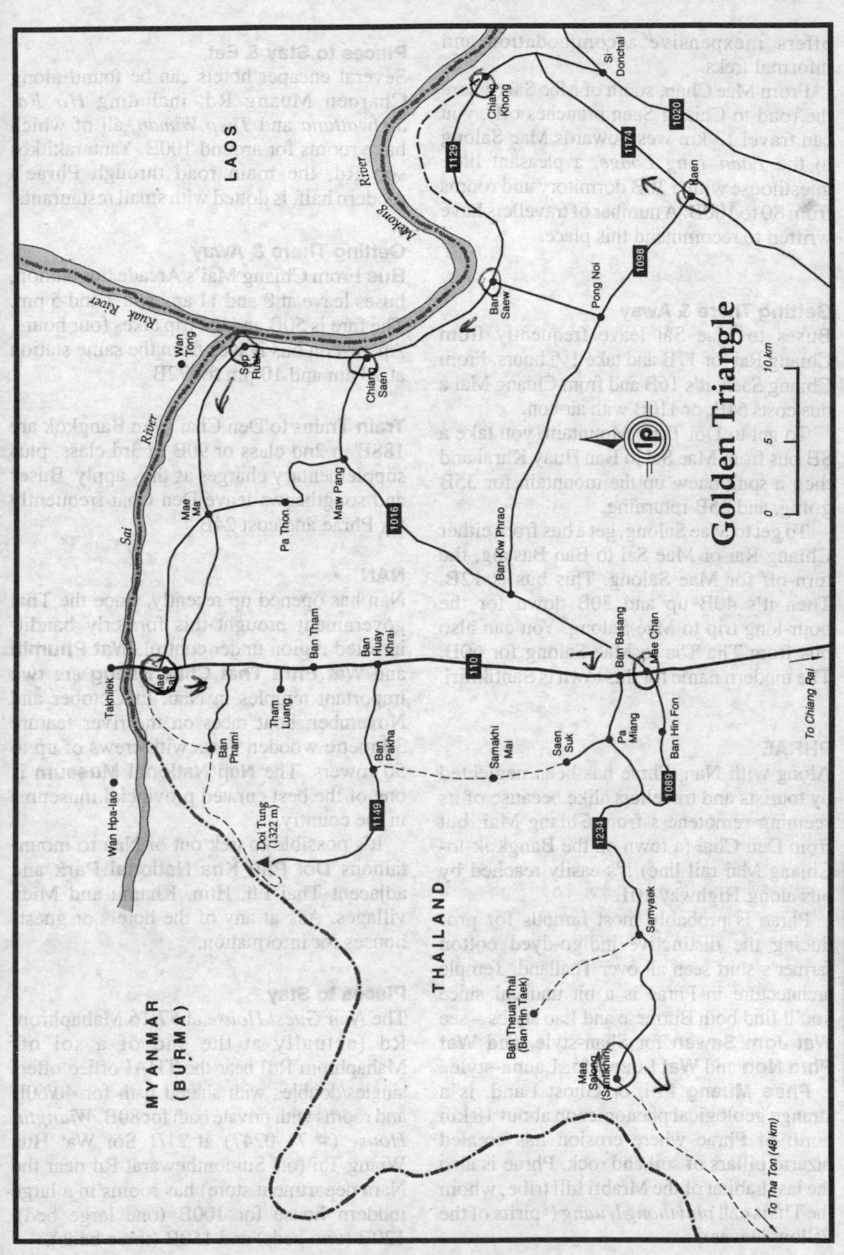
Golden Triangle
LAOS
MYANMAR (BURMA)
THAILAND
Mekong River
Ruak River
Sai River
Chiang Khong
Si Donchai
1129
1174
1020
Kaen
1098
Pong Noi
Ban Saew
Chiang Saen
Sop Ruak
Wan Tong
Mae Ma
Maw Pang
Pa Thon
1016
Ban Kiw Phrao
Ban Basang
Mae Chan
110
Ban Huay Khrai
Ban Tham
Tham Luang
Ban Phami
Takhilek
Wan Hpa-lao
Doi Tung (1322 m)
1149
Ban Pakha
Samakhi Mai
Saen Suk
Pa Miang
Ban Hin Fon
1089
1234
Samyaek
Ban Theuat Thai (Ban Hin Taek)
Mae Salong (Santikhiri)
To Tha Ton (48 km)
To Chiang Rai
0 5 10 km

THAILAND

offers inexpensive accommodation and informal treks.

From Mae Chan, south of Mae Sai (where the road to Chiang Saen branches off), you can travel 13 km west towards Mae Salong to the *Laan Tong Lodge*, a pleasant little guesthouse with a 30B dormitory and rooms from 80 to 100B. A number of travellers have written to recommend this place.

Getting There & Away

Buses to Mae Sai leave frequently from Chiang Rai for 17B and take 1½ hours. From Chiang Saen, it's 16B and from Chiang Mai a bus costs 64B, or 110B with air-con.

To get to Doi Tung Mountain, you take a 8B bus from Mae Sai to Ban Huay Khrai and then a songthaew up the mountain for 35B going, and 25B returning.

To get to Mae Salong, get a bus from either Chiang Rai or Mae Sai to Ban Basang, the turn-off for Mae Salong. This bus is 12B. Then it's 40B up and 30B down for the hour-long trip to Mae Salong. You can also bus from Tha Ton to Mae Salong for 60B. The modern name for this town is Santikhiri.

PHRAE

Along with Nan, Phrae has been neglected by tourists and travellers alike because of its seeming remoteness from Chiang Mai, but from Den Chai (a town on the Bangkok-to-Chiang Mai rail line) it's easily reached by bus along Highway 101.

Phrae is probably most famous for producing the distinctive indigo-dyed cotton farmer's shirt seen all over Thailand. Temple architecture in Phrae is a bit unusual since you'll find both Burmese and Lao styles – see **Wat Jom Sawan** for Shan-style, and **Wat Phra Non** and **Wat Luang** for Lanna-style.

Phae Muang Phi, or Ghost Land, is a strange geological phenomenon about 18 km north of Phrae where erosion has created bizarre pillars of soil and rock. Phrae is also the last habitat of the Mrabri hill tribe, whom the Thais call *phii thong leuang* (spirits of the yellow leaves).

Places to Stay & Eat

Several cheaper hotels can be found along Charoen Muang Rd, including *Ho Fa*, *Siriwattana* and *Thep Wiman*, all of which have rooms for around 100B. Yantarakitkoson Rd, the main road through Phrae's modern half, is dotted with small restaurants.

Getting There & Away

Bus From Chiang Mai's Arcade bus station, buses leave at 8 and 11 am, and 3 and 5 pm. The fare is 50B and the trip takes four hours. An air-con bus leaves from the same station at 10 am and 10 pm for 72B.

Train Trains to Den Chai from Bangkok are 188B in 2nd class or 90B in 3rd class, plus supplementary charges as they apply. Buses and songthaews leave Den Chai frequently for Phrae and cost 24B.

NAN

Nan has opened up recently, since the Thai government brought this formerly bandit-infested region under control. **Wat Phumin** and **Wat Phra That Chae Haeng** are two important temples in Nan. In October and November, boat races on the river feature 30-metre wooden boats with crews of up to 50 rowers. The **Nan National Museum** is one of the best curated provincial museums in the country.

It's possible to trek out of Nan to mountainous **Doi Phu Kha National Park** and adjacent Thai Lü, Htin, Khamu and Mien villages. Ask at any of the hotels or guesthouses for information.

Places to Stay

The *Nan Guest House* at 57/16 Mahaphrom Rd (actually at the end of a soi off Mahaphrom Rd) near the THAI office offers singles/doubles with shared bath for 40/60B and rooms with private bath for 80B. *Wiangtai House* (☎ 71 0247) at 21/1 Soi Wat Hua Wiang Tai (off Sumonthewarat Rd near the Nara department store) has rooms in a large modern house for 100B (one large bed), 120B (two beds) and 150B (three beds).

THAILAND

Doi Phukha Guest House, (☎ (54) 771422), 94/5 Sumonthewarat Rd (actually on a soi off Sumonthewarat), offers rooms in an old teak house for 60 to 100B.

Among Nan's hotels, the least expensive is the *Amorn Si* at 97 Mahayot Rd, where very basic rooms go for 100B. *Sukkasem* at 29/31 Anantaworarittidet Rd has better rooms from 130B with fan and bath, 160B with air-con.

Getting There & Away

Buses run to Nan from Chiang Mai (75B, and 120B for air-con) and Sukhothai (65B). The most direct way to Nan is from Den Chai via Phrae. You can also fly there from Chiang Mai, Chiang Rai and Phitsanulok.

North-Eastern Thailand

The north-east is the least visited region of Thailand, although in many ways it is the most 'Thai'. There are a number of places of interest here. In part, the lack of tourists can be accounted for by the region's proximity to Laos and Cambodia and tales of hold-ups and Communist guerrilla actions. In fact, travel is generally fine in most areas and, if anything, is easier now than it was a few years ago.

Among north-easterners, this part of Thailand is known as Isaan, from the Sanskrit name for the Mon-Khmer Isana Kingdom – a pre-Angkor culture that flourished in the area of (what is now) north-eastern Thailand and Cambodia. A mixture of Lao and Khmer influences is a mark of Isaan culture and language. Points of major interest in the north-east include the scenic Mekong River and the many Khmer temple ruins, especially those from the Angkor period.

Getting There & Away

There are railway lines operating from Bangkok to Udon Thani and Nong Khai on the Lao border in the north-east or to Ubon Ratchathani, near the Cambodian border, in the east. You can make an interesting loop through the north-east by travelling first north to Chiang Mai and the other centres in the north and then to Phitsanulok, Khon Kaen, Loei and Udon Thani. Several north-eastern cities are also accessible by air from Bangkok.

NAKHON RATCHASIMA (KHORAT)

Although Nakhon Ratchasima, also known as Khorat, is mainly thought of as a place from which to visit the Khmer ruins of Phimai and Phanom Rung, it has a number of attractions in its own right. They include the **Mahawirawong Museum** in the grounds of Wat Sutchinda with a fine collection of Khmer art objects. It's open from 9 am to noon and 1 to 4 pm Wednesday to Sunday. The **Thao Suranri Memorial** is a popular shrine to Khun Ying Mo, a heroine who led the local inhabitants against Lao invaders during the reign of Rama III.

The TAT office in Nakhon Ratchasima will supply you with a map of the city and a list of hotels, restaurants and other useful information. The office is on Mitthaphap Rd at the western edge of town, beyond the railway station.

Places to Stay

At 68-70 Mukkhamontri Rd, near the railway station, the *Fah Sang* is clean and friendly with rooms from 85B. *Pho Thong* at 179 Pho Klang Rd, in the 80 to 120B bracket, is noisy but liveable. A couple of blocks west, the *Siri Hotel* is central and friendly. Rooms start from 90B. The *Tokyo Hotel* on Suranari Rd has good, big singles with bath for 100B.

The *Thai Phokhaphan* at 104-6 Atsadang Rd is inside the city moats and costs 100/150B for singles/doubles, more for air-con. The *Khorat Doctor's House* (☎ 25 5846) at 78 Seup Siri Rd Soi 4 is quiet and comfortable and has four large rooms for 40 to 120B.

Places to Eat

There are lots of good places to eat around the western gates to the town centre, near the Thao Suranari Memorial. At night, the *Hua Rot Fai Market* on Mukkhamontri Rd is a great place to eat with a wide selection and cheap prices. The infamous *VFW Cafeteria*, next to the Siri Hotel, has real American breakfasts plus steaks, ice cream, pizza and salads. Several inexpensive Thai-Chinese restaurants can be found along Ratchadamnoen Rd in the vicinity of the Thao Suranri Memorial.

Getting There & Away

Bus Buses depart every 20 minutes to half an hour from the Northern bus terminal in Bangkok – the fare is 54B. The trip takes 3½ to four hours. Buses to or from Khon Kaen cost 45B.

Train There are two expresses daily from Bangkok's Hualamphong station but they arrive at ungodly hours in the morning. The rapid trains are better; they depart at 6.50 am and 6.45 pm, arriving in Nakhon Ratchasima at 11.30 am and 11.51 pm respectively. The trip passes through some fine scenery.

AROUND NAKHON RATCHASIMA

Pakthongchai

This silk-weaving centre is 28 km south of

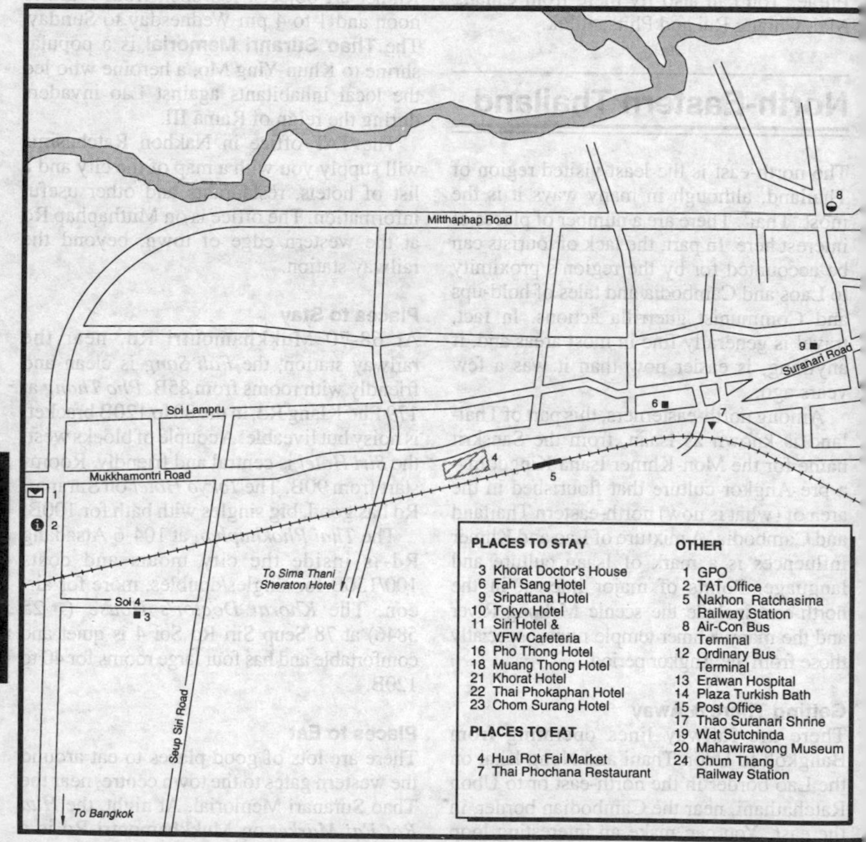

Nakhon Ratchasima. Buses go there every half an hour for 12B.

Phimai
This 12th-century Khmer shrine was constructed in the style of Cambodia's Angkor Wat and was once directly connected by road with Angkor. The main shrine has been restored and is a beautiful and impressive piece of work. There is also a ruined palace and an open-air museum. Admission to the complex is 20B. Phimai itself is nothing special but it's a pleasant enough place to stay.

Places to Stay There's just one hotel, the adequate *Phimai Hotel* with rooms from 80B without bath up to 260B for an air-con double with bath. The *Old Phimai Guest House*, in an alley off the main street, is comfortable enough for 60B in a four-bed dorm or 80/100B for single/double rooms with shared bath.

Getting There & Away There are buses every half an hour from Nakhon Ratchasima's main bus station behind the Erawan Hospital on Suranari Rd. The trip takes one to 1½ hours and costs 15B.

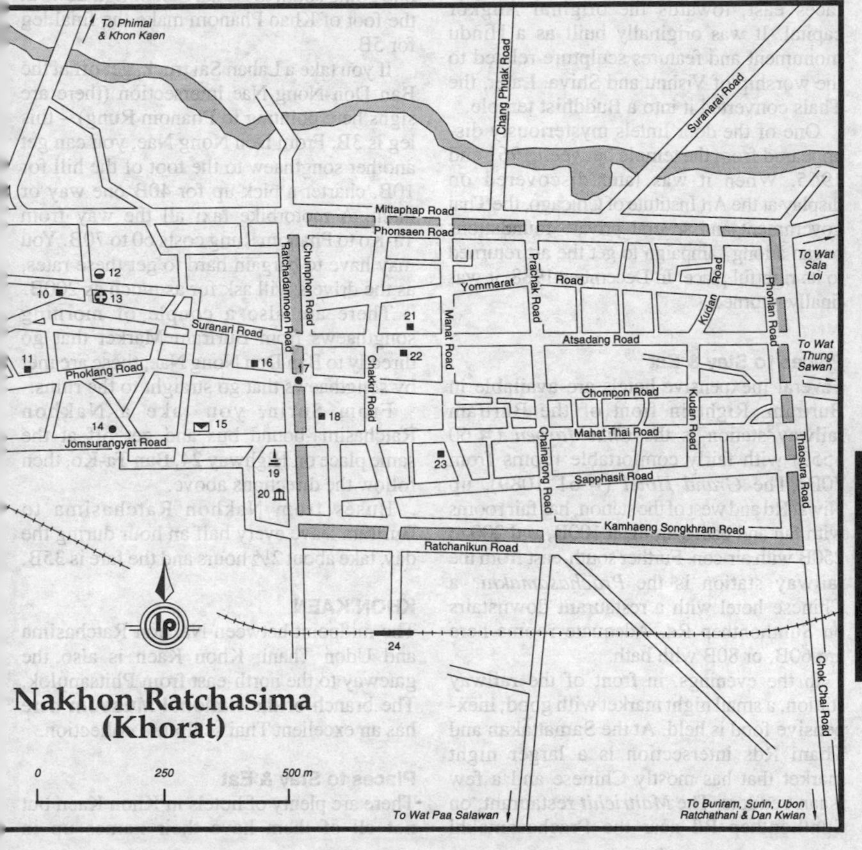

Prasat Phanomwan

Midway between Nakhon Ratchasima and Phimai, this is another impressive Khmer ruin. To get there, get off the Nakhon Ratchasima to Phimai bus at Ban Long Thong from where it's six km, via Ban Makha, to Prasat Phanomwan.

PRASAT PHANOM RUNG

The restored temple of Prasat Hin Khao Phanom Rung, around 50 km south of Buriram, is the most impressive of all Angkor monuments in Thailand. Constructed on top of an extinct volcano between the 10th and 13th centuries, the complex faces east, towards the original Angkor capital. It was originally built as a Hindu monument and features sculpture related to the worship of Vishnu and Shiva. Later, the Thais converted it into a Buddhist temple.

One of the door lintels mysteriously disappeared from the temple between 1961 and 1965. When it was later discovered on display at the Art Institute of Chicago, the Thai government and several private foundations began a long campaign to get the art returned to its rightful place. In December 1988, it was finally returned.

Places to Stay & Eat

Several inexpensive hotels are available in Buriram. Right in front of the Buriram railway station is the *Chai Jaroen* (☎ 60 1559) with fairly comfortable rooms from 70B. The *Grand Hotel* (☎ 61 1089), up Niwat Rd and west of the station, has fair rooms with fan and bath starting at 100B, and 200 to 250B with air-con. Further south-east from the railway station is the *Prachasamakhi*, a Chinese hotel with a restaurant downstairs on Sunthonthep Rd. Adequate rooms here are 60B, or 80B with bath.

In the evenings, in front of the railway station, a small night market with good, inexpensive food is held. At the Samattakan and Thani Rds intersection is a larger night market that has mostly Chinese and a few Isaan vendors. The *Maitrichit* restaurant, on Sunthonthep Rd near the Prachasamakhi Hotel, has a large selection of Thai and Chinese standards from morning till night.

There is one, cheap, friendly and noisy hotel in Nang Rong, on the way to Phanom Rung from Nakhon Ratchasima.

Getting There & Away

Prasat Phanom Rung can be approached from Nakhon Ratchasima, Buriram or Surin. From Nakhon Ratchasima, take a Surin-bound bus and get out at Ban Ta-Ko, which is just a few km past Nang Rong. The fare is about 20B. From the Ta-Ko intersection, occasional songthaews go as far as the foot of Khao Phanom Rung (15B) or catch any one going south to Lahan Sai. Songthaews at the foot of Khao Phanom make the final leg for 5B.

If you take a Lahan Sai truck, get off at the Ban Don Nong Nae intersection (there are signs here pointing to Phanom Rung) – this leg is 3B. From Don Nong Nae, you can get another songthaew to the foot of the hill for 10B, charter a pick-up for 40B one way or hitch. A motorbike taxi all the way from Ta-Ko to Phanom Rung costs 60 to 70B. You may have to bargain hard to get these rates, as the drivers will ask for as much as 200B.

There are also a couple of morning songthaews from Buriram Market that go directly to Ban Don Nong Nae; these are met by songthaews that go straight to the ruins.

From Surin, you take a Nakhon Ratchasima-bound bus and get off at the same place on Highway 24, Ban Ta-Ko, then follow the directions above.

Buses from Nakhon Ratchasima to Buriram leave every half an hour during the day, take about 2½ hours and the fare is 35B.

KHON KAEN

The midpoint between Nakhon Ratchasima and Udon Thani, Khon Kaen is also the gateway to the north-east from Phitsanulok. The branch of the **National Museum** here has an excellent Thai sculpture collection.

Places to Stay & Eat

There are plenty of hotels in Khon Kaen but not all of them have their names up in

THAILAND

English script. *Thani Bungalow* (☎ 22 1470), on Reun Rom Rd near the railway station and the market, is good value at 100 to 120B with fan and bath. The *Roma Hotel* (☎ 23 6276) at 50/2 Klang Muang Rd has rooms from 200B. Cheaper is the *Saen Samran* at 55-59 Klang Muang Rd, where rooms cost from 80 to 110B.

Next to the Roma Hotel is *Kai Yang Thiparot*, a good place for kài yâng (roast chicken) and other Isaan food. Khon Kaen has a lively *night market* with plenty of good foodstalls next to the air-con bus terminal.

Getting There & Away

From Nakhon Ratchasima, it's 2½ hours to Khon Kaen by bus and the fare is 44B. You can also do the trip by rail since Khon Kaen is on the Bangkok-Nakhon Ratchasima-Udon Thani rail line.

AROUND KHON KAEN

Kalasin

Kalasin, 80 km east of Khon Kaen, is a pleasant town and a good base for a visit to the **Phu Pan National Park**.

Places to Stay You can stay at the old wooden *Kalasin Hotel* from 80B, or at the slightly more expensive but very comfortable *Saengthawng Hotel* for 100 to 200B.

UDON THANI

This was one of the biggest US Air Force bases in Thailand during the Vietnam era – one of those places from where they flew out to drop thousands of tons of bombs into the jungle in the hope that somebody might be standing under one of the trees. It's got nothing much to offer apart from massage parlours and ice-cream parlours. **Ban Chiang**, 50 km east, has some interesting archaeological digs – the excavations at **Wat Pho Si Nai** are open to the public, and there's a recently constructed museum.

Places to Stay

The *Queen Hotel* at 6-8 Udon-Dutsadi Rd has rooms with fan and bath from 80B. In the centre of town, the *Tokyo* at 147 Prachak Rd has rooms of similar standard and price, and more expensive rooms with air-con. At 123 Prachak Rd, the *Si Sawat* has cheaper rooms in the old building from 80B.

Along Prachak Rd, you'll find several small, inexpensive hotels, including the *Mit Sahai* and the *Malasi Saengden*, both with rooms for 70 to 90B.

Places to Eat

Udon Thani has plenty of restaurants – many with Western food – but you can also find places that specialise in the Isaan food of the north-east region. *Yawt Kai Yang* at the corner of Pho Si and Mukkhamontri Rds is a good spot to try Isaan-style grilled chicken (kài yàang) with spicy papaya salad and sticky rice.

Try the *Rung Thong* at the west side of the clocktower for good curries. In the new *Charoensi Complex*, at the south-eastern end of Prajak Silpakorn Rd, there's a good food centre and a couple of modern coffee shops.

Getting There & Away

There's a daily express train from Bangkok which costs 228B in 2nd class, 128B in 3rd class and takes 11 hours overnight. Take a sleeper – it's worthwhile on this long trip. Buses from Bangkok depart frequently and cost 134B – the trip takes about nine hours. There are also regular flights to Udon Thani.

A bus from Nakhon Ratchasima to Udon Thani is 64B and takes four to five hours. There are regular buses between Udon Thani and Ban Chiang throughout the day for 22B.

NONG KHAI

Right on the Mekong River, this is the major crossing point to get to Vientiane in Laos. It's 624 km from Bangkok and only 55 km north of Udon Thani. The city is developing fast as it gears up for trade with Laos – a bridge now joins the two countries.

Visas for Laos are sometimes available from travel agencies here. These depend on the on-again, off-again policies of Lao Tourism (see Facts for the Visitor in the Laos chapter for more details). If you manage to get a visa, you can take the ferry across to Tha Deua, from where taxis run into Vientiane.

Places to Stay

Guesthouses *Mutmee (Mat-mii)* is on the river off Meechai Rd and has rooms from 60 to 120B. They have a pleasant garden restaurant overlooking the river. Also on Meechai Rd is the newer *Sawadee* with small but clean rooms for 80/100B and the *Mekong* with rooms overlooking the river for 60B/100B.

Several blocks further east off Meechai Rd on the river is *Tommy's* – dorm beds are 30B and rooms cost from 40 to 70B. They also rent bicycles and motorbikes and arrange river trips. By now, they may have a branch on the river as well. Other guesthouses are opening up in Nong Khai as more people are visiting Vientiane.

Hotels The *Prajak Bungalows* (☎ 41 1116) at 1178 Prajak Rd has rooms with fans from 150B. There are more expensive rooms with air-con and a cheap restaurant in front.

The *Sukhaphan Hotel* on Banthoengjit Rd is a nicely renovated old Chinese hotel with single/double rooms at 70/90B. *Pongwichit*, at 723 Banthoengjit Rd and right across the street, has clean 120/150B rooms with fan and bath.

Places to Eat

Overlooking the Laos ferry pier, *Udom Rot* has good food and a pleasant atmosphere. Another riverside choice is the *Rim Nam Khong* next to the Mekong Guest House. The French influence in Laos has crept over the border and into the local pastry shops.

Getting There & Away

Nong Khai is the end of the rail line which runs from Bangkok through Nakhon Ratchasima, Khon Kaen and Udon Thani. The basic fare is 215B in 2nd class and 103B in 3rd class, not including supplementary charges.

By bus, it's 146B (263B with air-con) from Bangkok and takes nine or 10 hours. From Nakhon Ratchasima, it takes four hours and costs 80B. Udon is only 1¼ hours away, and the fare is 23B.

AROUND NONG KHAI

Twelve km to the south-east of Nong Khai is **Wat Phra That Bang Phuan**. It is one of the most sacred temple sites in the north-east because of a 2000-year-old Indian-style stupa originally found here (it was replaced or built over by a Lao-style chedi in the 16th century). **Wat Hin Maak Peng**, 60 km north-west, is a quiet and peaceful place on the banks of the Mekong.

Nearer to town, **Sala Ku Kaew** is a strange Hindu-Buddhist sculpture garden. It's four or five km east of town.

NONG KHAI TO LOEI

Following the Mekong River from Nong Khai into Loei province, you'll pass through the towns of Si Chiangmai, Sangkhom, Pak Chom and Chiang Khan. Each of these small towns has a couple of guesthouses with accommodation from 50 to 80B. Although there are no major attractions along this route, it's a nice area to take a break from the road. Relaxing walks along the Mekong River are just the thing for frazzled nerves.

LOEI

From here, you can climb the 1500-metre **Phu Kradung** mountain, about 75 km south of Loei. The mountain is in a national park with trails and cabins available if you want to stay. The climb takes about four hours if you're reasonably fit.

Places to Stay

Guesthouses *Muang Loei Guest House* has two locations, both within walking distance of the bus terminal. Neither offer anything great, just basic and not particularly clean rooms for 50B per person.

A better choice is the *Friendship Guest House* (☎ 81 2399) at 257/12 Soi Boon Charoen. To get there from the centre of town, hop on a samlor for 15B or walk south on Charoen Rat Rd past the post office until you reach Wat Si Bunruang on your left.

Turn left on Soi Boon Charoen and follow the sign to the guesthouse. Rooms are 50/80B. Another rather new place is the similarly priced *Sri Pathum Guest House* at 12 Sathon Chiang Khan Rd.

Hotels The *Sarai Thong* on Ruamjit Rd has rooms from 90 to 130B, all with fan and bath. It's off the street, quiet and clean. The *Sri Sawat*, nearby on Ruamjit Rd, is similar but slightly cheaper. The *Phu Luang Hotel* (☎ 81 1532/570) at 55 Charoen Rat Rd near the market costs from 150B.

Places to Eat

The *market* at the intersection of Ruamjai and Charoen Rat Rds has cheap eats including some local specialities. Near the Bangkok Bank on Charoen Rat Rd, the *Chuan Lee* and the *Sawita* are two pastry/coffee shops that also sell a range of Thai and Western food.

Getting There & Away

Buses run directly from Bangkok to Loei, or you can get there from Udon Thani for 34B or from Phitsanulok via Lom Sak for around 80 to 90B, depending on the bus. Buses to Phu Kradung, 75 km to the south, leave the Loei bus station in the morning. Direct buses to Chiang Mai cost 121B.

LOM SAK

It's an interesting trip from Phitsanulok to this colourful small town on the way to Loei and Udon Thani. It's also a pleasant trip from here to Khon Kaen. There are several places to stay near the bus stop, including the *Sawang Hotel* which also has good Chinese food.

BEUNG KAN

This small dusty town on the Mekong River, 185 km east of Nong Khai, has a Vietnamese influence. Nearby is **Wat Phu Thawk**, a remote forest wat built on a sandstone outcrop.

NAKHON PHANOM

There's a great view across the Mekong River towards Tha Khaek in Laos from this otherwise dull city which has a large Lao and Vietnamese presence. **Renu Nakhon**, a village south of Nakhon Phanom (on the way to That Phanom), is renowned for its big Wednesday handicraft market.

Places to Stay

Charoensuk at 692/45 Bamrung Muang Rd is adequate at 80B for a room with fan and bath. The *Si Thep Hotel* (☎ 51 1036) at 708/11 Si Thep Rd costs from 120B up to around 250B for fancier air-con rooms.

The *First Hotel* at 370 Si Thep Rd is a good place with clean rooms from 100B with fan and bath. The *Windsor Hotel* at 692/19 Bamrung Muang Rd has very nice rooms at similar prices to the First, but it's not so quiet. Behind the Windsor, on the corner of Si Thep and Ruamjit Rds, is the *Grand* with rooms similar to the Windsor for 100B.

Places to Eat

Along Bamrung Muang Rd near the Windsor Hotel, there are several good and inexpensive restaurants. Try the *Tatiya Club* on the corner of Fuang Nakhon and Bamrung Muang Rds for a glittery Thai night out.

Getting There & Away

There are regular buses from Nong Khai to Nakhon Phanom via Sakon Nakhon for 55B. Direct buses are 76B.

THAT PHANOM

This remote north-eastern town, on the banks of the Mekong River, has the famous **Wat That Phanom** which is similar in style to Wat That Luang in Vientiane, Laos. There's also some interesting French-Chinese architecture around the town, again showing the Laotian influence. A Lao market convenes by the river every morning.

Places to Stay & Eat

The pleasant *Niyana Guest House* is on a soi near the That Phanom pier. Dorm beds are 30B, singles are 50 to 60B and a double is 80B. Niyana also does bicycle rentals and short boat trips on the river.

Chai Von (Wan) Hotel, on Phanom Phan-arak Rd to the north of the arch (turn left as you pass under the arch), is an old wooden hotel with rooms from 50 to 60B with shared bath, 70B with bath. There are a couple of Thai restaurants near the Chai Von Hotel.

Getting There & Away

Songthaews from Nakhon Phanom to That Phanom cost 15B and take about 1½ hours. Stay on until you see the chedi on the right. Sakon Nakhon is two to three hours north-west by bus at a cost of 22B. An air-con bus to Ubon Ratchathani is 99B.

YASOTHON

Although it's a bit out of the way if you're doing the Mekong circuit, the two-hour bus trip from Ubon Ratchathani is worth making to witness the annual **Rocket Festival** (from 8-10 May). This popular north-eastern rain-and-fertility festival is celebrated with particular fervour in Yasothon.

Places to Stay

The *Udomporn* at 169 Uthairamrit Rd has rooms from 70 to 80B. Or try the decent *Surawet Wattana* at 128/1 Changsanit Rd with rooms from 80 to 125B. The *Yothnakhon* (☎ 71 1122) at 169 Uthairamrit Rd costs from 100B for fan rooms, 200B with air-con.

Getting There & Away

A bus to Yasothon from Ubon Ratchathani costs 25B.

UBON (UBOL) RATCHATHANI

This was another major US Air Force base during Vietnam days. The **Wat Paa Nanachat** monastery at nearby Warin Chamrap has a large foreign contingent studying there. Ask for 'wat farang'! **Wat Thung Si Muang** in the centre of town and **Wat Phra That Nong Bua** on the outskirts are also interesting. The latter has a good copy of the Mahabodhi stupa in Bodh Gaya, India.

Places to Stay

Several of the cheaper hotels are along Suriyat Rd. The *Suriyat Hotel* at No 47/1-4 has basic rooms with fan for 80B, and rooms with air-con for 160B. The *Homsa-ad (Hawm Sa-at)* at No 80/10 Suriyat Rd is only 60 to 80B.

The *Racha Hotel* at 149/21 Chayangkun Rd, north of the city centre, starts at 120B for clean rooms with fan and bath. At 224/5 Chayangkun Rd, north of the Racha Hotel and municipal market and next to the flashy Pathumrat Hotel, is the *99 Hotel (Ubon Rat)*. All rooms have air-con and bath, and cost 90 to 160B – ask for a discount. The *Tokyo* is at 178 Uparat Rd, near the city centre. It's very nice, well-kept and single/double rooms with fan and bath cost 85B/120B, or 140B/ 160B with air-con.

At 220/6 Ratchabut Rd, in this same part of town, is the cheaper *Si Isan*, where rooms start at 80B with fan and bath.

Places to Eat

The *Loet Rot* at 147/13 Chayangkun Rd, near the Racha Hotel, has excellent noodle dishes. Several inexpensive rice and noodle shops can be found along Kheuan Thani Rd.

The family-run *Piak* on Jaeng Sanit Rd (next to a radio relay station) and *Suan Maphrao*, also on Jaeng Sanit Rd (next to Si Maha Pho Hospital), have the best Isaan food in Ubon. Try the knockout laap pet (spicy duck salad).

For breakfast, the *Chiokee* on Kheuan Thani Rd is very popular among local office workers. It's cheap and offers Thai, Chinese and Western-style breakfasts.

Getting There & Away

An express train and two rapid trains leave daily from Bangkok. Fares are 95B in 3rd class and 200B in 2nd class (not including rapid or express surcharges). By bus, there are frequent departures daily from the Northern bus station in Bangkok with fares of 160B on the regular buses, 290B air-con. Buses from Nakhon Phanom take six to seven hours and cost 65B.

SURIN

Surin is most well known for the elephant roundup held in late November every year.

There are elephant races, fights, tug-of-wars and anything else you can think of to do with a couple of hundred elephants. If you've ever had an urge to see a lot of elephants at one time, this is a chance to get it out of your system! Several minor Khmer ruins can also be visited nearby. There are a lot of day or overnight trips available from Bangkok during this time.

Places to Stay

Pirom's House (☎ 51 5140) at 242 Krung Si Nai Rd has dorm beds for 50B per person and singles/doubles for 70/100B. Pirom can suggest day trips around Surin, including excursions to nearby villages and Khmer temple sites.

Hotel prices soar during roundup time but normally the *Krung Si* (☎ 51 1037) on Krung Si Rd has rooms from 80 to 100B. The *New Hotel* (☎ 51 1341/22) at 22 Tanasarn Rd, next to the railway station, costs from 100 to 180B and has some more expensive air-con rooms.

Getting There & Away

Regular buses from the Northern bus terminal in Bangkok cost 108B. There are many special tour buses at roundup time. You can also get there on the Ubon Ratchathani express and rapid trains for 153B in 2nd class. Book seats well in advance in November.

Southern Thailand

The south of Thailand offers some of the most spectacular scenery in the country plus beautiful beaches, good snorkelling, fine seafood and a good selection of things to see. There are roads along the east and west coasts; the east-coast road runs close to the railway line.

The south is very different from the rest of Thailand in both its geography and people. Here, the rice paddies of the central area give way to the rubber and palm-oil plantations which you also see right down through Malaysia. Many of the people are also related to the Malays in both culture and religion. This 'difference' has long promoted secessionist rumblings and the Thai government still has to grapple with occasional outbreaks of violence in the south.

The two main attractions of the south are the beautiful islands of Phuket and Ko Samui. Both offer a wide range of accommodation (Phuket less so than Ko Samui) and some superb beaches. In fact, either island makes Pattaya look like a bad dream.

Other attractions of the south include the awesome limestone outcrops which erupt from the green jungle and the sea between Phang-Nga and Krabi, beyond Phuket. Chaiya has some archaeologically interesting remains while deep in the south is Hat Yai, a rapidly growing modern city with a colourful reputation as a weekend getaway from Malaysia.

Getting There & Away

You can travel south from Bangkok by air, bus or rail. The road south runs down the east coast as far as Chumphon where you have a choice of climbing over the narrow mountain range and going down the west coast (for Phuket) or continuing south on the east coast (for Ko Samui).

The railway line also follows the east-coast route and the two routes, east and west, meet again at the southern town of Hat Yai. From Hat Yai, you can continue on the western side into Malaysia to Alor Setar and then Penang. Or, you can head off to the eastern coast and cross the border from Sungai Kolok to Kota Bharu.

PHETBURI (PHETCHABURI)

Phetburi, 160 km south of Bangkok, has a number of interesting old temples. You can make a walking tour of six or seven of them in two or three hours. They include the old Khmer site of **Wat Kamphaeng Laeng**, the early Rattanakosin-era **Wat Yai Suwannaram** and others.

On the outskirts of town next to the Phetkasem highway is **Khao Wang**, a hill topped by a restored King Mongkut palace.

You can walk up the hill to the historical park or take a cable car for 10B one way. Entry to the park is 20B.

Places to Stay & Eat

The *Chom Klao* is on the east side of Chomrut Bridge and has rooms for 80 and 120B. The *Nam Chai*, a block further east, is similarly priced but not such good value. The *Phetburi* is on the next street north of Chomrut Bridge and behind the Chom Klao; it has overpriced rooms at 150B with fan and bath.

There are several good *restaurants* in the Khao Wang area, with a variety of standard Thai and Chinese dishes. The cheapest food with plenty of variety is at the night market at the southern end of Surinluechai Rd under the digital clocktower.

Getting There & Away

Buses leave regularly from the Southern bus terminal in Thonburi, Bangkok, for 36B or 65B with air-con. The bus takes about three hours. Buses to Phetburi from Hua Hin are 20B.

AROUND PHETBURI

The nearby **Kaeng Krachan National Park** is Thailand's largest. There is public transport from Phetburi as far as Kaeng Krachan village for 20B. From there, you must hitch or charter a truck for the four km to the park entrance.

HUA HIN

This town, 230 km south of Bangkok, is the oldest Thai seaside resort. Hua Hin is still a popular weekend getaway for Thais, but has recently been discovered by a rash of Europeans, who have brought high-rise hotels and Western restaurants. Rama VII had a summer residence here and the royal family still uses it.

The **Hotel Sofitel Central Hua Hin** is fronted by trees and shrubs trimmed into such shapes as roosters, ducks, women opening umbrellas, giraffes and snakes.

Places to Stay

Accommodation in Hua Hin tends to be a bit on the expensive side since it's so close to Bangkok. Rates are usually higher on weekends and holidays, so go during the week for the best deals.

The cheapest places are found along or just off Naretdamri Rd. Rooms at *Khun Daeng House* on Naretdamri Rd cost 100B with private bath. *Forum* and *Europa* each have rooms in the 150 to 200B range. Around Phetkasem Rd, there's the *Chaat Chai*, at No 59/1, with rooms from 140B, or the *Damrong*, at No 46, with slightly higher prices. The funky *New Hotel* (☎ 51 1108) at 39/4 Phetkasem is anything but new, but costs only 80 to 150B for fan-cooled rooms.

If you can afford it, the *Hotel Sofitel Central Hua Hin* (☎ 51 2021/40) is a fine experience. Formerly the Railway Hotel, this delightfully old-fashioned place was built by German railway engineers. It's just off the beach on Damnoen Kasem Rd. The rooms are big, the ceilings are high and the service is polished. Rooms have been expensive (1800B and up) by shoestring standards since a French conglomerate took over the hotel in 1986. Movie buffs may recognise the place as the Hotel Le Phnom from the film *The Killing Fields*.

Places to Eat

Hua Hin is noted for its seafood, available near the pier at the end of Chomsin Rd or at the *night market* (always settle the price before ordering). Along Naretdamri Rd are a number of touristy restaurants with touristy prices, such as the *Beergarden*, *Headrock Cafe* and *La Villa*.

Getting There & Away

Buses run from the Southern bus terminal in Bangkok. There are frequent departures for the four-hour trip and the cost is 51B or 92B with air-con. Trains en route to Hat Yai in the south also stop in Hua Hin. The trip takes around 4½ hours and costs 44B in 3rd class and 92B in 2nd class. The supplement on the three daily rapid trains is 20B and 30B for the express. Buses from Phetburi are 20B.

Getting Around

Samlor fares in Hua Hin have been set by the municipal authorities so there shouldn't be any haggling. As posted they are: from the railway station to the beach – 10B; from the bus terminal to Sofitel Central – 15B; and from Chatchai Market to the fishing pier – 10B.

PRACHUAP KHIRI KHAN

This provincial capital is sleepy compared to Hua Hin but some fine seafood can be found here. South of Ao Prachuap, around a small headland, is the small but scenic **Manao Bay**, ringed by limestone mountains and small islands. The Manao beach has recently been opened to the public; formerly it was off limits to foreigners because of the Thai Air Force base there.

A few kms north of town is another bay, **Ao Noi**, and a small fishing village with a few rooms to let.

Places to Stay & Eat

The centrally located *Yutichai* (☎ 61 1055) at 35 Kong Kiat Rd has fair rooms with fan and bath from 100 to 120B. Around the corner on Phitak Chat Rd is the cheaper *Inthira Hotel* with rooms in the 90 to 130B range, but it's noisier and has peepholes. The *King Hotel* (☎ 61 1170), further south on the same street, has rooms from 150 to 200B.

Facing Ao Prachuap is the *Suksan*, which has rooms with a fan from 160 to 200B, but it's very much one big brothel in the evenings. A better bayside choice is the plain but well-kept *Thaed Saban Bungalows* (Mirror Mountain Bungalows), which is owned by the city. A one-room bungalow (which sleeps two) is 200B a night with fan and bath; a two-room bungalow (which sleeps four) is 500B.

On Chai Thale Rd near the top-end Hadthong Hotel is a small *night market* that's quite good for seafood.

Getting There & Away

From Bangkok, buses are 72B and 130B with air-con. From Hua Hin, buses are 30B and they leave from the bus station on Sasong Rd every 20 minutes from 7 am to 3 pm.

It's also possible to catch a train from Hua Hin to Prachuap for 19B in 3rd class.

THAP SAKAE & BANG SAPHAN

South of Prachuap Khiri Khan, near the border with Chumphon Province, are these two districts. Both have minor beach areas that are fairly undeveloped.

The town of Thap Sakae is set back from the coast and isn't much – north and south of town, however, are the beaches of **Hat Wanakon** and **Hat Laem Kum**. There are a couple of guesthouses around and you can ask permission to camp at Wat Laem Kum, 3½ km from Thap Sakae. You can buy food at the fishing village of Ban Don Sai, nearby and to the north.

Bang Saphan isn't much either, but the long beaches here are beginning to attract some development. You can seek out the **beaches** of Hat Sai Kaew, Hat Ban Krut, Hat Ban Nong Mongkon, Hat (Ao) Baw Thawng Lang, Hat Pha Daeng, Hat Khiriway and Hat Bang Boet.

Getting around can be a problem since there isn't much public transport between these beaches. The manager at the Talay Inn in Thap Sakae can sometimes arrange transport to nearby beaches.

Places to Stay & Eat

Thap Sakae Near the seaside, in a small fishing village about 2½ km east of town, is the *Talay Inn* (☎ 67 1417). It's in a cluster of bamboo huts on a lake fed by a waterfall. It costs 60B per person and good food is available. Also in the vicinity are a few concrete-block places with 200 to 400B rooms, such as the *Chan Reua*.

Hat Khiriwong *Tawee Beach Resort* (also *Tawees, Tawee Sea)* has bungalows with private bath for 70 to 150B.

Bang Saphan Along the bay of Ao Bang Saphan, the *Hat Somboon Sea View* and *Wanwina Bungalows* are tourist bungalows in the 150 to 250B range. *Karol L's*, six km south of Bang Saphan, has 80B bungalows.

The new *Suan Luang Resort* (☎ (01) 2125687; fax (032) 691054) at 97 M 1 is 600 metres from the beach, just up from Karol's. They will pick up customers from the railway station if they give them a call. Their new and spacious bungalows with mosquito proofing are 150B for wooden ones, and concrete ones cost 300B. There are discounts for longer stays.

The *Krua Klang Ao* restaurant is a good place for seafood.

Getting There & Away

Buses from Prachuap to Thap Sakae are 12B and from Thap Sakae to Bang Saphan cost 9B. If you're coming from further south, buses from Chumphon to Bang Saphan are 27B.

You can also get 3rd-class trains between Prachuap, Thap Sakae and Bang Saphan for a few baht on each leg.

RANONG

Ranong is 600 km south of Bangkok and 300 km north of Phuket. Only the Chan River separates Thailand from Kawthaung (Victoria Point) in Myanmar at this point. There's a busy trade back and forth, supplying Burmese needs – the focus of the sea trade is the Saphaan Plaa Pier which is eight km south-west of town (5B on a No 2 songthaew).

Much of the town centre is Hokkien Chinese in flavour. Just outside of town is the 42°C (107°F) **Ranong Mineral Hot Springs** at Wat Tapotaram.

Places to Stay & Eat

Along Ruangrat Rd in Ranong are a number of cheap places, including the *Rattanasin* and the *Suriyanon* with single/double rooms for 60B, 80B with fan. The *Asia* (☎ 81 1113) and *Sin Tavee* (☎ 81 1213) on the same road are in the 120 to 450B range.

The somewhat expensive *Jansom Thara Hotel*, up on the main road, is the place to stay for mineral bathing since all the hotel's water is piped in from the hot springs. Rooms start at 1200B.

For inexpensive Thai and Burmese breakfasts, try the *morning market* on Ruangrat Rd. Also along Ruangrat Rd are several traditional Hokkien *coffee shops* with marble-topped tables.

Getting There & Away

Buses from Chumphon are 32B or 70B from Surat Thani. Buses from Takua Pa are 50B or 80B from Phuket. The bus terminal in Ranong is outside of town near the Jansom Thara Hotel.

AROUND RANONG

Along the coast at the southern end of Ranong Province is **Laem Son National Park**, a wildlife and forest preserve consisting of mangrove swamps, sandy beaches and uninhabited islands.

CHAIYA

Just north of Surat Thani and 640 km south of Bangkok, this is one of the oldest cities in Thailand and has intriguing remains from the Sumatran-based Srivijaya Empire. Indeed, one local scholar believes this was the real centre of the empire, not Palembang. The name is a Thai abbreviation of 'Siwichaiya', or Srivijaya. The restored **Borom That Chaiya** stupa is very similar in design to the *candis* (shrines) of central Java.

Outside of town, **Wat Suanmok** is a complete contrast, a modern centre established by Thailand's most famous Buddhist monk, the late Ajaan Phutthathat (Buddhadasa).

Places to Stay & Eat

There are guest quarters in *Wat Suanmok* for those participating in monthly 10-day meditation retreats, but most visitors make Chaiya a day trip from nearby Surat Thani. Too many travellers treat Suanmok and other forest wats as open zoos – visit it only if you are genuinely interested in Buddhism or meditation. Chaiya also has a nice old *Chinese hotel* just off the main road and close to the railway station. Rooms with a fan are 80B.

About 10 minutes from town, on the coast, there's a long pier with two *seafood restaurants.*

Getting There & Away

Chaiya is on the railway line only 20 km north of Surat Thani – you can get there by rail, bus or even taxi. Wat Suanmok is about seven km out of Chaiya. Buses run there directly from Surat Thani bus station so it isn't necessary to go right into Chaiya – you can get to the wat from the Chaiya railway station by motorbike for 15B.

SURAT THANI

This busy port is of interest for most travellers only as a jumping-off point for the island of Ko Samui, 30 km off the coast.

Places to Stay & Eat

A lot of Surat Thani's hotels are transient specialists, so you're quite likely to sleep better on the night ferry, without all the nocturnal disturbances as customers come and go. With the rail, bus and boat combination tickets, there's no reason to stay in Surat Thani at all.

There are quite a few places along Na Muang Rd, not far from Ban Don. The *Surat* (☎ 27 2243) is OK for 150 to 300B; better is the *Ban Don* (enter through the Chinese restaurant) which has rooms with fan and bath at 110 to 150B – it's one of the best bargains in Surat Thani. The *Lipa Guest House*, by the bus station, is a last resort if nothing else is available – rooms cost 100B.

In nearby Phun Phin, near the railway station, the *Tai Fah* and the *Sri Thani* hotels have rooms for around 100B.

The *market* near the bus station has good, cheap food or, in Ban Don, try the places on the waterfront.

Getting There & Away

Surat Thani is on the main railway and bus route from Bangkok to Hat Yai. By train the fare from Bangkok to Surat Thani is 125B in 3rd class and 244B in 2nd class. The Surat Thani train station is, however, 14 km out of town at Phun Phin. If you're heading south to Hat Yai, you may decide it is easier to take a bus rather than go to the station only to find there are no seats left.

From the Southern bus terminal in Bangkok, the trip to Surat Thani takes 11 hours and costs 158B or 285B for an air-con bus. Private tour buses cost from 222B. Departures are usually in the early morning or in the evening. From Surat Thani, buses run to Songkhla, Hat Yai and Phuket.

Getting Around

From the railway station to the pier for Ko Samui ferries, buses leave every five minutes and cost 7B. The buses that meet the night express are free, but if you arrive at a time when the buses aren't running, a taxi to Ban Don costs about 60 to 80B.

KO SAMUI

This beautiful island, off the east coast, is very much a travellers' centre well on its way to becoming a fully fledged tourist resort. An airport was finally completed here in 1987 and car ferries have been in operation for several years, so it's hardly as 'untouched' as it once was, but at least you can't drive there over a bridge (as you can to Phuket). For now, there's still accommodation at nearly every budget level.

Orientation

Ko Samui is the largest island on the east coast and the third largest in Thailand. It's about 25-km long, 21-km wide and is surrounded by 80 other islands, all except six of them uninhabited. The main town is Na Thon, and most of the population is concentrated there or at a handful of other towns scattered around the coast. Coconut plantations are still a primary source of income, and visitors go relatively unnoticed outside of the beach areas.

Information

The best time to visit Ko Samui is from February to late June. July to late October is very wet and from then until January it can be very windy. During the on season, from December to February and from July to August, accommodation can get a little tight.

There are several banks in Nathon, Chaweng and Lamai. Mail can be sent to poste restante at the GPO, Na Thon.

Things to See

The beaches are beautiful and, naturally, are the main attraction (the water is not as clear on the west coast of the island as the east). But Ko Samui also has a number of scenic waterfalls – particularly **Hin Lat**, three km east of Na Thon, and **Na Muang**, 10 km south-east of Na Thon in the centre of the island. Although Hin Lat is closer to Na Thon, Na Muang is the more scenic.

Near the village of Bang Kao, there's an interesting old chedi at **Wat Laem Saw** while the **Wat Phra Yai** (Big Buddha Temple), with its 12-metre-high Buddha image, is at the north-eastern end of the island, on a small rocky islet joined to the main island by a causeway. The monks are pleased to have visitors but proper attire (no shorts) should be worn on the temple premises.

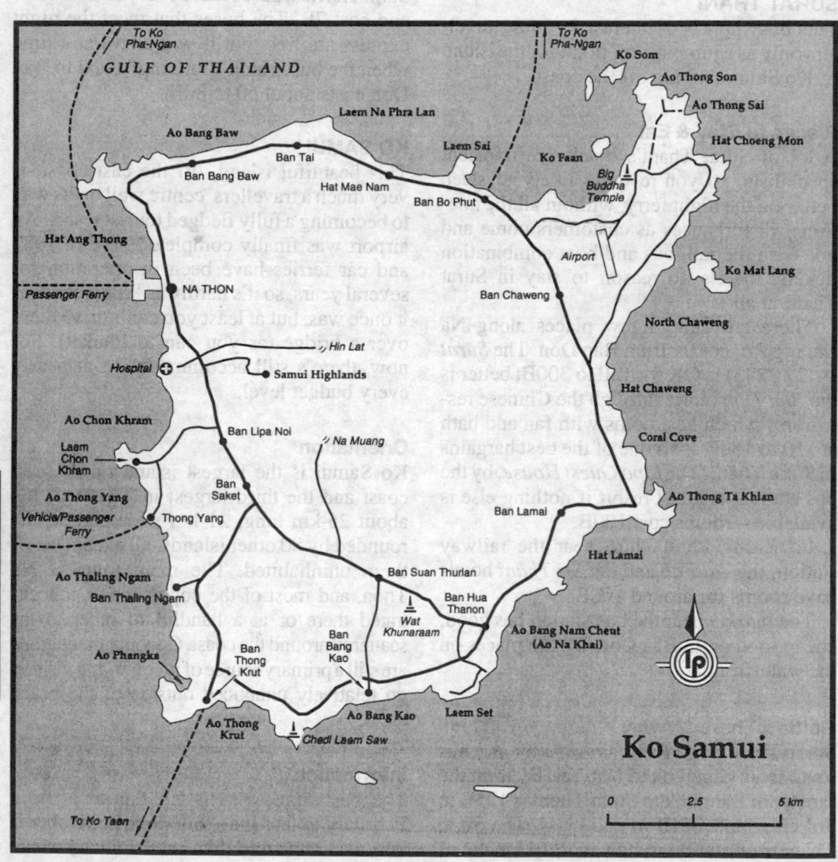

Places to Stay & Eat

There are literally hundreds of places to stay at the beaches, ranging in cost from 50B a night to 1000B and over. Hat Chaweng and Hat Lamai are the two most popular and both have beautiful sands and clear, sparkling water. Lamai has a great coral reef, while Chaweng is the largest beach with probably the best water and a small island opposite. Both are now dotted with discos/night clubs, so are not especially quiet during the high season.

Bo Phut and Big Buddha beaches are on the bay which encloses Ko Faan and the Big Buddha island, and these are rather quieter. Thong Yang is also very quiet, as are the little coves and tidal flats along the south shore. You can get further away from it all on the neighbouring islands of Ko Pha-Ngan and Ko Tao.

Na Thon If you want to stay in the town, there are a number of hotels to choose from. The *Palace Hotel* on the waterfront has clean, spacious rooms starting at 280B with fan or 400B with air-con. Less expensive is the *Seaview Guest House* on Wattana Rd, which has Khao San-style rooms with fan and bath for 150 to 200B.

Several restaurants face Na Thon's harbour and offer a combination of Western food and Thai seafood. One of the oldest and best is the *Chao Koh*. On the next street back from the waterfront are a couple of American-style *delis*, two or three *bakeries*, a *pizza joint*, a good *curry shop*, and a Hokkien *coffee shop* that has somehow managed to hold out in the tourist onslaught.

Chaweng There are over 80 bungalow 'villages' strung along here, the island's longest beach, and they are constantly upgrading themselves to drive room rates higher. The cheaper ones are all much the same and cost from 80B a night for a small bungalow – knock it down a bit for a longer stay or during the off season when some will go as low as 50B. In North Chaweng, you'll find *Matlang Resort, Blue Lagoon, Samui Island Resort, Marine, Moon, Family* and *K John Resort*.

Towards the centre of the beach, prices rise a bit. For example: *Lucky Mother* with rooms from 100 to 250B; *Coconut Grove* from 200 to 300B; and *Chaweng Garden* from 400 to 800B. At the south end of the beach around a headland is Chaweng Noi, where the more expensive resorts like the *Imperial*, with rooms from 2500B, and the *Tropicana*, with rooms from 800 to 1200B, are taking hold. Surviving backpacker standbys include the *Sunshine*, *Maew* and *Chaweng Noi*, all with bungalows from 100 to 140B.

Lamai Samui's second most popular beach is finally succumbing to bigger tourist developments and is feeling the price squeeze, although overall it's still less expensive than Chaweng. Cheaper huts at the north-east end of the beach are at *Comfort, No Name, Suan Thong Kaid, Royal Blue Lagoon Beach Resort* and, back from the beach, *My Friend* – all with huts at around 60 to 150B. More expensive and newer places include the *Island Resort*, *Rose Garden* and *Spanish Eyes*, in the 250 to 400B range.

Lamai's central section begins with a string of 100 to 600B places: *Mui*, *Magic*, *Coconut Villa* and the *Weekender*. The Weekender has a wide variety of bungalows and activities to choose from, including a bit of nightlife. The *Coconut Beach* is a find at the bay's centre – it still only charges from 80 to 200B. The *Lamai Inn* costs 300 to 800B.

Next comes *Marina Villa*, *Sawatdi*, *Mira Mare*, *Sea Breeze* and *Aloha*, 100 to 600B places with elaborate outdoor dining areas. At the southern end of central Lamai Beach is a mixture of 50 to 200B places, including the long-standing *White Sand*, *Palm*, *Nice Resort* and *Sun Rise*. The Sun Rise is upmarket with acceptable 100 to 200B huts.

Beyond a headland, between Hat Lamai and Bang Nam Cheut, are some of Ko Samui's cheapest digs, including *No 1*, *Swiss Chalets*, *Noi*, *Pine Beach* and *Rocky*, all with huts from 80 to 300B.

Big Buddha *Family Village* gets good reviews and costs from 200 to 700B. *Big Buddha Bungalows*, from 250 to 700B, is still OK. *Ocean View Resort* costs 200 to 1000B for simple huts. *Sunset* costs 70 to 120B and is also good. The rest are in the 100 to 200B range.

Bo Phut There are about 23 places to stay here, in spite of which the area manages to stay fairly quiet. At the north end, *Bo Phut Guesthouse*, *Sandy Resort*, *World Resort*, *Samui Palm Beach*, *Palm Garden*, *Calm Beach Resort* and *Peace* have bungalows in the 80 to 300B range.

Toward the village is *Boon Bungalows*, a small operation with 50B huts – the restaurant at this place is good. West of Boon's is *Ziggy Stardust*, a clean place with huts from 500 to 1500B. Cheaper in this area are *Smile House*, *Miami* and *Oasis*, all with huts in the 50 to 200B range.

The village has a couple of cheap local-style restaurants as well as a couple of farang places.

Others At Hat Mae Nam, 14 km north-east of Na Thon, the *Friendly*, *New La Paz Villa*, *Silent* and *Shady Shack Bungalows* are all economical beach places with huts in the 60 to 200B range. While the scene at Mae Nam is not quite as picturesque as at Chaweng or Lamai, the swimming and sand are quite OK.

Along the southern end of the island you'll find bungalows tucked away into smaller bays and coves. If the development along Chaweng and Lamai is too much for you, this area might be just the ticket – all you need is a motorbike and a Ko Samui map. As at Lamai, the places along the southern end are pretty rocky which means good snorkelling but not so good swimming.

Try Ao Na Khai and Laem Set, areas just beyond the village of Hua Thanon, for the best southern beaches. Other possibilities include Ao Thong Krut and Ao Bang Kao. Bungalows here start at 60 to 400B with bath.

At Ao Thong Yang and other seaside areas along Samui's west coast, bungalows are springing up everywhere as the car ferry from Don Sak docks on this side. None of them are anything special nor are they cheap, and the beaches tend to become mud flats during low tide.

Getting There & Away

You can fly directly to Ko Samui from Bangkok with Bangkok Airways, or there are three ferry companies. Altogether there are four ferry piers on the Surat coast (Ban Don, Tha Thong, Khanom and Don Sak – only three are in use at one time) and two piers on Ko Samui (Na Thon and Thong Yang). This can make things a bit confusing at times but if you just follow the flow of travellers everything will work out.

The State Railway of Thailand does rail, bus and ferry tickets straight through to Ko Samui from Bangkok or the reverse (eg 449B for a 2nd-class, lower berth). You end up paying about 50B more this way than if you book all the segments yourself.

Be cautious when using local agents to make mainland train and bus bookings – these don't always get made, or are not for the class you paid for. Several travellers have written to complain of rip-offs here.

Express Boats from Tha Thong From November to May, three daily express boats leave for Samui's Na Thon Pier from Tha Thong in Surat and take two to 2½ hours to reach the island. Departure times are usually 7.15 am, 11.30 am and 2.45 pm – these are subject to change according to weather conditions. From June to October, there are only two express boats a day at 7.15 am and 12.45 pm – the seas are usually too high in the late afternoon for a third sailing in this direction. Passage is 105B one way and 170B return.

From Na Thon back to Surat, there are departures at 7.15 am, noon and 2.30 pm from November to May, or at 7.30 am and 2.30 pm from June to October. The morning boat includes a bus ride to the train station in Phun Phin. The afternoon boats include a bus ride to the train station and to the Talaat Kaset bus station in Ban Don.

Night Ferry There is also a slow boat for Ko Samui that leaves the Ban Don Pier each night at 11 pm, reaching Na Thon around 5 am. This one costs 70B for the upper deck (with pillows and mattresses) and 50B down below (straw mats only). The night ferry back to the mainland leaves Na Thon at 9 pm and arrives at 3 am.

Jet Boat from Tha Thon The new jet boat on the Island Jet service takes 1½ hours from Tha Thong to Na Thon and costs 130B each way. Island Jet or Phanthip Travel can book the jet boat in Surat and in Na Thon. Considering the fare, it is worth paying the 25B more and saving one hour of travel time over the express boat. It departs for Samui from Surat Thani at 8 am and continues to Pha-Ngan at 10.20 am. On the return journey it departs to Samui at 12.30 pm and from there to Surat Thani at 2 pm.

Vehicle Ferry From Talaat Mai Rd in Surat Thani, you can get bus and ferry combination tickets straight through to Na Thon. These cost 70B or 90B for an air-con bus. Pedestrians, cars and motorbikes can also take the ferry directly from Don Sak. It leaves at 6.50 am, 8 am, 10 am and 2 pm and takes one hour to reach the Thong Yang Pier on Ko Samui. The fares are: pedestrians 40B, motorbikes and driver 70B, and a car and driver 180B.

Don Sak, in Surat Thani Province, is about 60 km from Surat Thani. A bus from the Surat bus station is 14B and takes 45 minutes to an hour to arrive at the Don Sak ferry. If you're coming north from Nakhon Si Thammarat, this might be the ferry to take, although from Surat, the Tha Thong ferry is definitely more convenient.

Tour buses run directly from Bangkok to Ko Samui, via the car ferry from Don Sak, for around 327B. From Ko Samui, air-con buses to Bangkok leave from near the pier in Na Thon twice daily, arriving in Bangkok in the early morning (there's a dinner stop in Surat the evening before). Or, for 50B, you can take a minibus from the ferry which gets you to the Surat Thani train station in time to catch the 6.30 pm express to Bangkok (you'd better book the train ticket in advance). Through buses are also available from Ko Samui to Hat Yai and other points south. Check with the travel agencies in Na Thon for the latest routes.

Getting Around

It's about 19 km from Na Thon to Bo Phut on the north coast, and 23 km to Chaweng in the east. Minibuses and songthaews operate all day. Official fares from Na Thon are 20B to Lamai, Mae Nam, Bo Phut or Big Buddha, and 25B to Chaweng.

Often you'll be met in Na Thon (even on the ferry at Ban Don) and offered free transport if you stay at the place doing the offering.

You can rent motorbikes on Ko Samui – these are better value at Na Thon than at the beaches. Smaller 100cc bikes cost 150B a day and larger ones are 200B – ask for discounts for multiday rentals.

KO PHA-NGAN

North of Ko Samui is the island of Ko Pha-Ngan, which is nearly as big as Ko Samui but generally more quiet and tranquil. It also has beautiful beaches, some fine snorkelling and the **Than Sadet Falls**.

The Songserm ferry boats from Surat and Ko Samui (Na Thon) dock at Thong Sala on Pha-Ngan's west coast, although there are also smaller boats from Mae Nam and Bo Phut on Ko Samui to Hat Rin on the island's southern end. Travellers are already searching for even more isolated islands beyond Ko Pha-Ngan.

Places to Stay

Near Thong Sala The beaches here are not among the island's best, but since they're close to Thong Sala, people waiting for an early boat back to Surat Thani or on to Ko Tao sometimes stay here. On Ao Bang Charu, the *Phangan Villa, Moonlight, Sun Dance* and *Chokkhana Beach* are all in the 60 to 300B range. Further south-east of here, towards Ban Tai, are a few other places from 40 to 60B, including the *Laem Tanote Resort* and *P Park*.

Just north of Thong Sala are the *Chan* and *Tranquil Resort* at 60B and up. *Siripun* and *Phangan* also have huts with baths from 80B. Further north of Thong Sala, at the southern end of Ao Wok Tum, are the basic *Tuk, Kiat, OK* and *Darin* from 40 to 80B. A little further down around the cape of Hin are *Porn Sawan, Cookies* and *Beach*, with the same rates and facilities.

Ban Tai to Ban Khai Between the villages of Ban Tai and Ban Khai is a series of sandy beaches with well-spaced collections of bungalows, all in the 40 to 100B range. They include *Pink, Wave House, Jup, Copa, Green Peace, Sun Sea, Thong Yang, Booms Cafe* and *Silvery Moon*.

Laem Hat Rin This long cape has beaches along both its westward and eastward sides. They're getting very crowded these days, especially on the eastward side (which has the best beach) – the all-night 'full moon' parties here are legendary and have recently begun attracting the attention of the local police. Here you'll find *Seaview, Tommy,*

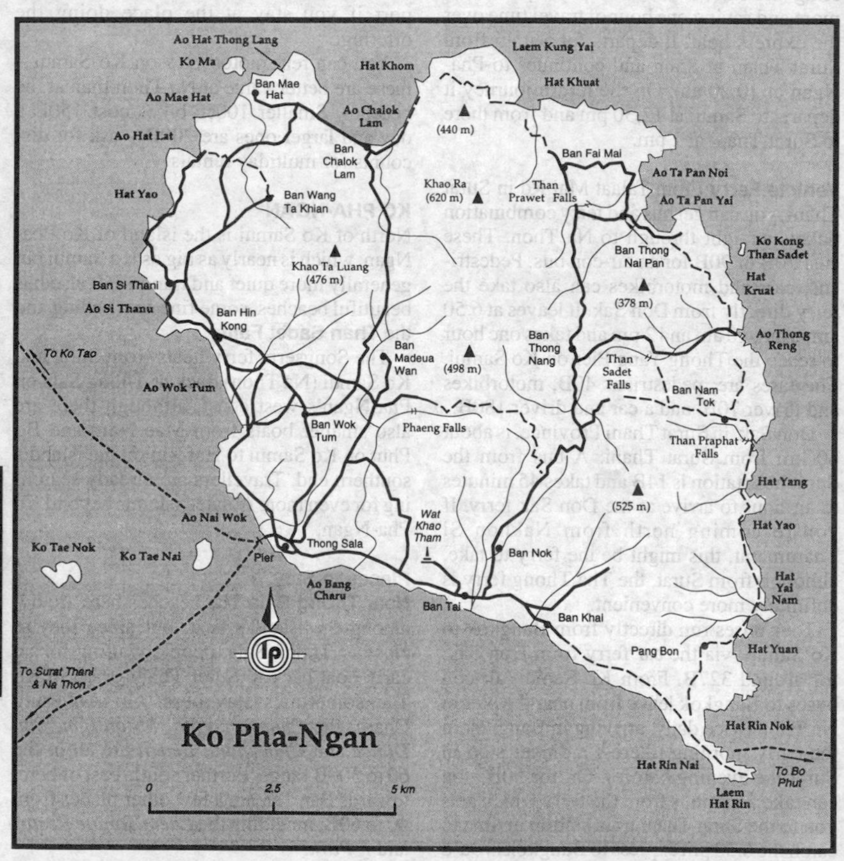

Sunrise, Hat Rin, Paradise, Palita Lodge and others in the 40 to 80B range, plus a few with bath from 100 to 150B, like the *Serenity* and *Pearl Resort*.

Along the western side are the long-runners *Palm Beach* and *Sunset*, both of which cost from 50 to 200B. Newer places that offer similarly priced accommodation are *Rainbow, Coral, Bang Son Villa, Sun Beach, Sea Side, Sook Som, Neptune's, Dolphin, Charung's, Family House* and, down near the tip of the cape, the *Lighthouse*. The *Rin Beach Resort* has a few larger huts with baths for 300B.

Ao Chalok Lam & Hat Khuat These two pretty bays on the northern end of Pha-Ngan are still largely undeveloped. Huts at the *Bottle Beach* are 60 to 250B, and 70 to 150B at the *Rock Beach*. West of Hat Khuat, 2½ km across Laem Kung Yai, is Hat Khom, where the *Coral Bay* charges 40 to 50B. The long Chalok Lam beach has *Thai Life, Try Tong* and *Fanta* at 40 to 200B.

Ao Si Thanu The *Laem Son* starts at 40B while the *Sea Flower, Seetanu* and *Great Bay* all have bungalows with baths from 60 to 150B.

Other On the beach at Ao Ta Pan Yai, near Ban Thong Nai Pan on the island's north-east coast, are the *White Sand* and *Nice Beach* for 60 to 300B. Up on Thong Ta Pan Noi are the very nicely situated and well-maintained *Panviman Resort* (300B up) and *Thong Ta Pan Resort* (80 to 150B).

Near Ban Mae Hat, on the north-west part of the island, are the *Mae Hat Bay Resort* and *Island View Cabana*. Both cost 40B for basic huts or up to 150B with bath. The beach here is rather coarse, however, like much of the west coast.

Getting There & Away

There are regular ferries from Na Thon, on Ko Samui, to Thong Sala for 60B and occasional boats from Bo Phut to Hat Rin for 50B. This latter boat trip requires wading in from the boat to the beach in hip-deep water. The crossing takes about 45 minutes.

The night ferry from Ban Don in Surat stops in Thong Sala – the fare is 80B on the upper deck and 70B on the lower deck for the six-hour trip.

From January to September, there is one boat a day between Mae Nam Beach on Ko Samui and Thong Nai Pan Bay on Pha-Ngan – the fare is 60B.

There is an express boat (once daily) from Surat Thani to Ko Pha-Ngan. The boat is operated by the Ferry Pha-Ngan Co (☎ 28 6461) which is located at 2-6 Chon Kasem Rd (near the Ban Don Pier) in Surat Thani; the fare is 105B each way. There is also a jet boat leaving Ko Samui at 10 am, taking half an hour and costing 60B.

KO TAO

Ko Tao, or Turtle Island, is only 21 sq km in area and lies 44 km north of Ko Pha-Ngan. Like Ko Pha-Ngan, the island is mostly mountainous with only a few dirt tracks here and there for roads.

Places to Stay

Simple hut accommodation on the island is 50 to 100B (avoid the huts on adjacent Ko Thian – the management evicts travellers who don't order enough food at the restaurant), while bungalows cost 150 to 600B. On Ao Mae beach, *Dam* has nice grassmat huts for 100B. There's also *Queen Resort* (100 to 200B) and *Tommy Resort* (80 to 500B). On Hat Sai Ri, the *Sai Ri Cottage, New-Way, Haad Sai Ree Villa* and *O-Chai* are all in the 80 to 250B price range.

During the peak season in 1994, it was difficult to find accommodation anywhere on the island. People were sleeping on the beaches or in restaurants for one or two nights until a hut became available. On arrival at Ban Mae it is best to find a tout as they will take you to the only places with any free huts, otherwise your chances of finding a place on your own are very slim. In the off season touts will take you to the open places, since not all open all year.

Getting There & Away

Depending on the weather, boats make the three-hour trip from Ko Pha-Ngan to Ko Tao daily. There are also boats daily from Chumphon's Tha Saphan Tha Yang (on the mainland). The trip takes five to seven hours, depending on the boat, and costs 200B. All boats dock at Ban Mae Hat on the island's west side.

There is also a new daily fast boat to Ko Tao from Chumphon, leaving at 8 am and arriving at 10.30 am for 400B per person.

NAKHON SI THAMMARAT

Situated 814 km south of Bangkok, Nakhon Si Thammarat has the oldest wat in the south, **Wat Phra Mahathat**. Reputed to be over 1000 years old and rebuilt in the mid-13th century, its 78-metre-high chedi is topped by a solid-gold spire. The town also has an interesting **National Museum** with a good 'Art of Southern Thailand' exhibit.

Nakhon Si Thammarat is also noted for its nielloware (a silver and black alloy-enamel jewellery technique) and for the making of leather shadow puppets and dance masks. The town is also supposed to produce the 'best' gangsters in Thailand!

Places to Stay

Most hotels are near the train and bus stations. On Yomarat Rd, across from the railway station, is the *Si Thong* with adequate rooms for 120B with fan and bath. Alternatively, try the *Nakhon* at 1477/5 Yomarat Rd or the *Yaowarat*, both similarly priced.

On Jamroenwithi Rd (walk straight down Neramit Rd opposite the station for two blocks and turn right), the *Siam* at No 1407/17 is a large hotel with rooms from 120 to 160B with fan and bath. Across the street is the *Muang Thong* at No 1459/7 with rooms from 100B. Near the Siam, on the same side of the street, is the *Thai Fa* which is good value as the rooms are equally good and 30B cheaper.

Places to Eat

Two very good and inexpensive Chinese restaurants, located between the Neramit and Thai Fa hotels on Jamroenwithi Rd, are the *Bo Seng* and the *Yong Seng* – neither have English signs. Among a cluster of restaurants near the intersection of Jamroenwithi and Watkhit Rd is *Ruam Rot*, which serves very good curries and khanõm jiin (curry noodles served with a huge tray of vegies).

Getting There & Away

From the Southern bus terminal in Bangkok, it takes 12 hours to Nakhon Si Thammarat and the fare is around 190B or 342B by air-con bus. Daily buses from Surat Thani cost about 70B. You can also get buses to or from Songkhla or Hat Yai.

By train, you usually have to get off at Khao Chum Thong, about 30 km to the west, since Nakhon Si Thammarat is not on the main southern trunk line. From there, you can continue by bus or taxi. The daily Nos 47 (rapid) and 15 (express) trains, however, make the trip all the way to Nakhon Si Thammarat via a small branch line. Either way, the fare is 133B in 3rd class and 279B in 2nd class.

PHATTALUNG

The major rice-growing centre in the south, Phattalung is also noted for its shadow puppets. The town has a couple of interesting wats, and **Lam Pang** is a pleasant spot for eating and relaxing beside the inland sea, on which Phattalung is situated. The **Thale Noi Waterbird Sanctuary** is 32 km north-east of Phattalung, and the cave **Tham Malai** is just outside the town.

Places to Stay

Most of Phattalung's hotels are along Ramet Rd, the main drag. The *Phattalung 2* at 34/1 Ramet Rd is not too bad for 100 to 180B. The *Thai Sakon* (the English sign reads 'Universal Hotel') is a little west and has adequate rooms at 80B. Across from the Grant cinema on the corner of Charoentham Rd, the *King Fah* is similar to the Universal. The *Thai Hotel* on Disara-nakarin Rd is the best place in town at 150B per double, more for air-con.

Places to Eat
The market off Poh-Saat Rd is a good place for cheap takeaway food. Other good eating places are along Pracha Bamrung Rd, just past the Thai Hotel.

Getting There & Away
Buses from Phattalung to Nakhon Si Thammarat or Hat Yai take 2 hours and costs around 30B.

SONGKHLA
This unexciting but quiet beach resort is about 30 km from Hat Yai – plenty of buses and share taxis operate between the two towns. Songkhla is on a peninsula between Thale Sap Songkhla (the inland sea) and the South China Sea.

Things to See
Offshore are two islands known as 'cat' and 'mouse'. Although the beach is not very interesting, Songkhla has an active waterfront with brightly painted fishing boats, an interesting **National Museum** (admission 10B), an **old chedi** at the top of Khao Tan Kuan hill and **Wat Matchimawat** with its frescoes, old marble Buddha image and small museum. The National Museum, open from 9 am to noon and 1 to 4 pm Wednesday to Sunday, has a collection of Burmese Buddhas and various Srivijaya artefacts. The building is an old Thai-Chinese palace.

Places to Stay
The popular and clean *Amsterdam* at 15/3 Rong Muang Rd has nice rooms with shared bath and toilet for 150 and 180B. It's run by a friendly Dutch woman. The *Suk Somboon II* (there's also a Suk Somboon I with similar prices) is fairly popular with travellers, although it's not that special. It's at 18 Saiburi Rd, a block from the clocktower and close to the museum. A double room is 140B but bargain as they're just wooden rooms, off a large central area.

On Vichianchom Rd is the *Songkhla Hotel*, across from the fishing station. Rooms cost 120B or from 160B with bath. At the foot of Khao Tan Kuan (the hill overlooking town), the *Narai Hotel* (☎ 31 1078), 12/2 Chai Khao Rd, is a long walk from the bus station (take a trishaw). It's a pleasant and friendly place and rooms start at 100/150B with shared bath.

Places to Eat
As you might expect, Songkhla has a reputation for seafood and there are a string of beach-front seafood specialists. None of them are particularly cheap and eating here is mainly a lunchtime activity. Try curried crab claws or fried squid.

At night, the food scene shifts to Vichianchom Rd in front of the *market* where there is a line of food and fruit stalls. *Raan Ahaan Tae*, on Tang Ngam Rd (south off Songkhlaburi Rd and parallel to Saiburi Rd), has the best seafood around, according to the locals.

Khao Noi Phochana, on Vichianchom Rd near the Songkhla Hotel, has a good lunchtime selection of Thai and Chinese rice dishes. Along Nang Ngam Rd in the Chinese section are several cheap Chinese noodle and congee shops.

Getting There & Away
Buses from Surat Thani to Songkhla cost 155B. Air-con buses from Bangkok take 19 hours and cost 425B. Regular buses are 224B but add a few baht to get to Hat Yai. By train, you have to go to Hat Yai first. There are buses and share taxis from Hat Yai to Songkhla – 15B by bus and 12B by taxi.

Although the usual route north from Songkhla is to backtrack to Hat Yai and then take the road to Phattalung and Trang, you can also take an interesting backroad route. There's a bus trip to Ranot, 63 km north at the end of the Thale Sap lagoon, and further buses connect to Hua Sai (32 km) and then Nakhon Si Thammarat (56 km).

Getting Around
Motorcycle taxis around Songkhla cost 5 to 10B and songthaews are 5 to 7B for anywhere on their routes.

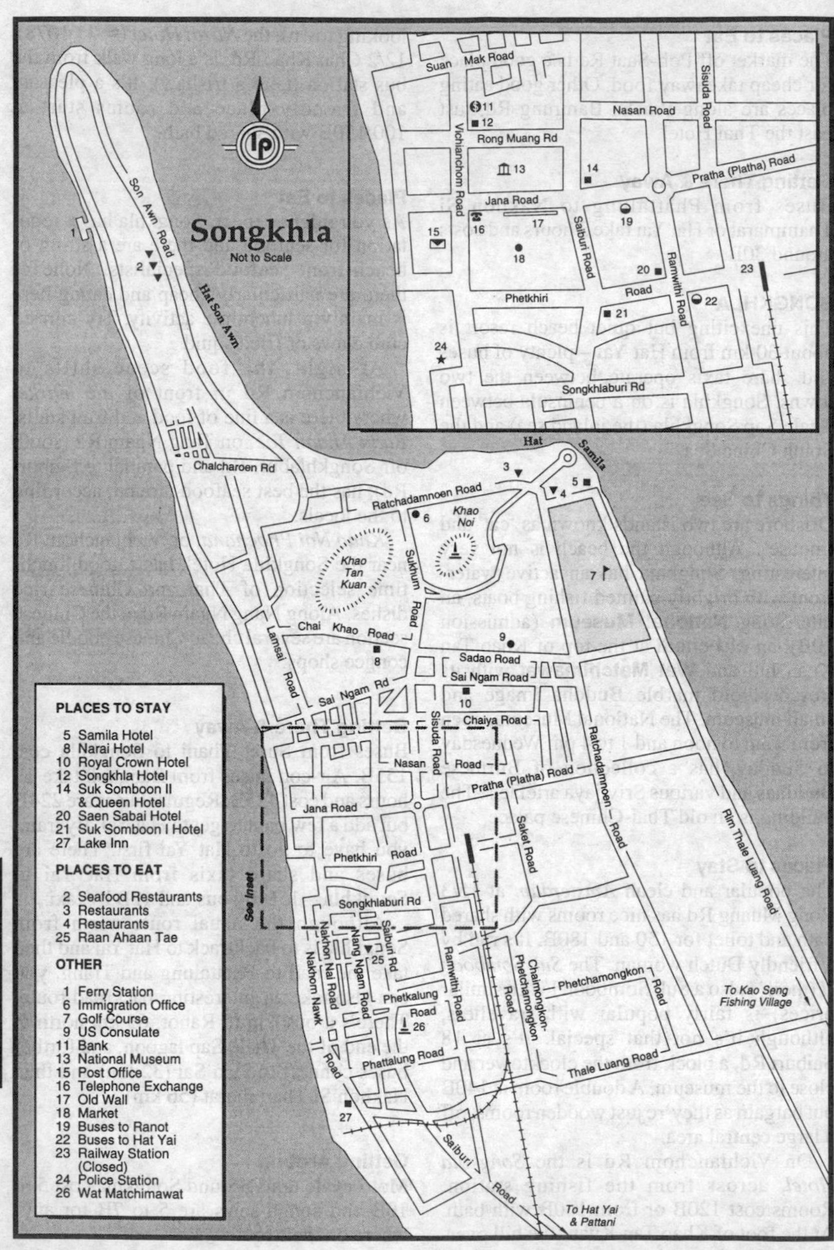
Songkhla
Not to Scale
Son Awn Road
Hat Son Awn
Chalcharoen Rd
Ratchadamnoen Road
Khao Noi
Khao Tan Kuan
Sukhum Road
Chai Khao Road
Lamsai Road
Sai Ngam Rd
Sadao Road
Sai Ngam Road
Chaiya Road
Sisuda Road
Nasan Road
Pratha (Platha) Road
Jana Road
Phetkhiri Road
Songkhlaburi Rd
Saket Road
Ratchadamnoen Road
Rim Thale Luang Road
Nakhon Nai Road
Nang Ngam Road
Saiburi Rd
Nakhom Nawk Road
Ramwithi Road
Phetkalung Road
Phattalung Road
Chaimongkon-Phetchamongkon Road
Phetchamongkon Road
Thale Luang Road
Saiburi Road
To Kao Seng Fishing Village
To Hat Yai & Pattani
Hat Samila
See Inset
Suan Mak Road
Nasan Road
Sisuda Road
Vichianchom Road
Rong Muang Rd
Pratha (Platha) Road
Jana Road
Saiburi Road
Ramwithi Road
Road
Phetkhiri
Songkhlaburi Rd
PLACES TO STAY
5 Samila Hotel
8 Narai Hotel
10 Royal Crown Hotel
12 Songkhla Hotel
14 Suk Somboon II & Queen Hotel
20 Saen Sabai Hotel
21 Suk Somboon I Hotel
27 Lake Inn
PLACES TO EAT
2 Seafood Restaurants
3 Restaurants
4 Restaurants
25 Raan Ahaan Tae
OTHER
1 Ferry Station
6 Immigration Office
7 Golf Course
9 US Consulate
11 Bank
13 National Museum
15 Post Office
16 Telephone Exchange
17 Old Wall
18 Market
19 Buses to Ranot
22 Buses to Hat Yai
23 Railway Station (Closed)
24 Police Station
26 Wat Matchimawat

THAILAND

AROUND SONGKHLA

On **Ko Yaw**, an island on the inland sea, you can see local cotton weaving and a **Folklore Museum** that emphasises Southern Thai culture. Buses to the island from either Songkhla or Hat Yai cost 8B.

The **Khu Khut Waterbird Park** is on the eastern shore of Thale Sap Songkhla near Sathing Phra, about 50 km north of Songkhla town. This 520-sq-km sanctuary is a habitat for about 140 species of waterbirds.

HAT YAI

A busy crossroads town, Hat Yai is 1298 km south of Bangkok where the east and west coast roads and the railway line all meet. Apart from being the commercial centre of the south, Hat Yai is also a popular 'sin centre' for Malaysians who pop across the border on weekends to partake of Thailand's freewheeling delights.

Orientation & Information

The three main streets – Niphat Uthit 1, 2 and 3 – all run parallel to the railway line. The TAT office is at 1/1 Soi 2 Niphat Uthit 3 Rd. Four of Hat Yai's cinemas have English-language sound rooms. Hat Yai is often spelt Haadyai.

Things to See

A few km out of town, towards the airport and just off Phetkasem Rd, **Wat Hat Yai Nai** has a large reclining Buddha image – get a samlor heading in that direction and hop off after the U Thapao Bridge. On the first and second Saturday of each month, bullfights (bull versus bull) are held at Hat Yai. It's always a heavy betting game for the Thai spectators.

The **Southern Cultural Village Show & Mini Zoo** (what a name) puts on an afternoon show several days a week for about 150B. It includes music, dances, ceremonies, sword and long-pole fighting and other entertainment. To get there, take a tuk-tuk down Phetkasem Rd towards Songkhla.

Places to Stay

There are a lot of places to stay in Hat Yai but most of them are there to cater for the Malaysian dirty-weekend trade – it's not a traveller's dream town. You can look for places in two categories – the remaining traditional places and the cheaper modern hotels. The old-style Thai hotels with their wood-partitioned rooms are gradually being torn down as Hat Yai develops.

Currently very popular with travellers is the *Cathay Guest House*, on the corner of Niphat Uthit 2 and Thamnoonvithi Rds. Rooms here start at 120B and there is also a 60B dorm. The management is quite helpful with information on local travel and travel to Malaysia or further north in Thailand.

The *Savoy* is 3½ blocks from the station on Niphat Uthit 2 Rd. It has adequate 120B rooms, although most rooms are 150B or more. The *Thai Hotel* on Rat Uthit Rd has rooms with fan for 130B, and cheaper rooms on the top floor for 100B.

The *King's Hotel* on Niphat Uthit 1 Rd is one of the older of the 'new' hotels in Hat Yai. Rooms start at 220B and are often full on weekends as it is a Malay favourite. Cheaper hotels include the Chinese *Tong Nam*, on Niphat Uthit 3 Rd (from 100B), and the newly upgraded *Rung Fah*, near the King's Hotel, which costs 170 to 200B with fan, 250 to 300B with air-con.

Places to Eat

Hat Yai has plenty of places to eat, including a lot of restaurants with appetising dishes and places selling cakes, confectionery, fruit and ice cream. Across from the King's Hotel, the popular *Muslim Ocha* is a particular hit with visiting Malaysians.

Jeng Nguan is a good, inexpensive Chinese restaurant at the end of Niphat Uthit 1 Rd (turn right from the station). The extensive *night market* along Montri 1 Rd, across from the Songkhla bus station, specialises in fresh seafood.

Getting There & Away

See the Thailand Getting There & Away section earlier in this chapter for details of travel between Hat Yai and Malaysia.

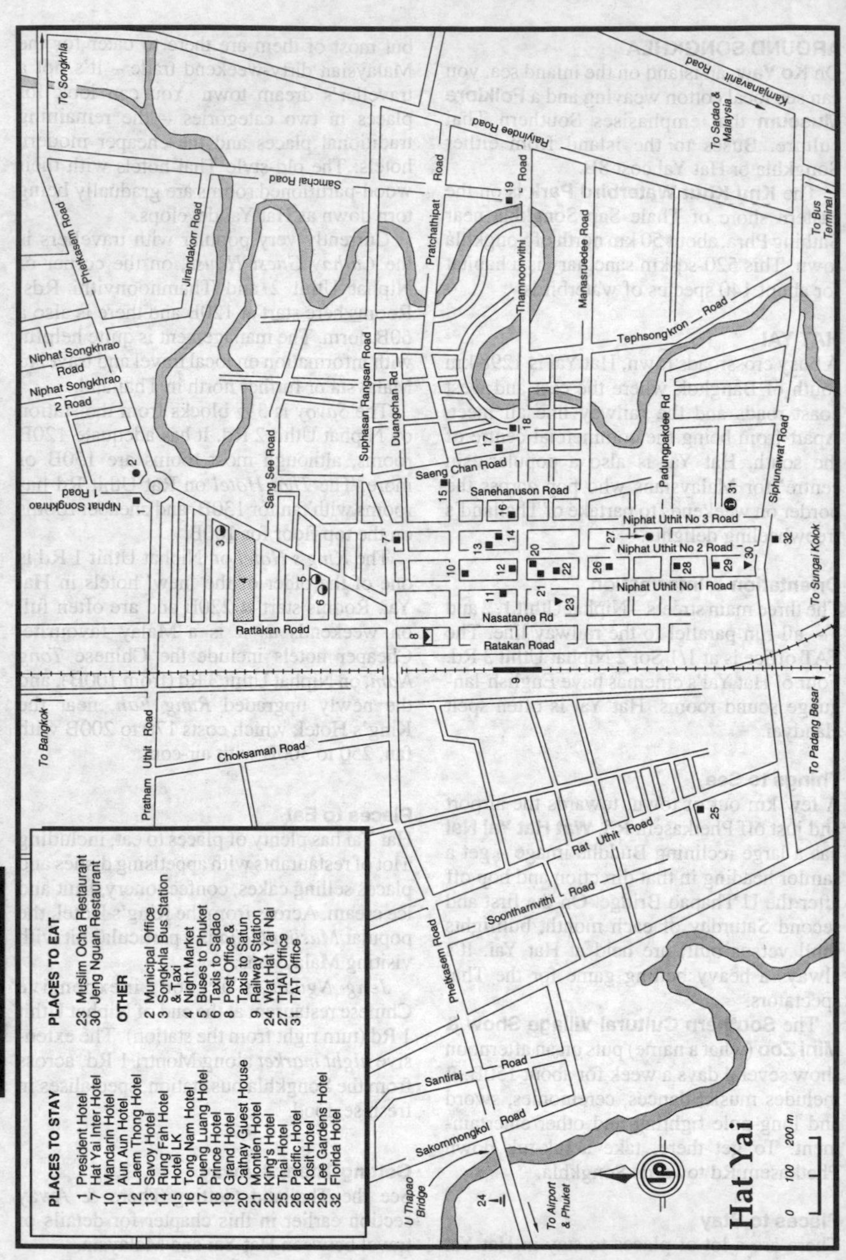

Hat Yai
0 100 200 m
PLACES TO STAY
1 President Hotel
7 Hat Yai Inter Hotel
10 Mandarin Hotel
11 Aun Aun Hotel
12 Laem Thong Hotel
13 Savoy Hotel
14 Rung Fah Hotel
15 Hotel LK
16 Tong Nam Hotel
17 Pueng Luang Hotel
18 Prince Hotel
19 Grand Hotel
20 Cathay Guest House
21 Montien Hotel
22 King's Hotel
25 Thai Hotel
26 Pacific Hotel
28 Kosit Hotel
29 Lee Gardens Hotel
32 Florida Hotel
PLACES TO EAT
23 Muslim Ocha Restaurant
30 Jeng Nguan Restaurant
OTHER
2 Municipal Office
3 Songkhla Bus Station & Taxi
4 Night Market
5 Buses to Phuket
6 Taxis to Sadao
8 Post Office & Taxis to Satun
9 Railway Station
24 Wat Hat Yai Nai
27 THAI Office
31 TAT Office
To Songkhla
Phetkasem Road
Jirandakorn Road
Samchai Road
Pratchathipat Road
Rajyindee Road
Kanjanavanit Road
To Sadao & Malaysia
Thamnoonvithi Road
Manasruedee Road
To Bus Terminal
Tephsongkron Road
Niphat Songkhrao Road
Niphat Songkhrao 2 Road
Niphat Songkhrao 1 Road
Suphasan Rangsan Road
Duangchan Rd
Saeng Chan Road
Sang See Road
Sanehanuson Road
Padungpakdee Rd
Siphunawat Road
Niphat Uthit No 3 Road
Niphat Uthit No 2 Road
Niphat Uthit No 1 Road
To Sungai Kolok
Nasatanee Rd
Ratakan Road
Rattakan Road
To Bangkok
Pratham Uthit Road
Choksaman Road
To Padang Besar
Rat Uthit Road
Soonthamvithi Road
Phetkasem Road
Santiraj Road
Sakornmongkol Road
U Thapao Bridge
To Airport & Phuket

Air There are at least two flights daily from Bangkok, and Hat Yai is also connected by air with Phuket and Penang.

Bus Buses from Bangkok cost 227B, or 428B with air-con. There are many agencies for buses to Bangkok and for taxis to Penang along Niphat Uthit 2 Rd towards the Thai Airways and MAS offices, or around the railway station. The travel agency below the Cathay Guest House also books tour buses and is reliable. Buses to Phuket are 220B with air-con. It's 20B for a bus to Padang Besar on the Malaysian border.

Train Straightforward fares from Bangkok (without rapid or express supplements) are 149B in 3rd class and 313B in 2nd class. There is no 3rd class on the daily International Express to Bangkok.

Getting Around

To/From the Airport The THAI van costs 40B per person for transport to the city; count on about 150B for a private taxi or about 50 or 60B for a songthaew.

Local Transport Songthaews cost 5B anywhere around town. The bus station for most departures is on Phetkasem Rd, a couple of hundred metres north of Thamnoonvithi Rd, which is the main road from the railway station.

AROUND HAT YAI

The **Ton Nga Chang Waterfall**, 24 km west of the city, features seven-tiered cascades in the shape of a pair of elephant tusks. October to December is the best time to visit.

SATUN

There's little of interest in this province in the south-west corner of Thailand but from here you can take boats to Kuala Perlis in Malaysia or visit the islands offshore.

Places to Stay

In Satun, the *Rian Thong Hotel* ('Rain Tong' on the English sign) is near the Rian Thong Pier and has large rooms for 100B. The more modern *Satun Thani* in the town centre is 150B but it's noisy. The *Udomsuk* (☎ 71 1006) near the municipal offices on Hatthakam Seuksa Rd is better value at 100B.

Places to Eat

Near the gold-domed Bambang Mosque in the centre of town are several cheap Muslim food shops. For Chinese food, wander about the little Chinese district near the Rian Thong Hotel.

Getting There & Away

Share taxis between Hat Yai and Satun cost 35B, while buses cost 27B. It's about RM5, say 30B, for a boat to Kuala Perlis in Malaysia.

KO TARUTAO NATIONAL PARK

Pak Bara, 60 km north of Satun, is the usual jumping-off point for Ko Tarutao National Park. This is the area's big attraction, just north of Malaysia's Langkawi. Nowadays, it's also possible to get boats direct from Satun.

Places to Stay

Park accommodation on Ko Tarutao is in several locations and costs 400B for a large 'deluxe' two-room bungalow, or 600B for one of the eight cottages that sleep up to eight people. A longhouse has ten-bed rooms for 280B each and sleeps four. All rooms and bungalows must be paid for in full even if only one person rents it. You may pitch your own tent for 5B per person. Camping is also permitted at Ao San and Ao Jak.

Getting There & Away

From Satun to Pak Bara, you first take a bus (11B) or share taxi (22B) to La-ngu and then a songthaew (8B) to Pak Bara. Boats to Tarutao cost 200B per person, or you can charter a boat large enough for eight to 10 people for 800B. They run between November and April – the park is closed for the remainder of the year.

PHUKET

Phuket is barely an island, since it's joined to the mainland by a bridge – yet conversely, it's more than just an island since it's surrounded by countless other smaller islands, some of them just swimming distance from the shore.

Phuket was a major tin-mining centre, but these days it's the rapidly expanding resort role that is most important. The town of Phuket is pleasant enough but it's the beautiful beaches and the offshore islands which are the main attraction, and there are plenty of them.

Virtually all transport radiates from Phuket town and the popular beaches are scattered all over the island. Phuket Island is very hilly, and often the hills drop right into the sea. Beach accommodation in Phuket is becoming downright high-class these days, with international-class resorts on nearly every beach.

Information

The TAT office, on Phuket Rd, has a list of standard songthaew charges to the various beaches. The Thai Airways office is on Ranong Rd and the post office is on Montri Rd.

In earlier days, Phuket was known for periodic thefts and muggings, but now it seems to be as safe or safer than most other places in Thailand. If there is a theft, the TAT is your best bet in catching the culprits. Be cautious in the water as there have been a number of drownings at Phuket beaches.

Phuket Beaches

Patong Development in Phuket has been rapid and relatively recent – the first time I came here in the early '70s Ao Patong had just one little restaurant where you could lay your sleeping bag on the floor. Now there are at least 70 hotels and guesthouses, and innumerable restaurants.

Ao Patong is still pleasant and has more variety of accommodation than most of the other beaches, although food is a little more expensive than at Ao Kata Yai or Ao Karon. There's also more going on at night here than at the other beaches. The beach itself is long, white, clean and lapped by the proper picture-postcard clear waters. Ao Patong is 15 km west of Phuket town.

Karon & Kata Only a little south of Ao Patong is Ao Karon, 20 km from Phuket town. This is really a triple beach: there's the long golden sweep of Ao Karon, then a small headland separates it from the smaller but equally beautiful Ao Kata Yai. Another small headland divides this from Ao Kata Noi where you'll find good snorkelling. Offshore, there's the small island of **Ko Pu**.

Most of the development is centred around the two Kata beaches and the southern end of Karon beach. Development is creeping north and, no doubt, there will eventually be a strip of hotels and guesthouses like Ao Patong. Ao Karon and the two Ao Katas are beautiful beaches with that delightful, squeaky-feeling sand.

Nai Han South again from Ao Kata Noi is Hat Nai Han, a pleasant small beach which was one of the last hold-outs for cheap bungalows until the Phuket Yacht Club moved in. Now it's more of a scene but still pleasant.

You can walk along a coastal track from Ao Karon to Hat Nai Han in about two hours. In fact, you could probably walk right around the island on coastal tracks. The roads radiate out from Phuket town and you have to backtrack into town and out again to get from one beach to another by road – even though they are just a couple of km apart along the coast. **Ao Saen** is a pleasant little place between Kata Noi and Nai Han.

Rawai If you turn round the southern end of the island from Hat Nai Han you'll come to Hat Rawai, another tourist development. Again these are mostly more expensive places and the beach is not so special. At low tide, there's a long expanse of mud exposed before you get to the sea. People staying at Rawai often travel out to other beaches to swim. Rawai is a good place to get boats out to the islands scattered south of Phuket. There is good snorkelling at **Ko Hae**.

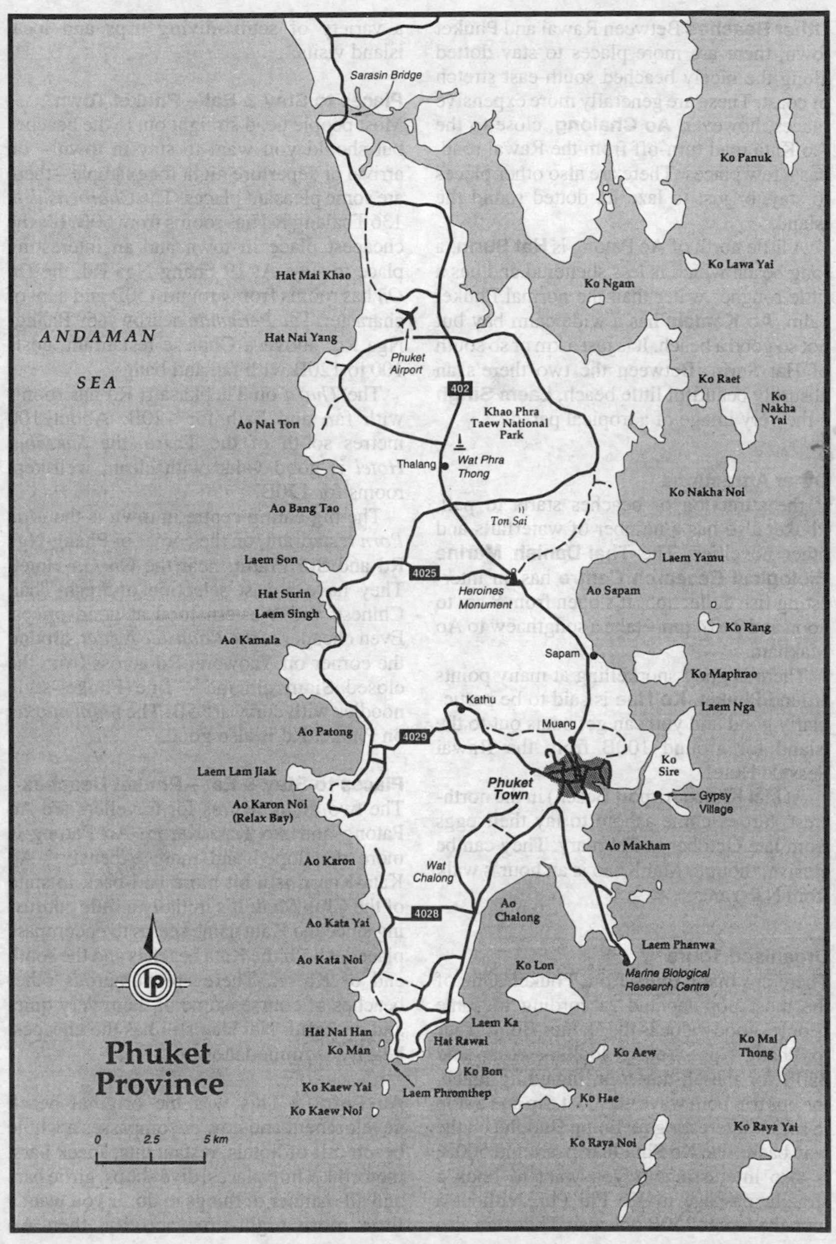

Sarasin Bridge
Ko Panuk
Ko Lawa Yai
Ko Ngam
Hat Mai Khao
ANDAMAN
SEA
Hat Nai Yang
Phuket Airport
402
Ko Raet
Ko Nakha Yai
Khao Phra Taew National Park
Ao Nai Ton
Thalang
Wat Phra Thong
Ko Nakha Noi
Ao Bang Tao
Ton Sai
Laem Son
Laem Yamu
4025
Heroines Monument
Ao Sapam
Hat Surin
Laem Singh
Ko Rang
Ao Kamala
Sapam
Ko Maphrao
Kathu
Laem Nga
Muang
Ao Patong
4029
Ko Sire
Laem Lam Jiak
Phuket Town
Gypsy Village
Ao Karon Noi (Relax Bay)
Ao Makham
Ao Karon
Wat Chalong
Ao Chalong
4028
Ao Kata Yai
Laem Phanwa
Ao Kata Noi
Marine Biological Research Centre
Ko Lon
Laem Ka
Hat Nai Han
Hat Rawai
Ko Man
Ko Aew
Ko Mai Thong
Ko Bon
Ko Kaew Yai
Laem Phromthep
Ko Hae
Ko Kaew Noi
Ko Raya Yai
Ko Raya Noi
0
2.5
5 km
Phuket Province

Other Beaches Between Rawai and Phuket town, there are more places to stay dotted along the nicely beached south-east stretch of coast. These are generally more expensive places, however. **Ao Chalong**, close to the Ao Kata road turn-off from the Rawai road, has a few places. There are also other places to stay, or just to laze in, dotted round the island.

A little north of Ao Patong is **Hat Surin**, a long beach which is less sheltered and has a little rougher water than the normal Phuket calm. **Ao Kamala** has a wide calm bay but not so good a beach. It is just a km or so south of Hat Surin. Between the two there's an absurdly beautiful little beach, **Laem Singh** – the very image of a tropical paradise.

Other Attractions

If the attraction of beaches starts to pall, Phuket also has a number of waterfalls and other novelties. The **Thai-Danish Marine Biological Research Centre** has an interesting fish collection. It's open from 8 am to noon and 2 to 4 pm – take a songthaew to Ao Makham.

There is good snorkelling at many points around Phuket. **Ko Hae** is said to be particularly good and you can get boats out to the island for around 100B from the Rawai Seaside Hotel.

At **Mai Khao** (Airport Beach) in the north-west, turtles come ashore to lay their eggs from late October to February. They can be elusive, though. Mai Khao is an hour's walk from Nai Yang.

Organised Tours

There are many tours from Phuket. One of the most popular and (according to some people) good value is the 'James Bond' Tour to Phang-Nga. You're looking at around 350B for the all-day tour, including lunch, the bus trip both ways, the boat trip and a stop to see an interesting reclining Buddha on the way back. The Ko Phi Phi trip, around 500B, is also interesting. If you want to book a straight passage to Ko Phi Phi, without a tour, the fare is 350B one way. There are also a variety of scuba-diving trips and local island visits.

Places to Stay & Eat – Phuket Town

Most people head straight out to the beaches but should you want to stay in town – on arrival or departure night for example – there are some pleasant places. The *Charoensuk* at 136 Thalang Rd has rooms from 60B. It's the cheapest place in town and an interesting place to stay. At 19 Phang-Nga Rd, the *On On* has rooms from around 150B and a lot of character. The *Pengman* nearby at 69 Phang-Nga Rd, above a Chinese restaurant, costs 100 to 120B with fan and bath.

The *Thara* on Thepkasatri Rd has rooms with fan and bath for 120B. About 100 metres south of the Thara, the *Suksabai Hotel* is good value with clean, well-kept rooms for 120B.

The big eating centre in town is the *Mae Porn* restaurant, on the corner of Phang-Nga Rd and Soi Pradit, near the On On Hotel. They have a vast selection of fresh Thai, Chinese and Western food at good prices. Even cheaper is the *Raan Jee Nguat*, around the corner on Yaowarat Rd across from the closed Siam cinema – fine Phuket-style noodles with curry are 5B. The *night market* on Phuket Rd is also good.

Places to Stay & Eat – Phuket Beaches

The two main centres for travellers are Ao Patong and Ao Kata/Karon. Ao Patong is more developed and more expensive; Ao Kata-Karon is a bit more laid-back in spite of the Club Med. It's initially a little confusing since the Kata name seems to encompass places at both the Kata beaches and the south end of Karon. There are numerous other beaches of course, some of them very quiet and peaceful. Nai Han still has the cheapest beach accommodation.

Ao Patong This was the original beach development and now encompasses a whole beach full of hotels, restaurants, snack bars, motorbike-hire places, dive shops, girlie bars and all manner of things to do. If you want a little more night-time activity, then Ao

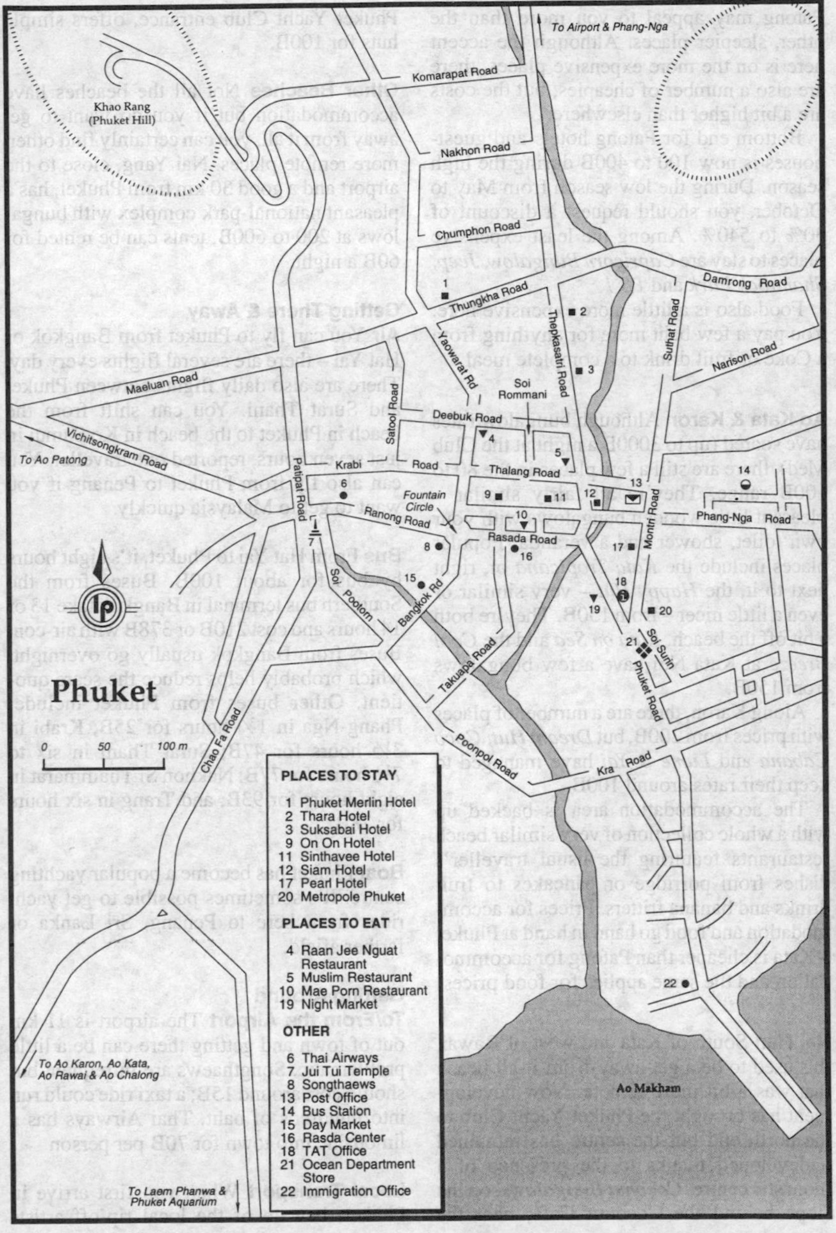

Phuket
To Airport & Phang-Nga
Komarapat Road
Khao Rang
(Phuket Hill)
Nakhon Road
Chumphon Road
Damrong Road
Thungkha Road
Thepkasatri Road
Suthat Road
Yaowarat Rd
Narison Road
Maeluan Road
Soi
Rommani
Deebuk Road
Satool Road
Vichitsongkram Road
To Ao Patong
Krabi
Road
Thalang Road
Patipat Road
Fountain
Circle
Phang-Nga
Road
Ranong Road
Rasada Road
Montri Road
Soi
Pootorn
Bangkok Rd
Soi Surin
Phuket Road
Takuapa Road
Chao Fa Road
Poonpol Road
Kra
Road
0
50
100 m
Ao Makham
To Ao Karon, Ao Kata,
Ao Rawai & Ao Chalong
To Laem Phanwa &
Phuket Aquarium
PLACES TO STAY
1 Phuket Merlin Hotel
2 Thara Hotel
3 Suksabai Hotel
9 On On Hotel
11 Sinthavee Hotel
12 Siam Hotel
17 Pearl Hotel
20 Metropole Phuket
PLACES TO EAT
4 Raan Jee Nguat Restaurant
5 Muslim Restaurant
10 Mae Porn Restaurant
19 Night Market
OTHER
6 Thai Airways
7 Jui Tui Temple
8 Songthaews
13 Post Office
14 Bus Station
15 Day Market
16 Rasda Center
18 TAT Office
21 Ocean Department Store
22 Immigration Office
THAILAND

Patong may appeal to you more than the other, sleepier places. Although the accent here is on the more expensive places, there are also a number of cheapies, but the costs are a bit higher than elsewhere.

Bottom end for Patong hotels and guesthouses is now 100 to 400B during the high season. During the low season from May to October, you should request a discount of 30% to 540%. Among the least expensive places to stay are *Capricorn Bungalow, Jeep, Shamrock Park* and *PS 1*.

Food also is a little more expensive here. You pay a few baht more for anything from a Coke or fruit drink to a complete meal.

Ao Kata & Karon Although bungalow rates have soared (up to 3000B a night at the Club Med), there are still a few places in the 80 to 100B range. They're all fairly similar – pleasant little wooden bungalows with your own toilet, shower and a veranda. Popular places include the *Kata Tropicana* or, right next to it, the *Happy Hut* – very similar or even a little nicer – from 150B. They're both a bit off the beach. *Kata on Sea* and the *Cool Breeze* at Kata Noi have a few bungalows from 150B.

Along Karon, there are a number of places with prices from 200B, but *Dream Hut, Coco Cabana* and *Lume & Yai* have managed to keep their rates around 100B.

The accommodation area is backed up with a whole collection of very similar beach restaurants featuring the usual traveller's dishes from porridge or pancakes to fruit drinks and banana fritters. Prices for accommodation and food go hand in hand at Phuket – Kata is cheaper than Patong for accommodation and the same applies for food prices.

Nai Han South of Kata and west of Rawai, this used to be a get-away-from-it-all beach that was a bit more remote. Now development has brought the Phuket Yacht Club to the north end but the centre has remained undeveloped thanks to the presence of a monastic centre. *Coconut Bungalows*, on the slope behind the Coconut Cafe, near the Phuket Yacht Club entrance, offers simple huts for 100B.

Other Beaches Not all the beaches have accommodation but if you do want to get away from it all, you can certainly find other, more remote places. Nai Yang, close to the airport and a good 30 km from Phuket, has a pleasant national-park complex with bungalows at 200 to 600B; tents can be rented for 60B a night.

Getting There & Away

Air You can fly to Phuket from Bangkok or Hat Yai – there are several flights every day. There are also daily flights between Phuket and Surat Thani. You can shift from the beach in Phuket to the beach in Ko Samui in just seven hours, reported one traveller. You can also fly from Phuket to Penang if you want to get to Malaysia quickly.

Bus From Hat Yai to Phuket, it's eight hours by bus for about 100B. Buses from the Southern bus terminal in Bangkok take 13 or 14 hours and cost 210B or 378B with air-con. Buses from Bangkok usually go overnight, which probably helps reduce the scare quotient. Other buses from Phuket include: Phang-Nga in 1¾ hours for 25B; Krabi in 3½ hours for 47B; Surat Thani in six to 7½ hours for 77B; Nakhon Si Thammarat in eight hours for 93B; and Trang in six hours for 78B.

Boat Phuket has become a popular yachting centre. It's sometimes possible to get yacht rides from here to Penang, Sri Lanka or farther afield.

Getting Around

To/From the Airport The airport is 11 km out of town and getting there can be a little problematic. Songthaews are infrequent but should cost around 15B; a taxi ride could run into hundreds of baht. Thai Airways has a limousine into town for 70B per person.

Local Transport When you first arrive in Phuket, beware of the local rip-off artists who will be on hand to tell you the tourist office is five km away, that the only way to get to the beaches is to take a taxi, or that a songthaew from the bus station to the town centre will cost you a small fortune.

Actually, songthaews run all over the island from a central area. The tourist office (which is also in the town centre) puts out a list of the standard charges to all the beaches and other popular destinations plus the recommended charter costs for a vehicle. Around town, the standard fare is 7B. Out of town, the standard fares to all the beaches vary from around 10B (Kata, Karon, Patong and Rawai) to 20B (Nai Yang and Nai Han).

You can also hire motorbikes (usually 100cc Japanese bikes) from various places at the beaches or in Phuket town from around 150 to 250B a day.

KHAO SOK NATIONAL PARK

Situated about midway between Phuket and Surat Thani, this national park has wonderful jungle and some crystal-clear rivers. You can stay at the national park lodge for 350B or in tree-house bungalows at *Tree Tops River Huts* or *AITS Jungle House* for 200 to 600B, or you can camp for 50B. To get there, take a Phuket-Surat Thani bus via Takua Pa and look for the Tree Tops sign at the Km 108 marker.

PHANG-NGA

Situated 94 km from Phuket town on the route to Hat Yai, Phang-Nga makes a good day trip from Phuket by motorbike. On the way to the town, turn off just five km past the small town of Takua Thung and visit the cave **Tham Suwan Kuha** which is full of Buddha images. Tha Don (with the Phang-Nga customs pier), between here and Phang-Nga, is the place where you hire boats to visit Phang-Nga Bay with its Muslim fishing villages on stilts, strangely shaped limestone outcrops soaring out of the sea and the water-filled caves. Yes, these are the James Bond islands from the film *Man with the Golden Gun*.

Places to Stay & Eat

There are a number of fairly nondescript hotels with rooms in the 80 to 150B range. Along Phetkasem Rd, Phang-Nga's main street, you'll find the *Rak Phang-Nga* and the *Lak Muang* (☎ 41 1125/288), two typical places with 80 to 150B rooms. The hotel with the most character and facilities is *Thawisuk*, the place with the blue facade in the middle of town with clean rooms for 80B.

You can buy good seafood and khanõm jiin at the stalls across from the movie theatre in Phang-Nga's main market.

KRABI

This small town offers similar offshore excursions to Phang-Nga but there are good local **beaches** to check out as well: Noppharat Thara, Ao Nang, Phra Nang and Raileh are currently popular. The longest beach is along Ao Nang, a lovely spot easily reached from Krabi. Phra Nang Bay is perhaps the most beautiful of all the beaches in this area.

Places to Stay & Eat – Town

Guesthouses New guesthouses are popping up all over town. Most offer little cubicles over shophouses for 60 to 80B. *B&B*, *Krabi Guest House* and *Su* are typical with rooms from 60 to 80B. Over on Ruen Rudee Rd are several other places with the usual upstairs rooms and slow plumbing, including *Walker*, *Coconut Home* and *KL*. Each charge 60B for rooms, or 80 to 100B if bath is included.

Guesthouses just south-west of town are quieter. Out on Jao Fa Rd is the *Chao Fa Valley* from 80 to 300B (it has a restaurant out the front). On the southern extension of Issara Rd, more or less parallel to Jao Fa Rd, are the *V&S Guest House* and *Lek's House*, both with rooms in old wooden houses for 60 to 80B. Lek's also has dorm beds for 30B. Others are tucked away along streets leading out of town – all similar.

Hotels The *New Hotel* (☎ 61 1318) on Phattana Rd has adequate rooms for 120B with fan and bath. The *Thai* on Itsara Rd is overpriced so give it a miss. The *Vieng Thong*

(☎ 61 1188/288) at 155 Uttarakit Rd has rooms from 250B.

Both the *Vieng Thong* and the *Thai* hotels have rather expensive coffee shops. At night, food vendors set up along the waterfront and there is a good morning market in the centre of town.

Places to Stay – Beaches

Ao Nang This has been a centre for budget accommodation, though rates are gradually increasing with demand. Near the turn-off for the pricey Krabi Resort are *Ao Nang Ban Leh* with 70B huts and the *Ao Nang Hill* from 40 to 60B. Going south along the beach, the *PS Cottage, Wanna's Place* and *Gift's* cost as low as 50B for simple huts or 150B for larger huts with bath.

Further along the beach, you'll come to a turn to the left which leads to the *Princess Garden* with 50B huts or 120B with bath. Back on the beach road next to the expensive Phra-Nang Inn, the *Ao Nang Villa* has a few roomy bungalows for 200 to 300B, more with air-con.

Further up the road is the *Krabi Seaview Resort* – 80B for simple huts and up to 450B for larger huts with air-con and bath.

Rai Leh Beach (West) Accessible by boat only. *Railay Village, Railae Beach* and *Sunset* have bungalows in the 200 to 300B range.

Phra Nang Beach Accessible by boat only. Staying here used to give access to three beaches: Phra Nang, West Rai Leh and East Rai Leh (or Nam Mao). Now all the bungalows on this beach have been moved out by the new *Dusit Beach Resort*.

Rai Leh Beach (East) There are four smaller bungalow operations here, *Queen*, *Sunrise*, *Ya-Ya* and *Coco Bungalows*, with rates from 50 to 150B. This beach tends toward mud flats during low tide.

Getting There & Away

Buses from Phuket to Krabi are 42B and leave twice a day from the terminal on Phang-Nga Rd. There are several buses a day from Phang-Nga to Krabi for 25B. From Surat Thani, it's 54B and the trip takes four hours. A bus and boat combo ticket to Ko Samui is an outrageous 250B.

Buses to and from Krabi arrive and depart at Taalat Kao, just outside Krabi proper – a songthaew into town is 2B.

Getting Around

Boats to the various beaches at Rai Leh and Phra Nang leave from the Jao Fa Pier on the Krabi waterfront and cost 35B per person. Noppharat Thara Beach and Ao Nang can be reached by songthaew for 15B.

AROUND KRABI

The **Than Bokkharani National Park**, a 10B songthaew ride from town near Ao Luk, makes for an interesting excursion with its forest and small waterfalls.

KO PHI PHI

Ko Phi Phi, four hours south of Krabi by boat, has white beaches, good diving and a huge cavern where the nests for bird's-nest soup are collected. There are actually two islands: Phi Phi Don is inhabited and has a small fishing village and a couple of groups of bungalows. Phi Phi Le is uninhabited and is the site for the licensed collecting of swallow nests – one of the nest caverns has some curious paintings.

Unfortunately, runaway growth has almost completely spoiled the atmosphere on Phi Phi Don, in spite of the fact that the island is part of a designated national marine park. Phi Phi Le remains protected not because it's part of the park (it isn't) but because the swallow's nest collectors make sure no one interferes with the ecology. Because all the accommodation is on Phi Phi Don, it can only be recommended these days if you're quite keen on snorkelling at nearby reefs. Otherwise, give it a miss.

Places to Stay & Eat

During high season, all accommodation on Phi Phi Don tends to be booked solid. At Ton Sai, the *Phi Phi Don Resort* has small bungalows for 100 to 300B. Over on Lo Dalam, the north side of the isthmus, are *Gift 2* and *Chong Kao* with simple huts from 100 to 300B.

On the other side of the peninsula at Hat Yao are *Long Beach, Viking Village* and *PP Paradise Pearl* with simple 90B huts, more with bath. The snorkelling is good here.

Getting There & Away

There is at least one boat a day, sometimes two or three, from Krabi's Jao Fa Pier. They only run regularly from November to May but during the monsoon it depends on the weather – the return fare is 200B. Today, commercialism is starting to catch up with Ko Phi Phi and there are frequent tours from Phuket. Although the distance is about the same from Phuket or Krabi the tours are much cheaper from Krabi.

There are also daily boats to Ko Phi Phi from Ao Nang, west of Krabi, from October/November to April/May for 100B per person.

TRANG

The town of Trang is a bustling little place between Krabi and Hat Yai with a history that goes back to the 1st century AD when it was an important centre for seagoing trade. Trang probably reached its peak during the 7th to 12th centuries at the height of the Srivijaya Empire.

Places to Stay & Eat

There are a number of places on the main street running down from the clocktower. The *Ko Teng* (☎ 21 8622) has rooms from 140B and a good restaurant downstairs. The *Wattana* (☎ 21 8184) is on the same stretch and is a little more expensive. Over on Ratchadamnoen Rd is the inexpensive *Petch (Phet) Hotel* (☎ 21 8002) with adequate rooms with fan and bath for 70 to 140B. They also have a restaurant downstairs. Moving upmarket, the *Queen Hotel* (☎ 21 8522) is great value at 200 to 300B for a big room with fan and a shower with hot water!

Adjacent to the Queen's Hotel, the *Phailin Restaurant* has a very broad selection of rice and noodle dishes, plus a few vegetarian specials. Trang is known for its coffee shops, which serve local Khao Chong coffee. Try the funky *Kafae Khao Chong* foodstall on Phattalung Rd or the *Sin Jiew* on Kantang Rd, which is open all night.

Getting There & Away

Buses from Satun, Hat Yai or Krabi to Trang are 35B. A share taxi from the same cities is around 60B. From Phattalung, it's 16B by bus and 25 by share taxi.

AROUND TRANG

The geography of the surrounding province is similar to that of Krabi and Phang-Nga but it's much less frequented by tourists. The Vegetarian Festival is celebrated fervently in September/October. Trang's coastline has several sandy beaches and coves, especially in the Sikao and Kantang districts. From the road between Trang and Kantang is a turn-off west onto an unpaved road that leads down to the coast. At the coast, a road south leads to Hat Yao, Hat Yong Ling and Hat Jao Mai. The road north leads to Hat Chang Lang and Hat Pak Meng. There are also several small islands just off the coast, including Ko Muk, Ko Kradan, Ko Ngai (Hai) and Ko Sukon.

SUNGAI KOLOK

This small town in the south-east is a jumping-off point for the east coast of Malaysia – its function is much like Hat Yai's for the busier west coast. Another border crossing has been added 32 km east in Ban Taba, a shorter and quicker route to Kota Bharu, Malaysia. Eventually, this crossing is supposed to replace Sungai Kolok's but, for the time being, both are functioning.

Information

There's a bank in the town centre, or Malaysian dollars can be changed at the bus station or in shops. It's easier to bring baht with you from Malaysia and you can change money at the border. There's a TAT office next to the immigration post on the Thai side.

Places to Stay

There are few English signs in this border town to the Malaysian east coast. In the centre of town, however, there are a number of places to stay although they are a bit grotty. The town is just a 10B trishaw ride from the border or a five-minute walk straight ahead from the railway station.

Cheapies include the *Savoy Hotel* and, next door, the *Thailieng Hotel* with rooms from 80 to 160B. Over on the corner of Arifmankha and Waman Amnoey Rds is the pleasant *Valentine* at 180B with fan, and 330B with air-con. There's a coffee shop downstairs and free fruit and coffee is provided to guests.

Places to Eat

There are lots of cheap *restaurants*. For a cheap and delicious breakfast, try coffee and doughnuts at the *station buffet*.

Getting There & Away

When you cross the border from Malaysia, the railway station is about a km straight ahead on the right-hand side. The bus station is a further km beyond the railway station, down a turning to the left.

Bus & Share Taxi Share taxis from Yala are 70B and the bus is 27B. From Narathiwat, the share taxi is 40B; the bus is 18B (air-con is 25B). There are no buses direct to Hat Yai from Sungai Kolok. Buses north go through Songkhla on their way to Bangkok.

Train From Hat Yai, the 3rd-class rail fare is 31B. From Bangkok, fares are 180B in 3rd class and 378B in 2nd class, before the rapid, express or sleeper supplements.

THAILAND

Vietnam

Since the 1960s, the name 'Vietnam' has come to signify to many Westerners a horrible war, a failure of American power, a socialist dictatorship and boatloads of refugees. When people thought about 'Vietnam', they thought of suffering – few considered it a place they'd want to visit.

Not that visiting was easy. Between 1975 and 1990, the few Western tourists who did visit encountered Draconian bureaucratic barriers at every turn. In the minds of Vietnamese officials, it seemed that the war had not ended.

All this has changed – Vietnam has flung open the doors to foreign tourists. This now-popular travel destination offers a rich and unique culture and outstanding scenic beauty.

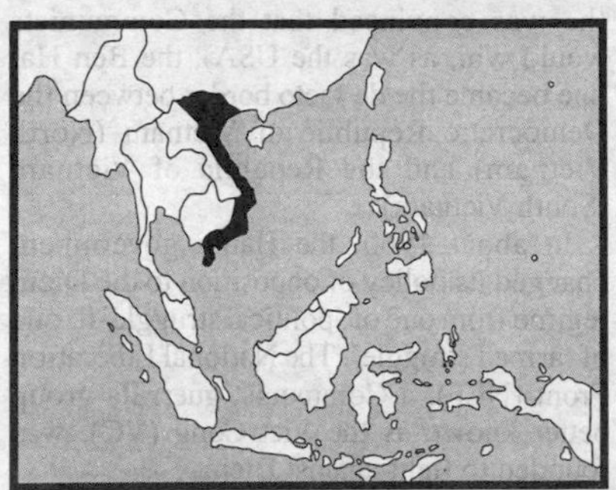

Facts about the Country

HISTORY

About 1000 years of Chinese rule over the Red River Delta (all of Vietnam at the time), marked by tenacious Vietnamese resistance and repeated rebellions, ended in 938 AD when Ngo Quyen vanquished the Chinese armies at the Bach Dang River.

During the next few centuries, Vietnam repulsed repeated invasions by China and expanded in a southward direction along the coast at the expense of the kingdom of Champa, which was wiped out in 1471.

The first contact between Vietnam and the West took place in Roman times. Recent European contact with Vietnam began in the 16th century, when European merchants and missionaries arrived. Despite restrictions and periods of persecution, the Catholic Church eventually had a greater impact on Vietnam than on any country in Asia except the Philippines.

In 1858, a joint military force from France and the Spanish colony of the Philippines stormed Danang after the killing of several missionaries. Early the next year, they seized Saigon. A few years later, Vietnamese Emperor Tu Duc signed a treaty that gave the French part of the Mekong Delta region and promised missionaries the freedom to proselytise everywhere in the country. In 1883, the French imposed a Treaty of Protectorate on Vietnam.

French rule often proved cruel and arbitrary. Ultimately, the most successful resistance came from the Communists. The first Marxist group in Indochina, the Vietnam Revolutionary Youth League, was founded by Ho Chi Minh in 1925.

During WW II, the only group that did anything significant to resist the Japanese occupation was the Communist-dominated Viet Minh. When WW II ended, Ho Chi Minh – whose Viet Minh forces already controlled large parts of the country – declared Vietnam independent. Efforts by the French to reassert control soon led to violent confrontations and full-scale war. In May 1954, Viet Minh forces overran the French garrison at Dien Bien Phu. This stunning and catastrophic defeat shattered public support in France for the war.

The Geneva Accords of mid-1954 provided for a temporary division of the country

VIETNAM

into two zones at the Ben Hai River. When the leader of the southern zone, an anti-Communist Catholic named Ngo Dinh Diem, refused to hold elections scheduled for 1956 (he was convinced that the Communists would win, as was the USA), the Ben Hai line became the de facto border between the Democratic Republic of Vietnam (North Vietnam) and the Republic of Vietnam (South Vietnam).

In about 1960, the Hanoi government changed its policy of opposition to the Diem regime from one of 'political struggle' to one of 'armed struggle'. The National Liberation Front (NLF), a Communist guerrilla group better known as the Viet Cong (VC), was founded to fight against Diem.

Diem was a brutal ruler and was assassinated in 1963 by his own troops. After Hanoi ordered regular North Vietnamese Army units to infiltrate the South in 1964, the situation for the Saigon regime became desperate. In 1965, the USA committed its first combat troops. They were soon joined by soldiers from South Korea, Australia, Thailand and New Zealand. By the spring of 1969 there were 543,000 US military personnel in Vietnam.

The Tet Offensive of early 1968 marked a crucial turning point in the war. As the country celebrated Tet, the Vietnamese New Year, the VC launched a deadly offensive in over 100 cities and towns. As the TV cameras rolled, a VC commando team temporarily took over the courtyard of the US Embassy building in the centre of Saigon. Many Americans, who had been hearing for years that the USA was winning, stopped believing their government and started demanding a negotiated end to the war.

The Paris Agreements, signed in 1973, provided for a cease-fire, the total withdrawal of US combat forces and the release by Hanoi of American prisoners of war. The agreement made no mention of approximately 200,000 North Vietnamese troops then in South Vietnam.

North Vietnam launched a massive conventional ground attack across the 17th Parallel in January 1975 – a blatant violation of the Paris Agreements. The South Vietnamese military leadership decided to make a 'tactical withdrawal' to more defensible positions. The withdrawal deteriorated into a chaotic rout as soldiers deserted in order to try to save their families. Whole brigades disintegrated and fled southward so fast the Communist troops could hardly keep up with them. Saigon surrendered to the North Vietnamese Army on 30 April 1975.

The takeover by the Communists was soon followed by large-scale repression. Despite repeated promises to the contrary, hundreds of thousands of people were rounded up and imprisoned without trial in forced-labour camps euphemistically known as 're-education camps'. Hundreds of thousands of southerners fled their homeland, creating a flood of refugees for the next 15 years.

A campaign of repression against Vietnam's ethnic-Chinese community – plus Vietnam's invasion of Cambodia at the end of 1978 – prompted the Chinese to attack Vietnam in 1979. The war lasted only 17 days, but Chinese-Vietnamese mistrust has lasted well over a decade.

The end of the Cold War and the collapse of the USSR in 1991 caused Vietnam and Western nations to seek rapprochement. The USA remains the only major power not to have established diplomatic relations with Vietnam, though this may change soon.

GEOGRAPHY

Vietnam stretches over 1600 km along the eastern coast of the Indochinese Peninsula. The country's land area is 329,566 sq km, making it slightly larger than Italy and a bit smaller than Japan.

The country's two main cultivated areas are the Red River Delta (15,000 sq km) in the north and the Mekong Delta (60,000 sq km) in the south. Three-quarters of Vietnam is hilly or mountainous.

CLIMATE

Vietnam has a remarkably diverse climate because of its wide range of latitudes and altitudes. The south is tropical but the north

Vietnam

CHINA
Red River
To Kunming
CHINA
Lao Cai
Lai Chau
Phongsali
Hoang Lien Mountains
Tam Dao
Thai Nguyen
Dong Dang
Nanning
Lang Son
Zhanjiang
Dien Bien Phu
Son La
Viet Tri
HANOI
Hong Gai
Halong Bay
LAOS
Nam Dinh
Cat Ba National Park
Sam Neua
RED RIVER DELTA
Haiphong
Luang Prabang
Cuc Phuong National Park
Ninh Binh
Thanh Hoa
Sam Son Beaches
GULF OF TONKIN
Hainan Island (CHINA)
VIETNAM
Vinh
Mekong
VIENTIANE
Tha Khaek
Dong Hoi
Vinh Moc
Former Demilitarised Zone (DMZ)
Dong Ha
River
Khe Sanh
Hué
Paracel Islands
Lao Bao
Savannakhet
Danang
THAILAND
Hoi An
My Lai (Son My)
Pakse
Quang Ngai
To Bangkok
Kontum
Central Highlands
SOUTH CHINA SEA
Pleiku
Angkor
CAMBODIA
Qui Nhon
Siem Reap
Battambang
Tonlé Sap
Tuy Hoa
Buon Ma Thuot
Nha Trang
Dalat
Cam Ranh Bay
PHNOM PENH
Tay Ninh
Moc Bai
Phan Rang
Cu Chi
Bien Hoa
Chau Doc
Sihanoukville
HO CHI MINH CITY (SAIGON)
Phan Thiet
Ha Tien
Long Xuyen
Mytho
Vung Tau
Phu Quoc Island
Vinh Long
Tien Giang River (Upper Mekong River)
Rach Gia
Cantho
MEKONG DELTA
GULF OF THAILAND
Camau
Hau Giang River (Bassac River)
0 150 300 km

VIETNAM

can experience chilly winters – in Hanoi, an overcoat can be necessary in January.

From April or May to October, the southwestern monsoon blows, bringing warm, damp weather to the whole country – except those areas sheltered by mountains, namely the central part of the coastal strip and the Red River Delta.

GOVERNMENT

The Socialist Republic of Vietnam (SRV) came into existence in July 1976 as a unitary state comprising the Democratic Republic of Vietnam (North Vietnam) and the territory of the defeated Republic of Vietnam (South Vietnam). Despite the rapid pace of economic reform in the 1990s, the government shows no sign of moving towards democracy and political control remains firmly in the hands of the Communist Party.

ECONOMY

Vietnam is poor, with an estimated per capita income of US$200 per year. The economy was devastated by war but even the government has admitted that the present economic fiasco is mainly the result of the collectivisation policies followed after reunification and bloated military budgets. Limited private enterprise was reintroduced in 1986. Since 1991, the loss of trade and aid from the former Eastern bloc has caused Vietnam to greatly accelerate the pace of free market economic reform.

POPULATION & PEOPLE

In 1993, Vietnam's population reached 72 million, making it the 12th most populous country in the world. There are virtually no government-orchestrated family planning policies and people may have as many children as they wish.

The population is 84% ethnic-Vietnamese and 2% ethnic-Chinese; the rest is made up of Khmers, Chams (a remnant of the once-great Champa Kingdom) and members of some 60 ethnolinguistic groups (also known as Montagnards, which means 'highlanders' in French).

ARTS & CULTURE

Conduct

Shoes are removed inside most Buddhist temples and often in people's homes, but this is not universal so watch what others do. Don't point the bottoms of your feet toward other people or toward Buddhist statues.

In general, shorts are considered inappropriate wear for all but children or men labouring in the sun. Vietnamese women never wear shorts no matter how hot the weather.

Leaving a pair of chopsticks sticking vertically in a rice bowl looks similar to the incense sticks which are burned for the dead. This powerful death sign is not appreciated anywhere in the Orient.

Ao Dais

The graceful Vietnamese national dress – these days worn almost exclusively by women – is known as the *ao dai*. It consists of a close-fitting blouse with long panels in the front and back that is worn over loose black or white trousers.

Water Puppetry

Water puppetry *(roi nuoc)* is a uniquely Vietnamese art form and can be seen at the Saigon Zoo and at Thay Pagoda near Hanoi.

RELIGION

Four great philosophies and religions have shaped the spiritual life of the Vietnamese people: Confucianism, Taoism, Buddhism and Christianity.

Popular Religion

Over the centuries, Confucianism, Taoism and Buddhism have fused with popular Chinese beliefs and ancient Vietnamese animism to form what is known collectively as the Triple Religion *(Tam Giao)*, which is sometimes referred to as Vietnamese Buddhism. The religious life of the Vietnamese is also profoundly influenced by ancestor worship, which dates from long before the arrival of Confucianism or Buddhism.

Christianity
Catholicism was introduced into Vietnam in the 16th century by missionaries from Portugal, Spain and France. Today, Vietnam has the highest percentage of Catholics (8% to 10% of the population) in Asia outside of the Philippines. Since 1954, in the North, and 1975, in the South, Catholics have faced restrictions on their religious activities.

Caodaism
Caodaism is an indigenous Vietnamese sect that was founded with the intention of creating the ideal religion by fusing the secular and religious philosophies of both East and West. It was established in the early 1920s based on messages revealed in seances to Ngo Minh Chieu, the group's founder. The sect's colourful headquarters is in Tay Ninh, 96 km north-west of Saigon. There are currently about two million followers of Caodaism in Vietnam. See the section on Tay Ninh for more information.

Islam
Muslims, mostly ethnic-Khmers and Chams, constitute about 0.5% of the population.

LANGUAGE
Greetings & Civilities
hello
Chào.
good night
Chúc ngủ ngon.
thank you
Cám ơn.
Thank you very much.
Cám ơn rất nhiều.
excuse me (often used before questions)
Xin lỗi.

Getting Around
I want to go to...
Tôi muốn đi...
bus
xe buýt
train
xe lửa
bus station
bến xe
railway station
ga xe lửa
post office
bưu điện
telephone
điện thoại
immigration police station
Phòng quản lý người nước ngoài.

Accommodation
hotel
khách sạn (Chinese construct)
hotel
nhà khách (Vietnamese construct)
cheap hotel
khách sạn rẻ tiền
air-conditioning
máy lạnh
fan
quạt
toilet
nhà vệ sinh
bathroom
phòng tắm
room key
chìa khóa phòng
I need to leave at (5) o'clock tomorrow morning.
Tôi phải đi lúc (năm) giờ sáng mai.
blanket
chăn (north) *mền* (south)
hot water
nước nóng
laundry
tiệm giặt quần áo
mosquito net
màn (north) *mùng* (south)
sheet
ra trải giường
toilet paper
giấy vệ sinh
towel
khăn tắm

Other Useful Words & Phrases
yes
Vâng. (north)
Có, Phải. (south)
no
Không.

VIETNAM

I don't understand.
Tôi không hiểu
How much (price)?
Cái này giá bao nhiêu?
expensive
đắt tiền
man
nam
woman
nữ
sanitary pads
băng vệ sinh
mosquito incense coils
hương đốt chống muỗi

Numbers

1	*một*
2	*hai*
3	*ba*
4	*bốn*
5	*năm*
6	*sáu*
7	*bảy*
8	*tám*
9	*chín*
10	*mười*
11	*mười một*
19	*mười chín*
20	*hai mươi*
21	*hai mươi mốt*
30	*ba mươi*
90	*chín mươi*
100	*một trăm*
200	*hai trăm*
900	*chín trăm*
1000	*một nghìn*
10,000	*mười nghìn*
100,000	*một trăm nghìn*
1 million	*một triệu*

Medical Emergencies
I'm sick.
Tôi bị bệnh.
doctor
bác sĩ
Please call a doctor.
Làm ơn gọi bác sĩ.
dentist
nha sĩ
hospital
bệnh viện
Please take me to the hospital.
Làm ơn đưa tôi đến bệnh viện.
pharmacy
nhà thuốc tây
diarrhoea
ỉa chảy
dizziness
chóng mặt
fever
cảm, cúm
headache
nhức đầu
malaria
sốt rét
stomachache
đau bụng
toothache
nhức răng
vomiting
ói, mửa

Other Emergencies
Help!
Cứu tôi với!
Thief!
Cướp, Cắp!
Pickpocket!
Móc túi!
police
Công an.

For a more complete selection of phrases, basic vocabulary and grammar, see Lonely Planet's *Vietnamese Phrasebook*.

Facts for the Visitor

VISAS & EMBASSIES

While Vietnamese bureaucracy is legendary, completing the necessary paperwork to obtain a visa is not all that daunting. Bangkok seems to be the fastest and most popular place to get a Vietnamese visa, though Hong Kong is a viable alternative. Keep plenty of visa photos handy – you need at least two to apply for a visa (in some places, six photos are needed!) plus a couple more photos for processing through immigration upon arrival in Vietnam.

Vietnamese visas specify where you are permitted to enter and leave the country – usually Ho Chi Minh City's Tan Son Nhut or Hanoi's Noi Bai airports, or sometimes the Chinese border at Huu Nghi Quan (Friendship Gate) or Lao Cai, or the Cambodian border at Moc Bai. Make sure this is made clear on your visa application. If you later decide to exit from a place not listed on your visa, amendments can be made at the Foreign Ministry in Hanoi or Ho Chi Minh City.

The visa is issued on a separate piece of paper. You can request that it be stamped into your passport, but this is *not* a good idea. The reason is that in most towns, hotels are required to register their guests – foreign and domestic – with the police. To do this, they need your visa and locals' identity papers. If the visa is stamped into your passport, you may need to hand it over, thus exposing yourself to the possibility of it getting lost. Sometimes you can get away with giving just a photocopy of your visa, but each police department makes its own rules and some will not accept photocopies.

In Bangkok, single-entry tourist visas cost US$60 at most travel agencies and can be issued in four days. An 'express visa' takes half the time and is arranged by fax to Hanoi – the drawback is a greater chance of things going awry (paperwork not being done properly on the Vietnamese end and the visa being declared 'invalid' on arrival).

Many travel agencies offer package deals costing US$365 to US$400 for both a visa and a round-trip air ticket (Bangkok-Ho Chi Minh City, returning Hanoi-Bangkok). In Bangkok, the place to look for competitive prices is Khao San Rd. Vista Travel at 24/4 Khao San Rd claims a large share of the budget traveller market. In Thailand, you *must* go to a travel agency rather than to the Vietnamese Embassy in order to secure a visa.

In Hong Kong, visas can be issued in five days and some agencies can get them as cheap as US$45, or US$85 if you are entering Vietnam overland from China. Three photos are required. One agent specialising in Vietnam travel is Phoenix Services (☎ 852-7227378; fax 852-3698884) in Room B, 6th floor, Milton Mansion, 96 Nathan Rd, Tsimshatsui, Kowloon. Phoenix offers a package deal – round-trip airfare plus visa for US$570.

Visas can also be obtained in Australia through STA Travel for around A$90 or from other travel agencies. They take about two weeks to issue.

We've had bad reports from travellers who have tried to obtain Vietnamese visas in Cambodia – bureaucratic delays and extra 'fees' have been tacked on. The Vietnamese embassy in Beijing is hit or miss – sometimes cooperative, but usually not.

Warning You might think that after you've obtained your visa and entered Vietnam, all is well. Unfortunately, Vietnamese immigration can be a very difficult lot – they may arbitrarily give you a shorter stay than what your visa calls for. Thus, your 30-day visa might only be validated for one week. No matter what it says on the front side of your visa, immediately after it's been stamped by the immigration officer, look on the back and see how many days they've given you. If you've only been given a week, sometimes you can get it changed right at the airport or border checkpoint – otherwise, you might be forced to visit the Ministry of Foreign Affairs and apply for an extension. Overstaying your visa by even one day can result in arrest, stiff fines and deportation!

Vietnamese Embassies Abroad

Cambodia

Son Ngoc Minh area (opposite 749 Achar Mean Blvd), Phnom Penh (☎ 25481)

China

32 Guangua Lu, Jianguomen Wai, Beijing (☎ 5321125)

Laos

1 Thap Luang Rd, Vientiane (☎ 2707, 5578)

Malaysia

4 Pesiaran Stonor, Kuala Lumpur (☎ (03) 2484036; fax 2483270)

Thailand

83/1 Wireless Rd, Bangkok (☎ (02) 2517201, 2515836)

Visa Extensions

If you've got the dollars, they've got the rubber stamp. Visa extensions are granted for 15 days at a time, and you can get extensions up to a maximum stay of three months. The cost is US$20 or US$30, depending on whether the relevant officials in charge of such matters need a new colour TV or a new refrigerator. Either way, visa extensions are not usually easy to handle yourself. Rather, a Vietnamese travel agent or your hotel can make the arrangements. Many hotels have a sign on the front desk indicating that they have a visa extension service. The procedure takes one or two days and one photo is needed. You can apply for your extension even several weeks before it's necessary.

This process is only readily accomplished in major cities – Hanoi, Ho Chi Minh City, Danang or Hué. At the time of this writing, the Hué office was the most friendly, but that can easily change when officials get reshuffled.

Re-Entry Permit

If you plan a side trip to Cambodia, you can use your original Vietnamese visa (if it hasn't expired) to re-enter Vietnam, but you must first secure a re-entry permit (US$10). Travel agents in Ho Chi Minh City or Hanoi can usually get these permits much faster than you can yourself, but if you're patient you can try applying directly to the Interior Ministry.

DOCUMENTS

Travel Permits

Formerly, foreigners had to have internal travel permits *(giay phep di lai)* to go anywhere outside the city in which they arrived. These were abolished in 1993, but beware of con artists who will insist you still need one and will happily sell you a fake internal travel permit.

That having been said, uncertainty still prevails in small towns and villages. Unfortunately, the police in many places seem to make up their own rules as they go along, no matter what the Interior Ministry in Hanoi says. In addition, more and more municipalities are chasing foreign dollars by charging for local travel permits. The bottom line is that you may have to inquire locally to see if a permit is needed.

For example, if you visit Dalat in the Central Highlands, no permit is necessary. However, to visit the nearby Lat Village (12 km away), you need to get a permit from the Dalat police (US$10).

Besides Lat Village, some other places currently requiring permits include Ban Don (near Buon Ma Thuot in the Central Highlands), the Cham Towers at My Son (near Danang), villages around the Demilitarised Zone (DMZ), My Lai (Son My subdistrict near Quang Ngai), Chau Doc (in the Mekong Delta) and Ha Tien (also in the Mekong Delta).

However, don't be absolutely sure that this information is correct because policies change frequently. The tendency to require extra permits seems to be escalating. Keep your ear to the ground to learn the latest erratic rules and regulations. Remember that being caught in an area without the necessary paperwork means a 'fine'.

CUSTOMS

Travellers have reported trouble with Vietnamese Customs. Most serious are the problems with video tapes – on both arrival and departure, you are supposed to get a certificate of clearance from the 'Cultural Department'. Of course, the Cultural Department doesn't have branch offices in the airports or at land border crossings. Some travellers have even been hassled over compact discs and music cassette tapes. Usually, the payment of a small 'fine' causes these problems to evaporate.

Jewellery is another problem area. The best advice we can give is that if you have jewellery, leave it at home.

MONEY

Currency

The dong is the currency of Vietnam. Banknotes in denominations of 200d, 500d, 1000d, 2000d, 5000d, 10,000d, 20,000d and

VIETNAM

50,000d are presently in circulation. There are no coins.

The US$ virtually acts as a second local currency. Other major foreign currencies are not readily accepted. Because of rapid inflation and continual devaluation of the dong, we quote prices here in US$.

Large-denomination bills (US$100) are preferred when changing into dong, but a small supply (say US$20 worth) of ones and fives will prove useful on arrival to hire a taxi into the city. US dollars are in such wide circulation now that many hotels and restaurants can accept a US$20 bill and give you change in US$.

Travellers' cheques in US$ can be exchanged for dong at certain banks – most hotels and airline offices will not accept travellers' cheques. Lost or stolen travellers' cheques cannot be replaced in Vietnam.

The black market pays about 3% more than the banks – not much better than the official rate. Jewellery shops are the best place to perform black market exchanges, but the front desks of some hotels do it too. Travellers who have changed money on the street (rather than in a shop) have fared poorly.

Be sure to bring enough US$ in cash (you can also use travellers' cheques) for your visit and to keep it safe, preferably in a money belt.

Exchange Rates

Australia	A$1	=	7895d
Canada	C$1	=	8127d
New Zealand	NZ$1	=	6501d
Britain	UK£1	=	16,568d
USA	US$1	=	10,945d
Japan	¥100	=	10,687d
Germany	DM1	=	6718d
France	FF1	=	1961d
Malaysia	M$1	=	4263d
Thailand	1B	=	443d

Visa, MasterCard and JCB credit cards are now acceptable in Ho Chi Minh City and Hanoi, but nowhere else (yet). Credit cards issued by US banks cannot be used in Vietnam, even if you are not a US citizen. And if you are a US citizen but have a credit card issued by a non-American bank, you are also not supposed to use it, though it's hard to see how the US government would catch you in that case. The Vietnamese know the rules and will read the fine print on the credit card carefully – if it's American-issued, the card will not be accepted. This is because of the lack of diplomatic relations between the USA and Vietnam.

Getting a cash advance from Visa, MasterCard and JCB is possible at Vietcombank in Ho Chi Minh City and Hanoi. Money can be cabled into Vietnam quickly and cheaply and the recipient can be paid in US dollars. However, sending money by wire is fast only if the overseas office is a 'correspondent bank' with Vietcombank. The list of correspondent banks is not extensive, but growing. Right now, only the branches of Vietcombank in Ho Chi Minh City and Hanoi are equipped to handle wire transfers.

Costs

Vietnam is very cheap compared to any Western country, but not so cheap compared to some travel bargains in Asia like Indonesia and India. It would be dirt cheap if you could pay the same as the locals, but special 'foreigners only' prices are often charged. In hotels, foreigners are charged at least double the price a Vietnamese would pay for the same room. For airline tickets, foreigners pay triple; for trains, foreigners are charged five times the Vietnamese price!

Nevertheless, since hotels, food and buses are so cheap, ascetics can get by on less than US$10 a day. For US$15, a backpacker can live fairly well.

Tipping

Tipping is not expected but it's enormously appreciated. For someone making US$20 per month, 10% of the cost of your meal can easily equal a day's wages.

Bargaining

Bargaining is common, even with the police if you are fined! Always be polite and smile when bargaining – nastiness will cause the other party to lose face, in which case they'll dig in their heels and you'll come out the loser.

TOURIST OFFICES

Vietnam Tourism (Du Lich Viet Nam) and Ho Chi Minh City's Saigon Tourist are state-run organisations which masquerade as tourist information offices. In fact, they have little information that they're willing to give for free – essentially, they are in business to book pricey tours. Booking tours through private agencies is cheaper, usually half the price or less.

Every province has a regional tourist office. These offices will cause you nothing but problems – for example, requiring you to get a special permit (US$50) to sit on an elephant's back for a photo. The best advice we can give about tourist offices in Vietnam is to avoid them.

BUSINESS HOURS & HOLIDAYS

Offices, museums etc are usually open from 7 or 8 am to 11 or 11.30 am, and from 1 or 2 pm to 4 or 5 pm. Most museums are closed on Monday.

Tet (Tet Nguyen Dan), the Vietnamese New Year, is the most important annual festival. Marking the new lunar year as well as the advent of spring, this week-long holiday falls in late January or in early February.

The date on which Saigon surrendered to Hanoi-backed forces in 1975, 30 April, is commemorated nationwide as Liberation Day.

POST & TELECOMMUNICATIONS

The international postal service from Vietnam is not unreasonably priced when compared to most countries. However, international telecommunications charges are among the highest in the world.

Sending Mail

Take your letters to the post office yourself and make sure that the clerk cancels them *while you watch* so that someone to whom the stamps are worth a day's salary does not soak them off and throw your letters away.

Receiving Mail

Poste restante works in the larger cities but don't count on it elsewhere. All post offices are marked with the words 'Buu Dien'.

Telephone

The cheapest and simplest way by far to make an international direct-dial (IDD) call is to buy a telephone card, known in Vietnam as a UniphoneKad. They are on sale at the telephone company. UniphoneKads can only be used in special telephones which are mainly found in Ho Chi Minh City, usually in the lobbies of major hotels. The cards are issued in two denominations: 30,000d (US$2.76) and 300,000d (US$27.64). The 30,000d card will only work for domestic calls, while the 300,000d card can be used to make both domestic and international calls.

Fax, Telex & Telegraph

Most GPOs and many tourist hotels in Vietnam offer domestic and international fax, telegraph and telex services. Hotels are likely to charge more than the post office.

BOOKS & MAPS

Lonely Planet's *Vietnam – a travel survival kit* has much more information about the country. Two classic books from the French colonial period are Graham Greene's novel *The Quiet American*, and Norman Lewis' account of travels in the region in the early 1950s, *A Dragon Apparent*. Among the many books on the Vietnam War, Jonathan Schell's *The Real War* and *Dispatches* by Michael Herr are among the best.

Maps of Vietnam are readily available in Hanoi and Ho Chi Minh City.

MEDIA

Most of Vietnam's English-language press is geared towards attracting the foreign investor and business traveller rather than peddling the news. It's great if you're interested in statistics on cement or fertiliser production, but it's hard to find reading matter with more widespread appeal.

The English-language *Vietnam News* is published daily in Ho Chi Minh City on a single sheet of paper. *Vietnam Weekly* comes from Hanoi. Other English periodicals include the *Vietnam Economic News*, *Saigon Times*, *Vietnam Business* and *Vietnam Foreign Trade*.

Foreign radio services such as the BBC World Service, Radio Australia and Voice of America can be picked up on short-wave frequencies. Vietnamese TV, which began broadcasting in 1970, consists of news and propaganda programming as well as sports and music.

FILM & PHOTOGRAPHY

Many Vietnamese airports are equipped with ancient X-ray machines that will severely damage or destroy *any* film. New film-safe machines have been installed at the airports in Ho Chi Minh City and Hanoi, but elsewhere it's dicey.

HEALTH

Malaria is a serious threat and chloroquine resistance has been widely reported in Vietnam.

DANGERS & ANNOYANCES

Since 1975, many thousands of Vietnamese have been maimed or killed by rockets, artillery shells, mortars, mines and other ordnance left over from the war. *Never* touch any relics of the war you may come across – such objects can remain lethal for decades. Remember, one bomb can ruin your whole day.

Although the amount pinched by snatch thieves and pickpockets pales in comparison to what is raked in by high-ranking kleptocrats, it's the street crime that most worries travellers. Drive-by bag-snatchers are common, especially in Saigon – thieves on motorbikes have been known to snatch bags through the open windows of cars and buses. Travellers on the trains report that on slow sections, gear has been grabbed straight through the windows.

The police in Vietnam are the best that money can buy. It's wise to avoid them, especially late at night:

> One woman I met was confronted by two cops late at night in Saigon and they insisted she pay US$20 for some fabricated law she broke like insulting the flag. She refused and didn't get her passport back (which of course they had asked to see) until she coughed up some dollars.
>
> The next evening around midnight, I was on the way back to my hotel in a cyclo when two cops waved us over and demanded my 'papers'. I gave them photocopies and told them they were all I had with me, and after a valiant effort to extort US$10 for riding in a cyclo without a licence, they let me go without paying anything. I told them (nicely!) they could keep the papers, and there was nothing they could do but shoot me with the AK-47 one of them was carrying. Anyway, carry copies in any case.

It should be pointed out that the Immigration Police are no better. One traveller reports being charged US$400 to have his lost visa replaced. A foreign woman was charged US$40 for a loss report which she needed to clear Customs because her ring was stolen.

To be fair, the problem of police corruption is not unique to Vietnam. The problems which plague many Third World police forces – very low pay, low morale and poor education – exist elsewhere.

Something to be wary of if you're travelling by rail are the rocks that children frequently throw at the trains – these can easily cause injury and you may have to keep the metal shields down. A similar hazard can be found in many rural communities, where locals tend to mistake foreign cyclists for Russians and throw rocks at them.

ACCOMMODATION

The good news is that the tourism boom has been accompanied by a boom in the construction of high-standard hotels. The bad news is that prices are rising. Foreigners are usually not permitted to stay in the really grotty dumps, but finding hotels priced at under US$10 is easy in the south. However, it costs at least double in the north, and Hanoi is particularly expensive.

FOOD

One of the delights of visiting Vietnam is the amazing cuisine – there are said to be nearly 500 traditional Vietnamese dishes – which is, in general, superbly prepared and very cheap. The Vietnamese bake the best bread in South-East Asia – a French-style *petit pain* loaf of bread costs just US$0.10. Buy some jam (ask for *confiture)* to make a cheap breakfast.

Some useful words include:

beef
thịt bò
chicken
thịt gà
crab
cua
fish
cá
shrimp
tôm

Condiments

Nuoc mam (pronounced something like 'nuke mom') is a type of fermented fish sauce, identifiable by its distinctive smell, which is found with all Vietnamese meals.

Soups

Pho is the Vietnamese name for the noodle soup that is eaten at all hours of the day, but especially for breakfast. It is prepared by quickly boiling noodles and placing them into a bowl along with greens (shallots, parsley) and shredded beef, chicken or pork. A broth made with boiled bones, prawns, ginger and nuoc mam is then poured into the bowl. Some people take their pho with chilli sauce or lemon.

Vegetarian Food

Because Buddhist monks of the Mahayana tradition are strict vegetarians, Vietnamese vegetarian cooking *(an chay)* is an integral part of Vietnamese cuisine. Tofu, mushrooms and raw, dried, cooked and fermented vegetables are used instead of meat. Because it does not include many expensive ingredients, vegetarian food is unbelievably cheap.

Menus

On restaurant *nha hang* menus, dishes are usually listed according to their main ingredient. For instance, all the chicken dishes appear together, as do all the beef dishes, and so on.

DRINKS

Whatever you drink, make sure that it's been boiled or bottled. Ice is generally safe in Ho Chi Minh City and Hanoi, but is not guaranteed elsewhere. Vietnamese coffee is fine stuff but the tea is disappointing. Imported beverages like Coca-Cola and San Miguel beer are widely available, and some of the domestic stuff isn't bad either.

Useful words include:

boiled water
nước sôi
mineral water
nước suối
carbonated water
nước sô-đa
lemon soda
sô-đa chanh
orange soda
sô-đa cam
tea
nước trà (south)
nước chè (north)
coffee
cà phê
coffee with milk
cà phê sữa
iced coffee
cà phê đá
iced coffee & milk
cà phê sữa đá
sugar
đường
beer
bia
ice
nước đá

VIETNAM

Getting There & Away

AIR

Bangkok, only 80 minutes flying time from Ho Chi Minh City, has emerged as the main port of embarkation for air travel to Vietnam. Bangkok-Ho Chi Minh City tickets are US$140 one way; round-trip tickets cost exactly double. There are also direct Bangkok-Hanoi flights (US$170 one way, US$338 round trip).

After Bangkok, Hong Kong claims second place. Hong Kong to Ho Chi Minh City costs US$293 one way, US$558 return. There are also Hong Kong-Hanoi flights (US$266 one way, US$503 return). The most popular ticket allows you to fly from Hong Kong to Ho Chi Minh City and return from Hanoi to Hong Kong; this ticket costs US$535. Many travel agents can arrange special discounts if you purchase a group ticket – you don't necessarily have to travel with a group, but you might be locked into fixed departure and return dates. For example, Hong Kong-Hanoi return can be as little as US$320.

Side trips from Vietnam to Cambodia are very popular. If you fly to Phnom Penh, you can get a Cambodian visa on arrival for US$20. See the Cambodian section of this book for details.

LAND

To/From China

It's become very popular to cross the border at Dong Dang (20 km north of Lang Son in north-east Vietnam). The nearest major Chinese city to this border crossing is Nanning, capital of Guangxi Province.

The other border crossing is at Lao Cai in north-west Vietnam, opposite the Chinese border town of Hekou. Lao Cai lies on the railway line between Hanoi and Kunming in China's Yunnan Province.

Entering Vietnam overland from China requires a special visa. It's not difficult to get, but costs twice as much and takes twice as long to issue as a standard visa. Travellers who have attempted to use a standard visa to enter Vietnam overland have fared poorly – some have managed it only after paying huge bribes, only to be given a one-week rather than one-month stay. Exiting overland poses no such problem, but the correct exit point must be marked on the visa – alterations can easily be made in Hanoi.

To/From Cambodia

Buses run daily between Phnom Penh and Ho Chi Minh City via the Moc Bai border checkpoint. The cost is around US$12 depending on bus size. For overland crossings, you need to apply for a Cambodian visa.

To/From Laos

Apparently it is possible to enter Laos from Lao Bao in north-central Vietnam, but this is questionable at the moment. If you're interested in trying this route, the best way to go about it would be to request a visa valid for Savannakhet entry from a Lao consulate in Saigon or Hanoi. Lao immigration would then be able to admit you at the border.

LEAVING VIETNAM

It's important to reconfirm your flight out of the country. Airport departure tax is US$6, which can also be paid in dong.

Travellers have reported things being pilfered from their luggage on departure.

Getting Around

AIR

All air travel within Vietnam is handled by Vietnam Airlines and Pacific Airlines. Flights fill up fast (some flights are literally standing room only) so reservations should be made at least several days before departure. Reservations and ticketing is something you usually take care of yourself – no travel agents have computer terminals in their office to book air tickets.

The international and domestic booking

offices of Vietnam Airlines are at separate locations in most cities. While the international booking offices are not generally crowded, the domestic booking offices tend to be an unruly mass of elbows and hands – no one stands in line. You will have little choice but to dive headlong into the vortex if you want to book a seat. Do not forget to bring either your passport or visa – you will need one or the other to buy an air ticket.

Vietnam Airlines has recently done a good job of overhauling its aging fleet: new Western-made engines have been installed.

BUS

Vietnam's extensive bus network reaches virtually every corner of the country. Prices are so cheap that it's almost free, but foreigners may be overcharged. Almost all Vietnamese buses suffer from frequent breakdowns, tiny seats or benches, almost no legroom and chronic overcrowding. Most intercity buses depart very early in the morning. There are also minibuses which are pricier, faster and more comfortable – you can pay for two seats on these if you want more legroom.

TRAIN

The 2600-km Vietnamese railway system runs along the coast between Saigon and Hanoi, and links the capital with Haiphong and points north. Odd-numbered trains travel southward; even-numbered trains go northward.

Even the fastest trains in Vietnam are extremely slow, averaging 30 km/h and slowing to five or 10 km/h in some sections. The quickest rail journey between Hanoi and Ho Chi Minh City takes 42 hours at an average speed of 41 km/h; the slowest trains take 48 hours, averaging 34 km/h.

Children frequently throw rocks at the trains – this can easily cause injury and conductors will insist you keep the metal shields down, which spoils the view.

There are five classes of train travel in Vietnam: hard-seat, soft-seat, hard-berth, soft-berth and super-berth. Conditions in hard-seat and soft-seat can be horrible, often worse than the bus. Hard-berth has three tiers of beds (six beds per compartment). Because the Vietnamese don't seem to like climbing up, the upper berth is cheapest. Soft-berth has two tiers (four beds per compartment) and all bunks are priced the same. These compartments have a door. Super-berth compartments have two beds in a room with a door. See the table at the bottom of the page for sample prices for foreigners.

CAR

Given the dilapidated state of public transport, hiring a car isn't such a bad idea, especially if you gather a small group of travellers to share the cost. Of course, some of the cars for rent are also in dilapidated condition. Vietnam Tourism and Saigon Tourist will hire out new Japanese cars with drivers for US$0.33 per km. You can get it for half that price from private travel agents, but costs vary and you have to shop around.

HITCHING

Westerners have reported great success at hitching. In fact, the whole system of passenger transport in Vietnam is premised on people standing along the highways and flagging down buses or trucks. To get a bus, truck or other vehicle to stop, stretch out your arm and gesture towards the ground with your whole hand. Drivers will expect to be paid for picking you up – negotiate the fare before getting on board.

Station	*Distance from Saigon*	*Hard Seat*	*Soft Seat*	*High Berth*	*Mid Berth*	*Low Berth*	*Soft Berth*	*Super Berth*
Nha Trang	411 km	$13	$15	$21	$23	$25	$27	$29
Danang	935 km	$27	$32	$46	$50	$55	$60	$64
Hué	1038 km	$29	$35	$50	$55	$61	$66	$71
Hanoi	1726 km	$48	$56	$82	$91	$99	$108	$117

BOAT

The extensive network of canals in the Mekong Delta makes getting around by boat feasible in the far south. It's slow going and conditions can be grim, but it's certainly cheap.

LOCAL TRANSPORT

Bus

Inner-city bus transport is so poor in Vietnam that you can just about forget it.

Taxi

Western-style taxis with meters are just beginning to make their appearance in Ho Chi Minh City, but not elsewhere.

Motorbike

Motorbikes (50cc or under) and motorcycles (over 50cc) are a common form of transport, but accidents are also common. Traffic drives on the right-hand side of the road (usually).

No driver's licence is needed to drive a motorbike. To drive a motorcycle you'll need an international driver's licence endorsed for motorcycle operation. In practice, many people operate motorcycles without a licence. But beware – the police are known to be strict, though for a fee they can decide to forgive your transgressions. Motorcycles can be rented in Ho Chi Minh City and Hanoi from some travel agencies and shops for around US$5 to US$10 per day. Cheapest of all are the Russian-made motorcycles – these are usually 175cc.

Honda Om

The *Honda om* is an ordinary motorbike on which you ride seated behind the driver. Getting around this way with luggage is quite a challenge. There is no set procedure for finding a driver willing to transport you somewhere. You can either try to flag someone down (most drivers can always use a bit of extra cash) or ask a Vietnamese to find a Honda om for you. The fare is a bit more than a cyclo for short trips and about the same as a cyclo for longer distances.

Bicycle

While bikes seem to be an accepted mode of transport for getting around large cities, long-distance biking is fraught with problems (bad roads, mean dogs, mean police etc). In many rural communities, the locals mistake all foreigners on bikes for Russians and throw rocks!

Cyclo

Travelling by cyclo (pedicab) is the most practical and fun way to get around cities. Always agree on a price before setting off.

TOURS

Vietnam has a number of cafes which have jumped into the business of offering budget tours. These are good value – you'd pay five to 10 times more for the same thing if you booked via the government-run tour agencies. For example, some cafes in Saigon have three-day tours to the Mekong Delta for US$25; a 10-day trip to Dalat, Nha Trang, Hoi An and Hué for US$65; and a 10-day trip to the Central Highlands and Hué for US$80. From Hanoi, cafes book overnight trips to Halong Bay for US$15, and four-day trips to Sapa for US$50.

Ho Chi Minh City

Vietnam's largest population centre, Ho Chi Minh City (population 3.5 million) covers an area of 2056 sq km, but it's a cartographer's creation – 90% is rural. The 'real city' is downtown (District 1), also known as Saigon, a name still used by most people to refer to the whole city. Cholon (District 5) is the Chinese section. Cholon means Big Market, an indication of the important role the Chinese have traditionally played in Vietnam's economy.

The huge numbers of people and their obvious industriousness give Saigon, capital of South Vietnam from 1956 to 1975, a bustling, dynamic and vital atmosphere.

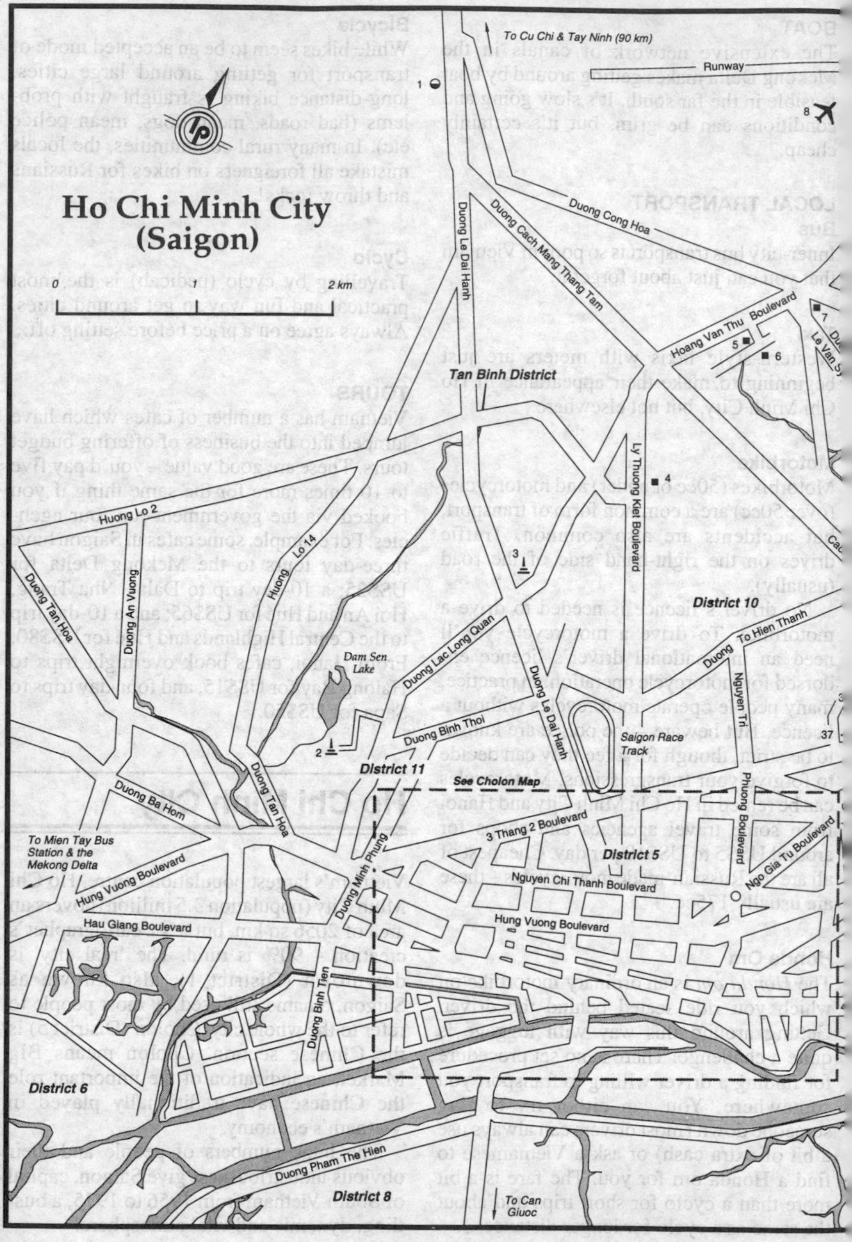

Ho Chi Minh City (Saigon)

0 2 km

To Cu Chi & Tay Ninh (90 km)
Runway
1
8
Duong Le Dai Hanh
Duong Cach Mang Thang Tam
Duong Cong Hoa
Hoang Van Thu Boulevard
Le Van Sy
5
6
7
Tan Binh District
Ly Thuong Kiet Boulevard
4
3
Huong Lo 2
Huong Lo 14
Duong Tan Hoa
Duong An Vuong
District 10
Duong To Hien Thanh
Nguyen Tri
Duong Lac Long Quan
Duong Le Dai Hanh
Dam Sen Lake
Duong Binh Thoi
Saigon Race Track
37
2
District 11
See Cholon Map
Duong Ba Hom
Duong Tan Hoa
3 Thang 2 Boulevard
Phuong Boulevard
Ngo Gia Tu Boulevard
To Mien Tay Bus Station & the Mekong Delta
Duong Minh Phung
District 5
Nguyen Chi Thanh Boulevard
Hung Vuong Boulevard
Hung Vuong Boulevard
Hau Giang Boulevard
Duong Binh Tien
District 6
Duong Pham The Hien
District 8
To Can Giuoc

VIETNAM

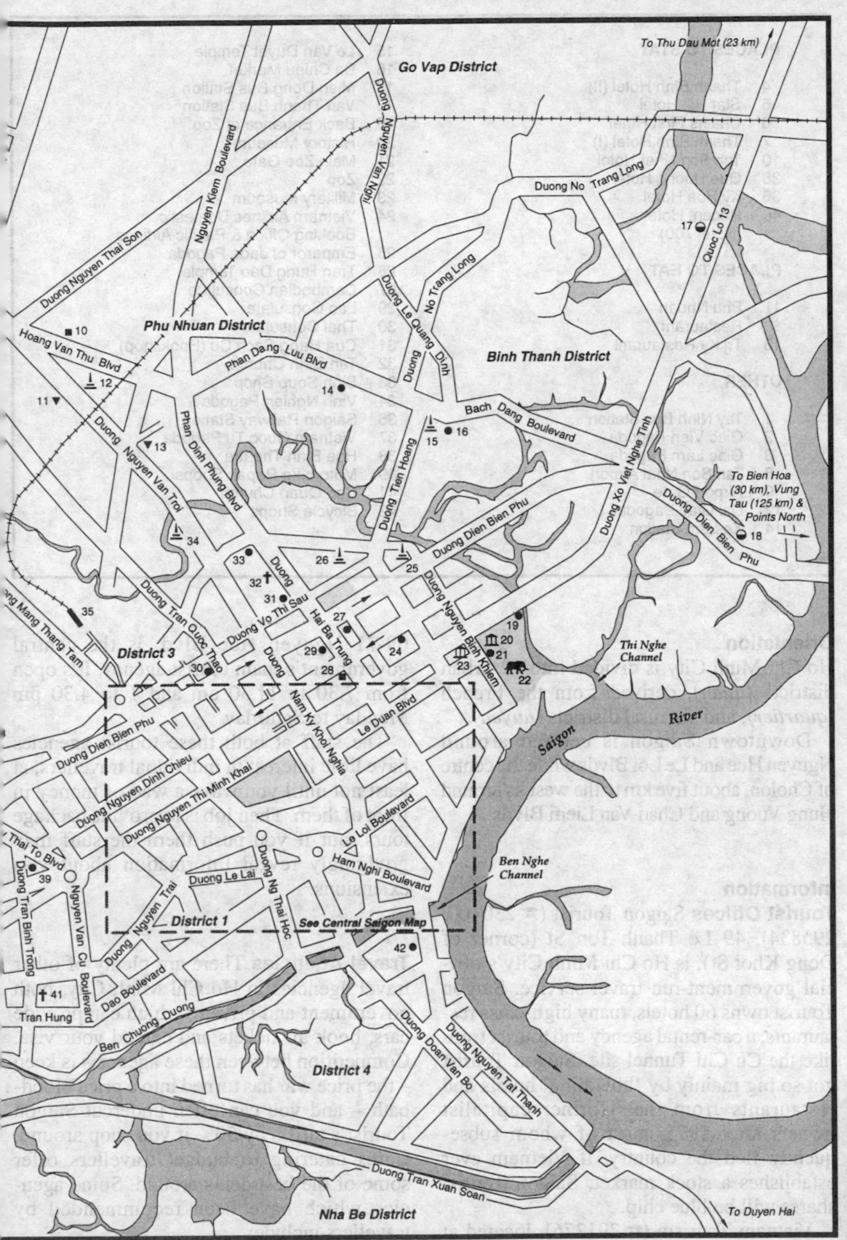

To Thu Dau Mot (23 km)
Go Vap District
Duong Nguyen Van Nghi
Nguyen Kiem Boulevard
Duong Nguyen Thai Son
Duong No Trang Long
Quoc Lo 13
17
No Trang Long
Duong Le Quang Dinh
Phu Nhuan District
10
Hoang Van Thu Blvd
12
11
Phan Dang Luu Blvd
Binh Thanh District
14
Duong Nguyen Van Troi
Phan Dinh Phung Blvd
13
15
16
Bach Dang Boulevard
Duong Tien Hoang
Duong Xo Viet Nghe Tinh
To Bien Hoa (30 km), Vung Tau (125 km) & Points North
Duong Dien Bien Phu
18
34
33
26
25
Duong Dien Bien Phu
32
Duong
Duong Nguyen Binh Khiem
Duong Tran Quoc Thao
31
Duong Mang Thang Tam
35
Duong Vo Thi Sau
Hai Ba Trung
27
19
District 3
30
29
24
20
21
23
22
28
Thi Nghe Channel
Duong
Nam Ki Khoi Nghia
Le Duan Blvd
Saigon
River
Duong Dien Bien Phu
Duong Nguyen Dinh Chieu
Duong Nguyen Thi Minh Khai
Le Loi Boulevard
Thai To Blvd
Duong Ng Thai Hoc
Ham Nghi Boulevard
39
Duong Le Lai
Ben Nghe Channel
Duong Tran Binh Trong
Nguyen Van Cu Boulevard
Duong Nguyen Trai
District 1
See Central Saigon Map
42
41
Dao Boulevard
Tran Hung
Ben Chuong Duong
Duong Doan Van Bo
Duong Nguyen Tat Thanh
District 4
Duong Tran Xuan Soan
Nha Be District
To Duyen Hai

VIETNAM

PLACES TO STAY

4 Thanh Binh Hotel (II)
5 Star Hill Hotel
6 Chains First Hotel
7 Thanh Binh Hotel (I)
10 Tan Son Nhat Hotel
28 Que Huong Hotel
36 Ky Hoa Hotel
40 Regent Hotel (Hotel 700)

PLACES TO EAT

11 Phu Nhuan Restaurant
13 Tri Ky Restaurant

OTHER

1 Tay Ninh Bus Station
2 Giac Vien Pagoda
3 Giac Lam Pagoda
8 Tan Son Nhat Airport
9 Airport Gate
12 Dai Giac Pagoda
14 Xe Lam Station
15 Le Van Duyet Temple
16 Ba Chieu Market
17 Mien Dong Bus Station
18 Van Thanh Bus Station
19 Back Entrance of Zoo
20 History Museum
21 Main Zoo Gate
22 Zoo
23 Military Museum
24 Vietnam Airlines Domestic Booking Office & Pacific Airlines
25 Emperor of Jade Pagoda
26 Tran Hung Dao Temple
27 Cambodian Consulate
29 Lao Consulate
30 Thai Consulate
31 Cua Hang Sach Cu (Bookshop)
32 Tan Dinh Church
33 Binh Soup Shop
34 Vinh Nghien Pagoda
35 Saigon Railway Station
37 Vietnam Quoc Tu Pagoda
38 Hoa Binh Theatre
39 Motorbike Repair Shops
41 Cho Quan Church
42 Bicycle Shops

Orientation

Ho Chi Minh City is divided into 12 urban districts *(quan)*, derived from the French *(quartier)*, and six rural districts *(huyen)*.

Downtown Saigon is centred around Nguyen Hue and Le Loi Blvds while the centre of Cholon, about five km to the west, is around Hung Vuong and Chau Van Liem Blvds.

Information

Tourist Offices Saigon Tourist (☎ 230100, 295834), 49 Le Thanh Ton St (corner of Dong Khoi St), is Ho Chi Minh City's official government-run travel service. Saigon Tourist owns 60 hotels, many high-class restaurants, a car-rental agency and tourist traps like the Cu Chi Tunnel site. Saigon Tourist got so big mainly by 'liberating' hotels and restaurants from their former capitalist owners after 1975, most of whom subsequently fled the country. If Vietnam ever establishes a stock market, Saigon Tourist shares will be blue chip.

Vietnam Tourism (☎ 291276), located at 69-71 Nguyen Hue Blvd, is the central government's main tourist agency. It's open from 7.30 to 11.30 am and 1 to 4.30 pm Monday to Saturday.

The staff at both these tourist agencies have little interest in individual travellers, at least not until you wave a wad of money in front of them. Their job is to provide package tours, but if you push them the staff may grudgingly reveal information about visa extensions.

Travel Agencies There are plenty of other travel agencies in Ho Chi Minh City, both government and private, which can provide cars, book air tickets and extend your visa. Competition between these agencies is keen – the price war has turned into a price bloodbath – and you can often undercut Saigon Tourist's tariffs by 50% if you shop around. Cafes catering to budget travellers offer some of the best deals around. Some agencies which have been recommended by travellers include:

Ann Tourist
58 Ton That Tung St, District 1 (☎ 332564; fax (84-8) 323866)
Cam On Tour
62 Hai Ba Trung St, District 1 (☎ 222166; fax (84-8) 298540)
CESAIS Lam Son Travel
Lam Son Square (behind the Municipal Theatre), District 1
CESAIS Tourism Service Centre (Trung Tam Dich Vu Du Lich CESAIS)
17 Pham Ngoc Thach, District 3 (☎ 296750)
Easiway (Pham Bac Hoa & Christine Hong)
34 Pham Ngoc Thach, District 3 (☎ 231337)
Kim's Cafeteria
270 De Tham St (☎ 398177)
Oscan Enterprises
2D Pham Ngoc Thach St, District 3 (☎ 231191; fax (84-8) 231024)
Peace Tours (Cong Ty Du Lich Hoa Binh)
60 Vo Van Tan, District 3 (☎ 298707)
Phoenix Services
199 Nam Ky Khoi Nghia, District 3 (☎ 224076, 224509; fax 291328)
Sinh Café
6 Pham Ngu Lao St (☎ 251842)

Another example of the price war is that cafes in Saigon can book 10-day trips which include Kontum for US$80 while Saigon Tourist charges US$1500 for the same thing.

Hotels and travel agencies can arrange visa extensions – shop around for the best price but figure on around US$20 for 15 days. For more information, see under Visas & Embassies in the Facts for the Visitor section.

Money The airport bank gives the legal exchange rate. The only problem is that the staff work bankers' hours, which means the bank is closed when at least half of the flights arrive. For this reason, you'd be wise to have sufficient US$ notes in small denominations to get yourself into the city.

Vietcombank (☎ 4252831), also known as the Bank for Foreign Trade of Vietnam (Ngan Hang Ngoai Thuong Viet Nam), is at 29 Ben Chuong Duong St on the corner of Nguyen Thi Minh Khai St (Pasteur St). It is open from 7 to 11.30 am and 1.30 to 3.30 pm daily, except Saturday afternoon and the last day of the month. Here you can change US cash, other major hard currencies and travellers' cheques at the official rate. Bring your passport (or a photocopy of it) for identification.

Vietcombank does cash advances for holders of MasterCard. If you need a cash advance against a Visa card, the place to go is Banque Française du Commerce Extérieur, 10 Ham Nghi St.

Post & Telecommunications Saigon's French-style GPO (Buu Dien Thanh Pho Ho Chi Minh) is at 2 Cong Xa Paris, next to Notre Dame Cathedral. Postal services are available daily from 7.30 am to 7.30 pm.

Foreign Consulates The addresses and telephone numbers of Ho Chi Minh City's consulates are as follows:

Cambodia
43 Phung Khac Khoan St, District 1 (☎ 292751, 292744)
Laos
181 Hai Ba Trung St, District 3 (☎ 297667)
Malaysia
53 Nguyen Dinh Chieu St, District 3 (☎ 299023)
Thailand
77 Tran Quoc Thao St, District 3

Medical Services Cho Ray Hospital (Benh Vien Cho Ray; ☎ 254137, 258074; 1000 beds), one of the best medical facilities in Vietnam, is at 201B Nguyen Chi Thanh St, District 5 (Cholon). There is a section for foreigners on the 10th floor. About a third of the 200 doctors speak English. You might also try Nhi Dong 2 Hospital (Grall Hospital) on Ly Tu Trong St opposite the Franco-Vietnamese Cultural Centre.

There are hundreds of pharmacies *(nha thuoc)* around the city.

Temples & Pagodas

Giac Lam Pagoda This pagoda dates from 1744 and is believed to be the oldest in the city. The architecture and style of ornamentation have not changed since the 19th century.

The best way to get there is to take Nguyen Chi Thanh Blvd or 3 Thang 2 Blvd to Le Dai Hanh St. Go north-west on Le Dai Hanh St

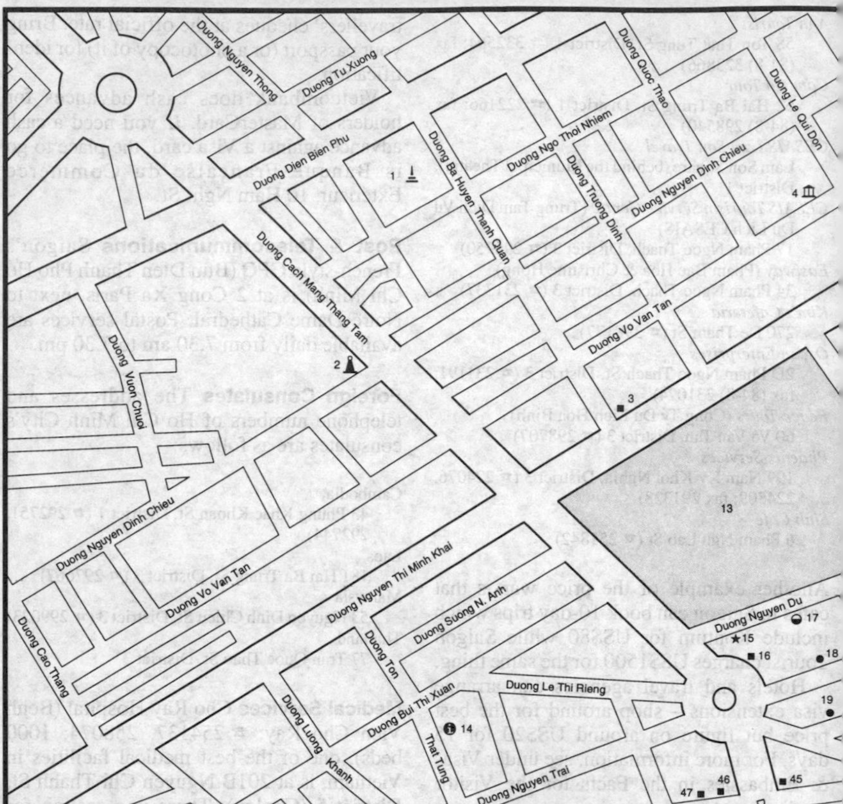

Central Saigon

0 150 300 m

Duong Nguyen Thong
Duong Tu Xuong
Duong Quoc Thao
Duong Le Qui Don
Duong Ngo Thoi Nhiem
Duong Dien Bien Phu
Duong Ba Huyen Thanh Quan
Duong Truong Dinh
Duong Nguyen Dinh Chieu
Duong Cach Mang Thang Tam
Duong Vo Van Tan
Duong Vuon Chuoi
Duong Nguyen Dinh Chieu
Duong Vo Van Tan
Duong Nguyen Thi Minh Khai
Duong Suong N. Anh
Duong Nguyen Du
Duong Cao Thang
Duong Ton
Duong Le Thi Rieng
Duong Bui Thi Xuan
Duong Luong Khanh
That Tung
Duong Nguyen Trai
Duong Pham Viet Chanh
Duong Cong Quynh
Duong Le Lai
Duong Nguyen Thai Hoc
Duong Pham Ngu Lao
Duong Do Dau
Duong Nguyen Trai
Duong Bui Vien
Tran Hung Dao Boulevard
Duong De Tham
Duong Nguyen Cu Trinh
Duong Co Bac
To Cholon

1 2 3 4 13 14 15 16 17 18 19 45 46 47 48 49 50 51 52 53 54 55 56 57 58

To Tan Son Nhat Airport (5.5 km)
To Zoo (300 m)
Duong Vo Van Tan
Duong Nguyen Thi Minh Khai
Duong Hai Ba Trung
Duong Nguyen Du
Duong Chu Manh Trinh
Duong Ton Duc Thang
Duong Thai Van Lung
Duong Nam Ky Khoi Nghia
Le Duan Boulevard
Duong Pasteur
Duong Han Thuyen
Duong Nguyen Du
Duong Dong Khoi
Duong H Tr Cong Chua
Duong Le Thanh Ton
Thi Sach
Duong Don Dat
Duong Ly Tu Trong
Duong Nguyen Trung Truc
Thu Khoa Huan
Ly Tu Trong
Duong Truong Dinh
Duong Le Thanh Ton
Phan Boi Chau
Le Loi Boulevard
Duong Nam Ky Khoi Nghia
Duong Nguyen Thiep
Duong Dong Du
Mac Thi Buoi
H H Nghiep
Duc Ke
Ton That Thiep
Nguyen Hue Boulevard
Thuc Khang
Duong Ho Tung Mau
Duong Ton That Dam
Duong Pasteur
Huynh
Duong Le Lai
Duong Pham Ngu Lao
Duong
Ham Nghi Boulevard
Ngo
Duong
Duong Ton Duc Thang
Duong Le Thi Hong Gam
Pho Duc Chinh
Duong Calmette
Cong Tru
Duong Nguyen
Duong Nguyen Cong Tru
Ben Chuong Duong
Duong Nguyen Tat Thanh
Duong Nguyen Thai Binh
Duong Ky Con
Duong Yersin
Ben Nghe Channel
Duong Ben Van Don
Saigon River

PLACES TO STAY

3 Saigon Star Hotel
16 Hoang Gia Hotel
21 Tao Dan Hotel
22 Embassy Hotel
26 Orchid Hotel
28 Continental Hotel
34 Rex Hotel (Ben Thanh Hotel)
38 Norfolk Hotel
45 Le Lai Hotel
46 Palace Saigon Hotel
47 A Chau & Le Suong Hotels
49 Prince Hotel (Hoang Tu Hotel)
51 Hoang Vu Hotel
52 Guest House #70 & 72
53 Vien Dong Hotel
54 Thai Binh Hotel
55 Peace Mini-Hotel
61 Thai Binh Duong Hotel
66 Vinh Loi Hotel
69 Century Saigon Hotel
70 Palace Hotel
72 Bong Sen Hotel
73 Mondial Hotel
74 Huong Sen Hotel
75 Saigon Hotel
78 Khach San 69 Hal Ba Trung
79 Caravelle Hotel & Air France
85 Saigon Floating Hotel
88 Riverside Hotel
90 Dong Khoi Hotel
93 Majestic Hotel

PLACES TO EAT

11 Madame Dai's Restaurant
31 Givral Ptisserie & Caf
36 Kem Bach Dang
39 Kem Bach Dang
41 Saigon Intershop & Minimart
48 Sinh Caf
50 Kim's Cafeteria
57 Lam Vien Restaurant
58 Fruit & Vegetable Market
62 Tin Nghia Vegetarian Restaurant
68 My Canh 2 Restaurant
71 Brodard Caf
81 Yellow Umbrella Restaurant
87 Restaurant 13
91 City Restaurant
92 Nha Hang 32 Ngo Duc Ke
95 Nha Hang 51 Nguyen Hue

OTHER

1 Xa Loi Pagoda
2 Thich Quang Duc Memorial
4 War Crimes Exhibition
5 Foreign Affairs Ministry
6 French Consulate Compound
7 Former US Embassy (1967-75)
8 GPO
9 Notre Dame Cathedral
10 Stamps & Coins Market
12 Reunification Hall
13 Cong Vien Van Hoa Park
14 Ann Tourist
15 Immigration Police Office
17 Buses to Cambodia
18 Motorbike Shops
19 Bicycle Shops
20 Mariamman Hindu Temple
23 Municipal Library
24 Revolutionary Museum
25 Hotel de Ville (Town Hall)
27 Municipal Theatre
29 Saigon Tourist
30 Vietnam Airlines International Booking Office
32 Philippine Airlines
33 Aeroflot
35 Phnom Penh Bus Garage
37 Cua Hang Bach Hoa (Tax Store)
40 Bookshop
42 Leather Goods & Shoe Stores
43 Ben Thanh Market
44 Bikes, Motorbikes & Sporting Goods
56 Thai Binh Market
59 Phung Son Tu Pagoda
60 War Surplus Market
63 Art Museum
64 Ben Thanh Bus Station
65 Tran Nguyen Han Statue
67 District 1 Post Office
76 Hard Rock Caf
77 Saigon Central Mosque
80 Ton Duc Thang Museum
82 Apocalypse Now
83 Shake's Pub
84 Me Linh Square & Tran Hung Dao Statue
86 Small Motorised Boats for Rental
89 Dining Cruise
94 Minibus Office (Cong Ty Dich Vu Du Lich Quan 1)
96 Vietnam Tourism
97 Huynh Thuc Khang Street Market
98 Pre-1967 US Embassy
99 Boats to Mekong Delta & Vung Tau
100 Boats across Saigon River
101 National Bank Building
102 Vietcombank
103 An Duong Vuong Statue
104 Wedding Taxis
105 Ho Chi Minh Museum

and turn right onto Lac Long Quan St. Walk 100 metres and the pagoda gate will be on your left. It is open to visitors from 6 am to 9 pm.

Giac Vien Pagoda The pagoda is right next to Dam Sen Lake in District 11, a more rural setting. Giac Vien was founded by Hai Tinh Giac Vien about 200 years ago. Today, 10 monks live here.

Because of the impossibly confusing numbering on Lac Long Quan St, the best way to get to Giac Vien Pagoda is to take Nguyen Chi Thanh Blvd or 3 Thang 2 Blvd to Le Dai Hanh St. Turn left (south-west) off Le Dai Hanh St on to Binh Thoi St and turn right (north) at Lac Long Quan St. The gate leading to the pagoda is at 247 Lac Long Quan St.

Pass through the gate and go several hundred metres down a dirt road, turning left at the 'tee' and right at the fork. The pagoda is open from 7 am to 7 pm but come before dark as the electricity is often out.

Emperor of Jade Pagoda This pagoda, known in Vietnamese as Phuoc Hai Tu and Chua Ngoc Hoang, was built in 1909 by the Canton congregation and is a gem of a Chinese temple. Filled with colourful statues of phantasmal divinities and grotesque heroes, it's one of the most spectacular pagodas in the city. The statues represent characters from both the Buddhist and Taoist traditions and are made of reinforced papier-mâché.

The Emperor of Jade Pagoda is at 73 Mai Thi Luu St in a part of Saigon known as Da Kao (or Da Cao). To get there, go to 20 Dien Bien Phu St and walk half a block north-westward (to the left as you head out of Saigon towards Thi Nghe Channel).

Notre Dame Cathedral The Notre Dame Cathedral, built between 1877 and 1883, is in the heart of Saigon's government quarter. Its neo-Romanesque form and two 40-metre-high square towers, tipped with iron spires, dominate the skyline. If the front gates (at the north-western terminus of Dong Khoi St) are locked, try at the door on the side of the building that faces Reunification Hall.

Mariamman Hindu Temple Mariamman Hindu Temple, the only Hindu temple still in use in the city, is a little piece of southern India in central Saigon. There are only 50 to 60 Hindus here, all Tamils, but the temple (referred to in Vietnamese as Chua Ba Mariamman), is also considered sacred by many ethnic Vietnamese and Chinese. The temple is at 45 Truong Dinh St, only three blocks from Ben Thanh Market. It was built at the end of the 19th century and dedicated to the Hindu goddess Mariamman. It is open daily from 7 am to 7 pm.

Saigon Central Mosque Built by south Indian Muslims in 1935 on the site of an earlier mosque, the Saigon Central Mosque is an immaculately clean and well-kept island of calm in the middle of bustling central Saigon. In front of the sparkling white and blue structure at 66 Dong Du St, with its four nonfunctional minarets, is a pool for ritual ablutions before prayers. As with any mosque, take off your shoes before entering the sanctuary.

Tam Son Hoi Quan Pagoda This pagoda, known to the Vietnamese as Chua Ba Chua, was built by the Fujian Chinese congregation in the 19th century. It retains much of its original rich ornamentation. The pagoda is dedicated to Me Sanh, the Goddess of Fertility. Both men and women – but more of the latter – come here to pray for children. The pagoda is at 118 Trieu Quang Phuc St, Cholon, very near 370 Tran Hung Dao B Blvd.

Nghia An Hoi Quan Pagoda This pagoda, built by the Trieu Chau Chinese congregation, is noteworthy for its gilded woodwork. It is at 678 Nguyen Trai St, Cholon, and is open from 4 am to 6 pm.

Quan Am Pagoda At 12 Lao Tu St, Cholon, one block off Chau Van Liem Blvd, this pagoda was founded in 1816 by the Fujian Chinese congregation. The roof is decorated with fantastic scenes, rendered in ceramic, from traditional Chinese plays and stories. The tableaus include ships, houses, people and several ferocious dragons. The front doors are decorated with very old gold and lacquer panels.

Phuoc An Hoi Quan Pagoda Built in 1902 by the Fujian Chinese congregation, this pagoda is one of the most beautifully ornamented in the city. Of special interest are the many small porcelain figures, the elaborate brass ritual objects, and the fine wood carvings on the altars, walls, columns and hanging lanterns.

From outside the building, you can see the ceramic scenes, each made up of innumerable figurines, which decorate the roof. It is at 184 Hung Vuong Blvd (near the intersection of Chau Van Liem Blvd), Cholon.

Phung Son Pagoda This is a Vietnamese Buddhist pagoda which is extremely rich in statuary made of hammered copper, bronze, wood and ceramic. It is in District 11 at 1408, 3 Thang 2 Blvd, Cholon, which is a block from Hung Vuong Blvd. The side entrance (to the left as you approach the building) is open from 5 am to 7 pm.

Museums

War Crimes Exhibition Once known as the Museum of American War Crimes, the name has been changed so as not to offend the sensibilities of American tourists. However, the pamphlet handed out at reception pulls no punches: it's entitled 'Some Pictures of US Imperialist's Aggressive War Crimes in Vietnam'.

This museum, housed in the former US Information Service building, is the most popular with foreigners. It's on the corner of Le Qui Don and Vo Van Tan Sts, near central Saigon.

Reunification Hall Built in 1966 to serve as South Vietnam's Presidential Palace, it was toward this building – then known as Independence Hall – that the first Communist tanks in Saigon rushed on the morning of 30 April 1975, the day Saigon surrendered. The building has been left just as it looked on that momentous day.

Reunification Hall is open for visitors from 7.30 to 10.30 am and 12.30 to 3.30 pm daily, except Sunday afternoon and when official receptions or meetings are taking place. The visitors' office and one of the entrances is at 106 Duong Nguyen Du (☎ 290629). The entrance fee for foreigners is US$3.25. Groups can make reservations in person or by phone and this is supposed to be done a day in advance to be sure a guide is available.

Revolutionary Museum Housed in a white neoclassical structure built in 1886 and once known as Gia Long Palace, the Revolutionary Museum is at 27 Ly Tu Trong St. There are displays of artefacts from the various periods of the Communist struggle for power in Vietnam. The museum is open from 8 to 11.30 am and from 2 to 4.30 pm, Tuesday to Sunday.

History Museum Built in 1929 by the Société des Études Indochinoises, and once the National Museum of the Republic of Vietnam, the History Museum displays artefacts from 3300 years of human activity in what is now Vietnam. Located just inside the main entrance to the Zoo (on Nguyen Binh Khiem St at Le Duan Blvd), it is open from 8 to 11.30 am and from 1 to 4 pm daily except Monday.

Parks & Gardens

Zoo & Botanical Garden The Zoo and its surrounding gardens, founded by the French in 1864, are a delightful place for a relaxing stroll under giant tropical trees. There are sometimes water-puppet shows here. The main gate is on Nguyen Binh Khiem St at the intersection of Le Duan Blvd.

Cong Vien Van Hoa Park Situated next to the old Cercle Sportif, an elite sporting club during the French period, the bench-lined walks of Cong Vien Van Hoa Park are shaded by avenues of enormous tropical trees.

This place is still an active sports centre but now you don't have to be French to visit. There are tennis courts, a swimming pool and a clubhouse which have a grand colonial feel about them. It's worth a look for the pool alone. There are Roman-style baths with a coffee shop overlooking the colonnaded pool.

The antique dressing rooms are quaint but there are no lockers! There are facilities for table tennis, weight lifting, wrestling and ballroom dancing, plus a gym.

Cong Vien Van Hoa Park is adjacent to Reunification Hall. There are entrances across from 115 Nguyen Du St and on Nguyen Thi Minh Khai St.

Binh Quoi Tourist Village Built on a small peninsula in the Saigon River, the Binh Quoi Tourist Village (Lang Du Lich Binh Quoi; ☎ 991833) is a slick tourist trap operated by Saigon Tourist. The 'village' is essentially a park featuring boat rides, water-puppet shows, a restaurant, swimming pool, tennis courts, camping ground, a guesthouse and amusements for the kids. The park puts in a plug for Vietnam's ethnic minorities by staging traditional-style minority weddings accompanied by music.

On Tuesday and Saturday evening from 5 to 10 pm, there is a traditional music performance and boat rides along the river. This might be worthwhile.

Binh Quoi Tourist Village is eight km north from downtown Saigon in the Binh Thanh district. The official address is 1147 Xo Viet Nghe Tinh St.

Places to Stay – bottom end

There is enormous variety ranging from the luxurious to truly grungy dives available by the hour. Prostitution is supposedly banned in government-owned hotels (unless the army or police run the hotel), creating an enormous opportunity for the new privately owned 'mini-hotels'.

Not all hotels are permitted to serve 'capitalist tourists'. While there are some really grotty dumps that will take foreigners, the tendency is to force foreigners upmarket. However, you can still find a room for US$5 a night.

Touts from private hotels hang around the airport looking for business. If you haven't got a clear idea of where you want to stay, you can at least talk to them.

Central Saigon (District 1) Pham Ngu Lao St in District 1 has emerged as the city's main centre for budget travellers. The *Hoang Vu Hotel* (☎ 396522, 396552) at 265A Pham Ngu Lao St is extremely popular with backpackers. Prices for rooms are US$7 to US$16.

The Hoang Vu fills up quickly and much of the overflow winds up staying in the nearby *Prince Hotel* (Hoang Tu in Vietnamese) at 193 Pham Ngu Lao St. Many travellers have reported the theft of valuables from their rooms in the Prince – lock your door with your own padlock. Rooms are priced the same as the Hoang Vu.

Many backpackers head down the street to the nearby *Thai Binh Hotel* (☎ 399544) at No 325, where doubles are only US$6.

Around the corner on Bui Vien St are two very clean and safe private hotels, *Guest House 70* (☎ 330569) and *Guest House 72* (☎ 330321); both charge US$7 for a room with fan or US$12 for air-conditioned comfort.

On a quiet alley behind Thai Binh Market is the very peaceful *Peace Mini-Hotel* (☎ 396544), 373/20 Pham Ngu Lao St. Doubles with fan are US$8 to US$12, and air-con will cost you US$12 to US$16.

A Chau Hotel (☎ 331571), 12 Le Lai St, is a popular place 50 metres from the fancy Palace Saigon Hotel. Singles/doubles cost US$5/7. Just next door is another current best seller, the *Le Suong Hotel* (☎ 334137) where singles/doubles are US$5/7 (with fan) and US$10/12 (with air-con).

Tao Dan Hotel is in a narrow alley just behind the snazzy Embassy Hotel on Nguyen Trung Truc St. Doubles with fan/air-con are US$8/15. The Japanese guidebooks give this place a good plug so it's often filled with Japanese backpackers.

Khach San 69 Hai Ba Trung (☎ 291513) is, as its name suggests, at 69 Hai Ba Trung St. Triples with fans are US$10; air-con pushes the tariff to US$15 while 'special' doubles cost US$20.

The *Dong Khoi Hotel* (☎ 294046), 12 Ngo Duc Ke St (corner with Dong Khoi St), is a grand old French-era building. It's quite a bargain with singles from US$10 to US$14 and doubles for US$18.

Cholon (District 5) Relatively few Westerners stay in Cholon, but it's cheap. This is the neighbourhood of choice for overseas Chinese visitors, and though not much English is spoken, you can brush up on your Mandarin and Cantonese.

The *Phuong Huong Hotel* (☎ 551888), 411 Tran Hung Dao B Blvd, is also known as the Phenix Hotel. Rooms cost US$11 to US$22.

Just up Chau Van Liem St at 111-117 is the *Truong Thanh Hotel* (☎ 556044). None of the rooms have air-con, but the hotel provides 'other services', namely prostitution. Singles/doubles cost US$4/5, other services not included.

Half a block away, at 125 Chau Van Liem St, is the *Thu Do Hotel* (☎ 559102). It looks very much like a dump, but what do you expect for US$4/5.

The *Trung Mai Hotel* (☎ 552101), 785 Nguyen Trai St, is just off Chau Van Liem Blvd. It's definitely a 'lower end' hotel but you'll probably survive. Singles/doubles with fan cost US$5/6 while air-con rooms are US$10/11.

The *Bat Dat Hotel* (☎ 555817) is a good choice at 238-244 Tran Hung Dao B Blvd (near the pricey Arc En Ciel Hotel). Rooms with fan cost US$7 for a single, while air-con ups the damage to US$16. This place is a candidate for renovation.

The *Hoa Binh Hotel* (☎ 355113), 1115 Tran Hung Dao Blvd, is looking a bit tattered around the edges but is otherwise OK. Singles/doubles with fan are US$5/7; with air-con and refrigerator it's US$12/15.

Khach San Quoc Thai (☎ 351657), 41 Nguyen Duy Duong St, is a dump but cheap. Singles/doubles with private bath and fan go for US$7/8.

Places to Stay – middle & top end

Central Saigon (District 1) Some places to stay in this neighbourhood include:

Bong Sen (☎ 291516), 117-119 Dong Khoi St, air-con singles/doubles US$25/35 to US$120/140

Caravelle (☎ 293704), 19-23 Lam Son Square (Saigon's most French hotel), singles/doubles US$46/57 to US$149

Century Saigon (☎ 231818), 68A Nguyen Hue Blvd, singles/doubles US$110/175 to US$475

Continental (☎ 294456), 132-134 Dong Khoi St, singles US$66 to US$132, doubles US$88 to US$154

Embassy (☎ 291430), 35 Nguyen Trung Truc St, doubles US$70 to US$120

Hoang Gia (☎ 294846), 12D Cach Mang Thang Tam St, singles/doubles US$27/33

Huong Sen (☎ 291415), 70 Dong Khoi St, air-con singles/doubles US$34/44 to US$50/60

Le Lai (☎ 291246), 76 Le Lai St, singles/doubles/triples US$22/29/37 to US$68/81/94

Majestic (☎ 295515), 1 Dong Khoi St, singles/doubles US$45/57 to US$120/140

PLACES TO STAY

3 Phu Tho Hotel
4 Goldstar Hotel
10 Thu Do Hotel
11 Truong Thanh Hotel
12 Phuong Huong (Phenix) Hotel
14 Trung Mai Hotel
24 Arc En Ciel (Rainbow) Hotel
25 Tan Dan Hotel
26 Bat Dat Hotel
30 Dong Khanh 5 Hotel
31 Cholon Tourist Mini-Hotel
32 Cholon Hotel
34 Andong Hotel
35 Khach San Quoc Thai (Hotel)
36 Dong Khanh Hotel
38 Hoa Binh Hotel
39 Tokyo Hotel
40 Hanh Long Hotel

PLACES TO EAT

23 My Le Hoa Restaurant
37 Tiem Com Chay Phat Huu Duyen (Vegetarian Restaurant)

OTHER

1 Phung Son Pagoda
2 Khanh Van Nam Vien Pagoda
5 An Quang Pagoda
6 Binh Tay Market
7 Cholon Bus Station
8 Cha Tam Church
9 Ong Bon Pagoda
13 Post Office
15 Quan Am Pagoda
16 Phuoc An Hoi Quan Pagoda
17 Cho Ray Hospital
18 Electronics Market
19 Thien Hau Pagoda
20 Nghia An Hoi Quan Pagoda
21 Tam Son Hoi Quan Pagoda
22 Cholon Mosque
27 Taxi Stand at Pham Ngoc Thach
28 Nga Sau Church
29 Consumer Goods Market
33 Andong Market

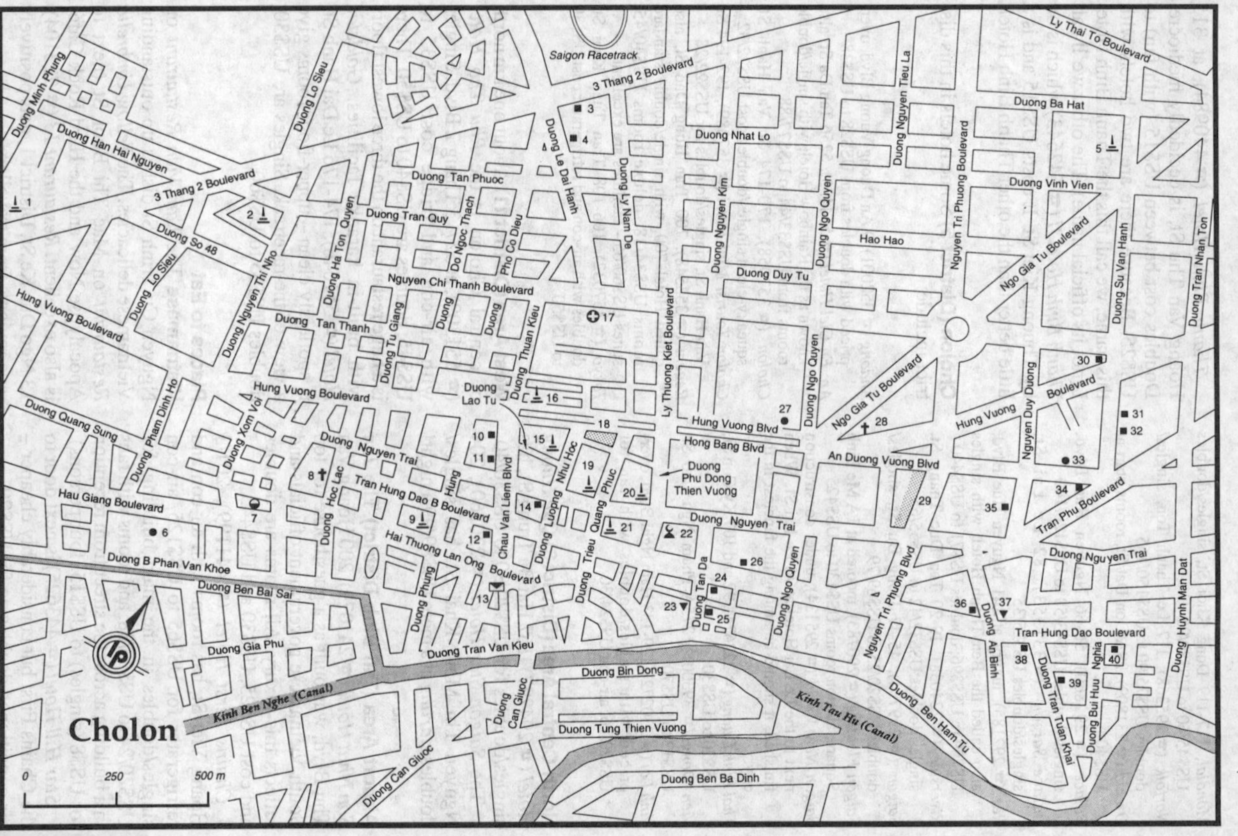
Cholon
0
250
500 m
Kinh Ben Nghe (Canal)
Kinh Tau Hu (Canal)
Saigon Racetrack
3 Thang 2 Boulevard
Ly Thai To Boulevard
Duong Minh Phung
Duong Han Hai Nguyen
Duong Lo Sieu
Duong So 48
Duong Nguyen Thi Nho
Hung Vuong Boulevard
Duong Quang Sung
Duong Pham Dinh Ho
Duong Xom Voi
Hau Giang Boulevard
Duong B Phan Van Khoe
Duong Ben Bai Sai
Duong Gia Phu
Duong Tan Phuoc
Duong Tran Quy
Duong Ha Ton Quyen
Do Ngoc Thach
Pho Co Dieu
Nguyen Chi Thanh Boulevard
Duong Tan Thanh
Duong Tu Giang
Duong Thuan Kieu
Duong Lao Tu
Duong Le Dai Hanh
Duong Ly Nam De
Duong Nhat Lo
Duong Nguyen Kim
Duong Ngo Quyen
Duong Duy Tu
Duong Nguyen Tieu La
Nguyen Tri Phuong Boulevard
Hao Hao
Duong Ba Hat
Duong Vinh Vien
Ngo Gia Tu Boulevard
Duong Su Van Hanh
Duong Tran Nhan Ton
Ly Thuong Kiet Boulevard
Hung Vuong Blvd
Hong Bang Blvd
An Duong Vuong Blvd
Hung Vuong
Nguyen Duy Duong
Boulevard
Tran Phu Boulevard
Duong Nguyen Trai
Duong Hoc Lac
Tran Hung Dao B Boulevard
Hung
Chau Van Liem Blvd
Duong Luong Nhu Hoc
Duong Trieu Quang Phuc
Duong Phu Dong Thien Vuong
Hai Thuong Lan Ong Boulevard
Duong Phung
Duong Tran Van Kieu
Duong Tan Da
Nguyen Tri Phuong Blvd
Duong An Binh
Tran Hung Dao Boulevard
Duong Huynh Man Dat
Duong Bui Huu Nghia
Duong Tran Tuan Khai
Duong Ben Ham Tu
Duong Bin Dong
Duong Can Giuoc
Duong Tung Thien Vuong
Duong Ben Ba Dinh
1
2
3
4
5
6
7
8
9
10
11
12
13
14
15
16
17
18
19
20
21
22
23
24
25
26
27
28
29
30
31
32
33
34
35
36
37
38
39
40

VIETNAM

Mondial, 117-119 Dong Khoi St, singles/doubles US$45/60 to US$80/95
Norfolk (☎ 295368), 117 Le Thanh Ton, singles/doubles US$75/90 to US$150/165
Orchid (☎ 231809), 29A Don Dat St, rooms start at US$40
Palace (☎ 292860), 56-66 Nguyen Hue Blvd, singles/doubles US$43/58 to US$120/140
Palace Saigon (☎ 331353), 82 Le Lai St, singles/doubles US$25/35
Rex (☎ 292185), luxury at 141 Nguyen Hue Blvd, also called the Ben Thanh Hotel, with singles US$59 to US$396; doubles US$71 to US$440
Riverside (☎ 224038), 19-20 Ton Duc Thang St, singles/doubles US$32/42 to US$55/65
Saigon (☎ 299734), 45-47 Dong Du St, singles/doubles US$20/25 to US$69/79
Saigon Floating (☎ 290783), moored at 1A Me Linh Square, air-con rooms US$130 to US$425
Saigon New World (☎ 295134), under construction next to the Le Lai Hotel at 76 Le Lai St. When finished, it should be among the fanciest in the city.
Thai Binh Duong (☎ 222674), 92 and 107 Ky Con St, US$20 to US$30
Vien Dong (☎ 393001), 275A Pham Ngu Lao St, US$12 to US$70
Vinh Loi (☎ 230272), 129-133 Ham Nghi Blvd, overpriced with singles/doubles with fan for US$20/26, air-con US$24/30

North-Central Area (District 3) *Que Huong Hotel* (☎ 294227), 167 Hai Ba Trung St, has singles/doubles for US$20/30 to US$30/40.

The *Saigon Star Hotel* (☎ 230260), 204 Nguyen Thi Minh Khai St, has singles/doubles *starting* at a mere US$89/99 a night!

Airport Area (Tan Binh District) The *Tan Son Nhat Hotel* (☎ 241079), 200 Hoang Van Thu Blvd, was built as a guesthouse for top South Vietnamese government officials and reflects this luxury. All rooms are doubles and cost US$25, US$30 and US$44.

Chains First Hotel (☎ 441199), 201/3 Hoang Viet St, has rooms with air-con and refrigerator for US$65 to US$125, air-con singles/doubles in the main building for US$20/24 to US$33/38, and rooms with fans in a building across the street from reception for US$8 (singles) to US$15 (four persons).

Star Hill Hotel (☎ 443625) is next door to the Chains First but considerably cheaper – air-conditioned doubles go for US$20.

Thanh Binh Hotel (☎ 440984), at 315 Hoang Van Thu St, is decidedly mediocre. Doubles cost between US$15 (with fan) to US$25. Because there are two hotels with this name, we call this the Thanh Binh Hotel I (not its official name). The other we'll call *Thanh Binh Hotel II* (☎ 642643) which is on Ly Thuong Kiet St. It costs US$15 and is a little better than the other Thanh Binh Hotel.

Cholon (District 5) Some hotels in this district include:

Andong (☎ 352001), 9 An Duong Vuong Blvd, overpriced with doubles from US$28 to US$38
Arc En Ciel Hotel (☎ 554435), 5256 Tan Da St, also known as the Rainbow Hotel, with single/double rooms from US$33/44 to US$77/88.
Cholon (☎ 357058), 170-174 Su Van Hanh St, squeaky-clean singles/doubles cost US$22/32
Cholon Tourist Mini-Hotel (☎ 357089), 192-194 Su Van Hanh St, singles/doubles for US$22/28
Regent (☎ 353548), 700 Tran Hung Dao St, also called Hotel 700, with single/double standard rooms US$34/38, deluxe rooms US$40/45, suites US$60/65 – facilities are excellent
Tokyo (☎ 357032), 106-108 Tran Tuan Khai St, doubles with air-con and refrigerator cost US$30 to US$50

West Area (District 11) About one km north of central Cholon is the *Phu Tho Hotel* (☎ 551309), at 527, 3 Thang 2 Blvd. Singles with air-con and fridge cost US$35 to US$45; doubles are US$40 to US$50. There is a huge restaurant on the three lowest floors with built-in karaoke facilities. *Goldstar Hotel* (☎ 551646), 174-176 Le Dai Hanh St, is spotlessly clean – upper-floor rooms give a view of the racetrack. Singles are US$30, doubles US$35 to US$60.

Places to Eat

Vietnamese The *Lam Vien Restaurant* on Nguyen Cu Trinh St dishes up outstanding Vietnamese delicacies. The *Yellow Umbrella Restaurant* on Mac Thi Buoi St (next to Apocalypse Now and the Hard Rock Café) is also excellent. *Restaurant 13* (☎ 223104), 13 Ngo Duc Ke St, District 1, gets positively rave reviews from travellers.

Chinese Cholon is Chinatown, the logical place to find Chinese restaurants. *My Le Hoa Restaurant* opposite the Tan Dan Hotel dishes up moderately priced Chinese meals.

Cafes For light Western-style meals or something to drink, there are a number of cafes featuring decent food at dirt-cheap prices. A popular hang-out for budget travellers staying at the Prince and Hoang Vu hotels is the *Sinh Café* (☎ 251842), 6 Pham Ngu Lao St. This is a very good place to meet people and get travel information. The cafe also arranges low-priced tours and can introduce you to English-speaking Vietnamese guides.

Kim's Cafeteria (☎ 398177), 270 De Tham St, provides similar service and similar prices. Don't confuse this place with the Kim Café almost next door to the Sinh Café (that Kim caters to Vietnamese) – Kim's Cafeteria is right around the corner from the Prince Hotel.

Vegetarian *Tin Nghia Vegetarian Restaurant* is a small place about 200 metres from Ben Thanh Market at 9 Tran Hung Dao Blvd. Meals cost less than US$1. Special vegetarian meals are also available at Kim's Cafeteria.

On the first and 15th days of the lunar month, foodstalls around the city – especially in the markets – serve vegetarian versions of non-vegetarian Vietnamese dishes.

Ice Cream The best ice cream (kem) in Ho Chi Minh City is served at the two shops called *Kem Bach Dang* (☎ 292707), which are on Le Loi St on either side of Nguyen Thi Minh Khai St (Pasteur St). Kem Bach Dang 2 is at 28 Le Loi Blvd. Both are under the same management and serve ice cream, hot and cold drinks and cakes for very reasonable prices. A US$0.50 speciality is ice cream served in a baby coconut with candied fruit on top (kem trai dua).

Dozens of little ice cream and yoghurt (yaourt) places line Dien Bien Phu St between numbers 125 and 187.

Self-Catering Simple meals can easily be assembled from fruits, vegetables, French bread and other basics sold in the city's markets. Try not to get short-weighed or overcharged. Fruit vendors can be found all over the city.

The best bread bakery in town is, according to many Saigonese, *Nhu Lan Bakery* at 66 Ham Nghi St. Fresh eggs are sold in the pastry shop of *Givral Pâtisserie & Café* at 169 Dong Khoi St.

Find yourself daydreaming about Kellogg's Frosties, Pringle's potato chips, Twining's tea or Campbell's soup? If you have an insatiable craving for plastic foods, by far the best place to go in Ho Chi Minh City is the *Minimart* (☎ 298189 ext 44) on the 2nd floor of the Saigon Intershop, 101 Nam Ky Khoi Nghia St. To enjoy the proffered delights, you must pay in US dollars.

Entertainment

Downtown Saigon is *the* place to be on Sunday and holiday nights. The streets are jam-packed with young Saigonese, in couples and groups, cruising the town on bicycles and motorbikes, out to see and be seen.

There is disco dancing on most nights at the *Rex*, *Caravelle*, *Majestic* and *Saigon Floating* hotels and at other spots around town. Karaoke has taken off in a big way – you'll have a hard time avoiding it.

One of the most popular places with foreigners is *Apocalypse Now* at 29 Mac Thi Buoi St near the Huong Sen Hotel. Action starts at 6 pm and keeps rolling until at least 2 am. Just across the street is the *Hard Rock Café* which also draws a predominantly foreign crowd. *Shake's Pub* is named after Shakespeare and appeals to the more well-dressed business traveller set than the 'shorts & thongs' set – Shake's is on Me Linh Square (near the Saigon River).

Things to Buy

In the last few years the free market in tourist junk has been booming – you can pick up a useful item like a lacquered turtle with a clock in its stomach or a ceramic Buddha that whistles the national anthem. And even if you're not the sort of person who needs a wind-up mechanical monkey that plays the cymbals, keep looking – Saigon is a good shopping city and there is sure to be something that catches your eye.

Not surprisingly, Saigon Tourist is trying to milk this market; the Saigon Tourist Art Gallery (☎ 293444) is at 55 Dong Khoi St.

Pick up a chic gas mask or flak vest at the Dan Sinh Market, 104 Nguyen Cong Tru St (next to Phung Son Tu Pagoda). The front part of the market is stalls selling motorbike parts, but behind the pagoda you can find out what happened to some of the billions of dollars the USA spent losing the Vietnam War. Fake Zippo lighters seem to be the hottest item.

Everything commonly eaten, worn or used by the average resident of Saigon is available in the city's markets. Biggest of the bunch is Ben Thanh Market (Cho Ben Thanh), 700 metres south-west of the Rex Hotel at the intersection of Le Loi Blvd, Ham Nghi Blvd, Tran Hung Dao Blvd and Le Lai St.

Binh Tay Market is Cholon's main marketplace, just off Hau Giang Blvd. Cholon's other indoor market, Andong, is very close to the intersection of Tran Phu and An Duong Vuong Blvds.

Getting There & Away

Air Vietnam Airlines acts as sales agent for Lao Aviation (Hang Khong Lao), Cambodia Airlines (Hang Khong Cam Bot) and Korean Air (Hang Khong Trieu Tien).

Aeroflot
(Hang Khong Nga), 4H Le Loi Blvd, District 1 (☎ 293489)

Air France
(Hang Khong Phap), 130 Dong Khoi St (Caravelle Hotel), District 1 (☎ 290982)

Cathay Pacific
(Hang Khong Ca-thay Pa-ci-fic), 49 Le Thanh Ton St, District 1 (☎ 223272)

China Southern Airlines
(Hang Khong Nam Trung Hoa), 52B Pham Hong Thai St, District 1 (☎ 291172)

Garuda Indonesia
(Hang Khong In-do-ne-xia), Room 67 & 68, Tan Son Nhat Airport (☎ 442696)

Lufthansa
(Hang Khong CHLB Duc), Tan Son Nhat Airport (☎ 440101)

Malaysian Airline System
(Hang Khong Ma-lay-sia), 116 Nguyen Hue Blvd, District 1 (☎ 230695)

Pacific Airlines
(Hang Khong Pa-ci-fic), 76D Le Thanh Ton St, District 1 (☎ 222614)

Philippine Airlines
(Hang Khong Phi-lip-pin), 4A Le Loi Blvd, District 1 (☎ 292113)

Singapore Airlines
(Hang Khong Sin-ga-po), 6 Le Loi Blvd, District 1 (☎ 231583)

Thai Airways International
(Hang Khong Thai Lan), Room 7 & 8, Tan Son Nhat Airport (☎ 446235)

Vietnam Airlines
Domestic: (Phong ve Quoc noi Hang Khong Vietnam), 27B Nguyen Dinh Chieu (☎ 299980)
International: (Phong ve Quoc Te Hang Khong Vietnam), 116 Nguyen Hue Blvd, District 1 (☎ 292118)

Bus Buses to points south of Ho Chi Minh City are based at Mien Tay (Ben Xe Mien Tay), which is about 10 km west of Saigon in An Lac.

Buses to places north of Ho Chi Minh City depart from the Mien Dong bus station (Ben Xe Mien Dong) in the Binh Thanh District, six km from central Saigon on Quoc Lo 13 (National Highway 13) – Quoc Lo 13 is the continuation of Xo Viet Nghe Tinh St.

Tay Ninh bus station (Ben Xe Tay Ninh) serves points north-east of Saigon – it is about 1½ km past where Cach Mang Thang Tam and Le Dai Hanh Sts merge.

Van Thanh bus station (Ben Xe Van Thanh) serves destinations in Song Be and Dong Nai provinces – it's in Binh Thanh District at 72 Dien Bien Phu St, about 1½ km east of the intersection of Dien Bien Phu and Xo Viet Nghe Tinh Sts.

Daily buses to Phnom Penh, Cambodia, leave from Nguyen Du St near the Immigration Police. However, you must buy tickets from the garage (☎ 293754) at 155 Nguyen Hue Blvd, next to the Rex Hotel. A one-way ticket costs about US$4.

Train The Saigon railway station (Ga Sai Gon; ☎ 245585) is in District 3 at 1 Nguyen Thong St. The ticket office is open from 7.15 to 11 am and from 1 to 3 pm daily.

Boat Passenger and goods boats to the Mekong Delta depart from a dock at the river end of Ham Nghi St near the Majestic Hotel. Hydrofoils to Vung Tau depart from the same wharf.

Getting Around

To/From the Airport Tan Son Nhat international airport is seven km from the city centre. The taxis for hire outside the customs hall will try to grossly overcharge, so bargain (a fair price into town is about US$5 to US$7). Cyclos can be hailed outside the gate to the airport, which is a few hundred metres from the terminal building – a ride to central Saigon should cost about US$1.

Cyclo Cyclos are the best way of getting around town and can be hired by distance or by time. Always agree on fares beforehand.

Bicycle Rental bicycles are becoming increasingly common in Saigon. You can hire bicycles from many budget hotels.

Around Ho Chi Minh City

CU CHI TUNNELS

The tunnel network of Cu Chi District, now part of Greater Ho Chi Minh City, became legendary during the 1960s for its role in facilitating Viet Cong control of a large rural area only 30 km north-west of Saigon. At its height, the tunnel system stretched from the South Vietnamese capital to the Cambodian border.

In the district of Cu Chi alone, there were over 200 km of tunnels. After ground operations against the tunnels claimed large numbers of casualties and proved ineffective, the Americans turned their artillery and bombers on the area, turning it into a moonscape.

Parts of this remarkable tunnel network have been reconstructed in the interests of promoting Vietnamese patriotism and mass foreign tourism.

Getting There & Away

Minibuses operated by budget cafes in Ho Chi Minh City charge around US$5 per person. Tourist hotels and Saigon Tourist run minibus tours to the area and charge more than if you hired your own rental car with driver!

TAY NINH

Tay Ninh town, capital of Tay Ninh Province, serves as the headquarters of one of Vietnam's most interesting indigenous religions, Caodaism. The **Caodai Great Temple** was built between 1933 and 1955.

The Religion of Cao Dai

Caodaism is the product of an attempt to create the ideal religion through the fusion of secular and religious philosophies from both East and West. The result is a colourful and eclectic potpourri that includes bits and pieces of Buddhism, Confucianism, Taoism, Hinduism, native Vietnamese spiritism, Christianity and Islam. Among the Westerners that the Caodai especially revere is Victor Hugo (look for his likeness at the Great Temple).

Caodaism was founded in 1926 after messages were communicated to the group's leaders by spirits. By the mid-1950s, one in eight southern Vietnamese was a Caodai. Today, the sect has about two million followers. All Caodai temples observe four daily ceremonies, which are held at 6 am, noon, 6 pm and midnight.

Getting There & Away

Tay Ninh is 96 km north-west from Ho Chi Minh City. The Caodai Holy See complex is four km east of Tay Ninh. Many travellers book a one-day minibus tour from the cafes in Saigon, which includes both Tay Ninh and the Cu Chi Tunnels.

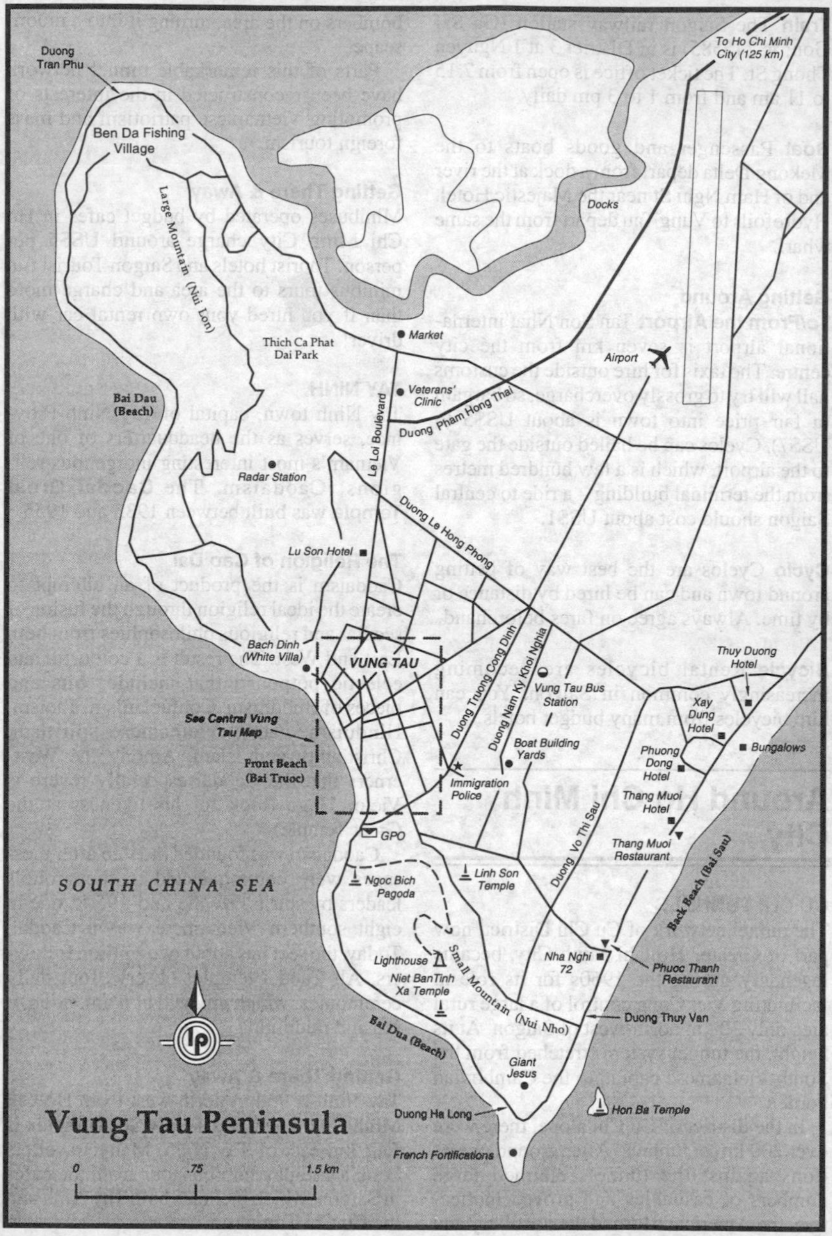

Vung Tau Peninsula

0
.75
1.5 km

Duong Tran Phu
Ben Da Fishing Village
Large Mountain (Nui Lon)
To Ho Chi Minh City (125 km)
Docks
Market
Thich Ca Phat Dai Park
Airport
Veterans' Clinic
Bai Dau (Beach)
Le Loi Boulevard
Duong Pham Hong Thai
Radar Station
Duong Le Hong Phong
Lu Son Hotel
Bach Dinh (White Villa)
VUNG TAU
Duong Truong Cong Dinh
Duong Nam Ky Khoi Nghia
Vung Tau Bus Station
Thuy Duong Hotel
Xay Dung Hotel
Bungalows
See Central Vung Tau Map
Front Beach (Bai Truoc)
Boat Building Yards
Immigration Police
Phuong Dong Hotel
Thang Muoi Hotel
Thang Muoi Restaurant
GPO
Duong Vo Thi Sau
Back Beach (Bai Sau)
Ngoc Bich Pagoda
Linh Son Temple
SOUTH CHINA SEA
Lighthouse
Niet BanTinh Xa Temple
Small Mountain (Nui Nho)
Nha Nghi 72
Phuoc Thanh Restaurant
Duong Thuy Van
Bai Dua (Beach)
Giant Jesus
Duong Ha Long
Hon Ba Temple
French Fortifications

VIETNAM

If you want to initiate yourself to the horrors of the Vietnamese bus system, buses from Ho Chi Minh City to Tay Ninh leave from the Tay Ninh bus station in Tan Binh District and the Mien Tay bus station in An Lac.

VUNG TAU

Vung Tau (population 100,000) is a beach resort 128 km south-east of Saigon. Vung Tau's beaches are not Vietnam's best, but are the most accessible from Ho Chi Minh City and therefore very popular.

Beaches

The main bathing area on the peninsula is **Back Beach** (Bai Sau, also known as Thuy Van Beach), an eight-km stretch of sun, sand and Soviets (Vung Tau was once the headquarters of a Soviet-Vietnamese oil rig operation) a couple of km east of the town centre. **Front Beach** (Bai Truoc, also called Thuy Duong Beach), which is rather dirty, rocky and eroded, borders the centre of town.

Bai Dau, a quiet coconut palm-lined beach, is probably the most relaxing spot in the Vung Tau area. The beach, which is about three km north of town, stretches around a small bay nestled beneath the verdant western slopes of Large Mountain (Nui Lon). **Bai Dua** (Roches Noires Beach) is a small beach about two km south of the town centre off Ha Long St.

Walks

The six-km circuit around Small Mountain (Nui Nho), known to the French as *le tour de la Petite Corniche*, begins at the southern end of Front Beach and continues on Ha Long St along the rocky coastline. The 10-km circuit around Large Mountain begins at the northern end of Front Beach.

Other Sights

The **Hon Ba Temple** is on a tiny island just south of Back Beach. It can be reached on foot at low tide. **Niet Ban Tinh Xa**, one of the largest Buddhist temples in Vietnam, is on the western side of Small Mountain. Built in 1971, it is famous for its five-tonne bronze bell, a huge reclining Buddha and intricate mosaic work.

Reminiscent of Rio de Janeiro is the 30-metre-high figure of **Jesus** (Thanh Gioc) with arms outstretched, which gazes across the South China Sea from the southern end of Small Mountain.

The 360-degree view of the entire peninsula from the 197-metre-high **lighthouse** *(hai dang)* is truly spectacular, especially at sunset. The narrow paved road up Small Mountain to the lighthouse intersects Ha Long St 150 metres south-west of the GPO.

Bach Dinh, the White Villa, is a former royal residence set amidst frangipanis and bougainvilleas on a lushly forested hillside overlooking the sea. The main entrance to the park surrounding Bach Dinh is just north of Front Beach at 12 Tran Phu St.

Thich Ca Phat Dai, a must-see site for domestic tourists, is a hillside park of monumental Buddhist statuary built in the early 1960s. Thich Ca Phat Dai is on the eastern side of Large Mountain at 25 Tran Phu St.

Places to Stay

Bai Dau is lined with inexpensive guesthouses, as is Bai Dua. The majority of visitors stay at either Back Beach or Front Beach.

Back Beach Cheapest is the *Nha Nghi 72*, close to the beach with large spacious grounds. Rooms are also large and complete with terrace and private bath; doubles cost US$8 with fan only, or US$15 with air-con.

Thang Muoi Hotel (☎ 452665), 4-6 Thuy Van St, is one of the older places in Back Beach but also one of the most beautiful. Doubles cost between US$15 and US$30.

Thuy Duong Hotel (☎ 452635) is a new and attractive place on Thuy Van St. Also known as the Weeping Willow Hotel, all rooms have air-con and hot water and cost between US$15 and US$30.

Xay Dung Hotel is at the northern end of Back Beach. Rooms in the hotel proper cost US$15 to US$30. The hotel also rents bun-

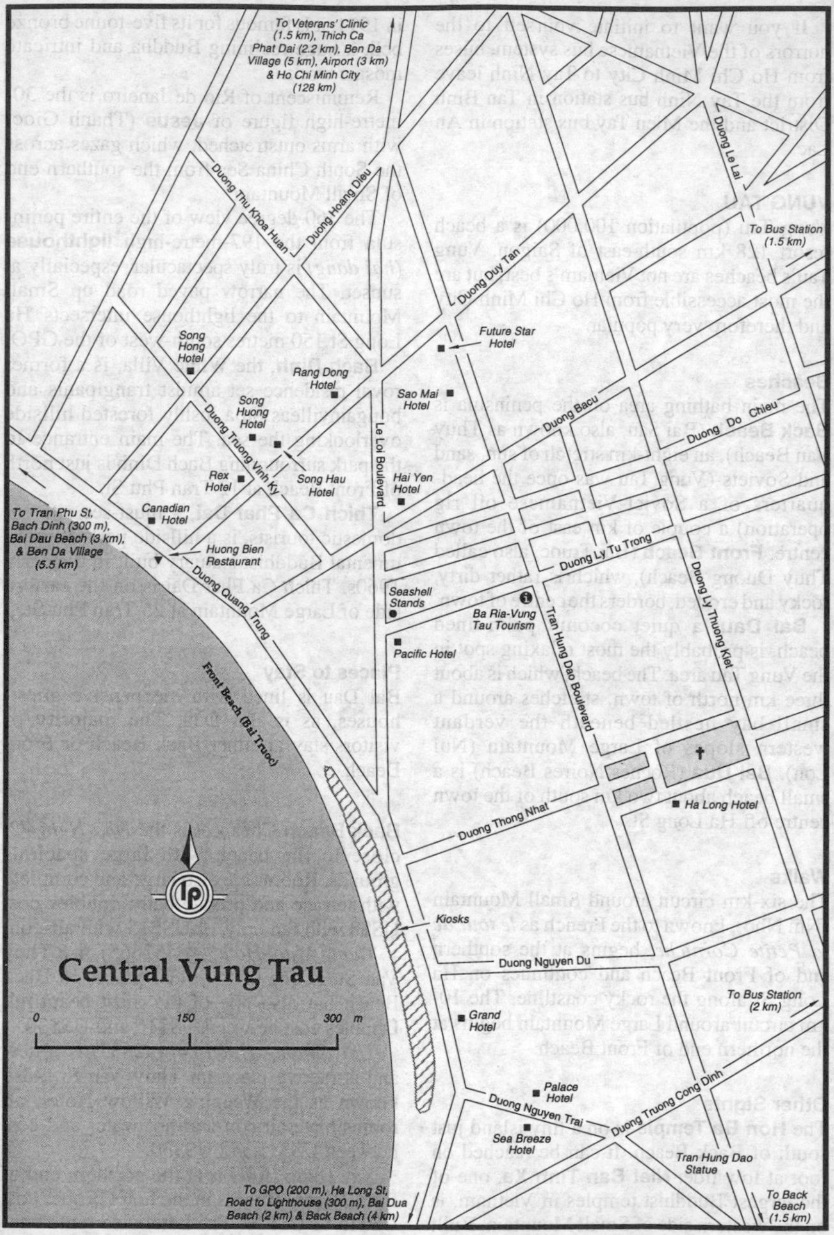

Central Vung Tau

To Veterans' Clinic (1.5 km), Thich Ca Phat Dai (2.2 km), Ben Da Village (5 km), Airport (3 km) & Ho Chi Minh City (128 km)

Duong Le Lai

To Bus Station (1.5 km)

Duong Thu Khoa Huan

Duong Hoang Dieu

Duong Duy Tan

Future Star Hotel

Song Hong Hotel

Rang Dong Hotel

Sao Mai Hotel

Song Huong Hotel

Duong Bacu

Duong Do Chieu

Le Loi Boulevard

Duong Truong Vinh Ky

Song Hau Hotel

Rex Hotel

Hai Yen Hotel

Canadian Hotel

To Tran Phu St, Bach Dinh (300 m), Bai Dau Beach (3 km), & Ben Da Village (5.5 km)

Huong Bien Restaurant

Duong Ly Tu Trong

Duong Quang Trung

Seashell Stands

Ba Ria-Vung Tau Tourism

Duong Ly Thuong Kiet

Tran Hung Dao Boulevard

Pacific Hotel

Front Beach (Bai Truoc)

Ha Long Hotel

Duong Thong Nhat

Kiosks

Duong Nguyen Du

To Bus Station (2 km)

0 150 300 m

Grand Hotel

Palace Hotel

Duong Nguyen Trai

Duong Truong Cong Dinh

Sea Breeze Hotel

Tran Hung Dao Statue

To GPO (200 m), Ha Long St, Road to Lighthouse (300 m), Bai Dua Beach (2 km) & Back Beach (4 km)

To Back Beach (1.5 km)

galows for US$15 with fan and US$25 with air-con.

Front Beach *Lu Son Hotel* (☎ 452576) is north of town (and far from the beach) at 27 Le Loi Blvd. Double rooms with private bath and air-con cost US$10.

Sao Mai Hotel (☎ 452462), 89 Tran Hung Dao Blvd, has doubles with air-con for US$10 to US$15. It's good value.

Song Huong Hotel (☎ 452491), 10 Truong Vinh Ky St, has singles with shared bath for US$12 which are not worth it. Doubles with private bath go for US$20. Overall, it's poor value.

Rang Dong Hotel (☎ 452133), 5 Duy Tan St, is reasonably priced at US$10/16 for singles/doubles with air-conditioning.

Next door you'll find the *Song Hau Hotel* (☎ 452601) at 3 Duy Tan St. It was once a Russian dormitory and still looks it. All rooms have attached bath and cost US$8 with electric fan or US$12 with air-con.

The *Ha Long Hotel* (☎ 452175) is an older place at 45 Thong Nhat St, across the street from the church. Singles cost US$10. Express buses to Saigon leave from here.

Other places in Front Beach are decidedly upmarket, with room prices starting at US$20 and escalating to US$80 or so. Amongst the hotels in this league are the *Hai-Au* (at 100 Halong Street, on the southern end of Front Beach), *Song Hong*, *Grand*, *Hai Yen*, *Future Star*, *Rex*, *Canadian*, *Palace* (Hoa Binh), *Sea Breeze* and *Pacific* hotels.

Places to Eat

For excellent seafood, try *Huong Bien Restaurant*, which is along Front Beach at 47 Quang Trung St. There are several places to eat nearby and quite a few more along Tran Hung Dao St. Hotels with decent restaurants include the *Palace* and the *Grand*.

At the southern end of Back Beach is the *Phuoc Thanh Restaurant*, which does a mean salad and splendid seafood, yet charges low prices. The largest restaurant along Back Beach is the *Thang Muoi Restaurant* (☎ 452515) at 7-9 Thuy Van St.

At Bai Dua, there are restaurants at 88 Ha Long St and 126 Ha Long St.

Getting There & Away

Bus Buses to Vung Tau from Ho Chi Minh City leave from the Mien Dong and Van Thanh bus stations.

Boat The best way to reach Vung Tau is by hydrofoil. These depart Saigon from the pier near the Majestic Hotel, cost US$12 and take 80 minutes to complete the journey.

Mekong Delta

Flat as a billiards table but lusciously green and beautiful, the Mekong Delta is the southernmost region of Vietnam. It's a rich agricultural region, the breadbasket (or perhaps 'ricebasket') of the nation. The delta is a thick patchwork of rice paddies, swamps and remnant forests interlaced with canals and rivers – an intriguing place to explore.

MYTHO

Mytho is a quiet city of 90,000 easily reached as a day trip from Saigon, yet very near some of the most beautiful rural areas of the Mekong Delta.

Island of the Coconut Monk

Until his imprisonment by the Communists for anti-government activities and the consequent dispersion of his flock, the Coconut Monk (Ong Dao Dua) led a small community on Phung Island (Con Phung), a few km from Mytho. In its heyday, the island was dominated by a fantastic open-air sanctuary that looked like a cross between a cheap copy of Disneyland and Singapore's Tiger Balm Gardens. The best way to get from Mytho to Phung Island is to hire a motorised wooden boat at around US$3 per hour.

Tan Long Island

The longan *(nhan)* orchards of Tan Long Island are a five-minute boat trip from the dock at the southern end of Le Loi Blvd.

Mytho

1 Tien Giang Tourism
2 Mytho Church & Bishopric
3 Khach San 43
4 Bicycle Shops
5 Food Stalls
6 Mytho People's Committee Building
7 Central Market
8 Grand Hotel (Khach San Song Tien)
9 Thanh Binh Hotel
10 Cheap Restaurants
11 Huong Duong Hotel
12 Lien Doan Lao Dong Tien Giang (Khach San Cong Doang)
13 Thien Thanh Restaurant
14 Mytho Hotel
15 Ferry Landing (Boats for Hire)
16 Boats to Tan Long Island
17 Cuu Long Restaurant
18 Statue of Nguyen Huu Huan

Footbridge
To Mytho Bus Station & Ho Chi Minh City (70 km)
Duong Nguyen Tri Phuong
Duong Truong Vinh Ky
Duong Ap Bac
Duong Tran Quoc Tuan
Duong Phan Hieu Dao
Duong Huynh Tinh Cua
Duong Nguyen Trai
Duong Nguyen Hue
Duong Ngo Quyen
Duong Tet Mau Than
Hung Vuong Boulevard
Le Loi Boulevard
To Vinh Trang Pagoda (1 km)
Duong Chau Van Tiep
Duong Le Dai Hanh
Footbridge
Duong Nam Ky Khoi Nghia
Duong Le Van Duyet
Thu Khoa Huan Boulevard
Duong Ly Cong Van
To Vinh Trang Pagoda (1 km)
Duong Dinh Bo Linh
Duong Do Huu
Le Loi Boulevard
Duong Nguyen Binh Khiem
Duong Rach Gam
Bao Dinh Channel
Duong Phan Thanh Gian
Duong Trinh Hoai Duc
Duong Thien Ho Duong
Duong Le Thi Hong Gam
To Ben Tre Ferry (500 m)
Duong 30 Thang 4
Duong Huyen Toai
Duong Trung Trac
Mekong River (Tien Giang River)

VIETNAM

Mytho Central Market

Mytho Central Market, along Trung Trac and Nguyen Hue Sts, has stalls selling everything from fresh foods and bulk tobacco to boat propellers.

Places to Stay

Most budget travellers stay at *Lien Doan Lao Dong Tien Giang* (☎ 72166), also known as Khach San Cong Doang. Rooms cost US$4 (baths and toilets are outside). It's on the corner of 30, Thang 4 St and Le Loi Blvd.

The *Thanh Binh Hotel*, 44 Nguyen Binh Khiem St, is a dilapidated dump which amazingly still accepts foreigners. The tariff is US$3 for doubles.

The *Huong Duong Hotel* (☎ 72011), 33 Trung Trac St, has doubles with fans and attached bath for US$8. Air-con doubles cost US$10 and US$12.

Khach San 43 (☎ 72126) is a clean and airy place at 43 Ngo Quyen St. Triple rooms with fan and attached bath cost US$6 while a double with air-con costs US$7.

The *Grand Hotel* (☎ 72009), also known as the Khach San Song Tien, is the largest in town. A double with fan and attached bath costs US$5. Air-con makes it US$12 and US$15.

Places to Eat

Thien Thanh Restaurant is at 65, 30 Thang 4 St. Across the street, next to the Tan Long Island ferry dock, is *Cuu Long Restaurant*. There are about half-a-dozen good places along Trung Truc St.

Getting There & Away

Bus Mytho is served by nonexpress buses which leave Ho Chi Minh City from Mien Tay bus station.

The Mytho bus station (Ben Xe Khach Tien Giang) is several km west of town – take Ap Bac St westward and continue on to National Highway 1.

Boat A passenger ferry to Mytho leaves Ho Chi Minh City daily at 11 am from the dock at the end of Ham Nghi Blvd; the trip should take about six hours.

Getting Around

Motorised seven-metre boats can be hired at an unmarked ferry landing on Trung Trac St at the foot of Thien Ho Duong St. Ferries to points across the river also dock here. Wooden rowboats to Tan Long Island leave from the pier at the foot of Le Loi Blvd, next to Cuu Long Restaurant.

VINH LONG

Vinh Long, the capital of Vinh Long Province, is a medium-sized town along the banks of the Mekong River about midway between Mytho and Cantho.

What makes a trip to Vinh Long so worthwhile is not the town itself, but the beautiful, small agricultural islands in the river.

Chartering a small motorboat to the islands costs about US$1 per hour. Some of the more popular islands to visit include Binh Hoa Phuoc and An Binh Island, but there are many others.

Places to Stay

Most travellers coming to Vinh Long overnight in the *Cuu Long Hotel*, which costs US$15 for a double with air-con.

Getting There & Away

Bus Buses to Vinh Long leave Ho Chi Minh City from Mien Tay bus station in An Lac. Nonexpress buses take four hours.

OTHER AREAS

Other places to consider visiting include: **Cantho**, the political, economic, cultural and transportation centre of the Mekong Delta; **Ben Tre**, renowned for its rich agricultural lands and network of waterways; **Tan An**; **Long Xuyen**, whose modern Catholic Church is one of the largest in the Delta; **Chau Doc**, with a well-known mosque across the river in Chau Giang District and a number of pagodas and temples at Sam Mountain; **Rach Gia**, on the Gulf of Thailand; and **Ha Tien**, a coastal town almost on the Cambodian border near which are a number of grottos and beaches. **Phu Quoc Island** is a large island 45 km west of Ha Tien.

All these places have cheap accommodation and are served by buses and, in some cases, scheduled ferry services. Phu Quoc Island has air service from Ho Chi Minh City. A permit is needed to visit Ha Tien – it's obtainable from the police in Rach Gia.

Central Highlands

The Central Highlands cover the southern part of the Truong Son Mountain Range. The areas most attractive to foreigners include Dalat and Kontum. The region, which is home to many ethnolinguistic minority groups (Montagnards), is renowned for its cool climate, beautiful mountain scenery and innumerable streams, lakes and waterfalls.

DALAT

Dalat (elevation 1475 metres) is in a temperate region dotted with lakes and waterfalls and surrounded by evergreen forests. Dalat is often called the City of Eternal Spring – days are pleasant and nights are cool enough for wearing a light jacket. The economy is based on tourism and some agriculture, and it's Vietnam's most favoured honeymoon spot.

During the Vietnam War Dalat was, by the tacit agreement of all parties concerned, largely spared from the fighting. Indeed, it seems that while South Vietnamese Army officers were being trained at the city's Military Academy and affluent officials of the Saigon regime were relaxing in their villas, VC cadres were doing the same thing not far away in *their* villas.

The city's population of 125,000 includes about 5000 members of ethnolinguistic minorities.

Markets

Dalat's **Old Central Market** is in the Mai Building – the street level is the place to find dried fruits and upper levels are a great place to buy clothing. Behind the Mai Building, a new shopping centre is under construction. The **Vegetable Market** once occupied this site but has now moved to a location next to Xuan Huong Dam – this market boasts the finest vegetables in Vietnam (as well as cut flowers and the usual merchandise).

Xuan Huong Lake

Xuan Huong Lake in the centre of Dalat was created in 1919 by building a dam. Paddleboats that look like giant swans can be rented near Thanh Thuy Restaurant, which is 200 metres north-east of the dam. A golf course occupies 50 hectares on the northern side of the lake near the Flower Gardens.

Crémaillère Railway

About 500 metres east of Xuan Huong Lake is a railway station, and though you aren't likely to arrive in Dalat by train, the station is worth a visit. The crémaillère (cog railway) linked Dalat and Thap Cham (Phan Rang) from 1928 to 1964, when it was closed because of repeated Viet Cong attacks. The line has now been partially repaired and is operated as a tourist attraction. You can't get to anywhere useful (like Ho Chi Minh City) on this train, but you can ride five km down the tracks to the suburbs of Dalat and back again. The fee for this journey is US$2 for the round trip.

Flower Gardens

The gardens (Vuon Hoa Dalat) were established in 1966 by the South Vietnamese Agriculture Service. The gardens front Xuan Huong Lake at 2 Phu Dong Thien Vuong St, which leads from the lake to Dalat University; they are open from 7.30 am to 4 pm.

Valley of Love

Named the Valley of Peace by Emperor Bao Dai, the Valley of Love (Thung Lung Tinh Yeu, or Valleé d'Amour in French) had its name changed in 1972 by romantically minded students from Dalat University.

The place has since taken on a carnival atmosphere: tourist buses line up to regurgitate visitors, boats line up to accommodate them and tourists line up by the side of the boat to regurgitate lunch if the water is rough. Paddleboats cost US$0.50 per hour;

Central Dalat

PLACES TO STAY

1 Thanh The II Hotel
2 Cam Do Hotel
3 Phu Hoa Hotel
15 Thuy Tien Hotel
16 Anh Dao Hotel
18 Thanh Binh Hotel
20 Haison Hotel
23 Ngoc Lan Hotel

PLACES TO EAT

4 Pho Tung
5 Café Tung
6 Shanghai Restaurant
11 Stop 'n Go Café
14 Long Hoa Restaurant
17 La Tulipe Rouge Restaurant
19 Nhu Hai Restaurant
21 Viet Hung Café
22 Thanh Thuy Restaurant

OTHER

7 Intra-Provincial Bus Station & Minibus Stand
8 Shopping Centre
9 Old Central Market (Mai Building)
10 Clothing Shops
12 Rap 3/4 Cinema
13 Vietnam Airlines Office
24 Xe Lam & Taxi Offices
25 Petrol Station
26 Foodstalls & Vegetable Market
27 Taxi Stand
28 Xuan Huong Dam

To Mimosa Hotel, Thanh The I Hotel, Lat Village (12 km) & Lang Bian Mountain
Phan Dinh Phung
Nguyen Van Troi
Tang Bat Ho
Truong Cong Dinh
Phan Boi Chau
To Small Guesthouses (250 m) & Valley of Love (5 km)
Pedestrian Overpass
Hoa Binh Square
Duy Tan
To Golf Course & Flower Gardens
Small Guesthouses
Nguyen Chi Thanh
Khoi Nghia Nam Ky
Nguyen Thi Minh Khai
Le Dai Hanh
Nguyen Thai Hoc
Xuan Huong Lake
0 50 100 m
To Thuy Ta Restaurant, Lam Dong Province Tourism & Lake of Sighs
Le Dai Hanh
To Dalat Cathedral, Palace Hotel, Dalat Hotel & GPO

15-person canoes cost US$4 an hour; obnoxious noise-making motorboats cost US$5 for a whirlwind tour of the lake.

This is a good place to see the 'Dalat Cowboys' (no relation to the American 'Dallas Cowboys' football team). The 'cowboys' are in fact Vietnamese guides dressed as American cowboys (come back in another year and they'll have the Montagnards dressed up as Indians). The cowboys rent horses to tourists for US$2 to US$4 per hour and can take you on a guided tour around the lake.

The Valley of Love is five km north of Xuan Huong Lake out Phu Dong Thien Vuong St.

Cam Ly Falls

Cam Ly Falls is one of those must-see spots for domestic visitors. The grassy areas around the 15-metre-high cascades are decorated with stuffed jungle animals which Vietnamese tourists love to be photographed with. Many of the cowboys you see around here aren't guides, but tourists – for a fee you can get dressed as a cowboy and have your photo taken. The waterfall is between numbers 57 and 59 on Hoang Van Thu St.

Places to Stay

Demand for hotel rooms is heavy and it is often difficult to find a room after 5 pm, especially on Saturday. Unless you like icy showers, be sure the place has hot water at night.

Two places have emerged in Dalat as unofficial backpacker guesthouses. One is the *Mimosa Hotel* (☎ 2656, 2180), 170 Phan Dinh Phung St. Single rooms cost US$5 to US$7 while doubles are US$8 to US$15. The hotel has hot water.

Cam Do Hotel on Phan Dinh Phung St is the other notable budget place in town. All rooms come with attached bath and hot water. Singles cost US$7 to US$12, doubles US$12 to US$17.

Two other places worth considering are the *Thanh The I* and *Thanh The II* on Phan Dinh Phung St. Both charge US$7/12 for singles/doubles.

Other selections on the hotel menu include the following:

Anh Dao Hotel (☎ 2384), Nguyen Chi Thanh St, singles US$30 to US$45, doubles US$35 to US$55

Dalat Hotel (☎ 2363), 7 Tran Phu St, singles US$12 to US$14, doubles US$17 to US$20

Duy Tan Hotel (☎ 2216), 82, 3 Thang 2 St, singles US$7 to US$24, doubles US$12 to US$30

Haison Hotel (☎ 2379), 1 Nguyen Thi Minh Khai St, singles US$10 to US$35, doubles US$15 to US$40

Lam Son Hotel (☎ 2362), 5 Hai Thuong St, singles US$7 to US$12, doubles US$12 to US$17

Minh Tam Hotel (☎ 2447), 20A Khe Sanh St, doubles US$40, villas US$25

Ngoc Lan Hotel (☎ 2136), 42 Nguyen Chi Thanh St, cold water singles for US$10, or US$14 with hot water; doubles with hot water US$14 to US$20

Palace Hotel (☎ 2203), overlooking Xuon Huong Lake, singles/doubles US$18/23 to US$37/45

Phu Hoa Hotel (☎ 2194), 16 Tang Bat Ho St, singles US$7 and US$12, doubles US$12 and US$17

Thanh Binh Hotel (☎ 2394), 40-42 Nguyen Thi Minh Khai St, singles US$7 to US$12, doubles US$12 to US$17

Thuy Tien Hotel (☎ 2444), corner of Duy Tan and Khoi Nghia Nam Ky Sts, singles/doubles overpriced at US$18/25

Places to Eat

The *Mimosa Hotel* at 170 Phan Dinh Phung St has a decent restaurant boasting low prices, good food and friendly service. The *Hoang Lan Restaurant* at 118 Phan Dinh Phung St serves excellent Western and Chinese food and also attracts many backpackers.

The *Shanghai Restaurant* is on the other side of Rap 3/4 cinema from the Old Central Market; the address is 8 Khu Hoa Binh Quarter. They serve Chinese, Vietnamese and French food from 8 am to 9.30 pm.

The *Long Hoa Restaurant* on Duy Tan St is also popular with travellers and even cheaper than the Shanghai Restaurant.

Close to the Shanghai Restaurant is *Pho Tung*, which is not a bad restaurant and also an outstanding bakery. It's hard to resist all those delectable pastries and cakes in the windows.

If it's fresh Vietnamese vegetables you want, the place to find them is the *Nhu Hai*

Restaurant on the traffic circle in front of the Old Central Market.

La Tulipe Rouge Restaurant (☎ 2394) is across the square from the Old Central Market. The fare includes Vietnamese, Chinese and European dishes.

There are dozens of foodstalls in the *Vegetable Market* – those signposted 'com chay' serve vegetarian food.

The *Thuy Ta Restaurant* (☎ 2268), formerly *La Grenouillère* (roughly translated, The Froggery), is built on piles over the waters of Xuan Huong Lake. Across the lake is *Thanh Thuy Restaurant* (Cua Hang Thanh Thuy), which is on the water 200 metres along Nguyen Thai Hoc St from the Xuan Huong Dam.

Stop 'N Go Café, across from the Rap 3/4 Cinema, is an intriguing place to sip coffee and talk to the chatty owner (a part-time poet) who has some incredible stories to tell.

Things to Buy

In the past few years, the Dalat tourist kitsch-junk market has really come into its own. Without any effort at all, you'll be able to find that special something for your loved ones at home – perhaps a battery-powered stuffed koala bear that sings 'Waltzing Matilda' or a lacquered alligator with a light-bulb in its mouth.

Getting There & Away

Air At present there are flights to and from Ho Chi Minh City on Monday, Wednesday and Saturday (US$30 one way).

Bus The Dalat bus station is two km from the centre. The best way to get there is by chartering a motorbike (easily done).

Minibuses to Dalat can be booked from the cafes on Pham Ngu Lao St in Saigon. The ticket office at Dalat bus station (Ben Xe Dalat) is open from 4.30 am to 5.30 pm – it's advised that you purchase more than one ticket as they will otherwise seat six across – departures are at the ridiculous hour of 4 am! More comfortable minibuses from Dalat to Nha Trang and Ho Chi Minh City can be booked at the Mimosa Hotel and depart at 6 am.

Getting Around

Taxi Rentable Peugeot 203s and motorbike taxis are parked next to the Old Central Market and near Rap 3/4 cinema.

Bicycle & Horse The best way to enjoy the forests and cultivated countryside around Dalat is on horseback or pedalling a bicycle. Horses can be rented from tourist sites, while bicycles are available from the hotels.

AROUND DALAT

Lake of Sighs

The Lake of Sighs (Ho Than Tho) is a natural lake enlarged by a French-built dam. There are several small restaurants up the hill from the dam. Horses can be hired near the restaurants for US$2 an hour.

The Lake of Sighs is six km north-east of the centre of Dalat off Phan Chu Trinh St.

Datanla Falls

The nice thing about Datanla is the short and pleasant walk to get there – the falls are 350 metres from the highway on a path that first passes through a forest of pines and then continues steeply down the hill into a rainforest. To get to this path, turn off Highway 20 (which runs south-east) about 200 metres past the turn-off to Quang Trung Reservoir.

Prenn Falls

This is one of the largest and most beautiful falls in the Dalat area, but it is also starting to suffer the effects of commercial exploitation.

Prenn Waterfall consists of a 15-metre free fall over a wide rock outcrop. A path goes under the outcrop, affording a view of the pool and surrounding rainforest through the curtain of falling water. An ominous sign of possible abominations to come are the 'Dalat Tourist Sailboats' now plying the waters of the tiny pool at the waterfall's base.

The entrance to Prenn Falls is near the Prenn Restaurant, which is 13 km from Dalat towards Phan Rang; the entrance fee is US$0.10 but there is a US$0.50 'camera fee'.

Lat Village

The nine hamlets of Lat Village (population 6000) are about 12 km from Dalat at the base of Lang Bian Mountain. The inhabitants are ethnic minorities.

There is a serious obstacle to visiting the Lat Village – the Dalat police! It's not illegal to visit the village, it's just that the Dalat municipal government has discovered a way to milk foreigners of some cash. To visit the village, you must first go to the Immigration Police in Dalat to obtain a permit for US$10.

Lang Bian Mountain

This mountain, known in Vietnamese as Lam Vien, has five volcanic peaks ranging in altitude from 2100 to 2400 metres. The hike up to the top of Lang Bian Mountain – the view is truly spectacular – takes three to four hours from Lat Village. The path begins due north of Lat and is easily recognisable as a red gash in the green mountainside. It is possible to hire young locals as guides.

Lang Dinh An

Also known as the 'chicken village', this is a minority area which attracts Westerners who don't want to pay the US$10 extortion fee to visit Lat Village. It's moderately interesting. It's 18 km from Dalat and you can get there by minibus.

BUON MA THUOT

Buon Ma Thuot (or Ban Me Thuot) has a population of 65,000, an elevation of 451 metres, and is the capital of Dac Lac (Dak Lak) Province. A large percentage of the area's population is made up of ethnic minorities.

Things to See

The **Army Tank Monument** in the centre of the town symbolises Buon Ma Thuot's 'liberation' in March 1975. Just next to that is the **Hill-Tribe Museum**, with displays of traditional Montagnard dress as well as agricultural implements, fishing gear, bows and arrows, weaving looms and musical instruments. The **Stadium** sometimes has elephant races and the **Cultural Centre** has been known to put on minority dances. The **Buon Ma Thuot Market** at the southern end of Quang Trung St is worth a look.

Places to Stay

The *Thanh Loi Hotel* (☎ 52322), 3 Phan Chu Trinh St, is the upmarket place (there is an in-house tourist office) and doubles cost US$24 to US$30.

Three km north of the centre is the *Union Hotel* (☎ 52415), or Nha Nghi Dulich Cong Doan in Vietnamese. It's inside a rubber plantation, surrounded by trees and is very quiet.

The *People's Committee Hotel* (☎ 52407) on Hai Ba Trung St is comfortable and has rooms for US$10 to US$20.

Hoang Gia Hotel (☎ 52161) at 2 Le Hong Phong St costs US$6, and the *Hong Kong Hotel* at 30 Hai Ba Trung St is US$8.

The fancy *Bao Dai Palace Hotel* (☎ 52177) at 4 Nguyen Du St is pleasant but doubles cost US$25.

Getting There & Away

Air Vietnam Airlines has flights between Buon Ma Thuot and Ho Chi Minh City on Monday, Wednesday and Saturday for US$45.

Bus There is a bus service to Buon Ma Thuot from most major towns and cities between Ho Chi Minh City and Hanoi.

AROUND BUON MA THUOT

Ban Don

The best sight near Buon Ma Thuot, Ban Don is sometimes called the 'elephant village' by foreigners. The villagers are mostly M'nong, a matrilineal tribe. The M'nong hunt wild elephants using domesticated elephants, dozens of which live in Ban Don.

Sitting on an elephant's back for a photo has almost become a requirement of every visitor, but inquire about the price first. The government tourist agency has started encouraging the locals to demand US$50 for this service!

Ban Don village is 45 km north-west of Buon Ma Thuot. The local authorities have started requiring foreigners to get a travel permit in Buon Ma Thuot before proceeding to the village.

PLEIKU

Pleiku (or Playcu) is a market town in the centre of a vast, fertile plateau whose red soil is of volcanic origin. Many of the 35,000 inhabitants of the city are members of ethnic minorities. At 785 metres above sea level, the climate can be bracing, especially since it's often windy.

Places to Stay

Yaly Hotel (☎ 24843), 89 Hung Vuong St, has rooms with fan and hot water for US$15; air-con doubles are US$20 to US$35.

The *People's Committee Hotel* is comfortable if you forget who owns it. Doubles cost US$20.

Pleiku Hotel (☎ 24628), 124 Le Loi St, is where you can find the tourist office. Rooms are very comfortable with doubles from US$18 to US$25.

Hotel 86 Nguyen Van Troi is good value at US$6 for a single. *Vinh Hoi Hotel* is another good mid-range place to stay. *Hotel 215 Hong Vuong* (☎ 24270) is dirt-cheap with rooms from US$1.50 to US$3, but it might be placed off-limits to foreigners soon unless renovated.

Places to Eat

My Tam Restaurant on the corner of Le Loi and Quang Trung Sts is cheap and excellent. There is a line-up of cheap cafes on Nguyen Van Troi St.

Getting There & Away

Air Vietnam Airlines has flights connecting Pleiku to Ho Chi Minh City on Monday and Thursday (US$65 one way). Flights to/from Hanoi fly on Tuesday and Friday (US$110) one way. Flights to/from Danang are every Tuesday and Friday (US$30) one way.

Bus There is a nonexpress bus service to Pleiku from most coastal cities between Nha Trang and Danang.

The road between Pleiku and Buon Ma Thuot is rough in spots, but the highway from Pleiku to Kontum is in good nick.

KONTUM

The jewel of the Central Highlands, Kontum (population 35,000; elevation 525 metres) is the place where most travellers head to. The town is in a region inhabited primarily by ethnic minority groups, including the Bana (distinguished by their black clothing), Jarai, Rengao and Sedeng. The old French colonial architecture adds another touch of elegance to this attractive highland village.

Places to Stay

Hotel 42 Le Hong Phong (☎ 62632) is the cheapest in town, with dumpy doubles for US$6.

The *People's Committee Hotel* (☎ 62249) on Ba Trieu St is upscale with doubles for US$20 to US$23.

A good alternative is the cosy *Bank Hotel* (☎ 62610), 88 Tran Phu St, where triple rooms cost US$20.

Getting There & Away

Buses connect Kontum to Danang, Pleiku and Buon Ma Thuot. By land from Kontum it is 246 km to Buon Ma Thuot, 896 km to Ho Chi Minh City, 436 km to Nha Trang, 46 km to Pleiku, and 198 km to Qui Nhon.

South-Central Coast

NHA TRANG

Nha Trang (population 200,000) has what is probably the nicest municipal beach in all of Vietnam. The turquoise waters around Nha Trang are almost transparent, making for excellent fishing, snorkelling and scuba diving.

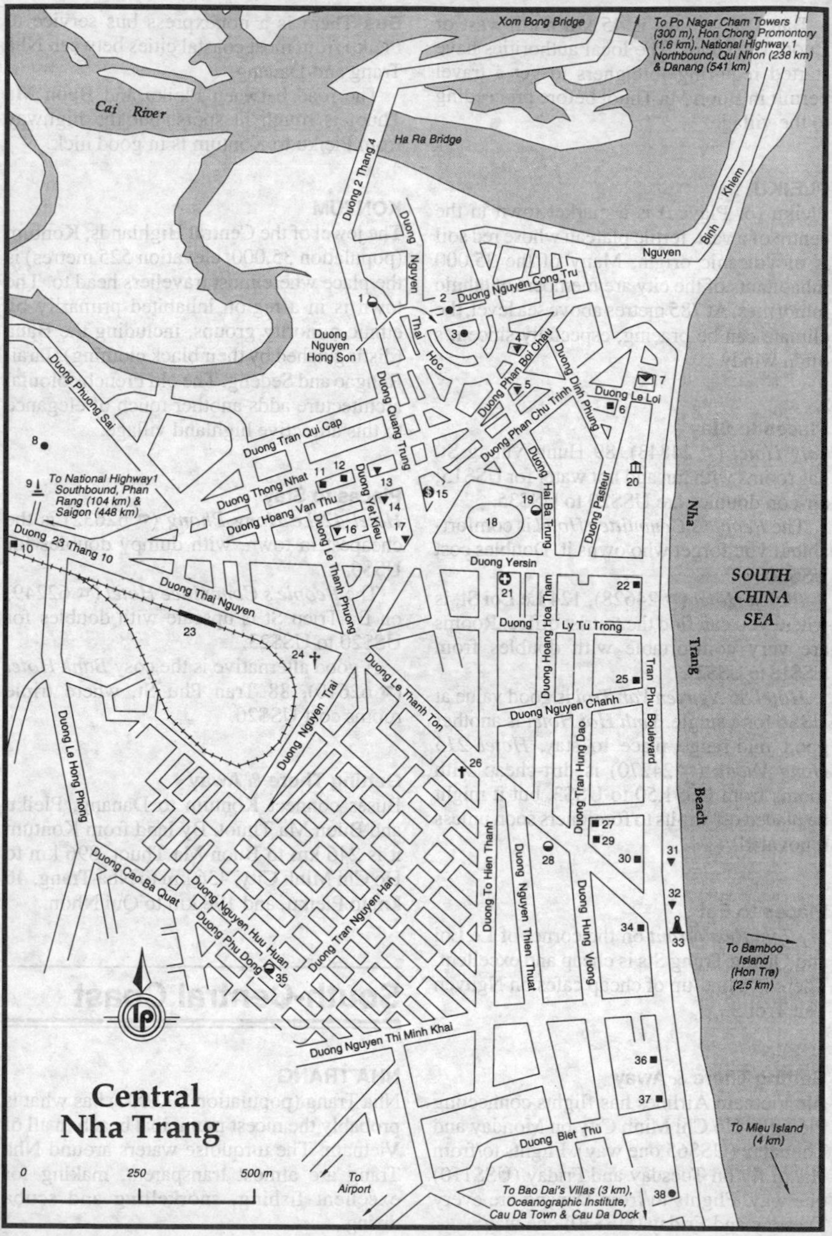

Central Nha Trang

Xom Bong Bridge

To Po Nagar Cham Towers (300 m), Hon Chong Promontory (1.6 km), National Highway 1 Northbound, Qui Nhon (238 km) & Danang (541 km)

Cai River

Ha Ra Bridge

Duong 2 Thang 4

Duong Nguyen Thai Hoc

Nguyen Binh Khiem

Duong Nguyen Cong Tru

Duong Nguyen Hong Son

Duong Phuong Sai

Duong Quang Trung

Duong Phan Boi Chau

Duong Dinh Phung

Duong Le Loi

Duong Phan Chu Trinh

Duong Tran Qui Cap

Duong Thong Nhat

Duong Yet Kieu

Duong Hoang Van Thu

Duong Le Thanh Phuong

Duong Hai Ba Trung

Duong Pasteur

To National Highway1 Southbound, Phan Rang (104 km) & Saigon (448 km)

Duong 23 Thang 10

Duong Thai Nguyen

Duong Yersin

Duong Ly Tu Trong

Duong Hoang Hoa Tham

Tran Phu Boulevard

Nha Trang Beach

SOUTH CHINA SEA

Duong Le Thanh Ton

Duong Nguyen Trai

Duong Le Hong Phong

Duong Nguyen Chanh

Duong Tran Hung Dao

Duong To Hien Thanh

Duong Nguyen Thien Thuat

Duong Hung Vuong

Duong Cao Ba Quat

Duong Nguyen Huu Huan

Duong Phu Dong

Duong Tran Nguyen Han

Duong Nguyen Thi Minh Khai

Duong Biet Thu

To Bamboo Island (Hon Tre) (2.5 km)

To Mieu Island (4 km)

To Airport

To Bao Dai's Villas (3 km), Oceanographic Institute, Cau Da Town & Cau Da Dock

0 250 500 m

1 2 3 4 5 6 7 8 9 10 11 12 13 14 15 16 17 18 19 20 21 22 23 24 25 26 27 28 29 30 31 32 33 34 35 36 37 38

lp

VIETNAM

PLACES TO STAY

6 Thang Loi Hotel
10 Viet Ngu Hotel
11 Nha Trang Hotel II
12 Nha Trang Hotel
22 Thong Nhat Hotel
25 Nha Khach 24
27 Hung Dao Hotel
29 Vien Dong Hotel
30 Hai Yen Hotel
34 Nha Khach 44
36 Nha Khach 58
37 Nha Khach 62

PLACES TO EAT

4 Lac Canh Restaurant
5 Nha Hang 33 Le Loi
13 Binh Minh Restaurant
14 Restaurant Lys
16 Ngoc Lau Restaurant
17 Ice Cream Shops
31 Hai Yen Café
32 Green Hat Café

OTHER

1 Short-Haul Bus Station
2 Dam Market Xe Lam Station
3 Dam Market
7 GPO
8 Giant Seated Buddha
9 Long Son Pagoda
15 Vietcombank
18 Stadium
19 Youth Tourism Express Bus Office
20 Pasteur Institute & Yersin Museum
21 Bien Vien Tinh (Hospital)
23 Nha Trang Station
24 Nha Trang Cathedral
26 Church
28 Express Bus Station
33 War Memorial Obelisk
35 Lien Tinh Bus Station
38 Nha Trang Ship Chandler Company

Things to See

The **Po Nagar Cham Towers** were built between the 7th and 12th centuries on a site used by Hindus for worship as early as the 2nd century AD. Shoes should be removed before entering the towers. The towers are two km north of Nha Trang, on the left bank of the Cai River.

Hon Chong Promontory is a scenic collection of granite rocks jutting out into the South China Sea. The promontory is 3.5 km north of central Nha Trang.

Long Son Pagoda is about 500 metres west of the railway station, opposite 15, 23 Thang 10 St. The **Giant Seated Buddha** is on the hill behind the pagoda. As you climb up to the buddha, veer left to enter the temple, which is stunning inside.

The **Oceanographic Institute** has an aquarium (ho ca) and specimen room. It's six km south of Nha Trang in the port village of Cau Da (also called Cau Be). The nearby **Bao Dai's Villas** (Cau Da Villas) is also worth a visit.

A **boat cruise** to the offshore islands is one of the highlights of Nha Trang. The best place to hire boats is the Cau Da fishing-boat dock (Ben Do Cau Da) or the Green Hat Café.

Places to Stay

The *Vien Dong Hotel*, 1 Tran Hung Dao St, looks upmarket but has some budget rooms – it's excellent value. Rooms on the 4th floor with fan and attached bath cost only US$10; air-con rooms are US$16 to US$25. According to the Vien Dong's pamphlet, 'weapons and objects with offensive smell should be kept at the reception desk'.

Hung Dao Hotel (☎ 22246), 3 Tran Hung Dao St, is next to the Vien Dong Hotel. It's a good deal at US$6/7 for singles/doubles with fan.

Along the beach on Tran Phu Blvd just to the south of the foregoing is *Nha Khach 58*, a large hotel with doubles for US$7. Next door is *Nha Khach 62*, which is relatively small but nicer with doubles for US$6 to US$7.

Other places to stay include:

Viet Ngu Hotel, 23 Thang 10 St (near the railway station), tattered doubles with fan cost US$6
Thang Loi Hotel (☎ 22241), 4 Pasteur St,

VIETNAM

singles/doubles with fan are US$5/10, with air-con US$20/24

Thong Nhat Hotel (☎ 22966), 18 Tran Phu Blvd, a beautiful place near the beach, singles/doubles/triples with fan are US$7/10/15; with air-con US$17 to US$25

Nha Khach 24 (☎ 22671), 24 Tran Phu Blvd, US$10 to US$35

Nha Khach 44, 44 Tran Phu Blvd, is a large place with a beach view. Rooms with fan are US$10; with air-con, US$18 to US$42.

Hai Yen Hotel (☎ 22828), 40 Tran Phu Blvd, singles/doubles with fan are US$7/10, air-con rooms US$15/20 to US$30/40

Nha Trang Hotel (☎ 22347), 133 Thong Nhat St, rooms with fan are US$8, with air-con US$10 to US$20

Nha Trang Hotel II (☎ 22956), 21 Le Thanh Phuong St, doubles with fan cost US$8 and US$12, with air-con US$15

Places to Eat

The restaurant in the *Vien Dong Hotel* is almost as big a bargain as the rooms.

The *Hai Yen Café* is on the beach opposite the Hai Yen Hotel.

Somewhere along the beach south of the Hai Yen Café, look for the *Green Hat Café*. We can't give a permanent location; at the time of this writing, the government kicked the tenants out of their leased building to make way for the Vinagen Café (a place *not* recommended). As a result, the staff have formed a sort of roving street market until a new permanent place can be found. This is *the* place to book cheap boat trips, minibuses, enjoy good food, beach parties etc. Just ask around – everyone knows about this place.

If you can find the Green Hat Café (or what remains of it), this place can book minibuses to Hoi An, Dalat and Saigon. Failing this, look for Mama Linh in the Hai Yen Café.

Getting There & Away

Air Vietnam Airlines has flights connecting Nha Trang with Ho Chi Minh City daily except Monday (US$45 one way). There are flights to/from Hanoi every Thursday and Sunday (US$105) one way.

Vietnam Airlines' Nha Trang office (☎ 21147) is at 74 Tran Phu St (not far from the GPO).

Bus The Lien Tinh bus station (Ben Xe Lien Tinh) is Nha Trang's main intercity bus terminal. It's opposite 212 Ngo Gia Tu St.

Train The Nha Trang railway station is across the street from 26 Thai Nguyen St. The ticket office is open from 7 am to 2 pm only. Many hotels can book train tickets for you.

HOI AN (FAIFO)

Hoi An (Faifo) was one of South-East Asia's major international ports during the 17th, 18th and 19th centuries. Today, parts of Hoi An look exactly as they did a century and a half ago. Hoi An was the site of the first Chinese settlement in southern Vietnam.

Warning Like their neighbours in Danang, the Hoi An police are bad news. Do all you can to avoid them.

Chinese Assembly Halls

Founded in 1786, the **Assembly Hall of the Cantonese Chinese Congregation** is at 176 Tran Phu St and is open daily from 6 to 7.30 am and from 1 to 5.30 pm.

The **Chinese All-Community Assembly Hall** (Chua Ba), founded in 1773, was used by all five Chinese congregations in Hoi An: Fujian, Cantonese, Hainan, Chaozhou and Hakka. The main entrance is on Tran Phu St opposite Hoang Van Thu St, but the only way in these days is around the back at 31 Phan Chu Trinh St.

The **Assembly Hall of the Fujian Chinese Congregation**, opposite 35 Tran Phu St, is open from 7.30 am to noon and from 2 to 5.30 pm.

The **Assembly Hall of the Hainan Chinese Congregation** was built in 1883. It's on the north side of Tran Phu St, near the corner of Hoang Dieu St.

The Chaozhou Chinese in Hoi An built the **Chaozhou Assembly Hall** in 1776. It's across from 157 Nguyen Duy Hieu St (near the corner of Hoang Dieu St).

Pagodas & Churches

Serving Hoi An's Caodai community is the small **Caodai Pagoda** (built in 1952) between numbers 64 and 70 Huynh Thuc Khang St (near the bus station).

The only tombs of Europeans in Hoi An are in the yard of the **Hoi An Church**, which is at the corner of Nguyen Truong To St and Le Hong Phong St.

Chuc Thanh Pagoda was founded in 1454, making it the oldest pagoda in Hoi An. To get to Chuc Thanh Pagoda, go all the way to the end of Nguyen Truong To St and turn left. Follow the sandy path for 500 metres.

Phuoc Lam Pagoda was founded in the mid-17th century. To get there, continue past Chuc Thanh Pagoda for 350 metres.

Cua Dai Beach

The beach is five km east of Hoi An. Go out on Cua Dai St, which is the continuation of Tran Hung Dao St.

Places to Stay

There are several hotels, but the only place authorised to accept foreigners is the *Hoi An Hotel* (☎ 373) at 6 Tran Hung Dao St. This hotel is a grand colonial-style building and was a US Marine base during the Vietnam War.

Singles/doubles/triples with shared bath cost US$5/8/9; with attached bath and electric fan it's US$8/10/15. The hotel's restaurant is known for overcharging – ask about prices before you eat, to avoid indigestion later.

Places to Eat

Hoi An's contribution to Vietnamese cuisine is cao lau, which consists of doughy flat noodles mixed with croutons, bean sprouts and greens, and topped with pork slices. It is mixed with crumbled crispy rice paper immediately before eating. A good place to try this is at the *Cao Lau Restaurant*, 42 Tran Phu St.

Restaurant Quan An 22 at 22 Nguyen Hue St is outstanding – English menu, pleasant English-speaking waitress and superb food. This place also serves cao lau.

Getting There & Away

The Hoi An bus station (Ben Quoc Doanh Xe Khach; ☎ 84) at 74 Huynh Thuc Khang St is one km west of the town centre. The ride (via the Marble Mountains and China Beach) to Danang takes an hour.

Buses from Danang to Hoi An leave from both the intercity bus station and the short-haul pick-up truck station in Danang.

Getting Around

The best way to get around Hoi An and to surrounding areas is by bicycle. The Hoi An Hotel rents out bicycles for US$1 per day or US$0.10 per hour, but first priority goes to their guests.

AROUND HOI AN

My Son

My Son, which is 60 km south-west of Danang, is Vietnam's most important Cham site. During the centuries when nearby Simhapura (Tra Kieu) served as the political capital of Champa, My Son was the most important Cham intellectual and religious centre and may also have served as a burial place for Cham monarchs. My Son is considered to be Champa's counterpart to the grand cities of other Indian-influenced civilisations to be found in South-East Asia: Angkor (Cambodia), Bagan (Burma/Myanmar), Ayuthaya (Thailand) and Borobudur (Java, Indonesia).

You can get a good view of the outlines of Simhapura, the capital of Champa from the 4th to the 8th centuries, from the Mountain Church (Nha Tho Nui), which is on the top of Buu Chau Hill in the town of Tra Kieu.

Unfortunately, a travel permit is now required to visit My Son. Inquire at the Hoi An Hotel – hopefully this idiotic regulation will be axed.

About the only way to reach My Son is by car or rented motorbike.

Marble Mountains & China Beach

Along the road from Hoi An to Danang are the Marble Mountains. These consist of five marble hillocks which were once islands. Local children make enthusiastic and unso-

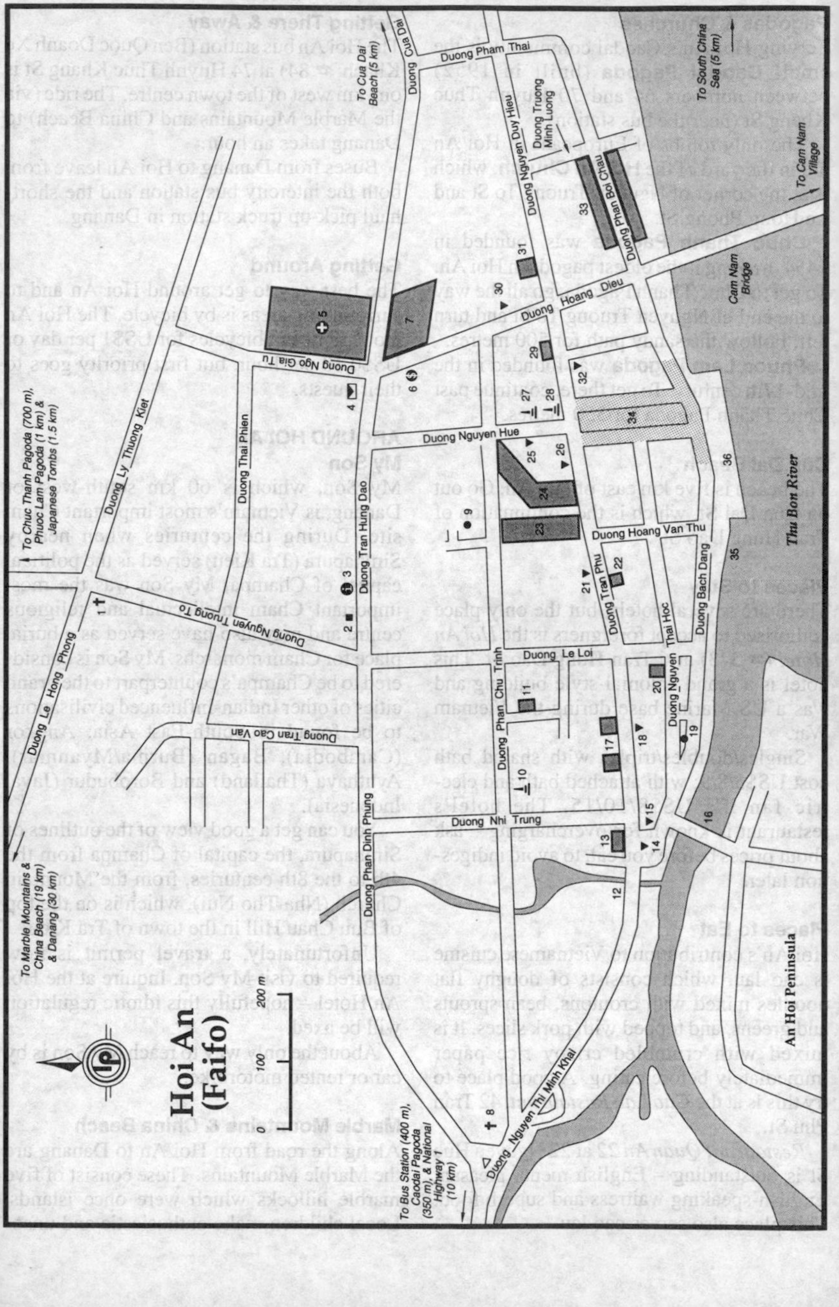

Hoi An
(Faifo)
0
100
200 m
To Marble Mountains & China Beach (19 km) & Danang (30 km)
To Chuc Thanh Pagoda (700 m), Phuoc Lam Pagoda (1 km) & Japanese Tombs (1.5 km)
To Cua Dai Beach (5 km)
To Bus Station (400 m), Caodai Pagoda (350 m), & National Highway 1 (10 km)
To South China Sea (5 km)
To Cam Nam Village
Cam Nam Bridge
Thu Bon River
An Hoi Peninsula
Duong Le Hong Phong
Duong Ly Thuong Kiet
Duong Thai Phien
Duong Nguyen Truong To
Duong Tran Cao Van
Duong Ngo Gia Tu
Duong Tran Hung Dao
Duong Phan Dinh Phung
Duong Cua Dai
Duong Pham Thai
Duong Nguyen Hue
Duong Phan Chu Trinh
Duong Nhi Trung
Duong Le Loi
Duong Nguyen Thi Minh Khai
Duong Tran Phu
Duong Hoang Van Thu
Duong Nguyen Thai Hoc
Duong Bach Dang
Duong Hoang Dieu
Duong Nguyen Duy Hieu
Duong Truong Minh Luong
Duong Phan Boi Chau
1 2 3 4 5 6 7 8 9 10 11 12 13 14 15 16 17 18 19 20 21 22 23 24 25 26 27 28 29 30 31 32 33 34 35 36

PLACES TO STAY

2 Hoi An Hotel

PLACES TO EAT

14 Caf Gia Khat Che
15 Nguyen Hue Café
18 Caf Dong Thi
21 Nha Hang 92 Tran Phu
25 Restaurant Quan An 22
26 Cao Lau Restaurant
30 Nha Hang So Nam (Restaurant No 5)
32 Coconut Milk Café

OTHER

1 Hoi An Church
3 Hoi An Tourism Service Company
4 GPO
5 Hospital
6 Bank
7 Hoi An People's Committee
8 Church
9 Ba Le Well
10 Gate of Ba Mu Pagoda
11 Truong Family Chapel
12 Japanese Covered Bridge
13 Cantonese Chinese Congregation Assembly Hall
16 An Hoi Footbridge
17 Cotton Mills
19 Tan Ky House
20 Diep Dong Nguyen House
22 House at 77 Tran Phu Street
23 Chinese All-Community Assembly Hall
24 Fujian Chinese Congregation Assembly Hall
27 Quan Am Pagoda
28 Quan Cong Temple
29 Hainan Chinese Congregation Assembly Hall
31 Chaozhou Chinese Congregation Assembly Hall
33 French Architecture
34 Central Market
35 Rowboat Dock
36 Hoang Van Thu Street Dock

licited tour guides and souvenir pushers – expect to be surrounded. But the kids are generally good-natured, and some of the caves are difficult to find without their help.

China Beach, made famous in the US TV serial of the same name, stretches for many km north and south of the Marble Mountains. During the Vietnam War, American soldiers were airlifted here for 'rest and relaxation' before being returned by helicopter to combat. The *China Beach Hotel* (☎ 21470), also known as the Non Nuoc Hotel, is right on China Beach. Singles/doubles cost US$15/18, US$18/22 or US$35/37. You can have a room with a terrace facing the sea. The hotel has two good restaurants – both charge very reasonable prices.

Getting There & Away Buses and minibuses running between Hoi An and Danang can drop you off at the entrance to the Marble Mountains and China Beach. From Danang, it's also possible to reach this area by bicycle and motorbike.

DANANG

Vietnam's fourth-largest city (population 400,000), Danang is chiefly of interest to travellers as a transit stop. A useful reason to visit Danang would be to cash travellers' cheques. The Foreign Trade Bank, Vietcombank (Ngan Hang Ngoai Thuong Viet Nam), is at 46A Le Loi St near the corner of Haiphong St.

The local mafia – otherwise known as the Danang police force – has a bad reputation and is known for stopping foreigners and levying arbitrary on-the-spot fines. The fines can usually be negotiated down to a trivial amount, but the safest advice we can give about Danang is to pass through it quickly.

Things to See

The best sight in Danang city is the **Cham Museum** (Bao Tang Cham). The museum is near the intersection of Tran Phu St and Vuong St and is open daily from 8 to 11 am and 1 to 5 pm.

Places to Stay

Several popular hotels are located, rather inconveniently, in the residential area at the northern tip of the Danang city peninsula. The *Danang Hotel* (☎ 21986) at 3 Dong Da St is home to many budget travellers. Singles/doubles with fan cost US$5/6; with air-con, US$6/8 to US$15/20. The hotel has an acceptable in-house restaurant.

A few doors down at 7 Dong Da St is the *Dong Da Hotel* (☎ 42216), also known as

Danang

Bay of Danang

Thanh Binh Beach

Han River

Stadium

Duong Tran Quy Cap
Duong Ly Thuong Kiet
Duong Le Loi
Duong Nguyen Chi Thanh
Duong Tran Phu
Duong Bach Dang
Duong Nguyen Du
Duong Ong Ich Khiem
Duong Dong Da
Duong Ly Tu Trong
Duong Quang Trung
Duong Tran Cao Van
Nguyen Thi Minh Khai
Duong Haiphong
Duong Ngo Gia Tu
Duong Le Duan
Duong Hoang Hoa Tham
Duong Phan Dinh Phung
Duong Pasteur
Duong Phan Chu Trinh
Duong Hung Vuong
Duong Ly Thai To
Duong Trieu Nu Vuong
Tri Phuong
Duong Yen Bai
Duong Tran Quoc Toan
Tram Binh Trong
Nguyen Trai
Nguyen
Duong Thai Phien
Duong Le Hong Phong
Duong Hoang Van Thu
Duong Pham Ngu Lao
Duong Le Dinh Duong
Duong Huynh Thuc Khang
Duong Hoang Dieu
Duong Phan Chu Trinh
Duong Trung Nu Vuong

To Dien Bien Phu St (500 m), Intercity Bus Station (1 km), National Highway 1, Hai Van Pass (30 km), Hué (108 km) & Ho Chi Minh City (972 km)

To Ho Chi Minh Museum (1.5 km), My Khe Beach (5 km), Marble Mountains/China Beach (10 km) & Hoi An (29 km)

0 250 500 m

1 2 3 4 5 6 7 8 9 10 11 12 13 14 15 16 17 18 19 20 21 22 23 24 25 26 27 28 29 30 31 32 33 34 35 36 37 38 39 40 41 42 43 44 45 46 47 48

VIETNAM

PLACES TO STAY

1 Nha Nghi Du Lich Thanh Binh
3 Dong Da Hotel (Khach San Huu Nghi)
4 Marble Mountains Hotel (Khach San Ngu Hanh Son)
5 Danang Hotel
6 Thu Bon Hotel
7 Peace Hotel
9 Hai Van Hotel
10 Song Han Hotel
13 Bach Dang Hotel
34 Thu Do Hotel
37 Hai Au Hotel
42 Orient Hotel (Phuong Dong Hotel)
43 Pacific Hotel (Thai Binh Duong Hotel)

PLACES TO EAT

2 Small Cafés
12 Kim Dinh Restaurant
15 Thanh Lich Restaurant
22 Tuoi Hong Café
23 Phi Lu Restaurant
25 Seamen's Club (Café)
28 Nha Hang 72
29 Thanh Huong Restaurant
31 Chin Den Restaurant
35 Dac San Restaurant
39 Ice Cream Cafés
40 Tiem An Binh Dan Restaurant
41 Tu Do & Kim Do Restaurants
44 Quan Chay Vegetarian Restaurant

OTHER

8 Market
11 People's Committee of Quang Nam-Danang Province
14 Vietnam Airlines Booking Office
16 GPO
17 Vietcombank
18 Caodai Temple
19 Railway Station
20 Market
21 Ancient Renault Buses
24 Danang Tourism & Tourist Shop
26 Ferries across the Han River
27 Former US Consulate
30 Municipal Theatre
32 Con Market
33 Short-Haul Pickup Truck Station
36 Cho Han (Market)
38 Danang Cathedral
45 Phap Lam Pagoda (Chua Tinh Hoi)
46 Cham Museum
47 Tam Bao Pagoda
48 Pho Da Pagoda

Khach San Huu Nghi. This is an acceptable alternative to the Danang Hotel. Rooms with fan cost US$6 and with air-con US$8 to US$10.

Sandwiched between the Dong Da and Danang hotels is the *Marble Mountains Hotel* (☎ 23258), 5 Dong Da St, also known as Khach San Ngu Hanh Son. This place is clean and is not a bad deal; all rooms have air-con or fan and hot water and cost from US$5 to US$18.

Just around the corner is the *Thu Bon Hotel* (☎ 21101), 10 Ly Thuong Kiet St. It's not a bad place, but at US$22 for a double, it's overpriced for a hotel of this standard.

Closer to the railway station is the *Hai Van Hotel* (☎ 21300), 2 Nguyen Thi Minh Khai St. It's an old place but has rooms with private bath and air-con. The toll is US$5 to US$18. Other cheapies include:

Thu Do Hotel, Duong Ly Thai To St, US$3 to US$8 with fan or US$10 with air-con
Song Han Hotel (☎ 22540), 36 Bach Dang St, singles/doubles US$12/16 and US$18/21
Thanh Thanh Hotel, Phan Chu Trinh St near Tran Quoc Toan St (near the Orient Hotel), US$6 to US$8 with fan, US$12 with air-con
Pacific Hotel (☎ 22137), also called Thai Binh Duong Hotel, Phan Chu Trinh St, singles/doubles US$7/24 to US$12/30

Places to Eat

Most hotels, even the budget ones, have restaurants. There are lots of sit-down ice-cream shops on Tran Quoc Toan St near the junction with Tran Phu St.

Danang's best is the *Tu Do Restaurant* (☎ 21869) at 172 Tran Phu St. The food is first-rate but some of the prices are a lot higher than you'd expect to pay. Next door is the *Kim Do*, a slightly fancier place where the food is 'number one' as the Vietnamese say. Also nearby at 174 Tran Phu St is the *Tiem An Binh Dan Restaurant*, a modest place with reasonable prices.

Getting There & Away

Air One of the main reasons to come to Danang is to fly out of it. There are daily flights to Hanoi and Ho Chi Minh City.

Vietnam Airlines (☎ 21130) is at 35 Tran Phu St. Service is sleepy, queues (if you want to call them that) are long, so allocate plenty of time (a few hours) for booking a flight here.

Bus The Danang Intercity bus station (Ben Xe Khach Da Nang) is about three km from the city centre. The ticket office for express buses is across the street from 200 Dien Bien Phu St; it's open from 7 to 11 am and 1 to 5 pm.

An express bus service is available to Buon Ma Thuot (17 hours), Dalat, Gia Lai, Haiphong, Hanoi (24 hours), Ho Chi Minh City (24 hours) and elsewhere.

Short-Haul Pickup Truck Station *Xe Lams* (tiny three-wheeled trucks used for short-haul passenger and freight transport) and small passenger trucks going to places in the vicinity of Danang leave from the Short-Haul Pickup Truck Station opposite 80 Duong Ly Thai To, which is about a block west of Con Market (Cho Con).

Train Danang Train Station (Ga Da Nang) is about 1.5 km from the city centre on Haiphong St, at the northern end of Hoang Hoa Tham St.

HUÉ

Hué (population 200,000) served as the political capital of Vietnam from 1802 to 1945 under the 13 emperors of the Nguyen Dynasty. Traditionally, the city has been one of Vietnam's cultural, religious and educational centres. Today, Hué's main attractions are the remains of the Citadel, the splendid tombs of the Nguyen emperors and several notable pagodas. A significant amount of cultural relics (not to mention lives) were lost in the heavy fighting of the 1968 Tet Offensive.

Most of the city's major sights have an admission charge of at least US$3. Many of these spots are open from 6.30 am until 5.30 pm.

Citadel

Construction of the moated Citadel (Kinh Thanh), whose perimeter is 10 km, was begun in 1804 by Emperor Gia Long. The emperor's official functions were carried out in the **Imperial Enclosure** (Dai Noi, or Hoang Thanh), a citadel-within-the-citadel whose six-metre-high wall is 2½ km in length.

Within the Imperial Enclosure is the **Forbidden Purple City** (Tu Cam Thanh), which was reserved for the private life of the emperor.

The 37-metre-high **Flag Tower** is Vietnam's tallest flagpole. During the VC occupation of Hué in 1968, the Viet Cong flag flew defiantly from the tower for 3½ weeks. Just inside the Citadel ramparts to either side of the Flag Tower are the **Nine Holy Cannons**, symbolic protectors of the palace and kingdom, which date from 1804.

The principle gate to the Imperial Enclosure is **Ngo Mon Gate** (Noontime Gate), which faces the Flag Tower. **Thai Hoa Palace** was used for the emperor's official receptions and other important court ceremonies, such as anniversaries and coronations. The **Nine Dynastic Urns**, weighing 1900 to 2600 kg each, symbolise the power and stability of the Nguyen throne.

The beautiful hall which houses the **Imperial Museum** was built in 1845 and restored in 1923.

Royal Tombs

The Tombs of the Nguyen Dynasty (1802-1945) are seven to 16 km south of Hué, reachable by car or bicycle.

Nam Giao (the Temple of Heaven) was once the most important religious site in Vietnam. Every three years, the emperor solemnly offered elaborate sacrifices here to the All-Highest Emperor of the August Heaven.

Dong Khanh's Mausoleum, the smallest of the Royal Tombs, was built in 1889. Construction of the **Tomb of Thieu Tri**, who ruled from 1841 to 1847, was completed in 1848.

Perhaps the most majestic of the Royal Tombs is the **Tomb of Minh Mang** who ruled from 1820 to 1840. The tomb is 12 km from Hué on the west bank of the Perfume River (there's a ferry from a point about 1½ km south-west of Khai Dinh's Tomb).

The **Tomb of Tu Duc**, a serene and impressive structure set amidst frangipani trees and a grove of pines, is probably the most popular and easily reached of the Royal tombs. It was constructed between 1864 and 1867 and is seven km from Hué.

The gaudy and crumbling **Tomb of Emperor Khai Dinh**, who ruled from 1916 to 1925, was begun in 1920 and completed in 1931.

Pagodas, Temples & Churches

The **Thien Mu Pagoda** (also called Linh Mu Pagoda) is one of the most famous structures in all of Vietnam. Its 21-metre-high octagonal tower, the seven-storey Thap Phuoc Duyen, was built by Emperor Thieu Tri in 1844 and has become the unofficial symbol of Hué. Founded in 1601, the pagoda is on the banks of the Perfume River, four km south-west of the Citadel. To get there from Dong Ba Market, head south-west (parallel to the river) on Tran Hung Dao St, cross the railway tracks and keep going on Kim Long St.

The **Bao Quoc Pagoda** was founded in 1670. To get to the pagoda, head south from Le Loi St on Dien Bien Phu St; turn right immediately after crossing the railway tracks.

Notre Dame Cathedral (Dong Chua Cuu The) at 80 Nguyen Hue St is an impressive modern building. If you find the gate locked, ring the bell of the yellow building next door.

There are many pagodas and Chinese congregational halls in Phu Cat and Phu Hiep subdistricts, which are across the Dong Ba Canal from Dong Ba Market. The entrance to **Dieu De National Pagoda** (Quoc Tu Dieu De), built under Emperor Thieu Tri (ruled 1841-47), is along Dong Ba Canal at 102 Bach Dang St. During the 1960s, it was a stronghold of Buddhist and student opposition to the South Vietnamese government and the war. Hué's Indian Muslim community constructed the **mosque**, at 120 Chi Lang St, in 1932.

Chieu Ung Pagoda (Chieu Ung Tu), opposite 138 Chi Lang St, was founded by the Hainan Chinese congregation in the mid-19th century and was rebuilt in 1908.

The **Cantonese Chinese Congregation Assembly Hall** (Chua Quang Dong), founded almost a century ago, is at 176 Tran Phu St.

Tang Quang Pagoda (Tang Quang Tu), which is just down the road from 80 Nguyen Chi Thanh St, is the largest of the three Hinayana (Theravada) pagodas in Hué.

Thuan An Beach

Thuan An Beach (Bai Tam Thuan An), 13 km north-east of Hué, is on a splendid lagoon near the mouth of the Perfume River. Xe Lams and old Renaults from Hué depart for Thuan An from the Dong Ba bus station. You might also try hiring a sampan to make the trip by river. At Thuan An, you can stay at the Tan My Hotel.

Places to Stay

Among the most delightful accommodation to be had in Hué are five small houses called the *Hué City Tourism Villas*, run by Hué City Tourism. The most popular villa is at 2 Le Loi St (☎ 22153), which has budget accommodation for US$5, US$6 and US$10, but it is possible that this villa will be renovated and the price ratcheted upwards. The other four villas can be found at 11, 16 and 18 Ly Thuong Kiet St and 5 Le Loi St. The four upmarket villas feature homey living rooms and bedrooms. All rooms cost US$20 and can accommodate three persons, and meals are prepared on request.

The *Nha Khach 18 Le Loi* (☎ 3720) at 18 Le Loi St is run by Hué City Tourism; doubles go for US$6 to US$8. It's a nice place and one of the better deals in the budget range.

A very popular place with budget travellers is the *Ben Nghe Guesthouse* on Ben Nghe St near Tran Cao Van St. Doubles cost US$5 with attached bath and hot water.

The *Khach San Thuong Tu*, 6 Dinh Tien Hoang St, is an old dump but the cheapest place in town. Rooms are just US$3, but in the future it's possible that they will not be permitted to accommodate foreigners.

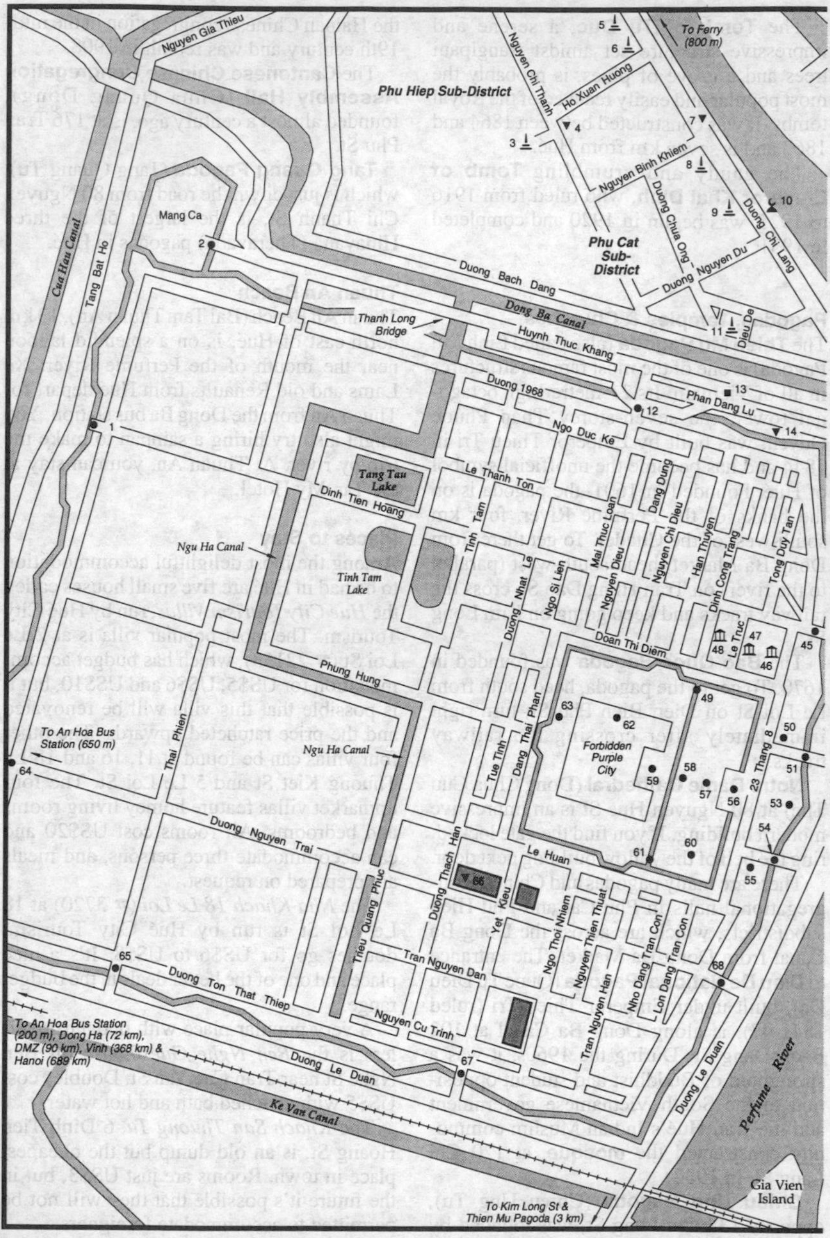

Phu Hiep Sub-District
Phu Cat Sub-District
To Ferry (800 m)
Nguyen Gia Thieu
Nguyen Chi Thanh
Ho Xuan Huong
Nguyen Binh Khiem
Duong Chua Ong
Duong Chi Lang
Duong Nguyen Du
Mang Ca
Cua Hau Canal
Tang Bat Ho
Duong Bach Dang
Dong Ba Canal
Thanh Long Bridge
Huynh Thuc Khang
Dieu De
Duong 1968
Phan Dang Lu
Ngo Duc Ke
Le Thanh Ton
Tang Tau Lake
Dinh Tien Hoang
Tinh Tam
Dang Dung
Mai Thuc Loan
Nguyen Chi Dieu
Han Thuyen
Dinh Cong Trang
Tong Duy Tan
Nguyen Dieu
Ngo Si Lien
Duong Nhat Le
Ngu Ha Canal
Tinh Tam Lake
Doan Thi Diem
Le Truc
Phung Hung
Thai Phien
Tue Tinh
Dang Thai Phan
Forbidden Purple City
23 Thang 8
To An Hoa Bus Station (650 m)
Ngu Ha Canal
Duong Nguyen Trai
Trieu Quang Phuc
Duong Thach Han
Le Huan
Yet Kieu
Ngo Thoi Nhiem
Nguyen Thien Thuat
Nho Dang Tran Con
Lon Dang Tran Con
Tran Nguyen Dan
Tran Nguyen Han
Duong Ton That Thiep
Nguyen Cu Trinh
Duong Le Duan
To An Hoa Bus Station (200 m), Dong Ha (72 km), DMZ (90 km), Vinh (368 km) & Hanoi (689 km)
Ke Van Canal
Perfume River
Gia Vien Island
To Kim Long St & Thien Mu Pagoda (3 km)

VIETNAM

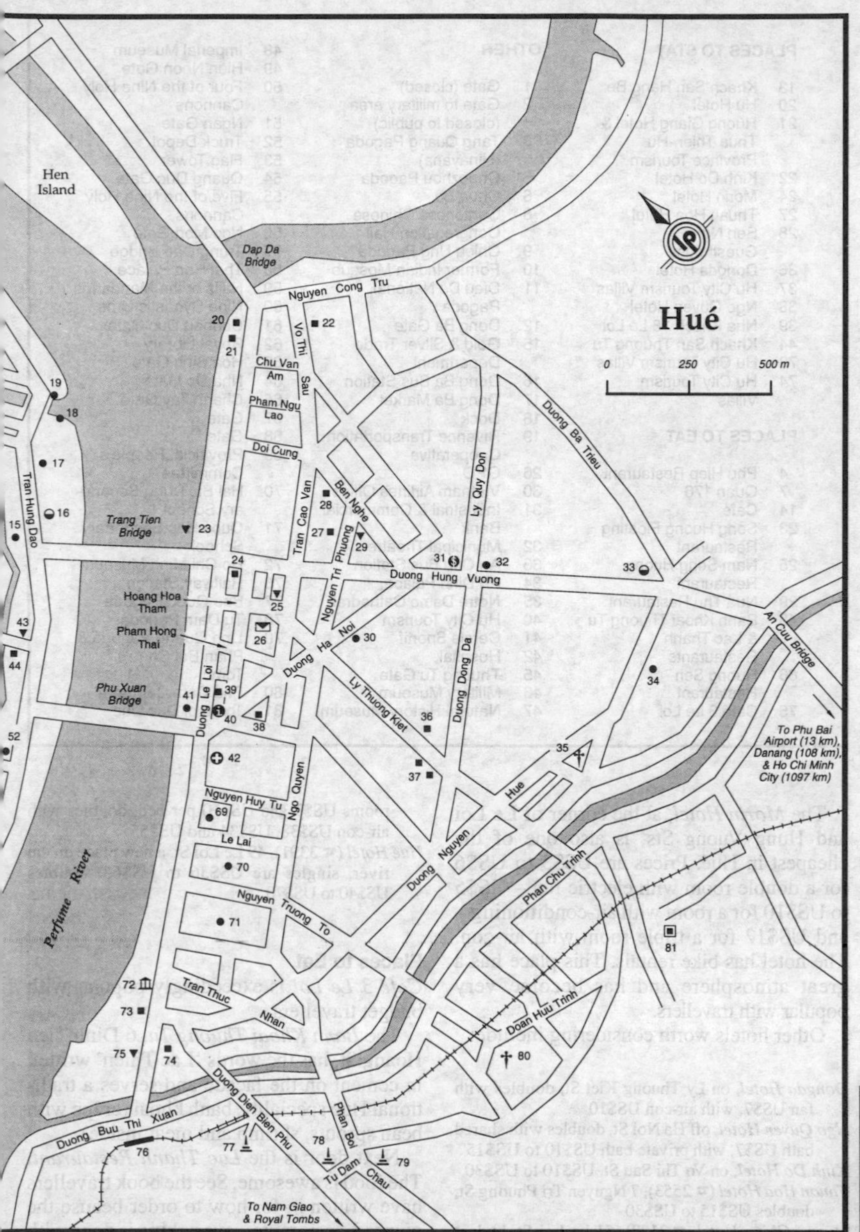
Hué
0
250
500 m
Hen Island
Dap Da Bridge
Nguyen Cong Tru
Vo Thi Sau
Chu Van Am
Pham Ngu Lao
Doi Cung
Tran Cao Van
Ben Nghe
Nguyen Tri Phuong
Duong Hung Vuong
Ly Quy Don
Duong Ba Trieu
Tran Hung Dao
Trang Tien Bridge
Hoang Hoa Tham
Pham Hong Thai
Phu Xuan Bridge
Duong Le Loi
Duong Ha Noi
Ly Thuong Kiet
Duong Dong Da
Ngo Quyen
Nguyen Huy Tu
Le Lai
Nguyen Truong To
Duong Nguyen Hue
Phan Chu Trinh
An Cuu Bridge
To Phu Bai Airport (13 km), Danang (108 km), & Ho Chi Minh City (1097 km)
Perfume River
Tran Thuc Nhan
Doan Huu Trinh
Duong Dien Bien Phu
Duong Buu Thi Xuan
Phan Boi Chau
Tu Dam
To Nam Giao & Royal Tombs

VIETNAM

PLACES TO STAY

13 Khach San Hang Be
20 Hu Hotel
21 Huong Giang Hotel & Thua Thien-Hu Province Tourism
22 Kinh Do Hotel
24 Morin Hotel
27 Thuan Hoa Hotel
28 Ben Nghe Guesthouse
36 Dongda Hotel
37 Hu City Tourism Villas
38 Ngo Quyen Hotel
39 Nha Khach 18 Le Loi
44 Khach San Thuong Tu
73 Hu City Tourism Villas
74 Hu City Tourism Villas

PLACES TO EAT

4 Phu Hiep Restaurant
7 Quan 176
14 Café
23 Song Huong Floating Restaurant
25 Nam Song Huong Restaurant
29 Nua Thu Restaurant
43 Banh Khoai Thuong Tu & Lac Thanh Restaurants
66 Huong Sen Restaurant
75 Café 3 Le Loi

OTHER

1 Gate (closed)
2 Gate to military area (closed to public)
3 Tang Quang Pagoda (Hinayana)
5 Chaozhou Pagoda
6 Chua Ba
8 Cantonese Chinese Congregation Hall
9 Chieu Ung Pagoda
10 Former Indian Mosque
11 Dieu De National Pagoda
12 Dong Ba Gate
15 Gold & Silver Trade Department
16 Dong Ba Bus Station
17 Dong Ba Market
18 Dock
19 Riverine Transportation Cooperative
26 GPO
30 Vietnam Airlines Office
31 Industrial & Commercial Bank
32 Municipal Theatre
33 An Cuu Bus Station
34 An Dinh Palace
35 Notre Dame Cathedral
40 Hu City Tourism
41 Cercle Sportif
42 Hospital
45 Thuong Tu Gate
46 Military Museum
47 Natural History Museum
48 Imperial Museum
49 Hien Nhon Gate
50 Four of the Nine Holy Cannons
51 Ngan Gate
52 Truck Depot
53 Flag Tower
54 Quang Duc Gate
55 Five of the Nine Holy Cannons
56 Ngo Mon Gate
57 Trung Dao Bridge
58 Thai Hoa Palace
59 Halls of the Mandarins
60 Nine Dynastic Urns
61 Chuong Duc Gate
62 Royal Library
63 Hoa Binh Gate
64 Nha Do Gate
65 Chanh Tay Gate
67 Gate
68 Gate
69 Provincial People's Committee
70 Hai Ba Trung Secondary School
71 Quoc Hoc Secondary School
72 Ho Chi Minh Museum
76 Railway Station
77 Bao Quoc Pagoda
78 Tu Dam Pagoda
79 Linh Quang Pagoda & Phan Boi Chau's Tomb
80 Phu Cam Cathedral
81 Tomb of Duc Duc

The *Morin Hotel*, at the corner of Le Loi and Hung Vuong Sts, is also one of the cheapest in Hué. Prices are US$3 to US$6 for a double room with electric fan – US$5 to US$10 for a room with air-conditioning – and US$12 for a triple room with air-con. The hotel has bike rentals. This place has a great atmosphere and has become very popular with travellers.

Other hotels worth considering include:

Dongda Hotel, on Ly Thuong Kiet St, doubles with fan US$7, with air-con US$10
Ngo Quyen Hotel, off Ha Noi St, doubles with shared bath US$7, with private bath US$10 to US$15
Kinh Do Hotel, on Vo Thi Sau St, US$10 to US$30
Thuan Hoa Hotel (☎ 2553), 7 Nguyen Tri Phuong St, doubles US$15 to US$30
Huong Giang Hotel (☎ 2122), 51 Le Loi St, budget rooms US$7 and US$10 per bed, doubles with air-con US$38, US$34 and US$55
Hué Hotel (☎ 3391), 49 Le Loi St, a new place on the river, singles are US$36 to US$63, doubles US$40 to US$70

Places to Eat

Café 3 Le Loi is exceedingly popular with budget travellers.

The *Banh Khoai Thuong Tu*, 6 Dinh Tien Hoang St, has the words 'Lac Thien' written in cement on the facade and serves a traditional Hué speciality, banh khoai (crêpe with bean sprouts, shrimp and meat inside).

Next door is the *Lac Thanh Restaurant*. The food is awesome. See the book travellers have written in for how to order beause the owner, Lac, is mute – everything is done with sign language. However, Lac's daughter, Lan Anh, can speak a bit of English.

Lac took us by rented motorbike around the DMZ. What a day! He is the best tour guide we've ever had – a treat to be with!

Delicious sweet soups (che) made with such ingredients as beans and bananas are served either hot or iced in shops at numbers 10 and 12 Dinh Tien Hoang St, just up from the Khach San Thuong Tu.

The *Quan 176* is a small place in Phu Cat subdistrict at 176 Chi Lang St. They serve traditional Hué pastries, including banh nam (a flat cake of rice flour, meat and shrimp fried in a banana leaf).

The *Hang Be Restaurant* (☎ 3752) is on the ground floor of the Khach San Hang Be at 73 Huynh Thuc Khang St. This place gets mixed reviews.

Within the Citadel, the *Huong Sen Restaurant* (☎ 3201) is at 42 Nguyen Trai St (corner of Thach Han St). This 16-sided pavilion is built on pylons in the middle of a lotus pond.

The *Phu Hiep Restaurant* (☎ 3560) in Phu Hiep District is at 19 Ho Xuan Huong St (opposite 53 Nguyen Chi Thanh St).

The *Café* is in an interesting old building at 51 Phan Dang Lu St, a few blocks north-west of Dong Ba Market; only drinks are served.

Stalls in the marketplaces serve vegetarian food on the first and 15th days of the lunar month.

Getting There & Away

Air The Vietnam Airlines booking office (☎ 2249) is at 12 Ha Noi St and is open Monday to Saturday from 7 to 11 am and 1.30 to 5 pm.

There are flights connecting Hué to Ho Chi Minh City (US$85 one way) every Tuesday, Friday and Sunday. There are flights to/from Hanoi (US$80 one way) every Tuesday and Friday.

Bus Buses to places north of Hué depart from An Hoa bus station (Ben Xe An Hoa or Ben Xe So 1; ☎ 3014), which is at the western tip of the Citadel across from 499 Le Duan St (on the corner of Tang Bat Ho St). Almost all buses depart at 5 or 5.30 am.

Buses to points south of Hué leave from An Cuu bus station (☎ 3817), which is opposite 46 Hung Vuong St (on the corner Nguyen Hue St).

Train Hué railway station (Ga Hué) is on the east bank at the south-west end of Le Loi St. The ticket office is open from 6.30 am to 5 pm.

Getting Around

Many sights in the vicinity of Hué, including Thuan An Beach, Thien Mu Pagoda and several of the Royal Tombs, can be reached by river. You might try hiring a boat behind Dong Ba Market or at the Riverine Transportation Cooperative (Van Tai Gioi Duong Song), whose office is right across Dong Ba Canal from Dong Ba Market.

Bicycles can be hired from the Nha Khach Hué Hotel at 2 Le Loi St, and the Morin Hotel.

DMZ & VICINITY

From 1954 to 1975, the Ben Hai River served as the demarcation line between the Republic of Vietnam (South Vietnam) and the Democratic Republic of Vietnam (North Vietnam). The Demilitarised Zone (DMZ) consisted of an area five km to either side of the demarcation line.

Most of what you can see nowadays in the DMZ are places where historical things happened. For it to all make sense, you really need a guide who can explain just what you're looking at. Guides can readily be found in Hué, and sometimes in Dong Ha. The Morin Hotel and the Lac Thanh Restaurant (see under Hué) are good places to arrange trips to the DMZ.

Information

Travel Permit The local government in Quang Tri Province requires that foreigners secure a separate travel permit to visit any places in the DMZ off National Highway 1. The charge for the permit is US$10, plus you must rent a car from the local government.

Cars cost US$30, or you can rent a minibus for US$40. This rule applies even if you already have your own rental car from elsewhere. You can secure these permits in the town of Dong Ha. It is possible that this idiotic rule will be rescinded, so make local inquiries.

Warning The war may be over, but death is still relatively easy to come by in the old DMZ. At many of the places listed in this section you may find live mortar rounds, artillery shells and mines strewn about. White phosphorous shells – whose contents burn fiercely when exposed to air – are remarkably impervious to the effects of long exposure to rain and sun and can remain deadly for decades. These shells even scare the hell out of Vietnamese scrap metal collectors, who won't touch them. In short, be careful. Don't become a candidate for plastic surgery, or another war statistic.

Things to See

The remarkable **Tunnels of Vinh Moc** are similar to the ones at Cu Chi, but these are the real thing, not rebuilt for mass tourism. In 1966, the villagers of Vinh Moc, facing incessant US aerial and artillery attacks, began tunnelling by hand into the red clay earth. After 18 months of work, the entire village of 1200 persons was relocated underground. The whole 2.8 km tunnel network, which remains in its original state, can be visited with a guide. Bring a torch (flashlight). The turn-off to Vinh Moc from National Highway 1 is 6½ km north of the Ben Hai River, in the village of Ho Xa. Vinh Moc is 13 km from National Highway 1.

Truong Son National Cemetery (Nghia Trang Liet Si Truong Son) is a memorial to the tens of thousands of North Vietnamese soldiers killed along the Ho Chi Minh Trail. Row after row of white tombstones stretch across the hillsides in a scene eerily reminiscent of the endless lines of crosses and Stars of David in US military cemeteries. The road to Truong Son National Cemetery intersects National Route 1 13 km north of Dong Ha and nine km south of the Ben Hai River. The distance from the highway to the cemetery is 17 km. A rocky cart path, passable (but just barely) by car, links Cam Lo (on National Route 9) with Truong Son National Cemetery.

The gargantuan 175-mm cannons at **Camp Carroll** were used to shell targets as far away as Khe Sanh, over 30 km away. These days, there is not much to see here except a few overgrown trenches and the remains of timber roofs. The turn-off to Camp Carroll is 11 km west of Cam Lo, 24 km east of the Dakrong Bridge and 37 km east of the Khe Sanh bus station. The base is three km from National Highway 9.

Set amidst beautiful hills, valleys and fields at an elevation of about 600 metres, the town of **Khe Sanh** (Huong Hoa) is a pleasant district capital once known for its French-run coffee plantations. **Khe Sanh Combat Base**, site of the most famous siege of the Vietnam War, sits silently on a barren plateau surrounded by vegetation-covered hills often obscured by mist and fog. In early 1968, about 500 Americans and uncounted thousands of North Vietnamese and local people died violently here. To get to Khe Sanh Combat Base, turn north-westward at the triangular intersection 600 metres towards Dong Ha from Khe Sanh bus station. The base is on the right-hand side of the road 2½ km from the intersection.

Lao Bao, 18 km from Khe Sanh, is right on the Tchepone River (Song Xe Pon), which marks the Vietnam-Laos border. Towering above Lao Bao on the Lao side of the border is Co Roc Mountain, once a North Vietnamese artillery stronghold. Two km towards Khe Sanh from the border crossing (recently opened to foreigners) is the lively Lao Bao Market.

Hanoi

A city of lakes, shaded boulevards and verdant public parks; where beggars fight over a plate of discarded noodles; where prosperous shopowners exemplify Vietnam's new economic reforms; the seat of power; where absolute power corrupts absolutely.

Hanoi (population 925,000), capital of the Socialist Republic of Vietnam, is different things to different people. Most foreigners on a short visit find Hanoi to be slow-paced, pleasant and even charming. Physically, it's a more attractive city than Ho Chi Minh City – there is less traffic, less noise, less pollution, more trees and more open space. But it's changing fast. The number of motorbikes increases daily. Perhaps a more telling sign that the north is determined to catch up with the progressive south is that prostitution – which the Communists once claimed was stamped out – is now one of Hanoi's leading growth industries.

Information

Tourist Offices The Hanoi Tourism Service Company, known as TOSERCO (Cong Ty Dich Vu Du Lich Ha Noi; ☎ 263541), is at 8 To Hien Thanh St (corner of Mai Hac De St). Vietnam Tourism (☎ 257080) is at 54 Nguyen Du St, and also has a branch office (☎ 255552) at 30A Ly Thuong Kiet St.

Travel Agencies There are plenty of travel agencies in Hanoi, both government and private, which can provide cars, book air tickets and extend your visa. Some of these places charge the same high prices as TOSERCO and Vietnam Tourism, while others will only charge half that. Cafes that cater to foreigners also offer these services, and often at incredibly cheap prices. Some agencies which have been recommended by travellers include:

Ann Tourist
20 Dien Bien Phu St (☎ 234680)
Darling Café
4 Hang Quat St
Ecco Vietnam
50A Ba Trieu (☎ 254615)
Especen Tourist Company
79 Hang Trong (☎ 266856)
Oscan Enterprises
60 Nguyen Du St (☎ 252690, 265859; fax (84-4) 257634)
Pacific Tours
58B Tran Nhan Tong St (☎ 267942; fax (84-4) 254437)
Queen Café
65 Hang Bac St (☎ 260860)
Tourist Meeting Café
59 Ba Trieu St (☎ 258812)

Money The Foreign Trade Bank (Ngan Hang Ngoai Thuong Viet Nam), also known as Vietcombank, is off Ly Thai To St. Another branch is on the corner of Tran Binh Trong and Nguyen Du Sts, near Thien Quang Lake.

Jewellery shops near the shoe market (at the north-east corner of Hoan Kiem Lake) are the best place to seek the black market.

Post & Telecommunications The GPO (Buu Dien Trung Vong; ☎ 257036; fax 253525), which occupies a full city block facing Hoan Kiem Lake, is at 75 Dinh Tien Hoang St (between Dinh Le St and Le Thach St). Telex and domestic telephone services are available from 6.30 am to 8 pm; telegrams can be sent 24 hours a day.

Visa Modifications If you want to exit Vietnam from a point other than what is indicated on your visa, changes can be readily made in Hanoi. The office handling this is in Room 202 of the Boss Hotel (☎ 252690) at 60-62 Nguyen Du St.

Immigration Police This is at 87 Tran Hung Dao St – open Monday to Saturday from 8 to 11 am and 1 to 5 pm.

Medical Services The International Hospital (Benh Vien Quoc Te; ☎ 243728), where foreigners are usually referred, is on the western side of Giai Phong St a bit south of the Polytechnic University (Dai Hoc Bach Khoa). To get there, take bus No 4, 7 or 15 from the city centre. In winter, the hospital's outpatient clinic is open from 8 am to 12.30 pm and 1 to 4.30 pm; in summer, it is open from 7.30 am to noon and 1 to 4.30 pm.

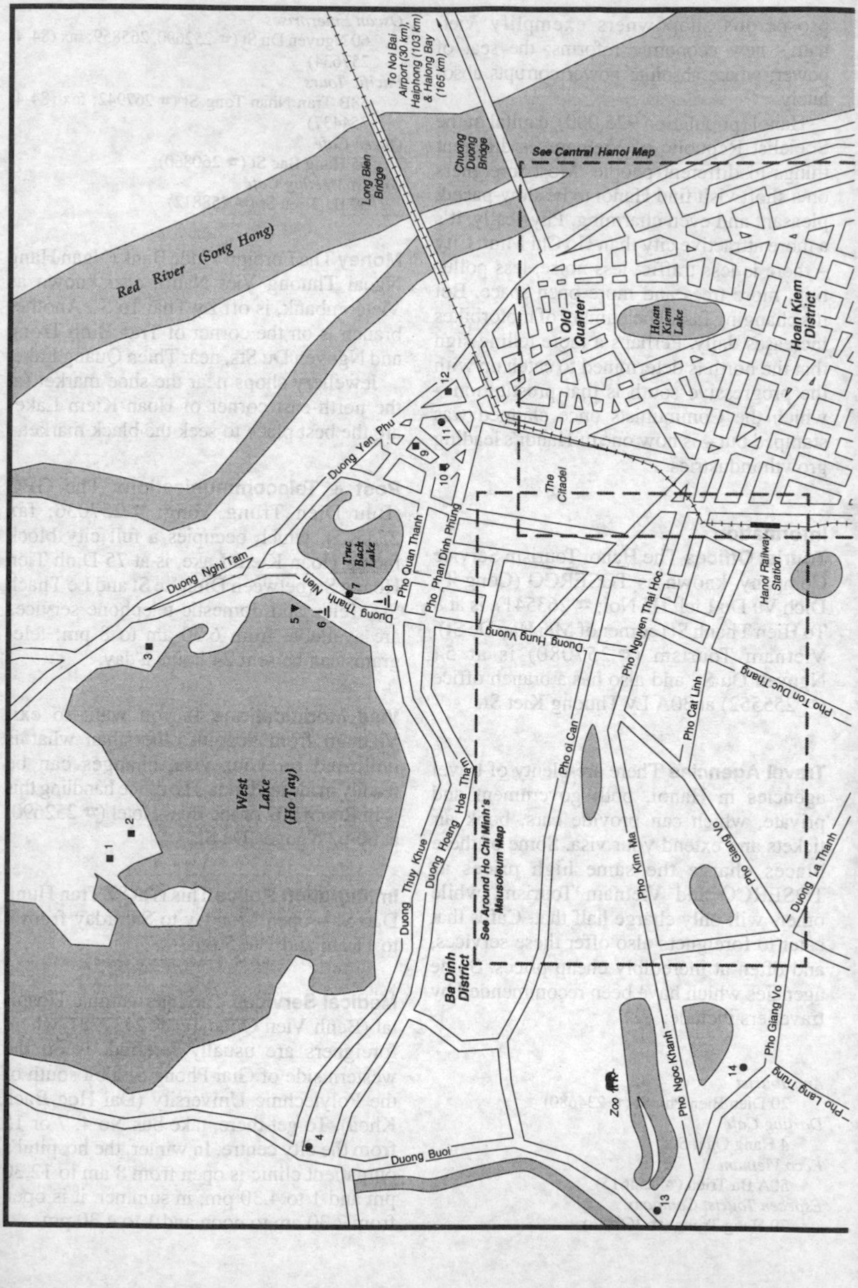

To Noi Bai Airport (30 km), Haiphong (103 km) & Halong Bay (165 km)
See Central Hanoi Map
Chuong Duong Bridge
Long Bien Bridge
Red River (Song Hong)
Old Quarter
Hoan Kiem Lake
Hoan Kiem District
The Citadel
Hanoi Railway Station
Duong Yen Phu
Truc Bach Lake
Pho Quan Thanh
Pho Phan Dinh Phung
Duong Nghi Tam
Duong Thanh Nien
Duong Hung Vuong
Pho Nguyen Thai Hoc
Pho Cat Linh
Pho Ton Duc Thang
West Lake (Ho Tay)
See Around Ho Chi Minh's Mausoleum Map
Duong Hoang Hoa Tham
Duong Thuy Khue
Ba Dinh District
Pho oi Can
Pho Kim Ma
Pho Giang Vo
Duong La Thanh
Pho Ngoc Khanh
Zoo
Pho Lang Trung
Duong Buoi
1
2
3
4
5
6
7
8
9
10
11
12
13
14

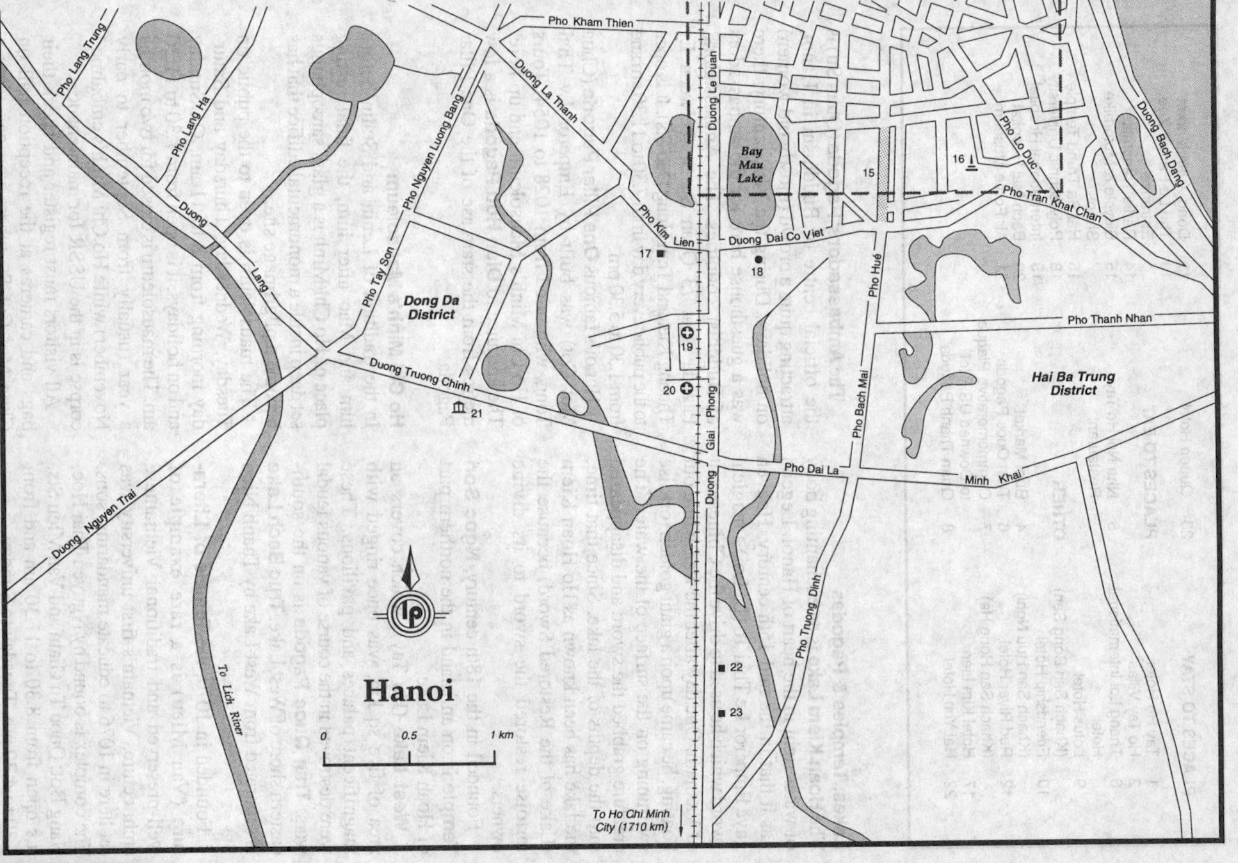
Pho Kham Thien
Pho Lang Trung
Pho Lang Ha
Duong
Lang
Duong La Thanh
Pho Nguyen Luong Bang
Pho Tay Son
Dong Da District
Duong Le Duan
Bay Mau Lake
Pho Kim Lien
17
18
Duong Dai Co Viet
15
16
Pho Lo Duc
Pho Tran Khat Chan
Duong Bach Dang
Pho Hué
Pho Thanh Nhan
Hai Ba Trung District
19
20
Giai Phong
Duong Truong Chinh
21
Pho Bach Mai
Pho Dai La
Minh Khai
Duong
Duong Nguyen Trai
Pho Truong Dinh
22
23
To Lich River
Hanoi
0
0.5
1 km
To Ho Chi Minh City (1710 km)

PLACES TO STAY

1 Tay Ho Hotel
2 Ho Tay Villas
3 Thang Loi International Hotel
9 Lotus Hotel (Khach San Bong Sen)
10 Friendship Hotel (Khach San Huu Nghi)
12 Red River Hotel (Khach San Hong Ha)
17 Hotel Kim Lien
22 Hai Yen Hotel
23 Queen Hotel

PLACES TO EAT

5 Nha Noi Ho Tay Restaurant

OTHER

4 Buoi Market
6 Tran Quoc Pagoda
7 Commemorative Plaque to Downed US Pilot
8 Quan Thanh Pagoda
11 Dong Xuan Market
13 Thu Le Park & Zoo Entrance
14 Radio Transmitter
15 Bicycle & Motorbike Shops
16 Hai Ba Trung Temple
18 Polytechnic University
19 International Hospital
20 Bach Mai Hospital
21 Air Force Museum

Lakes, Temples & Pagodas

The **Hoan Kiem Lake** is an enchanting body of water right in the heart of Hanoi. Legend has it that in the mid-15th century, Heaven gave Emperor Le Thai To (Le Loi) a magical sword which he used to drive the Chinese out of Vietnam. One day after the war, while out boating, he came upon a giant golden tortoise swimming on the surface of the water. The creature grabbed the sword and disappeared into the depths of the lake. Since that time, the lake has been known as Ho Hoan Kiem (Lake of the Restored Sword) because the tortoise restored the sword to its divine owners.

Founded in the 18th century, **Ngoc Son Temple** is on an island in the northern part of Hoan Kiem Lake.

West Lake (Ho Tay), which covers an area of five sq km, was once ringed with magnificent palaces and pavilions. These were destroyed in the course of various feudal wars. **Tran Quoc Pagoda** is on the south-eastern shore of West Lake. **Truc Bach Lake** is separated from West Lake by Thanh Nien St.

Founded in 1070, the **Temple of Literature** (Van Mieu) is a rare example of well-preserved and traditional Vietnamese architecture. Vietnam's first university was set here in 1076 to educate mandarins' sons. The complex is bound by Nguyen Thai Hoc, Hang Bot, Quoc Tu Giam and Van Mieu Sts. It,s open from 8.30 to 11.30 am and from 1.30 to 4.30 pm, Tuesday to Sunday.

The **Ambassadors' Pagoda** (Quan Su) is the official centre of Buddhism in Hanoi, attracting quite a crowd (mostly old women) on holidays. During the 17th century, there was a guesthouse here for the ambassadors of Buddhist countries. The Ambassadors' Pagoda is at 73 Quan Su St (between Ly Thuong Kiet and Tran Hung Dao Sts). It is open to the public every day from 7.30 to 11.30 am and from 1.30 to 5.30 pm.

Hanoi's famous **One Pillar Pagoda** (Chua Mot Cot) was built by Emperor Ly Thai Tong, who ruled from 1028 to 1054. Tours of Ho Chi Minh's Mausoleum end up here. The entrance to **Dien Huu Pagoda** is a few metres from the staircase of the One Pillar Pagoda.

Ho Chi Minh's Mausoleum

In the tradition of Lenin and Stalin before him and Mao after him, the final resting place of Ho Chi Minh is a glass sarcophagus set deep inside a monumental edifice that has become a pilgrimage site.

The mausoleum is open to the public on Tuesday, Wednesday, Thursday and Saturday morning from 8 to 11 am. On Sunday and on holidays, it is open from 7.30 to 11.30 am. The mausoleum is closed for two months a year (usually from September to early November) while Ho Chi Minh's embalmed corpse is in the USSR for maintenance.

All visitors must register and check their bags and cameras at the reception hall on Chua Mot Cot St, where you can view a

20-minute video, in English and other languages, about Ho Chi Minh's life and accomplishments.

The following rules are strictly applied to all mausoleum visitors:

- People wearing shorts, tank-tops etc will not be admitted.
- Nothing (including day packs and cameras) may be taken into the mausoleum.
- A respectful demeanour must be maintained at all times.
- For obvious reasons, photography is absolutely prohibited inside the mausoleum.
- It is forbidden to put your hands in your pockets.
- Hats must be taken off inside the mausoleum building.

Although the rules do not explicitly say so, it is suggested that you don't ask the guards, 'Is he dead'?

After exiting from the mausoleum, the tour will pass by the **Presidential Palace**, constructed in 1906 as the palace of the Governor General of Indochina. **Ho Chi Minh's house**, built of the finest materials in 1958, is next to a carp-filled pond. Nearby is what was once Hanoi's botanical garden and is now a park. The tour ends up at the One Pillar Pagoda. The new Ho Chi Minh Museum is nearby.

Museums

The **History Museum**, once the museum of the École Française d'Extrême Orient, is one block east of the Municipal Theatre at 1 Pham Ngu Lao St. The **Army Museum** is on Dien Bien Phu St. It is open daily, except Monday, from 7.30 to 11.30 am. The displays include scale models of various epic battles from Vietnam's long military history, including Dien Bien Phu and the capture of Saigon.

The **Ho Chi Minh Museum** is divided into two sections, 'Past' and 'Future'. You start in the past and move to the future by walking in a clockwise direction downwards through the museum, starting at the right-hand side at the top of the stairs. The displays are very modern and all have a message (eg peace, happiness, freedom etc). Some of the symbolism is hard to figure out (did Ho Chi Minh have a cubist period?). The 1958 Ford Edsel bursting through the wall (an American commercial failure used to symbolise America's military failure) is a knockout. The museum is the huge cement structure near Ho Chi Minh's Mausoleum. Photography is forbidden. Upon entering, all bags and cameras must be left at reception.

Many of the exhibits at the **Air Force Museum** are outdoors. They include a number of Soviet MIG fighters, reconnaissance planes, helicopters and anti-aircraft equipment. Inside the museum hall are other weapons including mortars, machine guns and some US-made bombs (hopefully defused). There is a partially truncated MIG with a ladder – you are permitted to climb up into the cockpit and have your photo taken. The museum is on Truong Chinh St in the Dong Da District (south-western part of the city). From the railway station it's almost five km, a rather long cyclo ride.

The works in the **Fine Arts Museum** (Bao Tang My Thuat) are revolutionary in style and content, depicting heroic figures waving red flags, children with rifles, a wounded soldier joining the Communist Party, innumerable tanks and weaponry, and grotesque Americans. The museum is at 66 Nguyen Thai Hoc St (corner of Cao Ba Quai St), across the street from the back wall of the Temple of Literature. It's open from 8 am to noon and 1.30 to 4 pm Tuesday to Sunday.

St Joseph's Cathedral

Stepping inside St Joseph's Cathedral (inaugurated in 1886) is like being instantly transported to medieval Europe. The cathedral is noteworthy for its square towers, elaborate altar and stained-glass windows. The first Catholic mission in Hanoi was founded in 1679.

The main gate to St Joseph's Cathedral is open daily from 5 to 7 am and from 5 to 7 pm, the hours when masses are held. Guests are welcome at other times of the day but must enter via the compound of the Diocese of Hanoi, the entrance to which is a block away at 40 Nha Chung St. After walking

through the gate, go straight and then turn right. When you reach the side door to the cathedral, ring the small bell high up to the right of the door and the priest will let you in.

Hanoi Hilton

The 'Hanoi Hilton' is the nickname given to a prison in which US prisoners-of-war – mostly aircraft crewmen – were held during the Vietnam War. The high walls of the forbidding triangular building, officially known as Hoa Lo Prison, are pierced by precious few barred windows. The structure is bound by Hai Ba Trung, Tho Nhuom and Hoa Lo Sts.

Places to Stay

Unlike Saigon with its numerous large-sized cheap hotels, Hanoi suffers from a serious lack of budget accommodation.

Hanoi, of course, did not enjoy the wartime economic boom that spurred hotel development in the former South Vietnam. Accommodating foreigners is a recent phenomenon in Hanoi, and the sudden invasion of backpackers since the Chinese border was opened in 1993 has resulted in a serious shortage of low-priced accommodation, especially during the peak (June through August) tourist season. To fill the gap, budding entrepreneurs have set up budget hotels, each consisting of a few rooms set aside in somebody's house. These small, French-built townhouses are charming places to stay, but finding a room takes patience – you may have to walk from house to house, only to find that most are full.

On the other end of the scale are huge mansions built as official state rest and recreation centres for high-ranking Communist Party officials. These places are palatial – high ceilings, chandeliers, huge dining halls and well-tended gardens surrounded by high fences. These places are now being converted into upmarket hotels – foreign tourists

PLACES TO STAY

9 La Thanh Hotel
13 Giang Vo Hotel
14 Thang Long Hotel
26 Hai Yen Mini-Hotel
28 Mai Anh Hotel
29 Dong Loi Mini-Hotel
30 Sao Mai Hotel

PLACES TO EAT

11 Restaurant 79
15 Dong Do Restaurant
18 Phuong Nam Restaurant

OTHER

1 Presidential Palace
2 Ho Chi Minh's Mausoleum
3 Ba Dinh Square
4 National Assembly Building
5 One Pillar Pagoda & Dien Huu Pagoda
6 Ho Chi Minh Museum
7 Reception for Ho Chi Minh's Mausoleum
8 Ministry of Foreign Affairs
10 Belgian, Malaysian, Myanmar & Swedish Embassies
12 Finnish Embasssy
16 Exhibition Hall
17 Kim Ma Bus Station
19 Chinese Embassy
20 Lenin Statue
21 Flag Tower
22 Army Museum
23 Fine Arts Museum
24 Mongolian Embassy
25 Hanoi Stadium
27 Entrance to Temple of Literature
31 Market
32 Railway Station

with hard currency are welcomed. There has also been a recent spate of upmarket hotel construction by foreign joint-ventures, but this is of little help to budget travellers.

Places to Stay – bottom end

The *Queen Café* (☎ 260860) at 65 Hang Bac St operates a small guesthouse upstairs above the restaurant. If full, the staff may be able to direct you to another place.

A similar deal is offered at the *Bodega Café & Guesthouse*, 57 Trang Tien St, or at their annexe *(Bodega II)* several blocks away at 41 Hang Bai St.

There are about 15 rooms available at the *Ta Hien Hotel* (☎ 255888) at 22 Ta Hien St. Doubles are US$10 with fan or US$15 with air-con.

The *Trang Tien Hotel* (☎ 256115, 256341), 35 Trang Tien St (just south-east of Hoan Kiem Lake) costs US$7 for a double with shared bath, or US$10 to US$15 for a room with private bath. Don't be put off by the entrance which is along a dark alley – there is a security guard at the end of the alley at the hotel entrance and the alley is quite busy.

Next to St Joeseph's Cathedral is *Guest House 8 Nha Chung* (☎ 268500). The friendly owner speaks good English. Rooms start at US$8.

The *Sophia Hotel* (☎ 255069) is at 6 Hang Bai St, up the stairs from the restaurant. It is adequate but overpriced at US$20 for a double, with bathroom and hot water. The staff are friendly but fairly incompetent and seem somewhat averse to cleaning the rooms. If the hotel is full, they will direct you to their other place, *Sophia II*, about three km away; prices there are about the same.

The *Dong Do Hotel* (☎ 233275), 27 Tong Duy Tan St, is a popular place with budget travellers. Rooms cost from US$10 to US$40.

Guest House Culture (☎ 253044), or Nha Khach Van Hoa, is at 22A Hai Ba Trung St. Doubles with attached bath cost US$15 and there are bicycles for rent here.

The *Hoan Kiem Guest House* (☎ 268944; four rooms), 76 Hai Ba Trung St, should not be confused with the much pricier Hoan Kiem Hotel. Suite-like rooms with attached bath, hot water, colour TV and air-con cost US$20 for a double. The rooms are squeaky clean and the manager is very friendly.

The *Hoa Binh Hotel* (☎ 253315; 112 rooms), 27 Ly Thuong Kiet St, is centrally located. This old place has a certain crumbling elegance to it, though there are plans to do renovation work soon. Singles/doubles cost from US$18/22 to US$57/65. As for the in-house restaurant, the hotel's glossy brochure promises 'excellent cook-chiefs who won gold medal'.

The *Hai Yen Hotel* (☎ 291024; seven rooms) is at 126 Giai Phong St in the far

Central Hanoi

To West Lake (Ho Tay)
Duong Tran Nhat Duat
Chuong Duong Bridge
To Noi Bai Airport (30 km), Haiphong (103 km) & Halong Bay (165 km)
Red River
Hang Luoc
D Xuan
Hang Chieu
Hang Ga
Hang Ma
Cha Ca
H Duong
H Giay
Dao Duy Tu
Buom
Hang
Phuc Tan
Hang Vai
Thuoc Bac
H Can
H Ngang
OLD QUARTER
The Citadel (military area)
Pho Ly Nam De
Hang Bac
H Mam
Hang Bo
Pho Bat Dan
Luong V Can
Hang Dao
Hang Be
Duong
H Thiec
H Quat
Pho Phung Hung
Cau Go
H Thung
Tran Duong Quang Khai
Duong Bach Dang
Yen Thai
Hang Gai
Dinh Tien
Lo Su
To Ho Chi Minh's Mausoleum
Ngo Tram
Thanh
Ly Quoc Su
Hang Trong
Hang Dau
Duong Tran Phu
Duong Dien Bien Phu
Hang Bong
Le Thai To
Hoan Kiem Lake
Pho Nguyen Thai Hoc
Hang Da
Pho Phu Doan
Tran N G Han
Pho Nha Chung
Pho Ly Thai To
Le Lai
Pho Trang Thi
Le Thach
Dinh Tien Hoang
Pho Phan Boi Chau
Pho Quan Su
Pho Hai Ba Trung
Dinh Le
Tho
Pho Hoa Lo
Hang Khai
Trang Tien
Pho Quang Trung
Pho Ly Thuong Kiet
Pham Ngu Lao
Le Thanh Tong
Pho Phan Chu Trinh
Ngo Quyen St
Hang Bai
Pho Nhuom
Duong Le Duan
Pho Yet Kieu
Pho Ba Trieu
Pho Tran Hung Dao
Pho Tran Binh Trong
Ng Gia Thieu
Pho Tran Quoc Toan
Pho Ham Long
Phan Huy Chu
Pho Nguyen Du
N T Hien
Le Van Huu
Pho Han Thuyen
Thien Quang Lake
N Quyen
Pho Hang Chuoi
Pho Tang Bat Ho
Pho Tran Thanh Tong
Pho Tran Nhan Tong
Pho Bui Thi Xuan
Pho Trieu Viet Vuong
Pho Hué
Pho Mai Hac De
Pho Tue Tinh
Lenin Park
Nguyen Binh Khiem
Pho Ba Trieu
Pho To Hien Thanh
Bay Mau Lake
To International Hospital, Bach Mai Hospital & Ho Chi Minh City
0 250 500 m
1 2 3 4 5 6 7 8 9 10 11 12 13 14 15 16 17 18 19 20 21 22 23 24 25 26 27 28 29 30 31 32 33 34 35 36 37 38 39 40 41 42 43 44 45 46 47 48 49 50 51 52 53 54 55 56 57 58 59 60 61 62 63 64 65 66 67 68 69 70 71 72 73

VIETNAM

PLACES TO STAY

5 Phung Hung Hotel
14 Nam Phuong Hotel
16 Energy Service Centre
17 Binh Minh Hotel & China Southern Airlines
19 Dong Do Hotel
21 Phu Gia Hotel
25 Hoan Kiem Guest House
26 Dong Loi Hotel
28 Rose & Saigon Hotels
31 Khach San 30-4
32 Capital Hotel
41 Sophia Hotel & Restaurant
45 Hotel Bac Nam
46 Dan Chu Hotel
48 Hotel Pullman Metropole (Thong Nhat Hotel)
54 Hoa Binh Hotel
62 Hoan Kiem Hotel
67 Boss Hotel & VIP Club

PLACES TO EAT

1 Piano Restaurant
2 Cha Ca Restaurant
3 Chau Thanh Restaurant
4 Restaurant 22
6 Darling Café
7 Caf Darling Hanoi
8 Queen Café
11 Thuy Ta Restaurant
13 Bittek Restaurant (Le Franais)
24 Huong Sen Restaurant
43 Bodega Café & Guesthouse
53 Small Restaurants
55 Small Restaurants
61 Tourist Meeting Café
71 Restaurant 202
72 Hoa Binh Restaurant

OTHER

9 Hanoi City Water Puppet Theatre
10 Shoe Market
12 Ngoc Son Temple & The Huc Bridge
15 ANZ Bank
18 Ann Tourist
20 St Joseph's Cathedral
22 Palace Restaurant & Dancing
23 Aeroflot Office
27 German Embassy
29 Australian Embassy
30 Railway Station
33 Ambassadors' Pagoda
34 'Hanoi Hilton' Prison
35 19th December Market
36 National Library
37 Vietnam Airlines International Office & Air France
38 GPO & DHL
39 International Telephone Office
40 Traditional Medicines Pharmacy
42 State General Department Store
44 Foreign Language Bookshop
47 Thong Nhat Book Store
49 Foreign Trade Bank
50 Revolutionary Museum
51 Municipal Theatre
52 History Museum
56 Indonesian Embassy
57 Vietcochamber
58 Immigration Police
59 Cambodian Embassy
60 French Embassy
63 Vietcombank
64 Lao Embassy
65 Kim Lien Bus Station
66 Lao Embassy Consular Section
68 Vietnam Airlines Domestic Booking Office
69 Japanese Embassy
70 TOSERCO
73 Bicycle & Motorbike Shops

south of Hanoi. Singles/doubles/triples cost US$12/15/17. It's good value but inconveniently far from the centre.

The *Giang Vo Hotel* (☎ 253407; about 300 rooms) consists of several five-storey apartment blocks in a large compound. One entrance to the hotel, which is 3.5 km west of the city centre, faces Giang Vo Lake; there is another entrance on Ngoc Khanh St. This is *the* most popular place with Vietnamese budget travellers, but foreigners are welcome if there is space. The dumpier rooms will cost you from US$5 to US$6; rooms with air-con, fridge and hot water cost US$20.

The *Phung Hung Hotel* (☎ 265555) is a bit over one km north-east of the railway station at 2 Duong Thanh St. Though not dirt-cheap, it has become fairly popular with backpackers. The hotel has a restaurant and bicycles for rent. Rooms cost US$16 with fan, or US$25 to US$30 with air-con.

The *La Thanh Hotel* (☎ 254123, 257057; 100 rooms) is a French-era renovated structure located two km west of Ho Chi Minh's Mausoleum at 218 Doi Can St. The lobby is interesting, filled with slot machines and billiard tables. This place is popular with Chinese tourists; the staff speak some English but they speak Chinese better. Budget rooms cost US$8 and US$12; rooms with TV cost US$14 to US$25.

The *Red River Hotel* (☎ 254911), or Khach San Hong Ha, is at 78 Yen Phu St. This is a good place in the budget category. Doubles cost US$5, US$20, US$25 and US$35. It's close to the Long Bien Bridge which crosses the Red River.

The *Phu Gia Hotel* at 136 Hang Trong St has a pleasant location next to Hoan Kiem

Lake. Not much English is spoken, but it seems to be a popular place and is often full. Double rooms cost US$12 to US$45.

The *Sao Mai Hotel* (☎ 255827), 16-18 Thong Phong Alley, off Ton Duc Thang St, is a pleasant mid-sized place less than one km south of the Ho Chi Minh Mausoleum. Double rooms cost US$20/25.

The *Dong Loi Mini-Hotel* (☎ 259173), 70 Nguyen Khuyen St, is very conveniently located for access to the railway station. This privately run guesthouse costs US$20 for a double.

The *Khach San 30-4* (☎ 252611; six rooms), 115 Tran Hung Dao St, is conveniently located opposite the railway station. It used to be a budget hotel, but at the time of this writing it was closed for renovation. When it reopens, it is possible the name will change and prices will escalate. Next door on Trang Hung Dao St is the *Capital Hotel*. Like Khach San 30-4, it was under renovation at the time of our visit.

Places to Stay – middle

Accommodation in the mid-range includes:

Binh Minh Hotel (☎ 266441), 27 Ly Thai To St (same building as China Southern Airlines), doubles US$26 to US$40

Dong Loi Hotel (☎ 255721), 94 Ly Thuong Kiet St, singles/doubles US$44/66

Energy Service Centre (☎ 253169), 30 Ly Thai To St (opposite China Southern Airlines), top-floor rooms cost US$30, other rooms are US$40 to US$50

Friendship Hotel (☎ 253182), or Khach San Huu Nghi, 23 Quan Thanh St, singles US$38 to US$42, doubles US$46 to US$54

Hai Yen Mini-Hotel (☎ 265803), 48 Hang Chao St, doubles US$30

Ho Tay Villas (☎ 258241), on the shore of West Lake, 5.5 km from the centre, singles/doubles are US$37/44 to US$44/50

Hoan Kiem Hotel (☎ 254204), 25 Tran Hung Dao St, singles/doubles US$30/35 to US$44/48, triples US$44 to US$57

Hotel Bac Nam (☎ 257067), 20 Ngo Quyen St, doubles US$20 to US$55

Lotus Hotel (☎ 4254017), or Khach San Bong Sen, 34 Hangbun St, singles/doubles US$38/44

Mai Anh Hotel (☎ 232702), 109A Nguyen Thai Hoc St, plush doubles US$25

Nam Phuong Hotel, 16 Bao Khanh St, doubles US$35

Queen Hotel (☎ 291237, 291238), 189 Giai Phong St (tacky south side of town), doubles US$30 to US$40

Rose Hotel (☎ 254438), or Khach San Hoa Hong, 20 Phan Boi Chau St, singles/doubles US$25/30 to US$48/52

Saigon Hotel, corner of Phan Boi Chau and Ly Thuong Kiet Sts, doubles US$40

Tay Ho Hotel (☎ 232380), north shore of West Lake, singles/doubles US$40/45 and US$50/55

Places to Eat

Hanoi is disappointing after Ho Chi Minh City. Restaurants in the capital tend to be more expensive than in the south, the food lousier and the service lethargic, but you won't starve.

Darling Café at 4 Hang Quat St has emerged as the favourite with backpackers. This is the top venue in Hanoi for banana pancakes and fruit shakes, not to mention spring rolls and other Vietnamese dishes. The Darling Café also organises day trips to various places like Halong Bay.

Café Darling Hanoi (☎ 269386), 33 Hang Quat St, is not related to the preceding – indeed, the two Darlings are bitter competitors. The competition probably benefits the customers – the food is good and this place also offers budget tours.

The selection of food is decidedly limited at the *Queen Café* (☎ 260860), 65 Hang Bac St. Nevertheless, it's a good place for breakfast, sandwiches and drinks, and a popular place with Westerners. The extremely friendly staff are a wealth of information on things to see and do in Hanoi, and they organise low-cost bus trips.

One other place that deserves an honorable mention is the *Tourist Meeting Café* (☎ 258812) at 59 Ba Trieu St. Food is reasonable, and as their namecard says, it's 'probably the perfect rendezvous spot'. This place also has motorbikes for rent.

The restaurants in the *Dan Chu Hotel* and the *Thong Nhat Hotel* are quite decent and the prices are surprisingly moderate (meals start at US$2). The *Hoan Kiem Hotel* has a limited menu, but the food is good and cheap. There is also an in-house restaurant in the *Hoa Binh Hotel*.

The *Sophia Restaurant* (☎ 255069) is at 6 Hang Bai St (between Hai Ba Trung St and Hoan Kiem Lake). Downstairs is a cafe; the restaurant proper is on the 2nd floor. The food is edible and priced in the mid-range. The menu is simple but a big selling point is the French cheese. Deafening music drifts through the walls from the adjacent stereo shop.

The *Bodega Café* is down the street at 57 Trang Tien St. This place serves pastries and drinks.

Restaurant Bistrot (☎ 266136) at 35 Tran Hung Dao St is an excellent French restaurant with almost obscenely low prices. This place has a great ambience and is really in vogue with budget travellers.

Restaurant 202 (Nha Hang 202) is 1.5 km south of Hoan Kiem Lake at 202 Pho Hué. It's one of the best restaurants in the city and a favourite of the diplomatic community. The atmosphere is vaguely French, the menu all-European and the serving sizes are small. Across the street at 163 Pho Hué is the *Hoa Binh Restaurant*.

At 92 Le Duan St, near the railway station, is the *Huong Sen Restaurant* (☎ 252805), run by Hanoi Tourism.

Restaurant 22 (also known as Quang An Restaurant) is at 22 Hang Can St. The entrance is through a narrow passageway and up the stairs. It has menus in Vietnamese, English, French, Italian and Swedish. One satisfied customer wrote:

> ...the best restaurant I found in Vietnam. Clean, tidy, with silver cutlery, tablecloths, friendly staff who speak English plus good meals and cheap prices.

Another favourite of the expat community is *Cha Ca Restaurant* at 14 Cha Ca St. Cha ca is not the name of a dance but means 'fried fish', which is in fact the restaurant's speciality. Cha Ca St, which is a two-block-long continuation of Luong Van Can St, begins about 500 metres north of Hoan Kiem Lake. The *Nha Thinh Restaurant* is at 28 Luong Van Can St.

Not far away at 50 Hang Vai St is the *Piano Restaurant* (☎ 232423). Chinese and Vietnamese food are on the menu, and one speciality is boiled crab. It's a fun place with live music every evening starting at 7 pm.

The *Chau Thanh Restaurant*, a favourite of visiting journalists, is at 48 Hang Ga St. The food is excellent but the menu is all French – good luck!

Bittek Restaurant, also known as Le Français, is off Hang Gai St at 17 Ly Quoc Su St; bittek means 'beefsteak'.

The *Thuy Ta Restaurant* at 1 Le Thai To St is a two-storey place overlooking Hoan Kiem Lake. It is about 200 metres south of the intersection of Le Thai To and Hang Gai Sts. The fare is limited to Vietnamese food, including what can best be described as Vietnamese chop suey.

Restaurant 79 is at 79 Ngoc Khanh St, which is a few hundred metres west of the Swedish Embassy.

The excellent *Phuong Nam Restaurant* is on Giang Vo St, less than 200 metres west of Hanoi stadium and not far from the Ho Chi Minh Mausoleum.

The *Dong Do Restaurant* is on Giang Vo St next to the Exhibition Hall (Trien Lam Giang Vo); the food is mediocre. There are several small places to eat across Giang Vo St from the Exhibition Hall.

The *Nha Noi Ho Tay Restaurant* (☎ 257884) floats on West Lake (Ho Tay) just off Duong Thanh Nien St near Tran Quoc Pagoda. The atmosphere is very pleasant but the food is so-so and the prices are high for what you get.

For some of the best French pastries and coffee in Vietnam, visit the *Pastry & Yogurt Shop* at 252 Hang Bong St, near the centre.

There are lots of ice cream *(kem)* cafes along Le Thai To St by Hoan Kiem Lake.

Fresh vegetables can be purchased at the 19th of December Market (Cho 19-12). The market has two entrances, one opposite 61 Ly Thuong Kiet St and one next to 41 Hai Ba Trung St. Dog meat is available from curbside vendors a few hundred metres north of the History Museum on Le Phung Hieu St near Tran Quang Kha St.

In Dong Xuan Market, just west of Friendship Hotel, there are foodstalls and fresh produce.

Entertainment

Municipal Theatre The 900-seat *Municipal Theatre* (☎ 254312), which faces eastward up Trang Tien St, was built in 1911 as an opera house. Performances are held here in the evenings.

Water Puppets This fantastic art form is unique to Vietnam and Hanoi is one of the best places to see it. The *National Water Puppet Theatre* (Nha Hat Mua Roi Trung Uong) is eight km south of the centre at 32 Dong Truong Trinh – some of the cafes catering to foreigners book tours and shows start at 7.30 or 8 pm.

Just on the shore of Hoan Kiem Lake is the *Hanoi City Water Puppet Theatre* (Roi Nuoc Thang Long) – check to find out when performances are given.

The Vietnam Stage Artists Association is a private organisation which books water puppet performances on request, but this place currently has no stable address.

Disco The *VIP Club* (☎ 252690), in the Boss Hotel at 60-62 Nguyen Du St, Hai Ba Trung District, is a thoroughly modern disco with thumping music, strobe lights and large-screen video. The VIP Club also has slot machines and karaoke cubicles. There is no cover charge but beer costs US$3 a glass while gin and tonic goes for US$5.50!

Pubs *Apocalypse Now* at 46 Hang Vai St calls itself a 'restaurant and dive bar'. It's about as good a dive as you'll find in Hanoi. It opens at 5 pm and closes when the customers trickle away. *Tintin Pub* at 14 Hang Non St is run by the same family that operates the Darling Café. This popular place serves only drinks, no food, though the management has plans to introduce snacks. It's open from 8 pm until 2 am.

Things to Buy

Lots of Western customers seem to like the Ho Chi Minh T-shirts. However, it might be worth keeping in mind that neither Ho Chi Minh T-shirts nor VC headgear are popular apparel with Vietnamese refugees and certain war veterans living in the West. Wearing such souvenirs while walking down a street in Los Angeles or Melbourne might offend someone, possibly endangering your relationship with the overseas Vietnamese community, as well as your dental work.

Greeting cards with traditional Vietnamese designs hand-painted on silk covers are available around town for US$0.10 or so.

Attractive gold-on-scarlet banners, usually given as awards for service to the Party or State, can be ordered to your specifications (with your name or date of visit, for instance) at shops at 13 and 40 Hang Bong St, north-west of Hoan Kiem Lake. Souvenir patches, sewn by hand, can also be commissioned at 13 Hang Bong St.

Hang Gai St and its continuation, Hang Bong St, are good places to look for embroidered tablecloths and hangings. Hanoi is a good place to have informal clothes custom tailored. There are also a number of antique shops in the vicinity.

There is an outstanding shoe market along Hang Dau St at the north-east corner of Hoan Kiem Lake. However, it's difficult to find large sizes for big Western feet.

Souvenir water puppets, costumery and paraphernalia can be purchased from all the theatres which do these performances.

The government-run Vietnamese Art Association at 511 Tran Hung Dao St is where aspiring young artists display their paintings in hopes of attracting a buyer. Prices are in the US$30 to US$50 range after bargaining.

Tapes of Vietnamese music are available at Sun Ashaba, at 32 Hai Ba Trung St. There is a pharmacy (Hieu Thuoc Quan Hoan Kiem; ☎ 254212) specialising in traditional medicines – including Gecko Elixir – at 2 Hang Bai St (corner of Hang Khai St).

For philatelic items, try the philatelic counter at the GPO (in the main postal services hall).

Watercolour paints and brushes are available at a store at 216 Hang Bong St (corner of Phung Hung St). Musical instruments can be purchased from shops at 24 and 36 Hang Gai St, and 76 and 85 Hang Bong St.

Getting There & Away

Air Vietnam Airlines has nonstop international flights between Hanoi and Bangkok, Guangzhou (Canton), Nanning (China), Hong Kong and Vientiane. There are other international flights (via Ho Chi Minh City) that include the following destinations: Kuala Lumpur, Manila, Paris, Phnom Penh and Singapore.

Vietnam Airlines acts as sales agent for Lao Aviation (Hang Khong Lao) and Cambodia Airlines (Hang Khong Cam Bot). Domestic and international airline offices found in Hanoi are as follows:

Aeroflot
: 2 Quang Trung St (☎ 256184)

Air France
: 3 Quang Trung St (☎ 253484)

China Southern Airlines
: Binh Minh Hotel, 27 Ly Thai To St, Hoan Kiem District (☎ 269233, 269234; fax (84-4) 269232)

Pacific Airlines
: 81 Tran Hung Dao St, Hoan Kiem District (☎ 265350)

Thai International Airways
: 1 Quang Trung St (next to Vietnam Airlines)

Vietnam Airlines
: Domestic: (Phong ve Quoc Noi Hang Khong Vietnam), 60 Quang Trung St (☎ 255194, 253577)
: International: (Phong ve Quoc Te Hang Khong Vietnam), 1 Quang Trung St (☎ 255284, 253842, 255229)

Bus Hanoi has several main bus terminals. Kim Lien bus station serves points south of Hanoi. Kim Ma bus station serves destinations that are north-west of the capital. Buses to points north-east of Hanoi leave from Long Bien bus station, which recently moved to the east bank of the Red River.

Kim Lien bus station (Ben Xe Kim Lien; ☎ 55230) at 100 Le Duan St (on the corner of Nguyen Quyen St) is 800 metres south of the railway station. The express bus *(toc hanh)* ticket office, which is open every day from 4.30 am to 5 pm, is across the street from 6B Nguyen Quyen St.

Kim Ma bus station (Ben Xe Kim Ma; ☎ 52846) is opposite 166 Nguyen Thai Hoc St (on the corner of Giang Vo St).

Train The Hanoi railway station (Ga Ha Noi; ☎ 52628) is opposite 115 Le Duan St (at the western end of Tran Hung Dao St). The ticket office is open from 7.30 to 11.30 am and from 1.30 to 3.30 pm only.

Getting Around

To/From the Airport Hanoi's Noi Bai airport is about 35 km north of the city, which means you aren't going to get there by cyclo.

Buses from Hanoi to Noi Bai Airport depart from the Vietnam Airlines international booking office on Quang Trung St, around the corner from Trang Thi/Hang Khai Sts. The schedule depends on the departure and arrival times of domestic and international flights, but in any case the buses do not go very frequently. The schedule has not very definite departures at 4.30 am and sometimes at 6, 7, 8 and 9 am and noon as well. The trip to Noi Bai takes 50 minutes in light traffic, more during busy hours. Bus tickets are sold inside the international booking office and cost US$2 for buses and US$4 for minibuses. Taxis also congregate here and you can bargain with the drivers – US$15 is a typical price.

At the airport itself, people will approach you at the luggage carousel with offers for taxi rides to Hanoi costing US$25. As soon as you step outside the door of the terminal building, the price drops to US$15. Sharing a taxi makes sense if you have luggage – beats the bus any old day.

Bus The tourist map you get in Hanoi includes bus lines in red. Services on most of the bus routes are infrequent.

Cyclo & Bicycle Cyclos are the main form of transport around town. They're slightly cheaper than in Saigon but the drivers typically try to charge foreigners about five times the going rate (or more). The best way to get around Hanoi is by bicycle. More and more hotels are now offering these for rent; try the Phung Hung Hotel if your hotel doesn't have any. Bike rentals cost about US$1 per day.

There are dozens upon dozens of bicycle (and motorbike) shops along Pho Hué (Hué

St) south of Restaurant 202, which is at 202 Pho Hué.

The North

Stretching from the Hoang Lien Mountains (Tonkinese Alps) eastward across the Red River Delta to the islands of Halong Bay, the northern part of Vietnam (Bac Bo), known to the French as Tonkin, includes some of the country's most spectacular scenery.

The mountainous areas are home to many distinct hill tribes, some of which remain relatively untouched by Vietnamese and Western influences.

SAM SON BEACHES

The two Sam Son Beaches, among the nicest in the north, are 16 km south-east of Thanh Hoa. They are a favourite vacation spot of Hanoi residents who can afford such luxuries. Accommodation ranges from basic bungalows to multi-storey hotels.

TAM DAO HILL STATION

Tam Dao hill station (elevation 930 metres), known to the French as the Cascade d'Argent (Silver Cascade), was founded by the French in 1907 as a place of escape from the heat of the Red River Delta. Today, the grand colonial villas are a bit run-down, but Tam Dao retains its refreshing weather, hiking areas and superb views. Not many travellers come here because Sapa draws foreigners like a magnet, but Tam Dao is closer to Hanoi (85 km north-west) and therefore more accessible.

HOA LU

Hoa Lu was the capital of Vietnam under the Dinh Dynasty (ruled 968-980) and the Early Le Dynasty (ruled 980-1009). The ancient citadel of Hoa Lu, most of which has been destroyed, covered an area of about three sq km. The outer ramparts encompassed temples, shrines and the place where the king held court. The royal family lived in the inner citadel.

Today, there are two sanctuaries at Hoa Lu. Dinh Tien Hoang, restored in the 17th century, is dedicated to the Dinh Dynasty. The second temple, Dai Hanh (or Dung Van Nga), commemorates the rulers of the Early Le Dynasty.

Bic Dong Grotto is in the village of Van Lam, a short boat trip away. The three sanctuaries here date from the 17th century. Also worth seeing are the Tam Coc Caves and Xuyen Thuy Grotto.

Reaching Ninh Binh, turn west for 20 km. On the right there's a hut with a bar. Pay a toll, go ahead and then you can take a tiny rowboat. It's a beautiful landscape: high rocks, green with vegetation, rice paddies. The boat sails along a narrow canal amongst the fields. The silence is pure. Three times we passed grottos. The trip may take two or more hours. Someone in our group compared this place to Halong Bay.

Mauro Grusovin

Getting There & Away

Hoa Lu is at the southern edge of the Red River Delta in Ninh Binh Province. By car, the trip from Hanoi to Hoa Lu is 120 km due south and takes about two hours.

PERFUME PAGODA

The Perfume Pagoda (Chua Huong) is a complex of pagodas and Buddhist shrines built into the limestone cliffs of Huong Tich Mountain.

Great numbers of pilgrims come here during a festival that begins in the middle of the second lunar month and lasts until the last week of the third lunar month. Pilgrims and other visitors spend their time here boating, hiking and exploring the caves.

The Perfume Pagoda is about 60 km south-west of Hanoi in Hoa Binh Province, accessible by road or river.

HAIPHONG

Haiphong, Vietnam's third most populous city, is the north's main industrial centre and one of the country's most important seaports. There isn't much to see here, though it's a

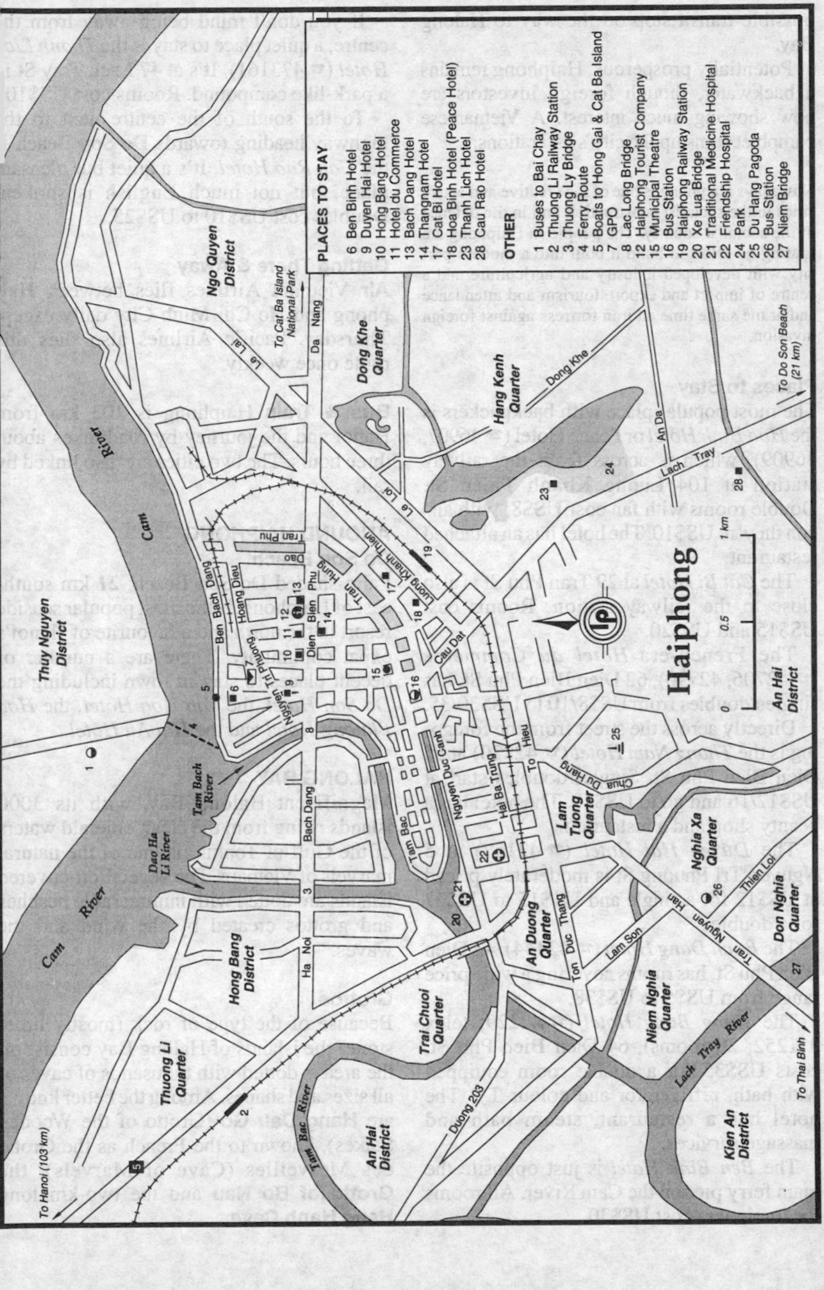

Haiphong
PLACES TO STAY
6 Ben Binh Hotel
9 Duyen Hai Hotel
10 Hong Bang Hotel
11 Hotel du Commerce
13 Bach Dang Hotel
14 Thangnam Hotel
17 Cat Bi Hotel
18 Hoa Binh Hotel (Peace Hotel)
23 Thanh Lich Hotel
28 Cau Rao Hotel
OTHER
1 Buses to Bai Chay
2 Thuong Li Railway Station
3 Thuong Ly Bridge
4 Ferry Route
5 Boats to Hong Gai & Cat Ba Island
7 GPO
8 Lac Long Bridge
12 Haiphong Tourist Company
15 Municipal Theatre
16 Bus Station
19 Haiphong Railway Station
20 Xe Lua Bridge
21 Traditional Medicine Hospital
22 Friendship Hospital
24 Park
25 Du Hang Pagoda
26 Bus Station
27 Niem Bridge
Thuy Nguyen District
Ngo Quyen District
Dong Khe Quarter
Hang Kenh Quarter
Hong Bang District
Thuong Li Quarter
An Hai District
Trai Chuoi Quarter
An Duong Quarter
Lam Tuong Quarter
Nghia Xa Quarter
Niem Nghia Quarter
Don Nghia Quarter
Kien An District
Cam River
Tam Bach River
Dao Ha Li River
Tam Bac River
Lach Tray River
To Hanoi (103 km)
To Cat Ba Island National Park
To Do Son Beach (21 km)
To Thai Binh
Ben Bach Dang
Hoang Dieu
Nguyen Tri Phuong
Dien Bien Phu
Tran Hung Dao
Tran Phu
Luong Khanh Thien
Le Loi
Le Lai
Da Nang
Dong Khe
Lach Tray
An Da
Cau Dat
Nguyen Duc Canh
Hai Ba Trung
To Hieu
Chua Du Hang
Bach Dang
Tam Bac
Ha Noi
Ton Duc Thang
Lam Son
Tran Nguyen Han
Thien Loi
Duong 203
0
0.5
1 km

possible transit stop on the way to Halong Bay.

Potentially prosperous, Haiphong remains a backwater, though foreign investors are now showing much interest. A Vietnamese pamphlet sums up the city's aspirations:

> Nowadays Haiphong is one of the creative and active cities in the socialist construction and in the defence of the socialist country. The people in Haiphong are sparing no effort to build it both into a modern port city with developed industry and agriculture and a centre of import and export, tourism and attendance and at the same time an iron fortress against foreign invasion.

Places to Stay

The most popular place with backpackers is the *Hoa Binh Hotel* or Peace Hotel (☎ 46907, 46909), which is across from the railway station at 104 Luong Khanh Thien St. Double rooms with fan cost US$8; with air-con they're US$10. The hotel has an attached restaurant.

The *Cat Bi Hotel* at 29 Tran Phu St is also close to the railway station. Rooms cost US$15 and US$20.

The French-era *Hotel du Commerce* (☎ 42706, 42790), 62 Dien Bien Phu St, has singles/doubles from US$8/10 to US$30/35.

Directly across the street from the foregoing is the *Thang Nam Hotel* (☎ 42820) at 55 Dien Bien Phu St. Singles/doubles start at US$12/16 and go to US$20. The hotel has a beauty shop and a restaurant.

The *Duyen Hai Hotel* (☎ 42157) at 5 Nguyen Tri Phuong St is moderately priced at US$12 for a single and US$15 to US$27 for a double.

The *Bach Dang Hotel* (☎ 42444), 42 Dien Bien Phu St, has rooms covering a wide price range from US$5 to US$38.

The *Hong Bang Hotel* (☎ 42229; telex 311252; 28 rooms), 64 Dien Bien Phu St, costs US$35 for a double room equipped with bath, refrigerator and colour TV. The hotel has a restaurant, steam bath and massage services.

The *Ben Binh Hotel* is just opposite the main ferry pier on the Cam River. All rooms for foreigners cost US$30.

If you don't mind being away from the centre, a quiet place to stay is the *Thanh Lich Hotel* (☎ 473161). It's at 47 Lach Tray St in a park-like compound. Rooms cost US$10.

To the south of the centre next to the highway heading towards Do Son Beach is the *Cau Rao Hotel*. It's a quiet but pleasant place, but not much English is spoken. Doubles cost US$10 to US$25.

Getting There & Away

Air Vietnam Airlines flies between Haiphong and Ho Chi Minh City daily except Thursday. Pacific Airlines also flies this route once weekly.

Bus & Train Haiphong is 103 km from Hanoi and the journey by road takes about three hours. The two cities are also linked by rail.

AROUND HAIPHONG

Do Son Beach

Palm-shaded Do Son Beach, 21 km southeast of Haiphong, is the most popular seaside resort in the north and a favourite of Hanoi's expat community. There are a number of decent places to stay in town including the *Do Son Hotel*, the *Van Hoa Hotel*, the *Hoa Phuong Hotel* and the *Hai Au Hotel*.

HALONG BAY

Magnificent Halong Bay, with its 3000 islands rising from the clear, emerald waters of the Gulf of Tonkin, is one of the natural marvels of Vietnam. The vegetation-covered islands are dotted with innumerable beaches and grottos created by the wind and the waves.

Grottos

Because of the type of rock (mostly limestone) the islands of Halong Bay consist of, the area is dotted with thousands of caves of all sizes and shapes. Among the better known are **Hang Dau Go** (Grotto of the Wooden Stakes), known to the French as the Grotte des Merveilles (Cave of Marvels), the **Grotto of Bo Nau** and the two-km long **Hang Hanh Cave**.

Places to Stay

Almost everyone making an excursion to Halong Bay spends at least one night in the town of Bai Chay.

The *Nha Nghi Cong Doan* (Workers' Guest House) is the cheapest place in Bai Chay and the most popular with budget travellers. Rooms cost US$3 to US$5 per night.

Following the main road of town up the hill brings you to the *Tien Long Hotel* (☎ 46372) where very comfortable singles/doubles cost US$6/8.

Other places include the *Vuon Dao Hotel* and *Hai Quan Hotel* (Navy Hotel). The *Van Hai Hotel* is central, but at US$8 to US$10 it's not great for the standard of accommodation that you get (fan, shared bath and free cockroaches).

The *Bach Dang Hotel* is near the ferry pier and is one of the more upmarket places in town. The *Halong Hotel* costs US$35 per night.

Alternatively, you can take a ferry over to Hong Gai which also has accommodation.

Getting There & Away

The 165-km trip from Hanoi to Halong Bay takes about five hours by bus. The Bai Chay bus station is about one km from the Ha Long Hotel. Buses from Hanoi to Halong Bay depart from the Long Bien bus station. Many travellers book a tour costing around US$20 from one of the cafes in Hanoi – these tours include bus transport, boat trip, one night's accommodation and a couple of meals.

Getting Around

If you're booked into a tour, no doubt a boat will already be provided. If you're on your own, it's easy enough to hire a motorised launch to tour the islands and their grottos. You can probably round up other foreigners to share the boat or even go with a group of Vietnamese tourists. A mid-sized boat can hold six to 12 persons and costs around US$6 per hour. Larger boats can hold 50 to 100 persons and cost US$10 to US$20 per hour. To find a boat, ask around the quays of Bai Chay or Hong Gai. Note that there has been at least one reported robbery from a small boat – the foreign passengers lost all their money, passports etc.

If you've got the cash to burn, helicopters can be chartered for whirlwind tours of the bay. Of course, it's hard to imagine how you're going to get a good look at the grottos from a helicopter unless the pilots are *really* skilled.

CAT BA NATIONAL PARK

About half of Cat Ba Island (total area of 354 sq km) and 90 sq km of adjacent inshore waters were declared a national park in 1986 in order to protect the island's diverse ecosystems. These include tropical evergreen forests on the hills, freshwater swamp forests at the base of the hills, coastal mangrove forests, small lakes, sandy beaches and offshore coral reefs. Unfortunately, at the present time a trip to the island is not a pleasant experience:

> The charm of Cat Ba is spoilt a little by a woman who seems to monopolise the place. We had to negotiate with her about the hotels, the food in the restaurant, the price of the bus to the ferry and the boat to explore Halong Bay. For the boat we paid US$70 for the whole day with seven people. Be sure to agree on an itinerary before you leave. The monopolist position of the woman is not in itself to be condemned. Had she had some degree of compassion, it would have been bearable. The fact is that this person was a walking contradiction to the word 'compassion'.
>
> **Twan van de Kerkhof**

Getting There & Away

Cat Ba National Park is 133 km from Hanoi and 30 km east of Haiphong. A boat to Cat Ba departs from Haiphong every day at 1.30 pm and returns the next day at 6 am; the trip takes about 3½ hours and costs US$1.40. The park headquarters is at Trung Trang.

LANG SON

Lang Son (elevation 270 metres), capital of mountainous Lang Son Province, is in an area populated largely by ethnic minorities. There are caves 3.5 km from Lang Son, near the village of Ky Lua.

However, the real attraction of Lang Son is neither ethnic minorities nor scenery. The town has long served as an important trading post and crossing point into China. The border was closed after the 1979 Sino-Vietnamese war, but it was reopened to traders in 1991 and foreigners have been permitted to cross since 1992. Although the border region is heavily guarded, international trade seems to be in full swing again and Lang Son has become a booming market town.

There's a thriving black market in Lang Son. Not only is the unofficial banking system able to exchange US dollars and dong, but Chinese renminbi is also on the menu. While it is possible to bargain a little, the exchange rates offered are usually not bad at all. In case you've still got leftover dong, it is possible to change money on the Chinese side too.

See under Land in the Getting There & Away section at the start of this chapter for additional details on entering Vietnam this way.

Getting There & Away

Bus Buses to Lang Son depart Hanoi's Long Bien bus station around 6 am. The cost is US$5 and the journey takes roughly six hours over a bone-jarring road.

There are two checkpoints along the way and locals can get searched very thoroughly though police usually go easy with foreigners. The situation seems even worse when going the other way (towards Hanoi) – the police are known to rip luggage open with knives and confiscate 'contraband' from China. Even if you are personally spared, the searches can cause long delays and it's really a depressing sight – Vietnamese people in tears pleading with the police. On the other hand, it's an educational experience – just think of how much worse it was in the old days before 'reform' and 'openness'.

From Lang Son to the border at Dong Dang is another 20 km with yet another police checkpoint along the way. The cheapest way to cover this distance is to hire a motorbike for US$1. There are also army jeeps willing to take you. Make sure they take you to Huu Nghi Quan – there are a few other checkpoints but this is the only one where foreigners can cross. The exit point marked on your visa must also read Huu Nghi (of course, if you're entering Vietnam this way, your visa entrance point must say Huu Nghi). Dong Dang presently has no place to stay, so if you need to overnight, do so in Lang Son – otherwise stay at the cheap Nanxiang Hotel in Pinxiang on the Chinese side of the border.

Train There is one train departing Hanoi daily at 9.30 pm and arriving in Lang Son at 3.30 am. These inconvenient hours make the bus a preferred mode of transport. As with the bus, arriving by train in Lang Son leaves you 20 km from the border and you'll need to hire a motorbike.

There is much talk of running an international train directly from Hanoi to Nanning, China. Presently, the Chinese and Vietnamese are arguing over who should pay to rebuild the train line which was damaged in the 1979 Sino-Vietnamese war.

Car The 150-km highway between Hanoi and Lang Son is in lousy condition and most passenger cars do not have sufficient high-ground clearance to negotiate this road safely. For this reason, jeeps, trucks and minibuses are the vehicles of choice. Chartering a jeep costs around US$80 to US$90. A minibus costs around US$120 but could well prove cheaper if you can get together five or six passengers to share the cost. While trucks are capable of making the journey, this seems like an uncomfortable alternative.

Despite the expense, renting a private vehicle is not a bad idea since you can be driven right to the border crossing at Dong Dang.

To/From China No matter what means of transport you use to reach the Vietnamese border, there is a walk of 600 metres from the Vietnamese border post to Friendship Gate on the Chinese side. Expect to be searched thoroughly at the border – there's quite a problem with drug smuggling. After you've crossed into China and cleared all customs hassles, it's a 20-minute drive to

Pinxiang by bus or share taxi (US$3) from where you can get a train to Nanning, capital of China's Guangxi Province. Trains to Nanning depart Pinxiang at 8 am and 2 pm. More frequent are the buses (once every 30 minutes) which take four hours to make the journey and cost US$3.

LAO CAI

Lao Cai is a small town near the Chinese border at the end of the railway line. This place is of keen interest to travellers because it's on the route between Hanoi and Kunming in China's scenic Yunnan Province (see under Land in the Getting There & Away section at the start of this chapter for additional details). Lao Cai is also visited by many travellers heading up to Sapa, a prime scenic attraction in the northern part of Vietnam.

The scenery around Lao Cai is beautiful and the people very friendly, but the town itself is only a transit stop. It must say Lao Cai on your visa if you want to enter or exit Vietnam by this route.

The bordertown on the Chinese side is called Hekou, separated from Vietnam by a river and a bridge. The bridge and border crossing is open every day from 8 am until 5 pm.

Places to Stay

There are no hotels in Lao Cai or nearby villages, though this is liable to change due to the rapidly expanding trade across the border. Foreigners who have shown up are usually offered a place to stay in a local person's house. Of course, some sort of payment is expected, but it will usually be cheap.

There is a *hotel* in Pho Lu adjacent to the small square in front of the railway station. While it looks reasonably clean from the outside, it's pretty grim on the inside – large but dirty rooms, no shower and just one toilet for the whole place. Rooms cost US$5.

In Hekou, on the Chinese side, budget accommodation is available at the old *Hekou Hotel* or the new, relatively upmarket *Dongfeng Hotel*.

Getting There & Away

Train Probably for security reasons, passenger trains currently do not go all the way to Lao Cai but terminate at Pho Lu, 40 km away. While there are trains going all the way to Lao Cai from Hanoi, these are only for hauling freight.

There are three trains daily from Hanoi to Pho Lu, but one arrives in the middle of the night and another at dawn. The safest train departs Hanoi at 7 am and arrives in Pho Lu at 5.30 pm. Most popular with travellers seems to be the night train departing Hanoi at 7.30 pm, but many people have reported that their luggage or moneybelts were slit open and contents removed while they slept!

In Pho Lu, you can transfer to another train that is waiting at the station. This is a very basic train with only small wooden benches on the long sides of the carriages. This train takes about an hour to get to a tiny village about 10 km from Lao Cai. The best way to get from Pho Lu to Lao Cai is to hire a motorbike for about US$1.50 or a truck for US$3.

Going the other way, a train departs Kunming's northern railway station at 3.30 pm for Hekou. Buses depart Kunming at 10 pm and arrive in Hekou the next morning. A train departs Pho Lu at 6.20 pm and arrives in Hanoi at 4 am; another departs Pho Lu at 8.20 pm and arrives in Hanoi at 5 am.

Motorbike More and more travellers are renting motorcycles in Hanoi and taking off for Lao Cai, then continuing onwards to Sapa. If getting there proves too exhausting, it is entirely possible to put the motorcycle on the train for the ride back to Hanoi.

Roads in this part of Vietnam are dismal, particularly during the rainy season (summer). When the roads are flooded, there are sometimes deep spots where bridges are needed but don't exist, and you can't drive across without immersing the engine. In this case, the accepted procedure is to find some locals with bamboo poles to carry the motorcycle across the deep spots on their shoulders!

SAPA

Sapa is an old hill station built in 1922 in a beautiful valley (elevation 1600 metres). Don't forget your winter woollies – Sapa is known for its cold, foggy winters (sometimes down to 0°C). Thanks to the chilly climate, the area boasts temperate-zone fruit trees (peaches, plums etc) and gardens for raising medicinal herbs. The dry season for Sapa is approximately January through June – afternoon rain showers in the mountains are frequent.

Surrounding Sapa are the Hoang Lien Mountains, nicknamed the Tonkinese Alps by the French. These mountains include **Fansipan**, which at 3143 metres is Vietnam's highest peak. Fansipan's summit is increasingly attracting visitors – some foreigners and the few adventurous Vietnamese who have the financial resources for mountaineering holidays. Fansipan is nine km from Sapa and reachable on foot.

The market in Sapa on Saturday is a major attraction. Check out some of the hats on sale.

Some of the more well-known sights around Sapa include **Thac Bac** (Silver Falls) and **Cau May** (Cloud Bridge), which spans the Muong Hoa River.

Due to its proximity to the Chinese border, Sapa was the scene of some fighting during the Chinese invasion of 1979. Some buildings in town were damaged and haven't been properly repaired yet.

At the moment Sapa sees only a handful of foreign travellers, but it is steadily growing in popularity. On the other hand, there are rumours that the Vietnamese authorities want to close Sapa to foreigners again, but who knows! Make local inquiries before setting off.

Getting There & Away

The gateway to Sapa is Lao Cai, 30 km from Sapa. Buses do make the trip (two hours) but are not reliable. Motorbikes are available for hire in Lao Cai at US$4 per day. Driving a motorbike from Hanoi to Sapa takes two days over shocking roads.

Some of the cafes in Hanoi now offer four-day bus trips to Sapa for US$50.

DIEN BIEN PHU

Dien Bien Phu was the site of that rarest of military events, a battle that can be called truly decisive. On 6 May 1954, the day before the Geneva Conference on Indochina was set to begin half a world away in Europe, Viet Minh forces overran the beleaguered French garrison at Dien Bien Phu after a 57-day siege, shattering French morale and forcing the French government to abandon its attempts to re-establish colonial control of Indochina.

Dien Bien Phu (population 10,000) is in one of the remotest parts of Vietnam. The town is only 16 km from the border with Laos, and is set in the flat, heart-shaped Muong Thanh Valley, which is about 20 km long and five km wide and surrounded by steep, heavily forested hills. The area is inhabited by by hill tribe people, especially Tai and Hmong.

For centuries, Dien Bien Phu was a transit stop on the caravan route from Burma and China to northern Vietnam. The town was esablished by the Nguyen dynasty to prevent raids on the Red River delta by bandits.

Except for a small museum marking the site of the battle and a memorial to the Vietnamese who were killed in the battle, there is not all that much to see at Dien Bien Phu these days.

Getting There & Away

A minimum of five days is required for an overland expedition from Hanoi to Dien Bien Phu (420 km each way): two days to get there, a day to visit the area and two days to come back. Most of the roads are in atrocious condition; if it's been raining recently even a 4WD vehicle will encounter difficulty on some stretches. Taking a two-wheel drive car is not advisable even when it's dry.

Some travellers rent motorbikes and do a loop trip – Hanoi to Dien Bien Phu, onwards to Sapa and then back to Hanoi. This takes about 10 days and it's rough going over some abysmal roads, but it is possible to put the motorcycle on the train from Lao Cai to Hanoi. The most scenic part of the journey is between Dien Bien Phu and the village of Phong Tho.

Along the route you pass near a hydroelectric station – keep away from it as the police are paranoid about 'spies' and have a reputation for harassing (and fining) foreigners. The route also passes through a number of towns where the majority of the population are hill tribes (notably the Black Tai and Hmong) who still live as they have for generations.

Appendices

RELIGIONS OF SOUTH-EAST ASIA

Buddhism

Buddhism was founded by Siddartha Gautama, an Indian prince, in the 6th century BC. After years of ascetic wanderings and contemplation he became the 'enlightened' or 'awakened one', the Buddha. His message is that the cause of life's suffering is the illusory nature of desire, and that by overcoming desire we can free ourselves from suffering. Desire can be conquered by following the Eightfold Path, consisting of right understanding, thought, speech, conduct, livelihood, effort, attentiveness and concentration. The ultimate goal is *nirvana*, the escape from the endless round of births and rebirths and their lives of suffering.

Buddhism is essentially a Hindu reform movement, and its philosophy owes much to the Hindu notions of *maya* (the illusory nature of existence) and *moksha* (enlightenment). The big difference is that Buddhism shunned the Hindu pantheon of gods and the caste system. It was initially not a religion but a practical, moral philosophy free from the priestly Brahman hierarchy.

Buddhism gained wide adherence in India with its adoption by Emperor Ashoka in the 3rd century BC, but later split into two sects: Mahayana (greater path) and Hinayana (lesser path), also known as Theravada (teaching of the elders). Mahayana Buddhism showed greater mysticism and the *bodhisattva*, or saint who attains nirvana, reintroduced the idea of divinity to Buddhism. It spread north to Tibet, China and Japan, and then down to Vietnam. The more scholarly, philosophical Theravada sect found less favour in the royal courts, but continued to thrive in Sri Lanka and lower Burma even after a resurgent Hinduism virtually eliminated Buddhism in India by the end of the first millennium AD.

In South-East Asia, Buddhism, along with Hinduism, was adopted by kingdoms in Indochina, Sumatra and Java in the first millennium. The major change came in the 11th century when the Burmese adopted Theravada Buddhism, and this later spread to Thailand, Laos and Cambodia. Theravada

Buddhism remains the dominant faith in these countries today while Vietnam, with its strongly Chinese influence, follows a form of Mahayana Buddhism.

Hinduism

Today, the tiny island of Bali is the only place in the region where Hinduism dominates, but Hinduism has strongly influenced the other cultures of South-East Asia.

Hinduism is a complex religion, but at its core is the mystical principle that the physical world is an illusion *(maya)* and until this is realised through enlightenment *(moksha)* the individual is condemned to a cycle of rebirths and reincarnations. Brahma is the ultimate god and universal spirit, but Hinduism has a vast pantheon of gods that are worshipped on a day-to-day level.

The two main gods are Shiva, the Destroyer, and Vishnu, the Preserver. Shivaism represents a more esoteric and ascetic path, and with Shiva's *shakti* or female energy (represented by his wives Kali and Parvati), destruction and fertility are intertwined. Shivaism found greater acceptance in South-East Asia, perhaps because it was closer to existing fertility worship and the appeasement of malevolent spirits. Vishnuism places greater emphasis on devotion and duty, and Vishnu's incarnations, Krishna and Rama, feature heavily in South-East Asian art and culture through the stories of the *Ramayana* epic.

Hinduism and Buddhism were often intertwined in South-East Asia and many empires accepted the principles and iconography of both religions. Hinduism's rigid caste system had much less relevance in South-East Asia, but the notions of the god-king and the elitist nature of Hindu society were readily accepted by South-East Asian rulers.

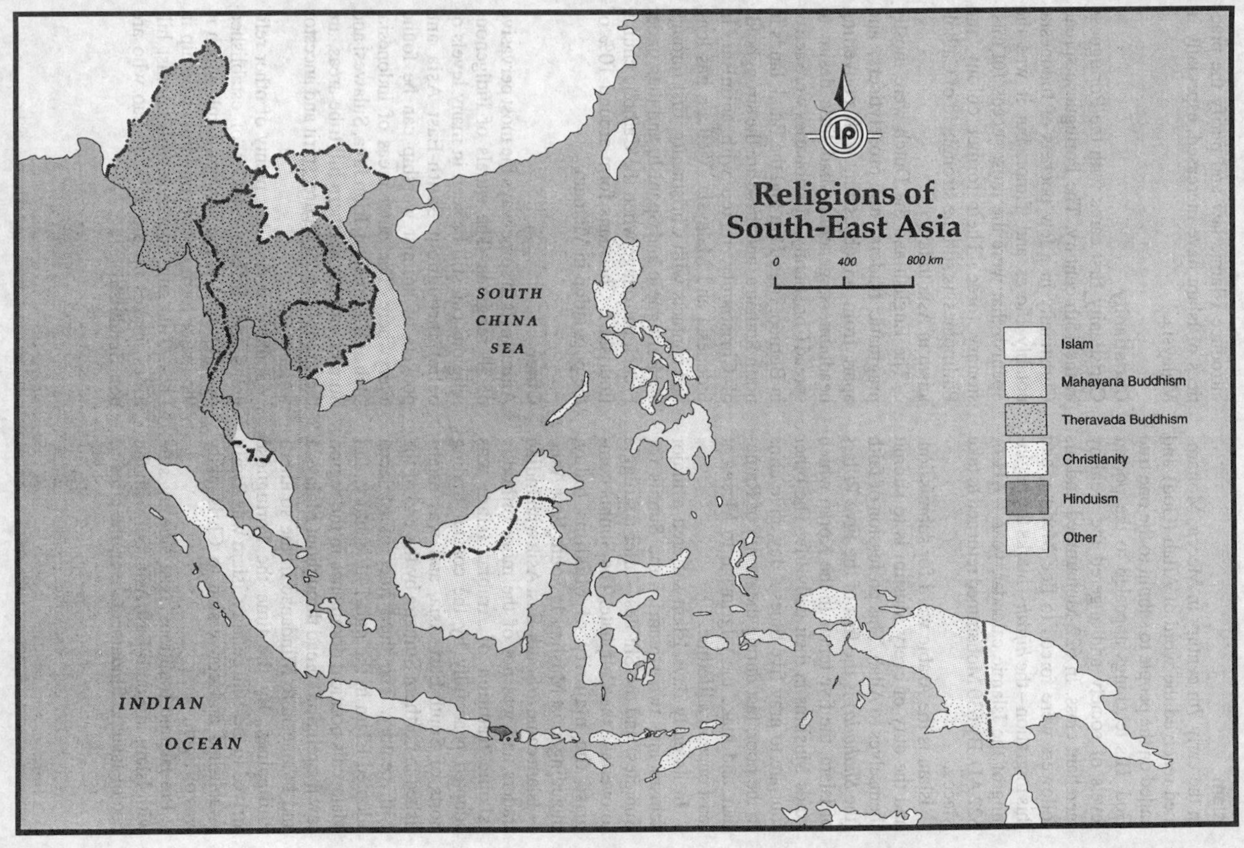
Religions of South-East Asia
0
400
800 km
Islam
Mahayana Buddhism
Theravada Buddhism
Christianity
Hinduism
Other
SOUTH CHINA SEA
INDIAN OCEAN

Islam

In the early 7th century in Mecca, Mohammed received the word of Allah (God) and called on the people to submit to the one true God. His teachings appealed to the poorer levels of society and angered the wealthy merchant class. In 622 Mohammed and his followers were forced to flee Medina, and this migration – the *hijrah* – marks the beginning of the Islamic calendar, year 1 AH or 622 AD. By 630 Mohammed returned to take Mecca.

Islam is the Arabic word for submission, and the duty of every Muslim is to submit themselves to Allah. This profession of faith (the *Shahada*) is the first of the Five Pillars of Islam, the five tenets in the Koran which guide Muslims in their daily life. The other four are to pray five times a day, give alms to the poor, fast during the month of Ramadan, and make the pilgrimage to Mecca at least once in a lifetime.

In its early days Islam suffered a major schism into two streams – the Sunnis (or Sunnites) and the Shi'ites – after a struggle to overtake the Caliphate. The Sunnis comprise the majority of Muslims today, including most Muslims in South-East Asia.

Islam came to South-East Asia with Indian traders and was not of the more orthodox Islamic tradition of Arabia. Islam was adopted peacefully by the coastal trading ports of South-East Asia, and was established in northern Sumatra by the end of the 13th century. The third ruler of Malacca adopted Islam in the mid-14th century, and Malacca's political dominance in the region saw the religion spread throughout Malaysia and Indonesia to Mindanao in the southern Philippines. By the time the Portuguese arrived in the 16th century, Islam was firmly established and conversion to Christianity was difficult.

Pre-Islamic traditions exist side by side with Islam in South-East Asia, but with the rise of Islamic fundamentalism, the cries to introduce Islamic law and purify the practices of Islam have increased, especially in Malaysia.

Christianity

Christianity first came with the Portuguese in the 15th century. The Portuguese spread Christianity in a few pockets of Indonesia, notably Flores and Timor, but it was the Spanish that were the most successful missionary force. Their former colony, the Philippines, is still the stronghold of Catholicism in Asia today.

The English and the Dutch were mostly pragmatic traders, not proselytisers, and apart from an obsession with converting headhunters, generally had little desire to spread Christianity. Missionaries were active in Borneo, Irian Jaya and the Batak lands in north Sumatra, and these are the strongholds of Christianity, mixed with animism, in Indonesia and Malaysia. Vietnam has long had contacts with Christianity, first through the Portuguese and Spanish, and then under French patronage when the Catholic church flourished. Christians form around 10% of the population in Vietnam.

Other

Animism is in some ways the most pervasive of all religions. The rituals of indigenous religions can still be seen in many levels of belief throughout South-East Asia and pockets of animist worship can be found everywhere. The outer areas of Indonesia, such as Kalimantan, Irian Jaya, Sulawesi and Sumba, and the northern hill tribe areas, are the strongholds of nature, spirit and ancestor worship.

South-East Asia has plenty of other religions and different shades of established ones. Of note is the *phii* spirit cult which is the major form of non-Buddhist worship in Laos. This cult, together with animist hill tribes, makes up the 37% of Lao who are non-Buddhist.

	Indonesia	***Malaysia***	***Thailand***	***Myanmar (Burma)***	***Vietnam***	***Cambodia & Laos***	***Philippines***
BC	Java Man 500,000 BC	Proto Malay migration from China 2500 BC		Mons arrive 2000 BC Asoka's Buddhist missionaries arrive 3rd c BC	Rise of Dong Son culture 300 BC Chinese rule 111 BC - 938 AD		
AD 0				Burmans arrive from Tibet 3rd c	Hindu Champa kingdom 2nd c Mahayana Buddhism	Hindu Funan kingdom 1st - 6th c	
500	Hindu-Buddhist Srivijaya empire in Sumatra 7th c Buddhist Sailendras in Java 8th c – Borobudur built 782-824 Hindu Mataram kingdom Java 9th c	Malay peninsula under loose control of Srivijaya		Pagan founded 849	Chinese overthrown – 1st Viet dynasty 939	Chenla kingdom 6th c Sailendras invade Chenla Angkor founded 889 – Hindu rule	
1000	Srivijaya defeats Mataram 1006 Cholas attack Srivijaya 1025 Srivijaya declines 13th c Majapahit empire founded in Java 1292 – Gajah Mada prime minister 1331-64 Rise of Islam and decline of Majapahits 15th c	Islam comes to Sumatran and Malay peninsular ports Malacca founded 1402 Malacca sultanate converts to Islam	Sukhothai kingdom 1238-1376 – Theravada Buddhism and Thai script adopted Ayuthaya founded 14th c Thais attack Khmers and control Malay states 15th c	Pagan dynasty 1044-1287 – Theravada Buddhism adopted Mongols sack Pagan 1287	Ly dynasty 1010-1225 – Theravada Buddhism promoted Tran dynasty 1225-1400 – Mongol invasion repelled	Angkor Wat built 1112-52 Theravada Buddhism replaces Hinduism 14th c Angkor occupied by Thais 1431, Phnom Penh becomes capital	

	Indonesia	***Malaysia***	***Thailand***	***Myanmar (Burma)***	***Vietnam***	***Cambodia & Laos***	***Philippines***
1500	Fall of Majapahits 1520 Portuguese in Ternate 1521 Javanese Mataram empire 1582	Portuguese conquer Malacca 1511	Burmese invasions				Magellan arrives 1521 Spanish settle Cebu 1565 Legaspi conquers Manila 1571
1600	Dutch VOC founded 1602 – Macassar, Moluccas, Java conquered	Dutch conquer Malacca 1641			French missionaries arrive		
1700	Dutch divide Mataram into Solo and Yogyakarta 1755	Francis Light arrives in Penang 1786	Burmese sack Ayuthaya 1767		Tay Son rebellion 1771-1802		British occupy Manila 1762-63
1800	British occupy Java 1811-16 Dipenogoro's Java War 1825-30 Ethical Policy 1870-1900	Raffles founds Singapore 1819 British intervention in sultanates Malay Federation 1895	Mongkut (1851-68) and Chulalongkorn (1868-1910) reforms and modernisation	British wars of 1824, 1852 and 1885 sees Britain annexe Burma	French attack Saigon (1859), occupy Cochinchina (1862) then Annam and Tonkin (1885)	Cambodia becomes French protectorate 1863	Rizal executed 1896 Independence from Spain then US annexation 1898
1900	Nationalist movements of Sarekat Islam (1912), PKI (1920) and PNI (1927)	Rubber introduced	Coup sees end of absolute monarchy1932		Nationalism suppressed	French gain Lao and Mekong territories from Thais 1904	Internal self-government 1935
	World War II and Japanese interregnum 1939-45						
	Republic of Indonesia proclaimed 1945 War against Dutch 1946-49 Untung coup and massacre 1965 Suharto president 1965-	Federation of Malaya 1948 Communist Emergency 1948-1960 Independence 1957 Singapore goes it alone 1965	Elections restored 1946 but civilian government interrupted by military coups Student riots 1973 Military coup 1991	Independence 1948, accompanied by communist and Karen rebellions Ne Win seizes power in left-wing army coup 1962 Democracy movement crushed 1988	Ho Chi Minh declares north independent 1945 Franco-Viet Minh War 1946-54 Vietnam divided 1955 US bombing of North 1965 Saigon falls 1975	Khmer Rouge 'killing fields' 1975-78 Vietnam invades Cambodia 1978 UN-sponsored elections 1993	Independence 1946 Marcos president 1965-86 Marcos ousted, Aquino becomes president 1986

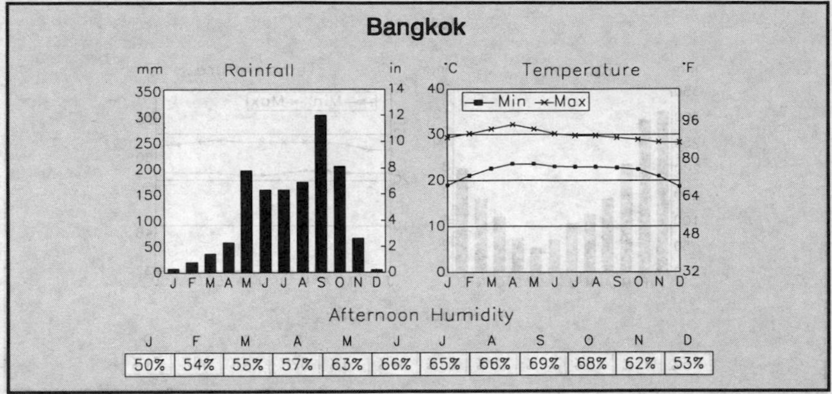
Bangkok
mm
Rainfall
in
350
300
250
200
150
100
50
0
14
12
10
8
6
4
2
0
J F M A M J J A S O N D
°C
Temperature
°F
Min
Max
40
30
20
10
0
96
80
64
48
32
J F M A M J J A S O N D
Afternoon Humidity
J F M A M J J A S O N D
50% 54% 55% 57% 63% 66% 65% 66% 69% 68% 62% 53%

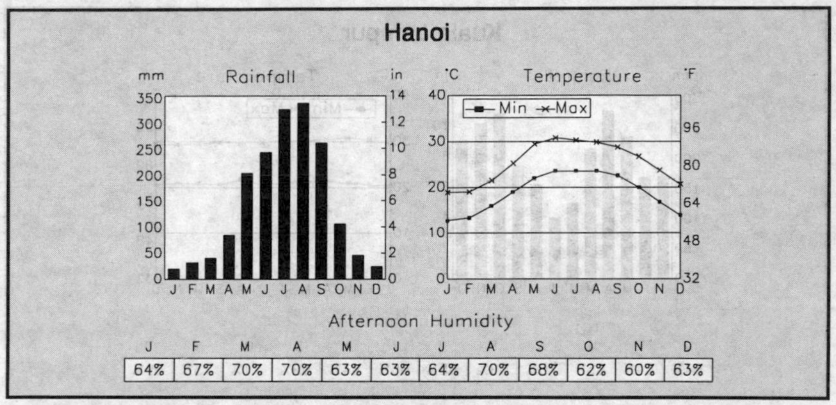
Hanoi
mm
Rainfall
in
350
300
250
200
150
100
50
0
14
12
10
8
6
4
2
0
J F M A M J J A S O N D
°C
Temperature
°F
Min
Max
40
30
20
10
0
96
80
64
48
32
J F M A M J J A S O N D
Afternoon Humidity
J F M A M J J A S O N D
64% 67% 70% 70% 63% 63% 64% 70% 68% 62% 60% 63%

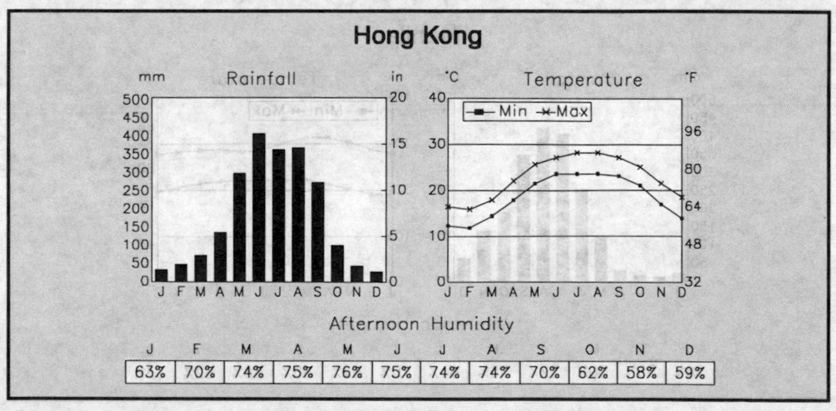
Hong Kong
mm
Rainfall
in
500
450
400
350
300
250
200
150
100
50
0
20
15
10
5
0
J F M A M J J A S O N D
°C
Temperature
°F
Min
Max
40
30
20
10
0
96
80
64
48
32
J F M A M J J A S O N D
Afternoon Humidity
J F M A M J J A S O N D
63% 70% 74% 75% 76% 75% 74% 74% 70% 62% 58% 59%

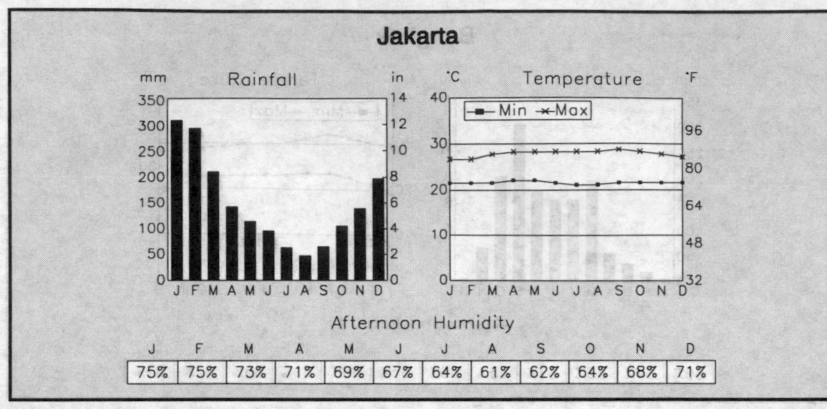

J	F	M	A	M	J	J	A	S	O	N	D
75%	75%	73%	71%	69%	67%	64%	61%	62%	64%	68%	71%

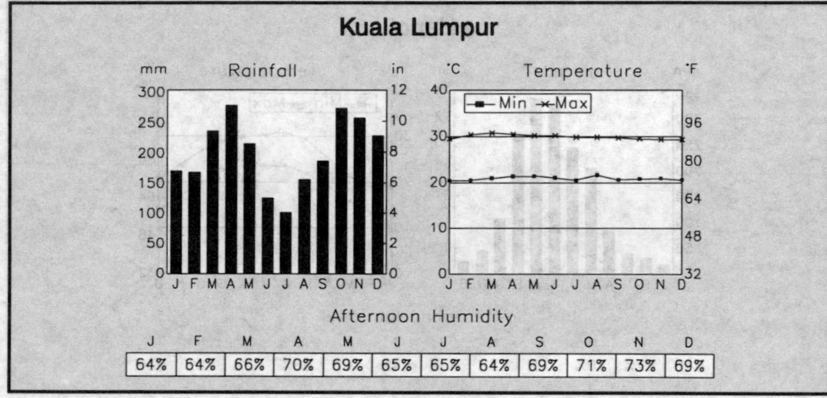

J	F	M	A	M	J	J	A	S	O	N	D
64%	64%	66%	70%	69%	65%	65%	64%	69%	71%	73%	69%

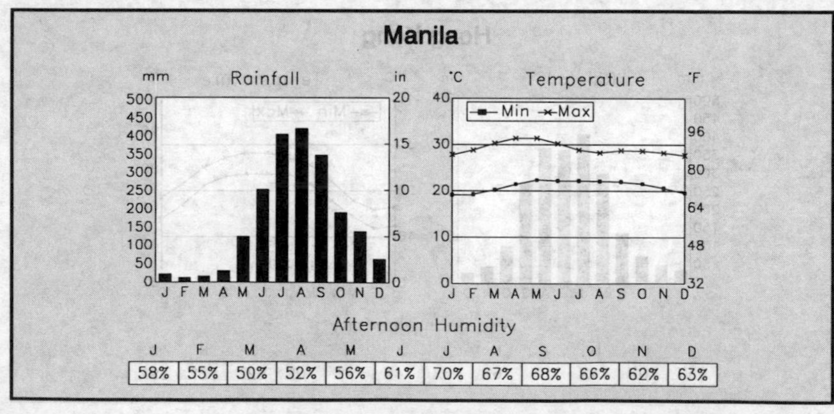

J	F	M	A	M	J	J	A	S	O	N	D
58%	55%	50%	52%	56%	61%	70%	67%	68%	66%	62%	63%

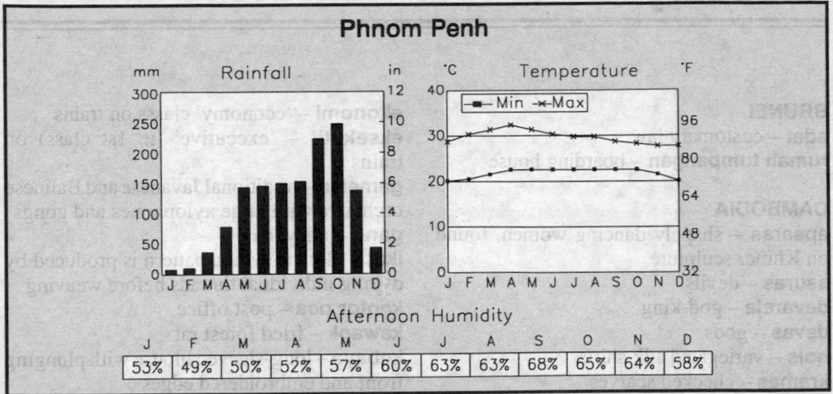

J	F	M	A	M	J	J	A	S	O	N	D
53%	49%	50%	52%	57%	60%	63%	63%	68%	65%	64%	58%

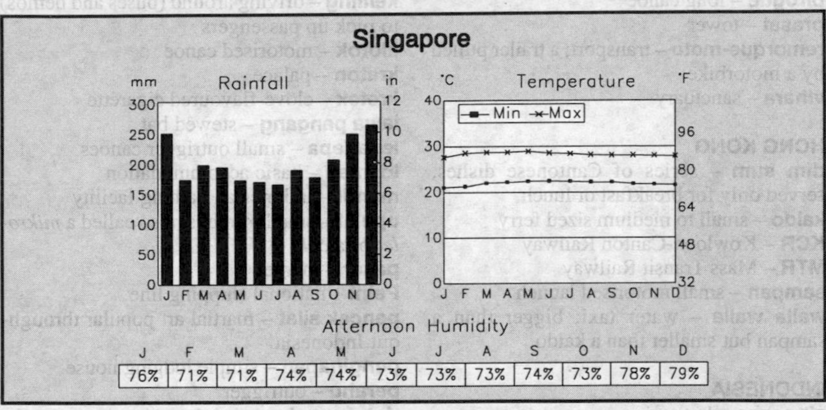

J	F	M	A	M	J	J	A	S	O	N	D
76%	71%	71%	74%	74%	73%	73%	73%	74%	73%	78%	79%

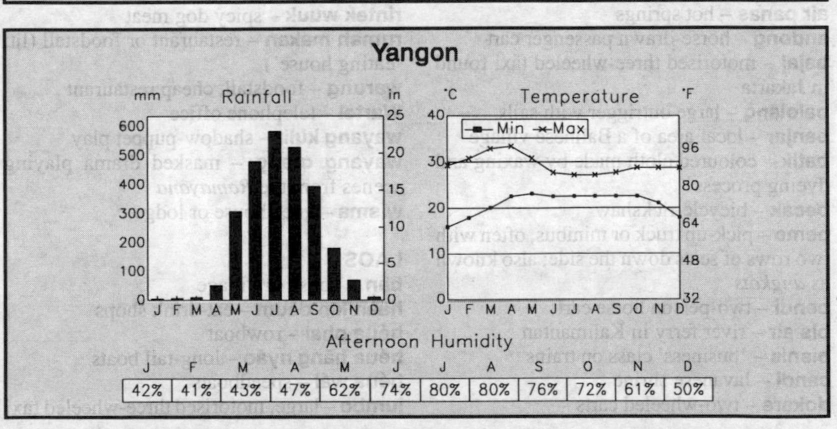

J	F	M	A	M	J	J	A	S	O	N	D
42%	41%	43%	47%	62%	74%	80%	80%	76%	72%	61%	50%

Glossary

BRUNEI
adat – customary law
rumah tumpangan – boarding house

CAMBODIA
apsaras – shapely dancing women, found on Khmer sculpture
asuras – devils
devaraja – god-king
devas – gods
hols – variegated silk shirts
kramas – checked scarves
pirogue – long canoe
prasat – tower
remorque-moto – transport; a trailer pulled by a motorbike
vihara – sanctuary

HONG KONG
dim sum – series of Cantonese dishes, served only for breakfast or lunch
kaido – small to medium sized ferry
KCR – Kowloon-Canton Railway
MTR – Mass Transit Railway
sampan – small motorised launch
walla walla – water taxi; bigger than a sampan but smaller than a kaido

INDONESIA
air panas – hot springs
andong – horse-drawn passenger cart
bajaj – motorised three-wheeled taxi found in Jakarta
balolang – large outrigger with sails
banjar – local area of a Balinese village
batik – coloured cloth made by waxing and dyeing process
becak – bicycle-rickshaw
bemo – pick-up truck or minibus, often with two rows of seats down the side; also known as *angkots*
bendi – two-person horse cart
bis air – river ferry in Kalimantan
bisnis – 'business' class on trains
candi – Javanese shrine
dokars – two-wheeled carts
ekonomi – 'economy' classs on trains
eksekutif – 'executive' (ie 1st class) on trains
gamelan – traditional Javanese and Balinese orchestra with large xylophones and gongs
gang – alley, lane
ikat – cloth in which pattern is produced by dyeing individual threads before weaving
kantor pos – post office
kawaok – fried forest rat
kebaya – long-sleeved blouse with plunging front and embroidered edges
keliling – driving around (buses and bemos) to pick up passengers
klotok – motorised canoe
kraton – palace
kretek – clove-flavoured cigarette
lawa pangang – stewed bat
lepa-lepa – small outrigger canoes
losmen – basic accommodation
mandi – Indonesian bathing facility
opelet – small minibus; also called a *mikrolet* or a *colt*
pasar – market
Pelni – national shipping line
pencak silat – martial art popular throughout Indonesia
penginapan – simple lodging house
perahu – outrigger
rintek wuuk – spicy dog meat
rumah makan – restaurant or foodstall (lit. 'eating house')
warung – foodstall, cheap restaurant
Wartel – telephone office
wayang kulit – shadow-puppet play
wayang orang – masked drama playing scenes from the *Ramayana*
wisma – guesthouse or lodge

LAOS
ban – house or village
hâan kin dëum – eat-drink shops
héua phai – rowboat
héua hãng nyáo – long-tail boats
héua wái – speedboats
jumbo – large, motorised three-wheeled taxi

khwaeng – province
muang – Lao-Thai city state; district
paa – fish
phii – spirits; the other main religion of Laos
sim – main sanctuary in a Lao Buddhist monastery where monks undergo ordination
talaat – market
thàek-sii – 'taxi', passenger trucks with two benches in the back; also known as *sawng-thâew*
thâat – Buddhist stupa or reliquary
thanon – street

MACAU

lorcha – type of sailing cargo-vessel
pastelarias – little cake shops
vila – cheap hotel; often called *hospedaria* or *pensao*

MALAYSIA

arak – rice wine
kain songket – hand-woven fabric
kampung – village
kongsi – clan house
pasar malam – night market
silat – Malay martial art; also known as *bersilat*
tambang – small ferry boat
tuai rumah – longhouse chief
tuak – rice wine

MYANMAR

cheroot – Burmese cigar
chinthe – mythical beasts that guard temple gateways
hti – pronounced 'tee', the umbrella or decorated top of a pagoda
longyi – Burmese sarong
nats – guardian spirit beings
pagoda – traditional Buddhist temple
pwe – festival
stupa – pagoda containing relics of Buddha
tonga – two-wheeled, horse-drawn vehicle

PHILIPPINES

abaca – a local plant; its leafstalks are the source of Manila hemp
banqueros – boatmen
calesas – two-wheeled horse carriages; known as *tartanillas* in Cebu City
mestizos – Filipino-Spanish or Filipino-American people
MNLF – Moro National Liberation Front; Muslim guerilla army in Mindanao
NPA – New Peoples Army; communist guerrilla movement

SINGAPORE

MRT – Mass Rapid Transit metro system
Peranakan – Straits-born Chinese
wayang – Chinese opera

THAILAND

ao – bay or gulf
bot – central sanctuary or chapel in a Thai temple
chedi – stupa; monument erected to house a Buddha relic
farang – foreigner of European descent
hat – beach
khlong – canal
muang – city
prang – Khmer-style tower on temples
samlor – three-wheeled pedicab
soi – lane or small street
songthaew – small pick-up truck with two benches in the back, used as buses/taxis
talaat nam – floating market
tuk-tuk – motorised samlor
wang – palace
wat – Buddhist temple-monastery

VIETNAM

ao dai – Vietnamese national dress
Buu Dien – post office
Caodaism – Vietnamese religious sect
cyclo – pedicab
Honda om – motorbike taxi
kem – ice cream
khach san – hotel
Lien Xo – literally 'Soviet Union'; generic term for foreigners
nha hang – restaurant
nha khach – guesthouse
nuoc mam – fish sauce
pho – noodle soup
Tet – lunar New Year
toc hanh – express bus
xe lam – three-wheeled motorised vehicle

Index

ABBREVIATIONS

B – Brunei
C – Cambodia
H – Hong Kong
I – Indonesia
L – Laos
M – Malaysia
Mc – Macau
My – Myanmar
P – Philippines
S – Singapore
T – Thailand
V – Vietnam

MAPS

TEXT

Map References are in **bold** type

Thanks

Thanks to all the travellers who wrote in to share their entertaining stories of life on the road. Writers (apologies if we've misspelt your name) who we'd like to acknowledge include:

E Abernethy (USA), Govind Acharya, Jadwiga Adamczuk (PL), N Addison (UK), James Adutt (UK), Martina Akeson (S), Einar Andersen (Dk), Afton Anderson (USA), T Anderson (USA), Jivan Arshinau, Dawn Asking (Aus), Charlotte Bacon (UK), Scott Baggoley (UK), Ramon Baker (F), Gordon Balderston (UK), Martin Baldry (UK), Chris Barkham (UK), Katya Bazley (NZ), Marc Becher-Floris (D), Ted Beck (C), Franz Beckanbauer (D), Alistair Bell (UK), Denise Belley (USA), Ernest Beyl (USA), Andreas Blersch (D), Robert Boardman (USA), Ysabelle Boatfield (UK), Thomas Borberg (Dk), Peter Bossew (A), Steve Bougerolle (C), David Breznick (USA), Iain Brodie (UK), Ann Brooks (UK), Wenche Bruhn (N), Mette Bruman (N), Rhona Buckingham (UK), R & I Butzer (CH), Woodman Caldwell (C), M Carson (Aus), Graeme Carter (UK), Andrea & Mike Carvill (USA), Kendal K Castleman (USA), J Cavlkett (UK), Matt Chabot (Aus), Cathy Chepil (C), Peter Choa (Sin), Andrew & Natali Chyba (UK), Stephen Close (Aus), Peggy Coates (UK), Kurt Cobain (USA), Kimberley Cook (USA), Nigel Corbett (UK), Martin Corbett (Irl), L Coulstock (UK), Bob & Terrie Cowley

R Dauncey (UK), Walther de Nijs (NL), Alexander Decker (A), Suellen Delahunt (Aus), Dominique Deligny (F), R van Det (NL), Andrea Doyle, Kris Durra (Aus), Hans Durrer (CH), David Dye (Aus), Ian Edwards (USA), Linda Edwardson (USA), Anita Ericson (A), Melanie Evans (UK), Hilary Evans, Anne Fahey (Aus), Doug Farber (USA), R Feitkenhauer (D), Jenny Firkin (Aus), Paul Fitzpatrick, Douglas Flemington (UK), Karen Flory, Melissa Fong (M), Mats Fornbrick (S), Erik M Forsgren (S), Christopher Foster (USA), Luca Franceschi (I), Ian Gason (Aus), Kym Gerner (Aus), Eddie Gilbert (UK), E Gilbert, S Gillis (Aus), John Glue (Aus), Robert Goble (C), Linda Gould (USA), Barbara Green (Aus), Alistair Greene (UK), Paul Greening (UK), Greg Guest (D), Alan Guimelli (Aus), E A Hackett (UK), Robert & Dale Hajek (USA), Patrick Hammond (D), Nick Hare (UK), Jim Harper, Louise Harvey, Tom Haug (Sin), Mark Haughton (UK), Emma Hawes, Mark Hayman (USA), Peter M Heckler, Dave Heckman, Stuart Henderson (UK), Dave Hill (UK), Chris Hitching (UK), Desiree Hoeke (USA), Steven Hoh, Nick Holmden (UK), Claudia Hudspeth (C), Chew Huei Ting (Sin), Craig & Lioija Hunt (Aus), Ian Hunter (UK)

Kate Ingham (UK), Helmut Jansch (Aus), Fina Johnson, Angela Johnson (Aus), Hartley Johnson (USA), Jan-Jaap Jonker (NL), Katja Jourdan (D), Sanna Kangasharju (Fin), Annabel Kapp (UK), Michael Jacqui Kearney (UK), Tara Kelly (USA), Mark Kendal (Aus), Chris Kendall (UK), Peter Kerby, David King (UK), Geoff Kingsmill (Aus), Andy & Jackie Kirk (UK), Roger Koenen (NL), Kiros Kokkas (G), Jens Krause (D), Thomas Kring (Dk), Frank Kriz (C), Christian Krueger (S), Hans-Joachim Kullmann (D), Wayne La Flamboy, Beulah Landslide (USA), Eric Lanthiez (F), Gert Larsson (S), Chris Lawson (Aus), John Lee (NZ), Richard Levy (USA), Michael Lewis, Hermes D Liberty (C), Kevin Lief (UK), John R Lilburne (Aus), Catarina Lilliehook (S), Marcus Lim (Aus), Cassio Lima (Bra), Mikael Lindstrom (S), Lorena Lirussi (I), Nico Lorenzutti (C), David & Fiona Loveday (UK), Terence Low (Aus), Carl Luer (USA)

Paul R Maguire (Aus), Jackie Maguire (UK), Anne-Emmanuelle Maire (F), Kenneth Mairs (C), Henry Mancini (USA), Dion Mant (NZ), John Marum (USA), Alexander Matskevich (USA), H Mayall (UK), C McCaffrey (UK), David McCarthy, Darren & Wendy McCormick (UK), Callum McInnes (Aus), Liza McKenna (Aus), Tracy McMenim (UK), Holly McNutt (USA), Michael Meijer (NL), Guido Merighi (I), Paul Miller (C), Marchen Moeller (Dk), Reidun Moen (N), Stuart Moles (UK), Mauro Montaldo (I), Danilo M Morales (Phl), Michael Mortensen (USA), B Murphy (Aus), Camilla Nestor (USA), Tony Newfield (Aus), Paul Newman (UK), Jonathan Newton (Aus), R H Newton (Aus), Jimmy Ng (Sin), Sanne Niazy (Dk), Julie Nicholls (UK), Glen Norris (USA), Lisa A Nye (USA), Tamsin O'Connell (UK), Michael O'Connell, Ben O'Hear (CH), Petra O'Neill (Aus), Mikko Ojala (Fin), Bjorn Olofson (S), Henry Oscar (Aus), James Patterson (USA), Jennie Peabody (USA), Giles Pearson (NZ), Lisa Penney (C), Florian Peter (D), Clare & Ivan Pollock (UK), Bud Porter (USA), A J Preston (UK), Bev Price (S), Greg Pugsley (UK), Matther Quinn (UK), Wolfgang Rakitsch (A), Neil Ranasinghe (UK), P & J Randall (Aus), Pawan & Parveen Rander (UK), A Ratcliffe (UK), Willi Rekowski (Aus), Gwyan Rhabyt (USA), David Rodgers (UK), W Romanowicz (Aus)

Tim Schey (USA), Gerard Schlund (F), Axel Schubert (D), Mark Schwarz (UK), Ralph Schwer (Aus), Deborah Scully (C), Ann B Searl (USA), Marta Seda-Poulin (USA), Eileen Seymour (Irl), Claudia Shepperd (C), Brian Shonamon (USA), Anna Sinclair (UK), Christopher Skase (Sp), Mari Skavhang (N), Carl Petter F Sky (N), Rupert Smedley (UK), Rhona Smith (UK), Sarah Smith (UK), James Snowden (USA), John Soar (NZ), Arne Staones (N), Luc & Sabine Steenssens (B), Jan Sternberg (Dk), Nick Stone (Aus), Judi Suter (Aus), Jasu & Leila Suvantola (Aus), Chantelle Svard (Aus), Setta Svensson (S), K J Swinburn (UK), Frederick Tan (Sin), Espen Tancen (N), Ryan Taplin (Aus), Isabelle Tardeglio (F), Garth Taylor (Aus), Aline & Al Thorsen (C), Michael &

Tracy Toal (Aus), J W Ton (NL), Martin Troun (Aus), Roger Turner (UK), Ellen Twiname (USA), David Twine (USA), Armin Uhlig (D), Liz Unwin (Aus), Regi Valar (CH), Peer Veldhinzen (NL), Michael von Beetzen (Fin)

Paul Wagner (Aus), Elaine Walker (UK), Neil Wall (Aus), Alexandra Wall (USA), Tracey Ward (UK), David Wayne (UK), Dave Wheeler (Aus), David White (UK), Andrew White-Hide (UK), Roger Wicks (UK), Robert Wilkinson (USA), Anne Marie Williams (UK), Anne Vita Willink (NL), Marian Willis (UK), Timothy Wilson, Charles Winokoor (USA), Tony Grote (B), Joanne Wise (NZ), L M Woods (Aus), Jeffery D Wright (USA), Anne Wyatt (USA), Philip Wylie (UK), Agustin Yague (Sp), Dr & Mrs Yale (USA), Pat Yale (UK), Darunee Yenjai, Stuart Young (Aus), Roxanne Youssef

A = Austria, Aus = Australia, B = Belgium, Bra = Brazil, C = Canada, CH = Switzerland, D = Germany, Dk = Denmark, F = France, Fin = Finland, G = Greece, I = Italy, Irl = Ireland, M = Malaysia, N = Norway, NL = Netherlands, NZ = New Zealand, Phl = Philippines, S = Sweden, Sin = Singapore, Sp = Spain

PLANET TALK

Lonely Planet's FREE quarterly newsletter

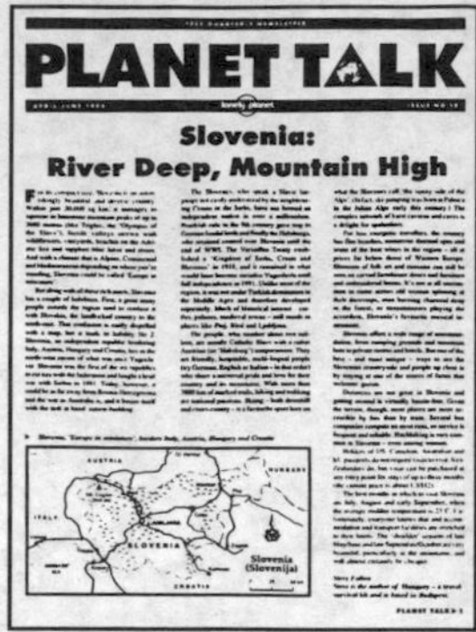

PLANET TALK

Slovenia:
River Deep, Mountain High

We love hearing from you and think you'd like to hear from us.

When...*is the right time to see reindeer in Finland?*
Where...*can you hear the best palm-wine music in Ghana?*
How...*do you get from Asunción to Areguá by steam train?*
What...*is the best way to see India?*

For the answer to these and many other questions read PLANET TALK.

Every issue is packed with up-to-date travel news and advice including:

- *a letter from Lonely Planet founders Tony and Maureen Wheeler*
- *travel diary from a Lonely Planet author - find out what it's really like out on the road*
- *feature article on an important and topical travel issue*
- *a selection of recent letters from our readers*
- *the latest travel news from all over the world*
- *details on Lonely Planet's new and forthcoming releases*

To join our mailing list contact any Lonely Planet office (address below).

LONELY PLANET PUBLICATIONS

Australia: PO Box 617, Hawthorn 3122, Victoria (tel: 03-819 1877)
USA: Embarcadero West, 155 Filbert St, Suite 251, Oakland, CA 94607 (tel: 510-893 8555)
TOLL FREE: (800) 275-8555
UK: 10 Barley Mow Passage, Chiswick, London W4 4PH (tel: 0181-742 3161)
France: 71 bis rue du Cardinal Lemoine – 75005 Paris (tel: 1-46 34 00 58)

Also available: Lonely Planet T-shirts. 100% heavyweight cotton (S, M, L, XL)

THE LONELY PLANET TRAVEL ATLAS

Tired of maps that lead you astray?

Sick of maps that fall apart after a few days' travel?

Had enough of maps that get creased and torn in all the wrong places?

Lonely Planet is proud to announce the solution to all these problems – the Lonely Planet travel atlas!

Produced in conjunction with Steinhart Katzir Publishers, a range of atlases designed to complement our guidebooks is now available to travellers worldwide.

Unlike other maps and road atlases, which look good on paper but often lack accuracy, LP's travel atlases have been thoroughly checked on the road by Lonely Planet's experienced team of authors. All details are carefully checked to ensure that the atlas conforms with the equivalent Lonely Planet guidebook.

The handy book format means that the atlas can withstand months of rigorous travelling adventures. So whether you're struggling through an Icelandic gale or packed like a sardine on a back-country bus in Asia, you'll find it easier to get where you're going with a Lonely Planet travel atlas. (Ideal for armchair travellers too!)

- full colour
- travel information in English, French, German, Spanish and Japanese
- place names keyed to LP guidebooks; no confusing spelling differences
- one country - one atlas. No need to buy five maps to cover large countries
- multilingual atlas legend
- comprehensive index

Available now:
Thailand and India

Coming in 1996:
Zimbabwe, Botswana & Namibia, Vietnam, Turkey, Laos and Chile.

Guides to South-East Asia

Bali & Lombok – a travel survival kit
This guide will help travellers to experience the real magic of Bali's tropical paradise. Neighbouring Lombok is largely untouched by outside influences and has a special atmosphere of its own.

Cambodia – a travel survival kit
As one of the last nations in the region opens its doors to travellers, visitors will again make their way to the magnificent ruins of Angkor. Another first for Lonely Planet!

Indonesia – a travel survival kit
Some of the most remarkable sights and sounds in South-East Asia can be found amongst the 13,000 islands of Indonesia – this book covers the entire archipelago in detail.

Laos – a travel survival kit
From the fertile lowlands of the Mekong River Valley to the rugged Annamite highlands, Lao hospitality, natural scenery and the attractive capital of Vientiane have survived decades of war and now offer travellers an unparalled glimpse of old Indochina.

Malaysia, Singapore & Brunei – a travel survival kit
Three independent nations of amazing geographic and cultural variety – from the national parks, beaches, jungles and rivers of Malaysia, to the tiny oil-rich Brunei and the urban prosperity and diversity of Singapore.

Myanmar (Burma) – a travel survival kit
Myanmar is one of Asia's most interesting countries. This book shows how to make the most of a trip around the main triangle route of Yangon–Mandalay–Bagan, and explores many lesser-known places such as Bago and Inle Lake.

Philippines – a travel survival kit
The friendly Filipinos, colourful festivals and superb natural scenery make the Philippines one of the most interesting countries in South-East Asia for adventurous travellers and sun-seekers alike.

Thailand – a travel survival kit
This authoritative guide includes Thai script for all place names and the latest travel details for all regions, including tips on trekking in the remote hills of the Golden Triangle.

Vietnam – a travel survival kit
From the wide avenues and pavement restaurants of Hanoi and Saigon to the spectacular verdant countryside, travelling in Vietnam is packed with challenges and surprises. A comprehensive and informative guide to one of the region's most popular destinations.

Singapore – city guide
Singapore offers a taste of the great Asian cultures in a small, accessible package. This compact guide will help travellers discover the very best that this city of contrasts can offer.

Bangkok – city guide

Bangkok has something for everyone: temples, museums and historic sites; an endless variety of good restaurants, clubs, international culture and social events; a modern art institute; and great shopping opportunities. This pocket guide offers you the assurance that you will never be lost...or lost for things to do in this fascinating city!

Also available:

Lao phrasebook, ***Thai*** phrasebook, ***Thai Hill Tribes*** phrasebook, ***Burmese*** phrasebook, ***Pilipino*** phrasebook, ***Indonesian*** phrasebook, ***Papua New Guinea Pidgin*** phrasebook, ***Mandarin Chinese*** phrasebook and ***Vietnamese*** phrasebook.

Lonely Planet Guidebooks

Lonely Planet guidebooks cover every accessible part of Asia as well as Australia, the Pacific, South America, Africa, the Middle East, Europe and parts of North America. There are five series: *travel survival kits*, covering a country for a range of budgets; *shoestring guides* with compact information for low-budget travel in a major region; *walking guides*; *city guides* and *phrasebooks.*

Australia & the Pacific
Australia
Australian phrasebook
Bushwalking in Australia
Islands of Australia's Great Barrier Reef
Outback Australia
Fiji
Fijian phrasebook
Melbourne city guide
Micronesia
New Caledonia
New South Wales
New Zealand
Tramping in New Zealand
Papua New Guinea
Bushwalking in Papua New Guinea
Papua New Guinea phrasebook
Rarotonga & the Cook Islands
Samoa
Solomon Islands
Sydney city guide
Tahiti & French Polynesia
Tonga
Vanuatu
Victoria
Western Australia

North-East Asia
Beijing city guide
China
Cantonese phrasebook
Mandarin Chinese phrasebook
Hong Kong, Macau & Canton
Japan
Japanese phrasebook
Korea
Korean phrasebook
Mongolia
North-East Asia on a shoestring
Seoul city guide
Taiwan
Tibet
Tibet phrasebook
Tokyo city guide

Middle East
Arab Gulf States
Egypt & the Sudan
Arabic (Egyptian) phrasebook
Iran
Israel
Jordan & Syria
Middle East
Turkey
Turkish phrasebook
Trekking in Turkey
Yemen

South-East Asia
Bali & Lombok
Bangkok city guide
Cambodia
Indonesia
Indonesian phrasebook
Jakarta city guide
Laos
Lao phrasebook
Malaysia, Singapore & Brunei
Myanmar (Burma)
Burmese phrasebook
Philippines
Pilipino phrasebook
Singapore city guide
South-East Asia on a shoestring
Thailand
Thailand travel atlas
Thai phrasebook
Thai Hill Tribes phrasebook
Vietnam
Vietnamese phrasebook

Indian Ocean
Madagascar & Comoros
Maldives & Islands of the East Indian Ocean
Mauritius, Réunion & Seychelles

Ma

Lonely Planet guidebooks are distributed worldwide. They are also available by
Lonely Planet, so if you have difficulty finding a title please write to us. US and Ca
should write to Embarcadero West, 155 Filbert St, Suite 251, Oakland CA 94607,
residents should write to 10 Barley Mow Passage, Chiswick, London W4 4PH;
other countries to PO Box 617, Hawthorn, Victoria 3122, Australia.

Europe

Baltic States & Kaliningrad
Baltics States phrasebook
Britain
Central Europe on a shoestring
Central Europe phrasebook
Czech & Slovak Republics
Dublin city guide
Eastern Europe on a shoestring
Eastern Europe phrasebook
Finland
France
Greece
Greek phrasebook
Hungary
Iceland, Greenland & the Faroe Islands
Ireland
Italy
Mediterranean Europe on a shoestring
Mediterranean Europe phrasebook
Poland
Prague city guide
Scandinavian & Baltic Europe on a shoestring
Scandinavian Europe phrasebook
Slovenia
Switzerland
Trekking in Spain
Trekking in Greece
USSR
Russian phrasebook
Vienna city guide
Western Europe on a shoestring
Western Europe phrasebook

Indian S

In
Hindi/Urd
Trekking in the Ind
Karakor
Kashmir, Ladakh
Trekking in the Nepal Hi
Nepali phrase
Pakis
Sri Lanka
Sri Lanka phrasebook

Africa

Africa on a shoestring
Central Africa
East Africa
Trekking in East Africa
Kenya
Swahili phrasebook
Morocco
Arabic (Moroccan) phrasebook
North Africa
South Africa, Lesotho & Swaziland
Zimbabwe, Botswana & Namibia
West Africa

Central America & the Caribbean

Baja California
Central America on a shoestring
Costa Rica
Eastern Caribbean
Guatemala, Belize & Yucatán: La Ruta Maya
Mexico

North America

Alaska
Backpacking in Alaska
Canada
Hawaii
Honolulu city guide
USA phrasebook

South America

Argentina, Uruguay & Paraguay
Bolivia
Brazil
Brazilian phrasebook
Chile & Easter Island
Colombia
Ecuador & the Galápagos Islands
Latin American Spanish phrasebook
Peru
Quechua phrasebook
South America on a shoestring
Trekking in the Patagonian Andes
Venezuela

...y Planet Story

...lanet published its first book in ...esponse to the numerous 'How did ... it?' questions Maureen and Tony ...er were asked after driving, bussing, ...ng, sailing and railing their way from ...and to Australia.

...Vritten at a kitchen table and hand col-...ed, trimmed and stapled, *Across Asia on ...e Cheap* became an instant local bestseller, ...nspiring thoughts of another book.

Eighteen months in South-East Asia resulted in their second guide, *South-East Asia on a shoestring*, which they put together in a backstreet Chinese hotel in Singapore in 1975. The 'yellow bible' as it quickly became known to backpackers around the world, soon became *the* guide to the region. It has sold well over half a million copies and is now in its 8th edition, still retaining its familiar yellow cover.

Today there are over 140 Lonely Planet titles in print – books that have that same adventurous approach to travel as those early guides; books that 'assume you know how to get your luggage off the carousel' as one reviewer put it.

Although Lonely Planet initially specialised in guides to Asia, they now cover most regions of the world, including the Pacific, South America, Africa, the Middle East and Europe. The list of *walking guides* and *phrasebooks* (for 'unusual' languages such as Quechua, Swahili, Nepali and Egyptian Arabic) is also growing rapidly.

The emphasis continues to be on travel for independent travellers. Tony and Maureen still travel for several months of each year and play an active part in the writing, updating and quality control of Lonely Planet's guides.

They have been joined by over 50 authors, 110 staff – mainly editors, cartographers & designers – at our office in Melbourne, Australia, at our US office in Oakland, California and at our European office in Paris; another five at our office in London handle sales for Britain, Europe and Africa. Travellers themselves also make a valuable contribution to the guides through the feedback we receive in thousands of letters each year.

The people at Lonely Planet strongly believe that travellers can make a positive contribution to the countries they visit, both through their appreciation of the countries' culture, wildlife and natural features, and through the money they spend. In addition, the company makes a direct contribution to the countries and regions it covers. Since 1986 a percentage of the income from each book has been donated to ventures such as famine relief in Africa; aid projects in India; agricultural projects in Central America; Greenpeace's efforts to halt French nuclear testing in the Pacific; and Amnesty International.

Lonely Planet's basic travel philosophy is summed up in Tony Wheeler's comment, 'Don't worry about whether your trip will work out. Just go!'